BOONE AND CROCKETT CLUB'S

27th Big Game Awards
2007-2009

▼   ▼   ▼   ▼   ▼   ▼   ▼

Boone and Crockett Club's 27th Big Game Awards, 2007-2009
Edited by Eldon L. "Buck" Buckner, Jack Reneau, and Justin Spring

Copyright © 2010, by the Boone and Crockett Club

ISSN: 1939-4527
Hardcover ISBN: 978-0-940864-68-9
Paperback ISBN: 978-0-940864-71-9
Published October 2010

Published in the United States of America
by the
Boone and Crockett Club
250 Station Drive
Missoula, Montana 59801
Phone (406) 542-1888
Fax (406) 542-0784
Toll-Free (888) 840-4868 (book or merchandise orders only)
www.booneandcrockettclub.com

BOONE AND CROCKETT CLUB'S

27th Big Game Awards
2007-2009

▼ ▼ ▼ ▼ ▼ ▼ ▼

A Book of the Boone and Crockett Club
Containing Tabulations of Outstanding North American
Big Game Trophies Accepted During the
27th Awards Entry Period of 2007-2009

Edited by
Eldon L. "Buck" Buckner
Jack Reneau
Justin Spring

2010

Boone and Crockett Club

Missoula, Montana

BIG GAME
MEASUREMENTS

Boone and Crockett Club

STANDARD

FOREWORD

▼ ▼ ▼ ▼ ▼ ▼ ▼ ▼

LOWELL E. BAIER
President of the Boone and Crockett Club

The Boone and Crockett Club's public recognition of trophy heads and horns can be traced back to 1895 at the 1st Annual Sportsmen's Exposition in New York City when Club members Theodore Roosevelt, George Bird Grinnell, and Archibald Rogers served as competition judges. A review of their early scoring techniques and challenges is detailed in a chapter of the Club's 1895 book *Hunting in Many Lands* titled "Head Measurements of the Trophies at the Madison Square Garden Sportsmen's Exhibition."

In 1902, the Club established a Committee on Game Measurements, comprised of Roosevelt, Rogers, and Caspar Whitney, to determine the exact method by which antlers and other dimensions of North American big game should be measured that could become the Club's official criteria. In 1906, the Club published *Big Game Measurements: Game Book of the Boone and Crockett Club*, which was authored by Club member James Hathaway Kidder, who later chaired the Committee on Game Measurements. Consisting of 107 unnumbered pages, this pocket-size book provided Boone and Crockett Club's first criteria for measuring 17 categories of North American big game.

In 1906, Club member William T. Hornaday, who was then director of the New York Zoological Society Park, donated his private collection of 131 heads and horns of the world's representative species to establish the National Collection of Heads and Horns (NCHH). Boone and Crockett Club established the New York Zoological Society (NYZS) in 1895, and supported Hornaday's efforts to establish a world-wide collection of the world's ungulates arranged zoologically and geographically. By 1912, the collection contained 798 specimens. Deacquisitioned in 1978, the North American specimens from this collection today are owned by the Boone and Crockett Club and are on display at the Buffalo Bill Historical Center in Cody, Wyoming. Continually being upgraded, the collection features 38 heads including 4 World's Record trophies.

In 1932 a new standard of measurement was developed and published titled *Records of North American Big Game*, a product of the Boone and Crockett Club's Heads and Horns Committee, chaired by Prentiss N. Gray under the auspices of the NCHH and the NYZS. The measurement system was initially conceived and the book published to record perceived vanishing North American big-game trophies, and to heighten awareness in North America of the plight of wildlife's declining populations. The 1932 book, and its 1939 successor, were richly illustrated by Boone and Crockett Club member and artist Carl Rungius, and contained 27 and 28 game categories, respectively.

The 1932 records book, limited to 500 copies, was popular and controversial, precipitating much argument and criticism over the scoring system and formulae used. The measurements were quite simple, the length of the skull, or the longer antler or horn, plus a basal circumference. Accordingly, Chairman Gray was asked to prepare a more comprehensive treatment of the subject establishing a system of measurement that could secure broad approval. His untimely death prevented this, and the sequel, *North American Big Game*, was published in 1939 by Boone and Crockett Club's Records of North American Big Game Committee, with the cooperation of the NCHH, the NYZS, and the American Museum of Natural History. It adhered to the measurement method for scoring trophies Prentiss Gray adopted for the 1932 records book, thus perpetuating the agitation among sportsmen for a universally acceptable formulae of measurement and tabulation, which finally evolved in 1950.

A solution to the two-decades-long measurement controversy was a product of a special Committee on Revisions chaired by Samuel B. Webb, and consisting of Boone and Crockett Club members James L. Clark, Harold E. Anthony, Milford Baker, and Frederick K. Barbour, and non-member Grancel Fitz. At the Club's annual meeting in December 1950, the new scoring system for trophy measurement was adopted for 30 big game categories, which remains relatively intact today. Quoting from a 1997 article by the former Director of Big Game Records, Emeritus Club Member William H. Nesbitt: "With the newly established system in place [and copyrighted], the Club set about rescoring those trophies previously recognized in the 1932 and 1939 records books. The results, along with other trophies qualifying under the new system, were published in 1952 in *Records of North American Big Game*. This is then the "first" all-time records book that used the Club's copyrighted scoring system adopted in 1950." Successive all-time records books, the 12th edition published in 2005, have provided the strongest single vehicle the Boone and Crockett Club utilizes to communicate the ethics and principles of Fair Chase to the American hunter, and given the professional game management and scientific community an invaluable database to measure animal population trends (from which game seasons and bag limits are set), genetics, nutrition, age, and habitat characteristics unavailable elsewhere in the world.

To encourage hunters to submit their trophies for measurement and to ensure the Club's records books were accurate and up-to-date, Club President Archibald B. Roosevelt

(Theodore Roosevelt's son) began a series of public Big Game Competitions, which later became known as Awards Programs, beginning with the 1st Competition in 1947, to recognize top-ranking trophy heads as determined by the Club's 1932-39 measurement criteria. These were held on an annual basis from 1947 through 1951; thereafter (utilizing the 1950 scoring system), on a two-year interval for seven competitions, and since 1968 on a three-year basis, all totaling 27 Awards Programs to date.

At the end or each three-year entry period, top-ranking trophies are invited to the North American Big Game Awards Program where they are measured by two separate independent teams of two judges each. Trophy scores are verified by the Judges Panel, and each trophy is examined for split skulls, breakage, repair, etc., utilizing x-rays where necessary, in the final evaluation before awards are presented. If an entry is later discovered to have been illegally taken, it is purged from the records. Boone and Crockett Club's records today constitute the "gold standard" for records of native North American big game because of its long history of tedious development over the last century, and the disciplines built into the system to protect its integrity and sanctity. To appropriately recognize and honor the awards made every three years, in 1984 following the 18th Awards Program, the Club began to publish a special Awards Record book, listing and ranking only those trophies for the three years of the Awards Entry Period.

The Club's big-game records-keeping program has been a continuing barometer of wildlife management across the country. Entries in 1980 totaled about 300 per year. The 27th Awards Program celebrated in 2010 in Reno, Nevada, had 4,906 accepted entries over a three-year period from which 98 were recognized with awards in 33 big game categories.

The highlight of any North American Big Game Awards Program is the potential awarding of Boone and Crockett Club's highest award, the Sagamore Hill Award, for an outstanding trophy worthy of great distinction. This award, which consists of a medal and a certificate, is given by the Roosevelt family in memory of the Club's founder and first President, Theodore Roosevelt, and two of his sons, Theodore Roosevelt, Jr., and Kermit Roosevelt. This year's 27th Big Game Awards honored Paul T. Deuling with the Sagamore Hill Award for his new World's Record mountain caribou. Theodore Roosevelt's great-great grandson, and Kermit's great grandson, Club member Simon Roosevelt, presented the award on behalf of the Roosevelt family. The Sagamore Hill Award for an outstanding big game trophy has been made only 16 times since 1948, and can only be awarded during a Big Game Awards Program. It remains one of the most coveted honors a hunter can collect in North America. ▲

ABOUT THE AUTHOR: Lowell E. Baier is President of the Boone and Crockett Club, and has been a Club member since 1980. He was recognized by the National Fish and Wildlife Foundation and Anheuser-Busch Companies, Inc. as the 2008 Conservationist of the Year, and similarly recognized by *Outdoor Life* magazine in 2010. Baier has been an attorney and investment builder in Bethesda, Maryland, for over 45 years, and engaged with the wildlife conservation community at the national level throughout this time.

RECORDS OF NORTH AMERICAN BIG GAME COMMITTEE

Eldon L. "Buck" Buckner, Chair
Baker City, Oregon

Gilbert T. Adams
Beaumont, Texas

James F. Arnold
Austin, Texas

Mark O. Bara
Hemingway, South Carolina

George A. Bettas
Stevensville, Montana

Vernon C. Bleich
Dickinson, North Dakota

Tommy L. Caruthers
Denton, Texas

Craig A. Cook
Anchorage, Alaska

John O. Cook III
North Bend, Washington

Ernie Davis
Cotulla, Texas

H. Hudson DeCray
Bishop, California

Richard T. Hale
Ottawa, Kansas

Robert H. Hanson
Wapiti, Wyoming

Kevin Hisey
Chatfield, Minnesota

Vernon D. Holleman
Temple, Texas

Frederick J. King
Gallatin Gateway, Montana

Kyle C. Krause
Richmond, Texas

Jay A. Lesser
Glenrock, Wyoming

William C. MacCarty III
South Boston, Virginia

Butch Marita
High Bridge, Wisconsin

Earl E. Morgenroth
Missoula, Montana

Jack S. Parker
Carefree, Arizona

John P. Poston
Helena, Montana

Jack Reneau
Missoula, Montana

David P. Rippeto
Fairbanks, Alaska

Mark B. Steffen
Hutchinson, Kansas

Wayne C. van Zwoll
Bridgeport, Washington

Paul D. Webster
Wayzata, Minnesota

TABLE OF CONTENTS

Award Winning Trophy Stories Continued...

Award Winning Trophy Stories Continued...

Tabulations of Trophies Accepted in the 27th Awards Program 447

Boone and Crockett Club's Official Score Charts 619

Color Field Photographs of Trophies Accepted in the 27th Awards Program 655

Acknowledgments 686

B&C Photo Archives

The 27th North American Big Game Awards Program Judges' Panel and Panel Assistants are pictured above in Reno, Nevada. Standing from left: Paul D. Webster, Justin Spring, William A. Keebler, Patrick H. McKenzie, Mark O. Bara, Glenn E. Hisey, Frederick J. King, Robert H. Hanson, Curtis R. Siegfried, Homer Saye, and L. Victor Clark. Kneeling from left: Eldon L. "Buck" Buckner, Kyle C. Krause, Gilbert Hernandez, Craig A. Cook, Larry C. Lack, Richard T. Hale, and Jack Reneau.

27TH NORTH AMERICAN BIG GAME AWARDS

PANEL OF JUDGES
Reno, Nevada – 2010

CHAIRMAN
Mark O. Bara
Hemingway, South Carolina

Eldon L."Buck" Buckner
Baker City, Oregon

Glenn E. Hisey
Chatfield, Minnesota

Craig A. Cook
Anchorage, Alaska

William A. Keebler
Happy Jack, Arizona

Larry C. Lack
Thompson Falls, Montana

Patrick H. McKenzie
Regina, Saskatchewan

Richard T. Hale
Ottawa, Kansas

Homer Saye
Cypress, Texas

Gilbert Hernandez
Elko, Nevada

Curtis R. Siegfried
Whitecourt, Alberta

CONSULTANTS

L. Victor Clark
Verdi, Nevada

Frederick J. King
Gallatin Gateway, Montana

Robert H. Hanson
Wapiti, Wyoming

Paul D. Webster
Wayzata, Minnesota

ASSISTANTS

Kyle C. Krause
Richmond, Texas

Jack Reneau
Missoula, Montana

Justin Spring
Missoula, Montana

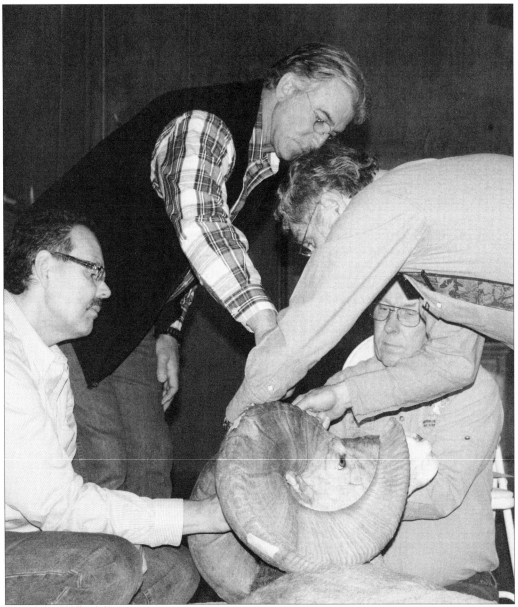

Members of the 27th Awards Judges Panel worked together to verify the scores of the 98 trophies sent to Reno, Nevada, for the event. Above Patrick H. McKenzie (left), L. Victor Clark, and Eldon L. "Buck" Buckner, assist fellow measurer Larry C. Lack as he takes a base measurement on Toni L. Sannon's bighorn sheep. Sannon harvested the sheep in Fergus County, Montana. With a score of 204-2/8 points, it's the largest ram ever harvested by a woman accepted in the Club's Records Program.

INTRODUCTION

▼ ▼ ▼ ▼ ▼ ▼ ▼ ▼ ▼

KYLE C. KRAUSE
Deputy, Boone and Crockett Club Publications Committee

Welcome to the 27th Big Game Awards book, the 10th edition published since the Boone and Crockett Club's Awards book series began in 1984. The trophies listed in this book were entered between January 1, 2007, and December 31, 2009, and have not previously been published in an Awards or All-time book. This book is unique because the minimum scores are lower than the minimums set for the All-time records book, and for the trophies that do not make the All-time minimum, this is the only records book in which many are listed.

At the end of 27th Awards Period, all entries that had been accepted were evaluated, and the top-five trophies from each category were identified. These individuals were invited to ship their trophies to Reno, Nevada, to be verified by the Judges Panel and displayed at the 27th Big Game Awards Banquet. A special word of thanks needs to be given to the Reno-area volunteers from the Nevada Wildlife Record Book Committee and Nevada Bighorns Unlimited for helping unload, unpack, and repack the trophies. The 27th Awards Judges Panel, which convened in Reno in April 2010, spent five days verifying and scoring the 98 trophies that are featured within these pages.

The judges and consultants for the panel were selected by the Chairman of the Records Committee, Eldon L. "Buck" Buckner, and the Director of Big Game Records, Jack Reneau. These gentlemen select from the approximately 1,200 Official Measurers who serve as volunteers for the Boone and Crockett Club, and whose level of experience, record of long-standing service to the Club, and exposure to a variety of big-game animals are an important part of the criteria for selection. Most important is their ability to resolve problems and disputes in a professional manner. The panel consists of a chairman, ten judges and four consultants, typically including at least one representative from the Pope and Young Club and two from Canada, with the rest of the members coming from as broad a geographic variation as possible.

To be chosen as a judge or consultant for a Judges Panel is an incredible honor. The sacrifices made by each of the measurers when they accept a position on the Judges Panel go largely unnoticed by those of us who enjoy using the records book as a snapshot of the past, so we extend our gratitude here. Each member spends a week away from their families and their jobs, and they experience the physical and mental strain of reviewing and scoring trophies for 10-12 hours a day for at least five days. They understand the significance of the decisions they make—their final decisions become set into the records books forever. At the end of the week for the 27th Awards Program Banquet activities, the judges no doubt were tired, but left for home gratified, knowing they had helped preserve and strengthen the validity of big-game records for another triennium.

The 27th Award's Program Banquet and related activities was a three-day event in Reno,

Photographs from B&C Photo Archives

Pictured above are the 16 youth hunters who traveled to Reno, Nevada, to be recognized at the Club's inaugural Generation Next Awards Banquet. Pictured from left to right in the back row: Jordan B. Phillips (non-typical mule deer – 242-4/8), Griffin M. Terrell (non-typical whitetail – 224-2/8), Adam J. Bouch (typical whitetail deer – 162-7/8), Rylan Rudebusch (Shiras' moose – 180-2/8), Brandon R. Kurkierewicz (black bear – 21-3/16), Kyle Lopez (non-typical mule deer – 306-3/8), Jacob L. Billman (black bear – 20-2/16), Cole M. Martinsen (black bear – 22), James P. Hamik (typical whitetail deer – 172), Cody C. Sanders (Roosevelt's elk – 307-4/8), Wesley S. Brown (black bear – 21-9/16), and Jakob P. Olsen (pronghorn – 84); Left to right in the front row: Kalee C. Teel (typical mule deer – 191-4/8), Morgan T. Daugherty (cougar – 15-2/16), Jolayne M. Collings (cougar – 15-1/16), and Kelsey A. Smith (typical Columbia blacktail – 135-6/8).

Nevada, in June 2010. It was the most well-attended Awards Program in Boone and Crockett Club's history, which is a tribute to the hard work of the Boone and Crockett Club's staff, committees, committee chairmen, and volunteers who put the show and display together. One of the most exciting things to come out of the weekend was Friday evening's inaugural Youth Recognition Awards Program, called the Generation Next Program. These awards were given to young men and women who were 16 years old or younger at the time they harvested their records-book trophies. The level of excitement and satisfaction in the young people's faces was something special for everyone in attendance at dinner that evening. There were 73 youth entries during the three years of the 27th Awards Program, with 16 of those on hand in Reno to be recognized for their achievements. Of those 16 individuals, two hunters had exceptional trophies that would also be recognized the following evening at the 27th Big Game Awards Banquet. Kyle Lopez was 14 years old when he harvested his award-winning non-typical mule deer. The buck, with a final score of 306-3/8 points, received the 1st Place Award. The other youth hunter recognized at the banquet was Rylan Rudebusch. He was 15 years old when he harvested his Shiras' moose, scoring 180-2/8 points, earning him a 2nd Place Award.

From January 1, 2010, the beginning of the 28th Awards Program, to July 2010, the Club's Records Department had already accepted more than 23 youth trophy entries. This is going to be an exciting program to watch grow. As you browse through the trophy lists at the back of this book, keep an eye out for trophies with the special youth logo beside them. I think you'll be impressed with what this group of young hunters has achieved.

ABOUT THE AUTHOR: Kyle C. Krause of Richmond, Texas, is a Regular member of the Boone and Crockett Club, as well as one of the Club's Lifetime Associates. He serves on the Club's Big Game Records Committee and is the deputy chairman of the Publications Committee. Krause was appointed as an Official Measurer in 2009 and attended the 27th Big Game Awards Judges Panel in Reno, Nevada, as a panel assistant.

BOONE AND CROCKETT CLUB'S

27th Big Game Awards
2007-2009

Photographs from B&C Photo Archives

Three highlights of the Club's 27th Big Game Awards Program in Reno, Nevada, include the new World's Record non-typical American elk taken by Denny Austad; the announcement by Simon Roosevelt of the prestigious Sagamore Hill Award given to Paul T. Deuling for his new World's Record mountain caribou; and the Club's first-ever youth awards program.

REVIEW OF THE
27TH AWARDS PROGRAM

▼ ▼ ▼ ▼ ▼ ▼ ▼ ▼ ▼

ELDON L. "BUCK" BUCKNER
Vice President of Records and
Records of North American Big Game Committee, Chair

AND

JACK RENEAU
Director, Big Game Records

Boone and Crockett Club's 27th Big Game Awards Program (2007-2009) closed December 31, 2009, with the greatest number of entries ever accepted during a three-year entry period. A total of 4,906 trophies were accepted in 35 of the 38 big-game categories recognized by the Club, which represents a 6 percent increase over the 26th Awards Program (2004-2006) three years ago. No entries were received and/or accepted for Atlantic walrus, jaguar, and non-typical Sitka blacktail deer.

The Grand Sierra Resort was host to the Club's 27th Big Game Awards Program Banquet and related activities Tuesday through Saturday, June 22-26. Hunters and visitors alike enjoyed the convenience of having all the associated activities on the ground floor and adjacent to the magnificent display of award-winning trophies.

Following a special Thursday evening welcome reception for hunters and their guests on June 24, the Club held its first-ever recognition dinner Friday evening to honor all the young hunters age 16 and under who had trophies accepted in the 27th Awards Program. After a lively auction of special hunts on Saturday afternoon, a record number of nearly 400 trophy owners and guests witnessed 66 hunters receive Boone and Crockett Medallions as photos of their trophies were projected onto two giant Diamond screens. The climax of the event occurred when Simon Roosevelt presented Paul T. Deuling with the Club's highest honor—the Sagamore Hill Award, for his new World's Record mountain caribou taken during an exemplary fair-chase hunt.

There were 98 trophies honored at the 27th Awards Program Banquet, and there aren't enough superlatives in the English language to describe the quality of these trophies. In addition to two new World's Records that were recognized with B&C Medallions and certificates, there were many other trophies that rank in B&C's All-time top-10 for their category, as well as many new state and provincial records. Following is a summary of the highlights of some of the finest North American big-game trophies that have ever been accepted and recorded by Boone and Crockett Club. These trophies are proof positive that hunter-supported, wildlife management is working in North America.

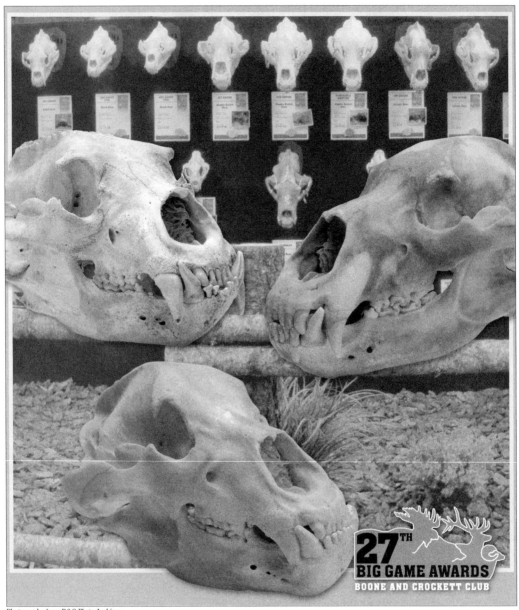

The skull display at the 27th Big Game Awards was an impressive sight with 14 bear and cat skulls in the main trophy display area. Pictured above are three of the First Award winners (clockwise from top left): Robert J. Evans' black bear scoring 22-13/16; Rodney W. Debias' grizzly bear scoring 27-3/16; and Robert Castle's Alaska brown bear scoring 29-9/16. James D. Unrein's award-winning polar bear skull scoring 27-5/16 (opposite page) was also on display.

BEARS AND COUGAR

BLACK BEAR

Robert J. Evans has taken two B&C black bears in the last few years in Manitoba that made B&C records. His most recent bear, scoring 22-13/16 points, was a 615-pound boar for which he received the 1st Place Award in this category. He harvested it with a bow from a tree stand near Riding Mountain during the 2008 spring season. It ties for eighth place in B&C and is the new No. 2 in Manitoba, as well as the new No. 2 trophy in Pope and Young Club.

With four black bears in the All-time top-10, Pennsylvania is well-known for producing trophy bruins. The boar that Joseph W. Paulo took in Lehigh County in 1997 scores 22-11/16 points and currently ties for 11th place in the All-time records book. Had Paulo entered this bear in B&C back in 1997, it would have ranked No. 5 at that time, giving a clearer indication of the quality of this trophy.

The black bear Donald L. Corrigan took in 2009 in Newaygo County, Michigan, is the new state record. It scores 22-11/16.

GRIZZLY BEAR

The huge boar that Rodney W. Debias took with a bow in 2009 near the Unalakleet River, Alaska, is the largest grizzly taken since 1976 and will go down as the largest hunter-taken trophy ever recorded in B&C's records book. It scores 27-3/16 and is second only to the current World's Record that was found dead on Lone Mountain, Alaska. Debias shot his trophy with an arrow at 29 yards after it passed within 10 yards of him. He held his shot until he couldn't see the bear's eye, correctly figuring that the bear couldn't see him move. The grizzly was so close to Debias as it passed that he could smell its breath every time it exhaled.

ALASKA BROWN BEAR

The legendary brown bears of Alaska are among some of the most sought-after big-game animals in North America. The largest one recognized in this category was a big boar scoring 29-9/16 points taken by Robert J. Castle at Uganik Lake on Kodiak Island in 2006. It ties for 40th place out of nearly 800 trophies accepted by B&C.

POLAR BEAR

The polar bear entered by James D. Unrein is only the third one accepted from Alaska since 1973 when they became protected by the Marine Mammal Protection Act (MMPA), which permits only Native Americans to hunt them. While Unrein's bear was taken in 2007, the other two were harvested prior to the MMPA taking effect on October 21, 1972. Unrein

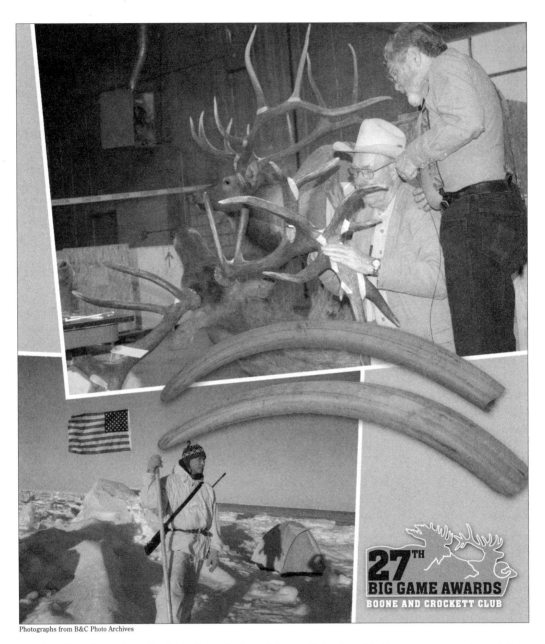

Judges Panel members Buck Buckner (left) and Larry C. Lack verify the measurements on John A. Shirk's non-typical American elk. The bull has a final score of 441-6/8 points and is the new state record from Pennsylvania. Two other unique trophies on hand at the 27th Big Game Awards Program were the Pacific walrus tusks picked up by Richard Van Blaricom in 1963 and James D. Unrein's polar bear taken on the frozen Chukchi Sea in Alaska in 2007.

took this unique trophy that scored 27-5/16 points as it was hunting him and a friend on the ice of the Chukchi Sea.

COUGAR

The 1st Place Award cougar was taken by Rod E. Bradley in Idaho County, Idaho, in 2007. It scores 15-14/16 points and ranks number 10 in B&C's records book and No. 2 in Idaho. It is second only to Gene Alford's tom taken 15 years ago that received the coveted Sagamore Hill Award.

PACIFIC WALRUS

The only Pacific walrus invited to an Awards Program are those that rank in the All-time top-10 because they are not eligible for a Place Award. In 1963 Richard Van Blaricom picked up a set of walrus tusks near Platinum Creek, Alaska. These tusks received a Certificate of Merit. Since passage of the MMPA in October 21, 1972, only walrus trophies hunted by or purchased from native hunters, or picked up and subsequently permitted by the U.S. Fish and Wildlife Service can be legally owned. The Judges Panel verified Van Blaricom's tusks at 135 points.

ELK

AMERICAN ELK

While taking a B&C bull elk is a once-in-a-lifetime accomplishment for most serious elk hunters, Dan J. Agnew took both a typical bull (399-4/8) in Arizona and a non-typical bull (436-4/8) in Washington in 2008. Both were invited to the 27th Awards Program and the latter, taken in Columbia County, is the new state record.

Pennsylvania is not a state most hunters would consider for a record-class elk hunt. However, the state's efforts to reintroduce elk there have started to pay big dividends for a handful of lucky hunters. John A. Shirk added to Pennsylvania's success story in 2006 when he harvested a massive bull, scoring 441-6/8 points in Clinton County. It is the largest non-typical bull ever taken in Pennsylvania and the ninth-largest non-typical ever recorded.

Denny Austad's World's Record non-typical American elk, which scores 478-5/8 points was on display in Reno where it received the 1st Place Award. It was taken in Piute County, Utah, in 2008 and declared the Worlds' Record in January 2009 after it was scored by a Special Judges Panel that convened at Denny's home. A stipulation for trophies scored by a Special Judges Panel is that the trophy must be sent to the next Awards Program to be displayed for the public's enjoyment.

ROOSEVELT'S ELK

The most notable bull in this category is one collected in 2009 by Allen M. Shearer near the Powell River of British Columbia that scored an impressive 362-5/8 points. It is the largest Roosevelt's elk certified by the 27th Judges Panel and is the first bull taken on

Photographs from B&C Photo Archives

Trophy owners, both young and old were recognized in Reno. The Columbia blacktail shown top left was taken in Shasta County, California, in 1962 by Gene Bland and David Boddy. Kyle Lopez (top right) received the 1st Place Award for this non-typical mule deer at the Awards Banquet, as well as a B&C Youth Award presented the previous evening at the Generation Next dinner. Trophy owners, such as James C. Johnson (woodland caribou), enjoyed viewing the various trophies on display.

British Columbia's mainland after the category boundary was expanded in late 2009. Allen's bull is the culmination of extensive conservation efforts of fish and game personnel and sportsmen to restore a native big-game animal to an area from which it was extirpated in the early 20th century.

TULE ELK

The four tule elk sent to Reno for certification and recognition by the Judges Panel are representative of another conservation success story that brought an endangered species back from the brink of extinction. They were first hunted in 1995 after removal from the endangered species list. The 1st Place Award trophy scored 322-5/8 points, taken by Andrew J. Wood in San Luis Obispo County, California, in 2007.

DEER

MULE DEER

The most spectacular mule deer in Reno was a non-typical taken by 14 year old Kyle Lopez in Douglas County, Colorado, in 2007, scoring 306-3/8 points. One of only 21 bucks that have ever exceeded 300 points, it is the largest taken since 1972. Kyle received the 1st Place Award for this magnificent buck at the 27th Awards Banquet on June 26, as well as a B&C Youth Award presented the previous evening at B&C's first Generation Next dinner for junior hunters. Unlike many who take a B&C trophy later in life, Kyle will be able to enjoy his trophy for many years to come.

COLUMBIA BLACKTAIL DEER

The larger of only two typical Columbia blacktails displayed in Reno was an older trophy, scoring 160-6/8 points. It was taken in Shasta County, California, in 1962 by Gene Bland and David Boddy while hunting on the Bland Ranch. B&C will list two hunters for a trophy so long as both hunters sign the Entry Affidavit certifying it was taken in Fair Chase and provide a copy of their hunting license.

SITKA BLACKTAIL DEER

Sitka blacktail deer can be deceiving because they are so much smaller than either of their close cousins—the mule deer and the Columbia blacktail. Without a doubt, one of the finest trophies on display was the typical Sitka blacktail taken by Joseph R. Jeppsen on Prince of Wales Island in 2007. With a score of 126-5/8 points, it is the largest Sitka taken since 1985. It ranks No. 3 in the world and No. 2 in Alaska. Jeppsen received the 1st Place Award for his outstanding trophy.

WHITETAIL DEER

Illinois and Oklahoma were both well-represented at the 27th Awards Program by two outstanding typical trophies. On the last day of Illinois' 2006 shotgun season, Charles Q. Rives used a one-ounce slug to drop a Greene County buck which scored 198-1/8—the

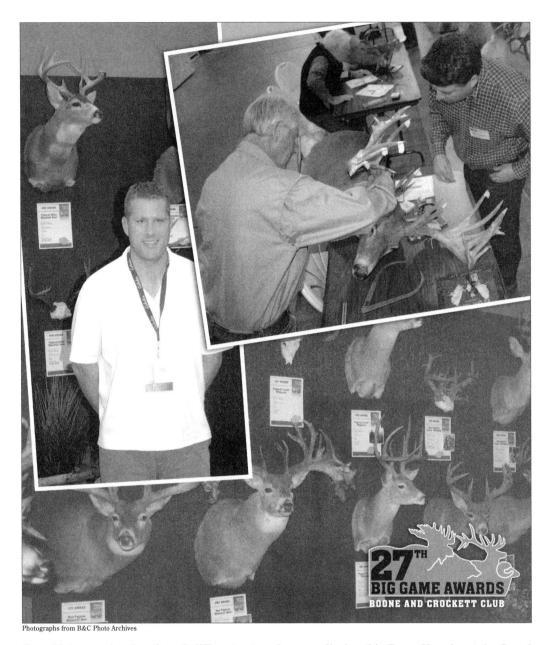

Over 20 top-scoring deer from 9 different categories were displayed in Reno, Nevada, at the Grand Sierra Resort. Judges Panel members Frederick J. King (left) and Richard Hale are shown here measuring Kyle M. Simmons' non-typical whitetail deer, which has a final score of 275-5/8 points. Dan Schulberg stands below the magnificent Sitka blacktail buck taken by his grandfather Arthur Schulberg in Alaska in 1961.

fourth largest ever taken in his state. Jason L. Boyett knew immediately that he would have his 2007 trophy mounted when he walked up to it in tall grass after dropping it with a single shot. His buck scored 192-5/8 points and is Oklahoma's new state record typical.

To give a perspective of the quality of the three non-typical whitetails displayed in Reno, all rank in the top 20 of the 4,242 entries that have been accepted in that category since the Club's current records system began in 1950. Kyle M. Simmons' bow-killed buck taken 2008 in Jackson County scored 275-5/8 and is the fourth-largest ever taken in Iowa. Helgie H. Eymundson had no doubts the massive buck with incredible palmated antlers in his sights in 2007 would make B&C's records book. However, it wasn't until its score was verified by the Judges Panel that it would be recognized as the third-largest non-typical ever taken in Alberta at a score of 274 points. The massive buck (272-2/8) taken by newly appointed B&C Official Measurer Gerald E. Rightmyer in Morris County, Kansas, in 2006 is the largest taken in that state since 1987. It is the second-largest non-typical ever recorded from Kansas.

COUES' DEER

Mexico was apparently the "go-to" place for trophy Coues' deer during the 27th Awards Program. Five of the eight Coues' deer in Reno were taken in Mexico from 2006 to 2009. Most incredible of them all was the non-typical taken by Gary A. Zellner in Sonora in 2009. With a total of 33 scoreable points, it scored 177-1/8. It is Mexico's new No. 1 non-typical and the largest taken since 1971. Zellner's buck is not the buck-of-a-lifetime; it is the buck-of-many-lifetimes.

MOOSE
CANADA MOOSE

British Columbia produced all five of the moose sent to Reno. The largest, scoring 224-6/8 points, was taken in 2008 by Keith A. Grant along the Tatshenshini River. It is the 12th-largest ever taken in North America, and the ninth-largest recorded for that province.

In the same area Grant hunted, Fred E. Dodge took a brace of bulls with a muzzle-loader that scored 220-7/8 and 213-3/8 during the 2009 and 2008 seasons, respectively. They are currently the two-largest Canada moose ever recorded by the Longhunter Society that keeps records of native North American big-game trophies taken with a muzzleloader.

ALASKA-YUKON MOOSE

With racks that can easily weigh 70 pounds, Alaska-Yukon moose are the largest of the three subspecies recognized by the Club. Even its scientific name, *Alces alces gigas*, is an obvious reference to its size. The bull (247-5/8) Craig S. Spencer took in Alaska's Selawik Hills in 2008 is the 17th-largest moose ever recorded and ranks 16th in Alaska.

SHIRAS' MOOSE

While all the trophy Shiras' moose in Reno were spectacular, 15 year old Rylan Rude-busch's was especially exceptional. The fact that there is a huntable moose population in

Photographs from B&C Photo Archives

One of the most impressive components of the 27th Big Game Awards display were the eleven moose trophies representing the three different categories recognized by the Boone and Crockett Club. Pictured above are Fred Dodge's two award-winning Canada moose scoring 213-3/8 (top left) and 220-7/8 (top right). Also shown the Shiras' moose harvested by youth hunter Rylan Rudebusch. Rylan was also recognized at the Generation Next dinner prior to the Awards Banquet.

Colorado is another conservation success story attributable to hunters and the Colorado Division of Wildlife, as they were extinct in Colorado prior to their reintroduction in 1976. Rylan's bull, which he took in Larimer County in 2007, is one of four bulls taken in Colorado that year. At 180-2/8 points, it is the fifth-largest of 60 Colorado bulls entered in B&C since the first one in 1987.

CARIBOU

MOUNTAIN CARIBOU

The most notable mountain caribou was a bull (459-3/8) taken by Paul T. Deuling in the Pelly Mountains, Yukon Territory, in 1988 that received the coveted Sagamore Hill Award. Paul entered his trophy in the 20th Awards Program but was not able to have its score verified by a Judges Panel until 2010. Only a B&C Final Awards Program Judges Panel or a Special Judges Panel can declare a trophy a new World's Record. Upon review of the hunting story by the Judges, it became the 17th trophy awarded the Sagamore Hill Award medal since 1948 when Robert C. Reeve received the first for an Alaska brown bear.

While there have been noticeable declines in a couple of caribou categories in recent years, mountain caribou have been averaging around 46 entries for the last seven Awards Programs. R. Bruce Moon took the finer of the two mountain caribou on display in Reno. Taken in the Mackenzie Mountains, Northwest Territories, in 2007, it scored 422-7/8 points and ties for 38th place on the All-time list.

WOODLAND CARIBOU

Concerned about a dramatic decline in numbers of woodland caribou harvested in Newfoundland during the last few years, the game and fish department has dramatically reduced the number of caribou permits. While the reasons for the decline are not totally apparent, this category was well represented in Reno with four specimens displayed. The bull James C. Johnson took in 2007 at Middle Ridge took the 1st Place Award with a final score of 325-6/8 points. Johnson has made the records book in four of five caribou categories.

BARREN GROUND CARIBOU

Barren ground caribou entries have exhibited the most dramatic reduction of the five different categories. The total number accepted during the 27th Awards Program was 21, including five taken before 1995. That's significantly down from the 147 accepted in the 22nd Awards Program just 18 years ago. The 1st Place Award was presented to Jack L. Wilson for a bull he took on the Seward Peninsula in 2008 that scored 419-4/8. It ranks 270 on the All-time list out of 1,088 in the category.

CENTRAL CANADA BARREN GROUND CARIBOU

The number of trophies accepted for this category in the last three Awards Programs has averaged around 34. This is down from a high of 100 bulls accepted in the 23rd Awards

Photographs from B&C Photo Archives

The caribou pictured above was harvested by James C. Johnson in 2007 took the 1st Place Award with a final score of 325-6/8 points. Johnson has made the records book in four of five caribou categories. There were two bighorn sheep on display in Reno, both harvested by women from Montana. The ram taken by Toni L. Sannon (left) scores 204-2/8 points and Debby L. Perry's bighorn has a final score of 202-7/8 points. Jack Reneau (right), the Club's Director of Big Game Records, visits with trophy owner Art D. Tong. The bison that Tong harvested scores 129-2/8 points.

Program 15 years ago. While the reason for this decline remains a mystery, fish and game authorities in the affected areas have drastically reduced the number of permits. However, Thonokied Lake, Northwest Territories, produced a very respectable bull for Nyla K. Swast in 2006 that scored 396-4/8 points. It is the 18th-largest bull ever recorded since this category originated in 1983.

QUEBEC-LABRADOR CARIBOU

A number of years ago, Quebec-Labrador caribou changed their historic migration pattern and continue to change it every year. Thus, guides and outfitters have a difficult time locating the migrating animals. The number of entries in this category has fluctuated from a low of 23 for the 23rd Awards Program to a high of 60 for the immediate past triennium, the 26th Awards Program. The nicest specimen sent to Reno was a bull that scored 423-6/8 points taken by Bret J. Wood in 2006 near Riviére Du Gué. It currently ranks No. 19 on the All-time list.

HORNED BIG GAME

PRONGHORN

Larry J. Landes' and Michael J. Wheeler's pronghorns are now the second-largest "speed goats" ever taken in each of their respective states of New Mexico and Wyoming. Landes took his buck (91-4/8) in 2006 in Harding County and Wheeler took his (91-2/8) in 2008 in Natrona County.

BISON

Bison probably came closer to extinction than any other native North American big-game animal. And, while their return to huntable populations is another true success story attributable to hunters, they will obviously never again number in the tens of millions that inhabited the Great Plains when Lewis and Clark trekked across North America in 1804. Bison have been restored to huntable numbers in several locations, including 15 areas where they are eligible for listing in B&C. Edward D. Riekens harvested his bull, scoring 133-2/8, from the Teton County, Wyoming, herd in 2007. It ranks No. 7 in B&C's records book. Custer State Park, South Dakota, produced the 15th-largest bull recorded in B&C for Art D. Tong during a hunt in 2007. He carefully looked over several bulls before taking one that scored 129-2/8.

ROCKY MOUNTAIN GOAT

A.C. Smid ended his quest for a record Rocky Mountain goat at Kalum Lake, British Columbia, in 2008 when he took a billy scoring 54 points. It ties for 15th place in British Columbia.

MUSKOX

Muskox populations have expanded incredibly in both Nunavut and Northwest

Territories, Canada, since 1974. Prior to that, only 20 specimens had been recorded in B&C, and most of those were historical records from museums with some dating back to the late 1800s. Since then, 336 trophies have been accepted and the population continues to expand. Tags are $25 each and there is no limit in the number of tags a hunter can purchase. Ben L. Mueller's 2007 muskox received the 1st Place Award and is tied for sixth place of 597 trophies.

Ben L. Mueller's musk ox shown above is the sixth largest out of 597 musk ox trophies accepted by the Club. His bull has a final score of 127 points and was taken near Kugluktuk, Nunavut.

BIGHORN SHEEP

Two spectacular trophies that received great admiration from attendees were a pair of bighorn rams taken by two women in Montana's Missouri Breaks during the 2008 hunting season. Both rams scored over 200 points. Toni L. Sannon's ram, at 204-2/8, is the largest bighorn ever taken by a woman, and it ranks No. 2 in Montana and No. 8 in North America. Debbie L. Perry's ram, at 202-7/8, is the third-largest ram ever taken by a woman. Her ram ranks No. 4 in Montana and No. 10 in North America.

STONE'S SHEEP

Don South's No. 1 priority for nearly 10 years and several hunts was to harvest a trophy Stone's sheep that made B&C's records book. His efforts were rewarded in 2008 when he tagged an incredible ram near the Stikine River in British Columbia. At 180-4/8 points, it is the largest of its kind taken in the last 18 years and was recognized with the 1st Place Award in Reno.

As you can see from the synopsis above, hunters/conservationists have a lot to be proud of since Boone and Crockett Club was founded in 1887. The 27th Awards Program was a resounding success from start to finish because of Theodore Roosevelt, early Club members, and their successors' support of conservation efforts in North America with blood, sweat, tears, and dollars. Our generation is reaping the rewards of their and subsequent conservationists' work. As a result, we are actually now living "the good old days." However, sportsmen and sportswomen can't rest on their laurels. There are many new and difficult challenges to face right now and in the foreseeable future. ▲

ABOUT THE AUTHORS

Eldon L. "Buck" Buckner is the current Vice President of Big Game Records and Chairman of the Boone and Crockett Club's Records of North American Big Game Committee. First appointed an Official Measurer in 1968 while serving as a U.S. Forest Service range conservationist in Arizona, Buck has served as Judges Panel Chairman, Consultant, and Judge for Boone and Crockett Club's Awards Programs since 1989. He is also a co-founder and member of the board of directors of the Jack O'Connor Hunting Heritage and Education Center in Lewiston, Idaho. He is also the Oregon State Director for the NRA Youth Hunter Education Challenge Program.

Jack Reneau is a certified wildlife biologist and the director of big-game records for the Boone and Crockett Club, a position he has held since January of 1983. He holds a B.S. in wildlife management from Colorado State University and a M.S. in wildlife management from Eastern Kentucky University. He was responsible for the day-to-day paperwork of the Boone and Crockett Club's records-keeping program from 1976 through 1979 as a hunter information specialist for the Hunter Services Division of the National Rifle Association (NRA) when NRA and the Boone and Crockett Club cosponsored the North American Big Game Awards Program, as it was known during that time. He is the co-author of the book, *Colorado's Biggest Bucks and Bulls*, and the co-editor of and/or contributor to 40 Boone and Crockett Club books and publications. He has also written a column, titled "Trophy Talk," for Fair Chase magazine and its predecessors since 1986.

AWARD-WINNING TROPHY STORIES

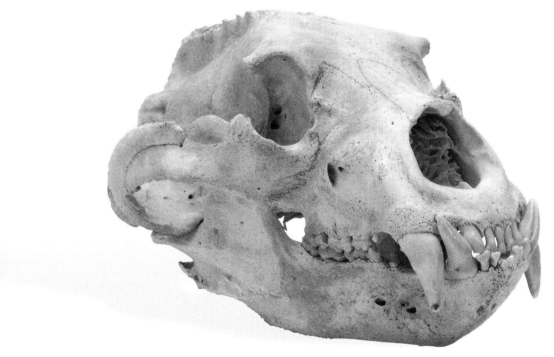

TROPHY STATS
▼ ▼ ▼ ▼ ▼

CATEGORY
Black Bear

SCORE
$22^{13}/_{16}$

SKULL LENGTH
$14^{1}/_{16}$

SKULL WIDTH
$8^{12}/_{16}$

LOCATION
Riding Mt., Manitoba – 2008

HUNTER
Robert J. Evans

BLACK BEAR
1st Award – 22 ¹³/₁₆

▼ ▼ ▼ ▼ ▼ ▼ ▼ ▼

ROBERT J. EVANS

Spring is my favorite time for bear hunting. The rut is on, the biggest bears do most of the mating, and hides are in pristine condition.

Every year I do my annual pilgrimage to E&D Outfitters of Olha, Manitoba, and this year was no different. It was a great and uneventful trip to camp, full of anticipation that doesn't seem to diminish over time.

While driving to camp, I recalled a trip to E&D where a hot little sow came in on the second day with a big boar—the biggest trophy bear I have ever taken. He followed her

Photograph courtesy of Robert J. Evans

Robert J. Evans harvested this award-winning black bear from the same stand he had taken another trophy bear just two years earlier. Evans' bear, which scores 22-13/16 points, received a First Place Award at the Club's 27th Big Game Awards Program in Reno, Nevada.

in and when he presented the shot, he took the carbon arrow like a champ. That was in 2006. The big boar weighed in at 630 pounds and officially scored 21-15/16 points, which currently ties him for 21st place in Pope and Young's trophy list. He currently ranks 135 of 2,489 black bears listed in B&C's records book.

Two years later, in 2008, it was much the same—a nice, uneventful trip to camp full of anticipation. Again on the evening of day two at the same stand, a hot sow came through the brush and behind her was another giant. It was, in the immortal words of Yogi Berra, "like déjà vu all over again." The brush parted like the Red Sea as the big boar followed his quest for that special moment.

> IT WAS, IN THE IMMORTAL WORDS OF YOGI BERRA, "LIKE DÉJÀ VU ALL OVER AGAIN." THE BRUSH PARTED LIKE THE RED SEA AS THE BIG BOAR FOLLOWED HIS QUEST FOR THAT SPECIAL MOMENT.

Unfortunately, that moment never came to fruition. The sow brought the big brute past my stand twice, but I didn't have a shot either time, at least not an ethical one. I watched them disappear for the second time into the thick brush.

Then, 10 minutes later, she appeared in the two-track leading to the stand. The big boar was in pursuit. I watched the brush parting again as he walked through it, his hulking frame snapping twigs and branches.

I readied myself, came to full draw, and held my breath. It seemed like a week before he stepped out onto the two-track, but step out he did, giving me a broadside shot at 24 yards. The arrow struck true, and 60 yards later I laid my hands on the new Manitoba archery record black bear and P&Y's new No. 2 All-time archery record. He weighed in at 615 pounds, and after final drying and official measuring, he scored 22-13/16 inches.

What an amazing run over a short span—two trophy bears in P&Y's top 20 with bow and arrow; two full-body mounted black bears from the same stand only two years apart; and 1,245 pounds of bear. It just doesn't get any better than this! ▲

Award-Winning Moments

B&C Photo Archives

Dr. James H. "Red" Duke exiting stage right after accepting the sponsorship recognition award for the Wild Sheep Foundation. Red is past president of both the Boone and Crockett Club and Wild Sheep Foundation.

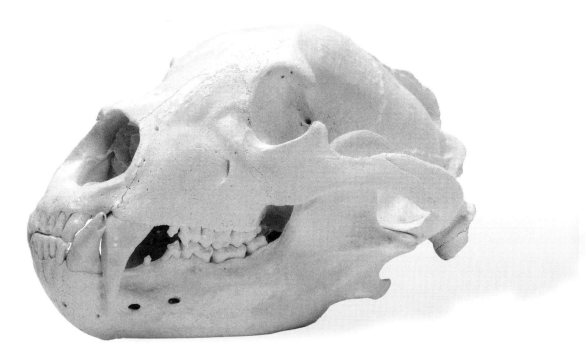

TROPHY STATS

▼ ▼ ▼ ▼ ▼

CATEGORY
Black Bear

SCORE
$22^{11}/_{16}$

SKULL LENGTH
14

SKULL WIDTH
$8^{11}/_{16}$

LOCATION
Lehigh Co., Pennsylvania – 1997

HUNTER
Joseph W. Paulo

BLACK BEAR
2nd Award (Tie) - 22 $^{11}/_{16}$

▼ ▼ ▼ ▼ ▼ ▼ ▼ ▼ ▼

JOSEPH W. PAULO

A little bit of sacrifice during the three-day black bear season in 1997 paid huge dividends to Joseph W. Paulo—685 pounds worth—when the New Tripoli, Pennsylvania, resident harvested one of the largest bears ever taken in the southeastern region of the state.

Paulo, who works for AmeriCold in Fogelsville, shot the large bear around 7:45 a.m., just a few hours after he had gotten off work.

"This Is Unbelievable"

The Carbon County native explains he had worked from 5-11 a.m. on Sunday, then came home and was awake all day. He said he went back at "8 p.m. and worked until 4:30 a.m., so I could have Monday off."

Paulo and two friends, Glenn Wright of Lansdale, Montgomery County, and Jim Walsh of Slatington had decided to hunt State Game land 217 near Leaser Lake in Lynn Township. After making their way along the Appalachian Trail for a mile or so, the three men stopped to discuss what they were going to do.

Paulo said to the guys, "I'm going straight down, down to the base of the mountain." About halfway down Paulo noticed a big black ball.

"As I got closer it stood up on all four legs."

He fired one shot from his .300 Winchester Magnum before the bruin took off.

"It looked like I never even hit the bear. The bear turned to its right and started running, and I put another shot in the left side, a foot and a half behind the shoulder." Paulo lost sight of the animal after it ran through some vines and briars, but he only had to trail it about 40 yards before the two met up again.

"The bear stood up on its hind legs with its back toward me," recalls Paulo looking up at the bear, just 10-15 feet away. "If it was going to turn and look at me, I was going to plug it again."

Fortunately, the bear fell over and Paulo used one more well-placed shot to keep the bear down for good.

Even then, the 33-year old knew he'd taken a fairly large bruin. "I was like, 'this is unbelievable.' I never thought in my life I'd shoot a bear in Pennsylvania, and to get a big bear like this one is incredible."

Pennsylvania's black bear population, which was estimated at around 8,500 animals prior to the 1997 season, has been expanding over the past few decades into new areas, including the southeastern and southwestern portions of the state. The first bear ever killed in Lehigh County was taken five years earlier. Since then, the annual bear harvest ranged from zero to five animals.

On the following Wednesday, Lehigh County wildlife conservation officer Michael Beahm said he was aware of four being taken in the county in 1997. "I know that three of them came from Lynn Township behind Leaser Lake," he said.

> **"THEY TOOK IT OFF THE TRUCK WITH A FORKLIFT AND WEIGHED IT," PAULO RECALLS. OFFICIALS ALSO PULLED A TOOTH AND CHECKED TAGS THAT WERE IN THE ANIMAL'S EARS. BEAHM SAYS THE BEAR WAS TAGGED BY BIOLOGIST GARY ALT ABOUT A MONTH AND A HALF EARLIER AT HAWK MOUNTAIN. "THEY TOLD ME HIS NAME WAS 'BUBBA' AND IT WAS A PROBLEM BEAR IN THE PAST," PAULO RECALLED, NOTING THE ANIMAL ALSO HAD A TATTOO INSIDE ITS LIP.**

Once the large bear was down, the three men still had the long, hard job of getting it out of the woods ahead of them. Paulo says he didn't field dress the animal because he was unsure of the regulations. "We actually rolled it until it got to the bottom where it was level," he said.

Wright and Paulo did the actual dragging, while Walsh helped out by carrying the equipment and guns. Once on the truck, the bear was taken to the Pennsylvania Game Commission's Southeast Regional Office near Reading where it was officially checked in by PGC staff.

"They took it off the truck with a forklift and weighed it," Paulo recalls. Officials also pulled a tooth and checked tags that were in the animal's ears. Beahm says the bear was tagged by biologist Gary Alt about a month and a half earlier at Hawk Mountain.

"They told me his name was 'Bubba' and it was a problem bear in the past," Paulo recalled, noting the animal also had a tattoo inside its lip.

After he got home, Paulo made arrangements with Dave Gazzara, a Breinigsville taxidermist, to create a life-sized mount of the bruin. And while he may have been dead-tired by Monday night, it's a safe bet that Paulo was glad he buckled down and forced himself to get into work the previous day. ▲

Story by correspondent Mark Demko of The Express-Times *is reproduced here with permission with some editing to update it.*

Moments in Measuring

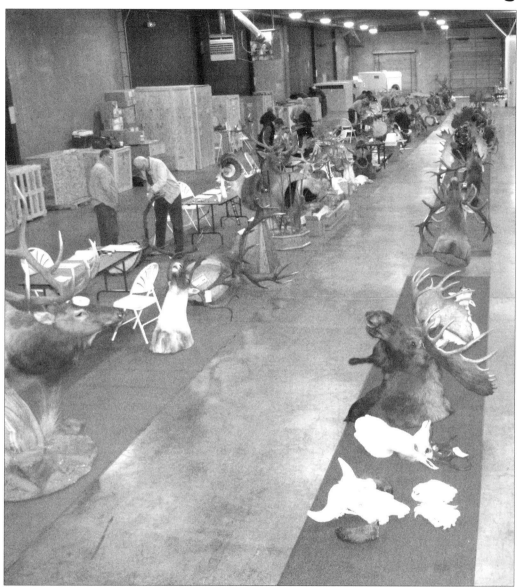

B&C Photo Archives

Boone and Crockett Club Regular Member Robert M. Lee generously gave B&C permission to use one of his warehouses to receive, score, and store trophies invited to the 27th Awards Program activities. The trophies are lined up here and ready to be measured by the Judges Panel. All trophies were measured twice to finalize their score. The Judges then certified them for B&C medallions and certificates.

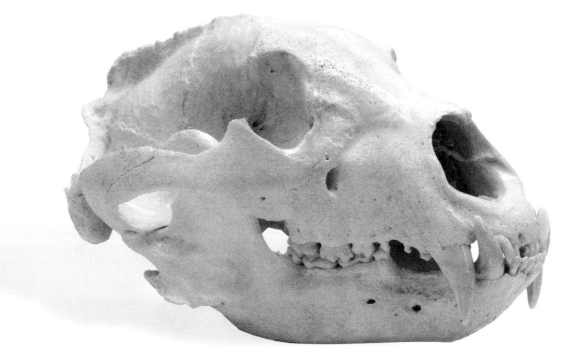

TROPHY STATS

▼ ▼ ▼ ▼ ▼

CATEGORY
Black Bear

SCORE
$22^{11}/_{16}$

SKULL LENGTH
14

SKULL WIDTH
$8^{11}/_{16}$

LOCATION
Newaygo Co., Michigan – 2009

HUNTER
Donald R. Corrigan

BLACK BEAR
2nd Award (Tie) - 22 ¹¹/₁₆

▼ ▼ ▼ ▼ ▼ ▼ ▼ ▼ ▼

DONALD R. CORRIGAN

If you told the residents of Newaygo County, Michigan, that they had a population of 300-400 bears living in their woods, most of them would not believe you. I have hunted in the county my entire life and had never seen a bear. When the Michigan Department of Natural Resources (DNR) decided to open a bear season in our area, which is just 20 miles north of Grand Rapids, I was skeptical. The lure of being the first hunter to take a "local" bear intrigued me. After looking at the DNR research and possible hunting areas, I applied, and applied, and applied. After nine seasons, I finally drew a permit.

With my permit in hand, I called my good friend Mike Perrin, the first person to take a bear in the county, to find out if he knew of any big bears in the area. Turns out he had trail camera pictures of a large bear that had been on his 40 acres for the last two years. He said that with a week of baiting, we should be in luck.

Opening day is always exciting, whether it's for deer, elk, or bear. My ten-year-old son Jake was going to accompany me on opening day, and we could hardly wait. The first night out we had a big bear come to our bait, but it was well after legal hunting hours. The next three days were the same. We saw bears, but they always came in too late. On the fifth night out, Jake suggested we put "bear bomb" scent on the bait pile. He had seen it mentioned on TV, and was confident it would work.

We were hunting in a swampy, wet, wooded area, and the bear suddenly appeared without a sound. I don't remember pulling the trigger when the bear was within 30 yards, but I was confident it was a good shot as the animal crashed away through the swamp. Our hearts were pounding so hard it was almost surreal; it all happened so fast. After waiting in the blind for about 30 minutes, Jake and I walked over to where the bear was standing when I fired to see if we could find any sign. Following a futile search, darkness was fast approaching, so we

Photograph by Jack Reneau

Donald R. Corrigan accepting his plaque and medal from Buck Buckner, Vice President and Chairman of the Big Game Records Committee.

Photograph courtesy of Donald R. Corrigan

Donald R. Corrigan and his son with his award-winning black bear taken in Newaygo County, Michigan, during the 2009 season. Corrigan's bear, which scores 22-11/16 tied for a Second Place Award at the 27th Big Game Awards Program in Reno, Nevada.

went back to the truck and called Mike Perrin for help.

Mike arrived after dark with lights and lanterns. We headed into the swamp and found the bear's trail right away.

I looked at Mike and said, "You baited the bear, so you go first."

He said, "You shot it, so you go first."

After about two minutes on our hands and knees pushing through the heavy undergrowth, pistols in hand, Jake's fear got the best of him and he decided to wait in the truck. Mike and I continued to track the bear and found him 30 yards from where he was shot. A bear's size is hard to judge, but this one looked huge. It took more than three hours to get him in the truck.

Jake was very excited and was sure I had shot a new World's Record. Both of us had a hard time sleeping that night. The next day we checked the bear at the local department of natural resources station. The big boar was 7.5 years old and field dressed at 500 pounds. His estimated live weight was over 600 pounds. The bear wasn't a World's Record like Jake had hoped, but with a skull measurement of 22-12/16, he was the second largest bear ever shot in Michigan. I have a lot of great hunting memories so far in my life, but to be able to take such a quality bear in my hometown with my son tops them all. Jake and I will never forget that cool, cloudy September 22, 2009 night. It truly was a hunt of a lifetime. ▲

Award-Winning Moments

Simon Roosevelt presents Buck Knives' president and CEO, C.J. Buck, with a sponsor recognition plaque during the Awards Banquet ceremony. This is the first year Buck Knives participated in an Awards event. C.J. Buck was also the emcee and sponsor of the Generation Next Youth Awards Banquet held the previous night.

TROPHY STATS
▼ ▼ ▼ ▼ ▼

CATEGORY
Grizzly Bear

SCORE
27³/₁₆

SKULL LENGTH
16¹³/₁₆

SKULL WIDTH
10⁶/₁₆

LOCATION
Unalakleet River, Alaska – 2009

HUNTER
Rodney W. Debias

GRIZZLY BEAR
1st Award – 27-3/16

▼ ▼ ▼ ▼ ▼ ▼ ▼ ▼ ▼

RODNEY W. DEBIAS

As the midnight sun inches its way along the horizon, a luminous glow engulfs the tundra, more beautiful than any tropical sunset I have ever seen. A shadow appears, which quickly manifests itself in the shape of a gigantic bruin. I whisper to my guide, "Bear. Don, there is a bear."

As we quickly move into position, Don ranges it at 385 yards. As I'm tightening my release strap, Don softly states, "It's the big

The Pinnacle

guy." He's now at 175 yards. We kneel on the soft, dried grass surrounded by driftwood that had washed deep onto the tundra by storm surges, giving us ample cover. I am in front, and Don is so close behind me I can feel his elbow touching my shoulder. With his right hand he continues to range and with his left hand over my left shoulder, we wind-check with a squeeze bottle of white powder. Don mumbles, "Look at that noggin."

I reply, "Just keep ranging. I'm gong to let him walk past us before I draw. If I draw now, he's going to see me."

The moment is almost here. The culmination of a lifetime of dreaming and after nearly a half dozen other grizzly hunts, I ask myself, *Is this finally happening?*

This saga started when I was a very young boy and my dad gave me his Bear Grizzly recurve. I started shooting it seriously when I was 11 years old. After a couple years, the limb split, so I mowed a gentleman's lawn for a full summer and the man paid me with an old fiberglass Ben Pearson bow, both of which I have today. After that bow came a $99 Bear Whitetail. I was 15, and my best friend Lou Mihalko and I painted his grandmother's house for—you guessed it—$100 each. I have since been addicted to archery hunting.

My goal since childhood was to take a

Photograph by Jack Reneau

Rodney W. Debias accepting his plaque and medal from Buck Buckner, Vice President and Chairman of the Big Game Records Committee.

Photograph courtesy of Rodney W. Debias

Rodney W. Debias (right) and his guide sit behind his award-winning grizzly bear taken near Unalakleet River in Alaska during the 2009 season. His bear, which scores 27-3/16 inches, received a First Place Award at the 27th Big Game Awards Program in Reno, Nevada.

grizzly with a bow. I have been fortunate enough to have taken many nice animals, including a very nice brown bear several years ago. The grizzly, however, eluded me almost to the point of conceding.

After months of talking with my booking agent about hunts, the question finally presented itself. Sheep hunt? Moose hunt? Elk hunt?

The consultant said, "How about the grizzly. I have an outfitter, Hunt Alaska, owned by Vergil Umpanour and his son Eric. They will not only take bowhunters for grizzly, but they actually want them."

After booking, the game planning was underway. I started to collect my gear. The weather could be 70°F one day and 0°F the next, so my equipment had to be versatile. I scheduled shoulder surgery in September to fix bone spurs that had developed from sports and drawing heavyweight bows. After Christmas, I would start shooting. The cold and windy days were the ones I would shoot on the most to get used to shooting with heavy clothes under all conditions.

May soon rolled around, and I found myself on a plane landing in Unalakleet. I couldn't figure out why anyone would want to live in this barren, unforgiving land. After a short time, we were on a snowmobile headed for camp. The hunters were Jaun, Bruce, Randy, and me. Vergil, Eric, Don, and Shawn were our guides. Also, we had a 14-year old camp helper named Shiler who had as many outdoor skills as anyone I have ever met. Shiler's uncle Paul joined us later.

GRIZZLY BEAR
1st Award – 27 $^3/_{16}$

▼ ▼ ▼ ▼ ▼

RODNEY W. DEBIAS

Camp was set up miles short of the area we wanted to hunt, as weather conditions would not allow passage of boats or snowmobiles. Each of us was assigned a guide and mine was Don Stiles.

Day 1: As we left camp and Don and I got to know each other, I informed him that I would be the easiest hunter he ever had.

"I will not question your ability and you will not need to question my heart. I have done my best to get in shape, and I'll hunt 24 hours a day if we can." Believe me when I say that my ability and endurance would both be tested. For two days Don and I pushed further and further from camp.

Day 3: 5:30 a.m. Don spotted a bear as we were glassing on high ground while heading back to camp. The bear was 300 yards away, coming right to us. It was almost too easy. The wind was blowing from the east. The bear was coming north. But as the big bruin closed, the wind started moving southeast. Don ranged him at 69 yards, and the wind was now on the right side of my neck blowing right towards the bear—bad news! He stopped, turned, and ran. We watched him, with the grace of a racehorse, run across the same tundra we could barely walk across.

We shouldered our heavy packs and headed back to camp. When we crossed the track of the running bear, Don noticed the front right paw had blood on the middle toe and remarked that the bear must have cut it on a rock or another bear bit him. This track would identify him in the days ahead.

Upon arriving at camp, we learned the ice blew out and boats were able to make it to the next camp. However, Don and I would stay. We were left a tent, supplies, and a Zodiac (a small inflatable boat and motor). After a nap, followed by pancakes and bacon, we inflated the Zodiac and boated up the coast several miles where we eventually beached it on a small stream that emptied into Norton Sound.

Day 4: 1:30 a.m. Don spotted a beautiful blonde bear 600 yards away. I noticed another, this one about 100 yards below Blondie. Don guessed the blonde to be 7.5 feet, the other one at 7 feet. Either would be a trophy in anybody's book. As we watched them, a huge chocolate bear appeared and ran between them. He dwarfed them as if they were Honda Civics and he was a Mack truck. As all three bears ran off, I said to Don, "If they were 7 and 7.5 feet, how big is he?"

Don said, "I don't know what to say—8 feet, maybe more. I don't know what to say. I mean, I just never seen anything like him. At any rate, he's gone now."

Day 5: Brought us to within 100 yards of a huge bear sleeping on the tundra with his squeeze, Blondie. We tried to make a stalk but the wind was not in our favor. At that point, you know how tightly wound your guide is when he doesn't slide his rifle to you and say, "Take him," knowing he would have guided a top 10 Boone and Crockett grizzly. We simply slipped out of there.

Day 6: As morning came, Don said we better check the sea, as the wind changed and ice may be blowing back in. He was right. The ice was half a mile from us and moving fast. We were out of food and would be unable to make it back to camp. Don said, "Let's pump up the Zodiac and make a run for town." So, we loaded our gear, pumped, and pushed off into the rough sea. The waves were tossing us left and right, and the crushing ice pack was pushing its way closer and closer to the boat. Don said if the ice catches us, it will crush us. But if it doesn't, the sea is calmer near the ice and he could speed up. I decided to get the life vests ready and only saw one. Don said the other was under his backpack. I tried to pull it out as he grinned and said he did not need it. "Up here, we call those body bags. You'll freeze to death long before you make the shore. Vests just make it easier for them to find the bodies."

Thankfully, Don proved to be very skilled in reading the waves, and we eventually made our way to Unalakleet.

Upon arriving, Don used his satellite phone and called his cousin Middy to pick us up. Middy fed us, gave us supplies and drove us to high ground to check the amount of ice that blew into shore. We were iced in as far as the eye could see. Middy suggested taking his and his brother Paul's snow machines along the coast and then packing our way back to the happy hunting grounds. The days ahead would be very cold, with 25 mph winds to the north and not a single bear track

Day 8: 1 a.m. Don was so tired, I could have poked him in the eye and he wouldn't have blinked. After a good bit of convincing, he finally said he would take a nap. As Don slept, I glassed several miles of tundra again and again. At 2:50, I noticed something running towards us. I woke Don and we realized it was two wolves hunting. What a sight. They came to within 25 yards and never knew we were there.

After they left, I was thinking, Three days without cutting a track is just too long. *We need a new plan.* So I suggested to Don we move to another area. Three days without cutting a track is just too long. Just as Don began to nod his head in agreement, I whispered, "Bear. Don, there's a bear."

I immediately assumed a shooting position. Don ranged him, saying, "He's the big guy."

As the giant approached, I whispered to Don to range a small stick in front of me. Don Softly replied "17 yards." I think he's coming to that stick, but there's not enough cover to draw. I made the decision to let him pass me, a tough call, but I felt certain he would spot me if I drew.

He came closer and closer. When he reached the stick, he was 17 yards away and getting closer.

GRIZZLY BEAR
1st Award – 27 ³/₁₆

▼ ▼ ▼ ▼ ▼

RODNEY W. DEBIAS

At 10 yards, he suddenly stops. He raises his nose. His nostrils flare, and I can hear him draw a deep breath. He exhales, and I can smell him. He draws another breath, this time curling his lips outward. I'm amazed at his size. He exhales again. I smell him. He knows something is up. With the wind at my nose, I know he cannot smell us. It must be a sixth sense. He takes two steps, stands straight up and looks down on us. With my bow on my knee at rest, I think, *Shoot him with the gun, Don!* Just as quickly as the thought entered my mind, he turns his head and looks the other way. Flabbergasted, relieved, and now determined, I say to myself, "He doesn't know where we are, and I'm going to get him." He drops down on all fours and begins to walk past us. I watch his eye. When I can no longer see his eye, I know he can't see me.

I draw. He pauses, and then continues to walk. For the third and final time in less than a minute he has abandoned that sixth sense that served him well for so many years. He stops, perfectly broadside. I'd really like to watch him more, but I don't know if there's time.

Don whispers, "29 yards." I center the peep on my outer sight ring and place my 30-yard pin just behind the shadow of his right shoulder. I squeeze my release trigger. The arrow flies true, the nock glowing as the arrow penetrates his chest. He growls, bites at the wound, turns, and runs. He only makes it a short distance before falling hard. I nock another arrow and ask Don to range him. "Sixty yards."

I adjust my sight and say, "Don, brace our binoculars on my shoulder. If he's breathing, I'm going to shoot again." Don replied, "He's already dead Rod, you did it!" While photographing the bear, we noticed a cut on his right paw. Turns out, he was the bear that had busted us on day three.

This would be the pinnacle of any hunter's life. However, it wasn't the trophy that made this hunt so memorable for me. During the fifth day, on what could be considered the low point of the hunt, I decided this was my favorite adventure because of the other hunters, Vergil and Eric Umpenhour, and Don. My appreciation would continue to grow as I would get to know the people of Unalakleet. William "Middy" Johnson (whose grandfather was one of the original mushers on the serum run to Nome, now known as the Iditarod) who, in his grandfather's memory, was planning to (and did) complete the 2010 Iditarod (He finished 33ʳᵈ). His entire family: his wife and children, brother Paul, Shawn, John, and so many others. What they have is so special.

When everything has you down, and you think there is no good in the world, buy a plane ticket to Unalakleet and walk down the dirt street lined with humble homes. Strangers will invite you into their homes to enjoy their best fish and share stories of their culture, and expect in return, only that you share stories of your own. The people of Unalakleet are the most wonderful, giving people I have ever met. ▲

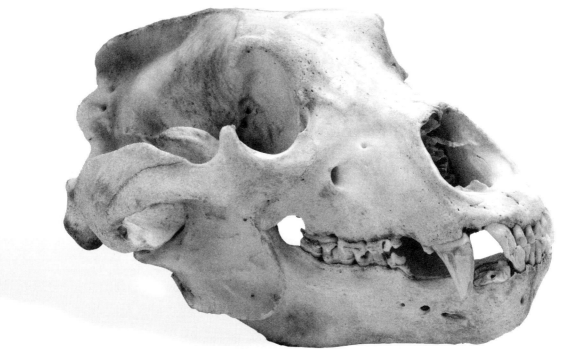

TROPHY STATS

▼ ▼ ▼ ▼ ▼

CATEGORY
  Grizzly Bear

SCORE
  $26^4/_{16}$

SKULL LENGTH
  $16^2/_{16}$

SKULL WIDTH
  $10^2/_{16}$

LOCATION
  Stikine River, British Columbia – 2007

HUNTER
  Blaine E. Nelson

GRIZZLY BEAR
Second Award – 26 4/16

▼ ▼ ▼ ▼ ▼ ▼ ▼ ▼ ▼

BLAINE E. NELSON

It was late September 2007 when I accompanied my dad, Clifford, brother Brandon, and Uncle Dennis on what was my second big bear hunt. After a long, cramped 14-hour drive in one truck with four grown men, we arrived at our destination. This, however, was only the starting point available for what would be an all-day boat ride to our undisclosed location on the Stikine River.

The Big Bear Hunt

The weather was against us from the moment we launched our boat. It started to rain, which would prove relentless throughout our hunt. After a very long, wet boat ride, we reached what would be our home for the next ten days and set up camp. We ate what would have to pass for supper that night and crawled into bed.

The following days proved to be more of the same routine, wake up, eat breakfast, and start trekking through the backcountry trying to navigate the much-detested devil's club. We spent our days searching along the maze of zigzagging streams and creeks, tracking, with no success, the occasional bear sign we came across. We would take the boat out every couple days, hoping to find that magic spot, but really just being satisfied with a break from the horrendous devil's club. Our nights were spent around the campfire listening to the tall tales of the older men—while pretending that we weren't sitting in the rain soaking wet—and enjoying every minute of it.

The day I took my bear was near the end of our hunt. When we awoke that morn-

ONCE WE RETURNED TO CAMP, WE DECIDED TO TRY OUR LUCK AT FISHING THAT NIGHT, HOPING THAT IF WE CAUGHT SOME FISH WE AT LEAST WOULDN'T GO HOME EMPTY-HANDED. WE GRABBED OUR RODS AND GUNS AND HEADED TO ONE OF THE MANY CREEKS IN OUR AREA TO LOOK FOR A GOOD FISHING HOLE. AFTER A WHILE, I HEARD SPLASHING IN THE CREEK AHEAD.

ing, it was the same routine with no mystic feelings that day would be any different than previous days. We ate breakfast, cleaned up camp, and prepared to face the daily tortures of the devil's club.

That day we had decided to explore an area where we hadn't yet been. We spent all day hiking in the new territory and came across nothing but a few tracks. A little disappointed, we decided the new spot was not the right one to find a bear, so we headed back to camp.

Once we returned to camp, we decided to try our luck at fishing that night, hoping that if we caught some fish we at least wouldn't go home empty-handed. We grabbed our rods and guns and headed to one of the many creeks in our area to look for a good fishing hole. After a while, I heard splashing in the creek ahead. We snuck through the willows and devil's club ahead until the creek came into view, and then we saw him. We were all fairly excited to come across a bear, and then it started to sink in that he was a fairly good-sized bear!

He was frolicking in the creek, catching fish for supper and had not yet noticed us. After a brief discussion on the best shot placement, I used my .338 Winchester Magnum to quickly finish the job.

It was still pouring rain, and although we were excited about the kill, we were not looking forward to the long process of field dressing my bear in the rain. It wasn't until we were examining the bear and getting ready to dress him out that we realized he may be a record bear. That thought helped to block out the rain.

It never stopped raining during that hunt, and we couldn't escape the devil's club. But it was all worth it to be able to come away from a hunt with my first records-book animal and tall tales I don't have to make up. ▲

B&C Photo Archives

Boone and Crockett Club hosted its first Youth Recognition Banquet for 16-year-old or younger hunters with a trophy accepted in the 27th Awards Program. Sixteen of the 73 youths invited to Reno attended the festivities with their families, and 14 of them displayed their trophies. All were recognized for their unique accomplishment at such a young age. Here, one of the youths checks out the youth trophy display.

TROPHY STATS

▼ ▼ ▼ ▼ ▼

CATEGORY
Grizzly Bear

SCORE
$26^2/_{16}$

SKULL LENGTH
$16^1/_{16}$

SKULL WIDTH
$10^1/_{16}$

LOCATION
Nulato Hills, Alaska – 2009

HUNTER
Eugene F. Segrest

GRIZZLY BEAR
Third Award – 26 ²/₁₆

▼ ▼ ▼ ▼ ▼ ▼ ▼ ▼

Eugene F. Segrest

In 2008 my son Caleb and I, along with some friends, experienced a wonderful and successful grizzly hunt in Alaska's Talkeetna Mountains. On that trip, both Caleb and his friend shot nice grizzlies. Caleb, my friend Bob Corcoran and I decided to rebook another grizzly hunt with Lance Kronberger in 2009.

On June 5, 2009, Caleb, Bob, and I boarded a plane headed north from Dallas to Alaska. We arrived in Anchorage that afternoon

A Real Brute

and stopped at the historic Millennium Alaskan Hotel. We enjoyed a good meal and viewed all of the incredible mounts. After a sleepless night, we headed to the airport and caught a

Photograph courtesy of Eugene F. Segrest

Eugene F. Segrest with his award-winning grizzly bear taken in Nulato Hills, Alaska, during the 2009 season. Segrest's bear, which scores 26-2/16, received a Third Place Award at the 27th Big Game Awards Program in Reno, Nevada.

plane to Unalakleet. After arriving, we trimmed down our packs even further and waited for the flight into hunting country. We headed out in mid-afternoon and landed on a flat ridge on one of the Nulato Hills. Considering the hiking that we had done during the hunt the year before, I was glad to see that we would be working from the top down rather than from the bottom up. When we arrived, we found that Lance, Shane, and Johnny had the tents and camp already set up.

After greetings and unpacking our gear, we hiked a short distance from camp to shoot our guns to make sure they were still on target. After a couple of verification shots, we headed back to camp, grabbed our spotting scopes and binoculars and headed to the nearest vantage point to glass and pass the afternoon while waiting to start our hunt the next day. That evening we saw five or six bears in the distance as well as one old bull musk ox, my first time to see a musk ox in the wild. What an incredible animal! Plus the scenery was truly awesome. We could see the blue thread of a river in the distance, surrounded by picturesque mountains. Breathtaking! Late that evening we saw a boar and a sow about a mile and a half away. Everyone became very excited, as you could see that it was a huge bear. Lance asked if Bob and I had decided who would take first shot. We had not, so Lance flipped a coin. I called tails and, lo and behold, I won. Little did I know how important that coin flip would become.

EVER SINCE I WAS A YOUNG BOY READING *OUTDOOR LIFE*, I HAVE DREAMED OF GOING ON A GRIZZLY HUNT IN ALASKA. MY DREAM FINALLY CAME TRUE. I AM THANKFUL THAT I HAD THE OPPORTUNITY TO EXPERIENCE SUCH AN AWESOME HUNT FOR SUCH A MAJESTIC ANIMAL IN SUCH GRAND COUNTRY. AT THE SAME TIME I WAS ABLE TO SHARE THIS EXPERIENCE WITH MY SON AND ONE OF MY DEAREST FRIENDS, ALONG WITH A FANTASTIC PROFESSIONAL GROUP OF GUIDES.

After glassing for a couple of hours, catching up on the previous year's activities and sharing our latest and greatest jokes, the lack of sleep caught up to us. We headed back to the tent to grab a bite, then catch some sleep. After a short, sleepless night dreaming of big bears, Lance stuck his head in the tent and said it was time to get up. We dressed, ate a quick breakfast, packed our bags, grabbed our rain gear, and headed to a preselected spot to start glassing.

Soon we spotted the big bear again. The huge boar and a sow were about three quarters of a mile from where we had seen them the day before. The fog and drizzle, compared to the beautiful sunshiny day we'd enjoyed the day before, made visibility difficult but didn't dampen our enthusiasm. We grabbed our packs and rifles and headed out to find that big bear.

After about a three-hour hike, Lance, Shane, Bob, and I hiked down from the mountaintop and onto a sloping tundra flat. I didn't think we would be able to get much closer to our quarry, but Lance kept finding little depressions where we were hidden from sight. Caleb and Johnny stayed higher up on the mountain to watch the scene unfold through waves of drizzle and fog. Lance, Shane, Bob, and I crept as near as we could get without spooking the bears, then set up for a shot.

GRIZZLY BEAR
Third Award – 26²/₁₆
▼ ▼ ▼ ▼ ▼

Eugene F. Segrest

Both animals were about 350 yards away, quartering toward us. I dropped my pack and got into position. I was shooting a Remington 300 Winchester Magnum, with Federal Premium® 180-grain bullets. After what seemed like an eternity, the boar wandered to within 250 yards. I took steady aim and squeezed off a round that passed through the front shoulders.

The boar began spinning, but, after a couple of excited shots, the big bear was down for good and I was shaking from excitement. As we approached the bear, I realized what a monster he was.

The bear's hide was beautiful. To date, I have not received the animal's age from game and fish, but Lance guessed he was an old bear, given his size and the condition of his teeth, a couple of which were missing. He measured nine feet four inches, a real brute! After pictures and skinning, we all headed back to camp for food and sleep. What a day!

Ever since I was a young boy reading *Outdoor Life*, I have dreamed of going on a grizzly hunt in Alaska. My dream finally came true. I am thankful that I had the opportunity to experience such an awesome hunt for such a majestic animal in such grand country. At the same time I was able to share this experience with my son and one of my dearest friends, along with a fantastic professional group of guides. By the way, Bob shot a beautiful eight footer two days later. ▲

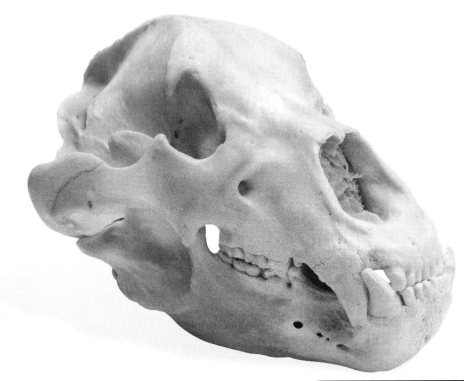

TROPHY STATS

▼ ▼ ▼ ▼ ▼

CATEGORY
  Alaska Brown Bear

SCORE
  29⁹/₁₆

SKULL LENGTH
  17¹⁴/₁₆

SKULL WIDTH
  11¹¹/₁₆

LOCATION
  Uganik Lake, Alaska – 2006

HUNTER
  Robert J. Castle

Photograph by Jack Reneau

Robert J. Castle accepting his plaque
and medal from Buck Buckner, Vice
President and Chairman of the Big Game
Records Committee.

ALASKA BROWN BEAR
First Award – 29 $^9/_{16}$

▽ ▽ ▽ ▽ ▽ ▽ ▽ ▽ ▽

ROBERT J. CASTLE

In 2005 I did a spring and fall bear hunt on Chichagof Island in southeast Alaska, and between the two hunts we spotted over 150 bears. Though some looked pretty big, none were as big as the bear I was looking for. It was very hard to keep passing up bears most hunters would have taken, and while I was getting tired and dejected, I had promised myself if I was going to shoot a brown bear, it had to be at least a 9-footer. I didn't want to shoot an animal as special as a brown bear and come away with something that wasn't what you envision when you think of a big brown bear. With this goal in mind, my attitude was such that if it wasn't to be, then so be it.

When I first returned home from the Chichagof Island hunts, I was tired of Alaska and wanted no part of returning. But as most hunters know, once you get rested, the itch starts to come back. I figured if I get an opportunity to hunt the right place, I might give it one more swing of the bat.

After finally settling on hunting Kodiak Island where the majority of the top-ranking Boone and Crockett Alaska brown bears have been taken over the years, I did some research for the best brown bear guides on Kodiak and found that nearly all of them were booked out three to four years in advance. I decided I was not going to wait that long. As far as I was concerned, it was now or never.

When I found out that Rohrer Bear Camp Outfitters annually donate a brown bear hunt to the Wild Sheep Foundation, formerly called the Foundation for North American Wild Sheep, I got set up to bid by telephone. I was lucky enough to win the hunt through the auction, which enabled me to be hunting brown bear on Kodiak Island on May 4, 2006.

Upon arriving at Rohrer Bear Camp, there were five hunters in camp, and Kodiak Island was everything you would expect it to be. On the first day of my hunt, we settled down on a good spotting point, and it didn't take long before we were seeing big bears. The biggest difference on this hunt was that if you decided to go on a stalk, you could easily lose a half day with the amount of ground you had to cover, so you wanted to really make sure the bear was big enough and that you could get to him in time for a good shot before the day ended.

On the second day we spotted a bear that my guide Sam said was well over 9 feet. The bear had a rub spot on his back that I didn't like, but he looked huge. After too much thinking, I said, let's go, but our stalk came up empty because we had waited too long. It was late in the day when we decided the stalk was fruitless, so we returned to camp. When we arrived back at camp, we found out one hunter had shot a really nice bear that went about

Photograph courtesy of Robert J. Castle

Robert J. Castle was elated when he finally harvested his trophy Alaska brown bear after a combined 33 days of hunting. The bear has a final score of 29-9/16 points.

9 feet 5 inches, which got me pumped up.

The next day we made another stalk and were just getting in range when the bear busted us and took off. Again it was late in the day, so we went back to camp and heard that another hunter had shot a big bear that went 9 feet 8 inches. At this point I had just a little doubt starting to creep into the back of my mind.

On day five we made a third stalk that failed once again. The next day, the hunter with whom I shared a cabin shot a monster bear that went 10 feet 3 inches. As we sat around the dinner table the next day, our outfitter, Dick Rohrer called in the floatplane for the following day. One hunter who had not shot a bear had to leave, and the other three who all had nice bears jumped on the plane with him and took off, leaving me at camp alone with all the guides. We all began to wonder what was up with my luck. With 22 days at Chichagof, plus eight days at Kodiak and nothing to show for all this effort, I was at the point of mental exhaustion and was pretty tired physically, to say the least. My outfitter was a great guy and on days 9 and 10, he kept me going, plus he had three of the other guides in addition to Sam coming along with us each day so we had five sets of eyes glassing.

On day 11, my second-to-last day, it seemed as if I was just going through the motions at times and was getting discouraged. It was about 8:30 p.m. when we caught just a glimpse of a bear near the top of a mountain. Dick had us move about 400 yards to get a different angle. We looked for a while and got another glimpse of the same bear. After we discussed it, Dick suddenly said, "You have to get up there to take a look."

I said to myself, "Wait a minute! It's 9 p.m., we don't have a very good idea how big the bear is, and it's way up there on the

ALASKA BROWN BEAR
First Award – 29 $^9/_{16}$

▼ ▼ ▼ ▼ ▼

ROBERT J. CASTLE

mountain." Then with one look from Dick and a few words, I knew that there was one more day of hunting left and we needed to take a gamble. I called it a "Hail Mary" effort. So up we went as fast as we could.

There was a lot of huffing and sweating, but as we neared the top of the ridge we slowed down and finally reached the exact spot Sam had in mind where he thought the bear was located. We sat for just about three or four minutes before we could hear a bear walking. I immediately started to get pumped.

Out came a bear and the first thing I could see was a face and body of a very ugly … sow! I took one look at my guide, Sam, and we both were thinking, "You have to be kidding. We came all the way up here for that?" That sow walked about 50 yards in front of us and kept on going right out of sight.

At this point I had the mindset that I was jinxed and was not going to kill a brown bear. Then, after another minute or two, I heard a noise and looked back to where the sow had emerged from the brush and I saw this big fat head of a bear. I elbowed my guide, Sam, and when he looked over I saw the look in his eyes and immediately knew it was something big. I said, "What do you think?"

Without hesitation he said, "Shoot him!"

He said it in such a way that I knew to just shut up and shoot. The bear was following the sow, so when he was about 50 yards away and broadside, I fired a round right behind the shoulder. He roared and took off into the brush. We knew he wasn't going to go very far.

After we all went crazy for a minute, I asked Sam, "Well, how big do you think he is?"

All he said was, "Real big!"

We found the bear only about 70 yards from where I shot him. Sam measured his front pad at 8-1/4 inches.

It was late in the day, so after we skinned him, we went back the next day to get him out. He ended up squaring a little smaller than we thought at 9 feet 5 inches. But I was thrilled to death. Then came the bonus. We talked a bunch about how huge his head was, but for some reason the thought of this being a records book bear never came into my mind until we got back to camp. The first thing Dick did back at camp was to grab the skull to measure it. Then it hit me, and I was like a little kid. I kept asking, "Well? Well? Well?"

Dick looked at me and said the bear's skull was over 29-4/8 inches, which just floored me. When I got back home, and after the 60-day drying period, the bear measured 29-9/16. It took 33 days of hunting (which my guides kept reminding me of throughout this hunt) and a "Hail Mary" stalk at the end, but wow, was it ever worth it. ▲

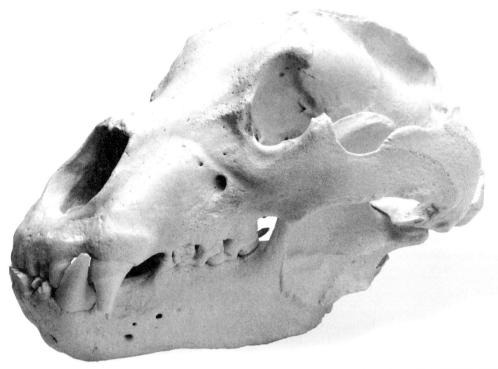

TROPHY STATS
▼ ▼ ▼ ▼ ▼

CATEGORY
Alaska Brown Bear

SCORE
29 $^6/_{16}$

SKULL LENGTH
17 $^{12}/_{16}$

SKULL WIDTH
11 $^{10}/_{16}$

LOCATION
Alaska Peninsula, Alaska – 2009

HUNTER
Mikkel Sørensen

Photograph by Jack Reneau

Mikkel Sørensen accepting his plaque
and medal from Buck Buckner, Vice
President and Chairman of the Big Game
Records Committee.

ALASKA BROWN BEAR
Second Award – 29 6/16

▼ ▼ ▼ ▼ ▼ ▼ ▼ ▼ ▼

MIKKEL SØRENSEN

After traveling for more than 32 hours from Denmark, I finally arrived in Anchorage, Alaska, on September 29, 2009. I still had another five hours of travel ahead of me before landing in Cold Bay on the Alaska Peninsula.

Coming from the tiny country of Denmark—Alaska is more than 39 times bigger—I was looking forward to the adventure of hunting the big coastal bears in the Alaskan wilderness on the Peninsula. I was first captivated with

The Last Frontier

bears 25 years earlier, when I was an agricultural trainee student in British Columbia. During that seven-month visit, I shot my first big game animal with a rifle—a black bear. In Anchorage, my expectations intensified when I saw the life-sized bear mounts displayed in the airport.

My plane landed in Cold Bay at 2:30 p.m. In the crowded lobby of the airport, I was greeted by Richard Guthrie who drove me and another European hunter, Ron Robat of the Netherlands, to Cold Bay Lodge where we were greeted by Mary and Bill Martin, the lodge owners.

I had purchased some essential hunting equipment from Cabela's and had it shipped to Cold Bay to await my arrival. Included were a number of items that I either can't buy in Denmark or they are far more expensive—if I can even find them. After taking a shower, I started to pack my gear for the hunt. Later, Ron and I talked about our expectations for the hunt, and I completed the last of the necessary paperwork with Richard.

The next day, Richard drove us to the airport and flew us to the hunting area near Muffett Lagoon in his Super Cub. We landed on a riverbank and were picked up by my guide, Spencer Pape. We loaded my gear into the boat and motored upriver to the camp that was located on a little island.

Camp consisted of two Bombshelter tents in the alders. After settling in, we ate, sighted in our rifles, and finished the day with a little fishing.

Ron's guide was delayed by one day at a moose camp, so Ron went with Spencer and me on the first day of the hunt. He, of course, offered an extra day of hunting as compensation.

I must say it was with great expectations of the hunt ahead of me for the next ten days when I went to sleep that night listening to fish jumping out of the water in the river, geese honking, and ducks quacking as they passed overhead.

On the first day of the hunt, I awoke at 7 a.m. and made my way to Spencer's tent for some breakfast. Then off we went. It was a beautiful morning with a light breeze and

Sørensen was treated to spectacular views during his hunt on the Alaska Peninsula.

a crimson sunrise to the east as we headed upriver—a good omen for the day ahead of us. After cruising upstream for half a mile, we tied the boat to some bushes on the riverbank. From there we hiked to a hilltop with a spectacular view to the north, east, and west. Below us was a vast area of mushy tundra, and a mile to the north, a creek drained from the hillside into the river.

At first light, we spotted a few bears traveling from the creek to the alders on the hillsides. Later in the morning, the sky was nearly cloudless. To the far north, we caught a glimpse of the Bering Sea and the Aghileen Pinnacles covered with snow that sparkled in the sunlight.

One bear on the creek especially caught our attention. It was dark colored and moved like a big bear. Spencer checked him out with his spotting scope and said he was a shooter. He asked me if we should go after it.

I thought it was a little early on the first day of a ten-day hunt to shoot my bear—it was only 10:30 a.m. On the other hand, if it was a big bear, I figured we might as well take him. Spencer and I moved down the hill, found one of the many bear trails and started walking towards the creek. When we reached the creek bank, we realized that we were too far west of where we had last seen the bear. Going east, we had to backtrack a little to cross a minor stream in our way. Immediately after crossing it, a bear jumped up from the riverbank and ran about 60 yards, stopped, and stared at us. We agreed that this bear was lighter colored and smaller than the one we saw from our earlier vantage point, so we didn't pursue him.

At our earlier vantage point, Spencer explained that the first big bear a hunter sees here on the Peninsula often seems bigger compared to the bears in the interior. Spencer has been out in camps since August 4, guiding hunters for Dall's sheep, grizzlies, and moose. I got to know him very well during my hunt, and he was a very nice guy and competent guide. He figured the bear we spooked was about an 8-footer.

In the afternoon, Spencer and I went back up the hill to spot for bears. We saw the bear that we had spooked that morning back along the creek again. We also saw other bears, including sows, cubs, and single bears moving down the hillsides.

ALASKA BROWN BEAR
Second Award – 29 $^6/_{16}$

▼ ▼ ▼ ▼ ▼

MIKKEL SØRENSEN

Shortly after 8 p.m., in the twilight, Spencer said, "There he is, and he is big. That's the one you want!" A huge bear lumbered down the alder-covered hillside towards the creek and disappeared in the tall grass and alders on the creek bank.

Back in the tent, we told Ron and his guide Nate Turner, who had arrived while we were gone, about the huge bear we had seen. Now we had to learn his routines and move in on him.

During the night and early morning we had a rainstorm, so the weather was not suitable for hunting in the morning. Ron and Nate left us around noon and headed upriver to set up their camp.

Late afternoon, Spencer and I went back to our lookout, but we did not see the big bear again. Spencer wanted to go up the creek and spend a night there so we would be close to the area where we had last seen the big boar. But, the wind was bad and we wanted to see the bear once again to learn more about his daily routines.

We spent the following days glassing, hoping to see him again or another big bear. However, we only saw three wolves and, of course, lots of small bears. We also saw a bull moose with a 60-inch spread. What a sight! I have hunted moose in Norway, but the Alaska moose is considerably larger.

On day four, we saw good-sized bears on the creek in both the morning and evening. The last one was slowly following the creek and heading east. At 8:20 p.m., the big bear came out of the alders at the same place we had seen one on the first day. Halfway down the creek he turned and went back into the alders. We wondered why he acted that way. After all, the bear on the creek seemed smaller than him and much further away.

Back in the tent we discussed the situation. Spencer suggested that we could head upriver and set up a camp on the riverbank in an area he was familiar with that had a lot of bears. However, we agreed to give our area another day and then decide if we should move camp.

The next day we did not see any of the bigger bears that we had been seeing, so we made plans to move camp the following day. Bad weather moved back in during the night, so we didn't hunt in the morning. Instead, we packed all our gear into the boat and left around noon.

The weather was still bad when we started upriver against the wind with rain pelting our faces. It was so bad that I wasn't able to take a lot of scenic photographs. I wished I could have had my camera when we went around a bend in the river and surprised two bears standing 80 yards from us on a sandbar in the middle of the river. Spencer idled the

Mikkel Sørensen and his guide Spencer Pape pose with Sørensen's award-winning Alaska brown bear. The bear, which scores 29-6/16 points, received a Second Place Award.

boat against the current as we watched them. Even though they weren't trophy-class bears, they looked very impressive as they stood there on their hind legs. After a brief pause, they ran for the riverbank and stopped in the grass and alders, where they watched us for a while before leaving the scene.

Two hours later we reached the spot where Spencer planned to make camp. We pitched our tent, got out of the rain, and grabbed a bite to eat before taking a brief rest. At 6 p.m. Spencer opened the tent, and 30 yards from us, a sow with two cubs was walking along the riverbank. They took off to the north as soon as they saw us. It was still raining a little and the visibility was not good for glassing for bears, so after a short walk, we returned to the tent.

The next morning the weather was better except for a cold wind. We hiked one and a half miles and found a good vantage point to glass from. We saw 16 bears that morning and three of them were good ones. One bear left the creek at first light and went for the alders, while the other two were still on the river delta when we decided to return to camp around 11:30 a.m. We planned to move into the area where we had seen the bear that left the creek in the morning.

After a brief nap, I woke up at 3 p.m., sweating. The weather had changed, and the sun was shining from a cloudless sky. It was a beautiful autumn afternoon. We packed our backpacks with the most essential supplies needed to spend the night on the creek near the bear's trail.

We headed upriver for a couple more miles, beached the boat, and hiked until we found a little ridge where we had a good view over the river delta and the hillside where the bear had disappeared that morning. We soon spotted a couple of smaller bears, and after a while Spencer spotted one of the big bears from the morning. It was slowly meandering along the river, occasionally diving into the water for a fish. He was fully exposed as he crossed a bend on the river and gave Spencer an excellent opportunity to judge his size. "He's over 9 feet. Do you want to go for him?" he asked. I decided to give it a go.

We left our backpacks and started our stalk into the delta at 7 p.m. The bear was more than a mile away when we saw him cross the river, so we walked as fast as we could in the tall grass between the bogs and the creeks. As we closed the distance, I chambered my Schultz & Larsen in .358 Norma Magnum with a 225-grain Barnes-X round.

Over halfway there, we paused to relocate the bear, but it was difficult. Eventually, Spencer spotted him lying on a sandbar in the middle of the river about 500 yards away. This was our chance to close in on him. At 86 yards, the bear started to move his head. "Any time you are ready!" Spencer said. The bear stood up broadside to us.

It's now or never, I thought. With one knee on the ground, I got above the tall grass and squeezed off a shot at his right shoulder, and my bullet hit him dead-on. At the impact he just turned and snapped at his shoulder. "Shoot again! Shoot again!" Spencer yelled. I took a couple more shots as Spencer backed me up and the bear went down. I reloaded a new clip, but it wasn't needed. He was done. He had run only about 15 yards after the first bullet hit him. It had all happened in 20 seconds or so. My dream had just come true. I had just shot a big bear on a fair-chase hunt and had seen many other bears in a wild and beautiful setting.

As we crossed the river, Spencer filmed me with my video camera as I walked up to the bear to make sure he was dead. I sat down and a lot of thoughts went through my head as my fingers ran through the fur on his neck. I later held his paw up for the camera.

"We have to leave him and come back tomorrow to skin him out because it's already 8:30 p.m. and it will be dark soon. This river will be full of bears during the night," Spencer said. I did not like the idea of leaving my bear, but I could see his point. We headed back to our backpacks and returned to our main tent upriver. We were back in camp at midnight.

The next day we returned to skin the bear. After admiring the magnificent animal and taking lots of photographs and video footage, we skinned him and packed him the "long" 30 yards back to the boat. We then headed back to our tent, packed up our spike camp, and headed downriver to our first camp on the island.

The next day Spencer started to flesh the bear hide. Shortly after noon we heard a boat coming. It was Ron and Nate returning from a successful hunt. Ron had also taken a big boar. The guides finished preparing the hides the next day and we measured them. Both of our bears were 10-footers.

Back in Cold Bay, Ron and I prepared to fly to Anchorage on October 12th. After thanking our guides for a fantastic hunt, as well as saying goodbye to Bill and Mary at the lodge, my adventure came to an end. But, Alaska is now in my blood, and I hope to hunt again in the "Last Frontier" someday soon. ▲

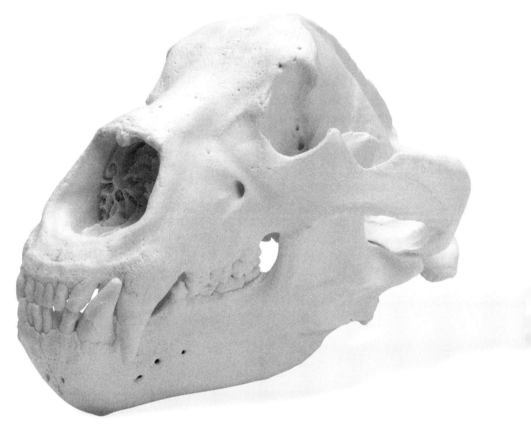

TROPHY STATS
▼ ▼ ▼ ▼ ▼

CATEGORY
Alaska Brown Bear

SCORE
$28^9/_{16}$

SKULL LENGTH
$17^7/_{16}$

SKULL WIDTH
$11^2/_{16}$

LOCATION
Olga Lake, Alaska – 2008

HUNTER
Peter J. Bausone

ALASKA BROWN BEAR
Honorable Mention – 28 9/16

▼ ▼ ▼ ▼ ▼ ▼ ▼ ▼ ▼

PETER J. BAUSONE

It all started with an unexpected phone call from my friend, asking if I would be interested in a brown bear hunt on Kodiak Island. Sam Fejis, a reputable hunting guide, had a November hunt cancellation and was looking to fill it. It was September 2008 at the time, the economy was falling, and my business was slower than ever. It was an easy decision to go on the hunt.

I arrived in Kodiak on November 7, 2008, **Hey Bear! Hey Bear!** and flew out to the camp in a floatplane with my guide Buck and his assistant. When we arrived, we unloaded our gear into a four-man cabin on the side of a mountain. As we were unloading our gear, the guide pointed to a 6-foot-tall bear some distance away behind the cabin. Later that day, looking through a spotting scope, I saw four large bears, a sow with cubs, and many other, smaller bears. I knew then that I had a very good chance of getting a great bear.

I defined a "great bear" as anything over 9 feet. I wasn't interested in shooting a bear that was anything less, since I had been on previous bear hunts and already had a nine-and-a-half-foot grizzly. I explained to my guides that I was okay with leaving without a bear should the opportunity to take a 9-foot-plus bear not present itself.

Around 7 a.m. the next morning, we left the cabin and walked up the mountain in order to glass across the lake and beyond. The young bear behind the cabin from the day before was still there about 300 yards away and started coming toward us. Thankfully, Buck managed to scare him off. We spent the next 45 minutes observing three bears quite a ways away. After careful scrutiny, we deemed them not worth any additional effort. Suddenly, Buck spotted a bear across the lake that he said was big. The bear laid down on the shoreline, which Buck found unusual. While I watched him through the spotting scope, the bear sat up again and

Photograph by Jack Reneau

Peter J. Bausone accepting his plaque from Buck Buckner, Vice President and Chairman of the Big Game Records Committee.

Peter J. Bausone (left) sits behind his Alaska brown bear with his guide Buck and the guide's assistant. They discovered the bear had been feeding on a half-eaten bear carcass near Olga Lake, Alaska. Bausone's bear skull has a final score of 28-9/16 points.

began pawing the ground as if looking for food. Buck believed that this bear was worth a closer look.

We began walking down the mountain through saw grass which was about four feet high. We decided to change our course and walk the shoreline instead, which was slightly easier, but very slippery because the rocks were coated in algae making it similar to walking on ice. About a half mile into our stalk, I saw a bear poke his head in and out along one of the impressions of the shoreline about 125 yards away. We realized that it would be safer for us to climb up the mountain and cross in order to have a vantage point where we could look down on the bear. We stopped several times to look at the bear as we got closer on our stalk. Buck saw the bear lying down and said that it was definitely a shooter. We estimated that the bear was around a 9-footer and was absolutely beautiful.

ALASKA BROWN BEAR
Honorable Mention – 28 9/16

▼ ▼ ▼ ▼ ▼

PETER J. BAUSONE

At 1:30 p.m., we ranged the bear at 180 yards. With only 12-inch shoreline grass between us and the bear, we decided we couldn't get any closer. I got in the prone position, looked through my scope, and was amazed at the magnificent size of this bear, even while the bear was lying down on his stomach. I told Buck that I was unable to get a shot on him while he was in that position. Buck said that he would try to rile the bear with some deer distress calls. The bear merely lifted his head without a care and then lowered it. Buck tried another call with similar results, then use the old stand-by call, "Hey bear…hey bear…hey bear!" The bear raised up, looked to his left, and I fired my .375 Holland and Holland.

The bear spun around in a circle, I fired two more times, and both times hit my mark. He then ran and disappeared into a high area between us where we had no visibility. We waited about an hour before proceeding into that area to search for him. We found a tank of a bear down for good, as well as another surprise. The bear was lying down in a pile of grass, rock, and dirt—a 10-by-15-by-2-feet area—with a half-eaten bear carcass in the center. Buck estimated the eaten-on bear carcass to be an 8-footer. My trophy bear squared at 10 feet, 6 inches and is a beauty!

I will forever savor the memories of this hunt. My burning desires and dreams for the ultimate bear and hunting experience have been realized. I thank my friend Sam Fejis for notifying me of the trip and Buck and his assistant guide for a great hunt. ▲

TROPHY STATS

▼ ▼ ▼ ▼ ▼

CATEGORY
Polar Bear

SCORE
$27^5/_{16}$

SKULL LENGTH
$16^{15}/_{16}$

SKULL WIDTH
$10^6/_{16}$

LOCATION
Chukchi Sea, Alaska – 2007

HUNTER
James D. Unrein

POLAR BEAR
First Award – 27 ⁵/16

▼ ▼ ▼ ▼ ▼ ▼ ▼ ▼ ▼

JAMES D. UNREIN

2007 was my sixth year of hunting polar bears near the Chukchi Sea in Alaska. Since I am a native Alaskan who lives in Seward, I take advantage of the opportunity that only Alaska natives dwelling in coastal areas are allowed to harvest polar bears. Most of the time, I hunt alone, but on this particular hunt I was with a friend and longtime Alaska native resident Vance Spaulding. In the previous six years on the ice after bears, I have only encountered about a half dozen other local Alaska native hunters.

13 Bears with Darkness Approaching

The area I hunt is approximately seven miles off the coast of Cape Lisburne, 800 miles northwest of Anchorage. We started the hunt on February 8, 2007, heading out onto the frozen ocean on foot. The bears are found on the edges of the open water hunting for seals, so the first order of business is to glass the area searching for ravens cleaning up anything the bears may have left. After locating a good section of open water, we set up a tent and sat all day looking for a good polar bear. The temperature was around -25°F, and the wind was out of the northeast at about 15 knots. It is a very unique and demanding landscape to hunt with many interesting factors to deal with. One, for example, is the strong water currents that are present around the cape; you can actually feel the water and ice moving below your feet. If you start to feel the ice under your feet grinding, that usually means another ice shelf has moved under the ice you are on. To verify thickness of the ice, I use a homemade walking stick with a metal spike on the bottom to probe with. If the metal spike goes through the ice, I know it is too thin.

Some of the largest polar bears in Alaska are found at Cape Lisburne. This is attributed to the presence of so many seals and such good conditions for the bears to hunt them. As

Photograph by Jack Reneau

James D. Unrein accepting his plaque and medal from Buck Buckner, Vice President and Chairman of the Big Game Records Committee.

Photograph courtesy of James D. Unrein

James D. Unrein uses a homemade walking stick with a metal spike on the bottom to probe the thickness of the ice while hunting off the coast of Cape Lisburne, 800 miles northwest of Anchorage.

evening approached, we started seeing lots of bears. They were competing for the best hunting grounds, diving in the water after seals, and mock-fighting. Around 7 p.m., as the sun started to set, we began walking back towards the mainland and came across some massive 12-inch-wide paw prints that weren't there earlier in the day.

We had seen 13 different bears within a one-mile radius of the hunting grounds, and at this point, one bear in particular started following us. The bear circled around behind us to get downwind and slowly started to approach. When he was within 75 feet, I decided to take him. Usually only juvenile bears or an older starving bear will charge. We were positive this bear definitely was not a juvenile. It had all the aspects of a big bear with huge front paws, long legs, ears down off to the side of his head, and a long tail.

I placed the first shot from my custom 7.82 Lazzaroni Warbird right on the front shoulder. The second shot was right at the base of the skull.

Within 15 minutes of killing the bear, it got so dark that I had to get my headlamp just to see the bear. And my friend Vance couldn't find his gun for a few minutes that he had put down a few feet away, which made for some very tense moments as he tried to locate his gun in the dark, knowing that 12 other polar bears were within 800 yards of us. We hauled the bear back to camp with a heavy duty sled.

When we returned, I used a digital scale to weigh this bear at 1,400 pounds. The other bears I have harvested weighed around 1,000 pounds. This bear squared 10 feet, 6 inches, and had a final Boone and Crockett score of 27-5/16 points. ▲

Photograph courtesy of James D. Unrein

Alaska native James D. Unrein with his award-winning polar bear taken on the frozen Chukchi Sea of Alaska, during the 2007 season. Unrein's bear, which scores 27-5/16, received a First Place Award at the 27th Big Game Awards Program in Reno, Nevada.

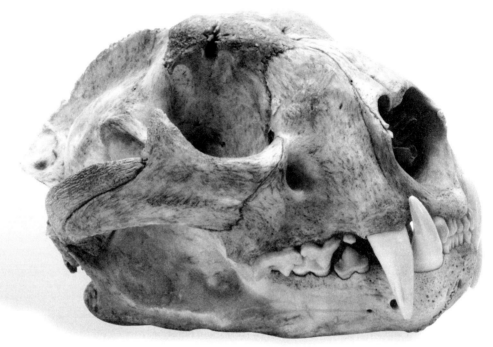

TROPHY STATS
▼ ▼ ▼ ▼ ▼

CATEGORY
Cougar

SCORE
$15^{14}/_{16}$

SKULL LENGTH
$9^{4}/_{16}$

SKULL WIDTH
$6^{10}/_{16}$

LOCATION
Idaho Co., Idaho – 2007

HUNTER
Rod E. Bradley

COUGAR
First Award – 15 ¹⁴/₁₆

▼ ▼ ▼ ▼ ▼ ▼ ▼ ▼ ▼

ROD E. BRADLEY

After 26 years of avid big-game hunting, I had never seen a single mountain lion during any of my hunting trips. For that reason, the elusiveness of these big cats has always intrigued me.

Last fall I was talking hunting with my dad and a good friend, Tim Craig, of Boulder Creek Outfitters. I asked Tim about his cougar hunts and then Dad and I sat listening as Tim told us story after story of hunting the big cats

Good Fortune

of the West. Tim asked us if we had ever been interested in hunting one. Without hesitation, we said, "Yes!" He told us to be ready and he would call us when he had an opening.

The call came the evening of December 10th, 2007. Tim wanted to know if we could be at camp the next morning. My wife agreed I could go—after a lot of begging—but I'd have to be back in town three days later on Thursday night. I agreed and started gathering all of my hunting gear.

Dad and I were on the road at 6 a.m. Tuesday, headed to Boulder Creek Outfitters' camp in Idaho's rugged north country. We met up with our guides, Chris and Lee, grabbed some lunch, and set off to find a cat. We covered a lot of ground while searching for a track. Both guides were very knowledgeable and tried to educate us about the animal we would be pursuing.

That afternoon and evening turned out to be fairly uneventful. We did cross one set of tracks and I was thinking, *Here we go*. There was a little snow on top of the track. Lee got one of the dogs out and it turned out that the track just wasn't all that hot. With darkness approaching and a questionable track, it wasn't a good time to let the dogs loose.

The next morning was overcast and we were greeted with four inches of new snow. Conditions were perfect for looking for fresh

Photograph by Jack Reneau

Rod E. Bradley accepting his plaque and medal from Buck Buckner, Vice President and Chairman of the Big Game Records Committee.

Rod E. Bradley and two of his guides hold Bradley's award-winning cougar taken in Idaho County, Idaho. The tom, which scores 15-14/16 inches, is the second largest cat ever taken in Idaho.

tracks. Dad and Chris went to cover some of the same ground we had looked at the evening before, while Lee and I headed out to check some different country a little farther back. Our plan was to take a 30-mile loop that would return us back to the main road.

About halfway through the loop, we finally found exactly what we were looking for—a fresh cat track. After a closer look, Lee determined that the cat had a kitten with her, and we'd have to pass on that one. As we finished the loop, we saw many deer and elk tracks, but no more lion tracks.

We met up with Chris and my dad back at camp to have some lunch and put together a plan for the afternoon. During the morning hunt, Chris and Dad had also crossed many deer and elk tracks and even saw a couple of wolves, but found no cats. We covered a lot of ground that afternoon, inspecting every track we crossed in the snow. Unfortunately, none of them were from a lion.

On Thursday morning, I was getting antsy. It was my last day to hunt. We were again greeted with snow—six inches this time. We couldn't have asked for any better conditions. Again, the plan was to travel some of the roads looking for fresh tracks. If nothing turned up, we would move several miles downriver and use snowshoes on roads closed to motorized vehicles. We didn't turn up any cat tracks during the morning, so we loaded up and headed downriver. Chris and I grabbed a dog and took off snowshoeing up a closed road while Lee and Dad traveled downriver to do the same. After a 45-minute walk, Lee and Dad returned to the truck with news similar to earlier reports: more deer, elk, and wolf tracks, but no cat tracks.

Chris and I made our way up the road. I had never walked in snowshoes before, and it certainly took a little getting used to. Half a mile up the road we found a very large cat track and my excitement immediately skyrocketed. As we inspected the track, the dog started baying and trying to follow it. Chris was holding the dog back, but the leash broke and the dog was off, with no tracking collar. Not being experienced with using hounds, I was thinking, *How are we ever going to find that dog?*

Chris and I walked back to the main road to meet Lee and Dad. After telling Lee what happened, he quickly unloaded two more dogs, fitted them with collars, and we headed back up the road to where the track was.

When we approached the track, the first dog was running back down the hill toward us. The guides weren't sure what to think about that. The track shouldn't have been too cold. They collared him and then turned all three dogs loose. The dogs took off like a rocket, working their way up the hill.

As we stood there listening to the dogs, the tone of the barks changed. Lee and Chris looked a little puzzled. Could the dogs be barking "treed" already? It had only been 15 minutes since they had been released.We listened to them bark for another ten minutes with no change in their location or in the type of bark. Lee said, "I guess it's time to go see what we've got."

It took us quite some time to climb up to where the dogs were. This was no small feat because it was nearly straight up, with 18 inches of snow on the ground. Much of our climb was done on all fours.

Arriving at the tree, what I saw was absolutely amazing and unforgettable. When a mountain lion—especially a huge male—is in a tree glaring down at you, it's very intimidating. The guides kept saying, "Look at the size of that cat!"

The atmosphere was charged with the dogs barking and us staring into the eyes of an ultimate predator. We spent some time admiring the animal and talking about how best to get a good, clean shot. Once that decision was made, the dogs were tied up. At the report of the rifle, the majestic cat came right out of the tree, landing in the fresh powder. We were cautious on the approach, knowing this was an animal that could rip a person to shreds with one swipe. Once we determined it was safe, the celebration began.

As we continued to stare in awe of this incredible creature, we knew without question it was a giant tom. The head was so massive it nearly defied description. How massive, though, we weren't exactly sure. All I knew was that this cat was as big as me, and I instantly had a deep and personal newfound respect for these stealthy predators.

After the 60-day drying period, Boone and Crockett Club Official Measurer Ryan Hatfield scored this great trophy at 15-14/16 inches. After scoring it, Ryan said it was the second-largest cat ever taken in the cougar-rich state of Idaho, behind only the 16-3/16 monster taken by legendary cougar hunter Gene Alford some 19 years earlier, whose trophy tom won the Boone and Crockett Club's coveted Sagamore Hill Award.

My trophy is now tied for 10th on the All-time list. There was a lot of good fortune involved in the hunt, and I feel very privileged just to have been able to see, let alone take, such a great animal. ▴

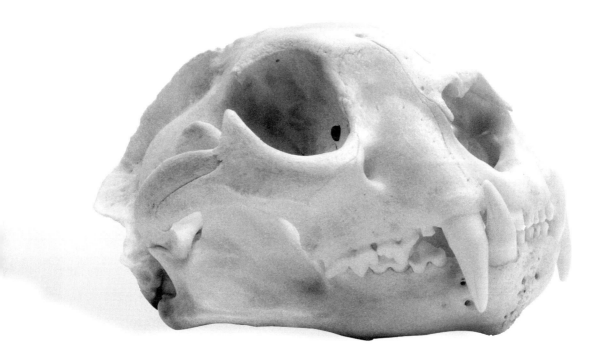

TROPHY STATS

▼ ▼ ▼ ▼ ▼

CATEGORY
Cougar

SCORE
15 $^{11}/_{16}$

SKULL LENGTH
9 $^{7}/_{16}$

SKULL WIDTH
6 $^{4}/_{16}$

LOCATION
Rio Blanco Co., Colorado – 2008

HUNTER
Gregory W. Wisener

COUGAR
Second Award – 15 ¹¹/₁₆

▼ ▼ ▼ ▼ ▼ ▼ ▼ ▼

GREGORY W. WISENER

In 2008, we had one of those epic snowfall years in Colorado. The skiing was out of this world, but it was hard on our local wildlife. The snow also made for one of the best years in recent memory for running hounds and chasing lions.

My good friend John Kobald lives in Meeker. He helps local legend Paul Janke, of Lone Tom Outfitting, with guide duties. I have always wanted to hunt lions with hounds and had been warned that it is very addictive. John had been emailing me pictures of great cats they'd been locating for Paul's clients, and I made the mistake of saying, "Jeez, I sure would like to do that sometime!"

Snarling and Growling

It was early March, and usually we're beginning to thaw out a bit and readying ourselves for spring. However, the snow just wouldn't let go of its grip that year.

On Sunday evening, March 9, John gave me a call at home and asked, "Can you be here tomorrow morning?" John told me they had cut tracks on one of the biggest cats they have ever seen, and the client that was supposed to be there couldn't make it.

Fortunately, I live in Aspen, which is only a couple of hours from Meeker. I told John that the following day was a Monday and I had work to do. He insisted that I needed to come up and chase this lion, no ifs or buts about it. Knowing full well that Monday was out of the question, I said, "Well, if you cut those tracks again the next afternoon, I can be up there at first light on Tuesday." Paul called Monday evening, saying he had the cat in a canyon and I needed to be there the next day at first light.

The next morning I met Paul, John, and another gentleman named Travis Flarthery. We took a short snowmobile ride up to see the tracks. I'm a cougar neophyte, but I knew these were extraordinary. Each track was the size of a small dinner plate.

Photograph by Jack Reneau

Gregory W. Wisener accepting his plaque and medal from Buck Buckner, Vice President and Chairman of the Big Game Records Committee.

Gregory W. Wisener with his award-winning cougar taken in Rio Blanco Co., Colorado, during the 2008 season. Wisener's tom, which scores 15-11/16, received a Second Place Award at the 27th Big Game Awards Program in Reno, Nevada.

Paul cut the hounds loose and soon they were hot on the trail. Paul and Travis headed up to the ridge while we waited down below to see which way the hounds would go. It was awesome to hear the hounds on the run all over the place, back and forth for a while, then up and down. At one point Travis even got a glimpse of another lion, but he said it wasn't the one we were after. John and I headed north to a spot two canyons up from where we started. This short relocation required a couple of hours spent breaking trail. Finally, at noon, the hounds had the tom treed. It took John and me another 30 minutes to claw through deep snow to get to the big cat. I even lost an arrow off my quiver going through all the thick brush.

When we finally reached the tree I was amazed at how big the cat looked. The big tom was plenty upset, both snarling and growling at us. As Paul tied up the hounds I tried to catch my breath and get my adrenalin under control. I figured the range between me and the cat was about 22 yards, but I was standing on a steep slope and shooting straight up through a hole in the branches about 18 inches in diameter. Normally a shot of that distance is easy for me, but shooting straight up and quivering from all the excitement made it tough! I tried to control my breathing as I nocked an arrow on my Matthews Switchback. Still shaking, I drew a deep breath, pulled the string back, and let fly.

In an instant I heard the awful noise of an arrow clipping a branch! My heart sank as the big cat moved over to another limb. This time I felt completely composed and confident as I nocked another arrow. The tom's new position was perfect for shot placement, with no obstructions. I let the Trophy Ridge expandable fly, resulting in a clean pass through shot.

Before I could get another arrow off my quiver the big cat was dead and freefalling down the tree. The tom slid down the hill about 50 yards before coming to rest. Paul checked to make sure the arrow had indeed gone through before he let his hounds loose to get at the cat. When we pulled the tom out of the brush, we all just stood there with our mouths open. When I tried to pick up the cat for the obligatory "bear hug" picture, I couldn't budge it! I'm 6 feet tall and 180 pounds, and I could not lift that cat up! Paul was giving me some grief as he came over to help lift him up. When he grabbed that cat, I saw in his eyes that he was amazed at the weight of this lion.

After pictures we tied a rope around the cat's neck and started pulling. It took all four of us, giving all we had, to drag that cat out to where we could get a truck to it. I called my friend Leland at Big Cat Taxidermy in Craig, and he sent someone to meet us and pick up my trophy. As I was headed home from my wonderful experience, I got a call from Leland.

COUGAR
Second Award – 15 ¹¹/₁₆
▼ ▼ ▼ ▼ ▼
GREGORY W. WISENER

He asked if we'd bothered to weigh this cat. I said we hadn't, but that he sure was heavy. Leland said, "Greg, I have had only one other lion that big in the shop, and it weighed 227 pounds. This cat is every bit that big!"

I am a Boone and Crockett Club Official Measurer and you always wonder if you will someday have a trophy of your own that is good enough to make the records book. In many cases you have to be satisfied to just handle trophies of this caliber and listen to the fortunate hunters tell their stories. As it turned out, I had no idea what a blessing had been bestowed on me.

My cougar ended up netting 15-10/16 points in Boone and Crockett and Pope and Young. The 27th Awards Program Judges Panel confirmed the score at 15-11/16. The lion tied the number three all time Pope & Young, tied the number ten B&C, and tied for first place in SCI's bow category. I may never kill another animal that makes the "book," but after this cougar that's just fine with me.

President Theodore Roosevelt killed his former World's Record cougar in 1904, which scored 15-12/16, just a few miles from my lion's territory. I would like to think my lion is a descendant of President Roosevelt's fine cougar. ▲

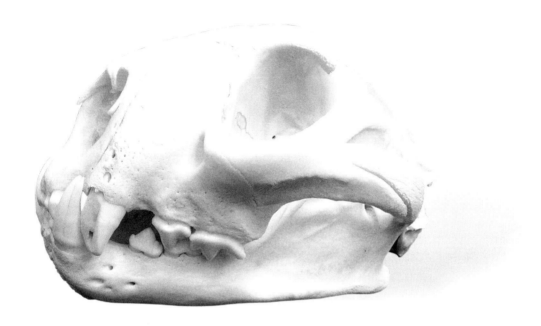

TROPHY STATS

▼ ▼ ▼ ▼ ▼

CATEGORY
Cougar

SCORE
$15^{10}/_{16}$

SKULL LENGTH
$9^{5}/_{16}$

SKULL WIDTH
$6^{5}/_{16}$

LOCATION
Drayton Valley, Alberta – 2006

HUNTER
Tim R. Gazankas

COUGAR
Third Award (Tie) – 15 ¹⁰/₁₆
▼ ▼ ▼ ▼ ▼ ▼ ▼ ▼

TIM R. GAZANKAS

It all started for me in 2005 with a chance meeting while fueling my truck in Red Deer, Alberta. The fellow filling his truck next to me had dog boxes on his truck, and after some idle conversation, I found out he spent the winters hunting cougars in the Rockies and foothills of western Alberta. We soon became friends, and by December we were out spending weekends hunting cats.

It took us six days of hunting before we turned loose on a large track and after six hours of up-and-down canyons, we were able to tree a

Hooked on Cougar Hunting

cat. I was so excited to reach the tree and see the cat, but on close inspection, we realized the cat was a young male with only half its tail. I had set my sights on only shooting one cougar, so I wanted a mature male with good fur. This one appeared to have frozen his tail, so we let him go. While no shots were fired at him, we did get some excellent photos.

Unfortunately my season ended without taking a cat. To make matters worse, my new friend was unable to keep his dogs and had to sell them to an out-of-province hunter. I was so hooked on cougar hunting, so I had to find another way. A friend suggested I talk to a local Drayton Valley outfitter who was becoming well-known for catching big cats. I contacted Byron Stewart of Tracks N Trails Outfitting, and after a couple calls, he put my name on his list. I hoped he would have an opening for me in 2006, though he was unsure due to his bookings.

Hunting season was soon upon us, and I got out after deer and elk in our local area, though my mind was always on cats. They were beginning to earn some notoriety in our area due to their abundance and frequent sightings. Regular big-game season closed at the end of November, then cougar season started. I called Byron to confirm I was on the list. He stated

Photograph by Jack Reneau

Tim R. Gazankas accepting his plaque and medal from Buck Buckner, Vice President and Chairman of the Big Game Records Committee.

Tim R. Gazankas sits behind his award-winning cougar taken in Drayton Valley, Alberta, during the 2006 season. Gazankas' tom, which scores 15-10/16, tied for a Third Place Award at the 27th Big Game Awards Program in Reno, Nevada.

that I was, but there were numerous hunters ahead of me, but he would hopefully be able to get to me by the end of December. During this conversation, Byron did ask me if I would be able to get away on a moment's notice if a previously booked hunter could not come. I told him that I was very flexible and had many holidays still remaining.

On December 3, 2006, my cell phone rang. It was Byron asking if I could hunt this week as his hunter was unable to come. I told him I could make it happen and he stated he had found tracks of a good tom. He wanted me to meet him the next morning 30 minutes west of Drayton Valley. It snowed heavily that night and I was suffering from insomnia. The conditions could not have been better; we hiked through the timber sorting out the tracks and soon realized there was also a female with kittens in the area. While waiting for Byron to get a couple dogs, I actually saw a cougar bolt across an opening in front of me, but I was unsure if it was the male or female. Shortly thereafter, Byron arrived and quickly identified the track as the female. He instructed me to follow him since he had cut the male track and it was very large. It was starting to get late in the afternoon, and if we were going to try to tree him, it had to be soon. The tracks were fresh, so off we went. At the day's conclusion, we were beat after running through snow and working to cut the tom's area down. We called the hunt until the next morning.

The following day was spent trying to sort out which direction the tom had gone and where he was heading. By lunch, the tom had moved about eight miles from where he was first found to the Paddy Creek area. I was starting to feel the opportunity was slipping away

COUGAR
Third Award (Tie) – 15 $^{10}/_{16}$

▼ ▼ ▼ ▼ ▼

TIM R. GAZANKAS

for me as I would have to return to work the next day. All of a sudden, Byron felt the track was hot enough and turned the dogs loose. Off we went, following the sweet baying sound through the heavy timber. Soon we heard the distinctive barking signaling a treed cat, so we worked our way down Paddy Creek, breaking through ice a couple of times, always closing the distance.

Byron bolted ahead and I moved as fast as I could to keep up—wet, but excited. Soon enough, I could see dogs and heard Byron calling that the cat was a very large tom and to hurry. By the time I reached the spot and saw the cat up a long overhanging tree above the creek, I had started to shake with excitement. I tried to take a picture but the adrenalin was extreme. Quickly, I passed the camera to one of our guides and he started taking pictures while I worked to free my rifle from its wet case.

I quickly regained my nerves and put the crosshairs on the cat's shoulder. All I could see was his enormous pumpkin head and large muscular shoulder. Byron encouraged me to shoot fast as the cat was getting nervous and one dog was working up the tree, getting too close.

At the sound of the shot the cougar vaulted out of the tree down into the tied dogs and bolted through them and across the creek bank. I fired a second shot as he went up the far bank before he vanished into the timber. Byron asked me how the shots felt, and I said they felt good. We tethered two dogs and slowly followed the tracks with rifle ready, but it was soon apparent this was not necessary. The cat grew larger and larger as we approached it.

I asked Byron what he thought, and he said, "You shot yourself one very large B&C cat."

It took another hour to get the cat by sleigh and snowmobile out to the road. I was very grateful for this once-in-a-lifetime experience. ▲

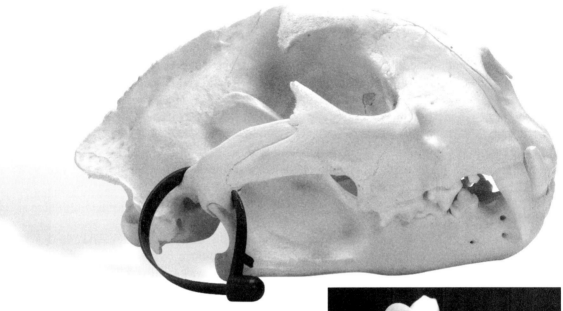

TROPHY STATS

▼ ▼ ▼ ▼ ▼

CATEGORY
Cougar

SCORE
$15^{10}/_{16}$

SKULL LENGTH
$9^{6}/_{16}$

SKULL WIDTH
$6^{4}/_{16}$

LOCATION
Owyhee Co., Idaho – 2007

HUNTER
Justin D. DeCroo

Photograph by Jack Reneau

Justin D. DeCroo accepting his plaque
and medal from Buck Buckner, Vice
President and Chairman of the Big Game
Records Committee.

COUGAR
Third Award (Tie) – 15 ^{10}/₁₆
▼ ▼ ▼ ▼ ▼ ▼ ▼ ▼

JUSTIN D. DeCROO

I had been on several cougar hunts before I received the opportunity to connect with this magnificent animal. Fortunately for me, my first cougar was a B&C tom that scored 15-9/16 points seven months after I took it. It weighed in at a hefty 179 pounds and was nearly 8-1/2 feet long.

The location of my hunt was near Jordan Creek in Owyhee County, Idaho. It was snowing extremely hard on the day of the hunt with about a foot of fresh snow on the ground. In fact, every track we saw was snowed in to the point that you could not even determine what kind of an animal had left it.

Then, we hit an extremely fresh track that had no snow in it at all. Not only was it a fresh track, but it was clearly a big cougar. We knew immediately that this was going to be as good as it would get.

After following the tracks for awhile, we spotted the animal feeding on a mule deer. I was able to get within 22 yards of this wonderful trophy and harvest it with my .22-250, shooting 55-grain bullets. After congratulations and photographs, we packed it back to the vehicle.

It was invited to B&C's 27th Awards Program Judges Panel in Reno, Nevada, where it was re-scored by the judges at 15-10/16 points. I attended the 27th Awards Program Banquet in Reno on June 26, 2010, and received the Third Place Award for my tom. It actually tied for third place with another tom taken in Drayton Valley, Alberta, in 2006 by Tim Gazankas. ▲

Photograph courtesy of Justin D. DeCroo

Justin D. DeCroo hunted during a snowstorm when he harvested this award-winning cougar in Owyhee County, Idaho. The tom scores 15-10/16 points.

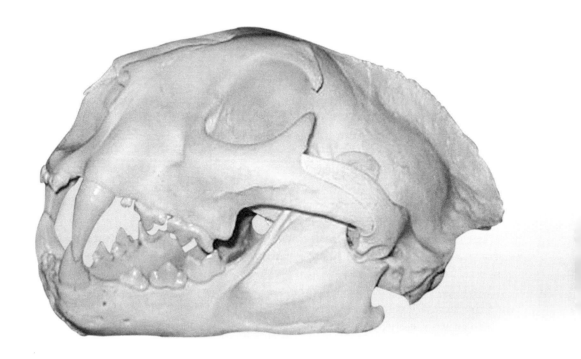

TROPHY STATS

▼ ▼ ▼ ▼ ▼

CATEGORY
Cougar

SCORE
15 $^8/_{16}$

SKULL LENGTH
9 $^3/_{16}$

SKULL WIDTH
6 $^5/_{16}$

LOCATION
Trout Creek, Alberta – 2008

HUNTER
Brice D. Folden

COUGAR
Honorable Mention – 15 $^8/_{16}$

▼ ▼ ▼ ▼ ▼ ▼ ▼ ▼ ▼

BRICE D. FOLDEN

My legs were rubbery, my lungs were burning and the sound of blood was rushing in my ears. In order to locate where my treed cougar was, I had to hold my breath for a few moments to hear the haunting sounds of the baying hounds echoing across the mountainsides.

"Ok, there they are, and I'm getting much closer. They sound like they must be just ahead in that patch of heavy spruce," I panted out loud in the thin mountain air.

Fat Elvis

A heavy shot of adrenaline pushed me onward and upwards, with heavy emphasis on the upwards. Wearily I climbed towards where my friend and outfitter Paul Pierunek of Timberline Guiding was impatiently waiting for me — the client he jokingly refers to as, "Fat Elvis."

Before I continue, however, allow me a moment to describe the events leading up to this hunt and to explain my dubious new nickname. I did not receive this wonderful handle as a result of being overweight, nor for my prowess on stage. It was earned the previous year on my first cougar hunt with Timberline Guiding. Climbing steep foothills in insulated hunting clothing made me sweat as much as the King himself did while performing in concert.

I had first inquired about a mountain lion hunt 13 years earlier while still in college. The price of a hunt represented a fortune for a 23-year-old student saddled with rent, tuition, and a vehicle payment. However, the conversations I had with the outfitter only deepened my resolve to collect a big cougar.

Fast forward 13 years. The college student gets a little older and more financially secure. Despite dwindling wall space, there was still space for a life-size cougar mount in my trophy room, plus the desire to collect one still burning deep within me. Apparently, however, the mountains got a little steeper during the last 13 years.

I did my research and kept hearing about Paul at Timberline Guiding and his reputation for results. I spoke with Paul numerous times, and the hunt was booked for 2008. I can attest to the fact that you will not find a more honest or harder working guy to book a hunt with. Paul conducts traditional-style hound hunts. He runs experienced and highly trained hounds and possesses a high success rate for big cats.

Our first hunt had originally been planned as a horseback hunt deep in Alberta's Rocky Mountains. We intended to camp in wall tents for a week, while bowhunting for an elusive mountain lion. Plans changed when Paul phoned me one evening three weeks before our scheduled hunt. I could tell by the excitement in his voice that he had found an exceptionally nice track.

"Brice, can you come tomorrow?" he asked. "This tom has a 23-inch stride and toes bigger than a loonie." A loonie is the nickname for the Canadian one dollar coin.

"So does this mean he's a nice cat, Paul?" I inquired, as the dimensions he provided really meant nothing to me.

"He's an absolute Boone and Crockett mountain lion, Brice," he replied.

And just like that our mountain lion horseback hunt was scrapped. I jumped from behind my desk and immediately left my office for home to pack my bow and hunting gear and head for Sundre, Alberta, that very night.

Take my advice, don't go straight from a desk job to trying to climb mountains with your hunting guide, as you will discover in short order how good of shape you ARE NOT in. Invest some time improving your cardio or you may well end up with a dubious nickname like the one I received.

We hunted hard for five thoroughly enjoyable days. The scenery was breathtaking, and the hunt was highly informative. I learned to tell the difference between male and female cougars by the shape of their toes, as well as other traits concerning mountain lion behavior. It was exciting to watch the hounds work and to listen to them bay as they trailed the cougar.

We chased the big tom daily for several miles, but he just kept running and refused to tree. My guide and his excellent hounds did their best for me, and in all fairness to Paul and the dogs, we did pass on lesser cats. Prior work and family commitments put an end to our initial attempt for my trophy. I immediately booked a hunt for the following year.

I do not measure the success of a hunt with a tape measure. The memories and experience of that hunt are priceless to me. One long year and several hours on a treadmill later, I finally received that greatly anticipated phone call.

"Fat Elvis, drop everything and get in your truck and leave now! We've cut a huge track, another giant of a cat. Can you get here tonight? He is huge with toes like 'toonies,'" which is a reference to the Canadian two dollar coin. "This may be the biggest cat I've ever found; it's certainly in the top three!"

Paul sounded quite excited about this cat, but I felt he might have been pulling my leg a bit, as we've become good friends and we enjoy giving each other the gears.

"C'mon Paul, don't kid me. How big is he really? Is he about the size of the big one we hunted last year?"

"I'm telling you Brice, if you don't get here tonight, I intend to shoot this cat myself tomorrow. It's huge. Last year's cat was likely a 'Booner' as well, but this one is a truly exceptional cat. He doesn't even walk properly. His body sways like a big old bear waddles, and he smears his tracks. It's a giant, so get your bow and get down here!"

Paul has helped put several cats in the records book and into people's trophy rooms. He has treed well over a hundred mountain lions and has yet to harvest one for himself. I knew this had to be a particularly special cougar to have him excited enough for him to want to harvest it himself. To say that I was now truly pumped would have been a dreadful understatement.

It is still a family joke and the topic of great amusement about how I sped around the house like a madman finding my hunting gear and leaving my supper un-eaten at the table. It felt like the longest hour of my life, but my family is certain I was packed and gone in about 10 minutes. They also assure me I went a little crazy while doing so.

The following morning, Paul, Tyson, and I were on the big cat's track in the snow at first light. Glancing at the tracks, I knew what all the fuss was about. This track was clearly larger than the tom we chased the previous year, and it was very apparent that this was an enormous mountain lion.

Words cannot describe my anticipation, the beauty of the surrounding mountains, or how grateful I was for the opportunity to be there. It is something that is only understood by other hunters who have experienced the grandeur of Alberta's Rockies while pursuing the noble cougars that dwell there.

I also can't describe how hard Paul and his fellow outfitter Tyson Mackin worked for me that day. We followed the cougar's huge tracks over one ridge after another. The chase went on for several miles. The wily tom would climb a tree, and then jump several feet through the air to the ground in an effort to shake the dogs off his scent.

COUGAR
Honorable Mention – 15 8/16
▼ ▼ ▼ ▼ ▼
BRICE D. FOLDEN

AT THE FIRST SHOT ABSOLUTE PANDEMONIUM BROKE LOOSE IN THE TREE ABOVE ME. BRANCHES BEGAN BREAKING, TREE BARK RAINED DOWN, DOGS WENT BALLISTIC AND WITH AN ANGRY SNARL THE BIG TOM BEGAN DESCENDING BACKWARDS DOWN THE TREE.

In desperation the big tom wound his way around the mountainside, hooked up with a female and treed with her. When the hounds arrived at the tree, the crafty tom would bail out, leaving the female treed in an effort to ditch the hounds. Paul's experienced dogs would have none of it. They quickly sorted out his track and continued pursuit of the tom we were now referring to as "toonie-toes."

Repeatedly the old tom would circle, re-tree with the female, and then bailout trying to escape Paul's determined hounds. The day waned, and I began to think we would never tree the tom before dark. Then suddenly disaster struck.

We were out of hearing range of the hounds, so Paul suggested that Tyson and I return to the Ski-Doos and circle well ahead to see if we could hear them.

Meanwhile, Paul remained on foot trailing his hounds and our elusive quarry.

We were dropping down a steep slope into a gorge when Tyson's Ski-Doo slid out of control and rolled. I was following behind him and upon hitting the brakes my Ski-Doo also

Photograph courtesy of Brice D. Folden

Brice D. Folden is pictured above with his cougar scoring 15-8/16 points. Folden was hunting near Trout Creek in Alberta when he took this tom during the 2008 season. The cougar weighed 192 pounds and was given an Honorable Mention at the 27th Big Game Awards in Reno, Nevada.

began a sideway's slide down the mountain. I was picking up speed and hurtling towards him. We can laugh about it now, but the look of concern on Tyson's face clearly indicated he thought he was about to meet his untimely demise by being run over by "Fat Elvis." I gunned the engine, roared off the trail into the trees and wrecked myself.

Our sleds damaged and pride bruised, we picked up gear strewn about the mountainside. Unfortunately, my Mathews bow had been heavily damaged in the wreck and was unusable. There is a lesson to be learned here about having your bow in a hard case for a hunt of this nature.

The hounds had treed the cat further up the mountain, meaning a long, hard climb up the steep, timbered slope in deep snow. I approached the large spruce tree where the hounds were baying and looked up at the sight I had anticipated for so long. The muscular cat was crouched in the thick spruce, glaring disdainfully down at the noisy dogs and two humans that had been pursuing him relentlessly the entire day. Paul tied up the dogs as I prepared to collect my trophy with a .30-.30 in lieu of my damaged bow.

At the first shot absolute pandemonium broke loose in the tree above me. Branches began breaking, tree bark rained down, dogs went ballistic and with an angry snarl the big tom began descending backwards down the tree.

COUGAR
Honorable Mention – 15 8/16

▼ ▼ ▼ ▼ ▼

BRICE D. FOLDEN

I certainly do not feel the big cat intended to attack us. He was badly hurt and was simply trying to escape. Nevertheless, the moment was quite intense as he locked his unwavering gaze on us and did not so much as blink as he rapidly descended the tree.

I was standing only eight feet or so from the tree, trying to thread my next shot through the thick branches into his vitals. A split second later, I had an angry mountain lion at eye level with me. My final shot at uncomfortably close range left the mighty cougar in a heap.

Following some hearty handshaking we excitedly relived the hunt. Next Mick and Ginger were allowed to worry the tom's hide as a reward for their day-long chase and outstanding trailing job. Paul informed me that the stocky cat should exceed 180 pounds and was definitely a Boone and Crockett contender. He also declared it was quite likely the second largest cat he had ever taken.

It was then that we realized that in my haste I had left my camera and skinning knives in my hunting pack back at the Ski-Doo. Imagine my sheer delight at having to scorch my legs and sear my lungs on another trip down to the snowmobiles for my gear, and then back up the mountain. The picture taking session took place in near darkness. My long-awaited trophy far exceeded my expectations. The cougar ended up weighing in at 192 pounds and placed well into Boone and Crockett Club's records book with an official entry score of 15-9/16 points after the mandatory 60-day drying period. The score was later verified at 15-8/16 when it was re-scored by the 27th Awards Program Judges Panel in Reno, Nevada.

Incidentally, the big tom actually edged out Paul's previous largest cat to date. That monster scored 15-7/16 points

In closing I'd like to thank Paul and his talented hounds Mick and Ginger for all their hard work that resulted in our trophy of a lifetime. The entire experience is one I highly recommend to others.

Each time I look at the huge cougar on my wall, I recall the planning, the effort, the sights and sounds of that hunt. I still chuckle when I remember the look of concern on Tyson's face as I bore down on him with the Ski-Doo. The memories and friendships created on my quest for my cougar mean as much to me as the mountain lion itself and will be treasured for the rest of my life. ▲

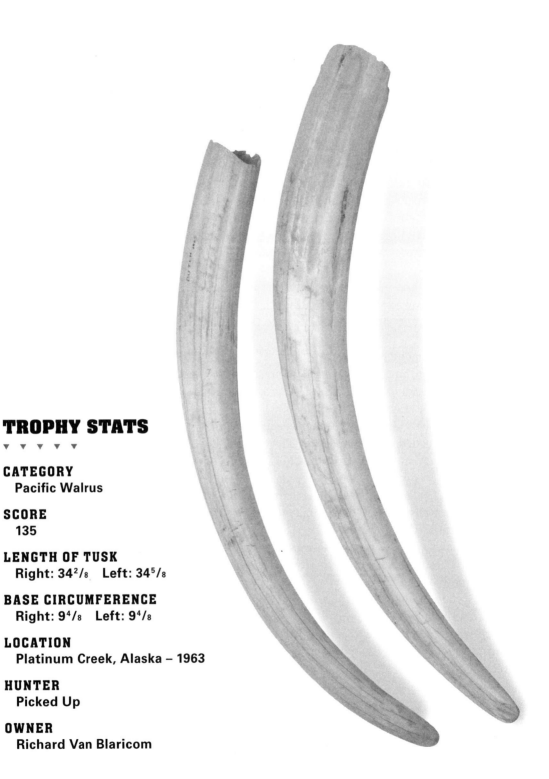

TROPHY STATS
▼ ▼ ▼ ▼ ▼

CATEGORY
Pacific Walrus

SCORE
135

LENGTH OF TUSK
Right: 34^2/$_8$ Left: 34^5/$_8$

BASE CIRCUMFERENCE
Right: 9^4/$_8$ Left: 9^4/$_8$

LOCATION
Platinum Creek, Alaska – 1963

HUNTER
Picked Up

OWNER
Richard Van Blaricom

PACIFIC WALRUS
Certificate of Merit – 135

▼ ▼ ▼ ▼ ▼ ▼ ▼ ▼ ▼

RICHARD VAN BLARICOM

I acquired these tusks in July 1963 while I was working in a small mining camp in Platinum, Alaska, near the village of Goodnews Bay. I was working there on a summer job while attending college.

There was an extremely strong storm in the Kuskokwim Bay area, after which several whales, sea lions, and walrus carcasses were blown ashore. After a full day's work, I decided to go to the beach to see what I could find. One of the fellows at camp was kind enough to drive me to the mouth of the Platinum River, where I started walking south along the beach. After about a quarter of a mile, I discovered a dead walrus that washed ashore during the storm. An examination of the carcass revealed a large abscess on the upper jaw that penetrated into its right tusk. I assumed that was the cause of his death.

I cut the tusks free from the putrefied skull and packed them back to camp that night. Most of the people in camp wouldn't have anything to do with me for several days, as I seemed to have acquired a stench when I cut the tusks out of the rotten head. I had a cold so I was not aware of the strong odor. I also had a local native named Ed who lived in Goodnews Bay to scrimshaw my nickname, Dutch, on both tusks and the date on one. He offered to do some more work on the tusks but his skills were lacking and I did not want to do any more damage to them.

I did walk the beach several times afterwards and found nothing of interest. I soon realized that these were a find of a lifetime. Several years ago I was at the local Big Horn Show in Spokane, Washington, and I asked a fellow who was measuring whitetail antlers if they had a class for walrus tusks. He said they did, and I visited him shortly thereafter. He scored them, and we were all surprised as to the size of the tusks that I have had with me the last 47 years. The 27th Awards Program Judges Panel verified their score at 135 points. ▲

TROPHY STATS

▼ ▼ ▼ ▼ ▼

CATEGORY
Typical American Elk

SCORE
404 1/8

LENGTH OF MAIN BEAM
Right: 57 4/8   Left: 59 5/8

**CIRCUMFERENCE BETWEEN
FIRST AND SECOND POINTS**
Right: 7 7/8   Left: 8 7/8

NUMBER OF POINTS
Right: 6   Left: 6

INSIDE SPREAD
41 3/8

LOCATION
Graham Co., Arizona – 2007

HUNTER
Duane Chapman

TYPICAL AMERICAN ELK
First Award – 404 ¹/₈

▼ ▼ ▼ ▼ ▼ ▼ ▼ ▼ ▼

DUANE CHAPMAN

To anyone familiar with the pursuit of big bull elk, the San Carlos Apache Reservation is a very familiar location. I am very fortunate in the fact that I reside on San Carlos Apache Reservation in San Carlos, Arizona. I have been hunting for several years and most of my hunting experience is on San Carlos. For local residences, we must qualify to get drawn on a lottery basis. I have been applying for several years in both hunting units of Dry Lake and Hilltop, the two top-producing units

What are Brothers for

for world-class bulls. I was finally drawn for a trophy bull elk tag in the Dry Lake unit in December 2007. I never dreamed that I would have the opportunity to kill a 400-plus bull elk, especially in December.

After I purchased my tag, I was excited and could not wait for December to come. I was thinking of what type of rifle, ammunition, and other types of equipment I should be preparing for the hunt. I had started a daily exercise regiment because I knew how tough the rough country is around the Dry Lake unit. I also called my brothers, Commander Chapman, Jr., and Danny Chapman, to see what days they could get off work to assist me on this once-in-a-lifetime hunt. I wanted to have everything lined up and ready prior to opening day.

Once December 2, 2007, the first day of my hunt, arrived, I was so excited. I was up and out of bed at 2:45 a.m. I ensured that all of my equipment was loaded in the truck, then had a huge breakfast. After breakfast, I headed off to pick up my brother. The drive from home to Dry Lake was a good two and a half hours.

When my brother and I hunt together, we try to get onto a ridge top to look down into the canyons where we have had our best success finding the big bulls. The two of us prefer this type of hunting since we can cover more ground just by spotting and glassing for hours

Photograph by Jack Reneau

Duane Chapman accepting his plaque and medal from Buck Buckner, Vice President and Chairman of the Big Game Records Committee.

Duane Chapman poses with his award-winning typical American elk taken in Graham County, Arizona, during the 2007 season. Both of Chapman's brothers were on hand to help him with the hunt. The bull scores 404-1/8 points and received a First Place Award at the 27th Big Game Awards Program in Reno, Nevada.

than just walking. Over the next couple days we spotted several bulls but none of them were the caliber of bull I was looking for.

My brother was still sure we could find something over 400 inches but my hope was starting to fade as the hunt continued. As a late season hunt, the biggest issue we faced was that many of the bulls had already broken off tines, and with points missing, it is nearly impossible to attain the 400-inch mark. I could feel the pressure mounting since my window of opportunity was closing and the odds of getting drawn for a bull elk again were slim to none.

We had spotted one bull that my brother estimated would reach 400 inches, but dense brush prevented us from closing the distance to where I felt confident taking the shot.

The two of us were hunting everyday, getting up at 2:45 a.m. and coming home at 8:30

every evening. Commander Jr. was the brother that I had been hunting with until that point, but work commitments required him to return home. I called my other brother Danny and asked if he could come with me to hunt and he agreed.

TYPICAL AMERICAN ELK
First Award – 404 $^1/_8$

▼ ▼ ▼ ▼ ▼

Duane Chapman

When Danny arrived, we continued with the same regimen, getting up early in the morning and coming off the mountain late. I was getting exhausted but the motivation to take a world-class bull kept me going. Tuesday evening, Danny and I saw a nice bull down in a canyon. After looking him over, I decided that he was a good bull worth some effort but I was just so exhausted, I couldn't make the two-hour hike into the canyon to try for a better look or shot. I took the next day off since my brother had to return to work and I needed some rest.

I slept in late that day and took my time getting ready to head into town. I couldn't get the thought of that big bull we had seen the night before out of my mind. I knew Commander Jr. would have the day off so I called him and he agreed to go with me for an afternoon hunt.

On the 90-minute drive up there, I told him about the bull Danny and I had seen the day before. We parked the truck where the road ended, got our gear ready, and checked our batteries in the GPS and flashlight. We started working up the trail, slowly and carefully glassing into the canyons on both sides of us. After about a half mile, we spotted the bull we thought we had seen the night before. He was on the upper third of the ridge and had seen us before we had gotten onto him. The bull started walking up and over the ridge but Commander Jr. calmed me by saying it was out of range and didn't even appear to be that good of a bull.

This slowed our pace considerably. The sun was dropping quickly and there was a storm forecast for the next two days. We continued on to a little over a mile from the truck. There was about an hour and a half of daylight left and we stopped to take a break for a minute. While standing there, we heard the distinctive sound of an elk hoof breaking a twig. We began carefully scanning the surrounding area and quickly picked up a good bull on the top portion of a close ridge. Commander Jr. pulled out the spotting scope just to verify that the bull would break 400 as he had predicted. After judging the bull through the scope, Commander Jr. told me it was near the 420 mark. I was so excited, but I knew it wasn't an ethical shot due to the fading light and distance. We sat and watched as the bull calmly fed across the ridge. We discussed a plan for the next morning and how I will have to hike up an extremely steep slope to get into position. We hiked out of the canyon at dark and went home.

I called Danny that night and asked him if he was ready to pack a 400-plus bull elk for me. He laughed and thought I was joking, but said okay. That night I couldn't sleep. I kept thinking this was a once-in-a-lifetime opportunity. I just could not wait until morning.

I only slept for three and a half hours that night and was up early for my huge breakfast. My brothers and I met at my dad's house and hooked up the Rhino (UTV). After arriving at the end of the road, I turned on my GPS and set it to lead me back to where I had left the bull the night before. We had left some of our gear there to make sure we could locate the spot in the morning, and after finding the stashed equipment, we knew we were in the correct spot. Commander Jr. and Danny set up there to watch as I hiked up the ridge to try and get into position. Darkness prevented me from being able to see anything other than my GPS unit that I could illuminate with my flashlight

As I climbed and fought my way through the brush, I was trying my best not to make a lot of noise. My heart was pounding and chest was heaving both from the strenuous climb and excitement as I neared the spot where I thought I needed to be. I found a nice rock to place my bag on and loaded my 7mm Remington Magnum. The sun was slowly rising over the next ridge across from me when the bull stepped out into a little opening where I could identify him. I put down my binoculars and picked up my rangefinder and ranged it at 230 yards. I found the bull's shoulder in the crosshairs of the scope and slowly squeezed the trigger. As the bull expired I couldn't help but think, please don't fall and break any points. The bull was down with one shot. I was so happy, I was yelling to my brothers, "I got it! I got it!" Commander Jr. asked if I was sure. I told him I definitely had the bull elk down.

I made my way over to the bull, not sure if he was as big as we had thought. When Commander Jr. got over to it, he confirmed that his original guess of a 420 bull was correct. After all the pictures were taken, we caped and quartered the elk. I'm glad Commander Jr. and Danny were there helping me pack the elk out. It took six trips down to the Rhino and back up the hill.

After we returned home I called a friend of mine, Julius Hostetler, to come over and give me a rough score of the bull. He came up with 413 points, it was definitely the class of bull I wanted.

I took the bull over to a taxidermist in Payson, Arizona, and it was officially scored at 404 1/8, the score that was verified by the 27th Awards Judges Panel in Reno, Nevada. I also received the bronze award from the Arizona Wildlife Federation.

I would like to give a huge thank-you to my hunting partners, Commander Chapman Jr. and Danny Chapman. They were both a great help during the whole hunt, especially helping me pack the bull elk out. Also, thanks to Mogollon Taxidermy who completed the measurements and did a great job with the shoulder mount. ▲

B&C Photo Archives

Denmark native and trophy owner Mikkel Sørensen (center) and his wife Tina take time during the 27th Awards Program festivities to share his hunting story with Official Measurer Gerald Rightmyer. Sørensen's Alaska brown bear, scoring 29-6/16, received the Second Place Award, and Rightmyer's once-in-a-lifetime non-typical whitetail, scoring 272-2/8, received the Third Place Award. Sørensen and his wife traveled the longest distance to participate in the Reno activities.

TROPHY STATS
▼ ▼ ▼ ▼ ▼

CATEGORY
Typical American Elk

SCORE
$399^4/_8$

LENGTH OF MAIN BEAM
Right: $54^6/_8$ Left: $56^5/_8$

**CIRCUMFERENCE BETWEEN
FIRST AND SECOND POINTS**
Right: $8^6/_8$ Left: $9^2/_8$

NUMBER OF POINTS
Right: 6   Left: 6

INSIDE SPREAD
$43^4/_8$

LOCATION
Gila Co., Arizona – 2008

HUNTER
Dan J. Agnew

TYPICAL AMERICAN ELK
Honorable Mention – 399 ⁴/₈

▼ ▼ ▼ ▼ ▼ ▼ ▼ ▼ ▼

DAN J. AGNEW

I arrived at elk camp on the San Carlos Indian Reservation on August 26, 2008, hoping to take advantage of some early rutting activity that Homer Stevens, my tribal guide, had told me was already going on. While my tag allowed me to start hunting August 15, the temperature hovered around 85°F every day, which I don't consider ideal fall elk-hunting weather. With that in mind, I decided to give it ten days and hopefully it would cool down a little. Once I finished unpacking my gear, Homer said, "I've got some video footage of a nice 6x6 bull that you might be interested in."

What a Thrill

Wow, I was definitely interested! He was a beauty—one of those rare, almost "perfectly" configured 6x6 bulls that had it all. I told Homer, "Let's go hunting."

I also told Homer we'd have to find the bull in the next five days, as I had another elk hunt in Washington that I was committed to for a week beginning September 2nd. Well, as luck would have it, we hunted and searched for that 6x6 bull for the next five days and never saw him. Disappointed, I told Homer I would be back in about ten days and resume my hunt as I had to leave for my Washington hunt, which, in retrospect, ended up creating an incredible opportunity for me to harvest a tremendous bull with that tag. (See story on page 107.)

I returned to the San Carlos on September 6 and was fortunate that my youngest son could accompany me. When we arrived in camp, Homer told me he had seen the bull we were after a couple of times while I was gone and that the rutting activity was still strong with the bulls bugling like crazy. This was music to my ears.

The first couple of days were uneventful, and the bull was nowhere to be found. The morning hunts were over early because it was still warming up into the eighties during the day, and the elk headed to their bedding areas earlier than usual. Homer advised me to be patient and that my bull would eventually show up.

Photograph by Jack Reneau

Dan J. Agnew accepting his plaque from Buck Buckner, Vice President and Chairman of the Big Game Records Committee.

Dan J. Agnew's son was with him on his hunt for this tremendous typical American elk taken in Gila County, Arizona, during the 2008 season. The bull, which scores 399-4/8 points received an Honorable Mention at the 27th Big Game Awards Program in Reno, Nevada.

Homer was right. We arrived at the Dry Lake area of the reservation before daylight on the morning of the 10th. It was chilly, and we listened to lots of bulls in the area as the rut continued. Homer picked out one bugle and said, "I think that's him."

We trekked in the dark toward the bugle and patiently waited for daylight. We found my bull in the middle of a large meadow with about a dozen cows. We almost missed them, as they were already headed for the timber. Homer estimated the distance at about 150 yards. It was perfectly calm, so the wind was not an issue.

The bull had no clue we were there. One carefully placed shot from my McMillan Brothers .30-.378 Weatherby, and the bull was down. He was a beauty and all that I had hoped for! What a thrill for me, especially because my son was with me to share that moment and a week's worth of memories. I have years of memories on the San Carlos, but this one is the best, thanks to my guide Homer and the wildlife department on the San Carlos that does a tremendous job of managing their incredible wildlife resources. ▲

B&C Photo Archives

A couple of visitors check out Denny Austad's new World's Record non-typical American elk (foreground) from Utah that scores 478-5/8, and Duane Chapman's typical American elk from Arizona that scores 404-1/8.

New World's Record

TROPHY STATS
▼ ▼ ▼ ▼ ▼

CATEGORY
Non-typical American Elk

SCORE
478⁵/₈

LENGTH OF MAIN BEAM
Right: 46⁴/₈   Left: 46⁶/₈

**CIRCUMFERENCE BETWEEN
FIRST AND SECOND POINTS**
Right: 9⁷/₈   Left: 9²/₈

NUMBER OF POINTS
Right: 14   Left: 9

INSIDE SPREAD
36⁵/₈

LOCATION
Piute Co., Utah – 2008

HUNTER
Denny Austad

NON-TYPICAL AMERICAN ELK
First Award – 478 ⁵/₈

▼ ▼ ▼ ▼ ▼ ▼ ▼ ▼

DENNY AUSTAD

I was the successful bidder for a Utah governor's elk tag in January 2008. A short time later, I contracted with Doyle Moss of Mossback Outfitters to guide me on the hunt.

In early July, Doyle sent me a video shot a day or so earlier of a bull elk in velvet known as the "spider bull." From that point on, I underwent a rigorous exercise routine to get in shape for the hunt and finished building a new version of my .300 SA III.

Photograph courtesy of Denny Austad

Denny Austad is pictured above with his non-typical American elk scoring 478-5/8 points. Austad was hunting in Piute County, Utah, when he harvested this World's Record bull during the 2008 season. He received a First Place Award at the 27th Big Game Awards in Reno, Nevada.

Guide Wyatt Bowles accepting Denny Austad's plaque from Buck Buckner, Vice President and Chairman of the Big Game Records Committee.

On August 31, I drove to Utah's Monroe unit and started hunting the next day. I quickly realized how difficult the hunt was going to be. The terrain was steep and visibility in the dark and downed timber ranged from 20-50 yards most of the time.

We first spotted my bull on the morning of September 12th at the top of a very steep mountain about one mile away. By the time we finally arrived at the spot where we had last seen the bull, he had disappeared into the timber. We set up for a shot, but we were unsuccessful at calling him in.

We spotted him again on the way out in a small opening in the trees. I set up a hurried shot and missed him. We located his escape route and checked for blood but didn't find any — it was a clean miss. We hiked off the mountain, ate lunch, and hunted that evening without sighting him again.

On September 13th, we hunted a different side of the mountain, but I really wasn't feeling well, so we went back to camp. I decided I was too sick to hunt anymore, folded up camp, and headed home. I was so sick, I wasn't sure if I would even make it home. I later found out that I had carbon monoxide poisoning.

Doyle called me on September 29 and convinced me to drive all night back to Richfield for another attempt at the bull. With less than an hour's sleep, we set out for an area where Doyle had last seen the bull and waited for daylight. About 8:30 a.m. on September 30th we spotted him, and I dropped the new World's Record non-typical American elk with one shot from my newly designed rifle. Its final score and status as the new World's Record were verified by a B&C Special Judges Panel that convened at my home on January 2, 2009. ▲

Award-Winning Moments

B&C Photo Archives

Intermedia Outdoors was the media partner for the 27th Big Game Awards using their print, Internet, and television assets to spread the word about the events in Reno and inform sportsmen and sportswomen across the country about this celebration of successful conservation and big game hunting. Intermedia's Jim Bequette accepted their plaque from Simon Roosevelt.

TROPHY STATS

▼ ▼ ▼ ▼ ▼

CATEGORY
Non-typical American Elk

SCORE
441$^6/_8$

LENGTH OF MAIN BEAM
Right: 55   Left: 50$^3/_8$

**CIRCUMFERENCE BETWEEN
FIRST AND SECOND POINTS**
Right: 8$^2/_8$ Left: 7$^5/_8$

NUMBER OF POINTS
Right: 11   Left: 10

INSIDE SPREAD
37

LOCATION
Clinton Co., Pennsylvania – 2006

HUNTER
John A. Shirk

NON-TYPICAL AMERICAN ELK
Second Award – 441 ⁶/₈

▼ ▼ ▼ ▼ ▼ ▼ ▼ ▼ ▼

JOHN A. SHIRK

I answered the phone on September 23, 2006, and the voice on the other end said, "Hello! I'm looking for a John Shirk from Goodville, Pennsylvania. I hope I have the right party. Well, I guess I do if you had sent in for an elk permit. I want to congratulate you for having your name drawn for a bull elk tag!"

I don't know how many times I listened to that message before it really began to sink in. My name, which was one of 52,087 applicants,

New Pennsylvania State Record

was drawn that year for one of the 40 elk tags (15 bulls and 25 cows) available. That call was soon followed by a couple more from outfitters offering their services.

Earlier in the summer I had filled out an application and sent it along with $10 to the Pennsylvania Game Commission for a chance at having my name drawn for a coveted Pennsylvania elk tag. I had gone through that same ritual every year since the Game Commission first started issuing elk tags in 2001.

Elk were reintroduced in Pennsylvania back in the 1930s, but by the mid 1970s these herds had almost become extinct once again. So the Game Commission, with the help of the Rocky Mountain Elk Foundation, initiated an elk management plan to restore the elk population in the Keystone State. By providing the habitat, food plots, and health needs of the herd, their numbers have grown to an estimated 800 animals today. It is quite an awesome sight to see beautiful elk in my home state of Pennsylvania.

I live in the small town of Goodville in Lancaster County, which is midway between Harrisburg and Philadelphia. My wife Susie and I have six children, Floyd, Wanda, Steve, Ruthie, Michael, and Damian, ranging from 32 to 9 years old, and four grandchildren. We have several vans and provide transportation for the Amish and Mennonites who do not have

Photograph by Jack Reneau

John A. Shirk accepting his plaque and medal from Buck Buckner, Vice President and Chairman of the Big Game Records Committee.

vehicles themselves. Their transportation needs take us all over the country, which allows me to do a lot of hunting in other counties and states.

My wife and four oldest children have all taken deer. We love to hunt together as a family. We own a small hunting camp in Juniata County where we enjoy hunting and also stay for weekend retreats. I have hunted over 40 years already, but I never shot anything bigger than a whitetail until this hunt. I have shot many a trophy (buck and doe), which to me, is the hunt itself and how everything unfolds, such as the excitement that comes from a deer or turkey coming within range. The anticipation of that once-in-a-lifetime monster buck walking in under my tree stand is what hunting is all about to me.

From September to November that year, we made several trips to Elk County where we saw lots of elk. There was one special 8x7 bull with a bunch of cows that I videotaped bugling as he herded them back into the timber.

My wife and I, plus our two youngest sons, Michael and Damian, spent an enjoyable weekend with Jeff and Janet Calwell from Hicks Run Outfitters who I had hired as my guides. Jeff's brother Chuck, Charlie Hess, and Janet's sister Elaine, who was our cook, made up our outfitter crew. My son-in-law Dana Hoover came along as the cameraman, and Clair Zimmerman, a good friend of mine, came along to guide and help locate elk.

Saturday, November 4, two days before the hunt, we headed north with a packed truck. We arrived about four hours later, unloaded our gear, and then sighted in my firearms. The rifle I used was my .30-06 Springfield, Remington 7600 carbine, pushing 180-grain Barnes red-tip bullets. I also had my Astra .44 Magnum revolver. After getting settled in, we left to do some more scouting for elk the rest of the day.

The next day we checked out quite a few different areas and saw a lot of elk, but it wasn't until the afternoon that we spotted a big bull. That was going to be my new challenge for opening day.

Monday, November 6, 2006, is a day I'll never forget. After getting up around 3 a.m. and eating a good breakfast, we headed to the area where we had seen the bull the evening before. We waited until daylight, and then headed toward the area where we had last seen the bull, but he was not there. We checked out other areas, but it wasn't until late afternoon when we spotted him feeding in a grassy area.

I stalked to within 300 yards of him, keeping a clump of trees and brush between us. At about 110 yards, I prepared myself for a shot and waited for him to take about two more steps for a good broadside shot. Instead, he just turned and laid down so that I was looking at his rear end. I didn't want to shoot him in the neck because the Game Commission had given me a DVD to watch, and it really discouraged neck-shots. So we decided to move off to one side and take cover behind some thick bushes and trees.

After moving to the edge of our thick cover, we stirred him up with a cow call. Instead of turning to see where the cow was, as we expected, he jumped up running. I shot, but it must have only grazed him.

We then spread out to see if we could spot him again and came across his fresh, deep tracks in a swampy area. We saw him standing, looking back at us, but I was hiding behind some thick underbrush. I had a small opening through the weeds and fired a shot that connected. A couple of shots later, the handshakes and backslapping started, especially after seeing the size of the antlers and realizing that none of my shots had done any damage to the antlers. I was awestruck.

After the excitement settled down a bit, we field dressed him. We had to take liver and lung samples, plus two bottles of blood for testing by the Game Commission. They also provided a box for the head to send it in for further testing after the taxidermist was done skinning it out.

Jeff left to get more help, ropes, and a tarp to use to drag it out. We wrapped the tarp around the body to keep the hide from being damaged while dragging it the 300 yards or so to the trailer, which was about the closest Jeff could get to the bull.

We then proceeded back toward the lodge. After traveling about 15 miles or so, the trailer axle snapped, and we had to park the trailer at Jeff's friend's house until we could come back with another vehicle. We were about six miles from Jeff's place when a whitetail buck ran out in front of our van, and Jeff swerved to miss it. He lost control of the van, and it overturned on its right side, spun around, and slid down the road a distance.

I was immediately knocked out and lying where the side window had been. All the glass had been knocked out of the right side of the van. When we stopped moving, my right arm was under the van, my wrist was crushed, a finger broken, and I had a nasty concussion. Also, my right elbow and wrist were badly cut, and my arm had been brush-burned right through the jacket I was wearing.

Instead of going back to the lodge to celebrate, I ended up spending that night and part of the next day in the hospital. The doctor gave me an option of having surgery right away or splinting my finger so I could have surgery done at our home area hospital, which is, of course, what I wanted to do because I wanted to be at the check station when my elk was brought in. There was quite a crowd of people there who knew we were coming. It was exciting to see the people's reaction when they saw the size of my bull. At the scales, the field-dressed animal weighed in at 656 pounds, which means the live weight of this bull was around 850 pounds.

My bull created quite a stir among the people and also the news media. I did two interviews for television, which were on the 6 p.m. news that evening. It seemed crazy to watch myself on the news, but it didn't stop there. I received calls from Cabela's and Bass Pro Shops and from people as far away as Wyoming, Utah, Colorado, and Montana, to mention only a few.

There are lots of people to thank, but I would first like to thank the Pennsylvania Game Commission for making this hunt possible through their elk conservation and management efforts. Thanks also goes to the folks who run the state records banquet and awards

John A. Shirk is pictured above with his non-typical American elk taken during the 2006 season in Clinton County, Pennsylvania. The bull, which has a B&C score of 441-6/8 points, is the largest elk taken in Pennsylvania since the state opened their elk hunting season in 2001.

ceremony in Carlisle, Pennsylvania; to the Rocky Mountain Elk Foundation for all their conservation efforts; to the newly founded Pennsylvania Elk Country Alliance Chapter for helping to finish the beautiful visitors center in Winslow Hill in the midst of the elk area; and to the National Rifle Association for making it possible for us to still own and hunt with guns. As a lifetime member of the NRA, I find it hard to believe that so many hunters do not find it necessary to join the only voice against the anti's that are trying to strip us of our freedoms.

Last but not least, thanks again to Chuck, Jeff, and Janet Calwell, Charlie, Elain, Dana, Clair, and Mervin for helping to make this a once-in-a-lifetime hunt and experience that I'll cherish and remember for the rest of my life.

Boone and Crockett Club's 27th Awards Program Judges Panel verified the score of my bull at 441-6/8 points. I'm pleased to say that it is Pennsylvania's state record for non-typical American elk. ▲

B&C Photo Archives

Judges Panel members Frederick J. King (left) and Richard T. Hale constituted one of the teams of judges who verified the final score of Kyle M. Simmons' non-typical whitetail that scores 275-5/8. The 15 judges and consultants were selected from B&C's cadre of 1,200 Official Measurers for their long-time service as B&C scorers and their expertise scoring various categories of big game.

TROPHY STATS

▼ ▼ ▼ ▼ ▼

CATEGORY
  Non-typical American Elk

SCORE
  436$^4/_8$

LENGTH OF MAIN BEAM
  Right: 49$^4/_8$ Left: 50$^6/_8$

**CIRCUMFERENCE BETWEEN
FIRST AND SECOND POINTS**
  Right: 8$^4/_8$ Left: 8$^1/_8$

NUMBER OF POINTS
  Right: 10   Left: 9

INSIDE SPREAD
  42$^7/_8$

LOCATION
  Columbia Co., Washington – 2008

HUNTER
  Dan J. Agnew

BOONE AND CROCKETT CLUB'S

NON-TYPICAL AMERICAN ELK
Third Award – 436 $^4/_8$

▼ ▼ ▼ ▼ ▼ ▼ ▼ ▼ ▼

DAN J. AGNEW

I purchased my Washington eastside auction elk tag at the Rocky Mountain Elk Foundation's 2008 convention after seeing pictures of a tremendous bull's shed antlers, which were found during the spring of 2007. I knew this bull had been actively and unsuccessfully hunted by many during the 2007 hunting season, and I could see why they were unsuccessful during a summer 2008 scouting trip to the area south of Dayton, Washington. The canyons and terrain are steep with lots of dark timber for the bull to hide in. I waited with great anticipation and excitement for the 2008 hunting season to arrive.

First Day Luck

When I arrived in camp around 10 p.m. on September 2, 2008, to prepare for my hunt, I was pleasantly surprised when my guide told me he had spotted this bull just prior to sunset earlier that evening. However, he was cautious and told me he was over a mile away and that the following day's hunt was going to be difficult if he stayed where he was. Consequently, I didn't sleep much that night.

With nervous anticipation, we left camp at 5:20 the next morning and headed for the general area where the bull had been seen the previous evening. Within 30 minutes, we spotted a large herd of elk feeding on an open hillside about a half mile from the road we were on. With our binoculars locked in on the herd, we waited for daylight and soon realized that the bull I had come to hunt was there. During the night, he and a large harem of cows had moved to an open ridge—an area where my guide had never previously seen him.

After parking our rig and a brief stalk through a sliver of timber separating the road from the open ridge, I took a shot from about 250 yards with my .30-.378 Weatherby. The bull buckled, but did not go down. I knew I had hit him hard, but I couldn't get off another shot

Photograph by Jack Reneau

Dan J. Agnew accepting his plaque and medal from Buck Buckner, Vice President and Chairman of the Big Game Records Committee.

Dan J. Agnew harvested this award-winning non-typical American elk in Columbia County, Washington, during the 2008 season. The bull, which scores 436-4/8 points, is the Washington state record and received a Third Place Award at the 27th Big Game Awards Program.

because he had moved and was milling about his cows. As the cows got more nervous, the lead cow began running down the steep hillside headed for the bottom of a ravine. The bull was following the cows, but he was obviously in distress and lagged behind. I finally got in a position to take a second shot that ended the hunt and my quest for this incredible bull.

Sometimes luck simply falls in our laps. While I've spent days, weeks, and even months successfully and unsuccessfully hunting elk throughout the West for many years, I shot the "Red Stag" bull, which is the bull of a lifetime, on public land within an hour after I left camp on the first day of my hunt. My bull scores 436-4/8 points and grosses 446-6/8 points. It is the new Washington State record. I've never had such a short hunt in my life, and it's likely to never happen to me again, but that's really okay with me. ▲

Award-Winning Moments

B&C Photo Archives

27th Awards Program trophy owners John W. Rodius (left) and Joseph C. Bitzan view the 12 spectacular elk in the trophy display at the Grand Sierra Resort. Rodius received the Third Place Award for his Roosevelt's elk, scoring 338-1/8, and Bitzan received the Second Place Award for his barren ground caribou, scoring 417-5/8, that he took in 1978.

TROPHY STATS

▼ ▼ ▼ ▼ ▼

CATEGORY
Roosevelt's Elk

SCORE
$362^5/_8$

LENGTH OF MAIN BEAM
Right: $40^4/_8$ Left: $41^7/_8$

**CIRCUMFERENCE BETWEEN
FIRST AND SECOND POINTS**
Right: $10^5/_8$ Left: $10^6/_8$

NUMBER OF POINTS
Right: 9   Left: 9

INSIDE SPREAD
$38^7/_8$

LOCATION
Powell River, British Columbia – 2009

HUNTER
Allen M. Shearer

ROOSEVELT'S ELK
First Award – 362 ⁵/₈

▼ ▼ ▼ ▼ ▼ ▼ ▼ ▼

ALLEN M. SHEARER

This story started in 2003 when the British Columbia Ministry of Wildlife decided to put up a Roosevelt's elk permit for auction. The Foundation for North American Wild Sheep was selected to auction the permit at its National Convention. This permit caught my interest as a mature Roosevelt's elk was high on my wish list. I've bid on this permit every year, but it always went for more than I could justify spending. Finally, in 2009, at the Hunter's Convention in Salt Lake City, I was the lucky high bidder.

Crowning of the King

Buying the tag is one thing; finding the right outfitter that would allow me to hunt the way I wanted was another. I talked with a couple of the outfitters on Vancouver Island, but I did not like their programs. Then, through a longtime friend of mine named Tom Stanway, I got hooked up with Brad Lister of Coastal Inlet Adventures. Brad is based out of Powell River, located on the Sunshine Coast, and is part of the mainland of British Columbia. This is an unbelievably beautiful piece of coastline with countless miles of inlets that this permit allowed us to hunt. Brad and I put together a great program that allowed me to show up four days early, do some scouting and even attend the Coastal Inlet annual barbeque. What a great time with great people.

Photograph by Jack Reneau

Allen M. Shearer accepting his plaque and medal from Buck Buckner, Vice President and Chairman of the Big Game Records Committee.

September 1 finally arrived and Brad, Tom, and I were able to start hunting. We were staying in one of Brad's float houses at the end of an inlet. The first morning, we rose early and headed out to glass some logging units and check some areas where we had seen fresh sign. We quickly found a bull with five cows but decided that he needed a few years to grow. That evening, the group took the boat and looked at a logging unit out in the main inlet. There were three bulls there, but they were also too small. After returning to the float

Allen M. Shearer was the successful bidder for a British Columbia Roosevelt's elk tag in 2009, which he'd been trying to get for years. After a substantial effort, he harvested this award-winning bull with his muzzleloader. The bull scored 362-5/8 and received a First Place Award at the 27th Big Game Awards Program held in Reno, Nevada.

house, we had the opportunity to enjoy Tom's amazing culinary expertise, and his prowess guaranteed we would not go hungry! It was truly a great first day!

Day two found us back out on the water again. Tom dropped Brad and me off where we had observed the three bulls the night before. We wanted to verify that there weren't more in this area than the three we had seen from the water. Brad and I hiked the logging unit and only found the same three small bulls. When Tom returned to pick us up, we headed north where there was plenty of sign, but no more elk.

The weather was starting to turn on us and we decided to head back to the float house. After a two-hour boat ride in wind and rough water and the forecast calling for rain and high winds, we decided to pack up and head for Brad's house in Powell River.

Tom and I went back to Sechelt and took care of his boat, then loaded all our gear in my pickup and headed north to catch a ferry to Powell River. That evening, Brad pulled out a video of some elk that he had taken the year before. Tom and I were blown away! One of the bulls was amazing. I asked Brad if he had seen that bull this year, but he had not been

ROOSEVELT'S ELK
First Award – 362 5/8

▼ ▼ ▼ ▼ ▼

ALLEN M. SHEARER

back to that area to look. I knew where I wanted to go first thing in the morning, and the others agreed.

The 2008 video showed the bull as a 7x7 with great mass and point lengths. I did not sleep too much that night with that video playing in my head. The fact that I had chosen to hunt this tag with a muzzleloader made sleep even harder as I questioned whether I had made the correct decision.

My setup consists of an Ultimate Muzzleloader .50 cal. Stealth, equipped with a Christensen Arms barrel and stock. It's topped with a Swarovski 4-12 x 50 BT and likes a 275-grain Fury bullet pushed by three triple 7 magnum pellets. The binoculars I use are Leica 10x42 Geovids, a combination that has proven itself in the field over and over again.

The next morning again found us up early for the one-hour drive to get close to where Brad had taken the video in 2008. At daybreak, we crept up over a rise and were shocked to see the bull right in front of us with 12 cows. Words cannot express the sight of the bull standing there before us! Brad was quick to get the video going as Tom and I looked through our binoculars to size him up. This bull had gone from a 7x7 to a 9x10 and had incredible mass; the Boone and Crockett score would later reveal 66 inches, along with great point length. The unique crowning of Roosevelt's bulls was well-established, affirming his status as the king.

By the time we confirmed his size and decided to attempt a shot, the bull had had enough of us and took off with his cows. We were feeling both excitement and regret as we watched him disappear. Breakfast was ready back at Brad's house, and we had video footage of this bull to study so we retreated to his home to formulate our next plan.

The video confirmed our initial impressions of the size and mass of the bull. We knew he was a true trophy Roosevelt's elk and entertained the thought that his impressive antlers could very well surpass the muzzleloader World's Record held at the time by Jim Shockey. Early in the afternoon, we returned to the area we had seen the bull and got in position to glass where the herd had vanished that morning.

As I laid against a comfortable stump and the warm sun shone down on me, I drifted off to sleep. I awoke to Brad saying, "Hey Al, the elk are out." Those two hours flew by while snoozing on the mountain dreaming about huge elk.

The herd had come out about 500 yards further up the logging unit from where they had left that morning. We glassed and filmed but never were given an opportunity with favorable wind to try a stalk. As darkness consumed the elk, our group backed out hoping they would be close in the morning.

Daybreak found us back on the mountain, but the morning light didn't reveal any elk. We hunted all day without seeing the bull we were looking for and I figured that we had blown the opportunity to harvest this monster. Brad just smiled and said, "Al, he lives right here and we will find him again."

The morning of day five brought the wind and hard rain the Pacific Northwest is famous for. On the return trip up to the logging unit, we spotted a couple of blacktail deer and a small bull, but not the big guy and his girls. With plenty of time left in the morning, we decided to go look in a different clearing a couple of miles away. While enroute, we spotted some elk in a swamp.

It was the bull and his cows, 20 yards off the main road bedded in the swamp. We bailed out and tried to get on the bull, but I didn't dare shoot through the thick brush and sheets of rain for fear of not being able to recover this magnificent animal. The elk eventually got up and moved off into the timber and out of sight. We couldn't relocate the bull that night or the next morning and I started to get nervous again. However, Brad was still sure we would run into the big bull again soon.

On the evening of September 6, I was sneaking through the clearing above the swamp. The clouds parted, the rain stopped, and the sun was setting brilliantly in the west when Tom whispered, "Hey boys! There's an elk!"

Brad soon spotted another cow feeding below us. We sneaked up a little further around a big stump and saw the monster bull feeding at 100 yards. I quickly set up on the shooting sticks and took the shot. The bull instantly went down. I started reloading with Tom helping pick up my tools. I then moved down to a big log for a better rest. Suddenly, the bull stood back up. Even with a naked eye, it was very apparent that the bull was hit well. Not wanting to take any chances in the wet and heavy cover, I put a couple follow-up shots into the bull.

We were excited beyond words to have had the opportunity to hunt and harvest such a great trophy Roosevelt's elk. We started to take care of the bull and took some pictures and video before it got dark, but the task of getting this behemoth out of the woods would have to wait until morning.

The final morning was a great one to be on the mountain, especially spending time with new and old friends who were kind enough to help pack out such a tremendous bull.

I want to thank Brad Lister of Coastal Inlet Adventures for his hospitality, great guide territory and Johnny. I'd also like to thank Tom Stanway, my longtime friend, who put me in touch with Brad. You're a great cook there, buddy, and you motivated me to buy this permit—I could not have done it without you. I owe thanks as well to the British Columbia Ministry of Wildlife for putting together such a great Roosevelt's elk management program. ▲

Moments in Measuring

Mark O. Bara (center) was chairman of the 27th Awards Program Judges Panel. Prior to scoring, Mark discusses procedures the judges and consultants will follow in the days ahead. In addition to the chairman, the panel is composed of 10 judges and four consultants. Two of the judges are Canadians, and one is from the Pope and Young Club.

TROPHY STATS

▼ ▼ ▼ ▼ ▼

CATEGORY
Roosevelt's Elk

SCORE
338^5/$_8$

LENGTH OF MAIN BEAM
Right: 47^4/$_8$ Left: 48^4/$_8$

**CIRCUMFERENCE BETWEEN
FIRST AND SECOND POINTS**
Right: 8^4/$_8$ Left: 9^4/$_8$

NUMBER OF POINTS
Right: 7   Left: 7

INSIDE SPREAD
40^6/$_8$

LOCATION
Del Norte Co., California – 2008

HUNTER
Fred D. Ruggaber

ROOSEVELT'S ELK
Second Award – 338 ⁵/₈

▼ ▼ ▼ ▼ ▼ ▼ ▼ ▼ ▼

FRED D. RUGGABER

Apparently California's preference point system, which was implemented in 2001, worked for Fred D. Ruggaber. He had applied for a Roosevelt's elk permit for nearly 20 years without success, but he hit the jackpot in 2008 when he drew one of California's 20 either-sex tags for zone 483 with eight preference points, the maximum number a hunter could have at that time.

The literature mailed with the tag included the telephone number of a local fish and game employee and suggested hunters call it to find out were the elk are located. As a result of the subsequent inquiry, Fred hunted the first four-and-a-half days of the season near Orick, a small coastal town 41 miles north of Eureka. Fred was accompanied by his longtime hunting companion, Jim Martin. They spotted a number of elk during this portion of his hunt, but none were in his zone, so they took a break and headed home.

Fred used his time during this break in the action to make a few more phone calls, at-tempting to locate a better hunting area. When the sun came up a few days later, both were hunting a brush-covered hillside a few miles east of Eureka off Highway 299. They hunted all morning without any luck, so they headed back to the truck at noon to grab a bite to eat and strategize for the afternoon hunt.

They decided to take a drive and glass some hillsides in hopes of locating a bull and quickly spotted a couple of cows on a brush-covered hillside. It was the middle of the rut, so they took a closer look to see if there was a bull with them. Sure enough, they quickly located a bull hanging back in the brush. They didn't get a clear view of the antlers, but that wasn't a problem at this point. As the end of the 12-day season was fast approaching, Fred had already made up his mind that he would settle for any legal bull.

Fred and Jim then made their way up the densely covered hillside. The going was tough

Photograph by Jack Reneau

Fred D. Ruggaber accepting his plaque and medal from Buck Buckner, Vice President and Chairman of the Big Game Records Committee.

and the visibility was poor, but they caught a glimpse of the cows as the pair of them passed through an opening about 150 yards away. Fred and Jim were watching the opening when the bull stepped out of the brush and paused broadside to them.

At the shot, the bull spun around and headed into the brush. Fred heard the solid impact of the bullet, and took a quick second shot that turned out to be a clear miss. After waiting 30 minutes, they eagerly surged uphill through the brush.

Fred did not find any blood, but he had no doubts in his mind that he had made a good shot on the bull. They zigzagged back and forth through the brush a few minutes and quickly located his trophy about 30 yards from where it was standing when Fred took his first shot.

Once his bull was back at the truck, Fred took out the measuring tape from the scoring kit he purchased from B&C and followed the scoring instructions to come up with a rough, green score of 350 points. It was then that he realized he had taken a much better bull than either of them expected.

B&C Official Measurer Rich McDrew officially scored it after the 60-day drying period at 337-5/8, and the 27th Awards Program Judges Panel confirmed the score at 338-5/8. It is the fourth-largest bull ever taken in Del Norte County, California. Fred said he is once again actively working on building up his preference points. ▲

Award-Winning Moments

Mike Schoby, Editor of *Petersen's Hunting* **accepted the sponsor recognition plaque from Simon Roosevelt on behalf of Remington Arms and Ammunition. This was Remington's fourth consecutive sponsorship of a B&C Awards Program dating back to the 24th Big Game Awards held in Springfield, Missouri.**

TROPHY STATS

▼ ▼ ▼ ▼ ▼

CATEGORY
Roosevelt's Elk

SCORE
$338^1/_8$

LENGTH OF MAIN BEAM
Right: $52^2/_8$ Left: $51^6/_8$

**CIRCUMFERENCE BETWEEN
FIRST AND SECOND POINTS**
Right: 10   Left: $9^7/_8$

NUMBER OF POINTS
Right: 7   Left: 7

INSIDE SPREAD
$39^3/_8$

LOCATION
Clallam Co., Washington – 2005

HUNTER
John W. Rodius

ROOSEVELT'S ELK
Third Award – 338 ¹/₈

▼ ▼ ▼ ▼ ▼ ▼ ▼ ▼ ▼

JOHN W. RODIUS

Every hunter has a story about a particularly difficult hunt, about the one that got away, or about that trophy bull they took on opening day. This is my story.

When I was seven, my father took me on my first elk hunt. I was too young to hunt but certainly able to watch and learn. All it took was one weekend of hard hunting, the crack of my father's rifle, and the magnificent animal that lay before my father's feet, and I was forever hooked.

At the End of the Day

I was born in Shelton, Washington, and have lived on the Olympic Peninsula my entire life. I'm a logger by profession, but it is the hunt that defines me. Opening morning in 2005 came just in time; we'd emptied the last of my 2004 elk from the freezer just days before. As usual, my huntin' buddies, Nick Iversen and Chad Olsen, accompanied me in the hope that at least one of us would bag a bull on opening day. The way I see it, hunting is a team sport. You share the workload, the glory, and the meat. At least that's the way it is in my circle.

With our normal spot littered with other hunters, we decided to head to another location where I'd located tracks while scouting a couple of months earlier. Unfortunately, it was a 25-minute drive around the valley just to get there. After checking the area for any elk sign and finding none, we finally started out around 10 a.m. I sent Nick and Chad around the bottom of the valley, while I stayed on top trying to push some elk their way.

Tracking elk through the rainforest is tough. The woods are thick with devil's club, pucker brush, and soggy grass. It takes a lot of experience and guesswork, and you've got to be able to read between the lines. Always remember that elk like to walk in easy spots too, and they're always looking for food. With that in mind, I stayed on the old tracks until 2

Photograph by Jack Reneau

John W. Rodius accepting his plaque and medal from Buck Buckner, Vice President and Chairman of the Big Game Records Committee.

John W. Rodius is pictured above with his award-winning Roosevelt's elk taken during the 2005 season. The bull was taken in Clallam County, Washington, and has a final score of 338-1/8 points.

p.m. when I found a spot where the tracks looked fairly fresh. Game on!

I tried reaching my buddies on the two-way radio, but no one answered. They were onto some elk of their own, so I hiked about a quarter-mile up the mountain, over dead-falls and through the devil's club, until I hit an old logging road. From there, I went into a full sprint for about half a mile. There was only three hours of daylight left, and it was no time to fool around. When I reached the spot where I figured the elk would be, they were not there.

I caught my breath and worked my way back to Nick to find that he had just downed a nice four-pointer. Apparently, he'd missed a giant bull only moments earlier. Being so tight on the elk herd I had been after, I hadn't even heard the blast from his muzzleloader. I congratulated him on his bull, snapped a few pictures, and asked him which way the herd had gone. With Nick busy dressing his bull and Chad on his way to lend a hand, I continued tracking the herd looking for that monster.

About an hour before dark, I caught up to the herd, catching only glimpses of them through the thick salmon berries and devil's club. I watched in silence from only 10 yards away as a monster bull charged a beautiful five-pointer, stabbing it in the neck with that giant rack of his. As the five-pointer staggered off, I positioned myself for a shot at it.

At this point, you're probably wondering why on earth I'd pass up a monster for a big five-pointer. I'm a meat-hunter. I take the first open shot I get because I might not get a second. And, at the end of the day, they all taste the same.

Sadly, I missed the five-pointer from about 15 yards with my muzzleloader. He was too close and facing me, to boot! The only shot I had was a neck-shot. As soon as the muzzle cracked, he jumped, and I missed. He ran off unharmed but was ultimately killed during rifle season by a buddy of mine who showed me the crease my errant shot had made in his neck.

I took a few minutes, put my pack back on and resumed tracking the monster. Twenty minutes later, I caught up with the herd, which had regrouped on the river, but I couldn't see that well through all the salmon berries. There I was, standing knee-deep in the river when I spotted a cow about a hundred yards off. No time to duck for the bushes—I just dropped straight down in the river, my legs splayed out with water rushing over my pants and boots, my chest sunken in the muddy bank. Eyes up, I scanned the area. About 45-50 yards off stood a large moss-encrusted tree with two sets of oversized antlers jutting out from either side.

I kept staring at this tree, just waiting for the right moment. There were about 25 cows within a stone's throw barking at me, trying to blow my cover. One cow in particular barked every 10 seconds the entire 15 minutes I lay face down in the muddy riverbank. I couldn't move, so I had to be patient. I sure wished I had a cow tag right about then.

Between the barks, the monster turned to leave. He took two steps from the tree and looked at me. With one leg still in the river and the other knee pressed tight in the soft bank, I leveled off and hit him square in the right front shoulder. Instead of falling like I'd hoped, the bull took about ten steps forward, stopped, and looked at me again. I reloaded in seven seconds and hit him in the exact same spot. This time, he ran off. I spun, grabbed my pack, and got to my feet. After lying motionless for nearly 15 minutes, my legs were a bit cramped.

With light fading fast and my aching legs unable to move, I watched the herd dart up the mountain, the bull limping along well behind. I tracked him for half an hour into

ROOSEVELT'S ELK
Third Award – 338 1/8

▼ ▼ ▼ ▼ ▼

JOHN W. RODIUS

AT THIS POINT, YOU'RE PROBABLY WONDERING WHY ON EARTH I'D PASS UP A MONSTER FOR A BIG FIVE-POINTER. I'M A MEAT-HUNTER. I TAKE THE FIRST OPEN SHOT I GET BECAUSE I MIGHT NOT GET A SECOND. AND, AT THE END OF THE DAY, THEY ALL TASTE THE SAME.

the night when I stopped. It was pitch-black, so I hung ribbon and headed back to the rig with the intention of finishing the job the next day.

We returned the following morning and made quick work of Nick's elk. With the meat headed back to the cooler with Nick, Chad and I headed upriver to find the herd. After six hard hours meandering through waist-high grass and sticker-infested reprod and logging slash, we finally heard a calf squeal and knew that we were close.

I wanted my buddy to share in some of the action Nick and I had seen, so I asked Chad, "Do you want a shot at that big bull?" He nodded anxiously.

I figured I could take about 15 steps to my left and let the herd scent me. They'd take off away from me and right into my buddy's crosshairs. At least, that was the plan. And that's sort of the way it happened.

I was quietly stalking upwind when the herd got a whiff of me and spun around in Chad's direction. Unfortunately, they weren't headed in Chad's direction so much as they headed directly for Chad. The lead cow literally stopped only inches from Chad's face as the ground rumbled under her weight. She was standing there eyeball to eyeball with Chad when she gave out another loud "bark." As Chad flinched, she spun the herd around again. Chad later told me that her breath was awful.

The herd was now headed back towards me. Luckily, they ran off 20 yards or so to my left, so I could concentrate on spotting the monster. Eyes scanning the thick forest, I spotted the bull as he limped out from behind some reprod. He stood about 60 yards almost vertical from my position as I leveled off and hit him right behind the shoulder. This time, he lumbered another 15 yards, leaned up against a big fir tree and collapsed. The hunt of my life was finally over. It was now time to enjoy the spoils of war. ▲

Panel Judge Eldon L. "Buck" Buckner (left) computes the score for the score chart that he and his team partner Larry Lack just completed for Frank Lawrence's typical Coues' whitetail. Since their score was within the predetermined shrinkage allowance for this category, the entry score of 126 points remained the same. Buckner is chairman of B&C's Records Committee, which is the governing body for the Club's records-keeping activities.

TROPHY STATS

▼ ▼ ▼ ▼ ▼

CATEGORY
Tule Elk

SCORE
$322^5/_8$

LENGTH OF MAIN BEAM
Right: $38^4/_8$ Left: $41^2/_8$

CIRCUMFERENCE BETWEEN FIRST AND SECOND POINTS
Right: $8^1/_8$ Left: $7^6/_8$

NUMBER OF POINTS
Right: 7   Left: 8

INSIDE SPREAD
$38^4/_8$

LOCATION
San Luis Obispo Co., California – 2007

HUNTER
Andrew J. Wood

TULE ELK
First Award – 322 ⁵/₈

▼ ▼ ▼ ▼ ▼ ▼ ▼ ▼

ANDREW J. WOOD

As a California youngster, I had heard my father's and uncles' hunting stories as they returned from elk hunting trips in Colorado and Wyoming. I figured that some day I would have the resources and time to put elk hunting on the top of my list of priorities. With 13 preference points in Nevada, I finally drew an American elk tag and harvested a great bull with the help of Western Wildlife Adventures.

I then used some friendship points to hunt and take an excellent Roosevelt's Elk on Santa Rosa

The Golden Bull

Island off the California coast. I then literally turned my sights on tule elk.

There are several opportunities to draw tule elk tags on game reserves and public land, but with my poor luck, plus a combination of high application numbers and low tag quotas, I figured my chances of drawing a tag were slim to none. I determined that my best chance to hunt one of these animals, while I was still young enough to enjoy the chase, was

to purchase California's equivalent of a land-owner's tag. I contacted long-time friend, Ron Lara of Western Wildlife Adventures and told him of my wish to hunt tule elk, and he put me in touch with Nick Tacito. I spent the next 18 months anticipating the hunt that would take place just outside of Paso Robles in the central coast region of the state. The plan was to start the hunt prior to the rut, which is a plus if a complete set of antlers is the goal, as tule bulls often break off all or part of their antlers each year during the annual brawl.

The middle of July 2007 found me driving the valley with the air-conditioner on full blast and my hunting gear whittled down to light-weight khakis in tan. Traditional camouflage would have stuck out like a sore thumb in the golden countryside. With predicted daytime temperatures in the 90°F range and shade consisting of an occasional scrub oak or fence post, hunting was going to be limited to an hour

Photograph by Jack Reneau

Andrew J. Wood accepting his plaque and medal from Buck Buckner, Vice President and Chairman of the Big Game Records Committee.

Photograph courtesy of Andrew J. Wood

Andrew J. Wood harvested this award-winning tule elk in San Luis Obispo County of his home state of California, during the 2007 season. The bull, which scores 322-5/8 points, received a First Place Award at the 27th Big Game Awards Program in Reno, Nevada.

or so in the morning and an equally short time period just before sunset.

I met my guide Clint White before daylight in Shandon, a small community east of Paso Robles. Clint's family owned and farmed the property we would be hunting. He had seen a bull he thought I should take a look at, but in typical cowboy fashion, he didn't give any details.

Dawn found us sitting high on a hill watching the sun's first rays touch the wheat fields. To our left, a bachelor group of 15 to 20 bulls filed along a ridge top. There were several spikes, but the largest of the bunch was certainly not the quality bull I was looking for.

"Hey, there he is," Clint whispered as he pointed out three heads silhouetted above the grass in a shaded part of the valley below.

I knew instantly I had found my bull. My mouth dried out and my heart tried jumping out of my chest. With no cover to speak of, we took the opportunity to survey the situation while the three bulls unconcernedly wandered up the hill and dropped out of sight on the far side. We were soon in hot pursuit, trying to catch a glimpse of the bulls before they could make us out.

TULE ELK
First Award – 322 5/8

▼ ▼ ▼ ▼ ▼

ANDREW J. WOOD

Unfortunately we circled around a knob and came face to face with the fellows staring down their noses at us from about 75 yards. Unable to get a shot, we watched as they snorted and wheeled in unison. The last we saw of them were their rumps and antlers headed over the horizon.

We spent the remainder of the morning glassing and spotting elk. But, needless to say, any animal that Clint presented to me during the rest of the day paled in comparison. At lunch we decided to let things settle down and try our luck in a different part of the ranch. We planned to try again for the big bull in the morning.

Dawn found us hunkered down, waiting to see if the threesome would return, I believe I mentioned my penchant for bad luck before, and the trend was holding true. There was no sign of the bull I had decided I had to have. With the sun already starting to heat things up, we hiked to the watering hole. There was some scat, but no elk.

Then Clint put his glasses up and said, "I think I've got him! He's out on the fallow ground and we can get pretty darn close."

Following the contour of the land we belly-crawled through dirt clods and rocks to within 300 yards. I took a rest on my pack and let the .300 Weatherby Magnum bark. Stunned, I thought I missed.

The three bulls took off at a dead run for a short distance, then turned back to look at us as if to say, "What's going on?"

"He stopped!" I said as I jacked another round into the chamber and let fly.

This time I heard the words, "You shot under him!"

I watched in disbelief as the bull topped the rise and disappeared. I consider myself a pretty good shot, although I'm not quite sure my guide would agree.

We made our way to a vantage point and spotted the bull again. This time I hit him hard but by now he had adrenalin pumping and something as small as a bullet wasn't going to stop him in his tracks. Using the contours of the land to his advantage now, the bull once again disappeared from sight. His buddies had long since decided that discretion is the better part of valor and headed off to parts unknown.

As we topped the last hill, I looked down the long slope and there was my bull, his crown pointed to the sky. One more well-placed shot and he was down for good.

As we made our way down the hill, I had time to think about what had just happened. I had taken a bull of a lifetime in the golden fields of my home state of California to complete my version of an elk slam. I had just taken the Golden Bull! I want to thank everyone who made this hunt possible, but most of all, I want to thank my wife who puts up with my obsessions and was there to enjoy this moment with me. Yes, everything is golden when you're hunting elk! ▲

TROPHY STATS

▼ ▼ ▼ ▼ ▼

CATEGORY
Tule Elk

SCORE
$322^3/_8$

LENGTH OF MAIN BEAM
Right: 46   Left: $43^4/_8$

**CIRCUMFERENCE BETWEEN
FIRST AND SECOND POINTS**
Right: $8^6/_8$ Left: $8^4/_8$

NUMBER OF POINTS
Right: 7   Left: 7

INSIDE SPREAD
$41^2/_8$

LOCATION
Colusa Co., California – 2008

HUNTER
Thomas B. Gordon

TULE ELK
Second Award – 322 ³/₈

▼ ▼ ▼ ▼ ▼ ▼ ▼ ▼ ▼

THOMAS B. GORDON

Most all big game hunters in California watch the mail closely. At the end of June each year we start looking for that envelope proclaiming success in the big game draw.

I was one of the lucky ones in June of 2008, receiving that much anticipated letter from the California Department of Fish and Game. In big, bold, black letters the letter read: Elk Drawing Notice - Successful. The hunt zone I had drawn was 461, East Park Reservoir, Period 1, General Bull.

A Classic Tule Elk

This particular hunt zone is only about 50 miles from my home near Princeton in the Sacramento Valley. The hunt was to take place in early September, and was open to any legal method except for Bureau of Reclamation lands in the vicinity of East Park Reservoir, where only muzzleloaders are allowed. This meant I would have to sharpen my skills with both my .50 caliber TIC Omega, as well as my center-fire rifle, just in case the elk were by the lake during the upcoming season. My son Tom had fished at East Park many times, and told me of hearing bull elk bugling near the lake during the fall rutting season.

Even though the zone was close to home and I knew there were elk around the lake, I also realized what a unique and valuable opportunity this was. I found the hunt zone encompassed U.S. Forest Service lands, Bureau of Land Management lands, private land, and the Bureau of Reclamation area (BOR) around the lake. Because of this, I wanted all the information I could gather about the zone, the property owners and the animals' habits. All these questions were answered when I received a phone call from a man in mid July. His name was Pat Callahan, and he lived in Stonyford, a small town on the northeast side of East Park Reservoir. Pat proceeded to tell me he knew the East Park elk herd better than anyone, pointing out that he watched the animals about 360 days

Photograph by Jack Reneau

Thomas B. Gordon accepting his plaque and medal from Buck Buckner, Vice President and Chairman of the Big Game Records Committee.

Photograph courtesy of Thomas B. Gordon

Thomas B. Gordon is pictured with his guide Brian Stonyford and the tule elk he harvested scoring 322-3/8 points. The award-winning bull was taken in Colusa County, California, during the 2008 season, and received a Second Award at the 27th Big Game Awards Program.

during the year. I would soon find out this was an understatement. Pat invited me to come to Stonyford to view some bull elk he had been watching.

The next evening I met Pat, his wife Erin, and son Brian at their home in Stonyford. Pat showed me a number of elk that evening, including one bull he had field scored at 330 points. That bull really excited me, and fueled a desire to scout as much as I could before the season arrived in September.

There were two bull tags given for the hunt, and I soon met the other lucky hunter, Brian Lohse. Brian lives in a town about 17 miles from me, and also would be hunting with Pat. He'd seen the 330 point bull, and liked what it offered. Both Brian and I had been scouting the bull when Pat informed us that an even bigger bull had entered the area where the elk were gathering. Brian took a look at the bigger bull and decided he wanted to harvest him. This worked out well for me, since the 330 bull was the one I was most interested in. The bigger bull had antlers with characteristics more like those of an American elk than a tule elk in my opinion. Plus the palmation with multiple points on top of the 330 bull was classic tule elk.

TULE ELK
Second Award – 322 ³/₈
▼ ▼ ▼ ▼ ▼

THOMAS B. GORDON

The evening before the hunt we watched the bulls bugle and fight until dark. That's when we noticed that the bull Brian wanted to harvest had some broken antler points on his left side near the top. Brian told Pat that he still wanted to harvest the bull, even though it wouldn't score as well with the missing points.

Brian and I studied the 330 bull just before dark, and confirmed his antlers were still intact with the exception of one point tip missing on the left side. Broken antlers on tule elk are very common, and can keep a big bull from scoring well. When we left the elk at dark they were on BOR land, which meant we would be hunting with our muzzleloaders in the morning.

The next morning at 5:30 I met Pat, and his son and Brian Lohse at the walk-in entrance to the BOR tract on East Park Reservoir. As we loaded our daypacks and prepared our muzzleloaders, Brian and I decided which bulls we would each pursue.

We agreed if the animals spooked and scattered, we would take whichever of the two bulls that presented a good shot. This was important because the season was only four days long, and spooked animals could disappear into one of several steep and brushy canyons and be difficult to relocate.

I was to hunt with Pat's son Brian. We all hiked to a good vantage point above where the elk had been seen the previous evening, then sat down to wait for enough light to glass. Not long after arriving we heard a battle between two bulls through the early morning darkness. The noise of antlers clashing continued for some time before we could gain enough light to focus on the event taking place before us. When we finally found the animals in our binoculars, our hearts sank. The two fighting bulls were the same two we were pursuing, and Brian's bull had broke even more antler from his left side.

The low light and large dust cloud prevented us from seeing if the 330 bull's antlers were still intact or not. The bigger bull pushed the 330 bull across a small opening in the brush, then ran him through a stand of willows and into a large patch of tules, where he sulked for some time. By now we had plenty of light to get into position for an ambush when the animals moved to their bedding area. Pat figured the elk would leave the low tule area when the sun rose over the ridge and head for the cool, steep canyons to bed for the day.

It seemed to take forever for the herd to feed toward our ambush point. When they finally did, we discovered that they would be moving through another ravine rather than the one we were set up on. Brian and I quickly ran to the next ravine and readied for the shot.

We found a small oak tree with a low limb perfect for a solid rest. The herd had split, and my bull was in the first group poised to enter the ravine.

The bull was moving slowly uphill behind the lead cows. When the elk stopped in a clearing at 165 yards, I squeezed the trigger and the .50 caliber slug slammed into the right shoulder. The bull never even flinched at the shot, so I glanced back for confirmation from Brian that it had been good. Brian gave me a thumbs-up, but indicated that the shot may have been further back than I thought.

While I was reloading the muzzleloader the bull took a few steps and went down behind a large, dead oak tree. The bull kept his head in an alert position for several minutes, but I couldn't get a second shot. Both Brian and I knew the bull was mortally wounded, but to our dismay the animal regained his footing and slowly stepped beyond the dead oak tree, finally giving me an opportunity for that second shot.

The bull fell at the sound of the second shot, and was down for good at 7:30 that morning. We walked the short distance to the bull and stood there admiring the animal for a few minutes until Pat and Brian Loshe appeared. They glanced at the bull then quickly left to intercept the second bull before he made it to the canyon to bed.

Pat and Brian found their quarry, and Brian made good on his plan to harvest him. Soon both bulls were down and the Bureau of Reclamation gate opened to bring in a vehicle to retrieve the two elk. To my astonishment, six pickups soon were on the scene, along with a total of 13 people to help load the bulls on a flatbed truck and haul them to Pat's house for skinning and processing. Included in this group was my wife Tina, my son Tom, a game warden, a sheriff's deputy, a Fish and Game biologist, other elk hunters and many local people, all there to admire the bulls we had taken. Obviously it's a special event when bull elk season opens in Stonyford.

After the 60-day drying period, my bull was scored at 326-5/8 points. Had he not broken the small piece of antler on his left side, the score would have been right at 330 points, exactly what Pat Callahan told me when we first spotted the bull. The 27th Awards Program Judges Panel confirmed the score of my bull at 322-3/8 points in April 2010 and honored it with the Second Place Award Medal, which I received at the Awards Banquet in Reno, Nevada, on June 26, 2010. ▲

B&C Photo Archives

A visitor views the non-typical whitetail deer section of the trophy display. Included is Gerald
E. Rightmyer's buck (foreground) that scores 272-2/8. There are 27 scorable points on this
rack, including a substantial drop tine on the right antler that measures 11-1/8 inches long. The
combined lengths of the abnormal points, which add into the score of non-typicals, total 101-2/8
inches on this rack.

TROPHY STATS

▼ ▼ ▼ ▼ ▼

CATEGORY
Tule Elk

SCORE
312⁵/₈

LENGTH OF MAIN BEAM
Right: 45   Left: 36⁴/₈

**CIRCUMFERENCE BETWEEN
FIRST AND SECOND POINTS**
Right: 9²/₈   Left: 9⁵/₈

NUMBER OF POINTS
Right: 6   Left: 9

INSIDE SPREAD
37⁵/₈

LOCATION
Colusa Co., California – 2007

HUNTER
Richard L. Garrison

TULE ELK
Third Award – 312 ⁵/₈

▼ ▼ ▼ ▼ ▼ ▼ ▼ ▼

RICHARD L. GARRISON

In July 2007, I received the incredible news from the California Department of Fish and Game (CDFG) that I had been awarded the East Park tule elk tag near Stonyford, California. I knew the area well, since I had been hunting the Snow Mountain area for over 30 years. It was only a matter of hours before I had my weekend's trip planned for scouting out the area that I would soon be hunting.

When I got to East Park Reservoir, I was informed by a local sheriff's deputy that I was very lucky to have drawn this tag. He also said that the best-known outfitter for tule elk happened to be a local rancher named Pat Callahan. Pat, from Snow Mountain Outfitters, was not only the local guide in the Stonyford area, but he also had been studying tule elk in the area for many years. His knowledge about the herd was unbelievable.

Following my initial call to Pat, we met and scouted for elk in the Stonyford area that following weekend. Pat used photographs, video, and notes to document the sizes and location of all of the biggest bulls we saw. On many occasions I told Pat that I would take any of the bulls we had seen, but his reply was always, "Those were only dinks. You'll eventually see a real Boone and Crockett bull."

As the season drew closer, I was seeing bigger and better bulls each weekend. Pat made weekly calls to update me on the different bulls he had seen, as well as emails that included pictures of bulls that his wife, Erin, had photographed. As opening day of the season drew near, Pat and I had found two or three bulls that we felt would easily make the B&C minimum.

Three weeks before the hunt date, Pat called and said he had seen one of the best bulls of the year. His excitement was cautioned with the warning that the rut had started and that bulls were starting to fight, which meant there would likely be some antler breakage.

The following week I received a call from Joe Hobbs, the Fish and Game biologist, who

Photograph by Jack Reneau

Richard L. Garrison accepting his plaque and medal from Buck Buckner, Vice President and Chairman of the Big Game Records Committee.

Richard L. Garrison and his wife Cherice stand beside Garrison's award-winning tule elk taken during the 2007 season in Colusa County, California. The bull has a final score of 312-5/8 points.

informed me of a mandatory orientation required for the hunt. After confirming that Pat Callahan was my guide, Joe said that explaining the hunt boundaries would be easy because of Pat's local knowledge of the hunt area.

Due to a drought and the proximity of elk to water, it was relatively easy to pattern elk movement. Since East Park Reservoir's water had receded, the cows were constantly feeding at the lake bottom, which meant the bulls were right behind them. Seeing all these cows and bulls together made for an unbelievable sight, too. The downside was that the bulls were so congregated, the fighting was intense!

We were down to our last week before the season opened when I received a call from Pat saying the bull we had been watching had broken off a portion of his left antler while fighting and that we needed to rethink our strategy. The search for the next best bull started immediately with only a few days remaining until opening day.

On our next drive to Stonyford to hookup with Pat, I saw a bull on private land that had the size and mass I was looking for. I couldn't get a good look at him through the spotting scope, but it looked as though there was a break on his right side. Pat followed up and confirmed that the bull was not broken but rather had very unique palmation on his right antler. It was the day before opening day before I finally saw that elk again. He was on a ridge with cows and still on private land. All I could do was hope he would make it to the lake bottom the following day.

TULE ELK
Third Award – 312 5/8

▼ ▼ ▼ ▼ ▼

RICHARD L. GARRISON

Later that evening, my friend Mike Bonanno came up to accompany me on the hunt. We went to the lake and found that the bull I liked had indeed made it to the lake bottom. Now my biggest hope was that he wouldn't fight and break any of his regal rack during the night or move off again to private land.

On opening morning, Pat and I hiked a mile before daylight to set up on the west shore of the reservoir where we had watched the elk crossing each morning and evening. After we set up in a draw on the west side of the lake, we watched in amazement as each and every cow and bull—except the bull I was looking for—walked around us within 100 yards of where we were set up. Thinking the bull must have left before light, Pat and I decided to back out and go to the truck to talk about revising our strategy. Shortly afterward, my wife Cherice and Mike told us that as they had been watching the bull through a spotting scope, the bull had actually pushed his cows to the far side of the lake and swam around behind us.

Pat's best guess was that the bulls had headed to a part of the lake called Middle Ridge, a small peninsula of land where the elk often bed down during the day. We decided to try a spot-and-stalk approach to see if we could get within muzzleloader-range. After setting up a spotting scope, we spotted the bull I was after on a west-facing ridge surrounded by his cows.

We began the stalk, working our way downwind and crawling within 100 yards of the herd. The bull was busy tending to his cows and finally gave me a good shot. I took advantage of it and touched off a 295-grain Hornady round from my .50 caliber Knight muzzleloader. When the smoke cleared, he was still standing, so I reloaded and fired a second round. The bull dropped but quickly regained his footing and started stumbling down toward the valley below, where he expired.

With the bull down, Pat returned to get Cherice, Mike, the biologist, and Pat's sons, Brian and Scott, to help pack my bull out. Brian and Scott had their packhorses and mule set up to pack out the bull, but as luck would have it, the bull just happened to drop within 50 yards of the only road that was legally accessible by vehicle. The warden allowed us to drive into the area and we were able to get right up to the bull, making for an easy pack out.

I would like to thank all the people that helped me with this hunt—my wife Cherice; Pat and Erin Callahan of Snow Mountain Outfitters; their sons, Brian and Scott; my friend, Mike Bonanno; the warden from the CDFG; the state biologist; and Joe Hobbs from CDFG. I would also like to dedicate this special hunt in memory of Scott Callahan. ▲

TROPHY STATS

▼ ▼ ▼ ▼ ▼

CATEGORY
Tule Elk

SCORE
311

LENGTH OF MAIN BEAM
Right: 42^4/$_8$ Left: 42^6/$_8$

CIRCUMFERENCE BETWEEN FIRST AND SECOND POINTS
Right: 7^3/$_8$ Left: 7^1/$_8$

NUMBER OF POINTS
Right: 8   Left: 7

INSIDE SPREAD
40^3/$_8$

LOCATION
Solano Co., California – 2006

HUNTER
Steven S. Bruggeman

TULE ELK
Fourth Award – 311
▼ ▼ ▼ ▼ ▼ ▼ ▼ ▼
STEVEN S. BRUGGEMAN

My first thought as I started glassing for tule elk was, *This can't be right!* I have hunted elk many times in various mountain states, but never in a swamp with ten-foot tall bulrushes and very few trees. My guide, Richard Cox, assured me that this was, indeed, prime habitat in the Grizzly Island Wildlife Management Area where my tule elk tag was valid.

My hunt officially began when Richard picked me up at the Sacramento airport and we immediately drove to the hunting area to begin scouting. As the afternoon wore on, elk began to emerge from the tules and fed into the open areas. We spotted several bulls that evening, but none big enough to get excited about tying my tag on.

In the Tules

We spent the next day—the day before the season opened—scouting the entire area. Late in the day we found two bulls that we believed would score well above a Boone and Crockett record and also contend for the top of the muzzleloader records book.

Opening day, August 5, dawned clear, and as the sky started to lighten, we were glassing the area where we had spotted the two largest bulls. We heard several bugles and anticipation was running high. As it got lighter, we could see several bulls and cows but neither of the two big bulls we were looking for. We hunted hard all day and saw dozens of elk, including several good bulls, but could not locate the biggest bulls from the day before. Late in the day, we did spot several elk but could not identify them in the fading light.

Day two found us glassing the area where we had spotted the elk the evening before. We soon found five bulls about 400 yards away, including the two big bulls we had been looking for. At this distance we studied the racks through the spotting scopes and agreed both bulls were B&C contenders, but one of

Photograph by Jack Reneau

Steven S. Bruggeman accepting his plaque and medal from Buck Buckner, Vice President and Chairman of the Big Game Records Committee.

Photograph courtesy of Steven S. Bruggeman

Steven S. Bruggeman is pictured above with his guide Richard Cox and the award-winning tule elk that Bruggeman harvested with his muzzleloader. The bull has a final score of 311 points and was taken during the 2006 season in Solano County, California.

the bulls had a short G-2 on his left side.

Because I was hunting with a muzzleloader, I needed to get much closer. Not long after we began our stalk, the bulls began to head toward the cover of the tules. Using available cover, we quickly closed the distance to 120 yards.

As the bulls passed through an opening, I took a quartering away shot at the best one. When the smoke cleared, we saw him disappear back into the tules. I reloaded as fast as possible, and we moved in to locate him. We found him standing about 80 yards away, and I quickly put another 250-grain Hornady behind his shoulder. At the shot, he took off again into heavy cover. We followed the trail of broken bulrushes and easily found our prize.

What a great bull and fantastic sight to walk up on! With a beautifully large rack, great mass, and many points on each side, we knew he would score well. After the required drying time, he was officially scored at 311, making it the No. 2 muzzleloader tule elk. His B&C gross score is 319-1/8 points.

I would like to thank California Department Fish and Game for their excellent management of the tule elk herd. This herd was nearly extinct, but has now been rescued and restored to a thriving, huntable population. ▲

Award-Winning Moments

Outdoor writer, television personality, and Boone and Crockett Club professional member, Wayne van Zwoll accepts the 27th Awards sponsorship on behalf of Leupold & Stevens. Van Zwoll authored Leupold's book celebrating the company's 100th Anniversary. This was Leupold's fourth sponsorship of a B&C Awards event.

TROPHY STATS

▼ ▼ ▼ ▼ ▼

CATEGORY
Typical Mule Deer

SCORE
209

LENGTH OF MAIN BEAM
Right: 28   Left: 27

**CIRCUMFERENCE BETWEEN
BURR AND FIRST POINT**
Right: $6^2/_8$ Left: $6^2/_8$

NUMBER OF POINTS
Right: 6   Left: 6

INSIDE SPREAD
$23^5/_8$

LOCATION
Garfield Co., Utah – 2008

HUNTER
Del R. Brady

TYPICAL MULE DEER
First Award – 209

▼ ▼ ▼ ▼ ▼ ▼ ▼ ▼ ▼

DEL R. BRADY

There he was, the buck of a lifetime, 197 yards away. My guide Kalan Lemon said, "You need to get a bullet into him now." It was early morning, and I was excited. I fired and missed.

I had previously applied for a deer permit in Utah's Book Cliffs area because it is close to my home in Vernal. However, in 2008, I decided to put in for the Henry Mountains Unit. While considering my options as a Utah resident, I decided to apply for the area I felt had the best deer in the state. When I received confirmation that I had indeed drawn a tag for the premium, limited entry season for buck mule deer in the Henry Mountains Unit, I knew immediately I had the tag of a lifetime in my hands.

The Buck of a Lifetime

I talked to Don Peay of Sportsman for Wildlife (SFW) and asked who he would recommend for a guide. He gave me two names and their phone numbers. I contacted both and settled on hunting with Doyle Moss from Mossback Guides and Outfitters of Elk Ridge, Utah. Doyle was hunting bear in Montana the first time I talked to him, but he said he would immediately have two videos sent to me showing some of the big bucks his hunters had taken over the last couple of years.

Two of my sons had general season, northeastern Utah deer tags. Lance had already committed to take a couple of other fellows hunting with him, so he could not go with me. My other son Todd wanted to go and decided to pass on his general season tag.

The day before the hunt, Todd and I met my guide, Kalan Lemon, in Hanksville, Utah. Kalan has hunted all his life with his dad Wade Lemon, a man who I had heard of many times before. I immediately felt very comfortable with Kalan, who led me to the hunting camp near the Henry Mountains.

The Henry Mountains are a unique

Photograph by Jack Reneau

Del R. Brady accepting his plaque and medal from Buck Buckner, Vice President and Chairman of the Big Game Records Committee.

Del R. Brady is pictured above with his award-winning typical mule deer scoring 209 points. The buck, which was taken in Garfield County, Utah, during the 2008 season, received a First Place Award at the 27th Big Game Awards Program in Reno, Nevada.

range located south of Hanksville, Utah. They rise from the desert floor to a height of 10,000 to 11,000-plus feet in elevation. It is also home to a well known herd of free-ranging buffalo acceptable for entry in Boone and Crockett. I had visited the area several years earlier and was fortunate to see the most beautiful, golden-blonde bull I could have possibly imagined. This is truly an amazing part of Utah.

The weather was warm for the third weekend of October. A bright, full moon illuminated the landscape that first cloudless night. Our camp was located on a sagebrush flat at the base of the mountains. It consisted of two trailers outfitted for the hunters, a few trailers set up for the guides, and a nice kitchen/dining trailer. The accommodations were top notch and very much appreciated.

On this particular hunt, I was using my MGA custom rifle, a .300 Remington Ultra Magnum with a 6-18 x 50 Swarovski scope. I was shooting Remington's Premier Power Level III, 180-grain Swift Sirocco Bonded bullets. The binoculars we were using were 10 x 42 Leica Geovid, and we used a 20-60 x 77 Leica and a 20-60 x 65 Swarovski for spotting scopes.

After getting settled in camp, Kalan and Wayne (the assistant guide) suggested that we go up the mountain and start looking for a buck. We started by focusing our attention on the piñon-juniper habitat around the lower part

TYPICAL MULE DEER
First Award – 209

▼ ▼ ▼ ▼ ▼

DEL R. BRADY

of the mountain. The two guides had spotted a big typical mule deer there earlier in the year that gave their muzzleloader hunters the slip on five different occasions. We were spotting from a position where the guides had previously seen the big typical. Even though we spotted quite a few deer, including a couple of nice four-pointers, that afternoon and evening, we didn't see anything worth getting too excited about. What I didn't know at the time was that Kalan and Wayne were specifically looking for the buck they had seen during the muzzleloader season.

On opening day, we left camp about one hour before daylight and drove up the mountain to the same area where we'd been glassing the previous afternoon. Several does and small bucks ran out in front of us as we climbed the mountain. Suddenly, a buck appeared on the hillside ahead of us. He was intent on eating and didn't seem too alarmed. I later learned that Kalan and Wayne easily recognized him because of the 3-1/2 inch kicker off the right antler. The guides immediately got very excited and said, "this is the buck we are after."

I looked at him through my binoculars and gauged him at nearly 150 yards. My first words were, "Wow, look how high he is!"

I MISSED THAT FIRST SHOT. THE BUCK RAN A SHORT DISTANCE DOWN THE RIDGE AND STOPPED BROADSIDE TO US. I REMEMBER SAYING, "LOOK HOW BIG HIS CHEST IS!" IT WAS LIKE SHOOTING AT A BARN DOOR.

The buck was easily identified by his 29-inch spread plus the kicker off the right beam, making him more than 32 inches wide. A large wild fire had swept through this area several years earlier, and the Utah Division of Wildlife Resources, with help of the BLM, had reseeded the burned area with a great seed mix that included alfalfa. It was in this reseeded area that we first located the buck.

He continued eating for a few moments, then bolted up over the top of the hill and out of sight. Assistant guide Wayne Brown watched where he ran and pointed him out on the far ridgeline, out of range for a shot. We continued to the top of the ridge where the buck had been standing.

As we crested the ridge, we quickly spotted the big buck standing in burnt junipers on the hill to the north, facing directly away from us. I quickly set up the shooting sticks for a kneeling shot. I could just see his white rump and part of his body. I was very excited and told Kalan that I couldn't settle down and hold right on him. Kalan said, "You need to get a bullet into him now."

I missed that first shot. The buck ran a short distance down the ridge and stopped broadside to us. I remember saying, "Look how big his chest is!"

It was like shooting at a barn door. I judged the range at 211 yards and finally felt comfortable. I calmly set the crosshairs on his chest and squeezed the trigger. I heard the bullet hit and knew that I finally had him. At the time, I didn't comprehend how big the buck really was, but Kalan and Wayne sure did.

We had the deer back to base camp by about 11 a.m. By noon, several people had stopped by camp to see my buck. Later in the afternoon, Mike Truman, another assistant guide, showed up in camp with some sheds he had found in April 2008. After studying the sheds and the buck, everyone was convinced that they were from this same buck. The sheds claimed a gross score of 207 points, allowing for a reasonable amount for the inside spread, which of course cannot be accurately determined.

Utah asks hunters taking a deer on a limited entry deer tag to submit a tooth for aging purposes. I was contacted in February 2009 and notified that my deer was 4 years old. Assuming those were his sheds from the previous year, he grossed 207 points as a three year old and 225-2/8 as a four year old.

I feel very fortunate to have drawn the tag and was very glad to have my son Todd with me. I want to thank Kalan Lemon and Wayne Brown, my guides, and Doyle Moss, the outfitter, for all they did in making this the hunt of a lifetime. ▲

Longtime Judges Panel member Paul D. Webster scores Allen M. Shearer's Roosevelt's elk with
Curtis R. Siegfried who is one of two Canadians that served on the Judges Panel. Shearer's
elk was taken on British Columbia's mainland, which was recently included in a boundary
expansion of the Roosevelt's elk category. Shearer's bull, which is the first entry from the newly
expanded area, scores 362-5/8.

TROPHY STATS

▼ ▼ ▼ ▼ ▼

CATEGORY
Typical Mule Deer

SCORE
$205^2/_8$

LENGTH OF MAIN BEAM
Right: $28^1/_8$ Left: 28

**CIRCUMFERENCE BETWEEN
BURR AND FIRST POINT**
Right: $5^4/_8$ Left: $5^4/_8$

NUMBER OF POINTS
Right: 6   Left: 7

INSIDE SPREAD
32

LOCATION
Sonora, Mexico – 2005

HUNTER
Jason J. Gisi

TYPICAL MULE DEER
Second Award – 205 $^2/_8$

▼ ▼ ▼ ▼ ▼ ▼ ▼ ▼ ▼

JASON J. GISI

We all live for the anticipation of the hunt. The promise of a new adventure makes the rest of the year bearable. As I boarded the flight to Hermosillo, Mexico, for my annual deer hunt, I smiled at the thought of seeing my outfitter and friend Agustin Hurtado. I knew that he was driving around Hermosillo, wound tighter than a clock, making last-minute preparations to ensure a smooth and successful trip for my father John Gisi and me.

Perfect Luck

Chad Smith, our guide, was probably down to the cuticle of his last fingernail worried to death about either: A) the big buck he had seen prior to our arrival, or B) the lack of a big buck to hunt the next morning. Chad takes enormous pride in doing his job well and as a result, he heaps tremendous pressure on himself to perform at the highest level possible. As a client, this is exactly what I want in a guide. As a friend, I sometimes wonder if his head is going to explode. His mind is not calm.

I had the pleasure of sitting next to a young endodontist from California who was headed south to hunt Coues' deer. He clearly had a passion for hunting and was quite knowledgeable about the overall trophy-hunting scene. As our conversation turned from elk to deer hunting, he made the comment that he was still searching for an opportunity to harvest a trophy mule deer. He asked my opinion after mentioning that he was on the waiting list of a high-profile ranch specializing in trophy mule deer. As I knew the property and those surrounding it, I commented that the chance to kill a big buck certainly exists and thought he would do just fine once his number came up. He then asked if my father and I hunted there anymore. I grinned and laid my standard reply on him, "Brian, I would mow lawns and walk to Hermosillo, if that is what it took to hunt deer in Sonora ever year!"

Photograph by Jack Reneau

Jason J. Gisi accepting his plaque and medal from Buck Buckner, Vice President and Chairman of the Big Game Records Committee.

Admittedly, I have far more experience hunting Coues' deer in Sonora than mule deer. In fact, this was the first time I ponied up for the cost of a mule deer hunt in the last five years. All informed hunters recognize that the opportunity to harvest a super buck in Sonora still exists. However, it exists at a hefty price. In years past, I could never get comfortable with the price of the hunt versus the opportunity I perceived to bag a big buck. I hoped that this hunt would be the pay-off for all the research I had conducted in years past.

WHAT IS IT ABOUT SUN-BLEACHED WHITE BONE THAT CAN SET A HUNTER'S IMAGINATION ON FIRE? IF YOU LOVE BIG DEER, YOU LOVE THEIR SHEDS AS MUCH OR MORE THAN THE BUCKS THEMSELVES. I THINK IT IS THE MYSTERY THAT EVERY LARGE SHED HOLDS—SO MANY QUESTIONS THAT CAN NORMALLY NEVER BE ANSWERED. HOW BIG? HOW OLD? WHAT WOULD HE LOOK LIKE TODAY? WHERE THE HECK COULD HE BE?

Chad played a vital roll as well. He understood my concerns and worked diligently at seeking an opportunity that would fit my desires and those of my father.

As I disembarked from the plane, my predatory juices started flowing. The smell of Hermosillo's air always reminds me of hunting seasons past and the promise of adventure to come. After a quick lunch at the finest Mexican seafood restaurant on the planet, Marco's Los Arbolitos, it was off to Agustin's father's ranch to hunt mule deer.

At the ranch house, I got a look at shed antlers from a giant typical buck. What is it about sun-bleached white bone that can set a hunter's imagination on fire? If you love big deer, you love their sheds as much or more than the bucks themselves. I think it is the mystery that every large shed holds—so many questions that can normally never be answered. How big? How old? What would he look like today? Where the heck could he be? We caress and rub them while asking these questions. It's almost like we think that if we hold them long enough and rub them just right, a genie will pop out and answer our questions. It hasn't happened for me yet but I'm sure I'll keep trying until I die!

Cochillo, the foreman of the ranch, is the one who found the big sheds. And of course, the buck had not been seen in the previous three days that Chad and Matt had scouted the ranch. The fact that the buck had not been seen was no surprise. Chad's gut instinct told him to keep looking. With sheds from the two previous years found on the ranch, he felt that the buck had to still be there.

As Chad and I glassed that evening, we discussed the odds of the buck being around. Our friends, all more knowledgeable than us about mule-deer hunting in Mexico, had informed us on multiple occasions that the bucks tend to travel far due to the wide open spaces and low deer densities. Oftentimes, it is a waiting game as a hunter persistently checks the same groups of does for days on end during the rut in hopes of catching a big buck in their vicinity. This could mean that the "shed ghost" could be on our ranch or rutting a hot doe five miles in any direction. I glassed the same six does Chad had told me about. The only buck around them was a small 3 x 3. The does were near the highest glassing point on the property where we planned to start in the morning.

TYPICAL MULE DEER
Second Award – 205 $^2/_8$
▼ ▼ ▼ ▼ ▼
Jason J. Gisi

Gray light found Chad and me high above the desert floor, waiting on enough light to begin glassing. As I puttered around getting set up to glass, I heard Chad snapping his fingers behind me. As I turned and looked at him, I knew in an instant that he had found the buck that had produced the huge sheds. Chad's eyes looked the size of saucers as he exclaimed, "I found the typical!"

I couldn't help but laugh out loud. I was still hacking from the exertion of the early morning hike. The day was five minutes old. I had been hunting mule deer in Sonora for just over 12 hours after five years of researching the right opportunity. The giant buck we had hoped to find was incredibly 550 yards below us and Chad was up my nose for laughing when it was time to get down to business! Sometimes things just come together.

The pre-game pep talk from my new drill instructor went something like this, "What's so funny? I don't want you looking at the buck! Get your stuff packed up quick. We're going right at him before he slips out onto the flats! Keep up with me and don't make any noise!"

I told Chad to head down the hill and I would catch up with him. I thought he needed a little time alone to decompress. Hiking down the hill was more like a controlled slide. It was steep and covered with basketball-sized, loose, mini-boulders. I did my best to cover ground with a minimum of noise but it was impossible. I rushed a bit in a slide area and dislodged a 100-pound rock. As I lay still on my back, I prayed to the hunting gods that I hadn't just ruined my opportunity. I looked down past my toes and could see no running deer. Chad wasn't yelling, so I figured I was okay to proceed.

When I caught up with Chad, he instructed me to range the buck. I picked up the buck in an arroyo with my new Leica Geovid 10x42 BRF-Y binoculars and pressed the button. Just as the LCD read 318 yards, the buck turned and fed straight away from me. His rack extended well past both sides of his body and I let out an audible gasp. I was quickly reprimanded for not following instructions, as usual. We decided that if we had made it this far undetected, we could make the next rim rock below, putting us as close as we were going to get.

At the rim rock, the rangefinder read 247 yards to the tree we expected him to pass by. Two rocks were hurriedly stacked on top of each other and my backpack was balanced on top. The makeshift rest on the steep slope was complete. In the meantime, the buck had moved into a brush-choked arroyo. We had to wait. In hindsight, this was the best thing that could have happened. It allowed time to get my breathing and emotions under control

Jason J. Gisi spent years researching his mule deer hunt in Sonora, Mexico, before he finally booked his trip for January 2005. On the first day of his long-awaited hunt, he harvested this award-winning buck with a final score of 205-2/8 points.

prior to taking a shot that I knew might only present itself once in my lifetime. I tried not to think about the fact that I had never dared to dream of seeing a trophy of this size, let alone be minutes from squeezing off a shot at such a specimen.

I let Chad know that I was ready but was not going to look at the buck in order to relax. I told him to let me know when the buck was clear. I looked away and he narrated as the buck came out of the wash, walked behind a tree, and stepped broadside in the open. It was time! The crosshairs settled on his shoulder and we both saw a doe directly behind him so I couldn't shoot. I mumbled some choice words but stayed off of the trigger. The buck walked on, then moved from behind another tree and stopped broadside, clear of all obstructions.

I remember reminding myself that the downward angle was steep and I needed to hold low. At the shot, my high quality rest shifted, and I couldn't see the buck. Frantically, I tried to cycle the bolt while searching for the buck. I was thinking there was no way he could've gotten out of there that fast. I couldn't cycle the bolt because my right arm was pinned to my rib cage. Chad was hugging me yelling, "He's down! You hammered him!"

TYPICAL MULE DEER
Second Award – 205 $^2/_8$

▼ ▼ ▼ ▼ ▼

JASON J. GISI

During the walk down to the buck I wondered if what had just happened was real or just another hunting addict's daydream. When we got close, I snapped back to reality. The buck was enormous! Chad asked how big I thought the buck was and I stammered incoherently that I didn't have a clue and it didn't matter. I was completely humbled by this magnificent buck, knowing full well that I could hunt a thousand lifetimes and never have this experience again. It was way too much to absorb at the time. His antlers were massive, long-tined, and taped 35 inches wide. Later, the rest of our party arrived on the scene. The whooping and hollering started immediately and then quickly subsided, as we all stood there in awe of the magnificent buck.

For the rest of my life, my friends and acquaintances will ask me about the events of January 8, 2005. I will never have a story heroic enough to match the size of the buck. I had done more homework than the average guy in hopes that it would increase the odds of replacing my daydreams with reality. My greatest contribution on that fateful day was making the shot and not folding under pressure like I have done in the past. The simple fact will always remain that I was in the right place at the right time. As in life, we are all only as good as the ponies in our stable. Without my father's guidance, the hard work of Chad and Agustin, the understanding of my wife Tammi, and the friendship of all, my experience on January 8, 2005, could not have been possible. Thank you. ▲

TROPHY STATS

▼ ▼ ▼ ▼ ▼

CATEGORY
Typical Mule Deer

SCORE
204$^3/_8$

LENGTH OF MAIN BEAM
Right: 26$^4/_8$ Left: 27$^3/_8$

**CIRCUMFERENCE BETWEEN
BURR AND FIRST POINT**
Right: 5$^7/_8$ Left: 5$^7/_8$

NUMBER OF POINTS
Right: 6 Left: 5

INSIDE SPREAD
26$^1/_8$

LOCATION
Old Wives Lake,
Saskatchewan – 2008

HUNTER
Warren M. Stadnyk

TYPICAL MULE DEER
Third Award – 204 ³/₈

▼ ▼ ▼ ▼ ▼ ▼ ▼ ▼

WARREN M. STADNYK

As a farmer in Southwestern Saskatchewan, I don't get a lot of pre-season opportunities for scouting and sizing up bucks for the upcoming season. My early season preparation consists of time on the combine or tractor along with my mental inventory of what is seen on the way to and from work. While I had seen numerous good mule deer bucks as the season approached, neither in reality nor my wildest dreams did I ever catch a glimpse of the buck I would be fortunate enough to harvest.

Maybe Next Year

It was November 13th. I had spent the last week of the season searching hard for a good buck and had all but conceded the thought that it might be time to take a doe for the freezer. Maybe next year would be my opportunity to take a monster Saskatchewan mule deer buck.

On the way to my intended hunting area near Old Wives Lake, I met up with a rancher who lives in the area. We started talking and admiring the nice 4x4 he had taken. The conversation turned to me inquiring as to how he was able to load the deer by himself. He had been hunting with his daughters and had loaded his deer with a tri-fold quad ramp. He said he had just dragged the deer up the ramp and into the back of his truck. He offered me the ramp if I wanted to borrow it, but I didn't think it would be necessary for loading a small buck or doe since I had all but given up on a large buck. After talking a while longer and considering how slick his method of loading his deer sounded, I decided that I should take it just in case.

I continued towards some pastures on the north side of the lake where I had seen some pretty good bucks in the past. On the way, I stopped by a bluff where I have seen mule deer before. I was a little surprised when two giant whitetails came running out—not surprised by

Photograph by Jack Reneau

Warren M. Stadnyk accepting his plaque and medal from Buck Buckner, Vice President and Chairman of the Big Game Records Committee.

the fact there were whitetails there, but the size of the two bucks was astonishing. The part of Saskatchewan that I am from typically does not produce bucks of their caliber. Trying to get a better look, I watched them with my binoculars until they eventually disappeared from sight.

After they disappeared, I continued west following the whitetails' escape route. After a while, I decided to head a little to the south. I stopped in the pasture where I had seen a good herd of deer on Monday. Nothing was there, so I continued around the edge of a hill. All of a sudden, there he was standing with a group of does.

I immediately crouched down, having already spooked the does. As they began running to the northwest I couldn't pick out the buck. I was expecting him to follow the does' retreat. I waited for him for what felt like an eternity, but he never re-appeared. I thought for sure he had gone down lower in the coulee and would be miles away by now.

Hoping my suspicions were wrong, I ran halfway up the hill and then belly-crawled to the crest of the hill. I was expecting to see him way off in the distance, but to my surprise, he was still standing at the bottom of the hill in some buck brush with a few more does. As I was trying to catch my breath to get a shot off I was extremely fortunate that he was facing away from me at approximately 140 yards. One of the does had spotted me but she couldn't quite make out what I was. I held off for a couple minutes until he turned and offered me a great broadside shot. I slowly squeezed the trigger and to my astonishment, missed cleanly! I really had no excuse other than a case of buck fever.

> **I HAD SPENT THE LAST WEEK OF THE SEASON SEARCHING HARD FOR A GOOD BUCK AND HAD ALL BUT CONCEDED THE THOUGHT THAT IT MIGHT BE TIME TO TAKE A DOE FOR THE FREEZER.**

I quickly reloaded, expecting him to be on a dead run when I put the scope on him again but the shot had just startled him a bit. He turned to run to the north, and I pulled the trigger again. This time my shot connected! He ran about 20 yards and down he went. I had to sit there for a few minutes to let my heart slow down a bit—it felt like it was beating out of my chest.

After making my way down to see him, I was pumped when I saw the thickness of his antlers. Needless to say, I am glad I borrowed the tri-fold ramp, because I definitely wouldn't have been able to load him into the truck myself.

Two thousand eight was a hunting season I will never forget. In March 2009, I attended the Saskatchewan Wildlife Federation Henry Kelsey 2008 Awards. I received the Ernie Paynter Memorial Award for the Best Overall Game Head taken in 2008. I also had an article printed in the Winter 2010 edition of *Big Buck Magazine*. Finally, I attended Boone and Crockett Club's 27th Awards Program Banquet in Reno, Nevada, in June 2010 where I received B&C's Third Place Award in the mule deer category. ▲

Award-Winning Moments

B&C Photo Archives

Add this up — Two 27th Awards attendees test their skills in trying to put a number on this non-typical mule deer as part of the Guess The Score Contest. Surprisingly, two guesses came in 1/8th of an inch under and 1/8th of an inch over the actual final score of 238.
Not bad for a complicated set of antlers.

TROPHY STATS

▼ ▼ ▼ ▼ ▼

CATEGORY
Non-typical Mule Deer

SCORE
306 3/8

LENGTH OF MAIN BEAM
Right: 26 3/8   Left: 27 3/8

CIRCUMFERENCE BETWEEN BURR AND FIRST POINT
Right: 5 2/8   Left: 5 1/8

NUMBER OF POINTS
Right: 26   Left: 17

INSIDE SPREAD
21 7/8

LOCATION
Douglas Co., Colorado – 2007

HUNTER
Kyle Lopez

NON-TYPICAL MULE DEER
First Award – 306 ³/₈

▼ ▼ ▼ ▼ ▼ ▼ ▼ ▼

KYLE LOPEZ

Beep, Beep, Beep! The alarm went off, signaling that my hunting season had finally arrived. I rolled over to my nightstand and silenced the alarm, then jumped out of bed. To no surprise, my dad was already up and ready, along with my uncle. I grabbed some breakfast and began to get ready. I had to make sure I had all my gear—rifle, knife, camo clothing, and, of course, my orange. When we were ready, I ran out to the truck and we were off. It took about 35 minutes, in the dark, to get to our hunting area.

On the first day we chose to go to a more popular area to see how many hunters were out in the unit. After a long and hard day of hunting, I came home empty-handed. However my uncle harvested a great buck, which Dad green scored at 194. We hunted hard the next day, including a trip into the area where I would eventually take my trophy. On this first trip into the area I missed a great buck and once again came home without filling my tag.

The next morning I had to go to school. I was still feeling frustrated and thinking about the buck I had missed. I was not able to hunt the next evening because of an after-school appointment to turn in football gear. That turned out to be an even more frustrating day; all I could think about was the buck that I had missed.

We were not able to hunt for the next two days, but finally on November 7, 2007, Dad and I were both able to take off early one day. Dad said he had a gut feeling that it would be our lucky hunt. We decided to make a trip back into the area where I had missed. However, we had a different plan of attack this time. We quickly and quietly maneuvered our way up a deep creek bottom surrounded by steep hillsides on both sides, weaving in and out through the tangled maze of burned timber to the base of the mountain.

It was a good three-mile hike. As we started to top out at the head of the creek, the hillsides became more visible. Dad paused for a

Kyle Lopez accepting his plaque and medal from Buck Buckner, Vice President and Chairman of the Big Game Records Committee.

Photograph courtesy of Kyle Lopez

Kyle Lopez is pictured above with his award-winning non-typical mule deer taken in Douglas County, Colorado, in 2007. The buck is the second largest mule deer ever harvested in Colorado and received a First Place Award at the 27th Big Game Awards Program in Reno, Nevada.

moment and pulled up his glasses to look ahead while we still had the cover of the creek. He quietly whispered that there were two young does up ahead. I looked at them through my binoculars to make sure they were does as well. I just couldn't draw antlers on either of them. So we snuck around to their left. As we did, the does spotted us. We paused for a moment to see what they were going to do. The excitement was starting to build. Just the sight of those deer and how close we were to them made it feel as if we had stepped into their bedroom.

In that moment we were struck with luck. The does curiously started walking toward us. As we held our position, I could only wonder what was going to happen next. Would the does finally realize what we were and blow out of the country, taking the rest of the forest life with them? Or would we be able to trick them and slip past to continue our quest for a buck? They paused about 50 yards from us, discovered that we weren't deer and quietly trotted off. They left in the direction from where they had come, which worked in our favor. Dad's plan was to move away from them and toward a steep hillside that had lush, green vegetation on it.

As we turned to start toward the hillside, Dad stopped and looked ahead again. He said, "Kyle, there is a buck looking right at us." As Dad was looking through his glasses he told me it was definitely a mature buck worth shooting. Dad was standing next to a burned tree, and as he stepped around it, he told me to rest my rifle against the side of the tree to take the shot. As I got my first look at the buck through the scope, it appeared to be just what Dad had said. He was facing us, looking in our direction with an intense stare.

I steadied my breathing, let out my breath, held it, and squeezed the trigger—Pow! The buck jumped a mile high as the shot went off. As he turned in mid-air, his head immediately hit the ground, and like a bulldozer, he plowed his way over a small bluff. He collapsed out of sight. Dad exclaimed, "You got him Kyle, good job!"

We hugged as Dad's gut feeling about me getting a deer that evening came true. We gave the buck a little time (what seemed like hours) of time before we went to find him. The adrenaline was definitely flowing and the excitement welled inside me. Dad told me to get another round ready as we took off to go track him. When we arrived at the spot where we last saw the buck standing, we immediately found blood and tracked him about 50 feet. He was in a small ditch. As we were approaching him, it looked like he had fallen into an old dead bush. My dad told me to get my gun ready. My heart was pumping; I could see the grey color of his body as Dad picked up a rock and tossed it toward the buck's belly. As the rock hit and bounced off the buck's body, Dad said, "He's done, Kyle."

That is when our luck took an enormous turn for the better. As I was securing my rifle, I heard my dad say, "Oh my God." He just kept saying, "Oh my God, Oh my God," over and over. Neither one of us was prepared for what we found lying at our feet. We assumed I had shot a good buck, but never in our wildest dreams thought it was that tremendous. As I stood next to my dad, looking at the buck, there were so many points coming off his antlers, it looked as if the bush that he had fallen into had overtaken him. His antlers were heavy. It seemed as if there were hundreds of points going in all different directions. From that point on, there would be no words to describe the buck—at least not that anyone would believe without seeing it with their own eyes.

Dad gave me a big hug. We had several high-fives before we dressed out my deer and got him ready for the journey back to the truck. Dad had decided to drag the buck out. We were losing light, making it too difficult to quarter the deer. What should have been an hour-long hike turned into a four-hour ordeal through a creek bed knotted with twisted, fallen, burned timber. It seemed as if we would drag for a hundred yards then clear debris for a hundred yards. Finally, we made it to the truck and loaded up my deer. We had done it, and now everything was over—so I thought.

Not too long after killing my deer, the phone calls, emails, and many other things began pouring in. It first started with offers to write magazine articles for such publications as *Eastman's*, *Hunting Illustrated* (then-owned by King's Outdoor World), *Muley Crazy*, and *Trophy Hunter*. (Many articles were written by Greg Merriam.) Then it escalated into offers to attend and present my deer at the various hunting shows. That's when I got a phone call from the man who made most of this possible, Roger Selner. He was the one who escalated my fame for me.

There is just no way to explain the excitement and emotion over what we were looking at that day. I am very proud of myself and what I accomplished. I would like to thank the entire Eastman family for all the work they have put into my deer, *King's Outdoor World* for its article and calendars, Mel Siefke at Wildlife Recapture Taxidermy, and Greg Merriam for the articles he has written. However the two most important people I would like to thank are Roger Selner and my dad. ▲

TROPHY STATS

▼ ▼ ▼ ▼ ▼

CATEGORY
Typical Columbia Blacktail

SCORE
$160^6/_8$

LENGTH OF MAIN BEAM
Right: $20^6/_8$ Left: 23

**CIRCUMFERENCE BETWEEN
BURR AND FIRST POINT**
Right: $4^6/_8$ Left: $4^5/_8$

NUMBER OF POINTS
Right: 6   Left: 5

INSIDE SPREAD
$20^6/_8$

LOCATION
Shasta Co., California – 1962

HUNTERS
G. Bland & D. Boddy

TYPICAL COLUMBIA BLACKTAIL
First Award – 160 $^6/_8$

▼ ▼ ▼ ▼ ▼ ▼ ▼ ▼ ▼

G. BLAND & D. BODDY

My uncle and I started hunting together in the fall of 1958 when I was 13-years old. My first buck fell that year to a Winchester Model 94 .25-35. The following year, I began guiding hunters on our ranch and took a couple more blacktails with that 94. It worked okay, but it became apparent that I needed a longer-shooting rifle. My grandfather Floyd E. Bland helped me pick out a Winchester Model 70 Featherweight .243. While it was expensive for me at that time, I managed to make the payments on it by hunting and trapping coyotes and bobcats.

Forty-Seven Years

In Shasta County, during the 1960s, we could get $10 for the nose of a coyote and $5 for a bobcat. If we happened to kill the coyote on the south side of the Middle Fork of Cottonwood Creek, we got $15 for the ears. I had a trap line and used the Coyote-getter, a cyanide-loaded .38 Special shell in a tube buried in the ground. We would bait a cotton ball on the end of the barrel with a foul smelling concoction my grandfather would make up and did fairly well. We did however disgust the people who were unfortunate enough to be in the county courthouse during one of our trips to town each month to collect our bounties and make my payment on the model 70.

I had been puttering around with different combinations for my rifle and had found a load which put my muzzle velocity just over 3,000 fps. It consisted of 42.6 grains of IMR-4350 powder, a Nosler Partition 100-grain bullet, and Winchester 120 primers. To date I have killed 26 blacktails, whitetails and mule deer bucks using this load with shots out to 400-plus yards.

That September in 1962, my grandmoth-

Photograph by Jack Reneau

Gene Bland and David Boddy accepting their plaques and medals from Buck Buckner, Vice President and Chairman of the Big Game Records Committee.

Photograph courtesy of Gene Bland

Gene Bland and David Boddy pose with their award-winning typical Columbia blacktail in this vintage photograph taken in 1962. The two hunters harvested the buck, which scores 160-6/8 points, in Shasta County, California, during the 1962 season.

er told me about some big bucks they had been watching on top of one of the bald hills on land between Howard Marks' and Joe McCauliffe's properties, a mile or two south of section 6. Section 6 was 640 acres that was not connected to the rest of the ranch. There were a couple of miles of the McCauliffe Ranch in between our ranch house and that section. Tar Bully Mountain was in the middle of Section 6 and we seldom hunted it since most of the blacktail deer were harvested along either Cottonwood or Beegum Creek on the main part of the ranch.

We felt there was a chance that one of these four or five big bucks she spoke about might stray over to Tar Bully. With this in mind, we decided to give this new area a try and planned our hunt there.

My uncle David J. Boddy and I were dropped off on the Bland Road and had hiked about a half mile when we heard a shot. It was my grandfather Floyd E. Bland, the owner of the Bland Ranch. When I first spotted the buck, he was running full tilt about 200 yards away across the top of the mountain. I dropped to a prone position and fired one shot with

BOONE AND CROCKETT CLUB'S

my .243 Winchester Model 70 Featherweight uphill at about 45 degrees. The 100-grain Nosler Partition bullet hit the deer, but the shot was a little further back than I had hoped. It had hit him hard though and he began to slide down a steep shale cliff in my direction. David fired a second shot with his .30-06

TYPICAL COLUMBIA BLACKTAIL
First Award – 160 6/8
▼ ▼ ▼ ▼ ▼
G. BLAND & D. BODDY

Springfield and the 150-grain Sierra bullet finished off the deer. The buck tumbled head-over-heels down the mountain and came to rest 70 yards away.

My grandfather and grandmother Edna Bland drove the jeep up to the deer and we loaded the field-dressed buck into the back. It took over an hour to drive back to the ranch house where we took photos and skinned out the buck for mounting. We finally had him scored by B&C Official Measurer Jennifer Barrow of Texas Parks and Wildlife 47 years later and the Shasta County buck came up with a final score of 160-6/8 points. ▲

TROPHY STATS

▼ ▼ ▼ ▼ ▼

CATEGORY
Typical Columbia Blacktail

SCORE
$160^1/_8$

LENGTH OF MAIN BEAM
Right: $21^2/_8$ Left: $21^3/_8$

**CIRCUMFERENCE BETWEEN
BURR AND FIRST POINT**
Right: $4^6/_8$ Left: $4^6/_8$

NUMBER OF POINTS
Right: 5 Left: 5

INSIDE SPREAD
$19^1/_8$

LOCATION
Trinity Co., California – 2001

HUNTER
Jerry L. Thissell

TYPICAL COLUMBIA BLACKTAIL
Second Award – 160 $^1/_8$

▼ ▼ ▼ ▼ ▼ ▼ ▼ ▼ ▼

JERRY L. THISSELL

Our hunt started just like every other hunt we had made into the Yolla Bolly Wilderness during hunting season. Four of us made plans to take our horses and ride into an area where we had seen good bucks in the last couple of years. Forest, Kevin, Scott, and I all agreed to meet at Kevin's cabin at Ruth Lake on Friday so we could drive to the trailhead first thing Saturday morning.

We left Kevin's about 4 a.m. Saturday and made the two-hour drive to the trailhead where we loaded the horses and Kevin's best mule, Bart, with the gear we thought we would need to last the weekend. We left the truck and the rest of civilization behind for a couple of days just as the sun was starting to rise. We spotted a coyote, a few does, and a couple small bucks on the hour-and-a-half ride to our campsite. We unloaded our gear from the animals and made sure we had the horses tied out where they could get plenty of food and water.

By the time we finished with the animals, it was almost 9 a.m. and starting to get pretty warm in the sun. We knew the deer would be headed for the timber to bed down for the day. With this in mind, we decided to go further out on the trail and then head down a ridge toward a basin. When we got there, we would spread out and hunt back toward our camp.

As we started down the ridge, Forest decided to stop about a hundred yards from the main trail to be the top person. The rest of us fell into line doing the same thing so we would be spread out about every 75 to a 100 yards—Forest at the top, then myself, Scott, and Kevin, who decided to be on the bottom closest to the river.

As we started side-hilling toward our camp, I spotted a small buck running down the next ridge, but could not tell what he had

Photograph by Jack Reneau

Jerry L. Thissell accepting his plaque and medal from Buck Buckner, Vice President and Chairman of the Big Game Records Committee.

for points. Kevin said later it was a small forked horn, and it had gone by him at about 50 yards.

After another hour of hiking, I decided to stop and get some water and a piece of jerky out of my pack. I sat on a small ridge so I could see out over an old burn area and look around. After taking a couple small swigs, I put my daypack back on and started walking again. I went about 50 yards and heard some sticks braking on the ridge in front of me. When I looked up, all I could see was a flash of gray, I knew it had to be a buck because all the does that we had seen were still a reddish color. As the deer came further down the ridge, I could see that it had a large set of antlers. I was not sure how big, but I could see he was a good buck.

When the buck was even with me on the ridge, I only had time to get a single shot at him before he was gone. After I shot, the buck gave no signal that he had been hit. I was slightly discouraged, yet everything felt right. I walked the 75 yards to the trail the buck had run down and could easily see his tracks in the dirt. I worked to the area where the buck had disappeared into the trees. I still couldn't find any sign of a hit but I figured I would follow the trail for a little bit just in case.

I went about 50 yards inside the trees and found him lying dead next to an old stump. By then, Forest, Scott, and Kevin were all working their way toward me hollering to see if I had killed a good buck. I just stood there with my mouth open, not believing how big this buck was. When I was finally able to yell for the other guys, it took them no time at all to get to me.

Forest was the first to find me. He told me he had seen the buck but was unable to get off a shot. When Kevin and Scott showed up, they could not believe how big the buck was.

Kevin and I started taking care of the buck while Scott and Forest went back to camp to saddle a couple of the horses and bring them down the hill to us. A couple hours later, when we finally made it back to camp, we were tired and worn out, but it was definitely worth it for the buck of a lifetime. ▲

Moments in Measuring

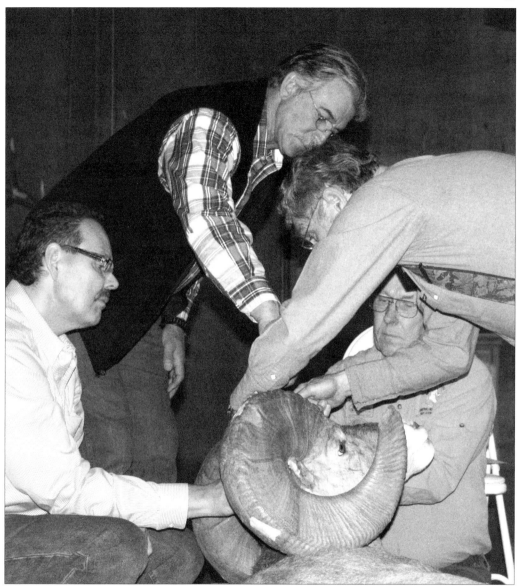

Judges Victor Clark and Larry Lack (standing, left to right) verify the score of Toni Sannon's bighorn ram that was taken in Montana's Missouri Breaks in 2008, while Pat McKenzie and Buck Buckner (seated, l-r) assist. Sannon's ram, which scores 204-2/8, is the largest ram ever taken by a woman. It is the sixth-largest ram ever recorded by B&C and the second-largest ever taken in Montana.

TROPHY STATS

▼ ▼ ▼ ▼ ▼

CATEGORY
Non-typical Columbia Blacktail

SCORE
$195^6/_8$

LENGTH OF MAIN BEAM
Right: $24^1/_8$ Left: $24^7/_8$

CIRCUMFERENCE BETWEEN BURR AND FIRST POINT
Right: $5^2/_8$ Left: $5^2/_8$

NUMBER OF POINTS
Right: 8   Left: 11

INSIDE SPREAD
$20^6/_8$

LOCATION
Benton Co., Oregon – Prior to 1901

HUNTER
James Ball

OWNER
Robert Suttles

NON-TYPICAL
COLUMBIA BLACKTAIL
Certificate of Merit – 195 $^6/_8$

▼ ▼ ▼ ▼ ▼ ▼ ▼ ▼ ▼

HUNTER – JAMES BALL   OWNER – ROBERT SUTTLES

Dave Heffner is a Boone and Crockett Club Official Measurer from Roseburg, Oregon. Because of his passion for hunting, Dave measures a lot of big game animals at his home and at taxidermy shops in southern Oregon. Additionally, he volunteers to measure trophies by working at sportsman's shows in Eugene, Roseburg, and Medford.

Incredible Twist of Fate

In February 2009 he was in Eugene meeting with proud owners of everything from forked-horn deer to trophy-sized elk, bear, cougar, etc. When a man named Bob Suttles walked up with a huge blacktail buck, Dave figured it might be the biggest he'd ever seen.

Bob wasn't the hunter who killed this deer in the woods of western Oregon. In fact, he hadn't even been born when this exceptional buck was taken. Grover Cleveland was president of the United States when the buck was harvested by a lucky Oregon hunter in 1895.

This awesome buck was given to Bob by a coworker in 1985. The buck had been relegated to the friend's garage and was destined for a Lane County landfill! Bob took it home so it could be enjoyed by his sons, both of whom were active hunters. After 90 years, the head mount was in understandably poor condition. Much to the chagrin of Bob's wife Lori, the nearly 100-year-old deer mount found a home above the fireplace in their living room. The boys thought it was awesome.

As the story goes, this buck was taken in the Alsea Unit about 14 miles west of Alpine, Oregon, and 30 minutes west of Interstate 5. The original mold or form for the head mount was made of wood, plaster, and square nails.

Photograph by Jack Reneau

Robert Suttles accepting his plaque from Buck Buckner, Vice President and Chairman of the Big Game Records Committee.

Over time, the hide and form had deteriorated, leaving the buck looking less than majestic. Bob's family wanted to treat this great animal with the respect it deserved, so it was placed onto a modern form and fitted with a new cape. Perhaps this buck will remain in the family and one of Bob's great, great grandchildren will proudly display it in their home in the next century.

Bob's son-in-law, Chris Travis, talked Bob into entering his buck into the show's head and horns competition. Sunday afternoon Bob found himself trekking across the parking lot of the expo center, packing the immensely awkward deer mount. Dave Heffner recognized the uniqueness of this enormous buck and encouraged Bob to enter it in Boone and Crockett Club.

> THIS AWESOME BUCK WAS GIVEN TO BOB BY A COWORKER IN 1985. THE BUCK HAD BEEN RELEGATED TO THE FRIEND'S GARAGE AND WAS DESTINED FOR A LANE COUNTY LANDFILL! BOB TOOK IT HOME... AFTER 90 YEARS, THE HEAD MOUNT WAS IN UNDERSTANDABLY POOR CONDITION. MUCH TO THE CHAGRIN OF BOB'S WIFE LORI, THE NEARLY 100-YEAR-OLD DEER MOUNT FOUND A HOME ABOVE THE FIREPLACE...

Pictures of a cable secured to the deer's antler were sent to Tod Lum, a biologist with Oregon's Department of Fish and Wildlife (ODF&W). Tod said that ODF&W had a deer check-in system in the late 1800s that often secured this type of cable to antlers.

In addition to telling him the year this deer was taken, Bob's friend had told him the buck was shot with a rifle and that the hunter was a man named James Ball. With so much time gone by, there is no way to prove or disprove that.

Bob says that for him, the most important thing is that the deer is treated with respect. He told me his children had grown up with this deer in their home, and it has become an irreplaceable possession. For generations to come, members of his family will hear the story of his saving this trophy from a less-than-honorable grave in a landfill.

Boone and Crockett Club invited Bob to send his trophy to the 27th Big Game Awards in Reno, Nevada, in June 2010. With an official score of 195-6/8, this is the third-largest buck ever accepted in the non-typical Columbia blacktail deer category. ▲

Written by Jim Gaskins of Roseburg, Oregon.

B&C Photo Archives

There were plenty of excellent opportunities in Reno to view and photograph some of the finest trophies ever recorded by B&C. A guest photographs Helgie H. Eymundson's non-typical whitetail buck that scores 274 points. Eymundson took this unique buck with palmated antlers near Cross Lake, Alberta, in 2007. It is the 18th-largest non-typical ever recorded by B&C.

TROPHY STATS
▼ ▼ ▼ ▼ ▼

CATEGORY
Typical Sitka Blacktail

SCORE
126⁵/₈

LENGTH OF MAIN BEAM
Right: 18¹/₈   Left: 18²/₈

CIRCUMFERENCE BETWEEN BURR AND FIRST POINT
Right: 4⁷/₈   Left: 4⁷/₈

NUMBER OF POINTS
Right: 5   Left: 5

INSIDE SPREAD
18¹/₈

LOCATION
Prince of Wales Island, Alaska – 2007

HUNTER
Joseph R. Jeppsen

TYPICAL SITKA BLACKTAIL
First Award – 126 ⁵/₈

▼ ▼ ▼ ▼ ▼ ▼ ▼ ▼ ▼

JOSEPH R. JEPPSEN

Boone and Crockett Club does not take its job lightly as the universally-recognized records keeper of native North American big game. When a subcommittee chaired by Samuel B. Webb created and introduced the world to B&C's scoring system in 1950, Sitka blacktail deer was not a viable category. It wasn't until 1984, or 35 years of records-keeping later, that the Club's Records of North American Big Game Committee created the category to recognize this unique subspecies of deer. An extensive study was conducted to establish boundaries and set a minimum score for accepting entries.

Sitka blacktails primarily live in southern Alaska, on Kodiak Island where they were transplanted, and the Queen Charlotte Islands of British Columbia. Since the category was established, 217 trophies have been accepted for the records book, indicating the decision to create the category was correct.

Prince of Wales Island, Alaska, which is where native Alaskan Joseph R. Jeppsen traveled to take this trophy, has produced more records-book specimens (38) than any other area of Alaska. Logging has been a significant contributing factor in producing records book animals and making the island accessible to hunters like Jeppsen.

Jeppsen was hunting the interior of Prince of Wales Island, glassing through his binoculars, when he watched this buck chase a doe straight towards him. The two deer were 50 yards away and quickly closing in on him when he exchanged his binoculars for his .280 Remington, sighted on the buck, and dropped it.

Three months later, Official Measurer James Baichtal scored it at 126-5/8 points. Its score was verified by the 27th Awards Program Judges Panel in 2010, which confirmed it is the largest Sitka recorded by B&C since 1985. It is the third-largest Sitka ever recorded by Boone and Crockett Club. ▲

Photograph courtesy of Joseph R. Jeppsen

Joseph R. Jeppsen is pictured above with his award-winning Sitka blacktail deer, which is the third largest ever recorded by B&C.

TROPHY STATS

▼ ▼ ▼ ▼ ▼

CATEGORY
Typical Sitka Blacktail

SCORE
118 1/8

LENGTH OF MAIN BEAM
Right: 19 3/8   Left: 18 5/8

CIRCUMFERENCE BETWEEN BURR AND FIRST POINT
Right: 4 2/8   Left: 4 2/8

NUMBER OF POINTS
Right: 5   Left: 5

INSIDE SPREAD
15 5/8

LOCATION
Alaska – 1961

HUNTER
Arthur Schulberg

OWNER
Dan Schulberg

Photograph by Jack Reneau

Dan Schulberg accepting his plaque and medal from Buck Buckner, Vice President and Chairman of the Big Game Records Committee.

TYPICAL SITKA BLACKTAIL
Second Award – 118 ¹/₈

▼ ▼ ▼ ▼ ▼ ▼ ▼ ▼ ▼ ▼

HUNTER – ARTHUR SCHULBERG   OWNER – DAN SCHULBERG

My grandfather Art Schulberg loved Alaska. He worked for Standard Oil Company for over 30 years and spent most of that time in Alaska. The stories he would spin of his experiences were graphic and very inspiring. He told of one very memorable deer hunt that took place on a fall morning along the shores of an unnamed fjord.

Grandpa said, "The mist hung heavy on the shoreline [with] fresh bear tracks in the sand. The hair on the back of my neck stood up when suddenly the brush started moving less than 50 yards in front of me. It didn't look good as there was no place to go but into the water. I figured I could get off one, maybe two, shots before the bear had me. I readied my .30-40 Krag for what I thought was my worst nightmare. Seconds seemed like minutes when out stepped a beautiful buck.

"My nerves were completely shot. I aimed, pulled the trigger, and cleanly missed. I thought, well shucks, but the buck only took a couple of steps and presented me with an easy neck shot. It wasn't until a few hours later, when I had the deer aboard my boat, that I could relax and enjoy this outstanding animal. That was back in 1961." ▲

Editor's Note: Boone and Crockett Club started big-game records keeping back in the early 1900s, though its current scoring system wasn't adopted until 1950. As with any database, it takes decades to compile the information necessary to establish a historical record that can be called upon to quantify the successes of Big Game management throughout North America. With this in mind, the Boone and Crockett Club's Records Program includes all trophies that are entered whose authenticity, including location of kill, can be confirmed. Not only do these trophies add very important data to the records, but the stories told by the hunters to family members give us a look into times past in which hunting was not as commercialized and gadget-laden as it is today. This magnificent Sitka blacktail buck was taken by Dan Schulberg's grandfather in Alaska. He was shooting a .30-40 Krag, a cartridge that was adopted by the U.S. army in 1892.

TROPHY STATS

▼ ▼ ▼ ▼ ▼

CATEGORY
Typical Sitka Blacktail

SCORE
114$^7/_8$

LENGTH OF MAIN BEAM
Right: 16$^6/_8$ Left: 16$^4/_8$

**CIRCUMFERENCE BETWEEN
BURR AND FIRST POINT**
Right: 3$^4/_8$ Left: 3$^5/_8$

NUMBER OF POINTS
Right: 5   Left: 5

INSIDE SPREAD
15$^3/_8$

LOCATION
Revillagigedo Island, Alaska – 2007

HUNTER
Darin L. Crayne

TYPICAL SITKA BLACKTAIL
Third Award – 114 7/8

▼ ▼ ▼ ▼ ▼ ▼ ▼ ▼ ▼

DARIN L. CRAYNE

Darin L. Crayne was five years old when his family moved to Alaska in 1971. His father, a commercial fisherman, preferred to hunt Rocky Mountain goats and moose, but introduced his son at age 14 to Sitka blacktail deer hunting on Admiralty Island. Because his father had serious concerns about that island's huge brown bears that came running at the sound of gunshots, he hunted Sitka deer alone during his junior and senior years in high school on Woewodski Island, which is located 75 miles south of their home in Wrangell.

Three Dollars

After spending three years at Fort Bragg in the 118th Airborne Corps, Darin returned to Wrangell and spent three more years hunting Sitkas on Woewodski Island. Eventually, he moved to Ketchikan, Alaska, where there are countless opportunities to hunt Sitkas on nearby Prince of Wales Island and numerous other neighboring islands.

During this time, Darin did a lot of trapping and commercial fishing. He also worked on a tug boat that set up and dismantled remote logging camps. Four years prior to taking his trophy buck, he helped set up a logging camp in Lucky Cove on Revillagigedo Island. When he helped take the camp out a year later, he noticed lots of does and immature bucks along the shoreline. He took a short hike inland and found some great rubs (blazes) that had to have been made by some huge bucks. All of these experiences gave him a good, basic knowledge of what Sitkas are all about, and he began formulating plans to return to Lucky Cove in three years for a Sitka deer hunt. He knew the buck that had made those blazes wouldn't be there, but he figured the immature bucks he saw would be "booners" by then.

The actual hunt for Darin's trophy Sitka started in Ketchikan where he hired Carson Lindli, the owner of the yacht Capella (formerly owned by heavyweight fighter Jack Dempsey) to take him and one friend to a remote location. Darin was very secretive about where he was going. Not only didn't he tell his friends were he was going, but he didn't even tell Carson where he was taking them until they dropped anchor in Lucky Cove. The only thing he told Carson was, "This is my Boone and Crockett hunt." Darin knew this was going to be his last Sitka deer hunt before his upcoming move to the lower 48 states, and he wanted to get his trophy of a lifetime.

On the first day of his hunt, he lowered the Capella's skiff into the water and headed for shore. He first looked for big rubs where the logging camp had been, but didn't find any. It was the rut, and if there were any big bucks in the area, there would be big blaze marks on the trees where they rubbed.

Darin hunted until about two hours before dark, when the weather turned nasty. The wind was blowing 50 mph, and the rain was coming down in horizontal sheets. He hadn't seen anything all day and was getting discouraged when he came upon a small muskeg opening with a pond in it. No deer were present, so he noted it and moved on with plans to check it out on the way back to the boat.

When Darin returned to the muskeg, he blew his deer call and brought in a three-pointer he promptly dropped with one shot. While traversing the muskeg to retrieve his buck, he spotted three does, two spikes, and a forked-horn buck off to his left. The bucks bolted, but the forked-horn returned after Darin grunted on his call. Darin dropped that buck, then field dressed and boned out both deer and was back on the boat at 6 p.m., which is about two hours after dark that time of year.

> **HOWEVER, THE MORNING WAS DIFFERENT THAN ANY OTHER. WHEN DARIN SCRAPED THE FROST OFF THE CABIN WINDOWS, IT WAS A CLEAR, SUNNY DAY. HE TOLD HIS PARTNER, "IT IS A BOONE AND CROCKETT MORNING!"**

The bad weather continued through the night. In fact, it was so bad that the yacht was blown off anchor twice, and they had to reset it closer to shore. It was still miserable when he headed out in the morning.

As the next day wore on, Darin became more discouraged. It was near dark when he was about to turn around and head back to the boat when a forked horn ran down the ridge to his left. He paused at 150 yards, and Darin dropped him with one shot. As he approached this buck, he looked off into the logged-over basin below him, and to his surprise, he could see buck blazes, huge buck blazes, and lots of them from the top of the basin to the bottom. There were so many, he quit counting at 32. After three days of hunting, he had finally found the hunting area he was looking for, but it was too late to hunt any more that day, so he dragged the forked-horn out and took the skiff back to the Capella.

That evening he made himself a doe deer call from two bamboo stirring sticks and a rubber band that came off a broccoli bunch in their refrigerator. He also started teasing his hunting companion who still hadn't even seen a deer saying, "I have found my Boonie."

The weather that night was more of the same as the previous night. The wind would blow the yacht off anchor and the captain would have to move it closer to shore and reset the anchor. However, the morning was different than any other. When Darin scraped the frost off the cabin windows, it was a clear, sunny day. He told his partner, "It is a Boone and Crockett morning!"

Once he was back on the mainland that morning, he jogged all the way back to where he had seen the blazes the night before. As he drew nearer, he slowed down to a walk so that his heart could slow down, and he could make a steady shot if the opportunity presented itself.

He tucked himself between a log and a stump about 50 feet up in the basin. There was about 10 years of second-growth in the basin with only one opening and a beaver pond off to his right. He blew his new call the first time and waited. Nothing happened so he blew it two more times at 10-minute intervals. He knew that if he didn't have any action after three tries, it was counterproductive to try a fourth time. In fact, more than three calls tend to spook deer.

TYPICAL SITKA BLACKTAIL
Third Award – 114 7/8

▼ ▼ ▼ ▼ ▼

DARIN L. CRAYNE

After the third call he turned his head slightly to the left and spotted a buck standing broadside on top of a rocky knob facing to the right just below him. He pulled the covers off his scope and slowly laid his .270 Remington across the log in front of him. He sighted right behind the armpit, flipped the safety off, squeezed the trigger, and heard the most deafening "click" he had ever heard. He slowly eased his rifle back over the log, chambered a round, and again laid the rifle across the log. To his great surprise, the buck was still standing there. He sighted again on the armpit and squeezed the trigger.

This time, there was no loud "click." At the sound of the shot, the buck turned and made two hops into the brush like he wasn't even hit. Darin's mouth was dry, his heart was racing, and he was mad at himself. He couldn't believe he missed.

A half-hour later, Darin walked down to the rocky knob where he found a piece of lung tissue the size of his thumb. There was no blood or any other evidence of a hit. However, he knew the buck was his. Now he just had to find him in the dense underbrush. The ferns and underbrush were all red because it was November, so he couldn't see any blood even if there was some. He started searching in the direction the deer had run, but the brush was so thick that he had to plow his way through it backwards.

For the better part of two hours, he was down on his hands and knees unsuccessfully crawling through the brush knowing that he was going to spend the rest of his life looking for his deer, if necessary. He knew it was there, and he wasn't leaving without it.

When he was about 200 yards from the rocky knob he decided to head back up to it. He was 20 yards from the knob when he stepped on the white belly of his buck lying totally concealed in the brush. He reached down, grabbed him by the nose, and pulled him up to get a good look at the antlers. It was the prettiest thing he had ever seen, and the rack had all the features he expected and wanted in a big rack.

It was a struggle to get his buck up the hill out of that basin, but it was all worth it. On the way back to the boat, he ran into his hunting companion who still hadn't seen a deer and promptly reached into his wallet and settled their bet by handing Darin three dollars for getting the first buck, the heaviest buck, and the largest antlers. As he handed him the money, he told Darin, "You got your Boonie!" ▲

TROPHY STATS

▼ ▼ ▼ ▼ ▼

CATEGORY
Typical Sitka Blacktail

SCORE
114⁵/₈

LENGTH OF MAIN BEAM
Right: 17⁵/₈   Left: 17¹/₈

**CIRCUMFERENCE BETWEEN
BURR AND FIRST POINT**
Right: 4   Left: 4²/₈

NUMBER OF POINTS
Right: 5   Left: 5

INSIDE SPREAD
14⁵/₈

LOCATION
Thomas Bay, Alaska – 2008

HUNTER
Rocky Littleton

TYPICAL SITKA BLACKTAIL
Fourth Award – 114 $^5/_8$

▼ ▼ ▼ ▼ ▼ ▼ ▼ ▼

ROCKY LITTLETON

Rocky Littleton was actually moose hunting the day he shot his Boone and Crockett records-book buck. He and his hunting partner Ladd Norheim live in Petersburg on Mitkof Island and have a hunting camp at Thomas Bay on the mainland. To get to the mainland, they take a speedboat across Frederick Sound from Petersburg to Point Agassiz Peninsula. From there, they ride their 4-wheelers about 15 miles up an old logging road to their camp that sits alongside the Muddy River. Camp consists of a canvas woodstove-heated wall tent set up on a 14x16-foot plywood platform.

Rocky and Ladd hunt on both sides of the river, which is 50-feet wide. To gain access to the opposite side of the river, they use a skiff attached to a cable-pulley system. To maneuver the skiff, there are two lines hanging from the pulley. One line is attached to the bow of the skiff and passengers hold on to the other one. The latter line enables passengers to hold the skiff at an angle to the current and the current pushes the skiff across the river.

In 2008, moose season closed on October 15. The morning before the season closed, Rocky and Ladd crossed the river in the hopes of filling their freezers with fresh moose meat. Ladd headed inland while Rocky headed upriver, following a series of trails and old logging roads for about two-and-a-half hours.

It was lightly raining when Rocky suddenly caught movement 50 yards ahead and immediately realized it was a deer. He started to reach into his pocket for a paper towel he always carries to wipe the water off his scope's lenses to prepare for a shot. This time however, Rocky realized that the buck facing him was so big that he didn't want to take the extra time. Instead, he shouldered his .300 Winchester Magnum, sighted through the rain-covered lenses on the buck's neck, and squeezed the trigger, instantly dropping the buck.

Rocky then field dressed his trophy and took an hour to bone out the meat in preparation for the trip back to camp. Once the meat was loaded into the pack he headed for camp. It took him two hours to reach the river where he placed his pack, antlers, and rifle into the skiff and crossed the river to the warmth and comfort of his tent.

Rocky had his buck scored after the required 60-day drying period by B&C Official Measurer James Baichtal. Jim scored Rocky's buck at a very impressive 114-7/8 points, which was verified by the 27th Awards Program Judges Panel in April 2010. Rocky's buck was awarded the Fourth Place Award on June 26, 2010, at the 27th Awards Program Banquet in Reno, Nevada. ▲

TROPHY STATS

▼ ▼ ▼ ▼ ▼

CATEGORY
Typical Whitetail Deer

SCORE
198 $^1/_8$

LENGTH OF MAIN BEAM
Right: 31 $^1/_8$ Left: 30 $^4/_8$

CIRCUMFERENCE BETWEEN BURR AND FIRST POINT
Right: 5 $^4/_8$ Left: 5 $^3/_8$

NUMBER OF POINTS
Right: 5   Left: 5

INSIDE SPREAD
20 $^7/_8$

LOCATION
Greene Co., Illinois – 2006

HUNTER
Charles Q. Rives

TYPICAL WHITETAIL DEER
First Award – 198 ¹/₈

▼ ▼ ▼ ▼ ▼ ▼ ▼ ▼ ▼

CHARLES Q. RIVES

Deer hunting for Charles Q. Rives is a family affair. He began tagging Illinois white-tails along with his father, Steve Rives, Sr., and two brothers, Steve, Jr., and Bill, as a young teenager. "Steve, Jr., is the serious deer hunter," Charlie said of his brother, who bowhunts as much as possible. However, he also hunts with firearms when hunting with the rest of the family.

When the whole family and a few friends met the night before Illinois' first shotgun sea-

I'll Take Luck Anytime

son in 2006, little did they realize that one of them was about to rewrite the record book of trophy bucks taken in the Prairie State.

"We are all just deer hunters, and we pretty much shoot whatever deer happens to show up," Charlie admitted.

On the first day of the shotgun season, the group killed a few does, but no one took a buck. The next morning before daylight, they all met and struck out again for their respective stands.

Charlie tells this story, pointing out he already had spent plenty of time in his tree stand without much to show for it. In fact, if he added his hunting hours from the previous year and the current year, he could have put up a mailbox and called it a homestead!

The 200-acre area the family hunts is located in central Illinois, and they've enjoyed remarkable hunting success there. They especially focus on a timbered tract of 25 to 30 acres which flanks two sides of the 200 acres and forms the runway, or bottleneck, between the larger pieces of timber. It seems that each year when the shooting starts, deer frequently use the small, timbered finger of land to move between the larger timbered areas on adjacent land.

Charlie says the hunting party follows what he called the "family rule." All the hunters are restricted to using some kind of a stand to hunt out of until the last day of each hunting season. On the last day, everyone hunts in a stand until late morning when they then all meet at his father's house to formulate a plan for a deer drive. He said they don't like to drive deer that much, so it's used as a last-resort on the final day of each Illinois gun season.

When that day arrived in 2006, the hunting party gathered at his father's home to plan the afternoon drive, following a morning of little deer activity seen from their stands. Despite his usual participation in the deer drive, and because he hadn't seen much at his stand during the season, Charlie had a gut feeling that his stand "must be overdue." So, he and his girlfriend Casey headed to his stand while hearing the now-infamous comment

Charles Q. Rives harvested his award-winning typical whitetail deer on the last day of the 2006 season in Greene County, Illinois. The buck has a final score of 198-1/8 points and received a First Place Award.

from his brother Bill, "There's no sense going to your tree stand. The deer are not going to come by there. We aren't driving them that way."

Charlie and Casey set up about 15 yards apart on each side of the narrow finger of timber, while all the other hunters started their drive. Within minutes, a doe came running across an open field. Both Charlie and Casey shot at it, but both missed their marks. About 15 minutes passed, when Casey suddenly turned to get Charlie's attention and quietly said, "There's a big buck coming across the field right at us."

Charlie slowly moved to Casey's side of the timber, not yet aware that the buck she was talking about was, indeed, truly a giant buck. When the buck reached the edge of the field, he was about 70 yards from Charlie and closing. Charlie immediately shouldered his 12-gauge, Remington Model 870, and lined up the open sights on the buck as he waited for it to get as close as possible before taking a shot. Like any hunter watching a heavy buck with large antlers run right at him, Charlie was a bit unnerved!

Charlie said when the buck was about 25 yards away and quickly closing the gap, he spotted both hunters and started to change directions while still moving at a pretty good clip. Charlie took his first shot as the deer turned, but the buck acted as though nothing had happened. Charlie shot again as the buck started heading away. He recalls seeing the second slug hit the deer a little further back than where he was aiming, and the buck went down.

An overload of adrenaline pumped through both Charlie and the buck. The buck tried to get up as Charlie realized he was out of slugs. He quickly took Casey's shotgun, moved to within a few yards, and dispatched the buck with a neck shot.

When the dust settled, Charlie was standing over the fourth largest typical buck ever recorded in Illinois. As he inspected his trophy, Charlie discovered his first shot had not missed the buck. He found that the first shot took a piece of antler off the bottom front part of the main beam without breaking away the antler, then his slug hit the base of the right antler blowing off the right brow tine, again without taking the main beam completely off.

Charlie's brother Steve soon showed up and backtracked to where the buck had been at the time of the first shot. Ten to 15 minutes later, he found the right brow tine that perfectly matched its location on the rack. It was lacking only one small chip. When they got the deer back to the house, a friend green scored it at 199 inches!

TYPICAL WHITETAIL DEER
First Award – 198 $^1/_8$

▼ ▼ ▼ ▼ ▼

CHARLES Q. RIVES

Charlie said he also decided to take the rack to the 2007 Illinois Deer Classic in Bloomington to see if they would officially measure it. He immediately told the officials that the antlers had been repaired. The official first responded that the rack could not be entered in the big-buck contest because it had been repaired. So, Charlie asked if someone would nonetheless score the antlers just to see what it would have scored.

While waiting and watching the antlers being measured, Charlie remembered he had brought along several "kill" photos. He talked to Tim Walmsley, an Official Measurer for Boone and Crockett Club and showed him the photos.

After looking at the antlers, sharing the photos and discussing the details of the kill with other measurers, Tim decided the buck could be officially scored. He told Charlie that B&C recently adopted a new rule that can qualify bucks like his for official measurement. Tim said deer racks that have a portion of an antler broken off can be scored so long as the pieces fit perfectly together without giving an advantage to the trophy.

The bottom line is, Charlie's buck was built to score. His magnificent 10-pointer had only 3-7/8 inches in deductions—one inch of which was from the difference between the G-4 tines. His buck also featured incredible main beams with both antlers measuring more than 30 inches long! The remainder of the rack featured good brow tines, fairly good G-2s, G-3s longer than 14 inches, and G-4s longer than 10 inches. It's easy to see how his buck ended up with a B&C gross score of 201-5/8. After deductions for side-to-side symmetry, the giant buck was entered in B&C at 197-6/8 points. The 27th Awards Program Judges Panel actually confirmed its score at 198-1/8 points

Charlie said his gut reaction—that his stand "must be overdue"—played a large part in the taking of his trophy whitetail. And, he added, "I'll take luck any time." ▲

This story is reprinted here (with minimal editing) with permission of the author and B&C Official Measurer Ron Willmore. It first appeared in the November 2007 issue of Illinois Game and Fish *magazine.*

TROPHY STATS

▼ ▼ ▼ ▼ ▼

CATEGORY
Typical Whitetail Deer

SCORE
192^5/$_8$

LENGTH OF MAIN BEAM
Right: 30^5/$_8$ Left: 29^4/$_8$

**CIRCUMFERENCE BETWEEN
BURR AND FIRST POINT**
Right: 5^2/$_8$ Left: 5^4/$_8$

NUMBER OF POINTS
Right: 9   Left: 12

INSIDE SPREAD
20^1/$_8$

LOCATION
Pushmataha Co., Oklahoma – 2007

HUNTER
Jason L. Boyett

TYPICAL WHITETAIL DEER
Second Award – 192 ⁵/₈

▼ ▼ ▼ ▼ ▼ ▼ ▼ ▼ ▼

JASON L. BOYETT

Nearly three hours southeast of Oklahoma City, Oklahoma, lies the town Rattan—a laid-back community of 764 folks who prefer the less-complicated life of a small town. At Howard's Café, the town's chief eatery, photos of a big buck harvested in 2007 generate some interesting conversation. The café's proprietor and namesake, Howard Boyett, is quick to point out that the big buck was taken by his son Jason.

Annual Gathering

Jason Boyett, Rattan's 30-year-old deer-hunting celebrity, grew up in Rattan before moving to Kansas in 2004, and since has returned to work in Oklahoma. Boyett did not have the luxury of moving back to Rattan, but instead lives near Tulsa. However, you can bet that he makes the commute to his hometown nearly every weekend to get away from the hustle and bustle of the big city.

Rattan is situated in the heart of timber country where large companies do extensive logging. Oklahoma's Cy Curtis listings show that Pushmataha County, where Rattan is located, has produced 241 bucks in the prestigious state record book. Nearly 86 percent of the record-class bucks taken there were typicals—a very interesting statistic!

Boyett has hunted deer for 18 years and humbly admits he hasn't taken many deer. "You could probably count the number of deer I've taken on one hand," Boyett stated. "I don't hunt as much as I used to when I lived in Rattan."

Nevertheless, each gun season Boyett goes to deer camp in the rugged southeast hills. The annual gathering takes place at a cabin built by the Boyetts and their friends in the early 1990s and attracts family, friends, and in-laws. The cabin is nestled within 430 acres of plantation pines, wooded ridges, creeks, and plenty of clear cuts. The spot has yielded a few bucks previously that qualified for the state's Cy Curtis Record Book.

Last fall, Boyett had high hopes after being informed by his aunt and uncle, and Mary Ann Arpealer of rumors of a big buck seen in the area of his hunting camp. The Arpealers operate a convenience store in Rattan and said a hunter told them the buck he saw was bigger than any other buck ever taken in this area.

Boyett was puzzled by the rumors; to his knowledge, the only big buck ever seen on the property was a buck he had missed several years earlier.

"I walked up on a big buck five or six years ago and missed a close shot at him with my .30-30," said Boyett. "We nicknamed the buck 'Ol' Mossyback.'"

Opening day of the 2007 gun season dawned to cool temperatures. Boyett was moving slow that morning after a late night in camp with his relatives and friends. At first light

Photograph courtesy of Jason L. Boyett

Jason L. Boyett kneels behind his award-winning typical whitetail deer taken during the 2007 season in Pushmataha County, Oklahoma. The buck has a final score of 192-5/8 points and received a Second Place Award at the 27th Big Game Awards Program.

he went to his deer stand but failed to see any deer. The other hunters from his camp also failed to spot any decent bucks as well.

The next morning Boyett insisted that David Evans, his friend from Texas, hunt his personal stand, while Boyett went elsewhere on the sprawling property. Boyett drove Evans to his hunting spot in his Polaris Ranger and then went to an area where a small drainage feeds into a larger creek.

Boyett returned to camp at 8 a.m. for breakfast and picked up another friend, Walter Mack. Boyett and Mack decided to drive around the perimeter of their property to make sure no one was trespassing. After making the rounds, Boyett decided to go pick up Evans to take him in for breakfast.

Just before arriving at Evans' spot, Boyett noticed a doe mingling with a herd of cows in a brushy clearing. While surveying the opening, Boyett and Mack spotted a buck as well. Mack grabbed Boyett's .30-06 to attempt a shot at the buck moving across the opening with a doe but lost it in the thick cover. Soon a third deer, another buck, ran over to join the pair, now standing 200 yards away.

The brush made viewing the deer so tough that Mack could no longer see the buck. "I told Walter to hand me my rifle, because I could see the deer clearly from where I was standing," said Boyett. "I put my scope on the deer and I could see one of the bucks in the waist-high grass."

Boyett fired and immediately thought he saw the brush moving where the deer had dropped. With adrenaline coursing through his veins in big doses, the pair hopped into the Polaris and drove in to locate the buck. The huge buck was lying right where Boyett had suspected he was, and the sight was something to behold.

"It was unbelievable," he said. "His antlers were sticking up, and he was bigger than any buck I had ever seen. I knew I was going to get this deer mounted." The buck had 21 amazing points and was wide.

Boyett hadn't realized what he had just accomplished, but nervously dialed his cell phone to tell his dad of his good fortune. "I've killed the biggest buck of my life," I told my dad. "But I think he thought I was exaggerating a bit."

After loading the buck, Boyett picked up Evans and drove back to the cabin, while calling Cecil Clark who was already at the cabin. After some high-fives at the cabin, Boyett and Mack drove to Hank's convenience store to check in the buck. Hank told Boyett the buck was the largest he had ever seen in all the years he had run the check station. A crowd of onlookers stopped by to see the buck and take photos.

TYPICAL WHITETAIL DEER
Second Award – 192 5/8

▼ ▼ ▼ ▼ ▼

JASON L. BOYETT

After washing off the buck at Boyett's dad's house, Boyett called his friend Jerry Thomas to come by and cape the buck, then Boyett and his dad took the buck to taxidermist Mike Haley in Ringold. Haley scored the buck and told Boyett that he may have a new state record.

Boyett's excitement was short-lived after malicious rumors began to swirl accusing him of taking the buck illegally. Oklahoma Department of Wildlife Conservation (ODWC) game wardens investigated Boyett, and after a four-hour interview, exonerated him of any wrongdoing. Warden Carlos Gomez stated, "The other two game wardens and I gladly gave Jason a thumbs-up."

In early February, Boyett attended an outdoor show in Claremore where ODWC scorer Dick Hoar was scoring whitetail trophies. Hoar is also an Official Measurer for Boone and Crockett Club, and he told Boyett the buck was the largest whitetail he had ever scored.

Hoar methodically scored the giant buck and then presented Boyett with two options: either he could classify his buck as a non-typical, which would tie it for eighth place in the Cy Curtis records book, or he could call it a typical buck with a B&C gross score of 244-5/8 and a final B&C score of 191-4/8—making the buck Oklahoma's new typical state record. Boyett obviously chose to list it in the typical category, and Boone and Crockett Club's 27th Awards Program Judges Panel verified the score of his buck at 192-5/8 points. ▲

Written by Mike Lambeth of Edmond, Oklahoma.

TROPHY STATS

▼ ▼ ▼ ▼ ▼

CATEGORY
Non-typical Whitetail Deer

SCORE
275 $^5/_8$

LENGTH OF MAIN BEAM
Right: 26 $^1/_8$ Left: 27 $^1/_8$

**CIRCUMFERENCE BETWEEN
BURR AND FIRST POINT**
Right: 5 $^1/_8$ Left: 5 $^1/_8$

NUMBER OF POINTS
Right: 13   Left: 15

INSIDE SPREAD
24

LOCATION
Jackson Co., Iowa – 2008

HUNTER
Kyle M. Simmons

NON-TYPICAL WHITETAIL DEER
First Award – 275 5/8
▼ ▼ ▼ ▼ ▼ ▼ ▼ ▼

KYLE M. SIMMONS

Hunting has always been a family affair for the Simmons family. Everything from choosing stand locations and hanging stands to shed hunting is experienced together. The first indication they had of Kyle's huge buck was a pair of sheds found in the spring of 2008. Lance, Kyle's younger brother, had found the sheds on property their father Todd has been hunting since 1984. When the sheds scored in the 190s, they knew their 2008 hunting season was going to be interesting and exciting.

Minutes Seemed Like Hours

In September, the family set up a few trail cameras on the land they knew so well, but the mystery monster never showed up. Early on the morning of Thursday, October 16, Kyle headed for a stand in the middle of the property, but never made it. A doe busted him, so he decided not to spook the whole area and went home.

Later that afternoon, Kyle took a climber stand and headed for a thickly wooded spot where two valleys converged. At 3:30 p.m., he heard something walking behind him. Half of a deer was visible through the brush, but Kyle could already tell it was a big buck. He grabbed his bow and took another look. This time he could see the buck's big rack—it was huge!

The buck stepped behind a tree, giving Kyle a chance to swing his bow around into position. The buck took a few more steps behind another tree and Kyle came to full draw. A few more steps and the buck was standing behind some brush. He held on at full draw. Two more steps and it was in his shooting lane. Settling the pin on the buck's vitals, Kyle let the arrow fly! He thought his shot was good, but maybe

Photograph courtesy of Kyle M. Simmons

Kyle M. Simmons took this award-winning non-typical whitetail deer scoring 275-5/8 points during the 2008 season in Jackson County, Iowa.

a little too far back. The buck turned and bolted about 50 yards and then abruptly stopped. Within 30 seconds, the giant went down.

Kyle immediately text messaged his brother with the news, as he sat and watched the buck. Fifteen minutes later, the buck stood up and started to walk away, only to quickly lie down again. The advice was to wait the buck out. After several hours, Kyle climbed down while there was still enough light, circled away from the buck, and headed home.

Minutes seemed like hours, but the Simmons family waited until 11 p.m. before going to search for Kyle's buck. Lights in hand, they found him only a short distance from where Kyle had last seen him. Kyle was speechless and with good reason. He didn't know it then, but he had just taken Iowa's new All-time non-typical buck. This wasn't just Kyle's first buck with a bow, it was his first deer ever. ▲

Award-Winning Moments

The Boone and Crockett Club welcomed Trijicon as a new Big Game Awards Program sponsor in Reno, Nevada. Tom Munson, the company's Director of Sales and Marketing, accepted the Club's thanks from Simon Roosevelt.

TROPHY STATS

▼ ▼ ▼ ▼ ▼

CATEGORY
Non-typical Whitetail Deer

SCORE
274

LENGTH OF MAIN BEAM
Right: $19^1/_8$ Left: $22^4/_8$

**CIRCUMFERENCE BETWEEN
BURR AND FIRST POINT**
Right: $4^5/_8$ Left: $4^6/_8$

NUMBER OF POINTS
Right: 16   Left: 20

INSIDE SPREAD
$27^7/_8$

LOCATION
Cross Lake, Alberta – 2007

HUNTER
Helgie H. Eymundson

NON-TYPICAL WHITETAIL DEER
Second Award - 274

▼ ▼ ▼ ▼ ▼ ▼ ▼ ▼ ▼

HELGIE H. EYMUNDSON

On November 29, 2007, in the early dawn light, I killed an Alberta giant.

It wasn't the first time I had seen him. The year before, on the very same field, my wife Gail and I both shot at, and missed, him. I can't speak for my wife, but last year this buck rattled me so severely that I had a hard time hitting the air around him! That was last year. This year was different—I was calm, cool, and collected. When the shot presented itself, I took my time and squeezed the trigger. Yeah, right! Now I know why they put that metal guard under the trigger, I pulled so fast and hard that if it hadn't been there, I would have broken it off!

I am going to give you all some advice. When you shoot something big, resist the urge to reach into your pocket to grab your cell and start calling your friends. Wait a few minutes until you calm down, because as much as you think you have it all together, you don't. The words that come out of your mouth are very loud gibberish punctuated by panting and heavy breathing. It doesn't sound good.

"I got him, I got him!" I yelled into the phone at my wife. It was barely daybreak when I called, and she was out with the kids and her brother a few miles away looking for a buck also. "That deer we missed last year—I got him! Gail, I just shot the biggest deer in Canada; he must score at least 250, maybe 275! Meet me at Mom and Dad's place with the kids." I think she was able to get a couple words in before I hung up and started calling more people.

I must have sounded quite strange as each person asked me if I was okay, and if I was having trouble breathing. Hell yes I was okay, and Hell yes I was having trouble breathing! I just ran over 200 yards in a foot of snow in minus -32°F weather to get a shot at this buck.

He was a sight—even at 500 yards, there was no mistaking that massive rack above his head. In fact, the webbing is so deep that when I saw him broadside, most of his face was obscured by antlers. It shocks you when you see that much bone in the binoculars. The area I was hunting was an abandoned hayfield consisting of brome, timothy, and a lot of clover. That's what attracted and held the does in there when the snow got deep and temperatures dropped. Behind the hayfield was an old pasture that gave way to big bush and swamp. Thousands of square miles of bush—the kind that could swallow an army, let alone one buck.

As soon as I saw the deer, I knew it was him and I knew I was going to have to act

Helgie H. Eymundson is pictured above with his award-winning non-typical whitetail deer scoring 274 points. The buck was taken near Cross Lake, Alberta, during the 2007 season

fast to get him. I had parked a half mile away at the field entrance and slowly made my way down the scrub brush to the edge, where I could get a good look at the field. There he was, standing with 10 does not 10 feet from the same rock pile on which I had frozen my butt for hours the night before. It didn't look good; the faint breeze was blowing almost directly to him and a couple does had already moved to the edge of the hayfield. They looked like they were ready to start heading along the old fence line that would lead them to their bedding area. I knew I had to get ahead of them and quickly.

You have no idea how hard it is to turn your back on the biggest buck you have ever seen and start walking off, making a large loop to try and intercept it. I got as tight to the brush as I could; I was hunched over, trying to walk as quickly and quietly as possible. I made it only a few yards before I couldn't take it anymore and looked back over my shoulder to see what he and the does were doing. That served to calm me down…not at all! They were still oblivious to my presence, so I told myself, keep walking, you idiot, and stop looking! Once I had covered about 400 yards, I decided it was time to cut across the wide open pasture to start closing the gap to that old treed-in fence line.

Luckily for me, the buck was heavy into the rut and was preoccupied chasing a doe. It kept him busy and was also keeping the does' attention focused over there and not on the hunched-over, 5-foot, 10-inch pile of snow moving across the pasture behind them. I was starting to feel pretty good about my odds once I had made it about 200 yards into the field undetected. That was short-lived, however, as some of the does were getting tired of this buck chasing everything in sight and were now leaving the field. Of course, they were on the opposite side of that old fence line, which was just a little too dense with poplars to shoot through.

I started to move faster! The does were almost across from me now, and the buck was trailing behind. I moved faster! We were now separated by 250 yards of pasture and a few poplars. I moved even faster! Now the lead doe was across from me, and the moment she cut my wind she blew and exploded to the north. They all followed her, tails waving high in the air and leaping through the snow like it wasn't there. There was only one thing to do; I charged! I was sprinting towards the tree line as hard as I could go, deer were running past me and I had lost sight of the buck and doe he was after. Tears were streaming out the corners of my eyes making it harder to see, and as I shed my mitts, the sinking feeling in my stomach was undeniable. It was not looking good, but I didn't slow down.

I hit that 40-year-old barbed wire fence going full speed; one hand on the top wire and over I went. Clutching my .30-06 to my chest, I put my left forearm up and crashed through the trees. It only took a few steps to break through, and when I did, I spotted a doe almost 300 yards away running wildly for the trees.

Then I heard him off to my right. He was following the doe and grunting loudly. With every jump, his head bobbed low to the ground and all I could see was antler extending way out past his body.

I quickly grabbed a tree for a rest and started to swing onto him. I didn't know whether to grunt, whistle, yell or just start shooting. No sooner had I thought, stop, and he did! He was grunting loudly and starting to spin around towards me as if in a challenge. As the crosshairs moved up his body, I briefly thought about aiming at the lungs but kept on moving. I put the crosshairs on his shoulder and squeezed. I wanted to pin him right there.

As the gun went off, I heard the loudest smack ever and when the recoil came down he was already on the ground. I quickly jacked out the empty and put another round in and instantly started running towards him. I had covered about 75 yards when I realized he wasn't moving and he was down for good. I stopped, bent over, put my hands on my knees, and started gasping for air. It was then that I realized my lungs were burning, cheeks were stinging, and fingers were numb. I didn't care; it was worth it! I stood up, raised my gun over my head, and tried to let out a whoop. It sounded more like a wheeze than a whoop, and I started to laugh. Oh my god, I was thinking. I can't wait to show Dad.

As I approached the fallen monarch, my knees were a little shaky. When I reached down to pull his head out of the snow, I reacted almost in shock. It was overwhelming. I dropped his head, stepped back, and sat down beside him. What I saw was indescribable—width, mass, points, length, and… a hole in the antler? Right smack dab through the middle of a long kicker, extending out the back, was a bullet hole. My bullet hole! When he was spinning around to face me, that sticker had been back over his shoulder and I had shot right through it.

I sat back, put my hand on him and said, "You and I were meant to be." ▲

TROPHY STATS

▼ ▼ ▼ ▼ ▼

CATEGORY
Non-typical Whitetail Deer

SCORE
$272^2/_8$

LENGTH OF MAIN BEAM
Right: $27^4/_8$ Left: $27^6/_8$

**CIRCUMFERENCE BETWEEN
BURR AND FIRST POINT**
Right: $7^7/_8$ Left: 7

NUMBER OF POINTS
Right: 14   Left: 13

INSIDE SPREAD
$23^2/_8$

LOCATION
Morris Co., Kansas – 2006

HUNTER
Gerald E. Rightmyer

NON-TYPICAL
WHITETAIL DEER
Third Award – 272 ²/₈

▼ ▼ ▼ ▼ ▼ ▼ ▼ ▼

GERALD E. RIGHTMYER

My hunt preparations began in early 2005. A good friend, Scott Fratter, gave me a call and asked if I was interested in a whitetail hunt in Kansas. I immediately said yes and prodded Scott for more details. He had met a fellow hunter on an Internet chat room and agreed to do a swap hunt. The gentleman's name was John Hower.

Grandpa

Scott lives in Colorado, and offered a pronghorn/mule deer hunt in exchange for John's whitetail hunt. After working out some of the details, Scott asked John if he could bring a friend along. John graciously obliged, and that is when Scott gave me a call.

I always wanted to hunt the Sunflower State and was eager to hear what Scott had to offer. Actually, I had applied for a Kansas whitetail tag two years in a row back in the late 1990s. Due to the lack of a preference point system, I wasn't lucky enough to draw one of their coveted tags.

The hunt was planned for 2006. We both decided it would be wise to apply for a preference point. The point would increase our odds of drawing a unit 14 tag. I knew the unit was one of the premier hunt areas in the state. *Huntin' Fool* magazine had ranked the unit second only behind unit 16, which is located in south-central Kansas.

The 2005 season went quickly. I killed a 124-inch (gross) whitetail in my home state of New York during the archery season and managed to eat "tag soup" in Alberta, Canada, during Thanksgiving week. The season was challenging, but that is deer hunting.

The following year started off with a literal bang, as I was able to harvest a beautiful

Photograph by Jack Reneau

Gerald E. Rightmyer accepting his plaque and medal from Buck Buckner, Vice President and Chairman of the Big Game Records Committee.

pronghorn in Gillette, Wyoming. Back home a few weeks later, I was fortunate to take another whitetail with my bow. This buck would gross 131 and would qualify for both the New York State Big Buck Club and Pope and Young Club records. The year was already turning into a dream season for me, and I still had a Kansas whitetail tag burning a hole in my pocket!

Whenever I travel to another state or province to hunt any species of big game, I try to keep my expectations low. If I can go into a hunt with reasonable goals, anything extra is just icing on the cake. I knew I was hunting a great area in Kansas but did not know how good an area it would turn out to be.

On November 27, I arrived at the Kansas City airport. Scott drove two hours out of his way to pick me up. Both of us were psyched to get into town and very excited to check out our hunting area. Later that same afternoon, we checked into our motel. While checking in, we met the owner, Emma. We told her that we were from out of town and there to hunt deer. Emma told us about a big old buck with a lot of points named "Grandpa", a local legend of sorts, and she told us that if we killed Grandpa, to make sure that we brought the buck back to the motel to show her. That was the first time I had heard about the mythical buck.

MY BUDDY SCOTT GOT A BIG KICK OUT OF THE STORY, AND I KIND OF SMIRKED ABOUT IT AND JUST PASSED IT OFF AS SOME LOCAL LORE. THE REST OF THAT NIGHT AND MOST OF THE FOLLOWING DAY, SCOTT WOULD INTERMITTENTLY JOKE ABOUT GRANDPA, AND I WOULD JUST LET IT GO IN ONE EAR AND OUT THE OTHER. I THOUGHT, DOES HE REALLY BELIEVE THAT STORY?

My buddy Scott got a big kick out of the story, and I kind of smirked about it and just passed it off as some local lore. The rest of that night and most of the following day, Scott would intermittently joke about Grandpa, and I would just let it go in one ear and out the other. I thought, *Does he really believe that story?*

On Tuesday, November 28, the weather was unseasonably warm. Temperatures hovered around 73°F, and an all-time record high was set in Council Grove. I was disappointed with the weather but also realized that weather patterns can change drastically this time of year. I hoped for the best, but expected the worst.

John showed me and Scott four different properties to hunt. We were also given maps of each property and told where we could and could not hunt. After scouting three of the four tracts, we decided that one wooded creek-bottom area was the most promising. The property was a perfect bottleneck. There were huge rubs, active scrapes, and deer trails both paralleling and intersecting the creek. A bedding area to the south funneled right down to where my stand was positioned. An intersecting strip of woods also bisected the creek bottom, which allowed deer to travel from point A to point B without exposing themselves. I felt really good about both the stand placement and the amount of sign present. I also made sure that I set up downwind from most of the deer activity. Now all I had to do was hope the weather turned and that the deer would cooperate. John also mentioned that a very big deer had been seen in the vicinity of my stand. He said that a local farmer had found a 110–inch shed (left side) while working a field recently.

Overnight the temperature dropped 50 degrees. A huge front had

NON-TYPICAL WHITETAIL DEER
Third Award – 272 $2/8$

▼ ▼ ▼ ▼ ▼

GERALD E. RIGHTMYER

traveled down from Canada and was wreaking havoc in the Midwest. The winds were howling. Gusts approaching 25 mph accompanied the plummeting mercury. The weather was definitely more seasonable.

Wednesday, November 29, was the opener of the Kansas rifle season. I had only been on stand for about 20 minutes when the first buck appeared. A small three pointer walked by at 15 yards. The buck had traveled downwind of my position. I could tell from the deer's body language that he was unaware of my presence. The Realtree Hardwoods HD camo I was wearing was effectively breaking up my outline. I also pay special attention to scent control. Some hunters may think I go a little overboard, but controlling human scent is one of the most critical aspects of hunting cagey deer, so I leave nothing to chance. I donned my Scent-lok suit while scouting and hanging my stand. I shower with scent-eliminating soap, and use scent-eliminating sprays to reduce any odors on the outside of my boots and clothing. I even eat apples before I go hunting to ensure that the chlorophyll neutralizes odors on my breath.

Shortly after seeing the small buck, a lone hunter donned in blaze orange appeared. I could tell that he saw me, and respectfully he turned and walked out of sight.

At 8:30 a.m. I had a lone doe walk by to the east. She hugged the strip of woods connecting the creek bottom and soon disappeared. I also noticed two other hunters walking side by side just south of my position. They were hunting a section of public ground. I lost sight of the two and again saw them a short time later. Twenty minutes later I noticed two different does being followed by a larger buck. I had difficulty seeing the buck's headgear. All three deer were obviously in a hurry and again they headed toward the strip of woods connecting the creek bottom.

As the morning wore on, the weather began to worsen. The wind chill approached zero degrees. Light rains began to fall, followed by sleet, and eventually, hail. It had been at least three hours since I had seen a deer, but I was used to long hours in the stand. I had mentally prepared myself for a long, nasty day on watch.

I decided to sip some half-frozen water, eat a couple of granola bars, and finish one of my turkey sandwiches. The food helped re-energize me and quite honestly, pass some time. It was now almost 12:30 p.m. and still nothing was moving. The woods were quiet with the exception of the hail beginning to pelt the forest floor.

Ten minutes later, I decided to turn around and scan the woods behind me when I noticed a buck. The deer had just climbed up out of the creek bottom, and I immediately

Gerald E. Rightmyer is pictured above with his award-winning non-typical whitetail deer scoring 272-2/8 points. The buck, which was taken in Morris Co., Kansas, during the 2006 season, received a Third Place Award at the 27th Big Game Awards Program in Reno, Nevada.

saw a very heavy set of antlers with many points sticking out. The buck had stopped behind a large tree trunk, and I was unable to see the entire rack. The buck's body was in full view with the exception of the rack. I almost had to pinch myself. As crazy as it sounds, I had to see the rack one more time just to verify what I thought I saw.

This buck was in no hurry. He began to walk broadside and was approximately 60 yards away. The wind was still howling, and I was downwind of the massive deer. I attempted to stop the brute with my best rendition of a doe bleat, but he was oblivious to the call and continued to walk broadside. I again bleated with my mouth, but this time a little louder. The buck definitely heard me on that attempt and he immediately stopped.

Fortunately, while all this was happening I managed to turn and squat on the tree stand platform. I had clicked the safety of the Remington .270 to the fire position. I jammed my shoulder against the tree trunk and braced my left elbow above my knee hoping for as solid a rest as possible. The buck was looking in my direction. Two trees bordered both the left and right side of the buck's vitals. I knew the time to shoot was now. I fired and the buck bolted from his position like a Brahma bull. In a matter of seconds, he was down. I was completely overwhelmed. It all happened so fast!

NON-TYPICAL WHITETAIL DEER
Third Award – 272 $^2/_8$

▼ ▼ ▼ ▼ ▼

GERALD E. RIGHTMYER

I quickly descended the tree and walked up the hill to my buck. Its rack was so immense, I could hardly believe my luck. I immediately knew that the behemoth was a 200-inch whitetail. I soaked up the moment and proceeded to call my friend Scott. My cell phone battery was running low as the extreme cold had run the battery down, but I managed to leave a message on his voicemail. I said "Scott, get over here. I just shot Grandpa!"

My next call was to my father, Ed Rightmyer. My dad had given me the .270 Remington, Model 700 recently, so the rifle had special meaning. After realizing the enormity of the moment, I broke down. My exact words were, "Dad, I just shot the buck of a lifetime!"

I managed to call my brother Pete with the good news before the cell phone battery went dead. Scott had heard the shot and ran over to my location. After many high-fives and photos, we field dressed the deer and dragged him back to the truck.

The word of "Grandpa" being killed spread quickly through town. Everyone was awestruck at the size of the deer's rack. The drop-tines, mass, and the number of points had the whole community buzzing.

After showing "Grandpa" to everyone, Scott and I had one last visit to make. We went back to the motel and showed Emma what "Grandpa" looked like up-close. The Polaroid photos are prominently posted in the lobby of the old motel for everyone to see. I guess the legend of "Grandpa" really was true after all! ▲

TROPHY STATS

▼ ▼ ▼ ▼ ▼

CATEGORY
Typical Coues' Whitetail

SCORE
127

LENGTH OF MAIN BEAM
Right: 19$^7/_8$ Left: 20$^1/_8$

**CIRCUMFERENCE BETWEEN
BURR AND FIRST POINT**
Right: 4$^1/_8$ Left: 4$^1/_8$

NUMBER OF POINTS
Right: 5   Left: 5

INSIDE SPREAD
15$^4/_8$

LOCATION
Coconino Co., Arizona – 2008

HUNTER
Brian C. Balmer

TYPICAL COUES' WHITETAIL
First Award – 127

▼ ▼ ▼ ▼ ▼ ▼ ▼ ▼ ▼

Brian C. Balmer

Brian C. Balmer was drawn for a November Coues' deer hunt in his home state of Arizona in 2008. He hadn't hunted for several years because of a number of commitments, nor had he ever hunted outside the rut. Therefore, he was understandably excited with the prospect that he was going to hunt Coues' deer again.

With only one week to hunt, he began his season by checking out his old familiar hunting spots with little success. He was able to stalk a couple of animals in the 90-points range, but ironically, one stalk was blown by a herd of elk.

On the fifth day of the hunt, he went to an area in Coconino County where he had harvested a nice typical in 1994 that barely missed B&C's minimum score. He arrived there early and set up to do some serious glassing, which is characteristic of Coues' deer hunters, when he quickly spotted two bucks feeding. He estimated the largest buck at around 90 points.

While working out a plan to go after the larger buck, he noticed that the smaller buck kept looking back over its shoulder up the hill behind him. The actions of the smaller buck reminded Brian that he had frequently heard that bucks at that time of the year travel in bachelor herds, and that smaller bucks often give away the presence of other, larger bucks by their actions. Even though it wasn't the rut, he knew that the larger bucks were still very wary and hung back in denser cover.

While watching the larger buck and formulating a plan to stalk it, he kept glancing back at the smaller buck, which kept looking up the hill over its shoulder. Suddenly, his patience paid off when a much larger buck stepped out into an opening from behind a juniper tree. He had an unobstructed view of the antlers at over 500 yards and immediately had no doubt he was looking at the buck of a lifetime. Prior to this moment, he had only dreamed of connecting with such an animal.

As he began to formulate his plan, he also developed a powerful case of buck fever. He tried to calm himself, but he was having serious troubles. He had never before seen such a huge set of antlers on a live deer in the wild!

The buck was on an opposite hillside across the canyon, so Brian started working his way downhill to narrow the distance between him and the object on which he focused his complete attention. At the same time, the bucks were quickly working their way to denser cover. He gained a hundred yards on the unsuspecting animals and began to set up for a shot. He was having trouble keeping track of the largest buck as the trio fed their way through thicker and thicker brush.

The largest buck finally stepped into an opening and paused, giving Brian an unprecedented opportunity. He managed to get his buck fever under control, and squeezed off a round. He wasn't sure of the lethality of his shot, but he clearly heard the bullet hit its intended target. At the sound of the shot, the three bucks immediately headed downhill. Twenty minutes later, only the two smaller bucks emerged from the dense brush. They headed uphill and disappeared though a saddle on the opposite ridge without the largest buck.

At this point, Brian was feeling pretty certain that the buck of a lifetime was his. However, he didn't want to take anything for granted. He began contouring around the rim, taking his time and constantly glassing the opposite hillside in case his shot wasn't fatal and the buck tried to escape. If he had taken the shortest route to his buck, he would have had to go down into the canyon bottom and work his way back up. This route would have taken him below his buck, where he would have made considerable noise going through the brush, and the buck could have easily escaped if it was only wounded.

WHILE WORKING OUT A PLAN TO GO AFTER THE LARGER BUCK, HE NOTICED THAT THE SMALLER BUCK KEPT LOOKING BACK OVER ITS SHOULDER UP THE HILL BEHIND HIM. THE ACTIONS OF THE SMALLER BUCK REMINDED BRIAN THAT HE HAD FREQUENTLY HEARD THAT BUCKS AT THAT TIME OF THE YEAR TRAVEL IN BACHELOR HERDS...

Brian continued on around the rim until he reached the opening where his buck was standing when he hit it and found hair and blood. Instead of following the blood trail, he continued contouring the hillside glancing down into the bottom with his binoculars looking for any sign of his buck. When he reached a point above where he had last seen the buck, he turned and headed back to pick up the blood trail and follow it. It was then that he almost stepped on his buck lying there partially hidden by a bush. On his first pass, he had passed within 20 feet of it.

Brian couldn't believe his eyes for quite a long time. Something like this only happens to other Coues' deer hunters.

Still three-quarters of a mile from his 4-wheeler in rugged terrain with only an hour of daylight, he quickly field dressed his buck and started to pack it out. He arrived back at his 4-wheeler shortly after dark, packed up, and headed home. On the way, he stopped by his father's house and woke him up. His father was a little groggy at first, but he is very familiar with Coues' deer and couldn't believe his eyes. He heartily congratulated Brian.

After the 60-day drying period, Brian contacted B&C Official Measurer and taxidermist Clay Goldman in Payson, Arizona, to have his trophy officially scored. Clay is an avid Coues' deer hunter himself with a large non-typical Coues' buck, scoring 148-6/8 points, that earned him the Second Place Award medal at B&C's 22nd Awards Program in Dallas, Texas, in 1995. Clay scored Brian's buck at 126-7/8 points, and the 27th Awards Program Judges Panel confirmed it at 127 points, qualifying it for the First Place Award. ▲

Past Boone and Crockett Club president, Earl Morgenroth had the ladies coveyed up at his table, including the winner of a B&C Field Scoring Kit door prize given out during the Welcome Reception held on Thursday night of the three-day event.

TROPHY STATS

▼ ▼ ▼ ▼ ▼

CATEGORY
Typical Coues' Whitetail

SCORE
126

LENGTH OF MAIN BEAM
Right: 16^6/$_8$　Left: 16^4/$_8$

CIRCUMFERENCE BETWEEN BURR AND FIRST POINT
Right: 4　Left: 4

NUMBER OF POINTS
Right: 6　Left: 5

INSIDE SPREAD
10^3/$_8$

LOCATION
Sonora, Mexico – 2006

HUNTER
Frank Lawrence

TYPICAL COUES' WHITETAIL
Second Award – 126

▼ ▼ ▼ ▼ ▼ ▼ ▼ ▼

FRANK LAWRENCE

Hunts for quality animals generally require careful planning, excellent direction, intensive work on the part of the hunter, and some of that elusive thing we call luck! My hunt for a trophy Coues' deer, which would turn out to be one of record-book quality, hardly followed equal parts of this tried-and-true formula.

It began when, for two reasons, my wife and I attended the Foundation for North American Wild Sheep Convention in San Antonio. I

Elusive Thing Called Luck

still hoped to be lucky enough to be drawn for a sheep hunt so I could complete my quest for the sheep Grand Slam (I had the three-quarter slam), and we both wanted to make a return visit to the city where we had lived during my basic medical training at Brooke Army Hospital during the late 1960s. A few days into the convention, I introduced my wife to Jeff Blair of Blair Worldwide Hunting, with whom I had booked several past hunts, and left her

talking with him while I stepped over to another booth. I had about decided by that time to pass on the sheep hunt because of its cost (unless I did, indeed, get lucky in a drawing). When I returned to the Blair booth, my wife had not only booked me for a desert sheep hunt but for a Coues' deer hunt with outfitter Kirk Kelso. Who was I to argue?

Our Mexico hunt was in December of 2006. Kirk had two ranches he was hunting. Fortunately for me, I was in the group which hunted in the more mountainous area, outside the town of Cananea in northern Sonora. I found beautiful country with oaks and minimal cactus other than the imposing saguaro. Accommodations, too, turned out well with a nice hacienda complete with hot showers and a fireplace. It was a great place to spend the cool evenings and talk about the hunt. I was to be guided by Beryl Kelso, Kirk's father, and a native Mexican guide named Noah (No-ay) Carlos. I had

Photograph by Jack Reneau

Frank Lawrence accepting his plaque and medal from Buck Buckner, Vice President and Chairman of the Big Game Records Committee.

Frank Lawrence is pictured above with his award-winning Coues' whitetail scoring 126 points. The buck, which was taken on a 2006 hunt in Sonora, Mexico, received a Second Place Award at the 27th Big Game Awards Program in Reno, Nevada.

hunted with both these men previously on a mule deer hunt. The atmosphere was enjoyable with Beryl's stories and his exuberant personality. I, too, had great confidence in Noah's excellent guiding skills.

On opening morning we drove to a ridge top and began to glass. Quickly, we spotted a nice buck on a far ridge about a half-mile distant. We watched him and spent quite some time deciding on the approach. To our left were open flats. We were on a ridge, which fell to our right and abutted another ridge where the buck was. The wind was blowing right to left. A right-hand approach, along the ridge top with some cover, would put us upwind of the buck. The guides decided on an approach over the ridge top, hoping that we could get close enough for a 300- to 400-yard shot. Noah moved out to try to locate a vantage point. About two thirds of the way to the ridge, he signaled us. My hunting partner was Dr. Jim Smith. The two of us started toward the guide. Jim was well ahead. My bad knees slowed me down, and for once, that was good. As I tried to work my way toward Noah and stay below the sight line, I was, by now, somewhat disoriented and did some stumbling around. A shot rang out. Jim and Noah had spotted another nice Coues' buck bedded down and Jim had taken his shot and was successful! His deer was impressive! We returned to camp for lunch and stories. I thought my knees had messed me up once more, but it had been lots of fun.

With afternoon, we returned to the same ridge and the same observation point. Again, after just a few minutes of glassing, we spotted the buck we had seen first that morning, now bedded only a few yards from where we had seen him earlier. The wind direction was unchanged, and we, again, decided to circle to the right, using the other ridge as cover and giving us an upwind approach. We engaged in some debate over using the vehicles. After all, this was a working ranch, animals were used to motorized equipment, the buck was bedded and, in short, we loaded up the vehicle and proceeded across the flat to the downwind edge of the ridge. When we stopped, we bailed out like a couple of commandos and proceeded up the ridge. I was forced to climb on my hands and knees to keep from stumbling over the very rocky terrain; I thanked heaven for the general scarcity of cactus! Noah went ahead and signaled that he saw the deer, bedded in tall sage-like grass. Ahead was a large oak, almost two feet in diameter. Noah tried to set me up on the left side of the tree, and I signaled him that I was a left-handed shooter. I immediately saw, provided by providence, I guess, a shooting knot on the right of the tree. As I positioned myself, it seemed to take forever for Noah to help me spot the deer again, now about 75 yards away. He was still bedded, looking in the opposite direction, missing all our arm signals and movement. I lined the vertical crosshair to bisect the middle of the antlers and brought down the horizontal hair to what I judged to be the base of his neck and fired. Because of the deer's position, my shot caught him as if it was a side-to-side chest shot.

Immediately, I knew I had harvested a good deer. He was one that even my friends back home in the Arkansas River Valley would find good! I was, in reality, a little familiar with the Coues' species and surprised at the reaction of the guides and other hunters to this deer. Only after seeing their reactions, was I aware of how tremendously lucky I was in taking such an animal!

Hunting, for me, has always been about the chance to be out-of-doors, meet great people, see new country, and harvest a nice specimen of the species I was stalking. Such a philosophy has given me great adventures in the U.S., Canada, Alaska, Mexico, and South America. Luck has always, of course, played its role. This hunt, however, seemed to be heavy on the luck! From my indulgent wife's booking the hunt, to my not getting to take the morning's first shot and, thus, waiting for the big deer in the afternoon, to my guides leading me to just the right spot, it was a lucky deal! The Sonoran Desert and its mountains provided me with an indelible memory. The beautiful snowfall which delayed our departure for home because of blocked mountain passes was a perfect ending to the hunt. By the way, later, Kirk Kelso's outfit also helped me complete that Grand Slam. I want to also recognize Weller Taxidermy for the fantastic job they did mounting my record-book Coues' deer. ▲

TYPICAL COUES' WHITETAIL
Second Award – 126

▼ ▼ ▼ ▼ ▼

FRANK LAWRENCE

TROPHY STATS

▼ ▼ ▼ ▼ ▼

CATEGORY
Typical Coues' Whitetail

SCORE
122^3/$_8$

LENGTH OF MAIN BEAM
Right: 20   Left: 18^5/$_8$

CIRCUMFERENCE BETWEEN BURR AND FIRST POINT
Right: 3^5/$_8$ Left: 3^6/$_8$

NUMBER OF POINTS
Right: 5   Left: 6

INSIDE SPREAD
13^4/$_8$

LOCATION
Sonora, Mexico – 2007

HUNTER
Jay Jones

TYPICAL COUES' WHITETAIL
Third Award – 122 ³/₈

▼ ▼ ▼ ▼ ▼ ▼ ▼ ▼

JAY JONES

My love of Coues' whitetail deer can be traced to my early childhood. I grew up in Douglas, Arizona, reading as many Jack O'Connor stories as I could get my hands on. As most O'Connor fans recall, one of his favorite game animals to hunt and write about was the Coues' whitetail. He felt they were one of the smartest game animals around, with a penchant for gambling with their lives to escape.

The mountains around southeastern Arizona are prime Coues' habitat and with the inspiration from O'Conner and the readily available hunting locations, I quickly became addicted to hunting Coues' bucks. I've been fortunate enough to hunt many big game animals worldwide and truly believe a trophy Coues' buck is the hardest to attain.

Gray Ghosts and Good Friends

I took my first Coues' buck at age 14. Since then, I have taken five bucks in the 100-110 Boone and Crockett class but could not break through the 110 barrier for inclusion into the All-time records book.

Over the last 10 years, I've hunted in Sonora, Mexico, on Rancho Mababi, a beautiful ranch in prime Coues' habitat owned by Roberto and Alice Valenzuela. It is composed of high ridges running off the Sierra Madre covered with ocotillo and scrub oak. The party on this December 2007 hunt included my brother-in-law Nick Forsythe and Ted Byfield. We had been hunting hard for two days but had not spotted the 110-plus trophy buck I was looking for.

Most successful Coues' deer hunters appreciate how significantly the use of quality, long-range optics—and patience—can increase your odds of success. Over the years, you finally learn that glassing, rather than walking, greatly increases your chances. This

Photograph courtesy of Jay Jones

Jay Jones is pictured above with his award-winning Coues' whitetail deer. The buck, which was taken during the 2007 season in Sonora, Mexico, has a final score of 122-3/8 points and received a Third Place Award at the 27th Big Game Awards Program.

particular hunt was no different. We had glassed for several hours the morning of the third day when Ted's patience began to waiver and his binoculars started to scan far away ridges and canyons. To the amazement of all of us, he spotted a group of deer high up in a bowl over two miles away and excitedly announced one was a huge buck. I strained to see the deer with my 15X binoculars and eventually spotted the buck. He looked big, even from that distance, and was in a bowl that we were familiar with. It was the same bowl where my hunting partners, Greg Lucero, Nick, Clint Hill, and I spotted a huge buck two years earlier. As we glassed him, we couldn't help but think this could be the same one.

The only problem: the bowl is guarded by several huge canyons and a very steep, thick mountain covered with manzanita. It's always amazing how much ambition can be mustered after seeing a huge buck! Ted and I quickly drove over and began the climb up the back of the bowl. We crawled up a steep face interspersed with manzanita and shale, while Nick covered the front of the bowl in case the buck tried to slip out. Ted and I crested the bowl at 1 p.m., careful not to get sky lined, and maneuvered into position to glass the dark north-facing slope. Within 10 minutes, Ted had spotted the buck bedded next to a feeding doe under a juniper. We quickly ranged the buck and I prepared for the shot. I extended the legs of my Harris bipod on my Weatherby .257 and found a comfortable sitting position to get a shot above the mountain grass. I adjusted the elevation turret to the correct yardage on my Leupold VX-III Long Range Tactical 6.5x20 outfitted with a Leupold bullet drop compensating dial and settled in. I put the crosshairs on the buck and tried to concentrate on a smooth trigger pull. I felt I was squeezing way too long and hard when I realized the safety was on. It happens to the best of us, I guess! I tried once again to compose myself. After a few deep breaths, I got off a good squeeze. The rifle cracked, sending the 115-Nosler ballistic tip on its way. Ted excitedly advised, "You hit him, but he's up and moving."

Two hours later, after some very anxious moments, we had my buck of a couple lifetimes. I was dumbfounded when I finally laid my hands on him. I have hunted Coues' for a lifetime and never have seen the tine length this buck possessed, especially the G-1s.

The green gross score was in the range of 138. In the end, my tremendous trophy netted 122-3/8.

I can't thank my hunting buddies Nick Forsythe, Ted Byfield, Greg Lucero, and Clint Hill enough. They all played a major role in helping make this possible. I have learned much from them. We are childhood friends who come together every fall to continue our quest and passion for chasing these little gray ghosts around the Chiricahua and Sierra Madre mountains creating very special lifetime memories. ▲

Award-Winning Moments

B&C Photo Archives

Trophy owners and guests at the welcoming reception had a unique and exclusive opportunity to view all 98 trophies honored in Reno with coveted B&C medallions and certificates. The moose display included 11 of the greatest trophies ever taken in all three categories recognized by the Club. Craig S. Spencer's bull, which is in the upper right of this photo, has a greatest spread measurement of 67-7/8 inches, 28 points, and scores 247-5/8.

TROPHY STATS

▼ ▼ ▼ ▼ ▼

CATEGORY
Typical Coues' Whitetail

SCORE
117^2/$_8$

LENGTH OF MAIN BEAM
Right: 17^2/$_8$ Left: 17^7/$_8$

CIRCUMFERENCE BETWEEN BURR AND FIRST POINT
Right: 4^5/$_8$ Left: 4^4/$_8$

NUMBER OF POINTS
Right: 4   Left: 4

INSIDE SPREAD
14

LOCATION
Coconino Co., Arizona – 2008

HUNTER
Frank A. Macias

TYPICAL COUES' WHITETAIL
Honorable Mention – 117 ²/₈

▼ ▼ ▼ ▼ ▼ ▼ ▼ ▼ ▼

FRANK A. MACIAS

Growing up hunting mule deer around my hometown in Arizona, I didn't give Coues' whitetail much thought. But as I started hunting elk in northern Arizona, I started locating Coues' deer often. I finally decided to give it a shot and put in for whitetail. My first two tags went unfilled, but my third tag in 2006 produced a buck scoring 94 points. The hook was set as many people know hunting this little deer becomes an addiction. In 2008, I drew a late-December tag in my favorite unit. I knew this year I was going to be able to spend a lot of time afield, so I was going to hunt hard for a "Booner" buck. The first five days I went out by myself locating does and checking if any rut activity had started. I found five groups of does and one buck in the 85-points range. I went home pleased with what I found, and got out just ahead of a big snowstorm.

Addicted to the "Little Deer"

That storm brought over two feet of snow and made most of the hunting unit inaccessible. The next weekend I had to hunt, two of my hunting buddies, Lavar Kendall and George Cordova, were along for the fun. We split up to cover more area but found out we would have to stay together to pull each other out of the snow since we were constantly getting stuck. After finally making it to one of the locations where I had seen does the week before, we glassed the canyons, but saw no deer. We decided to get around to lower elevations and that took the rest of the day just making it through, the snow. We did, however, see a herd of over 200 elk.

The next day we would try another spot that required an hour's walk through a foot of snow. We glassed and found a couple of does and a spike buck. Walking in and out of those canyons we saw a lot of tracks in the snow. Promising, we thought, and decided we would most likely return. We went off to another spot

Photograph by Jack Reneau

Frank A. Macias accepting his plaque from Buck Buckner, Vice President and Chairman of the Big Game Records Committee.

Frank A. Macias kneeling behind his typical Coues' whitetail deer taken during the 2008 hunting season in Coconino County, Arizona. The buck, which scores 117-2/8 points, received an Honorable Mention at the 27th Big Game Awards Program held in Reno, Nevada.

the rest of the day, but found the snow too deep to travel and too many fallen trees across the roads.

That Sunday we tried again to work our way through the snow to get to a spot I had found deer the first weekend. But again, we had to turn back. With the day almost halfway over our only option was to return to the spot we were the day before. As we neared the point from where we glass, I caught movement across the canyon. I stopped to glass as a massive buck was walking through some cedars. He was on a doe's scent, keeping his nose to the ground and moving like he was on a mission. He stopped just long enough to rake a tree, then disappeared over the ridge. It happened so fast I only had enough time to find a place to sit down, range him, and he was gone. We waited to see if he would come back over but it wasn't to be. I now had to do something that was extremely hard. I would have to leave this buck of a lifetime to return to work and then it would be time to celebrate Christmas with my family.

TYPICAL COUES' WHITETAIL
Honorable Mention – 117 $^2/_8$

▼ ▼ ▼ ▼ ▼

FRANK A. MACIAS

Those four days nearly drove me crazy. I kept wondering, Would he still be there? Did someone follow our tracks through the snow? Could I make the 500-yard shot across the canyon? Friday couldn't arrive quickly enough. After a great Christmas day, early Friday morning, Lavar and I left for the four-hour drive to our parking spot. The snow had melted somewhat, making the hike a little easier down to the point. As we set up to glass we could see a huge herd of elk had moved down and were right where I had spotted the buck last weekend. We glassed a few hours there but could not find him—or any other deer—so we worked our way back up the canyon to see if he had moved. We located three more bucks with does but not the big buck. We decided tomorrow we would try crossing the canyon to be able to glass both sides and hopefully find him if he had moved.

That next morning we left early on a four-hour hike across and down the other side. We found the elk had moved back up over night and the other deer were in the same spot as yesterday. As soon as we got to a vantage point I had picked from across the canyon, two does ran out ahead of us. A good sign I thought, so I found a spot to sit so I could see everything in front of me. After an hour, two does came running out to my right at about 400 yards with the big buck right behind them. The buck would stop every so often to smell the does allowing me to range different openings for the shot. The does kept on moving up and were headed directly in front of me at 180 yards. All I had to do was wait for the buck to catch up. Easier said than done—as he stopped and presented a shot, I missed. Telling myself to calm down, relax, and don't miss again, I dropped him on the next shot. The excitement was almost unbearable. As we walked up to my buck-of-a-lifetime, he seemed to grow even bigger on the ground. I had accomplished my goal by leaps and bounds, and my "booner" buck had really boosted my addiction!

I would like to thank my hunting buddies Lavar Kendall, George Cordova, my wife, Ranea and family for putting up with me being gone all the time hunting. You're the best. ▲

TROPHY STATS

▼ ▼ ▼ ▼ ▼

CATEGORY
Non-typical Coues' Whitetail

SCORE
177 $^1/_8$

LENGTH OF MAIN BEAM
Right: 20 $^1/_8$ Left: 19 $^5/_8$

**CIRCUMFERENCE BETWEEN
BURR AND FIRST POINT**
Right: 5 $^1/_8$ Left: 4 $^7/_8$

NUMBER OF POINTS
Right: 18   Left: 15

INSIDE SPREAD
13 $^4/_8$

LOCATION
Sonora, Mexico – 2009

HUNTER
Gary A. Zellner

NON-TYPICAL COUES' WHITETAIL
First Award – 177 ¹/₈

▼ ▼ ▼ ▼ ▼ ▼ ▼ ▼ ▼

GARY A. ZELLNER

My Hermosillo, Mexico, hunt began in early January 2009. It was set up from British Columbia by Gary Drinkall of Tracks BC. Our local outfitter, Javier Monge, met us at the airport and got us through security. It was a little later when he told us of a vaqueros who found the sheds of a massive Coues' deer. Of course I figured it was just a story to get us excited about our upcoming hunt.

Just a Story

The first morning of our hunt we headed into the hills and still-hunted most of the morning, gradually working our way to a waterhole. After sitting on a hillside above the waterhole for awhile, we saw a nice 10-pointer walk into the open. He was about 300 yards away but never provided a good shooting opportunity. There were others from our group hunting in this same vicinity, so the next day, my guide Cheno and I went to a different area. We hunted all morning and never saw anything interesting. That evening we went to a new waterhole, and as it started to get dark, we saw a couple of bucks that looked interesting.

The next morning, our third day of hunting, we were still-hunting the hillsides around this waterhole. Our plan was to be at the waterhole about noon and watch it the rest of the day. As we were getting close to it, we started to see deer—and lots of them. We started just creeping along, almost crawling. All of a sudden Cheno was pointing at an area about 50 to 75 yards away with some brush and a couple of trees. All we could see was part of the antlers and the head. The way he was standing prevented us from getting a good look at him for a decent shot. We must have watched for 15 to 20 minutes when he fell asleep and his head dropped.

Photograph by Jack Reneau

Larry Mike Smith accepting his friend Gary Zellner's plaque and medal from Buck Buckner, Vice President and Chairman of the Big Game Records Committee.

Guide Cheno and Gary A. Zellner kneeling behind Zellner's award-winning non-typical Coues'
whitetail deer taken during the 2009 hunting season in Sonora, Mexico. The buck, which scores
177-1/8 points, received a First Place Award and is the third largest Coues' deer in the Club's
Awards Program.

At this point, Cheno found an angle to get a good look at him. I could tell he was very excited as he was telling me to shoot. After I shot and we walked up to it, I have never seen anybody so excited as Cheno was.

After panel verification, my deer scored an amazing 177-1/8 points. It is the third-largest Coues' deer ever accepted into Boone and Crockett Club's records books. This is the largest Coues' deer entered in the last 38 years. ▲

B&C Photo Archives

Panel Judges Craig A. Cook (left) and L. Victor Clark verified the score of Jay Jones' typical Coues'
whitetail deer at its original entry score of 122-3/8. Jones took this buck in Sonora, Mexico, in
2007. Five of the eight Coues' deer trophies on display in Reno were taken in Mexico.

TROPHY STA

▼ ▼ ▼ ▼ ▼

CATEGORY
Non-typical Coues' whitetail

SCORE
133$^7/_8$

LENGTH OF MAIN BEAM
Right: 18$^5/_8$ Left: 18$^2/_8$

**CIRCUMFERENCE BETWEEN
BURR AND FIRST POINT**
Right: 4$^1/_8$ Left: 4$^1/_8$

NUMBER OF POINTS
Right: 9   Left: 7

INSIDE SPREAD
12$^5/_8$

LOCATION
Cochise Co., Arizona – 2008

HUNTER
Joshua J. Manning

NON-TYPICAL COUES' WHITETAIL
Second Award – 133 ⁷/₈

▼ ▼ ▼ ▼ ▼ ▼ ▼ ▼ ▼

JOSHUA J. MANNING

On November 8, 2008, the opening day of Arizona's Coues' deer hunting season, my dad Randy and I checked out our hunting area in Carr Canyon. We glassed for four hours or so and saw only one doe. Since we didn't see anything else, we decided to check out another area around Parker Canyon. At 10 a.m., we got onto a dirt road that would take us to Lyle Canyon in Cochise County.

First One for the Book

From that moment on, it seemed as if my luck was going downhill. We had a blowout and found that we didn't have a spare tire when we looked in the bed of the truck. We were in the middle of a canyon without a spare tire and even though we had two cell phones, we had no signal.

I headed uphill to find cell-phone coverage. That hill turned into more hills and ravines that I had to maneuver through to make it to the top where I was eventually able to use my cell phone. I called my brother Jeremy, but it appeared he was still sleeping because he works 24-hour shifts. I had to call him several times before he decided to answer his phone. I explained our situation and gave him directions so he could find us and bring us a spare tire.

My dad stayed with the truck while I was on my leisurely sightseeing tour looking for phone service. While sitting there, two gentlemen stopped to see if they could assist with our flat tire. My dad thanked them and mentioned I had gone off to get help. They were talking about hunting when one of the men told my dad about a prime hunting area. By the time my brother had arrived with the spare, it was too late to check out their suggestion, so we decided to leave and return the next morning.

Photograph by Jack Reneau

Joshua J. Manning accepting his plaque and medal from Buck Buckner, Vice President and Chairman of the Big Game Records Committee.

On the ride home I hoped that my luck would take a turn for the better the following day.

The next morning my dad and I were out the door at 5 a.m. This time we had two spare tires. We headed directly to the area suggested by our two would-be rescuers, and after parking our vehicle, I eagerly checked out the area and spotted a large deer after hiking for a half hour or so. The distance between me and that deer was so great that I couldn't tell if it had antlers, so I had to go back to the truck to grab some binoculars.

I asked my dad to come with me so he could take a look and verify what I had seen. When we both returned to the spot where I had seen the deer, we took turns with the binoculars and found that he was still grazing in the same spot. More importantly, the deer turned out to be a beautiful buck! We continued to watch him through the binoculars while we determined whether or not he was within range. In the meantime, he was oblivious to the fact that we were ascertaining his fate.

> **WHILE LEAVING THE HUNTING AREA WITH MY BUCK IN THE BED OF THE TRUCK, I FELT I HAD REALLY ACCOMPLISHED SOMETHING. THIS WAS MY FIRST KILL, AND IT WAS A CLEAN SHOT.**

My dad said it was about a 250-yard shot that I could easily make. By this time, my heart was pumping, and every time I brought my 7mm Remington Magnum up to look through the scope, my hands were shaking. This was the first time I had ever been hunting, and I was just hoping that if I did shoot that I would kill the buck instantly and not just wound it.

I asked my dad if I could use his shoulder to rest my rifle and steady my aim, and he said I could. The whole time I'm sizing up the buck and preparing myself for the shot, the buck continued to graze in the open. My heart was racing at this point, and I began to slowly squeeze the trigger. From that moment on, everything seemed to move in slow motion. I could see a small cloud of dust rise from the grazing buck's neck. He seemed to gently bend forward as if he was going to take another mouthful of grass. My dad said, "You hit him!" And the buck fell forward with his nose in the grass.

Though I mentioned the shot was 250 yards, I failed to mention that was the straight-line distance between me and the buck. To retrieve the buck, I had to walk up and down two small hills covered in thick brush and navigate my way through a set of rocky ravines. When I arrived at the buck, he was in the exact same position as when I had shot him. It took me over two hours to carry him out of the Huachuca Mountains. To make the situation a little more daunting, the temperature was reaching 70°F, and I had left my water in the truck.

While leaving the hunting area with my buck in the bed of the truck, I felt I had really accomplished something. This was my first kill, and it was a clean shot. On the way out we passed a truck going in the opposite direction and waved. A few moments later, the same truck was behind us so we pulled over to let it pass. Instead, they stopped and parked directly behind us and got out of their vehicle. They wanted to see my buck because they mentioned they could see its antlers when they passed us.

After all of the praise and high-fives were given, we passed on our information so they could find the location where I had taken my buck. As we continued our way out of the mountains, we were stopped by a few more hunters who wanted to see my buck. Later that evening, we took him to my dad's friend's house to be butchered. He put it in his walk-in cooler, and we were on our way home.

NON-TYPICAL COUES' WHITETAIL
Second Award – 133 7/8
▼ ▼ ▼ ▼ ▼
Joshua J. Manning

The next day the phone was ringing off the hook because my dad's friend had called people he wanted to see my deer. My dad had gone to get his hair cut later that day, and people at the barbershop had already heard about my buck. He sat there listening to the story and finally realized they were talking about the buck I had killed. ▲

TROPHY STATS
▼ ▼ ▼ ▼ ▼

CATEGORY
Non-typical Coues' Whitetail

SCORE
133 1/8

LENGTH OF MAIN BEAM
Right: 18 5/8   Left: 19 1/8

**CIRCUMFERENCE BETWEEN
BURR AND FIRST POINT**
Right: 4 3/8   Left: 4 4/8

NUMBER OF POINTS
Right: 7   Left: 7

INSIDE SPREAD
15 1/8

LOCATION
Sonora, Mexico – 2009

HUNTER
Thomas L. Thomsen, Jr.

NON-TYPICAL COUES' WHITETAIL
Third Award – 133 ¹/₈

▼ ▼ ▼ ▼ ▼ ▼ ▼ ▼ ▼

THOMAS L. THOMSEN, JR.

My Coues' deer hunting trip began on New Year's Day 2009. That's a great time to escape the cold and drizzle of Oregon and enjoy the sun and high-desert climate of Sonora, Mexico. Little did I know how much this trip was going to exceed my wildest dreams. However, when my guide's eyes lit up like a pinball machine a couple days later, I knew we had a chance for a big buck. Coues' deer are tough to spot in the brush and scrub trees of Sonora's mountains, so it took me awhile to get him in my spotting scope and confirm that we were looking at a real trophy. Yes, he was big indeed.

Escape to the High Desert

Earlier in the day, we had followed a nice buck up and over a ridge, only to lose him in the scrub. We saw a few smaller bucks, but nothing to get excited about. We decided that since it was lunchtime, we ought to have a bite to eat and a little siesta in the early afternoon sun. Afterward, we'd contemplate our next move.

Natacho Piño, or "Nacho" as we called him, is one of those guides with incredible eyesight. As soon as the siesta was over, he was up and glassing the canyon before us. Within minutes he had spotted the big guy more than 400 yards away bedded down and partially hidden by a bush.

Nacho told me that Coues' deer rut at night and sleep during the day. He said at around 4 p.m., the deer would begin to move and we'd have a chance for a better shot. Since we had a couple hours of waiting, we used the time to creep within 300 yards and set up a really solid rest with my jacket and pack. Since I'm far from the best shot in the world, I practiced

Photograph by Jack Reneau

Thomas L. Thomsen, Jr. accepting his plaque and medal from Buck Buckner, Vice President and Chairman of the Big Game Records Committee.

Photograph courtesy of Thomas L. Thomsen, Jr.

Guide Natacho Piño and hunter Thomas L. Thomsen, Jr., with Thomsen's award-winning non-typical Coues' whitetail deer taken in Sonora, Mexico. The buck was harvested during the 2009 season and has a final score of 133-1/8 points.

squeezing the trigger. I must have fired off a couple hundred imaginary rounds.

After what seemed like forever, 4 p.m. rolled around, and I was getting anxious to take my shot. The buck stayed tight, so we waited a few minutes, but because it was getting late in the afternoon, Nacho thought he could get him up with a whistle. Again the buck didn't move. I joked that the buck must be snoring and can't hear the whistle. Either that, or he had had a tough night with the ladies. Finally, I told Nacho that I was confident I could take the shot we had. One shot later, he was down to stay.

When we got to the animal, it was immediately apparent why Nacho got so excited. As a Texas buddy of mine would say, "This was a toad." I was even allowing myself to think that this could be my first animal to make Boone and Crockett.

We took a few pictures and proceeded to carry the deer back to the truck, some two miles away. The first half wasn't too bad, since we still had some light. The second half was in darkness and included a steep descent into an arroyo. From there it was a steep climb up to the top of the ridge where we had left the truck early that morning. Thankfully, when it got to be pitch black on that cloudy night, Nacho scrambled back to the truck and got the flashlight I'd left behind.

NON-TYPICAL COUES' WHITETAIL
Third Award – 133 1/8
▼ ▼ ▼ ▼ ▼
Thomas L. Thomsen, Jr.

When we arrived back in camp at Rancho Los Piños, everyone was excited—really excited—and it was then I realized this was the trophy of a lifetime.

I probably would not have gone on this hunt but for my hunting buddy, Dr. Jim Petersen. He arranged for everything. "Besides," he said, "it's a good time to get out of Oregon's rains. We can take our wives and leave them at a resort in Tucson." Suddenly, my wife was no longer disappointed she wasn't going hunting.

The outfitter and head guide, Aldo Garibay, did a superb job of supplying a nice camp, great food, and delightful company. Best of all, my guide Nacho worked hard and delivered. All in all, it was a perfect hunt. ▲

TROPHY STATS

▼ ▼ ▼ ▼ ▼

CATEGORY
Non-typical Coues' Whitetail

SCORE
$129^4/_8$

LENGTH OF MAIN BEAM
Right: $19^4/_8$ Left: $19^6/_8$

**CIRCUMFERENCE BETWEEN
BURR AND FIRST POINT**
Right: $4^2/_8$ Left: $4^2/_8$

NUMBER OF POINTS
Right: 6   Left: 7

INSIDE SPREAD
$14^3/_8$

LOCATION
Sonora, Mexico – 2007

HUNTER
John P. Westbrook

BOONE AND CROCKETT CLUB'S

NON-TYPICAL COUES' WHITETAIL
Fourth Award – 129 ⁴/₈

▼ ▼ ▼ ▼ ▼ ▼ ▼ ▼ ▼

JOHN P. WESTBROOK

I've been hunting since I was six years old. Waterfowl and venison were a big part of my family's menu while growing up. As I got older, we traveled to Idaho for elk and mule deer, and the latter became my favorite animal to hunt.

After I married my wife Carolyn, our hunting trips became the family vacation. Our sons Will and Matt were on all the hunts possible since they were only a few weeks old. As school took over our sons' priorities, my wife and I would take our ranch horses to areas in Idaho and Wyoming to chase trophy mule deer.

Love to Hunt!

We live on the edge of Redwood National Forest, which records over 100 inches of rain a year. As we got older, we found the thought of hunting in a warm place like Arizona very appealing. I received my Arizona Coues' deer tags for a special draw in December and couldn't wait to go to a drier climate. The dry weather and beautiful country is wonderful— we love glassing and looking at all the different wildlife. And the ability of Coues' deer to blend in and out of their surroundings really hooked us!

After several guided Coues' deer hunts, we were able to find Esteban from Bacatete Outdoors who helped us get hunting access to a ranch where we could guide ourselves. The first year we hunted this ranch, I missed a big trophy buck. But, watching them and hunting them was what we found fun.

The next year found us still enjoying our escape from the cold while chasing trophy Coues' deer. It was a clear morning after a few hours of light rain, which is always needed in the desert. We were on a point from which we liked to glass when my wife saw a buck standing in the sun, looking like he was soaking up its warmth. He was over a mile away, and after I took a quick look, we both agreed he looked big.

We jumped into our truck and headed toward that part of the ranch. I was calculating in my mind where he was and how I was going to hunt for him. We stopped the truck about 1,000 yards from where we had last seen him, and he was gone.

Coues' deer don't stay out in the open long and hardly ever stand still I decided we'd have to creep along a small rise opposite of where we had seen him. As we were creeping through the grass and mesquite trees, we saw movement lower down in the brush and trees. It was a nice buck with a doe. We couldn't see just how nice.

I calculated that if they kept heading in the direction they were going, they would be coming to a small opening where I had a chance to make a shot. I told my wife that I would wait for him to make the opening and asked her to keep watch.

My wife's hunting consists of looking for deer and trying to keep me from shooting "just any deer." She's looking for World's Records. And, she doesn't shoot or like to watch them being shot. She usually closes her eyes and plugs her ears as soon as I bring the rifle up. However, she felt like this could be a big deer and said she'd help me "as much as possible."

We watched movement in and around the brush for about an hour, as the deer were slowly making their way to a small opening. The doe stepped out first and nibbled around the brush. Then out came what I was hoping was the big one we were after. I saw one side was a big, heavy-beamed antler and asked, "Is that him?"

> **MY WIFE'S HUNTING CONSISTS OF LOOKING FOR DEER AND TRYING TO KEEP ME FROM SHOOTING "JUST ANY DEER." SHE'S LOOKING FOR WORLD'S RECORDS. AND, SHE DOESN'T SHOOT OR LIKE TO WATCH THEM BEING SHOT. SHE USUALLY CLOSES HER EYES AND PLUGS HER EARS AS SOON AS I BRING THE RIFLE UP.**

Carolyn answered after a brief hesitation, "Yes." Without any hesitation, I shot. There wasn't going to be a second chance where they were heading.

I looked at my wife and said, "Well, what do you think?" She said she only got a quick look before she shut her eyes, and she didn't think it was as big as she had originally thought. I headed to where I had last seen him. My wife was moving a little slower so that if the buck was only wounded, I would have a chance to quickly finish him off. Happily I found him lying right where I shot him.

When I got up close, I could hardly believe what I was looking at. What a beautiful buck! At first glance, I had not seen all his extra points. I hollered to Carolyn to come on over. She hollered back, "How did you do?" I told her he was a "very decent buck."

As she came up to the buck, she just started smiling and saying, "Oh my gosh!" This buck was as beautiful as they come; there were heavy, extra points with lots of character. He probably was soaking up the sun. From the condition of his teeth he appeared to be at least 8 or 9 years old. Most of them were missing. I felt very fortunate to have found him. Older Coues' deer have learned to hide very well, even during the rut. Every time we have gone hunting, my wife usually says, "This is the year for a World's Record."

Every year I tell her, "It doesn't matter if it's a record or not, as long as I get to see some quality animals!" I must admit, however, that this was a very fun hunt. ▲

Award-Winning Moments

B&C Photo Archives

Mule Deer Foundation executive director and Boone and Crockett Club professional member, Miles Moretti, receiving a handshake and thank you from Simon Roosevelt for the Foundation's support of the 27th Big Game Awards.

TROPHY STATS

▼ ▼ ▼ ▼ ▼

CATEGORY
Canada Moose

SCORE
224^6/$_8$

GREATEST SPREAD
68

LENGTH OF PALM
Right: 43^4/$_8$ Left: 44^5/$_8$

WIDTH OF PALM
Right: 14^6/$_8$ Left: 16^4/$_8$

NORMAL POINTS
Right: 15   Left: 12

LOCATION
Tatshenshini River, British
Columbia – 2008

HUNTER
Keith A. Grant

240

CANADA MOOSE
First Award – 224 ⁶/₈
▼ ▼ ▼ ▼ ▼ ▼ ▼ ▼ ▼
KEITH A. GRANT

Keith A. Grant and his guide Lance Goodwin of North West Big Game Outfitters headed out to their spike camp on the first day of Keith's 10-day Canada moose/Rocky Mountain goat combination hunt along the Tatshenshini River in British Columbia. The weather was exceptionally warm for mid-September, and the skies were clear. While they were hoping it would cool off so bull moose would start to move, conditions were ideal for glassing and locating goats at long distances, so they didn't waste any time heading down valley to see if they could locate a really nice billy for Keith.

After glassing for a few minutes, Lance started to pick out goats feeding on the far mountain range. He pulled out his 20-60X spotting scope to get a better look at the white objects in the distance to decide if there was a billy worth pursuing. As they got closer, they paused to glass again and relocate the goats. They located one exceptional billy away from the herd that they decided to go after. Keith was in good condition, so they made good time working their way uphill through the jungle of devil's club and alder bushes.

Breaking out of the timber about 250 yards from the feeding goats, Lance took a peek through the scope again to see if the one Keith wanted was still there. Keith never hesitated. He laid his pack down and settled in to make a good shot on a tremendous billy. After a four-hour climb, it was great to relax while admiring Keith's goat and looking over the country below from a birdseye view.

After the previous day's climb, the pair took it easy most of the following day caping out the billy and looking after the meat. Later that evening, they spotted a couple of younger bull moose moving around in the nearby swamps but didn't locate anything worth pursuing.

The next morning, the weather had cooled off so Lance led Keith to one of the lookouts he regularly used to glass for moose. Tas, Lance's black lab accompanied them. Most of Lance's lookouts have some sort of stand in a tree or bush to glass from, giving him a greater advantage when glassing. They watched for some time before they observed a very mature bull step out of the trees and into the swamp spread out below them. He started across the swamp, and at times, disappeared in the water and swamp grass.

Watching this particular bull through his scope gave Lance the shivers. He had spent several days two years earlier trying to get this bull for another hunter, but each time they got close, the bull had cows with him and was in about five feet of water, so the hunter never got a shot. This time, however, was different. He was by himself and meandering around the swamp, listening as only a bull in rut can do.

Photograph courtesy of Keith A. Grant

Keith A. Grant holds the antlers up on his award-winning Canada moose that he harvested during the 2008 season near Tatshenshini River in British Columbia. The bull, with a final score of 224-6/8 points, earned a First Place Award at the 27th Big Game Awards Program in Reno, Nevada.

When a bull hears something, he puts the best bird-dog pointer in the world to shame. It was cold enough that morning to see vapor plumes coming from his nostrils at every breath. Even if you can't hear a moose grunt in the distance, you can tell when they grunt by watching their head movement. Lance called a couple of times trying to get his attention when finely he looked in their direction. Lance called again and the bull didn't hesitate for a moment. He just started walking towards them and disappeared into the brush.

They waited at the lookout for an hour, but the bull never showed up, so they had a decision to make. They could either head downhill and cross into the swamp in search of the bull, or they could continue to wait him out. Before they could make their decision, however, the bull made it for them. They heard a faint grunt, and he emerged from the trees 500 yards away where they had been expecting him to show himself. As the moose moved

BOONE AND CROCKETT CLUB'S

off the hill and down to the creek, they waited and listened to him grunting as he continued walking towards them.

CANADA MOOSE
First Award – 224 6/8

▼ ▼ ▼ ▼ ▼

KEITH A. GRANT

There is no noise like a big bull moving through the trees and willows to get one's imagination going. Tas, the black lab, was shaking so hard in antici- pation that his teeth were clattering, and he's been present on a lot of hunts in his career. The big bull broke out of the alders about 80 yards away and walked right toward them.

Lance told Keith numerous times to just let him keep coming if he didn't stop. At 40 yards, Keith couldn't take it any longer and shot. He took his time chambering another round because he expected the bull to just drop. When it didn't, he took a second shot.

They admired Keith's tremendous animal that was laid out at their feet. It was the closest Lance had been to it after first spotting it two years earlier. Keith was especially pleased to take this bull of a lifetime that scores 224-6/8 points and took the First Place Award at B&C's 27th Awards Program in 2010. Lance hopes his genes are still alive and well out on the valley floor of the Tatshenshini River and the neighboring mountains. As they were field dressing and quartering Keith's bull, two other bulls stepped out of the trees and watched them, as if to give a final farewell. ▲

TROPHY STATS

▼ ▼ ▼ ▼ ▼

CATEGORY
Canada Moose

SCORE
221 2/8

GREATEST SPREAD
63 2/8

LENGTH OF PALM
Right: 43 3/8   Left: 42 6/8

WIDTH OF PALM
Right: 14 4/8   Left: 14 4/8

NORMAL POINTS
Right: 14   Left: 14

LOCATION
Dease Lake, British Columbia – 2008

HUNTER
Ross H. Mann

CANADA MOOSE
Second Award – 221 2/8

▼ ▼ ▼ ▼ ▼ ▼ ▼ ▼ ▼

ROSS H. MANN

When I was a young boy, I vividly remember my dad and his hunting partner coming home from a November mule deer hunt in the "Gang Ranch" grasslands of British Columbia. They had several large bucks tied to the top of the canopy on his truck. The picture of Dad and those big racks was forever etched in my memory. Ever since then, I've always had a strong compulsion to wait for large, mature animals on my hunting trips. From an early age, Dad took me hunting with him and taught me to respect and appreciate God's creation— both the animals and the awesome places they live in.

Great Antlers, Great Memories

In mid-September 2008, Brad Jackle, Dave Smith, and I chartered a plane with Bruce McNaughton of B.C.-Yukon Air Service to fly us into a remote northern British Columbia lake on our annual moose and caribou hunt. Once there, we spent a day setting up camp and cutting firewood.

Our method of hunting consists of climbing to a height of land about one-half mile above camp. We glass a vast area with our binoculars and inspect any game seen with our spotting scopes. Snow, rain, fog, and bone-chilling winds often make the "dawn to dusk" days a true endurance test. In addition to glassing, we cow-call in an effort to lure any bulls that might be in the area.

On the first full day of hunting, Brad spotted a 60-inch-plus bull about two miles away on the far side of a lake we call Lower Lake. He checked him out with the spotting scope and could see that he had good width, but he only had about six points per side, and his right palm was noticeably narrower and shorter than his left. Brad and I almost always have big antlers on the brain and don't mind if we fail to cut

Photograph by Jack Reneau

Ross H. Mann accepting his plaque and medal from Buck Buckner, Vice President and Chairman of the Big Game Records Committee.

our tags. Dave likes big antlers, too, but can't seem to resist all those cheeseburgers on average-sized bulls. Brad tried calling the bull in, but the breeze was too strong for him to hear at that distance.

As we watched him walk straight away, he would occasionally turn and look in our direction and thrash the brush with his rack. We watched him until he disappeared over the ridge. Dave would end up taking this bull a few days later.

An hour after that bull had left our sight, Brad happened to glass the closest shore of Lower Lake. His heart skipped a beat as he saw a huge bull standing in shallow water. He was easily over 60-inches wide, with lots of points and long, wide palms—a definite shooter. Even though he was only a mile away, Brad couldn't get him to come to the call. A cow and calf which were almost a half mile down the lakeshore held his attention.

Dave and Brad decided to move to a rocky hill we call "Grizzly Knob", which is about 400 yards above where the big bull was standing. The hike to Grizzly Knob took almost an hour because they had to climb down and up rocky ridges and slog through muskeg and arctic birch shintangle.

When they finally peeked over Grizzly Knob, their exhaustion and anticipation turned into disappointment; the cow and calf had moved down to the far end of the lake with the big bull in pursuit. The bull trailed the cow in the shallows until she urinated and he tested her scent. He then left the cow and disappeared over the same ridge as the other bull had earlier in the morning.

Ideally, we prefer to shoot our moose as close to our lake as possible, because backpacks and an inflatable boat are our only means of transporting them to the meat pole. Further pursuit of this huge bull was out of the question. Also, it was early in the hunt, so our hopes were high that we would see him again.

A couple of days after our encounter with the big bull, the three of us were on the lookout above camp for the evening hunt. We had seen a selection of moose throughout the day, but none of the bigger bulls were anywhere near close enough to try and make a stalk. In addition, strong winds made calling a waste of time.

Later, Brad spotted a big bull a mile away in the birch beyond a lake we call "Dave's Lake." I got him in the spotting scope as Brad grabbed his birch bark and gave a loud cow call. His rack swung in our direction when the sound finally reached him, so Brad gave another series of three long cow calls. He shook his rack and began trotting down the ridge bucking like a young colt. He crossed an open grassy area, stopped to smash a patch of willows, and then paused from wrecking trees to turn and listen in our direction. Brad gave him another series of calls and once again he shook his head and began trotting and bucking as he moved down the ridge. This pattern continued while I looked him over and confirmed he was a shooter. The bull continued to move along the lakeshore to our left as Brad continued to do his best to sound like a lovesick cow moose.

This is when we began to suspect that we might have a wind problem. When he finally waded in to swim across, he was close to being straight downwind but still close to 800 yards out. The backside of our lookout ridge is heavily timbered, so we can't see the near shore of Dave's Lake. We knew that the next time we saw him, he might be as close as 100 yards, or if he picked up our scent, we might not see him at all.

CANADA MOOSE
Second Award – 221 $^2/_8$

▼ ▼ ▼ ▼ ▼

Ross H. Mann

The big bull had been out of sight for 45 minutes when I spotted him again almost straight north of us. He was almost 900 yards out in a narrow clearing between the base of our ridge and a smaller ridge to our left. He would still turn and look toward us when Brad called, but he was gradually moving up the smaller ridge. He obviously had gotten a good whiff of us and didn't like it.

We quickly decided that I should hurry back to camp and move around to a location near our lake where I could call and try to turn him south. I set up in a good ambush spot where I could see several hundred yards to the west and to the north of where I had last seen him.

Meanwhile, Brad continued calling, smashing branches, and grunting. The bull was headed back in their direction when I finally saw those huge antlers gliding above the willows. He was 370 yards out when he went down on my second shot.

I hurried across the creek and up through the willows toward where I last saw him. By this time it was starting to get dark, and I managed to walk right past him in the thick willows. I soon figured out that I had gone too far and backtracked to where he was lying. When I saw him up close, I realized that he was significantly bigger than I had thought when I was watching him through the spotting scope three hours earlier.

I quickly field dressed and propped him open for cooling. By then it was totally dark, so I headed back to camp. When I got near our lake, I could see the headlamps of the guys bringing our inflatable boat down the lake to help me out. Unknown to me was the fact that they were able to watch the entire hunt from the top of the lookout hill and saw the bull go down.

The nights were getting cold, so we decided to leave him until daylight when we could do better and quicker work. We then returned to camp for a well-deserved rest and celebration.

After the 60-day drying period, the 63-2/8-inch-wide bull scored 221-2/8 points. My bull was the same one that Dave and Brad had seen below Grizzly Knob. Dave ended up taking the other wide bull we had seen by Lower Lake—a 62-inch bull that scored 181-4/8 points. Brad saw another huge bull on two separate occasions, but he was too far away to try for it.

Brad had a big bull coming in one evening from Lower Lake that began trotting and bucking as he came down the ridge just like my bull had. Brad told Dave that even if it came right in, he wasn't going to shoot because he had seen the other huge one plus another better one earlier that day. As it turned out, he should have taken it that evening because he ended up shooting it a few days later, when it was a lot farther from our lake. His 56-inch bull scored 198-1/8 points.

Ross H. Mann and his long-time hunting partner kneel beside Mann's award-winning Canada moose taken during the 2008 hunting season near Dease Lake, British Columbia. The bull, which scores 221-2/8 points, received a Second Place Award at the Club's 27th Big Game Awards Program held in Reno, Nevada.

We took three of the biggest bulls we saw on our three-week hunt. We will all remember 2008 for the great antlers, great memories, and a lot more cheeseburgers. Also, to top the hunt off nicely, I got a beautiful 350-class mountain caribou two days before the floatplane came to fly us out.

These bulls were all spotted from the same hill that my dad and I were hunting in 1991. The same hunt where he got his first and only mountain caribou. Dad is 89 years old now and has Parkinson's disease. He has finished his last hunt and is nearing the end of the trail, but I'll always have the memory of sitting beside Dad on that hill and watching for those big northern bulls! ▲

B&C Photo Archives

Donald R. Corrigan relaxes during the festivities with his wife Debra, stepson Alex Rudert (left) and son Jake. Corrigan was awarded the Second Place Award (tie) for a trophy black bear he took in Newaygo County, Michigan in 2009. Don's black bear, which scores 22-11/16 and field dressed at 500 pounds, is Michigan's new state record.

TROPHY STATS

▼ ▼ ▼ ▼ ▼

CATEGORY
Canada moose

SCORE
$220^7/_8$

GREATEST SPREAD
$66^5/_8$

LENGTH OF PALM
Right: 46   Left: $41^4/_8$

WIDTH OF PALM
Right: $16^2/_8$ Left: $16^2/_8$

NORMAL POINTS
Right: 12   Left: 12

LOCATION
Tatshenshini River, British
Columbia – 2009

HUNTER
Fred E. Dodge

BOONE AND CROCKETT CLUB'S

CANADA MOOSE
Third Award – 220 ⁷/₈
Fourth Award – 213 ³/₈

▼ ▼ ▼ ▼ ▼ ▼ ▼ ▼ ▼

FRED E. DODGE

The first time I met Fred Dodge was at the Wild Sheep Foundation's convention in 2009. This was shortly after he had taken his first of two Canada moose, which were accepted in Boone and Crockett Club's 27th Big Game Awards Program. He was there with the owner of Northwest Big Game Outfitters, Jack Goodwin, and Jack's master guide Lance Goodwin. Over a beer, the three of them gave me an abbreviated play by play story of Fred's recent moose hunt. To say the least, they had my undivided attention as they detailed the order of events.

Back to Back

To begin with, Fred does not necessarily fit the mold of what one might expect as one of the top moose hunters in North America. He calls Colorado home but is on the road working in the gold mining industry, traveling extensively throughout the western United States, Canada, and Alaska. I am not sure how much his travels have contributed to his passion for moose, but his love for *Alces alces* is apparent and undeniable.

At the most recent Wild Sheep Foundation convention in Reno, Fred was manning a booth and trying to recruit support for the North American Moose Foundation. He was so busy, it was tough to catch up to him, but finally we connected.

He has hunted big game extensively in Colorado, taking a once-in-a-lifetime Shiras' bull and also has an awards-book Alaska-Yukon moose from the Yukon, but Fred's knack for taking trophy-class Canada moose is unprecedented. While talking to him about the hunt, he told me he wanted to take the muzzleloader World's Record Canada moose. He had hunted the wild northwest country in British Columbia four times previously with Lance, Jack, and their other guides, taking home many species

Photograph by Jack Reneau

Fred E. Dodge accepting his plaques and medals from Buck Buckner, Vice President and Chairman of the Big Game Records Committee.

TROPHY STATS

▼ ▼ ▼ ▼ ▼

CATEGORY
Canada Moose

SCORE
213$^3/_8$

GREATEST SPREAD
62$^5/_8$

LENGTH OF PALM
Right: 47$^4/_8$ Left: 46$^5/_8$

WIDTH OF PALM
Right: 13$^2/_8$ Left: 12$^3/_8$

NORMAL POINTS
Right: 9   Left: 12

LOCATION
Tatshenshini River, British
Columbia – 2008

HUNTER
Fred E. Dodge

of trophy animals—including three other moose that would make the records book, but they wanted to step it up a notch or two.

For starters, the area he was hunting has proven in recent years to be head and shoulders above other Canada moose-hunting areas. For the most part, the records book reveals these moose can grow to world-class status across the majority of their range but at least three of the top-six Canada moose entered into the 27th Awards came from hunts guided by Lance in this area,.

Fred and Lance hunt the hard way. They hunt for days on end from horseback and pitch their tent wherever the horses may take them in their search for true world-class moose.

His first record-breaking muzzleloader bull was taken in October 2008. He arrived on October 22 and embarked on a nine-day hunt in some of the very worst weather that British Columbia could muster. Lance told Fred that it was the worst weather he could remember in the last 25 years.

After hunting as hard as possible during the first few days, they finally spotted a bull in the 210-range on October 30th. While they dealt with extreme weather, the only animals moving, except for a few sheep and a lone wolf, were moose. Very little other wildlife was seen through the falling snow. Lance first caught a glimpse of a bull at a considerable distance. However, there wasn't enough light to attempt a stalk. A bull of this caliber was definitely in the range Fred wanted, so the next day's hunt was already planned.

The following morning, the two of them spotted the bull within an hour of glassing. The conditions were extremely tough during the six-hour stalk with two feet of snow on the ground and a strong prevailing wind.

CANADA MOOSE
Third Award – 220 7/8
Fourth Award – 213 3/8

▼ ▼ ▼ ▼ ▼

FRED E. DODGE

The shot was fairly anti-climatic after the intense stalk. Fred dropped the bull with a single shot from his .50 caliber muzzleloader that fired a 300-grain slug. This bull scored an impressive 213-3/8 points that was verified by the Club's 27th Awards Program Judges Panel. It took the 4th Place Award in the Canada moose category.

After taking one great bull, it was a daunting task to try for another, let alone one to beat Fred's previous entry. However, he and Lance felt it could be done.

Fred returned to northern British Columbia at the end of September 2009 to again embark on another two-week horseback hunt in pursuit of some of the largest moose found

Photograph courtesy of Fred E. Dodge

Fred E. Dodge poses with his 2008 record-book Canada moose. This bull has a final score of 213-3/8 points and received a Fourth Place Award.

Fred E. Dodge poses with his 2009 Canada moose scoring 220-7/8 points. The bull was taken near Tatshenshini River, British Columbia, and received a Third Place Award.

anywhere in North America. His second trip was far more enjoyable as they were blessed with weather more conducive to moose hunting in the beautiful and untouched wilds of northern British Columbia. This hunt was much the same as before in terms of methodology. They hunted from horseback and camped wherever necessary to find big moose. Fortunately, moose were more prevalent on this trip, and they also saw numerous other wildlife species, including Dall's sheep, mountain goats, grizzly bears, black bears, and wolverine. The latter in particular was especially close, and they were able to get some great footage of the wolverine.

After locating and passing up numerous bulls, some approaching the 210-plus range, they finally spotted a good bull with several cows on the sixth day worth some work. This old boy was well over 65 inches wide with everything needed to go high in the records book. However, the herd spooked sometime during the stalk while Fred tried to get within range for his muzzleloader.

After spooking this guy, they decided to move completely out of the country. They figured he was obviously the top bull in the area based on the size of his rack and the number of cows with him. After arriving at their new area 30 miles away, Lance quickly spotted another tremendous bull over a mile away. As it was the peek of the rut, he immediately started calling. Two hours later, they finally caught up with the bull in an opening about a hundred yards away. Once again, Fred's .50 caliber muzzleloader slug found its mark, and Fred had a bull scoring an amazing 222-7/8 on the ground. It took them two full days of packing to get this giant back to their drop-off point. The 27th Awards Program Judges Panel verified the score at 220-7/8. ▲

Moments in Measuring

Panel Judges (left to right) Glenn E. Hisey, Craig A. Cook, Frederick J. King, and Buck Buckner verify the length of palm measurement for the left antler on Craig S. Spencer's Alaska-Yukon moose that scores 247-5/8 points. Spencer's bull was the highest-scoring moose in Reno. Hisey is vice president of the Pope and Young Club that uses B&C's scoring system with permission to record trophies taken with a bow.

TROPHY STATS

▼ ▼ ▼ ▼ ▼

CATEGORY
Canada Moose

SCORE
198$^5/_8$

GREATEST SPREAD
50$^1/_8$

LENGTH OF PALM
Right: 44$^7/_8$ Left: 42$^1/_8$

WIDTH OF PALM
Right: 14$^7/_8$ Left: 15

NORMAL POINTS
Right: 10   Left: 10

LOCATION
Telegraph Creek, British
Columbia – 2007

HUNTER
Richard M. Bock

CANADA MOOSE
Honorable Mention – 198 ⁵/₈

▼ ▼ ▼ ▼ ▼ ▼ ▼ ▼ ▼

RICHARD M. BOCK

Richard M. Bock's hunt of a lifetime for Canada moose and caribou started in 2008 with a two-and-a-half day drive from his home in the lower 48 states to Telegraph Creek, British Columbia, where he had signed on with Dempsey Callison of Golden Bear Outfitters for a combination trophy Canada moose/mountain caribou hunt. His hunting partner was his friend Tim Kunkel. They stayed in Highland Camp the first night where they rested up and used their time to organize their gear for the hunt ahead of them.

After a hearty and delicious breakfast the next morning, Richard and Tim helped load up the horses for their trip to Joe's Camp where they would spend the first leg of their hunt. They hunted two days out of that camp without seeing a moose large enough to fill either of their tags, so they moved to Beattie Camp on the third day.

As frequently happens between good friends, and to avoid confusion when the first shot presents itself, they agreed in advance that Tim would get the first shot at a mountain caribou and Richard would get the first shot at a moose. This was fortunate for Tim because the first animal they sighted was a caribou that he dropped on the second day hunting from Beattie Camp.

While Tim and their guide field dressed and quartered Tim's bull and prepared it for the horse pack trip back to Beattie Creek Camp, Richard stood guard in case the sound of gunfire or the smell of blood attracted a grizzly bear. It is a well-known fact in many areas that gunshots act as a dinner bell for grizzlies. Back at Beattie Camp, they hung Tim's caribou from the meat pole.

Things were looking up for Richard the next morning when they spotted two bull moose about a half mile out from camp. They attempted to follow them but they eventually lost their tracks without ever getting a good look or shot at either of the bulls. At least they were starting to see moose.

As they set up their scopes to do some serious glassing early the next morning, Tim told Richard and their guide that he thought he heard a bull moose grunt. Sure enough, they quickly spotted a couple of bulls from their vantage point, and it was immediately obvious that one was noticeably larger than the other.

Tim ranged the larger one at around 400 yards while Richard prepared his .300 Winchester Magnum for the shot. When he was ready, Richard carefully squeezed off his first shot, and Tim called it just behind the shoulder. While his shot was dead-on, it took a couple more quick shots to put down the moose for good.

When they reached Richard's bull, it was obvious to everyone that he had taken the

Richard M. Bock is pictured above with his Canada moose that received an Honorable Mention at the 27th Big Game Awards Program in Reno, Nevada. The bull, which has a final score of 198-5/8 points, was harvested near Telegraph Creek in British Columbia in 2007.

trophy of a lifetime. It took them an hour just to clear the dense, 4- to 6-foot-tall alders before they could take field photos to share with friends and to memorialize the hunt for years to come. After field dressing and quartering it, they packed it on the horses for the trip back to camp. Richard wasn't too excited about taking a caribou, so the hunt was over, and they headed home. ▲

B&C Photo Archives

Trophy owner Roger L. Leach (far right) and other attendees at the 27th Awards Program take the opportunity to check out the deals on some silent auction items and place their bids. Leach's woodland caribou, which scores 325-3/8, received the Second Place Award in Reno.

TROPHY STATS

▼ ▼ ▼ ▼ ▼

CATEGORY
Alaska-Yukon Moose

SCORE
247 5/8

GREATEST SPREAD
67 7/8

LENGTH OF PALM
Right: 52 1/8   Left: 49 7/8

WIDTH OF PALM
Right: 21 7/8   Left: 19

NORMAL POINTS
Right: 14   Left: 14

LOCATION
Selawik Hills, Alaska – 2008

HUNTER
Craig S. Spencer

ALASKA-YUKON MOOSE
First Award – 247 ⁵/₈

▼ ▼ ▼ ▼ ▼ ▼ ▼ ▼ ▼

CRAIG S. SPENCER

Anytime one travels into the bush pursuing Canada or Alaska-Yukon moose, just reaching camp is an adventure in itself, as Delaware hunter Craig S. Spencer found out on his 2008 Alaskan moose hunt. After flying into Fairbanks, he found himself in the back seat of a Super Cub headed for a remote camp.

Upon arrival, the gear was quickly un-packed, but due to Alaska's law prohibiting hunting on the same day as flying, a few hours

He's a Shooter

of grayling fishing became the first outdoor pursuit of this record hunt. The fishing excursion gave Craig his first exposure to the notorious hummock-covered landscape of Alaska's moose habitat. The experience yielded approximately 50 fish for Craig and his hunting companion Ed, in addition to a great distaste for walking the obstructive hummocks.

The next day, the pair found themselves in the field at first light, calling and glass-ing for moose. Dan, their guide, asked them who had first shot. Ed affirmed that Craig would have priority since he had put the hunt together, and Craig did not disagree. The calling produced one cow that came in, which got the blood flowing, but no bulls could be enticed. Later that day, while still trying to lure moose into range, the hunters heard a pack of wolves, and moose calls quickly gave way to wolf calls. Soon, the pack of five or six wolves headed their way, but when a couple shots at the wolves came up empty, Craig and Dan headed back to camp for dinner. It was dusk, and as they shed their hunting gear in favor of camp clothes, their guide did some last-minute cow calls. The next thing Craig knew, there they were, wearing blue jeans and lacking bug repellent, and in pursuit of a bull! They jogged over 500 yards from camp where they set up. Craig wanted a representative bull from the area and asked the guide to let him know if it was a trophy meeting

Photograph by Jack Reneau

Craig S. Spencer accepting his plaque and medal from Buck Buckner, Vice President and Chairman of the Big Game Records Committee.

Craig S. Spencer is pictured above with his award-winning Alaska-Yukon moose taken during the 2008 hunting season near Selawik Hills, Alaska. The bull, which scores 247-5/8 points, received a First Award at the 27th Big Game Awards Program held in Reno, Nevada.

his criteria. As the bull closed the distance, Ed was leaning over his shoulder saying he could see him, and from his expression Craig was certain that this was why they had made the trip. Dan mouthed the words with wide eyes, "He's a shooter."

By this time, Craig's nerves were shot. The bull appeared 175 yards away and took a moment or two to mutilate a bush. He closed the distance by 25 yards, finally stepping into a clear lane. After one good hit and a few follow ups, Craig Spencer stood over what the 27th Awards Judges Panel confirmed as a tie for the 17th largest Alaska-Yukon moose ever accepted into B&C's records books.

The bull has a greatest spread of 67-7/8 inches. The palm widths are 21-7/8 inches and 19 inches for the right and left antlers, respectively, and the palm lengths are 52-1/8 inches and 49-7/8 inches for the right and left antlers, respectively. ▲

Boone and Crockett Club partner organizations including Dallas Safari Club, Wild Sheep Foundation, Mule Deer Foundation, and Pope & Young Club all spent time talking hunting and conservation with visitors and attendees of the trophy exhibit.

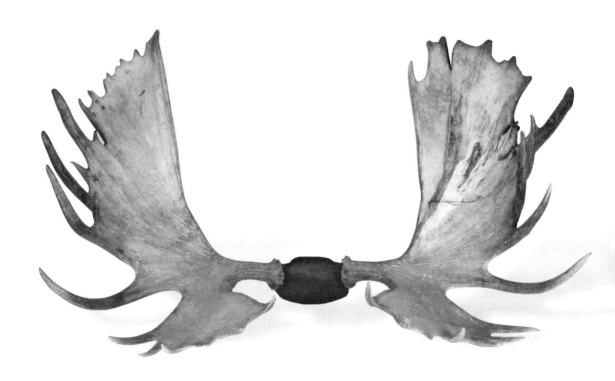

TROPHY STATS

▼ ▼ ▼ ▼ ▼

CATEGORY
Alaska-Yukon Moose

SCORE
242

GREATEST SPREAD
$65^2/_8$

LENGTH OF PALM
Right: $49^3/_8$ Left: $48^4/_8$

WIDTH OF PALM
Right: 18   Left: $17^4/_8$

NORMAL POINTS
Right: 15   Left: 15

LOCATION
Sheep Mt., Yukon Territory – 2009

HUNTER
Rob Springer

ALASKA-YUKON MOOSE
Second Award – 242

▼ ▼ ▼ ▼ ▼ ▼ ▼ ▼

ROB SPRINGER

This adventure started in the summer of 2006 when my good friend Chuck Lamar booked a combination hunt for both of us with Dan Reynolds Outfitting in Dawson City, Yukon Territory. Chuck had planned to hunt sheep and moose, and I was planning to hunt caribou and moose. Chuck had researched Dan Reynolds and knew his territory produced world-class moose annually, which piqued my interest. I had already taken a Shiras' moose and a Canada moose, but had yet to take an Alaska-Yukon moose.

Make Her Happen

After waiting a few years, the time had come to leave warm and sunny Florida for the distant cold wilderness of the Yukon. I arrived in Dawson City late on the evening of October 5, 2009, having driven 330 miles from Whitehorse due to inclement weather. Chuck was unable to make the hunt due to the success of the Philadelphia Phillies baseball team, for which he served as the assistant general manager.

Our hunt was delayed for two days because of continuous sleet and fog. After arriving at base camp on October 8, we had time to sight in my rifle and plan our first hunt away from base camp. I also met my guide Frank Ross. Frank and I discussed the type of moose I was looking for, the challenges we would face due to the approach of winter and the fact that the rut had all but ended.

Early on the morning of October 10th, we climbed atop a small knob above our cabin to glass for moose before departing for the day. Within the first 15 minutes of calling, Frank spotted a nice bull coming from the timber. It was my first exposure to the Alaska-Yukon moose subspecies, thus, I had no idea how good this bull actually was. We watched as it approached to within 100 yards, Frank guessed it to be around 65 inches wide, but felt it would

Photograph by Jack Reneau

Rob Springer accepting his plaque and medal from Buck Buckner, Vice President and Chairman of the Big Game Records Committee.

Rob Springer is pictured above with his award-winning Alaska-Yukon moose along with his guides Frank Ross and Dan Reynolds. The bull has a final score of 242 points and received a Second Place Award at the 27th Big Game Awards Program in Reno, Nevada.

not score well on one side. We elected to pass and then watched it walk down the runway for the Super Cub and out of sight back into the timber.

We then began our journey to an upper basin known to hold good numbers of moose with some large bulls. We arrived on foot around noon, and Frank immediately spotted several bulls herded together with cows in the willows along a timber patch. We moved several times attempting to get a better look—not an easy task due to the snow and the height of the willows.

It was around 2 p.m. when Frank reacted like a kid on Christmas morning after seeing a new bull that had just appeared from the timber. Frank and Dan discussed a plan to get a better look, and within minutes Frank and I were off to get closer before bad weather set in. The bull was traveling with three cows and eventually all four broke away from the other bulls and cows, which numbered around a dozen.

We watched for about two hours while the moose fed and then bedded down. Frank was getting concerned that darkness would eventually get us, but he insisted we should remain where we were. He sensed they would feed through the willows and back to the timber where he had originally spotted them. He was right.

ALASKA-YUKON MOOSE
Second Award – 242
▼ ▼ ▼ ▼ ▼
ROB SPRINGER

At 4:30 p.m., all four approached our position traveling through head-high willows. The cows were leading this bull right to us! My heart was beating so hard it felt like it was about to jump out of my chest. I was extremely cold, but warming up quickly as the bull approached. I rested my .300 Remington Ultra Mag into my shooting sticks and waited on Frank's famous words, "Make her happen, captain."

When he said that, I gently squeezed the trigger. At the report of the rifle, I watched as the massive bull collapsed at approximately 250 yards.

As we approached the bull, Frank and Dan erupted into jubilation. They knew we had just taken the bull of a lifetime. We later learned that my trophy bull green-scored close to 250 points and was nearly 70 inches wide—a true giant. The 27th Awards Program Judges Panel verified its final score at 242 points with a 65 2/8-inch spread.

I owe a Yukon-sized thank you to Frank Ross and Dan Reynolds for making this hunt a lifetime memory and for getting me out safely. They are the reason I was able to harvest such a trophy and both should be mentioned whenever this trophy is discussed.

I enjoyed my first visit to Yukon Territory—the vast terrain, the great people, and the incredible number of four-legged creatures roaming this great wilderness was amazing. I plan to return to hunt Dall's sheep with Dan and Frank in 2012, and I can't wait! ▲

TROPHY STATS

▼ ▼ ▼ ▼ ▼

CATEGORY
Shiras' Moose

SCORE
181$^6/_8$

GREATEST SPREAD
55$^6/_8$

LENGTH OF PALM
Right: 37$^2/_8$ Left: 36$^7/_8$

WIDTH OF PALM
Right: 9$^7/_8$ Left: 9$^6/_8$

NORMAL POINTS
Right: 10   Left: 11

LOCATION
Bonner Co., Idaho – 2006

HUNTER
Del J. Thompson

SHIRAS' MOOSE
First Award – 181 ⁶/₈

▼ ▼ ▼ ▼ ▼ ▼ ▼ ▼ ▼

DEL J. THOMPSON

After 16 years of applying for an Idaho moose tag, I was finally successful in 2006. This wouldn't be the first moose hunting trip for our family. Three years earlier, my son Garrett was fortunate enough to draw one of these coveted tags and harvested a bull. We were very excited to get to hunt Shiras' moose once again.

The next day at work, I found out that my friend Nadine had also been fortunate in the draw and pulled a tag as well. We made a bet for the biggest moose.

Patience Pays Off

I was able to make a few scouting trips before the season opened. With the moose I had seen and information from some friends, I decided to hunt the Lunch Peak. I elected not to hunt the first week of the season. Moose are historically still in velvet at this time of year and I wanted a hard-antlered bull. The second weekend, I was on Trestle Divide at daylight and tried some cow calling. Immediately, a bull started grunting. Another call and he was headed in, quickly closing the distance.

Within three minutes, the bull was at 75 yards, looking straight at me. Upon closer inspection I saw that he was a nice, 40 inch-plus, double eye-guard moose. Unfortunately he still was not quite as big as I was looking for.

My wife Lynne and I went out together on a few evening hunts. Nearly every trip we spotted moose, but still no shooters. One particular evening, my good friend Ron accompanied me. The two of us spotted a decent bull, though when we looked closely, we determined it was the double eye-guard bull that I had passed before.

This took me into October and the typical clear days and cool nights had arrived. The rut was in full swing and a Saturday morning hunt sounded promising. At 4 a.m., my friend Rob and I were on our way to what we hoped would

Photograph by Jack Reneau

Del J. Thompson accepting his plaque and medal from Buck Buckner, Vice President and Chairman of the Big Game Records Committee.

Del J. Thompson waited 16 years to draw his Idaho moose tag. He is pictured above with his award-winning Shiras' moose scoring 181-6/8 points. The bull was taken in 2006 in Bonner County and received a First Place Award.

be a successful hunt. In the first clearing we came to, we spotted three moose, but no bulls, so we moved on. Twenty minutes later, we got to another clearing and spotted two bulls at about 1,500 yards. After glassing, it looked like one may be a shooter bull so we started our stalk. As we neared the edge of the clearing where we had last seen the moose, I saw something move up ahead. There was the smaller of the two at about one hundred yards and right behind him was the big one. In front of me was a large rock that would make a good rest so we crawled up to it and got set up.

We sat for 15 minutes watching this bull. We estimated him to be at least 50 inches wide with six points per side and a double eye-guard on one side. A good moose but still not up to my expectations after my 16-year wait for the tag, so we moved on.

There were more after-work and weekend hunting trips, but I still could not find the big bull I was looking for. I was starting to wonder if I should have taken the 50-inch bull or maybe even one of the other ones earlier.

By now the rut was over, snow was getting deep, and Nadine, whom I had the bet with, had already taken a moose. With the snow and lack of rutting activity, hunting was getting tougher every day. It was like the bulls had all disappeared, I was wondering if I might be sending my tag back and applying again in a couple of years. With less than two weeks left to hunt, one evening after work I went to a spot that I knew moose liked to frequent in the winter. The first mile of my hunt, I found moose tracks and then a moose. It was a cow, but at least as she served as a good sign.

SHIRAS' MOOSE
First Award – 181 ⁶/₈

▼ ▼ ▼ ▼ ▼

DEL J. THOMPSON

I decided to take the following day off work and called my neighbor Rob to go along. At first light, we were at my newly discovered spot in the Cabinet Mountains. Thinking my luck might have changed, we spotted a moose at 75 yards. There was no field judging needed on this bull, I knew right away that he was what I had been waiting on. One shot with my Remington 700 chambered in 7mm Remington Magnum and the Federal Nosler 160-grain partitioned bullet did the job.

When my friend Dave came to help get the moose out, I told him I was hoping for a 48-inch greatest spread with lots of points. When he pulled a tape we were certainly surprised—just shy of 56 inches wide, wow! Needless to say, I won the bet. ▲

TROPHY STATS

▼ ▼ ▼ ▼ ▼

CATEGORY
Shiras' Moose

SCORE
$180^2/_8$

GREATEST SPREAD
$40^6/_8$

LENGTH OF PALM
Right: $39^2/_8$ Left: $38^5/_8$

WIDTH OF PALM
Right: $13^1/_8$ Left: $13^6/_8$

NORMAL POINTS
Right: 12   Left: 11

LOCATION
Larimer Co., Colorado – 2007

HUNTER
Rylan Rudebusch

SHIRAS' MOOSE
Second Award – 180 ²/₈

▼ ▼ ▼ ▼ ▼ ▼ ▼ ▼ ▼

RYLAN RUDEBUSCH

I knew we were close, but where was he? The willows were so dense that making out any-thing more than a few feet away was nearly impossible. Then, in a blink of the eye, he appeared. The first features that came into view were the incredibly long palms. They were a magnificent sight, reflecting the sun well above the willows. Next, the massive, dark body came into view at less than 50 yards. He was on a mission, making tracks for the other side of the drainage. I couldn't figure out why he was running. This was the only bull that Rylan had shown any interest during our entire summer of scouting. There was no way he could have seen or smelled us, so what was it?

High and Tight

"What happened? You didn't shoot," I said, half asking and half stating. Sometimes things happen pretty fast in the field, especially to a 14-year-old. My youngest son, Rylan, had drawn a coveted Colorado bull moose tag in 2007 at the age of 14—the first year he was eligible. I started putting him in for points when he was 11 and boy did it pay off! Here's Rylan's account of his hunt. — Gordon Rudebusch

My dad is really into hunting, and he got me into it too. One day I came home from school and Dad told me that I had drawn a moose license. It was only my third year hunting, but I knew that this was a once-in-a-lifetime op-portunity, literally. I was nervous. In the past, Dad had told me stories about people getting hard-to-get licenses but not getting anything or shooting something just to put a tag on it. If these experienced hunters couldn't find the animals they were looking for, then how was I supposed to? Luckily I had Dad to help.

One of the first people Dad called was a good friend, Scott Limmer, owner of Coman-che Wilderness Outfitters, (my dad guides for Scott). Scott and his crew have guided numer-ous moose hunters to their trophies in Colorado

Photograph by Jack Reneau

Rylan Rudebusch accepting his plaque and medal from Buck Buckner, Vice President and Chairman of the Big Game Records Committee.

Photograph courtesy of Rylan Rudebusch

Rylan Rudebusch and his father Gordon helped set up high-country elk camps for Comanche Wilderness Outfitters, which gave them time to learn the area and get in numerous days of scouting.

and he was pretty excited to hear of my good fortune. He knew the potential of this unit in Larimer County and told us of a big bull that had been eluding his hunters over the past two seasons. Scott also said he would loan us two of his guides, Mike Williams and Fred Sell, to help out.

Late that summer, Dad and I helped Scott pack in and set up high-country elk camps for the fall hunting season. While enroute to designated campsites, we would get the lay of the land and Scott would show us where he and his guides had seen some pretty nice bulls in the past. I'm not much into riding horses, so instead of riding, Dad and I hiked. This made for some pretty long, tiring days, but it was worth it.

We made several scouting trips into my unit. On one trip we hiked high up on a mountain together, and it wasn't long before I spotted a bull across a basin. Dad said, "That looks like one! What do you say we run over there to get a better look and some film of him?"

I thought for a second and said, "How about you run over there and I'll stay here and keep an eye on him in case he moves?" So off Dad went.

I kept an eye on Dad until he was out of sight. I then took in the scenery and glassed until I finally saw Dad making his way back. When he got back, he was excited, telling me how close he got and the film he took of the "good" bull. It always seemed like every bull Dad saw was a "good" bull—still is, for that matter.

The next morning, I slept in while Dad went out to check a new drainage. A few hours later he returned and was again pumped about what he saw. He showed me some film he took of a couple bulls and pointed out a "good" one! For the first time, I agreed with him. It really was a good bull, and I made this my number one choice. We later found out this was the bull that had eluded Scott and crew. They had named him "High & Tight." As his name suggested he wasn't the widest bull, but he had super long and wide paddles, a lot of points and huge brows.

SHIRAS' MOOSE
Second Award – 180 $^2/_8$

▼ ▼ ▼ ▼ ▼

RYLAN RUDEBUSCH

When hunting season finally arrived, the plan was for me to hunt for three days, then go back to school for two. Mom agreed to this part of the plan, but I didn't tell Mom the part about hunting the rest of the season if unsuccessful, and Dad wasn't about to say anything either.

We headed out early, two days before the season. It seems like every time we do anything outdoors like camping, fishing, scouting, hunting, or anything else, Dad seems to think we need to get there before daylight. This time, we arrived where we wanted to be right at daylight, but it was raining, so we drove around scouting until it stopped. Mike Williams went up a couple days earlier to secure our camping spot at the edge of a big park. This enabled us the opportunity to hunt right outside of camp.

Not much later, my Uncle Marlyn showed up to tag along for the hunt. He had never seen a moose but Dad said his strong back would be needed later. Marlyn's day job is construction, but he was going to be my cameraman. I later found out that he swings a hammer better than he runs a camera.

On Sunday morning, we still had one day of scouting left. Fred Sell rolled into camp, ready to do some scouting. Marlyn went with Fred to check out some of the areas with less hiking so he could get used to the altitude. It had snowed a few inches and it was still moving and blowing around the landscape.

We headed up the drainage into the hidden basin we had scouted in August. Once we were close to the head of the drainage, we started seeing moose. We glassed a bull until he went into the timber and Dad said (you guessed it), "That's a good bull. That could be your No. 1 bull."

After lunch, we brought Marlyn with us so he could see the bull. Out of nowhere, we came face-to-face with a bull. He dropped his head and gave it a shake at 30 yards. Dad stepped back and told us to get some pictures. I fumbled for the camera and Marlyn snapped a few with his while the bull came forward. Again, my dad instructed us to "Get some more pictures." I finally got my camera going and the bull took a couple more steps forward, cutting our distance to him in half. I turned around and saw Dad running for cover, so Marlyn and I decided that it was a good idea to follow. The bull proceeded to move past us at 15 steps. You guessed it, Dad said, "Hey that was a pretty good bull!"

Rylan Rudebusch and his father Gordon pose with Rylan's award-winning Shiras' moose. Rylan was recognized at the Club's first-ever Generation Next Youth Awards Banquet, which was followed the next night by the 27th Big Game Awards Program Banquet. His bull has a final score of 180-2/8.

Dad wanted to see the pictures so Marlyn set his camera up but found out his card was full and hadn't recorded one picture. He told us that he borrowed the camera from my other uncle, Larry. The thought of him being my cameraman didn't seem that great. Whose idea was this... Dad?

Opening day finally arrived. Mike and Fred headed to check a drainage not far from where Dad, Marlyn, and I were headed. The morning was cold, really cold.

The vegetation was very tall and made a lot of noise as we walked through it. Finally, we cut through a little section of timber and emerged into an open park. From there we moved up the drainage to where it narrowed, staying just inside the timber, popping out now and then to glass.

The sun was just beginning to rise above the mountaintops. After a few hundred yards of hiking the drainage, we stopped to glass. Immediately we saw the sun illuminating two huge palms just above the willow tops. We ducked into the timber, moved up another 100 yards, and the next thing I saw was a bull running across the drainage at close range.

SHIRAS' MOOSE
Second Award – 180 $^2/_8$
▼ ▼ ▼ ▼ ▼

RYLAN RUDEBUSCH

Dad set up the shooting sticks and said, "There you go! That's your bull!" I was caught off-guard.

Later, Dad said he knew the first time we glassed him that this was my bull, but he didn't want to tell me because he didn't want to get me all worked up. I quickly got the gun on the sticks and got him in the scope but the shot just didn't present itself. I didn't want to take a shot just to shoot, no matter how much I wanted him. I also had the sun in my shooting eye.

The bull made it across and into the timber. "What happened? You didn't shoot," Dad asked.

I told him and he said, "You did the right thing. Good job. It's okay. We'll move up a little and set up again."

A little further up the drainage, Dad said, "There's a cow and a calf. That's why the bull went running across, to check out that cow." Within a few seconds I heard Dad say "Here he comes, there's your bull Rylan." Dad ranged him at 167 yards. "Let him come. Get on him, 142 yards."

The bull stopped, turned, and looked right at us, his head held high and proud like he was king of the valley. Despite how cold I was, I was sweating. I put the crosshairs on target but I was shaking, so I took a breath and let it out easy. The sun was in my eyes, so Dad took a step forward and blocked the sun. Now I could see him clearly. I took another breath, let it out, and fired.

At the sound of the shot the bull was off and running. He only went 10 yards and stopped, so I shot again. This time the bull only took a step and lifted his front leg. I fired again and the bull did a 360 and down he went. I put another round in the chamber, ready to fire again, but he couldn't make it to his feet. All three of us watched intently to make sure he was done, but no one said a word. We just looked at each other in disbelief. Finally, Dad said, "You did it! That's your bull. That's the big bull. Great job!"

In no time Mike and Fred joined us, and Fred's first response was "Awesome! That's him, High and Tight."

The caping, quartering, and packing process were tough, but we had him all back to camp in two trips. Dad and I couldn't have been happier. I accomplished my goal and my dad was proud of me.

I would like to thank Scott Limmer of Comanche Wilderness Outfitters and two of his guides, Mike Williams and Fred Sell. Also, thanks to my uncle for taking time away from his job. He did a great job filming my hunt except for a couple sky shots. Finally, thanks to my dad, who made it all possible. ▲

TROPHY STATS

▼ ▼ ▼ ▼ ▼

CATEGORY
Shiras' Moose

SCORE
177^4/$_8$

GREATEST SPREAD
48

LENGTH OF PALM
Right: 38^2/$_8$ Left: 37

WIDTH OF PALM
Right: 12^4/$_8$ Left: 12^2/$_8$

NORMAL POINTS
Right: 9   Left: 10

LOCATION
Lincoln Co., Montana – 2006

HUNTER
Win D. Bock

SHIRAS' MOOSE
Third Award – 177 4/8

▼ ▼ ▼ ▼ ▼ ▼ ▼ ▼ ▼

WIN D. BOCK

Friday the 13th isn't always unlucky.

In June 2006, after applying for far too many years to mention, I finally received word that I had drawn a moose tag in my home state of Montana. My good friend and longtime hunting partner Jerome Johnson would be accompanying me and was nearly as excited as I was. For years, he and I had been hunting elk together and would see numerous moose every season with only an elk or deer tag in our pockets. We always wished we had a moose permit to take one. Now, I finally had my chance.

Injured Monarch

We figured with all our sightings over the years we would know right where to go. We quickly found out this wouldn't be the case! There wasn't much difficulty in finding moose, but after trying for so many years to just get the chance to harvest one, not just any moose would do. I think I passed on 23 cows and small bulls during my season.

On the "lucky morning", we left a little earlier than normal. We were going back up Boulder Creek where we had seen some cows. There was a good clear-cut we intended to glass at first light. The idea was solid since the cut contained cows and calves, but strangely, no good bulls. We decided to head back over the top and down Steep Creek towards another place where we had run across a few non-shooters earlier in the season. On the way there, to our amazement, a true trophy Montana brute stepped into the road not 40 yards away from the truck. We stopped and gawked as the bull stood broadside in the road,

As we sized up the bull, I noticed that an injury to his left eye had caused an infection of some sort, leaving a gray, cataract-looking fog and his lower eyelid hanging down. The larger of his two antlers was broken and rake-like lacerations ran down his side. Protruding from his skull between his eyes was a broken antler tip from a previous opponent.

As the battle-scarred bull stood there in the road, he eventually swung his head far enough to where the uninjured eye picked us up. As soon as he caught sight of us, the bull bolted up the bank and out of sight. Just like that, he was gone. While images of the bull stood out vividly in our minds, it felt as if time was standing still. It all happened so fast that neither of us really had any time to react. I looked over at Jerome and he asked, "Isn't that what you are looking for?"

I laughed and asked, "Yea—think we can sneak up on him?"

We had to try, he replied, so off we went. The bull had disappeared into alders so thick that we could only see a few yards ahead of us. We quickly found his trail and wondered in awe at how an animal the size of a horse with antlers as wide as the pickup was not far in front

Win D. Bock stands behind his Shiras' moose from Lincoln County, Montana. Bock harvested the bull, which scores 177-4/8 points during the 2006 season.

of us and we couldn't hear a sound of his movements. We had been hunting long enough to know that he might just up and leave us behind but we still pushed on. A few hundred yards above the road the alders started to open up. There was enough visibility to keep us going. After continuing a bit further, Jerome poked me with his cane and pointed to our right, where something was moving in the brush. I found a tree to use as a rest and waited. When the moose finally stepped into the clear, we could hardly believe it wasn't him. This bull's antlers were similar to bicycle handlebars, unlike the sheets of plywood that the bull we were after was carrying around.

Luckily, the wind was in our favor, so we watched him disappear and resumed our pursuit of the injured monarch. We carefully backtracked and found where the big bull had turned left and continued parallel to the road. We continued on, not sure if we would ever see him again. We climbed over a small rise to the top where we found an opening in the alders to look through. We were amazed to see him standing there. I found the bull's shoulder in the crosshairs and squeezed off a shot. He was close enough that the impact was visible with the naked eye, though the bull didn't even flinch. He slowly turned, offering the opposite broadside shot and I put a follow-up shot in him. Jerome and I both agreed that this bull was close to a skid road we had walked earlier and we didn't want him to go far. The second shot put him down for good.

When we got up to him, Jerome commented on how fortunate it was that we should be able to get the truck up the skid road. As I filled out my tag, I realized it was Friday the 13th and Jerome's birthday. So much for Friday the 13th being unlucky! I knew I had taken a good bull, but really had no clue what he would score. When I found out that Jim Williams with the Montana Fish Wildlife and Parks could score it for me, I had him put a tape on it more out of curiosity than anything. To my surprise, he scored an impressive 179-4/8 points and he is the largest bull ever entered from Lincoln County. ▲

Award-Winning Moments

B&C Photo Archives

Simon Roosevelt greets fellow Boone and Crockett Club member, Andrew Hoxsey who accepted the sponsorship plaque on behalf of the Rocky Mountain Elk Foundation. Hoxsey is a past Chairman of the Board for RMEF.

TROPHY STATS

▼ ▼ ▼ ▼ ▼

CATEGORY
Shiras' Moose

SCORE
172

GREATEST SPREAD
45 $^6/_8$

LENGTH OF PALM
Right: 34 $^4/_8$ Left: 34 $^4/_8$

WIDTH OF PALM
Right: 12   Left: 11 $^7/_8$

NORMAL POINTS
Right: 11   Left: 11

LOCATION
Caribou Co., Idaho – 2007

HUNTER
Susan A. Remer Shappart

SHIRAS' MOOSE
Honorable Mention – 172

▽ ▽ ▽ ▽ ▽ ▽ ▽ ▽ ▽

SUSAN A. REMER SHAPPART

One day in early spring 2007 my husband Darrel said, "Honey, I think we'll put you in for bull moose this year."

All I could think to say laughingly in reply was, "Oh, no. I don't think we will!"

Two weeks later I heard him telling his brother, Bret, "I think we'll put Susan in for bull moose this year."

I smiled. Then I looked at him through squinting eyes, shook my head, and again I said, "I don't think we will. We've already discussed that."

Fishing season came, so down we went to Doc's Gun Barn to get our licenses. My husband told Larry, his accomplice behind the counter, "While we're here, make both of our licenses combination licenses."

When I told my husband that I only needed a fishing license this year, he looked right past me and said to Larry, "Combination, and while we're here, put Susan in for bull moose."

Yet a third protest from me fell on deaf ears when Larry said, "Darrel's the boss."

Keep in mind that a couple of years prior, having drawn a cow moose hunt, I had come down with the flu. Hunting in the hills with a cold was a completely miserable experience. If it hadn't been for that, I probably wouldn't have been protesting so adamantly over trying for a bull. Well, that and the fact that I hadn't done much shooting in a while. I was afraid I would embarrass myself. All I could think about was that I might miss or ruin meat, if we even saw one at all.

The hunt I drew was near Soda Springs, Idaho, not too far from where we lived in Pocatello. Due to the timing of opening day, the plan was to be back home on the fifth day, September 25, for our one-year wedding anniversary.

After hunting for four days and not seeing a single moose (we'd seen plenty of cattle), we were headed back to camp to pack up. It

Photograph by Jack Reneau

Susan A. Remer Shappart accepting her plaque from Buck Buckner, Vice President and Chairman of the Big Game Records Committee.

was getting dusk when, at the base of the hill, I was sure that I saw him—a gorgeous bull moose. I asked my husband, "Is that a moose over there, or just another cow?"

He grabbed his binoculars and said, "Yeah, it sure is!" Sadly, it was almost dark and too late to shoot. All we could do was sit there and watch him, cussing the time of day.

This is where "best-laid plans" came into play, because, you know we couldn't go home now. It was the first and the only moose we'd seen in four days! After very little discussion, we decided that we'd stay another night and check this spot out first thing in the morning. If he was still there, we'd hunt; if not, we'd go on home and enjoy our anniversary.

The next morning we got back up on the hill bright and early. Darrel suggested that he would take his cup of coffee and walk one way and that after I finished getting bundled up, I would go the other direction. However, before I could even get going, he came running back. "Grab your gun! He's still here. Right back up over here!"

> **THIS IS WHERE "BEST-LAID PLANS" CAME INTO PLAY, BECAUSE, YOU KNOW WE COULDN'T GO HOME NOW. IT WAS THE FIRST AND THE ONLY MOOSE WE'D SEEN IN FOUR DAYS! AFTER VERY LITTLE DISCUSSION, WE DECIDED THAT WE'D STAY ANOTHER NIGHT AND CHECK THIS SPOT OUT FIRST THING IN THE MORNING. IF HE WAS STILL THERE, WE'D HUNT; IF NOT, WE'D GO ON HOME AND ENJOY OUR ANNIVERSARY.**

Being as short and round as I am, running was out of the question, but I never knew I could move so fast. The whole time, I kept repeating to myself, "Please let me get him."

It quickly became one of the most emotionally intense days of my life, and my husband was the greatest. He whispered to me to keep calm, go slow, and take my time aiming.

When I shot, that big ol' moose went right down. I was never so relieved in all my life! I'd done it! I could feel the tears in my eyes and was overcome with happiness and pride.

And that's when that big ol' moose got back up. I wasn't prepared for that, and tracking him through sagebrush, trees, deadfall, and thick foliage suddenly became the hardest part of the hunt. I had no idea that a moose could be so hard to find—a very large, brown moose.

Finally, totally exhausted, I had him down. Now, would you like to guess where our camera was? Yes, sitting where we'd accidentally left it—at home. After all, it's not like we were trophy hunting. I was going to shoot the first bull we saw—and I did.

So, while I rested on a fallen tree that was a couple of feet off the ground, with my rifle sitting upright next to me, I said to my husband, "Happy anniversary, honey! I hope it's what you really wanted! Now guess who gets to gut it?" ▲

Duane Chapman's typical American elk, which was taken on the San Carlos Indian Reservation in Graham County, Arizona, in 2007 scores a whopping 404-1/8. It was the center of attention, along with Denny Austad's new World's Record non-typical elk, when trophy owners and guests entered the trophy display room.

TROPHY STATS
▼ ▼ ▼ ▼ ▼

CATEGORY
Mountain Caribou

SCORE
422 $^7/_8$

INSIDE SPREAD
36 $^3/_8$

LENGTH OF MAIN BEAM
Right: 53   Left: 51 $^7/_8$

WIDTH OF BROW PALM
Right: 9 $^2/_8$ Left: $^1/_8$

NUMBER OF POINTS
Right: 19   Left: 15

LOCATION
Mackenzie Mts., Northwest
Territories – 2007

HUNTER
R. Bruce Moon

Photograph by Jack Reneau

R. Bruce Moon accepting his plaque
and medal from Buck Buckner, Vice
President and Chairman of the Big Game
Records Committee.

BOONE AND CROCKETT CLUB'S

MOUNTAIN CARIBOU
First Award – 422 $^7/_8$

▼ ▼ ▼ ▼ ▼ ▼ ▼ ▼ ▼

R. BRUCE MOON

I trudged along grimly until I neared the canyon rim. I was in a foul mood, and more than a little worried as each step took me farther from camp. Two days earlier I had been pushed to my physical limit on the granite-jumbled mountains while packing out a Dall's sheep, and my body had not yet fully recovered. I stopped and whistled softly to alert my guide that I was near. Moments later Cory appeared and waved me forward. The spotting scope was set up, and he motioned me to take a look. Through its lens I gazed upon the largest caribou I had ever seen as it fed leisurely on a bench almost a mile and a half away.

I looked at Cory in shock. He grinned and said, "I figured I needed to show you a nice caribou since you have been cussing me the last mile."

When I winced at the accusation, he looked at me seriously and said, "And don't tell me you haven't been."

It was true. Cory had wanted to check this drainage for caribou. Trouble was, it was four miles over rough country from camp, most of it downhill, and he had figured (correctly) that I would have declined the hike in favor of a second recovery day. After all, we were only on day three of a 10-day combination hunt and caribou was a distant second prize to my Dall's sheep, which was already in hand. So Cory did what good guides do: he figured out a way to get his hunter to go where he wanted the hunter to go.

Cory's stratagem was not to outright lie to me, but to merely mislead. That morning in camp he had first pointed to a flat a mile from camp—a relatively easy hike. "We may stay there all day, just glassing," he said. It sounded reasonable to me. Naturally, he decided we needed to move after we arrived and glassed a bit. The next stopping point, another mile further from camp, was apparently not optimum for glassing the valley below, and the next, another mile gone, was clearly not suitable. I was confused.

Cory finally came clean. "I just told you that to get you out here. I really want to look in that drainage over there," he pointed to a ridgeline another mile away. I had indeed been cussing him that last mile.

Now we had to decide what to do. If the caribou bedded down, we had an excellent opportunity for a stalk. If not, and we began the stalk, it would be both impossible to know if he moved off, and impossible to get ahead of him. Cory suggested we wait and see. I was glad to oblige.

We waited 45 minutes, watching the caribou through the spotting scope, talking, and enjoying the day. I had plenty of time to reflect upon my first caribou hunt nine years earlier.

R. Bruce Moon and his guide Cory made an impressive stalk on this old mountain caribou after a exhaustive four-mile hike. Moon's award-winning bull was taken in the Mackenzie Mountains of Northwest Territories during the 2007 season. It has a final score of 422-7/8 points, which earned it a First Place Award at the 27th Big Game Awards.

That Quebec-Labrador caribou hunt was billed as 98 percent successful on two caribou. Some friends and I had decided that we wanted as close to a sure thing as we could get on such a hunt—my first hunt outside the U.S., and only my third outside of Texas. Though considered an economy hunt, it was a ton of money to me.

I learned several things about hunting on that trip, which turned into an expensive sightseeing trip, and about myself. I reconfirmed that I hate to lose. I learned that if the animals aren't there, no amount of hard work will get you one. I learned that large hunting outfits catering to hunters in mass sometimes lose sight of the best interests of individual hunters. I learned that I was willing to go home empty-handed rather than shoot an immature animal.

But I also learned that memories of the wonder of nature remain vivid long after the bitterness of a frustrating hunt fades. I saw an eagle swoop and snag a fish from a lake and watched ravens harass it as the eagle struggled to fly with the fish in its talons. I heard my first wolf howl and my first ptarmigan chuckle. And perhaps best of all, I saw the Northern Lights in all their glory.

Now, nine years later, I had again seen the Northern Lights, this time hunting with Stan Simpson's Ram Head Outfitters in the Mackenzie Mountains of Canada's Northwest

Territories. I was again looking at a caribou, though I had never seen anything like this old bull.

The bull never did bed down. He would nibble at a plant and then move to another, but he never left the bench. Cory asked me what I wanted to do. He did not know why the caribou would not bed down, but the bull also didn't seem inclined to leave the bench, so he felt we had a good chance at a successful stalk. I told Cory that if he felt we had a 50 percent or better chance of success then I was for it. Cory said he was all for attempting the stalk, if I thought I could make it. That was all it took—testosterone can be a wonderful thing. Off we went.

The first mile was sharply downhill, and then we circled to put the wind in our face. We covered over a mile without knowing if the caribou had remained on the bench. He had and was now only a quarter mile away, still feeding, when we spotted him again. The wind in our face, we walked steadily, slowing when we were within 200 yards of him. The foliage was thick, so we would have to get close, and an off-hand shot would probably be necessary. Here is where I am supposed to write that we crawled the last 100 yards on my belly, and I made a spectacular, long-distance, off-hand shot with a howling crosswind at a caribou running through brush. Well, it was off-hand, and there was some brush. We crept stealthily to within 40 yards of the big bull. He was now feeding at the edge of the bench, a steep downhill into the next drainage only yards away. A light screen of limbs partially obscured his vitals. His head came up and I had to shoot right then or lose the opportunity. The bull, hit heavily, stumbled toward the edge of the bench. I did not want him going downhill and away from camp, so I quickly shot again. He dropped.

During processing, we discovered why he had not bedded down. His teeth were worn to the gums—he could eat only the tenderest plants and had to eat constantly to sustain himself. Either the approaching winter would have killed him, or the wolves would have pulled him down the next spring. A perfect animal, regardless of what his rack scored.

My exhaustion on the sheep hunt was due in large part to my failure to maintain nutrition and hydration. I did not make that mistake this time. I helped Cory as much as he would let me but had plenty of time to eat all the food I had brought in my pack and to drink my fill from a small stream nearby. I literally felt energy flowing back into my body as I rested and stretched in preparation for the work ahead.

We carried the head, antlers, hide, and meat about a quarter mile uphill to a small bench, then cached it for later retrieval where it would be hard for bears to find. We started the hike back to camp—five-plus miles, four of them uphill. It was a long, tough hike, but it was anything but grim, for I had my caribou at long last.

Postscript. Cory told me he thought the caribou was huge when he first saw it, but downplayed its size in talking with me as he had no idea if the stalk would be successful. He was right. My mountain caribou scored 422-7/8 B&C points, bettering the All-time records book minimum of 360 points to make the Awards book. It ties for 38th place out of 530 specimens listed in the category. ▲

TROPHY STATS

▼ ▼ ▼ ▼ ▼

CATEGORY
Mountain Caribou

SCORE
412⁴/₈

INSIDE SPREAD
38²/₈

LENGTH OF MAIN BEAM
Right: 50³/₈   Left: 48¹/₈

WIDTH OF BROW PALM
Right: 10³/₈   Left: ¹/₈

NUMBER OF POINTS
Right: 17   Left: 16

LOCATION
Prospector Mt., Yukon Territory –
2008

HUNTER
Jack E. Risner

MOUNTAIN CARIBOU
Second Award – 412 ⁴/₈

▼ ▼ ▼ ▼ ▼ ▼ ▼ ▼ ▼

JACK E. RISNER

I've been told that I'm a lucky (expletive) by a few jealous friends. My response is that I'll take all the good luck I can get.

In February 2007, my friend Lee Frudden called to tell me he was going caribou hunting in the Yukon in September. The trip was planned with Tim and Jen Mervyn of Mervyn's Yukon Outfitting. Lee said this was the place for the big ones. It sounded like a good hunt, so I called Tim. He didn't have any caribou hunts available in 2007 but he did have a moose hunt,

I'll Take All the Good Luck I Can Get

so I booked it. The hunt went very well. It was the type of hunting and outfit I like, so when Tim took me to the airport to leave, I asked him about caribou again. He told me he had two hunts left for 2008. I knew that my hunting buddy Shawn Hullinger had always wanted to hunt caribou, so I told Tim that we'd take the hunts. (I called Shawn later when I got cell service in Seattle to ask if he wanted to go.)

Eleven and a half months later, we were off, double-checking everything ten times—guns, gear, etc. When we got to Vancouver, none of our gear made it (now that's lucky), so we went on to Whitehorse without it. We had scheduled two extra days just in case something like this happened. After our planned buffer days expired and countless phone calls, we still had nothing, and it was time to go into the bush. Tim told us he had guns that he would loan us, but we had to get going to keep everything flowing.

We had our boots, but that was it. About $1,500 later (there are no bargains in White-horse) we headed to Tim's to pick up a gun. It was a nice Steyr Mannlicher .30-06. Tim had it out and had run some rounds through it confirming it was hitting two inches high at 100 yards. It was good enough, but not having your own gun takes something out of you—confidence!

Photograph by Jack Reneau

Jack E. Risner accepting his plaque and medal from Buck Buckner, Vice President and Chairman of the Big Game Records Committee.

Photograph courtesy of Jack E. Risner

Jack E. Risner was shooting a borrowed rifle on his mountain caribou hunt on Prospector Mountain, in Yukon Territory when he harvested his award-winning bull that scores 412-4/8 points.

The flight to camp was exciting like all bush flights. Shawn pinched holes in the back of the seat, but all for naught—we made it just fine. When we arrived, the guides and horses were waiting for us. It was a boggy one and a half miles to camp, and we were relieved to finally be there.

On September 14 at 5:30 a.m., I was up, chomping at the bit to go hunting. My guide Mike told me to chill out. Caribou hunting is similar to pronghorn hunting in that you can hunt all day long. After what seemed like far too long, we finally headed up the trail. About two miles up the creek we spotted a couple bulls about two miles away. We looked them over and decided they were immature bulls. Up to this point, the entire group had been together, but the canyon split into three different drainages. Shawn and his guide, Corey, took off up the right-hand fork and we went up the left. It was all uphill from there. Once we reached the top around 10 a.m., the view was spectacular—miles and miles of wilderness as far as the eye could see.

We hobbled the horses and headed down the ridge top on foot. In short order we had spotted seven or eight caribou about a mile away. There was what appeared to be a good bull in the bunch, but they fed over the top and out of sight. At that point, I really began missing my binoculars and spotting scope. Down the ridge, about a quarter mile across a canyon, we spotted caribou at the bottom. Mike set up his

MOUNTAIN CARIBOU
Second Award – 412 4/8
▼ ▼ ▼ ▼ ▼
JACK E. RISNER

spotting scope and began looking them over. All of a sudden he got really excited and said, "There is the stud duck!" I tried not to knock him over so I could look. There was no doubt, the bull was a hog.

His tongue was hanging out as he was circling the herd. He'd been fighting and gotten whipped. He proceeded all the way around the herd, and lay down. He was still about 1,500 yards away and we could see about 10 cows and a couple of small bulls.

He looked good to me, and Mike agreed, so I headed off the mountain and Mike stayed to give me signals in case the bull moved. I did have a pair of 8X binoculars with me, but no eye cups. I crossed the bottom and climbed up on the point that was between us and the bull. The basin was covered with blueberry bushes about 18 to 24 inches tall. When I peeked over the ridge, he was still lying there. I guessed him to be between 400 to 500 yards away—too far, having never shot the gun before. The group of 11 had transformed into about 25 caribou. The group was intermixed, feeding and lying down on the wide-open hillside. I decided that 200 yards would be my maximum shooting distance with this borrowed rifle. Considering they were all much farther than that, I started crawling down the hill. When I reached a point around 300 yards from them, I spotted another bull coming out from behind the hill. He appeared to be the boss and looked huge, but he was close to 450 yards and moving in and out of the cows. As I was trying to size him up with my borrowed 8X binoculars (and cussing the airlines), he turned around and headed back behind the hill. He stopped out of sight, but I could see the top of a tree whipping back and forth, so I kept crawling and slithered around the hill.

All this time, I was in plain sight of the first big bull and all the other caribou. I could just about see the second bull but some of the herd had spotted me. The first big bull stood up. I had already gone past him trying to get a good look at the other one. While he wasn't necessarily the biggest, he was still huge, and I decided I'd better take him before they all took off. It was at this point that I realized what a bad position I was in to take the shot. The hillside was too steep to sit down, so I lay down. This didn't work since there was too much brush to see facing downhill with my feet up, so I got on top of a bush and lay my arm out to rest the gun on top of. It was not the ideal position, but I had him in my crosshairs. Boom! He was down, and I was recovering from being scoped, but smiling through the blood.

Our gear showed up two days later. Shawn got to use his rifle to shoot his bull, also a 400-inch caribou. With my gun, I was fortunate enough to bag two wolves who were feeding on a kill of another 400-inch bull.

Good luck and a little bad luck—I'll take it all. My best luck is to be blessed with so many good friends and a wonderful wife, Lynette, who wishes me luck and tells me to shoot straight and be safe. I guess I am a lucky guy. ▲

TROPHY STATS

▼ ▼ ▼ ▼ ▼

CATEGORY
Woodland Caribou

SCORE
$325^{6}/_{8}$

INSIDE SPREAD
$33^{3}/_{8}$

LENGTH OF MAIN BEAM
Right: 40 Left: $42^{4}/_{8}$

WIDTH OF BROW PALM
Right: $15^{1}/_{8}$ Left: $5^{2}/_{8}$

NUMBER OF POINTS
Right: 20 Left: 17

LOCATION
Middle Ridge, Newfoundland – 2007

HUNTER
James C. Johnson

WOODLAND CARIBOU
First Award – 325 ⁶/₈

▼ ▼ ▼ ▼ ▼ ▼ ▼ ▼ ▼

JAMES C. JOHNSON

I have been blessed over the past 50 years with dozens of opportunities to hunt across most of North America. I am also grateful that during this time I have been fortunate enough to harvest 28 species of North American big game. With this woodland caribou, I have now received B&C medallions and plaques for four different categories of caribou recognized by the Club at Boone and Crockett Club's Awards Banquets.

My quest now is to harvest a barren ground caribou that will make Boone and Crockett Club's All-time records book. To my knowledge, J.J. McBride is the only hunter to have harvested a records book-qualifying specimen from each of the five caribou categories recognized by the Club. I look forward to joining him in this elite group of hunters in the near future.

Due to recent reductions in caribou populations across much of northern Canada and Alaska, this task has become much more difficult in recent years. I have been unsuccessful for the last three years of hunting Yukon Territory's Porcupine herd with Jim Fink of Blackstone Outfitters. I plan on returning there again this year and anticipate shooting the book bull that I'm after. If not, I suppose I'll just have to try again the following season.

As for this woodland caribou, which scores 325-6/8, I hunted with Bob Efford of Efford's Hunting Adventures, located in Port Blandford, Newfoundland. Bob runs a very good operation with highly qualified guides.

The first three days of this hunt, which took place in 2007, were fogged in at the base camp at Sam's Pond. On the fourth day, Bill Smith, another hunter from Reno, Nevada, and I finally made it to our spike camp via floatplane. That evening Bill stepped into a bog-hole and badly wrenched his hip. Luckily, Bill was able to harvest a nice bull the following day and left camp shortly thereafter.

On the floatplane flight into spike camp,

Photograph by Jack Reneau

James C. Johnson accepting his plaque and medal from Buck Buckner, Vice President and Chairman of the Big Game Records Committee.

James C. Johnson was hunting during the 2007 season near Middle Ridge in Newfoundland when he harvested his woodland caribou that scores 325-6/8 points. With the harvest of this bull, Johnson has successfully taken record-book qualifying bulls in four out the five caribou categories.

we observed approximately 300 to 400 head of caribou, with a few good bulls mixed in, approximately 20 miles west of camp. The first day my guide Frankie and I hunted about 10 miles from camp to take a look at some of the satellite groups to get a feel for what the caribou seemed to be doing that year. On the second day we decided to try to make it the rest of the way to the main herd. We started out about 7 a.m. and arrived at the main herd about five hours later. What a sight! The rut was in full swing, and caribou were visible in every direction. It was truly an awesome experience.

After selecting a herd of about 300 or so animals to focus on, Frankie and I skirted the caribou for about an hour and observed six to eight bulls that would make the book. After reviewing our options one last time, we selected what looked to be the best-scoring bull in this herd. One shot later, at approximately 175 yards, that bull was on the ground.

We immediately caped the animal, had a quick celebratory lunch, and then began the five or so hours' walk back to spike camp. We arrived there around 7:30 p.m., just after dark and totally exhausted! Thankfully, however, we had a tremendous bull to show for our efforts, and I had another lifelong memory and good hunting story to add to the list.

This area has not been hunted for a number of years and has developed a large population of moose. I look forward to exploring some new territory and hope to find another big bull. Special thanks go to Bob and the rest of the folks at Efford's Hunting Adventure. I look forward to another great trip with equally good results. ▲

At Friday afternoon's auction, recognition was given to those outfitters in attendance that graciously donated hunts to raise money for the Club's programs. Glenn Brown of Blue Bronna Outfitting from Alberta accepts his certificate of appreciation from B&C Marketing Director, Keith Balfourd. Glenn must know his mule deer. He was just 1/8th of an inch off and won the Guess the Score contest on a non-typical buck scoring 238 points.

TROPHY STATS

▼ ▼ ▼ ▼ ▼

CATEGORY
Woodland Caribou

SCORE
325$^3/_8$

INSIDE SPREAD
30$^6/_8$

LENGTH OF MAIN BEAM
Right: 38$^6/_8$ Left: 37$^4/_8$

WIDTH OF BROW PALM
Right: 11$^5/_8$ Left: 11$^1/_8$

NUMBER OF POINTS
Right: 17   Left: 15

LOCATION
Owl Pond, Newfoundland – 2009

HUNTER
Roger L. Leach

WOODLAND CARIBOU
Second Award – 325 ³/₈

▼ ▼ ▼ ▼ ▼ ▼ ▼ ▼ ▼

ROGER L. LEACH

I started my work on booking a moose hunt in December 2008. With Parkinson's disease, I have limited motor skills and have a hard time walking on uneven ground. After checking the Internet, I selected several outfitters, all of whom I contacted. I narrowed the hunt down to two camps and called references before I decided to go with Portland Creek in Newfoundland. Astor, the owner, was extremely good to work with and talked me into a caribou hunt as well. My good friend Jerry Clum was interested in going with me to film the hunt, so the two of us began our preparation.

It took three days to drive from Lake City, Michigan, to Portland Creek, Newfoundland. We found the trip beautiful with the fall colors and the people we met along the way all very friendly. The road was good, and we also took the time to see the tide at the Bay of Fundy, which was well worth the trip in itself. Every day 100 billion tons of water pass in and out of the bay.

When we arrived in Portland Creek, Astor filled out the paperwork for the hunt to start the next day, so we spent the night in a motel. On October 4 at 4 a.m., we had breakfast and drove approximately 160 miles to the camp pick-up point. We met one of the guides and loaded all our supplies into a trailer, ready to go into camp in a skidozer. The trip took us four hours, and we were fortunate enough to see several caribou on the way to the camp. We settled in, met my guide Ralph and the cook who treated us to a good meal, then we went to bed. The next morning we had a great breakfast at 5 a.m. and headed out across the lake around 7 a.m. As soon as we started hunting, we spotted several moose approximately 300 yards away. We moved through some tundra-like open areas and interspaced woodlots trying to close the distance. By 9 that morning, we had walked about two miles from the boat and through the woodlot. It was at this point that I spotted a couple cows and a bull

Photograph by Jack Reneau

Roger L. Leach accepting his plaque and medal from Buck Buckner, Vice President and Chairman of the Big Game Records Committee.

Photograph courtesy of Roger L. Leach

Roger L. Leach pictured with his award-winning woodland caribou scoring 325-3/8.

caribou on a distant hill. Again, we moved closer through the brush to get a better look. When we finally found a spot where the bull was visible through the brush, the guide informed me, "That's a big stag!"

I had to move to the side to get a clear view, but as soon as I did, I was impressed. Jerry was trying to focus the camera in a stiff wind with little success since the brush was getting blown around in front of the lens. There were about 20 cows milling around with one good mature stag and a couple younger ones. The group was getting fairly nervous, so I decided to take the shot before they got spooked.

My 7mm Remington Magnum dropped him in his tracks. The whole experience was only about three minutes long, though it seemed like an eternity. When we approached the animal, I was very happy with the antlers and especially his mass. The guide ranged the distance of the shot at 264 yards.

It was at this point that the work started. The guide caped the animal and Jerry and I worked on the meat. About halfway through the caping and butchering, a decent moose crossed a nearby opening. I got my rifle up and took a long shot, but the crosswind and excitement had me rattled and I missed. The gun jammed before I could get a second shot off.

After finishing the meat, we headed for the boat to go for help in transporting the meat. On our way there, about a half mile from the boat, Ralph and I saw a good bull moose with about a 60-inch spread. I tried to get a shot, but my Parkinson's wouldn't allow me to get a good-enough shot quickly enough. I gave a moose-call, but he was walking straight away from me, and I would not take a shot like that.

On October 6, we hunted a different area, while the other guide went looking for the big moose, but no one got anything that day. On October 7, we went back to the same area and spotted 24 caribou. Frank took a fine bull out of this bunch.

On October 8 and 9, the wind picked up to around 45 mph with gusts up to 60. The temperature was right around 45°F, but it appeared to be keeping the animals held up fairly tightly. At the end of the day on the 9th we came across a small moose and I managed to close the deal, ending my hunt.

I spent Saturday resting and enjoying the sun, which turned out to be the nicest day we had all week. Sunday we left camp and took the meat to a processor in town. He recommended I have it scored since it was one of the best he had ever seen. ▲

Award-Winning Moments

Visitors view Paul T. Deuling's mountain caribou that scores 459-3/8 and Aaron Kelly's Dall's sheep that scores 173-6/8. Deuling's bull was declared a new World's Record for its category and received the prestigious Sagamore Hill Award, which has been awarded on only 16 previous occasions since 1948. It is given in memory of Theodore Roosevelt and two of his sons if the judges feel there is a trophy worthy of such recognition.

TROPHY STATS

▼ ▼ ▼ ▼ ▼

CATEGORY
Woodland Caribou

SCORE
324 $1/8$

INSIDE SPREAD
33 $1/8$

LENGTH OF MAIN BEAM
Right: 43 $1/8$ Left: 38 $4/8$

WIDTH OF BROW PALM
Right: 15 $1/8$ Left: 6 $3/8$

NUMBER OF POINTS
Right: 16   Left: 16

LOCATION
Andrew Pond, Newfoundland – 2006

HUNTER
Tom Gallenbach

WOODLAND CARIBOU
Third Award – 324 ¹/₈
▼ ▼ ▼ ▼ ▼ ▼ ▼ ▼

Tom Gallenbach

In October 2007, my wife Jane, our friend Bill Russell, and I set out for our caribou/ moose hunting adventure in Newfoundland. The plan was to fly from Texas into Deer Lake, Newfoundland, on Friday evening and meet up with our outfitter, Kevin Decker of Woodland Lodges. He was to have a helicopter waiting to transport us over the last leg of the journey to a remote camp at Andrews Pond. As all frequent airline passengers know, plans and reality are sometimes very different. Our adventure was about to become a nightmare of sorts.

We were to change planes in New York then on to Montreal then to Deer Lake. I always schedule at least two hours between flights to give time for delays. A 30-minute delay in New York left us with an hour and a half to make our connection in Montreal. We knew we had to go through customs, but did not realize that we also had to clear our baggage—we thought it would go straight through to Deer Lake.

After being sent from customs to luggage retrieval then back to customs, we realized we were running short on time. We got to the check-in gate to go to Deer Lake and checked most of our luggage, but one big bag and our guns had to go completely over to another department. We rushed those over but couldn't get them on the plane because we didn't have a particular document that the airline was supposed to have given us. We missed getting the guns on the plane by 30 seconds. Our other luggage that we had checked at the first place went on through to Deer Lake. We were left with our guns in Montreal. We thought we would just catch the next plane over to Deer Lake. Wrong!

There were no seats available on the next flight a few hours later. There would not be another flight to Deer Lake for several days. The customer service guy told us that we could go standby to Halifax the next day but there were already several people ahead of us. Once in Halifax, we would then have to get standby to

Photograph by Jack Reneau

Tom Gallenbach accepting his plaque and medal from Buck Buckner, Vice President and Chairman of the Big Game Records Committee.

Tom Gallenbach, pictured above, endured an epic traveling adventure on his way to Newfoundland. Gallenbach harvested his award-winning bull early in his caribou/moose combo hunt. The bull has a final score of 324-1/8 points and received a Third Place Award.

Deer Lake. We seriously considered just returning home at this point, but fortunately there were some other hunters at the next help desk with the same situation. The customer service representative they were dealing with suggested they fly to St. Johns the next afternoon, rent a car, and drive across Newfoundland to Deer Lake. That seemed like a better option than returning home, so we decided to do the same thing.

After spending a long night at the hotel, we were back at the airport several hours early as not to have any problems. We checked our guns and luggage as soon as they would let us, and we just sat and waited. We visited with several people waiting for the flight to St. Johns, and without exception all of them advised us to wait until daylight to drive across Newfoundland to Deer Lake because of the moose on the highway at night. They had over 150 vehicle/moose accidents on that road in the past year. We were so tired and frustrated at that point, we did not do the smart thing. After landing we headed to the car rental, where only one car was available, and it was small. We stuffed our guns and luggage in the back seat but there was only room for two people in the front. Bill and Jane took turns scooting up under the guns and lying down for the duration of the trip across Newfoundland in the dark.

WOODLAND CARIBOU
Third Award – 324 $^1/_8$

▼ ▼ ▼ ▼ ▼

Tom Gallenbach

I drove with one of them riding shotgun to keep a lookout for moose on the road. Everyone had said they would just be there and you never see them. We drove a reasonable speed and in God's hands. We met only two vehicles on the 300-mile trek, and one of those was an 18-wheeler that had huge lights beaming out from the top of his truck. No doubt they were to spot moose at a distance. We arrived in Deer Lake at 8 a.m. and found our outfitter at the hotel. After retrieving our luggage at the airport that came from Montreal, we set out to the helicopter, excited to finally be on our way.

All day we sat there waiting to maybe get a ride out. We were two days late and we had no slot in his schedule. The last trip of the day, Mr. Decker went over and visited with the pilot and we loaded up. There were still people there that had to wait until the next day.

The ride out was awesome. We spotted moose and caribou lying down on hills and knolls. It was our first time to see tuckamore and muskeg, but by the end of our hunt we were very familiar with both. We flew into camp, which was a small cabin on Andrews Pond, a small lake that linked up to the river. Finally, we were at our destination. All the guides and cook were there to greet us, and we were so very happy to be there. It was getting dark, so we ate supper and unpacked our gear. We had only missed one day of hunting which was Saturday. Sunday is a no-hunt day. As luck would have it, Monday woke up with a vengeance. Rain came down in buckets. Later in the day we got stir-crazy, put on our rain gear, and ventured out for a look-see on the hill behind the cabin. Jane took her gun, just in case there might be a caribou or moose for the taking. There was a pretty nice bull and some cows lying down within 75 yards, but our guide advised us to wait. He told us there would be plenty to choose from and even bigger. As it turned out, we really needed that day to relax and decompress after all the frustration we had encountered the past few days. We were truly exhausted.

Our camp house was small but adequate. We had a generator that supplied electricity and hot water for a shower but had to go to the outhouse for our toilet. A wood heater kept the place warm and cozy. Many games of darts and hook the circle on the nail were played during that week. Joyce was a great cook and very pleasant, and she was excited to have another woman in camp. She and Jane became friends and still keep in touch. Her husband, Junior was one of the guides, along with Jasper and Jamey (my guide).

We set out on foot Tuesday morning to climb the big hill close to camp in search of our caribou or moose—whichever one we came upon first. Bill and Junior also set out on an adjacent hill. Jane and Jasper headed north to a location called Bob's Knob.

That first full day of hunting I saw a nice caribou—but he only had one good side—

and a really nice moose, but he was trotting away from us, and we could not get him to stop. There is no question that if he would have offered a shot, I would have taken him.

Back at camp, we all told our events of the day. No one else had seen anything of consequence. That night I went outside then came back in and told Jane to come outside and listen. It was the darkest and quietest that I had ever experienced. Not a bug, animal, wind, nothing. I have never experienced that sense of quiet before—or since. It was awesome. That is remote!

Wednesday came and Jamey decided that we should hit the river and go down a ways by boat, then climb one of the hills where we could glass. We spotted a moose following a cow on the other side of the river but could not tell how big he was. The two of us decided to cross the river and check it out. After trekking back across the river and getting a closer look, I decided to pass him up and wait for a more mature trophy, much to Jamey's dismay, who was not accustomed to having hunters pass up an animal. After the moose encounter, we went back to the other side of the river and hiked about two miles up a big hill. Around 11 a.m., we reached the top of the "mountain" and spotted six cows and one big stag about three miles away. Luckily they were headed in our direction. About an hour later, we were about 300 yards apart. At this point Jamey decided to stay behind, while I attempted to close the gap between me and that stag. At 150 yards, I took dead aim with my .300 Winchester Short Magnum loaded with a 180-grain, fail-safe bullet, and I brought him down with a perfect neck shot. Jamey was excited, since he knew the caliber of trophy I had just taken (though I had no idea how huge he was until later). I was one thrilled hunter with the trophy regardless of his score. We caped him out, loaded up the cape and horns on our backs, and called for the helicopter to airlift the meat.

We worked our way back to the boat, picked up Bill and Junior, and headed back to camp. Of course we took lots of pictures and I retold the hunt to the others at camp.

The rest of the hunt, I took a cow moose, Bill took a young bull moose and caribou. Jane passed up a couple of moose that Jasper brought in with a call made from a coffee can and string, but they were not as large as she wanted. She did see a big bull, possibly the same big one I saw but could not catch up with him with the tuckamore and muskeg. You cannot move across the tuckamore; you have to walk the trails of the animals. It is comparable to a small hedge but with intertwining branches about 2 feet high. The muskeg was like a sponge in the flats, making it just as hard to walk on and through. The moose was about 600 yards away and just disappeared. Jane ended up hunting the last day for a few hours but still came home empty-handed.

We did not know until the taxidermist saw the caribou that I probably had a Boone and Crockett animal. There was no scorer there in Deer Lake so I had him mounted without cutting the antlers in half to ship. I am certainly glad that I did because when he was scored, I was shocked. He was not only Boone and Crockett he was at the top of the list. The 27th Awards Program Judges Panel verified his score at 324-1/8 points.

Wow, what a trip! ▲

Moments in Measuring

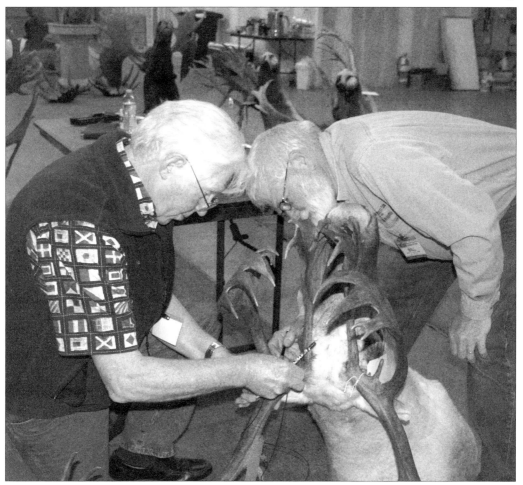

Panel Judge Glenn E. Hisey (left) holds a flexible steel cable in place while his partner William A. Keebler marks the base of the left bez on this caribou rack. The scores of 16 spectacular caribou, representing all five caribou categories recognized by Boone and Crockett Club, were verified in Reno.

TROPHY STATS
▼ ▼ ▼ ▼ ▼

CATEGORY
Woodland Caribou

SCORE
314$^6/_8$

INSIDE SPREAD
31

LENGTH OF MAIN BEAM
Right: 39$^3/_8$ Left: 36$^5/_8$

WIDTH OF BROW PALM
Right: 11$^3/_8$ Left: 9$^3/_8$

NUMBER OF POINTS
Right: 13   Left: 17

LOCATION
Owl Pond, Newfoundland – 2008

HUNTER
Richard W. Smith

WOODLAND CARIBOU
Honorable Mention – 314 ⁶/₈

▼ ▼ ▼ ▼ ▼ ▼ ▼ ▼ ▼

RICHARD W. SMITH

In 2008, Richard Smith and his hunting companion Sam Ricci signed up for a combination Canada moose/woodland caribou hunt with Aster Caines of Portland Creek Hunting and Fishing Outfitters in Portland Creek, Newfoundland. It was to be a 10-day hunt, but it took Sam and Richard an additional four days of traveling time to get to hunting camp and another four days to return home after the hunt.

The first leg of their trip to Newfoundland was a two-day, 1,100-mile drive from Delaware Bay, New Jersey, to North Sydney, Nova Scotia, where they caught a ferry boat across Cabot Strait to Newfoundland. Since this is a six-and-a-half-hour crossing, they took the nighttime ferry and booked a berth so that they could catch up on much-needed sleep prior to arriving in Newfoundland.

When they disembarked in Newfoundland the next morning, they drove another six hours to Daniel's Harbour where they met their outfitter Aster Caines and spent the night at a local hotel. After breakfast the next morning, they drove their truck down an old logging road to a wide spot where they parked and loaded their gear into the outfitter's snow cat for the last four-hour ride across dry and barren logging roads to their hunting camp at Owl Pond.

On opening day, Ralph Coles, their guide, took them by boat to the end of Owl Pond—which is more like a good-sized lake where Richard is from—where they spent the morning hiking eight miles or so looking for keeper moose because that's the time of day moose are most active. They only saw a couple of cows with calves. After eating lunch back at the boat, they spent an unfruitful afternoon searching for caribou.

Richard and Sam were starting to settle in after arriving back in hunting camp just before dark when Ralph yelled to Richard, "Grab your gun, and we'll go look at a nice caribou I just spotted on the other side of the lake."

Two other guides who had already returned with their clients from the day's hunt jumped into the boat to help if Richard shot something. After beaching the boat on the opposite shore, they headed to a prominent overlook to do some glassing. They just started glassing when Ralph excitedly whispered, "I've guided here eight years and he's really a dandy."

Richard had a chance to glance at the bull and knew immediately that it was better than any caribou bull he had seen on his two previous caribou hunts in Newfoundland. He also interpreted Ralph's statement as his cautious way of telling Richard he will probably never see a better one in his lifetime.

They ranged the bull at 500 yards from the knoll they were on. Richard didn't think it was a "fair-chase shot" so they headed downhill through the thick black spruce to cut the distance between them and a potential B&C bull. When they were within 200 yards of the bull, Richard laid his .30-06 across a black spruce branch he selected for a gun rest. The bull was quartering away on a nearby knob, but when Richard flipped off the safety, he turned and offered Richard a classic broadside shot. Richard fired and the bull hunched up. It was out of sight on the other side of the knob without giving Richard time for a second follow-up shot. Ralph was watching through his binoculars and said, "Richard, you hit him good! He's not going far."

They started downhill and cautiously looked over the knob, and immediately knew that a second shot was not necessary. The bull was bunched up 40-50 yards away in the scrubby black spruce.

It didn't take but a few seconds for Richard to realize that he had just shot the best trophy of his hunting career. After all the backslapping and handshaking, Richard reached for his camera, and quickly realized that he had left it back in camp in his haste to get into the boat. Ralph saved the day and took a couple of photos with his cell phone.

Dark was fast approaching, but they were able to quickly field dress and quarter his bull because of the two extra guides that came along just in case he filled his tag. They bagged the quarters and carried them back to the boat for the return trip to camp. It was dark by the time they reached camp where delicious pan-fried cod was on the menu for dinner that night.

Richard harvested his moose on the eighth day of his hunt, and they headed home with the meat in a large, commercial bait-sized cooler. They stopped in Rocky Harbour where they filled the cooler with ice and again in Maine where they topped it off with lobster.

The final score of Richard's bull, as determined by the 27th Awards Program Judges Panel is 314-6/8 points, and he gives all the credit for taking such an outstanding trophy to Ralph Coles his guide. He had such a good time on this hunt that he booked again with Portland Creek Hunting and Fishing Outfitters for the 2010 hunting season. He is really looking forward to this trip, not only because of the potential for taking another trophy-class bull, but because he'll get another opportunity to hunt with Ralph and visit all the other wonderful folks he's met in the past. He said, "Newfoundlanders are really genuine people. If they shake your hand, it's a done deal." ▲

Award-Winning Moments

Dallas Safari Club's Executive Director, Ben Carter, accepting their sponsorship plaque from Simon Roosevelt. Dallas Safari Club was a host sponsor of the Club's 26th Big Game Awards Program held in Fort Worth, Texas, in 2007. Ben Carter is also a Boone and Crockett Club professional member.

TROPHY STATS

▼ ▼ ▼ ▼ ▼

CATEGORY
Barren Ground Caribou

SCORE
$419^4/_8$

INSIDE SPREAD
$49^3/_8$

LENGTH OF MAIN BEAM
Right: 54   Left: $56^3/_8$

WIDTH OF BROW PALM
Right: $1^7/_8$ Left: $16^2/_8$

NUMBER OF POINTS
Right: 17   Left: 19

LOCATION
Seward Peninsula, Alaska – 2008

HUNTER
Jack L. Wilson

BARREN GROUND CARIBOU
First Award – 419 ⁴/₈

▼ ▼ ▼ ▼ ▼ ▼ ▼ ▼ ▼

JACK L. WILSON

As told by hunting partner, Chuck Stoddard.

Jack and I have been hunting, fishing, shooting, and storytelling most of our adult lives. As our camaraderie grows, so do the adventures. Hunting Alaskan barren ground caribou is, without exception, a true adventure.

If you have ever experienced the Alaskan wilds, you quickly realize how difficult things

A True Adventure

can become, especially in a do-it-yourself hunting situation. The effort, planning, and detriments are all part of the hunt. And the remote chance of bagging a bull the caliber of Jack's makes you want to do it all over again!

After setting up base camp the first morning, Jack and I headed west to a vantage point that fits our spot-and-talk style of hunting. Glassing across the distant rolling tundra, we both commented on the vastness when Jack spotted antlers at 12 o'clock. It was two bulls, moving fast. We positioned ourselves several hundred yards away. The bulls were feeding, yet still moving quickly. They truly appeared to be grazing on the run! We kept repositioning again and again, until our shadow was in front of us, and a slight breeze kept the mosquitoes from our face.

Even though we had given it our best effort, it appeared that we lost them. In order to cover more ground, we decided to move again and split up. I traversed up the slope while Jack worked his way down the ridge. As I struggled up the ridge, I stumbled and spotted the tops of Jack's bull. I quickly sat down and thought to myself, *He's huge!* And now before me, it becomes Jack's pursuit. Minutes seemed like hours as Jack moved into position. *Hurry Jack.* The bull knew something was askew. As Jack moved closer, the bull put his nose up and start-

Photograph by Jack Reneau

Jack L. Wilson accepting his plaque and medal from Buck Buckner, Vice President and Chairman of the Big Game Records Committee.

The award-winning barren ground caribou pictured above was taken by Jack L. Wilson during the 2008 season in Alaska. The bull, which has a final score of 419-4/8 points, received a First Place Award at the 27th Big Game Awards Program in Reno, Nevada.

ed to trot. After a short distance he made a fatal error and stopped to look back. I thought again, *Hurry-up Jack*. As the bull turned his head to escape, Jack made the shot.

For me, Jack, and the rest of our hunting party, this was a very special hunt. It was an experience responsible for numerous memories and a few more stories. I find this caribou bull truly impressive, and Jack would say they all are.

Jack's note: Chuck's storytelling ability is only exceeded by his modesty. He would downplay his part in this adventure. It was he who motioned to me the bull's location so I could take the shot. After my bull went down, he hustled down the ridge to harvest the other fine 360-plus bull.

As Chuck said, "A true adventure" with fantastic scenery, great hunting partners and a 419-4/8 bull. ▲

Award-Winning Moments

B&C Photo Archives

(l-r) William A. Keebler, Richard C. Berreth, Larry R. Carey, Jay A. Lesser, George A. Bettas, Paul D. Webster, David P. Rippeto, and Kyle C. Krause were among the Official Measurers from all over North America who attended the 27th Awards Program. Official Measurers who volunteer their time and talents to score trophies for B&C were honored at the first ever Field Generals luncheon.

TROPHY STATS

▼ ▼ ▼ ▼ ▼

CATEGORY
Barren Ground Caribou

SCORE
417 $^5/_8$

INSIDE SPREAD
35 $^5/_8$

LENGTH OF MAIN BEAM
Right: 47 $^5/_8$ Left: 49 $^5/_8$

WIDTH OF BROW PALM
Right: 11 $^5/_8$ Left: 9 $^2/_8$

NUMBER OF POINTS
Right: 20   Left: 20

LOCATION
King Salmon River, Alaska – 1978

HUNTER
Joseph C. Bitzan

BARREN GROUND CARIBOU
Second Award – 417 ⁵/₈

▼ ▼ ▼ ▼ ▼ ▼ ▼ ▼ ▼

JOSEPH C. BITZAN

The story for my trophy caribou hunt began in the fall of 1978, south of King Salmon, a small fishing town on the Alaska Peninsula. My two hunting companions and I arrived in late September in King Salmon where we had contracted with PenAir for a pilot with a twin-engine Widgeon to fly us into a small lake where we had spotted three caribou herds on an earlier scouting trip.

While setting up camp, I noticed a surveying tower overlooking the terrain. The next morning I climbed the tower and observed that the caribou were still where we had originally spotted them. One friend took off after one herd, while my other friend and I went after another herd of about 35 animals feeding on a dry lake bed. I had both a black powder rifle and a .30-06 Springfield, so I wanted to get as close to the herd as possible. We found a dry stream bed we used to get close to the herd and discovered that the dry lake bed was created by beaver dams.

Bullet Flip

After feeding all morning, the herd finally bedded down. There were so many antlers that it looked like a giant brush pile. A line of low willows about halfway between us and the herd concealed us as we low-crawled to get within range so I could use my black powder rifle. The never-ending wind was in our faces, causing movement of the willows that helped conceal us as we stalked the herd. We got within 35 to 50 yards of the herd and took our time glassing it for the largest bulls.

We eventually agreed on which one was the largest bull, and flipped a bullet to determine who would take him. I got the first shot of my choice and decided to use my .30-06 Springfield. Through the tangle of heads, antlers, necks, and bodies, I only had a neck shot. With the wind and no rest, it was a tough shot. My first shot missed but made a loud whopping sound in the mud on the far side of

Photograph by Jack Reneau

Joseph C. Bitzan accepting his plaque and medal from Buck Buckner, Vice President and Chairman of the Big Game Records Committee.

Joseph C. Bitzan stands behind his award-winning barren ground caribou taken in 1978. The bull scores 417-5/8 points.

the herd. Confused as to where the shot had come from, the herd jumped up and charged straight at us! As the caribou drew closer, I quickly chambered another round and settled the crosshairs on a bull with beautiful double shovels. I shot and down he went.

In the charging melee, my friend could not initially find the monster he was after. However, we spotted his bull about 350 yards away as the herd headed up a gradual slope. My friend had a good rest and dropped it instantly with his .300 Magnum. We were a pair of happy hunters!

It took me 32 years to get my bull officially measured for B&C and find out it scores 417-5/8. I received the Second Place Award for my bull at the 27th Awards Program Banquet in Reno, Nevada. ▲

B&C Photo Archives

Grant Kuypers of Buck Paradise Outfitters of Paradise Hills, Saskatchewan, accepts thanks from Keith Balfourd for his donation of a trophy whitetail hunt that sold at the Club's auction. Funds raised during Friday's auction provided a significant boost to the Club's mission-based programs.

TROPHY STATS

▼ ▼ ▼ ▼ ▼

CATEGORY
Central Canada Barren
Ground Caribou

SCORE
396 $^4/_8$

INSIDE SPREAD
41 $^2/_8$

LENGTH OF MAIN BEAM
Right: 54 $^3/_8$ Left: 55 $^2/_8$

WIDTH OF BROW PALM
Right: 17 $^3/_8$ Left: 11 $^1/_8$

NUMBER OF POINTS
Right: 18   Left: 12

LOCATION
Thonokied Lake, Northwest
Territories – 2006

HUNTER
Nyla K. Swast

CENTRAL CANADA BARREN GROUND CARIBOU
First Award – 396 4/8

▼ ▼ ▼ ▼ ▼ ▼ ▼ ▼ ▼

NYLA K. SWAST

In the summer of 2006, my father and I attended a Foundation for North American Wild Sheep meeting in Lancaster, Pennsylvania. Being the only daughter still at home, I began to tease him about going on a caribou hunt. When the hunts were auctioned off, I was on my way to getting my wish! The date of the hunt was set for October 2006.

Stories to Last

Starting at Pittsburgh International Airport, we ended in Yellowknife, Northwest Territories, Canada. From there we took a floatplane to a camp area set up near Lake Thonokied. The outfitter was Devin Aherne, and my guide was Kevin Armstrong. The method of hunting was simple: cruise the lake in a small motorboat, find a good spot to glass, and plan a stalk from that point. As with all big-game hunting regulations in that region, you are unable to kill an animal the same day you fly, so the first evening we settled into our tent, organized our gear, and enjoyed the tranquil landscape.

The Lake Thonokied hunting area was very interesting to me because of its location inside the Arctic Circle. In this area there are very few trees. One of the guides pointed out a few that he guessed were possibly over 100 years old and only 3 feet tall.

The day after we arrived in camp was a Sunday, and as I don't care to hunt on that day, my father and I spent it cruising the lake and glassing for signs of caribou activity on the tundra. Back in camp that night, we heard a story about a gigantic caribou bull that was stalked and consequently missed by another hunter.

"He was at least 370," enthused the guide. "Our shot was just a little off, but we'll get a chance tomorrow."

Photograph by Jack Reneau

Nyla K. Swast accepting her plaque and medal from Buck Buckner, Vice President and Chairman of the Big Game Records Committee.

Nyla K. Swast is pictured above with her father and her award-winning Central Canada barren ground caribou. Swast was hunting near Thonokied Lake in Northwest Territories when she harvested this bull, which has a final score of 396-4/8 points.

I looked the guide straight in the eye and said, "I will kill that bull tomorrow morning."

All the hunters and guides stared, and then the chuckling started. "What makes you think you'll kill him?" they said.

"That's my bull," I said. "And you can count him dead right now."

After a good night's sleep and a hurried breakfast, we motored out to where the caribou herd was last spotted. We had only glassed the area for an hour when the herd appeared on a ridge about a mile away. Kevin looked at me and said, "There they are Nyla. Let's go."

We shouldered our packs and started the hike. Although the tundra looks flat, I found out that wasn't the case as I struggled over hills and into holes deep enough to sprain your ankle with a wrong step. We made it across the valley and partway up the slope to a shooting range of about 250 yards from the main herd. Dad and Kevin placed my pack on a boulder. I took a deep breath and situated my .270 Ruger snugly against my shoulder. Following Kevin's directions, my first shot took down a nice bull with beautiful dark velvet still on the antlers.

Suddenly, Dad and Kevin were motioning to the left. "There he is. That's the bull, that's the bull! Second from the right, Nyla, shoot!" Not willing to let a rack like that get away, I shot. My prize took two steps and dropped. You've never seen quite a victory dance as we had on the tundra! I can't begin to describe the triumph I felt as I walked toward that beautiful trophy.

CENTRAL CANADA BARREN GROUND CARIBOU
First Award – 396 4/8

▼ ▼ ▼ ▼ ▼

NYLA K. SWAST

Later in the hunt, I was also able to get a rare trophy from Northwest Territories—a wolverine. I had just taken a shot at a white wolf that was feeding on another caribou kill, and we were checking the area for signs of blood when Kevin looked to the right and spluttered, "There, there, kill it!" My father and I both thought he was talking about the wolf I had just missed, but he kept on pointing and finally got out, "Wolverine! Get it—don't miss." I came home with three beautiful trophies and enough stories to last a year. I thank God and my father for the strength and opportunity to fulfill my dream of harvesting a trophy caribou. ▲

TROPHY STATS

▼ ▼ ▼ ▼ ▼

CATEGORY
Central Canada Barren
Ground Caribou

SCORE
$394^{1}/_{8}$

INSIDE SPREAD
$40^{5}/_{8}$

LENGTH OF MAIN BEAM
Right: $49^{6}/_{8}$ Left: $49^{7}/_{8}$

WIDTH OF BROW PALM
Right: $8^{7}/_{8}$ Left: 11

NUMBER OF POINTS
Right: 18   Left: 19

LOCATION
MacKay Lake, Northwest
Territories – 2007

HUNTER
Doran J. Lambson

CENTRAL CANADA BARREN GROUND CARIBOU
Second Award – 394 ¹/₈
▼ ▼ ▼ ▼ ▼ ▼ ▼ ▼ ▼

DORAN J. LAMBSON

My hunt started at the end of my undergraduate studies at Idaho State University. Whether out of pity or pride, I may never know why my father presented me with the gift of a week-long Central Canada barren ground caribou hunt for September 2007. After what seemed to be a lifetime of school and studying,

Wicked Awesome

I felt like I was about to have my first vacation as a free man. Unfortunately for me, my degree did not teach me anything about hunting caribou or even caribou in general. However, I was fortunate enough to have a great hunting party to go with—my older brother Dallen Lambson, my father, Hayden Lambson, and a friend of Dallen's.

We chose to drive from southeastern Idaho to Yellowknife, Northwest Territories, Canada—1,800 miles one way. We figured that way we could drive the distance for the price of one airline ticket each and haul a trailer so that we could bring meat, capes, and antlers home with us. At Yellowknife we hooked up with our outfitter, True North Safaris. From there we flew to camp at Mackay Lake. After disembarking from the plane and unloading our equipment in the lodge, I got a much-needed lesson about caribou and how to field judge trophy bulls. For those of you, like me, who are not skilled at judging caribou on the hoof, I will share with you the secret I learned while at Mackay Lake: Listen to your guide!

The first day at the lodge before the hunt, I was informed by some of the more learned hunters (from the school of hard knocks) not to shoot my caribou on the first day. I was told that if I was more patient than they had been and followed the advice of my guide, I would go home with a nice bull. So the next morning,

Photograph by Jack Reneau

Doran J. Lambson accepting his plaque and medal from Buck Buckner, Vice President and Chairman of the Big Game Records Committee.

Doran J. Lambson (right) is pictured above with his dad Hayden Lambson. Doran harvested his award-winning bull, scoring 394-1/8 points, while on a hunt in Northwest Territories that his dad gave him as a gift for completing his undergraduate studies.

my hunting partner, our guide, and I went scouting for that monster bull I dreamed about the night before. My dad had decided to switch hunting partners each day. He hunted with me one day and my brother the next. The first day, the guide assigned him to be with my older brother.

That first day was a true hunting utopia. While sitting next to a boulder, we watched what appeared to be trees growing on the skyline right before our eyes. It was one of the most amazing sights I had ever seen. The trees kept sprouting out of the horizon until the ridge was covered. And then the bodies came. A herd of about 50 animals came over the ridge and passed by us about 30 yards away. We heard them breathing and snorting. We could even hear their ankles clicking as they passed us. I was surprised that the sound of my heart thumping in my chest didn't scare them away. After viewing such a spectacular show, and as tempting as it was to allow such a beautiful animal walk past the crosshairs of my scope, we decided that we would hold out. The only advocate to our willpower was the ever-present words still ringing in our ears, "Don't shoot one on the first day."

After a full day of an hourly dose of natural, almost non-stop adrenalin for a straight eight hours, we hiked back to the boats and motored back to camp. At dinner, while eating the most delicious barbequed caribou ribs, all the hunters had their own unique experiences to share, which got us even more excited for the next day. After dinner, we finished the evening with a special show put on by Mother Nature herself. It was the Aurora Borealis. I felt like a child going to bed on Christmas Eve that night.

CENTRAL CANADA BARREN GROUND CARIBOU
Second Award – 394 ¹/₈

▼ ▼ ▼ ▼ ▼

DORAN J. LAMBSON

On the second day I had the privilege of hunting with my father and Malcolm, his guide. Malcolm was excited to take us to a place where he had seen some really nice bulls a few days earlier, so I, too, was excited. After a two-hour boat ride, we spotted a herd of caribou hanging out just off the shore of a peninsula jutting out into the lake. We saw a few mature bulls so we docked the boat on a nearby island to get a better look. After glassing the herd, Malcolm pointed out a bull lying down that appeared to have good potential. As we watched this bull, he finally decided to stand up. When he did, Malcolm turned to us and said, "That is a wicked awesome bull."

Now you're probably wondering what the information about my graduating from college had to do with this story. It was simply to illustrate a point. I'm no dummy. When I heard the excitement in Malcolm's voice, and with the unwritten "first day no harvest" rule expired, I whispered to Dad, "I'm going to take this one."

While my dad set up the video camera, I got into position with the perfect rest. The sky was overcast with a light sprinkling of rain. It appeared to be about a 160-yard shot, so the only thing left to do was take a deep breath, hold it, and squeeze the trigger.

After everything calmed down, except for my heart pounding in my chest, we hiked up to one of the most beautiful creatures I have ever harvested. After receiving hugs, handshakes, and chest bumps, our guide demonstrated the correct techniques for caping and quartering caribou. I then hiked back to the boat with my dad and a trophy caribou rack draped over my shoulders. With the excitement of taking a huge trophy with my dad, and the thought of more caribou ribs, this was one of the greatest highlights of my life (next to marrying my beautiful wife and the birth of my children).

My dad, brother, and I had rough-scored the antlers while still in camp, using a book found at the lodge, and a B&C score chart. Our best estimate was around 400 points. The 27th Awards Program Judges Panel scored this trophy at 394-1/8—not too shabby for three hunters who had never scored any heads before, let alone a caribou.

This creature is by far the largest trophy I have ever taken, but what made it a hunt-of-a-lifetime was the people I met and our hunting party.

Special thanks go to my dad for such a great gift and to my brother, who also harvested an exceptional bull. Both were just as excited for me and my trophy as I was, and all made this experience the hunt of lifetime. ▲

TROPHY STATS

▼ ▼ ▼ ▼ ▼

CATEGORY
Central Canada Barren
Ground Caribou

SCORE
392

INSIDE SPREAD
$39^2/_8$

LENGTH OF MAIN BEAM
Right: $51^2/_8$ Left: $51^5/_8$

WIDTH OF BROW PALM
Right: $10^5/_8$ Left: 13

NUMBER OF POINTS
Right: 20   Left: 17

LOCATION
Courageous Lake, Northwest
Territories – 2007

HUNTER
Loren B. Mickelson

CENTRAL CANADA BARREN GROUND CARIBOU
Third Award – 392

▼ ▼ ▼ ▼ ▼ ▼ ▼ ▼ ▼

LOREN B. MICKELSON

A hunt for Central Canada barren ground caribou in Northwest Territories had been a lifelong hunting dream of mine. The opportunity to witness one of the last great migrations on the North American continent would make this experience a lifetime highlight for me.

My mother Terri, stepfather Brad, and I left Laramie, Wyoming, on September 2, 2007, for the four-day trip to Yellowknife, Northwest Territories. Along the way, we traveled over Glacier National Park's Going to the Sun Road. We went through Calgary, Alberta, had a couple of delicious beers in Cranbrook, Alberta, then, traveled through both Banff and Jasper National Parks and saw both grizzly and black bears. We spent a fun-filled evening in High Level, Alberta, attending a free pizza party at our hotel before arriving in Yellowknife on September 5th.

We checked into our hotel, and the next day we met the rest of our immediate hunting party. We all spent the next couple of days sightseeing around Yellowknife. On September 8, our party included Terri, Brad, friends Reed and Sandy, Kevin, and me. We went to the Air Tindi hub to begin our great hunt up on the barren grounds of northern Canada. An airplane crew loaded all our gear onto a plane, and while they were loading, another floatplane returned from Courageous Lake, which was the same place we were going to be hunting. The plane was loaded to the brim with many caribou antlers and returning hunters were brimming with excitement from the hunts they had just experienced.

We climbed aboard our floatplane and taxied onto the Great Slave Lake. Within minutes, we were airborne, and my view of the landscape of sub-arctic Canada began to change. Trees and lakes dotting the ground soon became hundreds of lakes in a prairie-type

Photograph by Jack Reneau

Loren B. Mickelson accepting his plaque and medal from Buck Buckner, Vice President and Chairman of the Big Game Records Committee.

Loren B. Mickelson is pictured above with his award-winning Central Canada barren ground caribou. Mickelson was hunting with his mother Terri near Courageous Lake, Northwest Territories.

landscape covering everything. It was really cool to see parts of the world-famous ice road which lead to the arctic diamond mines.

About an hour later, we landed on Courageous Lake. We were greeted by Larry the camp manager and the rest of his crew, who immediately started to unload the plane. Once the plane was unloaded, Larry introduced himself and showed us to our tents. He assigned each tent a hunting guide. Kevin and I were assigned to Dan, a veteran guide for Shoshone Wilderness Adventures who was spending his first season at Courageous Lake.

Later, we had dinner and continued to introduce ourselves to the rest of the hunting party including a group from Vernal, Utah, who were great guys to have around during our hunt. My mom and Kevin decided to switch guides that night. Kevin would hunt with Brad, so she could hunt with me.

The next morning we awoke at 5 a.m. to a beautiful, but windy day. The lake had a little wave action going on, but nothing to be concerned about. Everyone ate breakfast and prepared their gear for the first day of their hunt. I went with my mom to our assigned boat where Dan was waiting with two life vests. Dan said we had to wear life vests for two reasons: 1) to keep us from drowning; and 2) to help the Royal Canadian Mounted Police identify our bodies should we capsize!

CENTRAL CANADA BARREN GROUND CARIBOU
Third Award – 392

▼ ▼ ▼ ▼ ▼

LOREN B. MICKELSON

We packed our hunting gear into the boat and climbed into our seats. Dan pointed the boat towards the east side of the lake, and a half hour later we pulled into shore. Dan, Mom and I hiked up a hill and started glassing the immediate area. Dan saw a high outcrop and decided that would be a better place to look for some caribou.

After nestling against a "comfortable rock" out of the wind, I started to view the caribou coming down the barren ground from the northwest. Watching caribou walk past you only 50 yards away is a cool sight. In fact, while glassing, we had one small herd come within 15 yards of us. The caribou seemed more curious about us than we were of them.

After glassing for a few hours, Dan decided we should go back to the boat and have a "Canadian lunch" (coffee, soup, and sandwiches). After hiking back to the boat on the spongy tundra, which feels like walking in 10 inches of snow, we had lunch then pushed the boat back onto the lake. Dan thought we should go further east and try our luck there.

After about 30 minutes of riding on choppy waters, Dan pulled the boat into shore and we unloaded our packs onto the small beach of a little cove. My mom's back was hurting her, so she decided not to take her pack or rifle during this excursion. It was around 1 p.m. when we started to hike east to climb a large hill and get a good view of the area. With the wind blowing in our faces and less agreeable weather, we glassed for about an hour until it got too cold. Dan started back down the hill and walked to the north, so Mom and I followed him. He took us through a nice, low, scrub-brush swamp, and then led us over to a little outcrop where we glassed the surrounding area. He spotted a herd of caribou coming our way with some good-looking bulls in it.

By this time, a good fall blizzard made it difficult to see. Dan wanted to get into a better position so I could have a chance at shooting one of the bulls. We hurried to a low-lying spot and watched as the herd continued our way. Dan looked through his binoculars and saw a couple of monster bulls. He excitedly told me to put a bullet in the chamber of my gun, and I quickly did as I was told. He said he wanted to put me in a better shooting position. So, we moved out of our low-lying area into clear view of the caribou so they could see us.

After Mom and Dan jostled me into the best shooting position possible, Dan eagerly pointed out the bull he liked. Mom put my backpack down in front of me to act as an impromptu brace. I looked through the scope and saw the bull Dan wanted me to shoot. Dan suggested I be patient and wait until the bull cleared the herd. The snow and wind were coming down hard, and at times it was difficult seeing the bull.

We waited for about 30 long seconds until the bull cleared the herd. I heard Dan say, "Take the shot! Take the shot!"

I looked through the scope, aimed at the bull, took a deep breath, held it, and squeezed the trigger. I saw the bull instantly drop to the ground and soon felt hands patting me on the back. I reloaded my gun in case the bull wasn't dead. I looked up from my scope and saw Dan and mom beaming with smiles.

I asked Dan how far he thought my shot was, and he said around 325 yards! I was shocked; I had never shot anything except targets that far away!

Dan, mom, and I got up and jogged over to the caribou. Dan checked to make sure it was dead. I had definitely made the perfect shot under difficult conditions. Dan started glowing at the size of the caribou's antlers and mentioned that it might make book, but it was most certainly a keeper. Since I had the only gun, I went off to watch for bears while mom and Dan dressed my bull. At about 4:30 p.m., I grabbed the antlers and my backpack while mom carried my rifle and Dan packed out the meat and cape. We made it back to the boat around 5:30 p.m. for a very cold, bumpy, windy ride back to camp.

When we got back to camp, everyone was excited to see us because we were the last boat in, and it was getting past sundown. Brad, Kevin, and some of the guys from Utah helped unload our gear and pull the boat back onto the beach. Everyone started saying how big my caribou was and how it will probably make the records book. I thanked them all but was too tired and hungry to enjoy the moment.

After a hot meal, I went over to my caribou and started to take in how big it really was compared to the others that had been harvested that day. Larry came up and shook my hand and congratulated me on a job well-done. He said Dan told him about how tough of a shot I'd taken. I relayed my little adventure, and he remarked that I should be proud of my accomplishment.

The trip to Courageous Lake caribou camp had many other highlights for me other than just shooting my caribou. A member from the Utah group shot an Arctic wolf. Plus, everyone saw two grizzly bears scuffle over a caribou carcass. The following morning, we saw some grizzly tracks less than 20 yards from our tents (we were protected by a 10,000-volt electric fence around our camp).

Back in Wyoming, my mom had my caribou officially measured in December 2007. It came back at 392 points. We were all stoked about the results. Brad looked in his records book and found it was in the top 50 All-time Central Canada barren ground caribou ever harvested. I had to wait two years—until December 2009—to find out that I had officially made the records book.

Overall, I found my hunting experience for a Central Canada barren ground caribou to be one I'll never forget. I took a record bull. I saw parts of one of the greatest migrations still on the North American continent. And, I had a great time hanging out with family and friends. ▲

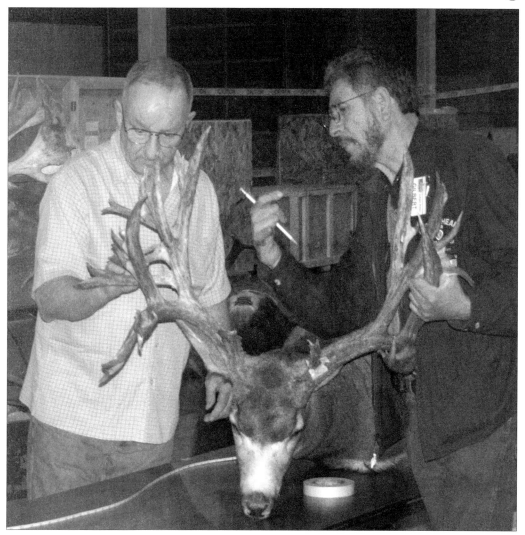

B&C Photo Archives

Homer Saye (l) and Gilbert Hernandez made up one of the two Judges Panel teams that verified the score of Kyle Lopez's non-typical mule deer. At 306-3/8, it is the largest mule deer entered in B&C since 1972 and only the 22nd buck that has ever scored 300 points or better. Kyle was 14 when he took this buck-of-a-lifetime in Douglas County, Colorado, in 2007.

TROPHY STATS

▼ ▼ ▼ ▼ ▼

CATEGORY
Central Canada Barren
Ground Caribou

SCORE
$389^2/_8$

INSIDE SPREAD
$26^1/_8$

LENGTH OF MAIN BEAM
Right: $50^2/_8$ Left: $50^4/_8$

WIDTH OF BROW PALM
Right: $15^5/_8$ Left: $9^7/_8$

NUMBER OF POINTS
Right: 20   Left: 16

LOCATION
Point Lake, Northwest
Territories – 2006

HUNTER
Steven R. Marr

CENTRAL CANADA BARREN GROUND CARIBOU
Fourth Award – 389 $^2/_8$

▼ ▼ ▼ ▼ ▼ ▼ ▼ ▼ ▼

STEVEN R. MARR

Our hunt for Central Canada barren ground caribou began on August 23, 2006. My son-in-law Justin Vavra and I boarded a floatplane out of Yellowknife for our destination, Peterson's Point Lake Lodge, which is located about 200 miles north in Northwest Territories.

A Tremendous Hunt

We were fortunate to be provided a very skillful guide, Grant St. Germaine. His knowledge of the caribou hunting area, as well as the history of Point Lake proved to be very beneficial for our hunt and education. To cover the distance from our camp, we used a boat. Anytime we were traveling, we kept a sharp eye out for any caribou we might see along the way. The scenery was spectacular, and if you weren't careful, you could find yourself enjoying the beauty and not looking for caribou.

The day after arriving in camp, I shot a respectable bull for the area we were in. The second day, things started to get a little more interesting. My son-in-law took a great bull that later scored 347-4/8 points. This bull earned Justin a listing in the Club's Triennial Awards book.

On the third day, we set off on a 30-plus-mile boat ride, having relinquished our hunting area to other guides. We spotted two bulls in the morning, but made the decision to pass on them. Around lunchtime, we beached the boat and climbed a hill. While we ate, Grant surveyed a small cove adjacent to us. He was looking for fresh tracks in the sand that might indicate animals in the area.

While he was checking the cove area, I happened to look up toward a saddle in the hills surrounding us and saw what looked like a large caribou bull standing in the middle of the saddle. Picking up the binoculars and glassing him, I told Grant, "Hey, there's a bull standing up there in the saddle."

Grant looked through his binoculars and said, "He looks promising. Let's just watch and see what he does."

There was a small stream coming into the cove and Grant thought he might follow that down. The bull did as hoped, making his way straight down until he came to an old game trail 40 yards from our position.

When he turned broadside, I took the shot. The bull ran parallel to me and died six feet from the cove—just 15 feet from me! Grant commented that he liked that kind of pack

Steven R. Marr (left) is pictured above next to his son-in-law, Justin Vavra, and his award-winning Central Canada barren ground caribou. Marr and Vavra were hunting near Point Lake, Northwest Territories during a 2006 hunt when he harvested the bull, which scores 389-2/8 points.

out. My bull's antlers were still in velvet, which we stripped for measuring. To our amazement, the bull officially scored 389-2/8, qualifying for the All-time records book.

On the fourth day, Justin took another nice bull, and on day five, we relaxed and fished for lake trout. It was an amazing and fulfilling adventure from beginning to end.

Unfortunately, Jim Peterson, the owner of Peterson's Point Lake Lodge, passed away from cancer only 18 months after our trip. Regardless, it remains a great facility with wonderful food, great people, and hot showers. This was a tremendous hunt, and we will remember it for the rest of our lives. ▲

Award-Winning Moments

One of the benefits and pleasures of attending one of B&C's Triennial Awards Programs is the opportunity to meet fellow hunters and share hunting stories. Buck Wahl, John Gisi, and G.T. Nunn (left to right) relax and share hunting experiences during one of the receptions in the trophy display area. Nunn is a renowned cougar outfitter and guide who donated a hunt that was auctioned off during the weekend activities.

TROPHY STATS

▼ ▼ ▼ ▼ ▼

CATEGORY
Quebec-Labrador Caribou

SCORE
423$^6/_8$

INSIDE SPREAD
35

LENGTH OF MAIN BEAM
Right: 47   Left: 49$^2/_8$

WIDTH OF BROW PALM
Right: 14$^1/_8$ Left: 10$^7/_8$

NUMBER OF POINTS
Right: 23   Left: 23

LOCATION
Riviére Du Gué, Quebec – 2006

HUNTER
Bret J. Wood

QUEBEC-LABRADOR CARIBOU
First Award – 423 ⁶/₈

▼ ▼ ▼ ▼ ▼ ▼ ▼ ▼ ▼

BRET J. WOOD

I can remember every time I have gone hunting in my life. Of course, being only 28 years old helps out. The strange thing is that it seems that no matter what happens, each time is more enjoyable than before. I love to hunt with my dad. Really that's why I go, because he is hunting. When he told me we were going to Canada caribou hunting, I said, "Sure, that sounds great!"

Little did I know I would come back with a trophy Quebec-Labrador caribou of a lifetime, or more realistically, many lifetimes.

Time with Dad

This was my first time hunting in Canada and my first time hunting caribou. I really had no idea what lay ahead, other than what my dad had told me. We flew to Schefferville, Quebec, and were picked up by our outfitters in an old school bus. I was the youngest member of our hunting party, which consisted of my father's friends and co-workers from our hometown. The bus took us to Club Chambeaux's headquarters where we checked in and were told we would be boarding a floatplane to take us to the hunting cabins.

As all of our gear was weighed and loaded into the plane, I was thinking, "How nice could the cabins be if we were flying to the middle of nowhere and if everything had to go out there via floatplane?" Once the loading was complete, it was time for my first floatplane take-off. All I really remember about the take-off was how incredibly loud it was. As we started off to fly to our new home for five days, I looked down, seeing nothing but lakes and brush. I remember thinking that never in my life had I been anywhere so remote.

We flew across the Canadian wilderness, looking down at numerous lakes and streams, circled twice over one of the lakes and started to descend. We were met at the water's edge by the hunters that were waiting to fly back. See-

Photograph by Jack Reneau

Bret J. Wood accepting his plaque and medal from Buck Buckner, Vice President and Chairman of the Big Game Records Committee.

Bret J. Wood is pictured on the bank of Riviére Du Gué in Quebec with his Quebec-Labrador caribou scoring 423-6/8 points. Bret was hunting with his dad during a 2006 hunt when he harvested the bull, which received a First Place Award at the 27th Big Game Awards Program.

ing all of the antlers of the departing hunters quickly gets you excited for the pending hunt. I was really surprised by the cabins; they were really nice—nothing like I had envisioned. There were two cabins with cots where everyone slept, one cabin for a kitchen and one cabin for a restroom with showers. Everyone stowed away their gear and met for dinner at the kitchen cabin to go over the plan for the next couple of days.

We had split up into hunting groups. I was teamed up with my dad and his longtime friend and hunting companion, Les Doll, or "Uncle Les." Having heard talk about the herds of caribou coming through the area, I thought this would be a short boat trip across the lake with our guide Paul Girard to quickly select and take my first caribou. No such luck.

The first couple of days, we sat. Dad said he had seen a caribou across the lake about 3,000 yards away, but Les and I were not so sure. As we sat on this mountaintop looking in all directions for caribou, the sun started to peak through the clouds. For a split second I remember thinking, *This isn't all bad. I might get a little nap in.* Before I could finish my thought, the mosquito hordes came. They were so thick that I couldn't have had enough

layers of spray on to even remotely protect me from them. As I was fighting the
urge just to get up and head down to the
boat, I looked over at my dad and Les.
Both of them had pulled their jackets up
over their heads with only an opening in
the front so one eye could peer out and
search the hillsides for caribou.

QUEBEC-LABRADOR CARIBOU
First Award – 423 6/8

▼ ▼ ▼ ▼ ▼

BRET J. WOOD

The next couple of days were more of the same, a lot of looking and sitting but no
caribou, and time was running out. We were still having a great time even with the lack of
caribou, and to me that was more important. I will admit, though, it would have been nice
to even see a caribou up close. After all the guides discussed the conditions at base camp,
they decided to fly us north to a river where caribou had been spotted. Dad, Les, Paul, and
I loaded up in the floatplane and took off. We flew just a couple of minutes to the landing
area, which was really just a wide spot in the river. We all waded to shore with our bags and
rifles and watched as the plane took off. I thought to myself, *I hope he comes back!*

Knowing the drill and thinking this was going to be like the four previous days,
we sat down just back from the river in the brush line and looked across the water to the
hillside scoping for caribou. I opened my lunch bag to see if there was something to snack
on when Dad tapped me on the shoulder and pointed across the river to the far hillside.
Caribou everywhere, not just one or two or 20, hundreds of them—and all coming our way!
Animal after animal funneling down the hillside all taking different trails disappearing for
a while then coming out in the open on the river's edge right across from us. Without hesitation, they jumped into the river and started across. They were everywhere—upstream,
downstream and more were still making their way down the hillside. Still amazed at the
unbelievable number of caribou coming down off the hill, we noticed that the first ones
were getting out of the river right in front of us, maybe 20 yards away. We were all dead
quiet as they started making their way to the brush line where we were sitting. I went from
not seeing a caribou the day before to almost being stepped on by one. It was one of those
once-in-a-lifetime experiences.

After almost being trampled by a caribou, our guide decided to move us down river
a bit. We were walking in mud that was 2 feet deep from the millions of caribou that had
traveled over the years on the trails we were hiking. While we made our way downstream,
periodically we would pop out to the river's edge to see what was coming down the hill. The
guide was in front of me, with my dad and Les a ways behind, navigating the deep mud. As
the guide turned and started downriver again, I looked straight ahead. Directly in front of
me, two large bulls were coming up the bank out of the river. I couldn't speak. I grunted
towards the guide but he didn't hear me. I turned and looked back, but Dad and Les were
too far back behind me in the mud to see. I threw my rifle up, found the front shoulder and
took the shot. Not really having much time to evaluate or even consider, I knew that I got a
good one, but really had no idea how big he really was. After I shot, Paul the guide wheeled

around to look at me. All he could see was a smoking gun and a caribou running off in the brush. By this time Dad and Les had made their way through the mud to me and I told them all, "I just shot a huge caribou!"

We made our way down to the river's edge and lying there in about six inches of water was my trophy. It was a perfect shot right through the front shoulder with my .300 Winchester Magnum, and I had just taken my first caribou. I knew from pictures that I had seen he was a good one, but really, I had no idea until our guide Paul in his broken English said, "Really good, big bou!" Les and my dad couldn't believe it. I couldn't believe it! They stood ten feet above me on the riverbank shaking their heads in disbelief.

It was getting late by the time we finished taking pictures. Dad and Les had pointed out several times the double shovels and the long rear points this caribou had. There may have been a couple of comments on luck but they were definitely outweighed by congratulatory slaps on the back and congratulations said all around.

The trophy was taken care of and brought back to the wide spot in the river to be picked up by the plane. We were all in high spirits from the day's events. When we reached camp with my trophy, everyone came to see what we got on that day's trip. It was a great time to share my dumb-luck story and my good fortune with the whole hunting camp. I enjoy hunting, but more so the people who I spend time with in the outdoors. It was a trip of a lifetime that I will never forget, not only for taking an animal that was good enough for the records book, but for the time I was able to share with my dad in the Canadian wilderness. ▲

Simon Roosevelt thanked Guy Eastman of *Eastman's Hunting Journal* and *Eastman's Bowhunting Journal*, not only for their sponsorship of the 27th Big Game Awards, but Guy was one of the featured seminar speakers in Reno. His seminar topic—Fair Chase—something Simon's great, great grandfather gave to us all.

TROPHY STATS

▼ ▼ ▼ ▼ ▼

CATEGORY
Quebec-Labrador Caribou

SCORE
422 $^3/_8$

INSIDE SPREAD
37 $^4/_8$

LENGTH OF MAIN BEAM
Right: 51 $^6/_8$ Left: 51 $^6/_8$

WIDTH OF BROW PALM
Right: 15 $^7/_8$ Left: 18 $^3/_8$

NUMBER OF POINTS
Right: 19   Left: 21

LOCATION
Lac Ribero, Quebec – 2006

HUNTER
Donald M. Vickers

344

QUEBEC-LABRADOR CARIBOU
Second Award – 422 ³/₈

▼ ▼ ▼ ▼ ▼ ▼ ▼ ▼ ▼

Donald M. Vickers

My father Joe Vickers, brothers Chad and Vince Vickers, and two close friends, Justin Ervin and Cliff Taylor, accompanied me on this hunt for Quebec-Labrador caribou in 2006. We stayed in a cabin near Lake Ribero in northern Quebec while hunting with Club Chambeaux Outfitters on a self-guided hunt. I had been hunting for three days without seeing any animals, but my dad scored a really nice caribou on September 15th. A few other people in our camp from Pennsylvania had also taken some small caribou.

Self-Guided Double

The day I took this trophy, I got up an hour before sunrise to 35°F weather and hiked a mile and a half to my hunting spot. It was very windy and cold on the plateau where I was hunting, but it was a great spot overlooking the lake and a few good caribou trails. To beat the wind, I used my pack saw and cut some branches off of a pine tree, then leaned against the tree and covered myself with the pine boughs. I figured I would be sitting there all day and was trying to stay warm and dry.

Cliff had just left me to join Justin and Chad who were fishing on a stream a half mile away. It was around 9 a.m. when I glassed a small herd of caribou bulls over 2,000 yards away. The herd was getting ready to cross the lake and then began swimming my way. I watched them for about 15 minutes and was able to pick out the best animals. When the herd reached the near shore, they were about 1,000 yards away, still too far to shoot. When they went through a small stand of trees and disappeared, I thought the hunt was over. About a half hour later, they appeared at 360 yards to my right. I wasn't able to get a shot at the best animal, so I reluctantly shot the second-best. I still wanted to get the biggest bull, so I watched the herd to see what they would do. They began running after the shot and were

Photograph by Jack Reneau

Donald M. Vickers accepting his plaque and medal from Buck Buckner, Vice President and Chairman of the Big Game Records Committee.

Donald M. Vickers is pictured above with the second of two Quebec-Labrador caribou bulls he harvested on his 2006 hunt near Lac Ribero, Quebec. The bull has a final score of 422-3/8 points.

running towards me. About 200 yards out, they calmed down, and I was able to get a shot at the big one. The big bull fell immediately, and I knew I had taken a Boone and Crockett-caliber trophy.

I knew it was a large caribou, but until I saw it up close, I had no idea how big it really was. Once my brothers and Cliff arrived, the real fun began. Six hours later, we had both animals quartered, caped, and on the boat. It would have been great to have both animals in the same photo but due to their size there was no chance of getting them together. I wish the entire hunting party would have been there with me. There were several nice animals in the herd and everyone would have had a chance at a trophy.

My older brother got a large caribou the following day. My younger brother came up empty-handed but was able to get a nice black bear. Cliff was able to get two caribou and my friend Justin never saw a live caribou the entire trip, but was able to bag a couple ptarmigan that I'm sure would have been Boone and Crockett qualifiers if there was a scoring system for them. All in all, it was a very memorable and exciting trip, and I was very fortunate to have had the opportunity to harvest such a beautiful animal. ▲

The 27th Awards Program trophy display was open to the general public free-of-charge from June 22-26, 2010. It was an unprecedented opportunity for thousands of people to view 98 of the finest North American big-game trophies, representing 33 different categories, accepted by B&C during 2007-2009. This couple discusses some of the finer details on this caribou's rack.

TROPHY STATS

▼ ▼ ▼ ▼ ▼

CATEGORY
Quebec-Labrador Caribou

SCORE
411 $^7/_8$

INSIDE SPREAD
39

LENGTH OF MAIN BEAM
Right: 51 $^2/_8$ Left: 49 $^6/_8$

WIDTH OF BROW PALM
Right: 15 $^6/_8$ Left: 5 $^2/_8$

NUMBER OF POINTS
Right: 19   Left: 19

LOCATION
Lac Roz, Quebec – 2006

HUNTER
Aaron Kelly

QUEBEC-LABRADOR CARIBOU
Third Award – 411 ⁷/₈

▼ ▼ ▼ ▼ ▼ ▼ ▼ ▼

AARON KELLY

Aaron Kelly's primary goal on this hunt was to take a trophy Quebec-Labrador caribou with a bow, but he was willing to use a rifle if there was a situation where a trophy bull presented itself, and he couldn't get close enough for a bow shot. In preparation for the hunt, he read everything he could find about judging big caribou bulls. His taxidermist told him that a good shooter bull would have double shovels, great bez points, and "bonus" rear points, if they're present, in addition to a great main frame.

No Regrets

He had all this useful information in the back of his mind when he headed into the field near Lac Roz, Quebec, in 2006 with a rifle, a bow, and two caribou bull tags. He quickly filled the first tag with a very respectable bull that he shot with his bow. It was a nice bull, but it wasn't a giant. Aaron was glad he had a second tag because that allowed him to hold out for a much bigger one the next time after he realized what it takes to make the book.

There wasn't much activity going on where Aaron harvested his first bull, so his outfitter moved him to an area in this vast, remote wilderness where the migration was in full swing. His first objective at his new hunting area was to find a stand where the caribou would naturally funnel right past him for an easy bow shot.

After glassing for a time, Aaron and his guide started moving towards a naturally constricted area where he thought he might be able to ambush a migrating bull. Before they could reach their stand and get in position, however, six cows with a rutting bull beat them to their potential stand. The cows were heading right at him but veered off at about 50 yards when they detected Aaron and his guide. When the bull emerged from the timber, Aaron could clearly

Photograph courtesy of Aaron Kelly

Aaron Kelly sits behind his award-winning Quebec-Labrador caribou that he harvested near Lac Roz in Quebec, during the 2006 season. The bull has a final score of 411-7/8.

see his rack had two well-developed shovels, two bezes, and one long "bonus" rear point on each antler. This bull had everything his taxidermist told him to hold out for.

Aaron quickly realized that the bull, which was obviously rutting, would also veer off and follow the cows before he could get in position for a bow shot and asked his guide to pass him the rifle he was carrying for just this situation. The bull was at 150 yards and moving away before Aaron fired and dropped him in his tracks.

Both Aaron and his guide were excited about the bull he had just harvested, but neither fully realized just how big it really was. The guide was especially pleased that Aaron decided to take it with his rifle. It was a long pack out, but the size of the antlers made it much easier.

There were two other very large-framed bulls in camp when they returned, and two very avid and knowledgeable caribou hunters who had just finished scoring them in the 400-class. Even though Aaron's rack had more antler material, no one paid much attention to it because it didn't appear to be as large as the two 400-point bulls. While Aaron had a gut feeling that his would score better, everyone in camp was surprised when the two other hunters scored his bull at about 420 points. The bottom line is that it scored 411-7/8 points after being judged by the 27th Awards Program Judges Panel.

After taking his bull, Aaron returned and sat near the ambush spot where he shot his B&C bull. Nearly 500 mature bulls passed within 20 yards of him. None were larger than the one he had taken, so he had no regrets about the one he picked. ▲

B&C Photo Archives

Panel Judges Buck Buckner (left) and Larry C. Lack teamed up to verify the score of Nyla K. Swast's First Place Award-winning Central Canada barren ground caribou at 396-4/8. The long main beams, tremendous inside spread, double shovels, bez points, and top palms all contributed greatly to the final score of Swast's trophy. The well developed double shovels were especially significant since there are no deductions for lack of symmetry between them.

TROPHY STATS

▼ ▼ ▼ ▼ ▼

CATEGORY
Quebec-Labrador Caribou

SCORE
407$^3/_8$

INSIDE SPREAD
40$^4/_8$

LENGTH OF MAIN BEAM
Right: 51$^3/_8$ Left: 50$^6/_8$

WIDTH OF BROW PALM
Right: 13$^7/_8$ Left: 2$^5/_8$

NUMBER OF POINTS
Right: 17   Left: 22

LOCATION
Caniapiscau River, Quebec – 2005

HUNTER
Frederick B. Davis

QUEBEC-LABRADOR CARIBOU
Fourth Award – 407 ³/₈
▼ ▼ ▼ ▼ ▼ ▼ ▼ ▼ ▼

Frederick B. Davis

I had done enough thinking about caribou hunting, and I finally decided that if I was going to go, I needed to start making some definite plans. It wasn't long before I was on the phone researching outfitters, and I soon had a hunt booked with Jack Hume Adventures.

My trip began in early September 2005 when I drove to Montreal where other hunters and I would board a plane to Schefferville, Quebec, a town from which several outfitters operated. Shortly after arriving, I met the other

Archery Trophy

hunters that I would be with for the next six days. We were all anxious to begin hunting after talking to other hunters returning from their adventures and seeing the caribou they brought back, including some nice bulls. The next morning, our hunting group boarded a floatplane that took us to a remote camp near the Caniapiscau River.

We had a camp helper, Alfred, and a cook for the week, which really helped things go smoothly since no one in camp had ever hunted caribou before. Our days began with a big breakfast, after which Alfred would take us by boat and drop us off at different crossings that caribou were known to use. In the evenings we would be picked up and brought back to another big meal at camp.

The first two days went by with only two bulls being taken by our group and very few sightings. The third morning was a cold sit by the lake, but I did see four bulls. The problem was that they had bedded on a distant ridge across the lake. When Alfred arrived at lunchtime to check on me, they hadn't shown any signs of moving, so I asked him for a ride across the lake so I could attempt a stalk. By the time I got to where the bulls had been, they were on their feet and just dropping below the ridge in front of me. I moved ahead to where I could see down the hill, expecting to see the four bulls nearby, but instead I saw another group of bulls working their way around the hill away from me. There was no cover to move directly in on them so I quickly backed off and swung around in an attempt to get in front of them. I was almost too late, but things started to get pretty exciting when I saw antler tops just in front of me. I just barely had time to move another couple of yards to a rock where I crouched down and nocked an arrow. In a matter of seconds I could hear the clicking sounds of moving caribou that until this hunt, I had only heard about, getting louder and louder, and I had several bulls coming into view. One was only ten yards away, but I held off knowing that more were approaching. I was enjoying the encounter, though itching for a shot opportunity knowing that I could be busted at any second. The next two bulls that came into view were considerably larger than the others, and the decision to shoot was easy. I picked what

Frederick B. Davis is pictured above with his award-winning Quebec-Labrador caribou taken in 2005. The bull, which scores 407-3/8 points, received the Fourth Place Award at the 27th Big Game Awards Program in Reno, Nevada.

I thought was the larger of the two, and when he stopped by a tree I had earlier ranged at 38 yards I made my move. He looked my way as I drew, but it was too late. My arrow was on its way. At the shot, he and the other 20 or so caribou bolted in as many different directions, but I kept my eye on him and I immediately knew the shot had been true.

I was excited and immediately got back to the top of the hill where I could radio back that I was going to need some help. I knew that I had shot a big bull, but I did not realize how big until we found him about 120 yards from where the blood trail started. Alfred was very surprised at the size of the bull and told me that it was very big. After stripping the velvet off back at camp we took some quick measurements, just to get an idea of the score. Even though I had limited knowledge of caribou antlers, I still realized that he was an exceptional bull. I never had him officially scored until three years later. I didn't personally know any measurers, and hauling him around was a hassle since I had a shoulder mount done as soon as I returned from my trip.

After the official scoring, I realized how fortunate I had been to take this bull. He ended up getting to be part of the display at the Pope and Young convention in Denver, Colorado, in 2009, and he was also sent to Boone and Crockett Club's 27th Awards Program Banquet in Reno, Nevada—both of which I expect to be once-in-a-lifetime honors. I may never get a shot at another animal as big as this; however, I will enjoy the memories from this hunt and the events that followed for the rest of my life. ▲

Award-Winning Moments

B&C Photo Archives

Terry French, the Minister of Tourism, Culture and Recreation for Newfoundland and Labrador, was instrumental in the auction donation of the woodland caribou hunt from Bob Efford's Hunting Adventures. Through the filming of this hunt for the Club's television series it is hopeful that more light will be shed on the growing concern of declining woodland caribou populations in Newfoundland.

TROPHY STATS

▼ ▼ ▼ ▼ ▼

CATEGORY
Pronghorn

SCORE
91$^4/_8$

LENGTH OF HORN
Right: 17$^2/_8$ Left: 17$^2/_8$

BASE CIRCUMFERENCE
Right: 7$^4/_8$ Left: 7$^3/_8$

PRONG LENGTH
Right: 6$^5/_8$ Left: 6$^4/_8$

LOCATION
Harding Co., New Mexico – 2006

HUNTER
Larry J. Landes

PRONGHORN
First Award – 91 ⁴/₈

▼ ▼ ▼ ▼ ▼ ▼ ▼ ▼ ▼

LARRY J. LANDES

Late August of 2006 found me and my good friend Robert Johnston in the Grass Range of northeastern New Mexico. We were trying to close the distance between us and the largest pronghorn I have ever had the opportunity to stalk. The temperature had to be in the 90s for the duration of the stalk, and we already finished the last of our water when we left Robert's truck two hours earlier. We were in plain sight of the big buck, and with our heads down and moving at a snail's pace,

A Banner Year

we were making progress. If the heat and cover issues weren't hard enough to deal with, we also had to hope that we didn't come face-to-face with any other critters that call this area home—scorpions and rattlesnakes had come to mind.

I had seen this buck the day before the season opened and knew then I would take him or go home with an unused tag. With a three-day season to hunt, and it being well into the second day, the pressure was on.

I had done some guiding for Jamie Baird of Circle Heart Outfitters in this part of New Mexico where he had access to some landowner permits. When a friend of mine, Steve York, who also guided for Jamie, called to tell me they had seen a huge buck on one of the properties, he asked if I would be interested in hunting him. Considering the last pronghorn tag in my home state of Arizona had been over 20 years earlier, I jumped at the chance. Later that year, Jamie called me with bad news: he hadn't been able to get permission to hunt the particular ranch with this big buck, and asked if I wanted my money back.

My reply was, "Of course not!" I was ready to hunt.

The big buck decided his nap was over and started to feed in our direction. Lying in the prone position with a bipod on my .25-06 Encore, I should have made a perfect shot but

Photograph by Jack Reneau

Larry J. Landes accepting his plaque and medal from Buck Buckner, Vice President and Chairman of the Big Game Records Committee.

Photograph courtesy of Larry J. Landes

Larry J. Landes is pictured above with his pronghorn scoring 91-4/8 points.

I didn't. He dropped in his tracks but needed a second shot. After the picture taking and field dressing were taken care of, the heat and no water had taken its toll.

Within 15 minutes we were back at the ranch house where we were staying. Cold drinks in the shade and I thought I might survive. In the meantime, Robert and Chester Kimber, the ranch owner, had a tape measure out and began to add up the numbers. Their score was within a quarter inch of what he officially scored later, a gross score of 92-3/8 and a net of 91-4/8. That was a banner year for big bucks. Out of four hunters, three of us killed pronghorn that make the records book. While we have hunted that area before and since that year—and always kill nice bucks—2006 was something special. ▲

Robert H. Hanson (left) and Patrick H. McKenzie were one of the teams of judges that diligently verified the score of Helgie H. Eymundson's non-typical whitetail deer at 274 points. Not only are the antlers uniquely palmated, but there are 16 and 20 measurable points on the right and left antlers, respectively. The lengths of the abnormal points alone total 102-4/8 inches. Eymundson took this trophy, which is Alberta's third-largest non-typical, at Cross Lake in 2007.

TROPHY STATS

▼ ▼ ▼ ▼ ▼

CATEGORY
Pronghorn

SCORE
$91^2/_8$

LENGTH OF HORN
Right: $14^2/_8$ Left: $14^5/_8$

BASE CIRCUMFERENCE
Right: $7^4/_8$ Left: $7^5/_8$

PRONG LENGTH
Right: $7^2/_8$ Left: $6^4/_8$

LOCATION
Natrona Co., Wyoming – 2008

HUNTER
Michael J. Wheeler

PRONGHORN
Second Award – 91 ²/₈
▼ ▼ ▼ ▼ ▼ ▼ ▼ ▼

MICHAEL J. WHEELER

Michael J. Wheeler felt that all-too-common disappointment of the unsuccessful draw notice at his home in Manchester, Michigan, after applying for deer and pronghorn permits in Wyoming. Undeterred, Mike checked the leftover tag lists showing units available for over-the-counter purchase. He and his hunting partner, David Rowe, contemplated their options and decided to return to the same area they hunted the previous year in Natrona County. While not the renowned Carbon County,

Over-the Counter Tag

Natrona has produced 122 records-book pronghorns, placing it in fourth place in Wyoming.

Two years earlier, Mike and Dave had taken two average pronghorn bucks, and in 2008 they were looking for big mule deer. They had decided that if they were to fill a pronghorn tag, it had to be something big—a "Wow!" buck in Mike's words.

Wyoming is a do-it-yourself hunter's paradise—evident from the success these two have achieved two years in a row. Mike and David planned to spend two weeks from late September to early October hunting with a few days set aside for setting up camp and making sure their firearms were sighted in.

Opening day, a shot at a respectable 6x5 mule deer presented itself to Mike, and he decided it was the trophy he was looking for. The next morning, David connected on the second respectable mule deer for the pair. Once their deer tags were filled, it was time to find a couple of pronghorns.

On the third morning, it didn't take long for the duo to get onto some pronghorns that met their criteria. After a few unsuccessful stalks, they broke for lunch. From camp, David spotted a herd of pronghorns on a nearby section of state land with a buck worth some effort. Using the topography to his advantage, Mike closed the distance but was still out of his comfort range. From the vantage point he

Photograph by Jack Reneau

Michael J. Wheeler accepting his plaque and medal from Buck Buckner, Vice President and Chairman of the Big Game Records Committee.

Michael J. Wheeler is pictured above with his massive, award-winning pronghorn scoring 91-2/8 points. The buck was harvested with an over-the-counter tag in Natrona County, Wyoming, in 2008.

was using for cover, he glassed the herd and determined they showed no signs of moving, so he dropped back behind the ridge and quickly cut the distance in half. The last few yards he crawled to a rock pile. From 175 yards, his .30-06 brought his stalk—and season—to a very successful conclusion.

At 91-2/8 points, Mike's buck ties with Wyoming's state record that was taken in renowned Carbon County in 1989 by Bill Boatman. The most unique parts of his record animal are the mass measurements. While most of the highest-ranking pronghorn trophies carry horn lengths of 16 to 18 inches, the length of Mike's buck's longer horn is a modest 14-5/8 inches; the shorter horn is 14-2/8 inches. These measurements immediately tell you, he had to make it elsewhere. Sixty inches of Mike's buck's horns come from the circumference and prong measurements. The larger base tapes an amazing 7-5/8 inches and the larger D-2 (second circumference) measures 9-1/8 inches. The left and right prongs (cutters) come in at an impressive 6-4/8 inches and 7-2/8 inches, respectively. There are only two inches of total deductions. ▲

B&C Photo Archives

Joe Bouch (left) and his son Adam share their story and photographs of Adam's B&C typical whitetail, scoring 162-7/8 points, with Canadian Official Measurer Rick Berreth (r). Adam was 14 years old at the time he took his trophy, so he was invited to participate in B&C's first Youth Recognition Program in Reno. He was one of 73 youths, age 16 and under, with a trophy accepted in B&C's 27th Awards Program.

TROPHY STATS

▼ ▼ ▼ ▼ ▼

CATEGORY
Bison

SCORE
$133^2/_8$

LENGTH OF HORN
Right: $17^6/_8$ Left: $18^5/_8$

BASE CIRCUMFERENCE
Right: $15^1/_8$ Left: $15^7/_8$

GREATEST SPREAD
$34^5/_8$

LOCATION
Teton Co., Wyoming – 2007

HUNTER
Edward D. Riekens, Jr.

BISON
First Award – 133 ²/₈

▼ ▼ ▼ ▼ ▼ ▼ ▼ ▼

EDWARD D. RIEKENS, JR.

Well it's about damn time, I thought to myself as I read the mail.

I had just opened my annually delivered confirmation letter from the Wyoming Game and Fish Department, this year letting me know that I was number 22 on the list for bison hunts. I had been applying for the limited bison hunt since around 1990 when I got out of the U.S. Navy. Wyoming takes all the applicants and randomly assigns a number to each hunter. They then work down the list with the available tags each year, starting with number one. After 16 years of the perpetual resignation that evolved from seeing that my draw number was too high, this time I knew that I had an almost-guaranteed chance to pursue one of the massive historical icons of the American West. I would only need the animal's cooperation to provide me with the opportunity of a lifetime.

The Mammoth

Since these sanctioned management hunts began here in Wyoming, a hunter has had to count on whether or not enough bison would migrate out of Yellowstone National Park in a timely manner. Their migration takes place annually onto the Bridger-Teton National Forest from Grand Teton and Yellowstone National Parks, where they may not legally be hunted. In most years, between 20 and 30 bulls made the trip in time and were available for the annual quota.

After I received my letter, the rest of the spring and summer months were spent in constant preparation for the chore that I was anticipating if I was to be good enough to get a shot at one of the enormous beasts. My other yearly pursuits for elk, deer, and pronghorn really took a back seat to this once-in-a-lifetime opportunity. I checked and double-checked my equipment, scavenged and borrowed extras, not sure what to expect after I had a massive animal on the ground.

In August, the federal government lifted

Photograph by Jack Reneau

Edward D. Riekens, Jr., accepting his plaque and medal from Buck Buckner, Vice President and Chairman of the Big Game Records Committee.

Edward D. Riekens, Jr., is pictured above with his award-winning bison taken in 2007. The bull is the seventh largest bison ever recorded by Boone and Crockett Club.

an injunction that for years had put an end to allowing bison to be hunted on the National Elk Refuge. This cleared the way for the issuance of more than 300 bison permits to reduce overgrazing.

That's just about par, I figured. I finally draw a nice, low number and they start handing tags out like candy. It wouldn't matter so much I reasoned, as I knew that tags would be issued in blocks to keep everyone from descending upon the area all at once. I knew I would be one of the first, and I aimed to make the most of it.

I scheduled my vacation time for the year and planned a scouting trip to the area for the second half of September. That way, I could casually hunt for deer and elk, which would be open, and judge the buffalo-harvesting situation for the cooler weather later in October. I was missing my archery elk and deer hunting in doing so, but for a one-tag-per-lifetime bison hunt, I was more than willing. As a committed bowhunter, I hadn't even carried a firearm while hunting in over 10 years.

My gear had been loaded up and ready to go for weeks, so after work on September 13th, I left for the Grand Teton region north of Jackson Hole. After many weeks of horribly dry, arid weather, as luck would have it, it was pouring rain when I left Cheyenne. Driving along, envisioning how this trip might turn out, I passed Laramie, and the rain suddenly let up. I was just as suddenly a witness to the most vivid, most brightly shining rainbow that I have ever seen. I took this as a most positive omen and started to feel very good.

I passed through numerous small thunderstorms as I approached the Teton Valley in the darkness. When I finally arrived to the area that was close to where I wanted to be, I unknowingly had parked my camper in such a position that provided me a second vision of pure Godliness and beauty. When I awoke and stepped outside, I saw the sunrise gleaming off of Grand Teton's east slope right in front of me.

Man, something special is gonna happen! I could tangibly feel it, just as I did when I saw the number 22 on my letter and when I saw the rainbow. I spent the rest of the day setting up camp near a secret area known to insiders as "where big buffalo bulls like to hang out away from the herds." I became enthralled watching two big boys catching the late-day sun that afternoon, about 80 yards below me.

I would have to wait until Monday morning to buy my tag anyway, so I spent the next two days scouting the entire secluded country, watching bull after bull for hours at a time, and getting antsy—many times wishing I was already tagged up and legal to take any one of the fine animals I had been watching. What a truly incredible weekend it was.

BISON
First Award – 133 $^2/_8$

▼ ▼ ▼ ▼ ▼

EDWARD D. RIEKENS, JR.

I bought my license Monday morning at the Jackson District Game and Fish office and went about my scouting in a couple different areas. Again, I looked over bull after massive bull, although many of them were still making residence in Grand Teton National Park, and therefore, were not fair game to hunt.

By Tuesday, September 18, I was more than excited. I made a call to a well-known local buffalo expert in Jackson because I was ambivalent about the chore to follow after downing a 2,000-plus pound animal. He told me to leave the bulls that I had been watching and go check out a big one in another "secret" drainage. I headed into that section of the forest and hunted the drainage all day, not seeing anything.

I decided to start over by going back out of the forest and working my way back in again. I was making my way around a large rock tailing pile and, *Oh my God, look at the size of that guy!* I backtracked slowly, trying to stifle my heavy breathing and my machine-gun heart rate. He had been within 25 yards of my last step, but I had no cover to work from there. I retreated back into the trees and started easing back toward where the monster had been. As I located him again, he started grazing, keeping his backside toward me with each lateral step I took. I carefully worked my way through the trees, trying to get him in my old-school Redfield scope. He finally lifted his head to look around, and I shot without hesitation. The bull went down with one quick shot from my .300 Weatherby Mark V Deluxe, perfectly placed six inches behind the horn base. The mammoth was on the ground even before I let off the trigger.

My forecasts were correct: when he fell, the real work would begin. The closer I got to him, the more he seemed to grow, beyond anything I had imagined possible before. My magnificent animal was green-scored as a potential World's Record at the butcher's in Jackson. He put the hanging equipment to the ultimate test, hanging just over 2,400 pounds dressed. I returned to Jackson three weeks later to pick up over 1,200 pounds of buffalo meat in 18 large coolers packed to their capacities. I took home the meat, skull, and hide and awaited the end of the 60-day drying period. On December 9, he was scored at 133-2/8 points. His score was verified by the 27th Awards Program Judges Panel, and he now ranks number 7 in B&C. I later received word from the Wyoming Game and Fish department that my monster buffalo was only 8 years old.

This once-in-a-lifetime hunt was everything and more than I could have asked it to be. It was a true blessing, and more than an honor to successfully hunt one of the descendants of the very few Yellowstone bison that still survived in the very early 1900s. Yet, unlike the slaughter of the late 1800s, my hunt helped manage herd numbers and keep it in balance with the carrying capacity of the land. ▲

TROPHY STATS

▼ ▼ ▼ ▼ ▼

CATEGORY
Bison

SCORE
129²/₈

LENGTH OF HORN
Right: 19⁷/₈   Left: 20

BASE CIRCUMFERENCE
Right: 14⁴/₈   Left: 14⁴/₈

GREATEST SPREAD
32

LOCATION
Custer Co., South Dakota – 2007

HUNTER
Art D. Tong

BISON
Second Award – 129 ²/₈

▼ ▼ ▼ ▼ ▼ ▼ ▼ ▼ ▼

ART D. TONG

This story really began in 2003 when my wife Cindy decided to surprise me and submitted an application on my behalf for a bison hunt at Custer State Park, South Dakota. When the results came out in July, I received the usual thanks, but no-thanks notice and a refund check.

This process repeated itself until 2007 when, to my amazement, I drew one of the coveted bull tags. While I was ecstatic at drawing

A Magnificent Beast

the tag, I had a serious conflict to resolve. A month earlier, my doctor had informed me that I needed total hip-replacement surgery, so I had to decide if I should have the surgery before or after the hunt. Neither prospect was great, but I opted to have the surgery after the hunt, realizing full well the difficulty I would have hiking during the hunt. At least there wouldn't be a risk of damaging a new hip by using it too soon.

After months of anticipation, a friend and I drove from northeastern California to South Dakota in early December. We both lived on the eastern slope of the Sierra Nevada range, which is known for its paralyzing, people-stopping snowfalls. We were comfortable with snowy driving conditions but totally underestimated the wrath of Mother Nature.

We entered the Wasatch Mountains in Utah at the same time ice and snow began to fall. Little did we realize, however, that we would soon be in the heart of the worst ice storm to hit the West in decades. From Utah to South Dakota we drove on a solid sheet of ice with howling winds and swirling snow. Much of the time visibility was limited to just a few feet.

About midnight of the second day, we were desperate for a place to stop for the night. Somewhere in mid-Wyoming, on the edge of the Red Desert, we spotted lights in the distance

Photograph by Jack Reneau

Art D. Tong accepting his plaque and medal from Buck Buckner, Vice President and Chairman of the Big Game Records Committee.

Photograph courtesy of Art D. Tong

Art D. Tong standing behind his award-winning bison taken in Custer County, South Dakota. The bull, which scores 129-2/8 points received a Second Place Award.

and turned off the highway. The only place we found open in this small town was the local pizza joint. Upon inquiring about rooms, we were informed there were none to be had.

The next town was Rawlins, which was a mere 45 miles away. What a wild ride those next few miles turned out to be. In one 10-mile stretch, we passed no less than 50 big rigs that had slid off the highway and were strewn about on their backs like children's toys carelessly cast aside.

We made Rawlins a little after 3 a.m., found a hotel and caught a few hours' sleep before heading out again. After another day and a half of very slow going, we finally arrived at our destination in South Dakota's Black Hills.

Opening morning, we were off to meet our guide Chad Kremer well before daylight. It was a balmy 7°F. The stars were out, and we thought that was a good omen. When we hooked up with Chad, we jumped in his truck and were off on our hunt for a trophy bison.

Chad planned the first day of the hunt to be a scouting mission to check out our opportunities. Then we'd spend the next few days closing the deal. As we made our way up the mountain, the sky began to lighten, and we witnessed a glorious sunrise without a cloud in sight. We were being smiled upon by the hunting gods!

We are both fairly adept at field judging deer and elk. However, neither of us have had any experience with bison. We relied solely on Chad's advice for a trophy-caliber interpretation and soon discovered that Chad really is a bison expert. He gave us a quick rundown on the basics of field judging. Realizing this was probably a once-in-a lifetime tag, I was hoping to harvest a bull that would make Boone and Crockett Club's records book, and I was willing to hold out to the bitter end if necessary.

A couple of hours into the hunt we spotted a solitary bull on a hillside in heavy timber. We were able to sneak within a 100 yards of him to take a good look. The sheer magnitude of his size was almost incomprehensible. He stood nearly 6 feet at the top of his hump, and his head was enormous. He was sporting a beautiful long, black shaggy winter hide, which made him appear even larger. Chad estimated this bull to be 10 to 12 years old. Upon closer scrutiny, we noticed he was missing a large chunk out of the middle of his right horn, so we decided to pass.

By the end of the first day, we had spotted 10 mature bulls. There was, however, only one bull that stood out above all the others. I decided this was the one I had to have. However, this bull was not in a place where I could make a good clean shot, so we decided to attempt to locate him the following day under better conditions.

BISON
Second Award – 129 $^2/_8$

▼ ▼ ▼ ▼ ▼

ART D. TONG

The next day, we located "my bull" at 2 p.m. He had joined several other bulls in the timber halfway up a hill. We managed to get within 125 yards of them undetected. As they moved around in the trees, it became extremely difficult to keep track of my bull. By this time, my hip was excruciatingly painful, and I was in no shape to track a wounded bison, so I wanted to make sure the shot was good and to drop the bull in place. We waited until the bull moved into a small clearing in the sun and presented a clear broadside shot. Ka-boom! One shot from my .300 Magnum and the bull dropped in its tracks.

What a feeling I had upon approaching this magnificent beast. His sheer size was indescribable. His hide was jet black, very dense, and in prime winter condition. The mass and length of his horns far exceeded our expectations. Chad estimated the bull to be 9 years old and weighing somewhere around 2,000 pounds. After the 60-day drying period, it was officially scored at 129-2/8.

At the 27th Big Game Awards Program in Reno, Nevada, I received the Second Place Award for my bison and dedicated it to the memory of my late wife Cindy. I am sad to say that she passed away a few months prior to the hunt. ▲

TROPHY STATS

▼ ▼ ▼ ▼ ▼

CATEGORY
Bison

SCORE
126⁶/₈

LENGTH OF HORN
Right: 18⁶/₈   Left: 18⁴/₈

BASE CIRCUMFERENCE
Right: 15²/₈   Left: 15¹/₈

GREATEST SPREAD
30

LOCATION
Custer Co., South Dakota – 2007

HUNTER
David W. Baxter

BISON
Third Award – 126 ⁶/₈

▼ ▼ ▼ ▼ ▼ ▼ ▼ ▼ ▼

DAVID W. BAXTER

Wild Bill Hickok, Calamity Jane, and Crazy Horse. Deadwood and the Homestake Mine, the Badlands and Wounded Knee. These names and places are familiar to most Americans for their role in the history of the expansion of the United States through the west and their appearance in literature and cinematography. What child hasn't memorized the names of the four American presidents whose images were coaxed with dynamite and jackhammer from the granite of Mount Rushmore: Washington, Lincoln, Jefferson, and that great American hunter and conservationist, Theodore Roosevelt? For decades, southwestern South Dakota has been, and continues to be, a popular vacation destination for innumerable families who come to enjoy the exquisite natural beauty and history of the Black Hills and its environs.

Sportsmen have long felt the allure of this area too. The abundant pheasant, deer, elk, and bighorn sheep found there are highly regarded, and the hunting seasons are looked upon with almost religious reverence by hunters, both resident and nonresident alike. With all the aforementioned attractions, it is hard to believe that South Dakota is home to another American treasure and has the honored distinction of being one of six states to be home to a huntable herd of bison.

Just south of Mount Rushmore lies Custer State Park. The trophy hunter in search of a bison will find one of the largest herds of bison in North America living in one of the nation's most impressive state parks. Some 1,500 bison roam the park's 73,000 acres, and each year, 10 to 12 older bulls are offered for hunting via a lottery drawing. These hunts not only offer a few very fortunate hunters an opportunity to pursue an icon of the American West, but also serve as a management tool to keep the herd at its optimal size for the available habitat.

A mature bison bull is the largest land animal indigenous to North America, often

Photograph by Jack Reneau

David W. Baxter accepting his plaque and medal from Buck Buckner, Vice President and Chairman of the Big Game Records Committee.

David W. Baxter with his award-winning bison taken in Custer County, South Dakota, during the 2007 season. The bull has a final score of 126-6/8 points and received a Third Place Award at the 27th Big Game Awards Program in Reno, Nevada.

exceeding one ton in weight, and Custer bulls get especially large. A glance at the trophy entries in the Boone and Crockett Club's records book will overwhelmingly confirm this fact. In my copy of the 12th edition of the Club's *Records of North American Big Game*, 16 of the top 50 trophies come from Custer County, South Dakota, meaning Custer State Park. In the years that sport hunting has been allowed in the park, over 80 percent of the trophy bulls harvested in the park have exceeded the minimum score of 115 points to qualify for inclusion in the records book. Custer State Park continues to be a location in which the harvesting of a truly record-class bison is attainable.

My three-day hunt in the park was scheduled for the first week of December 2007. That gave me a little time to chase some Texas whitetails and get my Mark X Whitworth .375 H&H sighted in. This gun likes heavy bullets and can print 1-1/2 inch groups all day long with the 300-grain Nosler partition bullets, so I felt plenty confident when I arrived in Rapid City the morning before the hunt. After a buffalo burger for lunch, I had an afternoon to myself to see Mount Rushmore and the snow-covered Black Hills. For dinner, I found a restaurant serving BBQ buffalo ribs. They were easily as good as any I've ever eaten back home and put me in the perfect frame of mind for the next day's hunt for a big bull.

My guide was Chad Kremer, the herd manager for Custer State Park's buffalo. He explained that in winter the old bulls tend to leave the cows and calves and hang out in the more remote canyons alone or in small bachelor groups. Conveniently, Chad knew all the honey holes and recommended that we spend the first day locating and sizing up several bulls before deciding on the one to try for later. This process was very entertaining, and I scored many photos of bighorn sheep, elk, whitetails, mule deer, and pronghorns in the picturesque foothills of the park. We admired several large bison bulls too, and while not tame by any means, they allowed us to approach fairly closely before moving away.

That first day, we found two mature 10-year-old bulls that were truly impressive. One was part of a group of three bulls in the Lost Canyon area. His horns possessed great length with bases that exceeded 15 inches in circumference. The second bull was a solitary individual that we found near the park boundary above Red Canyon. This guy had heavier horns, but they were a bit shorter and a little broomed at the tips. Both trophies would score well over 120 points, so which one did I like best? To put it in a sheep hunter's perspective, should I opt for the bison with especially long horns for a bull of that age, similar to the trait of the Chadwick ram whose intact lamb tips vaulted this amazing sheep to near un-attainability, or go with the classic mass and broomed tips of an old mature bull as seen on Guinn Crousen's 208-3/8 points Cadomin, Alberta, ram? Either way, it was a happy problem to have as there was no wrong answer. I told Chad that I would sleep on it and let him know in the morning.

The easy solution would have been to try for the bull that would score the best. But the difference between a head that will go high in B&C and one that will simply look great on the wall is only a quarter-inch here or an eighth-inch there. Chad was certainly as ex-perienced as they come in judging trophy bison, but even his expert evaluation was only general in nature, and offered up with no small degree of latitude.

Knowing that I couldn't go wrong with either bull, I finally decided that I'd like to try for the Lost Canyon bull with the longer horns. If we were unable to find him, we would spend the last day looking for the broomed bull.

The next morning we headed out for Lost Canyon. On the way to where we had last seen the bull, we admired more than a hundred pronghorns feeding in the open pastures there. By this point in my hunt, I had also come to realize that, while my primary objective was a buffalo, I was enjoying the often and unexpected sightings of other wildlife just as much.

Soon we were bumping up the rough track into Lost Canyon. And before long, we found the bachelor herd of three bulls not far from where we'd left them the day before. We closed the last few hundred yards on foot. At 53 yards, the shot was almost anticlimactic.

My bull unofficially green-scored in the mid-120s range. After the required 60-day drying period, he was officially scored at 126-6/8 points. After the Judges Panel verification, my bull was confirmed as tied for 35th place in the All-time records book at that score.

So where do the buffalo roam? Custer State Park! ▲

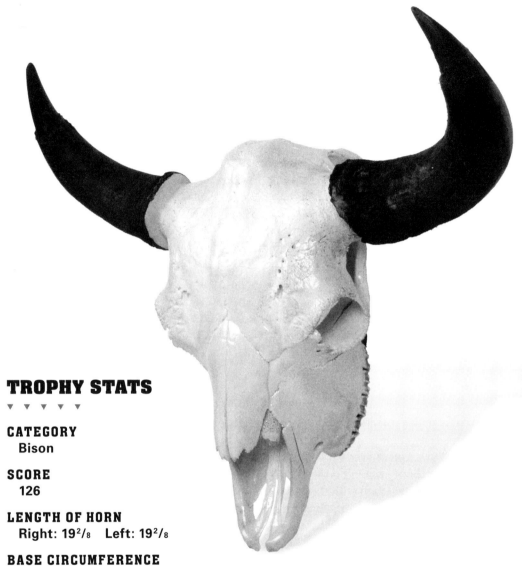

TROPHY STATS

▼ ▼ ▼ ▼ ▼

CATEGORY
Bison

SCORE
126

LENGTH OF HORN
Right: $19^2/_8$ Left: $19^2/_8$

BASE CIRCUMFERENCE
Right: 14   Left: $13^6/_8$

GREATEST SPREAD
$32^3/_8$

LOCATION
Teton Co., Wyoming – 2007

HUNTER
Gerald C. Newmeyer

BISON
Fourth Award – 126

▼ ▼ ▼ ▼ ▼ ▼ ▼ ▼ ▼

GERALD C. NEWMEYER

The beginning of my bison hunt actually started with a question of whether my older brother and I wanted to go bison hunting or deer hunting. After a lengthy debate, we eventually decided to head out for bison, and on October 13, we headed towards Jackson, Wyoming. I couldn't purchase my license until October 15, when the Jackson District Game and Fish office opened, so we planned to take advantage of the extra couple days to scout.

We'll Drag 'Em

The first night we stayed in Dubois, Wyoming, since we really didn't have any reason to rush. The following morning, we got up and headed for the Teton National Forest to unload the 4-wheeler and look around a bit before going into Jackson for the evening. While scouting, we found some very fresh sign, but no bison. We did, however, meet a couple from Dubois that had just seen a very nice bull in a meadow not a quarter mile from where we were sitting. From what they told us, he sounded content and we elected to let him be until the next day when I had my license.

First thing on the 15th we got up and went to the Wyoming Game and Fish office. I purchased my license at about nine in the morning and decided not to drive the 50-plus miles out to the area we had scouted the previous day. Instead, we would try an area called Shadow Mountain just outside the boundary of Teton National Park. While we were getting ready to head into the woods, another hunter and his granddaughter from Cheyenne were coming out. We got to talking and when we asked if they had seen any bison where they were hunting they said no, but they had seen a very nice one on the National Elk Refuge that morning. Then they offered to show us where they had seen him and naturally we agreed to follow them back to the refuge. Fortunately, they had opened the refuge in 2007 to bison hunting so he was definitely worth a look.

On our way to one of the designated parking areas, we spotted a large bull across Flat Creek, very near the national forest border. Once we made it to the designated parking area we started back in his direction trying to get a better look at him. When we got to the area where we had spotted him, he was no longer there. I worked my way down across the creek to try and relocate the bull. After getting across the creek I headed downstream. I pushed down about a half mile and then turned and headed up to the national forest boundary. Working my way up through the clearings, I would look down into the little depressions that I could see between myself and the creek. After another half mile or so, I topped a little rise and spotted the bull bedded down in a depression out of sight from the road. After quickly sizing him up, I decided that he was what I had been looking for and started working my way closer to ensure a clean, ethical kill. Finally, after crawling through a lot of sagebrush, I got to within 100 yards and prepared to take the shot. I put the crosshairs on the spot recommended in the pre-hunt brochures and squeezed the trigger. The bison stood up and just looked at me. I put two follow up shots into the vitals and one more straight on.

When I walked up to him and saw the size, I just couldn't believe it. I have hauled a lot of elk, moose, and other animals out of the woods and this guy was going to take more than my brother and I to get the meat out before spoilage started. He and I are 73 and 63 years old, respectively, and this bull was probably close to 2,000 pounds. We had an elk cart, thinking that we could get him out of the field as quickly as possible, but decided to call for some reinforcements, namely an outfit called "You Tag'em and We'll Drag'em." ▲

B&C Photo Archives

Danford Hunter and Tim Stevens from the San Carlos Apache Tribe awaiting the call for Auction LOT NO. 27LA14-B, a trophy Coues' whitetail and black bear hunt donated to the Club by the San Carlos Tribe. These tribal lands are mostly known for record-class bulls, but elk are not the only trophy opportunities offered by the tribe.

TROPHY STATS
▼ ▼ ▼ ▼ ▼

CATEGORY
Rocky Mountain Goat

SCORE
54

LENGTH OF HORN
Right: 11   Left: $11^{1}/_{8}$

BASE CIRCUMFERENCE
Right: $5^{7}/_{8}$ Left: 6

GREATEST SPREAD
$7^{3}/_{8}$

LOCATION
Kalum Lake, British Columbia – 2008

HUNTER
A.C. Smid

ROCKY MOUNTAIN GOAT
First Award – 54

▼ ▼ ▼ ▼ ▼ ▼ ▼ ▼ ▼

A.C. SMID

The first Rocky Mountain goat I ever harvested was in 2006. It was a beautiful goat, but it had a summer coat. So in September 2008, while hunting moose with my guide Roger, I mentioned to him that in some future year I would love to harvest a winter billy. He said that shouldn't be a problem, explaining that his good friend Bob Milligan, of Terrace, British Columbia, runs Milligan's Outfitting, and his area has some of the best goats in British Columbia.

A Goat for Pops

"Great!" I said. "See what you can do for some future year." End of conversation.

In November 2008, my phone rang, and it was Roger. He said Bob Milligan had called about a trophy goat he had spotted, and they had been unsuccessful in hunting it for the last couple of weeks due to poor weather conditions. Bob was scheduled to take some needed time off, but instead called Roger and asked if I could get up there—now! The rut was coming, and Bob knew the billy would hang in the same general area with the nannies. This was a once-in-a-lifetime trophy, and the pictures that he took through his spotting scope would verify that.

I explained to Roger that in five days I was headed to western Montana on an elk hunt with my good friend, Ray Godin of Superior, Montana; and then over to Lewistown in central Montana to celebrate Thanksgiving week with my wife Melissa and my in-laws. Roger knew that my father-in-law Richard, who I fondly refer to as Pops, was dying of cancer, and I didn't think he would make it to Christmas. Roger understood the dilemma I was in, and just asked me to think about it and to get back to him as soon as possible.

After hanging up the phone with Roger, I opened my email and downloaded the pictures. No doubt about it—a trophy goat of a lifetime!

"Timing is everything" they say, but this time, there was no time for delay. I explained the situation to my wife Melissa and she understood the meaning of a trophy of a lifetime. She encouraged me that if I was going to go that I should get my butt in gear and not dilly dally around. She also knew that calling off the elk hunt would not be hard, but the call to Pops would be the tough one. At first he understood, but then he didn't, and I'll just leave it at that.

On November 18, Roger picked me up at the Smithers Regional Airport. The next day we sighted in my rifle, gathered Roger's gear, and prepared for the journey. He said there was no way in hell that he was going to miss this trip. He dropped everything he was doing to be part of my hunt. On November 20th, we boogied west to Terrace, which is about 70 miles from the coast.

Upon arrival, we were greeted by Bob, his wife Michelle, and their two boys Bobby and Billy. There was also Brodie Cardinal, one of Bob's guides who would be on the hunt as well.

After settling in at their home for the night, and going through the customary small chat, we got right down to the business at hand. Bob explained that the hunt was going to be a tough one. The weather won't cooperate, the climb will be long and steep, and the snow will be about 6- to 8-feet deep. The plan is basic: drive the pickup until the snow gets too deep, unload the modified ATV with its snow tracks, and drive it to the end of the logging road, pulling a sled. Strap on the 12x14-inch snowshoes and hoof it from there.

IT WAS REALLY DIFFICULT TO DETERMINE WHO WAS WHO BECAUSE OF THE DISTANCE UNTIL OUR BILLY STEPPED FRONT AND CENTER. NOT ONLY DID HE HAVE THE HORNS, BUT THE MASS OF HIS BODY DOMINATED THE OTHERS. HE ALSO HAD A RED THROAT SASH THAT WAS LIKELY CAUSED BY ANOTHER BILLY DURING A DOMINANCE FIGHT.

The next morning, shortly after 5 a.m., we were headed down the road and executing the plan that we discussed the night before. Over the last couple of days, the snow had been coming down heavily, and today was no exception. If we didn't have a break in the weather by 10 a.m., we wouldn't strap on the snowshoes because the day would be done. There wouldn't be enough time to make it to the goats even if we got a break in the weather. We sat waiting in the snow. Before long, 10 a.m. arrived, and our day was done.

Day two was the same drill, down the road until the end, snowing again just like yesterday, however much lighter, and there was something in Bob's facial expression that led me to believe that something was amiss. Last night when we Googled the weather forecast, there was a hole forming that might give us a short break before a new storm would hit. As we looked up into the morning sky, Bob turned to us and said, "Gear up, put on the snowshoes, and we are outta here."

Brodie led, followed by Bob, Roger, and me. After hiking for about two hours up a steep, tree-lined ridge, we finally came to the first—and last—opening on our way up. It was about 300 yards long and interspersed with trees. It was here where we would first have an opportunity to glass up the mountain and look into the bowls for the goats. Just as Bob had predicted there they were—about 15 in all—nannies and kids feeding while the three billies went about their power struggle. We took out the spotting scopes to find the one we were after. It was really difficult to determine who was who because of the distance until our billy stepped front and center. Not only did he have the horns, but the mass of his body dominated the others. He also had a red throat sash that was likely caused by another billy during a dominance fight.

The game plan was easy to figure out, it was the execution that would prove difficult.

ROCKY MOUNTAIN GOAT
First Award – 54

▼ ▼ ▼ ▼ ▼

A.C. Smid

We needed to head to the thick tree-lined ridge that lay on the other side of this opening. The ridge looked like an inverted V, with bowls to the left and right. Our goats were in the bowl, above and to the left, and at the end of tree line. We estimated that the goats were over 1,200 yards horizontal distance and about 1,300 feet from the top of the mountain. Slowly we worked across the opening, trying to stay behind what trees we could, to avoid being spotted from above. After finally hitting the tree line, we headed straight up, angling to our right as we went, figuring the goats would be up and to our left.

It is hard to describe the entire journey, but the climb was surreal. It was like being on a StairMaster with snowshoes in eight feet of snow for over eight hours. Being fourth in line, I had the advantage of placing my foot in a preformed cast, while all of the snow that had accumulated on the tree branches was being knocked down by the others ahead. Brodie had it the worst. He was leading and of course had to break trail. Numerous times we all offered to switch, but we all felt safe knowing that his young ego would get in the way. It was during this long climb that I started to mentally prepare myself for a long shot and the importance of remaining calm. Bob said that generally the shots are between 150 and 250 yards. I felt today was going to be different. I regularly practice shots at 400 and 500 yards with my Blazer .270 Weatherby Magnum that is scoped with a Schmidt & Bender 3-12x42. I feel comfortable at that range but would definitely prefer closer. I do feel that I have a responsibility to the animal as well as to myself that if I'm going to shoot at that distance, I need to be confident and accurate.

By angling to our right, we kept the top of the ridgeline to our left and remained out of sight. As we finally broke through the tree line at the top of the inverted V, we found ourselves in scrub brush and stunted trees that stuck through the top of the snow. This was followed by small and large boulders as we continued up to a little knoll. We figured the bowl we had seen the goats in was to the left of the knoll, so we would stay to the right. As Brodie crested the knoll he immediately went prone, looked back at us and said, "The goats are 90 yards ahead in the bowl."

We all tried in vain to find them and we must have looked like bobbers in the ocean going up and down. Then over 500 yards away and about 100 feet higher in elevation, we spotted the off-white figures against the white snow. I guess I should have asked Brodie how he did in math, but in the end, it really didn't matter. The goats apparently drifted out of the bowl on our left and were now in the bowl to our right. Another group of about six goats appeared above us about 700 yards away, and they definitely had seen us. Fortunately, our billy was not among them. Bob crawled up and out to get a better view of the billy we were after. As Bob lay there and glassed, time went by and we could tell by his body language that he hadn't spotted our goat—no movement, no nothing.

Photograph courtesy of A.C. Smid

A.C. Smid (left) and outfitter Bob Milligan pictured with Smid's award-winning Rocky Mountain goat taken in the mountains near Kalum Lake, British Columbia, during the 2008 season. The billy has a final score of 54 points and received a First Place Award.

During the climb, the temperature hovered about 20°F with about a 20 mph wind, light snow, and overcast skies. The wind, thank goodness, had been blowing from our right to the left, so we knew they hadn't winded us. As we lay there, chill factor came into play, and I knew I would have to layer up. We all layered differently. Bob chose to stay fully dressed as he hikes from the bottom to the top and then change into dry clothes. On the other hand, I layer as I go, and now was the time to get warm so I wouldn't have the shakes when it would be my time to step up to the plate.

After getting the right amount of clothes on, we went back to the binoculars and continued to look at the goats that were on a little bench across from us. As we continued to glass, suddenly we saw tips of horns coming our way from the far side of the bench. As if on cue, there he was, with the red throat sash and significantly larger horns and body mass

BOONE AND CROCKETT CLUB'S

when compared to the other billy in the group. Bob immediately turned around and said, "Charles get ready. It's him."

Then Roger chimed in and said, "Please Bob, put the spotting scope on him and make sure." Bob complied and no doubt about it, this was our billy. We couldn't tell by their mannerisms if they had made us yet. They just kept pawing and feeding to the right.

ROCKY MOUNTAIN GOAT
First Award – 54
▼ ▼ ▼ ▼ ▼
A.C. Smid

We had to get closer, so Bob and I would go it alone. We couldn't go back around, then up and back down. It was already 3:30 p.m., and we would be out of light by the time we made it. Our only option was to angle up and to our right to the remnants of a scrub tree that lay about 100 yards away, and from there I could take the long shot. I turned and shook Brodie's and Roger's hands as they wished me luck, and off we crawled to about 40 yards away. There we paused to ensure that the goats would not go into panic mode by what we were doing. As I found out later, the only meltdown was happening with Roger who was having an anxiety attack over the improbability of success. Thankfully, Brodie shook him out of it.

We continued to crawl until we reached the 30-inch scrub tree. Trying to find a shooting position when the hill is so steep was a trick—thank goodness for the tree. I had to lay my pack on an angle against it so I could get a steady rest. As I was going through all these contortions, Bob kept fidgeting to my right.

"Bob, what are you doing?" I asked.

"I'm trying to get this damn video camera to work, but I think it is frozen."

"Forget the camera. I've got the distance, and let's get this goat," I said.

"Charles, are you on 12x power?"

"Yes I am, and he's in my crosshairs."

"Whenever you're ready, Charles."

The first shot rang out, and the goat buckled.

"Nice shot. Shoot him again—you got him in the guts," Bob said.

Second and third shots rang out. At the sound of the first shot, the goats were confused as to where the sound was coming from and what was going on. As they continued to move to the right, we lost sight of them once again because of the angle. Then all of a sudden they reappeared about 500 yards away as they were making their way up and out of the bowl going to our right. One by one they left, a few of the nannies would stop and look back to try and figure out what happened. When the billy wasn't among them, Bob and I knew for sure that our billy was hit well.

At the sound of the first shot, Roger and Brodie sprang to their feet and eventually made their way up to us. We informed them that we thought the billy was down over the bench and we needed to make our way through the bowl and up to him.

As we crossed the bowl, Brodie asked Bob if we were in an avalanche shoot. Bob said, "Just keep walking." I think we all got a bit more of a hitch in our giddy-up at that response.

As we neared the edge of the bench, Brodie was right in front of me and he professionally waited so we would go shoulder to shoulder and be ready for whatever would happen next. We just kept looking ahead and looking down for any sign of the goat. Then, just ahead, there he lay, completely still. We figured that he probably traveled no more than 30 yards before he expired, at an elevation of about 5,100 feet. No doubt about it, this billy was big, and his score in the records book would verify that.

After all the backslapping and picture taking, we settled into the task of caping and boning out the meat. As we figured, the red throat sash was caused by a dominance fight with another billy just missing his jugular by about a half inch. The chance of him surviving the winter was doubtful due to the severity of the wound. The shots all turned out to be well-placed, right behind the front shoulder. Our descent was the same way as we had come up, but now with head lamps on all the way down.

Before we left, and as I always do, I gave a prayer of thanks for having the opportunity to harvest such a beautiful animal.

I gave a special prayer for Pops.

We made it down in about half the time it took us to climb up. Basically we skied the whole way down with our snowshoes on. The only person that had difficulty was Roger, and seriously, he went end-over-end at least 40 times. Tired and exhausted, we finally made it back to Bob's domain.

After a good night's sleep, we said our good-byes with handshakes and hugs, just a bit more bonded by the experience. I cannot say thanks enough about Brodie and the effort he made in the hunt. He is a true professional guide with a lot of toughness. Roger is just Roger—a great man and an important person in my life. As for Bob, he is one talented individual with a deep respect and knowledge of the land and the animals. He is a very congenial person that makes one feel at ease in his home as well as in the mountains. It was a special journey, in a special place, with special people!

Roger got me back to the Smithers airport and back to Montana in time for Thanksgiving and special days with Pops. After telling the story to Pops, he relived the hunt with his numerous friends that came to visit and told the story like the hunt was his. In many ways it was. I believe that he now truly understood the meaning of a trophy of a lifetime!

Christmas came, and on that day, Richard T. Orr went to the higher spiritual hunting ground and I feel fortunate to say that "this goat was for Pops." ▲

B&C Photo Archives

Richard T. Hale (l) and Paul D. Webster pause for a photo with Debby L. Perry's bighorn sheep just after they verified its original entry score of 202-7/8. Debby's ram is the third-largest ram ever taken by woman. It is also the 10th-largest ram ever recorded by B&C, and the fourth-largest from Montana.

TROPHY STATS

▼ ▼ ▼ ▼ ▼

CATEGORY
Rocky Mountain Goat

SCORE
53$^6/_8$

LENGTH OF HORN
Right: 10$^7/_8$ Left: 11$^1/_8$

BASE CIRCUMFERENCE
Right: 6   Left: 6

GREATEST SPREAD
8$^4/_8$

LOCATION
Telegraph Creek, British Columbia – 2008

HUNTER
Robert L. Schermer

ROCKY MOUNTAIN GOAT
Second Award – 53 $^6/_8$

▼ ▼ ▼ ▼ ▼ ▼ ▼ ▼ ▼

ROBERT L. SCHERMER

After hiking over 150 miles up and down the Ozark Mountains in Missouri's Busiek State Park with an 80-pound backpack, I felt I was ready for my Rocky Mountain goat hunt. So, on August 5, 2008, I departed from Springfield, Missouri, to join Tim Metcalf from Lafayette, Louisiana, and guide Abe Dougan to hunt goats in the beautiful mountains near Telegraph Creek in northern British Columbia.

Abe picked us up at the airport, and we headed for Telegraph Creek. It took us all night to get to there, and after a day's wait, our bush pilot transported us to a remote lake at an elevation of 4,000 feet. By dropping us off at the lake, we only had to hike up another 2,500 feet to begin our goat hunt. Had we chartered a boat to take us up a river to our hunting area, we would have had to hike up 6,000 feet to get to occupied goat habitat.

After we landed, I fired my rifle to make sure it was still sighted in. Then we put on lighter clothes, loaded up our packs, and headed for the first peak at 6,000 feet. When we reached the top, we sat down to rest and glass for goats. I soon spotted one on the opposite ridge. Then we saw two more goats bedded on a snowfield. We had not been glassing for more than 15 minutes when we quickly spotted three goats that all looked like billies. I thought, we must be in a good spot!

Abe wanted to get up higher and get closer for a better view of the goats. After a couple more hours of strenuous hiking, we were finally set up to glass from the other side of the mountain.

From our new vantage point, we spotted eight goats that Abe thought were all billies, one which looked exceptional. We also saw 23 nannies and kids on the ridge to our south. I quickly realized that we were right in the middle of where the goats were on this mountain. Thus, we decided to drop down the mountainside to pitch camp for the night. It seemed as if we had hiked up and down for about 10 hours that first day.

Photograph by Jack Reneau

Robert L. Schermer accepting his plaque and medal from Buck Buckner, Vice President and Chairman of the Big Game Records Committee.

Robert L. Schermer (right) along with his hunting partner Tim Metcalf and guide Abe Dougan are pictured with Schermer's award-winning Rocky Mountain goat taken near Telegraph Creek in British Columbia. The billy has a final score of 53-6/8 points and received a Second Place Award.

We were up at daybreak on the second day, well-rested and excited about seeing all the goats we had seen the day before. I was shooting a .300 Winchester Magnum, and Tim was using his bow and arrow. Everything in these mountains is either straight up or straight down, and since this was my first backpack hunt, it turned out to be all that I expected—and more—for a 46-year-old man with an old football knee injury.

Soon after arriving at our vantage point in some rock outcroppings where we had spotted the goats the day before, I spotted three goats feeding and another huge goat bedded down. It was "game on." The plan was for Tim to make a stalk with his bow, while I set up with my rifle at the same time. Abe and I were about 150 yards from Tim as he stalked the goats. As he attempted to get around the goats on their left, Abe and I could see four goats that appeared to be billies. The one I focused on had noticeably larger horns than the others. We thought it was the goat Abe spotted the day before that he felt had Boone and Crockett potential. I was locked down on this goat with a good rest as Abe instructed me from behind.

We finally saw Tim from our left making his move on the goats. As he emerged from the rocks, the big billy I was focused on turned and spotted Tim. I was ready to pull the trigger and was thinking about all that I have heard about goats making a suicide dive if you don't anchor them on the first shot. I was ready to anchor him. I had him in my scope and was waiting for advice from my guide. When the biggest billy stood up and looked a little nervous, it was obvious Tim had been spotted. Abe gave me the okay to shoot, and at my shot the goat dropped in his tracks.

ROCKY MOUNTAIN GOAT
Second Award – 53 6/8
▼ ▼ ▼ ▼ ▼
ROBERT L. SCHERMER

The other goats didn't have a clue as to what had just happened so we sat quietly to see what they would do. Suddenly, more goats appeared on our right, and two of them ran close enough to Tim so he got off two shots with his bow. My big billy was down, but we didn't know if Tim had hit one or not.

We gathered our gear and went down to check out the goat. I could see he was a monster, as Abe measured one horn at 11 inches. Abe said he had put a tape on probably 50 goats, but never an 11-inch goat. He said it was for sure a Boone and Crockett goat with 11-inch horn lengths and 6-inch bases. This would be my first B&C animal. We gave high-fives all around and took plenty of photos to remember the occasion.

Mountain goats are magnificent animals; heavy through the shoulders and weighing upwards of 300 pounds. I was looking forward to and envisioning a life-sized mount of this great trophy in my "dead head" room, as my wife calls it.

Tim said there were nine goats in the group, but we only saw seven run off, so one goat was not accounted for. We looked for Tim's arrows and could only find one broken one. Tim was pretty sure he made a good hit.

Hours passed as Abe skinned and boned out my goat. We figured if Tim had hit one, we would give it some time before pursuing it. After my goat was skinned and boned out, we walked along the edge of the mountain where I spotted Tim's goat. It must have escaped to a ledge we couldn't see, finally died, and fell to the bottom. The longer horn on Tim's goat rough-scored at 10-7/8 and the base was 6-3/8. Abe estimated it at 13-years old.

"You guys just killed two Boone and Crockett mountain goats!" Abe exclaimed. Tim's would probably rank in the top three bow-kills ever recorded, according to Abe.

After skinning Tim's goat, the real work started, because we had to hike down 6,000 feet to the road with 100 pound packs on our backs.

I give our guide Abe a lot of credit for all he did to make this hunt possible. He worked extremely hard to get us on quality animals.

It took us two solid days of descending through the thickest alders and brush straight down with straight-up detours at times to get down the mountain. My feet hurt so badly, it was all I could do to put my boots on the last morning. (My big toenails turned black and later came off.) It was all worth it to have such an unbelievable experience in the beautiful coastal mountains of Telegraph Creek, British Columbia.

Killing two Boone and Crockett records-book mountain goats was a very special experience for both Tim and me. My goat was panel-scored by B&C at 53-6/8 points and is currently tied for 31st place in Boone and Crockett Club's All-time records. ▲

TROPHY STATS

▼ ▼ ▼ ▼ ▼

CATEGORY
Rocky Mountain Goat

SCORE
$53^4/_8$

LENGTH OF HORN
Right: $11^3/_8$ Left: $10^6/_8$

BASE CIRCUMFERENCE
Right: $6^2/_8$ Left: $6^1/_8$

GREATEST SPREAD
8

LOCATION
Revillagigedo Island, Alaska – 2008

HUNTER
Terry E. Meyers

ROCKY MOUNTAIN GOAT
Third Award (Tie) – 53 $^4/_8$

▼ ▼ ▼ ▼ ▼ ▼ ▼ ▼ ▼

TERRY E. MEYERS

In the summer of 2008, I booked a last-minute mountain goat hunt with Ed Toribio of Primo Expeditions out of Ketchikan, Alaska. Ed has quite a track record of getting clients on Boone and Crockett-class billies, and I was extremely excited about the opportunity.

I arrived at Ketchikan International on September 30th and was soon met by Ed and one of his packers, Kyle Berg. We left the airport and headed back across the Tongass Narrows in Ed's boat to his seaside house in Ward Cove. We spent the rest of the day and the following morning going through my gear and making sure I had brought everything I needed. Packer Charlie Ratzat arrived, and by mid-day we had our gear gathered on the dock for our 12:30 p.m. scheduled pickup. Ryan McCue of Alaska Seaplane Tours arrived on time to ferry us and our gear to our destination lake where we would set up base camp.

We arrived at the lake and found a nice spot along the shore to set up the wall tent and a couple of smaller tents for the packers and me. We were lucky to have one of the few short periods of no rain to set up base camp.

We awoke on the morning of October 2 to typical rainy southeastern Alaska weather. After a breakfast of sausage, eggs, and toast, we loaded our packs and began ferrying gear across the lake in the Zodiac to the mountain we would be hunting. By 12:30 p.m. we were ready to begin the 2,000-foot climb up the mountain. Of course, it began raining almost immediately and only got worse as we climbed. The amount of rain in that part of the country makes a climb with any sort of pitch interesting. It was without a doubt the hardest 2,000 feet I've ever climbed.

About three hours into the climb we encountered a band of rock that turned us back. We were extremely disappointed at the prospect of having to go all the way down and try another route. Charlie spotted a place he thought we might be able to sneak up through, and although it was difficult, the alternative spurred us on to make it work. We climbed up the cliff and pulled our packs up by rope.

By 5:30 p.m. we had reached the area where we hoped to set up spike camp and began searching for a place flat enough for our tents with a supply of firewood nearby. Charlie soon found the spot, and as luck would have it, the rain stopped just long enough to get tents and a kitchen fly rigged up.

It rained and blew all night and was still fogged in and rainy the next morning. We stayed in our tents until the rain let up around noon, then got up, prepared something to eat, and started a fire. Around 2:30 p.m. the clouds lifted enough to see the top of the mountain above us, so we grabbed our gear and hurried to the top. There was a great basin on top

Terry E. Meyers is pictured above with his award-winning goat taken on Revillagigedo Island in Alaska. The billy scores 53-4/8.

where a nursery band of goats had been hanging out, and we immediately found them bedded on a snow patch about 390 yards away. There was one long-horned nanny, two kids, and one 2-year-old billy.

We stayed hidden and searched in vain for a big billy. We wanted to take a look at the other side of the mountain, but with a short day and goats nearby, we decided not to push our luck. The four goats soon got up and headed straight away from us, across the valley. We headed back to camp as the sun sank into the horizon.

The weather that night was clear, and we got up early the following morning, October 4, to high overcast skies. We quickly ate breakfast and headed up the mountain to take advantage of the weather. When we arrived at our observation point from the previous evening, Kyle immediately spotted a single goat bedded on the far side of the canyon. We got a scope on him and were disappointed to find it was a young billy. This goat was soon joined by four others—the nanny, two kids, and young billy from the previous evening. They all worked their way across the far side of the basin, over the top and out of sight. We began to work our way around the upper side of the basin, mindful of the wind that continued to blow dangerously close to the direction of the goats.

We had no sooner started across when it began to rain. We stopped to don our rain-gear, but made the mistake of stopping in the open. Ed looked up and spotted a lone goat on the skyline far left of where the band of goats had disappeared. We were pinned down and couldn't get a scope on him, but we didn't think it was one of the same goats we had just seen go out of sight. The lone goat fed across the top of the ridge and soon went out of sight behind the ridge.

We quickly made our way around the basin, but as we neared the spot the lone goat had gone out of sight, we spotted the nursery band bedded on the opposite ridge. They had evidently circled around after going out of our sight and returned to the ridge where we had originally spotted them. They now had us pinned to our location, and the wind was blowing almost straight to them. We hunkered in to wait them out.

No sooner had we settled in for a wait, but the long-horned nanny quickly rose to her feet, bringing the rest of the herd to attention. They had obviously caught our wind, but thankfully bailed off the far side of the ridge, away from where the lone goat had disappeared. We quickly gathered our gear and crossed through the deep ravine and were soon standing in the notch over which the goat had fed out of sight over an hour earlier.

ROCKY MOUNTAIN GOAT
Third Award (Tie) – 53 4/8

▼ ▼ ▼ ▼ ▼

TERRY E. MEYERS

I took my rifle in hand as we began to traverse slowly along the opposite side of the ridgeline. Large clumps of brush reduced visibility to less than 30 yards in most places. As we eased along with Ed in the lead, me following, and the other two behind me, I glanced down to my right and spotted a white patch of hair behind a bush about 30 feet away. I hissed at Ed and pointed, and he instructed me to shoot quickly. I chambered a round, but all I could see of the bedded goat from my position were the hindquarters and a strip of his back. I raised my rifle and waited.

It didn't take long—the goat knew something was amiss and stood, exposing the top of his shoulder. He was down at the shot an instant later, and rolling down the hill. Luckily, he was stopped by a tree on a narrow bench a short distance down the hill. I finished him off and we all stood in amazement at what had transpired during the last minute.

We climbed down to the goat, and I was stunned when I got a good look at the horns. They looked long and extremely massive—bigger than I knew mountain goats grew! He was far more than I ever expected. We took a few photos where he was lying but there was no room to move on the small ledge where he had stopped, so we lowered him by rope to a larger ledge below.

The clouds and rain settled in on us as soon as we started preparing the goat for the hike out. We were amazed at our extremely good fortune to have found the billy and completed the stalk during our short weather window. With four of us working, we skinned the billy for a life-sized mount and de-boned it in no time. It was nice to have hard-working Kyle and Charlie along for the pack back to spike camp. Everyone was in good spirits, even when the trail was steep and wet. Back at spike camp, we made dinner and got a good fire going to help us dry out.

It wasn't raining the following morning, so we leisurely ate breakfast and drank coffee before packing up spike camp. We began the descent to the lake by 11 a.m. It began raining again almost as soon as we began our descent. We made it to the lake in a little over three hours. Other than having to lower our packs down by rope in about three tricky spots, the descent was uneventful. We ferried people and gear across the lake, built a fire in the woodstove, and changed into dry clothes. The following morning we had egg and sausage sandwiches for breakfast and then packed up base camp for our scheduled pickup at 1:30 p.m. Ryan McCue arrived right on time, and we quickly loaded gear and hunters onto the plane for the ride back to Ketchikan. The next morning was the best weather yet, giving Ed and me a chance to unpack and clean our gear.

My southeastern Alaska mountain goat hunt far exceeded my expectations. Ed Toribio's professionalism, attention to hunter safety, and knowledge of goat hunting in the rugged, wet terrain made the entire experience enjoyable. I came home with the trophy of a lifetime and memories that will last just as long. ▲

TROPHY STATS

▼ ▼ ▼ ▼ ▼

CATEGORY
Rocky Mountain Goat

SCORE
53⁴/₈

LENGTH OF HORN
Right: 11   Left: 11

BASE CIRCUMFERENCE
Right: 5⁶/₈   Left: 5⁶/₈

GREATEST SPREAD
7²/₈

LOCATION
Elko Co., Nevada – 2007

HUNTER
Don J. Dees

ROCKY MOUNTAIN GOAT
Third Award (Tie) – 53 ⁴/₈

▼ ▼ ▼ ▼ ▼ ▼ ▼ ▼ ▼

DON J. DEES

In Nevada, most of us diehard hunters wait in anticipation for that day in early June when the big-game tag results are posted. Many of us even start checking for hits on our credit cards. I found out mine had a charge for $30 and another for $130 from the Nevada Department of Wildlife. That meant I was for sure hunting (archery) mule deer in August—but what were the other two hits for?

Later that day, the results were posted on-line, and not in my wildest dreams did I expect

Double Draw

what I saw on the monitor. I drew one of nine Rocky Mountain bighorn sheep tags, as well as a once-in-a-lifetime mountain goat tag, and the hunts were in the same unit at the same time! After the shock diminished, I phoned my hunting buddies with the news. Everybody said I should be playing the California lottery that day with my kind of luck.

I am a do-it-yourself hunter and prefer not to use an outfitter, but the tags were for wilderness in the Ruby Mountains and I would need horses and someone with vast knowledge of the giant mountain range. I decided to hunt with Mitch Bussetti of Nevada High Desert Outfitters. Walt Gardner, with Secret Pass Outfitters, who works closely with Mitch would also be along.

As an archery hunter who does not own a rifle, my goal was to take both animals with my bow, but I was not about to go on this hunt-of-a-lifetime without a rifle. I borrowed my friend's .300 WSM and went out to the range to hone my skills.

My friend Casey Jones and I left Reno for Elko, Nevada, for my much-anticipated hunt. We met with my guides on the morning of August 31, packed all the horses and mules (20-plus) and headed into the rugged and magnificent Ruby Mountains. We also had the help of a certified sheep-hunting nut by the name of Kevin Peterson, much to my good fortune. It

Photograph by Jack Reneau

Don J. Dees accepting his plaque and medal from Buck Buckner, Vice President and Chairman of the Big Game Records Committee.

Photograph courtesy of Don J. Dees

View of the terrain during the 10-mile horseback ride into camp located in Nevada's Ruby Mountain range.

was a 10-mile horseback ride into camp. The plan on opening day, September 1, was to go after a good ram that was known to frequent the area.

At "0-dark-thirty," we left camp—pretty much straight up 1,500 feet to glass the next basin in hopes of finding the mysterious ram. We immediately spotted 20-plus goats. Seconds later, Kevin said, "I've got rams."

Over two miles away as the crow flies, we watched 10 rams feeding just below a ridge, one of which looked outstanding. We watched for several minutes, getting good video and still photos, until the rams moved around the face of the mountain.

It was time to move in. Four-plus hours later and after hiking what turned out to be well over four miles through two huge, gnarly canyons, we were looking at four of the rams bedded just on the edge of a patch of pine trees. The largest sheep in view looked to be about 165; the big one was nowhere to be found. We surmised he was bedded in the timber. Because of all the eyeballs on us and the steepness of the terrain, it would probably be impossible to get a shot with the bow, so out came the rifle.

Mitch and Casey stayed back with the spotting scope and Kevin and I moved in for a closer look. At 130 yards we watched the closest ram get up and start bee-lining down the face. The rest came out of the trees behind him. It was 12:45 p.m., and it appeared they were headed to a small lake below for a drink. The big ram was third from the last. I wasn't experienced at field-judging sheep, so I asked Kevin, "Is he big enough?"

ROCKY MOUNTAIN GOAT
Third Award (Tie) – 53 4/8
▼ ▼ ▼ ▼ ▼
Don J. Dees

I'm guessing he must have thought I was crazy by the way he said, "Shoot him." It was almost straight down and about 190 yards. My first shot missed and they started to pick up the pace. My next shot was true and we heard the telltale "thwack." The big ram walked about 10 yards and went down.

We celebrated and then gathered up our gear. Kevin and Mitch were the first to get to the ram and the celebrating started again. The ram was 40-4/8 inches on one side and 39-4/8 inches on the other, with a true full-curl. After pictures, caping, boning, and stuffing everything in our packs, the real work was about to begin. We thought we would be sleeping on the mountain until Dave showed up with two horses about a quarter of the way back to camp. We arrived back at camp at dark, and according to my GPS, we had walked 12 miles and climbed over 5,000 vertical feet. As good of shape as we all were in, we just lounged around camp the next day, letting our sore muscles rest up for the goat hunt.

As we headed out after a goat, my goal again was to harvest the animal with my bow. I asked my guide Walt, "Why don't we go after one of the goats we saw on the sheep hunt?"

He said no, because there was a billy he'd been trying to kill for four years that hunters had missed three separate times. He added that most of his clients couldn't get to where the big goat lived because of the difficulty of the terrain. I took that as a compliment.

Walt, Dave, Justin, Casey, and I went on a lovely three-hour horseback ride to find the monster billy. I thought to myself that even if I didn't get a goat, the hunt had been nothing less than epic. We arrived at our destination and began to glass. Lo and behold, bedded at the base of a cliff that reminded me of something you would see on a Discovery Channel show featuring Mount Everest, was the big billy goat.

We watched him for a while as he got up, moved higher into the basin and bedded down again. We got on the horses to close the gap to half a mile and scope him out again. I watched my master guide Walt get out his tape and field judge the billy through his spotting scope, stretching the tape, looking again and again and writing numbers. He said, "The billy is 11 inches tall and should go about 52-4/8." In the end, Walt's outstanding field judging would only be one inch off!

The goat was bedded under a small ledge in a very good spot for a sneak with the bow. Casey and Dave stayed back to video as the stalk began.

Because of the lay of the land, we had to cover some open ground and our billy spot-

Don J. Dees harvested a record-book bighorn sheep just 48 hours before he took this award-winning Rocky Mountain goat in Elko County, Nevada. The billy has a final score of 53-4/8 points and tied for a Third Place Award at the 27th Big Game Awards Program in Reno, Nevada.

ted us. He got up and took off, straight up about 1,000 feet over a ridge. We took off on a vertical sprint, climbing through boulders the size of SUVs in hopes of spotting him again. That was the fastest ascent I have ever made in my hunting career. Once we crested, we were looking into a giant bowl that turns into a sheer granite cliff 600-700 feet high. About 100 feet up on a ledge was our billy, bedded down all nice and comfy.

We ranged him at 650 yards. We sized up the situation and determined that the closest we could get to him would be about 400 yards, but any shot would likely send him off the cliff. After a lengthy discussion, including the option of coming back the next day, Walt said, "If I back out and climb up and around above him on the cliff and roll boulders, there's a small chance he will come down and present you with a shot."

Walt took off for the top while Justin and I backed out down and around and were able to sneak to within 383 yards of the giant billy. It took an hour, and just as we were setting up, down came the boulders. The goat sat there for several minutes, acting as if it were a daily occurrence. A few small rocks hit a few yards away from him and he finally stood up and proceeded to walk along a thin ledge for 100 feet or so and stopped directly behind a boulder that exposed his chest. The ledge was probably ten feet deep in front of him before it dropped 100 feet straight down. The billy just stood there for what seemed like eternity looking around and sizing up the situation. Justin said, "Don, if you feel comfortable enough to make a perfect shot and drop him in his tracks, the boulder he is standing behind should prevent him from sliding off the cliff."

ROCKY MOUNTAIN GOAT
Third Award (Tie) – 53 4/8

▼ ▼ ▼ ▼ ▼

DON J. DEES

I watched the goat through the scope and settled in, using a large boulder as my rest. I looked at him for several minutes, and he just stood there while I decided if I had enough confidence to make the shot. Finally, I placed the crosshairs above his shoulder, took a deep breath, and squeezed the trigger. I got the rifle scope back on him as quickly as I could and saw him fall forward. Justin said, "He's down. Put another one in him."

I shot another time and hit the boulder just next to him. He started to slide off the ledge but suddenly just stopped, inches short of falling off the cliff. The first shot had been true and he had expired in his tracks. The feeling was overwhelming. I couldn't believe what I had just done. I looked at my watch and noted it was almost exactly 48 hours since I had harvested my ram.

After the celebration, the Herculean job of getting to the goat was underway. A good 45 minutes of climbing later, we got to the spot where he had been bedded. We shed our packs and started to straddle that little ledge our billy had so effortlessly negotiated. I am terrified of heights, so getting to him was the most frightening thing I have ever done in my life. Justin got to him first and started whooping it up. I arrived a couple minutes later and was mesmerized by the animal. As luck would have it—and it seemed I'd had a lot of luck—the billy's horns caught in what little grass was growing on the ledge. Walt's estimation was right on—11-inch horns. We took some photos and then, while trying not to fall off the edge ourselves, we boned him out, moving the meat down off the ledge in several trips before heading down off the mountain.

I don't know what I did to deserve it, but the hunting gods were with me from the time I drew those remarkable tags until I took my second Boone and Crockett animal in 48 hours.

I want to thank Mitch Bussetti of Nevada High Desert Outfitters, Walt Gardner of Secret Pass Outfitters, Kevin Peterson, the "sheepaholic", and my good friend and hunting buddy Casey Jones—who sacrificed his Montana bowhunt to assist me. My sheep officially scored 187 points and my Rocky Mountain goat scored 53-4/8 points. ▴

Reprinted with permission from Eastmans' Hunting Journal.

TROPHY STATS

▼ ▼ ▼ ▼ ▼

CATEGORY
Musk Ox

SCORE
127

LENGTH OF HORN
Right: 29 1/8   Left: 29 1/8

BOSS WIDTH
Right: 11 2/8   Left: 10 6/8

GREATEST SPREAD
28 6/8

LOCATION
Kugluktuk, Nunavut – 2007

HUNTER
Ben L. Mueller

MUSK OX
First Award – 127

▼ ▼ ▼ ▼ ▼ ▼ ▼ ▼ ▼

BEN L. MUELLER

The hunt started like many others. On this occasion it was a call from my old business partner and friend Roy Brown that started with, "Ben, let's go on an adventure. A hunt to an untamed frontier."

Well this caught my interest and I responded, "Where is this adventure and hunt?"

Then he laid it on me. "Let's hunt musk ox in the Arctic!"

These words were spoken by a guy that couldn't care less about hunting. He's probably never killed more than two whitetails and a handful of doves and quail in his life, but he clearly loves an "adventure!" I expressed my sentiments mightily and then went on to comment about his intelligence and the likelihood of dying if there was the slightest mistake. Despite 15 or 20 minutes of his best sales pitch I gave him a flat no.

The pitch rocked on for months, mostly because he couldn't find anyone crazy enough to accompany him. After numerous calls, my resistance faltered and I told him that if I could hunt polar bear while he hunted the "ugliest creature on earth," I would consider it.

A couple of weeks later he called back and told me Webb Outfitters would not do bear and musk ox at the same time, so I declined again. Then, he hit me with the ultimate sales pitch, "I have already booked the hunt and paid for both of us and can't get a refund."

The earlier references concerning his intelligence were reasserted and delivered with pure expletives at this point.

"I've done the research and hired the best outfitter with the best musk ox in the Arctic," Roy said. "I have also found the best Arctic suit and gear and where to buy it."

Roy is one of those guys that can walk into any store and find clothes that fit. However,

Ugliest Creature on Earth

Photograph by Jack Reneau

Ben L. Mueller accepting his plaque and medal from Buck Buckner, Vice President and Chairman of the Big Game Records Committee.

Ben L. Mueller and his long-time friend Roy Brown called this camp in the Arctic their home during their 2007 musk ox hunt near Kugluktuk, Nunavut. Ben harvested an award-winning musk ox scoring 127 points, which makes it the sixth largest bull ever recorded by B&C.

my ample frame has problems with fit. Following a multitude of additional brow beatings, I finally relented, fully expecting to become frozen dessert for some grizzly in the spring.

Finally, the big day came in March 2007. Roy, his wife Dianne and I flew to Yellowknife, where we spent the night. In the Yellowknife airport there is a fabulous mount of a polar bear chasing seals. Once again, I told Roy that if we were going to be risking our lives, we should be going after polar bears.

The next day Roy and I departed for Kugluktuk, Nunavut Territory, in balmy -40°F weather while Dianne stayed in Yellowknife to see the Northern Lights. Obviously, she was the only one of us with brains.

Upon arrival in Kugluktuk, Webb met us and took us to his house to dress and depart for our "great adventure." Keep in mind, I still had not put on my Arctic clothing as I nearly suffocated in Houston's 85°F weather while attempting to try it on. Subconsciously, I was hoping it wouldn't fit.

Webb's outfit was efficient at loading the sleds and preparing for departure. He was handing out our licenses and explaining what to expect. They also made sure in no uncertain terms that we understood the Inuit guides were in complete control of all decisions. This is when I found out there was a polar bear hunter in our group.

With a look that could melt polar ice, I turned to Roy and said, "I thought there weren't any bear hunts when musk ox hunting."

Without a blink of an eye and absolutely no remorse, he looked back at me and replied, "I lied. I knew you wouldn't come, and I wasn't going to be out here alone."

MUSK OX
First Award – 127

▼ ▼ ▼ ▼ ▼

BEN L. MUELLER

That day we traveled about 60 miles by sled out onto the ice. Before dark, we stopped to make camp and prepare for the next day's hunt. While making camp, a wolverine came by to see what was going on. That is the only wolverine I have ever seen during many hunts in the North.

We didn't actually start hunting until three days later. The first two were spent in whiteout conditions in small tents big enough for one guide and one hunter. Time came to an absolute standstill. Roy and I are used to being on the move, and the down time weighed heavily on our minds. The weather finally broke on the third day, and the hunt was on.

We had traveled for a couple of hours looking for game when we came to a huge bowl that we glassed for what seemed an eternity. Finally, the guide said the magic words, "There are some musk ox!"

Surprisingly, they were harder to spot in the blowing snow than I had expected, even though they were the only black objects on the totally white landscape. Then, to my surprise, they just disappeared. Two hours later the guide and I came within 150 yards of a small herd of maybe eight bulls. We started glassing, and there were three bulls that I thought were very close to the same size, although my guide insisted that one was considerably larger. Eventually he pointed out what he considered was the best bull, and the rest is history. Later that day, Roy killed his bull, which also qualifies for Boone and Crockett.

I must take my hat off to these men of the North. They are tough and experts at what they do. Their advice and experience were crucial for survival on the polar ice.

My deepest thanks go out to Webb and the Inuits that made this hunt possible, and for making the intolerable conditions tolerable. I must also thank Roy Brown for browbeating me into submission for an adventure of a lifetime! ▲

TROPHY STATS
▼ ▼ ▼ ▼ ▼

CATEGORY
Musk Ox

SCORE
122⁶/₈

LENGTH OF HORN
Right: 29¹/₈   Left: 28³/₈

BOSS WIDTH
Right: 11³/₈   Left: 11¹/₈

GREATEST SPREAD
28⁷/₈

LOCATION
Kugluktuk River, Nunavut – 2008

HUNTER
M. Blake Patton

MUSK OX
Second Award (Tie) – 122 $^6/_8$

▼ ▼ ▼ ▼ ▼ ▼ ▼ ▼ ▼

M. BLAKE PATTON

After my bowhunting friends highly recommended outfitters Fred and Martin Webb for musk ox hunting, we decided to book a hunt with them for the last week of March 2008. Their outfitting area out of Kugluktuk, Nunavut, Canada, is known for producing some of the largest musk ox in the records books.

Due to logistics and the incredibly cold temperatures, this hunt took much more preparation than others. I purchased special clothing and boots to protect me from temperatures that could dip to -50°F.

Learning from Experience

I carried two Mathews bows with me—both in top condition—and I shot at least 30 arrows from them every day for months. I practiced shooting in the gloves, head cover, and heavy clothing that I planned to wear. After becoming more familiar with this setup, I determined that when the time came to make a shot, I'd first shed the big parka. While it would keep me warm, it was very bulky and made shooting a bow difficult.

After two days of air travel from Houston, I arrived at Kugluktuk and was met at the airport by Fred and Martin. We went to their house to get my license and tags, get the gear sorted and ready to go.

My Inuit guides for the hunt would be Charlie and George. I would hunt first on Victoria Island for Greenland or "white-face" musk ox—a smaller cousin of the barren ground musk ox.

The mode of transportation for the hunt would be a wooden sled pulled behind a snowmobile. It is a vast understatement to say that riding in that sled was rough. There were times when I thought my tailbone had hit me in the chin. The trip from Kugluktuk across Coronation Gulf to Victoria Island was 132 miles each way, not including the distance traveled while hunting on the island.

After more than four hours of travel and being only halfway there, the visibility deteriorated, so the guides found a suitable place to set up a tent and camp for the night. Caribou hides were placed on the ice under our sleeping pad and bag. I crawled into the sack early the first night to get warm.

I had fallen asleep while the guides were still awake and the stove was still burning and keeping the inside of the tent warm. When I woke up a while later, my face was numb! I realized quickly that going to sleep with my bare head exposed was a big mistake. It didn't take me long to learn that I needed to put on a stocking cap and get my noggin inside the bag.

M. Blake Patton and his guides stopped to warm up frequently during their trip to Victoria Island.

Despite a small weather delay the next morning, we reached Victoria Island by mid-day. During the trip, we stopped every hour or so to stretch and have coffee, tea, hot chocolate, or bullion to warm up (a relative term). The temperature was colder here than it was in Kugluktuk since we were 150 miles farther north. It was at least -35°F, with the wind chill factor approaching -60°F.

Once on Victoria Island, we located a couple herds of musk ox. I could only judge musk ox relative to each other, so I really didn't know how good the biggest bull in a herd was. One bull certainly looked good enough to take, so I peeled off my big parka and mitts in preparation for a shot. I stalked up to within 33 yards of the bull and it finally turned from head-on to mostly broadside. I figured it was a slam-dunk at that distance, but that would not be the case.

After a very frustrating episode of my release freezing to the bow string, I was finally able to release an arrow. It hit the bull, but my arrow rest snapped from the extreme cold and the bull was still standing. I had another bow, but it was at least a 16-hour roundtrip away in Kugluktuk. In retrospect, it wasn't very intelligent to drag a backup bow all the way from Texas and then leave it where it was of no use to me.

Ethically, I felt I needed to finish things as quickly as possible so I did what I had to do. I asked Charlie for the use of his .223 and finished the bull as quickly as possible.

It was a special moment to see this musk ox up close. He was a beautiful animal with excellent hair and nice horns. Charlie and George retrieved the sleds and pulled up next to the bull. We put up our shelter for the night right there and lit the Coleman stove in the tent. The wind picked up and it got extremely cold, which gave us a chance to take a break and warm up occasionally while skinning.

I didn't have a thermometer that would work, but it was brutally cold. Charlie figured it was -50°F before even figuring in a chill factor. An arctic fox came in to help himself to scraps that night, and I enjoyed being able to watch him.

I was happy to have taken a nice Greenland musk ox, but at the same time I was disappointed with the sequence of events that had occurred and that I hadn't been able to take the animal with archery tackle. The good news was that we were going back to town the next day and I would have time to repair my broken arrow rest and get my backup bow before embarking on a quest for a barren ground musk ox on the mainland.

MUSK OX
Second Award (Tie) – 122 6/8
▼ ▼ ▼ ▼ ▼
M. Blake Patton

After the long haul back to Kugluktuk, I checked in at the Coppermine Inn, cleaned up, reorganized my gear and spent a couple of hours making the necessary repairs to my broken arrow rest. Hoping to avoid making the same mistake twice, I also reinforced the rest on my other bow in the same way. I was now confident that I would have no more problems, at least with the arrow rest.

We regrouped at Fred's house the next morning and departed in the sled and snowmobiles. We would be heading east for about three hours to a cabin on the south shore of Coronation Gulf. The cabin was like a nice hotel when compared to sleeping on the ice in a tent.

After a good night's rest, we took off to hunt what Charlie referred to as "good musk ox country." He was correct. It didn't take but another couple hours to spot a herd of musk ox that consisted of 10 bulls, all good ones. There wasn't a cow or calf in the bunch. Even better, the majority appeared to be B&C-class animals.

We looked them over and focused on what appeared to be a really old bull. Using the rolling terrain, we were able to stalk into position so that the closest bull was only 35 yards. The bull I wanted to take was 50 yards away—still a very makeable shot. I nocked an arrow, put my 50-yard pin behind his shoulder and attempted to release my arrow. As had happened before, the release temporarily froze to the string, which altered the shot, and then the arrow flew harmlessly over the musk ox.

Determined to learn from my past mistakes, I again settled my pin just behind the shoulder and tripped the release. Anticipating the same thing happening as before (and being correct in that assumption), this time I carefully held the pin in place until the arrow was on its way.

The fatal shot hit the bull in the chest and he quickly fell behind the others as they ran. From there it wasn't difficult to approach him and finish the necessary job. After congratulatory handshakes and high-fives between the three of us, we admired the trophy animal and took pictures to capture the moment.

Charlie and George then discussed a plan for the rest of the day. They decided to put up a small tent and get the stove burning so that we could warm up during the skinning process. We would then try to make it back to the cabin before dark to spend the night more comfortably.

It took five hours to get everything done and begin the trip back. By then, the weather had deteriorated to very windy with almost whiteout conditions. I'm sure glad the guides

Patton is pictured above with his award-winning musk ox, the second bull he took on his archery trip to Nunavut. The bull has a final score of 122-6/8 points and tied for a Second Place Award.

knew where they were going. Under low light conditions in the snow, there is little or no depth perception. It was interesting when I looked up to see that I was passing the snow machine, only to realize that we were going down a pretty steep grade. We arrived back at the cabin just after dark and celebrated by partaking in musk ox tenderloin.

Equipment problems aside, I had a great Arctic adventure and feel very fortunate to have had the opportunity to harvest an exceptional musk ox. I was privileged and very appreciative to have hunted with a quality outfitter and two great Inuit guides with dependable equipment and a vast knowledge of the area.

My trophy was panel-judged for the Pope and Young Club's 26th Biennium Awards Banquet & Convention held in Denver, Colorado, in April 2009. It took top honors with a panel score of 122-6/8. That score was upheld by Boone and Crockett Club's 27th Big Game Awards Judges Panel, and my musk ox received a Second Place Award at the 27th Big Game Awards Program Banquet in Reno, Nevada, on June 2010. ▲

Moments in Measuring

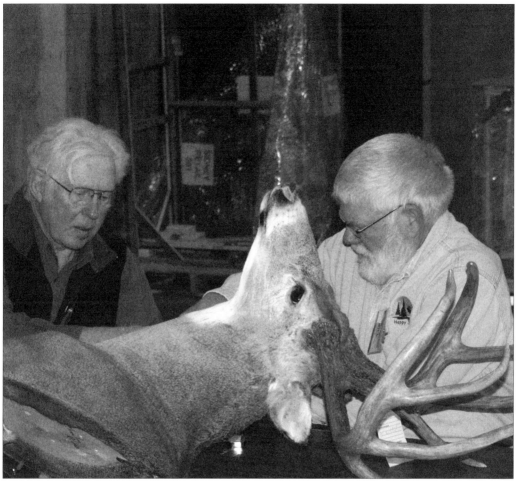

B&C Photo Archives

Panel Judge William A. Keebler (right) adds up the score chart that he and Glenn E. Hisey prepared for Charles Q. Rives' typical whitetail deer (foreground) that was in the top-five typical whitetails invited to Reno. The Panel verified Rives' buck's score at 198-1/8 points, which was higher than its entry score. It is the fourth-largest typical ever taken in Illinois.

TROPHY STATS

▼ ▼ ▼ ▼ ▼

CATEGORY
Musk Ox

SCORE
122 $^6/_8$

LENGTH OF HORN
Right: 27 $^3/_8$ Left: 27 $^6/_8$

BOSS WIDTH
Right: 10 $^4/_8$ Left: 10 $^1/_8$

GREATEST SPREAD
30

LOCATION
Gjoa Haven, Nunavut – 1995

HUNTER
James D. Mierzwiak

MUSK OX
Second Award (Tie) – 122 ⁶/₈

▼ ▼ ▼ ▼ ▼ ▼ ▼ ▼ ▼

James D. Mierzwiak

"Jim, that's the biggest *Oomingmak* (musk ox) that I have ever seen," said my guide Andy Kameemalik. These words didn't have the impact on me then that they would later.

The reason I didn't get too excited was really simple. I had hunted Central Canada barren ground caribou on eight previous occasions with Andy, and he, along with most of the other Inuit guides and hunters I have met, are wonderful, happy people. There were always praises for well-placed shots and the animals harvested. It wasn't until I found out later that I had taken a B&C musk ox that I fully understood the significance of his statement.

The Oncoming Beast

My partner for this hunt was Gary Solomon, a friend and hunting companion for many years. We were invited guests of our Inuit friends Andy Kameemalik and George Konana.

We left Los Angeles for the town of Yellowknife, Northwest Territories, Canada, on March 27, 1995. After an overnight stay in Yellowknife, we departed for the hamlet of Gjoa Haven, which is located on King Williams Island within the Arctic Circle. Due to the severity of the weather and frequent stops to deliver supplies to other outpost towns, we did not arrive in Gjoa Haven until March 30th. There are no direct flights to most of these hamlets.

Coming from Southern California, it is almost impossible to describe the Arctic cold in March. Let it suffice to say that after the plane landed in Gjoa Haven, it did not leave again for seven days due to the starter motor freezing solid, along with other moving parts on the plane. The temperature was -40°F, plus the wind-chill factor was significant. We had purchased the best clothing for Arctic exploration available, but nothing keeps you warm and comfortable in these extremes.

The best was yet to come. Our transportation on this hunt was a 16-foot wooden sled

Photograph by Jack Reneau

Joseph Chlebowski accepting his uncle's plaque and medal from Buck Buckner, Vice President and Chairman of the Big Game Records Committee.

James D. Mierzwiak harvested this award-winning musk ox, with a score of 122-6/8 points, during a hunt near Gjoa Haven, Nunavut, in 1995. His bull tied for a Second Place Award at the 27th Big Game Awards Program in Reno, Nevada

with a box attached to one end. There were no shocks or other attachments, and it was 10 hours of bone-jarring, teeth-crunching, back-breaking, skin-freezing hell to our camp!

What the heck were we thinking?

We finally arrived at our Hilton Hotel (igloo), much the worse for wear. After three days of isolation in our ice home, I became aware of this horrible feeling of doom in the form of claustrophobia coming over me. I casually informed our hosts that if they did not get me outside by tomorrow, I could not be responsible for my actions.

The next day dawned bright, clear, and of course, cold. After what seemed like hours, we arrived at an overlook with a view of forever. Way out there were several black dots in a sea of white. After looking through a spotting scope, Andy informed us there was indeed a herd of musk ox with some good bulls in the group. We immediately took off, arriving on the backside of the hill where the animals had been spotted. After a careful stalk, Andy set me up about 100 yards from the animals.

After some shifting of the herd, we both spotted what looked like an enormous bull. Keep in mind that I had never seen a live musk ox until this very minute, so they all looked big with shaggy coats of long hair! Only after Andy pointed out specific parts of their anatomy did I understand what to look for.

The .300 Winchester Magnum and the 180-grain Federal bullets did their job, and I had my first musk ox bull. The rest of the herd did not wait around and immediately got out of Dodge!

We made our way back to where our friends were waiting, and informed them my bull was down. Much celebrating and congratulations were exchanged, after which Andy and George took off with one of the sleds, both snowmobiles, and the only rifle to retrieve my bull.

This is when things began to get exciting. While we waited, Gary pointed out a dark shape moving towards our position with great haste. A look through the binoculars confirmed it was a musk ox bull running at full steam towards our position. We joked with each other about how we had heard that musk oxen are almost never aggressive unless provoked. Well it appeared that nobody had bothered to inform this oncoming beast of this fact!

This animal hit the box on our sled with such force that he put one of his horns through the plywood and almost knocked it off the sled. After chasing us around the sled a couple of times, he headed off into the white wilderness. Stunned, we looked at each other and started laughing hysterically.

As soon as Andy and George returned with my animal, George and Gary took off with the gun after the crazed musk ox. They followed him for quite some distance into a small valley where Gary was able to finally put an end to his rampaging. After some hot tea and a bite to eat, we packed up our animals and headed back to our ice Hilton.

During our hunt, we learned many survival techniques from our Inuit friends, including spear hunting seals through the ice; how to quickly build an igloo shelter; ice fishing for Arctic char with handmade soda pop-can lures; how to make emergency clothing, etc. I do not believe more caring, giving people exist on this earth. Hopefully, the Inuit people will continue to retain their current values as modern civilization invades their way of life in the far north.

One last thought: If you have a desire to hunt *Oomingmak* in his arctic home, go during the fall season before the snow and cold makes this hunt more of an exercise in survival than enjoyment! ▲

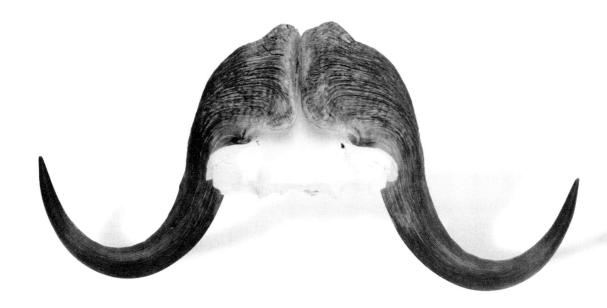

TROPHY STATS

▼ ▼ ▼ ▼ ▼

CATEGORY
Musk Ox

SCORE
$120^2/_8$

LENGTH OF HORN
Right: $27^6/_8$ Left: $28^2/_8$

BOSS WIDTH
Right: $10^6/_8$ Left: $10^1/_8$

GREATEST SPREAD
$30^7/_8$

LOCATION
Tuktoyaktuk, Northwest Territories – 2008

HUNTER
James M. Mazur

MUSK OX
Third Award – 120 ²/₈

▼ ▼ ▼ ▼ ▼ ▼ ▼ ▼ ▼

JAMES M. MAZUR

The temperature in the morning of the first day of my musk ox hunt was only -10°F. It was a relief from the -40°F we experienced during the first phase of my polar bear/musk ox combination hunt. This hunt took place 200 miles northeast of Tuktoyaktuk, Northwest Territories. Tuk, as the natives call it, is located at the mouth of the Mackenzie River where it flows into the Arctic Ocean and is about five miles north of the North American continent's tree line. All travel is by snowmobile.

In it for the Adventure

It took two, eight-hour days of hard riding across the frozen Arctic Ocean to reach our polar bear hunting area for the first phase of my hunt. The snow had drifted into 12- to 15-inch ridges separated by about 30 feet of ice. At 15-20 mph, the ride was as rough as a pickup truck driven at 30 mph over a washboard mountain road.

Inuits ride their snowmobiles as if they were wearing them; yet, at 20 mph, I was barely able to stay on the machine. The four snow machines, which carried three guides and me, towed six sleds with equipment, food, and dogs. The latter are required to hunt for polar bears.

After I harvested my polar bear, we traveled another 110 miles by snowmobile to the musk ox hunting area where the terrain consisted of endless miles of low-rolling hills covered with about 10 inches of snow. The scenery was a vast blue and white panorama where contour lines are barely visible. Visibility was unlimited, so we could see musk ox from two to eight miles away, depending on the height of the surrounding hills.

This part of the trip was a little smoother than the first leg of the trip because we were on land where the snow was fairly smooth. We were able to make about 25 miles per hour, but on the musk ox hunt, I did not have my own snowmobile. I rode on the back of my guide's machine.

Photograph by Jack Reneau

James M. Mazur accepting his plaque and medal from Buck Buckner, Vice President and Chairman of the Big Game Records Committee.

James M. Mazur was on the second half of a polar bear/musk ox combo hunt when he harvested his award-winning bull. It has a final score of 120-2/8 points and received a Third Place Award.

After traveling about an hour along a river's edge, we spotted a single bull grazing on the middle of a hill. Since the snow is only eight to ten inches deep, musk ox can easily paw away the snow and nibble on the grass that lies below. Every time we stopped, I would scrape away the snow with my foot and there would be grass. Clearly, musk oxen have no trouble surviving the winter.

The guide claimed that the herds are growing at an accelerated rate. This is not to say that there is a musk ox every two miles. In fact, we traveled a 50-mile loop looking for the bull I eventually took and only saw two herds. In that area, however, the native guide claimed there is now more musk ox than he had seen in 40 years.

We never saw any wolves or wolf tracks. Apparently, the only predators these animals have in this area at this time of year are humans. We could see a mountain range off in the distance, so grizzlies and wolves could be a problem in the summer and early fall.

MUSK OX
Third Award – 120 2/8

▼ ▼ ▼ ▼ ▼

James M. Mazur

After about four hours we came across musk ox tracks. Since there was no wind, we could follow the tracks until we caught up with the herd. The going was very slow as we had no snowshoes and the snow kept breaking with each step. When we spotted the herd, they formed into the typical phalanx formation. There were four cows, a bull, and two calves. After watching for about five minutes, the herd started to move off. Fortunately, the cows led the way and the bull followed. When he paused about 200 yards away and turned for a last look, I took him with my Model 70 Winchester chambered for .340 Weatherby Magnum.

As we approached him, I was in awe at the size of the bull. While he only stood about 36 to 40 inches tall at the withers, he was fully 36 inches wide. As he lay there he looked like a huge, hairy pig. The horns were massive. While I had never shot a musk ox before, and I had only seen one mounted musk ox and a few photographs, this one possessed the biggest horn bosses I had ever seen. As it turned out, he scored 120-2/8 points. At this score, he ties for 47th place of 602 animals listed in B&C's records book.

The trip home was truly eventful. We had just gotten started when one of the Polaris snowmobiles blew a piston. We were 200 miles from Tuk. We could either leave the sled or double up and tow a double with another person on the back. The machines would probably break down if we tried to double load them, and the recovery process would be tremendously tedious if we left the cargo sled, so the guides decided to repair the engine. To my amazement, we carried sufficient tools and spare parts to disassemble the engine and replace the piston. After a four-hour repair job in the middle of the Arctic Ocean, we were on our way.

We arrived back home in Tuk at 5 a.m. after 13 hours of hard traveling. That forced march was the most exhausting trip I have ever taken. The guides drove at the upper limit of their capabilities, and the constant pounding of the sled totally wore me out.

One consequence of that long ride was that my right foot got cold after traveling about 10 hours. The guides would not stop and told me to just walk it off at each of the hourly "smoke" breaks. I could not feel my toes on my right foot by the time we arrived in Tuk, and it was four months before the feeling came back. Thankfully, the weather had warmed up to zero that night so that I didn't suffer worse frostbite.

As an epilog, I could have flown in and out of the hunting grounds, but where would the adventure be in that? ▲

TROPHY STATS

▼ ▼ ▼ ▼ ▼

CATEGORY
Bighorn Sheep

SCORE
204^2/$_8$

LENGTH OF HORN
Right: 44^4/$_8$ Left: 44^2/$_8$

BASE CIRCUMFERENCE
Right: 16^4/$_8$ Left: 16^4/$_8$

GREATEST SPREAD
25^1/$_8$

LOCATION
Fergus Co., Montana – 2008

HUNTER
Toni L. Sannon

BIGHORN SHEEP
First Award – 204 ^{2}/$_8$

▼ ▼ ▼ ▼ ▼ ▼ ▼ ▼ ▼

TONI L. SANNON

After ten years of applying, 2008 was my year to be one of the lucky ones to receive a Montana bighorn ram permit for the much sought-after Missouri River Breaks. It was just two years earlier that I had drawn a coveted bull elk tag for the same area. While the Breaks tag for bulls isn't as desirable as the sheep permit, it is a very close second. After harvesting a six-point bull that year, I thought I had used up all of my luck. I knew this area has a well-deserved reputation for producing huge rams year after year, and to say I was excited would be a very big understatement.

Every Sheep Hunter's Dream

When it finally sunk in that I would be going on the hunt of my lifetime, the next three months were filled with much preparation. My hunting partner Randy Latterell and I spent countless hours obtaining landowner permission, purchasing and studying maps, talking to biologists and anyone else who had information on the sheep and this very unique country they inhabit. That summer, like several recent years, was extremely dry, and we figured the sheep would be concentrated close to the river. Access to this sheep area is limited at best, so we decided to put all our eggs in one basket and buy a river boat so that we could hunt from the water.

We knew there were outfitters that we could employ but I wanted this to be a true do-it-yourself hunt. I was confident that when the season was over, I would have a nice ram to show for all our efforts. I had arranged a full month off at the beginning of the season for the hunt, and more time later if necessary. I didn't really know how long it might take. My goal was to take a ram with my bow, though if I wasn't able to get a bow shot I would use a J.C. Higgins .270—a 1952 purchase for Randy's mother. He had killed his ram 12 years earlier with it, and

Photograph by Jack Reneau

Toni L. Sannon accepting her plaque and medal from Buck Buckner, Vice President and Chairman of the Big Game Records Committee.

Photograph courtesy of Toni L. Sannon

Toni L. Sannon is pictured above with her award-winning bighorn sheep taken in Fergus County, Montana, during the 2008 season. With a score of 204-2/8 points, it is the largest sheep ever taken by a woman in the Club's Records Program.

I had used it to take my bull in 2006.

We planned to camp as close to the sheep as possible, but a rainstorm just hours before our arrival made access to the camp area impossible. We would have to base camp 20 miles further downriver than we had planned. This would require two hours of unplanned travel time on the river each day. It did cut into the time that we had planned to be hunting, but we weren't going to let that get us down at the start of my bighorn adventure!

Montana recently began to allow a 10-day archery-only season prior to the regular season. Unfortunately I only had one day to hunt during this time. The rest of the season I would be hunting with both rifle and archery hunters.

The first morning, September 14, started out with extremely thick fog that didn't lift until 10 a.m. When it did, it was a beautiful sunny day that topped out around 70°F—not the type of weather that one thinks ideal for sheep hunting in Montana. This was our first look at this breathtaking country. Most of the river corridor is just as Lewis and Clark saw it 200 years earlier. The unique and varied rock formations throughout this badlands terrain were spectacular, as were the numerous other wildlife species we encountered. We saw deer, elk, eagles, badgers, beavers and thousands of geese and other waterfowl. We spotted a few rams the first day, with the biggest being about 180 points.

At 10 a.m. on my second day, we spotted two rams laid up under a ledge on a cliff. From 1,200 yards, we could tell one of them was worthy of closer inspection. We videoed and tried to judge him from 450 yards for an hour, but he would never turn his head. We needed to be closer. Just as we got to 250 yards, they stood and walked out of sight. As we waited for them to show again, three younger rams grazed on another nearby hillside. While we were watching them, much to our surprise the two big rams joined them at 600 yards. We conservatively estimated the biggest to be at least in the high 180s with both horns flared far to each side and appearing to be about the same length. He was a very pretty ram. We videoed and studied them with the spotting scope until they got up and grazed away from us. Not wanting to spook them out of the country, we decided that it would be best to find them the next morning. That evening at camp, we reviewed the footage, and I thought this was the one we should concentrate on getting within bow range.

On our way upriver the next morning, we spotted two mature rams in a group of eight. We studied them for a while but continued upstream to try to find the big flared ram from yesterday. We didn't find him and decided to put a sneak on the previous rams. The temperature was in the 90s, but we were able to get within bow range of the group. The two larger rams were pushing 190, but I couldn't get too serious about them this early in the hunt, especially since I needed to get a better look at the flared ram.

BIGHORN SHEEP
First Award – 204 2/8

▼ ▼ ▼ ▼ ▼

TONI L. SANNON

Each day we would see this group of eight, but we couldn't find the flared ram. I was quite concerned that maybe he had already been taken by another hunter, as we had seen sheep hunters every day in the area.

At 9:30 a.m. on September 21, the eighth day of my hunt, we finally found him. He was all alone near the top of a terribly steep ridge. After sizing up the terrain and taking into consideration the other hunters in the area, it was an easy decision to forego the archery equipment and take him with the .270. This was too nice of a ram to chance losing him again if the archery stalk spooked him out of the country. We had to motor across the river to his side and were scared that he might run. He continued to graze in the open while we closed the distance to 300 yards.

I wasn't used to shooting on such a steep incline so it took me about 15 minutes to get comfortable with the shooting sticks. Randy was busy filming and watching him through the spotting scope. My first shot hit him hard and a couple more anchored him. He rolled a good 100 yards down the hill before he hung up on sagebrush. It was a steep climb up to him, one filled with anticipation to see my ram. When we got up to him, we both knew instantly that I had just taken the ram of every sheep hunter's dreams. We put a quick tape on him and were sure that this was the largest sheep to ever come out of the Breaks. We had time for a couple dozen pictures but knew it would take the entire day to bone the meat, cape him for a life-sized mount, and get back to camp by dark.

The ram's Boone and Crockett entry score is 204-2/8 points. His horn lengths are 44-4/8 inches and 44-2/8 inches for his right and left horns, respectively. Both bases measure 16-4/8 inches. He has unbelievable symmetry with only a 1/8-inch deduction on one circumference measurement. Boone and Crockett Club's 27th Awards Judges Panel verified the entry score of the ram. This is the second largest bighorn ram ever taken in the United States and the largest bighorn sheep ever taken by a woman in Boone and Crockett Club records.

I feel truly blessed for the opportunity to hunt these magnificent animals in such a rugged and remote environment and to come away with such a truly remarkable trophy. ▲

TROPHY STATS

▼ ▼ ▼ ▼ ▼

CATEGORY
Bighorn Sheep

SCORE
202$^7/_8$

LENGTH OF HORN
Right: 43$^1/_8$ Left: 46$^2/_8$

BASE CIRCUMFERENCE
Right: 16$^7/_8$ Left: 16$^7/_8$

GREATEST SPREAD
24$^4/_8$

LOCATION
Blaine Co., Montana – 2008

HUNTER
Debby L. Perry

BIGHORN SHEEP
Second Award – 202 $^7/_8$

▼ ▼ ▼ ▼ ▼ ▼ ▼ ▼ ▼

Debby L. Perry

As the spring of 2008 approached, my partner Joe asked me where I wanted to apply for a bighorn sheep permit, and I told him Montana's Missouri River Breaks. I had heard many people talk about how beautiful this country is, and what a great place it is to hunt bighorn rams.

Two years earlier, Joe drew a sheep permit for unit 423 and shot a ram that scored 185 points. I participated in that hunt with him and found it to be very different compared to the hunting I was used to for elk, pronghorn and deer.

Rainbow Ram

The news of my permit seemed to spread like wildfire. All of a sudden, I had all these guys coming up to me and congratulating me saying, "Do you know how lucky you are to have drawn a sheep permit in unit 680?" Of course I had no idea at the time.

My next task was to learn about the land, and what was public and what was privately owned. By looking at maps and talking with various people, I found out who to contact for permission to hunt. It wasn't an easy task, getting in touch with landowners. They are very busy running their farms and ranches. Being farmers ourselves, Joe and I know how hectic July and August are.

I was limited to hunting weekends due to my job as an elementary school counselor. Joe and friends Randy Brenteson and Bruce Martin took a scouting trip to the breaks before the season began. Their goal was to contact landowners and also check out hunting areas.

My first weekend hunt was September 19–21. Our dear friend Amy Johnson accompanied Joe and me on this hunt. We left after school on Friday and drove 175 miles to our base camp. One of the landowners we contacted was gracious enough to let us use an old cabin

Photograph by Jack Reneau

Debby L. Perry accepting her plaque and medal from Buck Buckner, Vice President and Chairman of the Big Game Records Committee.

Debby L. Perry is pictured here with her award-winning bighorn sheep scoring 202-7/8 points. The ram was taken in Blaine County, Montana, during the 2008 season.

on his property, a primitive structure without running water or electricity. However it did provide warm, dry shelter. It was also home to a few pack rats that kept us company.

Most of the weekends in the remaining days of September and through October were spent hunting from dawn to dusk on Saturdays and Sunday mornings. We put many miles on our pickups and 4-wheelers. I especially enjoyed getting out and walking in this country. We spotted many sheep using this technique.

During this time my sheep spotting skills significantly improved. It was a thrill to see a herd of bighorns resting on a hillside or feeding. We saw many beautiful rams and worked hard at learning how to determine their size.

Late in October we spotted a very nice ram. He and several other rams were bedded down in a wheat field. Our friend Amy was with us on this hunt. We sat there for at least an hour watching him, taking pictures, and debating whether or not to take him. We decided to hold off until the next weekend. We were having so much fun. We really weren't in any hurry to end my hunt.

The following week I looked at the photograph we took of this magnificent ram. I called Joe and said, "Why again was it that I didn't shoot that guy? He's a beauty!"

I told Joe that if I saw him again I was going to go after him. Amy suggested that I should practice shooting. I followed her advice and went to our shooting range and practiced. Each time I shot, I had a vision of that ram in front of me.

We returned to the breaks the weekend of October 31 through November 2. Saturday morning we drove to the location where we'd spotted the ram the weekend before. We finally located him, but once again I passed up a shot. We still had an additional ranch we wanted to explore. As we were leaving the area, we ran into another sheep hunter who had permission to hunt this same property. I couldn't help but think to myself, "I blew it. That hunter is going to go in there, spot my sheep, and shoot him." We agreed that if it was meant to be, we still might have another chance at that ram.

That night I dreamed about shooting that ram. It was daylight savings time, and we turned our clocks back an hour. We woke up early, hoping to be at the spot where we'd seen the big ram before sunrise.

There was a lot of cloud cover that particular morning, and a beautiful sunrise. As it got brighter, a rainbow appeared in the west over the breaks. I told Joe I wanted a picture.

After taking the picture, I looked down and to my surprise saw the ram lying on the side of a hill. I got Joe's attention, but he'd already seen it. We made plans on how we would pursue this ram. We walked to a place where we could look over the bank. When I saw him, I knew it was going to be a challenge. I didn't feel comfortable shooting him from where we were, so we discussed our plan of action, and continued to glass.

BIGHORN SHEEP
Second Award – 202 7/8
▼ ▼ ▼ ▼ ▼
Debby L. Perry

The herd the ram was with suddenly spooked and headed towards the bottom of a huge draw. That's when the chase began. We stayed on top and followed the sheep as they moved along in the bottom. We traveled approximately one and a half miles before the animals started uphill. I knew that if I was going to take a shot, it had to be soon. I got situated, but decided it wasn't the right place and moved downhill a few feet.

I shouldered my rifle and placed the crosshairs on the ram. By this time my quarry and the other sheep had moved quite a ways up the hill. I had only seconds to take a shot before they would go over the hill and out of sight. Joe judged the range at 265 yards. I laid down on a flat rock on a spiny ridge, took my time, aimed, and fired.

Joe said, "You've got a hit."

The ram struggled uphill and went down just as I was pulling down on him a second time. Then he stood up and fell down the nearly vertical face. He bounced off boulders and ledges for at least 150 feet before reaching the bottom. I looked at Joe and said, "I got him, but I'll bet that fall didn't do his horns any good."

When we reached the ram he was at the absolute bottom of a very steep and narrow coulee. He had in fact broken a significant portion of his right horn. We caped and dressed him, and with the help of local ranchers who had become good friends, packed him out. We came out of the breaks in a rain. If it rains in the breaks, you need to be prepared to stay there or get out quickly, because the roads become impassible. We met Montana Fish, Wildlife, and Park Warden Ryan Linder in Big Sandy where we measured and checked my sheep.

I feel proud of the fact that Joe and I did this on our own. We didn't rely on guides and pay huge sums of money for this trophy. This is truly a story of people who enjoyed the whole experience of the hunt. For me, it was the hunt of a lifetime. When I look back on it, I have fond memories of every minute we spent in this magnificent country. We met wonderful landowners who were very gracious and, more importantly, saw many sheep in their historical habitat. ▲

TROPHY STATS

▼ ▼ ▼ ▼ ▼

CATEGORY
Stone's Sheep

SCORE
$180^4/_8$

LENGTH OF HORN
Right: $44^5/_8$ Left: $45^3/_8$

BASE CIRCUMFERENCE
Right: $13^6/_8$ Left: $13^7/_8$

GREATEST SPREAD
$29^2/_8$

LOCATION
Stikine River, British Columbia – 2008

HUNTER
Don South

STONE'S SHEEP
First Award – 180 ⁴/₈

▼ ▼ ▼ ▼ ▼ ▼ ▼ ▼ ▼

Don South

"I think you just took a Boone and Crockett ram!" was the first thing Jerry Geraci, owner of Upper Stikine River Adventures, said as we stood by my magnificent ram.

I replied, "I think we have!"

Taking a trophy Stone's sheep had become a priority for me that began with conversations I had with Jerry Geraci at the Foundation for North American Wild Sheep convention in 2000, which led to my first Stone's sheep hunt in 2001. After flying to Smithers, British Columbia, a floatplane took me to Toucho Lake, where Jerry and my guide Mark McKay were waiting to unload the plane and see off a successful sheep hunter who had just completed his hunt. There would be no such luck for me, even with a lot of very hard work by my guide. However, the 14-day adventure in the beautiful Cassiar Mountains was well worth the trip. I was hooked!

King of Sheep

In 2002, I signed on for another 14-day Stone's sheep hunt with Upper Stikine River Adventures. It was by far a more difficult hunt. We rode horses as far as they could take us and then backpacked for eight days into Jack Stone Creek. An eight-year-old ram was the prize for this journey of endurance.

I knew then that I wasn't finished with Stone's sheep hunting and my quest for an outstanding ram. To me, Stone's sheep had become the king of the four sheep—simply beautiful!

I hunted again with the same outfitter in 2006 with guide Glen Holmes. My 14-day hunt ended without even spotting a legal ram, so when I learned the next hunter had cancelled, I made a satellite phone call to my wife, Linda, and we decided that I should stay and continue. Still, I did not take a ram by the end of this extended hunt. When I returned home, I was reminded that I had been gone for 27 days.

Photograph by Jack Reneau

Don South accepting his plaque and medal from Buck Buckner, Vice President and Chairman of the Big Game Records Committee.

Don South (right) and his good friend and guide Jerry Geraci with Don's award-winning Stone's sheep taken during the 2008 season near the Stikine River in British Columbia. The ram received a First Place Award and has a final score of 180-4/8 points.

I continued to correspond with my now good friend Jerry Geraci, and returned to hunt with his guide service again for the beginning of the 2008 season. This time Jerry and I agreed we would hunt together out of his Stikine River Lodge. I was excited to be hunting with Jerry, knowing his great reputation as a master guide. I was also looking forward to hunting in an area where the country would not be quite as rough, which seemed important because I'm a lot older than the first hunt with this outfitter!

I flew into Smithers a day early to allow time to relax and wait for my luggage to catch up with me, which it turned out was needed! I checked into the Caribou Lodge to find that I would be sharing camp with friend Jerry Tyrrell from Washington state.

Two days later we flew to Dease Lake, then on to Hyland Park on the Stikine River, where we were picked up by a jet boat and taken to the lodge. Heavy rain the next day confined us to the spacious lodge. With two cooks, two guides, two wranglers, a handyman, and a photographer, as well as Jerry Geraci and Jerry Tyrrell, the time passed quickly. It was a good opportunity to get reacquainted with old friends and make new ones.

STONE'S SHEEP
First Award – 180 4/8

▼ ▼ ▼ ▼ ▼

DON SOUTH

The second day we rode more than 20 miles on horseback and spent the night at Grizzly Camp from which Jerry Tyrrell would hunt. The comfortable camp had a great meadow for the hobbled horses and was set up quickly.

In the morning, Jerry Tyrrell and I wished each other good hunting, then Jerry Geraci and I rode another seven miles to Hidden Valley Camp, which would be the base for our hunt. The horses were secured in a blocked box canyon where they had an excellent supply of food and water. A 70-foot waterfall cascaded down into the meadow, making quite a sight. Knowing that the horses were confined in this natural corral, I told Jerry that I would be responsible for "wrangling" the horses, so we began each day with me notifying him that the horses had been cared for and were doing fine.

Jerry talked of other successful hunts that had taken place in the area, like one sheep that had been harvested as it tried to walk through camp. I thought, "I should be so lucky!" He also mentioned the ram that scored 178-7/8 points that was taken last September in Sheep Pass—which we had ridden through that morning—by Terrell McCombs from Texas (See page 435). As we set up camp, we began to see sheep on the hillsides. Watching these small bands of ewes and young rams was a pleasant way to spend the evening.

The weather the following morning was cool and clear—perfect for hunting. After my wrangling duties and donning our backpacks, we hiked and glassed our way up the mountain behind camp. Near the top was a lake with a large open flat where a white ewe and lamb entertained us. Jerry told me to wait there while he checked an area around the ridge. He was soon back in sight, signaling me to join him. A not-quite-legal ram with a distinctive color pattern, one that we had watched on the opposite mountain the day before, was now on our side. He disappeared over a ridge, so we relaxed before heading back down. On the way down, we saw horns moving in the brush and soon had the same ram feeding within 20 feet. Jerry was able to take some great photographs of me with the ram in the background.

August 4 was another sunny, clear day. After camp chores, we donned our backpacks and headed up the mountain in front of camp to check a few basins. The ram we had seen the day before was feeding above camp—not far from where he had been when we last saw him.

About halfway up the mountain, I turned to glass behind us and discovered four more rams working across the hillside toward the lone ram. One of them was noticeably larger, with horns that carried a lot of mass. I asked Jerry if there were any other legal rams besides the largest one, and he said that there was one other legal one. I compared the two rams' horns to help me judge how much larger the first ram was.

We headed back down the hillside that was covered with tangled spruce. The big ram caught our movement at one point, but went back to feeding after staring at us for a considerable length of time.

We then had the opportunity to move to the bottom of the mountain, almost through our camp, and up a trail that led to where the four rams were last seen. A short time later, we had two rams just to our right. We carefully moved past these and had all four rams in sight just above the rim of Hidden Valley. I was able to get to a rock that was not quite tall enough to use for a rest, but it would have to do.

Jerry confirmed which ram was "the one", and after two quick shots at 150 yards, we walked up to this great ram. We took our time, enjoying the moment and congratulating each other. Following an extended photo session, we quartered the ram and packed the meat, horns, and whole cape back to camp. Words could not express my feelings knowing that I had just taken a B&C Stone's ram.

After the 60-day drying period, a B&C Official Measurer scored my 13-year-old ram at 180-4/8 points. The horn lengths were 44-5/8 and 45-3/8 inches, with bases of 13-6/8 and 13-7/8 inches.

Special thanks to Gerry Geraci and Upper Stikine River Adventures, and to my wife, Linda, for the opportunity to hunt in the rugged, picturesque Cassiar Mountains of Northern British Columbia.

Since then, recognition for this ram has taken my wife and me to many interesting and enjoyable places and conventions. We went to Victoria, British Columbia, where I received the Mountain Hunter Record Book Award from the Guides and Outfitters Association of British Columbia. We then traveled to Salt Lake City, Utah, in 2008 where I received the Wild Sheep Foundation's Gold Medal Award for Stone's sheep taken with a rifle, as well as the 2009 Rifle Award of Excellence. A trip to Las Vegas, Nevada, and the Grand Slam Club/Ovis convention added the Diamond Award and the Bouchard Summit Award, both for the 2006-2008 North American Sheep category. We then returned to Nevada to attend the Safari Club International convention in Reno, and received the 2008-2009 Major Award, 3rd place North America. We were invited to attend Safari Club, Italian Chapter National convention in Milano Marittima, Italy, where we received the Carlo Caldesi Award for one of the top six animals taken in the world in 2009. Finally, we attended B&C's 27th Awards Program in Reno, Nevada, June 2010, where my ram received the First Place Award for the Stone's sheep category. ▲

Award-Winning Moments

B&C Photo Archives

Not only did Toni L. Sannon (left) and Debby L. Perry both draw highly prized Montana bighorn sheep permits in 2008, but they each took a records-book ram in the Missouri Breaks that differs in score by just 1-3/8 inches. Toni's scores 204-2/8 and Debby's scores 202-7/8. The new-found friends pose with their rams, which both rank in the All-time top-10, in the trophy display at the Grand Sierra Resort.

TROPHY STATS

▼ ▼ ▼ ▼ ▼

CATEGORY
Stone's Sheep

SCORE
177^2/$_8$

LENGTH OF HORN
Right: 40^3/$_8$ Left: 42^3/$_8$

BASE CIRCUMFERENCE
Right: 14^7/$_8$ Left: 14^7/$_8$

GREATEST SPREAD
24^2/$_8$

LOCATION
Stikine River, British Columbia – 2007

HUNTER
R. Terrell McCombs

STONE'S SHEEP
Second Award – 177 ²/₈

▼ ▼ ▼ ▼ ▼ ▼ ▼ ▼ ▼

R. TERRELL McCOMBS

Sheep have always held a special fascination for me. Maybe it's because they live in such spectacular, harsh environments. Maybe it's because they represent such a tremendous physical and mental challenge. However, I think the real basis for my fascination is simple: It's those horns! I don't know many hunters who aren't in awe of holding a really good set of heavy, massive sheep horns in their hands.

It was in September 2007 that I set out to find a Stone's ram to add to a fine Dall's ram I

A Stone for the Ages

had harvested in Alaska's Chugach range. That was in 2004, and although I hunted these "rams of the rocks" in 2006, I had been unsuccessful. Now at 52, I can see the horizon of my sheep-hunting career much clearer than I could a decade earlier. We only have so much time to do what we love, and I was determined to take a good Stone's ram, arguably one of the most beautiful and coveted big-game animals in North America.

The final floatplane ride into Jerry Geraci's Stikine River Lodge was smooth and the scenery spectacular. After touching down, I ate a fine meal of sheep ribs prepared by Ruth, the lodge's cook, and sacked out for a good night's rest. The following morning would find me in the saddle for a 25-mile horseback ride with a pack string into some of the wildest country in North America.

My guide was Rod, a 33-year-old fireman and mountaineer from Vancouver, British Columbia. Rod enjoyed taking a month's vacation every year to guide for Jerry. He was athletic, offered intelligent conversation on a wide variety of subjects, and was well-versed in sheep behavior and ecology. While Rod had guided many hunters to moose, caribou, goat, and even grizzly, he freely admitted that this was his first opportunity to guide a sheep hunter. Normally this would concern me, but not with Rod. While I have a decent amount of sheep- and

Photograph by Jack Reneau

R. Terrell McCombs accepting his plaque and medal from Buck Buckner, Vice President and Chairman of the Big Game Records Committee.

goat-hunting experience, his attitude and confidence was infectious.

He said, "Terrell, all you and I have to worry about is the weather. We'll find a ram because I saw a real good one up here last week when I was glassing for moose down in the valley."

"How good was he?" I asked.

"Oh," Rod replied, "He was good alright. It looked to me like his horns came two or three inches above the bridge of his nose and he looked plenty heavy."

He curled above the bridge of his nose? What a ram! I thought. Now I was excited and in the game. Later that evening we arrived at our campsite, and I stole some time to glass for sheep while helping set up camp. Nothing motivates a sheep hunter like sighting a big ram.

The next morning Rod and I left Earl, our young wrangler, in camp as we backpacked two or three miles to a good spike camp location to glass for the ram. We hunted and glassed hard for nearly three days, climbing up to look over several basins and an untold number of shale slides. No sheep. The fourth and final day found us tent-bound as the weather cooled considerably and six inches of snow greeted us at dawn. It snowed all day.

> **ROD URGED ME TO HURRY BEFORE THE RAM DISAPPEARED OVER THE RIDGE. HOWEVER, I IGNORED HIS URGINGS, AS I CONCENTRATED FULLY ON THE SHOT. IT WAS STILL AND SILENT, NEARLY SOLEMN, LIKE BEING IN A CATHEDRAL. I WAS IN A DEEP ZONE OF CONCENTRATION NOW, AND MY WORLD WENT INTO SLOW MOTION.**

When you are 6-foot-5, spending the day cramped into a small backpack tent with your guide is a challenge to your commitment. Little doubts and questions enter your mind as to why you are really there. It also offers you too much time to think about your responsibilities back home. I tried to keep my mind busy by reading or simply sleeping. Bad weather is the curse of sheep hunting.

I have always thought the greatest challenge with hunting sheep is the mental aspect of it. You begin asking yourself too many questions when you are confined by the weather. How many days are left? Will I find a good ram? Will the weather ever clear up? Will that head cold turn into something worse? What if the shot is too far? How's my family? That is why I'll glass and trek to the top of every visible mountain before I'll spend one daylight hour in a tent. The problem is you never have any choice in the matter. Weather dictates everything. If you don't have the visibility to glass, you can't hunt sheep.

We glassed for an hour the next morning before bad weather descended upon us again. All we saw was one lone billy goat, but no sheep. At that point we decided to return to Earl and the horses. We at least had a larger tent there. We approached camp and called out for Earl around mid-morning. The 18-year-old was ecstatic to see us. I don't think Earl enjoyed those lonely days by himself! However, he offered good news. He had been riding up to a nearby pass early that morning and had seen a good ram feeding. We excitedly asked him for more details. After listening to Earl and asking several questions about the animal, Rod concluded that it was the same ram we had been looking for. The weather was clearing some, and we decided look for the ram that afternoon.

STONE'S SHEEP
Second Award – 177 $^2/_8$

▼ ▼ ▼ ▼ ▼

R. Terrell McCombs

We hunted very hard, glassing into high mountain basins, while sitting out wave after wave of snow and sleet descending upon us from the northwest. It was strange. There were periods you could see a mile or more, closely followed by periods where you could not see 100 yards, coupled with high winds. We stuck it out all afternoon in search of the ram. We glassed and hunted over the high mountain pass and the adjoining mountains and deep cirques for nearly seven hours. Only the approaching dusk pushed us back toward camp. While the scenic vistas had been beautiful, we hadn't seen any sheep.

That evening, a serious storm blew in, dumping more than a foot of snow on top of an already hefty accumulation. The temperature dropped into the high teens and the next day was spent in the tent. No one, as I mentioned earlier, likes being confined to a tent because of weather. The time passes slowly and cabin fever can build up in hunters and guides alike. Earl and Rod were singing the blues that evening. Now, with only two full days left to hunt, the warm fires of Jerry's Stikine River Lodge were becoming more and more appealing. In fact, the idea of heading back early was even mentioned. I can't blame the guys. We were all a little down over the weather. That's when I reminded them to maintain a positive attitude.

I said, "Many great animals have been taken on the last hour of the last day of the hunt. We are going to tough this thing out. Who knows? The weather could clear up tomorrow and we could climb up to that pass and take the ram of the century."

I had no idea how prophetic those words would become.

The next morning dawned with fog, snow, and a gray overcast but there was a hint of blue in the western sky. Sure enough, it cleared enough by 11 a.m. to hunt. We busily packed our gear and began climbing toward the pass.

The going was slow as we pushed through snow two to three feet deep. I was in the lead and stopped to glass often. After an hour, we were a little more than halfway to the head of the pass when I noticed something unusual about 1,200 yards away on a south facing slope. Any big-game hunter knows what I am talking about. It just looked out of place. Slowly and quietly I held up my hand to stop our progress. I pointed toward the slope, and three pairs of binoculars went up at once. My breathing stopped for a moment as I realized I was looking at a very good bedded Stone's ram. He had not seen us and we slowly dropped out of sight into a side canyon.

I can't exactly describe the next few moments except to say the debate over stalking strategy was heated and intense. Finally, Rod and I agreed on the most conservative approach to the ram. After my disappointing experience the prior year, I had developed a deep respect

Photograph courtesy of R. Terrell McCombs

R. Terrell McCombs sits behind his award-winning Stone's sheep harvested deep in the British Columbia mountains. The ram, which has a final score of 177-2/8 points, received a Second Place Award.

for the powerful vision of these animals. I would not make the same mistake twice.

We lunged through the deep snowdrifts, my lungs burning as we pushed up an adjacent slope to reach a good shooting position. Although we were only at a little over 6,000 feet, the steep slope and deep snow made every step feel like 30-pound weights were strapped to each leg. Earl was paralleling us, peeking around the edge from time to time to keep an eye on the ram as we ascended. Suddenly, he motioned that the ram was up. He could not have seen, heard, or smelled us. Regardless, he was headed straight up the slope toward the crest of the adjoining drainage. We shifted into high gear as we cursed the snow and the icy mountain as we slipped and struggled the last 50 yards to the crest.

I had wanted a shot under 300 yards, but there was no hope for that now. I flopped down into the snow and grabbed Rod's pack for a rest. I was still heaving from the hard climb and took several deep breaths to calm my nerves as I tried to prepare for the shot of my life. I settled down as the ram continued toward the crest of the ridge, now less than 25 yards ahead of him. He was moving with purpose and there would be no way to keep up with him under these conditions. It was now or never.

"Earl, give me the range."

"476 yards," he replied.

Rod urged me to hurry before the ram disappeared over the ridge. However, I ignored his urgings, as I concentrated fully on the shot. It was still and silent, nearly solemn, like being in a cathedral. I was in a deep zone of concentration now, and my world went into slow motion. I took two more slow, deep breaths and acquired a solid, steady sight picture. Earl was saying something to me, but I didn't hear him. Every ounce of concentration was on the ram. I slowly began my trigger squeeze and I remember being surprised as the loud report of the rifle disturbed the deep stillness of the wilderness.

I saw the ram fall as I recovered from the recoil. I was turning toward Earl, with a look of triumph on my face, when he screamed, "You killed him!"

Earl, his face showing a combination of shock and elation, leaped on me, driving us both down into three feet of snow. It was an act of pure joy. Suddenly, Rod joined the dog pile and the three of us laughed and shouted in victory as we rolled through the deep snow like schoolboys on winter vacation. We had been three men, thrown together as strangers in the intense crucible that is sheep hunting. Now we were laughing, screaming, and even shedding some tears in pure celebration of the hunt. It was a scene as old as mankind itself,

STONE'S SHEEP
Second Award – 177 ²/₈
▼ ▼ ▼ ▼ ▼

R. Terrell McCombs

and we continued to hug and shake hands, delirious over our success. We thought we might be shut out, but in the last inning, grasped victory! It is a feeling I cannot explain, but will never forget as long as I live.

We approached the ram together, for through this bonding experience we were now a team. I pulled the trigger but each of us owned a piece of that ram. No one had to say anything. We all knew it. I observed that his bases looked larger than 13 or even 14 inches. A tape measure was back at camp, but we weren't too concerned about it. We were just thrilled to have harvested such a fine animal. After plenty of pictures, we began the long pack down to camp.

I took out a vinyl tape measure in camp and casually measured the horns, mostly out of curiosity. The tape said 43 x 15 inches. Earl, ever the skeptic, insisted we measure them again. The results were the same. His horns didn't look that long due to their heavy mass. No one said anything for a few minutes as we began to realize the true size of this magnificent animal before us. I told Rod it was a heck of a way to begin his sheep guiding career and then kidded him that it would be all downhill from here.

Later, Jerry said it was the largest ram to come out of his area in nearly 25 years. No one had seen him before, strong testament to the fact that it is very hard to hunt every inch of a 4,000-square-mile hunting concession, even over 25 years. We carefully green-scored him at around 180 points. Roger Britton, the government inspector and a local taxidermist in Smithers, said it was the largest ram he had seen in more than 20 years on the job. He aged the ram at 13-1/2 years.

Large rams are where you find them. I have heard it said that all the great Stone's sheep were taken in the 60s and 70s and none are left in British Columbia and the Yukon today. Great sheep are still there and more probably die from worn teeth and wolves than most of us would care to admit. However, with recent commodity prices at historic highs, more resident hunting pressure is put on sheep today than in the past. Once-formidable wilderness is being carved up and penetrated with easily accessed mining roads. High prices, due to the world's growing demand for energy and minerals, are a fact of life today. No outfitter can control that fact. He can only work to gain the cooperation of these natural resource companies in order to respect the wildlife that is essential to his way of life. Let us hope this sense of cooperation in land-use management is successful. It is important because today more than ever, we need to know that great rams still roam wild and steep mountain basins.

Fortunately, this hunt proved to me they still do. ▲

TROPHY STATS

▼ ▼ ▼ ▼ ▼

CATEGORY
Stone's Sheep

SCORE
173 $1/8$

LENGTH OF HORN
Right: 39 $6/8$ Left: 39 $3/8$

BASE CIRCUMFERENCE
Right: 15 $4/8$ Left: 15 $4/8$

GREATEST SPREAD
26 $6/8$

LOCATION
Richards Creek, British Columbia – 2007

HUNTER
Michael D. Schauer

STONE'S SHEEP
Honorable Mention – 173 ¹/₈

▼ ▼ ▼ ▼ ▼ ▼ ▼ ▼ ▼

MICHAEL D. SCHAUER

I arrived in Fort St. John, British Columbia, midday on Tuesday, August 28, with instructions to call Kevin Olmstead, the proprietor of Prophet Muskwa Outfitting upon my arrival. The plan was to fly to the main lodge yet that afternoon. However, plans changed rapidly when Kevin explained how the lodge was socked in with rain and fog. Flying would be out on this day, so I took up residence at the Northern Grand in Fort St. John. Unfortunately, this became my home for the next two nights

Experiencing the Thrill

as well, as the weather would not let up. I, along with my new friends, two other Prophet Muskwa clients Mark and Bob, rose every morning, checked out of our rooms, waited all day in the lobby hoping for a phone call letting us know we were okay to fly and, upon not receiving the "okay to fly" call, subsequently checked into a different room each night.

Finally, Friday morning we got the much-anticipated call that the weather had cleared, and we would be flown to the main lodge, then on to spike camp at Richards Creek to begin our hunts: mine for sheep, Mark for elk and goat, and Bob for elk and moose. Thank God! To say we were getting a bit antsy would have been like saying the Canadian wilderness is kind of big!

Spike camp turned out to be far more luxurious than what I had expected. Instead of using tents like I had on previous sheep hunts, I had the pleasure of staying in a cabin, one with a working woodstove, no less. Another cabin housed the kitchen and eating area and was ably staffed by Kat. A third and fourth cabin held the guides and wrangler (Ed). All in all, a pretty comfortable set up for sheep camp.

My guide was a 55-year-old veteran sheep hunter named Garry. An off-season steel-worker from Toronto, Garry looked to be more than able to lead me up the mountains. And if looks were not enough, 60-70 successful sheep hunts convinced me that I had drawn an excellent guide. I was also impressed that he was packing a Swarovski spotting scope, further proof this guy was prepared.

After introductions, Mark, Bob, and I checked our gear into our cabin then headed for the shooting bench to check our rifles. All our rifles were on. However, there was not enough time remaining to hunt this day. Instead, we ate an excellent dinner of moose meat and turned in early with hopes of bagging the big one in the morning.

Five o'clock came quickly, and after spending several days in the "Northern Grand," I was thrilled to be finally going hunting. After a quick, hearty breakfast, lunch was packed, horses saddled, and Garry and I were off by roughly 6:15 a.m. It was September 1st. Roughly two hours later we reached a good vantage point to begin glassing.

It didn't take Garry long to spot two rams. Further study with the spotting scope led us to believe one of them might be worth checking out. Unfortunately, they were on a green, grassy slope some three to four miles back across the river we had just come from. We decided to leave the two rams alone for the time being and continue another 30-40 minutes to a basin that was our original destination. Upon reaching the basin, we dismounted, climbed a short distance, and quickly located a herd of several young rams. They were only 300 yards away but blended in amazingly well with their rocky surroundings. We decided to stay put and see if any other rams would show themselves. Unbelievably, a total of 12 more showed up over the next 45 minutes, but none of them met the full curl or 8-year-old requirement to be legal. It was now pushing noon.

Garry suggested we go back down the mountain, across the river, and hike up the other side in hopes of relocating the two rams we'd seen earlier in the day. We both agreed this would probably take the rest of our day.

THIS BECAME THE MOST DIFFICULT PART OF THE HUNT—WAITING. WE THOUGHT THEY WOULD FEED OUT INTO CLEAR SIGHT IF GIVEN A LITTLE TIME, BUT AFTER 10 MINUTES (OR WHAT SEEMED LIKE HOURS!) WE BECAME IMPATIENT AND STARTED CREEPING CLOSER TO THE EDGE OF THE ROCKSLIDE FOR A BETTER LOOK. FINALLY THEY WERE IN SIGHT, AND ONLY 150-175 YARDS AWAY.

After leading our horses down the steep mountain, we crossed the river only to discover our wind was going directly toward the area where we'd last seen the rams. In an attempt to neutralize this problem, we rode two drainages past where we'd seen the rams before we started to regain elevation. At this point, the horses were able to get us over a third of the way up the ridge. I'm guessing 800-1,000 feet of elevation up from the river. The rest would be up to us.

We ate a quick lunch at roughly 1:30 p.m. before starting our hike. To shield our wind, Garry suggested we go up a steep, narrow drainage that would bring us out on the ridge top roughly a mile from where the rams were feeding earlier in the morning. It was only a mile and a quarter to the top, but the hike was very tough. The terrain was steep, but more problematic was the footing that consisted of a steady diet of small stones, most no bigger than a baseball. Every step up resulted in a backward slide. Two steps forward, one back would have fairly described our progress. Further complicating the hike was my recently consumed lunch of fruit and a tuna sandwich, which was now sitting squarely in my throat and rising with every step.

I let Garry know that I'd make the top but that I'd be a little slow because I wasn't feeling well. So up I went—slowly. Finally, around 3:30 p.m., I reached the top of the ridge. What should have been a one-hour hike took nearly two, but I was on top. The problem now:

there were no sheep. Garry had been glassing for the last 15 minutes before I caught up with him and was unable to locate anything.

STONE'S SHEEP
Honorable Mention – 173 1/8
▼ ▼ ▼ ▼ ▼
MICHAEL D. SCHAUER

After assuring Garry I was feeling better, we headed along the ridge back towards where we had seen the rams. Our plan was to be above where we'd last seen them to ensure our scent blew up and over the ridge top. As we worked our way along the ridge, we peeked into every little hole along the way—still no sheep. Finally one big rockslide, this time with big rocks you could actually walk on, separated us from the green, grassy slope occupied by the two rams several hours earlier. It was now 4:15 p.m.

We peeked over the edge of the rockslide and were shocked. Two rams were running directly towards us. Although only 300-400 yards away, sizing them up was impossible due to the head-on angle and their hurry to get back on the green grass. In a few seconds they were out of sight, having reached a point close to us where the curvature of the rockslide shielded them.

This became the most difficult part of the hunt—waiting. We thought they would feed out into clear sight if given a little time, but after 10 minutes (or what seemed like hours!) we became impatient and started creeping closer to the edge of the rockslide for a better look. Finally they were in sight, and only 150-175 yards away. While the rams were unaware of our presence, Garry was instantly studying the larger one through his Swarovski scope, counting rings on the ram's horns to determine his age.

As he quietly counted, I was getting in position to shoot. I heard him get to seven two different times and wondered if he would give me the okay. Although the ram was visibly full-curl and legal, outfitters generally strive to shoot rams 8 years and older in an effort to perpetuate mature rams. Finally Garry gave me the green light.

I asked him for some quick size estimates. He guessed the big ram at 37 inches in length and 13-plus inches on the base. Although I was in no position to question his judgments, I truly believed the ram had more mass and decided to pull the trigger. The shot from my .300 Remington Ultra Mag entered just behind his near shoulder and exited through the far shoulder, a solid heart shot that dropped the big ram in his tracks. Unfortunately, due to the steep terrain, the ram started to roll down the hill, then cartwheel, then disappear entirely into a big draw. Of course I had lots of anxiety as Garry and I scrambled down to the sheep, now well over a quarter mile away.

As we approached the downed ram, I was relieved to see that he had weathered his fall pretty well. Neither horn was broken. Garry was quickly reassessing his estimate and now ventured the sheep would go 39 inches long and over 14 inches on the bases—truly a great ram.

After picture taking and butchering, Garry and I started down the mountain with two heavy packs of sheep meat, horns, and cape. We hiked roughly a mile to get to an area

Photograph courtesy of Michael D. Schauer

Michael D. Schauer harvested his Stone's sheep near Richards Creek in British Columbia during the 2007 season. The ram, which has a final score of 173-1/8 points, received an Honorable Mention at the 27th Big Game Awards Banquet in Reno, Nevada.

where we could get the horses. After leading the horses down another half mile, we were finally able to mount up and ride back to camp.

We arrived in camp at roughly 9 p.m. and were greeted with handshakes, backslaps, and all the five other forms of congratulations that follow a successful sheep hunt. A great dinner was waiting, but I admit it was a bit of a blur, as Garry and I were gulping our food so we could get back outside to cape and measure the big ram. Finally Garry put the tape on him. At nearly 40 inches in length and over 16-inch bases, the ram just kept getting bigger—no ground shrinkage here! Garry's green score totaled over 175 points, with an incredible 95-plus inches of mass. Words couldn't describe how thrilled I was! The 27th Awards Program Judges Panel confirmed a score of 173-1/8 with 15-4/8 inch bases on each side.

At the 2008 Wild Sheep Foundation (formerly FNAWS) banquet, my sheep received the Silver Award as the second largest Stone's sheep taken in the last year with a rifle. Although I appreciate the award, the true satisfaction comes from the hunt, the awe-inspiring scenery, and all the special people who help make sheep hunting possible. Special thanks goes out to my family, my friends, and the great guides and outfitters that have helped me experience the great thrill of hunting sheep. ▲

Moments in Measuring

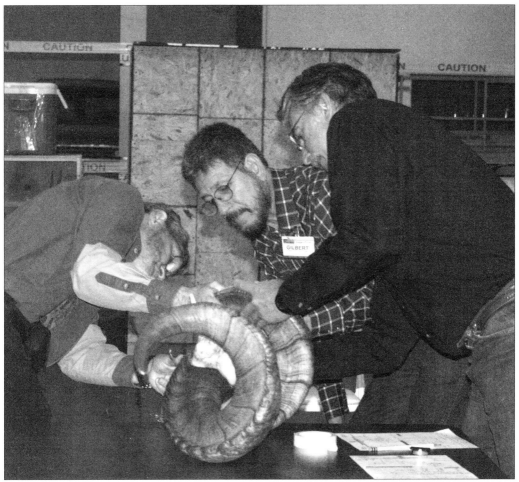

B&C Photo Archives

Judges Larry Lack, Gilbert Hernandez, and Victor Clark teamed up to score the horn lengths of the greatest Stone's sheep taken in the last 18 years. Harvested in 2008 by Don South near the Stikine River, British Columbia, its score was verified at 180-4/8 points. The lengths of the right and left horns are 44-5/8 inches and 45-3/8 inches long, respectively. This incredible ram was aged at 13-1/2 years old.

TABULATIONS OF RECORDED TROPHIES 27TH AWARDS PROGRAM 2007-2009

TABULATIONS OF RECORDED TROPHIES IN THE 27TH AWARDS ENTRY PERIOD

The trophy data shown herein has been taken from score charts in Boone and Crockett Club's Records Archives for the 27th Awards Program, 2007-2009. Trophies listed are those that meet minimum score and other stated requirements of trophy entry for the period.

The final scores and rank shown in the book are official, except for trophies shown with an asterisk. An asterisk is assigned to trophies accepted in this Awards Program with entry scores that were subject to verification by the 27th Awards Program Judges Panel but were not seen by the Panel. The asterisk can be removed (except in the case of a potential new World's Record) by submitting two additional, independent scorings by Official Measurers of the Boone and Crockett Club. The Records Committee of the Club will review the three scorings available and determine which, if any, will be accepted in lieu of the Judges' Panel measurement.

When the score has been accepted as final by the Records Committee, the asterisk will be removed in future editions of the All-time records book, *Records of North American Big Game*, and other publications by the Boone and Crockett Club. In the case of a potential new World's Record, the trophy must come before an Awards Program Judges Panel or a Special Judges Panel, which is convened between Awards Program Judges Panels, on an as-needed-basis to verify World's Record status in a timely manner. Only an Awards Program Judges Panel or a Special Judges Panel can certify a new B&C World's Record and finalize its score. Asterisked trophies are shown at the end of the listings for their category. They are not ranked, as their final score is subject to revision by a Judges Panel or by the submission of additional scorings, as described above.

"Party hunting" is a practice whereby one hunter tags an animal he or she has killed with the tag of another person in his or her hunting party. Party hunting for whitetail deer is a practice allowed in Wisconsin, Minnesota, and Iowa, and two Canadian provinces, Manitoba, and Ontario. The Club accepts all hunter-taken trophies where party-hunting is legal, so long as the animal is taken in Fair Chase. However, the hunter's name will only be listed in B&C publications for trophies killed by the hunter and tagged with the hunter's own tag(s). The hunter's name will be left blank for trophies tagged with the tag of another person.

Note that "PR" preceding the date of kill indicates "prior to" the year shown for kill.

This is the second B&C Awards book that lists a B&C gross score for antlered, horned, and tusked animals. B&C gross score for antlered animals is basically the typical frame, without deductions for lack of symmetry, plus the total of the lengths of the abnormal points. B&C gross score for horned and tusked animals is the total of the left and right sides without any deductions for lack of symmetry. Trophies will continue to be listed and ranked in B&C publications by their B&C final score, but the B&C gross score is listed for informational and comparison purposes.

The scientific and vernacular names and the sequence of presentation follows those suggested in the "Revised Checklist of North American Mammals North of Mexico," 1979 (J. Knox, et al; Texas Tech University, 14 December 1979.)

TROPHY BOUNDARIES

Many of the categories recognized in Boone and Crockett Club's North American Big Game Awards Program are based upon subspecies differences. In nature, subspecies freely interbreed where their ranges overlap, thus necessitating the setting of geographic boundaries to keep them, as well as hybrids, separate for records-keeping purposes.

Geographic boundaries are described for a number of categories. These include: Alaska brown and grizzly bear; Atlantic and Pacific walrus; American, Roosevelt's, and tule elk; mule, Columbia, and Sitka blacktail deer; whitetail and Coues' deer; moose; and caribou. Pertinent information for several of these boundaries is included in the trophy data listings that follow, but the complete, detailed description for each is to be found in *Measuring and Scoring North American Big Game Trophies,* 3rd Edition, revised 2009, or on the Club's web site at www.booneandcrockettclub.com.

In addition to category-specific boundaries, all trophies must be from North America, north of the south border of Mexico, to be eligible. For pelagic trophies such as walrus and polar bear, they must be from Canada, Greenland, and the USA-side of the International Date Line to be eligible.

Trophy boundaries are set by the Boone and Crockett Club's Records of North American Big Game Committee by working with the latest and best-available information from scientific researchers, guides, hunters, and other parties with serious interest in our big-game resources. Boundaries are set so that it is highly unlikely that specimens of the larger category or hybrids can be taken within boundaries set for the smaller category, thus upsetting the rankings of the smaller category. Trophy boundaries are revised as necessary to maintain this separation of the categories.

B&C's Records Committee is currently conducting extensive DNA research to identify genetic differences between mule deer, Columbia blacktail deer, and Sitka blacktail deer. Studies are also being conducted to determine if there are genetic differences between whitetail deer and its smaller cousin, the Coues' whitetail deer. These research efforts could be used to establish or modify category boundaries in the future. At a minimum, the results will enable us to verify the genetic purity of a trophy entered in these categories. ▲

BLACK BEAR

Ursus americanus americanus and related subspecies

Minimum Score 20   World's Record 23 10/16

Final Score	Greatest Length of Skull Without Lower Jaw	Greatest Width of Skull	Locality	Hunter	Owner	Date Killed	Rank
22 13/16	14 1/16	8 12/16	Riding Mt., MB	Robert J. Evans	Robert J. Evans	2008	1
22 11/16	14	8 11/16	Lehigh Co., PA	Joseph W. Paulo	Joseph W. Paulo	1997	2
22 11/16	14	8 11/16	Newaygo Co., MI	Donald R. Corrigan	Donald R. Corrigan	2009	2
22 9/16	14 2/16	8 7/16	Mesa Co., CO	Donald W. Foster	Donald W. Foster	2007	4
22 8/16	13 15/16	8 9/16	Haywood Co., NC	Thad Surrett	Thad Surrett	2008	5
22 7/16	13 9/16	8 14/16	Buncombe Co., NC	Picked Up	NC Wildl. Res. Comm.	2006	6
22 7/16	13 10/16	8 13/16	Pike Co., PA	Walter G. Rupnik	Walter G. Rupnik	2008	6
22 7/16	13 13/16	8 10/16	Leask, SK	Terry Shewchuk	Terry Shewchuk	2009	6
22 6/16	14 8/16	7 14/16	Huntingdon Co., PA	Paul W. Carothers, Jr.	Paul W. Carothers, Jr.	2001	9
22 6/16	13 14/16	8 8/16	Lincoln Co., WI	David J. Frahm	David J. Frahm	2007	9
22 6/16	14 4/16	8 2/16	Gila Co., AZ	Adam R. Powers	Adam R. Powers	2009	9
22 5/16	13 10/16	8 11/16	Peace River, AB	Kris S. Boivin	Kris S. Boivin	2006	12
22 5/16	14 4/16	8 1/16	Mifflin Co., PA	Jonas D. Glick	Jonas D. Glick	2007	12
22 4/16	14 5/16	7 15/16	Preston Co., WV	Earnest M. Schrock	Earnest M. Schrock	2001	14
22 4/16	13 7/16	8 13/16	Lake Manitoba, MB	Dana Harper	Dana Harper	2007	14
22 3/16	13 13/16	8 6/16	Lycoming Co., PA	Toby L. Hiestand	Toby L. Hiestand	2006	16
22 3/16	14 6/16	7 13/16	Qu'Appelle River, SK	Kevin D. Fonagy	Kevin D. Fonagy	2009	16
22 2/16	13 10/16	8 8/16	Wayne Co., PA	Donald L. Bush	Donald L. Bush	2008	18
22 1/16	13 11/16	8 6/16	Hyde Co., NC	Wilton C. Gay, Jr.	Wilton C. Gay, Jr.	2006	19
22 1/16	13 15/16	8 2/16	Orange Co., NY	Michael B. Maillet	Michael B. Maillet	2006	19
22 1/16	13 13/16	8 4/16	Rapid View, SK	Darcy J. Fehr	Darcy J. Fehr	2008	19
22	13 14/16	8 2/16	Peace River, AB	Kevin D. Martin	Kevin D. Martin	2005	22
22	13 6/16	8 10/16	Sussex Co., NJ	Mark A. Utter	Mark A. Utter	2005	22
22	13 10/16	8 6/16	Gates Co., NC	Travis J. Lilly	Travis J. Lilly	2006	22
22	14 2/16	7 14/16	Livingston Co., NY	Ronald P. Perham	Ronald P. Perham	2008	22
22	13 8/16	8 8/16	Bayfield Co., WI	Cole M. Martinsen	Cole M. Martinsen	2009	22
21 15/16	13 7/16	8 8/16	Clark Co., WI	Frederick W. Moen	Frederick W. Moen	2006	27
21 15/16	13 12/16	8 3/16	Indiana Co., PA	Donald L. Stear	Donald L. Stear	2006	27
21 15/16	13 8/16	8 7/16	Hudson Bay, SK	Gregory S. Hovey	Gregory S. Hovey	2007	27
21 15/16	14 4/16	7 11/16	Chippewa Co., WI	Greg R. Misfeldt	Greg R. Misfeldt	2007	27
21 15/16	13 12/16	8 3/16	Rio Arriba Co., NM	Robert J. Seeds	Robert J. Seeds	2007	27
21 15/16	13 10/16	8 5/16	Tehama Co., CA	Robert R. Henderson	Robert R. Henderson	2008	27
21 13/16	13 8/16	8 5/16	Tioga Co., PA	Thomas M. Oliver	Thomas M. Oliver	2007	33

			Locality	Hunter	Owner	Date	Rank
21 13/16	13 15/16	7 14/16	St. Croix Co., WI	Steve A. Parent	Steve A. Parent	2007	33
21 13/16	13 11/16	8 2/16	Langlade Co., WI	Joel W. Hoffman	Joel W. Hoffman	2008	33
21 13/16	13 9/16	8 4/16	Somerset Co., PA	Loren B. Murray	Loren B. Murray	2008	33
21 13/16	13 13/16	8	Sawyer Co., WI	Leonard D. Cutsforth	Leonard D. Cutsforth	2009	33
21 13/16	13 12/16	8 1/16	St. Walburg, SK	Gary Johnston	Gary Johnston	2009	33
21 12/16	13 10/16	8 2/16	Menominee Co., MI	Jason Welch	Jason Welch	2004	39
21 12/16	12 15/16	8 13/16	Slave Lake, AB	Gregory S. Spitzley	Gregory S. Spitzley	2006	39
21 12/16	13 8/16	8 4/16	Price Co., WI	David F. Hilgart	David F. Hilgart	2007	39
21 12/16	13 6/16	8 6/16	Pike Co., PA	William A. Savacool	William A. Savacool	2007	39
21 12/16	13 5/16	8 7/16	Garfield Co., CO	Eddie Elder	Eddie Elder	2008	39
21 12/16	13 10/16	8 2/16	Wexford Co., MI	Picked Up	Picked Up	2008	39
21 12/16	13 10/16	8 2/16	Jackson Co., OR	John Souza	John Souza	2008	39
21 12/16	13 5/16	8 7/16	Mesa Co., CO	John M. Bailey	John M. Bailey	2009	39
21 12/16	13 11/16	8 1/16	Marinette Co., WI	Daniel L. Clarksen	Daniel L. Clarksen	2009	39
21 11/16	13 3/16	8 8/16	Sanpete Co., UT	LuDene A. Hamilton	William M. Hamilton	1964	48
21 11/16	13 12/16	7 15/16	Bradford Co., PA	Eugene A. Smiley	Eugene A. Smiley	2006	48
21 11/16	13 2/16	8 9/16	Sawyer Co., WI	Kenneth J. Imm	Picked Up	2007	48
21 11/16	13 14/16	7 13/16	Chowan Co., NC	William L. Jackson	William L. Jackson	2007	48
21 11/16	14 1/16	7 10/16	Barron Co., WI	Rick J. Tokarski	Rick J. Tokarski	2007	48
21 11/16	13 10/16	8 1/16	Assiniboine River, MB	William B. Minshull	William B. Minshull	2008	48
21 10/16	13 10/16	8	Missaukee Co., MI	Jason L. Grimm	Jason L. Grimm	2005	54
21 10/16	13 10/16	8	Tioga Co., PA	Roger C. Gross	Roger C. Gross	2006	54
21 10/16	13 4/16	8 6/16	Bayfield Co., WI	Dennis E. Krueger	Dennis E. Krueger	2006	54
21 10/16	13 11/16	7 11/16	Piwei River, SK	M. Douglas Markham	M. Douglas Markham	2006	54
21 10/16	13 6/16	8 4/16	Lincoln Co., WI	Tony H. Yogerst	Tony H. Yogerst	2006	54
21 10/16	13 8/16	8 2/16	Pamlico Co., NC	Donald A. Boyd	Donald A. Boyd	2007	54
21 10/16	13 9/16	8 1/16	Douglas Co., WI	Shane M. Demulling	Shane M. Demulling	2007	54
21 10/16	13 10/16	8	Garrett Co., MD	Coty L. Jones	Coty L. Jones	2007	54
21 10/16	13 9/16	8 1/16	Barron Co., WI	Scott R. Kurth	Scott R. Kurth	2007	54
21 10/16	13 2/16	8 8/16	Ulster Co., NY	Kenneth J. Lord	Kenneth J. Lord	2007	54
21 10/16	13 4/16	8 6/16	Hamilton Co., NY	Arlene M. Peabody	Arlene M. Peabody	2007	54
21 10/16	13 11/16	7 15/16	Sawyer Co., WI	Lawrence T. Busse	Lawrence T. Busse	2008	54
21 10/16	13 10/16	8	Eau Claire Co., WI	Brian D. Freson	Brian D. Freson	2008	54
21 10/16	13 11/16	7 15/16	Stave Lake, BC	Uffe E. Herl	Uffe E. Herl	2008	54
21 10/16	13 6/16	8 4/16	Clark Co., WI	William H. Lewis	William H. Lewis	2008	54
21 10/16	13 2/16	8 8/16	Helen Lake, SK	Raymond J. Stebanuk	Raymond J. Stebanuk	2008	54
21 10/16	13 9/16	8 1/16	Bayfield Co., WI	John M. Tobiasz	John M. Tobiasz	2008	54
21 9/16	13 4/16	8 5/16	Bradford Co., PA	Mark Madden	Picked Up	2004	71
21 9/16	13 11/16	7 14/16	Taylor Co., WI	Benjamin M. Rakovec	Benjamin M. Rakovec	2005	71
21 9/16	13 12/16	7 13/16	Centre Co., PA	J. Emanuel Allgyer	J. Emanuel Allgyer	2006	71
21 9/16	13 9/16	8	McDowell Co., NC	Butch L. Parker	Butch L. Parker	2006	71
21 9/16	13 15/16	7 10/16	Hyde Co., NC	Gurnwood L. Radcliff, Jr.	Gurnwood L. Radcliff, Jr.	2007	71

BLACK BEAR

Ursus americanus americanus and related subspecies

Final Score	Greatest Length of Skull Without Lower Jaw	Greatest Width of Skull	Locality	Hunter	Owner	Date Killed	Rank
21 $^{9}/_{16}$	12 $^{10}/_{16}$	8 $^{15}/_{16}$	Plumas Co., CA	Dustin A. Vert	Dustin A. Vert	2007	71
21 $^{9}/_{16}$	13 $^{10}/_{16}$	7 $^{15}/_{16}$	Taylor Co., WI	David Gruny	David Gruny	2008	71
21 $^{9}/_{16}$	13 $^{13}/_{16}$	7 $^{12}/_{16}$	Chippewa Co., WI	Joshua C. Reed	Joshua C. Reed	2008	71
21 $^{9}/_{16}$	14 $^{2}/_{16}$	7 $^{7}/_{16}$	Pepin Co., WI	Daniel B. Seipel	Daniel B. Seipel	2008	71
21 $^{9}/_{16}$	12 $^{14}/_{16}$	8 $^{11}/_{16}$	Garfield Co., CO	Jared M. Street	Jared M. Street	2008	71
21 $^{9}/_{16}$	13 $^{6}/_{16}$	8 $^{3}/_{16}$	Prince of Wales Island, AK	Wesley S. Brown	Wesley S. Brown	2009	71
21 $^{8}/_{16}$	13 $^{7}/_{16}$	8 $^{1}/_{16}$	Bradford Co., PA	Rex L. Kingsley	Rex L. Kingsley	2000	82
21 $^{8}/_{16}$	13 $^{8}/_{16}$	8	Sullivan Co., PA	Bobby J. Simock	Bobby J. Simock	2005	82
21 $^{8}/_{16}$	13 $^{7}/_{16}$	8 $^{1}/_{16}$	Ashland Co., WI	Picked Up	Michael J. Bucheger	2006	82
21 $^{8}/_{16}$	13 $^{2}/_{16}$	8 $^{6}/_{16}$	Garfield Co., CO	Douglas M. Choate	Douglas M. Choate	2006	82
21 $^{8}/_{16}$	13 $^{6}/_{16}$	8 $^{2}/_{16}$	Whitefish Lake, SK	Ray Paslawski	Ray Paslawski	2006	82
21 $^{8}/_{16}$	13 $^{2}/_{16}$	8 $^{6}/_{16}$	Delaware Co., NY	Carl P. Davis	Carl P. Davis	2007	82
21 $^{8}/_{16}$	13 $^{7}/_{16}$	8 $^{1}/_{16}$	Qu'Appelle River, SK	Kevin D. Fonagy	Kevin D. Fonagy	2007	82
21 $^{8}/_{16}$	13 $^{10}/_{16}$	7 $^{14}/_{16}$	Searcy Co., AR	Donald R. Patterson	Donald R. Patterson	2007	82
21 $^{8}/_{16}$	13 $^{2}/_{16}$	8 $^{6}/_{16}$	Gila Co., AZ	Mindy B. Arthurs	Mindy B. Arthurs	2008	82
21 $^{8}/_{16}$	13 $^{8}/_{16}$	8	Barron Co., WI	Racheal L. Gifford	Racheal L. Gifford	2008	82
21 $^{8}/_{16}$	13 $^{14}/_{16}$	7 $^{10}/_{16}$	Burnett Co., WI	Lyle A. Klooster	Lyle A. Klooster	2008	82
21 $^{8}/_{16}$	13 $^{5}/_{16}$	8 $^{3}/_{16}$	Qu'Appelle Valley, SK	Alan M. Nicholauson	Alan M. Nicholauson	2008	82
21 $^{8}/_{16}$	13 $^{1}/_{16}$	8 $^{7}/_{16}$	Luzerne Co., PA	Larry W. Wolfe	Larry W. Wolfe	2008	82
21 $^{8}/_{16}$	13 $^{4}/_{16}$	8 $^{4}/_{16}$	Coffman Cove, AK	Dalton J. Wurm	Dalton J. Wurm	2009	82
21 $^{7}/_{16}$	13 $^{8}/_{16}$	7 $^{15}/_{16}$	Beaufort Co., NC	Edward D. Jones	Edward D. Jones	2006	96
21 $^{7}/_{16}$	13 $^{8}/_{16}$	7 $^{15}/_{16}$	Sawyer Co., WI	Randall B. Armsbury, Jr.	Randall B. Armsbury, Jr.	2007	96
21 $^{7}/_{16}$	13 $^{7}/_{16}$	8	Hubbard Co., MN	Harold F. Hartwig	Harold F. Hartwig	2007	96
21 $^{7}/_{16}$	13 $^{9}/_{16}$	7 $^{14}/_{16}$	Taylor Co., WI	Robert E. Kruger, Sr.	Robert E. Kruger, Sr.	2007	96
21 $^{7}/_{16}$	13 $^{6}/_{16}$	8 $^{1}/_{16}$	Lac La Biche, AB	Stephane R. Titley	Stephane R. Titley	2007	96
21 $^{7}/_{16}$	13 $^{1}/_{16}$	8 $^{6}/_{16}$	Garfield Co., CO	Robert C. Alcorn	Robert C. Alcorn	2008	96
21 $^{7}/_{16}$	13 $^{7}/_{16}$	8	Saline Co., AR	Donald A. Barnett	Donald A. Barnett	2008	96
21 $^{7}/_{16}$	13 $^{3}/_{16}$	8 $^{4}/_{16}$	Wexford Co., MI	Kevin L. Welp	Kevin L. Welp	2008	96
21 $^{7}/_{16}$	13 $^{9}/_{16}$	7 $^{14}/_{16}$	Sawyer Co., WI	Thomas R. Zimmer	Thomas R. Zimmer	2008	96
21 $^{7}/_{16}$	13 $^{5}/_{16}$	8 $^{2}/_{16}$	Gila Co., AZ	Johnny Basha	Johnny Basha	2009	96
21 $^{7}/_{16}$	13 $^{6}/_{16}$	8 $^{1}/_{16}$	Polk Co., WI	Peter D. Berger	Peter D. Berger	2009	96
21 $^{7}/_{16}$	13 $^{10}/_{16}$	7 $^{13}/_{16}$	Fort a la Corne, SK	Jefrey T. Thorlakson	Jefrey T. Thorlakson	2009	96
21 $^{6}/_{16}$	13 $^{10}/_{16}$	7 $^{12}/_{16}$	Taylor Co., WI	Dennis R. Winkler	Dennis R. Winkler	2003	108

			Location	Hunter	Owner	Year	Score
21 6/16	13 3/16	8 3/16	Cochise Co., AZ	Charles E. Hecox	Charles E. Hecox	2006	108
21 6/16	13 4/16	8 2/16	Blueberry Mt., AB	John W. Norris	John W. Norris	2006	108
21 6/16	12 14/16	8 8/16	Lane Co., OR	Robert Shank	Robert Shank	2006	108
21 6/16	13 2/16	8 4/16	Qu'Appelle River, SK	Mike Eckersley	Mike Eckersley	2007	108
21 6/16	13 3/16	8 3/16	Jackson Co., OR	Joel F. Gorman	Joel F. Gorman	2007	108
21 6/16	13 4/16	8 2/16	Raleigh Co., WV	Charles L. Simmons	Charles L. Simmons	2007	108
21 6/16	13	8 6/16	Carteret Co., NC	Randall D. Bowers	Randall D. Bowers	2008	108
21 6/16	13 10/16	7 12/16	Becker Co., MN	Katherine M. Dugger	Katherine M. Dugger	2008	108
21 6/16	13 9/16	7 13/16	Swan River, MB	Matthew A. Lipps	Matthew A. Lipps	2008	108
21 6/16	13 5/16	8 1/16	Dauphin, MB	Mark J. Perish	Mark J. Perish	2008	108
21 6/16	13 9/16	7 13/16	Sawyer Co., WI	Gary W. Pettis	Gary W. Pettis	2008	108
21 6/16	13 4/16	8 2/16	Prince of Wales Island, AK	Clayton J. Upshaw	Clayton J. Upshaw	2008	108
21 6/16	13 5/16	8 1/16	Hadashville, MB	Douglas Guthrie	Douglas Guthrie	2009	108
21 5/16	13 10/16	7 11/16	Beaufort Co., NC	Edward D. Jones	Edward D. Jones	2004	122
21 5/16	13 9/16	7 12/16	Broome Co., NY	Kimberly A. Moravcik	Kimberly A. Moravcik	2005	122
21 5/16	13 4/16	8 1/16	Pamlico Co., NC	Charles D. Tucker	Charles D. Tucker	2005	122
21 5/16	13 6/16	7 15/16	Marinette Co., WI	Craig D. Dolata	Craig D. Dolata	2006	122
21 5/16	13 6/16	7 15/16	Prince of Wales Island, AK	Perry L. Mills	Perry L. Mills	2006	122
21 5/16	13 9/16	7 12/16	Hyde Co., NC	Randy C. Frye	Randy C. Frye	2007	122
21 5/16	13 1/16	8 4/16	Kipahigan Lake, MB	Scott G. Hettinger	Scott G. Hettinger	2007	122
21 5/16	13 9/16	7 12/16	Rockingham Co., VA	David W. Kyger	David W. Kyger	2007	122
21 5/16	13 4/16	8 1/16	Prince of Wales Island, AK	Timothy J. Sherick	Timothy J. Sherick	2007	122
21 5/16	13 2/16	8 3/16	Pike Co., PA	Albert J. Smith	Albert J. Smith	2007	122
21 5/16	13 4/16	8 1/16	Sullivan Co., PA	William S. Chambers	William S. Chambers	2008	122
21 5/16	13 1/16	8 4/16	Barron Co., WI	Matthew M. Clark	Matthew M. Clark	2008	122
21 5/16	13 6/16	7 15/16	Bradford Co., PA	Kelly J. Devine	Kelly J. Devine	2008	122
21 5/16	13 5/16	8	Steuben Co., NY	Donald W. Snyder	Donald W. Snyder	2008	122
21 5/16	13 1/16	8 4/16	Essex Co., VT	Picked Up	VT Big Game Trophy Club, Inc.	2008	122
21 5/16	13 6/16	7 15/16	Dunn Co., WI	Brian T. Wellington	Brian T. Wellington	2008	122
21 5/16	13 14/16	7 7/16	Beltrami Co., MN	John W. McCulley, Jr.	John W. McCulley, Jr.	2009	122
21 4/16	13 5/16	7 15/16	Lycoming Co., PA	Barry J. Kile	Barry J. Kile	2005	139
21 4/16	13 2/16	8 2/16	Franklin Co., VA	R. Keith Peeples	R. Keith Peeples	2005	139
21 4/16	13 3/16	8 1/16	Eagle Co., CO	Ted Archibeque	Ted Archibeque	2006	139
21 4/16	13 1/16	8 3/16	Monroe Co., PA	Jeffrey Freeman	Jeffrey Freeman	2007	139
21 4/16	13 1/16	8 3/16	Apache Co., AZ	Cynda R. Lilly	Cynda R. Lilly	2007	139
21 4/16	13 6/16	7 14/16	Montgomery Co., VA	W. Wayne Cox	W. Wayne Cox	2008	139
21 4/16	13 7/16	7 13/16	Polk Co., WI	Mitchell J. Gebheim	Mitchell J. Gebheim	2008	139
21 4/16	13 4/16	8	Beaufort Co., NC	Elwood T. Godley, Jr.	Elwood T. Godley, Jr.	2008	139
21 4/16	13 7/16	7 13/16	Shawano Co., WI	Corey R. Meidl	Corey R. Meidl	2008	139
21 3/16	13 2/16	8 1/16	Gila Co., AZ	Brian A. Rimsza	Brian A. Rimsza	1983	148
21 3/16	13 5/16	7 14/16	Kuiu Island, AK	Michael T. Kinney	Michael T. Kinney	1994	148
21 3/16	13 8/16	7 11/16	Florence Co., WI	Zeke M. Peters	Zeke M. Peters	2005	148

BLACK BEAR

Ursus americanus americanus and related subspecies

Final Score	Greatest Length of Skull Without Lower Jaw	Greatest Width of Skull	Locality	Hunter	Owner	Date Killed	Rank
21 3/16	13 8/16	7 11/16	Sullivan Co., PA	Stanley Borascius, Jr.	Stanley Borascius, Jr.	2006	148
21 3/16	13	8 3/16	Mantagao Lake, MB	John W. Eckley	John W. Eckley	2006	148
21 3/16	13 2/16	8 1/16	Chippewa Co., MI	Brandon R. Kurkierewicz	Brandon R. Kurkierewicz	2006	148
21 3/16	13 7/16	7 12/16	Price Co., WI	Alan E. Rebedew	Alan E. Rebedew	2006	148
21 3/16	13 1/16	8 2/16	Orange Co., NY	Frank L. DeGennaro	Frank L. DeGennaro	2007	148
21 3/16	13 3/16	8	Pine Co., MN	Wayne R. Dehkes, Jr.	Wayne R. Dehkes, Jr.	2007	148
21 3/16	13 3/16	8	Sawyer Co., WI	Linda A. Gwinn	Linda A. Gwinn	2007	148
21 3/16	13 3/16	8	Duck Mt., MB	John R. Kerr	John R. Kerr	2008	148
21 3/16	13 3/16	8	Polk Co., WI	Kristen C. Lansin	Kristen C. Lansin	2008	148
21 3/16	12 12/16	8 7/16	Clark Co., WI	Roy J. Lato	Roy J. Lato	2008	148
21 3/16	13 1/16	8 2/16	Lackawanna Co., PA	James McDonough	James McDonough	2008	148
21 3/16	12 10/16	8 9/16	Lake Co., CO	D. Gordon Roberts III	D. Gordon Roberts III	2008	148
21 3/16	13 7/16	7 12/16	Burnett Co., WI	Joseph D. Tilton	Joseph D. Tilton	2009	148
21 2/16	12 15/16	8 3/16	Prince of Wales Island, AK	Joseph V. Caccamo, Jr.	Joseph V. Caccamo, Jr.	2004	164
21 2/16	13 4/16	7 14/16	Alcona Co., MI	James R. Doyle	James R. Doyle	2005	164
21 2/16	13 4/16	7 14/16	Bradford Co., PA	Matthew A. Russell	Matthew A. Russell	2005	164
21 2/16	13	8 2/16	Alcona Co., MI	Michael J. Traill	Michael J. Traill	2005	164
21 2/16	13 8/16	7 10/16	Vilas Co., WI	Dale C. Detampel	Dale C. Detampel	2006	164
21 2/16	13 3/16	7 15/16	Oconto Co., WI	Robert W. Magee	Robert W. Magee	2006	164
21 2/16	13 4/16	7 14/16	Marathon Co., WI	Timothy J. Romatowski	Timothy J. Romatowski	2006	164
21 2/16	12 13/16	8 5/16	Lake Co., CA	John Riley	John Riley	2007	164
21 2/16	12 14/16	8 4/16	Prince of Wales Island, AK	Darrin P. Brown	Darrin P. Brown	2008	164
21 2/16	12 15/16	8 3/16	Alstead Lake, SK	Nelson J. Capestany	Nelson J. Capestany	2008	164
21 2/16	12 13/16	8 5/16	Glenn Co., CA	Roy R. Ellis	Roy R. Ellis	2008	164
21 2/16	13 8/16	7 10/16	Union Co., OR	Jarom Hibbert	Jarom Hibbert	2008	164
21 2/16	12 12/16	8 6/16	South Brook, NL	Roger G. Laro, Jr.	Roger G. Laro, Jr.	2008	164
21 2/16	12 14/16	8 4/16	Mesa Co., CO	Marc T. Sanchez	Marc T. Sanchez	2008	164
21 2/16	13 1/16	8 1/16	Saddle Hills, AB	Michael J. Ukrainetz	Michael J. Ukrainetz	2008	164
21 2/16	13 7/16	7 11/16	Tyrrell Co., NC	Michael J. Wood	Michael J. Wood	2008	164
21 2/16	13 4/16	7 14/16	Bayfield Co., WI	Craig G. Cichanofsky	Craig G. Cichanofsky	2009	164
21 2/16	13 2/16	8	Alonsa, MB	Brenda L. Theoret	Brenda L. Theoret	2009	164
21 1/16	13 2/16	7 15/16	Beaufort Co., NC	James A. Buck	James A. Buck	1997	182
21 1/16	13 2/16	7 15/16	Shasta Co., CA	Randy L. Burger	Randy L. Burger	1999	182

			Locality	Hunter	Owner	Date	Rank
21 1/16	13 5/16	7 12/16	Doig River, BC	Hartley C. Blatz	Hartley C. Blatz	2002	182
21 1/16	12 15/16	8 2/16	Aroostook Co., ME	Gregg Holomakoff	Gregg Holomakoff	2002	182
21 1/16	13 5/16	7 12/16	Craven Co., NC	Elwood T. Godley, Jr.	Elwood T. Godley, Jr.	2005	182
21 1/16	13 2/16	7 15/16	Mifflin Co., PA	Bradley K. Leister	Bradley K. Leister	2005	182
21 1/16	13 4/16	7 13/16	Shawano Co., WI	Jason H. Augustyn	Jason H. Augustyn	2006	182
21 1/16	13 4/16	7 13/16	Ventura Co., CA	Clay D. Barbosa	Clay D. Barbosa	2006	182
21 1/16	13 1/16	8	Pitkin Co., CO	Loree McCardle	Loree McCardle	2006	182
21 1/16	12 15/16	8 2/16	St. John River, NB	David R. Sink	David R. Sink	2006	182
21 1/16	13 3/16	7 14/16	Graham Co., AZ	Bryce D.K. Stark	Bryce D.K. Stark	2006	182
21 1/16	13 1/16	8	Yamhill Co., OR	Derek W. Ellenwood	Derek W. Ellenwood	2007	182
21 1/16	13 6/16	7 11/16	Craven Co., NC	Larry Pollard	Larry Pollard	2007	182
21 1/16	13 2/16	7 15/16	Spirit River, AB	Michael J. Siegler	Michael J. Siegler	2007	182
21 1/16	12 13/16	8 4/16	Lac du Bonnet, MB	Edward A. Parker	Edward A. Parker	2008	182
21 1/16	13 2/16	7 15/16	Garfield Co., CO	Nathan D. Anderson	Nathan D. Anderson	2009	182
21 1/16	13 7/16	7 10/16	Burnett Co., WI	Leslie L. DeMarre	Leslie L. DeMarre	2009	182
21	12 12/16	8 4/16	Prince of Wales Island, AK	Jon A. Shiesl	Jon A. Shiesl	1990	199
21	12 10/16	8 6/16	Prince of Wales Island, AK	Ronald S. Kates	Ronald S. Kates	2005	199
21	13 2/16	7 14/16	Clearfield Co., PA	Ryan S. Mathews	Ryan S. Mathews	2005	199
21	13 2/16	7 14/16	Price Co., WI	James A. Vitella, Jr.	James A. Vitella, Jr.	2005	199
21	13 8/16	7 8/16	Schoharie Co., NY	Patrick S. Irwin	Patrick S. Irwin	2006	199
21	13 5/16	7 11/16	Hyde Co., NC	Charles R. Miller	Charles R. Miller	2006	199

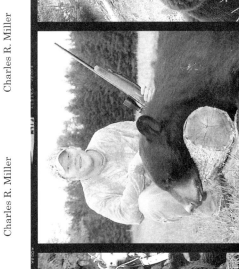

BLACK BEAR
FINAL SCORE: 21 4/16
HUNTER: Corey R. Meidl

BLACK BEAR
FINAL SCORE: 20
HUNTER: Darwin G. DeCroo

BLACK BEAR
FINAL SCORE: 21 10/16
HUNTER: Lawrence T. Busse

BLACK BEAR
FINAL SCORE: 20 3/16
HUNTER: Brian Henderson

BLACK BEAR

Ursus americanus and related subspecies

Final Score	Greatest Length of Skull Without Lower Jaw	Greatest Width of Skull	Locality	Hunter	Owner	Date Killed	Rank
21	13 $1/16$	7 $15/16$	Graham Co., AZ	Tyrone D. Nuessle	Tyrone D. Nuessle	2006	199
21	12 $15/16$	8 $1/16$	Wood Co., WI	Jacob D. Trierweiler	Jacob D. Trierweiler	2006	199
21	12 $12/16$	8 $4/16$	Thorne Bay, AK	Kelly J. Bailey	Kelly J. Bailey	2007	199
21	13	8	Rusk Co., WI	Michael R. Berres	Michael R. Berres	2007	199
21	13 $2/16$	7 $14/16$	Shell River, MB	Justin R. Brown	Justin R. Brown	2007	199
21	13	8	Presque Isle Co., MI	Patricia A. Dankers	Patricia A. Dankers	2007	199
21	13	8	Garfield Co., UT	Merlynn K. Jones	Merlynn K. Jones	2007	199
21	13 $1/16$	7 $15/16$	Prince of Wales Island, AK	Daniel R. Lilja	Daniel R. Lilja	2007	199
21	13 $4/16$	7 $12/16$	Juniata Co., PA	Raymond T. Long, Sr.	Raymond T. Long, Sr.	2007	199
21	12 $14/16$	8 $2/16$	Prince of Wales Island, AK	Bill A. Potts	Bill A. Potts	2007	199
21	13 $2/16$	7 $14/16$	Pennington Co., MN	Donnie R. Silmon	Donnie R. Silmon	2007	199
21	12 $14/16$	8 $2/16$	Manistee Co., MI	James W. Stevens	James W. Stevens	2007	199
21	12 $14/16$	8 $2/16$	Peace River, AB	George Williams, Jr.	George Williams, Jr.	2007	199
21	13 $2/16$	7 $14/16$	Huntingdon Co., PA	James R. Ziegler	James R. Ziegler	2007	199
21	12 $15/16$	8 $1/16$	Ashland Co., WI	William C. Klitzman	William C. Klitzman	2008	199
21	13 $4/16$	7 $12/16$	Delta Co., MI	Brandon J. Podolak	Brandon J. Podolak	2008	199
21	13 $1/16$	7 $15/16$	Koochiching Co., MN	Brett D. Riewer	Brett D. Riewer	2008	199
21	13 $5/16$	7 $11/16$	Rusk Co., WI	LaLonnie S. VanDenHeuvel	LaLonnie S. VanDenHeuvel	2008	199
21	13	8	Eriksdale, MB	Thomas O. Buenning	Thomas O. Buenning	2009	199
21	13 $1/16$	7 $15/16$	High Level, AB	Patrick Jones	Janiece Jones	2009	199
21	13	8	Hudson Bay Jct., SK	Daniel B. Rogers	Daniel B. Rogers	2009	199
21	13	8	Porcupine Mts., MB	Robert E. Webber	Robert E. Webber	2009	199
20 $15/16$	13	7 $15/16$	Lackawanna Co., PA	Robert A. Loeffler	Robert A. Loeffler	1996	227
20 $15/16$	13	7 $15/16$	Bradford Co., PA	Kevin E. Seifert	Kevin E. Seifert	2003	227
20 $15/16$	13 $6/16$	7 $9/16$	Beaver Lake, SK	Charles E. Lewis	Charles E. Lewis	2006	227
20 $15/16$	12 $13/16$	8 $2/16$	Prince of Wales Island, AK	Bill Hales	Bill Hales	2007	227
20 $15/16$	13 $3/16$	7 $12/16$	Price Co., WI	William R. Pickard	William R. Pickard	2007	227
20 $15/16$	12 $15/16$	8	Prince of Wales Island, AK	Bob R. Scarrow	Bob R. Scarrow	2007	227
20 $15/16$	13 $2/16$	7 $13/16$	Chippewa Co., WI	Timothy L. Trowbridge	Timothy L. Trowbridge	2007	227
20 $15/16$	12 $14/16$	8 $1/16$	Jackson Co., OR	Jeffrey J. Heil	Jeffrey J. Heil	2008	227
20 $14/16$	13 $1/16$	7 $13/16$	Bradford Co., PA	Timothy D. Leonard	Timothy D. Leonard	2003	235
20 $14/16$	13 $9/16$	7 $5/16$	Alpena Co., MI	Michael Filer	Michael Filer	2006	235
20 $14/16$	13	7 $14/16$	Lincoln Co., WI	Lori A. Pynenberg	Lori A. Pynenberg	2006	235

			Locality	Owner	Hunter	Year	Rank
20 14/16	12 15/16	7 15/16	Douglas Co., OR	Warren R. Weathers	Warren R. Weathers	2006	235
20 14/16	12 13/16	8 1/16	Lake Peribonca, QC	Walter C. Brown	Walter C. Brown	2007	235
20 14/16	13 4/16	7 10/16	Alonsa, MB	J. Jay Eubanks	J. Jay Eubanks	2007	235
20 14/16	12 13/16	8 1/16	Kern Co., CA	Jimmie Fox	Jimmie Fox	2007	235
20 14/16	13 1/16	7 13/16	Mahnomen Co., MN	Richard D. Wark	Richard D. Wark	2007	235
20 14/16	12 10/16	8 4/16	Upsala, ON	George T. Calvert	George T. Calvert	2008	235
20 14/16	13 6/16	7 8/16	Gila Co., AZ	Joshua M. White	Joshua M. White	2008	235
20 13/16	13 3/16	7 10/16	Blair Co., PA	Daniel P. Pettenati	Daniel P. Pettenati	2003	245
20 13/16	13 3/16	7 10/16	Itasca Co., MN	Troy F. Bode	Troy F. Bode	2006	245
20 13/16	13 5/16	7 8/16	Grant Co., WV	Oscar V. Keplinger	Oscar V. Keplinger	2006	245
20 13/16	13 6/16	7 7/16	Preeceville, SK	Thelma K. Markham	Thelma K. Markham	2006	245
20 13/16	12 11/16	8 2/16	Dolores Co., CO	Kalan N. Deavers	Kalan N. Deavers	2007	245
20 13/16	13 6/16	7 7/16	Beltrami Co., MN	Bruce A. Eckman	Bruce A. Eckman	2007	245
20 13/16	13 1/16	7 12/16	Kupreanof Island, AK	Andrew P. Gilbert	Andrew P. Gilbert	2007	245
20 13/16	13	7 13/16	Prince of Wales Island, AK	Lewis P. Henderson	Lewis P. Henderson	2007	245
20 13/16	13 2/16	7 11/16	Wicked Point, MB	Wendell Howes, Jr.	Wendell Howes, Jr.	2007	245
20 13/16	12 15/16	7 14/16	Green Lake, SK	Thomas J. Nega	Thomas J. Nega	2007	245
20 13/16	12 14/16	7 15/16	Grays Harbor Co., WA	Stephen D. Craig	Stephen D. Craig	2008	245
20 13/16	12 15/16	7 14/16	Tillamook Co., OR	Joseph E. Hulburt	Joseph E. Hulburt	2008	245
20 13/16	13	7 13/16	Oconto Co., WI	Joan J. Millard	Joan J. Millard	2008	245
20 13/16	13	7 13/16	Oconto Co., WI	Bruce C. Stanke	Bruce C. Stanke	2008	245
20 12/16	13 1/16	7 11/16	Bradford Co., PA	Kyle T. Borek	Kyle T. Borek	2006	259
20 12/16	13	7 12/16	Thorne Bay, AK	Ian K. Chase-Dunn	Ian K. Chase-Dunn	2006	259
20 12/16	12 13/16	7 13/16	Peace River, AB	Francis S. Plaisance, Jr.	Francis S. Plaisance, Jr.	2006	259
20 12/16	12 11/16	8 1/16	Dauphin Co., PA	Douglas S. Russo	Douglas S. Russo	2006	259
20 12/16	12 14/16	7 14/16	Allegany Co., NY	Bruce M. Stevens	Bruce M. Stevens	2006	259
20 12/16	12 15/16	7 13/16	Cowlitz Co., WA	Michael K. Wolf	Michael K. Wolf	2006	259
20 12/16	13 4/16	7 8/16	Riding Mt., MB	Julie L. Zopf	Julie L. Zopf	2006	259
20 12/16	12 15/16	7 13/16	Klamath Co., OR	Mark T. Heater	Mark T. Heater	2007	259
20 12/16	12 13/16	7 15/16	Bronson Lake, SK	Justin Hubert	Justin Hubert	2007	259
20 12/16	13	7 12/16	Lake of the Woods Co., MN	Brian C. Swenson	Brian C. Swenson	2007	259
20 12/16	12 13/16	7 15/16	Roscommon Co., MI	Russell C. Blake	Russell C. Blake	2008	259
20 12/16	12 14/16	7 14/16	Aroostook Co., ME	Shane DuFresne	Shane DuFresne	2008	259
20 12/16	13 2/16	7 10/16	Pulaski Co., VA	Fred T. Hale, Jr.	Fred T. Hale, Jr.	2008	259
20 12/16	13 6/16	7 6/16	Bradford Co., PA	Robert Traver	Robert Traver	2008	259
20 12/16	12 14/16	7 14/16	Taylor Co., WI	Stuart H. Young	Stuart H. Young	2008	259
20 12/16	12 15/16	7 13/16	Porcupine Forest, SK	David L. Biddle, Jr.	David L. Biddle, Jr.	2009	259
20 12/16	12 10/16	8 1/16	Douglas Co., OR	Dean A. Starr	Dean A. Starr	2009	259
20 11/16	12 11/16	8	Humboldt Co., CA	Jake D. Shuler	Jake D. Shuler	1999	276
20 11/16	12 12/16	7 15/16	Bayfield Co., WI	Nathan A. Hubbard	Nathan A. Hubbard	2002	276
20 11/16	12 13/16	7 15/16	Aroostook Co., ME	Jamie L. Voisine	Jamie L. Voisine	2002	276
20 11/16	12 13/16	7 14/16	Red Earth Creek, AB	Ian K. Chase-Dunn	Ian K. Chase-Dunn	2005	276

Ursus americanus and related subspecies

Final Score	Greatest Length of Skull Without Lower Jaw	Greatest Width of Skull	Locality	Hunter	Owner	Date Killed	Rank
20 11/16	12 11/16	8	Bayfield Co., WI	Gregory J. Neusen	Gregory J. Neusen	2006	276
20 11/16	12 15/16	7 12/16	Trinity Co., CA	John J. Vincent	John J. Vincent	2006	276
20 11/16	13 4/16	7 7/16	Barron Co., WI	Ernest P. Fankhauser	Ernest P. Fankhauser	2007	276
20 11/16	13 4/16	7 7/16	Shawano Co., WI	Alan W. Kocken	Alan W. Kocken	2007	276
20 11/16	13 1/16	7 10/16	Marshall Co., MN	Michael R. Powell	Michael R. Powell	2007	276
20 11/16	13 1/16	7 10/16	Gila Co., AZ	Jeremy L. Brandenburg	Jeremy L. Brandenburg	2008	276
20 11/16	13 3/16	7 8/16	Franklin Co., AR	David O. Hayes	David O. Hayes	2008	276
20 11/16	12 13/16	7 14/16	Ketchikan, AK	Clinton L. Morgan	Clinton L. Morgan	2008	276
20 11/16	12 15/16	7 12/16	Price Co., WI	Diane L. Pinter	Diane L. Pinter	2008	276
20 11/16	12 11/16	8	Lake of the Prairies, MB	Mark N. Rose	Mark N. Rose	2008	276
20 11/16	13 4/16	7 7/16	Chippewa Co., WI	Anthony M. Schemenauer	Anthony M. Schemenauer	2008	276
20 11/16	12 13/16	7 14/16	Fayette Co., WV	Jonathon A. Sorrell	Jonathon A. Sorrell	2008	276
20 10/16	13 1/16	7 9/16	Rio Blanco Co., CO	F. Rit Heller	F. Rit Heller	1969	292
20 10/16	12 13/16	7 13/16	Langlade Co., WI	Eugene P. Mancl	Eugene P. Mancl	2005	292
20 10/16	12 13/16	7 13/16	Ashland Co., WI	Gerald W. Doll	Gerald W. Doll	2006	292
20 10/16	12 12/16	7 14/16	Thunder Bay, ON	Theresa A. Woychik	Theresa A. Woychik	2006	292
20 10/16	12 11/16	7 15/16	Atikokan, ON	Rickey L. Ashman	Rickey L. Ashman	2007	292
20 10/16	12 14/16	7 12/16	Ignace, ON	Connie L. Agnew	Connie L. Agnew	2008	292
20 10/16	13 2/16	7 8/16	Lincoln Co., WI	Kyle J. Kulibert	Kyle J. Kulibert	2008	292
20 10/16	12 12/16	7 15/16	Teton Co., WY	James J. Farmer	James J. Farmer	2009	292
20 9/16	12 12/16	7 13/16	Prince of Wales Island, AK	James F. Baichtal	James F. Baichtal	2001	300
20 9/16	13 3/16	7 6/16	Langlade Co., WI	Mark J. Denis	Mark J. Denis	2004	300
20 9/16	12 9/16	8	Wrangell, AK	Thomas E. Butler, Sr.	Thomas E. Butler, Sr.	2006	300
20 9/16	12 15/16	7 10/16	Fayette Co., PA	Alex M. Grote	Alex M. Grote	2006	300
20 9/16	12 14/16	7 11/16	Cass Co., MN	Shea A. Lange	Shea A. Lange	2006	300
20 9/16	12 10/16	7 15/16	Porcupine Plain, SK	Andrew M. Blake	Andrew M. Blake	2007	300
20 9/16	12 12/16	7 13/16	Cowlitz Co., WA	Andrew S. Preston	Andrew S. Preston	2007	300
20 9/16	12 8/16	8 1/16	Lycoming Co., PA	Ryan D. Farley	Ryan D. Farley	2008	300
20 9/16	13	7 9/16	Carswell Lake, SK	Douglas A. Palecki	Douglas A. Palecki	2008	300
20 9/16	12 15/16	7 10/16	St. Louis Co., MN	Todd M. Sampson	Todd M. Sampson	2008	300
20 9/16	12 10/16	7 15/16	Kenora, ON	Rex A. Wolfsen	Rex A. Wolfsen	2008	300
20 9/16	13	7 9/16	Iron Co., MI	Larry H. Holsworth	Larry H. Holsworth	2009	300
20 8/16	12 9/16	7 15/16	Dickinson Co., MI	William O. Allender	William O. Allender	2004	312

Score	Locality	Hunter	Owner	Date Killed			
312	Shawano Co., WI	Allan L. Dorn	Allan L. Dorn	2005	20 8/16	13 2/16	7 6/16
312	Prince of Wales Island, AK	Heath D. Lewis	Heath D. Lewis	2005	20 8/16	12 13/16	7 11/16
312	Grant Co., NM	Richard B. Chavez	Richard B. Chavez	2006	20 8/16	13	7 8/16
312	Houston Co., GA	Picked Up	GA Dept. of Natl. Resc.	2006	20 8/16	12 14/16	7 10/16
312	Nipigon River, ON	Nathan R. Peitz	Nathan R. Peitz	2006	20 8/16	12 5/16	8 3/16
312	Bertie Co., NC	Jeremy I. Phelps	Jeremy I. Phelps	2006	20 8/16	13	7 8/16
312	Franklin Co., PA	Scott L. Spoonhour	Scott L. Spoonhour	2006	20 8/16	13	7 8/16
312	Springdale, NL	Thomas L. Steiner	Thomas L. Steiner	2006	20 8/16	12 12/16	7 12/16
312	Lake of the Woods, ON	Tom A. Williams	Tom A. Williams	2006	20 8/16	12 10/16	7 14/16
312	Bradford Co., PA	Clinton L. Crawford	Clinton L. Crawford	2007	20 8/16	12 15/16	7 9/16
312	Trinity Co., CA	Frankie T. Manfredonia	Frankie T. Manfredonia	2007	20 8/16	12 10/16	7 14/16
312	Kern Co., CA	Monte Rudnick	Monte Rudnick	2007	20 8/16	12 13/16	7 11/16
312	Price Co., WI	Joseph D. Stong	Joseph D. Stong	2007	20 8/16	12 10/16	7 14/16
312	Delaware Co., NY	Giovanni B. DiMaggio	Giovanni B. DiMaggio	2008	20 8/16	12 13/16	7 11/16
312	Sitka, AK	Glen W. Groenig	Glen W. Groenig	2008	20 8/16	12 15/16	7 9/16
312	Menominee Co., MI	Bradley C. Hall	Bradley C. Hall	2008	20 8/16	12 11/16	7 13/16
312	Kanawha Co., WV	Van E. Jenkins	Van E. Jenkins	2008	20 8/16	13 1/16	7 7/16
312	Van Buren Co., AR	Harry G. Snowden	Harry G. Snowden	2008	20 8/16	13 4/16	7 4/16
312	Florence Co., WI	Jason J. Sticka	Jason J. Sticka	2008	20 8/16	12 13/16	7 11/16
312	Point Leamington, NL	Robert A. Scidmore	Robert A. Scidmore	2009	20 8/16	12 12/16	7 12/16
312	Bennington Co., VT	Robert B. Costine	Robert B. Costine	1989	20 8/16	12 15/16	7 8/16
333	Jefferson Co., WA	Devan Ziara	Devan Ziara	2005	20 7/16	13 3/16	7 4/16
333	Sierra Co., CA	David C. Hoffman	David C. Hoffman	2006	20 7/16	12 10/16	7 13/16
333	Carlton Co., MN	Gregory S. Leschisin	Gregory S. Leschisin	2006	20 7/16	12 11/16	7 11/16
333	Marinette Co., WI	James R. Liska	James R. Liska	2006	20 7/16	13 2/16	7 5/16
333	Chippewa Co., WI	Jon D. Schroeder	Jon D. Schroeder	2006	20 7/16	13 4/16	7 3/16
333	Bayfield Co., WI	Suzette R. Tremblay	Suzette R. Tremblay	2006	20 7/16	12 5/16	8 2/16
333	Red Deer River, SK	Franklin R. Bucher	Franklin R. Bucher	2007	20 7/16	12 13/16	7 10/16
333	Hertford Co., NC	Steven L. Cooper	Steven L. Cooper	2007	20 7/16	12 14/16	7 9/16
333	Marwayne, AB	Walter T. Jones	Walter T. Jones	2007	20 7/16	13	7 7/16
333	Washburn Co., WI	Ricki L. Lambert	Ricki L. Lambert	2007	20 7/16	12 14/16	7 9/16
333	Iron Co., MI	Larry J. Pifke	Larry J. Pifke	2007	20 7/16	12 12/16	7 11/16
333	Chelan Co., WA	Eric Ross	Eric Ross	2007	20 7/16	12 13/16	7 10/16
333	Penobscot Co., ME	Joshua C. Callahan	Joshua C. Callahan	2008	20 7/16	12 14/16	7 9/16
333	Queen Charlotte Islands, BC	Peter J. Carlson	Peter J. Carlson	2008	20 7/16	12 11/16	7 12/16
333	Dufferin Lake, SK	John C. Casner	John C. Casner	2008	20 7/16	13 2/16	7 5/16
333	Aroostook Co., ME	Judy L. Drissel	Judy L. Drissel	2008	20 7/16	12 15/16	7 8/16
333	Price Co., WI	Ashley E. Grant	Ashley E. Grant	2008	20 7/16	12 14/16	7 9/16
333	Matheson, ON	Fred W. Illman	Fred W. Illman	2008	20 7/16	12 9/16	7 14/16
352	Okanogan Co., WA	James R. Hutson	James R. Hutson	2004	20 6/16	12 9/16	7 13/16
352	Whatcom Co., WA	David Zender	David Zender	2005	20 6/16	12 9/16	7 13/16

BLACK BEAR

Ursus americanus americanus and related subspecies

Final Score	Greatest Length of Skull Without Lower Jaw	Greatest Width of Skull	Locality	Hunter	Owner	Date Killed	Rank
20 6/16	12 12/16	7 10/16	Taylor Co., WI	Dennis C. Braun	Dennis C. Braun	2006	352
20 6/16	12 10/16	7 12/16	Teton Co., WY	Pep Brinkerhoff	Pep Brinkerhoff	2006	352
20 6/16	12 11/16	7 11/16	Price Co., WI	Timothy A. Dane	Timothy A. Dane	2006	352
20 6/16	12 9/16	7 13/16	Aitkin Co., MN	Danny O. Lundell	Danny O. Lundell	2006	352
20 6/16	12 11/16	7 11/16	Augusta Co., VA	John C. Shiflet	John C. Shiflet	2006	352
20 6/16	12 7/16	7 15/16	Prince of Wales Island, AK	Dean A. Hanson	Dean A. Hanson	2007	352
20 6/16	12 10/16	7 12/16	Pine Co., MN	Timothy J. Anderson	Timothy J. Anderson	2008	352
20 6/16	12 13/16	7 9/16	Tyrrell Co., NC	Ronnie E. Bruce	Ronnie E. Bruce	2008	352
20 6/16	12 11/16	7 11/16	Prince of Wales Island, AK	Jason L. Dombkowski	Jason L. Dombkowski	2008	352
20 6/16	12 11/16	7 11/16	Prince of Wales Island, AK	Robert S. Michael, Sr.	Robert S. Michael, Sr.	2008	352
20 6/16	12 11/16	7 11/16	Oconto Co., WI	Levi R. Missall	Levi R. Missall	2008	352
20 6/16	12 6/16	8	Albany Co., WY	Steven D. Peck	Steven D. Peck	2008	352
20 6/16	12 9/16	7 13/16	Albany Co., WY	Steven K. Perkins	Steven K. Perkins	2008	352
20 6/16	12 8/16	7 14/16	Cass Co., MN	Mark A. Pierog	Mark A. Pierog	2008	352
20 6/16	12 8/16	7 14/16	Marinette Co., WI	Brian J. Stammer	Brian J. Stammer	2008	352
20 6/16	12 12/16	7 10/16	Marinette Co., WI	Russell J. Wagner	Russell J. Wagner	2009	352
20 5/16	12 14/16	7 7/16	Bradford Co., PA	Sidney L. Hatch	Sidney L. Hatch	2001	370
20 5/16	13	7 5/16	Lycoming Co., PA	James H. Bear II	James H. Bear II	2002	370
20 5/16	12 13/16	7 8/16	Tioga Co., PA	Charles A. Duda	Charles A. Duda	2005	370
20 5/16	12 11/16	7 10/16	Iosco Co., MI	Martin R. Gayeski II	Martin R. Gayeski II	2005	370
20 5/16	12 14/16	7 7/16	Twiggs Co., GA	Picked Up	GA Dept. of Natl. Resc.	2005	370
20 5/16	12 11/16	7 10/16	Carter Co., TN	Daniel A. Vaughn	Daniel A. Vaughn	2005	370
20 5/16	12 9/16	7 12/16	Ignace, ON	Dale M. Dhuey	Dale M. Dhuey	2006	370
20 5/16	12 13/16	7 13/16	Coles Pond, NL	Raymond C. Grover	Raymond C. Grover	2006	370
20 5/16	12 8/16	7 13/16	Thaddeus Lake, ON	Karl J. Levisay	Karl J. Levisay	2006	370
20 5/16	12 15/16	7 6/16	Kuiu Island, AK	Mitchell A. Atkinson	Mitchell A. Atkinson	2007	370
20 5/16	12 13/16	7 8/16	Clearwater Co., MN	Raymond W. Burkhardt	Raymond W. Burkhardt	2007	370
20 5/16	12 12/16	7 9/16	Yell Co., AR	Larry Ennis	Larry Ennis	2007	370
20 5/16	12 12/16	7 9/16	Keweenaw Co., MI	Jacob L. Lambrix	Jacob L. Lambrix	2007	370
20 5/16	12 12/16	7 9/16	La Loche, SK	Willie L. Miles, Jr.	Willie L. Miles, Jr.	2007	370
20 5/16	12 6/16	7 15/16	Haywood Co., NC	Kasey A. Strganac	Kasey A. Strganac	2007	370
20 5/16	12 7/16	7 14/16	Prince of Wales Island, AK	Mark A. Todd	Mark A. Todd	2007	370
20 5/16	13	7 5/16	Lycoming Co., PA	Dean W. Berkheimer	Dean W. Berkheimer	2008	370

		Locality	Hunter	Owner	Date	Rank
20 5/16	12 8/16	Winnipeg River, MB	Raymond K. Firchau	Raymond K. Firchau	2008	370
20 5/16	12 9/16	Little Fishing Lake, SK	Christopher Jensen	Christopher Jensen	2008	370
20 5/16	12 15/16	Swan River, MB	Dan A. Jost	Dan A. Jost	2008	370
20 5/16	12 9/16	Teton Co., WY	William H. Murphy	William H. Murphy	2008	370
20 5/16	12 10/16	Nakina, ON	Paul F. Myers	Paul F. Myers	2008	370
20 5/16	12 11/16	Buchans Plateau, NL	William L. Oberkiser	William L. Oberkiser	2008	370
20 5/16	12 10/16	Lincoln Co., WY	Robert B. Point, Jr.	Robert B. Point, Jr.	2008	370
20 5/16	12 12/16	Thorne Bay, AK	Daniel J. Smith	Daniel J. Smith	2008	370
20 5/16	12 9/16	Marinette Co., WI	Ron W. Wontor	Ron W. Wontor	2008	370
20 5/16	12 7/16	Saint-Tite, QC	Kevin D. Pugh	Kevin D. Pugh	2009	370
20 4/16	12 14/16	Goshawk Lake, ON	Michael V. Cheek	Michael V. Cheek	1981	397
20 4/16	12 8/16	Elk Co., PA	Jerry L. Hechler	Jerry L. Hechler	1988	397
20 4/16	12 13/16	Aroostook Co., ME	William E. Finney	William E. Finney	1992	397
20 4/16	12 12/16	Umatilla Co., OR	Robert B. Qualey	Robert B. Qualey	1994	397
20 4/16	12 11/16	Windsor Co., VT	Raymond R. Forrest	Raymond R. Forrest	1996	397
20 4/16	12 10/16	Pierce Co., WA	Johnathan J. Sandin	Johnathan J. Sandin	2004	397
20 4/16	13	Clinton Co., PA	Carl D. Burrows	Carl D. Burrows	2005	397
20 4/16	12 12/16	Queen Charlotte Islands, BC	Bronko A. Terkovich	Bronko A. Terkovich	2005	397
20 4/16	12 4/16	Port Hardy, BC	Howard S. Topping	Howard S. Topping	2005	397
20 4/16	13 1/16	Hyde Co., NC	Hal S. Atkinson, Jr.	Hal S. Atkinson, Jr.	2006	397
20 4/16	12 15/16	Gogebic Co., MI	Ricketts R. Cable	Ricketts R. Cable	2006	397
20 4/16	12 10/16	Rusk Co., WI	Hannah M. Freymiller	Hannah M. Freymiller	2006	397
20 4/16	12 6/16	Beaupre Creek, SK	Judith A. Lamison	Judith A. Lamison	2006	397
20 4/16	12 14/16	Ontonagon Co., MI	Robert F. Wagner	Robert F. Wagner	2006	397
20 4/16	12 15/16	Saint-Janvier de Chazel, QC	Marcel Charrois	Marcel Charrois	2007	397
20 4/16	12 11/16	Queen Charlotte Islands, BC	Bryan K. Martin	Bryan K. Martin	2008	397
20 4/16	12 12/16	Lac Minto, QC	Arnold E. Allred	Arnold E. Allred	2008	397
20 4/16	12 10/16	Salmon Arm, BC	Michael S. Boehme	Michael S. Boehme	2008	397
20 4/16	12 14/16	Buck Lake, AB	Christy A. Christensen	Christy A. Christensen	2008	397
20 4/16	12 6/16	Humboldt Co., CA	Jace Comfort	Jace Comfort	2008	397
20 4/16	12 12/16	Aroostook Co., ME	Paul C. Critean	Paul C. Critean	2008	397
20 4/16	12 7/16	Aroostook Co., ME	Brady H. Haynes	Brady H. Haynes	2008	397
20 4/16	12 12/16	Bland Co., VA	Westly A. Hill	Westly A. Hill	2008	397
20 4/16	12 2/16	Lac Saint Jean, QC	Chris S. Krafft	Chris S. Krafft	2008	397
20 4/16	12 6/16	Yavapai Co., AZ	Travis A. Legler	Travis A. Legler	2008	397
20 4/16	12 14/16	Wexford Co., MI	Jacob C. Lueder	Jacob C. Lueder	2008	397
20 4/16	12 9/16	Windham Co., VT	Scott A. Rawson	Scott A. Rawson	2008	397
20 4/16	12 2/16	Warren Co., PA	Brian E. Ristau	Brian E. Ristau	2008	397
20 4/16	12 10/16	Oconto Co., WI	Robert J. School	Robert J. School	2008	397
20 4/16	12 7/16	Grandview, MB	Raymond Glastetter	Raymond Glastetter	2009	397
20 4/16	12 8/16	Morrison Co., MN	Stephen P. Hines	Stephen P. Hines	2009	397
20 4/16	12 8/16	Prince of Wales Island, AK	Sara L. Weythman	Sara L. Weythman	2009	397

BLACK BEAR

Ursus americanus and related subspecies

Final Score	Greatest Length of Skull Without Lower Jaw	Greatest Width of Skull	Locality	Hunter	Owner	Date Killed	Rank
20 3/16	12 14/16	7 5/16	Prince of Wales Island, AK	James F. Baichtal	James F. Baichtal	1997	429
20 3/16	12 6/16	7 13/16	Langlade Co., WI	Ronald A. Goldapske	Ronald A. Goldapske	2002	429
20 3/16	12 7/16	7 12/16	Prince of Wales Island, AK	Ian K. Chase-Dunn	Ian K. Chase-Dunn	2003	429
20 3/16	12 15/16	7 4/16	Douglas Co., WI	Eric A. Rasmussen, Sr.	Eric A. Rasmussen, Sr.	2003	429
20 3/16	12 8/16	7 11/16	Cass Co., MN	Jerome P. Crimmins	Jerome P. Crimmins	2005	429
20 3/16	12 15/16	7 4/16	Aitkin Co., MN	Daniel M. Niehoff	Daniel M. Niehoff	2005	429
20 3/16	13 1/16	7 2/16	Beaufort Co., NC	Bruce Clements	Bruce Clements	2006	429
20 3/16	12 11/16	7 8/16	Lewis Lake, MB	Jeffrey J. Ronspies	Jeffrey J. Ronspies	2006	429
20 3/16	12 9/16	7 10/16	Elma, MB	Joseph F. Schrader III	Joseph F. Schrader III	2006	429
20 3/16	12 9/16	7 10/16	Suemez Island, AK	Carroll L. Sherman	Carroll L. Sherman	2006	429
20 3/16	12 9/16	7 10/16	Hampden Co., MA	Phillip J. Sulewski	Phillip J. Sulewski	2006	429
20 3/16	12 3/16	8	Trinity Co., CA	Lyle Valador	Lyle Valador	2006	429
20 3/16	12 10/16	7 9/16	Oconto Co., WI	Dale M. Missall	Dale M. Missall	2007	429
20 3/16	12 8/16	7 11/16	Prince of Wales Island, AK	Timothy M. Murta	Timothy M. Murta	2007	429
20 3/16	13	7 3/16	Vancouver Island, BC	Gary A. Spina	Gary A. Spina	2007	429
20 3/16	12 9/16	7 10/16	Walla Walla Co., WA	Clyde Allen	Clyde Allen	2008	429
20 3/16	12 4/16	7 15/16	Humboldt Co., CA	Anjanette L. Dunn	Anjanette L. Dunn	2008	429
20 3/16	12 14/16	7 5/16	Mesa Co., CO	Wilma J. Files-Seriani	Wilma J. Files-Seriani	2008	429
20 3/16	12 8/16	7 11/16	Spirit River, AB	Jeremy E. Hach	Jeremy E. Hach	2008	429
20 3/16	13 1/16	7 2/16	Oakburn, MB	Brian J. McDermott	Brian J. McDermott	2008	429
20 3/16	12 4/16	7 15/16	Nukko Lake, BC	Gregory R. St. Amand	Gregory R. St. Amand	2008	429
20 3/16	12 7/16	7 12/16	San Bernardino Co., CA	Craig N. Davis	Craig N. Davis	2009	429
20 3/16	12 12/16	7 7/16	Prince Albert, SK	Ryan J. Harris	Ryan J. Harris	2009	429
20 3/16	12 5/16	7 14/16	Coos Co., OR	Brian Henderson	Brian Henderson	2009	429
20 2/16	12 9/16	7 9/16	Elk Co., PA	Lamont E. Gray	Lamont E. Gray	2005	453
20 2/16	12 8/16	7 10/16	Bennington Co., VT	Philip J. Trainor	Philip J. Trainor	2005	453
20 2/16	12 6/16	7 12/16	Mendocino Co., CA	Georg Aigeldinger	Georg Aigeldinger	2006	453
20 2/16	12 11/16	7 7/16	Iron Co., WI	Alvin M. Bellmer	Alvin M. Bellmer	2006	453
20 2/16	12 5/16	7 13/16	Rio Arriba Co., NM	Glenn A. Brungardt	Glenn A. Brungardt	2006	453
20 2/16	12 14/16	7 4/16	Presque Isle Co., MI	Daniel R. Chinavare	Daniel R. Chinavare	2006	453
20 2/16	12 6/16	7 12/16	Jackson Co., WI	Mark A. Gjerseth	Mark A. Gjerseth	2006	453
20 2/16	12 3/16	7 15/16	Grand Prairie, AB	Stephen A. Longo	Stephen A. Longo	2006	453
20 2/16	12 14/16	7 4/16	Van Buren Co., AR	Carl W. Rippy	Carl W. Rippy	2006	453

		Locality	Owner	Hunter	Date	Rank
20 2/16	12 6/16	Steepbank Lake, SK	Richard P. Smith	Richard P. Smith	2006	453
20 2/16	12 6/16	Culpeper Co., VA	Paul A. Wasyln	Paul A. Wasyln	2006	453
20 2/16	12 6/16	Nechako River, BC	David N. Campbell	David N. Campbell	2007	453
20 2/16	12 9/16	Iron Co., MI	Robert J. Carten	Robert J. Carten	2007	453
20 2/16	12 7/16	Chain Lakes, AB	Mark G. Damm	Mark G. Damm	2007	453
20 2/16	12 13/16	Itasca Co., MN	Timothy P. Elich	Timothy P. Elich	2007	453
20 2/16	12 2/16	Gouin Reservoir, QC	William M. Everett	William M. Everett	2007	453
20 2/16	12 10/16	Prince of Wales Island, AK	David A. Langrehr	David A. Langrehr	2007	453
20 2/16	12 13/16	Pine Co., MN	David L. Patterson	David L. Patterson	2007	453
20 2/16	12 7/16	Athabasca River, AB	Norman W. Bomer	Norman W. Bomer	2008	453
20 2/16	13 1/16	Jones Co., NC	Mitchell S. Deviney	Mitchell S. Deviney	2008	453
20 2/16	13 4/16	Converse Co., WY	Adam R. Fackelman	Adam R. Fackelman	2008	453
20 2/16	13 1/16	Houston Co., GA	GA Dept. of Natl. Resc.	Picked Up	2008	453
20 2/16	12 8/16	Fort McMurray, AB	Benjamin F. Hawke	Benjamin F. Hawke	2008	453
20 2/16	12 5/16	Caledonia Co., VT	Mathew R. Johnson	Mathew R. Johnson	2008	453
20 2/16	12 11/16	Hot Springs Co., WY	Curtis J. Kelstrom	Curtis J. Kelstrom	2008	453
20 2/16	12 11/16	Barron Co., WI	Gerald A. Kendzior	Gerald A. Kendzior	2008	453
20 2/16	12 9/16	Gallatin Co., MT	Steve R. Kuchinsky	Steve R. Kuchinsky	2008	453
20 2/16	12 6/16	Moberly Lake, BC	Phillip E. West	Phillip E. West	2008	453
20 2/16	12 12/16	St. Louis Co., MN	Jacob L. Billman	Jacob L. Billman	2009	453
20 2/16	12 10/16	Dubreuilville, ON	Michael J. Weber	Michael J. Weber	2009	453

BLACK BEAR
FINAL SCORE: 21 1/16
HUNTER: Edward A. Parker

BLACK BEAR
FINAL SCORE: 20
HUNTER: Ryan J. Graham

BLACK BEAR
FINAL SCORE: 21
HUNTER: Robert E. Webber

BLACK BEAR
FINAL SCORE: 21 2/16
HUNTER: Marc T. Sanchez

BLACK BEAR

Ursus americanus americanus and related subspecies

Final Score	Greatest Length of Skull Without Lower Jaw	Greatest Width of Skull	Locality	Hunter	Owner	Date Killed	Rank
20 1/16	12 11/16	7 6/16	Page Co., VA	Christopher D. Hensley	Christopher D. Hensley	2004	483
20 1/16	12 8/16	7 9/16	Berkshire Co., MA	Robert A. Arcott	Robert A. Arcott	2006	483
20 1/16	12 7/16	7 10/16	Clay Co., NC	Samuel D. Davis	Samuel D. Davis	2006	483
20 1/16	12 12/16	7 5/16	Lewis Co., WA	Patrick J. Obermire	Patrick J. Obermire	2006	483
20 1/16	12 7/16	7 10/16	Oconto Co., WI	Picked Up	Danny R. Siddons	2006	483
20 1/16	12 10/16	7 7/16	Dorion, ON	Gregory L. Surber	Gregory L. Surber	2006	483
20 1/16	12 8/16	7 9/16	Aroostook Co., ME	Jaret L. Carbone	Jaret L. Carbone	2007	483
20 1/16	12 4/16	7 13/16	Gilford Island, BC	Robert J. Clancy	Robert J. Clancy	2007	483
20 1/16	12 6/16	7 11/16	Washington Co., VT	Kyle Farnham	Kyle Farnham	2007	483
20 1/16	12 9/16	7 8/16	Rusk Co., WI	Donn W. Kubnick	Donn W. Kubnick	2007	483
20 1/16	12 12/16	7 5/16	Clinton Co., PA	William H. Thomas	William H. Thomas	2007	483
20 1/16	12 6/16	7 11/16	Chilkat Pen., AK	Fred W. Williams	Fred W. Williams	2007	483
20 1/16	12 2/16	7 15/16	Skead, ON	James M. Deckler	James M. Deckler	2008	483
20 1/16	12 6/16	7 11/16	Chelan Co., WA	Curtis Perry	Curtis Perry	2008	483
20 1/16	12 7/16	7 10/16	Fraser River, BC	Edwin H. Peterson	Edwin H. Peterson	2008	483
20 1/16	12 9/16	7 8/16	Langlade Co., WI	Brian M. Wolfe	Brian M. Wolfe	2008	483
20	12 9/16	7 7/16	Prince of Wales Island, AK	James F. Baichtal	James F. Baichtal	1995	499
20	12 8/16	7 8/16	Cass Co., MN	Eugene A. Peet	Eugene A. Peet	2000	499
20	12 14/16	7 2/16	Huntingdon Co., PA	Ronald L. Slee	Ronald L. Slee	2001	499
20	12 6/16	7 12/16	Valley Co., ID	Darwin G. DeCroo	Darwin G. DeCroo	2003	499
20	12 4/16	7 8/16	Yavapai Co., AZ	Brandt M. Lewis	Brandt M. Lewis	2005	499
20	12 8/16	7 11/16	Custer Co., CO	Picked Up	CO Div. of Wildl.	2006	499
20	12 5/16	7 8/16	Chelan Co., WA	Dallas D. Countryman	Dallas D. Countryman	2006	499
20	12 8/16	7 4/16	Prince of Wales Island, AK	L. Dwight Israelsen	L. Dwight Israelsen	2006	499
20	12 12/16	7 7/16	Tioga Co., PA	Bryn R. Kolbe	Bryn R. Kolbe	2006	499
20	12 9/16	7 12/16	Black Sturgeon Lake, ON	Richard L. Lilly	Richard L. Lilly	2006	499
20	12 4/16	7 7/16	Nueltin Lake, MB	Robert K. Petro	Robert K. Petro	2006	499
20	12 9/16	7 8/16	Caramat, ON	Dennis J. Sumbera	Dennis J. Sumbera	2006	499
20	12 8/16	7 8/16	Baker Co., OR	Brody L. Charpilloz	Brody L. Charpilloz	2007	499
20	12 8/16	7 10/16	Jackson Co., OR	Jeffrey R. Tucker	Jeffrey R. Tucker	2007	499
20	12 6/16	7 11/16	Presque Isle Co., MI	Gary O. Dix	Gary O. Dix	2008	499
20	12 5/16	7 5/16	Skootamatta Lake, ON	Rockie L. Ford	Rockie L. Ford	2008	499
20	12 11/16	7 5/16	Osilika Lake, BC	Ryan J. Graham	Ryan J. Graham	2008	499

20	12 $^{11}/_{16}$	7 $^{5}/_{16}$	Frank J. Hoeckl	Delta Co., MI	Frank J. Hoeckl	2008	499
20	12 $^{10}/_{16}$	7 $^{6}/_{16}$	Drake D. McClelland	Porcupine Plain, SK	Drake D. McClelland	2008	499
20	12 $^{9}/_{16}$	7 $^{7}/_{16}$	Lannon E. Nault	Loon Lake, SK	Lannon E. Nault	2008	499
20	12 $^{9}/_{16}$	7 $^{7}/_{16}$	Robert J. Witt	Worcester Co., MA	Robert J. Witt	2008	499
20	12 $^{10}/_{16}$	7 $^{6}/_{16}$	James P. Graf	Montrose Co., CO	James P. Graf	2009	499
20	12 $^{4}/_{16}$	7 $^{12}/_{16}$	Jerome J. Herron	Meagher Co., MT	Picked Up	2009	499
20	12 $^{5}/_{16}$	7 $^{11}/_{16}$	VT Big Game Trophy Club, Inc.	Orange Co., VT	Picked Up	2009	499
22 $^{13}/_{16}$*	14 $^{5}/_{16}$	8 $^{8}/_{16}$	Jesse L. Ritchey	Bedford Co., PA	Jesse L. Ritchey	2006	
22 $^{12}/_{16}$*	13 $^{14}/_{16}$	8 $^{14}/_{16}$	Douglas Kristiansen	Pike Co., PA	Douglas Kristiansen	2003	

* Final score subject to revision by additional verifying measurements.

BLACK BEAR
FINAL SCORE: 21 $^{8}/_{16}$
HUNTER: Mindy B. Arthurs

BLACK BEAR
FINAL SCORE: 21 $^{9}/_{16}$
HUNTER: Wesley S. Brown

BLACK BEAR
FINAL SCORE: 20 $^{5}/_{16}$
HUNTER: Ron W. Wontor

BLACK BEAR
FINAL SCORE: 20 $^{13}/_{16}$
HUNTER: Wendell Howes, Jr.

GRIZZLY BEAR

Ursus arctos horribilis

Minimum Score 23 · World's Record 27 13/16

Final Score	Greatest Length of Skull Without Lower Jaw	Greatest Width of Skull	Locality	Hunter	Owner	Date Killed	Rank
27 3/16	16 13/16	10 6/16	Unalakleet River, AK	Rodney W. Debias	Rodney W. Debias	2009	1
26 12/16	16 12/16	10	Unalakleet, AK	Jeffrey B. Brigham	Jeffrey B. Brigham	2009	2
26 4/16	16 2/16	10 2/16	Stikine River, BC	Blaine E. Nelson	Blaine E. Nelson	2007	3
26 2/16	16 1/16	10 1/16	Nulato Hills, AK	Eugene F. Segrest	Eugene F. Segrest	2009	4
26 1/16	16	10 1/16	Cache Creek, AK	Dennis B. Shennard II	Dennis B. Shennard II	2007	5
26 1/16	16 1/16	9 1/16	Buckland River, AK	Brian A. Robinson	Brian A. Robinson	2008	5
26	16 15/16	9 12/16	Kuskokwim River, AK	Nestor T. Norback	Nestor T. Norback	2001	7
25 14/16	16 2/16	10 5/16	Talkeetna Mts., AK	Chad B. Sherman	Chad B. Sherman	2006	8
25 12/16	15 7/16	9 14/16	Wood River, AK	Robert W. Witt	Robert W. Witt	2007	9
25 10/16	15 12/16	9 12/16	Otter Creek, AK	Scott E. Johnson	Scott E. Johnson	2009	10
25 9/16	15 13/16	9 13/16	Kantishna River, AK	James W. Dowdell	James W. Dowdell	2006	11
25 9/16	15 12/16	10	Darby Mountains, AK	David W. Baxter	David W. Baxter	2008	11
25 6/16	15 6/16	9 2/16	Seal Oil Creek, AK	Mark A. Wayne	Mark A. Wayne	2009	13
25 5/16	16 3/16	9 10/16	Seymour Inlet, BC	Darrell S. Lightfoot	Darrell S. Lightfoot	1992	14
25 5/16	15 11/16	8 14/16	Gisasa River, AK	Joel M. Brannan	Joel M. Brannan	2006	14
25 5/16	16 7/16	9 8/16	Bella Coola River, BC	Renato Uliana	Renato Uliana	2007	14
25 5/16	15 13/16	9 15/16	Koyukuk River, AK	James E. Schwartzhoff	James E. Schwartzhoff	2009	14
25 2/16	15 3/16	8 9/16	Bathurst Inlet, NU	John R. Gallimore	John R. Gallimore	2008	18
25 1/16	16 8/16	9 10/16	Kuskokwim River, AK	Nestor T. Norback	Nestor T. Norback	2004	19
25 1/16	15 7/16	9 1/16	Kispiox Mt., BC	Louis E. Leonor	Louis E. Leonor	2008	19
24 15/16	15 7/16	9 8/16	Bathurst Inlet, NU	J.P. Gallimore	J.P. Gallimore	2008	21
24 15/16	15 7/16	9	Mount Buckland, AK	Paul A. Gardner	Paul A. Gardner	2008	21
24 15/16	15 15/16	8 15/16	Norton Sound, AK	Frank S. Noska IV	Frank S. Noska IV	2009	21
24 14/16	15 15/16	9 12/16	Nulato Hills, AK	John C. Cunat	John C. Cunat	2007	24
24 14/16	15 2/16	9 1/16	Wright Bay, BC	Dan R. King	Dan R. King	2009	24
24 13/16	15 12/16	9 6/16	Koyukuk River, AK	John M. Gebbia	John M. Gebbia	2002	26
24 12/16	15 6/16	9 13/16	Skeena Mts., BC	John G. Niebur	John G. Niebur	2007	27
24 12/16	14 15/16	9 7/16	Mosquito Flats, AK	Robert E. Floyd	Robert E. Floyd	2008	27
24 12/16	15 5/16	9 3/16	Prince George, BC	Randy Kubbernus	Randy Kubbernus	2008	27
24 11/16	15 8/16	8 15/16	Tinsdale Creek, BC	Ab Bowden	Ab Bowden	2007	30
24 10/16	15 11/16	9 2/16	Alice Arm, BC	Tod W. Graham	Tod W. Graham	2007	31
24 10/16	15 8/16	9 2/16	Kingcome River, BC	Jerome D. Pyper	Jerome D. Pyper	2007	31
24 9/16	15 5/16	9 4/16	Koyuk River, AK	David L. Hussey	David L. Hussey	1999	33

466

BOONE AND CROCKETT CLUB'S

Score	Length of Skull	Width of Skull	Locality		Hunter	Year	Rank
24 9/16	15 1/16	9 8/16	Tuchodi River, BC	David W. Heeter, Jr.	David W. Heeter, Jr.	2008	33
24 9/16	15 4/16	9 5/16	White Mts., AK	Craig J. Schwanke	Craig J. Schwanke	2008	33
24 9/16	15 2/16	9 7/16	Shaktoolik River, AK	Douglas J. Roffers	Douglas J. Roffers	2009	33
24 8/16	15 6/16	9 2/16	Nadahini Creek, BC	Garry E. Merkwan	Garry E. Merkwan	2004	37
24 8/16	15 10/16	8 14/16	Wakeman River, BC	Robert J. Clancy	Robert J. Clancy	2007	37
24 8/16	15 10/16	8 14/16	Trapper Lake, BC	Randy Cuthbert	Randy Cuthbert	2007	37
24 8/16	15	9 8/16	Tok River, AK	Nadine L. Wilson	Nadine L. Wilson	2009	37
24 7/16	15 8/16	8 15/16	Chinchaga River, AB	James G. Steward	James G. Steward	2004	41
24 6/16	14 14/16	9 8/16	Salcha River, AK	Kenneth J. Lamers	Kenneth J. Lamers	2008	42
24 5/16	15 5/16	9	Ogilvie Mts., YT	Gerald J. Kane	Gerald J. Kane	1996	43
24 5/16	15 2/16	9 3/16	Norton Sound, AK	Terry E. Trexler	Terry E. Trexler	2008	43
24 5/16	15 8/16	8 13/16	Kinaskan Lake, BC	Richard G. Stelter	Richard G. Stelter	2009	43
24 4/16	15 1/16	9 3/16	Unalakleet, AK	Larry E. Ensign	Larry E. Ensign	2004	46
24 4/16	14 14/16	9 6/16	Koyuk River, AK	Philip B. Mancuso	Philip B. Mancuso	2007	46
24 2/16	15	9 2/16	Collins Creek, BC	Peter T. Rickard	Peter T. Rickard	2005	48
24 2/16	15 4/16	8 14/16	Meziadin Lake, BC	Steve E. Rakes	Steve E. Rakes	2007	48
24 2/16	15 5/16	8 13/16	McGregor River, BC	Christopher P. Speakman	Christopher P. Speakman	2007	48
24 2/16	15	9 2/16	Nabesche River, BC	Patricia M. Dreeszen	Patricia M. Dreeszen	2008	48
24 2/16	15 4/16	8 14/16	Chisana Glacier, AK	Roger A. Gunlock	Roger A. Gunlock	2008	48
24 1/16	15	9 1/16	Squirrel River, AK	Michael D. Taylor	Michael D. Taylor	2006	53
24	15	9	Kirbyville Creek, BC	Brian M. McDonald	Brian M. McDonald	2006	54
23 14/16	15	8 14/16	Moyie River, BC	Frank D. Nataros	Frank D. Nataros	1960	55
23 13/16	15 8/16	8 5/16	Kobuk River, AK	Michael G. Morton	Michael G. Morton	2007	56
23 13/16	14 13/16	9	Prince George, BC	Richard J. Anderson	Richard J. Anderson	2008	56
23 12/16	14 12/16	9	Wrangell Mts., AK	Nathan R. Cullum	Nathan R. Cullum	2007	58
23 11/16	14 13/16	8 14/16	Stikine River, BC	Boyd Wilson	Boyd Wilson	2007	59
23 10/16	14 7/16	9 3/16	Kaltag, AK	Ken Nelson, Jr.	Ken Nelson, Jr.	2006	60
23 9/16	15	8 9/16	Terrace, BC	Cliff Sheppard	Cliff Sheppard	2008	61
23 8/16	14 6/16	9 2/16	Taku River, BC	Kent Deligans	Kent Deligans	2005	62
23 7/16	14 8/16	8 15/16	Kwadacha River, BC	Bryan K. Martin	Bryan K. Martin	2006	63
23 5/16	14 5/16	9	Tuya River, BC	Gary A. Crowe	Gary A. Crowe	2008	64
23 3/16	14 11/16	8 8/16	Chandalar River, AK	Timothy L. Fullerton	Timothy L. Fullerton	2008	65
23 2/16	14 10/16	8 8/16	Anderson River, NT	Jack Keslar	Jack Keslar	2003	66
26 13/16*	16 8/16	10 5/16	McGrath, AK	Robert L. Magnuson, Jr.	Robert L. Magnuson, Jr.	2007	
26 2/16*	16 9/16	9 9/16	Apple River, BC	Gabriel Perez-Maura Garcia	Gabriel Perez-Maura Garcia	2008	

* Final score subject to revision by additional verifying measurements.

Ursus arctos middendorffi and certain related subspecies

Minimum Score 26 World's Record 30 12/16

Final Score	Greatest Length of Skull Without Lower Jaw	Greatest Width of Skull	Locality	Hunter	Owner	Date Killed	Rank
29 9/16	17 14/16	11 11/16	Uganik Lake, AK	Robert J. Castle	Robert J. Castle	2006	1
29 6/16	17 12/16	11 10/16	Alaska Pen., AK	Mikkel Sorensen	Mikkel Sorensen	2009	2
29 3/16	17 10/16	11 9/16	Karluk Lake, AK	Duane E. Dosser	Duane E. Dosser	2008	3
29 1/16	18 1/16	11	Hoodoo Lake, AK	David L. Stuart	David L. Stuart	2008	4
29	17 15/16	11 11/16	Thinpoint Lake, AK	Gary N. Ophaug	Gary N. Ophaug	2005	5
29	17 6/16	11 10/16	Terror Bay, AK	Murray J. Sorensen	Murray J. Sorensen	2008	5
29	17 8/16	11 8/16	Karluk Lake, AK	Steven G. Campbell	Steven G. Campbell	2009	5
28 15/16	18 3/16	10 12/16	Pilot Point, AK	Lester D. Giacomini, Jr.	Cabela's, Inc.	2006	8
28 15/16	17 8/16	11 7/16	Karluk Lake, AK	Picked Up	Mark A. Rusk	2009	8
28 14/16	17 10/16	11 4/16	Laura Lake, AK	Everett P. Muncy	Everett P. Muncy	2007	10
28 12/16	18	10 12/16	Port Heiden, AK	Wayne D. Simper	Wayne D. Simper	2009	11
28 11/16	17 4/16	11 7/16	Zachar River, AK	Lester M. Combs	Lester M. Combs	2006	12
28 10/16	17 6/16	11 4/16	Aliulik Pen., AK	Brooke E. Terkovich	Brooke E. Terkovich	2006	13
28 9/16	17 7/16	11 2/16	Olga Lake, AK	Peter J. Bausone	Peter J. Bausone	2008	14
28 9/16	18	10 9/16	Canoe Bay, AK	Jon B. Burrows	Jon B. Burrows	2008	14
28 8/16	17 2/16	11 6/16	Olds River, AK	Casey J. Jacobs	Casey J. Jacobs	2009	16
28 7/16	17 14/16	10 9/16	Becharof Lake, AK	Kelly G. Keithly	Kelly G. Keithly	2006	17
28 7/16	17 3/16	11 4/16	Karluk River, AK	Jerry Skeens	Jerry Skeens	2007	17
28 7/16	17 1/16	11 6/16	Kodiak Island, AK	Douglas W. Miller	Douglas W. Miller	2008	17
28 7/16	18 3/16	10 4/16	Wolf Lake, AK	Charles H. Rush	Charles H. Rush	2008	17
28 6/16	17 7/16	10 15/16	Egegik River, AK	Robert L. Friel	Robert L. Friel	2006	21
28 6/16	17 12/16	10 10/16	Puale Bay, AK	Jeffrey K. Chaulk	Jeffrey K. Chaulk	2007	21
28 6/16	16 13/16	11 9/16	Sturgeon River, AK	James R. Gabrick	James R. Gabrick	2007	21
28 6/16	18 5/16	10 1/16	Port Heiden, AK	Donald E. Perrien	Donald E. Perrien	2009	21
28 5/16	17 8/16	10 13/16	Portage Bay, AK	Raymond M. Hay, Jr.	Raymond M. Hay, Jr.	2008	25
28 4/16	16 9/16	11 11/16	Portage Bay, AK	Thomas Carlson	Thomas Carlson	2008	26
28 4/16	17 11/16	10 9/16	Canoe Bay, AK	Joshua B. Jones	Joshua B. Jones	2008	26
28 4/16	17 10/16	10 10/16	Port Heiden, AK	Robert E. Finn	Robert E. Finn	2009	26
28 3/16	17 1/16	11 2/16	Karluk River, AK	Gary E. Hoewe	Gary E. Hoewe	2006	29
28 3/16	17	11 3/16	Halibut Bay, AK	Denise J. Carter	Denise J. Carter	2008	29
28 3/16	17 3/16	11	Aliulik Pen., AK	Luke A. Terkovich	Luke A. Terkovich	2008	29
28 3/16	17 12/16	10 7/16	Olga Bay, AK	Fred J. Fanizzi	Fred J. Fanizzi	2009	29
28 3/16	17 6/16	10 13/16	Red Lake, AK	James L. Horneck	James L. Horneck	2009	29

Score	Length	Width	Hunter	Locality	Owner	Date Killed	Rank
28 2/16	17 4/16	10 14/16	William J. Daniel III	Tikchik Lake, AK	William J. Daniel III	2007	34
28 2/16	16 15/16	11 3/16	Breck A. Johnson	Spiridon Lake, AK	Breck A. Johnson	2009	34
28 2/16	17 12/16	10 6/16	Edward C. Joseph	Unimak Island, AK	Edward C. Joseph	2009	34
28 1/16	17 14/16	10 3/16	Edward B. Evans	Mendenhall Glacier, AK	Edward B. Evans	2006	37
28 1/16	16 12/16	11 5/16	Marty Markl	Sitkalidak Island, AK	Marty Markl	2009	37
28	16 15/16	11 1/16	Robert L. Hudman	King Salmon Creek, AK	Robert L. Hudman	2001	39
28	17 10/16	10 6/16	Dean R. Christian	Lake Kulik, AK	Dean R. Christian	2007	39
27 14/16	17 6/16	10 8/16	Ian K. Chase-Dunn	Alsek River, AK	Ian K. Chase-Dunn	2007	41
27 11/16	16 12/16	10 15/16	Ervin Borkenhagen	Cordova, AK	Jerry Smith	1964	42
27 11/16	17 5/16	10 6/16	James R. Doyle	Cold Bay, AK	James R. Doyle	2007	42
27 10/16	17 10/16	11 1/16	Ryan W. Fleishauer	Sharatin Bay, AK	Ryan W. Fleishauer	2007	44
27 10/16	16 9/16	11 3/16	Denise L. Spain	Kempf Bay, AK	Denise L. Spain	2008	44
27 9/16	17 5/16	10 4/16	Larry D. Napier	Alsek River, AK	Larry D. Napier	2009	46
27 7/16	17 5/16	10 2/16	Stephen D. Athman	Meshik River, AK	Stephen D. Athman	2005	47
27 7/16	17 9/16	9 14/16	David J. Brown	Grant Lake, AK	David J. Brown	2005	47
27 7/16	17 6/16	10 1/16	Jason W. Bakke	Meshik River, AK	Jason W. Bakke	2008	47
27 6/16	17 3/16	10 3/16	Dwayne E. Heikes	Cinder River, AK	Dwayne E. Heikes	2007	50
27 5/16	16 13/16	10 8/16	George E. Miller	Manby Stream, AK	George E. Miller	2008	51
27 4/16	17 9/16	9 11/16	Chris A. Dianda	Ivan Bay, AK	Chris A. Dianda	2006	52
27 3/16	17 1/16	10 2/16	Fred Moseley	Peters Hills, AK	Fred Moseley	1993	53
27 3/16	16 10/16	10 9/16	Mike A. Carpinito	Olga Bay, AK	Mike A. Carpinito	2005	53

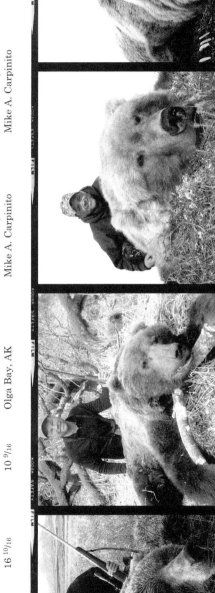

ALASKA BROWN BEAR
FINAL SCORE: 27 10/16
HUNTER: Denise L. Spain

ALASKA BROWN BEAR
FINAL SCORE: 28 8/16
HUNTER: Casey J. Jacobs

ALASKA BROWN BEAR
FINAL SCORE: 26 6/16
HUNTER: Michael W. Christopher

ALASKA BROWN BEAR
FINAL SCORE: 28 7/16
HUNTER: Jerry Skeens

ALASKA BROWN BEAR

Ursus arctos middendorffi and certain related subspecies

Final Score	Greatest Length of Skull Without Lower Jaw	Greatest Width of Skull	Locality	Hunter	Owner	Date Killed	Rank
27 1/16	17 1/16	10	Sandy River, AK	James E. Montgomery	James E. Montgomery	2007	55
27	17	10	Becharof Lake, AK	Charles E. Fenix	Charles E. Fenix	2003	56
26 14/16	16 8/16	10 6/16	Kupreanof Pen., AK	Gregory E. Olejniczak	Gregory E. Olejniczak	2004	57
26 13/16	16 10/16	10 3/16	Tokositna River, AK	Donald D. Holloway	Donald D. Holloway	2007	58
26 12/16	16 4/16	10 8/16	Johnson River, AK	Terry B. Neely	Terry B. Neely	2008	59
26 11/16	16 11/16	10	Hoholitna River, AK	Scott D. Ford	Scott D. Ford	2008	60
26 10/16	16 12/16	9 14/16	Olds River, AK	Todd D. Hoftiezer	Todd D. Hoftiezer	2007	61
26 10/16	17 4/16	9 6/16	Nelson Bay, AK	Brennan L. Potts	Brennan L. Potts	2007	61
26 10/16	16 9/16	10 1/16	Terror Bay, AK	Dennis Nemeth	Dennis Nemeth	2009	61
26 9/16	16 15/16	9 10/16	David River, AK	Stephen M. Porto	Stephen M. Porto	2008	64
26 8/16	16 5/16	10 3/16	Little Susitna River, AK	Damon Richardson	Damon Richardson	2004	65
26 7/16	16 6/16	10 1/16	Port Moller, AK	Bryan K. Martin	Bryan K. Martin	2006	66
26 7/16	16 10/16	9 13/16	Goodnews River, AK	Daniel W. Coats	Daniel W. Coats	2008	66
26 7/16	16 7/16	10	Dillingham, AK	Russell W. Mosier	Russell W. Mosier	2008	66
26 6/16	16 4/16	10 2/16	Iliamna Lake, AK	Michael W. Christopher	Michael W. Christopher	2006	69
26 5/16	16 3/16	10 2/16	Sunday Creek, AK	Steven L. Kiesel	Steven L. Kiesel	2006	70
26 5/16	16 9/16	9 12/16	Bering River, AK	Vincent L. Hazen	Vincent L. Hazen	2007	70
26 5/16	15 14/16	10 7/16	Kiliuda Bay, AK	James R. Trull	James R. Trull	2009	70
26 4/16	16	10 4/16	Mulchatna River, AK	William J. Kuntze	William J. Kuntze	2007	73
26 4/16	16 4/16	10	Kodiak Island, AK	John A. Martin	John A. Martin	2007	73
26 4/16	15 11/16	10 9/16	Zachar Bay, AK	Konnie W. Wheeler	Konnie W. Wheeler	2008	73
26 3/16	16 3/16	10	Chigmit Mts., AK	Michael F. Gosman	Michael F. Gosman	2006	76
26 2/16	16 7/16	9 11/16	Chilkat River, AK	Mark Wesen	Mark Wesen	2007	77
26	16 11/16	9 5/16	Port Heiden, AK	Joseph D. Wiggs	Joseph D. Wiggs	2007	78
26	16 1/16	9 15/16	Goodnews Bay, AK	Robert J. Beatty	Robert J. Beatty	2008	78
29 1/16*	18 2/16	10 15/16	Alaska Pen., AK	Fern R. Spaulding	Fern R. Spaulding	2006	

* Final score subject to revision by additional verifying measurements.

POLAR BEAR

Ursus maritimus

Minimum Score 27

Final Score	Greatest Length of Skull Without Lower Jaw	Greatest Width of Skull	Locality	Hunter	Owner	Date Killed	Rank
28 4/16	17 10/16	10 10/16	Kotzebue, AK	Robert B. Kullman	Cabela's, Inc.	1966	1
27 5/16	16 15/16	10 6/16	Chukchi Sea, AK	James D. Unrein	James D. Unrein	2007	2

COUGAR

Felis concolor hippolestes and related subspecies

Minimum Score 14 8/16   World's Record 16 4/16

Final Score	Greatest Length of Skull Without Lower Jaw	Greatest Width of Skull	Locality	Hunter	Owner	Date Killed	Rank
15 14/16	9 4/16	6 10/16	Idaho Co., ID	Rodney E. Bradley	Rodney E. Bradley	2007	1
15 11/16	9 7/16	6 4/16	Rio Blanco Co., CO	Gregory W. Wisener	Gregory W. Wisener	2008	2
15 10/16	9 5/16	6 5/16	Drayton Valley, AB	Timothy R. Gazankas	Timothy R. Gazankas	2006	3
15 10/16	9 6/16	6 4/16	Owyhee Co., ID	Justin D. DeCroo	Justin D. DeCroo	2007	3
15 8/16	9 2/16	6 6/16	Pembina River, AB	Robert W. Sydenham	Robert W. Sydenham	2007	5
15 8/16	9 3/16	6 5/16	Trout Creek, AB	Brice D. Folden	Brice D. Folden	2008	5
15 8/16	9 1/16	6 7/16	Elk River, BC	Bryce R. Kniert	Bryce R. Kniert	2008	5
15 8/16	9 2/16	6 6/16	Lincoln Co., MT	Mel K. Siefke	Mel K. Siefke	2008	5
15 7/16	9 4/16	6 3/16	Eakin Creek, BC	Andrew G. Dana	Andrew G. Dana	2007	9
15 7/16	9 5/16	6 2/16	Rio Arriba Co., NM	Robert J. Seeds	Robert J. Seeds	2008	9
15 7/16	9	6 7/16	Lewis & Clark Co., MT	Matthew C. Enrooth	Matthew C. Enrooth	2009	9
15 6/16	8 14/16	6 8/16	Valley Co., ID	Ken Nelson	Ken Nelson	1969	12
15 6/16	9	6 6/16	Gila Co., AZ	Johnny Basha	Johnny Basha	1994	12
15 6/16	9 1/16	6 5/16	Granite Co., MT	Peter Stertz	Peter Stertz	2006	12
15 6/16	9 1/16	6 5/16	Flathead Co., MT	Larry F. Dahlke	Larry F. Dahlke	2007	12
15 6/16	8 15/16	6 7/16	Idaho Co., ID	Robert A. Grant	Robert A. Grant	2007	12
15 5/16	9 2/16	6 3/16	Okanogan Co., WA	Steven Valley	Steven Valley	2007	17
15 5/16	9 1/16	6 4/16	Rio Arriba Co., NM	James S. Davis	James S. Davis	2009	17
15 4/16	9 2/16	6 2/16	Parker Creek, AB	Robert C. Bowlen	Robert C. Bowlen	2005	19
15 4/16	9	6 4/16	Columbia Co., WA	Daniel L. Maplethorpe	Daniel L. Maplethorpe	2006	19
15 4/16	9 1/16	6 3/16	Wolf Lake, AB	Nabil T. Sassine	Nabil T. Sassine	2006	19
15 4/16	9 2/16	6 2/16	Rocky Creek, BC	Ed S. Pearson	Ed S. Pearson	2008	19
15 4/16	9	6 4/16	Flathead Co., MT	Lillian E. Zach	Lillian E. Zach	2008	19
15 4/16	8 12/16	6 8/16	Powell Co., MT	Amanda M. Hastings	Amanda M. Hastings	2009	19
15 3/16	8 15/16	6 4/16	Sanders Co., MT	Bruce E. Hedetniemi	Bruce E. Hedetniemi	2005	25
15 3/16	8 15/16	6 4/16	Bryant Creek, AB	Adam Enfield	Adam Enfield	2006	25
15 3/16	9	6 3/16	Edson, AB	Kenneth E. Rudd	Kenneth E. Rudd	2007	25
15 3/16	8 15/16	6 4/16	Cibola Co., NM	Patrick H. Lyons	Patrick H. Lyons	2008	25
15 3/16	8 13/16	6 6/16	Bryant Creek, AB	Gordon P. Steppan	Gordon P. Steppan	2008	25
15 3/16	8 14/16	6 5/16	Ravalli Co., MT	Michael W. Bradt	Michael W. Bradt	2009	25
15 3/16	8 14/16	6 5/16	Idaho Co., ID	Brian T. Sifers	Brian T. Sifers	2009	25
15 2/16	8 14/16	6 4/16	Kittitas Co., WA	Clinton J. Knight	Clinton J. Knight	2005	32
15 2/16	8 12/16	6 6/16	N. Saskatchewan River, AB	David J. Campbell	David J. Campbell	2006	32

Score	Greatest Length of Skull	Greatest Width of Skull	Name	Locality	Name	Date	Rank
15 2/16	8 13/16	6 5/16	Matthew W. Serwa	Whiskey Creek, AB	Matthew W. Serwa	2006	32
15 2/16	9	6 2/16	Joe Hocevar	Cottonwood River, BC	Joe Hocevar	2007	32
15 2/16	8 12/16	6 6/16	Dean L. Kirkeby	Cynthia, AB	Dean L. Kirkeby	2007	32
15 2/16	8 15/16	6 3/16	Tom L. Sword	Quesnel River, BC	Tom L. Sword	2007	32
15 2/16	8 14/16	6 4/16	Morgan T. Daugherty	Las Animas Co., CO	Morgan T. Daugherty	2009	32
15 2/16	8 13/16	6 5/16	Harvey C. Swanson	Flathead Co., MT	Harvey C. Swanson	2009	32
15 1/16	8 15/16	6 2/16	Jesse L. Munch	Mason Co., WA	Jesse L. Munch	2005	40
15 1/16	8 13/16	6 4/16	Carl O. Clapp, Jr.	Mora Co., NM	Carl O. Clapp, Jr.	2006	40
15 1/16	8 11/16	6 6/16	Jolayne M. Collings	Dutch Creek, AB	Jolayne M. Collings	2006	40
15 1/16	9	6 1/16	Grant C. Edinger	Rio Blanco Co., CO	Grant C. Edinger	2006	40
15 1/16	8 14/16	6 3/16	Stephane R. Titley	Medicine Lake, AB	Stephane R. Titley	2006	40
15 1/16	8 15/16	6 2/16	David G. Collins	Mission Creek, BC	David G. Collins	2007	40
15 1/16	8 15/16	6 2/16	David R. Koeppen	Washington Co., ID	David R. Koeppen	2007	40
15 1/16	9	6 1/16	Frank D. Morgan, Jr.	Mora Co., NM	Frank D. Morgan, Jr.	2007	40
15 1/16	8 12/16	6 5/16	Thomas J. Peterson	Butte Co., ID	Thomas J. Peterson	2007	40
15 1/16	8 13/16	6 4/16	Travis R. Hunter	Shoshone Co., ID	Travis R. Hunter	2008	40
15 1/16	8 14/16	6 3/16	Donald C. MacGregor	Lyons Creek, AB	Donald C. MacGregor	2008	40
15 1/16	8 14/16	6 4/16	Richard W. Morrow	Grand Co., CO	Richard W. Morrow	2008	40
15 1/16	8 13/16	6 4/16	Randolph J. Tuhy	Carbon Co., MT	Randolph J. Tuhy	2008	40
15	8 13/16	6 3/16	Jeffrey S. French	Delta Co., CO	Jeffrey S. French	2006	53
15	8 14/16	6 2/16	Bill Brown	Apache Co., AZ	Todd Kokaly	2007	53

COUGAR
FINAL SCORE: 15 8/16
HUNTER: Bryce R. Kniert

COUGAR
FINAL SCORE: 15 2/16
HUNTER: Matthew W. Serwa

COUGAR
FINAL SCORE: 15
HUNTER: Richard B. Sapa, Sr.

COUGAR
FINAL SCORE: 14 15/16
HUNTER: Richard A. Case

COUGAR

Felis concolor hippolestes and related subspecies

Final Score	Greatest Length of Skull Without Lower Jaw	Greatest Width of Skull	Locality	Hunter	Owner	Date Killed	Rank
15	8 13/16	6 3/16	Wheeler Co., OR	Ryan A. Middaugh	Ryan A. Middaugh	2007	53
15	8 12/16	6 4/16	Carbon Co., WY	Dean R. Parker	Dean R. Parker	2007	53
15	8 11/16	6 5/16	Flathead Co., MT	Bill C. Sapa	Bill C. Sapa	2007	53
15	8 11/16	6 5/16	Asotin Co., WA	Gene R. Landrus	Gene R. Landrus	2008	53
15	8 14/16	6 2/16	Brewster Creek, AB	Picked Up	Paul L. Pierunek	2008	53
15	8 14/16	6 2/16	Missoula Co., MT	Billy Joe Weimer	Billy Joe Weimer	2008	53
15	8 13/16	6 3/16	Las Animas Co., CO	Steven L. Calhoun	Steven L. Calhoun	2009	53
15	8 13/16	6 3/16	Sanders Co., MT	Jeffrey D. Jedlicka	Jeffrey D. Jedlicka	2009	53
15	8 11/16	6 5/16	Flathead Co., MT	Richard B. Sapa, Sr.	Richard B. Sapa, Sr.	2009	53
14 15/16	8 13/16	6 2/16	Cowlitz Co., WA	David A. Denny	David A. Denny	2005	64
14 15/16	8 12/16	6 3/16	Lynch Creek, BC	Richard A. Case	Richard A. Case	2007	64
14 15/16	8 9/16	6 6/16	Boise Co., ID	Mark L. Hosick	Mark L. Hosick	2007	64
14 15/16	8 13/16	6 2/16	Utah Co., UT	Robert M. Heiner, Jr.	Robert M. Heiner, Jr.	2008	64
14 15/16	8 14/16	6 1/16	Clearwater Co., ID	John D. Bakale III	John D. Bakale III	2009	64
14 14/16	8 11/16	6 3/16	Chilcotin River, BC	Douglas J. Roffers	Douglas J. Roffers	2006	69
14 14/16	8 10/16	6 4/16	Flathead Co., MT	James L. Griffith	James L. Griffith	2007	69
14 14/16	8 12/16	6 2/16	Washakie Co., WY	Joel P. Hunt	Joel P. Hunt	2008	69
14 14/16	8 15/16	5 15/16	Boundary Co., ID	Thomas Mercier	Thomas Mercier	2008	69
14 13/16	8 12/16	6 1/16	Nakusp, BC	Tony J. Grabowski	Tony J. Grabowski	1983	73
14 13/16	8 10/16	6 3/16	Lincoln Co., WY	Michael Gaglia	Michael Gaglia	2004	73
14 13/16	8 10/16	6 3/16	Bannock Co., ID	Tim D. Horrocks	Tim D. Horrocks	2006	73
14 13/16	8 12/16	6 1/16	Rio Blanco Co., CO	Jimmy W. Smith	Jimmy W. Smith	2006	73
14 13/16	8 10/16	6 3/16	Idaho Co., ID	Dustin J. Decker	Dustin J. Decker	2007	73
14 13/16	8 11/16	6 2/16	Fremont Co., CO	Jeffrey A. Lute	Jeffrey A. Lute	2007	73
14 13/16	8 10/16	6 3/16	Idaho Co., ID	Frank A. Staab	Frank A. Staab	2007	73
14 13/16	8 12/16	6 1/16	Union Co., OR	Scott Mengis	Scott Mengis	2008	73
14 13/16	8 12/16	6 1/16	Missoula Co., MT	Peter Stertz	Peter Stertz	2008	73
14 13/16	8 15/16	5 14/16	Montezuma Co., CO	Paul R. Weyand	Paul R. Weyand	2008	73
14 13/16	8 9/16	6 4/16	Custer Co., SD	Brenden E. Hendrickson	Brenden E. Hendrickson	2009	73
14 12/16	8 11/16	6 1/16	Carbon Co., WY	Jon A. Williams	Jon A. Williams	2006	84
14 12/16	8 12/16	6	Elmore Co., ID	Krystal Schwartz	Krystal Schwartz	2007	84
14 12/16	8 12/16	6	Silver Bow Co., MT	Chad D. Gochanour	Chad D. Gochanour	2009	84

14 11/16	8 9/16	6 2/16	Kane Co., UT	Joshua B. Jones	Joshua B. Jones	2006	87
14 11/16	8 11/16	6	Skamania Co., WA	Clint R. Slocum	Clint R. Slocum	2006	87
14 11/16	8 12/16	5 15/16	Idaho Co., ID	Ryan P. Mader	Ryan P. Mader	2007	87
14 11/16	8 11/16	6	Nordegg, AB	Rodney N. Tetreault	Rodney N. Tetreault	2007	87
14 11/16	8 12/16	5 15/16	Carbon Co., WY	Jack L. Morey, Jr.	Jack L. Morey, Jr.	2008	87
14 11/16	8 12/16	5 15/16	Big Horn Co., WY	Harvey W. Nobles	Harvey W. Nobles	2008	87
14 10/16	8 8/16	6 2/16	Big Lake, BC	Kent Deligans	Kent Deligans	2004	93
14 10/16	8 12/16	5 15/16	Rio Arriba Co., NM	Dustin S. Boyd	Dustin S. Boyd	2006	93
14 10/16	8 8/16	6 2/16	Carbon Co., MT	Cody L. Kerr	Cody L. Kerr	2007	93
14 10/16	8 10/16	6	Washoe Co., NV	Todd D. Hoftiezer	Todd D. Hoftiezer	2008	97
14 9/16	8 10/16	5 15/16	Garfield Co., CO	Roy M. Goodwin	Roy M. Goodwin	1988	97
14 9/16	8 7/16	5 15/16	Nordegg River, AB	Bronko A. Terkovich	Bronko A. Terkovich	2006	97
14 9/16	8 10/16	6 2/16	Eureka Co., NV	Paul R. Downs	Paul R. Downs	2007	97
14 9/16	8 9/16	5 15/16	Lander Co., NV	Frank Iturriaga	Frank Iturriaga	2007	97
14 9/16	8 11/16	6	Valley Co., ID	Kevin S. Primrose	Kevin S. Primrose	2007	97
14 9/16	8 9/16	5 14/16	Washoe Co., NV	Eric D. Stanosheck	Eric D. Stanosheck	2008	97
14 9/16	8 7/16	6	Coos Co., OR	Brian Henderson	Brian Henderson	2009	97
14 9/16	8 10/16	6 2/16	Uintah Co., UT	Chris S. Jahnke	Chris S. Jahnke	2009	97
14 9/16	8 9/16	5 15/16	Huerfano Co., CO	Michael W. Stanley	Michael W. Stanley	2009	97
14 8/16	8 6/16	5 15/16	Cache Co., UT	Peter J. LoPiccolo	Peter J. LoPiccolo	2007	106
14 8/16	8 10/16	6 2/16	Sheridan Co., WY	Edwin T. Meredith	Edwin T. Meredith	2007	106
14 8/16	8 8/16	5 14/16	Washoe Co., NV	Clinton Reed	Clinton Reed	2007	106
14 8/16	8 8/16	6	Idaho Co., ID	Kirk M. MacDonald	Kirk M. MacDonald	2008	106
14 8/16	5 14/16	5 14/16	Colfax Co., NM	Charles A. Ferenchick	Charles A. Ferenchick	2009	106
14 8/16	8 9/16	5 15/16	Gunnison Co., CO	Brian J. Meilinger	Brian J. Meilinger	2009	106

PACIFIC WALRUS

Odobenus rosmarus divergens

Minimum Score 100

World's Record 147 4/8

The geographical boundary for Pacific walrus is: That portion of the Bering Sea east of the International Dateline; south along coastal Alaska, including the Pribilof Islands and Bristol Bay; extending eastward into Canada to the southwest coasts of Banks and Victoria Islands and the mouth of Bathurst Inlet in Nunavut Province (formerly the northwest portion of Northwest Territories).

Final Score	Gross Score	Entire Length of Loose Tusk R.	L.	Circumference of Base R.	L.	Circumference at the Third Quarter R.	L.	Locality	Hunter	Owner	Date Killed	Rank
135	135 7/8	34 2/8	34 5/8	9 4/8	9 4/8	6 3/8	6 2/8	Platinum Creek, AK	Picked Up	Richard Van Blaricom	1963	1
134 2/8	135 5/8	35 2/8	34 2/8	8 5/8	8 7/8	6 7/8	6 7/8	Port Heiden, AK	Picked Up	Daniel G. Montgomery	2005	2
122 6/8	128 4/8	29 5/8	34 4/8	8 3/8	8 1/8	6 7/8	6 4/8	Port Heiden, AK	Picked Up	Daniel G. Montgomery	2001	3
122 4/8	123 3/8	31 7/8	32 1/8	8 4/8	8 2/8	5 5/8	5 7/8	Cinder River, AK	Picked Up	Todd M. Walton	2005	4
121	126 6/8	34 6/8	29 6/8	8 2/8	8 1/8	6 1/8	5 7/8	Port Heiden, AK	Picked Up	Gordon Blair	2006	5
116 6/8	117 3/8	29 4/8	29 4/8	7 4/8	7 3/8	6	5 6/8	Port Moller Bay, AK	Picked Up	Steve Purviance	1995	6
111 2/8	114 6/8	25 1/8	27 7/8	8	7 6/8	6 5/8	6 3/8	Port Heiden, AK	Picked Up	Louis Finch	2005	7
111	113	28 4/8	27 6/8	6 4/8	6 6/8	6 5/8	6	Port Heiden, AK	Picked Up	Parker Hodges	2005	8
106 6/8	110	29 6/8	27 5/8	7 2/8	7 2/8	5 1/8	4 4/8	Port Heiden, AK	Picked Up	Henry Flatow	2005	9
136 *	137	36 7/8	36 2/8	9 2/8	9	5 7/8	6	Bering Sea, AK	Native American	George E. Cornell	PR 1965	

* Final score subject to revision by additional verifying measurements.

AMERICAN ELK - TYPICAL ANTLERS

Cervus elaphus nelsoni and certain related subspecies

Minimum Score 360   World's Record 442 5/8

Final Score	Gross Score	Length of Main Beam R.	L.	Inside Spread	Circumference at Smallest Place Between First & Second Points R.	L.	Number of Points R.	L.	Locality	Hunter	Owner	Date Killed	Rank
413 2/8	435 2/8	54 5/8	54 4/8	49	9 6/8	9 4/8	8	6	Coconino Co., AZ	William R. Dandy	Eric Olson	2008	1
404 1/8	411 5/8	57 4/8	59 5/8	41 3/8	7 7/8	8 7/8	6	6	Graham Co., AZ	Duane Chapman	Duane Chapman	2007	2
402 1/8	416 6/8	54 4/8	54 4/8	46 5/8	9 5/8	9 4/8	7	7	Wyoming	Unknown	Theresa Speake	PR 1910	3
400 4/8	417 7/8	62 4/8	60 2/8	48 6/8	8 5/8	8 6/8	7	7	San Miguel Co., CO	Dillon Z. Sanders	Dillon Z. Sanders	2007	4
399 4/8	406	54 6/8	56 5/8	43 4/8	8 6/8	9 2/8	6	6	Gila Co., AZ	Dan J. Agnew	Dan J. Agnew	2008	5
397 6/8	416 5/8	53 1/8	55	43 3/8	9 2/8	9 2/8	7	7	Lincoln Co., NV	Brandon L. Fordin	Brandon L. Fordin	2007	6
397 4/8	406 5/8	60 7/8	62 1/8	36 6/8	9 2/8	9 3/8	6	6	San Juan Co., UT	Kelly L. Beckstead	Kelly L. Beckstead	2007	7
394 7/8	409 2/8	56 1/8	53 7/8	42 7/8	8 4/8	8 3/8	7	7	Graham Co., AZ	John A. Cardwell	John A. Cardwell	2007	8
394 1/8	402 2/8	54 1/8	51 4/8	41 3/8	10 1/8	9 3/8	7	7	Navajo Co., AZ	Gregory D. Seay	Gregory D. Seay	2008	9
392 5/8	408 4/8	58	56 2/8	46 5/8	10 3/8	10 7/8	6	6	Garfield Co., UT	Richard L. Crawford, Jr.	Richard L. Crawford, Jr.	2009	10
391 6/8	401 7/8	56 1/8	55 3/8	36 2/8	9 4/8	9	7	7	Big Horn Co., MT	Salvatore Blancato	Salvatore Blancato	2008	11
390 1/8	405 3/8	51 4/8	48 7/8	39 7/8	8 5/8	8 7/8	7	6	Watrous, SK	Dwayne G. Miller	Dwayne G. Miller	2009	12
389 5/8	397 6/8	56	55 4/8	39 3/8	9	9 3/8	7	7	Coconino Co., AZ	Herman C. Meyer	Herman C. Meyer	2005	13
389 3/8	397 1/8	55 3/8	53 3/8	43 7/8	9 1/8	9	6	6	Billings Co., ND	Terry J. Doll	Terry J. Doll	2007	14
389 1/8	398 4/8	58	56 3/8	44 1/8	11 1/8	10 5/8	6	6	Beaver Co., UT	Travis J. Willden	Travis J. Willden	2006	15
388 6/8	396 3/8	52 4/8	51	47 6/8	9	9	6	6	Elko Co., NV	Brian D. Carone	Brian D. Carone	2007	16
388 6/8	393 5/8	51 1/8	52 1/8	37 4/8	8 7/8	8 6/8	7	7	Blaine Co., MT	Dave J. Bymaster	Dave J. Bymaster	2008	16
388 4/8	396 1/8	56 4/8	59 6/8	44 4/8	8 7/8	8 2/8	6	6	Park Co., MT	Nicholas M. Solari	Nicholas M. Solari	2006	18
388	394 7/8	58 6/8	58 3/8	41 2/8	8 5/8	8 5/8	6	6	Beaver Co., UT	Kevin T. Klumper	Kevin T. Klumper	2008	19
387	394 5/8	56	56	40	8 7/8	8 1/8	6	6	Edgerton, AB	Ray H. Cote	Ray H. Cote	2008	20
386	409 4/8	53 4/8	57	40 4/8	12 1/8	12 3/8	8	7	San Juan Co., UT	Tim C. Simonsen	Tim C. Simonsen	2006	21
386	403 3/8	57 7/8	56 6/8	38	8 5/8	8 3/8	7	6	Johnson Co., WY	Charlie C. Carter	Charlie C. Carter	2008	21
385 3/8	390 7/8	56 2/8	56	45 3/8	9	8 6/8	6	6	Garfield Co., UT	Morgan R. Einerson	Morgan R. Einerson	2007	23
385 2/8	407 5/8	51 4/8	54 3/8	39 6/8	10 2/8	10 2/8	7	7	Rosebud Co., MT	Tim W. Hite	Tim W. Hite	2007	24
385 2/8	390	58 3/8	58 4/8	50 2/8	9	8 6/8	6	6	Wayne Co., UT	Cody K. Gore	Cody K. Gore	2008	24
385 2/8	399 6/8	59 7/8	59 3/8	43 6/8	9 2/8	8 4/8	7	8	Powder River Co., MT	R. Chuck Shinabarger	R. Chuck Shinabarger	2009	24
384 1/8	396 7/8	55 7/8	52 3/8	44 5/8	10 3/8	10 7/8	6	6	Apache Co., AZ	R. Douglas Isbell	R. Douglas Isbell	2009	27
383 7/8	395 1/8	55	56 7/8	39 7/8	11 1/8	11 5/8	6	6	Cibola Co., NM	Arlene M. Holden	Arlene M. Holden	2006	28
383 6/8	395 2/8	54 6/8	56 2/8	46 2/8	10 1/8	9 7/8	6	6	Garfield Co., UT	Battista A. Locatelli	Battista A. Locatelli	2006	29
383 1/8	391 3/8	60 1/8	61 6/8	41 3/8	8 6/8	8 4/8	6	6	Navajo Co., AZ	Shea B. Morenz	Shea B. Morenz	2007	30
382 1/8	385 1/8	49 7/8	49 5/8	42 1/8	7 6/8	7 6/8	6	6	Powder River Co., MT	Oren L. Rosin	Oren L. Rosin	2007	31
381 6/8	400 2/8	59 2/8	58 2/8	46	7 5/8	7 6/8	7	6	Garfield Co., UT	Craig Kohler	Craig Kohler	2006	32

AMERICAN ELK - TYPICAL ANTLERS

Cervus elaphus nelsoni and certain related subspecies

Final Score	Gross Score	Length of Main Beam R.	L.	Inside Spread	Circumference at Smallest Place Between First & Second Points R.	L.	Number of Points R.	L.	Locality	Hunter	Owner	Date Killed	Rank
381 6/8	387 1/8	55 1/8	54 6/8	41 4/8	9 5/8	10 1/8	6	6	Lewis & Clark Co., MT	Victoria F. Forkin	Victoria F. Forkin	2007	32
381 6/8	394	56 6/8	56 3/8	38 6/8	10 2/8	9 4/8	6	6	Garfield Co., UT	Ron Sawyer	Ron Sawyer	2007	32
381 6/8	400 7/8	58 1/8	58 3/8	52 3/8	9 4/8	9 5/8	6	7	Wayne Co., UT	Duane A. Cook	Duane A.Cook	2008	32
381 5/8	387	52 1/8	52	38 5/8	9 1/8	9 2/8	6	6	Stillwater Co., MT	James A. Bailey, Sr.	James A. Bailey, Sr.	2006	36
381 3/8	395 7/8	59 4/8	58 3/8	43 1/8	10	9 6/8	6	7	San Juan Co., UT	James L. Kelly III	James L. Kelly III	2006	37
381 2/8	395 3/8	52 3/8	54	49	9 1/8	8 6/8	6	6	Custer Co., MT	Jammin D. Krebs	Jammin D. Krebs	2009	38
379 7/8	390 5/8	54	51 4/8	42 7/8	9 4/8	9 6/8	6	6	Sevier Co., UT	Gerald S. Laurino	Gerald S. Laurino	2006	39
379 5/8	390 7/8	63 1/8	64 4/8	40 1/8	7 7/8	8	6	7	Coconino Co., AZ	Randy W. Cosner	Randy W. Cosner	2009	40
379 4/8	390 5/8	58 4/8	59 4/8	43	8	8 4/8	6	6	Porcupine Hills, AB	Viggo Norgard	Darcy M. Alm	1946	41
379 2/8	393 3/8	50 6/8	48 2/8	43 4/8	10 5/8	10 4/8	6	6	Millard Co., UT	Craig L. Broadbent	Craig L. Broadbent	2006	42
379 2/8	388 3/8	56 2/8	57 5/8	42	9	9 4/8	6	7	San Juan Co., UT	Eli R. Ortiz	Eli R. Ortiz	2009	42
378 7/8	395 2/8	57 1/8	57 5/8	41 7/8	9 5/8	9	6	8	Apache Co., AZ	Bobby L. Beeman	Bobby L. Beeman	2007	44
378 7/8	386 7/8	57 4/8	54 1/8	45 1/8	6	5 7/8	6	6	Wildhay River, AB	Picked Up	Craig A. MacMillan	2007	44
378 4/8	385 1/8	52 6/8	52 6/8	35 4/8	10 2/8	10 3/8	7	7	Yavapai Co., AZ	Brian K. Crawford	Brian K. Crawford	2006	46
378 3/8	398 6/8	46 7/8	50 2/8	39 5/8	10 1/8	10 5/8	7	6	Park Co., WY	Jerry D. Blakeman	Jerry D. Blakeman	2006	47
377 7/8	385 5/8	56 6/8	55 6/8	38 1/8	8 3/8	8 1/8	6	6	Apache Co., AZ	Donnie B. Seay	Donnie B. Seay	2005	48
377 4/8	392 2/8	56 6/8	56 1/8	42 4/8	8 5/8	9 3/8	7	7	Big Horn Co., MT	Craig A. Overman	Craig A. Overman	2009	49
376 7/8	382 6/8	56 4/8	56 5/8	48 3/8	9 2/8	9 2/8	6	6	Rich Co., UT	Joe W. Hadley	Joe W. Hadley	2007	50
376 6/8	386 5/8	55 7/8	56	45 4/8	10 4/8	10 1/8	6	6	Beaverhead Co., MT	Johnny D. Christensen	Johnny D. Christensen	1968	51
376 6/8	393 7/8	55 4/8	56	44	8 4/8	8 7/8	6	6	Gila Co., AZ	James E. Reinert	James E. Reinert	2008	51
376 5/8	386 5/8	49 7/8	51 6/8	40 5/8	9 4/8	8 6/8	6	6	Catron Co., NM	Debra A. Jameson	Debra A. Jameson	2007	53
376 4/8	386 1/8	59 2/8	58 4/8	41 2/8	8 2/8	8 5/8	7	7	Golden Valley Co., ND	Barry L. Tescher	Barry L. Tescher	2004	54
376 3/8	385	53 1/8	53 6/8	45 5/8	8 6/8	9 1/8	7	7	Blaine Co., MT	Donald L. Boyce	Donald L. Boyce	2007	55
376 3/8	380 4/8	52	52 6/8	49 3/8	8	8 2/8	6	6	Moffat Co., CO	David G. Hamling	David G. Hamling	2009	55
376 2/8	397 2/8	56 7/8	57 5/8	41 2/8	12	10	7	7	Apache Co., AZ	Dale Hislop	Dale Hislop	2007	57
375 5/8	392 3/8	54 5/8	55 2/8	41 3/8	7 4/8	7 5/8	6	6	Gila Co., AZ	James P. Mellody	James P. Mellody	2006	58
375 4/8	381 5/8	53 7/8	52 4/8	43 6/8	10 4/8	9 7/8	6	6	Fergus Co., MT	Casey R. Robinson	Casey R. Robinson	2007	59
375 3/8	384 3/8	51 7/8	50 2/8	51 3/8	8 2/8	7 4/8	6	6	Sevier Co., UT	Brandon T. Wicks	Brandon T. Wicks	2008	60
375 3/8	391 3/8	52 3/8	52 2/8	39 7/8	8 5/8	8 2/8	7	6	Sanpete Co., UT	Joel J. Dingeldein	Joel J. Dingeldein	2009	60
375 1/8	387 2/8	55	54 2/8	42 5/8	9 4/8	9 5/8	6	6	White Pine Co., NV	Robert C. Durance	Robert C. Durance	2006	62
375 1/8	386 4/8	48 4/8	47 4/8	34 5/8	10 3/8	10 3/8	6	6	Bear Lake Co., ID	Friend C. Estus	Friend C. Estus	2007	62
375	380 2/8	53 4/8	53 2/8	41 6/8	9 1/8	8 4/8	6	6	White Pine Co., NV	Jeff R. Rogers	Jeff R. Rogers	2006	64
375	394 4/8	56 2/8	51 5/8	47 6/8	7 5/8	7 7/8	6	6	Golden Valley Co., MT	Brendan V. Burns	Brendan V. Burns	2008	64

Score	Length of Main Beam R	Length of Main Beam L	Inside Spread	Circ. R	Points R	Circ. L	Points L	Locality	Hunter	Owner	Date	Rank
374 6/8	59	56	39	9 2/8	7	9 2/8	7	Catron Co., NM	Mitchell R. Ballard	Mitchell R. Ballard	2007	66
374 4/8	55 3/8	54 6/8	45 4/8	8 3/8	7	8 3/8	7	Park Co., MT	Allen S. Miller	Allen S. Miller	2005	67
374 4/8	53	52 3/8	37 2/8	9 6/8	7	9 6/8	7	Johnson Co., WY	Larry W. Carr	Larry W. Carr	2007	67
372 2/8	55 6/8	56 3/8	41	9 5/8	7	9 1/8	7	Cascade Co., MT	Philip Y. Allegretti	Philip Y. Allegretti	2008	69
372 2/8	54 2/8	54 1/8	38 2/8	9 1/8	7	9	6	San Juan Co., UT	L. Garland Nelson, Jr.	L. Garland Nelson, Jr.	2008	69
372 1/8	54 7/8	55 1/8	41 5/8	8 6/8	6	9	7	Gila Co., AZ	Courtney M. Murry	Courtney M. Murry	2002	71
371 7/8	50 4/8	50 5/8	40 6/8	9 4/8	7	9 1/8	8	Park Co., WY	Frank R. Gallo	Frank R. Gallo	2007	72
371 2/8	52 7/8	52 2/8	42 4/8	7 6/8	8	7 5/8	6	White Pine Co., NV	Blake A. Bender	Blake A. Bender	2009	73
371 1/8	55 1/8	54 6/8	50 3/8	7 6/8	6	7 3/8	6	Elko Co., NV	Zachary J. Hastie	Zachary J. Hastie	2007	74
371	53 6/8	54 1/8	36 4/8	9	6	8 4/8	6	Sevier Co., UT	Chad T. Drake	Chad T. Drake	2007	75
371	49 5/8	52 2/8	39 2/8	10 5/8	6	10 5/8	7	Bell Co., KY	Greg L. Neff	Greg L. Neff	2007	75
371	53 1/8	53 3/8	40	8 3/8	7	8 3/8	7	Coconino Co., AZ	William L. Bruggeman III	Bruggeman III	2008	75
371	47 6/8	46 7/8	48 6/8	10 2/8	6	10 2/8	6	Cibola Co., NM	Frederick W. Bush	Frederick W. Bush	2009	75
370 7/8	54 2/8	52 5/8	46 1/8	8 2/8	6	7 6/8	6	Sanders Co., MT	James J. McLinden	John Harris	1966	79
370 7/8	52	52 5/8	41 5/8	9 1/8	6	8 7/8	6	Elko Co., NV	Daniel L. Evans	Daniel L. Evans	2008	79
370 3/8	53 1/8	52 2/8	39 5/8	9	7	8 1/8	7	Juab Co., UT	Michael J. Sperry	Michael J. Sperry	2006	81
370	54 3/8	48 3/8	39 4/8	8 7/8	6	8 5/8	6	Coconino Co., AZ	Robert E. Ronning	Robert E. Ronning	2006	82
369 4/8	49 6/8	48 1/8	40 4/8	9 7/8	6	9 3/8	6	Beaver Co., UT	Mark L. Wall	Mark L. Wall	2008	83
369 2/8	59 3/8	57 2/8	42 2/8	8	6	7 4/8	6	Coconino Co., AZ	George E. Flournoy, Jr.	George E. Flournoy, Jr.	1986	84
368 4/8	57 2/8	57 1/8	42 6/8	9	6	8 7/8	6	White Pine Co., NV	Kevin D. Peterson	Kevin D. Peterson	2008	85

TYPICAL AMERICAN ELK
FINAL SCORE: 375 5/8
HUNTER: James P. Mellody

TYPICAL AMERICAN ELK
FINAL SCORE: 397 6/8
HUNTER: Brandon L. Fordin

TYPICAL AMERICAN ELK
FINAL SCORE: 368 4/8
HUNTER: Kevin D. Peterson

AMERICAN ELK - TYPICAL ANTLERS

Cervus elaphus nelsoni and certain related subspecies

Final Score	Gross Score	Length of Main Beam R.	L.	Inside Spread	Circumference at Smallest Place Between First & Second Points R.	L.	Number of Points R.	L.	Locality	Hunter	Owner	Date Killed	Rank
368 3/8	374 3/8	54 4/8	53 4/8	51 7/8	8	7 7/8	7	7	Park Co., WY	Jack L. Morey, Jr.	Jack L. Morey, Jr.	2008	86
368 1/8	385 3/8	54 4/8	53 4/8	39 7/8	10	10 2/8	8	6	Sheridan Co., NE	Rose Mary Hollibaugh	Rose Mary Hollibaugh	2006	87
368 1/8	388 1/8	54 1/8	60 5/8	47 5/8	9 5/8	10	7	7	San Juan Co., UT	Steven L. Kiesel	Steven L. Kiesel	2008	87
367 7/8	379 7/8	53 5/8	52 5/8	41 1/8	9 4/8	8 4/8	6	6	Montezuma Co., CO	Calyn L. Allen	Calyn L. Allen	2007	89
367 4/8	375 7/8	57	55 5/8	41 4/8	8 7/8	8 7/8	7	7	Boise Co., ID	Jonathan D. Stosich	Jonathan D. Stosich	2007	90
367 4/8	379 4/8	50 5/8	50 5/8	42 2/8	7 3/8	7 2/8	7	7	Fremont Co., WY	Miles B. Shoun	Miles B. Shoun	2008	90
367 4/8	374 4/8	54 1/8	54 2/8	41	7 4/8	8	7	7	Garfield Co., UT	Slade Olson	Slade Olson	2009	90
367 2/8	379	55 5/8	57	35 6/8	9	8 1/8	6	6	Coconino Co., AZ	John G. Padilla	John G. Padilla	2008	93
367 1/8	379 5/8	50 7/8	49 6/8	47 1/8	9	8 3/8	7	6	Park Co., MT	Tom R. Desaveur	Tom R. Desaveur	2007	94
367 1/8	376 6/8	60 1/8	58 1/8	39 1/8	10 5/8	9 5/8	6	6	Grand Co., CO	William K. Denkins	William K. Denkins	2008	94
366 4/8	373 5/8	53 1/8	53 5/8	41 6/8	8 5/8	8 5/8	6	6	Sanpete Co., UT	Shawn R. Gregory	Shawn R. Gregory	2006	96
366 2/8	373 5/8	52 5/8	53	41	9 1/8	8 5/8	6	6	Duchesne Co., UT	Jackie A. LaRose	Jackie A. LaRose	2007	97
365 6/8	383 2/8	51 7/8	48 5/8	46 6/8	8 4/8	9	7	7	San Juan Co., UT	Steven L. Kiesel	Steven L. Kiesel	2006	98
365 6/8	372 2/8	52 5/8	52 7/8	38 6/8	9 2/8	8 6/8	6	6	Nye Co., NV	Nicholas G. Perchetti	Nicholas G. Perchetti	2008	98
365 4/8	373 7/8	55 1/8	54 3/8	42	8 6/8	8 4/8	7	6	White Pine Co., NV	Micheal S. Spillman	Micheal S. Spillman	2007	100
365 4/8	379 6/8	54 7/8	54 7/8	41 4/8	9 4/8	8 7/8	6	7	Columbia Co., WA	Scott Baysinger	Scott Baysinger	2006	100
365 4/8	383 1/8	52	49 4/8	51 2/8	10	10 2/8	6	6	Taos Co., NM	Donald J. Doyon	Donald J. Doyon	2009	100
365 2/8	377 3/8	58	57 4/8	45	8 5/8	8 7/8	6	6	Millard Co., UT	Matt E. Vaughn	Matt E. Vaughn	2006	103
365 1/8	371 2/8	56 6/8	56 3/8	50 5/8	9	8 7/8	6	6	Jenner, AB	Richard K. Thornton	Richard K. Thornton	2008	104
365	378 6/8	50 7/8	52 5/8	35 7/8	7 3/8	7 3/8	7	7	Lawrence Co., SD	Russ R. Roberts	Russ R. Roberts	2009	105
364 4/8	375 3/8	59 7/8	60 1/8	40 6/8	9 5/8	10 4/8	7	6	Millard Co., UT	Rocky P. Pack	Rocky P. Pack	2006	106
364 2/8	376 1/8	49 2/8	51 4/8	34 4/8	9 6/8	9 3/8	6	6	Lincoln Co., NV	Annette T. Mankins	Annette T. Mankins	2007	107
364 2/8	373 4/8	56 6/8	56 2/8	49	8	8 1/8	7	6	Rosebud Co., MT	Donald G. Shurr	Donald G. Shurr	2007	107
363 2/8	370 5/8	51 4/8	50 5/8	44 2/8	10 1/8	10 1/8	6	6	Teton Co., MT	Scott Ferguson	Scott Ferguson	1984	109
363 1/8	381 3/8	56 3/8	58 2/8	42 5/8	8 6/8	9 2/8	6	7	Gallatin Co., MT	Kevin T. Klumper	Kevin T. Klumper	2008	110
362 6/8	384 5/8	53 2/8	53 4/8	38	8 5/8	8	6	6	Ribstone Creek, AB	Bradley M. Rieland	Bradley M. Rieland	2005	111
362 6/8	376	56 1/8	57 6/8	38 4/8	10	10 2/8	6	6	Lincoln Co., NV	Steven L. Kiesel	Steven L. Kiesel	2007	111
362 6/8	374 4/8	51 1/8	51 5/8	38 4/8	8 6/8	8 2/8	8	7	Montmorency Co., MI	Arlis E. Fleshman, Jr.	Arlis E. Fleshman, Jr.	2009	111
362 4/8	368 5/8	62 1/8	63 3/8	48 4/8	8 4/8	9 2/8	6	6	Colorado	Unknown	Double H Ranch	PR 1899	114
362 2/8	369 3/8	53 7/8	54 5/8	43 4/8	10 1/8	10 1/8	6	6	Gila Co., AZ	Gary E. Biamonte	Gary E. Biamonte	2008	115
362 1/8	376 4/8	54 7/8	54	42 3/8	8 6/8	9	6	6	Beaver Co., UT	Robert C. Coulter	Robert C. Coulter	2006	116
362 1/8	377 5/8	56 4/8	53 4/8	42 1/8	10 1/8	10 3/8	7	6	Nye Co., NV	John L. Salois	John L. Salois	2007	116
362	400 3/8	58 4/8	56 2/8	43 1/8	10 3/8	9	8	7	Billings Co., ND	Robert W. Kennedy	Robert W. Kennedy	2007	118

Score									Locality	Owner	Hunter	Year	Rank
361 7/8	372	51 4/8	54 5/8	58	8 4/8	8 3/8	6	6	Sheridan Co., NE	Charles R. Rupp	Charles R. Rupp	2006	119
361 7/8	367 7/8	54 5/8	55 5/8	41 3/8	9	9 2/8	6	6	San Juan Co., UT	Bret K. Lowe	Bret K. Lowe	2008	119
361 7/8	382 2/8	52 2/8	48 7/8	46 7/8	7 4/8	7 6/8	7	7	Cheboygan Co., MI	Courtney Williams	Courtney Williams	2008	119
361 5/8	373 4/8	53 6/8	52 6/8	42 7/8	9 5/8	10	6	6	Bannock Co., ID	Lisa A. Guthrie	Lisa A. Guthrie	2006	122
361 4/8	376 5/8	51 5/8	56 4/8	46	8	8 4/8	7	7	Knott Co., KY	Franklin D. Scott	Franklin D. Scott	2006	123
361 3/8	371 5/8	56 4/8	58 1/8	43 1/8	10	10	6	6	Millard Co., UT	J. Tom Paluso	J. Tom Paluso	2007	124
361 3/8	366 7/8	55 5/8	55 3/8	42 7/8	8 7/8	9 3/8	6	6	Sheridan Co., WY	Warren D. Kennedy	Warren D. Kennedy	2008	124
361 2/8	371 4/8	58 5/8	55 2/8	39	8 3/8	8 1/8	6	6	Converse Co., WY	Stephen M. Ruttkamp	Stephen M. Ruttkamp	2008	126
360 6/8	380 6/8	46 5/8	50 4/8	42 2/8	7 7/8	8 4/8	7	7	Navajo Co., AZ	Jerry P. Weiers	Jerry P. Weiers	2007	127
360 3/8	376 6/8	56 4/8	59 1/8	47 3/8	8	8 4/8	6	6	Coconino Co., AZ	Mike L. Ronning	Mike L. Ronning	2005	128
360 3/8	369 7/8	52	52 5/8	47 7/8	9	9 3/8	6	6	Natrona Co., WY	Brad A. Stockman	Brad A. Stockman	2008	128
360 2/8	363 2/8	54 1/8	53 4/8	42 2/8	8 3/8	8 3/8	6	6	San Miguel Co., CO	Mark A. Soderlind	Mark A. Soderlind	2007	130
360 2/8	376	52 6/8	52 1/8	44 6/8	8 3/8	8 1/8	6	6	Wasatch Co., UT	Kimberly B. Arbogast	Kimberly B. Arbogast	2009	130
360 1/8	372 1/8	50 5/8	49 4/8	40 3/8	9 6/8	9 6/8	7	7	Lincoln Co., NV	Jimmy R. Younger	Jimmy R. Younger	2006	132
428 6/8*	434 7/8	55 6/8	58 1/8	34 4/8	9 6/8	10 3/8	6	6	Grand Co., UT	Ron F. Skoronski	Ron F. Skoronski	2006	
412 1/8*	422	60 2/8	60 3/8	56 5/8	8 6/8	8 3/8	7	7	Coconino Co., AZ	Kenneth S. Patterson	Kenneth S. Patterson	2005	
404 6/8*	413 4/8	51 7/8	53 3/8	42 6/8	9 2/8	9 4/8	7	7	Millard Co., UT	Stephen C. Broadbent	Stephen C. Broadbent	2006	

Final score subject to revision by additional verifying measurements.

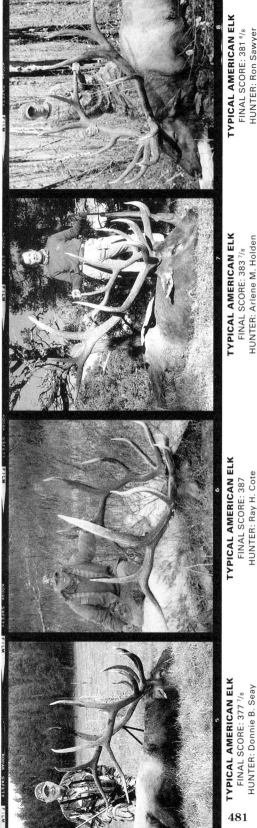

TYPICAL AMERICAN ELK
FINAL SCORE: 377 7/8
HUNTER: Donnie B. Seay

TYPICAL AMERICAN ELK
FINAL SCORE: 387
HUNTER: Ray H. Cote

TYPICAL AMERICAN ELK
FINAL SCORE: 383 7/8
HUNTER: Arlene M. Holden

TYPICAL AMERICAN ELK
FINAL SCORE: 381 6/8
HUNTER: Ron Sawyer

AMERICAN ELK - NON-TYPICAL ANTLERS

Cervus elaphus nelsoni and certain related subspecies

Minimum Score 385

New World's Record 478 5/8

Final Score	Gross Score	Length of Main Beam R.	Length of Main Beam L.	Inside Spread	Circumference at Smallest Place Between First & Second Points R.	Circumference at Smallest Place Between First & Second Points L.	Number of Points R.	Number of Points L.	Locality	Hunter	Owner	Date Killed	Rank
478 5/8	499 3/8	46 4/8	46 6/8	36 5/8	9 7/8	9 2/8	14	9	Piute Co., UT	Denny Austad	Denny Austad	2008	1
441 6/8	460 3/8	55	50 3/8	37	8 2/8	7 5/8	11	10	Clinton Co., PA	John A. Shirk	John A. Shirk	2006	2
436 4/8	446 6/8	49 4/8	50 6/8	42 7/8	8 4/8	8 1/8	10	9	Columbia Co., WA	Dan J. Agnew	Dan J. Agnew	2008	3
423 3/8	438	55 3/8	54 5/8	43 4/8	7 6/8	8 4/8	10	8	Gila Co., AZ	James R. Boldt	James R. Boldt	2007	4
423	434 1/8	57 5/8	58 6/8	49 3/8	9 7/8	10 1/8	7	7	Wayne Co., UT	Darrell Snedeger	Darrell Snedeger	2007	5
416 6/8	438	54 4/8	54 3/8	55	9 4/8	9	10	7	Beaver Co., UT	Mitch R. Carter	Mitch R. Carter	2008	6
413 6/8	421 7/8	59 2/8	58 2/8	45 7/8	10 2/8	9 2/8	8	7	Sheridan Co., WY	Gary D. Schock	Gary D. Schock	2008	7
411 1/8	416 1/8	50 3/8	49 5/8	36 4/8	9 5/8	10 2/8	6	7	Douglas Co., CO	James L. Ziemer	James L. Ziemer	2009	8
410 7/8	429 3/8	54 1/8	55 2/8	37 4/8	11	11 2/8	8	7	Lincoln Co., NV	Sam S. Jaksick, Jr.	Sam S. Jaksick, Jr.	2006	9
409 7/8	424 7/8	50 3/8	51 6/8	49 1/8	11 1/8	12 5/8	8	10	Garden Co., NE	Dana L. Foster	Dana L. Foster	2008	10
409 6/8	421 5/8	56 5/8	55 7/8	36 4/8	9 4/8	10 6/8	8	7	Park Co., WY	Chris C. Renner	Chris C. Renner	2009	11
408 3/8	417 7/8	56	56 2/8	36	11 4/8	11 3/8	8	7	Garfield Co., UT	Joshua S. Pollock	Joshua S. Pollock	2007	12
407 7/8	418 3/8	54 2/8	54 2/8	40 4/8	10 6/8	11 1/8	6	8	Custer Co., MT	Timothy M. Donnelly	Timothy M. Donnelly	2008	13
404 3/8	416 1/8	51 4/8	51 2/8	51 2/8	7 5/8	7 4/8	8	7	Beaver Co., UT	Mike J. Coelho	Mike J. Coelho	2006	14
403 7/8	415	59 4/8	58 1/8	33 6/8	9 2/8	9 3/8	7	7	Catron Co., NM	Charles J. Sillivent	Charles J. Sillivent	2006	15
403 6/8	414 4/8	56 4/8	57 4/8	54 4/8	8 6/8	8 6/8	7	7	Mora Co., NM	Zane T. Streater	Zane T. Streater	2008	16
402 6/8	409 4/8	51 2/8	52 2/8	42 3/8	7 7/8	7 5/8	7	7	Coconino Co., AZ	Dion M. Laney	Dion M. Laney	2007	17
402 5/8	416 4/8	55	55 4/8	35 6/8	9 3/8	8 5/8	8	6	Catron Co., NM	Adolfo Cordova	Adolfo Cordova	2003	18
401 1/8	426 2/8	51 7/8	48 1/8	47 5/8	10 5/8	10 3/8	7	7	Socorro Co., NM	Tod L. Reichert	Tod L. Reichert	2008	19
400 5/8	410 7/8	57 1/8	57 2/8	47 1/8	8 4/8	9 2/8	7	8	Millard Co., UT	Ron Mika	Ron Mika	2006	20
400 3/8	410 2/8	53 6/8	52 2/8	42	9 4/8	8 7/8	7	9	Saskatchewan River, SK	Jamie Freedman	Jamie Freedman	2008	21
399 3/8	414 1/8	54	53	40 7/8	10 3/8	11 1/8	8	7	Mount Evans, CO	Unknown	DLJM Collection	1948	22
398 4/8	407 1/8	49 3/8	52 4/8	39 2/8	9	9 3/8	9	7	Navajo Co., AZ	Don P. Barry	Don P. Barry	2008	23
398 4/8	419 2/8	58 2/8	53 2/8	33 2/8	8	7 7/8	10	8	Coconino Co., AZ	Robert E. Hallagan	Robert E. Hallagan	2008	24
398	408 2/8	48 2/8	52 2/8	43 1/8	8 5/8	8 3/8	8	7	Cassia Co., ID	K.C. A. Ramsey	K.C. A. Ramsey	2008	25
397 6/8	411 4/8	52	53 1/8	46 2/8	9 5/8	9 3/8	7	8	Flathead Co., MT	Douglas M. James	W.P. & D.M. James	1981	26
397 3/8	411 4/8	54 5/8	54 5/8	36 2/8	9 2/8	9 6/8	6	6	Cache Co., UT	Cory L. Meacham	Cory L. Meacham	2007	27
396 1/8	411 4/8	49 7/8	51	33 6/8	10 4/8	9 6/8	8	8	Nelson, BC	Andrew B. Walker	Andrew B. Walker	2008	28
395 7/8	404 7/8	57 6/8	57 4/8	44 6/8	8	8 4/8	7	7	Cibola Co., NM	David A. Young	David A. Young	2008	29
393 5/8	406 3/8	50 7/8	50 6/8	39 2/8	11 5/8	11 2/8	8	8	Kittitas Co., WA	Donald E. Myhre	Donald E. Myhre	2009	30
393 4/8	407 3/8	49	51	37 7/8	9 6/8	9 5/8	7	9	Beaver Co., UT	Garth K. Carter	Garth K. Carter	2006	31
391 4/8	400 4/8	53 4/8	54	33 2/8	9 5/8	9 7/8	9	7	Apache Co., AZ	Robert L. Hudman	Robert L. Hudman	2009	32
389 7/8	394 6/8	54 2/8	53 6/8	45 3/8	9 5/8	9 6/8	9	6	Weber Co., UT	Doug Hamblin	Doug Hamblin	2006	33

389 7/8	404 7/8	52 3/8	50 1/8	32 4/8	8 6/8	8 6/8	7	Mark A. Stewart	McKenzie Co., ND	9	Mark A. Stewart	2007	33
389 1/8	411 5/8	52 2/8	47 5/8	34 7/8	9 4/8	9 2/8	7	Picked Up	Las Animas Co., CO	10	Steve Montoya	2005	35
388 1/8	393 5/8	51 5/8	50 1/8	38	8 5/8	8 6/8	6	Russell G. Mingus	Pierce Co., WA	8	Marsha C. Mangan	1975	36
387 7/8	398 3/8	56 6/8	57 3/8	41 6/8	9 2/8	9	7	George J. Kueber	Windy Lake, AB	7	George J. Kueber	2007	37
387 4/8	402 7/8	52 5/8	50	43	8 7/8	8 7/8	7	A. Neal Barton	Garfield Co., UT	6	A. Neal Barton	2006	38
387 3/8	394 6/8	54 3/8	56 5/8	43 1/8	10 1/8	10 1/8	7	Charles F. Seibold	Garfield Co., UT	6	Charles F. Seibold	2006	39
387	402 6/8	51 5/8	52	37 1/8	10 2/8	10 1/8	7	Tona L. Lytle	White Pine Co., NV	7	Tona L. Lytle	2006	40
386 6/8	400	52 6/8	50 7/8	38 4/8	10 1/8	9 2/8	7	Garth K. Carter	White Pine Co., NV	7	Garth K. Carter	2008	41
386 6/8	406	51 7/8	54 4/8	45 1/8	8	7 4/8	6	Jesus M. Melendez	White Pine Co., NV	9	Jesus M. Melendez	2009	41
386 5/8	408	56 2/8	55 2/8	38 4/8	9 2/8	9 6/8	8	James P. Mellody III	Gila Co., AZ	8	James P. Mellody III	2008	43
386 4/8	399 1/8	48 6/8	48 5/8	46 6/8	9 2/8	9 2/8	7	DeWayne Hollibaugh	Dawes Co., NE	6	DeWayne Hollibaugh	2005	44
386 4/8	400 1/8	49 5/8	49 1/8	40 6/8	9 2/8	9 2/8	8	Mitchell V. Olsen	Uintah Co., UT	7	Mitchell V. Olsen	2007	44
385 7/8	395 4/8	52 5/8	51	39 6/8	9 1/8	10 1/8	6	Darcy Leffler	Red Deer River, SK	7	Darcy Leffler	2006	46
385 4/8	396 3/8	48 4/8	50	36 4/8	9 5/8	9 4/8	9	Robert O. Crow	Coconino Co., AZ	6	Robert O. Crow	2008	47
385 3/8	391 4/8	53 3/8	52 7/8	47 7/8	9 1/8	8 4/8	7	Verne C. Atwood	White Pine Co., NV	9	Verne C. Atwood	2006	48
460 1/8*	467 7/8	48 6/8	50 4/8	33 5/8	10 2/8	10	13	Frank Cameron	Unknown	13	David W. Dewees	1936	
441 3/8*	464 5/8	56 2/8	53 1/8	42	9 3/8	10 3/8	9	William H. Junell	Navajo Co., AZ	9	William H. Junell	2008	

Final score subject to revision by additional verifying measurements.

NON-TYPICAL AMERICAN ELK
FINAL SCORE: 409 7/8
HUNTER: Dana L. Foster

NON-TYPICAL AMERICAN ELK
FINAL SCORE: 400 5/8
HUNTER: Ron Mika

NON-TYPICAL AMERICAN ELK
FINAL SCORE: 395 5/8
HUNTER: David A. Young

NON-TYPICAL AMERICAN ELK
FINAL SCORE: 408 3/8
HUNTER: Joshua S. Pollock

ROOSEVELT'S ELK

Cervus elaphus roosevelti

Minimum Score 275

World's Record 404 6/8

Roosevelt's elk includes trophies from: west of Interstate Highway I-5 in Oregon and Washington; Del Norte, Humboldt, and Trinity Counties, California, as well as that portion of Siskiyou County west of I-5 in Northern California; Afognak and Raspberry Islands of Alaska; and Vancouver Island and the Powell River Area on the mainland of British Columbia.

Final Score	Gross Score	Length of Main Beam R.	L.	Inside Spread	Circumference at Smallest Place Between First & Second Points R.	L.	Number of Points R.	L.	Locality	Hunter	Owner	Date Killed	Rank
366 7/8	376	53 7/8	53	38 5/8	9 3/8	8 3/8	8	6	Clatsop Co., OR	Mr. Carlson	Louie Dix	1952	1
362 5/8	375 5/8	40 4/8	41 7/8	38 7/8	10 5/8	10 6/8	9	9	Powell River, BC	Allen M. Shearer	Allen M. Shearer	2009	2
353 7/8	368 3/8	53 4/8	54 1/8	40 3/8	9 3/8	10 1/8	7	8	Josephine Co., OR	Johnny Costello	Cabela's Inc.	2004	3
345 3/8	385 7/8	50 4/8	49 6/8	34 4/8	9 6/8	9 2/8	9	7	Douglas Co., OR	Travis J. Price	Cabela's, Inc.	2005	4
338 5/8	347 4/8	47 4/8	48 4/8	40 6/8	8 4/8	9 4/8	7	7	Del Norte Co., CA	Fred D. Ruggaber	Fred D. Ruggaber	2008	5
338 1/8	346 5/8	52 2/8	51 6/8	39 3/8	10	9 7/8	7	7	Clallam Co., WA	John W. Rodius	John W. Rodius	2005	6
336 3/8	343 2/8	51 3/8	52	41 2/8	10 2/8	9 3/8	6	6	Vancouver Island, BC	Tom Foss	Tom Foss	2007	7
332 4/8	342 3/8	54	52 2/8	36	8 3/8	9 3/8	7	7	Curry Co., OR	Mark J. Becker	Mark J. Becker	2009	8
326 7/8	333	48 3/8	47 6/8	37 4/8	9 4/8	9 3/8	7	7	Tillamook Co., OR	John L. Bishop III	John L. Bishop III	2008	9
326 4/8	332 5/8	46 7/8	45 5/8	39 2/8	9 2/8	8 7/8	6	7	Clallam Co., WA	Frank Oxenford	Patrick M. Lockhart	1936	10
324 7/8	350 3/8	42 5/8	44 6/8	34 2/8	9 3/8	8 5/8	9	8	Douglas Co., OR	Joseph O. Rutledge	Joseph O. Rutledge	2008	11
324 6/8	338 6/8	51 4/8	47 7/8	32 5/8	8 2/8	8 2/8	7	8	Humboldt Co., CA	Jim P. Thomas	Jim P. Thomas	2008	12
323 2/8	328 5/8	51 7/8	51 3/8	40 1/8	8 4/8	9	6	6	Tillamook Co., OR	Gregory L. McVittie	Gregory L. McVittie	2008	13
322 7/8	328 3/8	43	44 3/8	36 4/8	9 6/8	10 2/8	9	9	Clatsop Co., OR	James R. Bernards	James R. Bernards	2005	14
322 6/8	338 7/8	47 5/8	48 7/8	33 1/8	10 2/8	10 1/8	9	7	Humboldt Co., CA	Molly Heneks	Molly Heneks	2008	15
322	338 2/8	46 6/8	48 6/8	35	7 4/8	7 5/8	8	7	Humboldt Co., CA	Thomas P. Hardin	Thomas P. Hardin	2006	16
321 7/8	327 7/8	47 4/8	48 7/8	33 6/8	7 5/8	7 6/8	7	8	Humboldt Co., CA	Gary R. Haga, Jr.	Gary R. Haga, Jr.	2008	17
321 5/8	328 3/8	44 1/8	43 5/8	41 1/8	8	8 4/8	6	6	Port Renfrew, BC	Mark G. Russell	Mark G. Russell	2007	18
320 3/8	328 2/8	44 2/8	43 3/8	33 3/8	8 3/8	8 2/8	8	7	Vancouver Island, BC	Larry A. Meyer	Larry A. Meyer	2008	19
317 1/8	334 2/8	47 6/8	48 2/8	39 6/8	8 6/8	8 6/8	7	6	Coos Co., OR	Rob D. Miller	Rob D. Miller	2008	20
315 5/8	345 1/8	46 4/8	46 6/8	36 7/8	10	10 5/8	8	6	Trinity Co., CA	Mark C. Ogden	Mark C. Ogden	2007	21
314 7/8	324 7/8	45 4/8	45 4/8	32	8 1/8	8	6	6	Memekay River, BC	Raymond D. Neuwirth	Raymond D. Neuwirth	2007	22
314 4/8	322 6/8	46 4/8	48 5/8	36 3/8	8 5/8	9 2/8	7	7	Del Norte Co., CA	Casey Wooters	Casey Wooters	2005	23
314 3/8	324 3/8	45 1/8	44 1/8	37 6/8	8 5/8	8 7/8	7	7	Campbell River, BC	Casey P. Brooks	Casey P. Brooks	2006	24
314	322 4/8	41 4/8	44 2/8	33 7/8	9 4/8	9 2/8	6	6	Vancouver Island, BC	Brian H. Mason	Brian H. Mason	2006	25
313	323 7/8	47 4/8	45 3/8	34 5/8	8 5/8	9	6	7	Del Norte Co., CA	Lyle C. Foster	Lyle C. Foster	2007	26
312 2/8	323 3/8	41 6/8	43 6/8	37 2/8	9 4/8	9 2/8	8	6	Bacon Lake, BC	Glenn E. Francis	Glenn E. Francis	2008	27
308 3/8	316 1/8	47 7/8	49 5/8	33 1/8	8 2/8	7 7/8	7	7	Clatsop Co., OR	David S. Weiss	David S. Weiss	2008	28

307 4/8	310	46 5/8	46 7/8	41 3/8	9 2/8	9	6	6	Trinity Co., CA	Cody C. Sanders	Cody C. Sanders	2008	29
305 3/8	310 6/8	45 4/8	45 2/8	31 6/8	8 1/8	7 7/8	7	6	Del Norte Co., CA	Larry L. Schlenker	Larry L. Schlenker	2007	30
303 1/8	314 1/8	45 4/8	44 4/8	35 2/8	8 6/8	8 2/8	6	6	Polk Co., OR	Bryon D. Davidson	Bryon D. Davidson	2005	31
303	311	46 1/8	43 2/8	41 4/8	8 1/8	8	6	6	Humboldt Co., CA	LaDonna K. Haga	LaDonna K. Haga	2007	32
302 7/8	308 3/8	48 6/8	48 4/8	34 1/8	8 3/8	8 2/8	8	8	Coos Co., OR	Rob D. Miller	Rob D. Miller	2007	33
302	316 1/8	50 3/8	49 2/8	30 4/8	9 5/8	7 7/8	7	8	Humboldt Co., CA	Chester W. Holmes	Chester W. Holmes	2008	34
300 3/8	310 1/8	44	43 6/8	36	7 7/8	8	6	7	Humboldt Co., CA	Dean L. Burroughs	Dean L. Burroughs	2007	35
300 3/8	311 4/8	45	47 5/8	32 7/8	9 6/8	8 5/8	6	6	Memekay River, BC	Edward P. Pawlik	Edward P. Pawlik	2008	35
298 2/8	303	46	45 2/8	39 3/8	8 5/8	8 3/8	8	6	Port Renfrew, BC	Andrew A. Hill	Andrew A. Hill	2006	37
297 7/8	298 6/8	42 1/8	42	32 4/8	7 2/8	7 3/8	7	6	Humboldt Co., CA	Tessa R. Willburn	Tessa R. Willburn	2007	38
297 6/8	318 2/8	42 2/8	35 1/8	43 2/8	10 2/8	10 5/8	7	8	Vancouver Island, BC	David J. Turchanski	David J. Turchanski	2008	39
297 3/8	306 3/8	51 5/8	48 4/8	32 2/8	8 5/8	7 7/8	6	7	Tillamook Co., OR	Merle J. Kidwell	Merle J. Kidwell	1971	40
297	314 1/8	43 7/8	42 2/8	40 3/8	7 2/8	8 6/8	7	6	Tsitika River, BC	Kent Deligans	Kent Deligans	2005	41
294 6/8	319 3/8	47 3/8	49 6/8	34 6/8	10 4/8	10 3/8	8	7	Del Norte Co., CA	Robert L. Anderson	Robert L. Anderson	2008	42
294 4/8	301 6/8	43	45 2/8	42	7 3/8	7 4/8	6	6	Grays Harbor Co., WA	Picked Up	Cabela's, Inc.	2004	43
292 4/8	307	47 2/8	47 5/8	37 2/8	9 1/8	8 3/8	6	5	Clatsop Co., OR	Slade H. Taylor	Slade H. Taylor	2007	44
292 3/8	297 3/8	42 7/8	44 4/8	36 4/8	9 2/8	8 6/8	6	6	Siskiyou Co., CA	Robert W. Phares	Robert W. Phares	2008	45
291 7/8	333 4/8	51 1/8	49 6/8	36 6/8	8 5/8	8 4/8	8	8	Del Norte Co., CA	Glen J. Lockhart	Glen J. Lockhart	2005	46
291 4/8	298 3/8	48	46 5/8	44 6/8	6 6/8	6 5/8	8	6	Humboldt Co., CA	Trissha D. Juvenal	Trissha D. Juvenal	2007	47
290 7/8	302 3/8	39 5/8	39 5/8	32 4/8	7 5/8	6 7/8	7	7	Columbia Co., OR	Michael J. Pense	Michael J. Pense	2007	48
290 4/8	299 2/8	42 5/8	42 5/8	31 5/8	6 3/8	6 4/8	7	6	Campbell River, BC	Kevin T. Klumper	Kevin T. Klumper	2008	49
288 3/8	298 5/8	42 5/8	42 2/8	32 6/8	8 6/8	8 4/8	7	6	Wahkiakum Co., WA	Ed Engle	B. Engle & J. Engle	1950	50
286 7/8	293 3/8	47 3/8	47 5/8	35 7/8	8 3/8	8 2/8	6	7	Benton Co., OR	Christopher A. Wait	Christopher A. Wait	2007	51
282 2/8	295 5/8	45 3/8	45 4/8	36 2/8	8 2/8	8 1/8	7	7	Coos Co., OR	Mitchell W. Vincent	Mitchell W. Vincent	2007	52
282	284 4/8	40 1/8	39 3/8	34	9	8 6/8	7	7	Tillamook Co., OR	Kenneth R. Hurliman	Kenneth R. Hurliman	2006	53
281 6/8	326	44 4/8	45 5/8	39 4/8	11	10 7/8	7	8	Clallam Co., WA	Allen Pinkerton	Warren D. LaVille	1952	54
281 2/8	290 7/8	46 5/8	45 1/8	31 3/8	7 7/8	7 7/8	8	8	Humboldt Co., CA	Mike J. Coelho	Mike J. Coelho	2007	55
280	287 5/8	41 4/8	41 7/8	36 1/8	8	7 4/8	8	8	Clatsop Co., OR	Frank J. Twardoch	Frank J. Twardoch	2007	56
279 5/8	286	46	48 1/8	31 6/8	7 3/8	7 6/8	7	7	Humboldt Co., CA	Andy M. Cook	Andy M. Cook	2007	57
278 1/8	286 2/8	44 3/8	40 2/8	41 5/8	8 6/8	8 4/8	6	7	Grays Harbor Co., WA	Robert J. Mayton	Robert J. Mayton	2008	58
276 2/8	279 5/8	40 1/8	39 6/8	35	8	8 5/8	7	6	Yamhill Co., OR	Dennis A. McGanty	Dennis A. McGanty	2005	59
380 4/8*	386 1/8	54 3/8	53 1/8	39 5/8	9 4/8	9 2/8	7	7	Columbia Co., OR	Clifford M. Hayden	Clifford M. Hayden	1991	
347 2/8*	351 1/8	51 2/8	50 3/8	40	8 7/8	8 4/8	7	7	Siskiyou Co., CA	Clay E. Montgomery	Clay E. Montgomery	2009	

Final score subject to revision by additional verifying measurements.

TULE ELK

Cervus elaphus nannodes

Minimum Score 270

Tule elk are from selected areas in Calfiornia. For a complete description of the boundary, check the Official Measurer's manual, *Measuring and Scoring North American Big Game Trophies*, or visit the Club's web site at www.booneandcrockettclub.com.

Final Score	Gross Score	Length of Main Beam		Inside Spread	Circumference at Smallest Place Between First & Second Points		Number of Points		Locality	Hunter	Owner	Date Killed	Rank
		R.	L.		R.	L.	R.	L.					
322 5/8	330 3/8	38 4/8	41 2/8	38 4/8	8 1/8	7 6/8	7	8	San Luis Obispo Co., CA	Andrew J. Wood	Andrew J. Wood	2007	1
322 3/8	332 7/8	46	43 4/8	41 2/8	8 6/8	8 4/8	7	7	Colusa Co, CA	Thomas B. Gordon	Thomas B. Gordon	2008	2
312 5/8	326 4/8	45	36 4/8	37 5/8	9 2/8	9 5/8	6	9	Colusa Co, CA	Richard L. Garrison	Richard L. Garrison	2007	3
311	319 1/8	42 4/8	42 6/8	40 3/8	7 3/8	7 1/8	8	7	Solano Co, CA	Steven S. Bruggeman	Steven S. Bruggeman	2006	4
310 2/8	318	46	45 3/8	38	9 2/8	8 6/8	7	7	Colusa Co, CA	Brian W. Lohse	Brian W. Lohse	2008	5
310	323 6/8	40 4/8	40 1/8	44 2/8	7 6/8	7 1/8	8	9	Solano Co, CA	Walter Palmer	Walter Palmer	2009	6
305 5/8	311 5/8	41	41 2/8	41 4/8	8	7 7/8	7	7	Solano Co, CA	Ashlee M. Long	Ashlee M. Long	2009	7
300 3/8	303 1/8	42	42 4/8	44 6/8	7 1/8	7 1/8	8	8	Mendocino Co., CA	Mark A. Wayne	Mark A. Wayne	2009	8
285 1/8	296 1/8	39 1/8	42 6/8	42 3/8	7 6/8	8 4/8	7	7	Inyo Co., CA	Travis D. Schwartz	Travis D. Schwartz	2008	9
282	289	40 7/8	40	36 5/8	6 7/8	8	7	9	San Luis Obispo Co., CA	Raymond Mancuso	Raymond Mancuso	2008	10
281 7/8	286 5/8	37	37	39 3/8	7 2/8	6 5/8	7	8	San Luis Obispo Co., CA	Monte Rudnick	Monte Rudnick	2009	11
274 6/8	287 2/8	41 3/8	39	41	7 1/8	7 2/8	7	8	San Luis Obispo Co., CA	Mike J. Coelho	Mike J. Coelho	2005	12
321 4/8*	326	52 2/8	53 1/8	40	6 6/8	7 1/8	7	6	Mendocino Co., CA	William B. Mayta	William B. Mayta	2006	

* Final score subject to revision by additional verifying measurements.

MULE DEER - TYPICAL ANTLERS

Odocoileus hemionus hemionus and certain related subspecies

Minimum Score 180 World's Record 226 4/8

Final Score	Gross Score	Length of Main Beam R.	L.	Inside Spread	Circumference at Smallest Place Between Burr & First Point R.	L.	Number of Points R.	L.	Locality	Hunter	Owner	Date Killed	Rank
210 6/8	214 6/8	26 7/8	27 5/8	21 4/8	5 2/8	5 2/8	5	5	Swanson, SK	Glen Johnson	John B. McJannet	2007	1
209	235 3/8	28	27	23 5/8	6 2/8	6 2/8	6	6	Garfield Co., UT	Del R. Brady	Del R. Brady	2008	2
206 3/8	213 1/8	27	27 2/8	28 1/8	6	5 7/8	6	5	Mesa Co., CO	Aaron A. Behrens	Cabela's, Inc.	2006	3
205 2/8	218 3/8	28 1/8	28	32	5 4/8	5 4/8	7	7	Sonora, MX	Jason J. Gisi	Jason J. Gisi	2005	4
204 6/8	208 3/8	26 7/8	27	31 1/8	4 3/8	4 3/8	5	5	Sonora, MX	Johnny B. Grimes	Cabela's, Inc.	2006	5
204 3/8	213 4/8	27 3/8	27 1/8	26 1/8	5 7/8	5 7/8	6	6	Old Wives Lake, SK	Warren M. Stadnyk	Warren M. Stadnyk	2008	6
203 3/8	211 3/8	29 3/8	27 1/8	27 4/8	5 3/8	5 4/8	6	5	Mohave Co., AZ	Michael J. O'Brien	Michael J. O'Brien	2008	7
203 2/8	221	27 1/8	28 2/8	26 3/8	5 6/8	5 1/8	6	6	Rio Arriba Co., NM	Rod Pinkett	Rod Pinkett	2007	8
203 1/8	241 1/8	28 5/8	27 6/8	30 2/8	5 2/8	5 2/8	7	7	White River N.F., CO	Bill Barcus	Cabela's, Inc.	1979	9
203	208 1/8	25	24 3/8	20 4/8	5 3/8	5 2/8	5	5	Montrose Co., CO	Kenneth W. Canterbury	Kenneth W. Canterbury	2008	10
202 2/8	205 2/8	27 4/8	27 2/8	24	6 2/8	6 1/8	5	5	Antelope Lake, SK	John C. Slabik	John C. Slabik	2006	11
202 2/8	218 4/8	27 2/8	27 6/8	29	4 7/8	4 7/8	7	7	Mesa Co., CO	Gregory S. Hunt	Gregory S. Hunt	2008	11
200 6/8	217 3/8	26 1/8	26 1/8	18 5/8	5	5	6	6	Mesa Co., CO	Jennifer S. Teague	Jennifer S. Teague	2007	13
200 5/8	218 3/8	27 7/8	26 7/8	24 4/8	5	5	5	5	Outlook, SK	Gary K. Fidyk	Gary K. Fidyk	2007	14
200 3/8	202 4/8	28 4/8	28	28 3/8	4 6/8	4 6/8	5	5	Sioux Co., NE	Miles E. Lemley	Miles E. Lemley	2007	15
200 2/8	212 2/8	28 4/8	27 2/8	23 1/8	5 7/8	5 5/8	6	6	Siskiyou Co., CA	Wallace Bosworth	Stephen J. Bosworth	1929	16
200 2/8	204 4/8	28 1/8	27 1/8	26 6/8	5 2/8	5 5/8	5	5	Little Manitou Lake, SK	Frank Kondratowicz	Frank Kondratowicz	2006	16
200 1/8	206 5/8	26	26	24 3/8	4 7/8	4 7/8	5	5	Sonora, MX	Doyle C. Dale	Doyle C. Dale	2006	18
200	203 6/8	24 4/8	24 1/8	23 4/8	5	4 6/8	5	5	Coconino Co., AZ	Duane R. Richardson	Duane R. Richardson	1988	19
199 6/8	210 7/8	26 1/8	27	28 7/8	6	5 6/8	6	6	Saguache Co., CO	Jeremiah S. Roever	Jeremiah S. Roever	2008	20
199 5/8	210 1/8	27 5/8	26	29	6 1/8	5 7/8	6	6	Moffat Co., CO	Robert D. Vesely	Robert D. Vesely	2007	21
199 4/8	211 4/8	26	25 5/8	21 7/8	5 2/8	5 2/8	5	5	S. Saskatchewan River, SK	Murray W. Kasper	Murray W. Kasper	2005	22
199 2/8	212 4/8	27 4/8	27 3/8	25 7/8	5 5/8	5 3/8	7	6	Mohave Co., AZ	Robert A. Carlson	Robert A. Carlson	2006	23
199	205 3/8	23 2/8	23 4/8	25	5	5	5	5	Coconino Co., AZ	Brette N. Anderson	Brette N. Anderson	2007	24
198 3/8	202 2/8	28 4/8	28 5/8	26 1/8	4 6/8	5 5/8	7	5	Park Co., CO	Unknown	Robert M. Anderson	PR 1930	25
198	215	24 6/8	24 5/8	23	5 3/8	5 5/8	7	7	Las Animas Co., CO	W. Stephen Onstot	W. Stephen Onstot	2006	26
197 6/8	224 4/8	25 2/8	26 5/8	23 4/8	6 4/8	6	9	6	Lake Diefenbaker, SK	Gregory F. Taylor	Gregory F. Taylor	2007	27
197 4/8	200 7/8	25 4/8	26 2/8	23 6/8	5	5	5	5	Eagle Co., CO	Amy J. Carter	Amy J. Carter	2006	28
197 3/8	200 6/8	23 6/8	25 1/8	23 1/8	5	4 7/8	5	5	Eagle Co., CO	Dennis R. Wilson	Dennis R. Wilson	2007	29
197	221 7/8	25 5/8	26 3/8	27 4/8	5 6/8	5 7/8	6	9	Sonora, MX	Steve P. Bashista	Steve P. Bashista	2006	30
197	199 5/8	25 4/8	25 6/8	20 2/8	5 4/8	5 4/8	5	5	Halfway River, BC	Brad D. Wood	Brad D. Wood	2007	30

MULE DEER - TYPICAL ANTLERS

Odocoileus hemionus hemionus and certain related subspecies

Final Score	Gross Score	Length of Main Beam R.	L.	Inside Spread	Circumference at Smallest Place Between Burr & First Point R.	L.	Number of Points R.	L.	Locality	Hunter	Owner	Date Killed	Rank
196 4/8	212 1/8	26	23 7/8	23 5/8	5 1/8	5 2/8	5	6	Eagle Co., CO	Louis E. Martinelli	Angelo Martinelli	1962	32
196 4/8	200 5/8	24 4/8	27	24	5 2/8	5	5	5	Red Deer River, AB	Colin J. Campbell	Colin J. Campbell	2007	32
196 4/8	210 5/8	28 1/8	26 5/8	22 4/8	5	4 7/8	6	5	Lincoln Co., WY	Jack T. Kendall	Jack T. Kendall	2009	32
196 4/8	199 6/8	26 3/8	26 7/8	20 4/8	5 3/8	5 3/8	5	5	Garfield Co., CO	Richard L. Prather	Richard L. Prather	2009	32
196 3/8	201 7/8	23 7/8	24 3/8	23 7/8	5 6/8	5 4/8	5	5	Montrose Co., CO	R.L. Price & J.A. Argo	R.L. Price & J.A. Argo	2007	36
196 2/8	213 3/8	24 3/8	25 1/8	22	5 4/8	5 3/8	7	6	Garfield Co., CO	Gregory E. Beightel	Gregory E. Beightel	2009	37
196 1/8	202 4/8	26 6/8	27 2/8	23 2/8	5 1/8	5 1/8	5	6	Wasatch Co., UT	Daryl Grant	Daryl Grant	2006	38
196 1/8	223 5/8	26 3/8	27 1/8	27 4/8	5 3/8	5 3/8	8	7	Missoula Co., MT	Brink W. Kuchenbrod	Brink W. Kuchenbrod	2007	38
196 1/8	224 4/8	25 5/8	27 3/8	23 5/8	5 2/8	5 4/8	6	6	Bow River, AB	Peter Tsoulamanis	Peter Tsoulamanis	2007	38
196	199 6/8	26 5/8	26 1/8	24 4/8	5	5 1/8	5	5	Sonora, MX	Lou Kindred	Lou Kindred	2007	41
196	205 4/8	26	26 3/8	30 1/8	5 1/8	5	6	5	La Plata Co., CO	Randy W. Bongard	Randy W. Bongard	2008	41
195 7/8	201	24 2/8	24	22 6/8	4 3/8	4 4/8	5	6	Malheur Co., OR	Terry C. Hickson	Terry C. Hickson	2008	43
195 4/8	201 5/8	26	24 6/8	27 2/8	5 3/8	5 4/8	5	5	Garfield Co., UT	Sheldon S. Randall	Sheldon S. Randall	2006	44
195 4/8	198 5/8	25 2/8	25 7/8	23 2/8	4 4/8	4 4/8	5	5	Carbon Co., WY	Picked Up	Clay J. Evans	2008	44
195 3/8	215 4/8	26 7/8	26 7/8	29 6/8	5 3/8	5 2/8	6	7	Montezuma Co., CO	James S. Underwood	Clay Underwood	1971	46
195 2/8	207	25 4/8	24 4/8	27 2/8	4 6/8	4 5/8	7	5	Custer Co., ID	Paul Burtrum	Cabela's, Inc.	1957	47
195 1/8	202 7/8	23 3/8	23 5/8	20 3/8	4 7/8	4 7/8	6	6	Red Deer River, AB	Frank G. Foland	Jon K. Taylor	1931	48
195 1/8	204 3/8	25	27 1/8	23 7/8	4 6/8	4 6/8	5	5	Los Alamos Co., NM	Gary B. Tabor	Gary B. Tabor	1967	48
195 1/8	201 6/8	26 2/8	26 4/8	23 3/8	5 4/8	5 5/8	5	5	Unknown	Unknown	Mike DiLeo	PR 2006	48
195 1/8	212 1/8	24 2/8	25 4/8	22 6/8	4 7/8	5 3/8	6	7	Iron Co., UT	Lyf H. Erickson	Lyf H. Erickson	2009	48
195	202 6/8	26	23 6/8	22 2/8	4 5/8	4 5/8	5	6	Carbon Co., WY	James D. Graham	James D. Graham	2006	52
195	202 2/8	25 5/8	25 4/8	25 6/8	5 7/8	6	4	6	Mohave Co., AZ	Leon D. Searles	Leon D. Searles	2006	52
195	201	25 2/8	24 2/8	31 1/8	4 6/8	5	4	4	Mohave Co., AZ	Jeff M. Baird	Jeff M. Baird	2008	52
194 6/8	205 7/8	26 5/8	26 3/8	25 7/8	5 2/8	5	7	5	Bad Lake, SK	Marlowe B. Schmiess	Marlowe B. Schmiess	2007	55
194 5/8	207 3/8	27 7/8	27 7/8	21 5/8	5 7/8	6	5	5	Ferry Co., WA	Roland Carr	Sharon E. Carr-Hancock	1947	56
194 5/8	217 2/8	27	26 2/8	31 3/8	5 2/8	5 2/8	7	6	Shrimp Lake, SK	Kara Imlach	Kara Imlach	2006	56
194 4/8	198 7/8	25 7/8	25 7/8	21 4/8	4 5/8	5	5	5	Mesa Co., CO	John E. McBride	John E. McBride	2007	58
194 4/8	207 2/8	25 2/8	24 4/8	22 5/8	4 4/8	4 4/8	6	6	Union Co., OR	Jack M. Lowenstein	Jack M. Lowenstein	2009	58
194 3/8	202 4/8	24 2/8	25 1/8	29 7/8	5 1/8	5 1/8	5	5	Boise Co., ID	Karl Canright	Karl Canright	1977	60
194 3/8	196 6/8	26 1/8	25 6/8	20 5/8	4 7/8	5	5	5	Catron Co., NM	Michael A. Quintana	Michael A. Quintana	2007	60
194 3/8	201 4/8	27	27 1/8	21 7/8	5	4 7/8	6	5	Arrowwood, AB	Neil W. Friesen	Neil W. Friesen	2008	60
194 2/8	205 3/8	25 6/8	25 2/8	22 3/8	6	6	8	5	Pratt Lake, BC	Dennis L. De Leeuw	Dennis L. De Leeuw	2007	63

Score		Main Beam R	Main Beam L	Inside Spread	Circ. R	Circ. L	Pts R	Pts L	Locality	Hunter	Owner	Date	Rank
194 1/8	212 2/8	25 2/8	24 4/8	22 2/8	5 1/8	5	5	6	Delta Co., CO	Tony Banfield, Jr.	Tony Banfield, Jr.	2007	64
194 1/8	203 2/8	25 2/8	25	26 7/8	4 7/8	4 7/8	5	6	Mohave Co., AZ	George R. Richardson, Jr.	George R. Richardson, Jr.	2008	64
194	205 2/8	27 5/8	25 1/8	25 1/8	5 3/8	5 1/8	6	5	Grand Co., CO	Ronnie L. Ennis	Ronnie L. Ennis	1981	66
193 7/8	204 2/8	25 1/8	26 6/8	25 6/8	5 3/8	5 2/8	6	6	Jackson Co., CO	Steve R. Vesledahl	Steve R. Vesledahl	2007	67
193 6/8	217	24 6/8	24 1/8	23 7/8	5 3/8	5 1/8	7	6	Gem Co., ID	Earl P. Basso, Jr.	Earl P. Basso, Jr.	1972	68
193 6/8	201 2/8	26 3/8	26 7/8	24 7/8	4 5/8	4 6/8	6	5	Owyhee Co., ID	Mark B. Fullmer	Mark B. Fullmer	1987	68
193 6/8	198 3/8	26 5/8	26 2/8	24 2/8	5 5/8	5 5/8	5	5	Washington Co., ID	Gary Wageman	Gary Wageman	1987	68
193 6/8	203 3/8	27 2/8	26 4/8	22 5/8	5 3/8	5 3/8	5	6	Kane Co., UT	D. Shawn Shaw	D. Shawn Shaw	2008	68
193 4/8	196 7/8	24 4/8	23 3/8	22 2/8	4 7/8	4 7/8	5	5	Kane Co., UT	Jeffrey A. Zuniga	Jeffrey A. Zuniga	2005	72
193 3/8	209 5/8	24	24 4/8	27 1/8	5 4/8	5 5/8	5	8	Huerfano Co., CO	Carol L. Brown	Carol L. Brown	2006	73
193 3/8	199 2/8	26 5/8	27	26 7/8	4 7/8	4 7/8	7	5	Sonora, MX	Dennis D. Wintch	Dennis D. Wintch	2008	73
193 3/8	196 3/8	25 6/8	25 6/8	22 5/8	5 2/8	5 2/8	5	5	Carbon Co., WY	Van C. Myers	Van C. Myers	2009	73
193 2/8	199 2/8	25 4/8	25 4/8	24 2/8	5 1/8	5 1/8	5	5	Campbell Creek, BC	Christophe Chave	Christophe Chave	2007	76
193 2/8	199 6/8	26 2/8	23 6/8	22 2/8	4 7/8	4 7/8	5	5	Delta Co., CO	Jessie T. Outland	Jessie T. Outland	2008	76
193	202 4/8	24 1/8	22 4/8	19	4 6/8	4 6/8	6	6	Mesa Co., CO	Calvin C. Ackley	Calvin C. Ackley	2007	78
193	219 2/8	23 5/8	26 2/8	23 5/8	5	5	6	7	Beaton River, BC	Dan P. Cowger	Dan P. Cowger	2008	78
193	198 6/8	25 4/8	25 7/8	20 1/8	4 4/8	4 3/8	6	5	Fremont Co., WY	Patrick R. Garvin	Patrick R. Garvin	2008	78
193	198 7/8	25 4/8	26 3/8	20 5/8	4 7/8	4 7/8	5	6	Douglas Co., CO	Kenneth L. Peters	Kenneth L. Peters	2008	78
192 7/8	205 7/8	27 2/8	26 3/8	20	5 2/8	5 4/8	6	7	Idaho	Marc W. Babiar	Unknown	PR 1960	82
192 7/8	220 4/8	26 5/8	27 1/8	25 2/8	5	5	8	6	Duchesne Co., UT	Nathan W. Jacobson	Unknown	PR 1988	82

TYPICAL MULE DEER
FINAL SCORE: 190 7/8
HUNTER: Stacy L. Bolton

TYPICAL MULE DEER
FINAL SCORE: 180
HUNTER: Marty R. Jordens

TYPICAL MULE DEER
FINAL SCORE: 181 5/8
HUNTER: Heath Dreger

TYPICAL MULE DEER
FINAL SCORE: 185 3/8
HUNTER: William L. Nash

MULE DEER - TYPICAL ANTLERS

Odocoileus hemionus hemionus and certain related subspecies

Final Score	Gross Score	Length of Main Beam R.	L.	Inside Spread	Circumference at Smallest Place Between Burr & First Point R.	L.	Number of Points R.	L.	Locality	Hunter	Owner	Date Killed	Rank
192 7/8	198 6/8	23 5/8	23 4/8	26 7/8	5 2/8	5 3/8	5	5	Lake Diefenbaker, SK	Picked Up	Gordie A. Kimble	PR 2008	82
192 6/8	197 1/8	25 1/8	25 6/8	25 2/8	5 4/8	5 4/8	5	5	Unknown	Unknown	Don McLaughlin	PR 1954	85
192 6/8	198 7/8	23 5/8	24 5/8	22	5	4 6/8	5	5	Garfield Co., CO	Mark W. Smith	Mark W. Smith	2007	85
192 5/8	197 3/8	25 6/8	24 5/8	21 3/8	5	5	5	5	Rio Arriba Co., NM	Emily Ulabarri-Chavez	Emily Ulabarri-Chavez	2008	87
192 4/8	195 6/8	23 1/8	22 6/8	20 2/8	4 5/8	4 6/8	5	5	Mesa Co., CO	Tyler L. Achord	Tyler L. Achord	2007	88
192 4/8	213 5/8	27 3/8	26	27 1/8	5 2/8	5 2/8	5	7	Great Sand Hills, SK	Jim Clary	Jim Clary	2007	88
192 2/8	197 3/8	25 3/8	25 2/8	23	5	5 1/8	5	5	Kane Co., UT	Joe Grondona	Joe Grondona	2006	90
192 2/8	200	25 4/8	27 2/8	18 4/8	5 1/8	5 2/8	5	6	Rio Arriba Co., NM	Waylon R. Callado	Waylon R. Callado	2007	90
192 2/8	198 1/8	24 3/8	26	20 6/8	4 5/8	4 4/8	5	5	Jackson Co., CO	Daniel M. Vesledahl	Daniel M. Vesledahl	2007	90
192 1/8	205 3/8	24 6/8	25 5/8	22 2/8	5 4/8	5 5/8	6	7	Lincoln Co., MT	Bob McCollom	Bob McCollom	1959	93
192 1/8	198 1/8	25 6/8	26 4/8	24 5/8	5 1/8	5 1/8	5	5	El Paso Co., CO	James H. Richardson	James H. Richardson	2007	93
192 1/8	198 4/8	27 3/8	26 2/8	25 3/8	5 4/8	5 4/8	6	5	Coronation, AB	Morgan J. Williams	Morgan J. Williams	2008	93
192	203 3/8	25	25	19 5/8	5 3/8	5 2/8	7	6	Yuma Co., CO	Troy D. Welton	Troy D. Welton	2004	96
192	199 5/8	24 5/8	24 5/8	23 2/8	4 7/8	5	6	5	Custer Co., CO	Lance M. Gatlin	Lance M. Gatlin	2007	96
191 7/8	194 3/8	26	25 6/8	23 1/8	5	5	5	5	Boundary Co., ID	Red Sweet	Stan Sweet	1939	98
191 7/8	214	28 4/8	27 2/8	22 4/8	5 7/8	6	7	7	Sonora, MX	Paul M. Dickson, Jr.	Paul M. Dickson, Jr.	2009	98
191 6/8	204 4/8	25	25 5/8	26 4/8	5 6/8	5 5/8	6	5	Malheur Co., OR	Vernon Strong	Brian V. Strong	1952	100
191 6/8	196 3/8	27 4/8	27 6/8	28 2/8	5 2/8	5	5	5	Sonora, MX	George W. Wise III	George W. Wise III	2009	100
191 5/8	196 6/8	23 6/8	22 6/8	21 1/8	5 3/8	5	5	4	Uinta Co., WY	Keith Fraughton	Wendell Fraughton	1964	102
191 5/8	197 7/8	24 7/8	27 5/8	26 5/8	5	5	5	5	Rio Arriba Co., NM	Picked Up	Robert J. Seeds	PR 2002	102
191 4/8	203 6/8	24 7/8	25 6/8	27 1/8	5 1/8	5 2/8	5	7	Archuleta Co., CO	Bill Freeman	Bill Freeman	2006	104
191 4/8	197 4/8	21 7/8	23	26 6/8	5 6/8	5 5/8	5	5	Billings Co., ND	Robert D. Knote	Robert D. Knote	2006	104
191 4/8	195 5/8	25 3/8	26 2/8	25 2/8	5	5	5	5	Coconino Co., AZ	Roger D. Cook, Jr.	Roger D. Cook, Jr.	2008	104
191 4/8	200 1/8	25	24 2/8	22 1/8	4 5/8	4 5/8	6	6	Lincoln Co., NV	Kaylee C. Teel	Kaylee C. Teel	2008	104
191 3/8	221 5/8	28 4/8	27 7/8	24 1/8	5 4/8	5 4/8	8	8	Park Co., CO	Unknown	Randy Sandoval	1973	108
191 3/8	203 7/8	24 6/8	26	27 4/8	5 1/8	5	6	5	Montezuma Co., CO	Frayne Whiteskunk	Frayne Whiteskunk	2009	108
191 2/8	200 5/8	27 1/8	27	23 4/8	4 6/8	4 6/8	6	6	Grand Prairie, AB	Stephen A. Longo	Stephen A. Longo	2005	110
191 2/8	202 6/8	25 2/8	25 2/8	27 2/8	5 2/8	5 3/8	6	6	Dolores Co., CO	Michael E. LaLonde	Michael E. LaLonde	2006	110
191 2/8	202 7/8	23 5/8	24	24 2/8	5 1/8	5	6	6	Wasatch Co., UT	Jeremy E. Motley	Jeremy E. Motley	2006	110
191 2/8	196 3/8	24 6/8	22 4/8	26 1/8	5 2/8	5 1/8	6	5	Mohave Co., AZ	Roy E. Grace	Roy E. Grace	2008	110
191 1/8	206 5/8	25 1/8	26 6/8	21 4/8	5	5 2/8	6	6	Moffat Co., CO	Will L. Stone	Will L. Stone	1963	114
191 1/8	196	24 6/8	25 4/8	23 7/8	5 3/8	5 4/8	5	6	Crook Co., OR	Neal Halousek	Neal Halousek	1997	114

Score	Gross	Main Beam R	Main Beam L	Inside Spread	Circ. R	Circ. L	Pts R	Pts L	Locality	By Whom Killed	Owner	Date	Rank
191 1/8	206 1/8	26 5/8	26 1/8	27 1/8	5 1/8	5 1/8	5	6	Garfield Co., CO	Charles P. Atkinson	Charles P. Atkinson	2006	114
191 1/8	208 1/8	26 6/8	25 5/8	23	5 6/8	5 7/8	6	7	Lake Diefenbaker, SK	Darren Fichter	Darren Fichter	2007	114
191 1/8	197 6/8	25 1/8	26 4/8	23 7/8	4 1/8	3 7/8	4	4	Sonora, MX	Dave M. Westrum	Dave M. Westrum	2007	114
191 1/8	205 1/8	26 3/8	26 1/8	21 5/8	4 7/8	5	7	5	Battle River, AB	Donald D. Kraft	Donald D. Kraft	2008	114
191	194 2/8	24 5/8	25 2/8	23 6/8	5	5	5	5	Stanley Co., SD	Mark C. Harlow	Mark C. Harlow	2007	120
191	200	27 4/8	26 5/8	23 4/8	5 1/8	5 4/8	5	5	Fremont Co., CO	Raymond C. Swaringim, Jr.	Raymond C. Swaringim, Jr.	2007	120
190 7/8	198 6/8	25 4/8	25 4/8	19	4 4/8	4 3/8	6	6	Utah Co., UT	Donald Long	Dee W. Long	1959	122
190 7/8	201 6/8	24 5/8	24 3/8	25	5 7/8	5 6/8	7	5	Qu'Appelle River, SK	Blaine Depper	Blaine Depper	2006	122
190 7/8	198 3/8	27 4/8	27 4/8	27 1/8	5 3/8	5 3/8	6	5	Swift Current Creek, SK	Stacy L. Bolton	Stacy L. Bolton	2008	122
190 7/8	193 7/8	25 5/8	25 1/8	28 1/8	5 2/8	5 2/8	5	5	Elko Co., NV	Stanley A. Davis	Stanley A. Davis	2008	122
190 6/8	197 2/8	25 3/8	25 3/8	22 1/8	5	4 7/8	6	6	Sanpete Co., UT	E. Chad Johnson	E. Chad Johnson	1974	126
190 6/8	195 6/8	26 4/8	27 2/8	22 4/8	4 2/8	4 3/8	5	5	Montezuma Co., CO	Christopher L. Majors	Christopher L. Majors	2006	126
190 6/8	193 5/8	24 7/8	23 3/8	23	4 7/8	5	5	5	Rio Blanco Co., CO	William L. Boyd	William L. Boyd	2007	126
190 6/8	201 3/8	26 3/8	26 3/8	23 6/8	5 2/8	5 2/8	5	5	Sweetwater Co., WY	J.D. Hacking	J.D. Hacking	2007	130
190 5/8	198 6/8	24 4/8	24	22 1/8	4 6/8	4 5/8	6	6	Dolores Co., CO	William E. Garland, Jr.	William E. Garland, Jr.	1975	130
190 5/8	202 2/8	22 4/8	20 7/8	20	4 5/8	4 5/8	4	6	Coconino Co., AZ	Kristi S. Bennett	Kristi S. Bennett	2008	130
190 5/8	194 6/8	24 7/8	25 6/8	20 3/8	4 2/8	4 2/8	5	4	Johnson Co., WY	Jason O. Burns	Jason O. Burns	2008	133
190 4/8	208 3/8	26 5/8	26	22 3/8	4 4/8	4 5/8	7	7	La Plata Co., CO	Brandon L. Bell	Brandon L. Bell	2004	133
190 4/8	202 3/8	25 4/8	24 7/8	28 6/8	5	5	6	5	Fremont Co., CO	Devin L. Gulliford	Devin L. Gulliford	2006	133
190 3/8	197	25 3/8	24 6/8	20 7/8	5 6/8	5 6/8	5	6	Shoshone Co., ID	Justin W. Wilbur	Justin W. Wilbur	2007	136
190 3/8	196 4/8	24 6/8	24 2/8	21 4/8	4 7/8	4 6/8	5	6	Gunnison Co., CO	Lyle Smith	Randall L. Smith	1931	136
190 3/8	194 6/8	24 2/8	25 5/8	23 5/8	5	5	6	5	Adams Co., ID	Picked Up	Mike B. Brown	1992	136
190 3/8	198 5/8	25 5/8	24 7/8	20 4/8	6	6 1/8	5	6	Lake Diefenbaker, SK	Kenneth K. Johnson	Kenneth K. Johnson	2007	136
190 3/8	198 6/8	24 7/8	27 1/8	23 4/8	4 5/8	4 6/8	5	4	Eagle Co., CO	John V. LoFaro	John V. LoFaro	2009	140
190 2/8	210 5/8	27 4/8	23 6/8	21 7/8	5	4 7/8	6	7	Teton Co., WY	Patrick W. McAferty	Patrick W. McAferty	2006	140
190 2/8	191 6/8	25	25	22 2/8	4 3/8	4 4/8	4	4	Carbon Co., WY	Robert M. Walls	Robert M. Walls	2007	140
190 2/8	200 6/8	24 5/8	27 2/8	27 7/8	5 2/8	4 4/8	4	5	Pueblo Co., CO	David J. Askins	David J. Askins	2008	140
190 2/8	196 6/8	25 4/8	25 4/8	21 6/8	4 6/8	4 6/8	6	6	Mesa Co., CO	Ronald L. Petersen	Ronald L. Petersen	2008	145
190 2/8	197 5/8	24 5/8	24	18 3/8	4 7/8	4 7/8	5	6	Garfield Co., CO	Steve L. Woolsey	Steve L. Woolsey	2008	145
190 1/8	198 5/8	25 4/8	25 4/8	24	4 7/8	4 7/8	6	6	San Juan Co., NM	Raymond D. Chapman	Vernon R. Chapman	1968	145
190 1/8	213 5/8	24 3/8	24 3/8	24 4/8	4 6/8	4 6/8	7	7	La Plata Co., CO	Zachary M. Farnam	Zachary M. Farnam	2004	145
190 1/8	194 3/8	25 6/8	25 6/8	25 1/8	5 3/8	5 3/8	5	5	Peachland, BC	Jeremy Gooding	Jeremy Gooding	2005	145
190 1/8	205 7/8	23 6/8	23 4/8	19	4 6/8	4 6/8	7	6	Gunnison Co., CO	Derek R. Egbert	Derek R. Egbert	2006	145
190 1/8	194 4/8	25 4/8	25 4/8	23 3/8	5	5	5	5	Antelope Lake, SK	Dallas Leduc	Dallas Leduc	2006	145
190 1/8	217 3/8	25 6/8	25 6/8	23 5/8	5 6/8	5 5/8	8	6	Rio Arriba Co., NM	LaVonna R. James	LaVonna R. James	2007	145
190 1/8	201 3/8	26 4/8	26 4/8	25 5/8	4 5/8	4 6/8	4	5	S. Saskatchewan River, SK	Barry D. Miller	Barry D. Miller	2007	145
190	209 7/8	23 7/8	23 6/8	19 4/8	6	5 7/8	5	7	Fly Hill, BC	Michael S. Boehme	Michael S. Boehme	1994	152
189 6/8	199 1/8	26 6/8	25 7/8	25 6/8	5 2/8	5 2/8	5	6	Fergus Co., MT	Bryan L. Halpin	Bryan L. Halpin	2004	153
189 4/8	205 1/8	26 1/8	25 3/8	21 6/8	5	5	7	5	Garfield Co., CO	Tony DiGuglielmo	Tony DiGuglielmo	2006	154

MULE DEER - TYPICAL ANTLERS

Odocoileus hemionus hemionus and certain related subspecies

Final Score	Gross Score	Length of Main Beam R.	L.	Inside Spread	Circumference at Smallest Place Between Burr & First Point R.	L.	Number of Points R.	L.	Locality	Hunter	Owner	Date Killed	Rank
189 4/8	198 5/8	25 6/8	26 6/8	26 1/8	6 2/8	6 1/8	6	5	Rio Arriba Co., NM	Shannon V. Largo	Shannon V. Largo	2007	154
189 1/8	191 2/8	24 5/8	25	19 7/8	4 7/8	4 7/8	5	5	Nye Co., NV	Joseph L. Maslach	Joseph L. Maslach	1985	156
189 1/8	194	24 6/8	23 4/8	22 3/8	5 1/8	4 7/8	5	5	Jeff Davis Co., TX	Alberto Bailleres	Alberto Bailleres	2007	156
189	218 5/8	27 6/8	25 2/8	26 6/8	4 7/8	4 7/8	6	7	Jefferson Co., CO	Michael J. Griego	Michael J. Griego	1972	158
188 7/8	192	22 4/8	24 2/8	23 1/8	4 5/8	5	5	5	Sonora, MX	George C. Hein	George C. Hein	2006	159
188 7/8	191	26 4/8	25 4/8	21 7/8	5	5 1/8	5	5	Rio Arriba Co., NM	Rubena Velarde	Rubena Velarde	2007	159
188 7/8	197 4/8	23 5/8	23 7/8	20	4 7/8	4 6/8	5	5	Montezuma Co., CO	Terry R. Cook	Terry R. Cook	2008	159
188 6/8	195 3/8	27	26 6/8	24 5/8	4 4/8	4 4/8	5	6	Crooked Creek, AB	Les Riding	Gregory G. Sutley	1982	162
188 4/8	220	28 2/8	27 4/8	24 2/8	5 4/8	5 2/8	7	6	Ferry Co., WA	Charles A. Ross	Gary Thomas	PR 1945	163
188 4/8	202 6/8	27 1/8	25 6/8	18 6/8	4 4/8	4 4/8	7	7	Umatilla Co., OR	William L.Tolle	Bill Tolle	1976	163
188 4/8	190 6/8	24 5/8	24 6/8	21 2/8	4 5/8	4 6/8	5	5	Jeff Davis Co., TX	Bodie Means	Bodie Means	2006	163
188 4/8	192 4/8	26 2/8	25 7/8	28	4 3/8	4 4/8	5	5	Teton Co., WY	Stephen A. Munger	Stephen A. Munger	2007	163
188 3/8	195 2/8	25	22 7/8	23 1/8	4 4/8	4 5/8	5	5	Lemhi Co., ID	John C. Wilson	John C. Wilson	2007	167
188 3/8	194 1/8	24 7/8	24 6/8	25 1/8	4 5/8	4 6/8	5	5	Boise Co., ID	David V. Johnston	David V. Johnston	2008	167
188 2/8	192	24 2/8	25 2/8	25 2/8	4 5/8	4 7/8	5	5	Eagle Co., CO	Mike Duplan	Mike Duplan	2003	169
188 2/8	191 6/8	24 2/8	25	23 4/8	5	4 6/8	5	5	Rio Blanco Co., CO	Lawrence W. Cieslewicz	Lawrence W. Cieslewicz	2006	169
188 2/8	196 7/8	25 6/8	25 2/8	24 4/8	5 7/8	5 7/8	5	6	Delta Co., CO	Michael E. Benge	Michael E. Benge	2007	169
188 1/8	191	26 5/8	26 5/8	29 3/8	5 2/8	5 4/8	5	5	New Mexico	Ed Pediffer	Greg Anderson	1965	172
188 1/8	198 2/8	25 5/8	25 3/8	25 7/8	4 7/8	4 6/8	6	6	Sublette Co., WY	Unknown	Emmett A. Mavy	PR 2007	172
188	194 5/8	22 1/8	24 4/8	25 4/8	5 3/8	5 3/8	5	5	Las Animas Co., CO	Edward B. Hohnadel	Edward B. Hohnadel	1964	174
188	196 3/8	24 7/8	24 4/8	24 3/8	5 4/8	5 2/8	6	6	Rio Grande Co., CO	Bill Moye	Bill Moye	1979	174
188	195 1/8	26 2/8	26 2/8	27 2/8	4 2/8	4 3/8	5	5	Sonora, MX	Jason J. Gisi	Jason J. Gisi	2006	174
188	192 5/8	24 3/8	24 7/8	24 6/8	4 7/8	5 1/8	5	5	Pennington Co., SD	James L. Scull, Jr.	James L. Scull, Jr.	2007	174
187 7/8	194 5/8	27 1/8	25 5/8	28	5 1/8	5	5	5	Douglas Co., CO	Gary R. Hague	Gary R. Hague	2007	178
187 6/8	192 5/8	24 4/8	25 1/8	22	4 4/8	4 3/8	5	5	Eagle Co., CO	John J. Herzog	John J. Herzog	2005	179
187 4/8	190 5/8	24	24	22 6/8	4 6/8	4 4/8	5	5	Idaho Co., ID	Dan Comer	Dan Comer	2007	180
187 3/8	196 2/8	21 2/8	21 5/8	18 2/8	4 3/8	4 3/8	6	6	Delta Co., CO	Chris T. Thompson	Chris T. Thompson	2008	181
187 2/8	192 1/8	24 1/8	25	20 6/8	4 4/8	4 3/8	5	5	Emery Co., UT	Jay C. Bench	Robby D. Bench	1973	182
187 2/8	193 3/8	26 7/8	26 3/8	26 6/8	4 6/8	4 6/8	5	5	Grant Co., OR	Todd K. Hager	Todd K. Hager	1973	182
187 1/8	216 2/8	27 5/8	26	23	5 5/8	5 4/8	7	5	Weld Co., CO	Everett K. Thorpe	Everett K. Thorpe	1999	184
187 1/8	191 2/8	26	26 5/8	27 2/8	4 7/8	4 7/8	5	5	Ravalli Co., MT	Larry D. Reynolds	Larry D. Reynolds	2009	184
187	196 4/8	25 1/8	27	24 4/8	4 5/8	4 4/8	5	5	Gunnison Co., CO	Phillip L. Ehrlich	Phillip L. Ehrlich	2006	186

186 6/8	196 3/8	29 3/8	29 1/8	22 7/8	4 4/8	4 5/8	5	6	Boundary Creek, BC	John H. Hallstrom	John H. Hallstrom	2007	187
186 6/8	214 3/8	25 5/8	24 4/8	24 7/8	5 7/8	6 1/8	8	7	Coconino Co., AZ	L. Richard Pope	L. Richard Pope	2007	187
186 6/8	201 2/8	25 6/8	26 6/8	25 4/8	5 4/8	5 4/8	5	6	Elko Co., NV	Brady D. Shippy	Brady D. Shippy	2007	187
186 5/8	189 4/8	25 4/8	25 4/8	24 7/8	5 6/8	5 5/8	5	5	Frenchman River, SK	Scott Douglas	Scott Douglas	2007	190
186 5/8	194 1/8	27	25 2/8	26 7/8	4 6/8	4 6/8	5	6	Eagle Co., CO	Christopher J. Fedrizzi	Christopher J. Fedrizzi	2008	190
186 4/8	204 3/8	25 1/8	23 4/8	21 2/8	5 6/8	5 4/8	5	6	Rosebud Co., MT	David L. Bacon	David L. Bacon	1975	192
186 4/8	189 3/8	22 7/8	23 4/8	18 2/8	4 6/8	4 6/8	5	5	Rosebud Co., MT	Thomas J. Frane	Thomas J. Frane	2006	192
186 4/8	197 3/8	26	23 7/8	21 5/8	5	5 3/8	5	6	San Miguel Co., CO	Christian Huntington	Christian Huntington	2006	192
186 3/8	200 3/8	25 6/8	25 2/8	22 2/8	5 4/8	5 4/8	6	5	Sounding Creek, AB	John B. Powell	John B. Powell	2006	195
186 3/8	189 4/8	22 4/8	22 2/8	19 7/8	4 4/8	4 4/8	5	5	Boise Co., ID	Neil M. Hunter	Neil M. Hunter	2007	195
186 3/8	189 5/8	23 6/8	24 6/8	24 5/8	5 4/8	4 7/8	5	5	Carbon Co., UT	Christopher Marinelli	Christopher Marinelli	2008	195
186 2/8	195 6/8	24 2/8	24 2/8	24 3/8	5 4/8	5 6/8	7	5	Custer Co., CO	Anthony C. Martinez	Anthony C. Martinez	2006	198
186 1/8	190 5/8	23 3/8	23	29	5 5/8	5 4/8	5	5	Las Animas Co., CO	Dean D. Duran	Dean D. Duran	2007	199
186	194 4/8	24 4/8	24 2/8	19 3/8	5	5 1/8	6	5	Garfield Co., CO	Timothy J. Ashcroft	Timothy J. Ashcroft	2005	200
185 7/8	190 4/8	25 5/8	23 4/8	19 7/8	5 3/8	5	5	6	Platte Co., WY	Robert J. Bustos, Jr.	Robert J. Bustos, Jr.	2005	201
185 7/8	194 6/8	23 7/8	23 5/8	21 2/8	5	5 1/8	5	5	Rio Arriba Co., NM	Everett F. Wisener	Everett F. Wisener	2007	201
185 6/8	192 6/8	24 4/8	24 3/8	26 6/8	4 7/8	4 6/8	5	6	San Juan Co., NM	Eric J. Thornton	Eric J. Thornton	2007	203
185 4/8	198 2/8	23 6/8	24 6/8	25 1/8	4 7/8	4 7/8	6	6	Sonora, MX	Grady L. Miller	Grady L. Miller	2006	204
185 4/8	193 3/8	23 4/8	23 4/8	22	4 6/8	4 5/8	6	5	Mohave Co., AZ	Stanley W. Gaines	Stanley W. Gaines	2008	204
185 3/8	189 4/8	24	23 3/8	22 1/8	4 7/8	5	5	5	Lincoln Co., WY	Mike J. Coelho	Mike J. Coelho	2004	206
185 3/8	193 4/8	24 7/8	23 1/8	19 6/8	5 2/8	5 2/8	6	5	Battle River, AB	William A. Stock	William A. Stock	2007	206

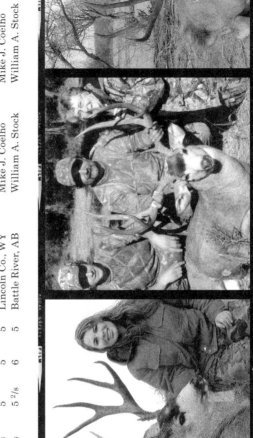

TYPICAL MULE DEER
FINAL SCORE: 191 7/8
HUNTER: Paul M. Dickson, Jr.

TYPICAL MULE DEER
FINAL SCORE: 181 4/8
HUNTER: Kelsey M. Seidle

TYPICAL MULE DEER
FINAL SCORE: 194 4/8
HUNTER: Jack M. Lowenstein

TYPICAL MULE DEER
FINAL SCORE: 193 3/8
HUNTER: Dennis D. Winch

MULE DEER - TYPICAL ANTLERS

Odocoileus hemionus hemionus and certain related subspecies

Final Score	Gross Score	Length of Main Beam R.	L.	Inside Spread	Circumference at Smallest Place Between Burr & First Point R.	L.	Number of Points R.	L.	Locality	Hunter	Owner	Date Killed	Rank
185 3/8	193 6/8	26 4/8	25 3/8	24 5/8	5 1/8	4 7/8	5	6	Rio Arriba Co., NM	William L. Nash	William L. Nash	2008	206
185 3/8	192 5/8	24	25 3/8	26 1/8	4 3/8	4 3/8	4	5	Taos Co., NM	Mark D. Smith	Mark D. Smith	2008	206
185 2/8	197 2/8	26 1/8	24 2/8	22 1/8	4 2/8	4 4/8	6	5	Fremont Co., CO	Joe H. Chess	Danny J. Chess	1961	210
185 2/8	196 7/8	24 4/8	24 7/8	22 1/8	4 6/8	4 6/8	6	6	Gunnison Co., CO	James P. Graf	James P. Graf	2004	210
185 1/8	188 1/8	24 1/8	24	22 3/8	5 2/8	5 1/8	5	5	Coconino Co., AZ	Jeremy A. Bohn	Jeremy A. Bohn	2007	212
185 1/8	205 7/8	27 7/8	27 5/8	26 3/8	4 5/8	4 6/8	6	6	Otero Co., CO	Ronald D. Pearce	Ronald D. Pearce	2007	212
185 1/8	198 3/8	26	25 2/8	24 6/8	5	4 5/8	6	6	Coconino Co., AZ	Andy J. Cast	Andy J. Cast	2008	212
185 1/8	188	24 3/8	25 1/8	22 7/8	4 7/8	4 7/8	5	6	Garfield Co., UT	Gary A. Durfee	Gary A. Durfee	2008	212
185	198 4/8	24 5/8	25 3/8	25	4 5/8	4 7/8	6	6	Grand Co., UT	Kevin G. Thayn	Kevin G. Thayn	2006	216
185	189 6/8	24 7/8	25 6/8	27	4 6/8	4 6/8	5	6	St. Mary River, AB	James M. Tardif	James M. Tardif	2007	216
184 5/8	188 4/8	25 2/8	24 7/8	19 1/8	4 5/8	4 6/8	5	5	Killarney Lake, AB	Michael T. Baker	Michael T. Baker	2006	218
184 4/8	199 2/8	23 1/8	23 7/8	22 1/8	4 3/8	4 2/8	6	7	Franklin Co., ID	Bernie C. Voyles	Bernie C. Voyles	1969	219
184 4/8	204 3/8	26 4/8	26 5/8	24 2/8	5 3/8	5 4/8	7	5	Chelan Co., WA	Michael C. Grubbs	Michael C. Grubbs	2006	219
184 3/8	186	24 6/8	24 2/8	19 3/8	4 2/8	4 2/8	5	5	Daggett Co., UT	Shaun M. Brgoch	Shaun M. Brgoch	2007	221
184 3/8	187 6/8	24 2/8	23 5/8	18 3/8	5 1/8	5 1/8	5	5	Okanogan Co., WA	Douglas A. Leese	Douglas A. Leese	2008	221
184 3/8	201 6/8	26 3/8	25	22 6/8	4 7/8	4 7/8	7	5	Montezuma Co., CO	Larry E. Thompson	Larry E. Thompson	2008	221
184 3/8	201	26 1/8	26	27	5	5	6	6	Harding Co., SD	Daniel Wright	Daniel Wright	2008	221
184 1/8	193 2/8	25 7/8	24 5/8	25 7/8	4 4/8	4 4/8	6	6	Dolores Co., CO	William C. Bain	William C. Bain	2006	225
184	187 2/8	25	25 3/8	20 6/8	4 5/8	4 6/8	5	5	Wallowa Co., OR	B.L. Zentner	Myrtle Zentner	1951	226
184	187 6/8	22	21 5/8	20 6/8	5 4/8	5 2/8	5	5	Knife Lake, AB	Robert P. Doyle	Robert P. Doyle	2006	226
184	186 1/8	24 6/8	24 5/8	21 4/8	5 2/8	5 3/8	5	5	Luck Lake, SK	John Morrison	John Morrison	2007	226
183 7/8	192 4/8	26 1/8	28 3/8	25 3/8	4 7/8	4 5/8	5	5	Meade Co., SD	James L. Feist	James L. Feist	2007	229
183 7/8	189 3/8	26 6/8	27 2/8	21 7/8	4 3/8	4 3/8	5	5	Lake Diefenbaker, SK	Tracy Preete	Tracy Preete	2007	229
183 6/8	188 1/8	24 3/8	22 3/8	20 4/8	5	4 6/8	5	5	Souris River, SK	Colby M. Halirewich	Colby M. Halirewich	2006	231
183 6/8	187	25	24 6/8	24	5	5 3/8	6	6	Haakon Co., SD	Gary Jaspers	Gary Jaspers	2008	231
183 5/8	194 2/8	23 5/8	24	22 2/8	4 5/8	4 5/8	6	6	Boise Co., ID	Michael Breske	Michael Breske	1992	233
183 5/8	213 4/8	22 6/8	23 6/8	22 2/8	5 2/8	5 3/8	6	6	Decatur Co., KS	Curtis C. Carman	Curtis C. Carman	2007	233
183 3/8	199 4/8	23 5/8	23 2/8	21 2/8	4 5/8	4 7/8	7	6	Lincoln Co., NV	Jesse W. Tatman	Jesse W. Tatman	2008	235
183 2/8	212 7/8	24 5/8	24 5/8	23 1/8	5 1/8	5 1/8	7	7	Ada Co., ID	Steve R. Kaufman	Steve R. Kaufman	1981	236
183 2/8	202	27 7/8	27	24 2/8	5	5 1/8	8	7	Eagle Co., CO	Christopher J. Fedrizzi	Christopher J. Fedrizzi	1996	236
183 1/8	187 2/8	26 7/8	26 5/8	23 5/8	4 3/8	4 2/8	5	5	Bow River, AB	Douglas C. Murray	Douglas C. Murray	2006	238
183 1/8	190 2/8	27 3/8	27 1/8	21 7/8	4 3/8	4 4/8	5	5	San Juan Co., NM	Jason A. Peace	Jason A. Peace	2009	238
183	196 4/8	25 5/8	25 3/8	27	4 4/8	4 4/8	5	7	Boise Co., ID	Kaleb L. Orcutt	Kaleb L. Orcutt	2004	240

								Locality	Hunter	Owner	Date Killed	Rank
182 7/8	206 5/8	26 7/8	24 5/8	5 3/8	5 2/8	7	6	Washoe Co., NV	Ralph R. Houk	Ralph R. Houk	2008	241
182 6/8	191	26 3/8	19	5 1/8	5 1/8	5	4	Fly Hill, BC	Albert Bianco	Albert Bianco	1972	242
182 6/8	184 1/8	26 2/8	22 4/8	4 2/8	4 2/8	5	5	Harney Co., OR	Lane A. Mastrud	Lane A. Mastrud	1986	242
182 6/8	190 2/8	24 1/8	24 6/8	5 2/8	5 2/8	6	5	Arras Creek, BC	Richard L. Huntley	Richard L. Huntley	2006	242
182 6/8	187 6/8	24 6/8	23	5	5	5	5	Elko Co., NV	Robert J. Grace	Robert J. Grace	2008	242
182 5/8	185	21 4/8	19 5/8	5 3/8	5 3/8	4	4	Park Co., CO	K.C. Woods	K.C. Woods	2006	246
182 4/8	189 1/8	21 6/8	23 2/8	4 6/8	4 7/8	5	5	Umatilla Co., OR	David L. Jarschke	David L. Jarschke	2004	247
182 4/8	192 6/8	25 3/8	24	4 7/8	5	5	5	Modoc Co., CA	Tim P. Hanna	Tim P. Hanna	2007	247
182 4/8	190 6/8	24 5/8	20 2/8	4 7/8	5	5	4	Moffat Co., CO	Nick J. Moyer	Nick J. Moyer	2008	247
182 4/8	186 3/8	22 4/8	22 2/8	4 7/8	4 7/8	5	5	Wood River, SK	Scott E. Smith	Scott E. Smith	2008	247
182 3/8	200	29 3/8	31 5/8	5	5	7	5	Custer Co., CO	Russell D. Berry	Russell D. Berry	1968	251
182 3/8	187 3/8	25 2/8	21 7/8	4 6/8	5	5	5	Chelan Co., WA	Charles E. Clayson, Sr.	Charles E. Clayson, Sr.	1999	251
182 3/8	190 4/8	25 6/8	27 2/8	5 1/8	5 1/8	6	5	Wayne Co., UT	Scott L. Grundy	Scott L. Grundy	2007	251
182 2/8	199 5/8	24 7/8	19	5 4/8	5 4/8	5	6	Chelan Co., WA	Parnell B. Joanis	Joanis Family	1947	254
182 2/8	186 6/8	26 4/8	20 6/8	5 3/8	5 4/8	5	5	Montezuma Co., CO	James M. Sparks III	James M. Sparks III	2003	254
182 2/8	187 4/8	23 7/8	18 6/8	5 1/8	4 7/8	5	5	Unknown	Unknown	David B. Van Osdell PR	2006	254
182 2/8	192 2/8	26 7/8	34 7/8	4 6/8	5	6	5	Decatur Co., KS	Steven G. Ranz	Steven G. Ranz	2007	254
182 1/8	185 2/8	23 3/8	22 1/8	4 3/8	5 4/8	5	5	Teton Co., MT	Kurt D. Rued	Kurt D. Rued	2004	258
182 1/8	200 5/8	25 1/8	25	5 4/8	5 5/8	6	5	Esther, AB	W. David Paplawski	W. David Paplawski	2006	258
182 1/8	212	27 2/8	19 4/8	4 2/8	4 2/8	6	6	Douglas Co., CO	Stephen O. Sprenger	Stephen O. Sprenger	2008	258
182	185 6/8	24 1/8	20 4/8	4 3/8	4 4/8	5	5	Shuswap Lake, BC	Terry J. Ridley	Terry J. Ridley	2008	261

TYPICAL MULE DEER
FINAL SCORE: 180
HUNTER: Slade S. Sanborn

TYPICAL MULE DEER
FINAL SCORE: 180 7/8
HUNTER: Rodney A. Lindsten

TYPICAL MULE DEER
FINAL SCORE: 192
HUNTER: Lance M. Gatlin

TYPICAL MULE DEER
FINAL SCORE: 185 1/8
HUNTER: Jeremy A. Bohn

MULE DEER - TYPICAL ANTLERS

Odocoileus hemionus hemionus and certain related subspecies

Final Score	Gross Score	Length of Main Beam R.	L.	Inside Spread	Circumference at Smallest Place Between Burr & First Point R.	L.	Number of Points R.	L.	Locality	Hunter	Owner	Date Killed	Rank
181 7/8	184 7/8	23 5/8	23 3/8	26 4/8	4 5/8	4 6/8	5	5	Garfield Co., CO	Kevin L. Walker	Kevin L. Walker	2005	262
181 7/8	187 2/8	24 4/8	25	22 3/8	5	4 6/8	6	5	S. Saskatchewan River, SK	Dave W. DePape	Dave W. DePape	2007	262
181 6/8	206 7/8	24 5/8	23 6/8	21 2/8	5 1/8	5	6	6	Mesa Co., CO	Troy W. McCoy	Troy W. McCoy	1976	264
181 6/8	190 6/8	26 4/8	25 6/8	24 7/8	5 2/8	5 4/8	6	5	Crook Co., OR	James D. McGovern	James D. McGovern	2004	264
181 6/8	186 6/8	25 2/8	24 7/8	25 2/8	5	5	5	5	Sounding Creek, AB	William J. Whittingham	William J. Whittingham	2008	264
181 5/8	196	26	27 1/8	23 5/8	5 1/8	5 4/8	6	5	Whitebear Lake, SK	Heath Dreger	Heath Dreger	2006	267
181 5/8	184 4/8	24 3/8	24	23 5/8	4 5/8	4 6/8	5	5	Eagle Co., CO	Peter A. Franzi	Peter A. Franzi	2007	267
181 5/8	185 7/8	25 2/8	25 1/8	18 2/8	5 3/8	5 3/8	5	6	Dowling Lake, AB	Wesley D. Schuett	Wesley D. Schuett	2007	267
181 5/8	198 5/8	24 4/8	24 3/8	22 7/8	4 5/8	4 6/8	8	6	Rio Blanco Co., CO	Michael T. Martinez	Michael T. Martinez	2008	267
181 4/8	209 2/8	24 7/8	25 6/8	22 4/8	5 4/8	5 4/8	7	7	Rio Arriba Co., NM	John M. Davidson	John M. Davidson	2006	271
181 4/8	190	24 2/8	23 7/8	21 7/8	4 1/8	4 2/8	5	6	Berry's Creek, AB	Ken R. Fels	Ken R. Fels	2008	271
181 4/8	197 6/8	24	23 4/8	20 3/8	5	5 1/8	6	7	Bigstick Lake, SK	Kelsey M. Seidle	Kelsey M. Seidle	2008	271
181 3/8	183 5/8	24 4/8	23 3/8	22 5/8	5	4 7/8	5	5	White Pine Co., NV	Jay A. Ambrose	Jay A. Ambrose	2006	274
181 3/8	186 1/8	23 1/8	22 3/8	21 5/8	4 4/8	4 4/8	6	5	La Plata Co., CO	J. Gregory Liddle	J. Gregory Liddle	2007	274
181 3/8	186 7/8	20 7/8	21 3/8	19 5/8	4 4/8	4 4/8	5	5	Delta Co., CO	Donald E. Perrien	Donald E. Perrien	2007	274
181 3/8	211 5/8	25 3/8	25 4/8	20	5 2/8	5 3/8	7	6	Ravalli Co., MT	Remi J. Warren	Remi J. Warren	2009	274
181 2/8	211 2/8	25 5/8	25 3/8	23 1/8	5 5/8	5 4/8	5	8	Soda Springs, ID	Unknown	Curtis P. Smiley	PR 1999	278
181 2/8	192 7/8	25 3/8	23 4/8	18 4/8	4 2/8	4 1/8	6	5	Eagle Co., CO	Mike Duplan	Mike Duplan	2004	278
181 2/8	206 6/8	28	27 7/8	25 5/8	5 2/8	5 3/8	8	7	Montezuma Co., CO	Bryan E. Lewis	Bryan E. Lewis	2005	278
181 2/8	184	23 7/8	25	23 6/8	4 6/8	4 6/8	7	5	Frenchman River, SK	Keegan D. Lafrentz	Keegan D. Lafrentz	2007	278
181 2/8	185 5/8	24 6/8	23 1/8	21 2/8	4 5/8	4 5/8	4	4	Grand Co., CO	Gary A. Durfee	Gary A. Durfee	2008	278
181 1/8	211 2/8	29 3/8	30 5/8	29 6/8	5 5/8	6 2/8	7	6	Utah Co., UT	James C. Grace	James C. Grace	1960	283
181 1/8	187	23 5/8	24 3/8	20 5/8	5	4 7/8	6	6	Lincoln Co., WY	V. Ronald Mancuso	V. Ronald Mancuso	2007	283
181	189 2/8	24 4/8	23 5/8	19 6/8	4 3/8	4 3/8	6	6	Goshen Co., WY	Joe R. Davis	Joe R. Davis	2007	285
180 7/8	183 4/8	23 5/8	24 1/8	20 5/8	5	5	5	5	Lemhi Co., ID	S. Blaine Grover	S. Blaine Grover	1987	286
180 7/8	185	25 2/8	24 1/8	21 7/8	4 7/8	4 6/8	5	5	Soles Creek, BC	Leonard A. Benty	Leonard A. Benty	2006	286
180 7/8	193	24	25	21 5/8	4 6/8	5 1/8	6	6	Cheyenne Co., KS	Rodney A. Lindsten	Rodney A. Lindsten	2008	286
180 6/8	192 5/8	24 3/8	24	23 6/8	5 1/8	5 2/8	5	5	White Pine Co., NV	Emilee A. Almberg	Emilee A. Almberg	2006	289
180 6/8	186 7/8	24	26 3/8	25	5 2/8	4 6/8	4	4	Grant Co., OR	Joan L. Larson	Joan L. Larson	2007	289
180 5/8	184	25 2/8	25 5/8	24 7/8	5	5	4	5	Coconino Co., AZ	David M. Britt	David M. Britt	2006	291
180 5/8	182 2/8	23 2/8	23 5/8	21 1/8	5 1/8	5 1/8	5	5	Bone Creek, SK	Lawrence J. Hansen	Lawrence J. Hansen	2006	291

Score									Locality	Owner	Hunter	Year	Rank
180 5/8	207 1/8	26 3/8	25 1/8	22 4/8	5 2/8	5	6	7	Rio Arriba Co., NM	Eric K. Ritter	Eric K. Ritter	2007	291
180 4/8	188	24 5/8	23 7/8	21 2/8	4 7/8	5	5	6	La Plata Co., CO	Scott R. DeBolt	Scott R. DeBolt	2006	294
180 4/8	186	26 4/8	25 5/8	28 3/8	5 4/8	5 3/8	5	5	San Juan Co., NM	Ted A. Black	Ted A. Black	2007	294
180 4/8	206 4/8	24	24	23 6/8	4 7/8	5 2/8	6	7	Gunnison Co., CO	Hunter S. Holmes	Hunter S. Holmes	2007	294
180 3/8	182 5/8	25 2/8	25 2/8	23 1/8	4 6/8	4 6/8	5	5	Red Deer River, AB	Darrell B. Schuett	Darrell B. Schuett	1991	297
180 3/8	192 5/8	22 5/8	25 6/8	30 6/8	5 5/8	5 3/8	6	5	Coconino Co., AZ	Joseph O. Spellman	Joseph O. Spellman	2005	297
180 3/8	187 2/8	24 1/8	24 3/8	29	4 6/8	4 6/8	4	5	Rio Blanco Co., CO	John C. Ward	John C. Ward	2006	297
180 3/8	182 2/8	25	24 7/8	23 5/8	4 7/8	5	5	5	Beaton River, BC	Jeremy Beliveau	Jeremy Beliveau	2008	297
180 3/8	183 5/8	24 5/8	24 6/8	22 3/8	4 4/8	4 6/8	5	5	Lincoln Co., NV	Joe R. Bennett	Joe R. Bennett	2008	297
180 3/8	204 2/8	25 7/8	25 6/8	19 5/8	4 5/8	4 5/8	7	6	Carbon Co., WY	Jnell L. Raymond	Jnell L. Raymond	2009	297
180 2/8	189 6/8	23 2/8	23	20 3/8	5 1/8	5 2/8	5	7	Custer Co., MT	Eric S. Siegfried	Eric S. Siegfried	2007	303
180 2/8	189 3/8	23 5/8	23 4/8	23 4/8	4 2/8	4 4/8	6	5	Chelan Co., WA	Aaron D. Bessonette	Aaron D. Bessonette	2008	303
180 2/8	195 5/8	24	23 4/8	19	5	5 1/8	6	5	Conejos Co., CO	Kyle C. Lopez	Kyle C. Lopez	2009	303
180 1/8	187 6/8	23 3/8	23 5/8	21 5/8	4 5/8	4 4/8	6	5	Coconino Co., AZ	Michael J. Blanchard	Michael J. Blanchard	2006	306
180 1/8	192	22 6/8	24 2/8	26 5/8	5	5	5	5	Lindale, AB	Jessica A. Prysko	Jessica A. Prysko	2008	306
180	183 2/8	24 2/8	23 6/8	20 4/8	5 2/8	5 3/8	5	5	Park Co., CO	Keeley H. Smith	Keeley H. Smith	2006	308
180	188 1/8	24 3/8	25 5/8	22 4/8	4 4/8	4 2/8	6	6	Lemhi Co., ID	Morgan J. Dingman	Morgan J. Dingman	2007	308
180	182 4/8	25 5/8	25 4/8	22 2/8	4 6/8	4 7/8	5	5	Souris River, SK	Marty R. Jordens	Marty R. Jordens	2007	308
180	191 4/8	24 4/8	23 5/8	22 5/8	5 4/8	5 4/8	5	7	Wasco Co., OR	Court R. Priday	Court R. Priday	2007	308
180	193	23 6/8	23 5/8	21 1/8	5 2/8	5 3/8	5	6	White Pine Co., NV	Slade S. Sanborn	Slade S. Sanborn	2007	308
180	187 5/8	23 5/8	23 5/8	22	5 6/8	5 6/8	6	5	Dolores Co., CO	Levi R. Sexton	Levi R. Sexton	2007	308
205 7/8*	217 6/8	25 6/8	26	25 6/8	5 3/8	5 4/8	7	5	Eagle Co., CO	Mike Duplan	Mike Duplan	2006	308
204 1/8*	206 2/8	26 3/8	26 4/8	22 7/8	4 4/8	4 6/8	5	5	Sonora, MX	Don M. Raddon	Don M. Raddon	2006	308

Final score subject to revision by additional verifying measurements.

MULE DEER - NON-TYPICAL ANTLERS

Odocoileus hemionus hemionus and certain related subspecies

Minimum Score 215

World's Record 355 2/8

Final Score	Gross Score	Length of Main Beam R.	L.	Inside Spread	Circ. at Smallest Place Between Burr & First Point R.	L.	Number of Points R.	L.	Locality	Hunter	Owner	Date Killed	Rank
306 3/8	311 2/8	26 3/8	27 3/8	21 7/8	5 2/8	5 1/8	26	17	Douglas Co., CO	Kyle Lopez	Kyle Lopez	2007	1
289 2/8	296 3/8	25 4/8	23 4/8	27 6/8	8	7 2/8	14	17	Unknown	Unknown	Cabela's Inc.	PR 2009	2
274 4/8	280 5/8	28 6/8	29	21 1/8	5	5 1/8	12	12	Lincoln Co., MT	Andrew Keim	Cabela's, Inc.	1978	3
271	279	22 6/8	21 5/8	20	4 4/8	4 5/8	14	15	Teller Co., CO	Bill Pannell	Jim Stout	1986	4
261 1/8	266 4/8	25	26 1/8	22 4/8	5 3/8	5 3/8	13	14	Wyoming	Garth Larkin	Kirk Stroda	1963	5
260 5/8	265 5/8	23 6/8	24 3/8	22 7/8	5 6/8	5 6/8	12	12	Valley Co., ID	Cecil E. Vassar	Dale Deitrick	1944	6
259 7/8	264 3/8	24 7/8	25 1/8	23 4/8	4 4/8	4 4/8	14	10	Yuma Co., CO	Gary D. Newton	Gary D. Newton	2007	7
258 5/8	265 3/8	25 3/8	26 4/8	21 2/8	4 7/8	4 4/8	8	10	Gem Co., ID	George H. Super	George H. Super	1941	8
256 7/8	261	23 2/8	23 2/8	22 4/8	5 3/8	5 3/8	13	14	Park Co., WY	Robert C. Buchanan	Robert Buchanan	1950	9
256 3/8	262 3/8	25 6/8	24 2/8	25 1/8	5 3/8	5 3/8	11	10	Socorro Co., NM	Don Schramm	Mark E. Chavez	1972	10
254	268 6/8	21 5/8	26 4/8	27 1/8	6 6/8	5 3/8	16	12	Park Co., CO	Salvador D. Harris	Salvador D. Harris	1985	11
253 7/8	258 2/8	29 2/8	28 5/8	27 7/8	5 7/8	6	9	9	Colorado	Unknown	William D. Lancaster	PR 1980	12
252 7/8	257	27 5/8	26 7/8	20 6/8	5 3/8	5 3/8	13	15	Rio Arriba Co., NM	Picked Up	Robert J. Seeds	1972	13
252 6/8	259 5/8	24 5/8	26	25 1/8	6	5 4/8	10	9	Coconino Co., AZ	Ty M. DeWees	Ty M. DeWees	2008	14
252 1/8	256 5/8	27 4/8	28	27 4/8	5	5 1/8	13	9	Bannock Co., ID	Howard Criddle	Scott W. Criddle	1953	15
252	255 1/8	25	25 6/8	22 4/8	5 6/8	5 6/8	12	10	Colorado	Stan Jacobsen	Christopher J. Trapnell	PR 1970	16
251 3/8	257 4/8	26 1/8	26 7/8	23 7/8	5 5/8	5 6/8	10	12	Eagle Creek, SK	Darryl B. McGladdery	Darryl B. McGladdery	2007	17
250 1/8	253 4/8	24 4/8	24	23 3/8	5 1/8	5 1/8	10	13	Colorado	Unknown	Christopher J. Trapnell	PR 1980	18
250	255 3/8	27	25	30 5/8	5 4/8	5 3/8	7	9	Bear Lake Co., ID	Henry H. DeValcour	Mark Davis	1947	19
249 6/8	255 6/8	28 2/8	27 7/8	27 2/8	4 6/8	5	11	12	Bonneville Co., ID	James C. Smith	James C. Smith	2007	20
249 4/8	256 3/8	28	29 2/8	25	5	5	13	9	Duchesne Co., UT	Sherman Sorenson	Jay Sorenson	1962	21
248 1/8	253 6/8	24 4/8	24 6/8	20 6/8	5	4 7/8	12	12	Oregon	Unknown	William D. Lancaster	PR 2007	22
247 5/8	258 3/8	34 5/8	30 1/8	25 3/8	6	6	11	7	Sevier Co., UT	Fredie Molocker	Cody Butterfield	1972	23
246 1/8	252 4/8	27 3/8	27 3/8	29	5 4/8	5 4/8	11	9	Coconino Co., AZ	Ted Riggs	Clay Simon	1942	24
245 5/8	254 5/8	27	24 6/8	27 6/8	5 4/8	5 4/8	12	11	Elmore Co., ID	Ralph G. McGrath	Ralph G. McGrath	1962	25
245	255 1/8	24	24 7/8	18 6/8	5 2/8	5 5/8	13	12	Pend Oreille Co., WA	Richard Brown	K. & C.N. Lewis	1940	26
244 4/8	250 2/8	25 1/8	25 7/8	20 6/8	5	5	10	7	Kyle, SK	Dean Schill	Dean Schill	2008	27
243 6/8	249 5/8	24 2/8	26 5/8	24	4 6/8	4 5/8	11	13	Wyoming	Unknown	William D. Lancaster	2008	28
243 5/8	250 5/8	21	22 1/8	16 5/8	4 7/8	4 7/8	10	9	Eagle Co., CO	Ignacio Archibeque	Ignacio Archibeque	2007	29

242 4/8	248	25 6/8	25 1/8	5 2/8	5 3/8	15	10	Outlook, SK	Jordan B. Phillips	Jordan B. Phillips	2007	30
242 3/8	244 3/8	24	21 7/8	4 6/8	4 4/8	11	14	Pocatello, ID	Unknown	Christopher J. Trapnell	PR 1960	31
242 1/8	245 4/8	25 5/8	22 7/8	5 4/8	5 2/8	8	10	Payette Co., ID	Harold Schmelzer	Christopher J. Trapnell	1977	32
241 3/8	249 5/8	28 3/8	32 2/8	5 5/8	5 6/8	9	11	Utah Co., UT	Pierre A. Moynier, Jr.	John Moynier	1958	33
241 3/8	252 5/8	23 5/8	24 6/8	5 6/8	6	14	11	Owyhee Co., ID	Lance Gardner	Christopher J. Trapnell	PR 1980	33
241 3/8	244	26	24 4/8	5 1/8	5	10	9	Rio Arriba Co., NM	John J. Gisi	John J. Gisi	2008	33
240 2/8	246 6/8	24	23 5/8	5	4 6/8	13	11	Pocatello, ID	Unknown	Christopher J. Trapnell	PR 1960	36
239	242 4/8	26 1/8	27 2/8	5 3/8	5 4/8	7	8	Mohave Co., AZ	Picked Up	Steven D. Monk	2003	37
239	243 4/8	26 4/8	28	4 6/8	4 6/8	11	9	Routt Co., CO	Richard W. Freeman	Richard W. Freeman	2007	37
238 7/8	242 5/8	21 6/8	20 2/8	5 2/8	5	13	11	Bannock Co., ID	Michael W. Hughes	William D. Lancaster	1983	39
238 6/8	246	25 3/8	26 2/8	5 7/8	6 2/8	13	9	Phillips Co., CO	Roger L. Gordon	Cabela's, Inc.	1989	40
238 6/8	244	25 4/8	26 2/8	6 1/8	6 1/8	15	12	Emery Co., UT	Guy C. Webster	Guy C. Webster	2007	40
238 5/8	243 7/8	27 6/8	24 2/8	4 7/8	5 1/8	9	9	Teton Co., MT	W.H. Stucker	William D. Lancaster	1931	42
238 5/8	245 6/8	26 1/8	22 4/8	5 1/8	5 2/8	9	17	Archuleta Co., CO	Tom A. Watson	Tom A. Watson	1977	42
238 4/8	247	22 5/8	19 3/8	5 2/8	6 1/8	11	11	Reed Lake, SK	Greg D. Illerbrun	Greg D. Illerbrun	2007	44
238 3/8	244 3/8	25 1/8	21 6/8	5 6/8	5 3/8	10	10	Rio Blanco Co., CO	William J. deVergie	William J. deVergie	2008	45
238	242 4/8	27 2/8	27 4/8	6 3/8	6 2/8	8	8	Rio Arriba Co., NM	Clifford Sandy	Clifford Sandy	1962	46
238	247 7/8	26 6/8	32 1/8	6 1/8	5 6/8	9	9	Rio Arriba Co., NM	Hayes Pitts	Hayes Pitts	1969	46

NON-TYPICAL MULE DEER
FINAL SCORE: 241 3/8
HUNTER: John J. Gisi

NON-TYPICAL MULE DEER
FINAL SCORE: 232 5/8
HUNTER: Gerry S. Imlach

NON-TYPICAL MULE DEER
FINAL SCORE: 236 1/8
HUNTER: Matthew C. Palmquist

NON-TYPICAL MULE DEER
FINAL SCORE: 243 5/8
HUNTER: Ignacio Archibeque

MULE DEER - NON-TYPICAL ANTLERS

Odocoileus hemionus hemionus and certain related subspecies

Final Score	Gross Score	Length of Main Beam R.	L.	Inside Spread	Circumference at Smallest Place Between Burr & First Point R.	L.	Number of Points R.	L.	Locality	Hunter	Owner	Date Killed	Rank
237 1/8	243 6/8	25 2/8	25 6/8	22 6/8	5 4/8	5 5/8	9	13	Noble Lake, BC	Mark D. Grant	Mark D. Grant	2007	48
236 6/8	240 4/8	24 1/8	24 3/8	18 6/8	4 5/8	4 2/8	12	10	Rosebud Co., MT	A. Jack Rosander	A. Jack Rosander	2006	49
236 5/8	242 1/8	27 2/8	25 2/8	22 1/8	5	5	11	10	Coconino Co., AZ	John Schnyder	Ron Russell	1949	50
236 5/8	245	22 4/8	24 2/8	24 5/8	5 3/8	5 2/8	10	12	Great Sand Hills, SK	Kevin R. Strunk	Kevin R. Strunk	2007	50
236 3/8	240 2/8	28 1/8	28 2/8	26 1/8	5 3/8	5 2/8	13	10	Rio Arriba Co., NM	Greg D. Vigil	Greg D. Vigil	2007	52
236 1/8	243 7/8	24	22 4/8	25 5/8	5 1/8	5 4/8	12	12	Gove Co., KS	Matthew C. Palmquist	Matthew C. Palmquist	2006	53
235 5/8	239 4/8	22 4/8	22 6/8	23 2/8	4 7/8	4 7/8	7	6	Sonora, MX	Chris W. Taylor	Chris W. Taylor	2009	54
235	241 3/8	27 3/8	26 4/8	22 7/8	6	5 7/8	7	12	Rio Arriba Co., NM	Larry Tafoya	Steve A. Trujillo	1962	55
235	239 5/8	25 7/8	24 6/8	22 6/8	5 6/8	5 4/8	9	15	Saskatchewan River, SK	Robert Penz	Robert Penz	2008	55
234 2/8	239	24 3/8	23 4/8	21 3/8	5 1/8	5 4/8	10	10	Okanagan Lake, BC	Kim Yamamoto	Kim Yamamoto	1979	57
234 2/8	238 2/8	25	25 4/8	25 6/8	5 2/8	5 2/8	11	10	Conejos Co., CO	David T. Martinez	David T. Martinez	2009	57
234 1/8	240 3/8	26 4/8	28 3/8	26 5/8	5 1/8	4 7/8	8	8	Unknown	Unknown	William D. Lancaster	PR 1979	59
233 5/8	237 5/8	25 5/8	26 6/8	23 5/8	4 7/8	5	11	10	Rio Arriba Co., NM	Leo R. Martinez	Leo R. Martinez	PR 1976	60
233 5/8	260 6/8	24 3/8	22 2/8	25 4/8	5 7/8	5 7/8	7	11	Mohave Co., AZ	James D. Hamberlin	James D. Hamberlin	2008	60
233 4/8	236 6/8	28 7/8	28	28 6/8	5 2/8	5 4/8	10	5	Wyoming	Picked Up	William D. Lancaster	PR 1990	62
233 3/8	240 2/8	25 4/8	25 6/8	25 6/8	5 2/8	5 2/8	9	9	South Dakota	Dresden Smith	Brian K. Alexander	1949	63
233 3/8	241 2/8	24	25	22 2/8	5	4 7/8	9	10	Coconino Co., AZ	John L. Roach	Tom McReynolds	1953	63
233 3/8	236 7/8	22 2/8	20 7/8	22 2/8	5 1/8	5	11	11	Great Sand Hills, SK	Braden L. Stan	Braden L. Stan	2009	63
233 2/8	242 1/8	27 7/8	25 5/8	24 3/8	6 1/8	6	7	9	Banner Co., NE	Dean Cruise	Robert D. Cruise	1951	66
232 7/8	237 1/8	24 4/8	24 7/8	24 4/8	5	5 1/8	10	9	Unknown	Unknown	Christopher J. Trapnell	PR 2006	67
232 5/8	238 3/8	24	25	27 7/8	5 3/8	5 5/8	9	10	Unknown	Unknown	William D. Lancaster	PR 1985	68
232 5/8	239 4/8	23 2/8	24 5/8	21 2/8	4 5/8	4 6/8	11	13	Shrimp Lake, SK	Gerry S. Imlach	Gerry S. Imlach	2008	68
232 3/8	242 3/8	26 1/8	26 6/8	23 3/8	5 3/8	5 4/8	11	11	Lake Co., OR	T.W. Dungannon	Duane E. Dungannon	1937	70
232	237 1/8	27	27 3/8	20 2/8	5 3/8	5 3/8	7	8	Clinton, BC	Richard G. Howe	Richard G. Howe	1953	71
231 3/8	239 3/8	23 2/8	24 2/8	23 2/8	5 5/8	5 6/8	14	15	Sounding Creek, AB	Conrad H. Scoville	Conrad H. Scoville	2006	72
231 3/8	235 2/8	25 3/8	24 3/8	20 2/8	4 5/8	4 6/8	10	13	Norton Co., KS	Justin T. Hogan	Justin T. Hogan	2007	72
231 2/8	237 5/8	24 7/8	25 1/8	16 7/8	5 6/8	5 4/8	9	12	Platte Co., WY	Brady Cochran	Brady Cochran	2008	74
231 1/8	238 2/8	27 5/8	28 1/8	29	5 6/8	5 7/8	13	10	Coconino Co., AZ	Robert E. Bennett	Robert E. Bennett	1985	75
231 1/8	238 1/8	28 5/8	26 7/8	25 7/8	4 7/8	5	10	9	Lincoln Co., WY	Ryan Z. Howell	Ryan Z. Howell	2007	75

Score	Gross	Length R	Length L	Inside Spread	Circ. R	Circ. L	Pts. R	Pts. L	Locality	Hunter	Owner	Date	Rank
230 6/8	236 5/8	25 2/8	25 6/8	23	4 3/8	4 3/8	8	8	Lake Diefenbaker, SK	Jason W. Neufeld	Jason W. Neufeld	2006	77
230 4/8	237 4/8	23 3/8	24 5/8	23 7/8	6 3/8	6 4/8	12	14	Cheyenne Co., KS	David L. Nelsen	David L. Nelsen	2007	78
230 2/8	245 3/8	23	21	26 7/8	5	4 7/8	15	15	Lake Diefenbaker, SK	David N. Yonge	David N. Yonge	2007	79
228 4/8	236	27 4/8	26 7/8	25 2/8	4 7/8	4 6/8	7	7	Custer Co., CO	Jerome L. DeGree	Jerome L. DeGree	1983	80
227 7/8	233 1/8	23 4/8	23 2/8	25 3/8	5 5/8	5 5/8	11	10	Lincoln Co., NV	John K. Koster	John K. Koster	2009	81
227 1/8	230 1/8	25 2/8	25 4/8	26 6/8	4 4/8	4 3/8	10	9	Union Co., NM	Victor V. Alderette	Victor V. Alderette	2008	82
227	232 1/8	25 1/8	25 6/8	25	4 7/8	4 7/8	10	11	Penticton, BC	Picked Up	BC Ministry of Environment	2007	83
226 6/8	234 3/8	25 7/8	27 4/8	30	5	5	9	9	Yuma Co., CO	Gregory C. David	Gregory C. David	2007	84
226 3/8	229 3/8	23 4/8	23 4/8	20 7/8	5 2/8	5 2/8	11	8	Klamath Co., OR	Unknown	Randy Sandoval	1978	85
226 1/8	234 1/8	26 4/8	24 4/8	30	5 6/8	5 4/8	9	9	Treasure Co., MT	Bernice Petersen	David G. Bodi	1958	86
226	236 3/8	28 6/8	27 6/8	22 2/8	5	5	5	12	Bannock Co., ID	Dean Harding	Earl P. Basso, Jr.	1992	87
225 6/8	232 2/8	27 2/8	26 7/8	24	5 2/8	5 2/8	9	11	Adams Co., ID	Horace H. Snider	Paul L.C. Snider	1939	88
225 6/8	233	24 4/8	24 4/8	18 1/8	4 6/8	4 7/8	10	8	Park Co., WY	Paul A. Kozisek	Paul A. Kozisek	2007	88
225 4/8	229 4/8	27 2/8	27 1/8	24 5/8	5 1/8	5	11	9	Elko Co., NV	John Sabin	NV Bighorns Unlimited - Midas	1963	90
224 5/8	232 5/8	26 5/8	26 4/8	24 2/8	6	6 2/8	8	9	Rio Arriba Co., NM	Katrina Davis	Roger Orthuber	2007	91
224 2/8	231 6/8	26 3/8	26 6/8	21 2/8	4 6/8	4 6/8	6	7	Umatilla Co., OR	Ellery Alexander	Phyllis A. Heidenrich	1938	92
223 7/8	228 3/8	24 5/8	24 6/8	21	4 4/8	4 3/8	10	9	Lake Co., OR	Chick K. Brugnoli	Ron Russell	1934	93
223 4/8	228 2/8	26 2/8	26 5/8	25 7/8	5 1/8	5 1/8	8	6	Sonora, MX	Trent B. Hartley	Trent B. Hartley	2009	94
223 2/8	227 5/8	23 2/8	25	19 5/8	4 6/8	4 5/8	8	13	San Juan Co., UT	Gregory Anderson	Gregory Anderson	2007	95
223	233 2/8	27 2/8	24 2/8	25 3/8	6 7/8	7 1/8	8	10	Battle River, AB	Robert J. Klinger	Robert J. Klinger	2007	96
222 1/8	240 6/8	28 1/8	29 2/8	29 1/8	5 1/8	5 1/8	9	10	Washington Co., UT	Landon H. Frei	Landon H. Frei	1969	97
221 5/8	225 6/8	25	25	19 7/8	5	5 2/8	9	10	Jefferson Co., OR	Jeremy L. Mackey	Jeremy L. Mackey	2006	98
221 1/8	230 7/8	21 6/8	24 2/8	20 6/8	6 2/8	6 4/8	11	8	Lincoln Co., NV	Tyler D. Kearney	Tyler D. Kearney	2007	98
220 6/8	223	25 4/8	25 4/8	19 1/8	4 4/8	4 4/8	10	11	Carbon Co., WY	Kyle L. Krejci	Kyle L. Krejci	2007	100
220	227 2/8	27 1/8	27 5/8	26 2/8	4 4/8	4 7/8	9	10	Garfield Co., CO	Gerald Fedrizzi	Gerald Fedrizzi	1971	101
219 7/8	227 2/8	25	24	19 6/8	4 6/8	4 7/8	14	14	Utah Co., UT	Randy N. Parry	Randy N. Parry	1964	102
219 5/8	223 1/8	25 1/8	25 6/8	22 7/8	5 1/8	5 2/8	9	11	Unknown	Unknown	Curtis P. Smiley	PR 1960	103
219 2/8	227	25 4/8	24 7/8	27 1/8	5 5/8	5 3/8	10	9	Chaffee Co., CO	Picked Up	CO Div. of Wildl.	2005	104
219	223 5/8	27 7/8	28 1/8	28 6/8	4 6/8	4 6/8	9	10	Fremont Co., WY	Kenneth R. Bunner	Kenneth R. Bunner	1968	105
218 2/8	225 4/8	27 4/8	27 4/8	20 2/8	5 3/8	5 3/8	7	10	Custer Co., CO	Steven E. Gauvin	Steven E. Gauvin	2009	106
217 7/8	227 7/8	26	26	27 4/8	5 6/8	5 4/8	11	7	Pueblo Co., CO	Dean B. Holcomb	Dean B. Holcomb	2007	107
217 2/8	227 2/8	26 1/8	26 1/8	24 7/8	5 5/8	5 4/8	8	6	Rio Blanco Co., CO	E.J. Snydal	Rodney Snydal	1934	108
217 6/8	222 4/8	28 3/8	28 4/8	29 7/8	6	5 6/8	7	5	Fawcett River, AB	Kevin M. Jackson	Kevin M. Jackson	2008	109
217 4/8	224	24	25 5/8	25 4/8	4 7/8	5	10	8	Montrose Co., CO	Anthony H. White	Anthony H. White	2006	110
217 2/8	225 4/8	25 5/8	24 4/8	21 5/8	4 6/8	4 7/8	9	5	Bonneville Co., ID	Nathan R. Taylor	Nathan R. Taylor	1988	111
217 2/8	223 4/8	24 4/8	24 7/8	22 7/8	4 2/8	4 6/8	8	8	La Plata Co., CO	Mark R. Oakes	Mark R. Oakes	2007	112
217 1/8	222 2/8	24 7/8	23 5/8	22	5 2/8	4 2/8	8	9	Gove Co., KS	Kiara C. Sharp	Kiara C. Sharp	2008	112
216 6/8	221 3/8	23 5/8	25 2/8	24 1/8	5 1/8	5 2/8	8	8	Magrath, AB	Dustin L. Beauchamp	Dustin L. Beauchamp	2008	114
216 5/8	226 5/8	25 2/8	27 3/8	24 3/8	4 4/8	4 5/8	10	11	Unknown	Picked Up	Gregory S. Rohr	PR 1997	115
216 5/8	222 1/8	27 1/8	21 6/8	21	5 5/8	5 4/8	10	13	Cheyenne Co., CO	M. Keith Almand	M. Keith Almand	2007	116

MULE DEER - NON-TYPICAL ANTLERS

Odocoileus hemionus hemionus and certain related subspecies

Final Score	Gross Score	Length of Main Beam R.	L.	Inside Spread	Circumference at Smallest Place Between Burr & First Point R.	L.	Number of Points R.	L.	Locality	Hunter	Owner	Date Killed	Rank
216 5/8*	223 4/8	26 2/8	23 5/8	27 3/8	5 1/8	5	9	10	McKenzie Co., ND	Timothy J. Sandstrom	Timothy J. Sandstrom	2008	116
216 3/8	218 6/8	24 2/8	24 3/8	22 4/8	5 1/8	5	10	7	Jackson Co., CO	John H. Feller	John H. Feller	2007	118
216 3/8	225	27 3/8	26 1/8	22 6/8	5 1/8	5 1/8	13	8	Chelan Co., WA	Todd M. Walker	Todd M. Walker	2009	118
216 2/8	228 3/8	23 1/8	23 2/8	21 7/8	4 7/8	4 6/8	7	8	Teller Co., CO	Edward M. O'Connell	Edward M. O'Connell	2007	120
216 1/8	224 4/8	22 2/8	20 4/8	18 3/8	4 6/8	4 7/8	14	17	Sheridan Co., KS	Robert G. Brewster	Robert G. Brewster	2008	121
215 7/8	226 5/8	23 7/8	23 1/8	20 7/8	5 4/8	5 7/8	10	9	Grizzly Bear Creek, AB	Laura Begg-McAllister	Laura Begg-McAllister	2006	122
215 6/8	222 7/8	27 2/8	26 6/8	22 5/8	4 6/8	4 4/8	10	10	Idaho Co., ID	T. Leroy West	T. Leroy West	1977	123
215 4/8	219 7/8	23 3/8	23 5/8	24 3/8	5 1/8	5 2/8	8	10	Mesa Co., CO	Unknown	Randy Sandoval	1971	124
215	221 2/8	23 5/8	24 1/8	18	4 6/8	4 5/8	6	8	Garfield Co., CO	Kenneth A. Scribner	Kenneth A. Scribner	1993	125
215	222 2/8	25 5/8	28	24 5/8	5 1/8	4 7/8	10	12	Bow River, AB	Terry L. Raymond	Terry L. Raymond	2007	125
273 1/8*	280	30 4/8	29 4/8	31 2/8	5 4/8	5 3/8	9	14	Arapahoe Co., CO	Fred C. Schulz	Fred C. Schulz	PR 1986	
271 5/8*	278 3/8	26 2/8	27 1/8	22 6/8	5 1/8	5 5/8	9	11	Adams Lake, BC	Eli J. Jules	E.J. Jules & A. Ono	2006	
264 1/8*	269 7/8	27 1/8	28 3/8	23 3/8	5 6/8	5 6/8	12	11	Delta Co., CO	Mack A. Gorrod	Mack A. Gorrod	1968	
262 4/8*	271 4/8	25 5/8	25 1/8	25 1/8	5 5/8	4 6/8	13	11	Coconino Co., AZ	Jason G. Carter	Jason G. Carter	2007	
261 1/8*	273 5/8	28 1/8	29 2/8	25 2/8	6 3/8	6 2/8	19	19	Fresno Co., CA	Jordan F. Fontana	Jordan F. Fontana	2008	

* Final score subject to revision by additional verifying measurements.

COLUMBIA BLACKTAIL - TYPICAL ANTLERS

Odocoileus hemionus columbianus

Minimum Score 125

World's Record 182 2/8

Final Score	Gross Score	Length of Main Beam R.	Length of Main Beam L.	Inside Spread	Circ. at Smallest Place Between Burr & First Point R.	Circ. L.	No. of Points R.	No. of Points L.	Locality	Hunter	Owner	Date Killed	Rank
162 5/8	167 1/8	26	25	23 5/8	4 5/8	4 6/8	5	5	Humboldt Co., CA	Picked Up	Tim Pricer	1993	1
160 6/8	171 5/8	20 6/8	23	20 6/8	4 6/8	4 5/8	6	5	Shasta Co., CA	G. Bland & D. Boddy	G. Bland & D. Boddy	1962	2
160 1/8	163 7/8	21 2/8	21 3/8	19 1/8	4 6/8	4 6/8	5	5	Trinity Co., CA	Jerry L. Thissell	Jerry L. Thissell	2001	3
159 1/8	163 3/8	22 3/8	22 2/8	19 7/8	4 4/8	4 4/8	5	5	Chilliwack, BC	G.R. Baker	Debra Nelson	1947	4
156 7/8	163 7/8	25	25 4/8	15 3/8	5 5/8	5 4/8	6	5	Mendocino Co., CA	Leroy Gilley	Earl P. Basso, Jr.	1958	5
155	158 7/8	22 5/8	21 6/8	20	5 1/8	5	5	5	Mendocino Co., CA	Stan W. Martenen	Stan W. Martenen	2009	6
154 3/8	160 4/8	20 2/8	20 5/8	17	4 6/8	5 1/8	6	5	Humboldt Co., CA	Darl L. Miller	Darl L. Miller	2004	7
153 2/8	160 1/8	23 6/8	23 4/8	19 6/8	4 1/8	4	4	5	Mendocino Co., CA	Jerame R. Sutton	Jerame R. Sutton	2008	8
153 1/8	165	22 3/8	22 5/8	16 6/8	4 5/8	4 5/8	6	5	Jefferson Co., WA	Picked Up	Greg Bray	PR 1940	9
152 7/8	161	25	25	15 1/8	4	4	5	5	Thurston Co., WA	Mel Tibbetts	Stacy Tibbetts	PR 1960	10
152 5/8	159	24	24 3/8	19 1/8	4 6/8	4 5/8	5	6	Humboldt Co., CA	Corrado R. Pinochi	Corrado R. Pinochi	2007	11
151 6/8	156 7/8	23 3/8	21 3/8	19 2/8	4 2/8	4 3/8	5	5	Jackson Co., OR	Erik G. Jensen	Erik G. Jensen	2007	12
150 4/8	161 4/8	22 7/8	21 7/8	21 5/8	4 6/8	5 1/8	5	5	Jackson Co., OR	Daniel S. Miske	Daniel S. Miske	1998	13
150 4/8	154 3/8	21 7/8	20 5/8	20 6/8	4 5/8	4 5/8	6	5	Mendocino Co., CA	Harry R. Spears	Harry R. Spears	2008	13
150	155 6/8	21 7/8	21 5/8	14 4/8	3 6/8	3 7/8	5	4	Tehama Co., CA	Picked Up	Murl C. McDonald	1990	15
149 2/8	152 2/8	21	22 3/8	18	4 1/8	4 2/8	5	5	Trinity Co., CA	Terra Albee	Terra Albee	2007	16
148 5/8	153 6/8	22 2/8	22	17 7/8	4 5/8	4 5/8	4	5	Jackson Co., OR	Gary D. Kaiser	Gary D. Kaiser	2007	17
147 7/8	153 2/8	23	21 4/8	17 7/8	4 3/8	4 3/8	5	5	Humboldt Co., CA	Picked Up	Robert N. Hansen	1987	18
147 7/8	153 7/8	21 7/8	23 2/8	20 1/8	4 7/8	4 6/8	6	5	Pitt Lake, BC	Norm McLaren	Norm McLaren	1999	18
146 3/8	151 6/8	21 7/8	21 5/8	18 5/8	5	4 7/8	5	5	Siskiyou Co., CA	Richard J. Sheats	Richard J. Sheats	2006	20
146 1/8	153	20 5/8	22 1/8	16 3/8	4 6/8	4 6/8	5	5	Trinity Co., CA	Arthur E. Benedetti	Arthur E. Benedetti	2008	21
145 6/8	152 6/8	22 6/8	22 7/8	17 6/8	4 6/8	4 7/8	6	5	Trinity Co., CA	Robert E. Pitas	Robert E. Pitas	2008	22
145 5/8	149 7/8	21 6/8	23 1/8	16 7/8	6 4/8	6 2/8	5	5	Skagit Co., WA	Travis Bullock	Travis Bullock	2007	23
145 3/8	150 3/8	25 1/8	24 6/8	19 5/8	4 6/8	4 6/8	5	5	Shasta Co., CA	Sherrill W. Turner	Sherrill W. Turner	2009	24
145 1/8	147 7/8	21	20	16 5/8	4 6/8	5 1/8	5	5	Whatcom Co., WA	LeRoy C. Harkness	LeRoy C. Harkness	2005	25
144 5/8	166 4/8	23 1/8	19 5/8	20 7/8	5 1/8	5 2/8	5	8	Clackamas Co., OR	Bill Linn	Bill Linn	1960	26
144 4/8	148 6/8	22 7/8	22 1/8	17 2/8	4	3 6/8	4	5	Siskiyou Co., CA	David A. Black	David A. Black	1977	26
144 4/8	148 4/8	21 3/8	20 7/8	16 2/8	4 4/8	4 6/8	5	5	Tehama Co., CA	Dwayne S. Tiffany	Dwayne S. Tiffany	1995	26
144 2/8	148 3/8	21 1/8	21 3/8	16 5/8	5	5	6	5	Jackson Co., OR	Clifford L. Skaggs	Clifford L. Skaggs	2007	29
143 5/8	152 6/8	24	24 1/8	15 5/8	4 3/8	4 6/8	5	6	Lewis Co., WA	Greg K. Dunham	Greg K. Dunham	2007	30
143 2/8	146 4/8	22 2/8	22 1/8	17 2/8	4 6/8	4 4/8	5	5	Chilliwack Lake, BC	Matt Isaak	Matt Isaak	2006	31
143 2/8	155 7/8	21 6/8	22 2/8	16 6/8	5 3/8	5 3/8	6	5	Clackamas Co., OR	Casey P. Brooks	Casey P. Brooks	2007	31
142 5/8	145 7/8	21 4/8	21 5/8	16 3/8	4 3/8	4 2/8	5	5	Siskiyou Co., CA	William B. Quisenberry	William B. Quisenberry	1979	33

COLUMBIA BLACKTAIL - TYPICAL ANTLERS

Odocoileus hemionus columbianus

Final Score	Gross Score	Length of Main Beam R.	L.	Inside Spread	Circumference at Smallest Place Between Burr & First Point R.	L.	Number of Points R.	L.	Locality	Hunter	Owner	Date Killed	Rank
142 2/8	143 5/8	24	23 6/8	15 6/8	3 7/8	4	4	4	Clackamas Co., OR	Kelly F. Baillie	Kelly F. Baillie	2007	34
142 2/8	149 3/8	21 4/8	22	19 2/8	3 6/8	4 4/8	4	5	Trinity Co., CA	Dennis A. Nilsen	Dennis A. Nilsen	2007	34
142 1/8	151 4/8	22 5/8	22 3/8	16 5/8	5 5/8	5 7/8	5	6	Lincoln Co., OR	Merle J. Kidwell	Merle J. Kidwell	1974	36
141 6/8	150 4/8	24 2/8	24	19 2/8	4 7/8	5 3/8	5	6	Humboldt Co., CA	Picked Up	Robert N. Hansen	1997	37
141 6/8	144 6/8	20 4/8	21 4/8	18	4	4	5	5	Trinity Co., CA	Nick Albert	Nick Albert	2006	37
141 4/8	162	22 6/8	21	18	4 7/8	5	7	5	Butte Inlet, BC	Jeff W. Pollock	Jeff W. Pollock	2006	39
141 4/8	143 7/8	22 1/8	22 2/8	18 4/8	4 3/8	4 3/8	4	5	Trinity Co., CA	Andrew J. Marx	Andrew J. Marx	2007	39
141	151 7/8	22 7/8	21 4/8	15 3/8	4 7/8	5	6	5	Jackson Co., OR	Veronica C. Dominguez	Veronica C. Dominguez	2006	41
140 7/8	144 6/8	21 6/8	21 6/8	15 1/8	4 4/8	4 6/8	5	5	Jefferson Co., WA	David L. Mosier, Jr.	David L. Mosier, Jr.	2008	42
140 4/8	142 2/8	21 2/8	20 6/8	14 6/8	5 1/8	5 1/8	4	4	Jackson Co., OR	Brian K. Samuel	Brian K. Samuel	2000	43
140 1/8	144 2/8	19 3/8	19 5/8	17 7/8	4 2/8	4 4/8	5	5	Trinity Co., CA	Ryan D. Nilsen	Ryan D. Nilsen	2007	44
140 1/8	142 5/8	20 1/8	20 4/8	19 7/8	4 2/8	4 1/8	5	5	Sonoma Co., CA	Alfred H. Petersen	Alfred H. Petersen	2008	44
139 4/8	146 7/8	22 4/8	21 3/8	19 4/8	4 3/8	4 3/8	5	5	Trinity Co., CA	Kevin E. Brett	Kevin E. Brett	2008	46
139 1/8	144 7/8	22 1/8	22 1/8	19 3/8	4 1/8	4	5	6	Jackson Co., OR	Dusty S. McGrorty	Dusty S. McGrorty	2005	47
138 7/8	143 1/8	20 5/8	20 5/8	16 5/8	4 5/8	4 5/8	5	4	Siskiyou Co., CA	Loren R. Kolu	Loren R. Kolu	2006	48
138 5/8	141 3/8	21 4/8	20 5/8	18 1/8	3 4/8	3 4/8	4	4	Colusa Co., CA	Michael R. Martin	Michael R. Martin	2006	49
138 4/8	142 6/8	22 6/8	21 6/8	21 2/8	5 1/8	5	4	4	Trinity Co., CA	Dee W. Sanders	Dee W. Sanders	2009	50
138 3/8	140	22 5/8	22 5/8	21 5/8	4 4/8	4 3/8	4	4	Mendocino Co., CA	Romolo R. Corsetti	Romolo R. Corsetti	2004	51
138 2/8	142 4/8	20 2/8	20 2/8	14 4/8	4 2/8	4 4/8	4	5	Marion Co., OR	William M. Kamrath	William M. Kamrath	1981	52
138 2/8	142 6/8	20 4/8	22 6/8	16 6/8	4 1/8	4 1/8	5	4	Trinity Co., CA	Autumn Brown	Autumn Brown	2007	52
138 1/8	140 2/8	22 1/8	22 2/8	19 1/8	4 6/8	4 7/8	4	4	Humboldt Co., CA	David W. Baxter	David W. Baxter	2008	54
137 6/8	145 6/8	23	22 7/8	20 6/8	4 5/8	4 4/8	5	4	Lake Co., CA	Howard L. Mabery	Howard L. Mabery	2008	55
137 3/8	148 4/8	21 5/8	21 4/8	15 5/8	4 2/8	4 2/8	6	5	Kitimat, BC	Larry R. Zilinski	Larry R. Zilinski	1997	56
137 2/8	140 7/8	20 3/8	20 7/8	16 4/8	4 1/8	4 1/8	5	5	Marion Co., OR	Jeffrey D. Peters	Jeffrey D. Peters	2007	57
137 2/8	141 6/8	17 5/8	20	14	4 6/8	4 6/8	5	5	Lane Co., OR	Timothy J. Jones	Timothy J. Jones	2008	57
137 1/8	143 1/8	20 7/8	20 1/8	19 3/8	5	5	4	5	Mendocino Co., CA	Richard L. Valladao	Richard L. Valladao	2009	59
137	142	22 2/8	21 3/8	21	4 3/8	4 3/8	5	5	Mendocino Co., CA	Phillip A. Celador	Phillip A. Celador	2007	60
137	148 5/8	21 6/8	20 4/8	21	4 2/8	4 6/8	5	5	Mendocino Co., CA	Stavros R. Pardini	Stavros R. Pardini	2008	60
136 7/8	147 2/8	21 1/8	20 3/8	15 5/8	4 2/8	4 4/8	6	6	Mendocino Co., CA	Cliff E. Jacobson	Cliff E. Jacobson	2002	62
136 5/8	142 6/8	23 5/8	24 1/8	21 5/8	4 5/8	4 5/8	4	3	Tehama Co., CA	Michael F. Spoon	Michael F. Spoon	2006	63
136 4/8	139 2/8	21 7/8	22 2/8	16	3 6/8	3 6/8	4	4	Glenn Co., CA	John Adams	Daryl C. Adams	1954	64
136 3/8	146 7/8	23	23 3/8	18	4 4/8	4 4/8	6	5	Jackson Co., OR	Teresa M. Samuel	Teresa M. Samuel	2006	65
136 1/8	139 4/8	21 7/8	20 6/8	15 5/8	5 1/8	5	5	5	Clackamas Co., OR	Jimmie L. Bauldree	Jimmie L. Bauldree	2008	66

Score	Main Beam R	Main Beam L	Inside Spread	Circ. R	Circ. L	Points R	Points L	Locality	Hunter	Date	Rank
135 6/8	20 7/8	20 4/8	20 2/8	3 6/8	3 6/8	5	4	Tehama Co., CA	Parrey F. Cremeans	2006	67
135 6/8	20 1/8	18 6/8	19 4/8	4 1/8	3 6/8	5	5	Linn Co., OR	Kelsey A. Smith	2008	67
135 5/8	19 6/8	20 4/8	16 3/8	5	5 4/8	5	5	Trinity Co., CA	Craig L. Brown	2009	67
135 5/8	22	23 6/8	18 1/8	5 1/8	5 3/8	4	5	Thurston Co., WA	Norman F. Jensen	1984	70
135 4/8	21	21	16 2/8	4 4/8	4 4/8	5	5	Benton Co., OR	Kenneth R. Forty	2008	71
135 2/8	20 6/8	20 3/8	15 4/8	4 5/8	4 5/8	5	5	Kitsap Co., WA	Daniel L. Waldbillig	2009	72
135 1/8	20 7/8	21	16 7/8	4 7/8	4 6/8	5	5	Tillamook Co., OR	Robert E. Smith	2006	73
135 1/8	19 1/8	20 2/8	17 4/8	4 6/8	4 6/8	5	7	Clackamas Co., OR	Jason M. Wille	2006	73
135	19	19 2/8	19 3/8	4 1/8	4 1/8	5	5	Mendocino Co., CA	Cliff E. Jacobson	2003	75
135	20 3/8	20 7/8	17	4 5/8	4 5/8	5	5	Kitsap Co., WA	Cheri M. Page	2008	75
134 3/8	19 2/8	20 3/8	17 5/8	4 2/8	4 2/8	5	5	King Co., WA	H.J. Havens	1973	77
134 2/8	22 4/8	22 6/8	19 4/8	4 6/8	4 7/8	6	6	Tillamook Co., OR	Gerald S. Johnson	1988	78
134 1/8	22 3/8	21 4/8	22 6/8	4 1/8	4 2/8	4	4	Mendocino Co., CA	Eddie W. Abrao, Jr.	2008	79
133 7/8	20 5/8	21 2/8	15 1/8	4 7/8	4 5/8	4	4	Lincoln Co., OR	Tracy Hobbs	1994	80
133 6/8	18 6/8	19 3/8	16 2/8	4 1/8	4 3/8	5	5	Glenn Co., CA	Daryl C. Adams	2007	81
133 4/8	19	18 2/8	18	4 6/8	4 4/8	5	5	Jackson Co., OR	James Davidson	2003	82
133 3/8	20 3/8	19 2/8	20	4 1/8	4 1/8	5	5	Trinity Co., CA	Autumn Slote	2009	82
133 2/8	20 4/8	21 1/8	15 6/8	4 4/8	4 4/8	5	5	Humboldt Co., CA	Gary L. Mayberry	1998	84
132 7/8	20 7/8	19 7/8	22 3/8	4 3/8	4 3/8	5	4	Sonoma Co., CA	William M. Somma	2008	85
132 6/8	21 3/8	22 5/8	15 1/8	4 3/8	4 3/8	6	5	Linn Co., OR	Allan C. Merrill	1973	86
132 5/8	21 5/8	21 1/8	17 3/8	4	3 7/8	4	5	Clackamas Co., OR	J. Scott Bailey, Sr.	1997	87

TYPICAL
COLUMBIA BLACKTAIL
FINAL SCORE: 141 6/8
HUNTER: Nick Albert

TYPICAL
COLUMBIA BLACKTAIL
FINAL SCORE: 125 6/8
HUNTER: Stanley J. Schmidt

TYPICAL
COLUMBIA BLACKTAIL
FINAL SCORE: 127 4/8
HUNTER: Tessa R. Willburn

TYPICAL
COLUMBIA BLACKTAIL
FINAL SCORE: 138 1/8
HUNTER: David W. Baxter

COLUMBIA BLACKTAIL - TYPICAL ANTLERS

Odocoileus hemionus columbianus

Final Score	Gross Score	Length of Main Beam R.	L.	Inside Spread	Circumference at Smallest Place Between Burr & First Point R.	L.	Number of Points R.	L.	Locality	Hunter	Owner	Date Killed	Rank
132 4/8	138 4/8	21 1/8	21 1/8	16 2/8	4 6/8	4 5/8	5	6	Clackamas Co., OR	Kyle J. Seal	Kyle J. Seal	2006	88
132 3/8	136 6/8	19 2/8	19 6/8	15 7/8	4	4	5	5	Mendocino Co., CA	Randy R. Houston	Randy R. Houston	1971	89
132 2/8	135 6/8	19 4/8	20 4/8	15 6/8	4 3/8	4 1/8	5	5	Sonoma Co., CA	William M. Somma	William M. Somma	2006	90
132 2/8	135 7/8	20 7/8	21 1/8	14 4/8	3 6/8	3 7/8	5	5	Clackamas Co., OR	Benjamin M. Norgren	Benjamin M. Norgren	2008	90
132 2/8	139 5/8	21 1/8	19 4/8	17 2/8	4 5/8	4 6/8	5	5	Glenn Co., CA	Kacey L. Simmons	Kacey L. Simmons	2009	90
132 1/8	137 5/8	19 3/8	19	16 3/8	5 5/8	5 3/8	5	5	Lewis Co., WA	Michael D. Hellem	Michael D. Hellem	2007	93
132	138 2/8	24	23 7/8	20 4/8	4 2/8	4 6/8	3	4	Trinity Co., CA	Jerry L. Thissell	Jerry L. Thissell	2001	94
131 6/8	138	21 5/8	21 5/8	18 6/8	4 2/8	4	5	5	Clallam Co., WA	Vance Birkland	Marilyn Lewis	1987	95
131 1/8	133 2/8	21 1/8	21 4/8	14 5/8	4	4 1/8	5	5	Trinity Co., CA	Darryl G. Lovato	Darryl G. Lovato	2007	96
130 7/8	133 5/8	20 2/8	19 4/8	17 3/8	4 4/8	4 4/8	5	5	Trinity Co., CA	Donald A. Dunn	Donald A. Dunn	2007	97
130 6/8	133	19	18 4/8	14 6/8	4 7/8	4 5/8	5	5	Clackamas Co., OR	Timothy W. Faist	Timothy W. Faist	2007	98
129 7/8	132 2/8	19 6/8	19 4/8	16 3/8	4 4/8	4 4/8	5	5	King Co., WA	H.J. Havens	H.J. Havens	1984	99
129 6/8	133 5/8	20 4/8	19 4/8	17	3 6/8	3 6/8	5	5	Mendocino Co., CA	Kenneth Stanley	Kenneth Stanley	2008	100
129 4/8	133 6/8	20 4/8	20	19 6/8	4	4 1/8	4	5	Humboldt Co., CA	Ira Alexander	Ira Alexander	2007	101
129 3/8	131 3/8	22 5/8	22 2/8	17 7/8	4 4/8	4 3/8	4	5	Clackamas Co., OR	J. Scott Bailey, Sr.	J. Scott Bailey, Sr.	1992	102
129	133 3/8	19 5/8	18 7/8	16	3 5/8	3 5/8	5	4	Mendocino Co., CA	Tony Tomasi	Tony Tomasi	2004	103
128 3/8	135 7/8	20 4/8	19 2/8	14 4/8	3 4/8	3 3/8	5	4	Lane Co., OR	Alan Wassom	Alan Wassom	1966	104
128 3/8	146 7/8	16 6/8	17 4/8	13 5/8	5 2/8	4 7/8	6	7	Clackamas Co., OR	Daniel A. Strom	Daniel A. Strom	2007	104
128 3/8	132 7/8	19 3/8	19 3/8	13 7/8	4 4/8	4 2/8	5	4	Island Co., WA	Chris O. Hallberg	Chris O. Hallberg	2008	104
128 2/8	139 7/8	20 5/8	19 7/8	14 6/8	4 7/8	5	6	6	Thurston Co., WA	Stephen A. Webley	Stephen A. Webley	2008	107
128 1/8	141	20 7/8	21	15 6/8	4 5/8	4 6/8	7	5	Clackamas Co., OR	Bill Linn	Bill Linn	1955	108
128 1/8	130 2/8	19 5/8	19 1/8	18 3/8	4 3/8	4 2/8	4	4	Trinity Co., CA	Albert Burton	Albert Burton	2008	108
127 4/8	134	21	21 1/8	18 2/8	4 3/8	4 3/8	5	4	Humboldt Co., CA	Tessa R. Wilburn	Tessa R. Wilburn	2007	110
127 3/8	147 4/8	21 3/8	19 7/8	12 6/8	5 1/8	4 3/8	6	6	Yamhill Co., OR	David Foster	David Foster	1994	111
127 2/8	134	19 2/8	19 7/8	17	3 7/8	4	5	7	Mount Woodside, BC	A. Larry Kahl	A. Larry Kahl	2006	112
127	132 1/8	21 6/8	22	15 6/8	3 5/8	5 1/8	4	5	Washington Co., OR	Merle J. Kidwell	Merle J. Kidwell	1995	113
126 7/8	129 1/8	18 2/8	17 5/8	12 3/8	3 7/8	3 7/8	5	5	Douglas Co., OR	Richard L. Baumgartner	Richard L. Baumgartner	2008	114
125 7/8	135 3/8	20 7/8	21 6/8	17 2/8	5 4/8	5 4/8	5	4	Pitt Lake, BC	Nils McLaren	Nils McLaren	2006	115
125 6/8	127 3/8	21 2/8	21 6/8	16 2/8	4 2/8	4 4/8	4	4	Humboldt Co., CA	Stanley J. Schmidt	Stanley J. Schmidt	2008	116
125 4/8	130 5/8	21 2/8	21	18 4/8	5 4/8	5 1/8	4	4	Pitt Lake, BC	Steve Strobel	Steve Strobel	2006	117
125 4/8	130 5/8	21	19 7/8	15 6/8	4 4/8	4 2/8	5	4	Coos Co., OR	Robert Marchant	Robert Marchant	2007	117
125 2/8	132	22 7/8	23 4/8	18 2/8	4 5/8	4 4/8	4	4	Mason Co., WA	Misty Bloomfield	Misty Bloomfield	1981	119

125 2/8	129 6/8	19 7/8	19 1/8	15 6/8	4 2/8		5	Humboldt Co., CA	Ron Carli	Ron Carli	1997	119
125 2/8	137 4/8	17	17	13 1/8	4		6	Yamhill Co., OR	Scott P. Beaudry	Scott P. Beaudry	2009	119
125 1/8	134 5/8	22 2/8	22 5/8	18 5/8	4 2/8	4 3/8	5	Clackamas Co., OR	Michael E. Oleson	Michael E. Oleson	2004	122
125 1/8	137 4/8	19 2/8	18 2/8	15 2/8	4 2/8	4	6	Humboldt Co., CA	Tessa R. Willburn	Tessa R. Willburn	2007	122
161 5/8*	168 7/8	25 5/8	25 2/8	20 3/8	5 3/8	5 2/8	5	Clackamas Co., OR	Jeffery Barry	Jeffery Barry	2005
158 5/8*	165 2/8	23 7/8	25 1/8	19 6/8	5	5 2/8	5	Pierce Co., WA	Donald E. Fehling, Jr.	Donald E. Fehling, Jr.	2005

Final score subject to revision by additional verifying measurements.

TYPICAL
COLUMBIA BLACKTAIL
FINAL SCORE: 128 3/8
HUNTER: Chris O. Hallberg

TYPICAL
COLUMBIA BLACKTAIL
FINAL SCORE: 138 4/8
HUNTER: Dee W. Sanders

TYPICAL
COLUMBIA BLACKTAIL
FINAL SCORE: 150 4/8
HUNTER: Harry R. Spears

TYPICAL
COLUMBIA BLACKTAIL
FINAL SCORE: 132 7/8
HUNTER: William M. Somma

COLUMBIA BLACKTAIL - NON-TYPICAL ANTLERS

Odocoileus hemionus columbianus

Minimum Score 155

World's Record 208 1/8

Final Score	Gross Score	Length of Main Beam R.	L.	Inside Spread	Circumference at Smallest Place Between Burr & First Point R.	L.	Number of Points R.	L.	Locality	Hunter	Owner	Date Killed	Rank
195 6/8	200 5/8	24 1/8	24 7/8	20 6/8	5 2/8	5 2/8	8	11	Benton Co., OR	James Ball	Robert Suttles	PR 1901	1
167 7/8	172 1/8	20 3/8	21 4/8	15 3/8	4 4/8	4 3/8	12	9	Siskiyou Co., CA	Adrian R. Graves	Adrian R. Graves	2007	2
213 7/8*	218 1/8	27 4/8	27 5/8	18 4/8	4 4/8	4 4/8	9	7	Clackamas Co., OR	Gordon Johnson	Gordon Johnson	1996	
200 *	203 6/8	24 6/8	23 4/8	17 6/8	5 2/8	4 7/8	8	8	Lane Co., OR	Bernard Hadley	Glenn Hadley	1979	
179 6/8*	184 2/8	24 7/8	23 4/8	19 3/8	5 6/8	5 6/8	7	7	Skamania Co., WA	Donald Golden	Tony G. Golden	1968	
169 1/8*	179 6/8	17 6/8	22 5/8	16 6/8	4 7/8	5	6	8	Lane Co., OR	Harold Kettleson	Harold Kettleson	1969	

* Final score subject to revision by additional verifying measurements.

SITKA BLACKTAIL - TYPICAL ANTLERS

Odocoileus hemionus sitkensis

Minimum Score 100

World's Record 133

Sitka blacktail deer includes trophies from coastal Alaska and the Queen Charlotte Islands of British Columbia.

Final Score	Gross Score	Length of Main Beam R.	Length of Main Beam L.	Inside Spread	Circumference at Smallest Place Between Burr & First Point R.	L.	Number of Points R.	L.	Locality	Hunter	Owner	Date Killed	Rank
126 5/8	129 3/8	18 1/8	18 2/8	18 1/8	4 7/8	4 7/8	5	5	Prince of Wales Island, AK	Joseph R. Jeppsen	Joseph R. Jeppsen	2007	1
118 1/8	123 6/8	19 3/8	18 5/8	15 5/8	4 2/8	4 2/8	5	5	Alaska	Arthur Schulberg	Dan Schulberg	1961	2
114 7/8	117	16 6/8	16 4/8	15 3/8	3 5/8	3 4/8	5	5	Revillagigedo Island, AK	Darin L. Crayne	Darin L. Crayne	2007	3
114 6/8	118 5/8	16 7/8	17	15 2/8	4 2/8	4 2/8	5	5	Prince of Wales Island, AK	Picked Up	Robert M. Meadows	2009	4
114 5/8	118 5/8	17 5/8	17 1/8	14 5/8	4	4 2/8	5	5	Thomas Bay, AK	Rocky Littleton	Rocky Littleton	2008	5
114 3/8	118 2/8	16 5/8	17 6/8	14 1/8	4	3 6/8	5	5	Prince of Wales Island, AK	Dan Arrant	Dan Arrant	2008	6
111 6/8	114 6/8	16 6/8	17 1/8	14 6/8	3 5/8	3 6/8	5	5	Prince of Wales Island, AK	Jason R. Richmond	Jason R. Richmond	2008	7
111 3/8	118	16 4/8	16 1/8	13 3/8	4	3 6/8	5	5	Kosciusko Island, AK	Spencer P. Richter	Spencer P. Richter	2008	8
110 1/8	113 7/8	17 3/8	17 4/8	14 1/8	4 1/8	4	5	5	Portage Bay, AK	Derek J. Boice	Derek J. Boice	2006	9
108 2/8	111	16 5/8	16 4/8	15 4/8	4 1/8	4	5	5	Prince of Wales Island, AK	Tobin E. Coate	Emily Coate	2005	10
108	114 6/8	17 5/8	18 4/8	14 6/8	4	4	5	4	Prince of Wales Island, AK	William H. Welton	William H. Welton	2006	11
107 1/8	111 2/8	17 1/8	17 1/8	14 1/8	3 6/8	3 5/8	5	5	Olga Bay, AK	Daniel C. Feeney	Daniel C. Feeney	1999	12
105 1/8	108 5/8	16 1/8	16 2/8	14 1/8	3 4/8	3 6/8	5	4	Kodiak Island, AK	John T. Schloeder	John T. Schloeder	2006	13
104 5/8	115 4/8	16 6/8	15 6/8	15	4 2/8	4 3/8	5	6	Uganik Passage, AK	Stuart Barrows	Stuart Barrows	2005	14
103 7/8	106 3/8	16 4/8	16 2/8	12 7/8	3 1/8	3 2/8	5	5	Portage Bay, AK	Mike S. Vincent	Mike S. Vincent	2006	15
103 6/8	106 3/8	15	15 4/8	14 2/8	3 3/8	3 3/8	5	5	Uganik Bay, AK	Richard J. Wristen	Richard J. Wristen	2007	16
101 4/8	104 4/8	15 6/8	15 3/8	15	3 4/8	3 3/8	5	6	Uganik Bay, AK	Jeffrey E. Byrne	Jeffrey E. Byrne	2006	17
100 4/8	110 5/8	16	15 1/8	12 7/8	3 7/8	3	5	5	Prince of Wales Island, AK	John C. Burick	John C. Burick	2007	18
100 3/8	103 6/8	16 6/8	16 2/8	13 1/8	3 2/8	3 3/8	5	5	Deadman Bay, AK	William F. Gorman	William F. Gorman	2007	19
123 5/8*	127 7/8	18 2/8	18 4/8	16 1/8	4	4 1/8	5	5	Prince of Wales Island, AK	Marty J. Martinez, Jr.	Marty J. Martinez, Jr.	2006	

* Final score subject to revision by additional verifying measurements.

WHITETAIL DEER - TYPICAL ANTLERS

Minimum Score 160   *Odocoileus virginianus virginianus* and certain related subspecies   World's Record 213 5/8

Final Score	Gross Score	Length of Main Beam R.	Length of Main Beam L.	Inside Spread	Circumference at Smallest Place Between Burr & First Point R.	Circumference at Smallest Place Between Burr & First Point L.	Number of Points R.	Number of Points L.	Locality	Hunter	Owner	Date Killed	Rank
200 3/8	224 4/8	28 1/8	27 2/8	24 7/8	4 4/8	4 6/8	8	9	Stevens Co., WA	James Cartwright	Bass Pro Shops	1992	1
198 6/8	215 5/8	28 5/8	27 1/8	20 1/8	4 4/8	4 2/8	9	8	White Co., IL	Joseph B. Girten	Cabela's, Inc.	2006	2
198 1/8	201 4/8	31 1/8	30 4/8	20 7/8	5 4/8	5 3/8	5	5	Greene Co., IL	Charles Q. Rives	Charles Q. Rives	2006	3
195 5/8	212 1/8	33 6/8	33 1/8	22 7/8	6 2/8	6 1/8	8	7	Indiana	Dave Roberts	Bass Pro Shops	1985	4
193 5/8	202 5/8	28 5/8	28 3/8	23 1/8	4 6/8	4 7/8	6	5	Des Moines Co., IA	Picked Up	Jerry A. Chubb	1962	5
193 2/8	201 2/8	27 5/8	25 6/8	19 4/8	5 4/8	5 2/8	5	5	Sanborn Co., SD	Glen McClane	Maine Antler Shed & Wildl. Mus.	1948	6
192 5/8	236 3/8	30 5/8	29 4/8	20 1/8	5 2/8	5 4/8	9	12	Pushmataha Co., OK	Jason L. Boyett	Jason L. Boyett	2007	7
192 3/8	199 6/8	28 6/8	28 4/8	21 5/8	5 4/8	5 4/8	6	5	Clinton Co., OH	Kenny Pickard	Kenny Pickard	2006	8
192	206 7/8	24 4/8	26 1/8	17	5 3/8	5 1/8	6	8	Lyon Co., KS	William M. Fickling, Sr.	William M. Fickling, Sr.	2007	9
191 7/8	202 6/8	26	25 7/8	18 6/8	4 6/8	5	6	7	Ribstone Creek, AB	Jason G. Klaus	Jason G. Klaus	2007	10
191 6/8	215	29 6/8	29 6/8	18 6/8	6 2/8	6 2/8	8	6	Brown Co., KS	Samuel L. Schuetz	Samuel L. Schuetz	2006	11
191 1/8	207 1/8	27	26 4/8	18 5/8	5 3/8	5 1/8	7	6	Jefferson Co., MO	Dwayne A. Labruyere	Dwayne A. Labruyere	2006	12
190 6/8	212 2/8	28 5/8	28 7/8	20 5/8	5	5	8	7	Van Buren Co., MI	Thomas R. Britenfeld	Thomas R. Britenfeld	2007	13
190 6/8	213 7/8	22 6/8	27 3/8	22 6/8	5 5/8	6 1/8	6	5	Randolph Co., IL	Joel D. Eggers	Joel D. Eggers	2007	13
189 6/8	219	25 4/8	24 5/8	20 1/8	5 2/8	5 4/8	6	8	Battle River, SK	Glen Manners	Glen Manners	2006	15
189 2/8	195 6/8	26 5/8	26	20 2/8	6 7/8	7	6	5	Green Co., WI	Picked Up	Todd Hefty	2007	16
188 7/8	207 3/8	28	28 2/8	23 4/8	4 6/8	4 6/8	6	6	Gage Co., NE	Unknown	Gale Sup	2000	17
188 7/8	201 2/8	25 3/8	27 2/8	22 7/8	4 7/8	4 6/8	8	6	Clark Co., IL	Mark Wakefield	Mark Wakefield	2007	17
188 3/8	191 5/8	26 6/8	27	26 3/8	4 7/8	4 7/8	6	6	Dimmit Co., TX	Allen R. Branch	Allen R. Branch	2007	19
188 3/8	191 7/8	26 2/8	26 2/8	19 1/8	5	5	6	7	Houston Co., MN	Gary A. Selness	Gary A. Selness	2007	19
188	190	26 1/8	26 5/8	18 2/8	5 4/8	5 5/8	5	5	Bradford Co., PA	Fritz C. Janowsky	Fritz C. Janowsky	1943	21
187 6/8	197 6/8	29 6/8	29 4/8	20 7/8	5	5	7	5	Dimmit Co., TX	Thomas D. Friedkin	Thomas D. Friedkin	2005	22
187 4/8	199 3/8	26 4/8	26 2/8	22 7/8	4 7/8	5	7	6	Meeting Lake, SK	Dean M. Brick	Dean M. Brick	2007	23
187 3/8	200 2/8	28	28 5/8	20 1/8	4 6/8	4 6/8	6	5	Van Buren Co., IA	Randy E. Phillips	Randy E. Phillips	2000	24
187 2/8	215	27 4/8	26 7/8	21 1/8	5 5/8	5 5/8	10	8	Jefferson Co., NE	Michael D. Hansmire	Michael D. Hansmire	2006	25
187 2/8	199 5/8	25 2/8	25 4/8	17 2/8	4	4	8	7	Merrimack Co., NH	John M. Klucky	John M. Klucky	2006	25
187 2/8	226 1/8	27 4/8	28	18 1/8	5 4/8	5 4/8	9	7	Dunn Co., WI	Barry A. Rose	Barry A. Rose	2006	25
186 7/8	200	27 5/8	26 7/8	19 2/8	4 5/8	4 7/8	7	6	Bonner Co., ID	Ronald M. McLamb	Ronald M. McLamb	2001	28
186 3/8	203	29 4/8	29 4/8	19 7/8	4 6/8	4 7/8	7	9	Sauk Co., WI	Paul A. Kujak	Paul A. Kujak	2006	29
186 2/8	204 2/8	30 4/8	28 7/8	20 5/8	4 2/8	4 1/8	5	6	Randolph Co., IN	Verlin H. Hale	Verlin H. Hale	2008	30
185 6/8	190 4/8	27 4/8	27 1/8	15 2/8	4 7/8	4 6/8	7	7	Sullivan Co., MO	Kenneth L. Dunlap	Kenneth L. Dunlap	2007	31

									Location	Hunter	Owner	Year	Rank
185	196 3/8	24 2/8	23 6/8	5	5	17 4/8	7	7	Jackson Co., IL	Craig D. Ahlers	Craig D. Ahlers	2008	32
185	207	28 2/8	30	4 5/8	4 7/8	24 1/8	7	6	Geary Co., KS	Jamie C. Farr	Jamie C. Farr	2008	32
184 4/8	193 4/8	27	25 4/8	4 4/8	4 4/8	19	6	6	Kleberg Co., TX	Terence Hall	Terence Hall	2008	34
184 3/8	193 6/8	26 2/8	25	5 2/8	5 2/8	19 1/8	6	6	High Level, AB	Philip W. Friesen	Philip W. Friesen	2008	35
184 2/8	196 3/8	27 7/8	27 1/8	5	5 1/8	20 5/8	7	6	Beaver River, SK	Marktavious Smith	Marktavious Smith	2006	36
184 2/8	192 5/8	29 4/8	28 2/8	6 1/8	6	22 4/8	5	7	Williamson Co., IL	John R. Graber	John R. Graber	2007	36
184 2/8	190 1/8	27 6/8	27	5 7/8	5 4/8	19 4/8	5	5	Waukesha Co., WI	Picked Up	Thom Connelly	2008	36
184 1/8	198 7/8	24 1/8	22 5/8	4 5/8	4 6/8	21 6/8	8	5	McPherson Co., KS	Joseph R. Lichti	Joseph R. Lichti	2000	39
183 7/8	192 5/8	28 6/8	29	5 3/8	5 1/8	24 2/8	6	8	Buffalo Co., WI	Daniel J. Bernarde	Daniel J. Bernarde	2009	40
183 6/8	192 5/8	29 7/8	28 6/8	5 4/8	5 3/8	22 7/8	6	6	L'Islet, QC	Raymond Jean	Raymond Jean	1987	41
183 6/8	185 5/8	27 6/8	28	4 7/8	5 4/8	22 4/8	6	6	Woodbury Co., IA	Gary T. Roan	Gary T. Roan	2006	41
183 6/8	198 2/8	29	28 5/8	5 4/8	5 4/8	21 1/8	5	5	Menominee Co., WI	Patrick T. Roberts	Patrick T. Roberts	2008	41
183 4/8	189	24 5/8	24 5/8	4 4/8	4 4/8	19	8	7	Republic Co., KS	Randy A. Miller	Randy A. Miller	2006	44
183 4/8	204 3/8	28 1/8	27 2/8	5 4/8	4 5/8	19 5/8	8	6	Sangamon Co., IL	Wesley A. Rogers	Wesley A. Rogers	2006	44
183 3/8	194 5/8	27	26 4/8	4 6/8	5	23 4/8	6	7	Charles Mix Co., SD	Garret Mellema	Cabela's, Inc.	1966	46
183 3/8	190 2/8	25 1/8	25 6/8	6 1/8	4 4/8	20 3/8	5	5	Pike Co., IL	Jack E. Medsker	Jack E. Medsker	2008	46
183 2/8	187 3/8	25 5/8	25 4/8	5	6 2/8	22	5	6	Dodge Co., WI	Michael L. Brummond	Michael L. Brummond	2007	48
183 1/8	190 2/8	26 5/8	25 6/8	4 7/8	5 1/8	18	6	5	Buffalo Co., WI	Walter Sitka	Walter Sitka	2007	49
183 1/8	187 7/8	27 1/8	28 1/8	5 7/8	5 5/8	17 7/8	7	5	Buffalo Co., WI	Mark A. Weber	Mark A. Weber	2009	49
183	197 3/8	26 5/8	27 2/8	5 1/8	5 1/8	18 3/8	5	5	Fayette Co., IA	Kevin F. Korman	Kevin F. Korman	2008	51
182 5/8	188 7/8	26	26	5 2/8	5 3/8	19 2/8	6	5	Miller Co., MO	Brody Ash	Brody Ash	2008	52
182 4/8	186 5/8	27 4/8	27 6/8	4 6/8	4 7/8	23 3/8	5	5	Fishing Lake, SK	Ted R. Bachynski	Ted R. Bachynski	2006	53
182 1/8	189 7/8	25 6/8	25 4/8	5 2/8	5 1/8	19 5/8	5	5	Dorintosh, SK	Jocelyn Dion	Jocelyn Dion	2007	54
181 7/8	192 3/8	26 7/8	28 2/8	4 5/8	4 5/8	18 7/8	5	6	Nemaha Co., KS	Nicholas Missler	Nicholas Missler	2007	55
181 6/8	188 2/8	23 6/8	25	4 4/8	4 4/8	19 4/8	8	5	Clark Co., KS	Greg L. Pike	Greg L. Pike	2005	56
181 4/8	187 6/8	26 3/8	26 3/8	5 2/8	5 4/8	19 4/8	7	5	Mercer Co., IL	Paul J. Corken	Paul J. Corken	2003	57
181 2/8	183 5/8	28 1/8	28 1/8	4 5/8	4 5/8	20 4/8	5	5	Licking Co., OH	Ronald E. Houdeshell	Ronald E. Houdeshell	2006	58
181 2/8	194 1/8	27 5/8	26 4/8	4 6/8	5	20 2/8	5	6	Lincoln Co., NE	Mark L. Christensen	Mark L. Christensen	2008	58
181 2/8	193 5/8	25 5/8	25 1/8	6	5 7/8	21 2/8	6	7	Wilkin Co., MN	James H. Komestakes	James H. Komestakes	2008	58
181 1/8	192	26 2/8	26 1/8	5 3/8	5 3/8	21 4/8	7	6	Elkhorn, MB	Nelson M. Farias	Nelson M. Farias	2008	61
180 7/8	197 3/8	25 4/8	27 1/8	5 6/8	5 4/8	18 7/8	5	7	Ottawa Co., KS	Jeffrey A. Crayton	Jeffrey A. Crayton	2007	62
180 6/8	194 6/8	29 7/8	28 7/8	6	5 5/8	22 4/8	6	5	Cannington Lake, SK	Kent T. Brown	Kent T. Brown	2006	63
180 6/8	197 2/8	25 1/8	25 3/8	4 7/8	5	19 4/8	7	7	Pike Co., KY	Larry R. Walters	Larry R. Walters	2006	63
180 4/8	184 4/8	27 5/8	27 4/8	5	5	20 4/8	5	5	Bear Hills, SK	Troy R. McCarty	Troy R. McCarty	2001	65
180 4/8	194 2/8	25 5/8	26 5/8	5 4/8	5 4/8	21 5/8	8	7	Breathitt Co., KY	Thomas P. Oaks	Thomas P. Oaks	2007	65
180 4/8	195 3/8	26 7/8	26 2/8	4 4/8	4 5/8	20 1/8	8	6	Harrison Co., MO	Troy Brafford	Troy Brafford	2008	65
180 4/8	196 3/8	29 2/8	28 2/8	5 7/8	5 5/8	21 7/8	6	6	Pierce Co., WI	Scott A. Kruse	Scott A. Kruse	2008	65
180 2/8	185 2/8	23 6/8	23 6/8	4 2/8	4 5/8	17 4/8	6	6	Lawrence Co., SD	Bat Ridley	Clint & Tee Ridley	1957	69
180 2/8	185 1/8	25 5/8	24 7/8	4 7/8	4 7/8	23 6/8	6	5	N. Battleford, SK	Mike Popelka	Diane Popelka	2005	69
180 2/8	185 1/8	29 4/8	28 4/8	5	5	21	5	5	Preble Co., OH	Timothy W. Grigsby	Timothy W. Grigsby	2007	69
180 2/8	203 7/8	28 4/8	28 2/8	5 2/8	5 1/8	24 2/8	6	6	Hubbard Co., MN	Picked Up	Warren Wilcox	2008	69
180 1/8	186 4/8	25	25 5/8	5	4 7/8	22 1/8	6	5	Webb Co., TX	Richard L. Jonas	Richard L. Jonas	2008	73

WHITETAIL DEER - TYPICAL ANTLERS

Odocoileus virginianus virginianus and certain related subspecies

Final Score	Gross Score	Length of Main Beam R.	L.	Inside Spread	Circumference at Smallest Place Between Burr & First Point R.	L.	Number of Points R.	L.	Locality	Hunter	Owner	Date Killed	Rank
180 1/8	191 1/8	27 1/8	27 1/8	19 4/8	5	5	6	5	Washington Co., KS	Mark C. MacNeil	Mark C. MacNeil	2008	73
180 1/8	193 2/8	30 4/8	27 6/8	25 1/8	5 6/8	5 3/8	6	6	Clermont Co., OH	Richard D. Kendle	Richard D. Kendle	2009	73
180	189 1/8	26 2/8	26 7/8	20	4 4/8	4 5/8	5	6	Brown Co., IN	Randall S. Dorton	Randall S. Dorton	2002	76
180	186 6/8	24 2/8	22 6/8	18	5	4 6/8	6	6	Maverick Co., TX	Ryan Friedkin	Ryan Friedkin	2006	76
180	187 3/8	29 4/8	29 7/8	22 4/8	5 2/8	5 2/8	6	6	Breathitt Co., KY	Brandon C. Henson	Brandon C. Henson	2006	76
180	207 5/8	29 7/8	29 2/8	19 1/8	5 3/8	5 4/8	9	9	Linn Co., IA	Kevin L. McDonald	Kevin L. McDonald	2007	76
179 7/8	191 6/8	25 4/8	25 6/8	17 3/8	5	5	7	6	Posey Co., IN	Terry W. Gibbs	Terry W. Gibbs	2006	80
179 7/8	193 2/8	25 5/8	25 7/8	21 6/8	5 6/8	5 3/8	6	6	Pine Lake, AB	James D. Jewell	James D. Jewell	2007	80
179 6/8	188 1/8	25 7/8	27 2/8	19 2/8	5 6/8	5 2/8	6	5	Hamilton Co., IL	Kevin E. Tinsley	Kevin E. Tinsley	2006	82
179 6/8	185 1/8	25 2/8	25 4/8	18 2/8	5 2/8	5 2/8	5	6	Iron Co., WI	Ronald J. Macak	Ronald J. Macak	2008	82
179 5/8	184 4/8	23 1/8	23 2/8	17 1/8	4 6/8	4 7/8	6	6	Shawano Co., WI	Russell R. Huebner	Russell R. Huebner	2006	84
179 5/8	193	24	24 3/8	18 1/8	5	5 1/8	6	6	Calhoun Co., IL	Joshua Brunaugh	Joshua Brunaugh	2007	84
179 5/8	186 5/8	26 7/8	27	20 5/8	4 3/8	4 4/8	6	6	Lincoln Co., WI	Kevin L. Kottke	Kevin L. Kottke	2007	84
179 5/8	185 3/8	26 6/8	25 4/8	20 3/8	4 7/8	4 7/8	5	5	Ford Co., KS	Anthony W. Stegman	Anthony W. Stegman	2008	84
179 4/8	183 2/8	26 6/8	25	22 2/8	4 7/8	4 7/8	5	5	Pratt Co., KS	Larry D. Honeman	Larry D. Honeman	2004	88
179 4/8	186 4/8	28 4/8	28 5/8	16 4/8	4 6/8	4 6/8	5	5	Ellsworth Co., KS	James S. Willems	James S. Willems	2007	88
179 4/8	185 6/8	27 1/8	26 5/8	19 4/8	5	5	6	5	Bear Hills, AB	George Flint	George Flint	2008	88
179 3/8	184 3/8	27 5/8	28 4/8	21 2/8	5 3/8	5 3/8	6	5	Clearwater Co., MN	Chad J. Fisher	Chad J. Fisher	2007	91
179 3/8	184 3/8	24 1/8	24 4/8	18	5	5	5	6	Texas Co., OK	Dane A. Weippert	Dane A. Weippert	2007	91
179 2/8	207	26 2/8	26	21 2/8	5 4/8	5 4/8	7	7	Whitesand Lake, SK	F.L. Hendrickson & D.S. White	F.L. Hendrickson & D.S. White	1985	93
179 2/8	205 2/8	25 7/8	24 7/8	21 4/8	6 2/8	5 7/8	6	7	Clark Co., MO	Tom Regot	J. Mark Arevalo	2006	93
179 2/8	184 5/8	26 2/8	26 1/8	22 2/8	4 6/8	4 6/8	5	5	Marion Co., IA	Bob Harsin	Bob Harsin	2007	93
179 1/8	184 1/8	26 2/8	27 3/8	18 3/8	5 5/8	5 5/8	5	5	Morgan Co., IL	Terry J. Day	Terry J. Day	2006	96
179 1/8	188 2/8	25 4/8	25 2/8	17	5 3/8	5 2/8	6	7	Wells Co., ND	Dustin J. Schander	Dustin J. Schander	2006	96
179	189 1/8	25 4/8	26	17 6/8	5	4 6/8	6	6	Pike Co., IN	Kurt L. Coleman	Kurt L. Coleman	2006	98
179	192 7/8	26 3/8	27	20 3/8	6 4/8	6 3/8	7	6	Macon Co., MO	Luke Shoemaker	Luke Shoemaker	2006	98
179	185	27 4/8	27	18	4 3/8	4 2/8	5	5	Haskell Co., TX	Matthew L. Goodfellow	Matthew L. Goodfellow	2007	98
178 7/8	206 7/8	31 1/8	30 6/8	22 3/8	4 4/8	4 6/8	9	7	Franklin Co., NE	Wayne Steinkruger	Rodney Steinkruger	1963	101
178 7/8	183 5/8	24 6/8	26	18 7/8	5 2/8	5 1/8	5	5	Kootenai Co., ID	Tony Siron	Tony Siron	1998	101
178 7/8	184 6/8	24 2/8	25	15 1/8	5	5	6	6	Putnam Co., MO	Kurt J. Bauer	Kurt J. Bauer	2006	101
178 7/8	195 3/8	27 6/8	26 1/8	22 1/8	5 6/8	5 4/8	7	5	Cameron River, BC	Glenn A. Harrold	Glenn A. Harrold	2006	101
178 7/8	196	23 6/8	24	19 6/8	5 3/8	5 3/8	7	8	Butler Co., IA	Brandy K. Magnuson	Brandy K. Magnuson	2006	101

Score	Gross Score	R. Main Beam	L. Main Beam	Inside Spread	R. Circ.	L. Circ.	R. Points	L. Points	Locality	Hunter	Owner	Date	Rank
178 7/8	185 5/8	28	27 1/8	20 3/8	5	5 2/8	5	5	Buffalo Co., WI	Joe S. Helwig	Joe S. Helwig	2007	101
178 6/8	181 7/8	25 1/8	25 1/8	14 6/8	4 5/8	4 7/8	5	5	Fir Mt., SK	Dan Chevrier	Dan Chevrier	2004	107
178 6/8	188 3/8	28	29	21 6/8	5 6/8	5 6/8	5	6	Paulding Co., OH	Larry L. Lamb	Larry L. Lamb	2007	107
178 5/8	182 2/8	27	26 5/8	19 7/8	5 7/8	6	5	5	Little Quill Lake, SK	Edward C. Hunter	Edward C. Hunter	2004	109
178 4/8	184 5/8	26	26 5/8	22 7/8	5 4/8	5 3/8	7	6	Long Lake, AB	Jeremy J. Cunningham	Jeremy J. Cunningham	2006	110
178 4/8	185 6/8	27 4/8	26 5/8	20 2/8	5 4/8	5 2/8	7	5	Henderson Co., KY	Jonathan R. Armstrong	Jonathan R. Armstrong	2007	110
178 4/8	181 7/8	25 6/8	25	17	4 6/8	4 6/8	6	6	Frontier Co., NE	Trampis R. Kasten	Trampis R. Kasten	2008	110
178 4/8	189	26	25	19 4/8	5 5/8	5 1/8	6	6	La Crosse Co., WI	Thomas R. Nedvidek	Thomas R. Nedvidek	2008	110
178 3/8	181 3/8	23 5/8	24	16 7/8	5 1/8	4 7/8	6	6	Buffalo Co., WI	Andy Arbs	Andy Arbs	2006	114
178 3/8	185 5/8	27 4/8	27	18 7/8	4 4/8	4 3/8	5	6	Oconto Co., WI	Chad A. DeBauch	Chad A. DeBauch	2006	114
178 3/8	183 3/8	25 1/8	25 4/8	18 3/8	5	5 3/8	6	5	Worth Co., MO	Samuel C. Martell	Samuel C. Martell	2007	114
178 2/8	184 7/8	26 3/8	22 5/8	22 3/8	5 2/8	5 3/8	5	6	Carroll Co., OH	Clifford L. Roberts	Clifford L. Roberts	2006	117
178 2/8	179 7/8	22 2/8	22 5/8	22 4/8	4 4/8	4 4/8	5	5	McCurtain Co., OK	Johnny E. Watkins	Johnny E. Watkins	2006	117
178 2/8	183 5/8	25 7/8	24 6/8	18 6/8	5 1/8	5	6	5	Ford Co., KS	Hal N. White	Hal N. White	2007	117
178 2/8	195 4/8	27 3/8	26 4/8	20 7/8	5 1/8	5 2/8	8	6	Keith Co., NE	Brandon R. Wilkie	Brandon R. Wilkie	2005	117
178 1/8	184 3/8	24 2/8	24 3/8	17 3/8	5 3/8	5 2/8	5	5	Whitesand River, SK	Kurt I. Madsen	Kurt I. Madsen	2006	120
178 1/8	193 6/8	23 4/8	23 2/8	17 2/8	5	5 1/8	9	6	Cass Co., IL	Robert L. Kizer	Robert L. Kizer	2007	120
178 1/8	194 3/8	25 7/8	26 3/8	18 2/8	5	4 6/8	6	6	Harford Co., MD	Mark Rogowski	Mark Rogowski	2007	120
178 1/8	193 3/8	25 7/8	26 2/8	19 7/8	5 2/8	5 1/8	7	6	Bonnyville, AB	Robert B. Sales	Robert B. Sales	2008	120
178	194 5/8	29 1/8	29 2/8	17 5/8	5 1/8	5	6	6	Warren Co., OH	Alexis N. Kemp	Alexis N. Kemp	2008	120
177 7/8	190 6/8	25 3/8	26	19	4 6/8	4 6/8	7	6	Jefferson Co., KS	Arthur R. Dilione	Arthur R. Dilione	2007	125
177 6/8	179 6/8	26 5/8	26 4/8	19 4/8	4 2/8	4 1/8	5	5	Morrison Co., MN	Ronald D. Court	Ronald D. Court	1996	126
177 5/8	182 5/8	24 4/8	23 6/8	18 1/8	5 2/8	5 1/8	5	5	Elk Co., KS	Randy D. Drake	Randy D. Drake	2006	127
177 5/8	196	29 7/8	29 3/8	21 5/8	5	4 4/8	7	6	Fairfield Co., OH	Christopher Shoemaker, Jr.	Christopher Shoemaker, Jr.	2006	128
177 5/8	181 4/8	27 4/8	27 5/8	17 7/8	5	5	5	5	Carter Co., KY	John D. Powell	John D. Powell	2007	128
177 4/8	188 2/8	27 1/8	27 3/8	20 4/8	4 6/8	4 6/8	6	6	Drumheller, AB	Kelly K. Dagenais	Kelly K. Dagenais	2008	128
177 4/8	187 4/8	27 1/8	27 3/8	20 7/8	5 1/8	5 3/8	6	7	Hart Co., KY	Kevin R. Cottrell	Kevin R. Cottrell	2007	132
177 3/8	181 5/8	23 3/8	22 6/8	19 6/8	5 2/8	5 2/8	6	6	Bankend, SK	Wayne Shewchuk	Wayne Shewchuk	2008	132
177 3/8	183 4/8	24 3/8	25	18 1/8	5 1/8	5 1/8	5	5	Whitewood Lake, SK	Marlin Wolitski	Marlin Wolitski	2006	134
177 3/8	183 1/8	25	26 2/8	17 7/8	4 5/8	4 4/8	6	6	Greenwood Co., KS	William N. Donges	William N. Donges	2007	134
177 3/8	180 7/8	26 6/8	26 2/8	21 1/8	4 3/8	4 3/8	5	5	St. Francis Co., AR	Robert D. Lemke	Robert D. Lemke	2008	134
177 3/8	182 2/8	27	26 2/8	22 3/8	4 5/8	4 7/8	5	5	Trempealeau Co., WI	Stephen P. Satterlund	Stephen P. Satterlund	2009	134
177 2/8	181 2/8	23 6/8	23 6/8	16 6/8	4 6/8	4 6/8	6	6	Mahnomen Co., MN	Timothy M. Danielson	Timothy M. Danielson	PR 1993	138
177 2/8	188	23 5/8	25	19 5/8	6 2/8	6	5	6	Fillmore Co., MN	Philip Yocum	Philip Yocum	2006	138
177 2/8	180 6/8	27 7/8	27 6/8	21 4/8	4 5/8	4 4/8	5	5	Desha Co., AR	Jeremy B. McMahan	Jeremy B. McMahan	2008	138
177 2/8	181 2/8	27 5/8	27 1/8	22 2/8	4 4/8	4 4/8	5	5	Grayson Co., TX	Steve Perkins, Jr.	Picked Up	2008	138
177 1/8	186 2/8	28 2/8	27 4/8	21 4/8	5 2/8	5 2/8	5	6	Randolph Co., IL	Jeremy D. Simpson	Jeremy D. Simpson	1994	142
177 1/8	184 4/8	26	26 1/8	17 6/8	5 3/8	5 4/8	7	5	Coles Co., IL	Dylan C. Johnson	Dylan C. Johnson	2006	142

WHITETAIL DEER - TYPICAL ANTLERS

Odocoileus virginianus virginianus and certain related subspecies

Final Score	Gross Score	Length of Main Beam R	L	Inside Spread	Circumference at Smallest Place Between Burr & First Point R	L	Number of Points R	L	Locality	Hunter	Owner	Date Killed	Rank
177 1/8	191 5/8	23	22 6/8	18 6/8	4 5/8	4 4/8	9	7	Red Deer, AB	Doug H. Noyes	Doug H. Noyes	2007	142
177	183 3/8	26 2/8	26	18 4/8	4 7/8	4 6/8	6	6	Pepin Co., WI	Alan J. Bechel	Alan J. Bechel	2007	145
177	187 3/8	25 1/8	27	20 2/8	5 1/8	5 1/8	5	6	Rock Island Co., IL	Jason M. Guthrie	Jason M. Guthrie	2007	145
176 7/8	200 7/8	24 6/8	25	21 5/8	5 4/8	5 4/8	7	7	S. Saskatchewan River, SK	Larry Beaulieu	Larry Beaulieu	2007	147
176 7/8	185	26 1/8	24 6/8	19 7/8	4 2/8	4 1/8	5	5	Perry Co., OH	David E. Kochensparger	David E. Kochensparger	2007	147
176 7/8	183 3/8	27 3/8	28	19 4/8	4 7/8	5 1/8	5	6	Fairfield Co., OH	Tom Lott	Tom Lott	2007	147
176 7/8	205 6/8	27 2/8	28 2/8	19 2/8	5 4/8	5 3/8	6	7	Racine Co., WI	Gregory A. Himebauch	Gregory A. Himebauch	2008	147
176 7/8	195 5/8	24 3/8	24 7/8	17 3/8	6	6 1/8	7	8	La Crosse Co., WI	Heath A. Tschumper	Heath A. Tschumper	2008	147
176 6/8	182 4/8	26 6/8	26 6/8	24 2/8	4 6/8	4 6/8	5	7	Van Buren Co., IA	Joseph S. Higdon	Joseph S. Higdon	2006	152
176 6/8	193 7/8	25	26 6/8	21	5 3/8	5 1/8	7	7	Dane Co., WI	Nicholas D. Ring	Nicholas D. Ring	2006	152
176 6/8	180	24 4/8	24 6/8	17 6/8	5 2/8	5 2/8	6	6	Bolivar Co., MS	Paul W. Warrington	Paul W. Warrington	2007	152
176 6/8	183 3/8	25 6/8	26 4/8	23 4/8	5 1/8	5 6/8	5	6	Edgar Co., IL	Clark N. Piper	Clark N. Piper	2008	152
176 5/8	183 5/8	24 3/8	26 1/8	20 1/8	5 3/8	5 2/8	5	6	Madison Co., KY	Donald C. Pedigo	Donald C. Pedigo	2006	156
176 5/8	178 4/8	25 4/8	25 4/8	19 5/8	4 5/8	4 4/8	5	5	Polk Co., AR	Andrew L. Butler	Andrew L. Butler	2007	156
176 5/8	189 7/8	24 1/8	25	18 7/8	4 4/8	4 4/8	6	7	Elk Co., KS	Thomas D. McFadden	Thomas D. McFadden	2007	156
176 5/8	195 1/8	28 4/8	28 2/8	21	5 3/8	5 4/8	7	5	Penobscot Co., ME	Stephen T. Jay	Stephen T. Jay	2008	156
176 5/8	182 3/8	28 3/8	28 1/8	21 1/8	4 6/8	4 4/8	5	5	Daviess Co., MO	Robert J. Machia	Robert J. Machia	2008	156
176 3/8	198 1/8	25 1/8	26 3/8	18 2/8	4 6/8	4 3/8	7	8	Saline Co., MO	Curtis W. Bright	Curtis W. Bright	2006	161
176 3/8	199 4/8	24 4/8	24 5/8	19	4 5/8	4 5/8	6	8	Sauk Co., WI	Anthony W. Cox	Anthony W. Cox	2006	161
176 3/8	188 1/8	27 7/8	28 2/8	18 3/8	4 3/8	4 3/8	6	5	Clinton Co., IA	Patrick C. Murphy	Patrick C. Murphy	2006	161
176 3/8	178 3/8	24 6/8	24 4/8	17 5/8	5	4 6/8	5	5	Whitesand River, SK	Dallas T. Rusnak	Dallas T. Rusnak	2006	161
176 3/8	195 6/8	26	24 4/8	18 2/8	4 7/8	4 7/8	7	8	Crawford Co., WI	Mark A. Giese	Mark A. Giese	2007	161
176 3/8	183	25 6/8	25 5/8	20 4/8	5 7/8	5 6/8	6	5	Estill Co., KY	Brandon Hall	Brandon Hall	2007	161
176 2/8	179 3/8	25 6/8	25 7/8	21 2/8	4 7/8	4 6/8	5	5	Wabasha Co., MN	Chad E. Schmit	Chad E. Schmit	2007	167
176 2/8	183 4/8	27 2/8	26 6/8	19 5/8	4 5/8	4 7/8	7	6	Cecil Co., MD	Patrick J. Simpkins	Patrick J. Simpkins	2007	167
176 2/8	181 4/8	25 4/8	26 3/8	23	5	5 4/8	5	5	Qu'Appelle Valley, SK	Riley F. Ottenbreit	Riley F. Ottenbreit	2008	167
176 2/8	180 6/8	26 3/8	24 7/8	19 4/8	5	5	5	5	Pepin Co., WI	David S. Prissel	David S. Prissel	2008	167
176 2/8	188	25 7/8	25 7/8	18 4/8	4 7/8	4 7/8	6	6	Stevens Co., MN	David E. Shelstad	David E. Shelstad	2008	167
176 2/8	183 4/8	26 3/8	26 3/8	19	5 1/8	5 1/8	5	5	Henderson Co., IL	Adam R. Silvers	Adam R. Silvers	2008	167
176 1/8	184 4/8	27 6/8	27 4/8	21 3/8	5	5 1/8	7	6	Colinton, AB	Ernie B. Stobee	Ernie B. Stobee	2006	173
176 1/8	178 5/8	24 6/8	25 6/8	18 1/8	4 7/8	4 7/8	5	5	Moose Mt., SK	Trent C. Carson	Trent C. Carson	2007	173

Score		L	R	Spread			R	L	Locality	Owner	Date	Rank
176 1/8	189 1/8	25 5/8	25	21	5 6/8	5 5/8	6	5	Barrier River, SK	Raymond L. Fredin	2007	173
176 1/8	180 7/8	25 3/8	26 3/8	20 5/8	4 4/8	4 3/8	5	5	Cherry Co., NE	Richard J. Schmidt	2007	173
176	177	25 1/8	25 2/8	19	5	5	5	5	Duck Mt., SK	Tyson S. Erhardt	2006	177
176	179 3/8	27 6/8	27 7/8	21 2/8	5 4/8	5 2/8	5	5	Mille Lacs Co., MN	Norman K. Lydeen	2006	177
176	180	27 2/8	27	20	5 2/8	5 1/8	5	5	Parke Co., IN	Denis A. Petit	2006	177
176	190 4/8	27 6/8	26 3/8	21 2/8	6 1/8	6 3/8	6	7	Grayson Co., KY	Hulen L. Sanders	2006	177
175 7/8	186 4/8	27 2/8	26	18	4 6/8	4 6/8	5	7	Nez Perce Co., ID	Joe Sparks	1987	181
175 7/8	180 2/8	27	28	20 1/8	4 6/8	4 6/8	5	5	Kosciusko Co., IN	Jeremiah A. Lotz	2000	181
175 7/8	181 6/8	23 4/8	24 4/8	18 3/8	5 3/8	5 5/8	6	5	Buffalo Co., WI	Lisa A. Brunner	2006	181
175 7/8	186 7/8	25 2/8	25	24 3/8	4 6/8	4 6/8	7	7	Muriel Lake, AB	Chris D. Davey	2006	181
175 7/8	179 1/8	24 7/8	24 2/8	21 1/8	4 2/8	4 3/8	6	6	Pike Co., IL	Brent Jones	2006	181
175 7/8	182 4/8	25 6/8	26 3/8	18 1/8	4 4/8	4 3/8	5	6	Meigs Co., OH	James D. Sayre	2006	181
175 7/8	192 5/8	26	28 3/8	22 3/8	4 4/8	4 4/8	6	8	Douglas Co., KS	Scott Davis	2007	181
175 7/8	195 5/8	27 3/8	26 7/8	21 7/8	4 4/8	4 6/8	6	5	Kosciusko Co., IN	Richard C. Gamber	2009	181
175 6/8	183 6/8	27 2/8	26 5/8	19 6/8	4 5/8	4 5/8	5	7	Sullivan Co., MO	Aaron L. Voyles	2005	189
175 6/8	181	27 7/8	27 3/8	21 6/8	4 7/8	4 6/8	5	5	McLean Co., IL	Chris D. Hawkins	2006	189
175 6/8	186 5/8	24 6/8	24 2/8	20 6/8	5	5 1/8	5	6	Ballard Co., KY	Wayne Batts	2007	189
175 6/8	188 6/8	25 4/8	24 7/8	18 5/8	4 7/8	5	7	6	Pipestone Creek, SK	Bradford D. Campbell	2007	189
175 6/8	189 7/8	24 4/8	25 1/8	20 5/8	5	5	5	7	King Co., TX	Ted A. Flowers	2007	189
175 5/8	202 7/8	27 3/8	27	21 2/8	5 7/8	5 6/8	7	9	Vermilion Co., IL	Richard Huckstadt	2006	194
175 5/8	180	23 6/8	24 2/8	18 1/8	4 7/8	5	6	6	Woodford Co., IL	Kyle L. Marquardt	2007	194

TYPICAL
WHITETAIL DEER
FINAL SCORE: 175 3/8
HUNTER: Edward A. Dierckman

TYPICAL
WHITETAIL DEER
FINAL SCORE: 176 7/8
HUNTER: Heath A. Tschumper

TYPICAL
WHITETAIL DEER
FINAL SCORE: 166 3/8
HUNTER: Chad T. McGuire

TYPICAL
WHITETAIL DEER
FINAL SCORE: 164 7/8
HUNTER: Mark T. Madison

Odocoileus virginianus virginianus and certain related subspecies

Final Score	Gross Score	Length of Main Beam R.	L.	Inside Spread	Circumference at Smallest Place Between Burr & First Point R.	L.	Number of Points R.	L.	Locality	Hunter	Owner	Date Killed	Rank
175 4/8	181 5/8	21 1/8	22 4/8	18 5/8	4 1/8	4 2/8	7	6	Hamilton Co., TX	Glenn D. Christian	Glenn D. Christian	2006	196
175 4/8	186 4/8	25 4/8	27	20 7/8	5 1/8	5 1/8	6	7	Woodford Co., IL	Rodney D. Fandel	Rodney D. Fandel	2006	196
175 4/8	195	25 7/8	25 3/8	25 6/8	6	6 3/8	7	6	White Co., IL	David D. Thompson	David D. Thompson	2006	196
175 4/8	189 5/8	25 1/8	23 3/8	20 2/8	5 2/8	5 3/8	6	6	Appanoose Co., IA	C. Allen Currin	C. Allen Currin	2008	196
175 4/8	180 2/8	25 5/8	26 2/8	20	5 5/8	5 5/8	5	5	Ross Co., OH	Michael Rang	Michael Rang	2008	196
175 4/8	201 2/8	27 1/8	27	17 6/8	5	5 1/8	5	6	Rice Co., KS	Scott A. White	Scott A. White	2008	196
175 3/8	179 5/8	25	24 7/8	20 1/8	5 5/8	5	5	5	Pueblo Co., CO	Ivan J. Muzljakovich	Ivan J. Muzljakovich	2005	202
175 3/8	188 2/8	24 1/8	25	17 6/8	4 5/8	4 7/8	6	7	Ripley Co., IN	Edward A. Dierckman	Edward A. Dierckman	2007	202
175 3/8	185 6/8	25	25 5/8	18	5	5	7	5	Becker Co., MN	Picked Up	James Hendrickson	2007	202
175 3/8	190 2/8	27 1/8	26 6/8	19 2/8	5 6/8	5 7/8	6	6	Coffey Co., KS	Donald W. Jameson	Donald W. Jameson	2008	202
175 3/8	182 5/8	26 2/8	26 7/8	22 3/8	4 6/8	4 6/8	6	5	Eagle Creek, SK	William T. Longman	William T. Longman	2008	202
175 2/8	191 6/8	26 7/8	24	17 5/8	4 4/8	4 3/8	7	7	Morgan Co., IL	Brett Hoots	Brett Hoots	2006	207
175 2/8	189 2/8	26 5/8	26 4/8	20	5 2/8	5 2/8	7	8	Chitek Lake, SK	Arthur E. Woolever	Arthur E. Woolever	2006	207
175 2/8	196 3/8	26 7/8	26	24 5/8	4 6/8	4 5/8	6	7	Delaware Co., OH	Sheryl A. Dew	Sheryl A. Dew	2007	207
175 2/8	180 2/8	28 2/8	28 6/8	23	5 1/8	5 3/8	5	5	Grayson Co., TX	James A. Lillis	James A. Lillis	2007	207
175 1/8	182 6/8	26 5/8	25 7/8	17 4/8	5 2/8	4 7/8	5	5	Outagamie Co., WI	Picked Up	Pat C. Flannery	2006	211
175 1/8	191 3/8	28 2/8	27 5/8	20 7/8	6 1/8	6 1/8	7	7	Fishing Lake, SK	Ken G. Kaban	Ken G. Kaban	2006	211
175 1/8	177 6/8	26 4/8	26 3/8	20 7/8	4 4/8	4 5/8	5	5	Whitesand River, SK	Brian M. Rusnak	Brian M. Rusnak	2006	211
175 1/8	188	26 3/8	25 3/8	20	6 1/8	6 1/8	6	5	Wadena Co., MN	Nathan R. Umland	Nathan R. Umland	2006	211
175 1/8	181 7/8	27 4/8	25 4/8	17 7/8	4 2/8	4 4/8	6	7	Grant Co., OK	Scott E. Sterling	Scott E. Sterling	2007	211
175	182 7/8	27 3/8	28 2/8	20 2/8	4 2/8	4 2/8	6	6	Adams Co., WI	Kevin J. Weber	Kevin J. Weber	2006	216
175	194	25 2/8	25 6/8	23	4 6/8	4 7/8	5	7	Greene Co., OH	Michael T. Beam	Michael T. Beam	2008	216
175	191 7/8	28 6/8	28 5/8	19 5/8	5 2/8	5 2/8	7	7	Jo Daviess Co., IL	Austin D. Fluhr	Austin D. Fluhr	2008	216
175	180 1/8	26 2/8	26 2/8	19	4 4/8	4 3/8	6	5	Kanabec Co., MN	Roland L. Nelson	Roland L. Nelson	2008	216
175	178 3/8	26 5/8	27 3/8	20 6/8	5	4 6/8	5	5	Rycroft, AB	Donald S. Spencer	Donald S. Spencer	2008	216
174 7/8	177 7/8	27 1/8	26 4/8	19 3/8	4 5/8	4 6/8	5	5	Harper Co., OK	Vance M. Barber	Vance M. Barber	2006	221
174 7/8	184 4/8	26 1/8	25 5/8	20 1/8	4 7/8	5	6	6	Leask, SK	Ronald G. Peake	Ronald G. Peake	2008	221
174 6/8	178 3/8	26 1/8	26	20 4/8	4 7/8	4 6/8	6	5	Van Buren Co., IA	David R. Miller	Delmar Weaver	2004	223
174 6/8	180	27	26 7/8	18 2/8	5 1/8	5 1/8	5	5	Miami Co., IN	Marcus L. Otto	Marcus L. Otto	2006	223
174 6/8	182 7/8	24	24 2/8	16 4/8	4 5/8	4 5/8	6	7	Dimmit Co., TX	Dan A. Hughes, Jr.	Dan A. Hughes, Jr.	2007	223
174 6/8	194 1/8	26 3/8	25 5/8	19 7/8	4 5/8	4 6/8	7	7	Pratt Co., KS	David P. Heeter	David P. Heeter	2008	223
174 5/8	179 4/8	26 4/8	27	20 7/8	5 3/8	5 3/8	6	6	Tazewell Co., IL	Marc S. Anthony	Marc S. Anthony	2007	227
174 4/8	179 4/8	23 6/8	23 2/8	18 4/8	5	4 6/8	6	6	Cass Co., MN	Troy D. Kelley	Troy D. Kelley	2007	228

Score	Gross Score	R. Main Beam	L. Main Beam	Inside Spread	Circ. R	Circ. L	Pts. R	Pts. L	Locality	Hunter	Owner	Date	Rank
174 4/8	184 5/8	27	25 7/8	19 5/8	4 3/8	4 4/8	5	7	Waupaca Co., WI	Lance R. Guerin	Lance R. Guerin	2008	228
174 4/8	181 4/8	26 7/8	26	19 2/8	4 1/8	4 1/8	6	6	Callaway Co., MO	Clark L. Zerr	Clark L. Zerr	2008	228
174 4/8	178 7/8	24 3/8	25 2/8	22	4 5/8	4 5/8	5	5	King Co., TX	Jeffrey F. Mitchell	Jeffrey F. Mitchell	2009	228
174 3/8	197 2/8	25 4/8	26 4/8	18 3/8	6	5 7/8	6	6	Dane Co., WI	Thomas A. Magnuson	Thomas A. Magnuson	2007	232
174 3/8	177 1/8	25 6/8	25 6/8	18 5/8	5 6/8	5 6/8	5	5	Mason Co., IL	Aaron P. Yetter	Aaron P. Yetter	2007	232
174 3/8	183 2/8	26 2/8	26 3/8	19 3/8	5 1/8	5 1/8	6	5	Waterhen River, SK	Mitch Baker	Mitch Baker	2008	232
174 3/8	186 3/8	25	26 7/8	17 1/8	4 5/8	4 6/8	6	6	Osborne Co., KS	Gary A. Middle	Gary A. Middle	2008	232
174 2/8	189 3/8	25 3/8	25 4/8	17 5/8	5 4/8	5 4/8	6	6	Fillmore Co., MN	Michael F. Mathison	Michael F. Mathison	2006	236
174 2/8	177 5/8	27 4/8	27	21	4 5/8	4 5/8	6	6	Langlade Co., WI	Christopher J. Pavek	Christopher J. Pavek	2006	236
174 2/8	177 3/8	24	23 6/8	16 6/8	4 4/8	4 4/8	5	5	Little Manitou Lake, SK	David F. Pongracz	David F. Pongracz	2006	236
174 2/8	182 3/8	25 1/8	24 6/8	19	4 4/8	4 3/8	5	7	Blaine Co., OK	Ryan S. Teply	Ryan S. Teply	2006	236
174 2/8	201 5/8	27 4/8	26 4/8	18 3/8	4 3/8	4 3/8	7	5	Scott Co., IN	Bobby Brock	Bobby Brock	2007	236
174 2/8	178 2/8	25 3/8	26 6/8	21 6/8	5 3/8	5 3/8	5	7	Battle River, SK	Michael J. Lessard	Michael J. Lessard	2007	236
174 2/8	186 3/8	27 7/8	27 5/8	24 4/8	5 2/8	5 2/8	8	8	Logan Co., OH	Jerry M. Resch	Jerry M. Resch	2007	236
174 2/8	179 2/8	25 2/8	25 2/8	16 7/8	5	4	7	7	Berrien Co., MI	Matthew L. Wheeler	Matthew L. Wheeler	2007	236
174 2/8	182 7/8	25 1/8	25 1/8	17 4/8	4 4/8	4 3/8	6	5	Polk Co., AR	Frank C. Foster	Frank C. Foster	2008	236
174 1/8	187 2/8	25 4/8	25 7/8	22	4 6/8	4 6/8	5	6	Maverick Co., TX	George R. Sellers	George R. Sellers	2003	245
174 1/8	179	21 6/8	20 3/8	18 1/8	6	5 7/8	6	6	Russell Co., KS	Robert P. Charlier	Robert P. Charlier	2007	245
174 1/8	200 3/8	26 6/8	25 5/8	22 4/8	5 3/8	6 1/8	7	6	Dickinson Co., KS	James R. Johnson	James R. Johnson	2007	245
174 1/8	181 4/8	26 6/8	26 5/8	19 3/8	5 1/8	4 7/8	5	6	Appanoose Co., IA	Bartt M. Carney	Bartt M. Carney	2008	245
174	181 5/8	26 7/8	26 7/8	17	4 2/8	4 6/8	5	6	Desha Co., AR	Jackie D. Privett	Jackie D. Privett	1978	249
174	175 7/8	23 4/8	23 4/8	18 2/8	5 1/8	5 1/8	5	5	Nez Perce Co., ID	Don W. Southern	Don W. Southern	1986	249
174	180 6/8	31 1/8	30 2/8	27	4 5/8	4 5/8	5	5	Crawford Co., OH	Mark A. Farina	Mark A. Farina	2006	249
174	191 1/8	23	23 6/8	21 4/8	4 5/8	4 4/8	5	5	Clark Co., KS	Dennis L. Noyes	Dennis L. Noyes	2006	249
174	179 7/8	24 5/8	25 1/8	21	5 2/8	5 2/8	5	6	Kingman Co., KS	Donald G. Burton II	Donald G. Burton II	2007	249
174	188	25 6/8	25 1/8	19 2/8	5	5	6	5	Will Co., IL	Richard S. Gicla	Richard S. Gicla	2007	249
174	177 5/8	25	25 1/8	17	4 3/8	4 4/8	6	6	Randolph Co., IL	William E. Hankammer	William E. Hankammer	2007	249
174	179 4/8	25	23 6/8	22 4/8	4 7/8	5	5	5	Cross Co., AR	Gregory B. McKnight	Gregory B. McKnight	2007	249
173 7/8	177	25 6/8	24 4/8	19 5/8	4 7/8	4 7/8	5	5	Fillmore Co., MN	Bradley C. Bremseth	Bradley C. Bremseth	2006	257
173 7/8	196 5/8	25 3/8	25 3/8	18 4/8	5 3/8	5 2/8	7	7	Putnam Co., IN	Christian S. Brotherton	Christian S. Brotherton	2006	257
173 7/8	195 7/8	28 2/8	27 7/8	21 4/8	5 7/8	5 5/8	8	6	Madison Co., IL	Nick J. Duncan	Nick J. Duncan	2006	257
173 7/8	180 1/8	26 3/8	25 4/8	21 2/8	5 4/8	5 4/8	5	6	Fayette Co., KY	William E. Rowe	William E. Rowe	2006	257
173 6/8	186 4/8	26 4/8	25 3/8	17 4/8	4 7/8	4 3/8	5	7	Van Buren Co., IA	William F. Winn	William F. Winn	1977	261
173 6/8	184 6/8	25 5/8	24 1/8	21	5 7/8	6	6	7	Clark Co., IL	Mindy S. Miller	Mindy S. Miller	2005	261
173 6/8	190 1/8	27 7/8	28 1/8	18 4/8	5 5/8	5 4/8	5	6	Muscatine Co., IA	Mark A. Seefeldt, Jr.	Mark A. Seefeldt, Jr.	2006	261
173 6/8	182 4/8	27 4/8	27 5/8	21 6/8	4 5/8	5 1/8	6	5	Fayette Co., IL	Craig A. Ulrici	Craig A. Ulrici	2006	261
173 6/8	186 6/8	28 6/8	27 5/8	22 2/8	5	5 1/8	6	5	Cass Co., MO	Aaron M. Norris	Aaron M. Norris	2007	261
173 6/8	186 2/8	28	28 3/8	18 4/8	4 3/8	4 3/8	7	6	Chisago Co., MN	Donald K. Kovach	Donald K. Kovach	2008	261
173 5/8	181 6/8	26 1/8	25 5/8	17 7/8	4 4/8	4 3/8	7	6	Clark Co., SD	James Dale	James Dale	2006	267
173 5/8	175 6/8	25 4/8	25 6/8	18 3/8	5	4 6/8	5	5	Outagamie Co., WI	Todd J. Van Hout	Todd J. Van Hout	2006	267

WHITETAIL DEER - TYPICAL ANTLERS

Odocoileus virginianus virginianus and certain related subspecies

Final Score	Gross Score	Length of Main Beam R	L	Inside Spread	Circumference at Smallest Place Between Burr & First Point R	L	Number of Points R	L	Locality	Hunter	Owner	Date Killed	Rank
173 4/8	185 2/8	24 6/8	25 6/8	18	4 3/8	4 4/8	7	5	Highland Co., OH	Michael D. Stroud, Sr.	Michael D. Stroud, Sr.	2003	269
173 4/8	180 1/8	26 5/8	27 2/8	18	4 7/8	4 6/8	6	6	Perry Co., AR	Tommy J. Bull	Tommy J. Bull	2007	269
173 4/8	176	26 1/8	25 4/8	20 6/8	5 1/8	5 1/8	5	5	Schuyler Co., MO	Travis A. McClanahan	Travis A. McClanahan	2007	269
173 4/8	179 7/8	26 3/8	27 1/8	17 2/8	4 6/8	4 6/8	5	5	Richland Co., OH	Kevin L. Heinberger	Kevin L. Heinberger	2008	269
173 3/8	186	27 1/8	27 7/8	24 1/8	4 6/8	5	6	6	Hamilton, ON	Bobby G. Haralampopoulo		2007	273
173 3/8	183 4/8	26	25 7/8	18	4 5/8	4 5/8	6	5	Jessamine Co., KY	Rick McGlothen	Rick McGlothen	2007	273
173 3/8	182 7/8	25 5/8	27 1/8	17 5/8	5 2/8	5 2/8	7	5	Prowers Co., CO	Kathryn K. Sanner	Kathryn K. Sanner	2007	273
173 3/8	190 1/8	24 2/8	24 2/8	18 5/8	5 1/8	4 7/8	8	7	Kensington Lake, SK	Steven Shackleton	Steven Shackleton	2007	273
173 3/8	183	23 5/8	23 1/8	19 1/8	4 6/8	4 6/8	8	6	Bayfield Co., WI	Rodney J. Hipsher	Rodney J. Hipsher	2008	273
173 3/8	180 2/8	24 7/8	24 4/8	23	4 7/8	4 7/8	5	6	Dimmit Co., TX	Wallace Rogers III	Wallace Rogers III	2008	273
173 2/8	179 3/8	23 7/8	24	22 2/8	4 2/8	4 5/8	5	6	Miller Co., MO	Cody Craddock	Cody Craddock	2007	279
173 2/8	178 3/8	25 3/8	25 2/8	17 2/8	4 5/8	4 5/8	6	6	Saline Co., KS	David A. Hammerschmidt	David A. Hammerschmidt	2007	279
173 2/8	191 2/8	26 3/8	27 4/8	21 4/8	5	5	8	6	Olmsted Co., MN	Eric B. Ronningen	Eric B. Ronningen	2007	279
173 2/8	190 3/8	25 6/8	25 6/8	18 7/8	5	4 7/8	7	5	Todd Co., MN	Marie A. Schultz	Marie A. Schultz	2007	279
173 1/8	182 5/8	24 4/8	26	19 2/8	4 7/8	4 6/8	7	6	Wolverine Lake, SK	Louis D. Knaus	Louis D. Knaus	2006	283
173 1/8	199 4/8	26 7/8	24 3/8	19 2/8	5 7/8	5 3/8	5	8	Kent Co., MD	Lawrence F. Croucher	Lawrence F. Croucher	2007	283
173 1/8	177 4/8	24 1/8	24 3/8	19 5/8	4 7/8	4 7/8	5	5	Martensville, SK	Michael P. Johnson	Michael P. Johnson	2007	283
173 1/8	180 3/8	23 6/8	25 5/8	22 1/8	5 7/8	5 6/8	6	5	St. Louis Co., MO	Kenny E. Harwell	Kenny E. Harwell	2008	283
173 1/8	180 3/8	25 5/8	25 7/8	16 4/8	5 3/8	5 4/8	7	5	Franklin Co., KS	Timothy D. Ott	Timothy D. Ott	2008	283
173	175 4/8	25 6/8	25 3/8	19 4/8	4 3/8	4 3/8	6	6	St. Louis Co., MN	Allen Holter	Allen Holter	1987	288
173	183 4/8	24 6/8	26	16	5	4 7/8	7	6	Washington Co., ME	Garth D. Fugel	Garth D. Fugel	2006	288
173	188 7/8	27 3/8	27	19 7/8	4 7/8	4 7/8	7	6	Pratt Co., KS	Jerry L. Hawrylak	Jerry L. Hawrylak	2006	288
173	191 2/8	27 2/8	27 3/8	20	4 7/8	4 6/8	8	6	Allamakee Co., IA	Craig A. Stange	Craig A. Stange	2006	288
173	187 1/8	25	25 2/8	18 4/8	5	4 5/8	9	6	Houston Co., MN	Dale R. Thesing	Dale R. Thesing	2006	288
173	180 1/8	24 7/8	24 7/8	20 4/8	5	5 1/8	5	6	Isanti Co., MN	Ward D. Pierson	Ward D. Pierson	2007	288
173	176 6/8	25	25	21 2/8	4 2/8	4 2/8	6	6	Tallahatchie Co., MS	Steven M. Simmons	Steven M. Simmons	2007	288
172 7/8	185 7/8	27 6/8	26 4/8	19 2/8	4 4/8	4 5/8	7	7	Spink Co., SD	Marvin Miller	Marvin Miller	2006	295
172 7/8	176 4/8	23 4/8	24 1/8	19 3/8	5	5	5	5	Morgan Co., CO	Bradley A. Hjelm	Bradley A. Hjelm	2007	295
172 7/8	195 2/8	24 3/8	26 6/8	16 4/8	5	4 7/8	9	7	Waterhen Lake, SK	Yves Martineau	Yves Martineau	2007	295
172 7/8	183 6/8	26 6/8	26 2/8	22 4/8	4 3/8	4 4/8	6	7	Perkins Co., NE	Travis D. Berg	Travis D. Berg	2008	295
172 7/8	198 5/8	27	26 5/8	19 1/8	5	5	7	8	Kleberg Co., TX	Charles A. Meloy	Charles A. Meloy	2008	295

Score									Locality	Owner	Hunter	Date	Rank
172 7/8	201	26 1/8	27 7/8	17 6/8	5 7/8	5 7/8	8	9	Hancock Co., IL	Alan N. Jenkins	Alan N. Jenkins	2009	295
172 6/8	201 2/8	23 2/8	24 1/8	20	6	6 1/8	9	8	Clay Co., MN	Clyde C. Nolan, Sr.	Alice Nolan	1953	301
172 6/8	185 1/8	26 7/8	26 7/8	19 4/8	4 1/8	4 1/8	6	5	Des Moines Co., IA	W. Blake Brindle	W. Blake Brindle	2006	301
172 6/8	184	25 3/8	25 1/8	17 3/8	5	5 1/8	6	6	Polk Co., WI	David L. Cran	David L. Cran	2006	301
172 6/8	176 4/8	25 4/8	25 4/8	23 1/8	4 7/8	4 5/8	5	6	Manitowoc Co., WI	Eric G. Riesterer	Eric G. Riesterer	2007	301
172 6/8	191 1/8	26 5/8	26 5/8	23 1/8	5 3/8	5 3/8	9	5	Rusk Co., WI	Gideon P. St. Aubin	Gideon P. St. Aubin	2008	301
172 5/8	183 7/8	22 5/8	24 4/8	19 6/8	5 3/8	5 3/8	6	5	Crawford Co., IL	Russell L. James	Russell L. James	2005	306
172 5/8	181 7/8	26 5/8	25 7/8	19 3/8	5 2/8	5 5/8	5	6	Buffalo Co., WI	Corinne L. Brenner	Corinne L. Brenner	2007	306
172 5/8	182 1/8	25 2/8	25 7/8	18 6/8	4 4/8	4 4/8	7	6	Pulaski Co., KY	Rickey L. Campbell	Rickey L. Campbell	2007	306
172 5/8	195	27	26	20 3/8	5 2/8	5 3/8	6	6	Grant Co., WI	Garrett J. Knapp	Garrett J. Knapp	2007	306
172 5/8	185 5/8	29 6/8	29 4/8	20 1/8	5	5	5	7	Geary Co., KS	Gregory S. Smith	Gregory S. Smith	2007	306
172 5/8	180 1/8	26 3/8	26 3/8	17 4/8	5	5	7	5	Burnett Co., WI	John L. Hennessey	John L. Hennessey	2008	306
172 5/8	177 5/8	25 4/8	25 4/8	16 3/8	5 3/8	5 1/8	5	5	Otoe Co., NE	Gary L. Myers	Gary L. Myers	2008	306
172 5/8	175 6/8	24 6/8	23 4/8	18 1/8	4 7/8	4 6/8	7	7	Riley Co., KS	David M. Sommers	David M. Sommers	2003	306
172 4/8	187 5/8	26 6/8	27 7/8	17 5/8	4 5/8	4 4/8	7	7	Cole Co., MO	Brian M. Rice	Brian M. Rice	2007	314
172 4/8	182	27	27 2/8	18 2/8	4 4/8	4 2/8	7	7	Switzerland Co., IN	Chris Gross	Chris Gross	2007	314
172 4/8	204	26 1/8	25 7/8	21 3/8	5 1/8	5 1/8	9	5	Neosho Co., KS	Johnny L. Kubacak	Johnny L. Kubacak	2008	314
172 4/8	176 2/8	25 6/8	25 4/8	18	4 7/8	5	5	5	Dimmit Co., TX	Rodney E. Meagher	Rodney E. Meagher	2008	314
172 4/8	175 2/8	25 7/8	26	18 2/8	4 5/8	4 5/8	5	5	Bear Lake, SK	Darrell Woytowich	Darrell Woytowich	2008	314
172 3/8	196	27 4/8	28 3/8	21 4/8	5 4/8	5 3/8	8	6	Peoria Co., IL	Michael J. Wozniak	Michael J. Wozniak	2006	320
172 3/8	192 5/8	27 3/8	27 1/8	22 4/8	6	6 1/8	7	7	Adair Co., MO	Steve R. Casey	Steve R. Casey	2006	320
172 3/8	181 4/8	24 1/8	24 1/8	22 1/8	4 7/8	4 5/8	6	6	McHenry Co., ND	Erica L. Clemens	Erica L. Clemens	2006	320
172 3/8	180 7/8	26	26 1/8	18 7/8	5 6/8	5 5/8	5	4	Harrison Co., OH	Thomas E. Newman	Thomas E. Newman	2008	320
172 2/8	186 2/8	27 3/8	28 3/8	22 1/8	4 5/8	5 4/8	7	5	De Kalb Co., IN	Dennis M. Treesh	Dennis M. Treesh	2005	324
172 2/8	174 1/8	25 5/8	25 6/8	18 2/8	5 3/8	5 3/8	5	5	Adams Co., WI	Dustin C. Kirsenlohr	Dustin C. Kirsenlohr	2006	324
172 2/8	182	27 1/8	27 1/8	22 6/8	5 2/8	5 1/8	5	5	Kleberg Co., TX	James P. Brady	James P. Brady	2007	324
172 2/8	176 7/8	26 5/8	26 5/8	18 3/8	5 6/8	5 6/8	5	5	Oldham Co., KY	Brandon Sullivan	Brandon Sullivan	2008	324
172 1/8	182 2/8	27 3/8	27 3/8	22 7/8	4 5/8	4 6/8	6	6	Moose Mt. Park, SK	Timothy A. Bowers	Timothy A. Bowers	1985	328
172 1/8	182 2/8	22	22	24 1/8	5	5	5	6	Loon Lake, SK	Dennis R. Mooneyham	Dennis R. Mooneyham	2006	328
172 1/8	184 1/8	27	27	19 7/8	5 5/8	5 6/8	5	6	Henry Co., IN	Jeffrey J. Roy	Jeffrey J. Roy	2006	328
172 1/8	186 3/8	25 2/8	25 4/8	19 5/8	4 5/8	4 7/8	8	6	Hart Co., KY	Jerry L. Walden	Jerry L. Walden	2007	328
172 1/8	174 4/8	26 6/8	26 6/8	20 7/8	4 7/8	4 7/8	5	5	Hartford Co., CT	Wade Meredith	Wade Meredith	2008	328
172 1/8	177 5/8	23 5/8	23 5/8	20 5/8	5 2/8	5 2/8	5	6	Pepin Co., WI	Christopher J. Belisle	Christopher J. Belisle	2008	328
172 1/8	182	25 1/8	25 1/8	22 5/8	5 6/8	5 6/8	5	6	Maverick Co., TX	Keith L. Brantner	Keith L. Brantner	2008	328
172 1/8	177 1/8	25 2/8	25 5/8	21 7/8	4 5/8	5	5	6	Linn Co., KS	Thomas D. Friedkin	Thomas D. Friedkin	2008	328
172 1/8	178 7/8	25 6/8	26 6/8	18 3/8	4 3/8	4 2/8	6	6	Dunn Co., WI	Alan H. Sifford	Alan H. Sifford	2008	328
172 1/8	179 5/8	25	25	22 5/8	5 1/8	5 1/8	7	7	Chautauqua Co., NY	Robert R. Joubert	Robert R. Joubert	2009	328
172	192 7/8	27 1/8	26 4/8	24 4/8	4 6/8	4 6/8	5	5	Barton Co., MO	Gilbert K. Freeman	Picked Up	1948	337
172	177	25 5/8	25 5/8	17 2/8	4 2/8	4 2/8	5	5	Camp Wainwright, AB	Matt A. Beard	Matt A. Beard	2007	337
172	175 7/8	26 1/8	26 1/8	19	5	5	5	7	Valhalla Centre, AB	Todd M. Zimmerling	Todd M. Zimmerling	2008	337
172	189 5/8	23 4/8	23 6/8	17 7/8	5 2/8	4 7/8	7	7		Duane A. Hagman	Duane A. Hagman	2008	337
172	175 2/8	28 3/8	28 2/8	23 2/8	4 7/8	5	5	4	Clay Co., NE	James P. Hamik	James P. Hamik	2008	337

WHITETAIL DEER - TYPICAL ANTLERS

Odocoileus virginianus virginianus and certain related subspecies

Final Score	Gross Score	Length of Main Beam R.	L.	Inside Spread	Circumference at Smallest Place Between Burr & First Point R.	L.	Number of Points R.	L.	Locality	Hunter	Owner	Date Killed	Rank
172	183 3/8	24 6/8	24 1/8	17 6/8	5 2/8	5 3/8	5	7	Pierce Co., WI	Van Howe	Van Howe	2008	337
172	178 3/8	26 1/8	26 3/8	18 6/8	4 5/8	4 6/8	5	5	Lucas Co., IA	Michael J. Howe	Michael J. Howe	2008	337
172	183 2/8	26 6/8	26 6/8	21	4 5/8	4 5/8	7	5	Houston Co., MN		David J. Pirkl	2008	337
171 7/8	192 3/8	25	24 7/8	18 2/8	5 1/8	5 1/8	9	8	Hempstead Co., AR	Travis C. Mitchell	Travis C. Mitchell	2006	345
171 7/8	178 2/8	25	25 6/8	18 7/8	4 7/8	5	5	5	Audrain Co., MO	John M. Armontrout	John M. Armontrout	2007	345
171 7/8	203 4/8	29 4/8	27 6/8	22 2/8	5 2/8	5 1/8	7	10	Busby, AB	Marty F. Faley	Marty F. Faley	2007	345
171 7/8	176 6/8	23 7/8	23 7/8	16 7/8	4 4/8	4 3/8	6	6	Stutsman Co., ND	Michael R. Struxness	Michael R. Struxness	2007	345
171 7/8	196 6/8	25 6/8	25 4/8	19 6/8	5	5 2/8	6	7	Pettis Co., MO	Steven C. Nesler	Steven C. Nesler	2008	345
171 6/8	178 6/8	26 5/8	27 6/8	18 6/8	5 6/8	5 6/8	6	5	Kendall Co., IL	Stephen S. Chivari	Stephen S. Chivari	2005	350
171 6/8	175	26 3/8	26 2/8	18 4/8	5	5	5	5	Sullivan Co., NY	Domenick A. DeMaria	Domenick A. DeMaria	2006	350
171 6/8	187 3/8	25 3/8	25 1/8	19 7/8	5 4/8	5 5/8	5	9	Fond du Lac Co., WI	Charles L. Wilke	Charles L. Wilke	2006	350
171 6/8	189 2/8	28 5/8	28	21 2/8	5 5/8	5 7/8	5	8	Tippecanoe Co., IN	Brian T. Brown	Brian T. Brown	2007	350
171 6/8	181 5/8	24	23 6/8	18 2/8	4 7/8	4 7/8	6	5	Cass Co., MI	Douglas J. Redder	Douglas J. Redder	2007	350
171 6/8	186 3/8	25 2/8	24 7/8	17 6/8	4 5/8	4 6/8	7	7	Maverick Co., TX	Thomas D. Friedkin, Jr.	Thomas D. Friedkin, Jr.	2008	350
171 6/8	186 6/8	26 1/8	26 3/8	17 3/8	5	5	6	6	Jerauld Co., SD	James E. Hines	James E. Hines	2008	350
171 6/8	179 3/8	25 4/8	25 7/8	19 6/8	4 7/8	4 6/8	6	5	Barrhead, AB	Ben A. Loitz	Ben A. Loitz	2008	350
171 6/8	175 3/8	23 4/8	23 6/8	18 6/8	5 2/8	5 4/8	5	5	Orleans Co., NY	Donald P. McKay	Donald P. McKay	2008	350
171 5/8	182 6/8	27 2/8	27 6/8	22 6/8	4 7/8	4 5/8	6	8	Richland Co., WI	Andrew J. Korducki	Andrew J. Korducki	2006	359
171 5/8	175	24 2/8	24 2/8	16 7/8	4 3/8	4 3/8	5	6	Bent Co., CO	Lance W. Barton	Lance W. Barton	2007	359
171 5/8	203 2/8	26 2/8	26	19 1/8	5 6/8	5 7/8	8	7	Christian Co., IL	Robert R. Carls	Robert R. Carls	2007	359
171 5/8	177	26 1/8	28	19 1/8	5 2/8	5 6/8	5	5	Boone Co., IA	Dennis E. Hidlebaugh	Dennis E. Hidlebaugh	2007	359
171 5/8	184 3/8	25 4/8	24 7/8	18 4/8	5	4 7/8	6	6	Cooper Co., MO	Chuck V. Hammers	Chuck V. Hammers	2008	359
171 5/8	174 2/8	24 6/8	24 4/8	17 7/8	4 7/8	4 7/8	7	5	McLean Co., ND	Kyle W. Haraseth	Kyle W. Haraseth	2008	359
171 5/8	197 1/8	25	26 2/8	19	5 1/8	5 2/8	6	7	Marshall Co., SD	Michael S. Lentsch	Michael S. Lentsch	2008	359
171 5/8	179 6/8	25 1/8	24 5/8	19 7/8	4 6/8	4 5/8	5	7	Robertson Co., KY	Jim D. Whisman	Jim D. Whisman	2008	359
171 5/8	186	24 4/8	24 4/8	17	4 5/8	4 7/8	7	7	Chippewa Co., WI	Bryan W. Zimmermann	Bryan W. Zimmermann	2008	359
171 4/8	182 5/8	24	25	18 4/8	5 2/8	5 2/8	7	6	Polk Co., WI	Thomas P. Coach	Thomas P. Coach	2006	368
171 4/8	173 3/8	24 6/8	25 3/8	21	4 7/8	5	5	5	Dane Co., WI	Wade M. Mapes	Wade M. Mapes	2006	368
171 4/8	183 2/8	24 5/8	24 1/8	18 3/8	5 3/8	5 3/8	5	7	Big Quill Lake, SK	Clayton D. Stefankiw	Clayton D. Stefankiw	2006	368
171 4/8	173 2/8	24 3/8	24 5/8	18 2/8	5 7/8	6	5	5	Sullivan Co., MO	John C. Marks	John C. Marks	2007	368
171 4/8	192 3/8	24 1/8	24 6/8	18 1/8	4 4/8	4 3/8	8	9	Holmes Co., MS	Paul T. Brown	Paul T. Brown	2008	368

Score									Locality	Owner	Hunter	Date	Rank
171 4/8	183	25 7/8	26 2/8	21 6/8	4	4 1/8	6	6	Forest Co., PA	Jeffrey A. Micco	Jeffrey A. Micco	2008	368
171 3/8	183 3/8	27 3/8	27 6/8	18 1/8	4 4/8	4 4/8	7	5	White Co., IN	Mark L. Culver	Mark L. Culver	2006	374
171 3/8	176 5/8	25	25 6/8	19 3/8	4 6/8	4 6/8	5	5	St. Charles Co., MO	Jeremy Fipps	Jeremy Fipps	2006	374
171 3/8	180 5/8	26 3/8	26 6/8	17 6/8	4 7/8	4 6/8	6	7	Hamilton Co., OH	Wayne A. Bolton	Wayne A. Bolton	2007	374
171 3/8	176 5/8	26 1/8	25 7/8	24 3/8	5	5	5	5	Clark Co., OH	Matthew R. Seibold	Matthew R. Seibold	2007	374
171 3/8	175 4/8	27 1/8	25	16 3/8	5	5	5	5	Maverick Co., TX	Ryan Friedkin	Ryan Friedkin	2008	374
171 3/8	198 3/8	26 2/8	25 6/8	19 5/8	5 3/8	5 4/8	8	9	Johnson Co., MO	Michael R. Henke	Michael R. Henke	2008	374
171 3/8	174 3/8	26	26 5/8	16 3/8	4 7/8	4 7/8	5	5	Moniteau Co., MO	Donald L. Welch	Donald L. Welch	2008	374
171 2/8	180 6/8	24 5/8	24 4/8	21 6/8	6	6	6	7	Old Wives Lake, SK	Cody L.H. Hutchinson	Cody L.H. Hutchinson	2005	381
171 2/8	179 3/8	25 1/8	24 5/8	16 2/8	4 4/8	4 4/8	5	6	Carroll Co., MO	Randy L. Serner	Randy L. Serner	2005	381
171 2/8	191 6/8	27 3/8	28 6/8	23 6/8	5	5 1/8	6	10	Coshocton Co., OH	Timothy W. Mullen	Timothy W. Mullen	2006	381
171 2/8	178 4/8	25 5/8	26 6/8	19 6/8	5 3/8	5 1/8	6	6	Warren Co., IA	Larry J. Caldwell	Larry J. Caldwell	2007	381
171 2/8	181 4/8	26 4/8	25	17 6/8	4 4/8	4 4/8	6	6	Cerro Gordo Co., IA	Jamie S. Busch	Jamie S. Busch	2008	381
171 1/8	194	28	29 2/8	22 2/8	4 7/8	4 7/8	6	9	Mille Lacs Co., MN	David W. Piatz	David W. Piatz	2006	386
171 1/8	175 4/8	26	25 7/8	22 5/8	4 6/8	4 5/8	5	5	Davis Co., IA	David R. Byrd	David R. Byrd	2007	386
171 1/8	179 6/8	24	24	18 5/8	4 7/8	5 3/8	7	6	McCurtain Co., OK	Keith B. Compton	Keith B. Compton	2007	386
171 1/8	179 1/8	25 7/8	26 1/8	18 4/8	4 5/8	4 4/8	6	6	Livingston Co., MO	Brett A. Dawkins	Brett A. Dawkins	2007	386
171 1/8	183 5/8	29 5/8	29 7/8	24	5 1/8	5	7	7	Oldham Co., KY	Stanley Huckaby	Stanley Huckaby	2007	386
171 1/8	200 3/8	28 3/8	29 1/8	24 2/8	5 5/8	6	6	7	Dubuque Co., IA	Mitchel McDermott	Mitchel McDermott	2007	386
171 1/8	173 2/8	23 1/8	23 2/8	18 5/8	4 6/8	4 5/8	5	5	Posey Co., IN	Ethan Paul	Ethan Paul	2007	386
171 1/8	191 1/8	24 6/8	25 4/8	16 2/8	4 6/8	4 6/8	9	9	Davis Co., IA	Greg R. Sims	Greg R. Sims	2008	386

TYPICAL WHITETAIL DEER
FINAL SCORE: 170
HUNTER: Chris A. Fischvogt

TYPICAL WHITETAIL DEER
FINAL SCORE: 170 2/8
HUNTER: Doug A. Doram

TYPICAL WHITETAIL DEER
FINAL SCORE: 170 4/8
HUNTER: Terry C. Clingingsmith II

TYPICAL WHITETAIL DEER
FINAL SCORE: 170 1/8
HUNTER: Kara A. Gowe

WHITETAIL DEER - TYPICAL ANTLERS

Odocoileus virginianus virginianus and certain related subspecies

Final Score	Gross Score	Length of Main Beam R.	L.	Inside Spread	Circumference at Smallest Place Between Burr & First Point R.	L.	Number of Points R.	L.	Locality	Hunter	Owner	Date Killed	Rank
171	184 5/8	26 3/8	26 3/8	18 5/8	5	5 1/8	6	5	Nemaha Co., KS	Kevin L. Kramer	Kevin L. Kramer	2005	394
171	177 3/8	24	25 4/8	15 4/8	4 3/8	4 3/8	6	6	Buchanan Co., MO	Russell Matt	Russell Matt	2005	394
171	199 6/8	27 7/8	27 4/8	21 3/8	5 4/8	5 4/8	7	10	Warren Co., OH	Timothy A. Bishop	Timothy A. Bishop	2006	394
171	180 6/8	26 5/8	27 5/8	21 4/8	6	5 7/8	6	5	Madison Co., MS	Kirk Hannon	Kirk Hannon	2007	394
171	189 2/8	21 5/8	21 5/8	19 6/8	5 5/8	5 5/8	9	8	Lac La Biche, AB	Serge O'Keefe	Serge O'Keefe	2008	394
170 7/8	194 6/8	26 5/8	26 7/8	20 6/8	5 1/8	5 3/8	7	7	Pepin Co., WI	John P. Biederman	John P. Biederman	2006	399
170 7/8	185 5/8	26 2/8	26 7/8	21 5/8	6 1/8	6	7	5	Saddle Lake, AB	Lorne C. Gill	Lorne C. Gill	2006	399
170 7/8	176 4/8	26	26	20 7/8	6	5	5	5	Clearwater River, AB	Shawn W. Gow	Shawn W. Gow	2006	399
170 7/8	183 1/8	24 4/8	24 5/8	20 2/8	5 2/8	5 1/8	8	5	Morin Creek, SK	Aime W. Zoufaly	Aime W. Zoufaly	2006	399
170 7/8	175 1/8	26 7/8	26 6/8	21 3/8	3 6/8	3 7/8	5	5	St. Clair Co., IL	Juanita J. Stein	Juanita J. Stein	2007	399
170 7/8	185 5/8	25 1/8	24 5/8	16 7/8	5	5 1/8	5	6	Richland Co., IL	Mike Wilson	Mike Wilson	2007	399
170 7/8	187	24 6/8	24 6/8	20 4/8	5 3/8	5 3/8	8	5	Decatur Co., IA	Michael T. Jensen	Michael T. Jensen	2008	399
170 7/8	174 7/8	23 6/8	23 7/8	20 3/8	4 5/8	4 4/8	6	6	Kenedy Co., TX	Sean P. Keenan	Sean P. Keenan	2008	399
170 7/8	172 7/8	24 5/8	24 6/8	22 5/8	5 2/8	5	5	5	Peace River, AB	Darrell B. Orth	Darrell B. Orth	2008	399
170 7/8	175 5/8	26 7/8	25 4/8	18 1/8	5	5	5	5	Huntington Co., IN	Mark K. Whitacre	Mark K. Whitacre	2008	399
170 6/8	190 4/8	25 7/8	26 7/8	22 6/8	4 5/8	4 6/8	8	7	Logan Co., OH	Stephen R. Elliott	Stephen R. Elliott	2005	409
170 6/8	191 4/8	23 4/8	25 5/8	17 6/8	4 5/8	4 5/8	9	7	Cedar Co., IA	Scott J. Shulista	Scott J. Shulista	2006	409
170 6/8	190 6/8	24 5/8	24 6/8	21 2/8	5	4 7/8	9	7	Johnson Co., KS	Kerry Williams	Kerry Williams	2007	409
170 6/8	174 1/8	25 4/8	24 7/8	18 6/8	5	5	5	5	Campbell Co., TN	David E. Woodward	David E. Woodward	2007	409
170 6/8	172 2/8	27 6/8	27 6/8	18 4/8	4 7/8	4 7/8	5	5	Otoe Co., NE	Jacob R. Mort	Jacob R. Mort	2008	409
170 6/8	176 6/8	25 6/8	25 4/8	18 2/8	5 1/8	4 7/8	5	5	Trempealeau Co., WI	Michael A. Pedersen	Michael A. Pedersen	2008	409
170 6/8	189 4/8	24	24 2/8	17 2/8	5 1/8	5 1/8	6	6	Butler Co., KS	David R. Rogers	David R. Rogers	2008	409
170 6/8	175	29	28 4/8	16 4/8	4 7/8	4 6/8	5	6	Monroe Co., IA	Kevin Yonkura	Kevin Yonkura	2008	409
170 6/8	189 4/8	25	24 6/8	19 6/8	5 3/8	5 4/8	7	7	Burt Co., NE	Joe G. Pennington	Joe G. Pennington	1993	409
170 5/8	187 1/8	28 5/8	28	18 7/8	5 3/8	5 3/8	6	7	Mason Co., IL	Doug Jallas	Doug Jallas	1994	417
170 5/8	194 3/8	26 6/8	27 2/8	21 7/8	5	5 3/8	6	6	Monroe Co., IA	Raymond R. Bain	Raymond R. Bain	2005	417
170 5/8	181 6/8	27 1/8	27 1/8	19 5/8	4 2/8	4 1/8	6	5	Waldo Co., ME	Bryan R. Jungels	Bryan R. Jungels	2006	417
170 5/8	183 5/8	24 6/8	24 4/8	17 2/8	4 7/8	4 6/8	6	8	Becker Co., MN	Matthew J. Olson	Matthew J. Olson	2006	417
170 5/8	177 2/8	27 4/8	29 3/8	18 1/8	5 2/8	5 2/8	5	6	Whitley Co., IN	Ryan G. Osbun	Ryan G. Osbun	2006	417
170 5/8	185 7/8	25 6/8	25 6/8	19 5/8	4 6/8	4 6/8	6	7	Lyon Co., KY	David L. Stevens	David L. Stevens	2006	417
170 5/8	181	29 7/8	30 6/8	23 3/8	6 1/8	5 4/8	5	4	Highland Co., OH	Bruce Thompson	Bruce Thompson	2006	417
170 5/8	181 5/8	22 3/8	26 4/8	21 1/8	5	5 1/8	5	7	Lampman, SK	Cam D. Gedak	Cam D. Gedak	2007	417
170 5/8	178 4/8	24 6/8	23	20 2/8	5 6/8	5 4/8	6	5	Jewell Co., KS	James D. Holt	James D. Holt	2007	417

Score	Gross	Main Beam R	Main Beam L	Inside Spread	Circ. R	Circ. L	Pts R	Pts L	Locality	Hunter	Owner	Date	Page
170 5/8	176 1/8	26 1/8	24 4/8	18 3/8	4 4/8	4 5/8	5	5	Jessamine Co., KY	Danny M. Preston, Jr.	Danny M. Preston, Jr.	2007	417
170 5/8	179 3/8	27 6/8	27 5/8	19 3/8	5 1/8	5 3/8	7	5	Shawano Co., WI	Ryan R. Wendt	Ryan R. Wendt	2007	417
170 5/8	181 5/8	26 3/8	27 4/8	23	4 2/8	4 2/8	6	5	La Salle Co., TX	Rene R. Barrientos	Rene R. Barrientos	2008	417
170 5/8	174 3/8	25 7/8	25 2/8	17 5/8	4 4/8	4 4/8	5	5	Sullivan Co., MO	Mustafa Besic	Mustafa Besic	2008	417
170 5/8	180 5/8	29 1/8	29 5/8	20	5 6/8	5 4/8	6	4	Morgan Co., IN	Michael L. Ikemire	Michael L. Ikemire	2008	417
170 5/8	176 2/8	25 1/8	25 3/8	17 5/8	5 1/8	5 2/8	5	5	Saskatoon, SK	Jim Shockey	Jim Shockey	2008	417
170 5/8	182 5/8	25 3/8	24 6/8	18 5/8	4 6/8	4 6/8	5	6	St. Brieux, SK	Chad Daubenfeld	Chad Daubenfeld	2009	417
170 5/8	173 7/8	27 7/8	27 7/8	25 1/8	4 7/8	4 6/8	5	5	Calvert Co., MD	Griff Hance	Griff Hance	2009	417
170 5/8	183	28 2/8	28 3/8	24 3/8	4 5/8	4 4/8	5	6	Jefferson Co., PA	Thomas P. Pisarchick	Thomas P. Pisarchick	2009	436
170 5/8	172 4/8	26 6/8	29 2/8	20	4 6/8	4 6/8	5	5	White Co., AR	Johnny T. Hendrix	Johnny T. Hendrix	1972	436
170 4/8	177 3/8	24 6/8	25 5/8	22 2/8	5	5	5	5	Maverick Co., TX	Terry C. Clingingsmith II	Terry C. Clingingsmith II	2004	436
170 4/8	175 3/8	24 1/8	24 7/8	18 6/8	5	5	6	6	Turtle Lake, SK	Mike R. Blankman	Mike R. Blankman	2006	436
170 4/8	182 6/8	28 4/8	29	21	4 7/8	5	5	7	La Salle Co., TX	Debbie H. Branch	Debbie H. Branch	2006	436
170 4/8	176 2/8	26 5/8	25 6/8	19	5 4/8	5 4/8	5	5	Morgan Co., IL	Bradley R. Fricke	Bradley R. Fricke	2006	436
170 4/8	188 3/8	26 2/8	25 5/8	20 6/8	4 5/8	4 3/8	5	7	Tuscarawas Co., OH	Ryan L. Strite	Ryan L. Strite	2006	436
170 4/8	185 2/8	25 5/8	26 2/8	23 6/8	4 5/8	4 4/8	6	7	Hocking Co., OH	John Westhoven	John Westhoven	2006	436
170 4/8	180 7/8	23 3/8	25 4/8	24 2/8	4 6/8	4 6/8	6	5	Shoshone Co., ID	George F. Bourgeois III	George F. Bourgeois III	2007	436
170 4/8	187	23	23 1/8	24 1/8	6 7/8	6 3/8	6	7	Trempealeau Co., WI	Matthew G. Galewski	Matthew G. Galewski	2007	436
170 4/8	175 3/8	28 5/8	28 4/8	20 1/8	5 1/8	5 1/8	6	5	Qu'Appelle River, SK	Emily Gust	Emily Gust	2007	436
170 4/8	187 7/8	25 7/8	25 3/8	23 2/8	6 4/8	5 7/8	5	6	Major Co., OK	Gary A. Jantzen	Gary A. Jantzen	2007	436
170 4/8	175 5/8	24 3/8	25 4/8	19 4/8	4 6/8	4 4/8	6	6	Neosho Co., KS	David L. Bailey	David L. Bailey	2008	436
170 4/8	186 3/8	28 2/8	28	23 5/8	5 1/8	5	6	7	Clay Co., KY	Adam Eversole	Adam Eversole	2008	436
170 4/8	175 2/8	26 5/8	28 1/8	20	4 7/8	4 7/8	5	5	Erie Co., NY	Stephen E. Hess	Stephen E. Hess	2008	436
170 3/8	175 1/8	24 4/8	24 5/8	17 6/8	5 1/8	5 1/8	6	6	Le Sueur Co., MN	Alexander S. Wesley	Alexander S. Wesley	2008	451
170 3/8	186 1/8	25 7/8	26 6/8	19 6/8	5 2/8	5 1/8	6	6	Brown Co., SD	Irvin Fliehs	Larry I. Fliehs	1948	451
170 3/8	176 3/8	26 7/8	26 2/8	17 7/8	4 6/8	4 6/8	5	6	Langlade Co., WI	Blake R. Brawner	Blake R. Brawner	2006	451
170 3/8	178 4/8	26 1/8	25 7/8	18 2/8	4 7/8	4 7/8	7	6	Clay Co., AR	Mark D. Craft	Mark D. Craft	2006	451
170 3/8	195 5/8	26	26	20 4/8	6 1/8	6 3/8	8	8	Barber Co., KS	David M. Downard	David M. Downard	2006	451
170 3/8	186 5/8	24 7/8	24 5/8	18 5/8	4 5/8	4 6/8	7	6	Otter Tail Co., MN	Scott D. Dunagan	Scott D. Dunagan	2007	451
170 3/8	178 2/8	24 3/8	23 3/8	18 5/8	4 7/8	4 7/8	6	6	Dubuque Co., IA	Scott L. McAtee	Scott L. McAtee	2007	451
170 3/8	199 6/8	26 4/8	26 2/8	20 2/8	5	5	11	7	Grant Co., WI	Ryan Olson	Ryan Olson	2007	451
170 2/8	190 2/8	25 2/8	25 2/8	15 5/8	4 3/8	4 3/8	9	8	Meade Co., KY	Craig Payne	Craig Payne	2007	451
170 2/8	176 6/8	24 6/8	24 4/8	18	4 4/8	4 6/8	7	6	Loon Lake, SK	Derek J. Wade	Derek J. Wade	2008	451
170 2/8	174 5/8	25 1/8	25 2/8	19 1/8	4 6/8	4 7/8	6	6	Lucas Co., IA	Donald Wyatt	Donald Wyatt	2008	451
170 2/8	197 2/8	24	24	17 4/8	5	5	9	9	Unknown	Benjamin Forziati	Bob Forziati	PR 1960	461
170 2/8	176 4/8	25 4/8	25 1/8	23	4 7/8	4 7/8	6	5	Hendricks Co., IN	Ray Eldridge	Ray Eldridge	2004	461
170 2/8	175	27 5/8	26	16 2/8	4 7/8	4 7/8	5	5	Crawford Co., WI	Van B. Jacobson	Van B. Jacobson	2004	461
170 2/8	189 6/8	26 5/8	25 3/8	19 7/8	5 4/8	5	7	5	Sioux Narrows, ON	Patrick Stone	Patrick Stone	2005	461
170 2/8	183 5/8	25 3/8	25 1/8	23 7/8	4 5/8	4 5/8	6	6	Belknap Co., NH	Alfred R. Bagley	Alfred R. Bagley	2006	461
170 2/8	173 5/8	25 6/8	25 4/8	17 4/8	4 6/8	4 6/8	6	5	Chisago Co., MN	Charles H. Boeck	Charles H. Boeck	2006	461
170 2/8	179 7/8	24 2/8	23 3/8	18 6/8	4 5/8	4 5/8	7	5	Wabaunsee Co., KS	Donald J. Hubbard	Donald J. Hubbard	2006	461

WHITETAIL DEER - TYPICAL ANTLERS

Odocoileus virginianus virginianus and certain related subspecies

Final Score	Gross Score	Length of Main Beam R.	L.	Inside Spread	Circumference at Smallest Place Between Burr & First Point R.	L.	Number of Points R.	L.	Locality	Hunter	Owner	Date Killed	Rank
170 2/8	176 4/8	26 5/8	27 3/8	19 6/8	4 7/8	4 7/8	5	5	Lewis Co., KY	Dale May	Dale May	2006	461
170 2/8	181 5/8	24 1/8	25 1/8	17	5 3/8	5 3/8	7	6	Wabasha Co., MN	Gerald P. O'Hanlon	Gerald P. O'Hanlon	2006	461
170 2/8	173	25 2/8	25 7/8	23 4/8	4 6/8	4 5/8	5	5	Long Island Lake, AB	Doug A. Doram	Doug A. Doram	2007	461
170 2/8	173 5/8	26 3/8	25 7/8	19	4 7/8	4 7/8	5	5	Old Wives Lake, SK	Blaine P. Miller	Blaine P. Miller	2007	461
170 2/8	180 5/8	22 4/8	22 7/8	16 5/8	4 7/8	4 7/8	6	5	Miller Co., MO	Henry T. Rallo, Jr.	Henry T. Rallo, Jr.	2007	461
170 2/8	179 4/8	28 4/8	28 3/8	23 5/8	4 4/8	4 2/8	4	6	Lawrence Co., OH	Gregory A. Sullivan	Gregory A. Sullivan	2007	461
170 2/8	172 2/8	27 2/8	27	20 4/8	4 3/8	4 3/8	5	5	Clark Co., MO	Adam K. Kuehn	Adam K. Kuehn	2008	461
170 2/8	181 5/8	26 1/8	26 3/8	21 2/8	5 3/8	5 3/8	5	7	Adams Co., MS	Alton R. Marlar	Alton R. Marlar	2008	461
170 1/8	176 4/8	24 2/8	23 5/8	20 5/8	4 4/8	4 6/8	6	6	Dawson Co., MT	Robert Storlie	Mike L. Storlie	1959	476
170 1/8	178	25 4/8	25 2/8	16 2/8	4 4/8	4 5/8	5	5	Latah Co., ID	Theodore Millick, Jr.	Theodore Millick, Jr.	1969	476
170 1/8	184 4/8	25 5/8	26 5/8	16 5/8	5 1/8	5 4/8	6	6	Allamakee Co., IA	David P. McGrew	David P. McGrew	2005	476
170 1/8	173 5/8	24 5/8	24 7/8	16 5/8	3 7/8	4	6	6	Ward Co., ND	Lawrence J. Hansen	Lawrence J. Hansen	2006	476
170 1/8	171 4/8	22 7/8	23 1/8	17 7/8	5 5/8	5 4/8	5	5	Cumberland Co., IL	Damon Zucco	Damon Zucco	2006	476
170 1/8	181 3/8	27 2/8	26 4/8	22 7/8	4 5/8	4 6/8	7	7	Wabasha Co., MN	Douglas A. Dubbink	Douglas A. Dubbink	2007	476
170 1/8	181 3/8	24 6/8	25 3/8	21 5/8	5 1/8	4 7/8	6	6	Eau Claire Co., WI	Kevin D. Schippers	Kevin D. Schippers	2007	476
170 1/8	177 6/8	27 3/8	27 3/8	20 1/8	5 2/8	5 3/8	5	7	Monroe Co., MO	Donald K. Thomas	Donald K. Thomas	2007	476
170 1/8	176 3/8	26 2/8	25 2/8	21 3/8	4 2/8	4 4/8	6	5	Bell Co., KY	Dustin Evans	Dustin Evans	2008	476
170 1/8	174 4/8	27 6/8	27 6/8	21 7/8	4 1/8	4 3/8	5	5	Talbot Co., MD	Kara A. Gowe	Kara A. Gowe	2008	476
170 1/8	174 2/8	26 1/8	26 4/8	20 1/8	4 5/8	4 4/8	6	5	Hidalgo Co., TX	G. Scott Jones	G. Scott Jones	2008	476
170 1/8	177 5/8	26 6/8	26 7/8	20 7/8	4 6/8	4 7/8	5	6	Buffalo Co., WI	Cody L. Marcelle	Cody L. Marcelle	2008	476
170 1/8	172 7/8	24 7/8	24 6/8	20 3/8	5	5	5	5	Clinton Co., KY	Richard L. Richardson	Richard L. Richardson	2009	476
170	191 1/8	26 2/8	26 5/8	18 3/8	4 4/8	4 5/8	7	8	Van Buren Co., IA	Picked Up	Allen Schrock	1994	489
170	175 3/8	26 1/8	25 7/8	20	4 3/8	4 2/8	5	6	Adams Co., OH	Boyd E. Stewart, Jr.	Boyd E. Stewart, Jr.	2003	489
170	186 7/8	29 6/8	29 2/8	19 2/8	4 4/8	4 3/8	5	6	Allamakee Co., IA	Owen S. Walleser	Owen S. Walleser	2005	489
170	194 2/8	24 2/8	24 4/8	18	5 6/8	5 7/8	8	8	Jennings Co., IN	Chris A. Fischvogt	Chris A. Fischvogt	2006	489
170	178 5/8	23 4/8	23 5/8	20	5	5 1/8	6	6	The Narrows, MB	Craig J. Lipsie	Craig J. Lipsie	2006	489
170	173 4/8	27 4/8	27 5/8	21 4/8	4 6/8	4 6/8	5	5	St. Joseph Co., MI	David R. Perry	David R. Perry	2006	489
170	183 6/8	26 1/8	28 2/8	22 5/8	5 5/8	5 5/8	6	6	Macon Co., IL	Phillip G. Tucker	Phillip G. Tucker	2006	489
170	178 1/8	25 7/8	27 6/8	21 5/8	6	6	6	6	Guthrie Co., IA	George K. Young	George K. Young	2006	489
170	174 6/8	25 4/8	25 5/8	16 2/8	5 6/8	5 7/8	5	5	Sangamon Co., IL	Mark A. Cheffy	Mark A. Cheffy	2007	489
170	176 7/8	26 1/8	25 1/8	21 4/8	4 3/8	4 2/8	5	5	Iowa Co., WI	Gary L. Johannsen	Gary L. Johannsen	2007	489
170	177 3/8	25 4/8	25 6/8	19	5 7/8	5 5/8	6	5	Lucas Co., IA	David C. Lockridge	David C. Lockridge	2007	489
170	180	24 5/8	25 5/8	19 6/8	4 3/8	4 3/8	7	6	Cowley Co., KS	Danny J. Rateliff	Danny J. Rateliff	2007	489

Score		R. Beam	L. Beam	Spread	R. Circ.	L. Circ.	R. Pts.	L. Pts.	Locality	Hunter	Owner	Date	Rank
170	211 1/8	28	27	19	4 5/8	5	9	7	Somerset Co., MD	Ben M. Wells	Ben M. Wells	2007	489
170	182 7/8	25 5/8	25 1/8	21	4 7/8	4 5/8	7	7	Branch Co., MI	Timothy S. Carper	Timothy S. Carper	2008	489
170	177 3/8	25	25	19 1/8	4 2/8	4 2/8	6	5	Kingman Co., KS	Robert T. Mertens	Robert T. Mertens	2008	489
170	179 6/8	24 1/8	25 4/8	19 3/8	5 1/8	4 6/8	6	7	Clark Co., MO	John R. Miller	John R. Miller	2008	489
170	177 4/8	23 4/8	24	18 2/8	5 1/8	5 2/8	6	5	Saddle Hills, AB	Marlow A. Watts	Marlow A. Watts	2008	489
169 6/8	186 4/8	24 1/8	24 7/8	20 4/8	6	6	7	6	Cochrane, AB	Bry Loyd	Bry Loyd	2006	506
169 6/8	188 7/8	26	25 5/8	20 4/8	5 1/8	5 2/8	6	5	Livingston Co., IL	Jeffrey A. Rieger	Jeffrey A. Rieger	2006	506
169 5/8	173 7/8	28 3/8	27 3/8	19 1/8	4 3/8	4 4/8	5	5	Pendleton Co., KY	Eddie Manning	Eddie Manning	2006	508
169 5/8	187 1/8	24 3/8	26	17 3/8	5	4 7/8	6	5	Union Co., KY	Christian Bennett	Christian Bennett	2007	508
169 5/8	175 3/8	25 4/8	24 5/8	19 5/8	5 1/8	5 2/8	5	5	Jefferson Co., NE	Robert R. Thurston	Robert R. Thurston	2008	508
169 4/8	184 5/8	26 7/8	26 4/8	25 4/8	5 4/8	5 3/8	5	6	Macoupin Co., IL	Brian G. Orf	Brian G. Orf	2006	511
169 4/8	174	28 5/8	29 2/8	20 7/8	4 3/8	4 3/8	5	4	Fillmore Co., MN	Gary L. Templin	Gary L. Templin	2007	511
169 3/8	187 7/8	26 4/8	25 7/8	17 7/8	4 7/8	4 3/8	5	7	Shawano Co., WI	Craig M. Gwidt	Craig M. Gwidt	2006	513
169 3/8	181 6/8	22 6/8	22 3/8	16 7/8	4 6/8	4 7/8	6	7	Ringgold Co., IA	Korey M. O'Day	Korey M. O'Day	2007	513
169 3/8	187 2/8	25 7/8	25 3/8	20 5/8	4 5/8	4 6/8	7	7	Madison Co., AL	Terry M. Miller	Terry M. Miller	2008	513
169 3/8	174 4/8	24 6/8	25 1/8	20 5/8	5 1/8	5	5	5	Wiwa Creek, SK	Greg D. Illerbrun	Greg D. Illerbrun	2009	513
169 2/8	180 6/8	26 7/8	26 4/8	18 3/8	4 7/8	4 7/8	7	5	Clark Co., IL	Raymond C. Kezler	Raymond C. Kezler	2006	517
169 2/8	193 5/8	27 7/8	26 7/8	15 7/8	5 6/8	5 4/8	7	8	Howard Co., MO	Michael A. Kustenbauder	Michael A. Kustenbauder	2006	517
169 2/8	174 7/8	21 2/8	22 4/8	17 6/8	4 4/8	4 5/8	5	5	Door Co., WI	Lance L. Nelson, Jr.	Lance L. Nelson, Jr.	2006	517
169 2/8	174 7/8	26 5/8	27 2/8	21	5	4 7/8	5	5	Warren Co., IL	Larry W. Shepard	Larry W. Shepard	2006	517
169 2/8	178 2/8	24 5/8	24 5/8	18	4 7/8	5	5	6	Rice Co., KS	David D. Cox	David D. Cox	2007	517
169 2/8	171 4/8	27 2/8	26 5/8	18 2/8	4 4/8	4 6/8	5	5	Allen Co., IN	Steven D. Welches	Steven D. Welches	2007	517
169 2/8	185 7/8	25 3/8	25 3/8	19 1/8	5 1/8	5 1/8	7	8	Christian Co., IL	Jason E. Heberling	Jason E. Heberling	2008	517
169 1/8	186	26 6/8	26 4/8	24 2/8	4 3/8	4 3/8	7	5	Lafayette Co., MO	Larry Hoeppner	Larry Hoeppner	2006	524
169 1/8	175 3/8	24 7/8	25 4/8	19 7/8	5 3/8	5 5/8	6	6	Moosehorn, MB	Darcy M. Kutzy	Darcy M. Kutzy	2006	524
169 1/8	194 2/8	24	24 1/8	19 5/8	5 2/8	5 3/8	6	9	Morton Co., ND	Justin D Sayler	Justin D Sayler	2008	524
169	181	23 7/8	23 7/8	17 1/8	4 2/8	4 2/8	6	7	Clark Co., MO	Steve K. Gross	Steve K. Gross	2007	527
169	172 4/8	25	24 6/8	18 4/8	4 7/8	4 7/8	6	5	Cooper Co., MO	Jerry L. Masek	Jerry L. Masek	2007	527
169	175 7/8	23	25 1/8	17 4/8	5 6/8	5 5/8	5	6	Manitowoc Co., WI	Tom Schneider	Tom Schneider	2008	527
168 7/8	186 7/8	25	24 6/8	16 2/8	5 2/8	5 2/8	6	6	Crittenden Co., KY	Nathan Corley	Nathan Corley	2007	530
168 7/8	182 4/8	24 4/8	24 2/8	19 1/8	4 4/8	4 5/8	5	5	Greeley Co., NE	Morgan S. Smith	Morgan S. Smith	2007	530
168 7/8	173 3/8	26	25 4/8	17 3/8	4 1/8	4 5/8	5	5	Houston Co., MN	Michael L. Vang	Michael L. Vang	2007	530
168 7/8	180 7/8	27 1/8	26 5/8	19 4/8	5	4 1/8	8	7	Pulaski Co., KY	Tanner McCalister	Tanner McCalister	2008	530
168 7/8	171 2/8	29 6/8	29	18 7/8	5	5	4	4	Rolette Co., ND	Darren F. Spaeth	Darren F. Spaeth	2008	530
168 6/8	183 6/8	30 3/8	30 2/8	21 4/8	5	5	5	5	Parke Co., IN	Steven W. Buckallew	Steven W. Buckallew	2006	535
168 6/8	177 5/8	25 2/8	25 7/8	17 1/8	3 5/8	5	8	6	Greene Co., IL	Patrick S. Mead	Patrick S. Mead	2007	535
168 6/8	192 3/8	26 1/8	25 6/8	24 3/8	5 2/8	3 5/8	6	9	Polk Co., IA	Glen E. Salow	Glen E. Salow	2008	535
168 5/8	176 2/8	24 3/8	25 6/8	19 1/8	4 4/8	4 4/8	6	5	Orleans Co., NY	William J. Surridge	William J. Surridge	2006	538
168 5/8	178 2/8	26 1/8	26 6/8	19 3/8	4 7/8	4 7/8	6	6	Barber Co., KS	Dwayne A. Boney	Dwayne A. Boney	2007	538
168 5/8	178 2/8	26 1/8	24 6/8	26 3/8	5 3/8	5 3/8	6	5	Fayette Co., IN	Jerry Rader	Jerry Rader	2007	538
168 5/8	170 4/8	28 5/8	28 5/8	22 7/8	5 1/8	5 1/8	4	4	Benton Co., IN	Jay E. Spitznagle	Jay E. Spitznagle	2007	538

WHITETAIL DEER - TYPICAL ANTLERS

Odocoileus virginianus virginianus and certain related subspecies

Final Score	Gross Score	Length of Main Beam		Inside Spread	Circumference at Smallest Place Between Burr & First Point		Number of Points		Locality	Hunter	Owner	Date Killed	Rank
		R.	L.		R.	L.	R.	L.					
168 5/8	174	25 4/8	25 4/8	19 1/8	4 7/8	4 7/8	5	5	Buffalo Co., WI	Daniel L. Ory	Daniel L. Ory	2008	538
168 5/8	175 4/8	26 6/8	27 1/8	21 7/8	4 4/8	4 5/8	5	5	Atascosa Co., TX	Justin A. Peeler	Justin A. Peeler	2008	538
168 5/8	188 4/8	29 5/8	29	23 3/8	4 6/8	4 6/8	7	6	Marion Co., IN	Casey J. Poer	Casey J. Poer	2009	538
168 4/8	174 5/8	25 5/8	25 6/8	22 2/8	5 3/8	5 3/8	5	5	Jo Daviess Co., IL	Robert Wand	Robert Wand	2004	545
168 4/8	179 5/8	27	26 3/8	18 6/8	5 2/8	5 1/8	5	6	Lincoln Co., SD	Justin Kelling	Justin Kelling	2006	545
168 4/8	171 2/8	27 1/8	26 6/8	20 4/8	5 4/8	5 2/8	4	4	Morrow Co., OH	Robby P. Lloyd	Robby P. Lloyd	2006	545
168 4/8	171 1/8	23 4/8	23 4/8	15 6/8	4 3/8	4 4/8	5	5	Huntington Co., IN	Lynn W. Gray	Lynn W. Gray	2008	545
168 4/8	179 3/8	25 4/8	25 5/8	20 4/8	5 2/8	5 3/8	6	5	Worth Co., MO	Rory F. Jackson	Rory F. Jackson	2008	545
168 4/8	177 2/8	25 4/8	25 6/8	22	4 6/8	4 7/8	6	7	Goose Lake, AB	Dean L. Kirkeby	Dean L. Kirkeby	2008	545
168 4/8	172 3/8	23 5/8	23 6/8	15 4/8	3 7/8	3 7/8	5	6	Webb Co., TX	William L. Nash	William L. Nash	2008	545
168 4/8	172 1/8	26	25 4/8	18 4/8	5 3/8	5 3/8	6	5	Clay Co., KY	Kevin L. Rice	Kevin L. Rice	2008	545
168 3/8	175 4/8	26 6/8	26 7/8	19	5 1/8	5 3/8	5	6	Jennings Co., IN	William L. Fields	William L. Fields	2006	553
168 3/8	179 3/8	29	28 5/8	18 5/8	4 7/8	4 7/8	7	6	Marshall Co., MN	Stephen L. Hanson	Stephen L. Hanson	2007	553
168 3/8	174 4/8	25 7/8	25 5/8	22 1/8	5 3/8	5 3/8	5	5	Wayne Co., IL	Ted W. Jones	Ted W. Jones	2007	553
168 3/8	188 6/8	29 1/8	28 5/8	21 1/8	5 1/8	5 2/8	5	7	Shelby Co., OH	Lucas A. Short	Lucas A. Short	2007	553
168 3/8	173 4/8	25 6/8	25 2/8	17 1/8	5 3/8	5 3/8	5	5	Ringgold Co., IA	Daniel L. Haney	Daniel L. Haney	2008	553
168 3/8	181	26	26	21 1/8	5 1/8	5 1/8	6	6	Mason Co., IL	Bradley B. Koke	Bradley B. Koke	2008	553
168 3/8	179 6/8	26 3/8	27	21 6/8	5 1/8	5 2/8	5	6	Morrison Co., MN	Zachary J. Woitalla	Zachary J. Woitalla	2008	553
168 1/8	181 2/8	27 5/8	28 2/8	24 1/8	5	5	6	8	Fremont Co., IA	Larry D. Forbes	Larry D. Forbes	2006	560
168 1/8	175 7/8	24 2/8	24 7/8	19 4/8	4 6/8	4 6/8	5	6	Union Co., IA	Jason W. Hellickson	Jason W. Hellickson	2007	560
168 1/8	170 6/8	29	29 2/8	21 7/8	5	5 1/8	4	4	Union Co., KY	Scott A. Pautler	Scott A. Pautler	2007	560
168 1/8	177 6/8	26 4/8	26 5/8	19 6/8	5 3/8	5 2/8	6	5	Lake Co., IN	Jason D. Harper	Jason D. Harper	2008	560
168 1/8	173 5/8	23 5/8	23 7/8	18 3/8	4 6/8	4 5/8	7	6	Dubois Co., IN	Ryan S. Morton	Ryan S. Morton	2008	560
168	191 5/8	26 5/8	25 3/8	20 2/8	5 4/8	5 2/8	7	7	Lewis Co., KY	Darrell Armstrong	Darrell Armstrong	2006	565
168	177 7/8	25 1/8	24 6/8	18 2/8	5	5	7	6	Casey Co., KY	Andy Miller	Andy Miller	2007	565
168	172 4/8	26 7/8	26 3/8	16 4/8	4 7/8	4 6/8	5	5	Polk Co., WI	Jason W. Tanner	Jason W. Tanner	2007	565
168	172 2/8	24 7/8	26 4/8	21	4 5/8	4 5/8	5	5	Perry Co., MO	Michael D. French	Michael D. French	2008	565
167 7/8	191 7/8	26 2/8	26 4/8	17	4 7/8	4 7/8	7	7	Pike Co., IL	Travis K. Duke	Travis K. Duke	2005	569
167 7/8	183	24 2/8	24 3/8	21 3/8	5	4 5/8	5	6	Hunterdon Co., NJ	Paul E. Jones	Paul E. Jones	2006	569
167 7/8	171 5/8	27 1/8	26 7/8	17 7/8	4 4/8	4 4/8	5	5	Worth Co., GA	Chris Brooks	Chris Brooks	2007	569
167 7/8	184 3/8	26 7/8	25 6/8	19 1/8	4 5/8	4 6/8	6	6	Chester-Nord, QC	Stephane Croteau	Stephane Croteau	2007	569
167 7/8	183 4/8	25 5/8	24 5/8	23 6/8	5 2/8	5 2/8	7	7	Owen Co., IN	J.D. Hall	J.D. Hall	2007	569
167 7/8	174 4/8	25 6/8	25 5/8	20 5/8	5 5/8	5 5/8	5	5	Pawnee Co., NE	Mark W. Sheldon	Mark W. Sheldon	2007	569

167 7/8	170	24 7/8	25 6/8	16 7/8	5	4 7/8	5	5	Parke Co., IN	Shane K. Wheeler	Shane K. Wheeler	2007	569
167 7/8	172 6/8	28 6/8	28 6/8	19 5/8	5	5	4	4	Winnebago Co., WI	Ronald C. Will	Ronald C. Will	2007	569
167 6/8	178 1/8	22 7/8	21 7/8	17 3/8	4 6/8	4 6/8	5	5	Natrona Co., WY	Darrell R. Hartsell	Darrell R. Hartsell	2007	577
167 6/8	177 6/8	26 5/8	27 3/8	19 6/8	5 1/8	5 2/8	6	6	Livingston Co., IL	Chris A. Kerber	Chris A. Kerber	2007	577
167 6/8	175 2/8	26 7/8	26 2/8	19 4/8	4 1/8	4 1/8	5	5	Highland Co., OH	Frank D. Paesler	Frank D. Paesler	2007	577
167 6/8	188 7/8	25 7/8	27	18 6/8	5 6/8	5 1/8	7	6	Iroquois Co., IL	Raymond J. Holohan	Raymond J. Holohan	2008	577
167 6/8	174 3/8	25 5/8	24 5/8	15 6/8	4 1/8	4 1/8	5	5	Trempealeau Co., WI	Mark J. Lange	Mark J. Lange	2008	577
167 6/8	173 6/8	27 2/8	27 3/8	20 5/8	5 5/8	5 6/8	5	4	Todd Co., KY	Emuel Sanford	Emuel Sanford	2008	577
167 5/8	176 5/8	25 6/8	25 6/8	19 3/8	5 7/8	5 6/8	6	6	Douglas Co., WI	Allen W. Michael, Jr.	Allen W. Michael, Jr.	2005	583
167 5/8	179 7/8	26 1/8	26 1/8	23	5 6/8	5 7/8	5	5	Montgomery Co., PA	Lewis A. Carmean	Lewis A. Carmean	2006	583
167 5/8	183	24 7/8	25 1/8	22 7/8	5 2/8	5 3/8	6	7	Lincoln Co., MO	Jeffrey F. DeKalb	Jeffrey F. DeKalb	2006	583
167 5/8	188 7/8	27 4/8	26 3/8	17 2/8	4 3/8	4 4/8	7	6	Kleberg Co., TX	J. Stephen Jones	J. Stephen Jones	2006	583
167 5/8	174 5/8	26 4/8	26	24 5/8	4 5/8	4 5/8	5	5	Beaver Co., PA	David J. Zagorski	David J. Zagorski	2008	583
167 4/8	186	24 5/8	24 6/8	18 1/8	5 2/8	5 5/8	9	8	Sheboygan Co., WI	Kim D. Keller	Kim D. Keller	2005	588
167 4/8	180 3/8	25 7/8	25 7/8	19 4/8	4 5/8	4 3/8	5	6	Bourbon Co., KY	Brad Biddle	Brad Biddle	2006	588
167 4/8	171 2/8	26 3/8	26 4/8	20 2/8	4 2/8	4 3/8	5	5	Trempealeau Co., WI	Robert W. Olson	Robert W. Olson	2006	588
167 4/8	171 5/8	24 7/8	24 1/8	16 6/8	5	5 1/8	5	5	Forest Co., WI	Robbie R. Schrader	Robbie R. Schrader	2006	588
167 4/8	173 7/8	24 4/8	26 3/8	16 6/8	5 2/8	5 4/8	5	5	Iroquois Co., IL	John W. Cox	John W. Cox	2007	588
167 4/8	180 1/8	24 1/8	24 5/8	20 7/8	5 6/8	5 4/8	6	8	Fielding, SK	Earl Kieper	Earl Kieper	2007	588
167 4/8	175 2/8	25 5/8	26	17 6/8	4 2/8	4 3/8	5	5	Jackson Co., MI	Todd L. See	Todd L. See	2008	588
167 3/8	170 5/8	27 6/8	28 2/8	16 1/8	5 1/8	5	5	5	Gatineau, QC	Gilles Galipeau	Gilles Galipeau	1987	595
167 3/8	175 4/8	26	26 3/8	18 5/8	5 3/8	5 2/8	5	5	Norbertville, QC	Roger Renaud	Roger Renaud	2006	595
167 3/8	189 7/8	29	28 3/8	26 1/8	4 5/8	4 5/8	6	8	Erath Co., TX	Jake J. Dearing	Jake J. Dearing	2007	595
167 3/8	187 3/8	26 3/8	26 7/8	18 2/8	4 4/8	4 4/8	9	6	Benton Co., IA	Zachary R. Parmater	Zachary R. Parmater	2007	595
167 3/8	182 3/8	25 5/8	25	18 5/8	5 7/8	5 4/8	5	6	Sioux Co., IA	Owen J. Sandbulte	Owen J. Sandbulte	2007	595
167 3/8	174 4/8	28	28 2/8	17 3/8	4 3/8	5 3/8	5	4	Grenada Co., MS	Robert C. Smith	Robert C. Smith	2007	595
167 3/8	171	28 4/8	27 5/8	22 7/8	5 4/8	5 4/8	5	5	Claiborne Co., MS	Danny P. Thompson	Danny P. Thompson	2007	595
167 3/8	175 3/8	27 1/8	26 2/8	16 3/8	5 4/8	5 4/8	4	5	Henry Co., TN	Kacy L. Watkins	Kacy L. Watkins	2007	595
167 3/8	171	25	25	18 7/8	4 4/8	4 5/8	5	5	Licking Co., OH	Kenneth B. Blankenship	Kenneth B. Blankenship	2008	595
167 2/8	183 1/8	25 5/8	25 6/8	16 4/8	5 2/8	4 7/8	6	6	Buffalo Co., WI	Jan V. Fedie	Jan V. Fedie	2006	604
167 2/8	186 4/8	27 1/8	28 2/8	19	4 1/8	4 1/8	9	5	Waupaca Co., WI	Gerald G. Torborg	Gerald G. Torborg	2006	604
167 2/8	168 7/8	23 3/8	23 4/8	16 2/8	4 7/8	4 6/8	5	5	Buffalo Co., WI	Trevor Adams	Trevor Adams	2007	604
167 2/8	172 2/8	28 4/8	27 2/8	22 6/8	4 4/8	4 7/8	4	4	Monroe Co., AR	James L. Heavner	James L. Heavner	2007	604
167 2/8	169 2/8	27 6/8	28	21	4 5/8	4 3/8	5	5	Tallahatchie Co., MS	Robert N. Stockett III	Robert N. Stockett III	2007	604
167 2/8	172 4/8	28 2/8	27 6/8	18 2/8	5	4 7/8	5	5	Henderson Co., KY	Jim Wolf	Jim Wolf	2007	604
167 2/8	187	25 4/8	26	18 3/8	4 7/8	4 6/8	6	6	Amherst Co., VA	Kenneth R. Crawford	Kenneth R. Crawford	2008	604
167 2/8	174 1/8	26 2/8	26 1/8	18 6/8	4 5/8	4 5/8	6	6	Rawlins Co., KS	Matthew S. Ryan	Matthew S. Ryan	2008	604
167 1/8	181 6/8	27 7/8	27 7/8	16 3/8	4 5/8	4 5/8	7	7	Mason Co., KY	Ronald A. Welch	Ronald A. Welch	2006	612
167 1/8	171 7/8	25 3/8	25 4/8	16 1/8	4 5/8	4 7/8	6	6	Rockcastle Co., KY	Larry D. Carter	Larry D. Carter	2007	612
167 1/8	174 5/8	23 3/8	23 6/8	16 1/8	4 6/8	4 6/8	6	5	Pawnee Co., NE	David L. Styskal	David L. Styskal	2007	612
167	171 2/8	27 5/8	29 3/8	21 2/8	5	5 1/8	5	5	Pulaski Co., GA	Lawrence W. McDaniel	Lawrence W. McDaniel	2008	615

WHITETAIL DEER - TYPICAL ANTLERS

Odocoileus virginianus virginianus and certain related subspecies

Final Score	Gross Score	Length of Main Beam R.	L.	Inside Spread	Circumference at Smallest Place Between Burr & First Point R.	L.	Number of Points R.	L.	Locality	Hunter	Owner	Date Killed	Rank
167	183	23 4/8	24 3/8	16 6/8	4 4/8	4 3/8	8	7	Davis Co., IA	Kerri K. Walker	Kerri K. Walker	2008	615
166 7/8	183 1/8	27 4/8	26 4/8	17 1/8	4 4/8	4 7/8	5	8	Holmes Co., MS	Dan E. Murff	Dan E. Murff	2006	617
166 7/8	173 6/8	25 5/8	24 6/8	18 7/8	4 7/8	5 1/8	5	7	Lucas Co., IA	Michael F. Carter	Michael F. Carter	2007	617
166 7/8	176 6/8	21 6/8	26 2/8	20 4/8	4 4/8	4 4/8	7	5	Pepin Co., WI	Billy J. Levers	Billy J. Levers	2008	617
166 7/8	184 5/8	26 7/8	26 6/8	24 5/8	5 6/8	5 5/8	7	5	Miller Co., MO	Brett M. Pendleton	Brett M. Pendleton	2008	617
166 7/8	172 3/8	24 4/8	24 4/8	17 4/8	4 6/8	4 7/8	6	5	Sheridan Co., NE	Darcie L. Thies	Darcie L. Thies	2008	617
166 6/8	172	26 1/8	26 3/8	20 4/8	4 5/8	4 5/8	5	5	Shawano Co., WI	Gary P. Gevaert	Gary P. Gevaert	2006	622
166 6/8	174 6/8	26	25 7/8	19 5/8	4 6/8	4 5/8	6	5	Newport Co., RI	Stephen C. Ponte	Stephen C. Ponte	2006	622
166 6/8	172 2/8	25 2/8	24 6/8	18 4/8	4 7/8	5 1/8	5	5	Columbia Co., WI	Maegan N. Schroeder	Maegan N. Schroeder	2006	622
166 5/8	179 5/8	25 1/8	23 6/8	15 4/8	5	5 3/8	7	7	Logan Co., KY	Mike Riley	Mike Riley	2006	625
166 5/8	169 6/8	25 4/8	25 6/8	15 3/8	4 4/8	4 4/8	5	5	Fairfield Co., OH	Steven J. Manalac, Sr.	Steven J. Manalac, Sr.	2008	625
166 4/8	172 4/8	25	25 6/8	18 4/8	4 4/8	4 4/8	5	5	Hennepin Co., MN	Mark E. Boll	Mark E. Boll	2005	627
166 4/8	182 4/8	25 4/8	24 5/8	18 4/8	5 6/8	5 6/8	7	6	Buffalo Co., WI	Dirk T. Derse	Dirk T. Derse	2006	627
166 4/8	173 6/8	26 2/8	25 2/8	22 4/8	5 1/8	5 3/8	5	5	Fond du Lac Co., WI	Scott C. Ketelhut	Scott C. Ketelhut	2006	627
166 4/8	174 7/8	24	23 2/8	18 6/8	5 2/8	5 3/8	6	5	Carroll Co., IN	Braydon A. Kitchel	Braydon A. Kitchel	2006	627
166 4/8	179 4/8	25	24 7/8	18 3/8	4 4/8	4 6/8	6	6	Mills Co., IA	Lloyd E. Barten	Lloyd E. Barten	2007	627
166 4/8	168 6/8	23 2/8	23 1/8	19 4/8	4 5/8	4 6/8	5	5	Jefferson Co., OK	Rick J. Ruzzamenti	Rick J. Ruzzamenti	2007	627
166 3/8	170 7/8	25 5/8	25 2/8	17 1/8	5 1/8	5 1/8	5	5	Clark Co., KS	Kelly C. Ison	Kelly C. Ison	2006	633
166 3/8	192 6/8	27 2/8	27	18 3/8	4 7/8	4 6/8	7	7	Belmont Co., OH	Chad T. McGuire	Chad T. McGuire	2006	633
166 3/8	177 6/8	28 2/8	28 5/8	26 4/8	5 1/8	5 2/8	5	5	Deep Creek, BC	Lance D. Mills	Lance D. Mills	2007	633
166 3/8	175	25 6/8	27 4/8	20 1/8	5 2/8	5 2/8	5	5	Marion Co., IN	Jeffrey D. Vaughan	Jeffrey D. Vaughan	2007	633
166 2/8	168 4/8	26 1/8	26	17 2/8	4 4/8	4 4/8	5	5	Chippewa Co., WI	Roger Heidtke	Roger Heidtke	2004	637
166 2/8	182 4/8	24 3/8	25 4/8	20 4/8	4 6/8	4 6/8	6	6	Quill Lake, SK	Steven Luciuk	Steven Luciuk	2005	637
166 2/8	173 3/8	25 3/8	26 1/8	19 6/8	5 1/8	5 1/8	5	5	St. Francis Co., AR	Picked Up	Jimmy R. Cook	2006	637
166 2/8	180 2/8	26 7/8	25 7/8	18 5/8	4 6/8	4 7/8	6	6	Marion Co., KY	Adam S. Gootee	Adam S. Gootee	2007	637
166 1/8	175 7/8	26 2/8	26 5/8	21 4/8	5 2/8	4 6/8	6	6	Stony Plain, AB	Marty F. Faley	Marty F. Faley	2004	641
166 1/8	190 3/8	24 6/8	24 7/8	20 7/8	5 2/8	5 1/8	7	5	Logan Co., OK	Fred N. Zachary, Jr.	Fred N. Zachary, Jr.	2006	641
166 1/8	171 4/8	23 5/8	23 4/8	20 1/8	4 6/8	4 6/8	5	6	Clark Co., IN	Bobby J. Foster	Bobby J. Foster	2007	641
166	170 2/8	25 3/8	24 2/8	21	5 1/8	4 7/8	5	5	Pasqua Lake, SK	Fred S. Benko	Fred S. Benko	2007	644
166	174 5/8	23 4/8	22 7/8	19 3/8	5 6/8	5 5/8	8	6	Bayfield Co., WI	Gloria E. Pasion	Gloria E. Pasion	2007	644
166	175 5/8	24 6/8	23 2/8	19 2/8	5 5/8	6 6/8	6	5	Boone Co., MO	Darin C. Turner	Darin C. Turner	2007	644
165 7/8	190	26 1/8	25 3/8	19 1/8	5 5/8	5 4/8	7	10	Lewis Co., KY	Picked Up	Floyd Bolander, Jr.	2006	647
165 7/8	170 6/8	24 7/8	23 7/8	19 3/8	4 6/8	4 6/8	6	5	Fayette Co., KY	Sam W. Cox	Sam W. Cox	2006	647

165 7/8	181 5/8	25	19 1/8	5 4/8	5 5/8	7	Livingston Co., MO	Shane L. Harkins	Shane L. Harkins	2006	647
165 7/8	179 5/8	26 1/8	17 7/8	6 4/8	6 2/8	5	Cass Co., NE	Nick L. Helzer	Nick L. Helzer	2006	647
165 7/8	170 7/8	25	20 3/8	4 4/8	4 3/8	6	Brown Co., WI	Marty J. Bruecker	Marty J. Bruecker	2007	647
165 7/8	171 3/8	23 6/8	20 3/8	4 5/8	4 6/8	6	Jefferson Co., IA	Matthew M. Orsargos	Matthew M. Orsargos	2007	647
165 7/8	177 3/8	26 2/8	15 6/8	6 3/8	6 1/8	6	Greene Co., IN	Gary L. Schlomer	Gary L. Schlomer	2007	647
165 7/8	174 2/8	26 5/8	18 5/8	4 3/8	4 3/8	6	Columbia Co., WI	Wayne A. Buckley	Wayne A. Buckley	2008	647
165 7/8	183 2/8	24 4/8	18 4/8	5 2/8	5 5/8	8	Fremont Co., IA	James A. Gross	James A. Gross	2008	647
165 7/8	173 2/8	26 2/8	19 5/8	4 6/8	4 6/8	6	Metcalfe Co., KY	Robert Sturgeon	Robert Sturgeon	2008	647
165 7/8	173 6/8	27	21 5/8	5 1/8	5 3/8	5	St. Louis Co., MN	Camron M. Vollbrecht	Camron M. Vollbrecht	2008	647
165 6/8	169 3/8	28 6/8	21 4/8	5	5	5	Mt. Ham Nord, QC	Gaetan Clement	Danielle Fréchette	1989	658
165 6/8	169 1/8	24 5/8	16 6/8	4 5/8	4 6/8	5	Lyon Co., KS	Brian L. DeWitt	Brian L. DeWitt	2007	658
165 6/8	175 5/8	26 7/8	17 6/8	4 3/8	4 4/8	4	Woodbury Co., IA	Michael A. Julius	Michael A. Julius	2007	658
165 6/8	188 5/8	26 1/8	19	4 5/8	4 4/8	7	Madison Co., KY	Blake Jeffries	Blake Jeffries	2008	658
165 6/8	169 2/8	26 3/8	21	5	5 1/8	5	Kanawha Co., WV	Ronald E. Myers	Ronald E. Myers	2008	658
165 5/8	179 1/8	27 7/8	19 1/8	4 4/8	4 3/8	6	Richardson Co., NE	Raymond R. Werner	Raymond R. Werner	2007	663
165 5/8	168 6/8	25 2/8	19 7/8	5 4/8	5 2/8	5	Greene Co., OH	Aaron S. Chaney	Aaron S. Chaney	2008	663
165 5/8	185 1/8	24 1/8	18	4 6/8	4 5/8	7	Monroe Co., WI	Kenneth A. Schmitz	Kenneth A. Schmitz	2008	663
165 4/8	168 7/8	26 5/8	19 2/8	5	5	5	Crooked Creek, AB	Gregory G. Sutley	Gregory G. Sutley	2004	666
165 4/8	169 6/8	26 3/8	18 2/8	4 5/8	4 5/8	5	Craig Co., VA	Starlin Galloway	Starlin Galloway	2005	666
165 4/8	188 7/8	28 4/8	18	4 7/8	4 7/8	8	Callaway Co., MO	Andy R. Cave	Andy R. Cave	2006	666
165 4/8	177 1/8	27 1/8	21	5		6	Pulaski Co., IN	Joseph W. Narantic	Joseph W. Narantic	2006	666
165 4/8	171 4/8	24 4/8	20 4/8	4 7/8	4 6/8	5	Allamakee Co., IA	Donald R. Larson	Donald R. Larson	2007	666
165 4/8	169 2/8	23	18 4/8	4 7/8	5 1/8	5	Franklin Co., NE	Jason A. Plank	Jason A. Plank	2007	666
165 4/8	183 3/8	25 3/8	22 6/8	4 6/8	5 3/8	7	Breckinridge Co., KY	J. Mark Stull	J. Mark Stull	2007	673
165 3/8	174 2/8	26 2/8	20 5/8	4 3/8	4 4/8	6	Pendleton Co., KY	Brandon K. Bruin	Brandon K. Bruin	2006	673
165 3/8	183 3/8	27 6/8	21	4 7/8	4 7/8	5	Washington Co., WI	Matthew J. Buchholz	Matthew J. Buchholz	2006	673
165 3/8	175	27 4/8	22 5/8	4 6/8	4 7/8	5	Southwold, ON	Shane R. Good	Shane R. Good	2006	673
165 3/8	174 5/8	25 6/8	17 7/8	4 6/8	4 6/8	5	Shelby Co., IL	William K. Lindsey	William K. Lindsey	2006	673
165 2/8	176	25 7/8	21 7/8	4 3/8	4 4/8	5	Trimble Co., KY	Rick L. Pelphrey	Rick L. Pelphrey	2006	679
165 2/8	170 2/8	26	15 5/8	4 4/8	4 5/8	7	Two Hills, AB	Douglas L. Butler	Douglas L. Butler	2008	679
165 2/8	178 5/8	26 2/8	18 1/8	6 5/8	6 4/8	6	Merrimack Co., NH	Tim Wunderlich	Tim Wunderlich	1990	679
165 2/8	181 2/8	28 7/8	15 2/8	4 4/8	4 4/8	6	Cape Girardeau Co., MO	Shelly Schamburg	Shelly Schamburg	2002	679
165 2/8	176 2/8	25 5/8	18 2/8	5 3/8	5 4/8	7	Boone Co., MO	Phillip B. Brooks	Phillip B. Brooks	2006	679
165 2/8	170 7/8	23 6/8	19 5/8	5	4 7/8	6	Washington Co., WI	William W. Evert	William W. Evert	2006	679
165 2/8	175	26 2/8	19 7/8	5	4 7/8	6	Howard Co., MO	David A. Hill	David A. Hill	2006	679
165 2/8	174 5/8	26 5/8	19	4 6/8	5	5	Buffalo Co., WI	Robert E. Toonen	Robert E. Toonen	2007	679
165 2/8	176	23 4/8	17 4/8	4 6/8	4 6/8	5	Morrill Co., NE	Rick Anacleto	Rick Anacleto	2007	679
165 2/8	170 2/8	28 2/8	19 7/8	4 4/8	4 4/8	6	Morrill Co., NE	Rick Hisey	Rick Hisey	2007	679
165 2/8	181 5/8	25 4/8	18 6/8	4 3/8	4 3/8	5	Carlton Co., MN	Wayne A. Lind	Wayne A. Lind	2007	679
165 2/8	172 2/8	27 6/8	19 1/8	4 6/8	4 6/8	6	Edgar Co., IL	Roy A. Lowe III	Roy A. Lowe III	2007	679
165 2/8	185 3/8	27 3/8	21 2/8	4 7/8	4 7/8	7	Le Sueur Co., MN	Charles D. Fenger	Charles D. Fenger	2008	679
165 1/8	173 7/8	27 7/8	20 7/8	5	5 1/8	6	Barrie, ON	Allen Henry	Allen Henry	1982	690

Two ✠ symbols appear in the right margin near the top of the page.

WHITETAIL DEER - TYPICAL ANTLERS

Odocoileus virginianus virginianus and certain related subspecies

Final Score	Gross Score	Length of Main Beam R.	Length of Main Beam L.	Inside Spread	Circumference at Smallest Place Between Burr & First Point R.	L.	Number of Points R.	L.	Locality	Hunter	Owner	Date Killed	Rank
165 1/8	171	23 4/8	23 5/8	18 1/8	5 5/8	5 4/8	5	5	Monroe Co., WI	Michael J. Betthauser	Michael J. Betthauser	2005	690
165 1/8	172 7/8	27 2/8	26 4/8	21 1/8	5 1/8	5 1/8	6	5	Geauga Co., OH	Fredrick R. Amport III	Fredrick R. Amport III	2006	690
165 1/8	168 1/8	23 7/8	23 4/8	19 1/8	4 3/8	4 3/8	5	5	Monona Co., IA	Umberto M. Cristina	Umberto M. Cristina	2006	690
165 1/8	180 1/8	25 6/8	25 4/8	19	5	5	7	7	Perry Co., IL	Kurt L. McHugh	Kurt L. McHugh	2006	690
165 1/8	170 2/8	24 2/8	23 3/8	18 7/8	4 2/8	4 1/8	5	5	Marion Co., IA	Mark E. McMurry	Mark E. McMurry	2006	690
165 1/8	168 5/8	26	27 5/8	22 3/8	5 1/8	5	5	5	Washington Co., OH	Mark E. Proctor	Mark E. Proctor	2006	690
165 1/8	181 6/8	27 5/8	28	19 6/8	5 1/8	4 7/8	7	7	Bell Co., KY	Charles Taylor	Charles Taylor	2006	690
165 1/8	180	25 5/8	26 3/8	19 5/8	4 6/8	5	6	6	Green Lake Co., WI	Richard A. Waters	Richard A. Waters	2006	690
165 1/8	167 6/8	22 5/8	22 4/8	20 1/8	5 2/8	5 2/8	7	5	Rosebud Co., MT	Patrick J. Bannon	Patrick J. Bannon	2007	690
165 1/8	170 7/8	26 2/8	25 7/8	16 7/8	4	4	5	5	Williamson Co., TN	Richard S. Beard, Jr.	Richard S. Beard, Jr.	2008	690
165	181 2/8	25 2/8	24 1/8	20 7/8	4 7/8	5 1/8	6	6	Christopher Lake, SK	Paul Frantz	Paul Frantz	2006	701
165	172 3/8	24	24 4/8	22 1/8	5	5 1/8	5	7	Columbia Co., WI	Brady L. Reigstad	Brady L. Reigstad	2006	701
165	171	25 2/8	25 4/8	16 6/8	5 1/8	5 1/8	6	5	Pike Co., KY	Bobby Thacker	Bobby Thacker	2006	701
165	169 2/8	26	24	19 4/8	4 7/8	4 6/8	5	5	Livingston Co., MI	Michel A. LaFountain	Michel A. LaFountain	2007	701
164 7/8	175 2/8	28 3/8	26 6/8	23 5/8	5 1/8	5 4/8	6	5	Caledonia Co., VT	Picked Up	John Gregory	1953	705
164 7/8	178 5/8	25 1/8	25 1/8	16 3/8	5 3/8	5 3/8	7	5	Butler Co., KY	Mark T. Madison	Mark T. Madison	2006	705
164 7/8	194 2/8	27	27 1/8	19 6/8	5 6/8	5 4/8	7	7	Clark Co., IL	Donald E. McWilliams, Jr.	Donald E. McWilliams, Jr.	2006	705
164 7/8	172 4/8	25 5/8	24 6/8	18 6/8	4 7/8	4 7/8	6	5	Powell Co., MT	Chris S. Dahl	Chris S. Dahl	2007	705
164 7/8	168 5/8	24 7/8	24 5/8	15 5/8	5 4/8	5 2/8	6	5	Phillips Co., AR	David A. Young	David A. Young	2007	705
164 7/8	171 4/8	25 6/8	25 7/8	16 7/8	5 2/8	5 3/8	6	5	Maries Co., MO	Pat J. Bauer	Pat J. Bauer	2008	705
164 7/8	174 2/8	26 3/8	25 4/8	18 5/8	5	4 6/8	6	6	Hart Co., KY	Joseph J. Miller	Joseph J. Miller	2008	705
164 6/8	171 6/8	24 7/8	24 2/8	19	4 7/8	4 5/8	5	5	St. Romain, QC	Sylvain Isabel	Sylvain Isabel	1998	712
164 6/8	175 4/8	27 1/8	26 3/8	21	4 5/8	4 6/8	5	6	Monroe Co., WI	James Belcher	James Belcher	2006	712
164 6/8	180 1/8	23 4/8	24 6/8	17 6/8	4 6/8	4 5/8	7	5	Lincoln Co., MO	Thomas R. Gibson	Thomas R. Gibson	2007	712
164 6/8	168 6/8	26	23 5/8	25 5/8	4 5/8	4 5/8	6	8	Clay Co., TX	Rodney L. Reese	Rodney L. Reese	2007	712
164 5/8	171 1/8	28 1/8	27 1/8	18 1/8	5	5 1/8	5	5	Parke Co., IN	Stephen J. Jones	Stephen J. Jones	1998	716
164 5/8	168 1/8	24 4/8	25 3/8	21 7/8	4 3/8	4 5/8	5	5	Henry Co., IN	W. Cole Fort	W. Cole Fort	2006	716
164 5/8	168 2/8	26 5/8	26 3/8	19 1/8	4 6/8	4 6/8	5	5	Vermilion River, AB	Joseph L. Johnson	Joseph L. Johnson	2006	716
164 5/8	173 6/8	24 6/8	26 2/8	21 5/8	4 2/8	4 2/8	5	5	Claiborne Co., MS	Miles Thomas	Miles Thomas	2007	716
164 5/8	168 5/8	23 2/8	23 5/8	18 2/8	4 6/8	4 6/8	6	5	Pettis Co., MO	William J. Breshears	William J. Breshears	2008	716
164 5/8	172	26 4/8	25 4/8	16 5/8	5	4 6/8	5	5	Pine River, BC	Randy Danilec	Randy Danilec	2008	716
164 4/8	172	25 4/8	25 4/8	21 4/8	4 5/8	5	5	5	Washington Co., RI	Picked Up	Donald A. St. Germain	2001	722

Score									Locality	Hunter	Owner	Date	Rank
164 4/8	177 1/8	28 2/8	26	19 3/8	4 4/8	4 5/8	5	7	Putnam Co., GA	Hank M. Johnson	Hank M. Johnson	2007	722
164 3/8	177 2/8	24 7/8	24 6/8	16 7/8	5 1/8	5 2/8	6	5	Hancock Co., IL	Todd M. Adams	Todd M. Adams	2006	724
164 3/8	172 2/8	25 5/8	25 7/8	19 1/8	4 6/8	4 4/8	5	6	Ontario Co., NY	Joseph A. Dammen	Joseph A. Dammen	2006	724
164 3/8	170 7/8	25 4/8	24 2/8	20 3/8	4 3/8	4 4/8	5	5	Shackelford Co., TX	John R. Bass, Jr.	John R. Bass, Jr.	2007	724
164 3/8	173 2/8	26 5/8	25	20 1/8	4 7/8	4 6/8	5	5	Bond Co., IL	Darrell V. Forsythe	Darrell V. Forsythe	2007	724
164 3/8	169 4/8	25 6/8	25 1/8	22 3/8	5 3/8	5 2/8	5	5	St. Joseph Co., IN	Michael A. Lauderback	Michael A. Lauderback	2007	724
164 3/8	171 3/8	25 2/8	25 5/8	19	5 3/8	5 1/8	6	5	Garrard Co., KY	Michael C. Noe	Michael C. Noe	2007	724
164 3/8	190 5/8	26 3/8	25 2/8	25 1/8	5 2/8	5 2/8	5	9	Jefferson Co., MS	Michael C. Burkley	Michael C. Burkley	2008	724
164 2/8	175 2/8	32 3/8	31 1/8	23 2/8	4 5/8	4 5/8	4	5	Van Buren Co., MI	Lori L. Mizwicki	Lori L. Mizwicki	2003	731
164 2/8	166 6/8	24	23 6/8	21 2/8	5	5	5	5	Hancock Co., IL	John L. Arnold	John L. Arnold	2006	731
164 2/8	171 5/8	27 4/8	26 3/8	22	4 1/8	4	4	4	Penobscot Co., ME	Carol A. Belanger	Carol A. Belanger	2006	731
164 2/8	167 6/8	24 6/8	26 2/8	20 4/8	4 6/8	4 7/8	5	5	Walworth Co., WI	Chad L. Hummel	Chad L. Hummel	2006	731
164 2/8	169 7/8	23 1/8	23 1/8	14 4/8	5 1/8	5 1/8	6	5	Morgan Co., MO	Anton M. Kalna, Sr.	Anton M. Kalna, Sr.	2006	731
164 2/8	176 3/8	26 1/8	27 2/8	16 4/8	5 1/8	5 2/8	5	6	Kent Co., DE	Victor Trietley	Victor Trietley	2006	731
164 2/8	168 7/8	25 4/8	25 4/8	19 2/8	4 5/8	4 5/8	4	4	Washtenaw Co., MI	Michael L. Klink	Michael L. Klink	2007	731
164 2/8	166 3/8	23 2/8	23 2/8	18 2/8	4 5/8	4 6/8	5	5	Grant Co., WI	Brian J. Koeller	Brian J. Koeller	2007	731
164 1/8	181 2/8	25	24 4/8	23 3/8	5	5	5	7	Will Co., IL	Frank J. Gavin	Frank J. Gavin	2002	739
164 1/8	168 3/8	24 6/8	24 4/8	18 3/8	5 1/8	5 1/8	5	5	Monroe Co., IA	Thomas D. DeMoss	Thomas D. DeMoss	2007	739
164 1/8	178 6/8	25	25 2/8	18 1/8	4 6/8	4 7/8	7	5	Brooks Co., GA	David J. Ferguson, Jr.	David J. Ferguson, Jr.	2007	739
164 1/8	175 3/8	24	25 4/8	17 7/8	4 4/8	4 4/8	6	6	Leake Co., MS	Danny R. Moore	Danny R. Moore	2008	739
164	181 3/8	24 1/8	24 6/8	19 7/8	5 4/8	5 4/8	6	4	Peace River, AB	Booner M. Beck	Booner M. Beck	2006	743
164	167 3/8	28 4/8	28 3/8	17 6/8	4 4/8	4 4/8	6	6	Ross Co., OH	Donald L. Eppert	Donald L. Eppert	2006	743
164	173 7/8	26 2/8	25	19 2/8	4 2/8	4 2/8	6	5	Waushara Co., WI	Jeremy C. Thull	Jeremy C. Thull	2006	743
164	172 6/8	24 4/8	24 6/8	19 2/8	4 6/8	4 5/8	5	6	Beaver Co., OK	Steve Purviance	Steve Purviance	2007	743
164	176 4/8	26 6/8	27 3/8	16	5 1/8	5 1/8	6	6	Pine Co., MN	Kyle S. Bowman	Kyle S. Bowman	2008	743
164	170 6/8	26 6/8	24 7/8	21 2/8	5	5	6	5	York Lake, SK	Heath L. Dreger	Heath L. Dreger	2008	743
164	194	25 7/8	28 6/8	19 2/8	5 5/8	5 4/8	9	9	Rainy Lake, ON	Thomas J. Kruszwicki	Thomas J. Kruszwicki	2008	743
164	166 7/8	22 6/8	21 6/8	17 4/8	4 4/8	4 3/8	5	5	Prairie Co., MT	Charles V. Long, Jr.	Charles V. Long, Jr.	2008	743
164	172 5/8	25 7/8	25 3/8	17	5 4/8	5 4/8	6	6	Chautauqua Co., KS	Lee Norman	Lee Norman	2008	743
164	173 5/8	25 5/8	25 7/8	20 4/8	4 2/8	4 1/8	6	6	Souris River, SK	Brent D. Olfert	Brent D. Olfert	2008	743
163 7/8	167 6/8	24 1/8	23 5/8	20 4/8	5 3/8	5 2/8	5	6	Randolph Co., IN	Verlin H. Hale	Verlin H. Hale	1987	753
163 7/8	175 7/8	28	28 1/8	17 3/8	5 5/8	5 5/8	6	5	Casey Co., KY	Michael G. Adams	Michael G. Adams	2006	753
163 7/8	181 6/8	26	26	19	4 4/8	4 3/8	8	6	Anderson Co., SC	Charles W. Owen, Sr.	Charles W. Owen, Sr.	2006	753
163 7/8	168 6/8	26	25 7/8	16 3/8	4 7/8	4 7/8	6	5	Clayton Co., IA	David J. Pfiffner	David J. Pfiffner	2007	753
163 7/8	166 6/8	23 5/8	23 6/8	16 5/8	4 4/8	4 5/8	5	5	Moose Mt. Park, SK	B.K. Van Damme & A.J. Galiz	B.K. Van Damme & A.J. Galiz	2007	753
163 6/8	184 2/8	25 6/8	25 6/8	20 1/8	5 2/8	5 4/8	8	8	Barren Co., KY	Picked Up	Ricky Pennington	2005	758
163 6/8	174 7/8	23 6/8	23 3/8	17	4 4/8	5 2/8	7	5	Saline Co., MO	John S. Ball	John S. Ball	2006	758
163 6/8	179 3/8	25 2/8	25 4/8	14 6/8	5	4 7/8	6	8	Todd Co., KY	Robert T. Cole	Robert T. Cole	2006	758
163 6/8	173	27	26 6/8	18 4/8	4 5/8	4 5/8	6	6	Garrard Co., KY	Jeff Rich	Jeff Rich	2006	758
163 6/8	168 5/8	27 4/8	26 4/8	15 4/8	4 7/8	5	5	5	Jackson Co., MO	Tom Dabbs	Tom Dabbs	2007	758
163 6/8	170 2/8	26 1/8	26 5/8	17	4 4/8	4 6/8	5	5	Marinette Co., WI	Ronald A. Peterson	Ronald A. Peterson	2007	758

WHITETAIL DEER - TYPICAL ANTLERS

Odocoileus virginianus virginianus and certain related subspecies

Final Score	Gross Score	Length of Main Beam R.	L.	Inside Spread	Circumference at Smallest Place Between Burr & First Point R.	L.	Number of Points R.	L.	Locality	Hunter	Owner	Date Killed	Rank
163 6/8	171 4/8	25 2/8	25	17 6/8	4 4/8	4 5/8	5	6	Sheboygan Co., WI	Michael W. Schaefer	Michael W. Schaefer	2007	758
163 6/8	182	27 5/8	26 7/8	24 4/8	5 6/8	5 4/8	6	6	Cumberland Co., TN	Tracy W. Derrick	Tracy W. Derrick	2008	758
163 6/8	166	26 7/8	26 3/8	20 2/8	4 7/8	4 7/8	4	4	Fillmore Co., MN	Stuart D. Hoel	Stuart D. Hoel	2008	758
163 6/8	173 3/8	23 6/8	24 7/8	18 3/8	4 4/8	4 4/8	7	5	Shawano Co., WI	Andrew Malueg	Andrew Malueg	2008	758
163 6/8	169 1/8	27 1/8	24 7/8	24 6/8	5 2/8	5 2/8	5	5	Nicolet, QC	Charles-Henri Dorris	Charles-Henri Dorris	2009	758
163 5/8	170 6/8	23 6/8	23 2/8	17	4 4/8	4 5/8	6	5	Saline Co., MO	Picked Up	Jerry W. Coleman	2003	769
163 5/8	168 5/8	24	25 1/8	18 5/8	4 7/8	4 7/8	5	5	Pulaski Co., KY	Picked Up	Justin Coots	2007	769
163 5/8	169 4/8	28 5/8	28 4/8	19 1/8	4 5/8	4 6/8	5	5	Aroostook Co., ME	Steven E. Little	Steven E. Little	2008	769
163 5/8	169 1/8	25 1/8	25 5/8	17 7/8	4 2/8	4 3/8	5	5	Putnam Co., MO	Erik J. Madison	Erik J. Madison	2008	769
163 5/8	182 5/8	25 3/8	25	20 2/8	5 1/8	5 1/8	7	7	Pope Co., MN	David C. Wrolson	David C. Wrolson	2008	769
163 5/8	175 1/8	24 6/8	23 6/8	18 1/8	4 3/8	4 4/8	5	5	Lincoln Co., WI	Thomas G. Schmeltzer	Thomas G. Schmeltzer	2009	769
163 4/8	178 6/8	22 1/8	22	20	5	4 6/8	7	8	Akuinu River, AB	Darrell A. Girard	Darrell A. Girard	2006	775
163 4/8	183 3/8	25 2/8	25 1/8	19	5 4/8	5 3/8	7	6	Melfort, SK	Michael D. Moore	Michael D. Moore	2006	775
163 4/8	187	24 1/8	25 1/8	21 2/8	5 2/8	6 3/8	6	10	Dubuque Co., IA	Robert J. Mueller	Robert J. Mueller	2006	775
163 4/8	168 7/8	23	23	18 2/8	4 4/8	4 5/8	6	7	Cooke Co., TX	Ashley D. Fisher	Ashley D. Fisher	2007	775
163 4/8	170 1/8	24 7/8	24 2/8	19 2/8	4 3/8	4 3/8	6	5	Monroe Co., AR	Issac L. Aldridge	Issac L. Aldridge	2008	775
163 4/8	176 5/8	25 6/8	25 4/8	18 5/8	5 1/8	5	7	7	Athabasca, AB	Hugh W. Newbraugh	Hugh W. Newbraugh	2008	775
163 4/8	171 5/8	24	23	18 4/8	4 7/8	4 5/8	7	5	Otoe Co., NE	Dustin T. Robinson	Dustin T. Robinson	2008	775
163 3/8	174 5/8	26 5/8	26 2/8	17 6/8	5	5	6	6	Price Co., WI	Karl A. Schwoch	Karl A. Schwoch	1959	782
163 3/8	169	24 7/8	24	20 1/8	4 5/8	4 2/8	5	5	Union Co., IA	Guillermo Garcia	Guillermo Garcia	2002	782
163 3/8	167 5/8	25 6/8	26	18 5/8	4 7/8	4 7/8	5	5	Scott Co., IN	Matt A. Smith	Matt A. Smith	2004	782
163 3/8	172 4/8	23	25 6/8	16 3/8	5 5/8	5	6	6	Saline Co., MO	Leo H. Grothaus, Jr.	Leo H. Grothaus, Jr.	2007	782
163 3/8	183 1/8	23 4/8	22 7/8	20 5/8	4 3/8	4 3/8	7	7	David Lake, AB	Geoffrey R. MacDonald	Geoffrey R. MacDonald	2007	782
163 3/8	173 7/8	22 3/8	24 1/8	17 7/8	5 4/8	5 2/8	6	7	Saline Co., KS	Albert J. Marklevits	Albert J. Marklevits	2007	782
163 3/8	178 4/8	20 4/8	27	18 4/8	4 3/8	4 5/8	7	6	Putnam Co., IN	Jonathan D. Chadd	Jonathan D. Chadd	2008	782
163 3/8	168 3/8	24 3/8	25 1/8	22 3/8	5 2/8	5 2/8	5	5	Polk Co., WI	Duane E. Fredrickson	Duane E. Fredrickson	2008	782
163 3/8	169 7/8	24	24 1/8	19 7/8	4 5/8	4 2/8	5	5	Shelby Co., TX	Jeffrey N. Schafer	Jeffrey N. Schafer	2008	782
163 3/8	167 7/8	24 3/8	24	20 4/8	4 4/8	4 4/8	6	5	San Saba Co., TX	David M. Perkins	David M. Perkins	2009	782
163 2/8	175 3/8	27	26 4/8	20	4 2/8	4 2/8	6	6	Washington Co., VT	Will C. Lyons	Alicia Bedell	1908	792
163 2/8	167 6/8	24 2/8	24 7/8	18 4/8	4 3/8	4 3/8	5	5	Sussex Co., DE	Michael G. Fannin	Michael G. Fannin	2005	792
163 2/8	179 4/8	26	26 6/8	23 3/8	5 6/8	5 4/8	7	5	Christian Co., IL	Michael W. Miloncus	Michael W. Miloncus	2005	792
163 2/8	182 6/8	24 7/8	26 2/8	22 4/8	4 7/8	4 7/8	6	5	Wabash Co., IN	Jimmy J. Wallen	Jimmy J. Wallen	2006	792
163 2/8	174 6/8	26 2/8	26 4/8	17 6/8	5 3/8	5 3/8	6	5	Plymouth Co., MA	Fernando A. Cristina	Fernando A. Cristina	2007	792

Score	Gross Score	Main Beam R	Main Beam L	Inside Spread	Circ. R	Circ. L	Pts R	Pts L	Owner	Hunter	Locality	Date Killed	Rank
163 2/8	166	24 4/8	25	17 4/8	4 4/8	4 3/8	5	5	David G. Edwards	David G. Edwards	Warren Co., IN	2007	792
163 2/8	171 3/8	25 5/8	25 5/8	17 6/8	4 4/8	4 4/8	6	6	Jason M. Egly	Jason M. Egly	Jennings Co., IN	2007	792
163 2/8	167 3/8	24	24	18	4 5/8	4 5/8	5	5	Lawrence G. Huenink	Lawrence G. Huenink	Lancaster Co., NE	2007	792
163 2/8	165 1/8	22 6/8	23 4/8	16 2/8	4 5/8	4 6/8	6	6	William J. Evans	William J. Evans	Tallahatchie Co., MS	2008	792
163 2/8	186 1/8	24 4/8	24 3/8	18 3/8	5	5	6	6	Wesley W. Smits	Wesley W. Smits	Waupaca Co., WI	2008	792
163 2/8	172 2/8	26 1/8	26 3/8	23	5 2/8	5 3/8	5	5	Erik N. Sorensen	Erik N. Sorensen	Aroostook Co., ME	2008	792
163 1/8	180 3/8	25 7/8	26 2/8	18	4 5/8	4 6/8	7	7	Harold H. Ableson	Dennison Ableson	Brandon, MB	1924	803
163 1/8	185 7/8	27 2/8	26 7/8	20 4/8	5	5	6	6	Robert E. Etter	Robert E. Etter	Parke Co., IN	2006	803
163 1/8	181 4/8	27	27	19 1/8	5 1/8	5 1/8	8	7	Daniel R. Troyer	Daniel R. Troyer	Portage Co., OH	2006	803
163 1/8	188 4/8	25 7/8	25 7/8	17 7/8	4 4/8	4 4/8	7	6	Eric M. Vaughn	Eric M. Vaughn	Gibson Co., IN	2007	803
163 1/8	173 5/8	23 5/8	24	17 3/8	5 2/8	5 2/8	6	6	Neal J. Hahn	Neal J. Hahn	Greeley Co., NE	2008	803
163 1/8	171	24 5/8	23 7/8	18 3/8	4 4/8	4 3/8	5	5	Blake A. Plattner	Blake A. Plattner	Peoria Co., IL	2008	803
163	168 1/8	25	25	20 5/8	4 3/8	4 2/8	6	5	Russell T. Steiner	Russell T. Steiner	Clarke Co., AL	2008	810
163	169 1/8	24 7/8	25	17	4 4/8	4 4/8	5	5	C. Ray Hummel	C. Ray Hummel	Vernon Co., WI	1999	810
163	166 1/8	25 1/8	25 1/8	20 4/8	4 5/8	4 5/8	6	6	Troy N. Garner	Troy N. Garner	Yell Co., AR	2006	810
163	176 1/8	28 4/8	28 6/8	20 2/8	4 4/8	5	6	5	David D. Waldschmidt	David D. Waldschmidt	Jo Daviess Co., IL	2006	810
163	169 4/8	24 3/8	24 3/8	20	5 3/8	4 5/8	5	5	Jacob A. Pettit	Jacob A. Pettit	Burt Co., NE	2007	810
163	180 4/8	25 4/8	25 3/8	18 5/8	4 5/8	5 6/8	6	6	Michael Woodward	Michael Woodward	De Kalb Co., IN	2007	810
162 7/8	171 4/8	25 1/8	25 1/8	20	4 3/8	4 5/8	5	6	William J. Oliver	William J. Oliver	Miami Co., OH	2008	818
162 7/8	176 2/8	26 7/8	26 7/8	17 2/8	5 4/8	4 3/8	7	7	Justin N. Scarborough	Justin N. Scarborough	Early Co., GA	2008	818
162 7/8	179 3/8	24 2/8	24 2/8	14 4/8	4 5/8	5 4/8	7	7	Casey L. Smith	Casey L. Smith	Hand Co., SD	2006	818
162 7/8	169 2/8	22 6/8	22 6/8	19 1/8	5 2/8	4 5/8	5	5	Kenneth R. Brimm	Kenneth R. Brimm	Knox Co., KY	2007	818
162 7/8	170 1/8	25 7/8	25 7/8	22 6/8	4 4/8	5 3/8	6	5	Jeremy C. Borden	Jeremy C. Borden	Lawrence Co., AL	2007	818
162 7/8	180 2/8	26 5/8	26 5/8	20 2/8	4 7/8	4 4/8	8	6	Adam J. Bouch	Adam J. Bouch	Mahoning Co., OH	2007	818
162 7/8	172 7/8	23 1/8	23 3/8	18 3/8	4 5/8	4 7/8	5	5	Cleveland D. Dobson	Cleveland D. Dobson	Knott Co., KY	2007	818
162 6/8	168 3/8	25 4/8	25 4/8	16	4 6/8	4 5/8	5	6	A.B. Hall	A.B. Hall	Worcester Co., MD	2007	826
162 6/8	170 1/8	24 5/8	24 5/8	17 7/8	5 5/8	5 3/8	7	5	Ben S. Kozak	Ben S. Kozak	Shawano Co., WI	2007	826
162 6/8	173 7/8	24 7/8	24 7/8	18 4/8	4 6/8	4 4/8	7	5	Mark E. Langford	Mark E. Langford	Pickaway Co., OH	2008	826
162 6/8	170 3/8	27 4/8	27 7/8	28	4 2/8	4 6/8	5	6	Dean R. Porter	Dean R. Porter	Hampden Co., MA	2008	826
162 6/8	174 3/8	26 7/8	28	16 4/8	5	4 2/8	6	6	John A. Landsburg	John A. Landsburg	Love, SK	2004	826
162 6/8	185 2/8	26 1/8	26 7/8	18 4/8	4 7/8	5	8	5	Mark A. Bivens	Mark A. Bivens	Anderson Co., KY	2006	826
162 6/8	170 2/8	23 4/8	26 1/8	18	4 2/8	4 7/8	5	5	Daniel J. Brezinski	Daniel J. Brezinski	Forest Co., WI	2006	826
162 6/8	170 4/8	23 6/8	23 6/8	18 4/8	5 1/8	4 2/8	5	5	Kevin L. Brown	Kevin L. Brown	Kosciusko Co., IN	2006	826
162 6/8	166	24 5/8	24 5/8	20 4/8	5	5	5	5	Donavan V. Robarge	Donavan V. Robarge	Washburn Co., WI	2006	826
162 6/8	167 1/8	26 4/8	26 4/8	20 4/8	4 3/8	5	5	5	Danny Sowards	Danny Sowards	Morgan Co., KY	2006	826
162 6/8	166 6/8	26 7/8	26 7/8	20	4 2/8	4 7/8	5	5	James H. Sutton	James H. Sutton	Benton Co., IA	2006	826
162 6/8	166 2/8	25 7/8	25 7/8	17 4/8	5	4 2/8	5	5	Delbert W. Carmer, Jr.	Delbert W. Carmer, Jr.	Linn Co., IA	2007	826
162 6/8	172 5/8	25 1/8	25 1/8	20 1/8	5 2/8	5	5	5	Eldon D. Holmes	Eldon D. Holmes	Buffalo Co., NE	2007	826
162 6/8	177 6/8	25 2/8	25 2/8	22 4/8	4 3/8	5 2/8	7	6	Dan D. Marking	Dan D. Marking	Atchison Co., MO	2007	826
162 6/8	166 7/8	26 7/8	26 7/8	21 3/8	5 2/8	4 3/8	6	5	Ralph Thompson	Ralph Thompson	Lawrence Co., IL	2007	826
162 6/8	170 3/8	25 1/8	25 1/8	19 4/8	5	5 2/8	5	6	Robert J. Stritch	Robert J. Stritch	Calhoun Co., IL	2008	826
162 5/8	171	28 5/8	26 5/8	19 1/8	4 4/8	4 4/8	5	6	John A. Drew, Sr.	Ethel Drew	Addison Co., VT	1953	838

WHITETAIL DEER - TYPICAL ANTLERS

Odocoileus virginianus virginianus and certain related subspecies

Final Score	Gross Score	Length of Main Beam R.	L.	Inside Spread	Circ. at Smallest Place Between Burr & First Point R.	L.	Number of Points R.	L.	Locality	Hunter	Owner	Date Killed	Rank
162 5/8	168 6/8	23	22 7/8	18 2/8	4 7/8	5	5	6	Green Lake Co., WI	Timothy A. Polcyn	Timothy A. Polcyn	1999	838
162 5/8	171 4/8	23 3/8	24 4/8	19	4 2/8	4 3/8	7	5	Hardin Co., KY	Jake J. McAlister	Jake J. McAlister	2001	838
162 5/8	172 1/8	24 7/8	24 2/8	16 7/8	5 1/8	4 7/8	6	6	Jo Daviess Co., IL	Timothy W. Brinkmeier	Timothy W. Brinkmeier	2005	838
162 5/8	174 5/8	27 3/8	27	18 3/8	5 2/8	5 2/8	5	6	Vigo Co., IN	Jack D. Fields II	Jack D. Fields II	2006	838
162 5/8	180 6/8	26 4/8	27	18 3/8	4 7/8	5	6	7	Oscar Lake, SK	David G. Rivers	David G. Rivers	2006	838
162 5/8	171 1/8	25 6/8	26 4/8	21 2/8	4 1/8	4 1/8	6	6	Hall Co., NE	Shay P. McGowan	Shay P. McGowan	2007	838
162 5/8	164 1/8	27 6/8	27 7/8	19 5/8	5	5	4	4	Wilcox Co., GA	Scott McGuinty	Scott McGuinty	2007	838
162 5/8	172 4/8	27 2/8	26 3/8	24 2/8	5 1/8	4 7/8	6	5	Sagadahoc Co., ME	Foster B. Meserve, Jr.	Foster B. Meserve, Jr.	2007	838
162 5/8	167 2/8	25 6/8	25 2/8	18 1/8	5 3/8	5 2/8	5	5	St. Louis Co., MN	Clint Vander Heyden	Clint Vander Heyden	2007	838
162 5/8	188 7/8	27	27 3/8	20 4/8	5 4/8	5 4/8	8	5	Woodbury Co., IA	Lee M. Williams	Lee M. Williams	2008	838
162 5/8	170 5/8	24 7/8	25 1/8	15 2/8	4 6/8	4 6/8	6	5	Kleberg Co., TX	Daryl D. Brown	Daryl D. Brown	2008	838
162 5/8	167	23 4/8	24 2/8	21 1/8	5	5	5	5	Tensas Co., LA	Barry J. Brown	Barry J. Brown	2008	838
162 4/8	189 7/8	26	26	16 3/8	5 5/8	6	10	6	Bourbon Co., KS	D. Shane Smith	D. Shane Smith	2006	851
162 4/8	175 3/8	28 1/8	27	17 7/8	5 6/8	5 6/8	7	5	Sherman Co., NE	Sam D. Sullivan	Sam D. Sullivan	2006	851
162 4/8	165 7/8	23 5/8	23 4/8	21	4 2/8	4 1/8	5	5	Strawberry Creek, AB	Picked Up	Bob Daudelin	2008	851
162 4/8	166 5/8	26 2/8	26 4/8	21 6/8	5	5	5	5	Monroe Co., IL	Jonathan E. Matzenbacher	Jonathan E. Matzenbacher	2008	851
162 4/8	189 5/8	22 5/8	21 7/8	17 1/8	5 2/8	5 2/8	9	9	Lewis Co., KY	Jack McEldowney	Jack McEldowney	2008	851
162 4/8	166 6/8	25 2/8	24 3/8	23 2/8	4 7/8	4 6/8	5	5	Marathon Co., WI	Heather D. Woodward	Heather D. Woodward	2008	851
162 3/8	172	24	25	19 2/8	4 7/8	4 5/8	6	7	Osage Co., MO	Russell R. Titus	Russell R. Titus	1995	857
162 3/8	165 4/8	23 3/8	22 2/8	16 3/8	4 7/8	5	5	5	Licking Co., OH	Gary L. Boling	Gary L. Boling	2006	857
162 3/8	166 2/8	21 2/8	20 4/8	18 3/8	5	4 6/8	6	6	Choctaw Co., AL	Garry E. Dewrell	Garry E. Dewrell	2006	857
162 3/8	169 3/8	25 5/8	26 1/8	19 3/8	5	5 1/8	6	5	Jo Daviess Co., IL	Joseph C. Hinderman	Joseph C. Hinderman	2006	857
162 3/8	176 2/8	24 2/8	24 2/8	19 7/8	4 5/8	4 4/8	5	7	Fort Frances, ON	Sherri L. Redford	Sherri L. Redford	2006	857
162 3/8	170 7/8	21 6/8	24 3/8	19 5/8	4 1/8	4	4	5	Sandusky Co., OH	Mark L. Dodson	Mark L. Dodson	2007	857
162 3/8	165 2/8	26 5/8	25 7/8	23 5/8	4 3/8	4 1/8	5	4	Brown Co., WI	Mitchell L. Miedema	Mitchell L. Miedema	2007	857
162 3/8	179 5/8	27 7/8	27 6/8	21 1/8	4 1/8	4 1/8	5	7	Coshocton Co., OH	Timothy W. Miller	Timothy W. Miller	2007	857
162 3/8	177 3/8	23 6/8	23 3/8	19 1/8	6 2/8	6 2/8	6	7	Bent Co., CO	Carl D. Lindauer	Carl D. Lindauer	2008	857
162 3/8	166 2/8	25 5/8	24 4/8	19 5/8	4 7/8	4 7/8	5	5	Lowndes Co., MS	Donald J. Emery	Donald J. Emery	2009	857
162 2/8	165 2/8	26 6/8	27	22	4 6/8	4 5/8	5	5	Lamoille Co., VT	Charles O. Brown, Sr.	Timothy J. Brown	1956	867
162 2/8	166	21 6/8	22 3/8	16 2/8	4 6/8	4 4/8	5	5	Oneida Co., WI	Mark A. Nelis	Mark A. Nelis	1987	867
162 2/8	166	24 6/8	23 7/8	20 4/8	5 4/8	5 4/8	5	5	Phillips Co., AR	Justin D. Privett	Justin D. Privett	2006	867

								Locality		Owner	Date	
162 2/8	166 4/8	26 2/8	25 5/8	17 2/8	4 6/8	4 6/8	5	Logan Co., OH	5	Gary L. Campbell	2007	867
162 2/8	180 1/8	27 1/8	27 3/8	22 1/8	4 5/8	4 3/8	6	Jackson Co., WI	6	Mathew Hess	2007	867
162 2/8	171 2/8	25 3/8	24 6/8	20 1/8	5 6/8	5 4/8	6	Greene Co., IL	5	Frank Lyerla	2008	867
162 1/8	174 6/8	24 1/8	24 1/8	22 2/8	4 6/8	4 5/8	6	Essex Co., VT	6	Philip E. Therrien	1961	873
162 1/8	165 3/8	25 2/8	25 4/8	16 5/8	5	5 1/8	5	Jo Daviess Co., IL	5	Randy L. Beyer	2004	873
162 1/8	178 3/8	24	25	19 5/8	5 1/8	5 2/8	7	Union Co., IA	6	Jason W. Hellickson	2004	873
162 1/8	167 3/8	25 1/8	26 2/8	17 7/8	4 5/8	4 5/8	5	La Porte Co., IN	5	Scott E. Banghart	2006	873
162 1/8	182 2/8	27 3/8	28	20 2/8	4 6/8	4 7/8	7	Licking Co., OH	5	Jay C. Larrison	2006	873
162 1/8	173 3/8	23 3/8	25	17 7/8	5 2/8	5 2/8	6	Meadow Lake, SK	6	Justin J. Paramzchuk	2006	873
162 1/8	188 5/8	25 6/8	25 3/8	19 6/8	4 7/8	5 1/8	8	Livingston Co., IL	6	Richard D. Bertsche	2007	873
162 1/8	167 6/8	26 5/8	25 6/8	19 6/8	4 4/8	4 2/8	6	La Porte Co., IN	5	Stephen E. Gourley	2007	873
162 1/8	179 1/8	27 1/8	26 5/8	19 6/8	4 5/8	4 5/8	5	Dubuque Co., IA	6	Michael J. Lyons	2007	873
162 1/8	192 6/8	24 3/8	22	22 3/8	5	5	8	Chautauqua Co., NY	8	Ronald D. Madison	2007	873
162 1/8	176 5/8	25 6/8	24	19 1/8	5 2/8	5	5	Calhoun Co., IL	6	Timothy D. Sickles	2007	873
162 1/8	174 7/8	24 2/8	24 7/8	21 2/8	4 2/8	4 1/8	6	Freeborn Co., MN	6	Scott E. Crabtree	2008	873
162	169 6/8	24	23 7/8	15	4 6/8	4 6/8	7	Kiowa Co., KS	6	Michael T. Boman	1995	885
162	167 3/8	23 5/8	23 6/8	18 5/8	4 7/8	4 6/8	5	Morgan Co., MO	5	Steven D. Vogt	2002	885
162	183 4/8	24 4/8	25 1/8	19 5/8	5 4/8	5 4/8	7	Cass Co., MN	6	Steven E. Caton	2006	885
162	180	24 3/8	24 2/8	16 1/8	5 3/8	5 2/8	6	Jefferson Co., NY	5	Charles R. Farney	2006	885
162	164 7/8	24 5/8	24 5/8	13	4 6/8	4 5/8	5	Jackson Co., KY	5	Mark L. Miller	2006	885
162	177 3/8	25	25	18 4/8	5	5	5	Tamaulipas, MX	5	Robert E. Betbeze	2008	885

TYPICAL WHITETAIL DEER
FINAL SCORE: 179
HUNTER: Matthew L. Goodfellow

TYPICAL WHITETAIL DEER
FINAL SCORE: 164
HUNTER: Booner M. Beck

TYPICAL WHITETAIL DEER
FINAL SCORE: 160 5/8
HUNTER: Bryan C. Boyer

TYPICAL WHITETAIL DEER
FINAL SCORE: 175 7/8
HUNTER: Lisa A. Brunner

WHITETAIL DEER - TYPICAL ANTLERS

Odocoileus virginianus virginianus and certain related subspecies

Final Score	Gross Score	Length of Main Beam R.	L.	Inside Spread	Circumference at Smallest Place Between Burr & First Point R.	L.	Number of Points R.	L.	Locality	Hunter	Owner	Date Killed	Rank
162	172 3/8	26 6/8	25 6/8	20 3/8	5	5	6	5	Montgomery Co., MO	Donald L. Epple	Donald L. Epple	2008	885
162	183 3/8	23 1/8	23 2/8	17 1/8	4 4/8	4 4/8	8	6	Claysmore, AB	Dean V. Manz	Dean V. Manz	2008	885
161 7/8	170 3/8	25 7/8	26 4/8	19 4/8	4 7/8	4 4/8	6	5	Hall Co., NE	Douglas V. Vogel	Douglas V. Vogel	2004	893
161 7/8	172 3/8	25 7/8	25 6/8	19 7/8	4 5/8	4 3/8	5	5	Gage Co., NE	Jay K. Nieveen	Jay K. Nieveen	2005	893
161 7/8	177	28 7/8	29 5/8	20 1/8	5 4/8	5 3/8	8	6	St. Louis Co., MN	Larry M. Kline	Larry M. Kline	2006	893
161 7/8	170 6/8	26 3/8	27 1/8	20 3/8	5	5	5	4	Door Co., WI	Eric J. Stocking	Eric J. Stocking	2006	893
161 7/8	181 4/8	27 2/8	26 5/8	17 5/8	5 1/8	5	6	6	Edmonson Co., KY	Donald W. Sullivan	Donald W. Sullivan	2006	893
161 7/8	164 3/8	25 3/8	24 7/8	19 3/8	5 1/8	5 1/8	5	5	De Kalb Co., MO	Michael D. Jager	Michael D. Jager	2007	893
161 7/8	172 7/8	25	25 4/8	17 7/8	4 7/8	5	6	6	Eagle River, BC	Aaron B. Willey	Aaron B. Willey	2007	893
161 7/8	162 7/8	25 3/8	25 5/8	20 5/8	4 6/8	4	4	4	Ness Co., KS	Brian R. Myers	Brian R. Myers	2008	893
161 7/8	165 1/8	24 2/8	24 2/8	17 5/8	4	4	6	6	Otter Tail Co., MN	Patrick D. Tobkin	Patrick D. Tobkin	2009	893
161 6/8	167 5/8	23 6/8	24 5/8	17 6/8	4 7/8	4 7/8	5	5	Hubbard Co., MN	Virgil Ellenson	Virgil Ellenson	1988	902
161 6/8	175 6/8	26 6/8	26 4/8	20 7/8	4 6/8	4 6/8	6	6	St. John River, NB	Rose Patterson	Rose Patterson	2006	902
161 6/8	184 6/8	26 4/8	24 7/8	21	5 1/8	5 1/8	6	6	Johnson Co., IN	Daniel C. Bell	Daniel C. Bell	2008	902
161 5/8	166 5/8	24	24 3/8	18 1/8	4 4/8	4 5/8	6	5	Pendleton Co., KY	James S. Borne	James S. Borne	1997	905
161 5/8	166 4/8	24 5/8	24	18 3/8	5	5	5	5	Lewis Co., KY	Charles T. Noble	Charles T. Noble	2003	905
161 5/8	168 6/8	24 3/8	24 1/8	18 7/8	4 4/8	4 5/8	5	6	Chippewa Co., WI	Thomas M. Sinclair	Thomas M. Sinclair	2006	905
161 5/8	177 1/8	21 4/8	23 6/8	17 4/8	4 7/8	4 7/8	7	7	Refugio Co., TX	Otto Schuster	Otto Schuster	2007	905
161 5/8	169 2/8	27 5/8	27 4/8	17 3/8	4 5/8	4 5/8	5	5	Morgan Co., MO	Naseef M. Azan	Naseef M. Azan	2008	905
161 5/8	164 6/8	23 4/8	23 4/8	15 3/8	5	4 6/8	5	5	Lake Co., IN	Timothy G. Weaver	Timothy G. Weaver	2008	905
161 5/8	166 5/8	25 4/8	25 3/8	17 4/8	4 6/8	4 6/8	5	6	Clayton Co., IA	Beau J. Winters	Beau J. Winters	2008	905
161 4/8	183 7/8	25 6/8	25 1/8	20 4/8	5 6/8	6	7	6	Union Co., KY	Robert N. Brown	Robert N. Brown	2006	912
161 4/8	187 5/8	24 6/8	24 3/8	20 7/8	5 1/8	5 3/8	5	7	Hamilton Co., IN	Timothy L. Mylin	Timothy L. Mylin	2007	912
161 4/8	163 1/8	27 6/8	28	18 6/8	5	5	4	5	McCreary Co., KY	Terry A. Shelton	Terry A. Shelton	2007	912
161 4/8	173 2/8	27	25 6/8	18	4 6/8	4 4/8	7	6	Monroe Co., NY	William E. Ladd	William E. Ladd	2008	912
161 4/8	166 2/8	25 6/8	26	16 4/8	5 1/8	5	5	5	Venango Co., PA	Daniel J. Sumosky	Daniel J. Sumosky	2008	912
161 3/8	164 3/8	24	24	17 5/8	4 3/8	4 1/8	6	6	Pulaski Co., KY	Brian W. Strunk	Brian W. Strunk	2004	917
161 3/8	171 2/8	25 4/8	25 4/8	16 4/8	5 4/8	5 5/8	5	5	Gentry Co., MO	John F. O'Leary	John F. O'Leary	2005	917
161 3/8	172 3/8	22 4/8	23 2/8	13 5/8	5 5/8	5 3/8	5	6	Fisher Co., TX	Les R. Owens	Les R. Owens	2007	917
161 3/8	174	27	28	20 1/8	5	5	6	5	Floyd Co., IA	Clay R. Schneckloth	Clay R. Schneckloth	2007	917
161 2/8	170	25 7/8	26	19 6/8	4 6/8	4 5/8	5	5	Madison Co., KY	Gary W. Langford	Gary W. Langford	2004	921
161 2/8	172 2/8	25 2/8	24 7/8	19 2/8	5 1/8	5 1/8	6	6	Columbia Co., WA	Junior Dedloff	Junior Dedloff	2006	921
161 2/8	178 1/8	25 5/8	25 6/8	19 3/8	5 6/8	5 4/8	9	5	Clay Co., KS	Kenneth W. Meadors II	Kenneth W. Meadors II	2006	921

Score							Pts	Pts	Locality	Hunter	Owner	Date Killed	Rank
161 2/8	162 4/8	26 3/8	26	18	3 7/8	3 7/8	4	4	Muscatine Co., IA	Stanley R. Thieman	Stanley R. Thieman	2006	921
161 2/8	163 6/8	23 6/8	23 4/8	18 2/8	5	5	5	5	Washtenaw Co., MI	Kurt A. Kopf	Kurt A. Kopf	2007	921
161 2/8	176 7/8	28 4/8	27 5/8	24 1/8	5 6/8	5 1/8	6	4	Henry Co., IN	Ronald D. Carey	Ronald D. Carey	2008	921
161 1/8	168 6/8	24 3/8	24 2/8	21 1/8	5	5 1/8	5	6	Brown Co., OH	Brian T. Gavin	Brian T. Gavin	2006	927
161 1/8	172	25	22 7/8	17 1/8	5 3/8	4 4/8	6	6	Greene Co., IN	Michael T. Smithey	Michael T. Smithey	2006	927
161 1/8	171 2/8	27	26 4/8	17 7/8	4 6/8	4 6/8	6	6	Marquette Co., WI	Scott A. Stephan	Scott A. Stephan	2006	927
161 1/8	167	25 6/8	25 5/8	16 4/8	4 7/8	4 7/8	4	5	Franklin Co., MO	Garry L. Busse	Garry L. Busse	2008	927
161 1/8	170 3/8	25 7/8	25 4/8	17 2/8	4 3/8	4 6/8	5	5	Knox Co., IL	Robert E. Otto, Jr.	Robert E. Otto, Jr.	2008	927
161	189 1/8	26 1/8	25 4/8	20 4/8	4 4/8	4 6/8	8	7	Marshall Co., MN	Virgil Bissener	Tony Bissener	1951	932
161	175	26 7/8	27 4/8	24	4 7/8	5	9	5	Lotbiniére, QC	Daniel Bilodeau	Daniel Bilodeau	2006	932
161	168 5/8	24 1/8	25 1/8	16 2/8	4 3/8	4 7/8	6	7	Shelby Co., MO	Raymond M. Faupel	Raymond M. Faupel	2006	932
161	170	25 2/8	24 4/8	16 6/8	5	5 1/8	6	5	St. Louis Co., MN	Steven M. Jezierski	Steven M. Jezierski	2006	932
161	173 1/8	24 1/8	25 1/8	18 2/8	5	5 1/8	5	6	Beltrami Co., MN	Glen W. Laginess	Glen W. Laginess	2006	932
161	162 5/8	26	25 6/8	18 2/8	4 6/8	4 7/8	6	5	Sherburne Co., MN	Greg A. Mealhouse	Greg A. Mealhouse	2006	932
161	165 7/8	25	25 1/8	18 2/8	4 7/8	4 7/8	5	6	Fairfax Co., VA	José Murillo	José Murillo	2006	932
161	164 2/8	26 7/8	27 6/8	19 2/8	4 6/8	4 5/8	5	5	Somerset Co., ME	Brian K. Reed	Brian K. Reed	2006	932
161	165	28 3/8	27 6/8	20 4/8	4 4/8	4 4/8	5	5	Berkshire Co., MA	William E. Tatro	William E. Tatro	2006	932
161	162 5/8	23 3/8	24 1/8	16 6/8	4 3/8	4 3/8	5	5	Turtle Lake, SK	Johnnie H. Werner, Jr.	Johnnie H. Werner, Jr.	2006	932
161	173 3/8	24 1/8	23 6/8	18 4/8	4	4	6	8	Seminole Co., OK	Joe D. Jones	Joe D. Jones	2007	932
161	164 7/8	23 3/8	23 4/8	18 6/8	6 7/8	6	4	4	Morris Co., KS	Stephen R. Kelley	Stephen R. Kelley	2007	932
161	172	22 6/8	23 1/8	18 6/8	5 2/8	5 4/8	6	5	Montgomery Co., MS	Kenneth G. Britt	Kenneth G. Britt	2008	932
161	165	26 7/8	26 2/8	15 6/8	4 3/8	4 3/8	5	5	Blackford Co., IN	Josh R. Light	Josh R. Light	2008	932
160 7/8	163 2/8	25 4/8	26 3/8	20 1/8	4 4/8	4 4/8	5	6	Ward Co., ND	Mark R. Hamilton	Mark R. Hamilton	2006	946
160 7/8	179 5/8	25 3/8	25 2/8	22 1/8	4 5/8	5	6	6	Rockingham Co., VA	Eric E. Lam	Eric E. Lam	2006	946
160 7/8	175 7/8	25 5/8	24 7/8	21 2/8	5 3/8	5 3/8	7	5	Clermont Co., OH	Kevin W. Estes	Kevin W. Estes	2007	946
160 7/8	167 1/8	25 7/8	26	20 1/8	5 3/8	5 2/8	5	6	Warren Co., MO	Ariel D. Schlenther	Ariel D. Schlenther	2007	946
160 7/8	162 7/8	24 4/8	24 5/8	22 5/8	5 2/8	5 2/8	5	5	Marathon Co., WI	Kim J. Schoessow	Kim J. Schoessow	2008	946
160 6/8	175 3/8	26	26 4/8	21	4 3/8	4 3/8	6	5	Lewis Co., ID	Bruce D. Ringsmith	Mike Madden	1992	951
160 6/8	166 7/8	26 5/8	26 4/8	17 2/8	5 1/8	5 2/8	6	8	Fillmore Co., MN	William F. Pich	William F. Pich	2006	951
160 6/8	178 6/8	24 1/8	24	17 5/8	4 4/8	4 5/8	8	7	Love Co., OK	Derek F. Hallum	Derek F. Hallum	2007	951
160 6/8	167 1/8	23 1/8	23 1/8	17 1/8	4 3/8	4 3/8	7	5	Hubbard Co., MN	Douglas D. Hookom	Douglas D. Hookom	2007	951
160 6/8	185 5/8	25 5/8	24 6/8	20 2/8	4 4/8	4 3/8	7	7	Lewis & Clark Co., MT	Thomas J. Skovron	Thomas J. Skovron	2007	951
160 6/8	170 5/8	27 6/8	26 6/8	21 2/8	4 2/8	4 2/8	5	7	Saddle Hills, AB	Bryan M. Watts	Bryan M. Watts	2008	951
160 5/8	164 4/8	23 3/8	23 4/8	14 5/8	5 2/8	5 1/8	5	5	Stillwater Co., MT	Ronald V. Giese	Ronald V. Giese	1982	957
160 5/8	167 4/8	24 3/8	24 6/8	17 2/8	5	5 1/8	6	6	Franklin Co., KS	Ronnie R. Rumford	Ronnie R. Rumford	1999	957
160 5/8	165	24 6/8	25 7/8	18 3/8	4 7/8	5	5	5	Christian Co., IL	Chuck R. Brown	Chuck R. Brown	2006	957
160 5/8	166 2/8	24 6/8	24 4/8	14 7/8	5	5	5	5	Choctaw Co., MS	Ricky H. Dendy	Ricky H. Dendy	2006	957
160 5/8	166 6/8	26 7/8	26	18 3/8	5 3/8	5 3/8	5	6	Dubois Co., IN	Matthew Eisenhut	Matthew Eisenhut	2006	957
160 5/8	169 3/8	27 2/8	26 6/8	19 3/8	4 5/8	4 5/8	6	6	Bedford Co., VA	John T. McQuade	John T. McQuade	2006	957
160 5/8	183	24 7/8	23	17 3/8	6 2/8	6	8	8	Pike Co., MO	Billy M. Boston	Billy M. Boston	2007	957
160 5/8	164	27 4/8	27 3/8	20 3/8	4 7/8	4 4/8	4	4	Queens Co., NB	Terry Saulnier	Terry Saulnier	2007	957
160 5/8	173 4/8	26 2/8	25	19	5 2/8	4 3/8	7	5	Bourbon Co., KS	Alvin C. Stamper	Alvin C. Stamper	2007	957

WHITETAIL DEER - TYPICAL ANTLERS

Odocoileus virginianus virginianus and certain related subspecies

Final Score	Gross Score	Length of Main Beam R.	L.	Inside Spread	Circ. at Smallest Place Between Burr & First Point R.	L.	Number of Points R.	L.	Locality	Hunter	Owner	Date Killed	Rank
160 5/8	172 2/8	24 6/8	24 4/8	19 1/8	4 6/8	4 7/8	7	7	De Kalb Co., MO	Bryan C. Boyer	Bryan C. Boyer	2008	957
160 5/8	185 1/8	27 4/8	24 7/8	24 4/8	5 2/8	5 6/8	6	7	Delaware Co., IA	Edward D. Gibbs	Edward D. Gibbs	2008	957
160 5/8	182	25 4/8	25	16 4/8	4 3/8	4 3/8	8	10	Forsyth Co., NC	Brent M. Marshall	Brent M. Marshall	2008	957
160 5/8	164 6/8	25 1/8	24 1/8	17 1/8	5	4 7/8	5	5	Ray Co., MO	Samuel A. Switzer	Samuel A. Switzer	2008	957
160 4/8	167	26	24 4/8	18 6/8	3 7/8	4 1/8	5	5	La Salle Co., TX	John W. Hodges	John W. Hodges	1976	970
160 4/8	171 3/8	25 5/8	24 7/8	18 4/8	4 6/8	4 6/8	7	5	Unknown	Picked Up	Robert S. Marszalek PR	1980	970
160 4/8	174 5/8	26 4/8	25 4/8	20 2/8	4 5/8	4 5/8	5	5	Waushara Co., WI	Bryan D. Cullen	Bryan D. Cullen	2002	970
160 4/8	167 1/8	25 3/8	25 4/8	16	4 5/8	4 6/8	5	7	Brown Co., IL	Douglas C. Ackerman	Douglas C. Ackerman	2005	970
160 4/8	181 3/8	22 7/8	23 6/8	15 6/8	5 3/8	5 4/8	5	5	Gentry Co., MO	Jarod E. Cox	Jarod E. Cox	2006	970
160 4/8	166 2/8	27	26 2/8	19	4 5/8	4 5/8	6	9	Bexar Co., TX	Gerald W. Jasik, Jr.	Gerald W. Jasik, Jr.	2006	970
160 4/8	170 5/8	24	23 5/8	19 4/8	4 1/8	4 3/8	5	6	Linn Co., KS	Jonathan M. Thornberry	Jonathan M. Thornberry	2006	970
160 4/8	183 1/8	25 6/8	24 6/8	15	4 7/8	4 7/8	8	9	Carroll Co., MO	David S. Clark	David S. Clark	2007	970
160 4/8	176 2/8	27 2/8	26 5/8	19 1/8	4 3/8	4 5/8	5	6	Otter Tail Co., MN	Chris A. Sumstad	Chris A. Sumstad	2007	970
160 4/8	164 5/8	25 2/8	26 5/8	20 2/8	4 5/8	4 6/8	4	4	Dubuque Co., IA	Chad P. Brandel	Chad P. Brandel	2008	970
160 4/8	174 2/8	24	24 1/8	15 4/8	4 2/8	4 2/8	8	6	Maverick Co., TX	Terry M. Howard	Terry M. Howard	2008	970
160 4/8	167 7/8	24 6/8	25 2/8	19 2/8	4 3/8	4 2/8	5	6	Winneshiek Co., IA	Brian J. McClintock	Brian J. McClintock	2008	970
160 4/8	183 5/8	23	25 1/8	18 4/8	5 2/8	5 3/8	6	7	Potter Co., SD	David M. Oberlitner	David M. Oberlitner	2008	970
160 4/8	180	26	25 5/8	17 6/8	5	5	6	6	Iroquois Co., IL	Darrin L. Warren	Darrin L. Warren	2008	970
160 3/8	169 3/8	26 4/8	26 2/8	21 5/8	5 5/8	5 2/8	5	4	Monroe Co., MS	Bobby Davis	Wayne Davis	1965	984
160 3/8	172 4/8	23 5/8	23 5/8	16	3 7/8	4	6	6	Queen Anne's Co., MD	Roy Bolling	Roy Bolling	1993	984
160 3/8	168 7/8	26	26	19 3/8	4 7/8	4 6/8	6	6	Todd Co., MN	Richard M. Cook	Richard M. Cook	2006	984
160 3/8	164 4/8	25 2/8	24 6/8	19 5/8	4 5/8	4 4/8	5	5	Worcester Co., MA	Brian M. Peary	Brian M. Peary	2006	984
160 3/8	168 4/8	27 5/8	27	16 3/8	6	5 2/8	6	6	Highland Co., OH	Darlene L. Smith	Darlene L. Smith	2006	984
160 3/8	172 4/8	26 3/8	26 6/8	20 4/8	4 6/8	4 6/8	6	6	Wabasha Co., MN	Robert A. Curran	Robert A. Curran	2007	984
160 3/8	172 2/8	24 7/8	23 7/8	18 3/8	4 4/8	4 4/8	7	6	Lake of the Woods, ON	Steve C. Economos	Steve C. Economos	2007	984
160 3/8	164 3/8	24 3/8	23 3/8	17 5/8	4 2/8	4 4/8	5	5	Franklin Co., TN	Chase D. Hensley	Chase D. Hensley	2007	984
160 3/8	165 3/8	26 5/8	26 1/8	21 3/8	5 4/8	5 4/8	5	5	Kent Co., ON	Melanie A. Long	Melanie A. Long	2007	984
160 3/8	174 3/8	27 4/8	25 6/8	18 3/8	5	5 1/8	6	7	White Co., IL	Trout T. Moser	Trout T. Moser	2007	984
160 3/8	166 3/8	22 5/8	22	19 5/8	4 7/8	4 6/8	7	6	Jackson Co., WI	Darrell L. Armbruster	Darrell L. Armbruster	2008	984
160 3/8	164 4/8	23 4/8	24	16 5/8	5 3/8	5 1/8	6	6	Todd Co., MN	Chad M. Crider	Chad M. Crider	2008	984
160 3/8	176 1/8	24 3/8	23 2/8	20 1/8	4 6/8	4 6/8	7	7	Frontier Co., NE	Jerimey J. Pace	Jerimey J. Pace	2008	984
160 3/8	183	24 5/8	25 7/8	18 5/8	6 3/8	5 3/8	6	6	Randolph Co., MO	Robert G. Rixon	Robert G. Rixon	2008	984
160 3/8	161 6/8	24 2/8	23 6/8	17 5/8	4 5/8	4 5/8	6	5	Stevens Co., WA	R.Tyler Vickrey	R.Tyler Vickrey	2008	984

Score								Locality	Owner	Hunter	Date Killed	Rank
160 2/8	165 4/8	25 2/8	25 4/8	17 2/8	4 5/8	5	4	McHenry Co., ND	Terry E. Cossette	Terry E. Cossette	1972	999
160 2/8	173 1/8	25 6/8	25 6/8	20 2/8	4 5/8	6	5	Richland Co., WI	Steven J. Borman	Steven J. Borman	2006	999
160 2/8	164 1/8	24 2/8	25	20	5 1/8	4	4	Clay Co., IN	Austin Harrison	Austin Harrison	2006	999
160 2/8	182 3/8	27 1/8	28 4/8	17 4/8	4 6/8	6	5	Custer Co., NE	William A. Gregory	William A. Gregory	2007	999
160 2/8	166	25 6/8	26 7/8	17 4/8	3 7/8	5	5	Madison Co., TN	Steven W. Harris	Steven W. Harris	2007	999
160 2/8	180 3/8	26 2/8	27 1/8	18 6/8	4 6/8	6	7	Newton Co., TX	Richard A. Kreger	Richard A. Kreger	2007	999
160 2/8	170 3/8	25	25	19	5 3/8	6	6	Cass Co., MI	Micheal J. Eash	Micheal J. Eash	2008	999
160 2/8	165 7/8	25 2/8	25 2/8	19 3/8	4 5/8	6	5	New Haven Co., CT	Paul B. Johnson	Paul B. Johnson	2008	999
160 1/8	166	24 6/8	23 7/8	16 6/8	4	5	6	Pendleton Co., WV	Gary G. Youngblood	Gary G. Youngblood	1982	1,007
160 1/8	183 5/8	25 6/8	25 7/8	21 5/8	4 7/8	6	8	Washington Co., IL	Thomas J. Toennies	Thomas J. Toennies	2005	1,007
160 1/8	165 3/8	26 1/8	25 2/8	19 1/8	5	6	6	Kleberg Co., TX	Daryl D. Brown	Daryl D. Brown	2006	1,007
160 1/8	178 6/8	25 1/8	24 2/8	19 2/8	6	7	5	Calhoun Co., IL	Alex J. Harbison	Alex J. Harbison	2006	1,007
160 1/8	178 1/8	26 5/8	26 7/8	20 6/8	5	6	6	McLean Co., KY	James G. Klump	James G. Klump	2006	1,007
160 1/8	173 7/8	26	25 4/8	19	4 6/8	7	6	Knox Co., KY	Kenneth Mills	Kenneth Mills	2006	1,007
160 1/8	170 6/8	24 2/8	23 2/8	19 7/8	4 1/8	7	5	Hunterdon Co., NJ	Samantha C. Pankow	Samantha C. Pankow	2006	1,007
160 1/8	165 4/8	24 5/8	24 3/8	18 6/8	4 3/8	5	6	Douglas Co., WI	Aric E. Tourville	Aric E. Tourville	2006	1,007
160 1/8	186 1/8	26 5/8	26 5/8	22 1/8	5 1/8	7	6	Highland Co., OH	Wes H. Davenport	Wes H. Davenport	2007	1,007
160 1/8	178 3/8	26 6/8	25 2/8	19 7/8	5 1/8	7	6	Polk Co., IA	Glen E. Salow	Glen E. Salow	2007	1,007
160 1/8	162 7/8	24 7/8	24 7/8	18 3/8	4 6/8	5	5	Madison Co., MS	Robert G. Dye, Jr.	Robert G. Dye, Jr.	2008	1,007
160 1/8	163 3/8	25 4/8	25 3/8	23 3/8	5 2/8	5	6	Carroll Co., OH	Eddie E. Mayle	Eddie E. Mayle	2008	1,007
160	163 5/8	26 2/8	25 6/8	20 2/8	5 1/8	5	5	Rutland Co., VT	Stanley E. Mills	Stanley E. Mills	1952	1,019
160	166 2/8	25 1/8	25	21 7/8	4 6/8	5	6	Burnett Co., WI	Brent Bristol	Brent Bristol	1995	1,019
160	167 1/8	25 4/8	24 4/8	17	5 3/8	5	5	Jefferson Co., IN	Tony L. Adams	Tony L. Adams	2004	1,019
160	172 5/8	24 6/8	24 3/8	19	5 3/8	7	6	Union Co., IA	Guillermo R. Garcia, Jr.	Guillermo R. Garcia, Jr.	2004	1,019
160	172 7/8	27 5/8	27	20 3/8	5	6	5	Noble Co., IN	Dwight Busche	Dwight Busche	2005	1,019
160	171 3/8	27 2/8	27 3/8	18 7/8	4 2/8	5	7	Newaygo Co., MI	Mark C. Hawley	Mark C. Hawley	2006	1,019
160	166 7/8	25 4/8	26 2/8	20	5 4/8	4	5	Hopkins Co., KY	Bo Hester	Bo Hester	2006	1,019
160	181 1/8	26 2/8	24 2/8	17 3/8	4 3/8	6	7	Walsh Co., ND	David E. Linstad	David E. Linstad	2006	1,019
160	164 5/8	23	23	19	4 5/8	6	5	Becker Co., MN	Ronald Perrine	Ronald Perrine	2006	1,019
160	164	23 6/8	24 5/8	19 3/8	4 4/8	6	5	Pine River, BC	Kody H. Tricker	Kody H. Tricker	2006	1,019
160	168 4/8	23 2/8	23 2/8	17	5	5	6	Union Co., KY	Troy E. Bunner	Troy E. Bunner	2007	1,019
160	173 5/8	26 1/8	28	16	5 7/8	6	7	Pratt Co., KS	Steve A. Tittsworth	Steve A. Tittsworth	2007	1,019
160	167 1/8	24 5/8	23 6/8	17 7/8	4 6/8	6	6	Langlade Co., WI	Richard E. Phillips	Richard E. Phillips	2008	1,019
160	167 2/8	24 5/8	26 1/8	19 6/8	4 1/8	5	5	Litchfield Co., CT	Mark J. Tutolo	Mark J. Tutolo	2008	1,019
160	162 3/8	25 3/8	25 2/8	21 6/8	5 1/8	5	5	Logan Co., OH	Julie E. Bodenmiller	Julie E. Bodenmiller	2009	1,019
202 3/8*	236 6/8	27 5/8	28 1/8	28 6/8	6 1/8	7	10	N. Saskatchewan River, SK	J. Tarala & M. Berezowski	J. Tarala & M. Berezowski	2006	
194 3/8*	202 1/8	28 1/8	28 1/8	19 5/8	6 2/8	5	5	Montgomery Co., IA	Mark A. Lewis	Mark A. Lewis	2008	
193 2/8*	195 7/8	27 1/8	27 3/8	15 2/8	4 5/8	7	7	Harper Co., KS	Keith J. Manca	Keith J. Manca	2007	

Final score subject to revision by additional verifying measurements.

WHITETAIL DEER - NON-TYPICAL ANTLERS

Minimum Score 185   *Odocoileus virginianus virginianus* and certain related subspecies   World's Record 333 7/8

Final Score	Gross Score	Length of Main Beam R.	L.	Inside Spread	Circumference at Smallest Place Between Burr & First Point R.	L.	Number of Points R.	L.	Locality	Hunter	Owner	Date Killed	Rank
275 5/8	290 2/8	26 1/8	27 1/8	24	5 1/8	5 1/8	13	15	Jackson Co., IA	Kyle M. Simmons	Kyle M. Simmons	2008	1
274	286 7/8	19 1/8	22 4/8	27 7/8	4 5/8	4 6/8	16	20	Cross Lake, AB	Helgie H. Eymundson	Helgie H. Eymundson	2007	2
272 7/8	289 2/8	27 4/8	27 6/8	23 3/8	7 7/8	7	14	13	Morris Co., KS	Gerald E. Rightmyer	Gerald E. Rightmyer	2006	3
271 7/8	276 2/8	29	28 6/8	24 3/8	6 6/8	6 4/8	19	12	Henry Co., KY	Picked Up	Brad Gsell	2004	4
252 7/8	263 4/8	29 3/8	28	29 4/8	5 2/8	5 3/8	10	15	Pawnee Co., NE	Unknown	DLJM Collection	1990	5
251 6/8	264 2/8	27 3/8	23 3/8	19	6	5 6/8	14	12	Kit Carson Co., CO	Joe Prinzi	Bass Pro Shops	2001	6
251	256 2/8	27 6/8	27 4/8	21 6/8	4 7/8	4 7/8	10	11	Sanders Co., MT	Brett Johnson	Randy Smith	1988	7
250 5/8	257 2/8	26	27	20 2/8	6	5 7/8	12	12	Macoupin Co., IL	Jess M. Gilpin	Jess M. Gilpin	2008	8
249 6/8	264 2/8	18 4/8	24 1/8	18 2/8	6 2/8	6	15	14	Butler Co., KY	Robert J. Taylor	Robert J. Taylor	2008	9
249 1/8	264 3/8	23 2/8	16	16	6	5 3/8	15	25	Wayne Co., IA	Scott L. McIntire	Scott L. McIntire	2006	10
248 7/8	256 1/8	26 6/8	28	20 1/8	5 6/8	5 5/8	15	10	Charles Co., MD	Donza L. Watson	Donza L. Watson	2007	11
246 5/8	251 5/8	23 7/8	24 5/8	20 6/8	6	5 7/8	13	13	Nance Co., NE	Unknown	Gale Sup	1960	12
246 3/8	254 2/8	30	30	20 3/8	6 1/8	5 6/8	10	9	Christian Co., KY	Dan U. Miller	Dan U. Miller	2006	13
246 2/8	255 2/8	26	27 5/8	19	5 4/8	5 3/8	18	13	De Kalb Co., MO	Jerald D. Utt	Jerald D. Utt	2007	14
244 6/8	263 5/8	24	23 1/8	20 1/8	5 7/8	10 7/8	13	20	Lucas Co., IA	Travis L. Hamilton	Travis L. Hamilton	2009	15
244	251 7/8	28 7/8	28 7/8	22 2/8	5 4/8	5 3/8	9	11	Barber Co., KS	Unknown	Brad Gsell	1978	16
243 6/8	255 7/8	26 5/8	27 1/8	20 5/8	5 1/8	5 1/8	14	15	Fond du Lac Co., WI	Wayne F. Schumacher	Wayne F. Schumacher	2009	17
242	251 7/8	27 1/8	27 1/8	18 1/8	6	6 2/8	13	13	Decatur Co., IA	Steven R. Binkley	Steven R. Binkley	2008	18
242	249 7/8	26 5/8	28 4/8	24 2/8	5 2/8	5 1/8	10	10	Douglas Co., KS	Chad M. Christie	Chad M. Christie	2008	18
241 7/8	252 4/8	27 2/8	26 3/8	17 3/8	4 4/8	4 4/8	13	12	Waupaca Co., WI	James F. Paalman	James F. Paalman	2008	20
240 2/8	247 5/8	22 4/8	23 4/8	15 2/8	4 7/8	4 6/8	13	12	Geary Co., KS	James Livingston	James Livingston	2007	21
238 5/8	245 6/8	23 7/8	24 4/8	17 2/8	7 1/8	6 4/8	17	10	Moultrie Co., IL	Nathan E. Webster	Nathan E. Webster	2009	22
238 2/8	241 1/8	25 7/8	25 3/8	19 1/8	5 1/8	5 2/8	12	14	Henry Co., IN	Steven R. Padgett	Steven R. Padgett	2007	23
238 2/8	245 6/8	26 7/8	27	19	6 4/8	6	13	15	Jasper Co., IL	Kevin L. Radke	Kevin L. Radke	2007	23
236 7/8	249 7/8	22 1/8	20 4/8	17 6/8	3 6/8	4 2/8	12	13	Chesterfield Co., VA	Lanny L. Bolen	Lanny L. Bolen	1967	25
234 2/8	240 1/8	24 4/8	24 2/8	19	5 6/8	6	13	11	Ripley Co., IN	Jeremy A. Eaton	Jeremy A. Eaton	2008	26
234 1/8	237 6/8	27 2/8	27 2/8	20 6/8	6 2/8	6 4/8	11	9	Delaware Co., OH	Gregory S. Hunt	Gregory S. Hunt	2008	27
233 3/8	241 7/8	23 4/8	26 4/8	16 1/8	5 1/8	5 1/8	12	10	Red Deer River, AB	Mark E. Altwasser	Mark E. Altwasser	2004	28
233 2/8	240 7/8	27 7/8	26 6/8	20 2/8	5 2/8	5 1/8	8	8	Buffalo Co., WI	Robert J. Decker	Robert J. Decker	2008	29
232 4/8	239 5/8	25	26 2/8	24 5/8	6	6	12	11	Big River, SK	Duane M. Becker	Duane M. Becker	2006	30
230 6/8	233 7/8	27 2/8	28	26 6/8	5 7/8	5 6/8	9	11	Benton Co., IA	Jeff A. Parker	Jeff A. Parker	2007	31
230 5/8	239	28 4/8	29 2/8	24 2/8	5 5/8	5 6/8	12	11	Fairfield Co., OH	Scott A. Esker	Scott A. Esker	2008	32
229 4/8	235 3/8	29 1/8	29	23	5 6/8	5 6/8	10	11	Carleton, ON	Frank C. Argue	Frank C. Argue	2006	33

Score									Locality	Owner	Hunter	Date	Rank
229 1/8	238 6/8	25 6/8	27 4/8	20	5 5/8	5 4/8	12	15	Phillips Co., KS	Russell L. Van Zoeren	Russell L. Van Zoeren	2006	34
228 5/8	241 6/8	24 5/8	20 6/8	17 5/8	5 7/8	6	14	12	McDonough Co., IL	Nathan R. Campbell	Nathan R. Campbell	2009	35
228 4/8	238 5/8	28 4/8	27 6/8	21 3/8	5 5/8	5 3/8	14	10	Pike Co., MO	Daren L. Walker	Daren L. Walker	2008	36
227 3/8	238 1/8	29 7/8	28	21 3/8	5 3/8	5 5/8	10	14	Lawrence Co., OH	Randy Delawder	Randy Delawder	2008	37
227 3/8	232 3/8	25	25 4/8	19 7/8	6 1/8	6 2/8	14	13	Morrison Co., MN	Scott M. O'Konek	Scott M. O'Konek	2009	37
227 2/8	238 4/8	26 2/8	26 2/8	20 5/8	5 7/8	5 5/8	11	15	Chariton Co., MO	Joseph L. Bryant	Joseph L. Bryant	2007	39
227 2/8	234 5/8	21 2/8	22 2/8	18 2/8	4	4	20	17	Haywood Co., TN	Henry N. Cannon	Henry N. Cannon	2007	39
226 3/8	236 5/8	26 7/8	26 6/8	23 7/8	7 4/8	7 4/8	12	12	Linn Co., IA	Matthew A. Yamilkoski	Matthew A. Yamilkoski	2006	41
226 3/8	233 3/8	26 5/8	23 4/8	23 4/8	5 4/8	5 7/8	12	11	Houston Co., MN	Benjamin W. Spanjers	Benjamin W. Spanjers	2008	41
225 4/8	240 2/8	31 4/8	28 4/8	23 3/8	5 7/8	6 2/8	11	11	Dubois Co., IN	Timothy E. Friedman	Timothy E. Friedman	2007	43
224 2/8	229 5/8	27 7/8	27 7/8	17 7/8	5 3/8	5 3/8	14	14	Greene Co., IN	Griffin M. Terrell	Griffin M. Terrell	2007	44
224 1/8	234 6/8	25 6/8	25 6/8	21 4/8	6	6 2/8	15	13	Madison Co., IL	Bill Klawitter	Bill Klawitter	1963	45
224 1/8	229 6/8	25 3/8	23 5/8	20 1/8	7 4/8	7 3/8	12	13	Jackson Co., IL	Carl D. Brooks	Carl D. Brooks	2007	45
223 3/8	232 1/8	21	19 4/8	19 4/8	6 2/8	6 2/8	14	10	Phillips Co., KS	Tracy L. Atchison	Tracy L. Atchison	2009	47
222 5/8	233 4/8	24 5/8	24 7/8	19 4/8	5 5/8	5 5/8	10	11	Montgomery Co., IL	Gregory D. Wilson	Gregory D. Wilson	2007	48
222 4/8	229 5/8	22 1/8	23 3/8	21 4/8	6 2/8	6	12	12	Ringgold Co., IA	Martin D. White	Martin D. White	2008	49
222 3/8	232 6/8	26 5/8	27 5/8	22 3/8	5 5/8	5 2/8	15	11	Jefferson Co., WI	Richard S. Goulder	Richard S. Goulder	2007	50
222 1/8	234 1/8	28 4/8	25 4/8	17 5/8	4 5/8	4 5/8	11	10	Fayette Co., IL	Jeremy E. Cauble	Jeremy E. Cauble	2008	51
221 7/8	231 3/8	26	25 3/8	19 4/8	6	6 4/8	12	12	Seward Co., NE	Gus Shy	Gus Shy	2006	52
221 4/8	228 7/8	26 6/8	26 6/8	20 5/8	5	4 7/8	13	11	Cudworth, SK	Tracy Trischuk	Tracy Trischuk	2008	53
221 2/8	236 5/8	22 2/8	22 2/8	19 2/8	6 5/8	6 5/8	21	13	Christian Co., KY	Rick Weatherford	Picked Up	2008	54
221 1/8	233 6/8	24 3/8	24 3/8	14 7/8	5 3/8	5 3/8	10	16	Moose Mountain Creek, SK	Tyson J. Geisel	Tyson J. Geisel	2006	55
221	231 2/8	26	25 6/8	19 3/8	5 3/8	5 3/8	11	11	Niagara Co., NY	Keith A. LeVick	Keith A. LeVick	2007	56
220 5/8	228 6/8	21 6/8	19 7/8	19 7/8	6 2/8	6 3/8	12	12	St. Clair Co., IL	Gary Hollen	Picked Up	2005	57
220 5/8	231	22 5/8	23 6/8	23 6/8	6 3/8	5 2/8	9	7	Qu'Appelle River, SK	Jack Lubachowski	Jack Lubachowski	2006	57
220 2/8	234 7/8	26 3/8	25 1/8	17 6/8	5 5/8	5 2/8	11	9	Andrew Co., MO	Cary L. Vaughn	Cary L. Vaughn	2007	59
219 7/8	232 5/8	25 6/8	26 3/8	21	6 6/8	6 2/8	11	14	Otoe Co., NE	Brian S. Bevil, Sr.	Brian S. Bevil, Sr.	2007	60
219 6/8	227 4/8	24 4/8	24 6/8	20 1/8	5 2/8	5 2/8	20	11	Marshall Co., MS	Brian K. Smith	Brian K. Smith	2006	61
219 4/8	228 7/8	22 3/8	22 1/8	17	5	5	10	12	Macon Co., MO	Randall C. Barnes	Randall C. Barnes	2007	62
219 3/8	224 2/8	25 3/8	25 3/8	26 2/8	5 3/8	5 2/8	8	10	La Salle Co., TX	Rene R. Barrientos	Rene R. Barrientos	2009	63
219 2/8	226 4/8	25 5/8	25 2/8	22 4/8	5 2/8	5 2/8	11	11	Maverick Co., TX	Thomas D. Friedkin	Thomas D. Friedkin	2006	64
219 1/8	226 1/8	29 3/8	29 4/8	18	5 6/8	5 4/8	13	9	McPherson Co., KS	Randy R. Bercume	Randy R. Bercume	2006	65
219	224 5/8	27 4/8	20 7/8	20 7/8	5 4/8	5 1/8	10	10	Ross Co., OH	Derek P. Thompson	Derek P. Thompson	2008	66
218 7/8	228 2/8	21 1/8	21 1/8	17 3/8	5 7/8	5 7/8	11	13	Sargent Co., ND	Bruce Bosse	Bruce Bosse	2007	67
218 5/8	225 1/8	23 2/8	23 2/8	20 5/8	5 2/8	5 6/8	12	10	Richland Co., IL	Ransom M. Brooks	Ransom M. Brooks	2008	68
218 3/8	230	25 3/8	25 2/8	19 2/8	5 6/8	5 7/8	14	13	Smith Co., KS	A. Bryan Davis	A. Bryan Davis	2008	68
218 2/8	230 1/8	21 2/8	19 1/8	19 4/8	5 1/8	5 6/8	10	18	Owen Co., KY	Ervin R. Vance	Ervin R. Vance	2007	70
218	222 5/8	24 6/8	22 3/8	22 3/8	5 3/8	5 4/8	12	12	Pendleton Co., WV	K.D. & C. Colvin	Morris Dahmer	1953	71
217 7/8	229 7/8	24 1/8	24	18 6/8	5 1/8	5 2/8	11	11	Fremont Co., IA	Andy J. Sheldon	Andy J. Sheldon	2008	72
217 6/8	220 6/8	27 1/8	27 5/8	23 4/8	5 4/8	5 2/8	9	9	Douglas Co., NE	Gary Winans	Gary Winans	2008	73

WHITETAIL DEER - NON-TYPICAL ANTLERS

Odocoileus virginianus virginianus and certain related subspecies

Final Score	Gross Score	Length of Main Beam		Inside Spread	Circumference at Smallest Place Between Burr & First Point		Number of Points		Locality	Hunter	Owner	Date Killed	Rank
		R.	L.		R.	L.	R.	L.					
217 5/8	228 2/8	27 3/8	27 1/8	20 7/8	5 4/8	5 6/8	9	11	Carroll Co., MO	Justin B. Adkison	Justin B. Adkison	2008	74
217 4/8	222 4/8	24 6/8	25 5/8	17 2/8	5 2/8	5 3/8	12	16	Brown Co., IL	Michael G. Hyma	Michael G. Hyma	2007	75
217 3/8	224 6/8	26 1/8	26	19 4/8	5 5/8	5	11	9	Fulton Co., IL	Parrish N. Brown	Parrish N. Brown	2006	76
217 2/8	228 3/8	25 6/8	24	19 1/8	5 6/8	5 6/8	12	13	Clarke Co., IA	Gregg E. Voegtlin	Gregg E. Voegtlin	2008	77
217	228 2/8	24 7/8	23 4/8	20 2/8	5	5	11	17	Nance Co., NE	Charles Rowland	Gale Sup	PR 1991	78
216 6/8	224 7/8	25 5/8	27 2/8	16 6/8	5 7/8	6	8	11	Henderson Co., KY	Picked Up	Carson Crafton	2007	79
216 3/8	223 5/8	22 7/8	24 2/8	14 5/8	5 3/8	4 4/8	13	8	Sully Co., SD	Picked Up	John T. Hughes	2009	80
216 2/8	225 2/8	22 6/8	25 2/8	22 2/8	5 1/8	4 7/8	11	12	Bonner Co., ID	Fred C. Colby	Fred C. Colby	2006	81
216 1/8	227 1/8	24 3/8	23 1/8	18 5/8	5	6 5/8	12	10	Jasper Co., IL	Rodney E. Williams	Rodney E. Williams	2008	82
215 5/8	220 2/8	24 5/8	23 2/8	18 7/8	5 3/8	5 4/8	11	8	Murray Lake, SK	G. Day & M. Day	G. Day & M. Day	2006	83
215 4/8	219 4/8	26 7/8	26 1/8	21	5 2/8	4 7/8	11	11	Chickasaw Co., IA	Angela R. Lenehan	Angela R. Lenehan	2007	84
215 2/8	218 5/8	29 1/8	27 7/8	25 3/8	5 4/8	5 3/8	8	8	Hancock Co., IL	Mike K. Belshaw	Mike K. Belshaw	2008	85
215 2/8	222 4/8	25 1/8	26 5/8	20 5/8	5 5/8	5 6/8	9	7	Boone Co., MO	William A. Lowrey	William A. Lowrey	2008	85
215 1/8	225	26 1/8	27	21 1/8	5 7/8	6 1/8	9	10	Calhoun Co., MI	Tim Tackett	Tim Tackett	2007	87
215	224 6/8	25 7/8	27 1/8	21 1/8	5 1/8	5 2/8	11	10	Bureau Co., IL	Alan O. Kaiser	Alan O. Kaiser	2006	88
215	222 5/8	26 6/8	26 1/8	19 6/8	4 5/8	4 5/8	11	10	Franklin Co., IN	Johnny L. Thacker	Johnny L. Thacker	2006	88
214 6/8	219 1/8	23 5/8	21 3/8	17 4/8	5 4/8	5 1/8	11	11	Le Flore Co., OK	Patricia A. White	Patricia A. White	2006	90
214 6/8	227 4/8	27 4/8	25 2/8	22 4/8	6 2/8	6 2/8	10	11	Shawano Co., WI	Boyd L. Dallmann	Boyd L. Dallmann	2007	90
214 5/8	220 2/8	25 7/8	26 3/8	18 6/8	5 7/8	5 6/8	9	10	111 Mile House, BC	Derek S. Robin	Derek S. Robin	2008	92
214 4/8	222 5/8	26 6/8	25 3/8	21 1/8	5 7/8	7 1/8	8	12	Jasper Co., IL	Brock A. Tarr	Brock A. Tarr	2008	93
214 2/8	219 5/8	30 2/8	28 7/8	29 4/8	5 7/8	5 5/8	10	8	Trempealeau Co., WI	John Filla	John Filla	2006	94
214 2/8	231 1/8	25 3/8	24 3/8	21 3/8	6 1/8	6 2/8	10	13	Schuyler Co., IL	Norman Gorsuch	Norman Gorsuch	2006	94
214 1/8	220 1/8	23 5/8	22	17 7/8	5 6/8	5 6/8	11	12	Sedgwick Co., KS	Herman C. Hamilton	Herman C. Hamilton	2008	96
214	220 5/8	27 6/8	28 3/8	20 5/8	5 5/8	5 7/8	11	8	Boone Co., IA	Casey M. Moorman	Casey M. Moorman	2006	97
214	218 5/8	25 6/8	26 6/8	19 6/8	5 2/8	5 2/8	12	8	Birch Lake, SK	Brett E. Seidle	Brett E. Seidle	2008	97
213 7/8	224 1/8	23 7/8	25 2/8	16 6/8	8 4/8	6 2/8	8	8	Jackfish Lake, SK	Jeffrey B. Rittenhouse	Jeffrey B. Rittenhouse	2006	99
213 7/8	221 3/8	23 3/8	23 5/8	18	5 2/8	5 4/8	9	9	Fayette Co., IA	Jim Avenson	Jim Avenson	2007	99
213 7/8	220 2/8	28 1/8	25 6/8	19 5/8	6 1/8	6 3/8	9	14	Randolph Co., IL	Donald R. Krull	Donald R. Krull	2008	99
213 6/8	224	27 6/8	26	20	4 1/8	4 7/8	10	10	Switzerland Co., IN	J. Chris Robbins	J. Chris Robbins	2006	102
213 5/8	227 2/8	26	27 4/8	24	5 6/8	6	11	12	Pawnee Co., NE	Matt P. Kalin	Matt P. Kalin	2007	103
213 4/8	229 3/8	28 6/8	22 7/8	16 5/8	5 4/8	6 1/8	15	19	Pushmataha Co., OK	John A. McDonald	John A. McDonald	2006	104
213 4/8	231 7/8	20 5/8	22	20 5/8	5 5/8	5 1/8	11	7	Fulton Co., GA	Jay Maxwell	Jay Maxwell	2007	104
213 3/8	222 2/8	22 5/8	22 7/8	17 7/8	4 5/8	4 6/8	10	12	Hidalgo Co., TX	David F. Coleman	David F. Coleman	2006	106

Score	Gross Score	Main Beam R	Main Beam L	Inside Spread	Circ. R	Circ. L	Points R	Points L	Locality	Hunter	Owner	Date	Rank
213 3/8	222 6/8	25 7/8	25 5/8	20 1/8	4 6/8	4 6/8	14	8	N. Battleford, SK	Todd S. Smith	Todd S. Smith	2008	106
213 2/8	220 6/8	25 6/8	25 6/8	18 4/8	5	5	10	12	Camden Co., MO	John H. Shelton	John H. Shelton	2007	108
213 2/8	226 5/8	26 2/8	26 6/8	25 4/8	5 2/8	5	9	14	Ashburn, ON	Alex W. MacCulloch	Alex W. MacCulloch	2008	108
213	215 6/8	25 2/8	25 2/8	22 4/8	5 4/8	5 3/8	12	8	Silver Beach Lake, SK	Bruce Stieb	Bruce Stieb	2006	110
212 7/8	219 4/8	26 3/8	27 1/8	22 4/8	5 7/8	5 3/8	9	10	Kawartha Lake, ON	Paul J. Clancy	Paul J. Clancy	2006	111
212 7/8	221 3/8	26 5/8	27 5/8	21 2/8	4 7/8	5 7/8	7	9	Houston Co., MN	Alex L. Edwards	Alex L. Edwards	2008	111
212 6/8	220 1/8	24 2/8	25	18 4/8	6 5/8	6 6/8	10	13	Vermilion River, AB	Joe Reck	Joe Reck	2007	113
212 5/8	221 2/8	27 4/8	27 2/8	21 6/8	5 3/8	5 1/8	10	9	Lancaster Co., NE	Jon R. Allen, Jr.	Jon R. Allen, Jr.	2007	114
212 5/8	220 3/8	25 1/8	26 2/8	17	5 2/8	5	10	13	Hancock Co., IL	Ohne L. Raasch	Ohne L. Raasch	2007	114
212 5/8	233 6/8	26 7/8	26 7/8	19	6 3/8	5 7/8	14	10	Muskingum Co., OH	William B. Ramsey	William B. Ramsey	2007	114
212 3/8	216 2/8	23 6/8	23 2/8	19	5	5	11	10	Livingston Co., MO	Brandon S. Thorne	Brandon S. Thorne	2008	117
212 1/8	222 6/8	29 3/8	28	21 3/8	6 3/8	6 7/8	9	10	Hendricks Co., IN	Allan L. Miller	Allan L. Miller	2006	118
212	216 5/8	26 6/8	27 3/8	19 6/8	4 7/8	4 7/8	9	10	Benton Co., MO	Boone W. Kroenke	Boone W. Kroenke	2008	119
211 5/8	216 4/8	22 3/8	23	19 1/8	5 2/8	5	13	11	Rockdale Co., GA	Devin D. Key	Devin D. Key	2008	120
211 4/8	218	22 6/8	22 5/8	19 3/8	5 1/8	5 6/8	10	12	Coshocton Co., OH	William D. Murphy	William D. Murphy	2007	121
211 4/8	220 6/8	24 5/8	25	21 5/8	5 6/8	5 7/8	11	12	Lyndon Creek, AB	Tyler E. Nauta	Tyler E. Neuta	2008	121
211 3/8	217 3/8	24	25	17 3/8	4 7/8	5	15	11	Renville Co., ND	Kent L. Block	Kent L. Block	2008	123
211 2/8	217 4/8	27 2/8	27 2/8	21 2/8	5 5/8	5 5/8	12	10	Noble Co., OH	Charles W. Tennant	Charles W. Tennant	2000	124
211 2/8	218 6/8	27 4/8	27	21 6/8	6 1/8	6 7/8	9	11	Greene Co., IN	Tom Johnson	Tom Johnson	2007	124
211 2/8	219 5/8	26 7/8	25 4/8	18	5 2/8	5 5/8	15	9	Clay Co., MO	Timothy D. Skidmore	Timothy D. Skidmore	2008	124
211 1/8	215 5/8	24 4/8	24	19 6/8	5 2/8	5	6	9	Knox Co., MO	Picked Up	Ernest Shotton	2007	127

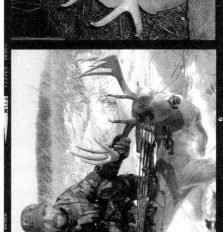

NON-TYPICAL WHITETAIL DEER
FINAL SCORE: 189 4/8
HUNTER: Thomas E. Pinyan, Jr.

NON-TYPICAL WHITETAIL DEER
FINAL SCORE: 188 3/8
HUNTER: Matthew C. Rehor

NON-TYPICAL WHITETAIL DEER
FINAL SCORE: 191 5/8
HUNTER: Dale L. Schulz

NON-TYPICAL WHITETAIL DEER
FINAL SCORE: 203 1/8
HUNTER: Daniel P. DesRosiers

WHITETAIL DEER - NON-TYPICAL ANTLERS

Odocoileus virginianus virginianus and certain related subspecies

Final Score	Gross Score	Length of Main Beam R.	L.	Inside Spread	Circumference at Smallest Place Between Burr & First Point R.	L.	Number of Points R.	L.	Locality	Hunter	Owner	Date Killed	Rank
210 7/8	220 3/8	24 6/8	25 6/8	19 2/8	5 1/8	5 3/8	13	8	Union Co., KY	Mason Hancock	Mason Hancock	2007	128
210 7/8	231 6/8	24 6/8	22 4/8	20	6 3/8	7 2/8	7	10	Pike Co., MO	Josh M. Schremmer	Josh M. Schremmer	2005	129
210 6/8	220 1/8	24 2/8	27 4/8	19 4/8	5	5 2/8	9	7	Iroquois Co., IL	Hanley H. Guy	Hanley H. Guy	2006	129
210 6/8	220 6/8	28 6/8	28 7/8	23	5	5 3/8	9	8	Green Co., WI	Derek D. Scheidegger	Derek D. Scheidegger	2007	129
210 6/8	216 1/8	27 2/8	26 6/8	19 2/8	6 2/8	6 1/8	9	6	Shelby Co., IL	Jack Jansen	Jack Jansen	2009	129
210 3/8	225 2/8	25	25 3/8	19 2/8	5	5	8	9	Taylor Co., WI	Jeffrey G. Gebauer	Jeffrey G. Gebauer	2007	133
210 3/8	217 2/8	25 5/8	26 1/8	17 7/8	4 7/8	6 4/8	9	10	Goodhue Co., MN	Donald C. Latch	Donald C. Latch	2007	133
210 3/8	231 5/8	29	27 4/8	23 7/8	5 5/8	5 3/8	10	19	Hancock Co., IL	Curtis W. Stevens	Curtis W. Stevens	2007	133
210	216	25 3/8	25 7/8	19 2/8	5 2/8	5 3/8	14	8	Ramsey Co., MN	Frank M. Frattalone	Frank M. Frattalone	2006	136
210	211 5/8	27 4/8	26 7/8	22 5/8	5 1/8	5 2/8	9	8	Bureau Co., IL	Picked Up	Dustin Erickson	2008	136
209 7/8	215 1/8	27	26 2/8	21 2/8	5 7/8	5 6/8	11	8	McLean Co., IL	Robert J. Vandeberg	Robert J. Vandeberg	2004	138
209 7/8	224 4/8	25 5/8	22 2/8	22 3/8	8 3/8	7 2/8	10	9	Randolph Co., IL	Mike C. Umbdenstock	Mike C. Umbdenstock	2006	138
209 6/8	217 6/8	26 4/8	24 6/8	18 6/8	5 4/8	5 3/8	9	11	Story Co., IA	Jesse L. Watters	Jesse L. Watters	2007	140
209 3/8	217 4/8	26 3/8	25 1/8	18 4/8	5	5 2/8	12	15	Koochiching Co., MN	Donald J. Seykora	David A. Jensen	1963	141
209 3/8	214 1/8	25 5/8	24 6/8	18 3/8	6 1/8	6	12	10	Cumberland Co., IL	Robert E. Green	Robert E. Green	2006	141
209 3/8	218 5/8	25 3/8	25 3/8	17 5/8	6 3/8	6	12	13	Allen Co., KS	Kortney L. McGraw	Kortney L. McGraw	2009	141
209 1/8	214 2/8	22 5/8	22 7/8	16 6/8	5 6/8	5 5/8	9	10	Chemung Co., NY	Robert L. Cuozzo	Robert L. Cuozzo	2006	144
209 1/8	214 1/8	26	24 7/8	22 7/8	5 2/8	5 5/8	11	10	Knox Co., IL	Troy D. Huffman	Troy D. Huffman	2007	144
209 1/8	212 6/8	23 7/8	23 4/8	17	5 2/8	5 2/8	15	21	Allegheny Co., PA	Gerald R. Simkonis	Gerald R. Simkonis	2007	144
209 1/8	217 5/8	33 6/8	32	21	5 1/8	5 3/8	7	8	Highland Co., OH	Nicholas D. Fauber	Nicholas D. Fauber	2008	144
209	212 5/8	23 7/8	23 5/8	21	4 5/8	4 7/8	11	11	Cass Co., MO	John G. Kagarice	John G. Kagarice	2007	148
209	215 3/8	29 2/8	29 4/8	22 3/8	5 5/8	5 4/8	12	12	Phillips Co., AR	Davis H. Smith	Davis H. Smith	2008	148
208 5/8	213 3/8	27	26 6/8	25 6/8	5 3/8	5 2/8	12	8	Renfrew, ON	Yves Chouinard	Yves Chouinard	2002	150
208 5/8	216 4/8	25 3/8	27	21 3/8	5 3/8	5	9	5	Rockingham Co., NC	Jonathon Reaser	Jonathon Reaser	2006	150
208 5/8	219 6/8	26 2/8	25 3/8	22 4/8	5 7/8	5 2/8	9	9	Kent Co., MD	Picked Up	Chesapeake Farms	2007	150
208 5/8	213 1/8	25 2/8	25 4/8	18 4/8	6	6	8	11	Dallas Co., IA	Kenny E. Head	Kenny E. Head	2008	150
208 3/8	217 4/8	24 7/8	23 7/8	16 1/8	5 6/8	5 7/8	10	12	Pike Co., IL	Chris M. Kauble	Chris M. Kauble	2006	154
208 3/8	215 1/8	23 1/8	24 4/8	16 1/8	5 3/8	5 4/8	12	14	Douglas Co., NE	Carl K. Bank	Carl K. Bank	2008	154
208	211 6/8	27 1/8	28 5/8	19 1/8	5	5 2/8	7	7	Shawano Co., WI	Robert E. Philbrick	Robert E. Philbrick	2006	156
207 7/8	222 7/8	27 7/8	27	19 6/8	5 7/8	6 3/8	10	10	Pike Co., MO	Melvin B. Meyer	Melvin B. Meyer	2007	157
207 6/8	218 5/8	25 3/8	22 5/8	17 2/8	5	4 7/8	8	13	Amite Co., MS	Shelby B. Tate	Shelby B. Tate	2007	158
207 6/8	217	26 1/8	26 2/8	18 4/8	7 1/8	5 6/8	9	7	Knox Co., IL	Jacob R. Landon	Jacob R. Landon	2008	158
207 5/8	214 4/8	24 7/8	26 1/8	19 5/8	4 7/8	4 7/8	9	8	Birch Hills, SK	Cory Sandness	Cory Sandness	2006	160

544

Score									Locality	Hunter	Owner	Date	Rank
207 5/8	231 5/8	28 4/8	30 2/8	24	5	6 1/8	12	4	Hamilton Co., IA	Brent W. Johnson	Brent W. Johnson	2007	160
207 4/8	214 7/8	24 4/8	23 3/8	17 2/8	4 5/8	4 4/8	13	15	Davis Co., IA	Joseph P. Bedell	Joseph P. Bedell	2006	162
207 3/8	216 7/8	26 2/8	26 2/8	20 3/8	4 6/8	5 1/8	15	10	Christian Co., MO	Larry S. McHaffie	Larry S. McHaffie	2008	163
207 2/8	214 2/8	27	25 6/8	19 7/8	5	5 1/8	11	10	Crawford Co., MO	Kristopher J. Havelka	Kristopher J. Havelka	2007	164
207 2/8	212 5/8	25 7/8	25 5/8	18 4/8	5 2/8	4 7/8	10	12	Clayton Co., IA	Gary L. Robbins	Gary L. Robbins	2007	164
207 2/8	209 2/8	26 4/8	26 4/8	19 5/8	5 1/8	5 3/8	9	11	Duck Mt., SK	Monte Erhardt	Monte Erhardt	2008	164
207	213	19 7/8		14 2/8	5 3/8	6 1/8	15	17	Callaway Co., MO	Steven R. Ward	Steven R. Ward	2006	167
206 7/8	210 4/8	26 5/8	25 3/8	16	5	5 5/8	10	9	Bureau Co., IL	Scott M. E.liott	Scott M. Elliott	2006	168
206 7/8	210 7/8	27 4/8	26 5/8	24 5/8	5 5/8	6 1/8	11	9	Mills Co., IA	Scott A. Warren	Scott A. Warren	2006	168
206 7/8	215 6/8	27 2/8	27 4/8	20 4/8	5 4/8	5 2/8	9	11	Lee Co., IL	Matthew C. Rehor	Matthew C. Rehor	2008	168
206 6/8	211 3/8	27 5/8	28	18 7/8	4 6/8	4 7/8	8	8	Brown Co., IL	Michael G. Hyma	Michael G. Hyma	2003	171
206 6/8	218 2/8	27	25	20 4/8	6 7/8	5 7/8	8	14	Tippecanoe Co., IN	Chad A. Compton	Chad A. Compton	2006	171
206 5/8	213 6/8	22 7/8	24 2/8	20 6/8	6 5/8	5 2/8	10	14	Douglas Co., KS	Edwin Bouton	Cabela's, Inc.	1996	173
206 5/8	217 3/8	26 6/8	26 1/8	25 5/8	5 7/8	5 5/8	9	10	Jasper Co., IL	Michael A. Kuhn	Michael A. Kuhn	2008	173
206 4/8	211 6/8	27 7/8	27 7/8	18	4 7/8	4 7/8	10	10	Ward Co., ND	James D. Kraft	James D. Kraft	1986	175
206 3/8	212 5/8	28 2/8	28 2/8	19 1/8	5 6/8	5 5/8	8	7	Todd Co., MN	David M. Meide	David M. Meide	2006	176
206 3/8	216 5/8	24 6/8	25	18	6 1/8	7 2/8	12	9	Montgomery Co., MO	Nicole Dawson	Nicole Dawson	2007	176
206 3/8	216 2/8	23 1/8	23 1/8	15	6	6 2/8	10	10	Lesser Slave Lake, AB	Daryl E. Anderson	Daryl E. Anderson	2008	176
206 3/8	213	23	27 2/8	15 7/8	5	5 1/8	7	11	Mercer Co., IL	Michael C. Steele	Michael C. Steele	2006	179
206 1/8	210 3/8	27 2/8	28 7/8	21 6/8	5 3/8	5 3/8	10	9	Harlan Co., KY	Shawn Fuson	Shawn Fuson	2007	179
206 1/8	212 2/8	28 3/8	25 3/8	18 2/8	6 2/8	6 2/8	9	11	Van Buren Co., MI	Robert A. Reits	Robert A. Reits	2007	179
206 1/8	214 1/8	24 6/8	26 4/8	20 7/8	5 5/8	5 5/8	9	9	Henry Co., IA	Phillip D. Coffin	Phillip D. Coffin	2008	179
206		27 5/8	25 3/8	20 6/8	5 4/8	5 4/8	8	12	Wilson Co., KS	John E. Shanbarger	John E. Shanbarger	2006	183
206	213 5/8	27 1/8	26 7/8	20 1/8	5 5/8	5 5/8	10	8	Washington Co., OH	Gregory A. Wagner	Gregory A. Wagner	2009	183
205 6/8	213 2/8	24 3/8	22 6/8	22 5/8	5 3/8	5 1/8	11	10	Fayette Co., IA	Matthew J. Lansing	Matthew J. Lansing	2004	185
205 6/8	214 7/8	23	23 3/8	15 3/8	5 2/8	4 6/8	8	9	Warren Co., MO	Jeffrey T. Wilson	Jeffrey T. Wilson	2007	185
205 5/8	217 4/8	26 1/8	22 7/8	26 5/8	6 6/8	6 3/8	11	11	Chickasaw Co., MS	Terry O. Cruse	Terry O. Cruse	2007	187
205 5/8	220 2/8	24 4/8	24 7/8	18 3/8	5 4/8	4 4/8	11	8	Denton Co., TX	Danny G. Preas	Danny G. Preas	2007	187
205 5/8	216 5/8	29 6/8	28 3/8	26 5/8	5 2/8	4 5/8	8	6	Chase Co., KS	Kent M. Wartick	Kent M. Wartick	2008	187
205 5/8	208 6/8	29 7/8	30 3/8	19 7/8	6 4/8	6 2/8	6	7	Vermillion Co., IN	Sean M. Lagacy	Sean M. Lagacy	2009	187
205 3/8	211 4/8	23 1/8	22 7/8	19 5/8	5 4/8	5 3/8	11	10	Clayton Co., IA	Scott J. Hefel	Scott J. Hefel	2007	191
205 3/8	211 5/8	25	24 3/8	19 5/8	5 4/8	5 4/8	11	7	Comanche Co., OK	Melton W. Wickens	Melton W. Wickens	2007	191
205 3/8	213 6/8	24	23 7/8	20 3/8	5 4/8	5 5/8	11	9	Carroll Co., MO	Terry L. Henavan	Terry L. Hanavan	2008	191
205 3/8	213 7/8	25 4/8	25 6/8	18 4/8	5 6/8	5 7/8	10	10	Cass Co., IN	Gregory D. Hartley	Gregory D. Hartley	2008	191
205 3/8	208 4/8	26 1/8	25 4/8	17 7/8	5 2/8	5 1/8	11	9	Egg Creek, AB	Picked Up	Garth W. Laturnus	2008	191
205 2/8	211 7/8	22 1/8	26 1/8	15 5/8	5 3/8	5	10	13	Sullivan Co., MO	Nicholas J. Waldo	Nicholas J. Waldo	2007	191
205 2/8	214 2/8	26 2/8	22 2/8	14 7/8	7 1/8	8 1/8	12	13	Kewaunee Co., WI	Mark D. Bohm	Mark D. Bohm	2008	197
205 2/8	213 6/8	22 3/8	21 2/8	15 1/8	3 7/8	3 6/8	17	21	Webster Co., MS	Jimmy D. Eaker	Jimmy D. Baker	2009	197
205 1/8	212 3/8	17 4/8	18 6/8	17 6/8	5 3/8	5 2/8	18	13	Kaufman Co., TX	Eric C. Minter	Eric C. Minter	2006	197
205	211 7/8	27	27 5/8	19 2/8	5 3/8	5 5/8	7	6	Lee Co., AR	David L. Jordening	David L. Jordening	2006	200
205	212 2/8	25 4/8	24 4/8	20 2/8	5 5/8	5 6/8	9	6	Atchison Co., KS	Jacob A. Koehler	Jacob A. Koehler	2006	201
205	210 2/8	28	28 6/8	23 3/8	5 6/8	5 6/8	10	7	Carroll Co., MO	Justin J. Godfrey	Justin J. Godfrey	2007	201

WHITETAIL DEER - NON-TYPICAL ANTLERS

Odocoileus virginianus virginianus and certain related subspecies

Final Score	Gross Score	Length of Main Beam R.	L.	Inside Spread	Circumference at Smallest Place Between Burr & First Point R.	L.	Number of Points R.	L.	Locality	Hunter	Owner	Date Killed	Rank
204 7/8	208 2/8	26 2/8	26 4/8	18 4/8	6 4/8	6 1/8	9	10	Brown Co., IL	Michael P. Postema	Michael P. Postema	2006	203
204 7/8	223 5/8	23 4/8	18 3/8	15 3/8	5 3/8	6 2/8	14	22	Dodge Co., WI	Casey Heine	Casey Heine	2007	203
204 5/8	212 1/8	22 7/8	25 2/8	20 1/8	7 4/8	5 6/8	16	7	Frenchman Butte, SK	Darcy A. Vetter	Darcy A. Vetter	2006	205
204 4/8	208 5/8	24 2/8	24 2/8	22 6/8	5 4/8	5 3/8	10	10	Grant Co., WI	Mark P. Rikli	Mark P. Rikli	2006	206
204 3/8	209 7/8	27 7/8	26 6/8	17 5/8	4 7/8	5 4/8	10	9	Tuscarawas Co., OH	Bruce E. Lane	Bruce E. Lane	2009	207
204 2/8	211 1/8	24 7/8	23 1/8	19 7/8	5 2/8	5 3/8	7	9	N. Saskatchewan River, SK	Kirk Gerich	Kirk Gerich	2006	208
204 2/8	212 6/8	25 4/8	25 4/8	26	5 1/8	5 2/8	10	7	Maverick Co., TX	Thomas D. Friedkin, Jr.	Thomas D. Friedkin, Jr.	2008	208
204 1/8	208 2/8	28 4/8	27 3/8	21 7/8	4 7/8	4 6/8	9	8	Fulton Co., IL	Howard W. Lock	Howard W. Lock	2007	210
204 1/8	212 1/8	23 1/8	24 4/8	19 3/8	5 7/8	5 4/8	10	7	Monroe Co., IA	Matthew E. Tyrrel	Matthew E. Tyrrel	2008	210
204	211 1/8	23 6/8	25 1/8	19 2/8	6	5 5/8	9	7	Harvey Co., KS	Alan K. Waltner	Alan K. Waltner	1999	212
203 7/8	208 7/8	25 1/8	24	16 2/8	4 4/8	4 4/8	7	9	Adams Co., WI	Robert J. Polewaczyk	Robert J. Polewaczyk	2007	213
203 7/8	212 5/8	24 6/8	24 7/8	17 5/8	4 6/8	4 4/8	9	11	Houston Co., MN	David W. McCabe	David W. McCabe	2008	213
203 6/8	209 2/8	25 5/8	24 7/8	22 2/8	4 4/8	4 6/8	9	8	Delta Co., TX	Jeffrey L. Preas	Jeffrey L. Preas	1986	215
203 6/8	209 2/8	26 4/8	26 4/8	21 6/8	5 5/8	5 5/8	12	9	Big River, SK	Adrien C. Proulx	Adrien C. Proulx	2006	215
203 5/8	221 3/8	22 4/8	21	15 2/8	5 2/8	5 3/8	16	14	Caddo Parish, LA	Christopher G. Campbell, Jr.	Christopher G. Campbell, Jr.	2007	217
203 4/8	220 2/8	27 2/8	28 3/8	20 6/8	5 2/8	5 2/8	9	11	Auglaize Co., OH	Josh L. Coffey	Josh L. Coffey	2007	218
203 4/8	210 1/8	23	23 3/8	18 4/8	4 6/8	4 6/8	11	9	Goodhue Co., MN	Kaleen A. Gustafson	Kaleen A. Gustafson	2008	218
203 3/8	206 2/8	23 7/8	23 7/8	19	4 3/8	4 3/8	11	11	Cooke Co., TX	Ernest M. Elbert, Jr.	Ernest M. Elbert, Jr.	2007	220
203 3/8	211	27 6/8	26 4/8	17 1/8	5 1/8	5 3/8	13	9	Licking Co., OH	Joseph F. Wayne	Joseph F. Wayne	2007	220
203 3/8	210 6/8	27 6/8	27 6/8	18 5/8	6	5 4/8	9	8	Crawford Co., IL	James A. Fink	James A. Fink	2008	220
203 2/8	208 7/8	26 5/8	26 3/8	20 3/8	5 6/8	4 5/8	7	11	Wabash Co., IN	Jeff L. Dale	Jeff L. Dale	2007	223
203 2/8	210 5/8	26 4/8	25	17 7/8	4 3/8	4 3/8	8	9	Lake Co., IN	Dale R. Huseman	Dale R. Huseman	2008	223
203 1/8	207 2/8	26 2/8	26 7/8	17 5/8	6 2/8	6 3/8	10	10	Buffalo Co., WI	Daniel P. DesRosiers	Daniel P. DesRosiers	2006	225
203 1/8	207 6/8	22 6/8	22 3/8	19 5/8	6 4/8	6 4/8	9	11	Pendleton Co., KY	James S. Borne	James S. Borne	2007	225
203	206 2/8	24 4/8	24 4/8	25 3/8	5 2/8	4 6/8	11	9	Hemphill Co., TX	Everette W. Newland	Everette W. Newland	2006	227
202 7/8	210 2/8	25 1/8	25 4/8	18 2/8	4 7/8	4 6/8	10	10	Nez Perce Co., ID	Eric R. Steigers	Eric R. Steigers	1973	228
202 7/8	211 5/8	29 5/8	28 1/8	23 1/8	5 5/8	5 6/8	7	9	Jennings Co., IN	Gregory A. Hopper	Gregory A. Hopper	2006	228
202 7/8	208 5/8	26	26 1/8	18 6/8	5 3/8	5 3/8	7	8	Fillmore Co., MN	Picked Up	Michael M. Opat	2007	228
202 7/8	208 5/8	27 1/8	28 1/8	20 6/8	5 3/8	5 6/8	6	10	Randolph Co., IL	Harry L. Spies	Harry L. Spies	2008	228
202 6/8	206 6/8	24	24	18 3/8	6 4/8	6 5/8	9	11	Sheridan Co., ND	Darnell E. Arndt	Darnell E. Arndt	2008	232

									Locality	Hunter	Owner	Year	Page
202 5/8	212 6/8	22 4/8	22 4/8	13 2/8	6 6/8	6 4/8	12	10	Lee Co., IA	Leo M. Schinstock	Leo M. Schinstock	2003	233
202 5/8	207 5/8	24 4/8	23 2/8	18 5/8	4 4/8	5 1/8	10	11	Sioux Co., NE	Joseph A. Perry III	Joseph A. Perry III	2006	233
202 5/8	213 2/8	22 2/8	23 2/8	16 4/8	4 6/8	4 7/8	10	9	Okfuskee Co., OK	Ricky L. Burden	Ricky L. Burden	2007	233
202 5/8	209 4/8	23 7/8	25 3/8	19 3/8	5 1/8	5	10	13	Grant Co., ND	Tyler S. Hartman	Tyler S. Hartman	2007	233
202 2/8	207 6/8	24 2/8	25 1/8	19 7/8	4 7/8	4 6/8	9	8	Washington Co., WI	George H. Harrison	George H. Harrison	2006	237
202 2/8	206 5/8	28 5/8	28 3/8	24 5/8	6 3/8	6 2/8	7	8	Last Mountain Lake, SK	Picked Up	Picked Up	2007	237
202 2/8	207 3/8	24 3/8	23	16 7/8	5 4/8	5 5/8	12	10	Mellette Co., SD	Mark Kayser	Mark Kayser	2008	237
202 1/8	208 6/8	28 2/8	30	18 6/8	5	5	12	8	Pulaski Co., KY	Rick E. Gosser	Rick E. Gosser	2006	240
202 1/8	211 5/8	26 2/8	26 2/8	18 6/8	6 4/8	6 1/8	10	9	Franklin Co., OH	Stephen E. Esker	Stephen E. Esker	2009	240
202	214	30 7/8	30 3/8	20	4 3/8	4 6/8	10	10	Westend Lake, ON	Darren Squire	Darren Squire	2007	242
202	204 6/8	23	22 5/8	16 4/8	5 2/8	5 2/8	10	9	Loon Lake, SK	Gary A. Taylor	Gary A. Taylor	2007	242
201 7/8	213 4/8	27 7/8	27 1/8	22 4/8	5 1/8	5 6/8	8	12	Culpeper Co., VA	James E. Taylor	James E. Taylor	2008	244
201 6/8	208 7/8	28 2/8	27 2/8	20 2/8	5	4 6/8	9	9	Mitchell Co., KS	Andy J. Becker	Andy J. Becker	2007	244
201 4/8	209 4/8	25 3/8	25 3/8	18 2/8	4 3/8	4 4/8	10	9	Oconto Co., WI	Adam F. Filz	Adam F. Filz	2006	245
201 4/8	209 5/8	27	27	20	5 6/8	5 6/8	11	10	Monona Co., IA	Allen A. Yarke	Allen A. Yanke	2007	246
201 3/8	208 1/8	24	22 6/8	17 1/8	4 4/8	4 4/8	7	12	Pushmataha Co., OK	Kelt M. Gibson	Kelt M. Gibson	2007	246
201 3/8	208 3/8	25 6/8	25 4/8	19	5 1/8	5 2/8	10	10	Vermilion River, AB	Anthony J. VanDitto	Anthony J. VanDitto	2006	248
201 2/8	210 4/8	24 5/8	27	19	6 4/8	6 3/8	10	10	Hancock Co., IN	Kendall L. Christopher	Kendall L. Christopher	2007	248
201 2/8	204 2/8	27 4/8	27	22 5/8	5 2/8	5 2/8	11	9	Grayson Co., TX	Spencer B. Benson	Spencer B. Benson	2006	250
201 2/8	222 4/8	24	19	20 6/8	5	4 6/8	11	13	Winneshiek Co., IA	Travis S. Massman	Travis S. Massman	2007	250
201 1/8	210 3/8	27 4/8	28 5/8	16 1/8	5 1/8	5 1/8	10	8	Bracken Co., KY	Dennis W. Sharp	Dennis W. Sharp	2007	250
201 1/8	206 3/8	26	26	23 6/8	5 5/8	5 5/8	6	13	Warren Co., MO	Steve M. Micke	Steve M. Micke	2008	253
201 1/8	206	23 7/8	24 2/8	18 6/8	5 1/8	5 1/8	9	9	Waupaca Co., WI	Earl H. Clement	Earl H. Clement	2009	253
201	212 2/8	26 7/8	26 7/8	16 4/8	6 1/8	5 5/8	12	12	Jennings Co., IN	Derik J. Vance	Derik J. Vance	2007	253
201	203 5/8	25	25	22	5 6/8	6 2/8	6	9	Reno Co., KS	Jason H. Kirkland	Jason H. Kirkland	2008	256
200 7/8	207 7/8	25 6/8	26 5/8	16 3/8	4 7/8	5	10	10	Garrard Co., KY	Ricky K. Baker	Ricky K. Baker	2007	256
200 6/8	208 5/8	28 4/8	27 5/8	20 7/8	5 4/8	5 6/8	9	12	Iroquois Co., IL	John S. Nichols	John S. Nichols	2006	258
200 6/8	210	26 4/8	26 2/8	16 4/8	5 6/8	6	12	8	Coshocton Co., OH	Justin Williamson	Justin Williamson	2006	259
200 5/8	203 5/8	23 7/8	22 6/8	22 5/8	5 7/8	5 6/8	11	7	Vermilion Bay, ON	Robert C. Niles	Robert C. Niles	2007	259
200 5/8	215 5/8	24 1/8	22 2/8	19 2/8	5 5/8	5 7/8	11	9	Cole Co., MO	Andrew W. Groose	Andrew W. Groose	2007	261
200 4/8	205 4/8	22 2/8	22 2/8	17 6/8	6 4/8	5 5/8	8	12	Dorchester Co., MD	Gregory A. Glos	Gregory A. Glos	2006	261
200 4/8	206 1/8	25	25	17	4 5/8	4 5/8	11	8	Jackson Co., IL	Darin P. Fager	Darin P. Fager	2007	263
200 4/8	205 5/8	26 5/8	26 7/8	17 5/8	4 6/8	6 2/8	10	12	Callaway Co., MO	Dennis L. Murphy	Dennis L. Murphy	2007	263
200 3/8	210	26 6/8	26 6/8	17 5/8	6	4 7/8	9	8	Richardson Co., NE	James F. McNealy	Cabela's, Inc.	2006	263
200 3/8	203 4/8	23 7/8	23 2/8	18 3/8	5 5/8	5 7/8	8	8	Breton, AB	Picked Up	Grant E. Lang	2008	266
200 2/8	205 5/8	26	25 7/8	20 1/8	5 3/8	5 2/8	8	8	Vinton Co., OH	Jason F. Williams	Jason F. Williams	2007	266
200 1/8	210 2/8	23 3/8	23 6/8	19 5/8	5 3/8	5 2/8	11	9	Dakota Co., MN	Dean M. Basch	Dean M. Basch	2006	266
200 1/8	204 5/8	27 5/8	25	18 2/8	4 7/8	5 7/8	6	8	Knox Co., IL	Dennis L. Easley	Dennis L. Easley	2006	268
200 1/8	203 1/8	20 7/8	21 4/8	16 5/8	5	5	12	13	Itasca Co., MN	Jack Rajala	Jack Rajala	2006	268
200 1/8	208 6/8	29	28	20 2/8	6 4/8	6 2/8	8	7	Estill Co., KY	Seth U. Lainhart	Seth U. Lainhart	2007	269
200 1/8	206 6/8	23 1/8	24 3/8	16 2/8	6 2/8	5 7/8	12	11	Monroe Co., WI	John P. Ollerdick	John P. Ollendick	2007	269
200 1/8	206 6/8	24 2/8	25 6/8	16 2/8	4 6/8	5 5/8	10	17	Marion Co., IL	Rodney L. Armstrong	Rodney L. Armstrong	2008	269

WHITETAIL DEER - NON-TYPICAL ANTLERS

Odocoileus virginianus virginianus and certain related subspecies

Final Score	Gross Score	Length of Main Beam R.	L.	Inside Spread	Circ. at Smallest Place Between Burr & First Point R.	L.	Number of Points R.	L.	Locality	Hunter	Owner	Date Killed	Rank
200 1/8	204 5/8	26 4/8	26 1/8	19 1/8	5	4 7/8	6	11	Adams Co., IA	Joshua D. Bowman	Joshua D. Bowman	2008	269
200	208 3/8	26	25 4/8	19 4/8	6 2/8	6	9	8	Fremont Co., IA	Harman E. Crawford, Jr.	Harman E. Crawford, Jr.	2006	276
200	202 3/8	26	25 4/8	19 6/8	5 3/8	5 3/8	12	8	Stephenson Co., IL	Shawn Tessendorf	Shawn Tessendorf	2007	276
200	217 2/8	28 6/8	27 6/8	19 7/8	5 3/8	5 6/8	5	6	Harper Co., KS	Kevin S. Albright	Kevin S. Albright	2008	276
200	207 7/8	27 1/8	27 1/8	19 2/8	6 1/8	6 2/8	11	9	Rockcastle Co., KY	Edward Barnett	Edward Barnett	2008	276
199 7/8	219 4/8	25 7/8	27 6/8	21 2/8	5 3/8	5 3/8	6	9	Athabasca River, AB	Alan J. Oswald	Alan J. Oswald	2006	280
199 7/8	208 5/8	26 3/8	25 3/8	18 5/8	6 2/8	6 2/8	8	10	Riley Co., KS	Kenneth E. Burnette	Kenneth E. Burnette	2007	280
199 6/8	208 5/8	25	26	22 2/8	5 1/8	5	10	10	Parke Co., IN	Brent L. Irelan	Brent L. Irelan	2008	282
199 4/8	209 2/8	25 7/8	26	19 2/8	4 7/8	5	12	10	Cowley Co., KS	Dana R. Hodges	Dana R. Hodges	2007	283
199 4/8	205 1/8	22 6/8	23 1/8	18	5 6/8	6 1/8	8	8	Clark Co., IL	Roscoe Tarry	Roscoe Tarry	2007	283
199 4/8	204 7/8	28 6/8	28 3/8	23 4/8	5 4/8	5 2/8	8	6	Wapello Co., IA	Junior Hemm	Junior Hemm	2008	283
199 3/8	205 5/8	26 3/8	25 4/8	20	5 6/8	6	7	10	Dodge Co., NE	Carrol L. Moseman	Carrol L. Moseman	1968	286
199 3/8	220 3/8	21 6/8	22 4/8	16 5/8	4 5/8	5 4/8	12	10	Saunders Co., NE	Unknown	Gale Sup	PR 2007	286
199 2/8	211 4/8	27	24 6/8	21 2/8	5 2/8	4 7/8	7	11	Kittson Co., MN	John Roman	Timothy J. Roman	1976	288
199 2/8	201 3/8	20 7/8	20 7/8	19 2/8	5	5	9	6	Sauk Co., WI	Daniel G. Kruchten	Daniel G. Kruchten	2006	288
199 2/8	206 4/8	26 3/8	26 3/8	20 2/8	5 6/8	5 1/8	7	8	Audrain Co., MO	G. Donald McCord	G. Donald McCord	2006	288
199 2/8	205 6/8	26 7/8	27	15 6/8	4 4/8	4 3/8	9	8	Lawrence Co., KY	Dallas R. Stacy	Dallas R. Stacy	2006	288
199 2/8	206 2/8	24 7/8	26 3/8	22	5 7/8	5 6/8	9	11	Henry Co., IL	Gregory T. Ahlgren	Gregory T. Ahlgren	2007	288
199 1/8	205 7/8	25 1/8	24 4/8	16 7/8	4 6/8	5	7	11	Loon Lake, SK	Jimmy D. Carpenter	Jimmy D. Carpenter	2006	293
199 1/8	204 2/8	27 4/8	26 5/8	20 6/8	6	6	11	13	Ripley Co., IN	Shawn E. Dilk	Shawn E. Dilk	2007	293
199 1/8	203 1/8	23 1/8	21 4/8	16 2/8	5 3/8	5 5/8	12	13	Posey Co., IN	Mark A. Lueder	Mark A. Lueder	2008	293
199	203 1/8	24 6/8	26 7/8	20 1/8	5 4/8	5 3/8	7	7	Leavenworth Co., KS	Jim W. Slapper, Jr.	Jim W. Slapper, Jr.	2006	296
199	213	27 1/8	25 6/8	20 2/8	5 7/8	6 1/8	10	10	Washington Co., IN	Picked Up	Billy J. Deaton	2007	296
198 7/8	209 4/8	27 1/8	27 5/8	18 3/8	4 4/8	4 5/8	10	7	Reno Co., KS	Greig A. Sims	Greig A. Sims	1987	298
198 7/8	208 7/8	25 2/8	26 4/8	24 2/8	5 6/8	5 6/8	9	10	Vernon Co., WI	Daniel L. Tollefson	Daniel L. Tollefson	2007	298
198 7/8	207 3/8	29 3/8	28 5/8	20 7/8	6	6 3/8	14	13	Van Buren Co., IA	Ivan J. Muzljakovich	Ivan J. Muzljakovich	2008	298
198 6/8	211 2/8	30 5/8	29 1/8	27 7/8	6 5/8	6 4/8	6	8	Greene Co., IL	Raymond E. Daniels	Raymond E. Daniels	2006	301
198 6/8	215 6/8	22 6/8	19 3/8	12 3/8	6 4/8	7 7/8	9	14	Morrill Co., NE	Robert J. Smalley	Robert J. Smalley	2007	301
198 6/8	213 2/8	25	26	22 4/8	7 7/8	6 2/8	12	9	Hardin Co., IA	Randall K. Smuck	Randall K. Smuck	2007	301
198 6/8	204 3/8	26 4/8	26 5/8	17 3/8	5 2/8	5 2/8	8	8	Licking Co., OH	Robert L. Wingeier	Robert L. Wingeier	2008	301
198 5/8	204 6/8	25	25 4/8	17 2/8	5	5	8	8	Vermilion River, AB	Blake D. Fafard	Blake D. Fafard	2007	305
198 5/8	201 5/8	24 6/8	24 7/8	19 1/8	5	4 5/8	12	10	Daviess Co., MO	Richard L. Page	Richard L. Page	2007	305

198 4/8	204 6/8	28 5/8	27 6/8	22 1/8	6 1/8	6 3/8	6	8	Washington Co., MN	Michael S. Versland	2009	307
198 3/8	203 3/8	21 2/8	23 2/8	20 3/8	4 4/8	4 3/8	12	9	Monroe Co., AR	Daniel W. Baxter	2006	308
198 3/8	206 3/8	25 3/8	26	17 2/8	4 7/8	5	8	8	Parke Co., IN	Chris J. Thomas	2006	308
198 3/8	207 7/8	24 5/8	25 4/8	20 7/8	6 6/8	6 3/8	9	9	Franklin Co., NE	Brian Lenneman	2007	308
198 2/8	204 2/8	28 4/8	26 4/8	21 3/8	5 6/8	5 7/8	7	11	Portage Co., OH	Andy C. Fisher	2007	311
198 2/8	206 1/8	22 5/8	23 5/8	17 7/8	5 6/8	5 4/8	12	7	Dodge Co., NE	Kerry L. Neumann	2007	311
198 2/8	204 4/8	26 3/8	26 4/8	20 2/8	4 7/8	4 7/8	7	10	Makwa River, SK	Donald R. Broughton	2008	311
198 2/8	205 5/8	25 1/8	23	21 2/8	4 4/8	4 1/8	10	10	Pawnee Co., OK	David E. Nance	2008	311
198	203 7/8	25 1/8	26 1/8	18 6/8	4 4/8	4 4/8	8	11	Unknown	Matt Smith	PR 1950	315
198	205 6/8	25 1/8	24 2/8	18 2/8	5	4 7/8	10	8	Livingston Co., MO	Michael A. Brown	2006	315
198	202 2/8	26	26	21 4/8	5 1/8	4 7/8	9	6	Ringgold Co., IA	David L. Williams	2006	315
198	203 7/8	30 7/8	30 4/8	20 6/8	5 5/8	5 4/8	8	11	Burnett Co., WI	Byron Hopke	2007	315
198	203 1/8	24 5/8	25 1/8	20 3/8	5 4/8	5 2/8	10	12	Cooper Co., MO	Steven A. Miltenberger	2007	315
198	207 1/8	23 3/8	21 2/8	18 6/8	5 4/8	7 1/8	7	13	Little Smoky River, AB	Dustin J. Seabrook	2007	315
198	203 3/8	24	24 7/8	21 3/8	5 1/8	5	9	9	Iroquois Co., IL	Albert J. Hering	2008	315
197 6/8	212 2/8	27	26 2/8	18 6/8	5 6/8	5 7/8	11	8	Decatur Co., IA	Russ C. Amundson	2004	322
197 6/8	202 6/8	24 6/8	25 7/8	20 1/8	5 3/8	5 2/8	10	8	Goodfish Lake, AB	Daniel A. Riggins	2006	322
197 6/8	201 4/8	25 2/8	25 1/8	21 1/8	5 4/8	5 1/8	10	8	Grey, ON	Michael N. Emke	2007	322
197 6/8	203 6/8	23 1/8	21 7/8	23 1/8	5 6/8	5 6/8	12	10	Benton Co., AR	Ronald G. Harp	2007	322
197 6/8	201 1/8	26	25 5/8	21 7/8	5	5	8	7	Maverick Co., TX	Timothy L. Kennedy	2009	322
197 5/8	204 7/8	25 6/8	25 4/8	16 2/8	5 2/8	5 2/8	10	10	Crawford Co., KS	Danny Brackett	2006	327

**NON-TYPICAL
WHITETAIL DEER**
FINAL SCORE: 199 7/8
HUNTER: Daniel G. Kruchten

**NON-TYPICAL
WHITETAIL DEER**
FINAL SCORE: 203
HUNTER: Everette W. Newland

**NON-TYPICAL
WHITETAIL DEER**
FINAL SCORE: 212 5/8
HUNTER: Jon R. Allen, Jr.

**NON-TYPICAL
WHITETAIL DEER**
FINAL SCORE: 242
HUNTER: Chad M. Christie

WHITETAIL DEER - NON-TYPICAL ANTLERS

Odocoileus virginianus virginianus and certain related subspecies

Final Score	Gross Score	Length of Main Beam R.	L.	Inside Spread	Circ. at Smallest Place Between Burr & First Point R.	L.	Number of Points R.	L.	Locality	Hunter	Owner	Date Killed	Rank
197 5/8	201 2/8	26 2/8	27 1/8	20 5/8	6 2/8	6 1/8	8	9	Knox Co., IL	Robin R. Harshbarger, Sr.	Robin R. Harshbarger, Sr.	2006	327
197 4/8	208	26 4/8	25 1/8	17 6/8	5 3/8	5 3/8	7	10	Monroe Co., MO	Randy Boulware	Randy Boulware	2002	329
197 4/8	203 1/8	23 4/8	22 7/8	15 6/8	6	6	11	12	Chickasaw Co., IA	Greg W. Richards	Greg W. Richards	2007	329
197 4/8	203 3/8	25	25 2/8	24 7/8	5 4/8	5	7	8	Maverick Co., TX	Thomas D. Friedkin	Thomas D. Friedkin	2008	329
197 4/8	210 2/8	24 4/8	25 4/8	19 3/8	5 4/8	5	10	8	Fairfield Co., OH	Richard S. Hutchison	Richard S. Hutchison	2008	329
197 3/8	205 3/8	23 4/8	25 7/8	20 6/8	5 2/8	5	9	7	Bonner Co., ID	Robert Z. Borysek	Robert Z. Borysek	2005	333
197 3/8	201 4/8	28 7/8	28	21 5/8	5 3/8	5 4/8	8	6	Cumberland Co., KY	William B. Bertram	William B. Bertram	2006	333
197 3/8	206 6/8	27 2/8	27 4/8	19 7/8	5 2/8	5 1/8	10	12	Henry Co., VA	Anthony L. Hodges	Anthony L. Hodges	2006	333
197 3/8	203 3/8	26	25 4/8	18 6/8	5 3/8	5 6/8	7	11	Union Co., IL	Mark A. Bundren	Mark A. Bundren	2008	333
197 3/8	199 7/8	26 4/8	26 7/8	20 7/8	5 3/8	5 4/8	8	6	Luce Co., MI	Bill R. Rushford	Bill R. Rushford	2008	333
197 2/8	202 4/8	24 7/8	24 2/8	20 3/8	6 3/8	4 7/8	10	8	Licking Co., OH	David A. Nichols	David A. Nichols	2007	338
197 2/8	212 3/8	27 2/8	22 7/8	17 7/8	5 4/8	5 3/8	10	13	Christian Co., KY	Michael Snyder	Michael Snyder	2007	338
197 2/8	199 7/8	25 1/8	25 4/8	18	5 5/8	5 3/8	7	10	Wayne Co., IA	Tanner Bradley	Tanner Bradley	2009	338
197 1/8	201 3/8	24 6/8	25 6/8	17 4/8	5 5/8	5 5/8	8	8	Crow Wing Co., MN	Craig A. Loehr	Craig A. Loehr	2007	341
197 1/8	204 1/8	23 7/8	24 7/8	16 6/8	6 7/8	6 4/8	11	10	Iroquois Co., IL	Steve Popovich	Steve Popovich	2008	341
197 1/8	204 2/8	25 3/8	24 6/8	17	4 4/8	4 3/8	9	8	Winfield, BC	Brent W. Saukarookoff	Brent W. Saukarookoff	2008	341
197	205 1/8	24	24	16 4/8	5 6/8	5 2/8	8	11	Grant Co., WI	Z.A. & B.D. Allen	Z.A. & B.D. Allen	2006	344
197	204 6/8	27	25 5/8	24 7/8	4 6/8	4 5/8	7	7	Grant Parish, LA	Shane R. Spears	Shane R. Spears	2006	344
197	208 1/8	23 3/8	23 5/8	19 1/8	6 3/8	6 2/8	11	11	Schuyler Co., IL	M. David Castleberry	M. David Castleberry	2007	344
197	200 4/8	24 4/8	25 2/8	20 7/8	5 7/8	5 6/8	7	7	Knox Co., OH	John E. Lowther	John E. Lowther	2007	344
196 7/8	208 1/8	24 6/8	22 6/8	18 4/8	5	6 3/8	8	10	Wells Co., ND	James R. Schmitz	James R. Schmitz	2006	348
196 6/8	206 3/8	23 6/8	23 7/8	17 5/8	4 5/8	4 6/8	12	11	Goshen Co., WY	Joseph M. Mladenik	Joseph M. Mladenik	2007	349
196 6/8	202 6/8	27	26 2/8	19 2/8	5 2/8	5 4/8	8	7	Morgan Co., IL	George R. Eck	George R. Eck	2008	349
196 6/8	199	26 4/8	27 3/8	20 5/8	5	5	7	7	Clayton Co., IA	Jeffrey E. Palmer	Jeffrey E. Palmer	2008	349
196 6/8	205 5/8	23	23 6/8	16	5 6/8	5 5/8	11	12	Caldwell Co., MO	Philip R. Stuedle	Philip R. Stuedle	2008	349
196 5/8	205 5/8	26 3/8	28 1/8	20 6/8	7 1/8	6 4/8	8	8	Sangamon Co., IL	Bradley W. Harden	Bradley W. Harden	2006	353
196 5/8	201 7/8	26 2/8	26	17 7/8	5 3/8	5 5/8	13	9	Waushara Co., WI	Brian L. Sanders	Brian L. Sanders	2006	353
196 5/8	201 4/8	25 2/8	25 3/8	21 2/8	5 7/8	6 2/8	9	7	Washington Co., MN	Todd C. Berry	Todd C. Berry	2007	353
196 5/8	201 4/8	22 3/8	23 3/8	13	4 4/8	4 5/8	12	12	Pope Co., AR	Preston R. Estes	Preston R. Estes	2007	353
196 5/8	203 5/8	27 5/8	28 7/8	19 6/8	5 3/8	5	7	8	Haldimand Co., ON	Leslie W. Lambert	Leslie W. Lambert	2007	353
196 5/8	206 4/8	29	29 1/8	23 3/8	6 2/8	6 2/8	8	7	Parke Co., IN	Roy L. Rhoads	Roy L. Rhoads	2007	353
196 5/8	203 3/8	24 2/8	25 1/8	17 5/8	4 5/8	4 4/8	8	7	Yankton Co., SD	Ryan Ulmer	Ryan Ulmer	2007	353

Score	Length of Main Beam R	Length of Main Beam L	Inside Spread	Circ. R	Circ. L	Points R	Points L	Locality	Hunter	Owner	Date Killed	Rank
196 5/8	25 6/8	24 7/8	23 6/8	5 5/8	5 2/8	7	7	Harper Co., KS	Cassidy E. Cate	Cassidy E. Cate	2008	353
196 4/8	27 2/8	26 6/8	20 1/8	4 6/8	4 7/8	8	7	Warren Co., IL	Shawn R. Guyer	Shawn R. Guyer	2007	361
196 4/8	22 7/8	22 2/8	16 3/8	5 4/8	5 5/8	7	8	Waupaca Co., WI	Jeremy L. Mengert	Jeremy L. Mengert	2007	361
196 3/8	21 6/8	21 7/8	18 7/8	4 7/8	4 6/8	9	7	Wilson Co., TX	Sam Kirkendall	Sam Kirkendall	2002	363
196 3/8	25 7/8	26 4/8	18 3/8	5	5	12	9	Harrison Co., MO	Jim L. Chamberlin	Jim L. Chamberlin	2006	363
196 3/8	22 3/8	27 2/8	18 6/8	5 4/8	5 4/8	9	7	Butler Co., IA	Bret R. Moore	Bret R. Moore	2006	363
196 3/8	30 2/8	30 1/8	25 4/8	5 2/8	5 1/8	5	8	Charles Co., MD	Robert L. Murphy, Jr.	Robert L. Murphy, Jr.	2006	363
196 3/8	24	24	15 3/8	4 5/8	4 4/8	10	8	Sauk Co., WI	Tod R. Fleming	Tod R. Fleming	2007	363
196 3/8	25 2/8	24 6/8	21 3/8	5 4/8	5 2/8	8	9	Macoupin Co., IL	Matthew D. Magers	Matthew D. Magers	2008	363
196 2/8	23 2/8	26 3/8	20 2/8	4 1/8	4 1/8	10	12	Suffolk Co., NY	Richard S. Gates	Richard S. Gates	2006	369
196 2/8	27 6/8	25 7/8	18 6/8	5 5/8	5 4/8	7	10	Jefferson Co., NE	George A. Russell, Jr.	George A. Russell, Jr.	2006	369
196 2/8	28 1/8	27 5/8	22 5/8	5	4 6/8	6	7	Breckinridge Co., KY	Tracy Butler	Tracy Butler	2007	369
196 2/8	23 4/8	26	19 7/8	5 5/8	5 4/8	10	8	Jackfish Lake, SK	Karch S. Cassidy	Karch S. Cassidy	2007	369
196 1/8	28 1/8	27 1/8	18 2/8	5 2/8	4 7/8	7	8	Vinton Co., OH	Brian Martin	Brian Martin	2007	369
196	24 6/8	24 2/8	22 4/8	5 1/8	5	7	8	Dane Co., WI	Picked Up	Todd Hefty	2004	374
196	24 4/8	21 6/8	16	5 7/8	5	9	26	Leavenworth Co., KS	Steven C. Pope	Steven C. Pope	2006	374
196	27 3/8	25	20	6 6/8	5 6/8	9	13	Edwards Co., IL	Randy L. Rice	Randy L. Rice	2006	374
196	21 6/8	22 6/8	19 5/8	5 4/8	4 6/8	11	12	St. Louis Co., MN	Richard W. Van Valkenburg	Richard W. Van Valkenburg	2007	374
195 7/8	26	26	20 6/8	5 3/8	5 4/8	9	10	Licking Co., OH	Stephen E. Bradley	Stephen E. Bradley	2006	378
195 7/8	23 6/8	23 6/8	19 5/8	5 2/8	5 4/8	11	11	Goodwin Lake, AB	Leonard G. Burt	Leonard G. Burt	2007	378
195 7/8	20 3/8	20 3/8	12 7/8	6 1/8	6	12	11	Madison Co., MS	Justin P. Malouf	Justin P. Malouf	2007	378
195 7/8	28	28 7/8	19 3/8	6 3/8	6	11	10	Champaign Co., IL	Benjamin J. Self	Benjamin J. Self	2007	378
195 7/8	24 2/8	24 7/8	19 7/8	5 6/8	5 2/8	8	11	Marshall Co., IL	Joe P. Dunphy	Joe P. Dunphy	2008	378
195 6/8	27 7/8	26 1/8	18 5/8	5 3/8	5 3/8	5	11	Marion Co., IA	Rick L. Dye	Rick L. Dye	2006	383
195 6/8	25 1/8	20 3/8	20 3/8	5 5/8	5 5/8	9	16	Davis Co., IA	Loras J. Steffen	Loras J. Steffen	2007	383
195 5/8	26 6/8	29 7/8	23	6 1/8	6 1/8	8	9	Benton Co., IN	Mark R. Stover	Mark R. Stover	1999	385
195 5/8	23	23 7/8	18 4/8	4 6/8	4 5/8	10	8	Adams Co., IL	Joseph A. Price	Joseph A. Price	2006	385
195 5/8	24 3/8	24 7/8	25 3/8	6 2/8	4 7/8	8	10	Creek Co., OK	Picked Up	Christopher J. Bailey	2008	385
195 5/8	24 5/8	26 3/8	20 3/8	4 2/8	4 2/8	8	11	Major Co., OK	Todd D. Gilchrist	Todd D. Gilchrist	2008	385
195 4/8	25 2/8	24 7/8	21 1/8	5	4 7/8	7	13	White Co., AR	Eric S. Jones	Eric S. Jones	2006	389
195 4/8	25 1/8	22 7/8	20 4/8	4 6/8	4 6/8	8	8	Columbia Co., WI	Daniel D. Klappstein	Daniel D. Klappstein	2006	389
195 4/8	24 4/8	24	17 5/8	4 4/8	4 4/8	8	8	Haywood Co., TN	Michael J. Wilbur	Michael J. Wilbur	2007	389
195 4/8	24 6/8	24	17 1/8	4 3/8	4 3/8	12	7	Grand Forks Co., ND	Mark I. Bry	Mark I. Bry	2008	389
195 4/8	26 4/8	26 4/8	17 2/8	5	5	11	9	Menard Co., IL	Dwaine E. Heyen	Dwaine E. Heyen	2008	389
195 3/8	25 6/8	27 5/8	19 3/8	4 7/8	4 7/8	8	9	Preble Co., OH	Mark A. Bassler	Mark A. Bassler	2006	394
195 3/8	26 1/8	26 1/8	20 4/8	4 2/8	4 2/8	6	8	Jo Daviess Co., IL	Craig J. Olson	Craig J. Olson	2007	394
195 3/8	25 6/8	27 2/8	17 7/8	6 2/8	6 2/8	9	8	Wabamun Lake, AB	Rick L. Pell	Rick L. Pell	2007	394
195 3/8	25	24 4/8	17 7/8	5 2/8	5 2/8	7	10	Allegheny Co., PA	C. Bruce Stickley	C. Bruce Stickley	2007	394
195 3/8	24 3/8	25	18 3/8	5 4/8	5 4/8	10	9	Baptiste Lake, AB	Derrick Tabaka	Derrick Tabaka	2007	394
195 3/8	20	21 6/8	16 7/8	5 4/8	6 2/8	8	9	Valley Co., MT	Sue A. Kinney	Sue A. Kinney	2008	394
195 2/8	21 6/8	23 3/8	22 1/8	6 2/8	5 3/8	9	12	Grayson Co., TX	Robert K. Kimberlin	Robert K. Kimberlin	2006	400

WHITETAIL DEER - NON-TYPICAL ANTLERS

Odocoileus virginianus virginianus and certain related subspecies

Final Score	Gross Score	Length of Main Beam R.	L.	Inside Spread	Circumference at Smallest Place Between Burr & First Point R.	L.	Number of Points R.	L.	Locality	Hunter	Owner	Date Killed	Rank
195 2/8	203 7/8	22 6/8	23	21 3/8	5 6/8	5 5/8	12	7	Dubuque Co., IA	Donald A. Meyer	Donald A. Meyer	2006	400
195 2/8	201 5/8	27 7/8	28	18 5/8	5 7/8	5 7/8	8	11	Martin Co., IN	Jason Bird	Jason Bird	2007	400
195 2/8	199 2/8	25 2/8	25 4/8	20	6	6 1/8	7	9	Hot Spring Co., AR	Edward J. Carey	Edward J. Carey	2007	400
195 2/8	208 1/8	26	26 3/8	19 3/8	4 6/8	5	9	9	Ray Co., MO	Samuel A. Switzer	Samuel A. Switzer	2007	400
195 2/8	200 3/8	26 6/8	26 4/8	17 1/8	6 4/8	6 4/8	7	6	Greene Co., OH	Victor S. Burton	Victor S. Burton	2008	400
195 2/8	199 4/8	23	24 6/8	18 4/8	4 5/8	4 5/8	9	7	Cherry Co., NE	Jason M. Kelber	Jason M. Kelber	2008	400
195 1/8	205 2/8	24 2/8	23 3/8	18 6/8	4 2/8	4 3/8	12	9	Kleberg Co., TX	Nancy C. Cavazos	Nancy C. Cavazos	1973	407
195 1/8	204 7/8	29 6/8	29 3/8	26 3/8	5 3/8	5 2/8	11	7	Davis Co., IA	Theodore P. Henderson	Theodore P. Henderson	2006	407
195 1/8	208 4/8	23 6/8	22 7/8	17 5/8	4 5/8	4 7/8	10	9	Yazoo Co., MS	Roger F. Burton III	Roger F. Burton III	2007	407
195 1/8	197 3/8	22 6/8	22 4/8	14 2/8	5 1/8	5 2/8	11	10	Audrain Co., MO	Joshua R. Dollens	Joshua R. Dollens	2007	407
195 1/8	203 2/8	26 3/8	26 6/8	19 5/8	4 5/8	4 5/8	10	6	Jack Co., TX	Jon M. duPerier	Jon M. duPerier	2007	407
195 1/8	201 7/8	25 3/8	24 2/8	18 3/8	5 5/8	5 4/8	13	7	Richardson Co., NE	Trevor J. Godemann	Trevor J. Godemann	2007	407
195 1/8	205 1/8	26 7/8	26 1/8	24 2/8	5 1/8	5 7/8	9	11	Clark Co., OH	Russell B. Shatto	Russell B. Shatto	2007	407
195 1/8	197 6/8	23 7/8	23 5/8	18 4/8	4 2/8	4 2/8	9	8	Zavala Co., TX	Alberto Bailleres	Alberto Bailleres	2008	407
195 1/8	198 7/8	27	27	17 5/8	5 5/8	5 5/8	7	9	Grant Co., WI	Roger E. Szudera	Roger E. Szudera	2008	407
195	201 5/8	27 3/8	25 7/8	18 6/8	5 5/8	5 4/8	9	6	Ringgold Co., IA	Lee H. Martin	Lee H. Martin	2004	416
195	200 4/8	24 4/8	24 1/8	18 7/8	4 3/8	4 3/8	7	10	Crow Wing Co., MN	Lance E. Wasniewski	Lance E. Wasniewski	2007	416
195	197 3/8	25 3/8	25 4/8	17 7/8	4 6/8	4 6/8	6	7	Linn Co., IA	John E. Eaton	John E. Eaton	2008	416
194 4/8	197 3/8	25 7/8	27	21 7/8	4 5/8	4 5/8	8	7	Clearwater Co., ID	Jacob D. Lott	Jacob D. Lott	2005	419
194 4/8	206 2/8	24 7/8	25 2/8	21 3/8	5 3/8	5 1/8	8	9	Marion Co., OH	Martin E. Hamm, Jr.	Martin E. Hamm, Jr.	2007	419
194 2/8	197 6/8	26 1/8	25 1/8	17	6	6	9	10	Traill Co., ND	Marlin W. Ingebretson	Marlin W. Ingebretson	1955	421
194 2/8	204	23 6/8	26 2/8	17 4/8	5 1/8	5 4/8	9	10	Aitkin Co., MN	Michael A. Flint	Michael A. Flint	2008	421
194 2/8	207 6/8	20 2/8	22 4/8	19 7/8	5 5/8	6 2/8	10	13	Nance Co., NE	Deanna C. Hellbusch	Deanna C. Hellbusch	2008	421
194	204 3/8	24 2/8	24 2/8	17 7/8	4 6/8	4 5/8	9	7	Portage Co., OH	George T. Cariglio	George T. Cariglio	2006	424
193 7/8	199 2/8	22 7/8	22 4/8	14 3/8	4 2/8	4 2/8	9	10	Hamilton Lake, AB	Remo R. Pizzagalli	Remo R. Pizzagalli	2007	425
193 6/8	199 4/8	23 6/8	24 5/8	20 4/8	5 1/8	5 3/8	9	9	Tate Co., MS	Kenneth R. Crockett	Kenneth R. Crockett	2006	426
193 6/8	204 5/8	24	23 3/8	20	5 3/8	5 5/8	10	14	Delaware Co., OH	William E. Lehnert	William E. Lehnert	2006	426
193 6/8	199	21 7/8	22 3/8	18 3/8	5 4/8	4 6/8	8	10	Assiniboine River, SK	Evan Steppan	Evan Steppan	2006	426
193 6/8	200	24 6/8	25 1/8	16 2/8	5 3/8	5 4/8	6	9	Buffalo Co., WI	James D. Jacobson	James D. Jacobson	2008	426
193 5/8	204 1/8	26	24 2/8	16 4/8	5 2/8	5 5/8	10	9	Cowley Co., KS	James A. Snyder	James A. Snyder	2007	430
193 5/8	199 6/8	24 2/8	23 6/8	19 3/8	6	6	11	8	Lafayette Co., MO	Kenneth P. Creech III	Kenneth P. Creech III	2008	430
193 4/8	204 6/8	27 4/8	27 1/8	16 6/8	6	6	7	9	Portage Co., OH	Picked Up	Greg W. Winland	2008	432
193 3/8	196 1/8	26 2/8	26	20 2/8	5 4/8	5 5/8	7	7	Saline Co., IL	Gary Arthur	Gary Arthur	2006	433

Score	Gross Score	R. Beam	L. Beam	Inside Spread	Circ. R	Circ. L	Pts. R	Pts. L	Locality	Hunter	Owner	Date	Rank
193 3/8	197 3/8	26 4/8	27 1/8	16 4/8	4 5/8	4 2/8	7	4	Johnson Co., TN	John H. Hammett	John H. Hammett	2006	433
193 3/8	204 1/8	25 4/8	27 1/8	24	5 3/8	5 2/8	7	8	Madison Co., IL	Terry Jenkins	Terry Jenkins	2006	433
193 3/8	196 5/8	26	26 4/8	21 4/8	5 6/8	5 5/8	7	7	Good Spirit Lake, SK	Alick McMillan	Alick McMillan	2007	433
193 3/8	205 4/8	23 3/8	21 4/8	15 4/8	5 3/8	6	10	12	Silver Lake, SK	Garth V. Romanovitch	Garth V. Romanovitch	2007	433
193 3/8	201 5/8	28 7/8	28	21 5/8	4 3/8	4 5/8	12	10	Rainy Lake, ON	Parry J. Vandenelzen	Parry J. Vandenelzen	2007	433
193 2/8	196	24 2/8	25	18 6/8	5	4 7/8	7	6	St. Clair Co., IL	Brandon J. Hovick	Brandon J. Hovick	2007	439
193 2/8	206 5/8	29 3/8	29 3/8	20 2/8	5 6/8	5 3/8	7	7	Champaign Co., OH	William E. Coe	William E. Coe	2008	439
193 1/8	199 2/8	30	29 4/8	21 1/8	5 2/8	5 2/8	8	6	Martin Co., IN	John H. Kenworthy	John H. Kenworthy	2003	441
193 1/8	196 6/8	23 6/8	23 2/8	15 4/8	5 6/8	5 6/8	10	10	Johnson Co., NE	Bradley M. Harm	Bradley M. Harm	2006	441
193 1/8	197 7/8	25 3/8	24 1/8	19 2/8	5 1/8	5	10	10	Frio Co., TX	David O. Traylor	David O. Traylor	2007	441
193	200 4/8	22 4/8	24	18 4/8	6 2/8	5 6/8	7	8	Union Co., IL	C. Allen Johnson	C. Allen Johnson	2005	444
193	197 4/8	26 1/8	26 4/8	18 2/8	4 7/8	5 2/8	8	10	Schuyler Co., IL	Melissa R. Bachman	Melissa R. Bachman	2007	444
192 7/8	196 5/8	27	27	20 7/8	4 3/8	4 2/8	6	7	Crawford Co., WI	Loral E. Hare	Loral E. Hare	2008	444
192 5/8	200 3/8	23 5/8	26	16 6/8	5 5/8	5 5/8	15	9	Oldham Co., KY	Mike LeClair	Mike LeClair	2006	447
192 5/8	197 5/8	25 3/8	25 3/8	18 7/8	5 2/8	5 2/8	7	11	Fayette Co., IA	Curt G. Boose	Curt G. Boose	2006	448
192 5/8	203 3/8	23 7/8	30	18 7/8	5 3/8	5 4/8	10	8	Ross Co., OH	Ronald W. Preston	Ronald W. Preston	2007	448
192 5/8	194 6/8	26	25 7/8	19 7/8	5 4/8	5 2/8	9	11	Waupaca Co., WI	Picked Up	Timothy C. Bellile	2008	448
192 5/8	196 7/8	23	23 7/8	20 2/8	4 6/8	4 5/8	8	10	Lincoln Co., MO	Dane T. Baldwin	Dane T. Baldwin	2008	448
192 5/8	200 1/8	26 1/8	25 2/8	18 5/8	5 2/8	5	8	7	Sussex Co., DE	Robin E. Short	Robin E. Short	2008	448
192 4/8	198 2/8	25 5/8	26 1/8	17 5/8	5 3/8	5 3/8	9	9	Jefferson Co., KS	Wayne E. Henry	Wayne E. Henry	2002	453
192 4/8	200 7/8	25 1/8	25 3/8	18 6/8	5 5/8	5 5/8	8	13	Maverick Co., TX	James L. Gallogly	James L. Gallogly	2005	453

NON-TYPICAL WHITETAIL DEER
FINAL SCORE: 197 4/8
HUNTER: Greg W. Richards

NON-TYPICAL WHITETAIL DEER
FINAL SCORE: 201 3/8
HUNTER: Anthony J. VanDitto

NON-TYPICAL WHITETAIL DEER
FINAL SCORE: 202 5/8
HUNTER: Joseph A. Perry III

NON-TYPICAL WHITETAIL DEER
FINAL SCORE: 186 3/8
HUNTER: Charles P. Journee

WHITETAIL DEER - NON-TYPICAL ANTLERS

Odocoileus virginianus virginianus and certain related subspecies

Final Score	Gross Score	Length of Main Beam		Inside Spread	Circumference at Smallest Place Between Burr & First Point		Number of Points		Locality	Hunter	Owner	Date Killed	Rank
		R.	L.		R.	L.	R.	L.					
192 4/8	207 4/8	26 1/8	23 5/8	18 6/8	5 7/8	5 5/8	8	10	Fulton Co., IL	William J. Major	William J. Major	2006	453
192 3/8	199 5/8	19 2/8	20 4/8	18 4/8	5	5	7	8	Winnebago Co., IL	D. Shane Perry	D. Shane Perry	1994	456
192 3/8	196 6/8	24 1/8	23 5/8	20 1/8	4 5/8	4 4/8	5	10	Big Hay Lake, AB	Daniel B. O'Brien	Daniel B. O'Brien	2007	456
192 2/8	195	24 5/8	25 4/8	18 1/8	5 4/8	5 4/8	7	10	Nelson Co., ND	Patrick W. Novak	Patrick W. Novak	2006	458
192 2/8	197 3/8	24 7/8	21 6/8	22 4/8	3 6/8	4	8	9	Carroll Co., OH	Daniel J. Filisky	Daniel J. Filisky	2007	458
192 1/8	214 7/8	28 1/8	20	19 7/8	5 2/8	6 1/8	8	9	Johnson Co., IA	Ronald W. Chramosta	Ronald W. Chramosta	2006	460
192 1/8	201 5/8	24 1/8	24 5/8	17	5	5	8	6	Lucas Co., IA	Brent C. Town	Brent C. Town	2006	460
192 1/8	198 4/8	26 3/8	27	20 2/8	6	6	11	8	Nackawic, NB	Stephen H. Eldridge	Stephen H. Eldridge	2008	460
192 1/8	202 5/8	25	25 5/8	18 2/8	4 7/8	5 2/8	9	9	Knox Co., MO	Matthew C. Richardson	Matthew C. Richardson	2008	460
192	198 7/8	25 7/8	26 4/8	25 5/8	5 7/8	6 2/8	7	9	Greene Co., IN	John R. Vowell	John R. Vowell	2006	464
191 7/8	201	21 1/8	22 7/8	20 3/8	6 5/8	6	15	12	Schuyler Co., IL	Picked Up	Donald L. Young	2005	465
191 7/8	201 5/8	25 5/8	26 2/8	21 6/8	6 3/8	5 7/8	7	6	Greene Co., IL	Stephen R. Bartelli	Stephen R. Bartelli	2006	465
191 7/8	202	24 3/8	23 6/8	19 5/8	6 2/8	6	7	9	Jefferson Co., WI	Jennie L. Fisher	Jennie L. Fisher	2007	465
191 7/8	198 7/8	23 6/8	22 2/8	18 3/8	6 7/8	6 5/8	11	13	Osborne Co., KS	Picked Up	Raymond M. Schneider	2008	465
191 6/8	200 2/8	24 4/8	22 3/8	22 1/8	5 6/8	6 6/8	8	9	Lenawee Co., MI	Scott D. Norkey	Scott D. Norkey	2006	469
191 6/8	198 2/8	26 6/8	26 5/8	22 1/8	5 3/8	5 1/8	10	8	Crawford Co., WI	Benjamin C. Wohland	Benjamin C. Wohland	2006	469
191 6/8	195 3/8	26 3/8	27	21	5 2/8	5	8	9	Sullivan Co., IN	Chad M. Nash	Chad M. Nash	2007	469
191 5/8	199 3/8	24 6/8	26 6/8	20 3/8	5 2/8	5 4/8	9	8	Barron Co., WI	Thomas J. Engebretson	Thomas J. Engebretson	2006	472
191 5/8	205 2/8	25 4/8	25	17 5/8	5 1/8	5 1/8	11	9	Iron Co., WI	Matthew D. Heuer	Matthew D. Heuer	2006	472
191 5/8	196 2/8	26	26 2/8	19 6/8	5	4 5/8	8	6	Wabasha Co., MN	Dale L. Schulz	Dale L. Schulz	2006	472
191 5/8	198 6/8	26 4/8	26 2/8	21 5/8	5 2/8	5 4/8	7	7	Morrison Co., MN	Robert L. Brown	Robert L. Brown	2007	472
191 5/8	207 3/8	23 2/8	27	19 1/8	4 7/8	5	10	9	Monroe Co., IA	Eldon D. Collingwood	Eldon D. Collingwood	2007	472
191 5/8	197	27 2/8	27 6/8	20 4/8	5	5 6/8	7	8	Ashley Co., AR	Ted S. Selby	Ted S. Selby	2007	472
191 5/8	198 1/8	25	25 7/8	16 1/8	4 7/8	4 7/8	13	11	Jackfish Lake, SK	William J. Sabatose	William J. Sabatose	2008	472
191 4/8	195 6/8	22	21 3/8	20 6/8	4 5/8	4 3/8	10	7	Miquelon Lake, AB	M. Dean Wheeler	M. Dean Wheeler	2006	479
191 3/8	196	26	25 5/8	17 7/8	5 4/8	5 5/8	7	8	Logan Co., KY	Terry Baldwin	Terry Baldwin	2008	480
191 3/8	199 3/8	26 2/8	26 1/8	20 7/8	4 6/8	4 5/8	6	7	Moose Mt. Prov. Park, SK	Brent Shelest	Brent Shelest	2008	480
191 2/8	195 1/8	23 3/8	23 1/8	18 1/8	5 5/8	5 6/8	9	8	Bonner Co., ID	Michael S. Emerson	Michael S. Emerson	2005	482
191 2/8	202 2/8	28 1/8	26 5/8	17 6/8	5 2/8	5 3/8	8	8	Adams Co., IL	Bradley J. Caro	Bradley J. Caro	2006	482
191 2/8	198 1/8	25	26 2/8	20 2/8	6	5 3/8	8	9	La Salle Co., IL	Robert W. Myers	Robert W. Myers	2007	482
191 2/8	192 6/8	24 3/8	24 4/8	18 6/8	4 7/8	5	9	8	Winona Co., MN	Larry D. Walters	Larry D. Walters	2007	482

Score								Locality	Owner	By whom killed	Date	Rank
191 2/8	197 2/8	25 2/8	18 4/8	5	5 3/8	8	9	Henry Co., KY	Shelton S. Roberts, Jr.	Shelton S. Roberts, Jr.	2008	482
191	197 1/8	23 3/8	18 5/8	6	5 5/8	9	10	Wapello Co., IA	Daniel G. Horgen	Daniel G. Horgen	2006	487
191	199 1/8	25	17 1/8	5 6/8	5 6/8	7	8	Goodhue Co., MN	Michael W. Preston	Michael W. Preston	2008	487
191	199 2/8	24 5/8	16	4 6/8	5	9	11	Kingman Co., KS	Steven T. Tetrick	Steven T. Tetrick	2009	487
190 7/8	198 5/8	25 3/8	19 5/8	5	5 4/8	7	8	Isanti Co., MN	Shane A. Hoskins	Shane A. Hoskins	2007	490
190 7/8	195 5/8	21 5/8	26 6/8	4 4/8	4 7/8	11	12	Pittsburg Co., OK	Ronny G. Lambeth	Ronny G. Lambeth	2008	490
190 6/8	194 7/8	26 3/8	21 7/8	5 1/8	4 4/8	8	9	Aitkin Co., MN	Timothy J. Dale	Timothy J. Dale	2006	492
190 6/8	197 7/8	24 6/8	20 7/8	5 7/8	5 1/8	9	8	Schuyler Co., IL	John C. Miner	John C. Miner	2007	492
190 6/8	196 7/8	24 1/8	16 6/8	5 2/8	5 2/8	6	12	Barton Co., MO	David W. Ailshire	David W. Ailshire	2008	492
190 5/8	200	25 7/8	18 4/8	5 2/8	4 7/8	8	8	Monroe Co., IA	Raymond R. Bain	Raymond R. Bain	2006	495
190 5/8	201 3/8	23 5/8	18	6	5 7/8	10	7	Brown Co., KS	Robert D. Hall	Robert D. Hall	2008	495
190 5/8	196 3/8	22 6/8	16	5	4 7/8	9	8	Meriwether Co., GA	James E. Hill	James E. Hill	2008	495
190 5/8	196 2/8	26	15 1/8	6 4/8	5 3/8	9	8	Hopkins Co., KY	Roger Long	Roger Long	2008	495
190 4/8	195 3/8	25 2/8	17 2/8	6 3/8	6 2/8	7	10	Warren Co., MO	Cathy L. Engelage	Cathy L. Engelage	2006	499
190 4/8	196 4/8	25 2/8	21 2/8	5 6/8	6	8	9	Hamilton Co., IL	Kevin E. Tinsley	Kevin E. Tinsley	2006	499
190 4/8	193 4/8	24 7/8	18 5/8	6 7/8	6 7/8	8	8	Carroll Co., MO	Jim L. Shatto	Jim L. Shatto	2008	499
190 3/8	196 4/8	25 6/8	20 2/8	5 1/8	5 3/8	10	9	Kaposvar Creek, SK	Michael J. Schwitzer	Michael J. Schwitzer	2005	502
190 2/8	203 3/8	25 3/8	25 3/8	5 3/8	5 2/8	8	10	Sangamon Co., IL	Sydney H. Letz	Sydney H. Letz	2002	503
190 2/8	196	25 5/8	16 5/8	5 2/8	5 3/8	8	8	Wells Co., ND	Brian M. Miller	Brian M. Miller	2008	503
190 1/8	195 2/8	24 5/8	17 5/8	4 5/8	5 1/8	7	9	Johnston Co., OK	Samuel I. Barrett	Samuel I. Barrett	2007	505
190 1/8	194 2/8	26 1/8	18 3/8	5 2/8	5 1/8	11	5	Atchison Co., KS	Linda K. Funk	Linda K. Funk	2007	505
190	200 4/8	23 7/8	15 4/8	6 2/8	5 7/8	9	11	Marshall Co., IN	Thomas L. Zimmer	Thomas L. Zimmer	2006	507
189 7/8	196	24 5/8	16 6/8	5 2/8	5 3/8	11	9	Adair Co., MO	Les V. Chapman	Les V. Chapman	2005	508
189 7/8	203 4/8	29 2/8	17	5 5/8	5 3/8	10	9	Randolph Co., IL	Jay K. Roudabush	Jay K. Roudabush	2007	508
189 7/8	198 6/8	26 2/8	15 4/8	5 2/8	5 4/8	12	13	Larue Co., KY	Jason Abell	Jason Abell	2008	508
189 6/8	196 3/8	25 3/8	20 1/8	5 4/8	5 2/8	9	5	Licking Co., OH	Gary W. Kirsch	Gary W. Kirsch	2006	511
189 6/8	197 3/8	23 7/8	19 2/8	4 5/8	4 6/8	7	7	Kenora, ON	Robert J. LeClair	Robert J. LeClair	2006	511
189 6/8	195	22 7/8	22 2/8	5 2/8	5 2/8	8	8	Red Deer River, AB	David E. Powell	David E. Powell	2007	511
189 5/8	196 2/8	24	16	6 4/8	6	8	11	Canadian Co., OK	Zach J. Birdsong	Zach J. Birdsong	2004	514
189 5/8	196 4/8	26 2/8	19 4/8	4 7/8	4 6/8	7	9	Noble Co., IN	Alan L. Lytle	Alan L. Lytle	2007	514
189 4/8	197 3/8	25 4/8	17 6/8	4 6/8	4 6/8	8	10	Clay Co., MN	Earl L. Hodson	Earl L. Hodson	1958	516
189 4/8	199 2/8	24 3/8	15 4/8	7 1/8	5 5/8	7	9	Schuyler Co., IL	Thomas E. Pinyan, Jr.	Thomas E. Pinyan, Jr.	2006	516
189 4/8	195 3/8	24 4/8	21 6/8	6 1/8	6	9	9	Pike Co., IL	Paul H. Roeber	Paul H. Roeber	2006	516
189 4/8	192 2/8	23 4/8	17 2/8	5 5/8	5 4/8	6	7	Cooper Co., MO	Darrell W. Schultz	Darrell W. Schultz	2007	516
189 4/8	193 2/8	23 5/8	19 6/8	6 4/8	6 6/8	9	10	Jersey Co., IL	William D. Dailey	William D. Dailey	2009	516
189 3/8	195 4/8	24 6/8	15 1/8	5	5	6	8	Cass Co., MO	Robert A. Jessup	Robert A. Jessup	2006	521
189 3/8	204	27 3/8	20 7/8	7	7 4/8	9	7	Picton, ON	Jamie P. Branscombe	Jamie P. Branscombe	2008	521
189 3/8	199 2/8	23 2/8	20 4/8	6 6/8	6 6/8	9	6	Alix, AB	Joshua J. Garrett	Joshua J. Garrett	2008	521
189 3/8	195 2/8	24 6/8	21 2/8	5 5/8	5 5/8	6	8	Pottawatomie Co., KS	Mark A. Mayle	Mark A. Mayle	2008	521
189 2/8	195 4/8	27 6/8	20 1/8	4 4/8	4 6/8	9	9	Caldwell Co., KY	Denny Crisp	James D. Crisp	1978	525
189 2/8	206 2/8	26 6/8	16 2/8	5 2/8	5 1/8	6	9	Story Co., IA	Herbert J. Fromm	Herbert J. Fromm	2006	525
189 2/8	192 7/8	25	17 7/8	5 4/8	5 4/8	8	10	Ribstone Creek, AB	Raymond G. Kelsey	Raymond G. Kelsey	2007	525

WHITETAIL DEER - NON-TYPICAL ANTLERS

Odocoileus virginianus virginianus and certain related subspecies

Final Score	Gross Score	Length of Main Beam R.	Length of Main Beam L.	Inside Spread	Circumference at Smallest Place Between Burr & First Point R.	Circumference at Smallest Place Between Burr & First Point L.	Number of Points R.	Number of Points L.	Locality	Hunter	Owner	Date Killed	Rank
189 1/8	194 4/8	24 7/8	25 1/8	20 2/8	4 4/8	5	8	8	Sheboygan Co., WI	Russell W. Spindler	Russell W. Spindler	2007	528
189 1/8	199 1/8	24 3/8	25	18 4/8	4 6/8	4 6/8	7	9	Winnebago Co., WI	Stuart C. Miller	Stuart C. Miller	2009	528
189 1/8	198	25 6/8	25	17 7/8	6	6	8	12	Cass Co., MI	Todd A. Seiler	Todd A. Seiler	2009	528
189	200 1/8	24 6/8	23 4/8	16 1/8	5 4/8	6	11	11	Washington Co., NE	Darold K. Fitz, Jr.	Darold K. Fitz, Jr.	2006	531
189	193 3/8	23 7/8	23 3/8	21 1/8	5 1/8	5	8	11	Grant Co., OR	Nancy A. Garrett	Nancy A. Garrett	2007	531
189	198	24 2/8	23 4/8	19 7/8	6 1/8	5 7/8	9	10	Schuyler Co., IL	Picked Up	Robert Van Munster	2007	531
189	201 3/8	27 2/8	27 1/8	24	5 3/8	5 6/8	7	7	Van Buren Co., IA	Douglas L. Moore	Douglas L. Moore	2008	531
188 7/8	195 3/8	25 2/8	25 2/8	15 7/8	5	5 3/8	12	9	Marinette Co., WI	Matthew W. Serwa	Matthew W. Serwa	1999	535
188 6/8	194 3/8	24	25 3/8	22 2/8	4 4/8	4 4/8	7	7	Clearwater Co., ID	David W. Carver	David W. Carver	1978	536
188 6/8	190 4/8	24 1/8	23 6/8	17 6/8	5 5/8	5 7/8	9	5	St. Louis Co., MN	Donald O. Neubarth II	Donald O. Neubarth II	2006	536
188 6/8	196	25 2/8	25 3/8	20 6/8	5 3/8	5 4/8	8	6	Fillmore Co., MN	Brian J. Becker	Brian J. Becker	2007	536
188 6/8	191 6/8	25 5/8	26	18 1/8	4 6/8	4 7/8	9	8	Clay Co., IN	W. Perry Shaw, Jr.	W. Perry Shaw, Jr.	2008	536
188 5/8	193 1/8	25 7/8	25 7/8	21 2/8	4 4/8	4 4/8	6	7	Marshall Co., TN	Joseph M. Furden	Joseph M. Furden	2007	540
188 4/8	198 3/8	24 5/8	26 2/8	20	5 7/8	5 7/8	8	6	Oneida Co., WI	Robert L. Gentz	Robert L. Gentz	2006	541
188 4/8	190 5/8	27 4/8	27 3/8	20	4 6/8	5	7	6	Gatineau, QC	Francis D. Sabourin	Francis D. Sabourin	2006	541
188 3/8	194 5/8	26	22 3/8	18	6	5 6/8	10	9	Allegheny Co., PA	James D. Edwards	James D. Edwards	2000	543
188 3/8	201 4/8	25	22 3/8	19 3/8	5	6 6/8	9	12	Coshocton Co., OH	R. Stanley Barnes	R. Stanley Barnes	2006	543
188 3/8	192 6/8	27 5/8	26 3/8	18 7/8	5 3/8	5 3/8	8	10	Northumberland Co., PA	Steven L. Butler	Steven L. Butler	2007	543
188 3/8	190	25 4/8	25 2/8	16 3/8	5 1/8	5 1/8	7	7	Linn Co., MO	James G. Chapman	James G. Chapman	2007	543
188 3/8	192 5/8	24 1/8	25	19 5/8	5 4/8	5 4/8	8	7	Kalamazoo Co., MI	Douglas E. Hamstra	Douglas E. Hamstra	2008	543
188 3/8	193	26 1/8	25 1/8	19 3/8	4 7/8	4 6/8	7	7	Lee Co., IL	Matthew C. Rehor	Matthew C. Rehor	2008	543
188 2/8	192 2/8	25 3/8	24 7/8	18 6/8	5 3/8	5 4/8	6	8	Pend Oreille Co., WA	Edward Moses	Mark R. Mebes	1982	549
188 2/8	196 3/8	25 5/8	25 2/8	19 7/8	5 2/8	5 3/8	6	9	Doniphan Co., KS	Raymond L. Hoverson	Raymond L. Hoverson	2007	549
188 1/8	197 1/8	25 7/8	25 3/8	18 4/8	4 5/8	4 7/8	14	17	Latimer Co., OK	Terence G. Young	Terence G. Young	2006	551
188 1/8	192	24	23 7/8	19 2/8	4 3/8	4 5/8	9	9	Clarion Co., PA	Eric J. Dobrowski	Eric J. Dobrowski	2007	551
188	190 6/8	24 1/8	23 5/8	18 4/8	5 1/8	5 1/8	9	7	Addison Co., VT	Ronald E. Moody	Mary Moody	1958	553
188	191 4/8	25 6/8	25 4/8	19 1/8	5 2/8	5 1/8	7	7	Montmorency Co., MI	Larry D. Chastain	Larry D. Chastain	2006	553
188	195	27 2/8	26 1/8	20 4/8	5 7/8	5 6/8	8	6	Cole Co., MO	Marvin D. Phillips	Marvin D. Phillips	2008	553
187 6/8	190 2/8	24 5/8	25 1/8	19 7/8	5 2/8	5 1/8	9	7	Todd Co., MN	Matthew C. Falzone	Matthew C. Falzone	2006	556
187 6/8	195 4/8	26 6/8	25 1/8	19 6/8	4 6/8	4 5/8	10	8	Hocking Co., OH	Robert L. Westhoven	Robert L. Westhoven	2006	556
187 6/8	191 3/8	25	25 5/8	22 4/8	6 2/8	4 5/8	9	10	St. Francois Co., MO	John C. Huff	John C. Huff	2007	556
187 6/8	192 5/8	25 5/8	26 2/8	19 2/8	4 4/8	4 4/8	9	11	Warren Co., OH	Chad W. Grote	Chad W. Grote	2008	556
187 6/8	191 3/8	27	28 3/8	21 7/8	4 7/8	4 6/8	10	8	Minaki, ON	James McKinney	James McKinney	2008	556

Score	Gross	Main Beam R	Main Beam L	Inside Spread	Cir. R	Cir. L	Locality	Pts. R	Pts. L	Owner	Hunter	Date	Rank
187 5/8	192 7/8	20 3/8	19 7/8	14 6/8	5 7/8	8 7/8	Red Deer River, AB	11	11	Joseph D. Wiggs	Joseph D. Wiggs	2007	561
187 5/8	191 7/8	24 5/8	25 1/8	17 6/8	4 4/8	4 5/8	Boone Co., KY	10	9	Christopher R. White	Christopher R. White	2009	561
187 4/8	195 1/8	24 3/8	26 6/8	19 4/8	5 2/8	5 4/8	Republic Co., KS	9	9	Paul C. Aughtry III	Paul C. Aughtry III	2007	563
187 4/8	195 6/8	25 3/8	23 4/8	15	5 1/8	5 6/8	De Kalb Co., GA	10	8	Rusty Osborne	Rusty Osborne	2008	563
187 3/8	191 3/8	24 4/8	23 6/8	17 7/8	4 6/8	4 5/8	Adams Co., IL	7	8	Mike Dougherty	Mike Dougherty	2006	565
187 3/8	199 6/8	25 6/8	25 6/8	24	5 6/8	6 1/8	Washington Co., MS	7	8	Angus L. Catchot	Angus L. Catchot	2007	565
187 3/8	198 2/8	28 1/8	27 1/8	18 4/8	4 6/8	4 4/8	Ashland Co., OH	7	6	Dennis L. Dininger	Dennis L. Dininger	2008	565
187 2/8	191 5/8	24 3/8	24 3/8	20	6 1/8	5 5/8	Coffey Co., KS	6	6	David C. Jordan	David C. Jordan	2006	568
187 2/8	193 3/8	25 6/8	25 2/8	20 4/8	5 2/8	6	Allegan Co., MI	10	6	Peter D. Prather	Peter D. Prather	2006	568
187 2/8	192	22 5/8	22 3/8	16	4 6/8	4 5/8	Lyon Co., IA	7	7	Kenneth D. Knoblock	Kenneth D. Knoblock	2007	568
187 2/8	196 4/8	24 6/8	25 1/8	16 4/8	5 2/8	5 2/8	Allamakee Co., IA	9	9	Darrell J. Moose	Darrell J. Moose	2007	568
187 2/8	194 6/8	21 5/8	23 1/8	18 4/8	5 2/8	5 2/8	Auglaize Co., OH	13	11	Jason J. Vanderhorst	Jason J. Vanderhorst	2009	568
187 1/8	193 4/8	26 6/8	26 3/8	22	5 3/8	5 3/8	Ripley Co., IN	8	11	Steven W. Brunner	Steven W. Brunner	2005	573
187 1/8	193 7/8	23	23	17 1/8	5 5/8	5 7/8	Iroquois Co., IL	12	7	Anthony D. Lucht	Anthony D. Lucht	2006	573
187 1/8	196 4/8	25 4/8	25 1/8	20 4/8	5 2/8	5 4/8	Barnes Co., ND	7	11	Brian D. Nelson	Brian D. Nelson	2006	573
187 1/8	194 7/8	23	23 7/8	22 3/8	8 4/8	6 2/8	Monroe Co., IA	12	7	William H. Kirkpatrick, Jr.	William H. Kirkpatrick, Jr.	2007	573
187 1/8	190 2/8	23 4/8	23	19 7/8	5 2/8	5 1/8	Buffalo Co., WI	9	8	Timothy S. Crawford	Timothy S. Crawford	2008	573
187	195 4/8	23 3/8	24 3/8	17 4/8	4 7/8	5 4/8	Ghost Lake, ON	8	7	Michael J. Haubert	Michael J. Haubert	2006	578
187	191 1/8	28	27 5/8	20 3/8	6 2/8	6 3/8	Winnebago Co., IL	8	7	David T. Marske	David T. Marske	2007	578
187	193 1/8	24 1/8	25	20 6/8	5 7/8	5 5/8	Brazeau Mts., AB	11	12	Aaron L. Mueller	Aaron L. Mueller	2008	578
186 7/8	192 5/8	25	25 6/8	16 1/8	5 2/8	5 2/8	Saline Co., NE	6	10	Benjamin J. Vilda	Benjamin J. Vilda	2008	582
186 7/8	190 7/8	25 6/8	24 6/8	20	6 6/8	6 2/8	Coal Creek, BC	7	6	Carl M. Gitscheff	Carl M. Gitscheff	2006	582
186 7/8	193 3/8	24 7/8	25 4/8	16 4/8	5 4/8	5 2/8	Monroe Co., IA	11	8	Picked Up	Robert Smith	2006	582
186 6/8	191 7/8	25 3/8	26 7/8	19 7/8	5 1/8	5 1/8	Ohio Co., KY	6	11	Ben Groves	Ben Groves	2007	585
186 6/8	195 2/8	27 2/8	25 7/8	18 2/8	5	5	Richland Co., OH	8	6	William Bowers	William Bowers	2002	585
186 5/8	192 2/8	25 7/8	26	18 6/8	4 7/8	4 7/8	Calloway Co., KY	8	8	Blake Munger	Blake Munger	2008	587
186 4/8	192	26 6/8	26 1/8	21 4/8	5	4 4/8	Koochiching Co., MN	9	7	Gregory A. Schneider	Gregory A. Schneider	2006	588
186 3/8	188 5/8	26 1/8	26	19 1/8	4 4/8	4 7/8	Itasca Co., MN	9	8	Jeffrey R. Houston	Jeffrey R. Houson	2007	589
186 3/8	190 3/8	28 6/8	28 6/8	15 6/8	4 6/8	4 6/8	St. Louis Co., MN	12	9	Dave Vukich	Mark K. Sieg	1976	589
186 3/8	196 7/8	24 7/8	24 7/8	24 6/8	6	6	Clearwater Co., MN	7	6	Alex O. Jesness	Alex O. Jesness	2008	589
186 2/8	190	22 6/8	22 6/8	20 4/8	4 1/8	4	Trinity Co., TX	9	7	Charles P. Journee	Charles P. Journee	2008	592
186 2/8	193 5/8	24 4/8	24 4/8	18 6/8	4 6/8	4 6/8	Barren Co., KY	9	9	James M. Binder	James M. Binder	2004	592
186 2/8	191 4/8	22	22	21 4/8	5 1/8	5 1/8	Pawnee Co., NE	10	8	Lennis L. Blecha, Jr.	Lennis L. Blecha, Jr.	2005	592
186 2/8	196 5/8	23 4/8	23 4/8	18 2/8	5 3/8	5	Jefferson Co., NE	15	12	Vernon D. Hampton	Vernon D. Hampton	2007	592
186 2/8	191 3/8	23 6/8	23 6/8	17	5 4/8	5 7/8	Coffey Co., KS	9	11	Anthony L. Burkett	Anthony L. Burkett	2008	592
186 2/8	190	26 3/8	26	21 7/8	5 2/8	4 3/8	Jessamine Co., KY	6	9	Jason Burkley	Jason Burkley	2008	592
186 1/8	196 1/8	28 4/8	27 7/8	18	4 3/8	5 5/8	Pike Co., OH	7	7	Keith D. Stubblefield	Keith D. Stubblefield	2008	598
186 1/8	190 3/8	26 5/8	26 4/8	18 6/8	5 5/8	4 5/8	Rimouski, QC	7	7	Jacques Lamontagne	Raynald Groleau	2004	598
186 1/8	190 3/8	22 6/8	23 5/8	15	4 5/8	5 4/8	Worth Co., MO	7	8	Rory F. Jackson	Rory F. Jackson	2006	598
186 1/8	190	23 3/8	22 4/8	16 6/8	5 4/8	5 7/8	Trempealeau Co., WI	13	11	Daniel J. Baer	Daniel J. Baer	2007	598
186 1/8	191 1/8	24 4/8	24 6/8	17 3/8	4 6/8	4 6/8	Moose Mt., SK	7	10	David W. Oldhaver	David W. Oldhaver	2007	598

WHITETAIL DEER - NON-TYPICAL ANTLERS

Odocoileus virginianus virginianus and certain related subspecies

Final Score	Gross Score	Length of Main Beam R.	L.	Inside Spread	Circumference at Smallest Place Between Burr & First Point R.	L.	Number of Points R.	L.	Locality	Hunter	Owner	Date Killed	Rank
186	195 7/8	25 6/8	23 5/8	15 4/8	5 3/8	5 6/8	8	13	Darke Co., OH	Bruce R. Henry	Bruce R. Henry	2006	602
186	193 5/8	25 6/8	27	19 5/8	5 1/8	4 7/8	9	9	Coffey Co., KS	Marc A. Glades	Marc A. Glades	2007	602
186	196 3/8	25 1/8	25 1/8	19 7/8	5 5/8	6	7	11	Warren Co., MO	Adam M. Hasenjaeger	Adam M. Hasenjaeger	2007	602
186	196 2/8	22 6/8	23 1/8	23 5/8	4 6/8	4 5/8	9	7	Reno Co., KS	Jason J. Applebe	Jason J. Applebe	2008	602
186	195 6/8	25 6/8	24	18 6/8	5 1/8	5 1/8	7	9	Vermilion Co., IN	Jeremy Cook	Jeremy Cook	2008	602
186	196 2/8	22 2/8	21 5/8	20 4/8	5 2/8	5 1/8	7	7	Wilson Co., KS	Jenessa D. Shinkle	Jenessa D. Shinkle	2008	602
186	190 2/8	26 5/8	26 5/8	16 6/8	5 5/8	5 5/8	7	7	Pulaski Co., KY	Hurley R. Combs, Jr.	Hurley R. Combs, Jr.	2009	602
185 7/8	191 2/8	26 3/8	26 4/8	18 5/8	4 5/8	4 4/8	6	7	Darke Co., OH	Randy M. Grisez	Randy M. Grisez	2003	609
185 7/8	191 4/8	26 1/8	27 1/8	17 2/8	5 4/8	5 2/8	6	7	Jackson Co., WI	Kyle R. McPherson	Kyle R. McPherson	2005	609
185 7/8	194 7/8	23	23 3/8	15 5/8	5	5 3/8	10	15	Comanche Co., KS	Gary K. Rice	Gary K. Rice	2007	609
185 6/8	189 3/8	25	24 7/8	19 4/8	6 1/8	6 1/8	10	9	Kingsbury Co., SD	Lorraine Steffensen	Lorraine Steffensen	1967	612
185 6/8	187 5/8	22 1/8	21 7/8	17 7/8	5 7/8	5 6/8	10	8	Henry Co., IN	David D. Simpkins	David D. Simpkins	2006	612
185 5/8	190 5/8	25	25 2/8	19	4 6/8	4 7/8	9	7	Waupaca Co., WI	Rose M. Bazile	Rose M. Bazile	2006	614
185 5/8	188 3/8	28 3/8	29	19 4/8	4 5/8	4 6/8	8	8	Livingston Co., MI	Jeanetta A. Flanery	Jeanetta A. Flanery	2006	614
185 5/8	193 1/8	25 4/8	25 7/8	18 2/8	5 2/8	5 3/8	8	8	Carroll Co., OH	Shane A. Elifritz	Shane A. Elifritz	2007	614
185 5/8	191 7/8	24 6/8	24 6/8	22 1/8	5 1/8	5	8	7	Nelson Co., KY	Robert L. Fenwick	Robert L. Fenwick	2008	614
185 5/8	193 1/8	24 3/8	24 2/8	21 4/8	5	5 1/8	8	11	Keya Paha Co., NE	Kelly L. Griffith	Kelly L. Griffith	2008	614
185 5/8	191 6/8	24 3/8	23 6/8	17 3/8	4 7/8	4 6/8	12	8	Shuswap River, BC	Mitchell C. Haller	Mitchell C. Haller	2008	614
185 4/8	190 1/8	24 2/8	25	16 1/8	5 4/8	5 2/8	9	7	Ralls Co., MO	Dale E. Hemme	Dale E. Hemme	2006	620
185 4/8	188	22 1/8	22 3/8	18	4 4/8	4 4/8	9	10	Dubuque Co., IA	Gerald M. Nickol	Gerald M. Nickol	2006	620
185 4/8	197 2/8	26 4/8	27 5/8	19 6/8	4 3/8	4 6/8	7	8	Warren Co., IL	Barry L. Robinson	Barry L. Robinson	2006	620
185 4/8	192	26 6/8	24 4/8	16 7/8	5	5	11	11	Marshall Co., MS	Joseph M. Lundine	Joseph M. Lundine	2007	620
185 4/8	191 3/8	25	24 3/8	17 1/8	5 5/8	5 6/8	10	12	Marquette Co., WI	Shawn M. Campion	Shawn M. Campion	2008	620
185 4/8	192	23 2/8	24 4/8	19 3/8	5 2/8	5	9	8	Livingston Co., MO	John C. Gilliland	John C. Gilliland	2008	620
185 4/8	191 2/8	25 5/8	25 7/8	19 7/8	4 7/8	4 6/8	8	8	Highland Co., OH	Timothy V. Schlater	Timothy V. Schlater	2008	620
185 3/8	196 7/8	24 6/8	25 4/8	18 4/8	5	5 1/8	11	7	Vermilion River, AB	Emil C. Kure	Emil C. Kure	1994	627
185 3/8	193 5/8	25 3/8	24 3/8	20	7 2/8	7 2/8	9	12	Stephenson Co., IL	Ron E. Kaderly	Ron E. Kaderly	2002	627
185 3/8	193 3/8	27	26 3/8	16 3/8	5 2/8	5 4/8	8	10	Logan Co., IL	Brad L. Beggs	Brad L. Beggs	2005	627
185 3/8	189 3/8	26 2/8	25	26 1/8	4 7/8	5 1/8	6	6	Fayette Co., IL	Michael J. Bianchi	Michael J. Bianchi	2006	627
185 3/8	194 4/8	26 2/8	25 4/8	19 3/8	6	5 7/8	12	9	Russell Co., KY	Jacob Pyles	Jacob Pyles	2008	627
185 2/8	194 4/8	26 6/8	25 5/8	23	4 3/8	4 4/8	10	8	Madison Co., VA	James E. Board	James E. Board	2007	632
185 2/8	194 5/8	22 2/8	21 7/8	14 6/8	4 4/8	5	9	11	Madison Co., IA	Robert J. Clifton	Robert J. Clifton	2007	632
185 1/8	192 3/8	23 5/8	24	17 6/8	5	5	6	6	Randolph Co., IL	Don Schulte	Don Schulte	2004	634

185 1/8	190	25 2/8	24 6/8	20	5	5 1/8	10	7	Harrison Co., MO	William C. Pollack	William C. Pollack	2006	634
185 1/8	197 7/8	29 7/8	28 7/8	18 5/8	5	4 7/8	8	11	Itasca Co., MN	Vince A. Weik	Vince A. Weik	2007	634
185 1/8	187 4/8	26 6/8	26 6/8	19 1/8	5 1/8	5 2/8	9	8	Finney Co., KS	Gary L. Brand	Gary L. Brand	2008	634
185 1/8	193 3/8	25 6/8	26 1/8	21 2/8	5 7/8	5 6/8	9	7	Woodward Co., OK	Diamon S. Miller	Diamon S. Miller	2008	634
185 1/8	195 4/8	26 2/8	27 7/8	16 7/8	5 3/8	5 2/8	5	5	Qu'Appelle River, SK	Douglas E. Trevena	Douglas E. Trevena	2008	634
185	188 3/8	25 2/8	25 4/8	16 6/8	4 7/8	4 7/8	7	6	Wadena Co., MN	Dan Carlson	Lauren E. Carlson	1980	640
185	194 6/8	21	22 6/8	17	4 3/8	4	10	7	Leslie Co., KY	Denver Brock	Denver Brock	2006	640
185	191 2/8	26 4/8	25 2/8	18 2/8	5	5 1/8	9	7	Jackson Co., IA	Eric C. Proshuto	Eric C. Proshuto	2007	640
185	189 3/8	25	24 6/8	16 3/8	5 1/8	5	6	8	Todd Co., KY	Devin A. Chastain	Devin A. Chastain	2008	640
268 1/8*	272 2/8	25 7/8	25 6/8	20 6/8	5 6/8	5 7/8	14	14	Charles Co., MD	Bill Crutchfield, Jr.	Bill Crutchfield, Jr.	2006	640
250 7/8*	256 2/8	27 3/8	27 4/8	21 5/8	5 5/8	6 3/8	12	11	Jewell Co., KS	Marc L. Barnes	Marc L. Barnes	2006	640

* Final score subject to revision by additional verifying measurements.

**NON-TYPICAL
WHITETAIL DEER**
FINAL SCORE: 195
HUNTER: Lance E. Wasniewski

**NON-TYPICAL
WHITETAIL DEER**
FINAL SCORE: 197
HUNTER: M. David Castleberry

**NON-TYPICAL
WHITETAIL DEER**
FINAL SCORE: 199 1/8
HUNTER: Jimmy D. Carpenter

**NON-TYPICAL
WHITETAIL DEER**
FINAL SCORE: 200 1/8
HUNTER: Dean M. Basch

COUES' WHITETAIL DEER - TYPICAL ANTLERS

Odocoileus virginianus couesi

Minimum Score 100

World's Record 144 1/8

Final Score	Gross Score	Length of Main Beam R.	L.	Inside Spread	Circumference at Smallest Place Between Burr & First Point R.	L.	Number of Points R.	L.	Locality	Hunter	Owner	Date Killed	Rank
127	128 3/8	19 7/8	20 1/8	15 4/8	4 1/8	4 1/8	5	5	Coconino Co., AZ	Brian C. Balmer	Brian C. Balmer	2008	1
126	133 6/8	16 6/8	16 4/8	10 3/8	4	4	6	5	Sonora, MX	Frank Lawrence	Frank Lawrence	2006	2
122 3/8	138 7/8	20	18 5/8	13 4/8	3 5/8	3 6/8	5	6	Sonora, MX	Jay Jones	Jay Jones	2007	3
121	124 4/8	18 7/8	19 5/8	14 4/8	3 6/8	3 5/8	5	5	Sonora, MX	Jack E. Risner	Jack E. Risner	2009	4
119 6/8	127 2/8	18 6/8	19 7/8	15	3 3/8	3 2/8	4	5	Sonora, MX	Kooper Mitchell	Kooper Mitchell	2007	5
118 4/8	122 5/8	19 4/8	19 4/8	13 6/8	4 2/8	4 3/8	5	4	Sonora, MX	Bart D. Hill	Bart D. Hill	2005	6
118 1/8	126 2/8	17 4/8	17 3/8	12 2/8	4	4	5	6	Sonora, MX	Donald E. Perrien	Donald E. Perrien	2009	7
117 4/8	127 6/8	21	20 5/8	16 4/8	4	4	6	5	Santa Cruz Co., AZ	Danny L. Crain, Jr.	Danny L. Crain, Jr.	2007	8
117 4/8	131 2/8	18 1/8	16 5/8	14 2/8	3 6/8	3 6/8	6	5	Sonora, MX	James A. Reynolds	James A. Reynolds	2008	8
117 2/8	120 5/8	17 2/8	17 7/8	14	4 5/8	4 4/8	4	4	Coconino Co., AZ	Frank A. Macias	Frank A. Macias	2008	10
116 6/8	118 2/8	19	18 5/8	13 4/8	3 6/8	3 5/8	4	4	Sonora, MX	Ronald J. Nadzieja	Ronald J. Nadzieja	2008	11
116 3/8	124	18 5/8	19 3/8	13 5/8	3 5/8	3 5/8	4	5	Sonora, MX	Steven L. Kiesel	Steven L. Kiesel	2009	12
116 2/8	119 4/8	20 2/8	21 2/8	14 2/8	3 7/8	3 7/8	4	4	Sonora, MX	Jason J. Gisi	Jason J. Gisi	2005	13
116 1/8	120 2/8	17 6/8	15 5/8	14 1/8	4 3/8	4 2/8	4	4	Sonora, MX	Bart D. Hill	Bart D. Hill	2008	14
115 4/8	117 1/8	18 6/8	18 6/8	15 4/8	3 7/8	3 6/8	4	4	Pima Co., AZ	Robert C. Stark	Robert C. Stark	2008	15
115 4/8	117 2/8	17 6/8	18 3/8	13 6/8	3 6/8	4	4	4	Sonora, MX	Rick D. Parker	Rick D. Parker	2009	15
115	117 4/8	17 4/8	17 2/8	14 4/8	4 6/8	4 6/8	4	4	Sonora, MX	Brant Hilman	Brant Hilman	2007	17
114 3/8	116 7/8	18 3/8	18	15 1/8	4 2/8	4 1/8	4	5	Yavapai Co., AZ	Dean L. Peterson	Dean L. Peterson	2007	18
114 2/8	118 6/8	19	17 5/8	14	4	4 1/8	5	5	Gila Co., AZ	Erin J. Bittner	Erin J. Bittner	2008	19
114 1/8	116 7/8	18	17 1/8	14 7/8	3 7/8	3 6/8	5	4	Pima Co., AZ	William C. Snyder	William C. Snyder	1999	20
114	117 2/8	19 1/8	19 6/8	14 2/8	3 7/8	3 7/8	4	4	Hidalgo Co., NM	Roger A. Roan	Roger A. Roan	2007	21
114	116 6/8	17 7/8	18 5/8	17 4/8	4	4 1/8	4	4	Hidalgo Co., NM	Patrick H. Lyons	Patrick H. Lyons	2008	21
113 5/8	118 3/8	17 6/8	19	14 5/8	3 6/8	3 6/8	4	4	Sonora, MX	Bethena C. Pugh	Bethena C. Pugh	2007	23
113 5/8	121 7/8	15 3/8	17 1/8	16	3 5/8	3 4/8	5	6	Gila Co., AZ	Jason R. Beck	Jason R. Beck	2008	23
113 4/8	115 5/8	18 4/8	18 2/8	13 2/8	3 7/8	3 7/8	4	4	Sonora, MX	Matt S. Pandol, Jr.	Matt S. Pandol, Jr.	2006	25
113 4/8	118 7/8	20 7/8	20 2/8	15 6/8	3 4/8	3 4/8	4	5	Sonora, MX	John P. Westbrook	John P. Westbrook	2008	25
112 4/8	121	19 4/8	18 4/8	14 2/8	4	4 2/8	5	5	Navajo Co., AZ	Picked Up	John E. Brown	1993	27
112 2/8	120 7/8	19 4/8	19 6/8	18 4/8	4 1/8	4 2/8	4	5	Pima Co., AZ	Kent J. Waller	Kent J. Waller	2007	27
112 2/8	118	17 7/8	18 7/8	13	4 4/8	4 5/8	5	4	Sonora, MX	Carroll E. Moran	Carroll E. Moran	2009	27
112	124 1/8	19 3/8	19 4/8	16	3 6/8	3 6/8	6	6	Sonora, MX	John P. Westbrook	John P. Westbrook	2000	30
111 7/8	118 7/8	18 3/8	17 5/8	12 7/8	3 7/8	3 7/8	5	4	Sonora, MX	Robert C. Sugg	Robert C. Sugg	2009	31
111 6/8	117 7/8	17 6/8	18 5/8	15 6/8	4 3/8	4 3/8	5	5	Pima Co., AZ	Jane A. Beck	Jane A. Beck	2007	32
111 5/8	117 5/8	18 6/8	19 2/8	14 4/8	4 1/8	4 1/8	5	4	Santa Cruz Co., AZ	Hayden G. Maclean	Hayden G. Maclean	2006	33
111 4/8	114 6/8	17 1/8	17	14 4/8	3 7/8	3 7/8	5	5	Pima Co., AZ	Mark C. Manning	Mark C. Manning	2008	34

Score							Points		Locality	Owner	By	Date	Rank
111 3/8	120 7/8	16	15 5/8	11 6/8	4 1/8	4	6	6	Pima Co., AZ	Jacob W. Hume	Jacob W. Hume	2007	35
111 3/8	121 4/8	16 6/8	19 7/8	12 7/8	3 6/8	3 7/8	5	4	Sonora, MX	Michael D. Bright	Michael D. Bright	2009	35
111 2/8	119 6/8	19 6/8	19 1/8	16 2/8	3 6/8	3 6/8	4	5	Sonora, MX	William D. Skor	William D. Skor	2009	37
110 6/8	121 1/8	18 4/8	17 6/8	16 1/8	4 5/8	4 4/8	7	4	Gila Co., AZ	Brian A. Rimsza	Brian A. Rimsza	2009	38
110 5/8	120	20 1/8	19 3/8	13 7/8	3 7/8	3 5/8	4	4	Sonora, MX	Michael A. Ronning	Michael A. Ronning	2008	39
110 4/8	112 5/8	20 3/8	20	13 4/8	4	3 7/8	3	3	Pima Co., AZ	Christopher M. Pena	Christopher M. Pena	2006	40
110 3/8	122 6/8	18 6/8	18 6/8	16 4/8	3 7/8	3 1/8	5	4	Sonora, MX	James A. Reynolds	James A. Reynolds	2009	41
110 2/8	118 6/8	16 1/8	16 5/8	12 4/8	3 5/8	3 5/8	5	6	Sonora, MX	David L. May	David L. May	2007	42
108 7/8	111 1/8	19 6/8	20	11 7/8	3 5/8	3 4/8	4	4	Sonora, MX	Chadley J. Blackhurst	Chadley J. Blackhurst	2009	43
108 3/8	111 6/8	18 7/8	18 6/8	13 7/8	3 6/8	3 5/8	4	4	Sonora, MX	Joseph B. Hollis	Joseph B. Hollis	2009	44
108	108	16 6/8	16 6/8	16 6/8	3 5/8	3 5/8	4	4	Sonora, MX	Gary A. Hayden	Gary A. Hayden	2008	45
107 4/8	118 7/8	18 4/8	18 6/8	18 4/8	3 7/8	4	6	6	Sonora, MX	John D. Todd	John D. Todd	2004	46
107 3/8	111 4/8	18 3/8	18 3/8	12 7/8	3 3/8	3 4/8	5	4	Cochise Co., AZ	David W. Janos	David W. Janos	1992	47
106 7/8	110 1/8	17 1/8	17 1/8	14	3 6/8	3 5/8	4	5	Sonora, MX	William H. McLean	William H. McLean	2007	48
106 3/8	109 2/8	17 1/8	17 1/8	15 1/8	3 3/8	3 4/8	4	4	Graham Co., AZ	Thomas L. Freestone	Thomas L. Freestone	1995	49
106 2/8	109 7/8	19	19	14 4/8	3 6/8	3 5/8	4	4	Sonora, MX	Charles I. Kelly	Charles I. Kelly	2006	50
106 1/8	108 4/8	17 1/8	16 7/8	13 7/8	4 1/8	3 7/8	4	4	Pima Co., AZ	Denny Tidaback	Denny Tidaback	2008	51
106	110 2/8	15 7/8	15 4/8	14 6/8	3 6/8	3 6/8	5	4	Pima Co., AZ	Mark D. Thomson	Mark D. Thomson	2007	52
105 6/8	110 4/8	15 7/8	16 2/8	14 6/8	4 1/8	5 2/8	5	5	Sonora, MX	Cathy S. Sloan	Cathy S. Sloan	2009	53
105 5/8	110 1/8	18 5/8	17 5/8	15 1/8	3 3/8	3 3/8	4	5	Yavapai Co., AZ	Richard E. Gurcius	Richard E. Gurcius	2008	54
105 4/8	108 3/8	17 2/8	17 5/8	13	3 4/8	3 4/8	4	4	Sonora, MX	Stan D. Guse	Stan D. Guse	2009	55
104 2/8	110 1/8	16 2/8	16 3/8	12 5/8	3 4/8	3 4/8	4	4	Chihuahua, MX	Tony Tomasi	Tony Tomasi	2005	56
104	110 3/8	16 5/8	17 5/8	15 2/8	4	4	5	5	Cochise Co., AZ	Robert E. Hallagan	Robert E. Hallagan	1992	57
103 6/8	110 5/8	19 3/8	19	18	3 4/8	3 5/8	4	4	Cochise Co., AZ	Melvin E. Williams	Russell Fletcher	1955	58
103 6/8	104 5/8	18	18	14	3 5/8	4	5	5	Sonora, MX	Nathan W. Jacobson	Nathan W. Jacobson	2008	58
103 6/8	112 6/8	18 4/8	18 3/8	12 2/8	4 1/8	4 4/8	5	4	Sonora, MX	Rick D. Parker	Rick D. Parker	2009	58
102 7/8	107 3/8	16 6/8	17 1/8	14 7/8	3 4/8	3 4/8	4	5	Sonora, MX	Lyle C. Foster	Lyle C. Foster	2008	61
102 5/8	108 2/8	17 4/8	17 4/8	12 7/8	3 6/8	3 4/8	5	5	Sonora, MX	Mark B. Steffen	Mark B. Steffen	2008	62
102 4/8	111 4/8	17 4/8	17 6/8	12 6/8	3 5/8	3 5/8	4	4	Sonora, MX	Frank S. Noska IV	Frank S. Noska IV	2009	63
102 1/8	107 1/8	16 4/8	16 2/8	11 5/8	4 6/8	4 6/8	5	5	Gila Co., AZ	Tracy H. Rushing	Tracy H. Rushing	2008	64
101 5/8	113 2/8	17 3/8	17 3/8	12	3 3/8	3 4/8	4	4	Sonora, MX	Jack E. Risner	Jack E. Risner	2002	65
101 4/8	109 6/8	16 3/8	16 6/8	13 2/8	3 5/8	3 6/8	5	5	Cochise Co., AZ	Bradley C. Scott	Bradley C. Scott	2008	66
101 2/8	108 4/8	16 5/8	16 5/8	15	4 3/8	4 2/8	5	5	Pima Co., AZ	Kevin Mitchell	Kevin Mitchell	2006	67
101 1/8	106 3/8	16 2/8	16 1/8	12 3/8	3 5/8	3 4/8	5	5	Sonora, MX	William R. Mitchell	William R. Mitchell	2009	68
100 6/8	108 2/8	17 3/8	16 5/8	14 2/8	3 7/8	3 7/8	5	5	Yavapai Co., AZ	Samuel L. Ferguson	Samuel L. Ferguson	1989	69
100 4/8	107 1/8	17 4/8	17 3/8	14 3/8	4 3/8	4 3/8	4	4	Sonora, MX	Mark W. Streissguth	Mark W. Streissguth	2006	69
100 1/8	107 3/8	18	17 7/8	12 7/8	3 1/8	3 1/8	5	5	Sonora, MX	Bryan L. McGregor	Bryan L. McGregor	2009	71
100 1/8	102 3/8	17 1/8	17	14 5/8	3 4/8	3 4/8	3	3	Pima Co., AZ	Eugene A. Beaudoin	Eugene A. Beaudoin	2007	72
100 1/8	105 1/8	15 4/8	15 5/8	12	4	3 7/8	5	5	Hidalgo Co., NM	Travis M. Edwards	Travis M. Edwards	2007	72
124 *	129 1/8	18 7/8	19 4/8	17 4/8	4 4/8	4 5/8	4	4	Graham Co., AZ	A.B. Blair	A.B. Blair	1981	

* Final score subject to revision by additional verifying measurements.

COUES' WHITETAIL DEER - NON-TYPICAL ANTLERS

Odocoileus virginianus couesi

Minimum Score 105

World's Record 196 2/8

Final Score	Gross Score	Length of Main Beam R	L	Inside Spread	Circumference at Smallest Place Between Burr & First Point R	L	Number of Points R	L	Locality	Hunter	Owner	Date Killed	Rank
177 1/8	181 5/8	20 1/8	19 5/8	13 4/8	5 1/8	4 7/8	18	15	Sonora, MX	Gary A. Zellner	Gary A. Zellner	2009	1
134 1/8	139 7/8	21 1/8	19 2/8	14	4 3/8	4 3/8	7	8	Pima Co., AZ	Ron Alley	Randy Sandoval	1988	2
133 7/8	141 1/8	18 5/8	18 2/8	12 5/8	4 1/8	4 1/8	9	7	Cochise Co., AZ	Joshua J. Manning	Joshua J. Manning	2008	3
133 1/8	140 3/8	18 5/8	19 1/8	15 1/8	4 3/8	4 4/8	7	7	Sonora, MX	Thomas L. Thomsen, Jr.	Thomas L. Thomsen, Jr.	2009	4
129 4/8	131 5/8	19 4/8	19 6/8	14 3/8	4 2/8	4 2/8	6	7	Sonora, MX	John P. Westbrook	John P. Westbrook	2007	5
128 1/8	130 3/8	18 1/8	17 5/8	17	4 4/8	4 6/8	7	5	Gila Co., AZ	Nathan LaCost	Nathan LaCost	2008	6
127 7/8	133 1/8	19 5/8	19	14 1/8	4 4/8	4 3/8	7	8	Pima Co., AZ	Kyle W. Craig	Kyle W. Craig	2008	7
127 1/8	132 2/8	16 5/8	17 3/8	13	4	3 6/8	10	9	Sonora, MX	Matthew P. Westbrook	Matthew P. Westbrook	2008	8
126 2/8	131 5/8	17 5/8	16 4/8	13 5/8	4 3/8	4 2/8	6	4	Sonora, MX	Mark W. Streissguth	Mark W. Streissguth	2009	9
123 4/8	129 5/8	17 1/8	16 6/8	15	3 2/8	3 4/8	9	8	Sonora, MX	Michael A. Corona	Michael A. Corona	2008	10
123 2/8	127 2/8	17 2/8	16 7/8	16 1/8	3 7/8	3 6/8	6	5	Pima Co., AZ	Lloyd W. McCraney	Lloyd W. McCraney	2007	11
120 6/8	126 3/8	18 4/8	16 6/8	14 6/8	4 4/8	5 2/8	5	5	Sonora, MX	Grady L. Miller	Grady L. Miller	2006	12
120 6/8	125 5/8	18 1/8	17 4/8	14 5/8	4 1/8	4 1/8	6	5	Sonora, MX	Clark D. Hurst	Clark D. Hurst	2008	12
120 3/8	122 5/8	17 4/8	17 2/8	12 3/8	3 6/8	3 5/8	5	5	Santa Cruz Co., AZ	Audria L. Dolan	Audria L. Dolan	2008	14
120 3/8	125	18 3/8	17 7/8	13 7/8	3 4/8	3 3/8	5	7	Chihuahua, MX	Jason L. Greer	Jason L. Greer	2009	14
120	131 2/8	19 7/8	19 1/8	13 5/8	4 7/8	5	6	7	Gila Co., AZ	Jacob S. Hanlin	Jacob S. Hanlin	2007	16
120	127	18 5/8	18 6/8	17	4 3/8	4 4/8	5	6	Gila Co., AZ	Jeremy D. Ulmer	Jeremy D. Ulmer	2008	16
117 7/8	123 3/8	15 7/8	18 2/8	12 1/8	4 7/8	4 6/8	6	4	Sonora, MX	C. Grady Dawe	C. Grady Dawe	2008	18
115 7/8	118 5/8	15 3/8	16	12 6/8	3 7/8	3 6/8	5	6	Pima Co., AZ	Roger D. Cook	Roger D. Cook	2006	19
115 3/8	122 5/8	17	17 4/8	14 1/8	3 6/8	3 6/8	6	6	Cochise Co., AZ	Gordon M. Clark	Gordon M. Clark	2006	20
114 4/8	120 2/8	18 2/8	18	14	3 6/8	3 7/8	6	6	Gila Co., AZ	Wayne R. Oberg	Wayne R. Oberg	2008	21
112	113 7/8	16 1/8	16 1/8	12 4/8	3 4/8	3 3/8	5	7	Santa Cruz Co., AZ	William F. Gorman	William F. Gorman	2008	22
111 3/8	113 1/8	17	17 1/8	14 3/8	4	4	6	5	Sonora, MX	Steven L. Kiesel	Steven L. Kiesel	2009	23
110 1/8	113 2/8	18 2/8	19 7/8	12 6/8	4	4 1/8	5	6	Sonora, MX	Keith A. Johnson	Keith A. Johnson	2009	24
109 6/8	114 2/8	17	17 4/8	13	3 6/8	3 6/8	5	6	Pima Co., AZ	Dean E. Lippert	Dean E. Lippert	2000	25
108 6/8	111 3/8	17 6/8	17 3/8	16 5/8	3 4/8	3 3/8	4	6	Sonora, MX	William T. Haney	William T. Haney	2008	26
130 5/8*	133 5/8	17 6/8	17 7/8	14 1/8	3 4/8	3 4/8	8	8	Sonora, MX	Jay Scott	Jay Scott	2009	

* Final score subject to revision by additional verifying measurements.

CANADA MOOSE

Alces alces americana and *Alces alces andersoni*

Minimum Score 185 — World's Record 242

Canada moose includes trophies from Newfoundland and Canada (except for Yukon Territory and Northwest Territories), Maine, Minnesota, New Hampshire, North Dakota, and Vermont.

Final Score	Gross Score	Greatest Spread	Length of Palm R.	Length of Palm L.	Width of Palm R.	Width of Palm L.	Circ. of Beam at Smallest Place R.	Circ. of Beam at Smallest Place L.	No. Normal Points R.	No. Normal Points L.	Locality	Hunter	Owner	Date Killed	Rank
224 6/8	230 5/8	68	43 4/8	44 5/8	14 6/8	16 4/8	8 1/8	8 1/8	15	12	Tatshenshini River, BC	Keith A. Grant	Keith A. Grant	2008	1
222	225 3/8	59 4/8	44	43 4/8	13 7/8	14 5/8	7	6 7/8	17	19	Eagle Creek, SK	Picked Up	Grant A. Seibold	2006	2
221 2/8	221 7/8	63 2/8	43 3/8	42 6/8	14 4/8	14 4/8	7 6/8	7 6/8	14	14	Dease Lake, BC	Ross H. Mann	Ross H. Mann	2008	3
220 7/8	225 5/8	66 5/8	46	41 4/8	16 2/8	16 2/8	7 5/8	7 3/8	12	12	Tatshenshini River, BC	Fred E. Dodge	Fred E. Dodge	2009	4
217 2/8	221 2/8	64 4/8	42 6/8	42	15 1/8	17 3/8	7 2/8	7 2/8	13	12	Somerset Co., ME	Roy M. Norton	Roy M. Norton	2008	5
213 3/8	218 2/8	62 5/8	47 4/8	46 5/8	13 2/8	12 3/8	7 3/8	7 4/8	9	12	Tatshenshini River, BC	Fred E. Dodge	Fred E. Dodge	2008	6
211	215 3/8	59	45 1/8	41 1/8	15 1/8	14 6/8	8 1/8	8 1/8	12	12	Tatshenshini River, BC	James P. Kramer	James P. Kramer	2008	7
210	214 4/8	74 6/8	34 5/8	38 3/8	14 2/8	13 5/8	7 4/8	7 3/8	12	12	Cactus Lake, SK	Harley C. Busse	Harley C. Busse	2009	8
209 6/8	211 5/8	55 6/8	39 6/8	39 4/8	15 3/8	13 6/8	6 6/8	6 6/8	17	17	Pasqua Hills, SK	David Parfitt	David Parfitt	1976	9
209 1/8	219 7/8	60 3/8	44	43 5/8	14	17 5/8	8	8 2/8	10	12	Ogoki River, ON	Richard A. Martin	Richard A. Martin	2006	10
208 5/8	213 6/8	62 1/8	36 6/8	37 5/8	15 2/8	15 2/8	8 4/8	8 4/8	13	14	Aroostook Co., ME	Ralph G. Miller, Jr.	Ralph G. Miller, Jr.	2008	11
208 4/8	212 3/8	62 5/8	41 2/8	45 1/8	13 2/8	12 7/8	6 5/8	7 1/8	13	14	Atlin Lake, BC	Robert MacDonald	Robert MacDonald	1998	12
208	211 3/8	57 6/8	44 7/8	39 7/8	13 3/8	14 3/8	7 2/8	7 7/8	11	10	Kawdy Mt., BC	Timothy M. Steiner	Timothy M. Steiner	2006	13
208	212 7/8	60 2/8	40 2/8	38 3/8	12 1/8	14 5/8	7 7/8	7 6/8	14	16	Eagle Creek, SK	Kyle Imlach	Kyle Imlach	2006	14
208	208 5/8	65 4/8	38 3/8	43 3/8	13 1/8	13 6/8	7 6/8	7 3/8	12	12	Shovel Creek, BC	Michael Trudeau	Michael Trudeau	2006	14
206 6/8	209 5/8	55 6/8	43 1/8	38 6/8	15 4/8	14 3/8	7 4/8	7 6/8	12	10	Dease Lake, BC	Larry A. Meyer	Larry A. Meyer	2000	16
205 7/8	213	60 1/8	43 5/8	44 3/8	14 4/8	12 7/8	7 7/8	6 7/8	12	14	Tuya River, BC	Luciano Dalla Lana	Luciano Dalla Lana	2007	17
205 2/8	209 7/8	57 6/8	42	40 4/8	13	14 1/8	7	7	14	12	Teslin Lake, BC	Judy A. Letendre	Judy A. Letendre	2005	18
204 5/8	205 6/8	59 3/8	41 4/8	44 1/8	14 2/8	17 3/8	7	8	11	11	Prophet River, BC	Peter J. Carlson	Peter J. Carlson	2006	19
204 5/8	209 1/8	54 5/8	42 4/8	44 2/8	16 4/8	14	8	7 5/8	10	8	Kinaskan Lake, BC	Rick G. Stelter	Rick G. Stelter	2009	19
204 4/8	208 1/8	55	44 6/8	43 1/8	12	13 7/8	7 4/8	6 7/8	12	11	Ketchum Lake, BC	Bill G. Hodson	Bill G. Hodson	2009	21
204	208 6/8	58 2/8	45 2/8	41 4/8	12 4/8	12 2/8	7	7 3/8	10	11	Alameda Dam, SK	Trent T. Dorrance	Trent T. Dorrance	2006	22
203 4/8	206 4/8	56 2/8	41 4/8	41 7/8	11 2/8	13 3/8	7	8 1/8	15	14	Tochieka Range, BC	Jack E. Risner	Jack E. Risner	2009	23
203 2/8	209 7/8	54	40 3/8	38 4/8	16 4/8	15	8	7 6/8	14	14	Cassiar Dist., BC	Chad Hamblin	Chad Hamblin	2008	24
203	205 4/8	56 4/8	39 5/8	41	14 6/8	15	8	8 1/8	12	13	Souris River, SK	Allan Sagin	Allan Sagin	2006	25
202 2/8	204 4/8	58	40 1/8	40 2/8	12 4/8	12 2/8	7 6/8	7 6/8	12	13	Hudson Hope, BC	Brian D. Coe	Brian D. Coe	2009	26
201 6/8	206 1/8	63 2/8	39 2/8	40 2/8	11 2/8	11 5/8	7 2/8	7 2/8	13	12	Lac a la Croix, QC	René Marquis	René Marquis	2005	27
200 6/8	210 1/8	57 6/8	39 3/8	36 4/8	13 5/8	15 2/8	6 7/8	9 6/8	15	15	Toad River, BC	Steven S. Bruggeman	Steven S. Bruggeman	2008	28
199 7/8	202	63 5/8	37 5/8	36 3/8	12 4/8	12 4/8	7 2/8	8 1/8	12	12	Beaver Lake, NB	Vaughan C. Nicholas, Jr.	Vaughan C. Nicholas, Jr.	2009	29

CANADA MOOSE

Alces alces americana and *Alces alces andersoni*

Final Score	Gross Score	Greatest Spread	Length of Palm R.	L.	Width of Palm R.	L.	Circumference of Beam at Smallest Place R.	L.	Number of Normal Points R.	L.	Locality	Hunter	Owner	Date Killed	Rank
199 6/8	204	59	38 1/8	40	14	13	7 2/8	8 5/8	12	12	Gataga River, BC	Greg Hutton	Greg Hutton	1998	30
198 5/8	202	50 1/8	44 7/8	42 1/8	14 7/8	15	7 2/8	7 6/8	10	10	Telegraph Creek, BC	Richard M. Bock	Richard M. Bock	2007	31
198 4/8	199 6/8	54 2/8	39 5/8	38 6/8	13 6/8	14 1/8	7 5/8	7 5/8	12	12	Fort St. John, BC	Denis Henchoz	Denis Henchoz	2009	32
198 2/8	205 7/8	58	38 6/8	43 3/8	11 4/8	14 4/8	6 7/8	6 7/8	13	13	Aroostook Co., ME	Picked Up	Robert M. Provencher	2002	33
198 1/8	199 5/8	56 1/8	42 1/8	40 7/8	13 7/8	13 7/8	7 4/8	7 2/8	9	9	Tuya River, BC	Bradley R. Jackle	Bradley R. Jackle	2008	34
198	202 4/8	61 6/8	40 1/8	42 4/8	13	12 3/8	7 5/8	8 1/8	9	8	Big Sand Lake, MB	Warren R. Hoehn	Warren R. Hoehn	2007	35
197 7/8	200 6/8	55 1/8	38 6/8	40	14 4/8	14	7 6/8	7 5/8	12	11	Moose Mt., SK	James A. Debruyne	James A. Debruyne	2005	36
197 6/8	199	54 2/8	37 6/8	37 5/8	15 1/8	15	7 1/8	7 1/8	13	12	Lake Co., MN	Keith A. Pollock	Keith A. Pollock	2007	37
197 5/8	203 2/8	55 5/8	43 6/8	39 6/8	12	12 5/8	7 2/8	7 2/8	13	12	Tatshenshini River, BC	Trey A. Poulson	Trey A. Poulson	2007	38
197 4/8	207	55 4/8	45 2/8	38 7/8	14	15 2/8	8 1/8	9	11	10	Inklin River, BC	Ronnie W. McGee	Ronnie W. McGee	2007	39
197 2/8	204 7/8	55 6/8	40	41 2/8	13 2/8	16 4/8	7 1/8	7	11	12	Cape Brenton, NS	Gary Leslie	Gary Leslie	2007	40
197 2/8	201 4/8	53 4/8	38 4/8	39 1/8	14 3/8	14 6/8	7 2/8	7	15	12	Sedgewick, AB	Ivo Profeta	Ivo Profeta	2007	40
196 7/8	204 3/8	62 7/8	35 4/8	37 7/8	13 6/8	14 5/8	6 6/8	7	11	15	Lac Mégantic, QC	Pierre Routhier	Pierre Routhier	2006	42
196 6/8	200 3/8	54	37 6/8	38 4/8	13 6/8	13	6 5/8	6 6/8	16	14	Pigeon River, MB	David O. Anaman	David O. Anaman	2006	43
196 6/8	199 7/8	55 2/8	40 4/8	41 4/8	11 1/8	12 5/8	7 1/8	7 6/8	12	12	Franklin Co., ME	Daniel P. Gallant	Cabela's, Inc.	2006	43
196 3/8	204 2/8	57 3/8	38 1/8	41 7/8	13 4/8	15 4/8	6 7/8	7	11	13	Pine River, BC	Kody H. Tricker	Kody H. Tricker	2006	45
196 2/8	197 4/8	55 2/8	38 4/8	38 6/8	15	15	7	7	10	11	Stikine River, BC	Lois H. Aylen	Lois H. Aylen	2006	46
196 1/8	200 4/8	53 1/8	39 2/8	41	13	13 2/8	7 2/8	7 5/8	12	14	Pine River, BC	William S. Bergen	William S. Bergen	2008	47
196	199 4/8	62 6/8	37 5/8	37 4/8	14 6/8	13 5/8	7 4/8	7 6/8	10	8	Cassiar, BC	William N. Beach	Shelburne Museum	1918	48
195 6/8	203 7/8	57 2/8	37 7/8	39 5/8	17 3/8	16	7 3/8	7 3/8	13	8	Pleasant Bay, NS	Christopher Tooker	Christopher Tooker	2001	49
195 6/8	199 1/8	52 6/8	42 2/8	40 7/8	13 3/8	14 2/8	7 2/8	7 3/8	11	10	Telegraph Creek, BC	Hope N. Crites	Hope N. Crites	2009	49
195 4/8	201 4/8	65 4/8	36 6/8	33	11 6/8	12 5/8	7 5/8	7 2/8	14	13	Battle River, AB	William J. Penner	William J. Penner	2006	51
195 3/8	210 7/8	64 3/8	40	35	16 6/8	14 3/8	7 1/8	7 2/8	10	14	Bennington Co., VT	Robert B. Dewey	Robert B. Dewey	2002	52
195 3/8	206 4/8	62 3/8	36 2/8	43 2/8	15 2/8	13 3/8	6 7/8	7 1/8	12	10	Coos Co., NH	Wayne E. Stevens	Wayne E. Stevens	2007	52
195 1/8	196 5/8	55 5/8	35 4/8	35 5/8	15 4/8	13 3/8	7 1/8	7	13	12	Clifton Lake, MB	Stephen K. Marshall	Stephen K. Marshall	2008	54
195 1/8	203 4/8	56 5/8	43 1/8	44 4/8	16 6/8	15 3/8	7 3/8	7 1/8	6	9	Muncho Lake, BC	R. Craig Willis	R. Craig Willis	2006	55
195	199 4/8	59	40 1/8	38 7/8	10 7/8	13	7 3/8	7 2/8	13	14	Kapuskasing, ON	Kirk H. Seddon	Kirk H. Seddon	2007	56
194 4/8	201 4/8	48	36 2/8	39 2/8	15 1/8	16 7/8	7 2/8	7 3/8	15	15	Swan Lake, BC	Michael B. Roche	Michael B. Roche	2005	57
194 2/8	196 4/8	63 2/8	38 1/8	37 4/8	12	12 5/8	7 5/8	7	13	9	Redwillow River, BC	Robert H. Buehler	Robert H. Buehler	2007	58
193 4/8	198 1/8	55 4/8	38 7/8	37 7/8	14	16 4/8	8 1/8	8 2/8	10	9	Kawdy Mt., BC	James Jurgensen	James Jurgensen	2008	59
193 1/8	194 6/8	51 1/8	36 3/8	37	14 1/8	15 1/8	7 4/8	7 4/8	13	13	Sikanni River, BC	Ben F. Carter III	Ben F. Carter III	2004	60

193	196	52 4/8	41 7/8	39 3/8	14	13 4/8	7 3/8	7 3/8	10	10	Penobscot Co., ME	Timothy D. Nelson	Timothy D. Nelson	2008	61
191 6/8	200 1/8	58	40 7/8	43	12 5/8	14 6/8	6 7/8	7	9	7	Maine	Unknown	Kevin A. Parah	PR 2002	62
191 3/8	192 7/8	55 7/8	38	37 4/8	10 3/8	10 3/8	6 7/8	6 7/8	13	14	Tachilta Lakes, BC	Brad D. Johnson	Brad D. Johnson	2008	63
191 1/8	202 3/8	59 3/8	36 1/8	40 7/8	13 3/8	12 7/8	7 3/8	7 3/8	14	10	Cloud Lake, ON	Peter Nunan	Peter Nunan	1987	64
191 1/8	200 5/8	64 5/8	37 2/8	40	12 3/8	10 1/8	7 3/8	6 7/8	9	13	Bennington Co., VT	Max A. Grout	Max A. Grout	2007	64
190 7/8	198 4/8	59 3/8	41	37 2/8	12 4/8	13 1/8	7	7 2/8	9	12	Piscataquis Co., ME	Peter B. Brassard	Peter B. Brassard	2006	66
189 7/8	192 3/8	55 3/8	37 5/8	38 5/8	12 4/8	13 7/8	7 1/8	7 2/8	10	10	St. Louis Co., MN	Mark W. Johnson	Mark W. Johnson	2008	67
189 5/8	197	53 5/8	35	35 2/8	15 2/8	16 4/8	7 2/8	8 1/8	11	14	Oxford Co., ME	Michael P. Collier	Michael P. Collier	2008	68
189 3/8	195 5/8	57 3/8	40 3/8	39	11 3/8	13 1/8	8 1/8	6 6/8	12	9	Economy Creek, AB	Romano Corrado	Angelo Corrado	1978	69
189	193 6/8	54 2/8	40 1/8	37	13	11 4/8	7	6 7/8	12	12	Aroostook Co., ME	Quinn A. Willmarth	Quinn A. Willmarth	2009	70
188 6/8	194 1/8	59 4/8	32 6/8	34 1/8	12 6/8	15 5/8	6 7/8	7 1/8	12	13	Lake Co., MN	Robert M. Rocheleau	Robert M. Rocheleau	2009	71
188 5/8	192 2/8	59 7/8	33 6/8	35 2/8	15	14	6 5/8	6 6/8	11	10	Essex Co., VT	Peter D. Grass	Peter D. Grass	2006	72
188	193 4/8	62 2/8	37 6/8	38 4/8	14 1/8	11 5/8	6 4/8	6 6/8	7	9	Lac de l' Est, QC	Jean-Paul Chouinard	Jean-Paul Chouinard	2006	73
187 6/8	190 4/8	57 2/8	34	36	12 1/8	12 5/8	7 1/8	7 3/8	12	12	Dease Lake, BC	Ross H. Mann	Ross H. Mann	2009	74
187 4/8	189 2/8	49 4/8	38 3/8	39 5/8	13 3/8	13 7/8	8 2/8	8 2/8	9	9	Stikine River, BC	Larry S. Hicks	Larry S. Hicks	2009	75
187 2/8	193 4/8	57 6/8	39 2/8	41 2/8	11 4/8	10 3/8	7 5/8	7 6/8	9	8	Orleans Co., VT	Fernand L. Beloin	Denis A. Beloin	2004	76
186 7/8	194 5/8	51 7/8	36 2/8	39 1/8	11 5/8	13 4/8	6 5/8	6 5/8	13	16	Kakwa River, AB	J. Seth Walter	J. Seth Walter	2006	77
186 6/8	190 4/8	57 4/8	34 7/8	36 1/8	13	13 4/8	7 6/8	7 6/8	9	11	Rainy River, ON	John C. DuCharme	John C. DuCharme	2006	78
186 6/8	199 6/8	55 4/8	40	38 6/8	11 6/8	13	7 1/8	7 1/8	10	12	Washington Co., ME	Arvid J. Laskey	Arvid J. Laskey	2006	78
186 6/8	190 2/8	56	40 1/8	40 5/8	12 4/8	11 4/8	7 6/8	7 6/8	8	6	Essex Co., VT	John A. LaFreniere	John A. LaFreniere	2007	78
186 1/8	191 7/8	61 2/8	37	34	12 3/8	12 2/8	7 4/8	7 4/8	9	11	Piscataquis Co., ME	Edward J. Kennedy	Edward J. Kennedy	2009	78

CANADA MOOSE
FINAL SCORE: 191 3/8
HUNTER: Brad D. Johnson

CANADA MOOSE
FINAL SCORE: 185 2/8
HUNTER: Adam H. Bartsch

CANADA MOOSE

Alces alces americana and *Alces alces andersoni*

Final Score	Gross Score	Greatest Spread	Length of Palm		Width of Palm		Circumference of Beam at Smallest Place		Number of Normal Points		Locality	Hunter	Owner	Date Killed	Rank
			R.	L.	R.	L.	R.	L.	R.	L.					
186 4/8	193 1/8	54 4/8	40 3/8	38 5/8	12 5/8	13 3/8	6 6/8	6 7/8	8	12	Atlin, BC	Robert MacDonald	Robert MacDonald	2000	82
186 3/8	191 3/8	56 1/8	35 7/8	33 2/8	16 5/8	16 3/8	7 4/8	7 5/8	10	8	Dick Lake, BC	Brian A. Hauck	Brian A. Hauck	1999	83
186 2/8	188 7/8	53 4/8	38 1/8	37 4/8	11 3/8	12 2/8	7 4/8	7 5/8	10	11	Omineca Mt., BC	Delbert L. Kerr	Delbert L. Kerr	2007	84
186 1/8	191 5/8	57 1/8	41 3/8	39 2/8	10 6/8	11 7/8	7 4/8	7 6/8	9	7	Piscataquis Co., ME	Steven E. Lacroix	Steven E. Lacroix	2006	85
185 2/8	189 4/8	51 2/8	36	35 7/8	14	17	7 2/8	7 1/8	11	10	Pink Mt., BC	Adam H. Bartsch	Adam H. Bartsch	2006	86
185 2/8	198 2/8	51	36 4/8	46	14 1/8	12 6/8	7 4/8	7 3/8	11	11	Somerset Co., ME	David A. Paape	David A. Paape	2008	86
185 1/8	188 2/8	51 1/8	39 6/8	40 1/8	12 6/8	14 3/8	7 4/8	7 5/8	8	7	Kechika River, BC	Bryan K. Martin	Bryan K. Martin	2006	88
185 1/8	187 3/8	57 7/8	38 5/8	38 1/8	10 6/8	11 4/8	7 6/8	7 6/8	8	7	Washington Co., ME	Michael G. Viviano	Michael G. Viviano	2006	88
185 1/8	189 1/8	51 5/8	38	40 2/8	10	11 4/8	7	6 6/8	12	12	Cold Fish Lake, BC	Casey G. Terry	Casey G. Terry	2007	88
185	190 6/8	63 2/8	35 6/8	36	11	14 3/8	7 1/8	7 2/8	7	9	Piscataquis Co., ME	Dale P. Powers	Dale P. Powers	2006	91
185	188	55 4/8	36 2/8	34 6/8	13 4/8	13 2/8	7	6 6/8	11	10	Toad River, BC	David B. Armstrong	David B. Armstrong	2007	91
185	188 3/8	53 4/8	38 3/8	39 2/8	10 5/8	10 2/8	7 1/8	7 2/8	12	10	Munroe Lake, MB	Irvin R. Savidge	Irvin R. Savidge	2007	91

ALASKA-YUKON MOOSE

Alces alces gigas

Minimum Score 210

World's Record 261 5/8

Alaska-Yukon moose includes trophies from Alaska, Yukon Territory, and Northwest Territories.

Final Score	Gross Score	Greatest Spread	Length of Palm R.	Length of Palm L.	Width of Palm R.	Width of Palm L.	Circumference of Beam at Smallest Place R.	Circumference of Beam at Smallest Place L.	Number of Normal Points R.	Number of Normal Points L.	Locality	Hunter	Owner	Date Killed	Rank
247 5/8	257	67 7/8	52 1/8	49 7/8	21 7/8	19	8	8 2/8	14	14	Selawik Hills, AK	Craig S. Spencer	Craig S. Spencer	2008	1
242	245 6/8	65 2/8	49 3/8	48 4/8	18	17 4/8	7 7/8	8 2/8	15	15	Sheep Mt., YT	Rob Springer	Rob Springer	2009	2
241	245 1/8	59	49 4/8	49 2/8	19 4/8	18 4/8	9 1/8	8 2/8	17	15	Hart River, YT	Wes S. McMillen	Wes S. McMillen	2007	3
240 7/8	244 1/8	71 1/8	51	52 7/8	15 2/8	15 5/8	7 5/8	7 5/8	12	11	Kemuk Mt., AK	Anthony J. Tamburelli	Anthony J. Tamburelli	2004	4
239 7/8	249 3/8	73 7/8	45 6/8	43 2/8	18 4/8	19 4/8	8 2/8	8 2/8	14	16	Huslia River, AK	Bradley L. Erickson	Bradley L. Erickson	2008	5
239 1/8	240 5/8	66 3/8	45 2/8	45 3/8	19	17 7/8	8 4/8	8 2/8	15	15	Nushagak River, AK	Michael L. Thompson	Michael L. Thompson	2006	6
238 2/8	239 5/8	63	45 7/8	46 6/8	17 3/8	17	7 7/8	7 6/8	17	17	Faro, YT	Richard C. Busby	Richard C. Busby	2007	7
238 2/8	240 5/8	70 4/8	47 4/8	45 4/8	18 4/8	18 3/8	8 2/8	8	12	12	Chitanana River, AK	Timothy S. Greener	Timothy S. Greener	2008	7
237 7/8	241 6/8	74 7/8	42	44 3/8	14 6/8	16 2/8	7 6/8	7 6/8	17	17	Kemuk Mt., AK	James F. Sullivan, Jr.	James F. Sullivan, Jr.	2006	9
236 2/8	261 2/8	77 4/8	51 5/8	45 7/8	22	15 5/8	8 1/8	8 4/8	16	12	Northwest Territories	Ted Manx	Cabela's, Inc.	PR 1982	10
235 1/8	244 7/8	66 7/8	48	46	18 4/8	23 1/8	7 6/8	7 5/8	12	15	Stokes Lake, YT	Charles R. Henne	Charles R. Henne	2008	11
234 7/8	241 5/8	67 1/8	47 1/8	48 1/8	17	19 6/8	7 6/8	7 6/8	12	15	Mosquito Fork, AK	Theodore P. Ward	Theodore P. Ward	2006	12
234 5/8	242 2/8	65 3/8	47 1/8	47 5/8	20 5/8	16 5/8	8 4/8	8 3/8	13	14	Mayo, YT	Rene Hardy	Rene Hardy	2008	13
234 5/8	241 2/8	72 5/8	52	50 1/8	13 4/8	12 6/8	8 1/8	8 1/8	10	14	Kobuk River, AK	Robert A. Kuntz	Robert A. Kuntz	2008	13
234 1/8	240 1/8	64 1/8	47 5/8	50 2/8	15 4/8	15 7/8	7 7/8	7 7/8	14	17	Hart Lake, YT	A.C. Smid	A.C. Smid	2008	15
233	237 2/8	70 4/8	43 4/8	45 6/8	17 3/8	19 1/8	8 3/8	8 5/8	12	12	McGrath, AK	Mark A. O'Brien	Mark A. O'Brien	2008	16
231 6/8	233 7/8	64 4/8	46	47 4/8	13 7/8	14 4/8	7 6/8	7 6/8	16	16	Alaska	Tom Fisher	John M. DeVriend	1977	17
230 7/8	236 3/8	62 3/8	43 2/8	46 3/8	16 6/8	18	8 2/8	8 3/8	17	16	Bonnet Plume River, YT	Patrick Beckwith	Patrick Beckwith	2007	18
230 1/8	230 6/8	73 5/8	45 5/8	41 6/8	13 1/8	12 6/8	7 7/8	8 1/8	12	12	King Salmon Creek, AK	Steven M. Cain	Steven M. Cain	2006	19
230 1/8	236 4/8	69 1/8	45 4/8	41 2/8	18	20 4/8	8 6/8	8 7/8	12	12	Pass Creek, AK	Richard F. Stonke	Richard F. Stonke	2009	19
230	231 3/8	71	44 3/8	43 4/8	17 3/8	17	8 1/8	8	11	11	MacMillan River, YT	Greg L. Poley	Greg L. Poley	2009	21
227 7/8	230 5/8	68 5/8	42 6/8	41 2/8	19	18	8 5/8	8 3/8	12	12	Iowithla River, AK	Joshua M. Peirce	Joshua M. Peirce	2006	22
227 3/8	235 5/8	74 1/8	44 1/8	47 2/8	15 3/8	16 4/8	8 1/8	8 1/8	9	13	Earn Lake, YT	Pierre Lamoureux	Pierre Lamoureux	2005	23
227 3/8	231 4/8	67 1/8	43 5/8	41 4/8	17 3/8	19 3/8	8 2/8	8 2/8	13	13	Bonnet Plume River, YT	Cliff W. Price	Cliff W. Price	2008	23
226 4/8	230 7/8	72 6/8	41 6/8	43 6/8	14	13 6/8	7 4/8	7 4/8	16	14	Allen River, AK	Chris M. Hanks	Chris M. Hanks	2007	25
226	237 1/8	70 4/8	52 4/8	46 7/8	14 7/8	16 7/8	8	8 4/8	11	8	Figure Eight Creek, AK	Christopher Hornak	Christopher Hornak	2008	26
226	236 5/8	63 4/8	46	46 5/8	14 1/8	17	7 1/8	7 2/8	14	21	Yukon River, AK	Gregory E. Olejniczak	Gregory E. Olejniczak	2008	26
225 6/8	230 1/8	68	42 6/8	45 2/8	17 1/8	16 7/8	7 2/8	7 7/8	12	13	Ugashik, AK	William E. Shoemaker	William E. Shoemaker	2005	28

ALASKA-YUKON MOOSE

Alces alces gigas

Final Score	Gross Score	Greatest Spread	Length of Palm R.	L.	Width of Palm R.	L.	Circumference of Beam at Smallest Place R.	L.	Number of Normal Points R.	L.	Locality	Hunter	Owner	Date Killed	Rank
225 4/8	233 7/8	68 2/8	45 2/8	47 1/8	16 7/8	15 4/8	8	7 7/8	15	10	Koyukuk River, AK	Angelo M. Caputo	Angelo M. Caputo	2008	29
225 2/8	229 6/8	60 2/8	43 4/8	44 5/8	21 3/8	20 2/8	8	7 6/8	13	11	MacMillan River, YT	Don F. Erbert	Don F. Erbert	2009	30
225	228 2/8	65 2/8	44	46	13 2/8	13	7 7/8	7 7/8	15	16	Mackenzie Mts., NT	Michael Black	Michael Black	2009	31
224 5/8	230 5/8	63 5/8	46 2/8	48	15 3/8	16 2/8	7 7/8	8 2/8	14	11	Twitya River, NT	Larry Bain	Larry Bain	2008	32
224 2/8	224 6/8	67 6/8	47 4/8	47	13	13	7 2/8	7 2/8	11	11	Nenana River, AK	John A. Parret	John A. Parret	2006	33
222 4/8	227 2/8	63 6/8	45 3/8	47	14 4/8	15 3/8	8 2/8	8	12	12	Robertson River, AK	Raymond J. Kosydar	Raymond J. Kosydar	2007	34
221 7/8	231 7/8	69 7/8	46 2/8	48	12 4/8	14 6/8	7 6/8	7 6/8	10	14	Mackenzie Mts., NT	Daniel M. Christmas	Daniel M. Christmas	2007	35
221 5/8	222 3/8	64 3/8	43 3/8	43	15	15 2/8	7 6/8	7 5/8	13	13	Innoko River, AK	Kelly F. White	Kelly F. White	2005	36
220 7/8	227 4/8	65 1/8	44 4/8	40	16 2/8	16 2/8	8 1/8	8 2/8	14	14	Caribou Hills, AK	Danny K. Presley	Danny K. Presley	2007	37
220 5/8	230 3/8	62 7/8	44 3/8	48 1/8	16 6/8	15 6/8	7 6/8	7 6/8	12	13	Marmot Pass, YT	Alfred A. Fusco III	Alfred A. Fusco III	2005	38
220 5/8	222 2/8	73 5/8	42 4/8	42 6/8	13 7/8	14 2/8	7 1/8	7 1/8	10	11	Koyukuk River, AK	William S. Phillips	William S. Phillips	2008	38
220 1/8	226 4/8	59 5/8	49	44 6/8	15 1/8	16 1/8	7 4/8	7 3/8	14	13	Stuyahok River, AK	Shaun R. Greear	Shaun R. Greear	2007	40
220	225 7/8	65 2/8	43 5/8	39 2/8	16 3/8	16 6/8	7 6/8	7 7/8	15	14	Bristol Bay, AK	Greg E. Diehl	Greg E. Diehl	2006	41
219	225 3/8	62 2/8	42	44 5/8	17	18	7 3/8	8 1/8	12	14	Nushagak River, AK	Jerry R. Dennis	Jerry R. Dennis	2008	42
218 2/8	223 2/8	67 2/8	39 4/8	41 5/8	14 7/8	14 1/8	7 7/8	8	16	14	Alaska	Mrs. J. Watson Webb	Samuel B. Webb, Jr.	PR 1935	43
217 7/8	221 2/8	59 3/8	44 3/8	44 4/8	16 1/8	16 2/8	7 6/8	7 7/8	11	14	Delta River, AK	Steven A. Hardy	Steven A. Hardy	2008	44
217 6/8	226 5/8	69	38 6/8	40 3/8	17 3/8	14 7/8	8 4/8	7 6/8	13	17	Squirrel River, AK	David C. Klauschie	David C. Klauschie	2008	45
217 4/8	222 2/8	69 6/8	44 5/8	43	14 6/8	15 6/8	8 1/8	8 2/8	10	8	Dillinger River, AK	Ernesto M. Santana	Ernesto M. Santana	2007	46
217 2/8	220 3/8	65 2/8	42 4/8	44 4/8	13 4/8	13 4/8	9 1/8	9	11	12	Tetlin River, AK	Ken Gloster	Ken Gloster	2006	47
216 7/8	224 1/8	67 7/8	52 1/8	47	10 5/8	12 4/8	8 1/8	7 7/8	9	9	Dillingham, AK	Verl P. Luckhurst	Verl P. Luckhurst	2006	48
216 7/8	219 7/8	59 5/8	41 6/8	43 2/8	15	15	8 2/8	8 1/8	14	14	Harrison Creek, AK	Mark F. Ryder	Mark F. Ryder	2006	48
216 4/8	221 1/8	60	39 4/8	41 4/8	18	18 5/8	8 2/8	8 1/8	13	13	Kenai Pen., AK	Harry H. Webb	Shelburne Museum	1931	50
216 3/8	220 7/8	66 3/8	41 1/8	41	17 5/8	16 3/8	7 5/8	7 6/8	10	13	Joseph Creek, AK	Donald C. Stuart	Donald C. Stuart	2007	51
216	222 1/8	65 4/8	38 4/8	40 2/8	14 7/8	14 5/8	7 1/8	7 2/8	16	16	Koyuk River, AK	Mary Jaynes	Mary Jaynes	2007	52
214 7/8	220 1/8	67 1/8	42 6/8	41 5/8	13 3/8	12 2/8	7	7	13	13	Wellesley Lake, YT	Fred E. Dodge	Fred E. Dodge	2008	53
214 3/8	223 4/8	62 3/8	47 1/8	50 4/8	11 1/8	10 6/8	9	8 5/8	10	12	Beluga River, AK	Tony Dawson	Tony Dawson	2004	54
214 2/8	219 2/8	50 2/8	48	46 4/8	20	18 4/8	7	7	13	13	Wrangell Mts., AK	Frank N. Lecrone, Jr.	Frank N. Lecrone, Jr.	2008	55
214 1/8	221 4/8	56 7/8	48 4/8	47	14 3/8	13 6/8	8 7/8	9 1/8	9	14	Moose Lake, YT	Gary D. Wrzosek	Gary D. Wrzosek	2006	56
213 2/8	218	63 6/8	45 1/8	42 7/8	12 6/8	14 1/8	7 1/8	7 2/8	13	12	Robertson River, AK	Robert H. Ferguson III	Robert H. Ferguson III	1987	57
213 2/8	217 1/8	64 6/8	42 7/8	41 2/8	15 2/8	16 3/8	7 7/8	7 6/8	11	10	Earn Lake, YT	Jean-Marie Veilleux	Jean-Marie Veilleux	2005	57
213 2/8	216 4/8	59 2/8	41 4/8	43	13	14 4/8	7 4/8	7 6/8	15	15	Nowitna River, AK	Todd L. Stroven	Todd L. Stroven	2007	57

212 7/8	217 3/8	66 3/8	42 2/8	43 3/8	14	14 3/8	7 4/8		10	11	North Lakes, YT	R. Kim Greene	R. Kim Greene	2009	60
212 2/8	217 2/8	58 2/8	42 1/8	40 6/8	15 6/8	17 2/8	7 5/8		15	13	No Name Creek, AK	Michael L. Niemants	Michael L. Niemants	2008	61
211 5/8	217 3/8	67 5/8	41 4/8	42 4/8	12 2/8	12 5/8	8 1/8		13	11	Cordova, AK	Jason G. Lenoir	Jason G. Lenoir	2008	62
210 6/8	221 5/8	60 2/8	44 2/8	45 3/8	14	18 5/8	7		12	11	Tustemena Lake, AK	Robert H. Ferguson III	Robert H. Ferguson III	1991	63
210 3/8	212	68 1/8	41 2/8	41 3/8	13 2/8	13 4/8	7 7/8		9	10	No Name Creek, AK	Kevin J. Lindsey	Kevin J. Lindsey	2006	64
210 2/8	214 1/8	60	44 3/8	46	12 3/8	14 4/8	7 3/8		11	11	Japan Hills, AK	Jack L. Morey, Jr.	Jack L. Morey, Jr.	2007	65
210 2/8	212	62 6/8	41 4/8	41 2/8	13 2/8	13 3/8	7 2/8		12	13	Kvichak River, AK	Robert W. Nash	Robert W. Nash	2009	65
210 1/8	216 4/8	57 5/8	43 1/8	43 5/8	18 4/8	15 6/8	7 3/8		13	10	Pelly River, YT	Donald Garrison	Curtis P. Smiley	1986	67
249 7/8*	259 1/8	68	51 1/8	51	20 2/8	20 3/8	8 7/8	9 4/8	12	15	Aishihik Lake, YT	Patrick Casey	Patrick Casey	2007	
249 *	255 2/8	75	51	48 1/8	19 7/8	17 4/8	8 3/8	8 3/8	14	13	Earn Lake, YT	Real Langlois	Real Langlois	2008	
247 2/8*	256 6/8	66 4/8	49 6/8	54 3/8	16 5/8	20 4/8	8	8	16	17	Nahanni River, NT	Jan Boenicke	Jan Boenicke	2008	
244 *	250 1/8	62 4/8	49 2/8	49 2/8	17 2/8	17 4/8	7 6/8	7 7/8	20	17	Koyuk River, AK	Gregory L. Parker	Gregory L. Parker	1990	

Final score subject to revision by additional verifying measurements.

ALASKA-YUKON MOOSE
FINAL SCORE: 221 7/8
HUNTER: Daniel M. Christmas

ALASKA-YUKON MOOSE
FINAL SCORE: 225 4/8
HUNTER: Angelo M. Caputo

SHIRAS' MOOSE

Alces alces shirasi

Minimum Score 140

World's Record 205 4/8

Shiras' moose includes trophies taken in Colorado, Idaho, Montana, Utah, Washington, and Wyoming.

Final Score	Gross Score	Greatest Spread	Length of Palm R.	L.	Width of Palm R.	L.	Circumference of Beam at Smallest Place R.	L.	Number of Normal Points R.	L.	Locality	Hunter	Owner	Date Killed	Rank
181 6/8	185 3/8	55 6/8	37 2/8	36 7/8	9 7/8	9 6/8	6 7/8	7	10	11	Bonner Co., ID	Del J. Thompson	Del J. Thompson	2006	1
180 2/8	182 4/8	40 6/8	39 2/8	38 5/8	13 1/8	13 6/8	7	7	12	11	Larimer Co., CO	Rylan Rudebusch	Rylan Rudebusch	2007	2
177 4/8	180	48	38 2/8	37	12 4/8	12 2/8	6 4/8	6 4/8	9	10	Lincoln Co., MT	Win D. Bock	Win D. Bock	2006	3
177 2/8	182	50 6/8	37	38 3/8	10 2/8	9 7/8	6 3/8	6 3/8	13	10	Sublette Co., WY	James B. Hattan	James B. Hattan	2009	4
176 3/8	182 4/8	48 1/8	35 3/8	32 7/8	11 1/8	13 5/8	6 1/8	6 2/8	14	15	Grand Co., CO	Weldon W. Flaharty	Weldon W. Flaharty	2009	5
173 4/8	176 1/8	49 2/8	32 2/8	33	12 2/8	11 5/8	6 2/8	6 4/8	13	12	Park Co., MT	Jeremiah Johnson	Jeremiah Johnson	2001	6
173 3/8	175 7/8	60 5/8	31	31 2/8	8 6/8	10 6/8	6 7/8	6 5/8	10	10	Idaho Co., ID	Thomas C. Saltarella	Thomas C. Saltarella	2007	7
173 1/8	176 7/8	48 3/8	37 6/8	35 6/8	10 6/8	9 2/8	6 5/8	6 3/8	11	11	Weber Co., UT	Lawrence M. Kochevar	Lawrence M. Kochevar	2007	8
172 3/8	181 3/8	49 1/8	34 1/8	41 3/8	12 1/8	13 6/8	6 3/8	6 4/8	9	9	Kootenai Co., ID	Larry D. Sieverding	Larry D. Sieverding	2008	9
172	172 1/8	45 6/8	34 4/8	34 4/8	12	11 7/8	5 6/8	5 5/8	11	11	Caribou Co., ID	Susan A. Remer Shappart	Susan A. Remer Shappart	2007	10
171	179 2/8	47	36 1/8	37 4/8	9 6/8	12 4/8	6 1/8	6 2/8	10	14	Teton Co., WY	David F. Bishop	David F. Bishop	2008	11
167 7/8	172 4/8	48 3/8	33 6/8	33 6/8	13 1/8	12 6/8	6 2/8	6 4/8	7	11	Boundary Co., ID	Bill R. Moe	Bill R. Moe	2007	12
167	172 2/8	51 6/8	32 2/8	35 3/8	9 4/8	9 4/8	7	6 7/8	9	11	Weber Co., UT	Michael R. Bronson	Michael R. Bronson	2006	13
166 6/8	170 5/8	53 4/8	34	32 2/8	10 5/8	9 5/8	5 6/8	5 7/8	9	10	Teton Co., ID	Robert W. Eason	Robert W. Eason	2007	14
166 2/8	170 4/8	44 2/8	35	38 4/8	9 2/8	10	6 6/8	6 6/8	10	10	Lincoln Co., WY	Ross M. Hinschberger	Ross M. Hinschberger	2008	15
166 1/8	169 4/8	49 3/8	34 1/8	32 2/8	10 6/8	10 2/8	6 7/8	6 7/8	9	10	Teton Co., WY	Robert W. Langdon	Robert W. Langdon	2007	16
165 7/8	178 3/8	46 3/8	32 6/8	37 5/8	11 6/8	13 1/8	6 2/8	6 4/8	9	15	Bingham Co., ID	Tony Saiz	Tony Saiz	2006	17
165 4/8	167	45 2/8	31 6/8	31 3/8	12 3/8	12 3/8	6 4/8	6 3/8	11	10	Carbon Co., WY	Charlie D. Todd	Charlie D. Todd	2007	18
164 1/8	165 5/8	45 1/8	31 4/8	32 1/8	12 1/8	11 3/8	6 5/8	6 6/8	10	10	Jackson Co., CO	Brad A. Knutson	Brad A. Knutson	2009	19
164	167 5/8	47 4/8	35	32 4/8	12 5/8	11 4/8	6 2/8	6 2/8	8	8	Idaho Co., ID	Judy A. Reilly	Judy A. Reilly	2006	20
163 7/8	168 1/8	45 5/8	36	34 2/8	10 2/8	10	7 1/8	6 7/8	8	10	Teton Co., WY	Ted W. Bade	Ted W. Bade	2007	21
163 3/8	168 7/8	50 5/8	33 1/8	33 4/8	8 1/8	10 1/8	6 1/8	6 2/8	9	12	Salt Lake Co., UT	Quincy R. Rindlisbacher	Quincy R. Rindlisbacher	2006	22
163 2/8	167 5/8	50 2/8	32 5/8	36	8 5/8	9 4/8	6 3/8	6 2/8	9	9	Stevens Co., WA	Travis M. LeCaire	Travis M. LeCaire	2007	23
162 3/8	165 2/8	46 1/8	34 1/8	33 4/8	9	8 7/8	6 7/8	6 6/8	9	11	Grand Co., CO	Dana W. Roe	Dana W. Roe	2009	24
162	168 2/8	53 2/8	30 6/8	32 3/8	10 5/8	10 1/8	6 4/8	6 5/8	8	8	Latah Co., ID	Helene M. Cummings	Helene M. Cummings	2008	25
161 4/8	162 5/8	41 6/8	32 6/8	33 2/8	11 6/8	11 1/8	7	7	9	9	Teton Co., WY	Robert J. Anderson	Robert J. Anderson	2008	26
161 4/8	168 3/8	44 2/8	28 5/8	31 6/8	15 2/8	12 4/8	6 4/8	6 4/8	12	11	Bonneville Co., ID	Michael J. Magalsky	Michael J. Magalsky	2009	26
161 3/8	163	44 3/8	33 6/8	34	9 2/8	9 5/8	6 4/8	6 4/8	10	9	Teton Co., WY	Tobi L. Brown	Tobi L. Brown	2009	28

161 3/8	164 6/8	32 2/8	32 2/8	11 3/8	11	6 4/8	6 4/8	11	12	Cache Co., UT	Walter L. Rochell	Walter L. Rochell	2009	28
161 2/8	167 1/8	32 3/8	30 6/8	11 4/8	11 4/8	6 6/8	7 4/8	11	10	Teton Co., WY	Lisa R. Harrington	Lisa R. Harrington	2007	30
160 7/8	164 2/8	30 7/8	51 1/8	9 2/8	10 5/8	6 4/8	6 6/8	9	10	Beaverhead Co., MT	Kurt D. Rued	Kurt D. Rued	2007	31
160 7/8	166 4/8	30 5/8	49 3/8	10 2/8	11 1/8	5 7/8	5 7/8	9	12	Pend Oreille Co., WA	Jacob T. Sadler	Jacob T. Sadler	2008	31
160 5/8	161 7/8	31 7/8	52 1/8	7 4/8	8 1/8	6 7/8	6 7/8	8	8	Cache Co., UT	Cindy L. Fronk	Cindy L. Fronk	2007	33
160 4/8	162 3/8	36	43 2/8	9 5/8	9 5/8	6	6 3/8	7	8	Mineral Co., MT	James E. Ratcliffe	James E. Ratcliffe	2007	34
160 2/8	161 1/8	30 2/8	47 6/8	10 1/8	10 2/8	5 7/8	5 7/8	10	10	Lincoln Co., MT	Kaily A. Baer	Kaily A. Baer	2007	35
160 1/8	165 6/8	30 4/8	50 3/8	9 4/8	10 1/8	7 1/8	6 3/8	8	10	Carbon Co., WY	Paul R. Parke	Paul R. Parke	2009	36
159 3/8	164 2/8	29 2/8	44 5/8	11 3/8	12 7/8	6 7/8	6 6/8	10	11	Pend Oreille Co., WA	Christopher Wilson	Christopher Wilson	2007	37
159 2/8	162 2/8	31 1/8	49 4/8	9 6/8	10 2/8	6 4/8	6 3/8	10	9	Benewah Co., ID	Michael R. Minier	Michael R. Minier	2007	38
159 2/8	166 4/8	30 2/8	47 4/8	11 3/8	10 5/8	7	8 2/8	9	8	Grand Co., CO	Michael A. Symanski	Michael A. Symanski	2007	38
159	162 4/8	33 2/8	44 2/8	8 4/8	8 4/8	6 5/8	6 6/8	11	9	Duchesne Co., UT	Woody Olsen	Woody Olsen	2003	40
159	161 2/8	30 5/8	45	10 7/8	11 2/8	6 4/8	6 5/8	11	10	Idaho Co., ID	Lori A. Alley	Lori A. Alley	2007	40
159	166	27 3/8	47	14 5/8	12	5 5/8	5 6/8	9	11	Morgan Co., UT	Dee N. Olson	Dee N. Olson	2007	40
158 4/8	161 6/8	33	47	7 6/8	9 1/8	6	6 1/8	11	9	Jackson Hole, WY	Harry J. Wilkinson	Harry J. Wilkinson	1949	43
158 4/8	162 6/8	30 5/8	44 6/8	12 4/8	9 2/8	6	6	9	11	Missoula Co., MT	Steven A. Slagle	Steven A. Slagle	2006	43
158 3/8	164	35 7/8	39 5/8	11 2/8	10 3/8	5 7/8	5 7/8	12	10	Ravalli Co., MT	Daniel L. Walker	Daniel L. Walker	2007	45
158 2/8	163	30 1/8	53 6/8	10	8 5/8	5 7/8	5 6/8	11	8	Kootenai Co., ID	Tamara M. Coleman	Tamara M. Coleman	2007	46
158 1/8	163 5/8	33 2/8	48 3/8	12 1/8	11 5/8	6 2/8	7	8	7	Meagher Co., MT	Rodney N. Kummer	Rodney N. Kummer	2006	47
158 1/8	160 5/8	28 6/8	45 7/8	12 1/8	11 5/8	5 7/8	5 6/8	11	10	Teton Co., ID	Diane B. Kinzie	Diane B. Kinzie	2008	47
157 7/8	159 5/8	30 2/8	48 3/8	10 6/8	10 1/8	6 4/8	6 3/8	8	8	Benewah Co., ID	Carlton G. Schenken III	Carlton G. Schenken III	2009	49
157 6/8	161 1/8	28	42	12 7/8	12 1/8	6 7/8	6 6/8	12	11	Park Co., WY	Jeffrey J. Lutz	Jeffrey J. Lutz	2006	50
157 6/8	169	30 4/8	56 6/8	8	12 4/8	7	7 6/8	7	11	Albany Co., WY	Benton G. Street	Benton G. Street	2008	50
157	168	30	45 2/8	9 3/8	11 4/8	6 4/8	6 7/8	10	13	Sanders Co., MT	Todd D. Barstow	Todd D. Barstow	2007	52
156 7/8	160 5/8	28	51 3/8	10 5/8	9 4/8	6 2/8	6 5/8	10	9	Stevens Co., WA	David J. Peoples	David J. Peoples	2006	53
156 6/8	164 3/8	31 6/8	44 6/8	13 1/8	10 1/8	7	7	9	8	Flathead Co., MT	James L. Friske	James L. Friske	2007	54
156 6/8	161 1/8	30 6/8	45 6/8	9 6/8	10	6 6/8	6 4/8	9	10	Uinta Co., WY	Sandra K. Fruchey	Sandra K. Fruchey	2007	54
156 6/8	159 5/8	32 7/8	42 6/8	11 3/8	11 3/8	6 3/8	6 5/8	9	7	Idaho Co., ID	Shawn G. Stewart	Shawn G. Stewart	2008	54
156 4/8	160 6/8	30 2/8	51 2/8	9	9 4/8	6 3/8	6 3/8	7	9	Weber Co., UT	Mark A. Green	Mark A. Green	2007	57
156 4/8	159 6/8	34	45 4/8	10 4/8	10 2/8	6 2/8	6 2/8	8	8	Sheridan Co., WY	Gary B. Mefford	Gary B. Mefford	2007	57
156 1/8	158 3/8	34	49 3/8	7 5/8	8 2/8	6 3/8	6 3/8	7	7	Bonner Co., ID	Jim G. McGlocklin	Jim G. McGlocklin	1997	59
156 1/8	158 4/8	33 1/8	42 3/8	9	8 4/8	6 4/8	6 2/8	9	10	Madison Co., MT	Corey J. Donahue	Corey J. Donahue	2008	59
156	161 3/8	32 2/8	46	11 2/8	11 4/8	6 5/8	6 4/8	10	10	Larimer Co., CO	Joseph A. Straley	Joseph A. Straley	2007	61
156	161 5/8	32 4/8	41 6/8	11 3/8	10 4/8	6 4/8	6 4/8	12	12	Lincoln Co., MT	Shay P. McGowan	Shay P. McGowan	2008	61
155 7/8	160 4/8	34	47 1/8	8 3/8	8	6 3/8	6 3/8	10	8	Bannock Co., ID	Jamie K. Roche	Jamie K. Roche	2006	63
155 5/8	158 2/8	30	46 3/8	8 4/8	9 7/8	6 7/8	7	6	9	Ravalli Co., MT	V. Wayne Rusk II	V. Wayne Rusk II	2008	63
155 6/8	160 6/8	33 7/8	46 2/8	9 2/8	10 6/8	6 1/8	6 1/8	9	8	Larimer Co., CO	Jean E. Branstetter	Jean E. Branstetter	2007	65
155 3/8	160	31 1/8	47 5/8	10 3/8	10 2/8	6	5 7/8	9	11	Pend Oreille Co., WA	Billie L. Ritchey	Billie L. Ritchey	2006	66
155 1/8	160 7/8	29 5/8	46 7/8	9 6/8	11	5 6/8	5 7/8	9	12	Lincoln Co., MT	Picked Up	Randy Sandoval	1967	67
155 1/8	163 5/8	32 5/8	46 1/8	13 3/8	9 1/8	6 4/8	6 3/8	7	9	Salt Lake Co., UT	Kaye Seeley	Kaye Seeley	2006	67
155 1/8	160 5/8	30	42 7/8	11 4/8	10 2/8	6	5 7/8	13	10	Madison Co., ID	Stephen W. Mistretta	Stephen W. Mistretta	2007	67

SHIRAS' MOOSE

Alces alces shirasi

Final Score	Gross Score	Greatest Spread	Length of Palm R	L	Width of Palm R	L	Circumference of Beam at Smallest Place R	L	Number of Normal Points R	L	Locality	Hunter	Owner	Date Killed	Rank
154 4/8	156	51 2/8	29 3/8	29 1/8	7 6/8	9	6 6/8	6 6/8	8	8	Grand Co., CO	Erinn S. Flaharty	Erinn S. Flaharty	2006	70
154 2/8	156 1/8	40	32 2/8	30 6/8	10 2/8	9 7/8	6 4/8	6 4/8	10	10	Sublette Co., WY	Oscar Eiden	Bruce A. Eiden	1979	71
154 2/8	159 5/8	44 2/8	30 7/8	30 2/8	10 7/8	11 2/8	6 2/8	5 7/8	12	8	Cache Co., UT	Glade H. Smith	Glade H. Smith	2006	71
153 6/8	158 5/8	46	29 6/8	32 2/8	10 7/8	10 5/8	6 4/8	6 5/8	7	9	Stevens Co., WA	Jason R. Uhls	Jason R. Uhls	2007	73
153 5/8	159 3/8	45 1/8	30 1/8	30 3/8	10 6/8	12 2/8	6 3/8	6 3/8	11	7	Madison Co., MT	Terrell L. Cotterell	Terrell L. Cotterell	2009	74
153 1/8	153 7/8	49 1/8	27 3/8	28	9	8 7/8	6 6/8	6 6/8	9	9	Beaverhead Co., MT	Jason L. Rorabaugh	Jason L. Rorabaugh	2007	75
152 5/8	156 6/8	43 3/8	27 4/8	29	10 7/8	10 7/8	6 2/8	6 7/8	10	12	Larimer Co., CO	Brent L. Dicks	Brent L. Dicks	2008	76
152 4/8	154 4/8	41 6/8	33 7/8	34 2/8	8 7/8	9 4/8	5 5/8	5 5/8	7	8	Missoula Co., MT	Mike T. Dellwo	Mike T. Dellwo	2007	77
152 1/8	159 4/8	47 7/8	32 3/8	27 7/8	11	12 6/8	6 2/8	6 3/8	8	7	Idaho Co., ID	Jeff L. Eacker	Jeff L. Eacker	2006	78
152	156 1/8	42	33	29 1/8	11 2/8	11	5 7/8	5 7/8	9	9	Weber Co., UT	Gary S. Miller	Gary S. Miller	2007	79
151 7/8	159 3/8	41 7/8	26	32	11 2/8	11 6/8	6 6/8	6 6/8	11	12	Stevens Co., WA	Ashton T. Wolfe	Ashton T. Wolfe	2007	80
151 5/8	155 7/8	45 6/8	29 5/8	29 4/8	8 6/8	11 3/8	6 6/8	7 1/8	8	9	Park Co., MT	Thomas W. Kitts	Thomas W. Kitts	1965	81
151 6/8	155 5/8	39	29 5/8	29 2/8	11 2/8	11	6 3/8	6 1/8	13	10	Caribou Co., ID	Betty G. Gentry	Betty G. Gentry	2007	81
151 1/8	154 5/8	43 3/8	30 2/8	28	11 4/8	11 4/8	6 3/8	6 5/8	9	8	Carbon Co., WY	Susan J. Malone	Susan J. Malone	2009	83
151	155	39 4/8	29	29 4/8	14 6/8	14 3/8	6 4/8	6 3/8	6	9	Jackson Co., CO	Jeffrey D. Rushlo	Jeffrey D. Rushlo	2008	84
150 7/8	155 2/8	44 1/8	29 7/8	26 5/8	11 5/8	11 4/8	6 2/8	6 2/8	10	9	Idaho Co., ID	J. Tom Mangold	J. Tom Mangold	2000	85
150 6/8	153 3/8	41 2/8	30 2/8	30 7/8	8 5/8	9 4/8	5 7/8	6	10	11	Cache Co., UT	Shane J. Hunt	Shane J. Hunt	2007	86
149 5/8	155	38 3/8	30 6/8	32 5/8	10 5/8	11	5 6/8	5 7/8	9	10	Clark Co., ID	Joe D. Rohrbacher	Joe D. Rohrbacher	1994	87
149 5/8	154 2/8	45 3/8	32 5/8	29 2/8	7 6/8	8 7/8	7 1/8	7 2/8	8	8	Sheridan Co., WY	Loren L. Green	Loren L. Green	2007	87
149 3/8	151 5/8	48 5/8	28 4/8	29 2/8	8 3/8	8	6 7/8	7	7	7	Lewis & Clark Co., MT	Ernie A. Lundberg	Ernie A. Lundberg	2007	89
149 1/8	157 1/8	43 1/8	33	31 2/8	10	11 2/8	6 2/8	6 2/8	6	9	Utah Co., UT	David A. Goodrich	David A. Goodrich	2009	90
148 7/8	154 7/8	43 7/8	29	32 5/8	9 3/8	9 5/8	6 1/8	6 2/8	10	8	Morgan Co., UT	Steven M. James	Steven M. James	2007	91
148 4/8	154 1/8	43 6/8	30 3/8	30 5/8	9 3/8	10 4/8	7 1/8	7 3/8	6	8	Sublette Co., WY	James P. Graf	James P. Graf	2006	92
148 4/8	151 5/8	47	30	32	7 4/8	6 4/8	6 2/8	6 3/8	8	8	Stevens Co., WA	C. Daniel Smith	C. Daniel Smith	2009	92
148 2/8	150 5/8	46 2/8	28 6/8	30 3/8	8 4/8	9 2/8	5 6/8	5 6/8	8	8	Granite Co., MT	Randy O. Schott	Randy O. Schott	2009	94
147 6/8	148 6/8	46 3/8	27 4/8	26 2/8	8	8 4/8	6	6 1/8	10	10	Mesa Co., CO	Thomas E. Gannon	Thomas E. Gannon	2009	95
146 5/8	149 7/8	48 5/8	28 4/8	29 1/8	9 1/8	6 4/8	6	6	8	8	Teton Co., WY	Steven V. Dwyer	Steven V. Dwyer	2006	96
146 4/8	155 4/8	43 2/8	28 6/8	36 5/8	7 3/8	7 5/8	6 5/8	6 5/8	9	10	Park Co., WY	John E. Webber	John E. Webber	2008	97
146 3/8	161 2/8	43 1/8	41 6/8	32 2/8	9 6/8	7 7/8	5 6/8	6	6	9	Pend Oreille Co., WA	Jacob Nichols	Jacob Nichols	2006	98
146 2/8	149 5/8	45 4/8	30 1/8	29 1/8	7 7/8	9 1/8	6 3/8	6 4/8	6	8	Flathead Co., MT	Brendan R. Beatty	Brendan R. Beatty	2006	99
146 2/8	150 2/8	46 4/8	27 3/8	30 1/8	9	8 6/8	5 6/8	5 6/8	7	9	Beaverhead Co., MT	Randy A. Baker	Randy A. Baker	2007	99
146	146 4/8	44 4/8	29 2/8	28 7/8	8 2/8	8 2/8	5 6/8	5 5/8	8	8	Pend Oreille Co., WA	Scott E. Gillis	Scott E. Gillis	2006	101
146	148	42 2/8	30 6/8	30 2/8	9 2/8	8 7/8	5 6/8	5 7/8	8	7	Pend Oreille Co., WA	Chad Miller	Chad Miller	2006	101

Score											Locality	Hunter	Owner	Date	Rank
145 6/8	150 4/8	42	28 2/8	28 3/8	11 7/8	12	5 6/8	6 2/8	6	10	Flathead Co., MT	Steven T. Herman	Steven T. Herman	2006	103
145 4/8	149 6/8	51	27 6/8	24 4/8	10 5/8	10 5/8	6 1/8	6 1/8	7	6	Idaho Co., ID	Richard L. Routh	Richard L. Routh	2006	104
145	152 1/8	42	28 6/8	30	12 1/8	10 3/8	5 7/8	6	7	9	Flathead Co., MT	Stephen T. Golliday	Stephen T. Golliday	2003	105
145	149 5/8	43	30 2/8	29 7/8	9 3/8	10 4/8	5 6/8	5 7/8	9	6	Beaverhead Co., MT	JoAnn Hibl	JoAnn Hibl	2008	105
144 5/8	151 3/8	44 3/8	29 2/8	29 6/8	10	10 7/8	6 2/8	5 7/8	6	7	Granite Co., MT	Ronald M. Pare	Ronald M. Pare	2009	107
144 4/8	148 1/8	44	28 2/8	28 5/8	7 3/8	9 3/8	6 5/8	6 7/8	8	9	Beaverhead Co., MT	Gary D. Loghry	Gary D. Loghry	2008	108
144 1/8	147 1/8	42 3/8	28	27 4/8	10 4/8	9	5 3/8	5 3/8	9	10	Lincoln Co., WY	George F. Sund, Jr.	George F. Sund, Jr.	2004	109
144 1/8	146 1/8	40 3/8	30 4/8	30 2/8	8 7/8	10 4/8	5 6/8	5 7/8	7	7	Lemhi Co., ID	Teri L. Thaemert	Teri L. Thaemert	2007	109
144 1/8	147 4/8	39 1/8	26 4/8	28 2/8	11 4/8	12	5 4/8	5 5/8	9	10	Sublette Co., WY	Kenneth C. Kieler	Kenneth C. Kieler	2008	109
144	148 5/8	40 4/8	28	29 7/8	11 2/8	9 5/8	6 1/8	6 2/8	9	8	Beaverhead Co., MT	Alexander S. Mackey	Alexander S. Mackey	2007	112
143 7/8	149 2/8	45 1/8	30 2/8	27 4/8	8 4/8	7 7/8	6	6	10	8	Albany Co., WY	Rene J. Suda	Rene J. Suda	2007	113
143 6/8	147	48 6/8	30	29 1/8	10 1/8	8	5 5/8	5 3/8	5	5	Boundary Co., ID	Lonny B. Spaulding	Lonny B. Spaulding	2008	114
143 5/8	148 3/8	45 7/8	24 2/8	27 2/8	9 6/8	10 4/8	5 7/8	5 7/8	9	10	Pend Oreille Co., WA	Michael T. Warn	Michael T. Warn	2006	115
143 5/8	149	44 7/8	30 5/8	26 6/8	9 6/8	11 1/8	5 7/8	6	7	7	Carbon Co., WY	Mike J. Coelho	Mike J. Coelho	2007	115
143 3/8	147 7/8	38 5/8	25 1/8	25 6/8	11 3/8	10 4/8	6 2/8	6 2/8	12	11	Madison Co., ID	Jana L. Yancey	Jana L. Yancey	2007	117
143	145 6/8	49 2/8	28 1/8	26 1/8	8 6/8	9 1/8	6 3/8	6	6	6	Grand Co., CO	Dennis M. Casey	Dennis M. Casey	2009	118
142 2/8	146	40 6/8	26 5/8	27 7/8	10 5/8	11 1/8	6 4/8	6 4/8	7	9	Hot Springs Co., WY	Curtis R. Griffith	Curtis R. Griffith	2006	119
142 2/8	146 7/8	43 2/8	30	27 4/8	8 2/8	8 2/8	6 7/8	6 6/8	9	7	Big Horn Co., WY	Timothy N. Winland	Timothy N. Winland	2006	119
142 2/8	144 3/8	39 6/8	28 6/8	28 1/8	9	8 4/8	5 5/8	5 5/8	9	10	Cache Co., UT	Nathan M. Larsen	Nathan M. Larsen	2009	119
141	143 6/8	42 2/8	26 7/8	26 4/8	9 2/8	10 4/8	5 5/8	5 6/8	8	9	Sublette Co., WY	John T. Philley	John T. Philley	2007	122
141	142	43 2/8	26 4/8	26 4/8	7 7/8	7 7/8	6 4/8	6 4/8	9	8	Kootenai Co., ID	Gary Manes	Gary Manes	2009	122
140 7/8	147 5/8	43 3/8	27 6/8	26 1/8	11 2/8	10 4/8	6 1/8	6 1/8	6	10	Johnson Co., WY	Mina S. Stewart	Mina S. Stewart	2008	124
140 7/8	143	46 1/8	27	26 6/8	7 6/8	7	5 6/8	5 5/8	9	8	Pend Oreille Co., WA	Peter W. Nelson	Peter W. Nelson	2009	124
140 4/8	142 1/8	46 4/8	23 7/8	25 3/8	9 2/8	9 3/8	5 7/8	5 7/8	8	8	Uinta Co., WY	Steven L. Gonsior	Steven L. Gonsior	2007	126
140 2/8	142	47 2/8	24 4/8	24 4/8	7 5/8	8 2/8	6 3/8	6 4/8	9	8	Beaverhead Co., MT	David A. Bowen	David A. Bowen	2008	127
179 *	181 6/8	48	33	33 1/8	11 7/8	13 3/8	6 6/8	6 5/8	15	14	Stevens Co., WA	Kirk T. Youngers	Kirk T. Youngers	2007	

Final score subject to revision by additional verifying measurements.

MOUNTAIN CARIBOU

Rangifer tarandus caribou

Minimum Score 360   World's Record 459 3/8

The mountain caribou category includes trophies from Alberta, British Columbia, southern Yukon Territory, and the Mackenzie Mountains of Northwest Territories.

Final Score	Gross Score	Length of Main Beam R	L	Inside Spread	Circ. at Smallest Place Between Brow and Bez Points R	L	Length of Brow Points R	L	Width of Brow Points R	L	Number of Points R	L	Locality	Hunter	Owner	Date Killed	Rank
422 7/8	434 6/8	53	51 7/8	36 3/8	6 4/8	8 2/8	17 4/8	7 1/8	9 2/8	1/8	19	15	Mackenzie Mts., NT	R. Bruce Moon	R. Bruce Moon	2007	1
412 4/8	426 7/8	50 3/8	48 1/8	38 2/8	8 1/8	6 5/8	17	10 4/8	10 3/8	1/8	17	16	Prospector Mt., YT	Jack E. Risner	Jack E. Risner	2008	2
411 3/8	428	53 2/8	49 1/8	39 7/8	5 7/8	6 1/8	17 1/8	20 7/8	11 4/8	13	18	23	Arctic Red River, NT	Gregory Menzies	Gregory Menzies	2009	3
410 6/8	426 5/8	43 3/8	41 5/8	36 1/8	6 4/8	6 4/8	13 7/8	14 6/8	9 6/8	10 6/8	26	26	Pelly Mts., YT	Mike R.J. Lamothe	Mike R.J. Lamothe	2008	4
408 7/8	423 1/8	45 6/8	46 3/8	34 1/8	5 6/8	5 6/8	19	14 1/8	9 6/8	16 3/8	20	15	Mackenzie Mts., NT	Anthony V. Hoots	Anthony V. Hoots	2008	5
408 3/8	423 3/8	55 4/8	59 4/8	37 4/8	6 4/8	6 4/8	16 7/8	15 7/8	17	1/8	13	12	Spatsizi Plateau, BC	Norman Simon	Norman Simon	2008	6
407 5/8	419 6/8	45	47 2/8	32	6 1/8	6	18 3/8	8 4/8	13	1/8	24	17	Cassiar, BC	William N. Beach	Shelburne Museum PR	1932	7
406 3/8	422 2/8	45 5/8	48 5/8	41 1/8	6 6/8	6 4/8	16 1/8	17	17 2/8	1 4/8	21	20	Spatsizi Plateau, BC	Fred P. Burd	Fred P. Burd	2008	8
404 3/8	420 2/8	43 1/8	41 6/8	43 6/8	8 2/8	9 4/8	2 4/8	18	10 1/8	13 2/8	19	17	Ketchum Lake, BC	Picked Up	Brooke Whitelaw	2008	9
401 1/8	410 5/8	47 5/8	51 1/8	38 2/8	5 5/8	5 7/8	15 3/8	16 5/8	14 1/8	1/8	19	18	Mackenzie Mts., NT	Rick D. Meritt	Rick D. Meritt	2007	10
400 6/8	415 6/8	49 3/8	50	42 6/8	7 3/8	7 2/8	4 3/8	15 2/8	4	8 7/8	16	18	Rancheria, YT	Matthew T. Kremer	Matthew T. Kremer	2008	11
399 5/8	414	42	41 1/8	38	7 2/8	7 1/8	4 6/8	16 2/8	1 2/8	10 2/8	20	15	Grass Lakes, YT	Jerry L. Beck	Jerry L. Beck	2007	12
398 7/8	407 5/8	55 1/8	51 7/8	32	8	7 7/8	15 6/8	12 2/8	13 5/8	2 4/8	24	18	Dease Lake, BC	Michael Kozin	Michael Kozin	2008	13
398 3/8	416 2/8	45 1/8	45 6/8	36 3/8	6 7/8	6 5/8	18 1/8	20 1/8	14 4/8	12	18	15	Aishihik Lake, YT	Michael W. Christopher	Michael W. Christopher	2007	14
398 2/8	413 5/8	49 7/8	42 4/8	35	7 3/8	7 3/8	18 5/8	18 5/8	4 6/8	12 6/8	15	14	Aishihik Lake, YT	Clint Sawicki	Clint Sawicki	2005	15
397 5/8	410 3/8	42 7/8	46 6/8	34 4/8	7 2/8	7 2/8	1 4/8	15 6/8	11 4/8	1/8	20	28	Dease Lake, BC	Mike A. Carpinito	Mike A. Carpinito	2008	16
394 4/8	400 4/8	40 2/8	42 2/8	32 5/8	7	7 3/8	2	7 6/8	9 3/8	1/8	17	21	Tagish Lake, BC	Ron A. Matt	Ron A. Matt	2006	17
394 2/8	409 5/8	44 5/8	41 6/8	34 2/8	6 5/8	6	12 2/8	17 1/8	11	1/8	11	17	Whitehorse, YT	Thomas J. Little	Thomas J. Little	2007	18
392 6/8	404 2/8	49 2/8	38 6/8	38 6/8	7 1/8	6	16 3/8	19 5/8	13 5/8	1/8	11	14	Apex Mt., YT	A.C. Smid	A.C. Smid	2007	19
392 5/8	402	48 4/8	50 3/8	36 6/8	8	8	20 6/8		—	12 7/8	12	17	Hart River, YT	John Beecher	John Beecher	2006	20
392 4/8	402 1/8	49	48 4/8	25 3/8	6 4/8	5 7/8	14	17	6 5/8	12 5/8	14	17	Dry Lake, BC	Randy L. Meyn	Randy L. Meyn	2008	21
391 7/8	405 1/8	49 3/8	51 1/8	47 4/8	7 1/8	6 4/8	20 2/8	19 4/8	12 2/8	14 3/8	14	16	Anvil Range, YT	Daryll D. Southwick	Daryll D. Southwick	2006	22
390	401 3/8	43 2/8	39 6/8	39	6 2/8	6 1/8	7 6/8	17 4/8	1/8	12 5/8	17	19	Mackenzie Mts., NT	David F. Jenkins	David F. Jenkins	2005	23
389 4/8	399 1/8	48 6/8	45 5/8	34 6/8	6 6/8	6 5/8	19 1/8	17 1/8	18 2/8	8 4/8	17	13	Mackenzie Mts., NT	Jerry Peebles	Jerry Peebles	1998	24
389 2/8	402 2/8	48 1/8	48 6/8	29 7/8	6 7/8	6 6/8	18 5/8	4	14 3/8	1/8	22	15	Mackenzie Mts., NT	Dee Opperman	Dee Opperman	2007	25
387 2/8	398	46 2/8	47 4/8	34 7/8	5 7/8	6	2 1/8	17 6/8	14 3/8	1/8	17	24	Sanabar Creek, BC	Ben L. Mueller	Ben L. Mueller	2006	26
385 6/8	392 2/8	49 3/8	49	34 7/8	7 4/8	7 4/8	13 6/8	13 6/8	6 1/8	12 5/8	16	15	Mackenzie Mts., NT	Trent B. Hartley	Trent B. Hartley	2008	27
385 2/8	397 5/8	46 7/8	46 2/8	32 6/8	6 1/8	6 5/8	13 7/8	16 4/8	1/8	13 6/8	22	28	Mountain River, NT	Steven Mulvihill	Steven Mulvihill	2007	28
383 4/8	392 1/8	42 3/8	44 4/8	24 6/8	6 1/8	6 1/8	12 4/8	18 6/8	17 5/8	1/8	23	26	North Lakes, YT	R. Kim Greene	R. Kim Greene	2009	29
383 2/8	392 5/8	46 3/8	46 2/8	33 1/8	6 4/8	6 4/8	14 3/8	13 3/8	1	13 5/8	12	13	McClure Lake, NT	Alan L. Friend	Alan L. Friend	2005	30

													Locality	Hunter	Owner	Date Killed	Rank
381 7/8	396 6/8	44	41 2/8	29 3/8	7 5/8	9 6/8	2	23	1/8	15 7/8	15	18	Long Lake, YT	David W. Laveck	David W. Laveck	2009	31
377 1/8	394 1/8	42	42 1/8	33 2/8	6	5 7/8	18 5/8	17 1/8	11 2/8	13 5/8	21	19	Mackenzie Mts., NT	James L. Thurston	James L. Thurston	2008	32
376 2/8	390 7/8	49	46 6/8	34 6/8	6 2/8	6 5/8	7 7/8	18 4/8	1/8	13 2/8	12	15	Cold Fish Lake, BC	Toby W. Terry	Toby W. Terry	2007	33
376	384 7/8	43 3/8	42 4/8	32 6/8	7 3/8	7 4/8	4 6/8	17 1/8	1/8	11 4/8	13	16	Mt. Nansen, YT	Dana G. Journeay	Dana G. Journeay	2009	34
374 3/8	390 5/8	51 2/8	52	42 2/8	6 5/8	6 5/8	2 5/8	17 7/8	1/8	13 4/8	12	16	Spatsizi Wilderness, BC	Timothy S. Geppert	Timothy S. Geppert	2008	35
374 1/8	382 4/8	43 3/8	44 4/8	33 5/8	5 7/8	6 1/8	1 1/8	15 2/8	1/8	8	18	19	Arctic Red River, NT	Glenn Bailey	Glenn Bailey	2008	36
373 5/8	397 3/8	44 1/8	46	29 7/8	7	6 7/8	16 6/8	11 2/8	9 1/8	2 7/8	20	16	Rabbit River, BC	Kanina M. Fulton	Kanina M. Fulton	2006	37
370 7/8	401 3/8	41 4/8	46 5/8	31 3/8	6 7/8	6 6/8	12 7/8	2	10 4/8	1/8	18	16	Rancheria River, BC	James G. Turner	James G. Turner	2006	38
369 2/8	379 2/8	44 4/8	43 1/8	33 3/8	7 2/8	7 6/8	16	16 2/8	5 7/8	6 4/8	16	18	Mackenzie Mts., NT	William D. Eshee, Jr.	William D. Eshee, Jr.	2007	39
368 3/8	382 2/8	48 2/8	46 5/8	38	6 6/8	7	20 6/8	16 6/8	9 4/8	1/8	18	13	Cassiar Mts., BC	Peter J. LoPiccolo	Peter J. LoPiccolo	2006	40
367 3/8	373 5/8	42 4/8	41 6/8	31 2/8	6 7/8	7 1/8	7/8	17	1/8	11 3/8	15	16	Weissener Creek, BC	Robert L. Gerstner	Robert L. Gerstner	2006	41
367 1/8	380 4/8	52 6/8	53 2/8	36	6 1/8	6 4/8	13 2/8	15	7/8	11 2/8	15	18	Pink Mt., BC	Marion G. Macaluso	Marion G. Macaluso	2008	42
365 2/8	384 2/8	48 4/8	45	30 6/8	6 3/8	6 3/8	17 2/8	10	14 5/8	12 4/8	23	15	Gundahoo River, BC	Earl Pulliam	Earl Pulliam	2008	43
365 1/8	384 3/8	48 4/8	48 5/8	28 6/8	5 5/8	6 1/8	8 1/8	16 5/8	1/8	11 6/8	15	14	Arctic Red River, NT	Jon D. Jencks	Jon D. Jencks	2008	44
363 5/8	370 5/8	47 6/8	48 5/8	39 1/8	6 3/8	6 1/8	12 6/8	17 5/8	1/8	12 4/8	14	13	Cold Fish Lake, BC	Casey G. Terry	Casey G. Terry	2007	45
361 1/8	376 1/8	47 7/8	47 4/8	35 6/8	5 4/8	5 4/8	4 3/8	20 2/8	1/8	13 5/8	14	13	Klaza River, YT	Eldon L. Buckner	Eldon L. Buckner	2009	46
360 3/8	369 3/8	49 5/8	50	37 1/8	6 6/8	6 5/8	8 5/8	14 2/8	8 1/8	13 2/8	18	19	Dease Lake, BC	Mike A. Carpinito	Mike A. Carpinito	2007	47
424 2/8 *	439 5/8	50 3/8	47 7/8	37 1/8	7 4/8	7 6/8	17 1/8	18 1/8	7/8	7 6/8	19	13	North Lakes, YT	Mike E. Broadwell	Mike E. Broadwell	2008	
416 *	428 7/8	52 5/8	51 1/8	38	6 5/8	6 4/8	21 2/8	22 7/8	15 6/8	9 7/8	13	18	Long Lake, YT	Leonard R. Beecher	Leonard R. Beecher	2007	
415 4/8 *	427 4/8	53 4/8	56 7/8	49 3/8	7	6 6/8	2 6/8	20 4/8	1	10 5/8	14	18	Klaza River, YT	Shayne D. Parker	Shayne D. Parker	2005	

Final score subject to revision by additional verifying measurements.

MOUNTAIN CARIBOU
FINAL SCORE: 374 3/8
HUNTER: Timothy S. Geppert

MOUNTAIN CARIBOU
FINAL SCORE: 374 1/8
HUNTER: Glenn Bailey

MOUNTAIN CARIBOU
FINAL SCORE: 361 1/8
HUNTER: Eldon L. Buckner

MOUNTAIN CARIBOU
FINAL SCORE: 397 5/8
HUNTER: Mike A. Carpinito

WOODLAND CARIBOU

Rangifer tarandus caribou

Minimum Score 265

World's Record 419 5/8

Woodland caribou includes trophies from Nova Scotia, New Brunswick, and Newfoundland.

Final Score	Gross Score	Length of Main Beam R	L	Inside Spread	Circumference at Smallest Place Between Brow and Bez Points R	L	Length of Brow Points R	L	Width of Brow Points R	L	Number of Points R	L	Locality	Hunter	Owner	Date Killed	Rank
325 6/8	340 5/8	42 4/8	40	33 3/8	5 3/8	5 2/8	19 2/8	14	15 1/8	5 2/8	20	17	Middle Ridge, NL	James C. Johnson	James C. Johnson	2007	1
325 3/8	336 2/8	37 4/8	38 6/8	30 6/8	6 5/8	6	14 2/8	14 3/8	11 5/8	11 1/8	17	15	Owl Pond, NL	Roger L. Leach	Roger L. Leach	2009	2
324 1/8	335 7/8	43 2/8	38 6/8	33	4 6/8	4 6/8	17	16 1/8	15 1/8	6 3/8	16	16	Andrew Pond, NL	Tom Gallenbach	Tom Gallenbach	2006	3
320 3/8	325	40 4/8	41 4/8	36 1/8	5 1/8	5 1/8	18	15 1/8	15	1/8	13	10	Gaff Topsail, NL	Michaelangelo P. Ripepi	Michaelangelo P. Ripepi	2007	4
317 7/8	333 5/8	39 7/8	37 2/8	32 2/8	6 2/8	5 7/8	15 1/8	15	14	4 4/8	17	13	Middle Ridge Pond, NL	John R. Thodos	John R. Thodos	1998	5
316 7/8	334 4/8	39 4/8	37 6/8	31 7/8	5 7/8	5	18 1/8	19 3/8	16	14 6/8	14	12	Gander River, NL	Rockey L. Hunt	Rockey L. Hunt	2006	6
315 4/8	324	37 6/8	36 5/8	30	5 2/8	5 2/8	15 1/8	17 2/8	6 7/8	14 6/8	15	17	Grey River, NL	Michael E. Manincor, Jr.	Michael E. Manincor, Jr.	2007	7
314 6/8	329 7/8	39 3/8	36 5/8	31	5 1/8	5 2/8	16	14 6/8	11 3/8	9 3/8	13	17	Owl Pond, NL	Richard W. Smith	Richard W. Smith	2008	8
314 4/8	330 4/8	41 4/8	38 6/8	41 4/8	5 2/8	5 7/8	16	15 6/8	9 2/8	11	12	15	Sam's Pond, NL	Bruce G. Ebbeson	Bruce G. Ebbeson	2007	9
307 7/8	326 3/8	41 3/8	38 7/8	33	4 7/8	5	17 2/8	17 3/8	5 2/8	12 4/8	14	13	Parson's Pond, NL	Everett M. Sharpe	Scott Sharpe	1979	10
307	315 4/8	36 2/8	34 6/8	22 2/8	5	5 1/8	16 7/8	18 7/8	8 7/8	8 5/8	12	14	Caribou Lake, NL	Steven S. Bruggeman	Steven S. Bruggeman	2007	11
304	317 5/8	36 1/8	39	32 2/8	4 6/8	5 1/8	17	19 5/8	11 6/8	11 3/8	14	14	Blue Pond, NL	Victor R. Cole	Victor R. Cole	2005	12
303 4/8	313 4/8	34 3/8	36 6/8	32 4/8	4 6/8	5 2/8	13 2/8	18 1/8	8 7/8	15 2/8	12	14	Dunn Hill Lake, NL	Brian D. Hicks	Brian D. Hicks	2006	13
303 3/8	320	37 6/8	43 3/8	26 4/8	5 4/8	5	16 5/8	17 1/8	8 7/8	14 5/8	16	18	Daniel's Harbour, NL	Danny L. Mellott	Danny L. Mellott	2006	14
297 7/8	307 6/8	39 4/8	38 7/8	35 5/8	5 6/8	6 2/8	16 6/8	7	15	1/8	11	11	Sunday Pond, NL	Charles D. Keri	Charles D. Keri	2007	15
296 3/8	306 1/8	33 5/8	33 1/8	27 5/8	5 4/8	6 1/8	14 5/8	12	11 5/8	7 4/8	13	14	Caribou Lake, NL	David J. Turchanski	David J. Turchanski	2008	16
286 2/8	293 4/8	35 2/8	35 2/8	20 2/8	4 4/8	4 4/8	15 3/8	18 6/8	10 5/8	16 6/8	12	18	Deer Lake, NL	Daniel Wyant, Jr.	Daniel Wyant, Jr.	2006	17
285 5/8	295 4/8	35 4/8	34 2/8	28 3/8	5 5/8	5 2/8	15 5/8	16 6/8	13 6/8	4 3/8	18	14	Deer Lake, NL	Larry L. Decker	Larry L. Decker	2008	18
284 5/8	292 6/8	39 7/8	40 6/8	36	4 5/8	4 6/8	12 4/8	12 6/8	5 6/8	8 3/8	10	10	Gander River, NL	John Lemondes	John Lemondes	2007	19
281 7/8	286 7/8	34 7/8	35 2/8	27 6/8	4 5/8	4 6/8	14 2/8	12	9 3/8	9 3/8	14	14	Dolland Pond, NL	Roy M. Goodwin	Roy M. Goodwin	2000	20
281 2/8	289 6/8	42 3/8	42 7/8	33 3/8	5 1/8	5 1/8	15	12 3/8	12 2/8	9 4/8	12	13	Deer Lake, NL	Paul J. Paquette	Paul J. Paquette	2007	20
280 6/8	292 6/8	32 6/8	34 7/8	30 6/8	4 3/8	4 4/8	13 4/8	14 5/8	5 7/8	10 6/8	11	13	Dolland Pond, NL	Roy M. Goodwin	Roy M. Goodwin	2006	22
275 6/8	281 5/8	37 1/8	37 6/8	22	5	4 6/8	14 4/8	14 7/8	11	1 7/8	13	10	Dolland Pond, NL	Roy M. Goodwin	Roy M. Goodwin	2005	23
272 7/8	287 3/8	36 5/8	36 5/8	32 2/8	4 5/8	4 5/8	12 1/8	13	6	10	12	15	St. Anthony, NL	Marion G. Macaluso	Marion G. Macaluso	2009	24
271 7/8	313 7/8	34 6/8	36 6/8	29 3/8	5 2/8	5 1/8	14 1/8	14 2/8	13 1/8	13	18	13	Cat Arm, NL	Thomas E. Clayton	Thomas E. Clayton	2006	25
271 2/8	279 1/8	35 2/8	36 5/8	28 1/8	5 4/8	5 6/8	11 7/8	3 4/8	8 5/8	1/8	10	13	Andrews Pond, NL	Joseph M. Aesif, Jr.	Joseph M. Aesif, Jr.	2008	26
270 3/8	284 1/8	30 7/8	34	23 6/8	4 2/8	4	13 2/8	9 7/8	11 1/8	6 3/8	19	16	Main River, NL	Dennis L. De Vore	Dennis L. De Vore	2007	27

265 4/8   285 2/8   34 2/8   40 6/8   28 4/8   4 7/8   5 1/8   15 6/8   16   4 3/8   11 1/8   12   11   Great Gull Lake, NL   Mark A. Wayne   John D. Todd   2008

330 *   337 6/8   44 5/8   40   5 2/8   5 3/8   16 6/8   18 1/8   2 1/8   15   11   16   Gull Lake, NL   Mark A. Wayne   John D. Todd   2008   28

Final score subject to revision by additional verifying measurements.

WOODLAND CARIBOU
FINAL SCORE: 303 3/8
HUNTER: Danny L. Mellott

WOODLAND CARIBOU
FINAL SCORE: 296 3/8
HUNTER: David J. Turchanski

WOODLAND CARIBOU
FINAL SCORE: 272 7/8
HUNTER: Marion G. Macaluso

WOODLAND CARIBOU
FINAL SCORE: 271 2/8
HUNTER: Joseph M. Aesif, Jr.

BARREN GROUND CARIBOU

Rangifer tarandus granti

Minimum Score 375   World's Record 477

The barren ground caribou category includes trophies from Alaska and northern Yukon Territory.

Final Score	Gross Score	Length of Main Beam R.	L.	Inside Spread	Circumference at Smallest Place Between Brow and Bez Points R.	L.	Length of Brow Points R.	L.	Width of Brow Points R.	L.	Number of Points R.	L.	Locality	Hunter	Owner	Date Killed	Rank
436 4/8	449 7/8	48 1/8	48 5/8	38 1/8	5 5/8	5 3/8	20 3/8	22 1/8	14 2/8	7 7/8	23	22	Alaska	Unknown	Curtis P. Smiley	1970	1
419 4/8	432 5/8	54	56 3/8	49 3/8	5 6/8	5 7/8	20 3/8	20 7/8	1 7/8	16 2/8	17	19	Seward Pen., AK	Jack L. Wilson	Jack L. Wilson	2008	2
417 5/8	428 2/8	47 5/8	49 5/8	35 5/8	5	5 1/8	18	22 1/8	11 5/8	9 2/8	20	20	King Salmon River, AK	Joseph C. Bitzan	Joseph C. Bitzan	1978	3
393	403 2/8	55	51 4/8	42 2/8	6 2/8	6 6/8	18	3 2/8	11 5/8	1/8	14	13	Delta River, AK	Keith A. Fredrickson	Keith A. Fredrickson	2007	4
392 2/8	405	44 2/8	46 4/8	33 7/8	6 5/8	5 6/8	15 6/8	16 4/8	9	11 3/8	18	19	Salcha River, AK	Chance W. Ott	Chance W. Ott	2009	5
391 2/8	408 4/8	56 6/8	56 5/8	33 3/8	6 3/8	7 1/8	20 6/8	2 6/8	17 2/8	1/8	20	15	Blackstone River, YT	Rich B. Queen	Rich B. Queen	2008	6
391 2/8	411 2/8	50 3/8	50 3/8	32 1/8	6 1/8	7 4/8	14	18 1/8	11 1/8	1/8	19	18	Salcha River, AK	Craig A. Meyer	Craig A. Meyer	2009	6
387 7/8	405 4/8	53 7/8	50 5/8	46	4 6/8	7 2/8	19 1/8	13 7/8	15 4/8	1/8	17	11	Ogilvie Mts., YT	Allan D. Koprowsky	Allan D. Koprowsky	2008	8
387 4/8	400 1/8	49 6/8	48 1/8	34 7/8	7	6 4/8	17 1/8	15 5/8	5	9 3/8	16	18	Adak Island, AK	Jon A. Shiesl	Jon A. Shiesl	2006	9
386 7/8	397 6/8	48 2/8	49 3/8	31 1/8	5 6/8	6 4/8	13 4/8	17	13	14 2/8	26	28	Singauruk Point, AK	Casey J. Kombol	Casey J. Kombol	2006	10
384 5/8	396 7/8	46 4/8	47	41 4/8	5 5/8	5 7/8	13 3/8	18 4/8	10 5/8	11 3/8	21	25	Shotgun Hills, AK	David O. Anaman	David O. Anaman	1995	11
384 5/8	391 2/8	52 3/8	52 1/8	30 4/8	5 4/8	5 5/8	19	20 4/8	9 3/8	16 6/8	18	24	Noatak River, AK	Stephen C. Sykora	Stephen C. Sykora	2007	11
384 3/8	402 1/8	44 7/8	48 7/8	38 1/8	7 1/8	7 2/8	17 4/8	3	14 3/8	1/8	21	21	Tay River, YT	William N. Beach	Shelburne Museum	1921	13
383 3/8	391 3/8	51 6/8	50 7/8	35 3/8	5 7/8	5 7/8	21 5/8	14 6/8	3 7/8	13	16	12	Firth River, AK	Nicholas R. Martin	Nicholas R. Martin	2009	14
382 6/8	393 1/8	48 6/8	47 1/8	42 3/8	4 4/8	4 6/8	17 5/8	15	10 1/8	6 5/8	19	19	Coleen River, AK	C. Richard Ferdig	C. Richard Ferdig	2001	15
380 3/8	390 2/8	45 1/8	46 2/8	34	5 5/8	5 4/8	19	18 1/8	10 2/8	15 6/8	17	19	Tok, AK	Howard M. Hursh	Howard M. Hursh	2008	16
379 6/8	398 4/8	58	53 6/8	43	5 7/8	6	17	19	17	10 6/8	20	19	Adak Island, AK	Jeffrey L. Matney	Jeffrey L. Matney	2005	17
378	390 3/8	49	49 5/8	29 7/8	5 6/8	5 7/8	14 4/8	12 5/8	12	7	20	15	White Mts., AK	James M. Peek	James M. Peek	2007	18
375 3/8	384 5/8	44 3/8	43 5/8	40 5/8	6	5 7/8	15	7 1/8	9 2/8	1/8	18	14	Alaska	Harry H. Webb	Samuel B. Webb, Jr.	PR 1960	19
426 5/8*	432	48 5/8	48 5/8	41 5/8	6	5 7/8	17 3/8	17 1/8	13 6/8	13 6/8	21	19	Seventy Mile River, AK	Richard J. Grossman	Richard J. Grossman	2007	
415 3/8*	423 4/8	51 5/8	53 5/8	37 7/8	5 6/8	5 6/8	17 4/8	18 4/8	9 4/8	11 6/8	21	21	Adak Island, AK	Corey J. Calderwood	Corey J. Calderwood	2006	
409 3/8*	431 2/8	53 3/8	50 5/8	40 1/8	6 2/8	6 1/8	20 2/8	5 3/8	15 6/8	1/8	23	15	Nelchina, AK	Robert G. Fuller	Robert G. Fuller	1988	

Final score subject to revision by additional verifying measurements.

CENTRAL CANADA BARREN GROUND CARIBOU

Rangifer tarandus groenlandicus

Minimum Score 345 — World's Record 433 4/8

Central Canada barren ground caribou occur on Baffin Island and the mainland of Northwest Territories, with geographic boundaries of the Mackenzie River to the west; the north edge of the continent to the north (excluding any islands except Baffin Island); Hudson Bay to the east; and the southern boundary of Northwest Territories to the south. The boundary also includes the northwest corner of Manitoba north of the south limit of township 87 and west of the Little Churchill River, Churchill River, and Hudson Bay.

Final Score	Gross Score	Length of Main Beam R.	L.	Inside Spread	Circumference at Smallest Place Between Brow and Bez Points R.	L.	Length of Brow Points R.	L.	Width of Brow Points R.	L.	Number of Points R.	L.	Locality	Hunter	Owner	Date Killed	Rank
396 4/8	405 2/8	54 3/8	55 2/8	41 2/8	5 1/8	5	21 4/8	19 2/8	17 3/8	11 1/8	18	12	Thonokied Lake, NT	Nyla K. Swast	Nyla K. Swast	2006	1
394 1/8	401 5/8	49 6/8	49 7/8	40 5/8	5 7/8	5 4/8	14 3/8	16 4/8	8 7/8	11	18	19	MacKay Lake, NT	Doran J. Lambson	Doran J. Lambson	2007	2
392	403 5/8	51 2/8	51 5/8	39 2/8	5	5	14 6/8	14 7/8	10 5/8	13	20	17	Courageous Lake, NT	Loren B. Mickelson	Loren B. Mickelson	2007	3
389 2/8	403 4/8	50 2/8	50 4/8	26 1/8	5 3/8	4 7/8	18 2/8	15 7/8	15 5/8	9 7/8	20	16	Point Lake, NT	Steven R. Marr	Steven R. Marr	2006	4
386 2/8	400 6/8	47 7/8	49	27 1/8	5	4 7/8	12	21 2/8	1/8	18	15	27	Point Lake, NT	Jerry Kottschade	Jerry Kottschade	1999	5
384 1/8	391 7/8	49 4/8	49	38 5/8	5 2/8	5	15 6/8	15 2/8	11 6/8	12 2/8	18	17	Glover Lake, MB	Robert Pankiewicz	Robert Pankiewicz	2007	6
383 6/8	391 5/8	53 5/8	54 4/8	39 2/8	5 3/8	5 2/8	18	20 2/8	8 1/8	14 1/8	21	19	Lake Providence, NT	Troy Faryna	Troy Faryna	2008	7

CENTRAL CANADA BARREN GROUND CARIBOU
FINAL SCORE: 377 1/8
HUNTER: Beau Parisi

CENTRAL CANADA BARREN GROUND CARIBOU
FINAL SCORE: 384 1/8
HUNTER: Robert Pankiewicz

CENTRAL CANADA BARREN GROUND CARIBOU
FINAL SCORE: 347 1/8
HUNTER: Chad Fuchs

BARREN GROUND CARIBOU
FINAL SCORE: 380 3/8
HUNTER: Howard M. Hursh

CENTRAL CANADA BARREN GROUND CARIBOU

Rangifer tarandus groenlandicus

Final Score	Gross Score	Length of Main Beam R.	L.	Inside Spread	Circumference at Smallest Place Between Brow and Bez Points R.	L.	Length of Brow Points R.	L.	Width of Brow Points R.	L.	Number of Points R.	L.	Locality	Hunter	Owner	Date Killed	Rank
381 2/8	389 2/8	46 4/8	46 3/8	25 5/8	4 6/8	5 6/8	18	17 6/8	9	15 5/8	21	22	Point Lake, NT	Dallas S. Muise	Dallas S. Muise	2009	8
380	388 1/8	54 2/8	53 2/8	30	5	5 1/8	19	19 3/8	6 1/8	15 2/8	12	16	Humpy Lake, NT	Jim Fuchs	Jim Fuchs	2006	9
378 3/8	389 7/8	45 7/8	49 1/8	31 6/8	5 5/8	5 6/8	11 2/8	14 7/8	2	11 2/8	18	20	Courageous Lake, NT	Mark Jergens	Mark Jergens	2006	10
377 1/8	383 6/8	45 1/8	45 6/8	32 3/8	5 4/8	5 5/8	16 6/8	1 4/8	13 7/8	1/8	20	14	Lac de Gras, NT	Beau Parisi	Beau Parisi	2008	11
375 7/8	388	56 4/8	57 3/8	36 6/8	5 3/8	5 3/8	20	18 4/8	4 4/8	14 5/8	17	17	Courageous Lake, NT	Timothy J. Weaver	Timothy J. Weaver	2006	12
374 2/8	386	44	42 4/8	26 5/8	6	6	16	17 7/8	10 1/8	14 1/8	19	17	Rendez-vous Lake, NT	Larry Johnson	Larry Johnson	2003	13
372 1/8	383 3/8	48 3/8	47 3/8	29 3/8	5 3/8	5 1/8	16 6/8	15 3/8	13 4/8	4 1/8	25	22	Point Lake, NT	Christopher J. Parfett	Christopher J. Parfett	2009	14
368 7/8	374 5/8	53 5/8	53 1/8	43 4/8	5	5	16 6/8	19 2/8	10 6/8	8 1/8	11	15	Yellowknife, NT	James E. Rolfe	James E. Rolfe	2008	15
368 1/8	381	48 5/8	48 3/8	23 7/8	4 2/8	4 2/8	19 1/8	18 5/8	14 3/8	14 1/8	19	22	Tadoule Lake, MB	Donald E. Byers	Donald E. Byers	2007	16
366	376 6/8	49 3/8	51	29 3/8	6 2/8	5 4/8	4 7/8	20 3/8	1/8	14 2/8	16	19	Courageous Lake, NT	Sandra F. Eike	Sandra F. Eike	2007	17
365 4/8	373 4/8	49	49 3/8	33 4/8	5 1/8	4 7/8	14 3/8	14 6/8	11	1/8	16	15	Humpy Lake, NT	Steve Hough	Steve Hough	2007	18
364 4/8	377 4/8	42	44 1/8	28 5/8	4 6/8	4 7/8	14 6/8	12 7/8	12 4/8	6 4/8	18	19	Courageous Lake, NT	Remo R. Pizzagalli	Remo R. Pizzagalli	2006	19
362 4/8	376 1/8	52 3/8	54 2/8	35 2/8	5 4/8	5	19 7/8	6 4/8	16 6/8	1/8	19	11	Bullock Lake, MB	Alexander R. Winram	Alexander R. Winram	2008	20
361 7/8	369 2/8	51	51 5/8	34 7/8	4 6/8	4 5/8	17 2/8	9	17 5/8	1/8	20	14	Thonokied Lake, NT	Susan B. Smith	Susan B. Smith	2006	21
357 7/8	366 3/8	52 1/8	52 7/8	24 7/8	5 2/8	5 2/8	10	15	1/8	10 7/8	20	20	Blevins Lake, MB	Darryl J. Vehige	Darryl J. Vehige	2007	22
355 2/8	373 4/8	52 6/8	52 7/8	31 3/8	4 7/8	5	16 7/8	17 3/8	11	14 1/8	17	19	Schmok Lake, MB	Mark J. White	Mark J. White	2008	23
351	356 4/8	52 5/8	53 3/8	35 5/8	4 6/8	4 6/8	8 4/8	14 1/8	4 1/8	9 1/8	15	14	Humpy Lake, NT	Timothy K. Rushing	Timothy K. Rushing	1999	24
349 5/8	358 4/8	50 7/8	48 5/8	33 5/8	4 6/8	5	18 2/8	—	13 4/8	8 5/8	18	9	Humpy Lake, NT	Brian Happ	Brian Happ	2006	25
349 2/8	371	48 6/8	47 2/8	26	6 2/8	5 6/8	14 1/8	14 3/8	7 7/8	9 6/8	16	22	Noname Lake, MB	Phil Orf	Phil Orf	2007	26
349 1/8	358 3/8	47 2/8	47	33	4 5/8	4 3/8	13 2/8	15	8 1/8	1/8	18	21	Blevins Lake, MB	Darryl J. Vehige	Darryl J. Vehige	2007	27
347 6/8	359 5/8	43 7/8	43 7/8	28 6/8	6 1/8	5 3/8	16	13	13 1/8	1/8	21	16	Courageous Lake, NT	Robert C. Twohy	Robert C. Twohy	2006	28
347 1/8	359 4/8	39 2/8	51 6/8	34 2/8	4 3/8	4 5/8	19 5/8	4 1/8	17	1/8	16	14	Humpy Lake, NT	Chad Fuchs	Chad Fuchs	2006	29
346 4/8	358 6/8	51	47 6/8	29 6/8	5 2/8	5	17 7/8	17	16 4/8	3 1/8	19	17	Point Lake, NT	Justin M. Vavra	Justin M. Vavra	2006	30
386 6/8*	398 1/8	52	50 6/8	38 3/8	5 1/8	5 5/8	23 3/8	21 4/8	17 3/8	2 1/8	16	14	MacKay Lake, NT	Michael E. Jeffries	Michael E. Jeffries	2006	

* Final score subject to revision by additional verifying measurements.

QUEBEC-LABRADOR CARIBOU

Rangifer tarandus

World's Record 474 6/8

Minimum Score 365

The Quebec-Labrador caribou category includes trophies from Quebec and Labrador.

Final Score	Gross Score	Length of Main Beam		Inside Spread	Circumference at Smallest Place Between Brow and Bez Points		Length of Brow Points		Width of Brow Points		Number of Points		Locality	Hunter	Owner	Date Killed	Rank
		R.	L.		R.	L.	R.	L.	R.	L.	R.	L.					
423 6/8	435 4/8	47	49 2/8	35	6 2/8	6 3/8	18 5/8	15 5/8	14 1/8	10 7/8	23	23	Riviére Du Gué, QC	Bret J. Wood	Bret J. Wood	2006	1
422 3/8	435 6/8	51 6/8	51 6/8	37 4/8	5	5	22	21 5/8	15 7/8	18 3/8	19	21	Lac Ribero, QC	Donald M. Vickers	Donald M. Vickers	2006	2
411 7/8	425 2/8	51 2/8	49 6/8	39	5 2/8	5 3/8	21 3/8	17 4/8	15 6/8	5 2/8	19	19	Lac Roz, QC	Aaron Kelly	Aaron Kelly	2006	3
407 3/8	419	50 3/8	50 5/8	51 6/8	5	5	20 4/8	17 2/8	14 4/8	6	23	14	Tudor Lake, QC	Michel M. Degenais	Michel M. Degenais	1980	4
407 3/8	422 7/8	51 3/8	50 6/8	40 4/8	4 5/8	4 7/8	19 4/8	16 5/8	13 7/8	2 5/8	17	22	Caniapiscau River, QC	Frederick B. Davis	Frederick B. Davis	2005	4
406 1/8	421 4/8	44 6/8	43 3/8	40 2/8	5 6/8	6 2/8	21 7/8	19 7/8	13 3/8	19	25	23	Lac Grand Rosoy, QC	Wayne Clem	Wayne Clem	2006	6
400 6/8	410 7/8	54 5/8	52 5/8	54 6/8	5	5	21 6/8	7 7/8	15 7/8	1/8	21	17	Nastapoka River, QC	John M. Daly	John M. Daly	2006	7
399	412 2/8	51 4/8	49 1/8	53	5 6/8	5 7/8	20 4/8	15 4/8	15 7/8	5 3/8	15	19	Andrea Lake, NL	Daniel R. Green	Daniel R. Green	2008	8

QUEBEC-LABRADOR CARIBOU
FINAL SCORE: 394 7/8
HUNTER: Todd D. Hansen

QUEBEC-LABRADOR CARIBOU
FINAL SCORE: 382 7/8
HUNTER: Matthew T. Mostad

QUEBEC-LABRADOR CARIBOU
FINAL SCORE: 398 4/8
HUNTER: William Gangel

QUEBEC-LABRADOR CARIBOU
FINAL SCORE: 389 1/8
HUNTER: Dean Dolenc

QUEBEC-LABRADOR CARIBOU

Rangifer tarandus

Final Score	Gross Score	Length of Main Beam R.	Length of Main Beam L.	Inside Spread	Circ. at Smallest Place Between Brow and Bez Points R.	Circ. L.	Length of Brow Points R.	Length of Brow Points L.	Width of Brow Points R.	Width of Brow Points L.	No. of Points R.	No. of Points L.	Locality	Hunter	Owner	Date Killed	Rank
398 4/8*	406 5/8	61 2/8	62 5/8	37 1/8	5 1/8	5	19	13 4/8	11 7/8	3	23	14	Caniapiscau River, QC	William Gangel	William Gangel	2006	9
396 5/8	416 5/8	51 5/8	46	32 4/8	6 7/8	4 7/8	18 5/8	20 3/8	11 7/8	10 2/8	16	15	Chateauguay River, QC	Mic E. Hampton	Mic E. Hampton	2005	10
394 7/8	410 1/8	44 5/8	44 7/8	35 5/8	6	5 7/8	18 1/8	11 3/8	15	6 6/8	22	19	Lac Réal, QC	Todd D. Hansen	Todd D. Hansen	2007	11
389 1/8	397 3/8	45	46 2/8	39 6/8	5 7/8	6 6/8	15 6/8	14 4/8	6 3/8	10	21	24	Leaf River, QC	Dean Dolenc	Dean Dolenc	2007	12
388 2/8	403	56 3/8	55 4/8	40 6/8	5	5	14	12 3/8	6 6/8	2 1/8	15	14	Ungava Bay, QC	Leighton A. Wildrick	Leighton A. Wildrick	1991	13
386 6/8	399 3/8	46 2/8	48 5/8	41 3/8	5 2/8	5 5/8	20 1/8	17 4/8	6 6/8	15 6/8	19	26	Messin Lake, QC	Frank A. Wagenhoffer	Frank A. Wagenhoffer	2005	14
386 2/8	395 2/8	54 7/8	52 7/8	39 7/8	6	5 3/8	19 1/8	19 3/8	11 3/8	16 6/8	23	21	Nastapoka River, QC	Bronko A. Terkovich	Bronko A. Terkovich	2006	15
382 7/8	397 1/8	51 1/8	49 1/8	44 1/8	5 1/8	4 7/8	13 5/8	18 5/8	7 2/8	14 4/8	21	19	Larch River, QC	Matthew T. Mostad	Matthew T. Mostad	2006	16
380 6/8	386 2/8	49 4/8	49 6/8	44 4/8	4 7/8	4 6/8	17 2/8	17 5/8	14 5/8	15	17	15	Andrea Lake, NL	Daniel R. Green	Daniel R. Green	2008	17
380 2/8	387 3/8	54 7/8	54 7/8	47 7/8	5 6/8	6	18	—	11 7/8	1/8	17	13	Lac Chaulieu, QC	Toney R. Sheppard	Toney R. Sheppard	2006	18
378 1/8	390 7/8	47 1/8	47 4/8	43	5 6/8	4 7/8	15 6/8	3 3/8	10 3/8	1/8	25	20	Minto Lake, QC	Tad E. Crawford	Tad E. Crawford	2005	19
377 4/8	394 5/8	48 2/8	47 1/8	39	4 7/8	4 7/8	18 2/8	16 3/8	11 4/8	9 1/8	18	17	Larch River, QC	Derek L. Pickett	Derek L. Pickett	2006	20
377 1/8	395 5/8	46 5/8	44 1/8	35 7/8	5 7/8	6 1/8	17	15	9 7/8	7 3/8	17	17	Petite Baleine River, QC	Paul Allard	Paul Allard	1997	21
370 7/8	382 6/8	51 4/8	52 4/8	35 4/8	5 5/8	5 2/8	16 1/8	2 7/8	14	1/8	25	25	George River, QC	Wayne La Douceur	Wayne La Douceur	2007	22
370 6/8	376 4/8	45 6/8	46 4/8	43	4 6/8	4 7/8	17 4/8	14 6/8	15	9 4/8	15	16	Lac Chateauguay, QC	Gerry L. Cowell	Gerry L. Cowell	2003	23
370	376 7/8	50 2/8	49 6/8	38 4/8	5 5/8	5 1/8	16 4/8	4 1/8	11 2/8	1/8	20	18	Mistinibi Lake, QC	William H. Daly	William H. Daly	2008	24
368 5/8	380 2/8	46 3/8	48 3/8	43 7/8	4 6/8	4 6/8	10 1/8	—	4 7/8	—	15	14	Lacs des Loups Marins, QC	John D. Bernath	John D. Bernath	1995	25
366 7/8	377 4/8	52	52 4/8	52 1/8	4 5/8	4 7/8	17 1/8	3	12 6/8	1/8	21	16	George River, QC	Roy M. Goodwin	Roy M. Goodwin	1989	26
366 1/8	381	55 1/8	58 6/8	42 4/8	5 1/8	4 7/8	16 6/8	18	7 5/8	10 4/8	15	18	Leaf River, QC	Ethan L. Annis	Ethan L. Annis	2006	27
414 3/8*	424	53 2/8	53 5/8	57 1/8	5 2/8	5 1/8	13 1/8	16 4/8	1	12 5/8	16	20	Lac Cambrien, QC	Eric Caouette	Eric Caouette	2005	

* Final score subject to revision by additional verifying measurements.

PRONGHORN

Antilocapra americana americana and related subspecies

Minimum Score 80   World's Record 95

Final Score	Gross Score	Length of horn R.	L.	Circumference of Base R.	L.	Circumference at Third Quarter R.	L.	Inside Spread	Tip to Tip Spread	Length of Prong R.	L.	Locality	Hunter	Owner	Date Killed	Rank
91 4/8	92 3/8	17 2/8	17 2/8	7 4/8	7 3/8	2 6/8	2 7/8	8	2 1/8	6 5/8	6 4/8	Harding Co., NM	Larry J. Landes	Larry J. Landes	2006	1
91 2/8	93 2/8	14 2/8	14 5/8	7 4/8	7 5/8	3 4/8	3 4/8	8 7/8	7 5/8	7 2/8	6 4/8	Natrona Co., WY	Michael J. Wheeler	Michael J. Wheeler	2008	2
90	90 4/8	16 1/8	16 4/8	7 2/8	7 2/8	2 3/8	2 3/8	12 6/8	7 2/8	8	7 7/8	Perkins Co., SD	Brian D. Simonson	Cabela's, Inc.	2006	3
90	90 6/8	17 1/8	17 2/8	6 6/8	6 7/8	3 2/8	3 2/8	11 6/8	9 2/8	6 1/8	6 4/8	Mora Co., NM	Dillon K. Baloun	Dillon K. Baloun	2007	3
89 6/8	90 6/8	16 6/8	16 6/8	7 5/8	7 5/8	2 6/8	2 4/8	13	9 5/8	6 2/8	6 6/8	Natrona Co., WY	John Hinricks	John Hinricks	2006	5
89 4/8	90	15 5/8	15 6/8	7 3/8	7 4/8	3 5/8	3 5/8	11 4/8	9 2/8	6 3/8	6 1/8	Yavapai Co., AZ	Kristin M. Currie	Kristin M. Currie	2005	6
89 4/8	93	16	16 6/8	7 1/8	7 2/8	3	2 6/8	9 6/8	6 4/8	7 3/8	7 5/8	Meade Co., SD	Mickey L. Ihnen	Mickey L. Ihnen	2007	6
89 4/8	90 1/8	18 1/8	18 2/8	6 5/8	6 4/8	3 1/8	3 1/8	10 6/8	6 4/8	5 4/8	5 6/8	Cibola Co., NM	James A. Bibler	James A. Bibler	2008	6
89 2/8	90	16 7/8	17	6 5/8	6 5/8	3	3 1/8	10 2/8	6 3/8	6 3/8	6 4/8	Lincoln Co., NM	Sherwin N. Scott	Sherwin N. Scott	2006	9
89	90 4/8	17 4/8	17	7 1/8	7 2/8	3 1/8	3	11	4 2/8	5	5 4/8	San Miguel Co., NM	Joel S. Kirkpatrick	Joel S. Kirkpatrick	2007	10
88 4/8	91 1/8	18	17 3/8	7 6/8	7 2/8	3 1/8	3	11 1/8	6 2/8	6	5 1/8	Fremont Co., WY	Patricia S. Brooks	Patricia S. Brooks	2007	11
88 4/8	89 7/8	15	15 3/8	7 2/8	7 1/8	3 3/8	3 5/8	8 3/8	6 2/8	6 4/8	6 7/8	Humboldt Co., NV	Maria A. Gaspari-Crawford	Maria A. Gaspari-Crawford	2007	11
88 4/8	89 1/8	17 1/8	17	7 1/8	6 7/8	2 7/8	2 6/8	10 3/8	4 4/8	6 5/8	6 6/8	Malheur Co., OR	Kenneth C. Barrows	Kenneth C. Barrows	2009	11
88 2/8	88 6/8	17	17	7 4/8	7 2/8	2 7/8	2 7/8	11 5/8	7 2/8	5 3/8	5 3/8	Morrill Co., NE	Daryl L. Scherbarth	Daryl L. Scherbarth	2008	14
88 2/8	88 7/8	15 5/8	15 7/8	6 3/8	6 3/8	3 3/8	3 2/8	9 5/8	7 7/8	7 2/8	7 1/8	Socorro Co., NM	Bronko A. Terkovich	Bronko A. Terkovich	2008	14
88	89 4/8	18 4/8	17 7/8	7 1/8	7	2 6/8	2 4/8	7 3/8	6	5 5/8	5 5/8	Catron Co., NM	Cade Salopek	Cade Salopek	2006	16
88	88 4/8	16 2/8	16 3/8	6 7/8	7	3 4/8	3 5/8	10	4 4/8	5 3/8	5 3/8	Coconino Co., AZ	Dillon C. Currie	Dillon C. Currie	2007	16
88	89 2/8	16 3/8	16 6/8	6 6/8	6 6/8	3	3 4/8	10 2/8	7 1/8	6 2/8	6	Lincoln Co., NM	Jerry L. Hamilton	Jerry L. Hamilton	2007	16
88	89	16 5/8	17	6 5/8	6 5/8	3 1/8	3 2/8	14 2/8	11 4/8	5 4/8	5 2/8	Hudspeth Co., TX	Danny R. Schultz	Danny R. Schultz	2009	16
87 6/8	88 5/8	17	17 2/8	7	6 7/8	3	3	12 4/8	10 1/8	6	5 7/8	Fremont Co., WY	Patricia S. Brooks	Patricia S. Brooks	2008	20
87 6/8	88 5/8	17	16 4/8	7 2/8	7 2/8	2 5/8	3	11 3/8	7 7/8	6 5/8	6 4/8	Carter Co., MT	Patrick R. Hansen	Patrick R. Hansen	2008	20
87 4/8	88 5/8	17 3/8	17 4/8	6 6/8	6 4/8	3 4/8	3 5/8	7 6/8	3	5 4/8	5	Lincoln Co., NM	Foster V. Yancey, Jr.	Foster V. Yancey, Jr.	2006	22
87 2/8	87 5/8	16 3/8	16 3/8	6 6/8	6 5/8	2 6/8	3	11 7/8	8 1/8	6	6	Socorro Co., NM	Joe R. Anderson	Joe R. Anderson	2006	23
87 2/8	87 5/8	16 1/8	16 2/8	7	6 7/8	3	3	8 5/8	5	6 4/8	6	Lincoln Co., NM	Len H. Guldman	Len H. Guldman	2006	23
87 2/8	88 6/8	16 5/8	16 2/8	6 5/8	6 5/8	2 7/8	2 6/8	10 6/8	8 4/8	6 3/8	6 4/8	Fremont Co., WY	Flint B. Smith	Flint B. Smith	2007	23
87 2/8	88 7/8	16 6/8	16 7/8	7 2/8	7 1/8	3 5/8	3 6/8	11	9 4/8	5 4/8	5 2/8	Lincoln Co., NM	Paul E. Wollenman	Paul E. Wollenman	2007	23
87 2/8	88 2/8	16 5/8	16 6/8	6 2/8	6 1/8	3 5/8	3 4/8	10 2/8	8 1/8	6	6 2/8	Hudspeth Co., TX	Robert M. Anderson	Robert M. Anderson	2008	23
87	87 3/8	17 7/8	18	6 3/8	6 2/8	2 4/8	2 5/8	12 6/8	7 1/8	6 4/8	6 4/8	Lake Co., OR	Donald F. Geer	Donald F. Geer	2006	28
87	87 7/8	16 6/8	16 4/8	6 5/8	6 3/8	2 5/8	2 4/8	10 3/8	3 6/8	6 3/8	6 6/8	Washoe Co., NV	Anita M. Ihrig	Anita M. Ihrig	2007	28
87	87 5/8	18	17 7/8	5 7/8	5 7/8	2 7/8	2 7/8	13 3/8	11 2/8	5 7/8	6	Coconino Co., AZ	Tim R. Tate	Tim R. Tate	2007	28
87	88 6/8	16 6/8	16 4/8	7	7	2 5/8	2 4/8	10 4/8	5	6 5/8	5 4/8	Humboldt Co., NV	Norman G. Beach, Jr.	Norman G. Beach, Jr.	2008	28
87	87 6/8	16 3/8	17	6 6/8	6 6/8	3	3	13	11	5 3/8	5 3/8	Humboldt Co., NV	Herman J. Menezes	Herman J. Menezes	2008	28

Antilocapra americana americana and related subspecies

Final Score	Gross Score	Length of horn R.	L.	Circumference of Base R.	L.	Circumference at Third Quarter R.	L.	Inside Spread	Tip to Tip Spread	Length of Prong R.	L.	Locality	Hunter	Owner	Date Killed	Rank
87	88	15 2/8	15 5/8	7 2/8	7 2/8	3 4/8	3 4/8	12	10 2/8	5 4/8	5 6/8	Yavapai Co., AZ	Scott R. Muzzy	Scott R. Muzzy	2009	28
86 6/8	87 3/8	17 6/8	17 5/8	6 6/8	6 5/8	3 1/8	3 1/8	8 7/8	1 3/8	5 5/8	5 4/8	Mora Co., NM	Grant A. Medlin	Grant A. Medlin	2006	34
86 6/8	87 3/8	16	15 7/8	7	7	2 7/8	2 6/8	10 7/8	6 4/8	6 3/8	6 2/8	Bennett Co., SD	Jon D. Gregg	Jon D. Gregg	2007	34
86 6/8	87 7/8	16 5/8	17	6 3/8	6 4/8	3	3	13	9 4/8	6 3/8	6 5/8	Socorro Co., NM	Stephen C. LeBlanc	Stephen C. LeBlanc	2008	34
86 6/8	87 4/8	16 4/8	16 6/8	6 3/8	6 4/8	3	3 1/8	11 6/8	9 4/8	6 2/8	6 1/8	Catron Co., NM	Ivy A. Hansen	Ivy A. Hansen	2009	34
86 4/8	88 1/8	18	17 6/8	6 4/8	6 5/8	3 3/8	3 4/8	6 4/8	2 5/8	5 2/8	4 4/8	Moffat Co., CO	Gary J. Morrow	Gary J. Morrow	2006	38
86 4/8	88 1/8	17 4/8	17 7/8	7 1/8	7	3 1/8	3	7	3 3/8	4 5/8	5 1/8	Sweetwater Co., WY	Levi J. Pope	Levi J. Pope	2007	38
86 4/8	87 5/8	17 4/8	17	6 7/8	6 6/8	2 3/8	2 3/8	12	7 2/8	7	6 6/8	Guadalupe Co., NM	Sean P. Hill	Sean P. Hill	2008	38
86 2/8	86 6/8	16 5/8	16 5/8	6 5/8	6 5/8	3 1/8	3 1/8	12 4/8	8 4/8	6 2/8	6 2/8	Torrance Co., NM	Jeffrey S. Emerling	Jeffrey S. Emerling	2006	41
86 2/8	88 2/8	17 1/8	17 4/8	6 3/8	6 2/8	3 1/8	3 2/8	12	7 6/8	6	5 1/8	Lincoln Co., NM	David R. Hewlett	David R. Hewlett	2007	41
86 2/8	86 7/8	15	15 2/8	6 6/8	6 6/8	3 2/8	3 2/8	9 3/8	5	6 1/8	6	Sweetwater Co., WY	Shawn M. Plemel	Shawn M. Plemel	2008	41
86 2/8	87 1/8	16 7/8	17 2/8	6 3/8	6 3/8	3 4/8	3 4/8	10 2/8	10 2/8	4 6/8	4 7/8	Hudspeth Co., TX	Robert M. Anderson	Robert M. Anderson	2009	41
86 2/8	88 6/8	18 6/8	18 7/8	6 7/8	6 4/8	3	3	10 3/8	5 2/8	4	5 2/8	Coconino Co., AZ	Cody L. Defer	Cody L. Defer	2009	41
86	87	16	16 2/8	6 5/8	6 4/8	3 6/8	3 5/8	7 4/8	3	5 4/8	6	Coconino Co., AZ	Richard L. Currie	Richard L. Currie	2004	46
86	86 3/8	15 2/8	15 2/8	7 3/8	7 2/8	3	3	10 7/8	7 4/8	5 5/8	5 4/8	Fremont Co., WY	Phillip S. Craft	Phillip S. Craft	2005	46
86	86 6/8	16 1/8	16 1/8	6 5/8	6 4/8	3 1/8	3 1/8	7 6/8	4	5 7/8	6 1/8	Moffat Co., CO	Len H. Guldman	Len H. Guldman	2006	46
86	86 5/8	16	15 6/8	7 2/8	7 2/8	3	3	11 3/8	7 1/8	5 6/8	5 5/8	Carbon Co., WY	Terry A. Mason	Terry A. Mason	2006	46
86	86 5/8	16 2/8	16	7 3/8	7 4/8	3 1/8	2 7/8	10 1/8	5 5/8	5	4 7/8	Natrona Co., WY	Eric W. McDonald	Eric W. McDonald	2006	46
86	86 6/8	16 1/8	16 2/8	7	7 1/8	2 7/8	2 7/8	15 3/8	11 6/8	5 7/8	6	Elko Co., NV	Israel I. Fimbres	Israel I. Fimbres	2007	46
86	87	15 6/8	15 5/8	6 4/8	6 2/8	3 5/8	3 5/8	12 6/8	9 2/8	6 1/8	5 5/8	Yavapai Co., AZ	Shaun D. Friesen	Shaun D. Friesen	2007	46
86	86 7/8	15 5/8	15 5/8	7 1/8	7 1/8	2 5/8	2 5/8	8 6/8	4 6/8	6 4/8	6 1/8	Carbon Co., WY	Ronald J. Hale	Ronald J. Hale	2007	46
86	87 3/8	15 4/8	15	7 5/8	7 2/8	3	3	8 1/8	6 4/8	6 3/8	6 3/8	Natrona Co., WY	Hunter L. Scott	Hunter L. Scott	2007	46
86	87	17 7/8	17 6/8	6 2/8	6 1/8	3	3	7 2/8	2 6/8	5 5/8	5 4/8	Yavapai Co., AZ	Walter Statler	Walter Statler	2007	46
86	87 3/8	15 7/8	15 5/8	8 1/8	8 2/8	2 6/8	2 4/8	8 6/8	4 4/8	6	6 4/8	Sweetwater Co., WY	Charles K. Williams	Charles K. Williams	2007	46
86	86 3/8	16 2/8	16 4/8	6 1/8	6 1/8	3 3/8	3 3/8	15	9 7/8	6 6/8	6 7/8	Hudspeth Co., TX	Tamara K. Trail	Tamara K. Trail	2008	46
86	86 7/8	16 6/8	17	6 2/8	6 2/8	3	3 2/8	9 1/8	3 7/8	6 2/8	6 4/8	Lincoln Co., NM	Joseph M. Vigneri	Joseph M. Vigneri	2008	46
86	86 6/8	15 3/8	15 4/8	7 2/8	7 2/8	2 4/8	2 4/8	10 1/8	6 3/8	7 1/8	6 7/8	Washoe Co., NV	Raymond L. Wood	Raymond L. Wood	2008	46
86	86 3/8	17	17	7	7	2 3/8	2 3/8	11	4 1/8	5 7/8	5 4/8	Park Co., CO	Norman S. Cavanaugh	Norman S. Cavanaugh	2009	46
85 6/8	88 2/8	17 2/8	17	6 4/8	6 3/8	3	3	14 4/8	11 2/8	4 2/8	6	Catron Co., NM	Robert L. Hudman	Robert L. Hudman	2009	46
85 6/8	88	15 5/8	15 4/8	7 4/8	7 4/8	2 7/8	2 5/8	6 5/8	1 1/8	6 4/8	7 5/8	Meade Co., SD	Shawn Powers	Shawn Powers	2006	62
85 6/8	86 7/8	14 5/8	15	7 4/8	7 3/8	2 6/8	2 6/8	9 4/8	4 3/8	6 1/8	6 3/8	Carbon Co., WY	Greg A. Salisbury	Greg A. Salisbury	2006	62
85 6/8	85 7/8	17 1/8	17	6 6/8	6 6/8	2 6/8	2 6/8	15 5/8	11 7/8	6	6	Cessford, AB	Alexander K. Barton	Alexander K. Barton	2007	62

Score												Locality	Hunter	Owner	Date	Rank
85 6/8	86 6/8	16 3/8	16 3/8	6 5/8	6 6/8	2 7/8	2 7/8	11 1/8	9 3/8	6 3/8	5 6/8	Carbon Co., WY	Larry S. Hicks	Larry S. Hicks	2007	62
85 6/8	86 6/8	15 7/8	15 5/8	7	7 1/8	2 6/8	2 6/8	14	10 4/8	5 4/8	5 1/8	Socorro Co., NM	Mike L. Ronning	Mike L. Ronning	2007	62
85 6/8	86 6/8	17	16 6/8	7 1/8	7 1/8	3	3	16	14 1/8	5 3/8	5	Humboldt Co., NV	Thomas P. Scoggin	Thomas P. Scoggin	2007	62
85 6/8	86 7/8	15 4/8	15 1/8	6 6/8	6 6/8	2 7/8	3	10 4/8	6 6/8	6 4/8	6 2/8	Rio Grande Co., CO	Reginald J. Lopez	Reginald J. Lopez	2008	62
85 6/8	86 6/8	17 6/8	18	6 2/8	6 2/8	2 5/8	2 5/8	8 1/8	5	5 6/8	5 7/8	Lincoln Co., NM	Dan E. McBride	Dan E. McBride	2009	62
85 6/8	86 3/8	16 6/8	16 6/8	6 4/8	6 6/8	2 4/8	2 4/8	10 2/8	5 4/8	6 1/8	6 3/8	Washoe Co., NV	Richard J. Retterath	Richard J. Retterath	2009	62
85 4/8	87 3/8	16 1/8	15 4/8	6 7/8	6 7/8	3 5/8	3 5/8	11 6/8	6 4/8	6 1/8	5 5/8	Coconino Co., AZ	Jeff A. Mott	Jeff A. Mott	2006	71
85 4/8	86 2/8	17 1/8	17	6 2/8	6 2/8	2 7/8	3 3/8	8 6/8	3 6/8	5 6/8	6 2/8	Lincoln Co., NM	Steven S. Bruggeman	Steven S. Bruggeman	2008	71
85 4/8	86 7/8	17	16 6/8	7 1/8	6 5/8	3 3/8	3 2/8	12 4/8	10	4 6/8	4 6/8	Yavapai Co., AZ	Andrew B. Pedroncelli	Andrew B. Pedroncelli	2008	71
85 4/8	87	15 6/8	16 2/8	7	7 2/8	2 3/8	2 3/8	13	9 6/8	6 6/8	6 6/8	Socorro Co., NM	Carl B. Walton	Carl B. Walton	2008	71
85 4/8	86 1/8	16 4/8	16 4/8	6 5/8	6 4/8	3 2/8	3 2/8	12 7/8	9	5	5	Lassen Co., CA	Melvin R. Todd	Melvin R. Todd	2009	71
85 2/8	85 2/8	17 1/8	17 1/8	6 3/8	6 2/8	2 6/8	2 6/8	9 4/8	4	5 6/8	5 6/8	Washoe Co., NV	Luke B. Anderson	Luke B. Anderson	2006	76
85 2/8	86	15 1/8	14 7/8	6 7/8	7 1/8	3 2/8	3 2/8	13 1/8	11 4/8	6 3/8	6 3/8	Mora Co., NM	Jimmy D. Davis	Jimmy D. Davis	2006	76
85 2/8	86 4/8	16 1/8	16 3/8	7	6 6/8	3 2/8	3 2/8	9 5/8	3 5/8	5 6/8	5 6/8	Sweetwater Co., WY	Len H. Guldman	Len H. Guldman	2007	76
85 2/8	86	15	14 4/8	7 2/8	7 2/8	3	3	9 2/8	6 5/8	6 4/8	6 4/8	Moffat Co., CO	Len H. Guldman	Len H. Guldman	2007	76
85 2/8	86 6/8	15 5/8	16	7 3/8	7 4/8	2 4/8	2 4/8	6 3/8	3 7/8	6 1/8	6 1/8	Carbon Co., WY	Patrick P. Jaure	Patrick P. Jaure	2007	76
85 2/8	86 2/8	15 1/8	15 5/8	7 3/8	7 2/8	3	3	11 2/8	8 7/8	5 4/8	5 4/8	Natrona Co., WY	Roger C. Krasnicki	Roger C. Krasnicki	2007	76
85 2/8	86	16 3/8	16 4/8	6 3/8	6 3/8	2 6/8	3	13 4/8	9 4/8	4 6/8	4 6/8	Rosebud Co., MT	Oren J. Dorris	Oren J. Dorris	2008	76
85 2/8	85 5/8	17	16 7/8	6 4/8	6 4/8	2 7/8	2 7/8	10 6/8	8	5 3/8	5 3/8	Las Animas Co., CO	Steven J. Montoya	Steven J. Montoya	2008	76
85 2/8	86 3/8	15 7/8	16 2/8	6 7/8	6 7/8	2 6/8	2 6/8	11 7/8	9 7/8	5 4/8	5 1/8	Catron Co., NM	Randall D. Newberg	Randall D. Newberg	2008	76
85 2/8	86	16 3/8	16 4/8	6 5/8	6 5/8	2 5/8	2 5/8	6 2/8	2 6/8	6 3/8	6 2/8	Lake Diefenbaker, SK	Martin B. Wiles	Martin B. Wiles	2009	76
85	85 3/8	16 4/8	16 3/8	6 2/8	6 2/8	2 7/8	2 7/8	9 6/8	3 4/8	5 4/8	5 4/8	Mora Co., NM	William D. Karnes	William D. Karnes	2006	86
85	85 3/8	16 6/8	16 6/8	6 3/8	6 3/8	2 5/8	2 5/8	12 3/8	9 3/8	5 5/8	5 3/8	Meade Co., SD	Jamie D. Spring	Jamie D. Spring	2006	86
85	85 4/8	17 1/8	17 2/8	6 6/8	6 7/8	2 7/8	2 7/8	9 6/8	1 5/8	5 2/8	5 2/8	Meade Co., SD	Tony L. Watson	Tony L. Watson	2006	86
85	85 7/8	16 7/8	16 3/8	6 2/8	6 2/8	3	3	12	6 7/8	6 1/8	6 2/8	Grant Co., NM	Dale Miller	Dale Miller	2008	86
84 6/8	84 6/8	16 1/8	15 5/8	6 7/8	6 6/8	3 1/8	3 1/8	12 5/8	10 3/8	6 3/8	6 3/8	Sierra Co., NM	Terry A. Mason	Terry A. Mason	1999	90
84 6/8	84 5/8	17	17 2/8	6 4/8	6 4/8	2 6/8	2 6/8	10	4	6	6	Custer Co., MT	Justin J. Goff	Justin J. Goff	2006	90
84 6/8	85 3/8	18 2/8	18 3/8	6 5/8	6 6/8	2 7/8	2 7/8	11 4/8	5 3/8	4 4/8	4 3/8	Coconino Co., AZ	Thomas C. Lassen	Thomas C. Lassen	2006	90
84 6/8	85 7/8	17 2/8	17 6/8	6 5/8	6 4/8	2 6/8	2 6/8	13 7/8	9	5 4/8	5 3/8	Malheur Co., OR	H.W. Buhrig	H.W. Buhrig	2007	90
84 6/8	85 2/8	15 7/8	15 5/8	7 1/8	7 1/8	2 5/8	2 4/8	11 1/8	6	6 3/8	6 3/8	Carbon Co., WY	Matt D. Schuele	Matt D. Schuele	2007	90
84 6/8	85 6/8	15 5/8	16 3/8	6 2/8	6 2/8	2 7/8	2 7/8	17 1/8	13 4/8	6	6	Grant Co., NM	Lee Frudden	Lee Frudden	2008	90
84 6/8	86 4/8	16 3/8	17 2/8	7	6 6/8	2 6/8	2 6/8	10 7/8	6 3/8	6 1/8	6 1/8	Blaine Co., ID	Robert L. Hartwig	Robert L. Hartwig	2008	90
84 6/8	85 4/8	17	17	6 3/8	6 2/8	3	2 7/8	8 6/8	4 5/8	6 4/8	6 4/8	Harding Co., SD	Pierrette T. Lyons	Pierrette T. Lyons	2008	90
84 4/8	85 4/8	16	16	6 5/8	6 5/8	2 7/8	2 7/8	4 5/8	21	6 5/8	6 5/8	Lincoln Co., NM	Arie Eric de Jong	Arie Eric de Jong	2006	98
84 4/8	85	16	14	7 2/8	7 2/8	2 7/8	3 1/8	20 6/8	12 1/8	6 2/8	6 2/8	Grand Co., UT	Mel L. Helm	Mel L. Helm	2006	98
84 4/8	85 6/8	17 4/8	18	5 7/8	6	2 4/8	2 4/8	11 5/8	7 6/8	7	7	Harney Co., OR	Timothy P. Brown	Timothy P. Brown	2007	98
84 4/8	85 1/8	16 3/8	16 3/8	6 2/8	6 1/8	3	3	12 3/8	4 6/8	5 6/8	5 4/8	Hudspeth Co., TX	James H. Duke, Jr.	James H. Duke, Jr.	2007	98
84 4/8	85 5/8	16	15 7/8	7 2/8	7	2 4/8	2 4/8	9 3/8	7 1/8	6 5/8	6 5/8	Valley Co., MT	William S. Erdmann	William S. Erdmann	2007	98
84 4/8	85 6/8	17 1/8	16 6/8	6 3/8	6 2/8	2 6/8	2 5/8	11 2/8	1 6/8	5 2/8	5 2/8	Meade Co., SD	Jim L. Hoogshagen	Jim L. Hoogshagen	2007	98
84 4/8	85 2/8	18	18 1/8	6 1/8	6	2 7/8	2 7/8	7 3/8	5 1/8	4 6/8	4 4/8	Lea Co., NM	Jimmie C. McIlroy	Jimmie C. McIlroy	2007	98

PRONGHORN

Antilocapra americana americana and related subspecies

Final Score	Gross Score	Length of horn R.	L.	Circumference of Base R.	L.	Circumference at Third Quarter R.	L.	Inside Spread	Tip to Tip Spread	Length of Prong R.	L.	Locality	Hunter	Owner	Date Killed	Rank
84 2/8	85	16	15 6/8	7 4/8	7 3/8	2 4/8	2 3/8	10 7/8	4 5/8	6	5 7/8	Carbon Co., WY	Brad A. Bartlett	Brad A. Bartlett	2007	105
84 2/8	85 2/8	16 7/8	16 5/8	6 4/8	6 4/8	2 6/8	2 5/8	7 4/8	5	5 2/8	5 4/8	Carbon Co., WY	Buckie F. Hulme	Buckie F. Hulme	2007	105
84 2/8	84 7/8	15 6/8	16 1/8	6 6/8	6 6/8	2 6/8	2 7/8	9 4/8	5 2/8	6	6	Lea Co., NM	Brandon O. Ray	Brandon O. Ray	2007	105
84 2/8	85 2/8	15 7/8	15 6/8	6 5/8	6 5/8	2 5/8	2 6/8	13 6/8	11	6 5/8	6 2/8	Fremont Co., WY	Mike Trevor	Mike Trevor	2007	105
84 2/8	85 4/8	15 5/8	15 4/8	7 1/8	6 7/8	2 5/8	2 4/8	9 6/8	5 4/8	6 5/8	6 4/8	Jackson Co., CO	Thomas J. Little	Thomas J. Little	2008	105
84 2/8	84 5/8	16 6/8	16 7/8	5 7/8	5 7/8	2 6/8	2 6/8	9 4/8	2 1/8	5 7/8	5 7/8	Coconino Co., AZ	Rodney J. Hoekert	Rodney J. Hoekert	2009	105
84 2/8	84 5/8	15	15 1/8	6 7/8	7	2 4/8	2 4/8	14 7/8	13	6 4/8	6 3/8	Park Co., WY	Thomas G. Obuhanych	Thomas G. Obuhanych	2009	105
84 2/8	85 3/8	16 1/8	16 2/8	6 6/8	6 4/8	2 6/8	3	4 6/8	9 4/8	6 1/8	6 1/8	Sheerness, AB	John J. Person	John J. Person	2009	105
84 2/8	85 3/8	15 7/8	15 4/8	7	7	2 5/8	2 4/8	13	8 6/8	6	6 3/8	Rosebud Co., MT	Kurt D. Rued	Kurt D. Rued	2009	105
84 2/8	85 2/8	15 4/8	15 4/8	7 2/8	7 4/8	2 5/8	2 6/8	11 1/8	6 5/8	5 4/8	5 6/8	Carbon Co., WY	Eric D. Stanosheck	Eric D. Stanosheck	2009	105
84 2/8	85 2/8	16	15 6/8	7	6 7/8	2 7/8	2 7/8	13 6/8	13 2/8	6	5 4/8	Moffat Co., CO	Earl L. Stout	Earl L. Stout	2009	105
84 2/8	85 2/8	16 6/8	16 6/8	6 1/8	6 2/8	3 1/8	3 1/8	10 2/8	7 1/8	6	5 4/8	Catron Co., NM	Hugh C. Williamson	Hugh C. Williamson	2009	105
84 2/8	85 5/8	16 5/8	16 1/8	6 6/8	6 5/8	2 5/8	2 3/8	5 5/8	2 1/8	5 7/8	6 3/8	Custer Co., MT	David E. Lyons II	David E. Lyons II	2006	117
84	84 4/8	15	14 7/8	6 6/8	6 7/8	3 2/8	3 2/8	8 2/8	5	5 2/8	5 4/8	Converse Co., WY	Jakob P. Olsen	Jakob P. Olsen	2006	117
84	84 5/8	16 4/8	16 3/8	6 3/8	6 3/8	3	3	11 6/8	13 3/8	5 5/8	5 7/8	Garfield Co., UT	Gary Schear	Gary Schear	2006	117
84	84 6/8	17 1/8	16 6/8	6 6/8	6 5/8	3	3	8 1/8	1 1/8	5	5	Lincoln Co., NM	John F. White	John F. White	2006	117
84	84 6/8	15 3/8	15 6/8	6 4/8	6 4/8	2 6/8	3	5 4/8	0 6/8	6	5 7/8	Hudspeth Co., TX	Marc L. Bartoskewitz	Marc L. Bartoskewitz	2007	117
84	84 2/8	15 2/8	15 2/8	7 3/8	7 3/8	2 4/8	2 4/8	9 7/8	5 1/8	5 7/8	6	Carbon Co., WY	Elizabeth S. Grainger	Elizabeth S. Grainger	2007	117
84	85 2/8	17 6/8	17 5/8	6 5/8	6 3/8	2 5/8	2 6/8	6 3/8	3	5 7/8	5 4/8	Perkins Co., SD	Ryan Sieveke	Ryan Sieveke	2007	117
84	84 7/8	15 2/8	15 2/8	6 3/8	6 5/8	3	3	11 2/8	8 1/8	6 2/8	6 6/8	Baca Co., CO	Robert W. Smith	Robert W. Smith	2007	117
84	86 3/8	17 4/8	18 2/8	6 4/8	6 4/8	2 7/8	3 1/8	12 6/8	9 3/8	4 2/8	5 3/8	Catron Co., NM	Rick A. Gonzales	Rick A. Gonzales	2008	117
84	84 3/8	15 7/8	15 7/8	6 2/8	6 2/8	2 7/8	2 7/8	9 2/8	5 6/8	6 1/8	6 1/8	Milk River, AB	Robert G. LaRue	Robert G. LaRue	2008	117
84	85	16	16	7 3/8	7 5/8	2 4/8	2 6/8	11	7 5/8	5 3/8	5 4/8	Carbon Co., WY	Mike R. Bailey	Mike R. Bailey	2009	117
84	84 6/8	15 2/8	15 4/8	6 4/8	6 4/8	3 4/8	3 4/8	7 5/8	3 3/8	5 4/8	5 6/8	Lincoln Co., NM	Aaron Nesbit	Aaron Nesbit	2009	117
83 6/8	84 7/8	16 2/8	16 3/8	7 4/8	7 1/8	2 7/8	3	13	9 3/8	5 1/8	4 7/8	Gunnison Co., CO	Douglas C. Cotten	Douglas C. Cotten	2006	129
83 6/8	84	16 3/8	16 3/8	6 6/8	6 5/8	2 7/8	2 7/8	8 7/8	3	5 2/8	5 1/8	Humboldt Co., NV	Nick K. Landis	Nick K. Landis	2006	129
83 6/8	85 1/8	15 4/8	15 6/8	6 7/8	6 7/8	2 7/8	2 7/8	11 4/8	8 3/8	5	5 4/8	Carbon Co., WY	Thomas J. Easton	Thomas J. Easton	2007	129
83 6/8	84	15 1/8	15 1/8	6 7/8	6 7/8	2 7/8	2 7/8	8 3/8	3 5/8	5 4/8	5 4/8	Dallam Co., TX	Mark A. Kalmbach	Mark A. Kalmbach	2007	129
83 6/8	84 4/8	16 4/8	16 1/8	7	6 7/8	2 6/8	2 5/8	13 7/8	11	5	5 3/8	Hudspeth Co., TX	Calvin K. LaGrone	Calvin K. LaGrone	2007	129
83 6/8	84 3/8	16	16 1/8	6 4/8	6 3/8	3	2 7/8	10 4/8	5 1/8	5 4/8	5 4/8	Catron Co., NM	Ronald J. Nadzieja	Ronald J. Nadzieja	2007	129
83 6/8	84 4/8	16	16 1/8	6 7/8	6 6/8	2 6/8	2 6/8	9 5/8	5 3/8	5	5 1/8	Converse Co., WY	Larry A. Napolitano	Larry A. Napolitano	2007	129
83 6/8	84 3/8	15 4/8	15 3/8	7 3/8	7 2/8	3	3	10 6/8	7 6/8	5 1/8	5	Carbon Co., UT	Boyd R. Roberts	Boyd R. Roberts	2007	129

83 6/8	84 2/8	15 6/8	6 5/8	6 6/8	2 7/8	2 7/8	6 5/8	10 3/8	5	5	Meade Co., SD	Thaine Strom	Thaine Strom	2007	129
83 6/8	85 3/8	17 1/8	6 3/8	6 4/8	2 6/8	2 6/8	10 6/8	13 6/8	5 2/8	5 4/8	Dallam Co., TX	Charles W. Wolcott	Charles W. Wolcott	2007	129
83 6/8	85 7/8	17 2/8	6 6/8	7	2 6/8	2 6/8	6 6/8	9 3/8	4 5/8	5 6/8	Rosebud Co., MT	Larry S. Hicks	Larry S. Hicks	2008	129
83 6/8	84 5/8	16 7/8	6 1/8	6 1/8	3	2 6/8	9 4/8	13 6/8	5	5 2/8	Pershing Co., NV	Scott E. Taylor	Scott E. Taylor	2008	129
83 6/8	84	16 4/8	6 4/8	6 4/8	3 1/8	3 1/8	8 4/8	12 3/8	5 2/8	5 1/8	Fremont Co., WY	Brent Z. Wilkes	Brent Z. Wilkes	2008	129
83 6/8	84 6/8	16	6 7/8	6 6/8	2 5/8	2 5/8	11 2/8	14 3/8	6 2/8	6	Mora Co., NM	Cole G. Medlin	Cole G. Medlin	2009	129
83 6/8	84 2/8	14 4/8	7 1/8	7 1/8	3	3	16	16 7/8	5 4/8	5 6/8	Sweetwater Co., WY	Trenton R. Meyer	Trenton R. Meyer	2009	129
83 6/8	84 2/8	16 2/8	6 2/8	6 2/8	3 2/8	3 3/8	4 6/8	9 2/8	5 3/8	5 3/8	Lincoln Co., NM	Phillip G. Steffens	Phillip G. Steffens	2009	129
83 6/8	84 4/8	15 5/8	6 2/8	6 3/8	3 1/8	3 1/8	7 6/8	12 3/8	5 4/8	5 6/8	Box Elder Co., UT	Elaine D. Tribelhorn	Elaine D. Tribelhorn	2009	129
83 6/8	84 6/8	17	6 6/8	6 7/8	2 7/8	2 7/8	12 5/8	16	5	4 5/8	Washakie Co., WY	Wade J. Wittkop	Wade J. Wittkop	2009	129
83 4/8	83 7/8	15 2/8	6 6/8	6 7/8	2 7/8	2 6/8	6 6/8	10 7/8	5 6/8	5 6/8	Fremont Co., WY	Micheal H. Eastman	Micheal H. Eastman	2005	147
83 4/8	84 1/8	13 7/8	6	6 5/8	2 5/8	2 4/8	7 5/8	10	7	6 7/8	Fremont Co., WY	Scott A. Brownell	Scott A. Brownell	2006	147
83 4/8	84 5/8	17 1/8	6 3/8	6 1/8	2 4/8	2 6/8	5 2/8	9 5/8	5 6/8	6 2/8	Humboldt Co., NV	Thomas J. Currid	Thomas J. Currid	2006	147
83 4/8	84 6/8	16 3/8	6 3/8	6 2/8	2 5/8	2 6/8	3 2/8	10 4/8	5 2/8	5 1/8	Washoe Co., NV	Kimberly Fenner	Kimberly Fenner	2006	147
83 4/8	84 2/8	15 7/8	7 2/8	6 2/8	2 7/8	3	8 3/8	11 2/8	6 3/8	6 2/8	Carbon Co., WY	Richard B. Evans, Jr.	Richard B. Evans, Jr.	2007	147
83 4/8	85 7/8	16 6/8	7 3/8	6 5/8	2 6/8	2 6/8	6 7/8	12	5 1/8	5 5/8	Yavapai Co., AZ	Mike P. Landgren	Mike P. Landgren	2007	147
83 4/8	84 4/8	15 4/8	7 3/8	7 3/8	2 5/8	2 4/8	7 7/8	10 6/8	5 1/8	5 6/8	Carbon Co., WY	Gregg S. Rothenberger	Gregg S. Rothenberger	2007	147
83 4/8	84 4/8	18	6 4/8	6 4/8	2 5/8	2 5/8	1 3/8	8 7/8	5 3/8	5	Dewey Co., SD	Jace A. Vrooman	Jace A. Vrooman	2007	147
83 4/8	84 1/8	17	6	5 6/8	2 2/8	2 2/8	2	7 4/8	6 4/8	6 4/8	Pershing Co., NV	Shirley M. Baird	Shirley M. Baird	2008	147
83 4/8	84 2/8	16 3/8	6 4/8	6 4/8	2 7/8	2 6/8	6 3/8	11 2/8	5 7/8	5 6/8	Big Horn Co., MT	Jason L. Buyse	Jason L. Buyse	2008	147

PRONGHORN
FINAL SCORE: 82 6/8
HUNTER: R. Jason Weeks

5

PRONGHORN
FINAL SCORE: 82 2/8
HUNTER: Becke E. Medlin

6

PRONGHORN
FINAL SCORE: 88
HUNTER: Danny R. Schultz

7

PRONGHORN
FINAL SCORE: 80 6/8
HUNTER: Kurt D. Rued

8

PRONGHORN

Antilocapra americana americana and related subspecies

Final Score	Gross Score	Length of horn R.	L.	Circumference of Base R.	L.	Circumference at Third Quarter R.	L.	Inside Spread	Tip to Tip Spread	Length of Prong R.	L.	Locality	Hunter	Owner	Date Killed	Rank
83 4/8	85	15 3/8	15 6/8	7	6 4/8	3 2/8	3 1/8	11 1/8	5 4/8	5 6/8	5 7/8	Hudspeth Co., TX	William G. Kyle	William G. Kyle	2008	147
83 4/8	84 4/8	17 2/8	17 4/8	7	6 7/8	2 5/8	2 4/8	17 5/8	13 3/8	4 7/8	4 4/8	Dewey Co., SD	Jace Long	Jace Long	2008	147
83 4/8	85	16 5/8	16	6 5/8	6 5/8	2 4/8	2 7/8	10 3/8	10 4/8	6 2/8	5 5/8	Harney Co., OR	Benjamin W. Cooney	Benjamin W. Cooney	2009	147
83 4/8	84	14 5/8	14 3/8	7 2/8	7 3/8	3	3	10 1/8	5 4/8	6	6	Humboldt Co., NV	Theodore W. Ohm	Theodore W. Ohm	2009	147
83 4/8	84 7/8	15 2/8	16	6 4/8	6 4/8	2 5/8	2 4/8	10 6/8	5 7/8	7	6 7/8	Mora Co., NM	Scott A. Peonio	Scott A. Peonio	2009	147
83 4/8	84	14 4/8	14 5/8	6 6/8	6 7/8	2 5/8	2 5/8	9	6 6/8	6 3/8	6 5/8	Natrona Co., WY	Glen H. Taylor	Glen H. Taylor	2009	147
83 2/8	83 5/8	14 6/8	14 6/8	7 5/8	7 5/8	2 6/8	2 7/8	12 5/8	11 5/8	5 7/8	5 7/8	Carbon Co., WY	Kelly W. Hepworth	Kelly W. Hepworth	2006	163
83 2/8	85 1/8	15 6/8	14 7/8	6 5/8	6 4/8	3	2 6/8	8 6/8	4 2/8	6 6/8	6 5/8	Carbon Co., WY	Brent B. Vosika	Brent B. Vosika	2006	163
83 2/8	83 6/8	15 6/8	15 5/8	6 7/8	7	3	3	11 4/8	8 7/8	5	5 1/8	Sheridan Co., WY	Lester P. Bush	Lester P. Bush	2007	163
83 2/8	84 1/8	15 3/8	15 4/8	7 1/8	6 7/8	2 4/8	2 5/8	11 5/8	8 2/8	6 2/8	6	Rosebud Co., MT	Todd D. Friez	Todd D. Friez	2007	163
83 2/8	83 3/8	17 1/8	17	6 2/8	6 7/8	2 4/8	2 4/8	7 3/8	3 7/8	5 7/8	5 7/8	Cutbank Creek, AB	James L. Gariano	James L. Gariano	2007	163
83 2/8	84 5/8	17 3/8	16 7/8	6 3/8	6 2/8	2 6/8	2 4/8	10 4/8	4 6/8	5 5/8	5 5/8	Hudspeth Co., TX	Sheldon Grothaus	Sheldon Grothaus	2007	163
83 2/8	83 6/8	13 7/8	14	7 5/8	7 4/8	3 5/8	3 4/8	9 3/8	5 5/8	4	4	Harney Co., OR	John Crafton	John Crafton	2008	163
83 2/8	84	13 7/8	14	6 6/8	6 6/8	3 4/8	3 4/8	8 7/8	7 6/8	5 4/8	5 6/8	Humboldt Co., NV	Gary B. Jensen	Gary B. Jensen	2008	163
83 2/8	84 6/8	17 2/8	17	6 2/8	6 1/8	2 5/8	2 5/8	12	6 4/8	6 5/8	5 5/8	Uinta Co., WY	John K. Jones	John K. Jones	2008	163
83 2/8	83 6/8	15 6/8	16	7 5/8	7 5/8	2 6/8	2 6/8	11 3/8	7 4/8	5	4 7/8	Powder River Co., MT	Brad L. Knutson	Brad L. Knutson	2008	163
83 2/8	83 5/8	15 2/8	15 1/8	7 4/8	7 4/8	2 5/8	2 6/8	10 7/8	8 2/8	5 3/8	5 3/8	Custer Co., SD	Steve R. Malone	Steve R. Malone	2008	163
83 2/8	84	16 7/8	16 6/8	6 7/8	6 6/8	2 6/8	2 6/8	11 4/8	7 5/8	5	5 2/8	Sweetwater Co., WY	Shyanne K. Peterson	Shyanne K. Peterson	2008	163
83 2/8	84 1/8	16 3/8	16	6 5/8	6 4/8	2 6/8	2 5/8	12 1/8	9 4/8	6 1/8	6 2/8	Lincoln Co., NM	Mike Stewart	Mike Stewart	2008	163
83 2/8	83 4/8	15 2/8	15 1/8	6 7/8	6 7/8	3	3	7	2 1/8	5 5/8	5 4/8	Meade Co., SD	Joseph J. Vogle	Joseph J. Vogle	2008	163
83 2/8	84	14 2/8	14 3/8	7 3/8	7 2/8	2 6/8	2 6/8	8 6/8	5 4/8	6 2/8	6	Natrona Co., WY	Mark A. Berg	Mark A. Berg	2009	163
83 2/8	84 3/8	16	16 2/8	6 4/8	6 3/8	3	3 1/8	11 2/8	6 4/8	5 1/8	5	Hudspeth Co., TX	Genessa R. Gerber	Genessa R. Gerber	2009	163
83 2/8	83 3/8	15	15	6 4/8	6 4/8	2 5/8	2 4/8	11 4/8	8 1/8	6 6/8	6 6/8	Lassen Co., CA	Brian J. Langslet	Brian J. Langslet	2009	163
83 2/8	83 5/8	16 7/8	16 6/8	6 3/8	6 3/8	2 6/8	2 6/8	11	6 7/8	5 5/8	5 6/8	Elko Co., NV	John C. McDowell	John C. McDowell	2009	163
83 2/8	84	16 1/8	15 6/8	6 1/8	6 1/8	3 2/8	3 2/8	10 4/8	6 5/8	5 5/8	5 4/8	Lincoln Co., NM	John C. Vanko	John C. Vanko	2009	163
83 2/8	83 6/8	15 3/8	15 2/8	6 3/8	6 3/8	3 2/8	3 3/8	9 7/8	6 7/8	5 4/8	5 3/8	Lincoln Co., NM	J.D. Woods, Jr	J.D. Woods, Jr	2009	163
83	84	15 5/8	15 1/8	6 6/8	6 6/8	3	2 7/8	10 5/8	9 2/8	6 2/8	5 7/8	Sweet Grass Co., MT	Lisa Blair	Arnold G. Blair	1974	183
83	83 2/8	16 2/8	16 2/8	6 7/8	6 7/8	2 3/8	2 2/8	12 7/8	9 6/8	6	5 7/8	Humboldt Co., NV	William O. Bradley	William O. Bradley	2006	183
83	83 4/8	15 3/8	15 1/8	5 7/8	6	2 3/8	2 3/8	8 7/8	4	7 6/8	7 6/8	Yellowstone Co., MT	Casey V.L. Hinkle	Casey V.L. Hinkle	2006	183
83	84 7/8	16 2/8	16 2/8	7 1/8	7	2 3/8	2 4/8	15 4/8	13 4/8	6 2/8	5 3/8	Carbon Co., WY	Kyle L. Krejci	Kyle L. Krejci	2006	183
83	84 1/8	16 6/8	16 1/8	6 3/8	6 4/8	2 6/8	2 6/8	10 5/8	5 3/8	5 4/8	5 5/8	Sioux Co., NE	Jeff C. Miller	Jeff C. Miller	2006	183

Score											Locality	Owner	Hunter	Date	Rank
83	83 4/8	16 3/8	16 3/8	6 3/8	6 3/8	2 4/8	2 4/8	9 5/8	7	5 7/8	Meagher Co., MT	Dayna L. Ogle	Dayna L. Ogle	2006	183
83	83 4/8	16 4/8	16 2/8	6 3/8	6 3/8	2 6/8	2 5/8	7 6/8	0 6/8	5 6/8	Carbon Co., WY	Bradley G. Schemmel	Bradley G. Schemmel	2006	183
83	83 6/8	15	14 6/8	6 7/8	7	2 3/8	2 3/8	12 4/8	6 5/8	7 4/8	Lake Co., OR	John P. Sheehy	John P. Sheehy	2006	183
83	83 3/8	16	16	6 7/8	6 7/8	2 7/8	2 6/8	12 3/8	7 6/8	5 7/8	Fremont Co., WY	Bret C. Dolph	Bret C. Dolph	2007	183
83	83 6/8	15 5/8	15 5/8	6 4/8	6 4/8	3 2/8	3 1/8	12 1/8	7 2/8	5 1/8	Harding Co., NM	Mike Little	Mike Little	2007	183
83	83 5/8	14 4/8	14 6/8	7 1/8	7 1/8	2 6/8	2 6/8	7 7/8	5 4/8	5 7/8	Carbon Co., WY	Jared J. Mason	Jared J. Mason	2007	183
83	83 5/8	16 7/8	16 5/8	6 1/8	6 1/8	2 5/8	2 6/8	13 3/8	8 4/8	5 7/8	Utah Co., UT	Chans R. Carson	Chans R. Carson	2008	183
83	84	14 7/8	14 5/8	7	7	3	3 1/8	9 2/8	5 6/8	6	Carbon Co., WY	James M. Clegg	James M. Clegg	2008	183
83	84 5/8	16 5/8	16 3/8	6 5/8	6 5/8	3 1/8	3	9 1/8	4 7/8	5 3/8	Natrona Co., WY	Douglas P. Hanenburg	Douglas P. Hanenburg	2008	183
83	84 2/8	15 3/8	15 3/8	6 3/8	6 1/8	2 4/8	2 4/8	9 7/8	5 4/8	6 1/8	Grant Co., NM	Arnold W. Klintworth	Arnold W. Klintworth	2008	183
83	83 7/8	15 4/8	15 2/8	6 7/8	6 7/8	2 6/8	2 5/8	9 4/8	4 2/8	5 5/8	Dallam Co., TX	Charles T. Miller	Charles T. Miller	2008	183
83	83 3/8	14 7/8	15	7 3/8	7 3/8	2 4/8	2 3/8	9 2/8	5 6/8	5 4/8	Humboldt Co., NV	Scott M. Rasmussen	Scott M. Rasmussen	2008	183
83	84 1/8	16 2/8	16	6 5/8	6 5/8	2 5/8	2 6/8	7 3/8	4 7/8	5 3/8	Carbon Co., WY	Larry S. Hicks	Larry S. Hicks	2009	183
83	85 1/8	14 6/8	15 3/8	6 7/8	6 7/8	2 5/8	2 5/8	12 1/8	7 6/8	6 7/8	Elko Co., NV	Howard R. McDonell, Jr.	Howard R. McDonell, Jr.	2009	183
83	83 4/8	15 3/8	15 4/8	6 5/8	6 5/8	2 4/8	2 4/8	9 5/8	6 1/8	6	Natrona Co., WY	Dana L. Olson	Dana L. Olson	2009	183
83	84	15 6/8	15 6/8	7	7 2/8	2 6/8	2 6/8	12	8	5 2/8	Natrona Co., WY	Jeffrey T. Rossiter	Jeffrey T. Rossiter	2009	183
82 6/8	83 7/8	15 7/8	15 7/8	7	7	2 3/8	2 4/8	12 7/8	9 3/8	6 1/8	Lincoln Co., NM	John C. Shaw	John C. Shaw	2000	204
82 6/8	83 3/8	16 6/8	16 5/8	6 5/8	6 5/8	2 5/8	2 5/8	10 4/8	5 4/8	5 4/8	Socorro Co., NM	Stephen C. LeBlanc	Stephen C. LeBlanc	2002	204
82 6/8	83 1/8	16 6/8	16 6/8	6 3/8	6 3/8	2 6/8	2 6/8	18 1/8	13 6/8	5 2/8	Rosebud Co., MT	Kurt D. Rued	Kurt D. Rued	2003	204
82 6/8	83	15 4/8	15 4/8	5 4/8	5 4/8	3 3/8	3 3/8	11 3/8	9 3/8	4 2/8	Union Co., NM	Larry D. Alderson	Larry D. Alderson	2006	204
82 6/8	83 3/8	16 3/8	16 4/8	6	6	2 4/8	2 4/8	9 1/8	3	6 2/8	Coconino Co., AZ	Robert B. Andersen	Robert B. Andersen	2006	204
82 6/8	83 6/8	15 6/8	16	6 5/8	6 4/8	2 3/8	2 4/8	13	11	6 3/8	Grant Co., NM	Lee Frudden	Lee Frudden	2006	204
82 6/8	83 3/8	15 3/8	15 3/8	6 3/8	6 2/8	3	3	10 4/8	6 4/8	5 6/8	Yavapai Co., AZ	Robert D. Griego	Robert D. Griego	2006	204
82 6/8	83	14 3/8	14 3/8	6 6/8	6 6/8	3 5/8	3 4/8	10 1/8	5 3/8	5 4/8	Hudspeth Co., TX	William T. Hanna	William T. Hanna	2006	204
82 6/8	83 6/8	17 6/8	17 5/8	5 6/8	6	3 1/8	3 1/8	8 5/8	4 2/8	5	Catron Co., NM	R. Douglas Isbell	R. Douglas Isbell	2006	204
82 6/8	83 1/8	16 3/8	16 3/8	6 3/8	6 3/8	2 6/8	2 6/8	11 4/8	9 4/8	4 4/8	Lea Co., NM	Alan Martinez	Alan Martinez	2006	204
82 6/8	83 3/8	16	16	6 5/8	6 5/8	2 5/8	2 5/8	11 5/8	5 6/8	5 4/8	Campbell Co., WY	Keith R. Moyer	Keith R. Moyer	2006	204
82 6/8	83 6/8	16 4/8	16 4/8	6 4/8	6 4/8	2 4/8	2 3/8	10 2/8	6 3/8	5 6/8	Elko Co., NV	Ronald R. Ricks	Ronald R. Ricks	2006	204
82 6/8	84 1/8	15 7/8	15 7/8	7 2/8	7 2/8	2 4/8	2 4/8	8 4/8	7	6 2/8	Custer Co., MT	Mark W. Streissguth	Mark W. Streissguth	2006	204
82 6/8	83 2/8	15 1/8	15	7 2/8	7 2/8	2 6/8	2 6/8	11 2/8	7 2/8	5 7/8	Emery Co., UT	Mark A. Carrillo	Mark A. Carrillo	2007	204
82 6/8	83 4/8	14 2/8	14	6 5/8	6 4/8	3 2/8	3 2/8	10 7/8	5 4/8	5 1/8	Meade Co., SD	Joe R. Gunderson	Joe R. Gunderson	2007	204
82 6/8	84 2/8	15 6/8	16	6 4/8	6 4/8	2 6/8	2 6/8	11 5/8	9 6/8	5 4/8	Carbon Co., WY	Michael J. Halter	Michael J. Halter	2007	204
82 6/8	83 1/8	15 4/8	15 4/8	6 4/8	6 4/8	3 1/8	3 2/8	9 5/8	5 4/8	5 5/8	Carbon Co., WY	Michael J. Reilly	Michael J. Reilly	2007	204
82 6/8	83 4/8	15 6/8	16	6 6/8	6 6/8	3 2/8	2 7/8	9 7/8	7 6/8	5 5/8	Johnson Co., WY	Stacy R. Smith	Stacy R. Smith	2007	204
82 6/8	83 1/8	15	15 1/8	6 6/8	6 6/8	3	3	9 1/8	4 5/8	5 3/8	Banner Co., NE	Thomas R. Zimmer	Thomas R. Zimmer	2007	204
82 6/8	83 4/8	15	15 1/8	6 5/8	6 5/8	2 5/8	2 5/8	10 5/8	4 6/8	5 4/8	Wardlow, AB	Gerald W.K. Conners	Gerald W.K. Conners	2007	204
82 6/8	83 1/8	16 1/8	16 1/8	6 5/8	6 6/8	2 5/8	2 4/8	15 1/8	10 4/8	6	Humboldt Co., NV	Carol S. Drake	Carol S. Drake	2008	204
82 6/8	83	15 4/8	15 4/8	6 6/8	7 1/8	2 4/8	2 4/8	15 1/8	2 5/8	6 3/8	Carbon Co., WY	Edmond V. Given	Edmond V. Given	2008	204
82 6/8	83 3/8	15 2/8	15 2/8	6 4/8	6 5/8	2 4/8	2 5/8	8 1/8	5 7/8	6 5/8	Elko Co., NV	Keven M. Hall	Keven M. Hall	2008	204
82 6/8	84 5/8	15 6/8	15 6/8	6 5/8	6 6/8	2 7/8	3	13 2/8	7 5/8	4 6/8	Colfax Co., NM	Brian A. Hauck	Brian A. Hauck	2008	204

PRONGHORN

Antilocapra americana americana and related subspecies

Final Score	Gross Score	Length of horn R.	L.	Circumference of Base R.	L.	Circumference at Third Quarter R.	L.	Inside Spread	Tip to Tip Spread	Length of Prong R.	L.	Locality	Hunter	Owner	Date Killed	Rank
82 6/8	83 4/8	14 5/8	14 3/8	7 3/8	7 3/8	2 5/8	2 6/8	11	6 5/8	6	5 7/8	Carbon Co., WY	Levi K. Heath	Levi K. Heath	2008	204
82 6/8	83 2/8	15 7/8	15 6/8	6 3/8	6 4/8	2 6/8	2 7/8	11 4/8	6 6/8	5 5/8	5 5/8	Humboldt Co., NV	Harold J. Humes	Harold J. Humes	2008	204
82 6/8	83 7/8	16 2/8	16 4/8	6 7/8	6 6/8	2 4/8	2 5/8	11 1/8	7 7/8	5 6/8	5 1/8	Harding Co., SD	Peter Lien	Peter Lien	2008	204
82 6/8	83 3/8	15 3/8	15 4/8	7 2/8	7 1/8	2 6/8	2 6/8	8	3 2/8	5 1/8	5 2/8	Sweetwater Co., WY	Stephen F. Adams	Stephen F. Adams	2009	204
82 6/8	84 2/8	15	14 7/8	6 6/8	6 6/8	2 7/8	2 6/8	16 1/8	14	5 7/8	6	Niobrara Co., WY	Joseph A. Benson III	Joseph A. Benson III	2009	204
82 6/8	83 3/8	15 2/8	15 1/8	7 1/8	7	2 6/8	2 5/8	11	7 4/8	5 6/8	5 5/8	Sweetwater Co., WY	Kevin C. Cook	Kevin C. Cook	2009	204
82 6/8	83 2/8	16 5/8	16 6/8	6 6/8	6 6/8	2 5/8	2 5/8	13 4/8	11 1/8	5 2/8	5 1/8	Washoe Co., NV	Melissa J. Humes	Melissa J. Humes	2009	204
82 6/8	83 3/8	16	16 1/8	6 4/8	6 4/8	2 5/8	2 5/8	8 2/8	2 2/8	5 5/8	6	Nye Co., NV	Robert F. Klug	Robert F. Klug	2009	204
82 6/8	84 6/8	16 2/8	16 5/8	6 5/8	6 3/8	3	3	9 4/8	3	5 3/8	4 7/8	Humboldt Co., NV	Natalie D. Norcutt	Natalie D. Norcutt	2009	204
82 6/8	83 2/8	16 4/8	16 2/8	6 6/8	6 6/8	2 6/8	2 6/8	11 5/8	6	5 1/8	5	Weld Co., CO	R. Jason Weeks	R. Jason Weeks	2009	204
82 4/8	84 1/8	16 6/8	16 3/8	6	5 7/8	2 6/8	2 5/8	8 4/8	3 3/8	5 5/8	6	Colfax Co., NM	John C. Shaw	John C. Shaw	1991	238
82 4/8	83 2/8	16 4/8	16 2/8	6 6/8	6 6/8	2 6/8	2 7/8	12	5	5 1/8	5	Mora Co., NM	Brittany R. Streissguth	Brittany R. Streissguth	2002	238
82 4/8	83 2/8	15 1/8	15 3/8	7	6 6/8	2 6/8	2 6/8	12 5/8	11 3/8	5 6/8	5 6/8	Natrona Co., WY	John T. Benbow	John T. Benbow	2004	238
82 4/8	83 5/8	14 6/8	15 6/8	6 4/8	6 4/8	3 1/8	3 2/8	10 3/8	9 2/8	6	6	Unknown	Shaun D. Friesen	Shaun D. Friesen	2005	238
82 4/8	83 5/8	18 1/8	18 3/8	6 2/8	6 1/8	3	2 7/8	16 4/8	13 2/8	4 7/8	4 5/8	Coconino Co., AZ	Wilson W. Allen, Jr.	Wilson W. Allen, Jr.	2006	238
82 4/8	83 5/8	16 2/8	16	6 4/8	6	3	2 6/8	10 6/8	5 7/8	5 5/8	5 6/8	Yavapai Co., AZ	Joe W. Bishop	Joe W. Bishop	2006	238
82 4/8	83 3/8	16 2/8	16 3/8	6	6	2 4/8	2 4/8	7 3/8	3 4/8	6 5/8	6 7/8	Cimarron Co., OK	Dewey M. Dalton	Dewey M. Dalton	2006	238
82 4/8	83 5/8	15 2/8	15 5/8	7 1/8	7	2 6/8	2 7/8	11 4/8	9 5/8	5 2/8	5 5/8	Carbon Co., WY	Jefre R. Bugni	Jefre R. Bugni	2007	238
82 4/8	83 2/8	15 6/8	15 4/8	6 3/8	6 3/8	2 6/8	2 6/8	9 2/8	7 1/8	5 7/8	6	Ziebach Co., SD	Robin Hulm	Robin Hulm	2007	238
82 4/8	83 5/8	15 7/8	16	7 2/8	7 1/8	3	2 6/8	12 3/8	6 2/8	5 1/8	4 6/8	Rosebud Co., MT	Dwayne R. Just	Dwayne R. Just	2007	238
82 4/8	83	16 3/8	16 3/8	6 4/8	6 3/8	2 6/8	2 7/8	9 3/8	5 7/8	5	4 7/8	Potter Co., SD	Devyn W. Lemler	Devyn W. Lemler	2007	238
82 4/8	83 1/8	17 2/8	16 7/8	6 6/8	6 5/8	2 5/8	2 4/8	7 6/8	4 4/8	4 3/8	4 3/8	Socorro Co., NM	Clifton S. Lewis	Clifton S. Lewis	2007	238
82 4/8	83	14 6/8	14 5/8	6 5/8	6 4/8	2 6/8	2 7/8	9 4/8	6 2/8	6	6	Las Animas Co., CO	Terrance S. Marcum	Terrance S. Marcum	2007	238
82 4/8	83	15 3/8	15 3/8	7	6 7/8	3 1/8	3	11 3/8	7 5/8	4 5/8	6	Fremont Co., WY	Steven M. Staten	Steven M. Staten	2007	238
82 4/8	83 2/8	16	16 1/8	6 7/8	6 5/8	2 6/8	2 6/8	13 6/8	8 3/8	5 4/8	5 6/8	Tide Lake, AB	Robert G. Stevens	Robert G. Stevens	2007	238
82 4/8	83 6/8	15 2/8	15	6 6/8	6 6/8	2 5/8	2 5/8	10 4/8	7 1/8	6 2/8	5 5/8	Harding Co., SD	Jess V. Wammen	Jess V. Wammen	2007	238
82 4/8	83 1/8	15 4/8	15 4/8	6 4/8	6 4/8	2 7/8	3	10 3/8	6 2/8	5 4/8	5 6/8	Sweetwater Co., WY	Picked Up	Randy A. Cragoe	2008	238
82 4/8	83 4/8	15 6/8	16	6 4/8	6 4/8	2 6/8	2 6/8	9	4 5/8	5 4/8	5 3/8	Catron Co., NM	Mark A. Dodson	Mark A. Dodson	2008	238
82 4/8	84 5/8	15 1/8	15 5/8	6 5/8	6 5/8	2 6/8	2 6/8	12 2/8	7 3/8	5 1/8	6	Grant Co., NM	Allen A. Ehrke	Allen A. Ehrke	2008	238
82 4/8	83 7/8	16 3/8	16	6 6/8	6 5/8	3	2 6/8	9 2/8	3 5/8	5 3/8	5 1/8	Emery Co., UT	Robert H. Etzel	Robert H. Etzel	2008	238
82 4/8	82 5/8	16 6/8	16 6/8	6 3/8	6 3/8	2 4/8	2 4/8	12 3/8	9 1/8	5 4/8	5 4/8	Carbon Co., WY	Frederick J. Gossman	Frederick J. Gossman	2008	238
82 4/8	83 7/8	17	17 3/8	6 1/8	6 1/8	3 1/8	2 7/8	9 7/8	3 4/8	5 3/8	5	Lea Co., NM	Dale Hislop	Dale Hislop	2008	238

Score												Locality	Hunter	Owner	Date	Rank
82 4/8	83 4/8	16 3/8	16 6/8	6 1/8	6 2/8	2 7/8	2 7/8	9 3/8	3 4/8	5 7/8	5 7/8	Yavapai Co., AZ	James M. Machac	James M. Machac	2008	238
82 4/8	84 2/8	16	15 6/8	7 2/8	7 2/8	2 5/8	2 5/8	8 3/8	3 6/8	6 1/8	6 1/8	Siskiyou Co., CA	Brent J. Miller	Brent J. Miller	2008	238
82 4/8	83 3/8	15 3/8	15 5/8	6 4/8	6 4/8	2 4/8	2 4/8	9 6/8	6	7 2/8	7 2/8	Humboldt Co., NV	Kenny H. Tavener	Kenny H. Tavener	2008	238
82 4/8	83 2/8	16	15 7/8	6 2/8	6 1/8	3 2/8	3 1/8	11 1/8	4 7/8	5 2/8	5 1/8	Mora Co., NM	Helen D. Van Dyke King	Helen D. Van Dyke King	2008	238
82 4/8	83 3/8	16 2/8	16 3/8	6 6/8	6 6/8	2 6/8	2 6/8	12 1/8	8 3/8	4 4/8	5	Emery Co., UT	Susan Ward	Susan Ward	2008	238
82 4/8	83 4/8	15 6/8	15 6/8	6 6/8	6 6/8	2 6/8	2 7/8	15 2/8	15 4/8	5 2/8	5 2/8	Sweetwater Co., WY	Charles K. Williams	Charles K. Williams	2008	238
82 4/8	84 2/8	15 3/8	15 6/8	6 5/8	6 5/8	2 6/8	2 7/8	9 3/8	6 2/8	6 4/8	6 4/8	Moffat Co., CO	Clay J. Evans	Clay J. Evans	2009	238
82 4/8	84 4/8	15 6/8	15 7/8	6	6	2 6/8	2 7/8	8 2/8	5 1/8	4 2/8	5	Huerfano Co., CO	Michael D. Gatlin	Michael D. Gatlin	2009	238
82 2/8	83 1/8	16	16	6	6	2 7/8	2 7/8	7 3/8	1 6/8	5	5	Navajo Co., AZ	W. Hays Gilstrap	W. Hays Gilstrap	2001	268
82 2/8	83 5/8	14	14 3/8	6 4/8	6 4/8	3	3	13 4/8	13 1/8	5 5/8	5 4/8	Fremont Co., CO	Chet Jones	Chet Jones	2002	268
82 2/8	82 5/8	16 4/8	16 1/8	7 4/8	7 4/8	3	3	10 2/8	5 5/8	5 4/8	5 4/8	Mora Co., NM	Becke E. Medlin	Becke E. Medlin	2006	268
82 2/8	83 1/8	16 4/8	16 4/8	6 2/8	6 2/8	2 6/8	2 4/8	7 5/8	3 2/8	5 4/8	5 4/8	Fox Valley, SK	Cary J. Bonogofski	Cary J. Bonogofski	2006	268
82 2/8	84 1/8	18 2/8	18 1/8	5 6/8	5 7/8	2 4/8	2 4/8	11 7/8	8 1/8	5 6/8	5 6/8	Harding Co., SD	Gentry Boswell	Gentry Boswell	2007	268
82 2/8	83 3/8	15 3/8	14 7/8	7 3/8	7 3/8	2 5/8	2 5/8	9 1/8	4 7/8	5 4/8	5 4/8	Natrona Co., WY	Owen J. Brown	Owen J. Brown	2007	268
82 2/8	83 7/8	16 2/8	16 2/8	6 2/8	6 1/8	2 5/8	2 6/8	12 2/8	8 7/8	6 2/8	6 1/8	Converse Co., WY	Steve R. Davis	Steve R. Davis	2007	268
82 2/8	85 6/8	15 7/8	15 4/8	6 5/8	6 6/8	2 6/8	2 5/8	10	4 4/8	5 4/8	5 4/8	Hudspeth Co., TX	Billy I. Dippel	Billy I. Dippel	2007	268
82 2/8	83 1/8	15 3/8	16 5/8	6 3/8	6 4/8	2 5/8	3 2/8	8 3/8	4 2/8	6 1/8	6 1/8	Moffat Co., CO	Len H. Guldman	Len H. Guldman	2007	268
82 2/8	83 3/8	15 2/8	14 7/8	6 6/8	6 6/8	3 1/8	2 6/8	15 6/8	14 5/8	4 6/8	4 6/8	Catron Co., NM	R. Douglas Isbell	R. Douglas Isbell	2007	268
82 2/8	83 7/8	17 3/8	17 4/8	6 2/8	6 2/8	3 1/8	3 3/8	13 3/8	10	5 2/8	5 2/8	Modoc Co., CA	Michael J. Mckoen	Michael J. Mckoen	2007	268
82 2/8	83 5/8	16 7/8	16 1/8	7	7	2 6/8	2 3/8	7 3/8	2 7/8	4 7/8	4 7/8	Yavapai Co., AZ	Bobby M. Priest	Bobby M. Priest	2007	268
82 2/8	84 2/8	16 2/8	16 6/8	6 6/8	7 5/8	3	2 5/8	11 3/8	8 5/8	5 6/8	5 6/8	Sweetwater Co., WY	Michael D. Swanson	Michael D. Swanson	2007	268
82 2/8	82 7/8	14 3/8	14 3/8	6 3/8	6 3/8	3	2 4/8	9 4/8	5 3/8	5 6/8	5 6/8	Elko Co., NV	Ron A. Toste	Ron A. Toste	2007	268
82 2/8	83 4/8	16 2/8	16 1/8	6 7/8	7 1/8	2 6/8	2 7/8	12 1/8	8 3/8	4 6/8	4 6/8	Colfax Co., NM	Michael F. Wieck	Michael F. Wieck	2007	268
82 2/8	82 5/8	15 3/8	15 1/8	6 2/8	6 2/8	3 3/8	3 2/8	11 7/8	9 3/8	5 7/8	5 7/8	Coconino Co., AZ	Blaine A. Dominy	Blaine A. Dominy	2008	268
82 2/8	82 4/8	14 6/8	14 6/8	6 4/8	6 4/8	3 3/8	3 3/8	9 6/8	6 6/8	5 2/8	5 2/8	Humboldt Co., NV	David D. Elizondo	David D. Elizondo	2008	268
82 2/8	83 6/8	15 5/8	15 5/8	6	6	2 5/8	2 5/8	10 1/8	6 3/8	3 6/8	3 6/8	Lassen Co., CA	Jeff A. Glenn	Jeff A. Glenn	2008	268
82 2/8	82 7/8	16	16	5 7/8	7 3/8	2 6/8	2 6/8	11 6/8	6 5/8	5 1/8	5 1/8	Sioux Co., NE	Ryan K. Hochstein	Ryan K. Hochstein	2008	268
82 2/8	83 5/8	15 7/8	15 6/8	7	7 1/8	2 7/8	2 7/8	11 4/8	6 1/8	4	4	Coconino Co., AZ	Michael D. Lassig	Michael D. Lassig	2008	268
82 2/8	83 3/8	18 5/8	18 4/8	7	6 1/8	2 6/8	2 4/8	7 7/8	2 5/8	6 4/8	6 4/8	Elko Co., NV	Louis M. Lemaire	Louis M. Lemaire	2008	268
82 2/8	82 6/8	15 7/8	15 7/8	6 7/8	6 2/8	2 4/8	2 5/8	10 4/8	5 2/8	5	5	Sublette Co., WY	Thomas A. Little	Thomas A. Little	2008	268
82 2/8	84	17	17	6	6 3/8	2 6/8	2 6/8	10 2/8	8 5/8	5	5	Fremont Co., WY	Kelly L. Britain	Kelly L. Britain	2009	268
82 2/8	83 3/8	14 6/8	14 6/8	7 3/8	6 5/8	2 7/8	2 7/8	9 4/8	7	6 7/8	6 7/8	Albany Co., WY	Chad Hoefs	Chad Hoefs	2009	268
82 2/8	83 4/8	13 2/8	13 6/8	7 1/8	6 3/8	2 6/8	2 4/8	12 6/8	10 2/8	5 5/8	5 5/8	Natrona Co., WY	Shawn L. Wagner	Shawn L. Wagner	2009	268
82	83 2/8	15 6/8	15 5/8	7	6 3/8	2 4/8	2 4/8	7 5/8	1 2/8	5 2/8	5 2/8	Catron Co., NM	Keith Appling	Keith Appling	2006	293
82	82 2/8	17 2/8	16 4/8	6 7/8	5 7/8	2 6/8	2 4/8	12 3/8	8 7/8	5 3/8	5 3/8	Carbon Co., WY	Willy F. Gill	Willy F. Gill	2006	293
82	82 2/8	15 6/8	15 6/8	6 1/8	7 3/8	2 7/8	2 5/8	10 5/8	5	5 2/8	5 2/8	Albany Co., WY	Tom Grygelko	Tom Grygelko	2006	293
82	83	16	16 1/8	6 3/8	7	2 5/8	2 4/8	10	6 2/8	6	6	Sweetwater Co., WY	Nathan D. Noble	Nathan D. Noble	2006	293
82	82 4/8	15 7/8	16 1/8	7 3/8	6 7/8	2 4/8	2 7/8	14 2/8	11 3/8	5 4/8	5 4/8	Carbon Co., WY	Steven O. Peterson	Steven O. Peterson	2006	293
82	82 5/8	15 7/8	14 6/8	6 4/8	7	2 7/8	2 4/8	9 6/8	8 2/8	5 2/8	5 2/8	Modoc Co., CA	Kevin J. Ward	Kevin J. Ward	2006	293
82	83 2/8	15 6/8	15 6/8	7 1/8	7 1/8	2 3/8	2 3/8	13 4/8	9	5 1/8	5 1/8	Malheur Co., OR	Anthony L. Barnett	Anthony L. Barnett	2007	293
82	83 4/8	14 7/8	15 1/8	6 4/8	6 4/8	3 3/8	3 3/8	9 3/8	7 3/8	5 4/8	5 4/8	Carbon Co., WY	Robert E. Bergquist	Robert E. Bergquist	2007	293

PRONGHORN

Antilocapra americana americana and related subspecies

Final Score	Gross Score	Length of horn R	L	Circumference of Base R	L	Circumference at Third Quarter R	L	Inside Spread	Tip to Tip Spread	Length of Prong R	L	Locality	Hunter	Owner	Date Killed	Rank
82	82 6/8	16 1/8	16 1/8	6 6/8	6 5/8	2 4/8	2 3/8	11 2/8	6 3/8	6	5 7/8	Lake Co., OR	Leighton K. Cornish	Leighton K. Cornish	2007	293
82	82 5/8	16 7/8	16 7/8	6 4/8	6 4/8	2 2/8	2 2/8	8 3/8	3 2/8	5 7/8	6 3/8	Natrona Co., WY	Eric M. Evenson	Eric M. Evenson	2007	293
82	82 4/8	16	15 7/8	6 7/8	6 7/8	2 4/8	2 5/8	10 1/8	9 4/8	4 7/8	5	Natrona Co., WY	J. Kyle Halford	J. Kyle Halford	2007	293
82	83 2/8	15 7/8	15 1/8	6 7/8	6 7/8	2 6/8	2 5/8	9 6/8	7 4/8	5 7/8	5 6/8	Sweetwater Co., WY	Richard M. Hartvigsen	Richard M. Hartvigsen	2007	293
82	84 7/8	16 7/8	15 7/8	6 4/8	7 2/8	2 1/8	2 5/8	14 1/8	10 6/8	6 4/8	6 4/8	Hudspeth Co., TX	Patrick K. Herring	Patrick K. Herring	2007	293
82	82 4/8	15 7/8	16	6 7/8	6 7/8	2 4/8	2 4/8	8 3/8	3 5/8	6 1/8	6 1/8	Reid Lake, SK	Bo Langer	Bo Langer	2007	293
82	83 5/8	15 6/8	15 4/8	6 7/8	6 7/8	2 6/8	2 5/8	11 7/8	9 3/8	6	5	Carbon Co., WY	Miguel Martinez	Miguel Martinez	2007	293
82	83 2/8	16 5/8	15 6/8	6 5/8	6 5/8	2 3/8	2 3/8	13 2/8	9 6/8	5 6/8	5 6/8	Park Co., WY	Paul A. Pearson	Paul A. Pearson	2007	293
82	83 5/8	15 5/8	16 2/8	6 3/8	6 4/8	2 5/8	2 6/8	12 2/8	9 4/8	5 4/8	5 7/8	Carbon Co., WY	Jack E. Risner	Jack E. Risner	2007	293
82	82 4/8	14 6/8	14 3/8	6 6/8	6 6/8	2 7/8	2 7/8	9 1/8	7 3/8	5 6/8	5 6/8	Converse Co., WY	Malcolm S. Wade, Jr.	Malcolm S. Wade, Jr.	2007	293
82	83 7/8	15	15	7 1/8	6 5/8	2 6/8	2 6/8	8 2/8	4	6 1/8	6 1/8	Fremont Co., WY	Steve M. Berrett	Steve M. Berrett	2008	293
82	83 5/8	16 3/8	16 1/8	6 3/8	6 3/8	2 5/8	2 5/8	11 3/8	7 3/8	5 1/8	5 3/8	Fremont Co., WY	Mark A. Blake	Mark A. Blake	2008	293
82	83 4/8	16 2/8	17 1/8	6 5/8	6 4/8	2 4/8	2 5/8	11 4/8	6 3/8	5 6/8	6	Natrona Co., WY	Chad D. Bohn	Chad D. Bohn	2008	293
82	83 6/8	16 3/8	16 3/8	6 1/8	6 2/8	3 1/8	3 2/8	12 1/8	7 7/8	4 1/8	5 3/8	Socorro Co., NM	Michael R. Carlson	Michael R. Carlson	2008	293
82	83	15 4/8	15 3/8	6 7/8	6 4/8	2 4/8	2 4/8	8 4/8	5 4/8	6 3/8	6 3/8	Success, SK	Christopher Garland	Christopher Garland	2008	293
82	82 4/8	16	16	6 2/8	6 1/8	3 2/8	3 2/8	11 2/8	7 2/8	5	4 7/8	Mora Co., NM	Grant A. Medlin	Grant A. Medlin	2008	293
82	83 1/8	15 6/8	16 2/8	6 3/8	6 3/8	2 2/8	2 2/8	13	10 1/8	6 4/8	7	Moffat Co., CO	Darrell D. Poulter	Darrell D. Poulter	2008	293
82	82 2/8	15	15	6 7/8	6 7/8	2 5/8	2 5/8	13	8 5/8	6	6 2/8	Carbon Co., WY	Duwayne Statzer	Duwayne Statzer	2008	293
82	82 5/8	16 6/8	16 6/8	6	5 6/8	2 6/8	2 6/8	9 3/8	2 6/8	6	5 6/8	Hudspeth Co., TX	Kevin R. Williams	Kevin R. Williams	2008	293
82	82 6/8	16	16 2/8	5 7/8	5 7/8	3 2/8	3 1/8	9 7/8	5 4/8	5 1/8	5 1/8	Hudspeth Co., TX	Jerome O. Chapman	Jerome O. Chapman	2009	293
82	82 4/8	16 2/8	16 3/8	6 5/8	6 5/8	2 6/8	2 6/8	12 4/8	8 4/8	4 4/8	4 3/8	Humboldt Co., NV	Wesley W. Edney	Wesley W. Edney	2009	293
82	82 6/8	16 4/8	16 4/8	6 4/8	6 4/8	2 4/8	2 5/8	10	4 6/8	5 5/8	5 2/8	Natrona Co., WY	Eddie J. Hinkle	Eddie J. Hinkle	2009	293
82	82 5/8	14 4/8	14 4/8	6 7/8	6 6/8	3 3/8	3 2/8	8 4/8	4 5/8	5 2/8	5	Carbon Co., WY	Jared J. Mason	Jared J. Mason	2009	293
82	82 4/8	15 5/8	15 7/8	7	6 6/8	2 5/8	2 5/8	6 3/8	3 7/8	5 6/8	5 4/8	Elko Co., NV	Jacob A. Reed	Jacob A. Reed	2009	293
82	83	14 7/8	14 6/8	6 6/8	6 6/8	3	3	5 5/8	4 6/8	5 6/8	5 4/8	Carbon Co., WY	Thomas A. Thompson	Thomas A. Thompson	2009	293
81 6/8	82 5/8	14 7/8	15 1/8	7 2/8	6 7/8	2 6/8	2 6/8	7 7/8	2 3/8	5 3/8	5 2/8	Niobrara Co., WY	Danny L. Chapman	Danny L. Chapman	2006	326
81 6/8	83	15 2/8	14 6/8	6 7/8	6 2/8	2 6/8	2 4/8	15	11 2/8	6	6 2/8	Lipscomb Co., TX	Carl W. Daubitz	Carl W. Daubitz	2006	326
81 6/8	82 7/8	14 6/8	15 1/8	6 3/8	6 2/8	3 3/8	3 1/8	10	5 7/8	5 4/8	5 4/8	Hartley Co., TX	Michael D. Fain	Michael D. Fain	2006	326
81 6/8	82 4/8	15 5/8	15 7/8	6 2/8	6 2/8	2 6/8	2 6/8	13 2/8	12 1/8	5 5/8	6	Fremont Co., WY	Larry A. Staten	Larry A. Staten	2006	326
81 6/8	82 1/8	15 3/8	15 2/8	6 6/8	6 6/8	2 6/8	2 6/8	12 5/8	10 4/8	5 3/8	5 2/8	Carbon Co., WY	Brian M. Jensen	Brian M. Jensen	2007	326
81 6/8	82 2/8	15 7/8	15 6/8	6 5/8	6 5/8	2 7/8	2 7/8	10 4/8	5 5/8	5	4 7/8	Powder River Co., MT	Les A. Williams	Les A. Williams	2007	326

81 6/8	82 2/8	15 1/8	15 1/8	6 4/8	6 4/8	2 7/8	3	9 3/8	7 2/8	5 1/8	5 1/8	Weld Co., CO	John-David C. Broderius	John-David C. Broderius	2008	326
81 6/8	82 6/8	15 6/8	16 1/8	6 2/8	6 1/8	2	1 7/8	10 3/8	7 2/8	7	7 2/8	Millard Co., UT	Greg S. Dalton	Greg S. Dalton	2008	326
81 6/8	83	16 1/8	16	6	6	2 6/8	2 5/8	10 7/8	7 4/8	5 6/8	6 2/8	Meade Co., SD	Scott M. Herbert	Scott M. Herbert	2008	326
81 6/8	82 2/8	16	15 1/8	6 5/8	6 5/8	2 5/8	2 5/8	11 4/8	6 2/8	4 6/8	5 2/8	Carbon Co., WY	Danette L. Perrien	Danette L. Perrien	2008	326
81 6/8	82 3/8	15 2/8	15 2/8	6 6/8	6 5/8	2 5/8	2 5/8	10 5/8	8 7/8	6	5 7/8	Natrona Co., WY	Raymond J. Zupancic	Raymond J. Zupancic	2008	326
81 4/8	83 1/8	14 6/8	14 6/8	7	7	2 7/8	2 6/8	10	4 7/8	5 2/8	5 2/8	Chouteau Co., MT	Gerald L. Brockpahler	Gerald L. Brockpahler	2005	337
81 4/8	82 2/8	14 4/8	14 4/8	6 4/8	6 3/8	2 6/8	2 6/8	11 2/8	10	5 2/8	5 6/8	Fremont Co., WY	Greg E. Fuechsel	Greg E. Fuechsel	2006	337
81 4/8	82 3/8	14 5/8	14 5/8	7 2/8	7 2/8	2 3/8	2 4/8	14 4/8	10 6/8	5 4/8	6 4/8	Natrona Co., WY	Craig S. Talbot	Craig S. Talbot	2006	337
81 4/8	82 7/8	15 5/8	15 7/8	6 6/8	6 6/8	3 3/8	2 7/8	13 5/8	11 3/8	5 4/8	5 4/8	Routt Co., CO	James O. Menger III	James O. Menger III	2007	337
81 4/8	82	16 5/8	16 5/8	6 5/8	6 2/8	2 6/8	2 5/8	9	2 5/8	5 2/8	5 4/8	Fremont Co., WY	Mike Portschy	Mike Portschy	2007	337
81 4/8	82 3/8	14 6/8	15	7 2/8	7 2/8	2 3/8	2 3/8	11 2/8	5 6/8	5 3/8	5 6/8	Washoe Co., NV	Kyle T. Massaro	Kyle T. Massaro	2008	337
81 4/8	82 2/8	16 2/8	16	6 2/8	6 2/8	2 7/8	2 5/8	20	20	5 5/8	5 3/8	Hudspeth Co., TX	Dan E. McBride	Dan E. McBride	2008	337
81 4/8	82 6/8	15 7/8	15 7/8	6 7/8	6 1/8	2 5/8	2 6/8	9 7/8	5 3/8	6 5/8	6	Fremont Co., WY	Robert J. McGreevey	Robert J. McGreevey	2008	337
81 4/8	82 2/8	14 5/8	14 5/8	6 6/8	6 6/8	2 6/8	2 6/8	6 7/8	3 5/8	5 6/8	5 1/8	McCone Co., MT	Chandra L. Nettles	Chandra L. Nettles	2008	337
81 4/8	82 3/8	15 2/8	15	6 1/8	6 5/8	2 6/8	2 5/8	10 1/8	5 7/8	6 5/8	6 6/8	Fremont Co., WY	Brian W. Steward	Brian W. Steward	2008	337
81 4/8	82 7/8	16 4/8	16 4/8	6 4/8	6 2/8	2 7/8	2 7/8	10 5/8	7 2/8	4 4/8	4 6/8	Socorro Co., NM	Pate Stewart	Pate Stewart	2008	337
81 4/8	82	16 2/8	16 2/8	6 5/8	6 4/8	3	2 7/8	12 2/8	8 4/8	4 7/8	5	Hudspeth Co., TX	Richard Strom	Richard Strom	2008	337
81 4/8	81 7/8	15 2/8	15 2/8	6 4/8	6 4/8	2 6/8	2 6/8	11	7 7/8	5 2/8	5 1/8	Union Co., NM	John D. Evans	John D. Evans	2009	337
81 4/8	82 3/8	15 2/8	15 2/8	6 3/8	6 3/8	2 5/8	2 5/8	12 2/8	3 7/8	6	5 3/8	Lassen Co., CA	Terri L. Mankins	Terri L. Mankins	2009	337
81 4/8	82 5/8	16 5/8	16 5/8	6 4/8	6 4/8	2 3/8	2 5/8	8 6/8	3 7/8	6	5 5/8	Natrona Co., WY	Joe P. Olson	Joe P. Olson	2009	337

PRONGHORN
FINAL SCORE: 82 4/8
HUNTER: Brittany R. Streissguth

PRONGHORN
FINAL SCORE: 83 6/8
HUNTER: Calvin K. LaGrone

PRONGHORN
FINAL SCORE: 84 4/8
HUNTER: William S. Erdmann

PRONGHORN
FINAL SCORE: 83 4/8
HUNTER: William G. Kyle

Antilocapra americana americana and related subspecies

Final Score	Gross Score	Length of horn R.	L.	Circumference of Base R.	L.	Circumference at Third Quarter R.	L.	Inside Spread	Tip to Tip Spread	Length of Prong R.	L.	Locality	Hunter	Owner	Date Killed	Rank
81 4/8	82 6/8	13 7/8	13 5/8	7 1/8	7	3	3	10 7/8	8 6/8	5 1/8	5 6/8	Chouteau Co., MT	Kirk D. Pederson	Kirk D. Pederson	2009	337
81 4/8	82 3/8	15 1/8	15	6 7/8	6 6/8	2 5/8	2 4/8	8 4/8	3 5/8	6	5 5/8	Sweetwater Co., WY	Thomas C. Wilson	Thomas C. Wilson	2009	337
81 2/8	82 6/8	14 7/8	15 3/8	6	6	2 7/8	2 6/8	11	7 1/8	6 4/8	7	Quay Co., NM	Dorothy J. Peiffer	Dorothy J. Peiffer	2006	354
81 2/8	82 1/8	15 5/8	15 6/8	6 5/8	6 4/8	2 6/8	3	9 3/8	3 4/8	5 6/8	5 6/8	Great Sand Hills, SK	Jack Clary	Jack Clary	2007	354
81 2/8	81 5/8	14 6/8	14 5/8	6 6/8	6 6/8	2 7/8	2 5/8	11 5/8	8	6 2/8	6 2/8	Phillips Co., MT	Stuart J. Farnsworth	Stuart J. Farnsworth	2007	354
81 2/8	82 1/8	16 4/8	16 1/8	7	6 7/8	2 4/8	2 3/8	9 4/8	5 4/8	4 7/8	4 5/8	Perkins Co., SD	Clint J. Gillespie	Clint J. Gillespie	2007	354
81 2/8	81 7/8	16 4/8	16 6/8	6 2/8	6 3/8	2 5/8	2 5/8	13 5/8	8	4 4/8	4 3/8	Mora Co., NM	William D. Karnes	William D. Karnes	2007	354
81 2/8	81 7/8	16 6/8	16 7/8	6	6	2 6/8	2 6/8	10 6/8	6 6/8	5 2/8	5 5/8	San Miguel Co., NM	Brad Leavell	Brad Leavell	2007	354
81 2/8	82 6/8	15 2/8	15 2/8	6 5/8	6 5/8	2 6/8	3 1/8	11 1/8	6 6/8	5 3/8	4 7/8	Chouteau Co., MT	James F. Voborsky	James F. Voborsky	2007	354
81 2/8	82	16 3/8	16 1/8	6	5 7/8	2 5/8	2 5/8	13 1/8	7 7/8	6 1/8	6 2/8	Garfield Co., UT	Jeffrey A. Anderson	Jeffrey A. Anderson	2008	354
81 2/8	82 1/8	16 2/8	16 2/8	6 4/8	6 2/8	3	3 2/8	10 2/8	9 3/8	4 6/8	5	Fremont Co., WY	Richard J. Brower	Richard J. Brower	2008	354
81 2/8	82 5/8	15 6/8	15 1/8	6 4/8	6 5/8	2 6/8	2 4/8	11	6 6/8	5 2/8	5 2/8	Humboldt Co., NV	Quinn A. Hesterlee	Quinn A. Hesterlee	2008	354
81 2/8	82 2/8	16 4/8	16 4/8	6	6	2 5/8	2 7/8	10 7/8	4 6/8	5 2/8	5 6/8	Hudspeth Co., TX	D. Heath McBride	D. Heath McBride	2008	354
81 2/8	81 6/8	15 4/8	15 4/8	6 4/8	6 4/8	2 3/8	2 4/8	11	9 6/8	5 7/8	5 6/8	Sweetwater Co., WY	Terry A. Reeves	Terry A. Reeves	2008	354
81 2/8	82 1/8	16 7/8	17 2/8	6 3/8	6 2/8	2 5/8	2 5/8	8 5/8	4 7/8	5 4/8	5 5/8	Crook Co., WY	Stuart N. Swenson	Stuart N. Swenson	2008	354
81 2/8	81 7/8	14 5/8	15 4/8	6 6/8	6 7/8	3	2 7/8	10 7/8	7 2/8	5 2/8	5 2/8	San Miguel Co., NM	Benny R. Wood	Benny R. Wood	2008	354
81 2/8	82 2/8	15 7/8	15 7/8	6 5/8	6 5/8	3 2/8	3	11	9 3/8	5	4 6/8	Beaver Co., UT	Larry Barnes	Larry Barnes	2009	354
81 2/8	82 4/8	16 4/8	16 2/8	6 4/8	6 2/8	3	2 7/8	10 2/8	3 2/8	5 2/8	4 7/8	Washoe Co., NV	Bernie S. Crooks	Bernie S. Crooks	2009	354
81 2/8	81 5/8	15	15	7 1/8	7 2/8	2 5/8	2 5/8	6 7/8	2 7/8	4 7/8	5	Fremont Co., WY	Palmer J. Mattson III	Palmer J. Mattson III	2009	354
81 2/8	82 4/8	16	15 6/8	7 1/8	7	2 3/8	2 3/8	9 7/8	5 3/8	6	5 4/8	Lincoln Co., WY	Patrick Rodenbaugh	Patrick Rodenbaugh	2009	354
81 2/8	81 6/8	14 7/8	15	6 3/8	6 3/8	2 6/8	2 6/8	12 2/8	8	5 4/8	5 2/8	Elko Co., NV	Paula Y. Sena	Paula Y. Sena	2009	354
81 2/8	82	15 5/8	15 7/8	6 4/8	6 4/8	2 4/8	2 5/8	11	10 3/8	5 6/8	6	Las Animas Co., CO	Barry J. Smith	Barry J. Smith	2009	354
81 2/8	82	14 7/8	14 7/8	6 1/8	6 1/8	2 7/8	3	10 1/8	8 3/8	5 5/8	5 6/8	Meade Co., SD	Chris E. Taylor	Chris E. Taylor	2009	354
81 2/8	82 1/8	15 4/8	15 3/8	6 3/8	6 5/8	3	3	6 6/8	2 4/8	5 4/8	5 6/8	Moffat Co., CO	Jacob D. Vanko	Jacob D. Vanko	2009	354
81 2/8	81 7/8	16 4/8	16 1/8	6 3/8	6 3/8	2 2/8	2 2/8	13 1/8	8 1/8	5 4/8	5 4/8	Modoc Co., CA	Matthew S. Wells	Matthew S. Wells	2009	354
81	82 1/8	15 1/8	15 3/8	7 2/8	6 6/8	2 2/8	2 7/8	9 6/8	5 6/8	5 4/8	5 2/8	Rio Grande Co., CO	Donna J. Crask	Donna J. Crask	2003	377
81	81 7/8	15 4/8	15 1/8	6 5/8	6 5/8	2 6/8	2 6/8	9 6/8	5	6 1/8	5 7/8	Meade Co., SD	Austin L. Jordan	Austin L. Jordan	2005	377
81	81 5/8	14 4/8	14 6/8	7 1/8	7 1/8	2 3/8	2 3/8	13 1/8	9 7/8	5 5/8	5 4/8	Carbon Co., WY	Francis J. Cuneo, Jr.	Francis J. Cuneo, Jr.	2006	377
81	82 3/8	13 5/8	13 5/8	6 6/8	6 6/8	3 5/8	3 3/8	12 3/8	12 3/8	5 6/8	6 3/8	Klamath Co., OR	Donald E. Lehrmann	Donald E. Lehrmann	2006	377
81	81 3/8	15 2/8	15 3/8	6 6/8	6 6/8	2 5/8	2 6/8	9 5/8	4 2/8	5 1/8	5 1/8	Carbon Co., WY	Gary R. MacBlane	Gary R. MacBlane	2006	377
81	81 6/8	17 1/8	16 7/8	6 3/8	6 2/8	2 4/8	2 4/8	8 5/8	2 2/8	4 4/8	4 6/8	Perkins Co., SD	Donald M. Cameron	Donald M. Cameron	2007	377
81	81 4/8	14	14	6 7/8	6 6/8	2 4/8	2 4/8	8 4/8	5	6 7/8	6 6/8	Moffat Co., CO	David J. Knight	David J. Knight	2007	377

Score											Locality	Owner	Hunter	Date	Page
81	81⁵/₈	14⁴/₈	7²/₈	2⁶/₈	7¹/₈	2⁶/₈	10¹/₈	7¹/₈	5⁶/₈	5⁵/₈	Carbon Co., WY	Donald E. Perrien	Donald E. Perrien	2007	377
81	81⁵/₈	18⁴/₈	5⁵/₈	2³/₈	5⁶/₈	2³/₈	13	9⁴/₈	5	5	Arizona	E.D. Doughart	Brad F. Pfeffer	PR 2007	377
81	83	16¹/₈	6³/₈	2⁴/₈	6³/₈	2⁴/₈	7⁴/₈	1²/₈	6³/₈	4⁵/₈	Elmore Co., ID	Scott D. Ramsay	Scott D. Ramsay	2007	377
81	81⁶/₈	16²/₈	6²/₈	3¹/₈	6³/₈	3	16⁴/₈	12¹/₈	5¹/₈	5¹/₈	Socorro Co., NM	Dave M. Westrum	Dave M. Westrum	2007	377
81	81⁵/₈	15³/₈	6⁵/₈	2⁶/₈	6⁴/₈	2⁶/₈	13⁶/₈	10¹/₈	5²/₈	5³/₈	Lake Co., OR	Fred W. Ashley	Fred W. Ashley	2008	377
81	81⁷/₈	14³/₈	7	2⁷/₈	7²/₈	2⁷/₈	9³/₈	6⁵/₈	5⁴/₈	5¹/₈	Natrona Co., WY	Robin E. Crisler	Robin E. Crisler	2008	377
81	81⁵/₈	14⁴/₈	6³/₈	3	6³/₈	3	11²/₈	8	5⁵/₈	5⁴/₈	El Paso Co., CO	Christopher M. Murray	Christopher M. Murray	2008	377
81	81²/₈	14⁶/₈	7	2⁴/₈	7	2⁵/₈	10⁴/₈	7²/₈	5⁴/₈	5⁴/₈	Fremont Co., WY	Lance A. Nading	Lance A. Nading	2008	377
81	82³/₈	14⁷/₈	7³/₈	2⁵/₈	7²/₈	2⁶/₈	8⁴/₈	4	5²/₈	4⁶/₈	Carbon Co., WY	Zachary S. Sherman	Zachary S. Sherman	2008	377
81	81⁷/₈	15³/₈	6⁶/₈	2³/₈	6⁵/₈	2³/₈	12⁶/₈	9⁶/₈	6	6²/₈	Carbon Co., WY	Ronald A. Lachini, Sr.	Ronald A. Lachini, Sr.	2009	377
81	81⁷/₈	16¹/₈	6³/₈	3¹/₈	6³/₈	3¹/₈	10¹/₈	5²/₈	4¹/₈	4⁵/₈	San Miguel Co., NM	Thomas F. Miles	Thomas F. Miles	2009	377
81	81³/₈	15⁷/₈	6³/₈	2⁷/₈	6³/₈	2⁷/₈	13³/₈	11²/₈	5¹/₈	5²/₈	Sweetwater Co., WY	Stephen N. Warner	Stephen N. Warner	2009	377
80⁶/₈	81³/₈	15⁶/₈	6⁵/₈	2⁵/₈	6⁴/₈	2⁵/₈	8	2⁷/₈	4⁷/₈	5¹/₈	Harding Co., SD	Mark A. Lembke	Mark A. Lembke	1999	396
80⁶/₈	81⁶/₈	16⁵/₈	6³/₈	2⁵/₈	6⁴/₈	2⁵/₈	8⁶/₈	6³/₈	6¹/₈	4⁷/₈	Adams Co., CO	Joseph A. Quaratino	Joseph A. Quaratino	2004	396
80⁶/₈	81⁴/₈	15⁶/₈	6⁴/₈	2³/₈	6²/₈	2²/₈	8³/₈	4²/₈	6¹/₈	6¹/₈	Rosebud Co., MT	Kurt D. Rued	Kurt D. Rued	2004	396
80⁶/₈	81⁵/₈	15²/₈	6⁵/₈	2⁶/₈	6⁵/₈	2⁷/₈	9⁵/₈	4⁷/₈	6³/₈	6¹/₈	Meade Co., SD	Karsten A. Jordan	Karsten A. Jordan	2005	396
80⁶/₈	81	14⁴/₈	6⁴/₈	2⁷/₈	6⁴/₈	2⁷/₈	10⁶/₈	8²/₈	6³/₈	6³/₈	Converse Co., WY	Sarah A. Anderson	Sarah A. Anderson	2006	396
80⁶/₈	81³/₈	15²/₈	7	2⁵/₈	6⁷/₈	2⁴/₈	11⁶/₈	8¹/₈	5¹/₈	6³/₈	Hudspeth Co., TX	Wanda H. Bazemore	Wanda H. Bazemore	2006	396
80⁶/₈	81³/₈	15²/₈	6⁶/₈	2⁶/₈	6⁷/₈	2⁶/₈	8	3⁶/₈	5⁴/₈	5²/₈	Converse Co., WY	Gregory C. Flynn	Gregory C. Flynn	2006	396
80⁶/₈	81⁶/₈	16²/₈	6³/₈	2⁷/₈	6⁵/₈	3	16⁴/₈	14¹/₈	5	5³/₈	Carbon Co., WY	Cooper L. Lauck	Cooper L. Lauck	2006	396
80⁶/₈	81⁶/₈	16	6	2⁶/₈	6	2⁵/₈	10⁶/₈	7²/₈	5⁵/₈	4⁵/₈	McPherson Co., NE	Dustin C. Noble	Dustin C. Noble	2006	396
80⁶/₈	82³/₈	16¹/₈	6⁴/₈	2⁶/₈	6⁴/₈	2⁷/₈	10²/₈	5⁶/₈	6⁴/₈	5³/₈	De Baca Co., NM	Merle L. Schreiner	Merle L. Schreiner	2006	396
80⁶/₈	81²/₈	15⁴/₈	7¹/₈	2⁶/₈	7¹/₈	2⁶/₈	6³/₈	1⁶/₈	5	6³/₈	Albany Co., WY	James C. Shindle III	James C. Shindle III	2006	396
80⁶/₈	81⁷/₈	15⁴/₈	6²/₈	2⁷/₈	6⁶/₈	2⁶/₈	15⁴/₈	15⁴/₈	5⁵/₈	5	Lipscomb Co., TX	Carl W. Daubitz	Carl W. Daubitz	2007	396
80⁶/₈	81⁶/₈	15	6³/₈	2⁵/₈	6³/₈	2⁵/₈	9	9	6	5⁵/₈	Cypress Lake, SK	Elvis Fink	Elvis Fink	2007	396
80⁶/₈	81³/₈	15⁷/₈	—	—	—	—	—	—	—	—	Carbon Co., WY	Patricia G. Hettick	Patricia G. Hettick	2007	396
80⁶/₈	—	—	—	—	—	—	—	—	—	—	Butte Co., SD	Christopher J. Jackson	Christopher J. Jackson	2007	396
80⁶/₈	81⁶/₈	15⁷/₈	6⁶/₈	2⁵/₈	6⁷/₈	2⁴/₈	15	6¹/₈	4⁶/₈	5⁵/₈	Perkins Co., SD	Jeff A. Lick	Jeff A. Lick	2007	396
80⁶/₈	81⁵/₈	16²/₈	6²/₈	2³/₈	6²/₈	2³/₈	12	6²/₈	6¹/₈	5⁶/₈	Sioux Co., NE	Jina L. Nemnich	Jina L. Nemnich	2007	396
80⁶/₈	81⁴/₈	15⁴/₈	6⁷/₈	2⁴/₈	6⁷/₈	2⁴/₈	10⁷/₈	7	5²/₈	5²/₈	Carbon Co., WY	Timothy W. Stanosheck	Timothy W. Stanosheck	2007	396
80⁶/₈	81⁵/₈	14⁷/₈	6⁴/₈	3²/₈	6⁵/₈	3	9	7	5³/₈	5³/₈	Moffat Co., CO	John C. Vanko	John C. Vanko	2007	396
80⁶/₈	82²/₈	16²/₈	6²/₈	2⁶/₈	6	2⁵/₈	8¹/₈	2³/₈	6²/₈	5⁴/₈	Meade Co., SD	Jesse L. Wheeler	Jesse L. Wheeler	2007	396
80⁶/₈	81⁴/₈	16	6³/₈	2⁶/₈	6³/₈	2⁶/₈	11¹/₈	5³/₈	5²/₈	5⁵/₈	Butte Co., SD	Charles P. Atkinson	Charles P. Atkinson	2008	396
80⁶/₈	81⁴/₈	17²/₈	6	3¹/₈	6	2⁷/₈	13⁶/₈	11	4¹/₈	4¹/₈	Hudspeth Co., TX	Sheldon Grothaus	Sheldon Grothaus	2008	396
80⁶/₈	81⁶/₈	16	6⁴/₈	2⁶/₈	6⁵/₈	3	16¹/₈	10⁷/₈	4⁴/₈	4⁶/₈	Luna Co., NM	Keith C. Halstead	Keith C. Halstead	2008	396
80⁶/₈	81⁶/₈	15⁵/₈	6⁵/₈	2⁷/₈	6²/₈	3²/₈	7⁶/₈	4²/₈	4²/₈	4⁴/₈	Campbell Co., WY	William P. Hanberry	William P. Hanberry	2008	396
80⁶/₈	81³/₈	14	7¹/₈	2⁷/₈	7	2⁷/₈	8²/₈	4⁵/₈	6	5⁶/₈	Niobrara Co., WY	Shawn E. Hickey	Shawn E. Hickey	2008	396
80⁶/₈	81³/₈	15⁶/₈	6³/₈	2⁴/₈	6²/₈	2⁴/₈	8⁵/₈	3⁷/₈	6	6²/₈	Emery Co., UT	Amanda D. Lake	Amanda D. Lake	2008	396
80⁶/₈	81⁵/₈	16⁷/₈	5⁶/₈	2⁷/₈	5⁷/₈	2⁷/₈	11	6³/₈	5⁵/₈	5¹/₈	Guadalupe Co., NM	Larry J. Lombard	Larry J. Lombard	2008	396

PRONGHORN

Antilocapra americana americana and related subspecies

Final Score	Gross Score	Length of horn R.	L.	Circumference of Base R.	L.	Circumference at Third Quarter R.	L.	Inside Spread	Tip to Tip Spread	Length of Prong R.	L.	Locality	Hunter	Owner	Date Killed	Rank
80 6/8	81 2/8	14 1/8	14 1/8	7 1/8	6 7/8	2 5/8	2 6/8	10	10 5/8	5 7/8	6	Natrona Co., WY	Duane F. Butler	Duane F. Butler	2009	396
80 6/8	81 6/8	14 6/8	14 7/8	6 4/8	6 5/8	2 4/8	2 5/8	9 5/8	5 6/8	6 3/8	6 3/8	Hudspeth Co., TX	Alexander W. Kibler	Alexander W. Kibler	2009	396
80 6/8	82 4/8	16 4/8	16 5/8	6 4/8	6 4/8	2 7/8	2 7/8	12 3/8	11 1/8	3 5/8	3	Lander Co., NV	Derrick J. Rader	Derrick J. Rader	2009	396
80 6/8	81 5/8	15 5/8	15 4/8	6 2/8	5 7/8	2 4/8	2 4/8	9 2/8	5 6/8	6 4/8	6 4/8	Fox Valley, SK	Warren S. Thompson	Warren S. Thompson	2009	396
80 4/8	81 2/8	15 6/8	15 4/8	6 2/8	6 2/8	3 2/8	3 2/8	15 6/8	16 3/8	3 5/8	4	Carbon Co., WY	John J. Corbett	John J. Corbett	1938	427
80 4/8	82	15	15 4/8	6 2/8	6 2/8	2 6/8	2 7/8	11 4/8	6 4/8	5 4/8	6	Elko Co., NV	Robert C. Carpenter	Robert C. Carpenter	2006	427
80 4/8	81 4/8	15 6/8	16 1/8	6 2/8	6 2/8	2 5/8	2 6/8	11	5 6/8	5 2/8	5 5/8	Moffat Co., CO	Roger D. Daves	Roger D. Daves	2006	427
80 4/8	81 4/8	15 6/8	15 3/8	6 3/8	6 4/8	2 5/8	2 5/8	9 7/8	5 6/8	5 2/8	5 4/8	Las Animas Co., CO	Terrance S. Marcum	Terrance S. Marcum	2006	427
80 4/8	81 4/8	16 1/8	15 6/8	6 2/8	6 2/8	2 5/8	2 5/8	8 2/8	2 3/8	5 5/8	5 3/8	Quay Co., NM	Dennison V. Peiffer	Dennison V. Peiffer	2006	427
80 4/8	81 4/8	15 5/8	15 5/8	6 2/8	6 3/8	2 5/8	2 4/8	11 4/8	9 7/8	5 3/8	5 7/8	Natrona Co., WY	John B. Price	John B. Price	2006	427
80 4/8	82	16 7/8	16	6 2/8	6 2/8	2 6/8	2 6/8	10 3/8	7 2/8	5 4/8	5 2/8	Sublette Co., WY	Jacob M. Traughber	Jacob M. Traughber	2006	427
80 6/8	80 6/8	15 4/8	15 4/8	6 4/8	6 4/8	2 6/8	2 6/8	12 4/8	9 1/8	5 1/8	4 7/8	Converse Co., WY	Gary W. Bolinger	Gary W. Bolinger	2007	427
80 6/8	81 6/8	15 6/8	16	6 6/8	6 4/8	2 4/8	2 4/8	8 3/8	4 1/8	5 4/8	5	Uinta Co., WY	Robert L. Bozzini	Robert L. Bozzini	2007	427
80 4/8	81	15 3/8	15	6 1/8	6 1/8	2 7/8	2 7/8	12	9 5/8	4 7/8	4 7/8	Hudspeth Co., TX	Thomas J. Buxton	Thomas J. Buxton	2007	427
80 4/8	81 3/8	15 1/8	15 3/8	6 5/8	6 5/8	2 4/8	2 5/8	11 6/8	7 1/8	5 4/8	5 5/8	Ziebach Co., SD	Matthew R. Grunig	Matthew R. Grunig	2007	427
80 6/8	80 6/8	14 4/8	14 4/8	6 5/8	6 5/8	3	3	10	5 4/8	4 7/8	5	Mohave Co., AZ	Clinton J. Harrold	Clinton J. Harrold	2007	427
80 4/8	81 7/8	15 6/8	15 3/8	6 2/8	6 2/8	2 3/8	2 3/8	14 3/8	13 2/8	5 6/8	6	Humboldt Co., NV	Tamara D. Isom	Tamara D. Isom	2007	427
80 4/8	81 2/8	15 3/8	15 3/8	6 6/8	6 6/8	2 6/8	2 4/8	9 5/8	8	5 3/8	5 1/8	Fremont Co., WY	William H. Lassiter	William H. Lassiter	2007	427
80 4/8	81 5/8	15 7/8	16 2/8	6 4/8	6 4/8	2 2/8	2 4/8	14 4/8	11 4/8	5 5/8	5 5/8	Sweetwater Co., WY	Thomas D. Lundgren	Thomas D. Lundgren	2007	427
80 4/8	82	15 3/8	15 4/8	6 4/8	6 3/8	3	3	9 2/8	6 4/8	5	4	Hudspeth Co., TX	Dan E. McBride	Dan E. McBride	2007	427
80 4/8	80 7/8	15	15	6 7/8	6 7/8	3	2 6/8	9 4/8	4 3/8	4 7/8	4 7/8	Meade Co., SD	Joseph E. Bares	Joseph E. Bares	2008	427
80 4/8	81 4/8	15 3/8	15 4/8	5 7/8	6 1/8	2 7/8	3	10 2/8	5 3/8	6 5/8	6 1/8	Guadalupe Co., NM	Richard J. Buller	Richard J. Buller	2008	427
80 4/8	81 1/8	15	15 1/8	6 3/8	6 1/8	2 6/8	2 6/8	10 2/8	5 6/8	5 7/8	5 6/8	Fremont Co., WY	Michael P. Clancy II	Michael P. Clancy II	2008	427
80 4/8	83 2/8	14 5/8	15 4/8	7 1/8	7	3 2/8	2 5/8	9 4/8	6 3/8	6 2/8	5 4/8	Natrona Co., WY	Steve M. Berrett	Steve M. Berrett	2009	427
80 4/8	81 4/8	14 5/8	14 2/8	6 4/8	6 5/8	2 5/8	2 6/8	8 6/8	5 7/8	5 7/8	6	Sweetwater Co., WY	Jody L. Meyer	Jody L. Meyer	2009	427
80 2/8	81 2/8	15 2/8	15 5/8	6 3/8	6 4/8	2 5/8	2 5/8	9 1/8	4 5/8	5 6/8	5 6/8	Butte Co., SD	Gary D. English	Gary D. English	1991	448
80 2/8	82	15 3/8	14 7/8	7 1/8	7 3/8	2 3/8	2 3/8	8 6/8	3 4/8	6 3/8	5 5/8	Uinta Co., WY	Jason D. Winters	Jason D. Winters	2004	448
80 2/8	81 5/8	17	17	6	6	2 3/8	2 2/8	8 3/8	4 5/8	6 2/8	5 1/8	Humboldt Co., NV	Heather M. Gingell	Heather M. Gingell	2006	448
80 2/8	81	14 1/8	14 2/8	7 2/8	7 2/8	2 7/8	3	8 5/8	3 7/8	5 3/8	5 2/8	Natrona Co., WY	J. Kyle Halford	J. Kyle Halford	2006	448
80 2/8	80 7/8	15 6/8	15 6/8	6 4/8	6 4/8	3	2 6/8	10 4/8	7	5	4 7/8	Las Animas Co., CO	Johnny J. McElley	Johnny J. McElley	2006	448
80 2/8	81 2/8	14 5/8	15 3/8	6 3/8	6 3/8	2 3/8	2 3/8	10 3/8	5	6	6	Natrona Co., WY	Matthew C. Swartz	Matthew C. Swartz	2006	448
80 2/8	80 6/8	15	15 1/8	6 7/8	6 5/8	2 5/8	2 5/8	11 3/8	8 5/8	5	5	Carbon Co., WY	J. Mike Clegg	J. Mike Clegg	2007	448

Score												Locality			Date	Rank
80 2/8	80 7/8	15 1/8	15 1/8	6 7/8	6 6/8	3	2 7/8	6 1/8	9 4/8	4 6/8	4 4/8	Carbon Co., WY	Michael E. Condict	Michael E. Condict	2007	448
80 2/8	80 6/8	14 6/8	15	6 6/8	6 6/8	3 7/8	3 7/8	1 7/8	6 2/8	4 4/8	4 5/8	Bennett Co., SD	Nathan J. Doblar	Nathan J. Doblar	2007	448
80 2/8	81 1/8	15 6/8	16	6 2/8	6 2/8	2 4/8	2 5/8	3 1/8	7 3/8	6	6	Elko Co., NV	Scott D. Fetters	Scott D. Fetters	2007	448
80 2/8	80 7/8	14 5/8	14 5/8	6 4/8	6 3/8	3 1/8	3 1/8	14	15 6/8	4 7/8	4 7/8	Colfax Co., NM	Kathy W. Haines	Kathy W. Haines	2007	448
80 2/8	80 7/8	15 6/8	16 1/8	6 3/8	6 3/8	2 3/8	2 3/8	6	10 3/8	5 1/8	5	Humboldt Co., NV	Peter C. Leonard	Peter C. Leonard	2007	448
80 2/8	81 3/8	15 2/8	15 4/8	6 2/8	6 2/8	2 4/8	2 4/8	8 3/8	11 2/8	5 5/8	5 7/8	Natrona Co., WY	Lee A. Liggett	Lee A. Liggett	2007	448
80 2/8	82 1/8	15	14 5/8	6 5/8	6 5/8	2 5/8	2 5/8	8 5/8	12 5/8	5 5/8	6 5/8	Harding Co., SD	Ryan L. Moncur	Ryan L. Moncur	2007	448
80 2/8	80 6/8	15 6/8	15 6/8	6 7/8	6 7/8	2 4/8	2 4/8	7 2/8	12 1/8	7 2/8	4 6/8	Carbon Co., WY	Detlef E. Sarbok	Detlef E. Sarbok	2007	448
80 2/8	81	16	16 6/8	6 4/8	6 4/8	2 5/8	2 5/8	5	9 1/8	5	5 5/8	Harding Co., SD	Gentry W. Boswell	Gentry W. Boswell	2008	448
80 2/8	81 4/8	17 4/8	14	5 6/8	5 6/8	2 5/8	2 5/8	5 6/8	7 2/8	5 6/8	5 4/8	Hudspeth Co., TX	Kenneth A. Stewart	Kenneth A. Stewart	2008	448
80 2/8	80 4/8	14 1/8	15 1/8	7 1/8	7 1/8	2 4/8	2 5/8	1 3/8	9 3/8	3 1/8	6	Lincoln Co., WY	Jodie M. Boley	Jodie M. Boley	2009	448
80 2/8	81 2/8	15	15 2/8	6 6/8	6 6/8	2 5/8	2 5/8	5 7/8	10 6/8	5 7/8	5 5/8	Valley Co., MT	Richard J. Winters	Richard J. Winters	2009	448
80	81 4/8	14 4/8	15 1/8	6 6/8	6 6/8	2 1/8	2 3/8	8 2/8	12 4/8	7	7 1/8	Moffat Co., CO	Bruce Brown	Bruce Brown	1985	467
80	81 4/8	15 4/8	15 6/8	6 5/8	5 6/8	3 1/8	3 1/8	5 2/8	9	6	5 3/8	Hudspeth Co., TX	Paul E. Wollenman	Paul E. Wollenman	2006	467
80	80 5/8	16 2/8	16	6 2/8	6 1/8	2 6/8	2 6/8	9	11 6/8	4 5/8	4 5/8	Catron Co., NM	Kenneth T. Calton	Kenneth T. Calton	2007	467
80	81 5/8	13 7/8	13 7/8	7 1/8	7 1/8	3 4/8	3 5/8	8 2/8	10 3/8	5 2/8	5	Natrona Co., WY	James W. DeLozier	James W. DeLozier	2007	467
80	80 6/8	15 2/8	15 2/8	6 3/8	6 3/8	2 5/8	2 4/8	6	9 4/8	5 6/8	5 3/8	Converse Co., WY	Scott M. Dobry	Scott M. Dobry	2007	467
80	81 1/8	16 6/8	17	7	6 2/8	2 4/8	2 5/8	14	16	4	4 4/8	Lincoln Co., NM	Johnny L. Lay	Johnny L. Lay	2007	467
80	80 5/8	15 6/8	15 4/8	6 3/8	6 3/8	2 4/8	2 4/8	9 5/8	12 6/8	6 3/8	6 1/8	Washoe Co., NV	Randall D. Newberg	Randall D. Newberg	2007	467
80	80 4/8	16 3/8	16 3/8	6 6/8	6 4/8	2 5/8	2 5/8	4 7/8	8 6/8	4 4/8	4 4/8	Lincoln Co., WY	J. Richard Stark	J. Richard Stark	2007	467
80	80 5/8	14 6/8	14 6/8	6 3/8	6 4/8	2 7/8	2 6/8	6 7/8	9 4/8	5 4/8	5 5/8	Carbon Co., WY	Duwayne Statzer	Duwayne Statzer	2007	467
80	80 7/8	15 7/8	15 7/8	6 4/8	6 4/8	2 4/8	2 4/8	8 2/8	12 1/8	5 2/8	5 2/8	Red Deer River, AB	John F. Bottomley	John F. Bottomley	2008	467
80	80 4/8	16 1/8	16 1/8	6 3/8	6 1/8	2 6/8	2 7/8	1 7/8	7 6/8	4 7/8	4 5/8	Stark Co., ND	Raymond W. Brew	Raymond W. Brew	2008	467
80	80 2/8	15 3/8	15 1/8	6 6/8	6 6/8	2 4/8	2 4/8	6 1/8	10 1/8	4 7/8	4 7/8	Carbon Co., WY	Hillary J. Condict	Hillary J. Condict	2008	467
80	80 7/8	15 7/8	15 7/8	6 7/8	6 7/8	2 5/8	2 5/8	2 4/8	8 1/8	4 7/8	4 6/8	Berry Creek, AB	Victor H. Dyck	Victor H. Dyck	2008	467
80	80 7/8	14 7/8	14 7/8	6 5/8	6 6/8	2 6/8	2 6/8	7	11 2/8	5 1/8	5 4/8	Converse Co., WY	Delmar W. Ferris	Delmar W. Ferris	2008	467
80	81 6/8	15 4/8	15 4/8	6 6/8	6 6/8	2 2/8	2 7/8	5 7/8	10 4/8	6 2/8	6 5/8	Converse Co., WY	Terry L. Froeber	Terry L. Froeber	2008	467
80	80 6/8	15 7/8	15 7/8	6 1/8	6 1/8	2 6/8	1 7/8	3 3/8	9 7/8	5	5 1/8	White Pine Co., NV	Hal M. Hollingsworth	Hal M. Hollingsworth	2008	467
80	80 4/8	13 7/8	13 7/8	6 6/8	6 6/8	2 6/8	2 6/8	7	11 3/8	5 3/8	5 2/8	Sweetwater Co., WY	Jamie L. Lyons	Jamie L. Lyons	2008	467
80	81	16	16	5 7/8	5 7/8	2 5/8	2 4/8	8 7/8	10	5 4/8	5 5/8	Elko Co., NV	Carl A. Ranger	Carl A. Ranger	2008	467
80	80 2/8	14 5/8	14 5/8	7	7	3	3	4 1/8	8 5/8	4 5/8	4 5/8	Box Butte Co., NE	Colby R. Slaymaker	Colby R. Slaymaker	2008	467
80	81 6/8	15 3/8	15 6/8	5 6/8	6 1/8	2 6/8	2 5/8	6 5/8	10 2/8	5 5/8	6 2/8	Lea Co., NM	Brady A. Sullivan	Brady A. Sullivan	2008	467
80	81 6/8	14 6/8	14 7/8	7	6 7/8	2 7/8	2 7/8	9 1/8	11 2/8	5 5/8	4 1/8	Manyberries, AB	Derrick Tabaka	Derrick Tabaka	2008	467
80	80 5/8	15 5/8	15 5/8	6 5/8	6 6/8	2 5/8	2 4/8	5 5/8	10	4 6/8	4 7/8	Converse Co., WY	James L. Weier	James L. Weier	2008	467
80	80 7/8	16 5/8	16 4/8	6 4/8	6 4/8	2 4/8	2 3/8	5 5/8	8 2/8	4 6/8	5 2/8	Custer Co., MT	Brendan R. Beatty	Brendan R. Beatty	2009	467
80	81 3/8	15 2/8	15 2/8	6 3/8	6 5/8	2 3/8	2 4/8	6 1/8	7 4/8	5 5/8	5 4/8	Carbon Co., WY	Clay J. Evans	Clay J. Evans	2009	467
80	80 6/8	14 4/8	14 4/8	6 3/8	6 5/8	3	3	4 4/8	7 6/8	5 7/8	6 1/8	Sioux Co., NE	Kerry G. Keane	Kerry G. Keane	2009	467
90 4/8*	91 2/8	18	17 7/8	6 3/8	6 2/8	3 1/8	3 2/8	10	12 4/8	7 1/8	7	Coconino Co., AZ	Jack K. Himes	Jack K. Himes	2007	467
90 4/8*	90 7/8	17 1/8	17 3/8	7	7	3	3	8 3/8	11 4/8	6	6	Otero Co., NM	Donald E. Perrien	Donald E. Perrien	2008	467

Final score subject to revision by additional verifying measurements.

BISON

Bison bison bison and *Bison bison athabascae*

Minimum Score 115

World's Record 136 4/8

Trophies are acceptable only from states and provinces that recognize bison as a wild and free-ranging game animal and for which a hunting license and/or big game tag is required for hunting.

Final Score	Gross Score	Length of horn R	L	Circumference of Base R	L	Circumference at Third Quarter R	L	Greatest Spread	Tip to Tip Spread	Locality	Hunter	Owner	Date Killed	Rank
133 2/8	135 2/8	17 6/8	18 5/8	15 1/8	15 7/8	8 4/8	8 3/8	34 5/8	26 5/8	Teton Co., WY	Edward D. Riekens, Jr.	Edward D. Riekens, Jr.	2007	1
129 2/8	129 4/8	19 7/8	20	14 4/8	14 4/8	7 2/8	7 1/8	32	25 2/8	Custer Co., SD	Art D. Tong	Art D. Tong	2007	2
126 6/8	127 5/8	18 6/8	18 4/8	15 2/8	15 1/8	6 5/8	6 2/8	30	24 2/8	Custer Co., SD	David W. Baxter	David W. Baxter	2007	3
126	127 3/8	19 2/8	19 2/8	14	13 6/8	7 2/8	7 6/8	32 3/8	27 7/8	Teton Co., WY	Gerald C. Newmeyer	Gerald C. Newmeyer	2007	4
125 2/8	126 3/8	19 2/8	19 4/8	14 5/8	14 6/8	6	6 2/8	29 3/8	20	Teton Co., WY	John P. Schreiner	John P. Schreiner	2007	5
125	127 3/8	19 5/8	20 2/8	15 5/8	15 5/8	5 1/8	5 6/8	30 2/8	24 2/8	Coconino Co., AZ	Patrick J. Cooley	Patrick J. Cooley	2007	6 COLOR
124 2/8	125 3/8	16 2/8	16	14 4/8	14 4/8	8 3/8	8 6/8	31 1/8	27 4/8	Teton Co., WY	Herbert W. Duerr	Herbert W. Duerr	2008	7
124	125 5/8	16 7/8	17 4/8	14 6/8	14 4/8	7 6/8	7 3/8	32 1/8	25 6/8	Custer Co., SD	Curtis J. Babler	Curtis J. Babler	2005	8
124	125 5/8	17 4/8	16 7/8	14 2/8	14 3/8	7 6/8	7 7/8	30	25	Teton Co., WY	Picked Up	A. Deeds & B. Deeds	2007	8
124	125 4/8	20 5/8	20 1/8	14 6/8	14 6/8	6 2/8	5 5/8	30 3/8	21 7/8	Teton Co., WY	Patrick J. Durcholz	Patrick J. Durcholz	2007	8
124	125 5/8	17 3/8	18	14 4/8	14 6/8	7 2/8	7 4/8	30 2/8	24 7/8	Teton Co., WY	Dean R. Parker	Dean R. Parker	2008	8
123 6/8	124 7/8	18 7/8	19 6/8	14 3/8	14 3/8	5 7/8	6	28 6/8	22 7/8	Custer Co., SD	Thomas D. Lund	Thomas D. Lund	2007	12
123 2/8	124 5/8	15 5/8	15 5/8	14 2/8	13 7/8	8 5/8	9 2/8	31 3/8	27 3/8	Teton Co., WY	LaCinda S. Tilton	LaCinda S. Tilton	2008	13
122 2/8	124 6/8	17	15 3/8	15	14 5/8	7	7	27 3/8	22 2/8	Custer Co., SD	David R. Lautner	David R. Lautner	2006	14
122 2/8	123 5/8	18 2/8	19 3/8	14 4/8	14 4/8	6 1/8	6 2/8	21	28 6/8	Teton Co., WY	John V. Sjogren	John V. Sjogren	2007	14
122	122 5/8	20	19 7/8	14 2/8	14 1/8	5 6/8	5 6/8	30 5/8	24 2/8	Custer Co., SD	Randy A. Foutch	Randy A. Foutch	2008	16
121 6/8	122 4/8	17	17	13 6/8	14	7 7/8	7 7/8	31 2/8	28	Teton Co., WY	Jerry D. Dye	Jerry D. Dye	2009	17
121 4/8	122 4/8	18	18 2/8	15	14 6/8	6 4/8	6 3/8	30 1/8	25 3/8	Teton Co., WY	John C. Sjogren	John C. Sjogren	2007	18
121 4/8	122 4/8	16 4/8	16 2/8	14 4/8	14 2/8	8 2/8	8	27 6/8	22 1/8	Grand Co., UT	Mike J. Coelho	Mike J. Coelho	2008	18
121 2/8	123 5/8	17 4/8	17	14 4/8	13 6/8	7 5/8	8	31 2/8	25 6/8	Teton Co., WY	Cleveland B. Holloway	Cleveland B. Holloway	2007	20 COLOR
121 2/8	122	17 2/8	17 4/8	13 5/8	13 5/8	7 2/8	7 2/8	29 7/8	25	Teton Co., WY	William F. Madasz	William F. Madasz	2008	20
121	121 5/8	14 5/8	14 6/8	14 3/8	14 2/8	8 1/8	8	28 7/8	26 4/8	Custer Co., SD	Michael J. Borel	Michael J. Borel	2007	22
120 6/8	121 4/8	17 1/8	16 6/8	15 3/8	15 4/8	6 2/8	6 3/8	29	23 7/8	Teton Co., WY	John E. Webber	John E. Webber	2007	23
120 6/8	122 7/8	19 2/8	17 6/8	13 7/8	14 1/8	6 2/8	6 3/8	32 5/8	27 5/8	Custer Co., SD	Erik D. Holum	Erik D. Holum	2008	23
120 2/8	121 4/8	20 3/8	19 4/8	14 6/8	14 6/8	5 1/8	5	27 3/8	18 2/8	Pink Mt., BC	Mark Einarson	Mark Einarson	2007	25
120	120 7/8	18 4/8	18 3/8	13 5/8	13 6/8	5 7/8	5 7/8	31	26	Custer Co., SD	Tina R. Gregor	Tina R. Gregor	2007	26
120	121 4/8	16 6/8	16 6/8	14 2/8	14 5/8	7 3/8	8	29 1/8	23	Big Horn Co., MT	John L. Lundin	John L. Lundin	2008	26
120	123 1/8	19 7/8	18 2/8	14 5/8	14	5 7/8	5 3/8	31 3/8	25 6/8	Custer Co., SD	Robert Rosenquist	Robert Rosenquist	2008	26
119 6/8	120 5/8	16 3/8	15 7/8	14 7/8	14 4/8	6 7/8	6 7/8	28	24	Custer Co., SD	Paul A. Lautner	Paul A. Lautner	2008	29
119 6/8	120 6/8	19 7/8	19 7/8	14 3/8	14	6	5 5/8	28 7/8	20	Halfway River, BC	Ashley B. Penner	Ashley B. Penner	2008	29

Score									Locality	Owner	Hunter	Date	Rank
119 6/8	122	17	15 3/8	15 1/8	6 6/8	6 1/8	27 4/8	20	Uintah Co., UT	Jeffrey M. Jones	Jeffrey M. Jones	2009	29
119 6/8	122 4/8	18 2/8	14 7/8	14 4/8	5 2/8	6 5/8	28 2/8	20 4/8	Zama Lake, AB	Colton J. Logue	Colton J. Logue	2009	29
119 4/8	122 3/8	17 5/8	14 3/8	13 4/8	6 7/8	6 2/8	33 5/8	31 7/8	Custer Co., SD	Steven R. Knuth	Steven R. Knuth	2006	33
118 6/8	119 4/8	17 5/8	12 4/8	12 4/8	8 2/8	8 1/8	27 4/8	21 7/8	Teton Co., WY	Brenda K. Thiele	Brenda K. Thiele	2007	34
118 4/8	119 3/8	17 2/8	14 2/8	14 4/8	6 4/8	6 6/8	28 1/8	21 1/8	Teton Co., WY	Corey W. Spilski	Corey W. Spilski	2007	35
118 4/8	118 6/8	18 3/8	15 2/8	15 3/8	5 1/8	5 1/8	27 4/8	17 2/8	Braeburn, YT	Ryan J. Christensen	Ryan J. Christensen	2008	35
118 2/8	120 5/8	18 1/8	13 6/8	13 6/8	7 2/8	7	29 6/8	23 1/8	Teton Co., WY	Fernando P. Escobedo, Jr.	Fernando P. Escobedo, Jr.	2006	37
118	121 3/8	18 4/8	14 6/8	15 3/8	6 1/8	5 6/8	29 4/8	20 7/8	Custer Co., SD	Daryll D. Southwick	Daryll D. Southwick	2006	38
118	119 7/8	18	13 2/8	13 1/8	7 1/8	6 7/8	29 6/8	23 4/8	Teton Co., WY	Jerrell F. Coburn	Jerrell F. Coburn	2007	38
118	119	17 2/8	14 6/8	14 4/8	6 4/8	6 5/8	31 2/8	28 2/8	Teton Co., WY	Debbie L. Crail	Debbie L. Crail	2007	38
118	118 5/8	16 2/8	14 6/8	15	6 3/8	6 2/8	28 4/8	22 6/8	Park Co., MT	Melodi E. Naasz	Melodi E. Naasz	2007	38
117 4/8	119 3/8	16 1/8	13 2/8	13 1/8	8 4/8	7 7/8	28 3/8	25	Teton Co., WY	Picked Up	Vernon E. Estes	2007	42
117 4/8	118 5/8	16 4/8	14	14 4/8	7	6 7/8	28 4/8	23 6/8	Teton Co., WY	Todd W. Bouley	Todd W. Bouley	2008	42
117 4/8	118 5/8	17 6/8	14 2/8	14 3/8	5 7/8	6	29 6/8	24	Teton Co., WY	Scott M. Buckingham	Scott M. Buckingham	2008	42
117 2/8	118 5/8	20	13 3/8	13 4/8	5 5/8	5 2/8	31 4/8	23 4/8	Custer Co., SD	Kurt W. Kohtz	Kurt W. Kohtz	2008	45
117 2/8	118 6/8	16 1/8	14	13 6/8	6 4/8	6 7/8	30 2/8	27 2/8	Teton Co., WY	Jeff A. Baker	Jeff A. Baker	2009	45
117	117 2/8	18 2/8	14 2/8	13 6/8	5 2/8	5 1/8	29 3/8	23 3/8	Halfway River, BC	Ronald C. Rockwell	Ronald C. Rockwell	2007	47
116 6/8	116 7/8	17 6/8	14 2/8	14 2/8	5 4/8	5 4/8	30 7/8	26 3/8	Teton Co., WY	Eric H. Boley	Eric H. Boley	2007	48
116 6/8	116 2/8	17 5/8	14 4/8	14 4/8	5 4/8	5 4/8	28	18 2/8	Aishihik River, YT	John W. Salevurakis	John W. Salevurakis	2005	49
116 2/8	116 5/8	17 7/8	13 2/8	13 1/8	5 3/8	5 3/8	29 6/8	25 5/8	Teton Co., WY	George S. Czapskie	George S. Czapskie	2008	49
116 2/8	117	16 5/8	13 4/8	13 4/8	6 5/8	6 2/8	29 1/8	25 6/8	Teton Co., WY	Shawn G. Sharkey	Shawn G. Sharkey	2008	49
116	118 2/8	16 3/8	15 6/8	15 6/8	4 6/8	5 3/8	30 1/8	25 2/8	Dry Pass, YT	John Beecher	John Beecher	2006	52
116	117	17 3/8	13	13 1/8	6 4/8	6 5/8	26 1/8	16 6/8	Davis Co., UT	Brad M. McCullough	Brad M. McCullough	2006	52
116	116 5/8	18	13 4/8	13 5/8	5	5 3/8	27 6/8	22 2/8	Garfield Co., UT	Wayne D. McGhie	Wayne D. McGhie	2007	52
116	116 5/8	18 6/8	13 6/8	13 4/8	5 3/8	5 2/8	27 4/8	19 2/8	Teton Co., WY	John M. Paladeni	John M. Paladeni	2007	52
115 6/8	119 3/8	19	14 1/8	14 2/8	7 3/8	6 6/8	30 2/8	26 2/8	Chitina River, AK	Lloyd Z. Crow	Lloyd Z. Crow	2008	56
115 4/8	116 1/8	18	13 2/8	13 2/8	5 1/8	5 2/8	28 6/8	19 1/8	Teton Co., WY	Christopher Goff	Christopher Goff	2005	57
115 4/8	116 3/8	19 4/8	13 5/8	13 6/8	5 1/8	5 4/8	29 1/8	26 4/8	Garfield Co., UT	John W. Arbon	John W. Arbon	2007	57
115 4/8	117	17	14 7/8	14 5/8	4 5/8	4 7/8	25 2/8	13 7/8	Coconino Co., AZ	James E. Stark	James E. Stark	2008	57
115 2/8	117 2/8	19 1/8	14 7/8	14	6 6/8	6 3/8	29 2/8	25	Custer Co., SD	Fred W. Williams	Fred W. Williams	2006	60
115 2/8	117 2/8	15 4/8	14 7/8	14 5/8	5 1/8	5 1/8	22 4/8	25 7/8	Teton Co., WY	Warren S. Gamble	Warren S. Gamble	2007	61
115	115 2/8	16 4/8	15	15	8 3/8	8 3/8	30 6/8	25 6/8	Teton Co., WY	Gil A. Winters	Gil A. Winters	2008	
125 4/8* 127		17 2/8	16 1/8	16									

* Final score subject to revision by additional verifying measurements.

ROCKY MOUNTAIN GOAT

Oreamnos americanus americanus and related subspecies

Minimum Score 47

World's Record 56 6/8

Final Score	Gross Score	Length of horn R.	L.	Circumference of Base R.	L.	Circumference at Third Quarter R.	L.	Greatest Spread	Tip to Tip Spread	Locality	Hunter	Owner	Date Killed	Rank
54	54 3/8	11	11 1/8	5 7/8	6	2	2	7 3/8	6 7/8	Kalum Lake, BC	A.C. Smid	A.C. Smid	2008	1
53 6/8	54 1/8	10 7/8	11 1/8	6	6	2	2	8 4/8	7 5/8	Telegraph Creek, BC	Robert L. Schermer	Robert L. Schermer	2008	2
53 4/8	53 4/8	11	11	5 6/8	5 6/8	2	2	7 2/8	6 6/8	Elko Co., NV	Don J. Dees	Don J. Dees	2007	3
53 4/8	54 4/8	11 3/8	10 6/8	6 2/8	6 1/8	2	2	8	6 3/8	Revillagigedo Island, AK	Terry E. Meyers	Terry E. Meyers	2008	3
53 2/8	53 6/8	11 1/8	10 6/8	5 6/8	5 6/8	2 1/8	2	7 6/8	7 1/8	Deer Mt., AK	Mark W. Deibert	Mark W. Deibert	2007	5
53 2/8	53 3/8	11 1/8	11 2/8	5 7/8	5 7/8	1 7/8	1 7/8	8 3/8	6 7/8	Sweetin River, BC	Timothy J. Vining	Timothy J. Vining	2007	5
53	53 2/8	10	10	6 1/8	6 1/8	2 1/8	2 1/8	7 3/8	6 6/8	Telegraph Creek, BC	Robert D. Thompson	Robert D. Thompson	2004	7
53	53 1/8	10 6/8	10 7/8	5 7/8	5 7/8	2	2	6 4/8	5 2/8	Deer Mt., AK	Andrew B. Powers-Toribio	Andrew B. Powers-Toribio	2007	7
53	53 3/8	10 5/8	10 7/8	5 6/8	5 7/8	2	2	8 4/8	8	Exstew River, BC	Robert MacDonald	Robert MacDonald	2009	7
52 6/8	53 3/8	10 2/8	10 4/8	5 6/8	5 7/8	2	2	7	6 4/8	Elko Co., NV	Tony J. Langdon	Tony J. Langdon	2007	10
52 4/8	52 7/8	10 6/8	10 3/8	6	6	1 7/8	1 7/8	7 2/8	6 7/8	Adams Co., ID	James D. Newton	James D. Newton	2006	11
52 4/8	52 5/8	10 1/8	10 2/8	6 1/8	6 1/8	2	2	8 1/8	7 7/8	Wallowa Co., OR	Terrence P. O'Loughlin	Terrence P. O'Loughlin	2007	11
52 2/8	52 4/8	10 4/8	10 4/8	5 7/8	5 7/8	1 7/8	1 7/8	8	7 2/8	Wallowa Co., OR	Scott J. LaRoque	Scott J. LaRoque	2007	13
52	52 4/8	10 4/8	10 5/8	5 7/8	5 7/8	1 7/8	1 7/8	7 2/8	6 6/8	Copper River, BC	Jimmy J. Liautaud	Jimmy J. Liautaud	2006	14
52	52	10 1/8	10 1/8	6	6	2	2	7 1/8	6 5/8	Piute Co., UT	Jim Shockey	Jim Shockey	2006	14
52	52 2/8	11	11	5 6/8	5 6/8	1 7/8	1 7/8	7 6/8	7 2/8	Chouteau Co., MT	David J. Muckey	David J. Muckey	2007	14
52	52 2/8	10 4/8	10 5/8	5 5/8	5 5/8	2	2	8	7 5/8	Nass River, BC	James G. Petersen	James G. Petersen	2008	14
51 6/8	52 4/8	9 6/8	10 2/8	5 6/8	5 7/8	2	2	8	7 3/8	Kitsumkalum Lake, BC	Timothy K. Krause	Timothy K. Krause	2006	18
51 6/8	52 7/8	11 1/8	10 4/8	6	6	1 5/8	2	8 1/8	8 1/8	Baker Co., OR	Matea K. Huggins	Matea K. Huggins	2009	18
51 4/8	52	10 4/8	10 5/8	5 6/8	5 6/8	1 7/8	2	6 4/8	6 4/8	Little Oliver Creek, BC	Michael G. Kovach	Michael G. Kovach	2007	20
51 4/8	51 6/8	10 5/8	10 5/8	5 5/8	5 5/8	2	2	8	8 1/8	Whatcom Co., WA	Stephen R. Parker	Stephen R. Parker	2007	20
51 2/8	51 6/8	10 1/8	9 7/8	6	6	2	2	7 2/8	6 2/8	Revillagigedo Island, AK	James F. Baichtal	James F. Baichtal	2007	22
51 2/8	51 6/8	10 4/8	10 5/8	5 6/8	5 7/8	1 7/8	1 7/8	7 4/8	6 6/8	Strohn Creek, BC	Gary K. Nehring	Gary K. Nehring	2007	22
51 2/8	51 4/8	10 2/8	10 1/8	5 4/8	5 4/8	2 1/8	2	6 6/8	6	Clear Creek Co., CO	Donald E. Perrien	Donald E. Perrien	2007	22
51 2/8	51 5/8	9 7/8	9 6/8	5 6/8	5 6/8	2	2	6 4/8	5 7/8	Misty Fjords Natl. Mon., AK	George A. Pickel	George A. Pickel	2007	22
51 2/8	51 6/8	10 5/8	10 5/8	5 5/8	5 6/8	1 7/8	2	7 4/8	6 6/8	Misty Fjords Natl. Mon., AK	L. Mark DeLong	L. Mark DeLong	2008	22

Score	Score	L. Horn R	L. Horn L	Circ. Base R	Circ. Base L			Greatest Spread	Tip to Tip	Locality	Hunter	Owner	Date Killed	Rank
51 2/8	51 2/8	10	10	6	6	2	2	7 1/8	6	Clore River, BC	Eduardo F. Negrete	Eduardo F. Negrete	2008	22
51	51 1/8	10 5/8	10 5/8	5 5/8	5 5/8	1 7/8	1 7/8	8 2/8	7 6/8	Kispiox Range, BC	Louis E. Leonor	Louis E. Leonor	2006	28
51	51 5/8	10	10 3/8	6	5 7/8	1 7/8	1 7/8	7	6 2/8	Summit Co., UT	James N. McDonald	James N. McDonald	2007	28
51	51 1/8	10 1/8	10 2/8	5 6/8	5 6/8	1 7/8	1 7/8	6 2/8	4 7/8	Aaltanhash River, BC	Ralph S. Hernandez	Ralph S. Hernandez	2008	28
51	51 1/8	10 2/8	10 2/8	5 4/8	5 4/8	2	2	8 4/8	8 1/8	Whatcom Co., WA	Chris C. Culbertson	Chris C. Culbertson	2009	28
51	51 1/8	9 7/8	9 7/8	5 4/8	5 4/8	1 7/8	1 7/8	6 5/8	5 7/8	Misty Fjords, AK	John C. Sawyer	John C. Sawyer	2009	28
50 6/8	50 7/8	9 7/8	10	5 6/8	5 6/8	2	2	9 3/8	9	Dry Lake, BC	David O. Anaman	David O. Anaman	1999	33
50 6/8	50 6/8	11 5/8	11 5/8	5 2/8	5 2/8	1 5/8	1 5/8	8 2/8	7 7/8	S. Castle River, AB	Colton D. Howells	Colton D. Howells	2007	33
50 6/8	50 7/8	10 5/8	10 5/8	5 5/8	5 5/8	1 6/8	1 6/8	6 6/8	6 2/8	Elk Valley, BC	C.W. & S.E. Weed	C.W. & S.E. Weed	2007	33
50 6/8	51	10 5/8	10 4/8	5 5/8	5 5/8	1 7/8	1 6/8	6 6/8	5 4/8	Cummings Creek, BC	Ken L.G. Yuill	Ken L.G. Yuill	2007	33
50 6/8	50 6/8	10 3/8	10 3/8	5 5/8	5 5/8	1 7/8	1 7/8	7 2/8	6 5/8	Scoop Lake, BC	James S. Davis	James S. Davis	2009	33
50 4/8	51	10 2/8	10 2/8	5 6/8	5 6/8	2	1 7/8	7 4/8	6 6/8	Baldy Mt., BC	William K. Sillaman	William K. Sillaman	2008	38
50 2/8	50 2/8	9 1/8	9 1/8	5 7/8	5 7/8	2	2	7	6 6/8	Wallowa Co., OR	Larry A. Spears	Larry A. Spears	2006	39
50 2/8	50 6/8	10 3/8	10 3/8	5 7/8	5 7/8	1 7/8	1 7/8	8	7 4/8	Lake George Glacier, AK	Kyle E. Neill	Kyle E. Neill	2007	39
50 2/8	50 3/8	10 1/8	10 1/8	5 4/8	5 4/8	1 7/8	1 7/8	5 4/8	4 6/8	Elko Co., NV	Ryan A. Perchetti	Ryan A. Perchetti	2007	39
50 2/8	50 3/8	9 6/8	9 6/8	5 5/8	5 5/8	1 7/8	1 7/8	5 6/8	6 4/8	Elko Co., NV	Doris A. Twichell	Doris A. Twichell	2007	39
50 2/8	50 3/8	9 2/8	9 2/8	5 5/8	5 5/8	2	2	5 5/8	6 7/8	Terrace, BC	Steven S. Bruggeman	Steven S. Bruggeman	2008	39
50 2/8	50 3/8	9 6/8	9 6/8	5 5/8	5 5/8	2 2/8	2	5 5/8	7 2/8	Day Harbor, AK	Matthew E. Hardwig	Matthew E. Hardwig	2008	39
50 2/8	50 3/8	10	10 1/8	5 5/8	5 5/8	1 6/8	1 6/8	5 5/8	6 6/8	Elko Co., NV	Russell R. Sillitoe	Russell R. Sillitoe	2008	39
50 2/8	50 2/8	9 7/8	9 7/8	5 6/8	5 6/8	1 7/8	1 7/8	5 6/8	6 1/8	King Co., WA	Michael T. Warn	Michael T. Warn	2008	39
50 2/8	50 4/8	9 7/8	9 7/8	5 7/8	5 7/8	1 7/8	1 6/8	5 7/8	5 1/8	Weber Co., UT	Blair R. Fogg	Blair R. Fogg	2009	39
50 2/8	50 6/8	10 3/8	10 4/8	5 6/8	5 5/8	1 6/8	1 6/8	5 5/8	8 1/8	Klahowya Lake, BC	James M. Mazur	James M. Mazur	2009	39
50 2/8	50 7/8	10 3/8	10 3/8	5 4/8	5 4/8	1 7/8	1 7/8	5 4/8	8 2/8	Skeena River, BC	Kent P. McKenzie	Kent P. McKenzie	2009	39
50 2/8	50 3/8	9 5/8	9 5/8	5 7/8	5 7/8	2	2	5 7/8	7 6/8	Portage Bay, AK	Brandon C. Otts	Brandon C. Otts	2009	39
50	50 1/8	10 6/8	10 5/8	5 4/8	5 4/8	2	1 7/8	5 4/8	7 1/8	Misty Fjords, AK	Donny N. Cross	Donny N. Cross	2007	51
50	50	10 1/8	10 1/8	5 5/8	5 5/8	1 7/8	1 7/8	5 5/8	6 5/8	Copper River, BC	Kelly W. Manning	Kelly W. Manning	2008	51
50	50 4/8	10 7/8	10 7/8	5 5/8	5 5/8	1 6/8	1 5/8	5 5/8	7 1/8	Sustut Lake, BC	Leaf Steffey	Leaf Steffey	2008	51
50	50 1/8	9 6/8	9 5/8	5 6/8	5 6/8	2	2	5 6/8	4 6/8	Elko Co., NV	Tina R. Buonamici	Tina R. Buonamici	2009	51
50	50 1/8	9 3/8	9 3/8	5 6/8	5 6/8	1 7/8	1 7/8	5 6/8	4 6/8	Elko Co., NV	Michael F. Porter	Michael F. Porter	2009	51
49 6/8	50 1/8	10 1/8	10 3/8	5 4/8	5 4/8	1 6/8	1 6/8	5 4/8	7	Pierce Co., WA	Anthony R. Nastansky	Anthony R. Nastansky	2008	56
49 6/8	50	10	10	5 4/8	5 4/8	2	2	5 4/8	6 5/8	Revillagigedo Island, AK	Richard D. Olmstead	Richard D. Olmstead	2008	56
49 4/8	50	9 2/8	9 5/8	5 6/8	5 6/8	2	2	5 6/8	5 7/8	Misty Fjords, AK	Ian K. Chase-Dunn	Ian K. Chase-Dunn	1983	58
49 4/8	49 6/8	9 7/8	9 6/8	5 6/8	5 6/8	1 7/8	1 7/8	5 6/8	7 3/8	Inklin River, BC	James W. Lloyd	James W. Lloyd	2006	58
49 4/8	49 5/8	9 5/8	9 4/8	5 6/8	5 6/8	1 7/8	1 7/8	5 6/8	6 6/8	Elko Co., NV	Mike S. Vincent	Mike S. Vincent	2009	58
49 4/8	50 3/8	9 7/8	9 3/8	5 5/8	5 5/8	1 7/8	1 7/8	8 2/8	7 5/8	Copper River, BC	Stephen R. Webb	Stephen R. Webb	2009	58
49 2/8	49 6/8	9 6/8	9 6/8	5 5/8	5 5/8	2 1/8	2 1/8	7 6/8	6 6/8	Skeena River, BC	Diana G. Adams	Diana G. Adams	2005	62
49 2/8	49 6/8	10 2/8	10 2/8	5 6/8	5 6/8	1 7/8	1 7/8	7 4/8	7	Cassiar Mts., BC	Howard Peppi	Howard Peppi	2005	62
49 2/8	49 3/8	9 3/8	9 3/8	5 7/8	5 6/8	1 7/8	1 7/8	7 1/8	6 6/8	Kalum Lake, BC	Michael F. Kwak	Michael F. Kwak	2008	62

ROCKY MOUNTAIN GOAT

Oreamnos americanus americanus and related subspecies

Final Score	Gross Score	Length of horn R.	L.	Circumference of Base R.	L.	Circumference at Third Quarter R.	L.	Greatest Spread	Tip to Tip Spread	Locality	Hunter	Owner	Date Killed	Rank
49 2/8	49 2/8	9 7/8	9 7/8	5 6/8	5 6/8	1 6/8	1 6/8	7 7/8	7 1/8	Knik Glacier, AK	Robert W. Nash	Robert W. Nash	2008	62
49 2/8	49 6/8	9 4/8	9 5/8	5 5/8	5 4/8	1 7/8	1 7/8	6 6/8	6 1/8	Ketchikan, AK	Bruce H. Hansen	Bruce H. Hansen	2009	62
49 2/8	49 6/8	10 3/8	10 4/8	5 3/8	5 3/8	1 7/8	1 6/8	7 1/8	5 7/8	Dease Lake, BC	Kenneth H. Jones	Kenneth H. Jones	2009	62
49	49 1/8	9 4/8	9 4/8	5 5/8	5 6/8	1 6/8	1 6/8	7 6/8	7 1/8	Center Mt., AK	Douglas D. Watson	Douglas D. Watson	2007	68
49	49 3/8	10 7/8	10 5/8	5	5 1/8	1 6/8	1 6/8	6 2/8	4 4/8	Misty Fjords, AK	Kevin D. Ash	Kevin D. Ash	2008	68
49	49	10 1/8	10 1/8	5 4/8	5 4/8	1 6/8	1 6/8	6 4/8	5 7/8	Leo Creek, BC	Charles M. Robson	Charles M. Robson	2008	68
48 6/8	48 7/8	9 6/8	9 6/8	5 4/8	5 4/8	1 7/8	1 7/8	7 3/8	6 7/8	Alaska	Unknown	Elliott Millione	1988	71
48 6/8	49 5/8	9 7/8	10 4/8	5 2/8	5 3/8	1 6/8	1 6/8	8 2/8	8 1/8	Bainbridge Glacier, AK	Michael J. Hentgen	Michael J. Hentgen	2006	71
48 6/8	49	9 2/8	9 2/8	5 4/8	5 4/8	2	1 7/8	5 6/8	5	Elko Co., NV	Michael J. Jurad	Michael J. Jurad	2006	71
48 6/8	49	10 1/8	10	5 3/8	5 4/8	1 6/8	1 6/8	7 1/8	6 2/8	Cascade Co., MT	Edward J. Merlo	Edward J. Merlo	2006	71
48 6/8	49	9 6/8	9 6/8	5 5/8	5 7/8	1 6/8	1 6/8	6 7/8	6 6/8	Yakima Co., WA	Tracy A. Sautner	Tracy A. Sautner	2007	71
48 6/8	49	8 7/8	8 7/8	5 7/8	5 7/8	1 7/8	1 7/8	6 1/8	5 6/8	Duchesne Co., UT	Hal J. Giles	Hal J. Giles	2008	71
48 4/8	48 7/8	9 6/8	10	5 3/8	5 4/8	1 7/8	1 7/8	7	6	Skeena River, BC	Daniel E. Hauck	Daniel E. Hauck	2006	77
48 4/8	48 6/8	9 2/8	9 2/8	5 5/8	5 5/8	1 7/8	1 6/8	6 4/8	6 1/8	Elko Co., NV	Kyle G. Powning	Kyle G. Powning	2008	77
48 4/8	49	10 1/8	10 4/8	5 1/8	5 2/8	1 7/8	1 7/8	7 3/8	6 6/8	Mt. Sidney Williams, BC	Richard Hoverter	Richard Hoverter	2009	77
48 4/8	48 6/8	9 4/8	9 3/8	5 5/8	5 4/8	1 6/8	1 6/8	8	7 7/8	Oliver Creek, BC	Scott A. Huebner	Scott A. Huebner	2009	77
48 4/8	48 7/8	8 7/8	8 7/8	5 6/8	5 6/8	1 7/8	2	6 3/8	6	Summit Co., UT	Gary K. Madsen	Gary K. Madsen	2009	77
48 2/8	48 3/8	10	10	5 3/8	5 3/8	1 5/8	1 5/8	7 1/8	6 7/8	Flathead Co., MT	Matt M. Marvel	Matt M. Marvel	2005	82
48 2/8	48 5/8	9 7/8	9 6/8	5 4/8	5 5/8	1 6/8	1 6/8	7 6/8	7 5/8	San Juan Co., CO	Rex H. Howard, Jr.	Rex H. Howard, Jr.	2007	82
48 2/8	48 3/8	9 3/8	9 3/8	5 3/8	5 3/8	1 7/8	1 7/8	7 4/8	7 3/8	Chouteau Co., MT	Joe R. Bennett	Joe R. Bennett	2008	82
48 2/8	48 4/8	9 5/8	9 4/8	5 4/8	5 4/8	1 6/8	1 7/8	7	6 2/8	Ice Mt., BC	John P. Hollmann	John P. Hollmann	2008	82
48 2/8	48 5/8	9 2/8	9 1/8	5 5/8	5 6/8	1 7/8	1 7/8	7	6 4/8	Wallowa Co., OR	Justin E. Spring	Justin E. Spring	2008	82
48	48 4/8	9 3/8	9 1/8	5 6/8	5 5/8	1 6/8	1 6/8	7	6 3/8	Kodiak Island, AK	Kevin B. Kreofsky	Kevin B. Kreofsky	2006	87
48	48	9 4/8	9 4/8	5 5/8	5 5/8	1 6/8	1 6/8	6 1/8	5 6/8	Kodiak Island, AK	Seth B. McKinnis	Seth B. McKinnis	2006	87
48	48 7/8	8 6/8	9 4/8	5 5/8	5 6/8	1 7/8	1 7/8	6 4/8	5 7/8	Copper River, BC	Michael S. Rex	Michael S. Rex	2007	87
48	48 5/8	10	10 2/8	5 2/8	5 4/8	1 6/8	1 7/8	6 5/8	5 6/8	Takla Lake, BC	Ryan N. Hutt	Ryan N. Hutt	2008	87
47 6/8	48 1/8	9 5/8	9 7/8	4 6/8	4 6/8	1 6/8	1 6/8	6 3/8	5 5/8	Snohomish Co., WA	Robert J. Fuchs, Sr.	Robert J. Fuchs, Sr.	1987	91
47 6/8	47 7/8	9 2/8	9 3/8	5 5/8	5 5/8	1 6/8	1 6/8	6 5/8	6	Elko Co., NV	Jim D. Heckman, Jr.	Jim D. Heckman, Jr.	2006	91
47 6/8	48 1/8	9 3/8	9 5/8	5 4/8	5 5/8	1 6/8	1 6/8	7 1/8	6 2/8	Eaglenest Range, BC	Mark T. Donovan	Mark T. Donovan	2007	91
47 6/8	48 3/8	9 6/8	9 4/8	5 2/8	5 2/8	1 7/8	1 7/8	7 6/8	7 1/8	Skeena River, BC	Tod W. Graham	Tod W. Graham	2008	91
47 4/8	48 3/8	9	9 5/8	5 4/8	5 4/8	1 7/8	1 7/8	6 5/8	5 5/8	Cleveland Pen., AK	Mary Lou Merrill	Mary Lou Merrill	1978	95

										Location	Hunter	Date	Score
47 4/8	47 7/8	10 2/8	9 7/8	5 3/8	5 3/8	1 5/8	1 5/8	6 4/8	5 7/8	Quarrie Creek, BC	Jeffrey G. Brummer	2005	95
47 1/8	47 7/8	9	9 1/8	5 4/8	5 4/8	1 7/8	2	6 2/8	5 6/8	Misty Fjords, AK	Donald A. Burleson	2007	95
47 4/8	47 6/8	9 4/8	9 5/8	5 2/8	5 3/8	1 6/8	1 6/8	7 6/8	7	Tochieka Range, BC	Jack E. Risner	2009	95
47 2/8	47 2/8	9 4/8	9 4/8	5 4/8	5 4/8	1 5/8	1 5/8	7 5/8	7 7/8	Eklutna River, AK	Joshua W. Wood	1995	99
47 2/8	47 2/8	9 1/8	9 1/8	5 3/8	5 3/8	1 6/8	1 6/8	8	5 6/8	Elko Co., NV	Emilee A. Almberg	2007	99
47 4/8	47 4/8	9 2/8	9 2/8	5 3/8	5 4/8	1 6/8	1 6/8	6 3/8	4 4/8	Powell Co., MT	Stephen E. Brown	2007	99
47 5/8	47 5/8	9 1/8	9 1/8	5 4/8	5 4/8	1 6/8	1 6/8	5 2/8	5 4/8	Beaver Co., UT	Kim D. Graham	2007	99
47 4/8	47 4/8	9	9 6/8	5 2/8	5 2/8	1 5/8	1 5/8	6 5/8	6 5/8	Chouteau Co., MT	Delmar E. Hayden	2007	99
47 5/8	47 5/8	9 3/8	9 4/8	5 2/8	5 3/8	1 6/8	1 6/8	6 7/8	6 5/8	Kitsumkalum River, BC	Stephen G. Bouck	2008	99
47 2/8	48 3/8	9 5/8	8 6/8	5 3/8	5 3/8	1 7/8	1 7/8	7 2/8	6 6/8	Chugach Mts., AK	Donald Z. Detwiler	2008	99
47 2/8	47 4/8	9 4/8	9 5/8	5 4/8	5 4/8	0 7/8	0 7/8	6	6 4/8	Skeena Mts., BC	Craig L. Kling	2008	99
47 2/8	47 6/8	9 5/8	9 7/8	5 2/8	5 3/8	1 6/8	1 6/8	7 2/8	7 2/8	Park Co., MT	Michael B. Bazan	2009	99
47	47 1/8	8 5/8	8 5/8	5 4/8	5 4/8	1 7/8	1 7/8	5 7/8	4 7/8	Cleveland Pen., AK	Lynn W. Merrill	1986	108
47	47 1/8	9 4/8	9 4/8	5 2/8	5 2/8	1 5/8	1 5/8	6 4/8	6	Elko Co., NV	Jeffrey M. Lilyhorn	2006	108
47 2/8	47 2/8	9 3/8	9 3/8	5 3/8	5 3/8	1 6/8	1 6/8	6 4/8	6	Summit Co., UT	George E. Walker, Jr.	2008	108
54 2/8*	54 6/8	10 2/8	10	6 3/8	6 4/8	2 2/8	2 2/8	7 5/8	6 7/8	Telegraph Creek, BC	David A. Young	2006	108

* Final score subject to revision by additional verifying measurements.

ROCKY MOUNTAIN GOAT
FINAL SCORE: 49
HUNTER: Charles M. Robson

ROCKY MOUNTAIN GOAT
FINAL SCORE: 47 4/8
HUNTER: Donald A. Burleson

ROCKY MOUNTAIN GOAT
FINAL SCORE: 51 6/8
HUNTER: Matea K. Huggins

ROCKY MOUNTAIN GOAT
FINAL SCORE: 50 2/8
HUNTER: Steven S. Bruggeman

MUSK OX

Ovibos moschatus moschatus and certain related subspecies

World's Record 129 (tie)

Minimum Score 105

Final Score	Gross Score	Length of Horn R.	L.	Width of Boss R.	L.	Circumference at Third Quarter R.	L.	Greatest Spread	Tip to Tip Spread	Locality	Hunter	Owner	Date Killed	Rank
127	128 2/8	29 1/8	29 1/8	11 2/8	10 6/8	6 4/8	6 3/8	28 6/8	26 4/8	Kugluktuk, NU	Ben L. Mueller	Ben L. Mueller	2007	1
122 6/8	123 6/8	27 3/8	27 6/8	10 4/8	10 1/8	6	6 1/8	30	28 7/8	Gjoa Haven, NU	James D. Mierzwiak	James D. Mierzwiak	1995	2
122 6/8	126	29 1/8	28 3/8	11 3/8	11 1/8	6 1/8	5 4/8	28 7/8	28 2/8	Kugluktuk River, NU	M. Blake Patton	M. Blake Patton	2008	2
120 2/8	123 1/8	27 6/8	28 2/8	10 6/8	10 6/8	5	5 6/8	30 7/8	30 3/8	Tuktoyaktuk, NT	James M. Mazur	James M. Mazur	2008	4
120	120 1/8	26 7/8	26 7/8	10 7/8	10 6/8	5 4/8	5 4/8	30 4/8	30	Kugluktuk, NU	Dennis Fletcher	Dennis Fletcher	2007	5
119 4/8	124 7/8	28 7/8	27 2/8	10	10 6/8	6 2/8	5 4/8	27 2/8	26	Kugluktuk, NU	Roy Brown	Roy Brown	2007	6
117	118 3/8	27 4/8	26 6/8	10 5/8	10 4/8	5 6/8	5 6/8	27 7/8	25 6/8	Inuvik, NU	John R. Thodos	John R. Thodos	2007	7
116 2/8	120 6/8	27 5/8	29 3/8	10 1/8	10 1/8	5 1/8	5 7/8	24 4/8	23 7/8	Kugluktuk River, NU	Thomas A. Puzas	Thomas A. Puzas	2008	8
116	117	27 7/8	27 5/8	10 1/8	10 1/8	5 6/8	5 5/8	28 5/8	27 2/8	Kugluktuk, NU	Michael R. Carlson	Michael R. Carlson	2006	9
116	116 6/8	27	27 1/8	10 1/8	10 2/8	5 3/8	5 5/8	27 4/8	27 1/8	Coronation Gulf, NU	Randy D. Oleson	Randy D. Oleson	2007	9
116	116 7/8	26 5/8	26 4/8	9 6/8	9 3/8	5 6/8	5 7/8	28 4/8	28 1/8	Kugluktuk River, NU	Brian A. Hauck	Brian A. Hauck	2008	9
115 2/8	117 3/8	28	28 5/8	10 1/8	9 7/8	5 2/8	5 5/8	29 7/8	28 6/8	Kugluktuk, NU	Edward D. Yates	Edward D. Yates	2009	12
115	116 7/8	28	27 2/8	10 3/8	10	4 7/8	4 6/8	26 7/8	25 1/8	Smoking Hills, NT	David O. Anaman	David O. Anaman	1998	13
114 2/8	116 1/8	27 7/8	27 1/8	9 6/8	10	5 3/8	5	28 6/8	27 6/8	Kivalliq, NU	Michael M. Girbav	Michael M. Girbav	2008	14
113	114 3/8	25 2/8	25 1/8	10 3/8	10 3/8	5 4/8	5 6/8	27 4/8	25 3/8	Kugluktuk, NU	John L. Enquist, Sr.	John L. Enquist, Sr.	2009	15
112 4/8	114 1/8	26 5/8	27 1/8	9 4/8	9 3/8	5	5 4/8	27 1/8	25 2/8	Mason River, NT	W. Boyd McNeilly	W. Boyd McNeilly	2009	16
111	113	25 1/8	26 2/8	8 6/8	8 4/8	6 2/8	6 3/8	26 7/8	25 1/8	Shishmaref, AK	Randy M. St. Ores	Randy M. St. Ores	2009	17
110 2/8	112 5/8	26 6/8	27 1/8	9 7/8	9 3/8	4 7/8	5 4/8	26 2/8	25 2/8	Mason River, NT	Joe S. Mull	Joe S. Mull	2009	18
110	111 5/8	28 5/8	27 6/8	8 6/8	8 6/8	5 2/8	4 6/8	26 1/8	25 6/8	Nelson Island, AK	Hunter J. Crace	Hunter J. Crace	2009	19
110	112 5/8	27 5/8	26 6/8	9 3/8	9 7/8	5 2/8	4 6/8	27 7/8	25 7/8	Rendez-vous Lake, NT	Cecil K. Files	Cecil K. Files	2009	19
109 6/8	114 1/8	30 1/8	28 4/8	9	9 5/8	5	4 1/8	24 4/8	20 7/8	Banks Island, NT	Colin F. MacRae	Colin F. MacRae	2000	21
109 6/8	111 5/8	27 6/8	26 6/8	8 7/8	8 6/8	5 4/8	5 1/8	27 1/8	27	Sarichef Island, AK	Jacques A. Kaune	Jacques A. Kaune	2005	21
109 4/8	112 4/8	25 2/8	26 4/8	10 1/8	10 1/8	5 3/8	5 6/8	27	24 5/8	Kugluktuk, NU	Michael R. Carlson	Michael R. Carlson	2006	23
109 2/8	111 3/8	26 5/8	26 2/8	9 1/8	9 1/8	4 7/8	5 2/8	29	28 1/8	Princess Mary Lake, NU	Christian E. Klar	Christian E. Klar	2007	24
109 2/8	111 2/8	26	26 5/8	9 5/8	9 1/8	4 7/8	5 3/8	28 4/8	28 1/8	Caribou Creek, AK	Mark W. Smith	Mark W. Smith	2009	24
109	114 3/8	26 5/8	28 3/8	9	8 5/8	4 6/8	6 1/8	27 6/8	27 4/8	Coyote Creek, AK	William A. Ladd	William A. Ladd	2005	26
109	113 1/8	25 4/8	27 1/8	8 3/8	9	5 6/8	6 2/8	27 3/8	27	Cambridge Bay, NU	Matthew E. Franks	Matthew E. Franks	2008	26
109	110 7/8	27 5/8	27 1/8	8 7/8	9	5 4/8	5	26 3/8	25	Nunivak Island, AK	William S. Duncan	William S. Duncan	2009	26
108 6/8	109 3/8	25 6/8	25 6/8	10 2/8	10 1/8	5 4/8	5 5/8	25 4/8	23 2/8	Coppermine River, NU	Larry E. Ensign	Larry E. Ensign	2003	29
108 2/8	110 1/8	25 5/8	24 5/8	8 3/8	8 3/8	6 2/8	6	27 4/8	27	Kougarok River, AK	Harvey J. Fiskeaux	Harvey J. Fiskeaux	2006	30

108 2/8	110 4/8	25 4/8	24 6/8	9 4/8	9 5/8	5 5/8	5	28	27 3/8	Ellice River, NU	Lanny S. Rominger	Lanny S. Rominger	2007	30
108 2/8	111 4/8	26 1/8	27 7/8	9	8 6/8	5 2/8	5 4/8	30 5/8	30 2/8	Shishmaref, AK	Myron P. Heil	Myron P. Heil	2009	30
107 6/8	109 7/8	26 3/8	26 4/8	8 4/8	8 4/8	5 7/8	4 6/8	40 3/8	40 2/8	Nunivak Island, AK	Raymond W. Hysom	Raymond W. Hysom	2007	33
107 6/8	109 2/8	26 7/8	27 1/8	8 4/8	8 4/8	5 2/8	5 2/8	25 7/8	25 3/8	Kougarok River, AK	Mark W. Smith	Mark W. Smith	2007	33
107 4/8	108 2/8	25 2/8	25	8 5/8	8 5/8	5 4/8	5 3/8	26 1/8	25 3/8	Coyote Creek, AK	William A. Ladd	William A. Ladd	2006	35
107	107 4/8	25 1/8	25	9 3/8	9 2/8	4 5/8	4 4/8	26 4/8	24 4/8	Rendez-vous Lake, NT	John W. Oberlitner	John W. Oberlitner	1996	36
106 6/8	111 1/8	28	25 5/8	8 2/8	8 2/8	6 2/8	5 1/8	23 7/8	23 6/8	Seward Pen., AK	Clifford R. Hugg	Clifford R. Hugg	2006	37
106 6/8	107 2/8	26 2/8	26 3/8	8 5/8	8 5/8	4 7/8	4 6/8	27 1/8	26 7/8	Nunivak Island, AK	Dan J. Helm	Dan J. Helm	2008	37
106 2/8	110 1/8	26 4/8	25 1/8	9 6/8	10 2/8	5 2/8	4 1/8	27	26 5/8	Ellice River, NU	Steven S. Bruggeman	Steven S. Bruggeman	1991	39
105 6/8	108 2/8	25 4/8	26 4/8	9	8 2/8	5 1/8	5 4/8	28 2/8	28	Shishmaref, AK	Justin M. Heil	Justin M. Heil	2009	40
105 2/8	106 5/8	24 7/8	25 3/8	8 6/8	8 5/8	5 3/8	5	27	27	Nunivak Island, AK	Mark W. John	Mark W. John	2009	41
105 2/8	107 3/8	24 7/8	26 1/8	8 5/8	8 5/8	4 6/8	5 2/8	23 6/8	22 4/8	Nunivak Island, AK	Robert A. Kramer	Robert A. Kramer	2009	41
105	109 3/8	23 5/8	25 6/8	9 6/8	9 5/8	4 5/8	5 2/8	26 2/8	23	Anderson River, NT	James L. Horneck	James L. Horneck	2008	43
123 4/8*	124 7/8	28	27 2/8	10 3/8	10 4/8	6 3/8	6	28 1/8	27 4/8	Kugluktuk, NU	Jerry Peebles	Jerry Peebles	2006	

* Final score subject to revision by additional verifying measurements.

MUSK OX
FINAL SCORE: 116 2/8
HUNTER: Thomas A. Puzas

MUSK OX
FINAL SCORE: 106 6/8
HUNTER: Dan J. Helm

MUSK OX
FINAL SCORE: 108 2/8
HUNTER: Lanny S. Rominger

MUSK OX
FINAL SCORE: 114 2/8
HUNTER: Michael M. Girbav

BIGHORN SHEEP

Minimum Score 175   *Ovis canadensis canadensis* and certain related subspecies   World's Record 208 3/8

Final Score	Gross Score	Length of horn R.	L.	Circumference of Base R.	L.	Circumference at Third Quarter R.	L.	Greatest Spread	Tip to Tip Spread	Locality	Hunter	Owner	Date Killed	Rank
204 2/8	204 3/8	44 4/8	44 2/8	16 4/8	16 4/8	10 5/8	10 6/8	25 1/8	25 1/8	Fergus Co., MT	Toni L. Sannon	Toni L. Sannon	2008	1
202 7/8	204	43 1/8	46 2/8	16 7/8	16 7/8	9 4/8	10 1/8	24 4/8	22 6/8	Blaine Co., MT	Debby L. Perry	Debby L. Perry	2008	2
196 7/8	197 5/8	41 5/8	40 4/8	16 6/8	16 6/8	9 7/8	9 2/8	22 3/8	14 5/8	Dutch Creek, AB	K. Steed & T. Bolokoski	K. Steed & T. Bolokoski	2009	3
196 2/8	196 5/8	41 4/8	43 6/8	15 6/8	15 6/8	10	10 2/8	24 6/8	19 3/8	Garfield Co., WA	John L. Amistoso	John L. Amistoso	2006	4
196	197	41 6/8	41 4/8	15 6/8	15 7/8	10 7/8	11 5/8	22	21	Elko Co., NV	William R. Balsi, Sr.	William R. Balsi, Sr.	2009	5
195 5/8	198 2/8	43 2/8	50 7/8	15 1/8	14 2/8	9 1/8	9 6/8	29 4/8	22 2/8	El Paso Co., CO	Picked Up	CO Div. of Wildl.	2005	6
195 4/8	197	41	43 6/8	15 5/8	16 1/8	10 3/8	10 5/8	21	20 4/8	Uintah Co., UT	Daniel Smith IV	Daniel Smith IV	2006	7
195	197 1/8	42 4/8	42 4/8	15 6/8	15 6/8	10 7/8	11 2/8	25 4/8	24 7/8	Fergus Co., MT	James R. Buckley	James R. Buckley	2007	8
194 4/8	195 1/8	43 6/8	39 6/8	16 1/8	16 2/8	9 1/8	9 3/8	26 3/8	25	Blaine Co., MT	Joel B. Scrafford	Joel B. Scrafford	2007	9
194 3/8	194 4/8	39 6/8	40 7/8	16 2/8	16 2/8	10 3/8	10 4/8	23	17 1/8	Greenlee Co., AZ	Edward L. Turner	Edward L. Turner	2007	10
194 2/8	194 7/8	40 1/8	39 1/8	16 6/8	16 6/8	10 3/8	10 4/8	22 3/8	21 3/8	Fergus Co., MT	Gary R. Schneider	Gary R. Schneider	2008	11
194 1/8	194 1/8	44 3/8	38	16 4/8	16 4/8	8 7/8	8 7/8	23 2/8	20	Blaine Co., MT	Shannell A. Halvorson	Shannell A. Halvorson	2008	12
193 5/8	193 7/8	43 1/8	43 4/8	16 1/8	16 2/8	8 5/8	8 5/8	22 1/8	21 6/8	Churn Creek, BC	Christopher W. Hodel	Christopher W. Hodel	2007	13
193 4/8	194 4/8	39 4/8	39	18	18	8 4/8	8 6/8	23	19 5/8	Uintah Co., UT	Mike Kemery	Mike Kemery	2007	14
193 4/8	194	40 5/8	40 5/8	15 3/8	15 4/8	11 4/8	11 2/8	23 2/8	15	Blaine Co., MT	Michael C. Spicher	Michael C. Spicher	2007	14
193 2/8	194	41 3/8	41 7/8	16 2/8	16 2/8	9 3/8	9	24 4/8	23 6/8	Ravalli Co., MT	Larry N. Lee	Larry N. Lee	2007	16
192 2/8	192 3/8	39 3/8	41 3/8	15 6/8	15 6/8	10	10 1/8	22 3/8	21 5/8	Fergus Co., MT	Robert Ethington	Robert Ethington	2007	17
192 2/8	192 7/8	40 4/8	40	16 3/8	16 4/8	9 5/8	9 6/8	23 6/8	22	Sanders Co., MT	Michael K. Runyan	Michael K. Runyan	2008	17
192	193 5/8	41 3/8	41 7/8	15 5/8	15 5/8	9 4/8	10 1/8	26 4/8	26	Fergus Co., MT	Stephen H. Keaster	Stephen H. Keaster	2008	19
191 6/8	192	42 2/8	40 4/8	16 2/8	16 2/8	9 1/8	9	24	22 4/8	Sanders Co., MT	Scott W. Wendling	Scott W. Wendling	2007	20
191 6/8	192 1/8	41	41	16 6/8	16 5/8	9 1/8	9	25 3/8	24 5/8	Deer Lodge Co., MT	Elizabeth L. Klunder	Elizabeth L. Klunder	2008	20
191 3/8	192	40 1/8	41	16 6/8	16 6/8	8 7/8	9 3/8	25 2/8	25 2/8	Fergus Co., MT	Jamie J. Fadness	Jamie J. Fadness	2008	22
190 7/8	191 6/8	42 4/8	39 5/8	16	16 1/8	9 2/8	9	22 2/8	22 2/8	Nez Perce Co., ID	Tim J. Shockley	Tim J. Shockley	2006	23
190 6/8	191 3/8	41	41	15 7/8	15 4/8	9 7/8	9 7/8	23 3/8	22 1/8	Blaine Co., MT	Jady A. Trangmoe, Jr.	Jady A. Trangmoe, Jr.	2005	24
190 6/8	191	42 5/8	40 7/8	14 7/8	14 7/8	10 3/8	10 3/8	20 6/8	19	Luscar Mt., AB	Richard B. Abbott	Richard B. Abbott	2007	24
190 6/8	191 2/8	40 4/8	40	16	15 7/8	9 7/8	9 6/8	22 3/8	17 6/8	Granite Co., MT	Paul N. Hutchinson	Paul N. Hutchinson	2007	24
190 6/8	191 2/8	39 4/8	39 2/8	15 7/8	15 6/8	10 3/8	10 4/8	20	19 1/8	Elko Co., NV	Gino J. Aramini	Gino J. Aramini	2008	27
190 1/8	191 2/8	41 2/8	40 1/8	15 2/8	15 4/8	10 1/8	10 3/8	24	17 6/8	Blaine Co., MT	Victor L. Lauer	Victor L. Lauer	2006	28
190 3/8	190 3/8	40 4/8	40 4/8	15 4/8	16 4/8	10	10 1/8	23 4/8	22 4/8	Lewis & Clark Co., MT	Eric R. Norby	Eric R. Norby	2006	29
190	191 1/8	41 3/8	39 3/8	16 2/8	16 2/8	9 4/8	10 2/8	24 5/8	24 2/8	Elko Co., NV	Nevin R. Jensen	Nevin R. Jensen	2008	29
189 6/8	189 7/8	40 4/8	42	15 4/8	15 4/8	9 3/8	9 2/8	25 4/8	24 6/8	Blaine Co., MT	Brent C. Smith	Brent C. Smith	2006	31
189 6/8	190 6/8	38 4/8	36	16 4/8	16 4/8	10 1/8	11	24	15 6/8	Huerfano Co., CO	Douglas L. Weller	Douglas L. Weller	2007	31

Score										Location	Hunter	Owner	Date	Rank
189 6/8	190 5/8	39	39 4/8	15 7/8	15 6/8	10 1/8	10 3/8	23 3/8	21 1/8	Cadomin, AB	William K. Meyer	William K. Meyer	2008	31
189 3/8	189 4/8	41 3/8	41 4/8	16 1/8	16 2/8	8 4/8	8 4/8	26 1/8	25	Deer Lodge Co., MT	Bryan K. Martin	Bryan K. Martin	2006	34
189	189 1/8	41 3/8	40 3/8	15 5/8	15 4/8	9 2/8	9 2/8	20 5/8	20 5/8	Sanders Co., MT	Terry L. Towner	Terry L. Towner	2008	35
188 2/8	188 2/8	38 6/8	39 6/8	16 2/8	16 2/8	9	9	21 7/8	19 6/8	Blaine Co., MT	Leonard L. Lawver	Leonard L. Lawver	2006	36
188 2/8	188 5/8	37 6/8	39 4/8	16	16	10 4/8	10 4/8	23 7/8	23	Elko Co., NV	Kenneth J. Wilkinson	Kenneth J. Wilkinson	2009	36
188 1/8	188 3/8	39 6/8	39 7/8	15 7/8	15 7/8	9 4/8	9 2/8	21 5/8	19	Ravalli Co., MT	Gerald A. Linneweh	Gerald A. Linneweh	2008	38
187 5/8	188 5/8	41 1/8	41 1/8	14 3/8	14 6/8	10 2/8	10 5/8	25	23 6/8	Columbia Co., WA	Matthew Bell	Matthew Bell	2007	39
187 2/8	187 6/8	39	39	15 2/8	15 6/8	10	10	23 4/8	21 2/8	Kamloops Lake, BC	Sean D. Connolly	Sean D. Connolly	2006	40
187 2/8	188 3/8	38 6/8	38 6/8	16 2/8	16	9 4/8	10	26	24 1/8	Granite Co., MT	Devin M. Khoury	Devin M. Khoury	2006	40
187 2/8	187 6/8	39 7/8	37 5/8	15 7/8	15 7/8	10	9 6/8	25 1/8	21 5/8	Blaine Co., MT	Richard D. Moseman	Richard D. Moseman	2007	40
187 2/8	189	40	39 6/8	15 2/8	15	10 3/8	11	21 3/8	20 5/8	Blaine Co., MT	Donald G. Wells	Donald G. Wells	2008	40
187	187 4/8	40 4/8	40 7/8	15 4/8	15 4/8	9 6/8	9 6/8	21 6/8	21	Elko Co., NV	Don J. Dees	Don J. Dees	2007	44
187	187 4/8	40 7/8	41 1/8	15 4/8	15 4/8	8 7/8	8 7/8	24 4/8	23 7/8	Sanders Co., MT	Jerald A. Kohne	Jerald A. Kohne	2007	44
186 7/8	187	39 1/8	38 4/8	15 1/8	15 1/8	10 3/8	10 3/8	21 4/8	18 2/8	Phillips Co., MT	Dale K. Hinckley	Dale K. Hinckley	2006	46
186 6/8	187 7/8	38 1/8	39 1/8	16 1/8	16 1/8	9 6/8	8 7/8	19 5/8	18 1/8	Nez Perce Co., ID	Scott D. Baldwin	Scott D. Baldwin	2006	47
186 6/8	187	40 1/8	42 5/8	14 6/8	14 6/8	9 2/8	9 1/8	23 1/8	20 4/8	Ravalli Co., MT	A. Jay Darrah	A. Jay Darrah	2007	47
186 4/8	187 1/8	38 6/8	37	16 4/8	16 4/8	9 4/8	9 6/8	22 7/8	21 2/8	Sanders Co., MT	Chad W. Benson	Chad W. Benson	2006	49
186 4/8	186 6/8	41 6/8	39 4/8	15 7/8	15 7/8	8 4/8	8 4/8	23 4/8	20 4/8	Wallowa Co., OR	Joshua D. Simmons	Joshua D. Simmons	2006	49
186 4/8	186 4/8	39 4/8	40	14 7/8	14 7/8	10 1/8	10 1/8	24	21 3/8	Powell Co., MT	Randall G. Nichols	Randall G. Nichols	2008	49
186 3/8	187 5/8	37 6/8	37 5/8	15 7/8	15 7/8	10 4/8	9 4/8	20 7/8	18 7/8	Greenlee Co., AZ	Louis R. Saide	Louis R. Saide	2006	52
186 2/8	186 7/8	41 2/8	40 2/8	15	15	9 3/8	9 6/8	22 1/8	20 4/8	Luscar Mt., AB	Douglas L. Butler	Douglas L. Butler	2006	53
186 1/8	187 1/8	35 3/8	39	16 6/8	16 6/8	9 7/8	9 1/8	22 6/8	19 3/8	Missoula Co., MT	Will R. Schott	Will R. Schott	2006	54
186	187 1/8	39 4/8	38 4/8	15 7/8	15 7/8	10	9 4/8	21 6/8	19 5/8	Taos Co., NM	Jim C. Tyler	Jim C. Tyler	2009	55
185 6/8	185 6/8	40 6/8	41 2/8	15 3/8	15 3/8	8 7/8	8 7/8	25 5/8	24 6/8	Granite Co., MT	Dale R. Manning	Dale R. Manning	2008	56
185 5/8	185 4/8	41 7/8	40	15 5/8	15 5/8	9 2/8	8 3/8	22 1/8	20	Baker Co., OR	Rayden C. Dodson	Rayden C. Dodson	2007	57
185 5/8	185 4/8	38 3/8	38 3/8	15 4/8	15 4/8	10 3/8	10 3/8	20 5/8	19 4/8	Elko Co., NV	Dan L. Papez	Dan L. Papez	2009	57
185 3/8	186	39 5/8	38 4/8	16	16 1/8	8 6/8	8 4/8	28 7/8	28 2/8	Ravalli Co., MT	Elgin R. Forbes	Elgin R. Forbes	2006	59
185 3/8	185 7/8	40 1/8	38 6/8	16 5/8	16 4/8	7 5/8	7 4/8	21 4/8	20 7/8	Granite Co., MT	Kenneth W. Goerz	Kenneth W. Goerz	2009	59
185 2/8	185 3/8	40 3/8	40 3/8	16	16	8	8	26 3/8	26 3/8	Wallowa Co., OR	Mike A. Carpinito	Mike A. Carpinito	2007	61
185 2/8	185 2/8	39 4/8	39 4/8	16	16	8 2/8	8 2/8	24 2/8	24	Teton Co., MT	Troy D. Steffes	Troy D. Steffes	2007	61
185 2/8	185 7/8	42	42	14 6/8	14 6/8	8 6/8	9 1/8	22	20 6/8	Columbia Co., WA	Jay E. Link	Jay E. Link	2008	61
185 1/8	185 3/8	36 4/8	37 3/8	16 3/8	16 4/8	9 1/8	9 2/8	25	22 6/8	Las Animas Co., CO	Kris M. Asbell	Kris M. Asbell	2008	64
185	185 7/8	37 6/8	39 6/8	16 1/8	16	9	8 4/8	21 4/8	15 4/8	Highwood River, AB	Dewy D. Matthews	Dewy D. Matthews	2006	65
184 7/8	185 2/8	37 6/8	39 3/8	16	16	9 2/8	9 2/8	21 6/8	15 5/8	Granite Co., MT	Christopher L. McHugh	Christopher L. McHugh	2007	66
184 7/8	185 2/8	37 6/8	39 3/8	16 2/8	16 2/8	9 2/8	9 2/8	23 2/8	19 1/8	Lewis & Clark Co., MT	Dean L. Pearson	Dean L. Pearson	2007	66
184 7/8	185 6/8	38 1/8	38	15 4/8	15 4/8	9 6/8	9 5/8	23	23	Nez Perce Co., ID	Tamara M. Coleman	Tamara M. Coleman	2008	66
184 6/8	185 6/8	38	38 4/8	16 5/8	16 3/8	8 6/8	9	22	18 4/8	Sanders Co., MT	Warren A. Illi	Warren A. Illi	2006	69
184 6/8	185	41 4/8	42	15 4/8	15 4/8	8 2/8	8	26	25 5/8	Sanders Co., MT	JoAnn G. Illi	JoAnn G. Illi	2007	69
184 6/8	185	38 2/8	38 2/8	15 1/8	15 1/8	9 6/8	9 6/8	23 2/8	15 5/8	Hinsdale Co., CO	Denver D. McCabe	Denver D. McCabe	2009	69
184 4/8	184 5/8	39 2/8	41	15 7/8	15 7/8	8 1/8	8 2/8	23 6/8	23 3/8	Sanders Co., MT	Dennis M. Rehbein	Dennis M. Rehbein	2006	72
184 4/8	186	37 3/8	39 1/8	16 3/8	16 5/8	7 6/8	8 4/8	21 2/8	16	Bull River, BC	Christopher D. Hill	C.D. Hill & D Hoyt	2007	72

BIGHORN SHEEP

Ovis canadensis canadensis and certain related subspecies

Final Score	Gross Score	Length of horn R.	L.	Circumference of Base R.	L.	Circumference at Third Quarter R.	L.	Greatest Spread	Tip to Tip Spread	Locality	Hunter	Owner	Date Killed	Rank
184 4/8	185 1/8	39 4/8	39	15 2/8	15 1/8	9 3/8	9 4/8	21 7/8	19	Kamloops Lake, BC	Robert W. Shatzko	Robert W. Shatzko	2008	72
184 3/8	184 6/8	43 5/8	39 2/8	15 4/8	15 4/8	7 4/8	7 2/8	23 4/8	23 4/8	Ravalli Co., MT	Earl L. Morgan, Jr.	Earl L. Morgan, Jr.	2008	75
184 2/8	184 4/8	39 4/8	40 2/8	15 7/8	15 6/8	8 5/8	8 5/8	20 6/8	15 5/8	Sanders Co., MT	Bernard M. Bosch	Bernard M. Bosch	1985	76
184 2/8	184 6/8	40	38 6/8	15 4/8	15 2/8	9 2/8	9 1/8	21 4/8	20 6/8	Columbia Co., WA	Chris A. Dianda	Chris A. Dianda	2008	76
184 2/8	185 1/8	37 2/8	37 2/8	15	15 2/8	10 6/8	10 6/8	22 3/8	16	Taos Co., NM	Greg A. Strait	Greg A. Strait	2009	76
184 1/8	184 2/8	40 6/8	41 1/8	14 2/8	14 3/8	9 4/8	9 4/8	21	19 7/8	Taos Co., NM	John K. Koster	John K. Koster	2006	79
184	185 1/8	38 6/8	38 2/8	15 2/8	15 3/8	10 4/8	10 2/8	24	16 2/8	Taos Co., NM	Terry J. Fricks	Terry J. Fricks	2007	80
184	185 4/8	40 4/8	39 4/8	15 4/8	15 4/8	8	9	21 4/8	19 5/8	Lewis & Clark Co., MT	Larry L. Wiseman	Larry L. Wiseman	2008	80
183 7/8	184 4/8	37 2/8	38 1/8	15 6/8	15 6/8	10	10 2/8	23 2/8	22	Deer Lodge Co., MT	Roger A. Smithson	Roger A. Smithson	2006	82
183 7/8	184	36 7/8	37 4/8	15 1/8	15 1/8	11	10 7/8	22 7/8	17	Las Animas Co., CO	Picked Up	Roger Schalla	2009	82
183 6/8	184 5/8	41 3/8	40 5/8	15 6/8	15 4/8	8	7 6/8	25 6/8	25 6/8	Sanders Co., MT	Dale M. Peters	Dale M. Peters	2007	84
183 6/8	184 1/8	37 5/8	38 7/8	14 7/8	15	10 4/8	10 2/8	21 7/8	18 5/8	Granite Co., MT	Lars J. Engelhard	Lars J. Engelhard	2009	84
183 3/8	184 3/8	41 1/8	40 6/8	15	14 7/8	8 2/8	8 4/8	23 6/8	23 3/8	Sanders Co., MT	Terence L. Andres	Terence L. Andres	2007	86
183 2/8	183 5/8	38 4/8	38	16 4/8	16 4/8	8 5/8	8 5/8	23 4/8	23	Missoula Co., MT	Philip M. Ripepi	Philip M. Ripepi	2008	87
183 1/8	183 7/8	37 6/8	36 5/8	16	15 7/8	9 5/8	9 3/8	21 2/8	15 7/8	Grand Co., UT	Robert B. Strasburg	Robert B. Strasburg	2007	88
183	184 3/8	35 2/8	39 2/8	16 3/8	16 5/8	8 6/8	8 4/8	22 1/8	20 2/8	Chouteau Co., MT	Charles E. Bryant, Jr.	Charles E. Bryant, Jr.	2006	89
182 6/8	183 6/8	39 7/8	37 7/8	15 3/8	15 2/8	8 6/8	9 2/8	25 3/8	17 7/8	Pennington Co., SD	Donald W. Hill	Donald W. Hill	2006	90
182 6/8	183 2/8	38 5/8	38 3/8	16	16 1/8	8 2/8	8 3/8	21 3/8	22 3/8	Lewis & Clark Co., MT	Larry R. Johns	Larry R. Johns	2007	90
182 6/8	183 6/8	36	39	15 3/8	15 4/8	9 6/8	10 2/8	23	19	Jasper, AB	Vint Varner	Vint Varner	2008	90
182 5/8	182 7/8	37 1/8	39	14 4/8	14 4/8	10 3/8	10 5/8	21 6/8	13 3/8	Taos Co., NM	Robert J. Stallone	Robert J. Stallone	2006	93
182 5/8	182 7/8	36 3/8	36 2/8	15 6/8	15 6/8	10 6/8	10 6/8	20 4/8	16 5/8	Granite Co., MT	Jeffery D. Watkins	Jeffery D. Watkins	2008	93
182 3/8	182 4/8	37 2/8	38 3/8	15 6/8	15 5/8	8 7/8	8 7/8	22 5/8	21	Kananaskis, AB	Michael W. Mudie	Michael W. Mudie	2005	95
182 3/8	182 5/8	36 6/8	36 7/8	15 7/8	15 7/8	9 4/8	9 3/8	22	22	Grand Co., UT	Tyler Serawop	Tyler Serawop	2007	95
182 1/8	183 5/8	42 2/8	39 3/8	15 1/8	15	9 2/8	8 5/8	23 1/8	21	Park Co., WY	Susan B. Smith	Susan B. Smith	2007	97
182	182 4/8	39 6/8	40	16 1/8	16 1/8	7 6/8	7 5/8	23 3/8	22 7/8	Ravalli Co., MT	Ronald D. Knowles	Ronald D. Knowles	2006	98
182	182 5/8	37 2/8	37	15 5/8	15 6/8	9 3/8	9 3/8	21 1/8	16 3/8	Missoula Co., MT	Jason S. Nordberg	Jason S. Nordberg	2006	98
182	183 2/8	38 2/8	38	15 2/8	15 1/8	9 3/8	10 2/8	21 5/8	19 5/8	Teton Co., MT	Timothy Taranto	Timothy Taranto	2006	98
182	182 3/8	37 6/8	37	15 1/8	15 1/8	10 1/8	10 1/8	22	18 1/8	Blaine Co., MT	Tim D. Kolstad	Tim D. Kolstad	2009	98
181 7/8	182 3/8	42	41 5/8	15 3/8	15 3/8	7	7 2/8	22	15 1/8	Castlegar, BC	James B. Giles	James B. Giles	2009	102
181 7/8	182 6/8	36 4/8	36 3/8	15 6/8	15 7/8	9 6/8	9 2/8	24 1/8	18	Garfield Co., CO	John C. Krueger	John C. Krueger	2009	102
181 6/8	182 6/8	38 7/8	38 5/8	14 7/8	14 7/8	10 1/8	9 4/8	24 3/8	24 3/8	Powell Co., MT	Ben F. Harrison	Ben F. Harrison	2006	104

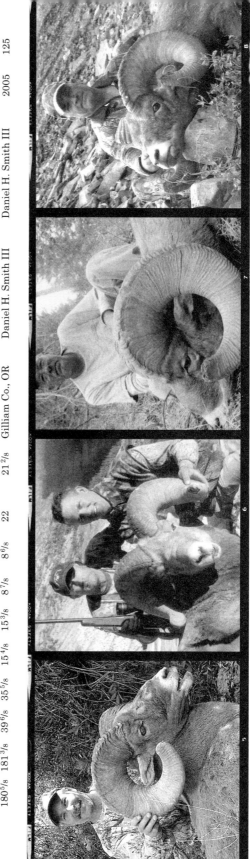

181 6/8	182 4/8	38 5/8	38 5/8	15 7/8	8 2/8	8 1/8	19 6/8	Roman R. Roberts	Pennington Co., SD	Roman R. Roberts	2006	104
181 6/8	182 4/8	39 3/8	38 3/8	15 5/8	8 6/8	8 3/8	17 2/8	Angela L. Butler	Baker Co., OR	Angela L. Butler	2008	104
181 6/8	182 4/8	40 2/8	39 2/8	14 6/8	9 5/8	9 3/8	17	Jason R. Pierson	Taos Co., NM	Jason R. Pierson	2008	104
181 5/8	182 3/8	36 6/8	40 1/8	15 3/8	8 7/8	9 1/8	22	James C. Shannon	Grande Cache, AB	James C. Shannon	2009	108
181 4/8	181 6/8	37 5/8	37 7/8	14 6/8	10	10	19 1/8	L. Crate	McBride, BC	Maurice Bonneville	PR 1970	109
181 4/8	181 7/8	37 6/8	38 4/8	15 1/8	9 2/8	9 3/8	18 1/8	Bradley M. Gremaux	Fergus Co., MT	Bradley M. Gremaux	2006	109
181 4/8	181 7/8	39 5/8	38 7/8	15	9 1/8	8 7/8	21 2/8	Kirk C. Clinkingbeard	Park Co., WY	Kirk C. Clinkingbeard	2008	109
181 4/8	182	38 6/8	38 6/8	16 2/8	8 2/8	8 4/8	20 5/8	Darrell S. Lendrum	Castle River, AB	Darrell S. Lendrum	2008	109
181 3/8	181 6/8	38 5/8	37	15 7/8	8 5/8	8 3/8	16 2/8	Russell S. Holcomb	Wallowa Co., OR	Russell S. Holcomb	2005	113
181 2/8	181 6/8	36 3/8	38 5/8	15 7/8	8 3/8	8 6/8	18	Thomas I. Grabowski	Kananaskis, AB	Thomas I. Grabowski	2007	114
181 2/8	182	37 2/8	36 2/8	15 4/8	10	9 6/8	18 3/8	John E. Legnard	Huerfano Co., CO	John E. Legnard	2008	114
181 2/8	181 4/8	38 1/8	38 1/8	16	8 5/8	8 4/8	20	Gary E. Eudaily	Granite Co., MT	Gary E. Eudaily	2009	114
181 1/8	181 4/8	43	37 1/8	15	8 3/8	8 2/8	23 2/8	Dennis R. Jenkins	Missoula Co., MT	Dennis R. Jenkins	1997	117
181	181 3/8	36 4/8	36 1/8	14 6/8	11 2/8	11 2/8	15 3/8	Mark K. Simas	Taos Co., NM	Mark K. Simas	2008	117
180 7/8	181 4/8	38 4/8	36 6/8	15 3/8	9 4/8	9 2/8	17 4/8	Douglas J. Leech	Elk Valley, BC	Douglas J. Leech	2007	119
180 7/8	181 4/8	37	38 5/8	15 2/8	9	9 3/8	15 2/8	Bradford G. McDavid	Graham Co., AZ	Bradford G. McDavid	2006	120
180 7/8	181 1/8	35 2/8	35 5/8	16	9 2/8	9 3/8	17 4/8	Leslie C. Wall	Mt. Allen, AB	Leslie C. Wall	2007	120
180 7/8	182 1/8	39 6/8	37 7/8	15 2/8	8 6/8	8 2/8	22 2/8	Bernadette H. Clevenger	Ravalli Co., MT	Bernadette H. Clevenger	2008	120
180 7/8	181 2/8	38	37 7/8	14 6/8	9 3/8	9 6/8	17 2/8	Kent P. Stevinson	Las Animas Co., CO	Kent P. Stevinson	2008	120
180 6/8	181 1/8	35 7/8	37 1/8	15 2/8	10 1/8	10	20 1/8	Vincent L. Fiscus	Blaine Co., MT	Vincent L. Fiscus	2004	124
180 5/8	181 3/8	39 6/8	35 5/8	15 4/8	8 7/8	8 6/8	21 2/8	Daniel H. Smith III	Gilliam Co., OR	Daniel H. Smith III	2005	125

BIGHORN SHEEP
FINAL SCORE: 180 7/8
HUNTER: Bradford G. McDavid

BIGHORN SHEEP
FINAL SCORE: 180 5/8
HUNTER: Sean D. Griffith

BIGHORN SHEEP
FINAL SCORE: 189
HUNTER: Terry L. Towner

BIGHORN SHEEP
FINAL SCORE: 182 6/8
HUNTER: Vint Varner

BIGHORN SHEEP

Ovis canadensis canadensis and certain related subspecies

Final Score	Gross Score	Length of Horn R.	Length of Horn L.	Circumference of Base R.	Circumference of Base L.	Circumference at Third Quarter R.	Circumference at Third Quarter L.	Greatest Spread	Tip to Tip Spread	Locality	Hunter	Owner	Date Killed	Rank
180 5/8	182 4/8	34 3/8	34 2/8	15 6/8	15 4/8	10 6/8	12	24 3/8	20 7/8	Union Co., OR	Sean D. Griffith	Sean D. Griffith	2008	125
180 4/8	181 4/8	38 6/8	39	14 6/8	14 6/8	9 4/8	10	24 6/8	24 6/8	Lewis & Clark Co., MT	Landon Koteskey	Landon Koteskey	2006	127
180 3/8	180 7/8	40	40 3/8	15 1/8	15 2/8	7 5/8	7 6/8	22	21 7/8	Sanders Co., MT	Corey R. Johnson	Corey R. Johnson	2007	128
180 2/8	182 5/8	39 5/8	39 1/8	15 1/8	15 1/8	9 5/8	8 3/8	21 4/8	14 4/8	Blaine Co., MT	Mark R. Copenhaver	Mark R. Copenhaver	2009	129
180 1/8	180 7/8	36 7/8	38	15 5/8	15 4/8	9 2/8	9	22 6/8	21 6/8	Phillips Co., MT	Walter D. Pekovitch	Walter D. Pekovitch	2006	130
180 1/8	180 6/8	38 1/8	37	16 4/8	16 5/8	7 6/8	8	23	22 7/8	Granite Co., MT	Mitchell C. Johnson	Mitchell C. Johnson	2007	130
180 1/8	180 5/8	39 1/8	38 4/8	15 7/8	15 7/8	7 2/8	7 4/8	22 3/8	20	Kananaskis, AB	Gerhard Osbitsch	Gerhard Osbitsch	2007	130
180 1/8	180 6/8	39 5/8	37 2/8	14 7/8	14 7/8	9 2/8	9 3/8	22 4/8	18 6/8	Taos Co., NM	Vincent E. Schneider	Vincent E. Schneider	2007	130
180 1/8	180 4/8	37 7/8	39	15 3/8	15 3/8	9	8 6/8	21 4/8	19 6/8	Lake Co., MT	Craig A. Padilla	Craig A. Padilla	2008	130
180 1/8	180 3/8	36 5/8	36 4/8	15 4/8	15 4/8	9 4/8	9 4/8	20 4/8	17 7/8	Sanders Co., MT	William E. Wilson	William E. Wilson	2009	130
180	180 5/8	38 4/8	38 4/8	14 3/8	14 5/8	10 2/8	10 2/8	20 2/8	19 4/8	Fremont Co., WY	James V. Butkovich	James V. Butkovich	2008	136
179 7/8	179 7/8	40 4/8	41	15 1/8	14 7/8	7 4/8	7 4/8	23 4/8	23	Ravalli Co., MT	Joseph D. Fragnito	Joseph D. Fragnito	2006	137
179 4/8	180 3/8	41 2/8	37 4/8	14	14	9 7/8	10	23 2/8	21 2/8	Blaine Co., MT	Jacob C. Dahl	Jacob C. Dahl	2008	138
179 4/8	180 3/8	40 4/8	41 2/8	14 7/8	15 1/8	7 3/8	7 7/8	20 5/8	20 2/8	Sanders Co., MT	Donald F. Walton	Donald F. Walton	2008	138
179 3/8	179 5/8	36 6/8	35 1/8	15	15	11 1/8	10 4/8	21 1/8	18 7/8	Albany Co., WY	Shawn M. Wilson	Shawn M. Wilson	2009	140
179 2/8	179 7/8	38 6/8	38 6/8	14 4/8	14 3/8	9 4/8	9 4/8	21 2/8	19 4/8	Sanders Co., MT	Alan W. Anderson	Alan W. Anderson	2008	141
179 2/8	179 4/8	35 3/8	37 7/8	15 1/8	15 2/8	9 6/8	9 4/8	24 4/8	20 6/8	Huerfano Co., CO	Chris Furia	Chris Furia	2009	141
179 1/8	180 6/8	37 1/8	37 6/8	14 6/8	14 7/8	10	10	20 2/8	17 4/8	Ravalli Co., MT	Charles R. Johnson	Charles R. Johnson	2007	143
179	179	38	39	14 4/8	14 6/8	10 2/8	10 2/8	24 3/8	17 4/8	Gila Co., AZ	James L. Ludvigson	James L. Ludvigson	2006	144
178 1/8	178 4/8	36 7/8	38 4/8	15 1/8	15 1/8	8 5/8	8 5/8	25 2/8	24 5/8	Sherman Co., OR	Timothy P. Brown	Timothy P. Brown	2004	145
178	179	38 2/8	34 4/8	15 2/8	15 2/8	9 5/8	9 5/8	23 6/8	16 2/8	Chaffee Co., CO	Picked Up	CO Div. of Wildl.	2000	146
178	178 3/8	38 5/8	38 7/8	14 3/8	14 3/8	9 1/8	8 7/8	21 2/8	16 4/8	Lewis & Clark Co., MT	Emilee P. DeKam	Emilee P. DeKam	2006	146
177 7/8	178 3/8	38 7/8	39 4/8	15 2/8	15 2/8	7 6/8	7 6/8	23 7/8	23 7/8	Granite Co., MT	Gregory A. Hewitt	Gregory A. Hewitt	2008	148
177 7/8	177 7/8	37	39 1/8	14 5/8	14 5/8	9	8 7/8	20 4/8	20 3/8	Granite Co., MT	Beau M. Means	Beau M. Means	2008	148
177 4/8	177 5/8	37 2/8	35 6/8	15	14 7/8	9	9	24 1/8	15 6/8	Park Co., WY	Picked Up	William S. Trapp	1995	150
177 3/8	177 4/8	37 4/8	41 7/8	15	15	7 7/8	7 7/8	25 7/8	25	Teton Co., MT	Edward C. Darfler	Edward C. Darfler	2007	151
177 3/8	177 6/8	38 5/8	34 6/8	15	15 1/8	9	9	21	15 5/8	Blaine Co., MT	Jeff J. Sundheim	Jeff J. Sundheim	2008	151
177	177 3/8	36 5/8	36 7/8	14 7/8	14 7/8	9 3/8	9 3/8	20 3/8	19	Broadwater Co., MT	Cal F. Bender	Cal F. Bender	2006	153
176 6/8	177	38	38 4/8	15 2/8	15 1/8	8 1/8	8 1/8	22 3/8	22	Teton Co., MT	Robert B. Swartz	Robert B. Swartz	2008	154
176 5/8	177 2/8	35 6/8	35 7/8	14 6/8	14 7/8	9 5/8	9 4/8	19 5/8	18 6/8	Fremont Co., CO	John F. Alderton	John F. Alderton	2008	155
176 5/8	177 1/8	35 7/8	36 2/8	15 6/8	15 6/8	8 1/8	8 3/8	21 4/8	19 4/8	Granite Co., MT	Justin C. Winz	Justin C. Winz	2008	155

Score										Locality	Hunter	Owner	Date Killed	Rank
176 4/8	177	35	35	16 4/8	16 4/8	8 4/8	8 3/8	23	21 3/8	Packhorse Creek, BC	J.D. Fitterer	J.D. Fitterer	2009	157
176 3/8	177 3/8	35 5/8	37 2/8	14	14	10 6/8	10 5/8	18	18	Park Co., WY	Picked Up	Casey R. Brazelton	2006	158
176	176 3/8	35 3/8	35 3/8	14 6/8	14 5/8	9 7/8	9 7/8	23 2/8	20	Gilliam Co., OR	Phillip E. Sherrell	Phillip E. Sherrell	2006	159
176	176 5/8	39 1/8	39 3/8	14 5/8	14 6/8	7 5/8	8	25 6/8	25 6/8	Missoula Co., MT	Connor E. Kowalski	Connor E. Kowalski	2008	159
175 6/8	176 6/8	37 6/8	36	15 2/8	15 1/8	8 6/8	8 2/8	23 4/8	20 5/8	Lake Co., OR	Derek K. Ward	Derek K. Ward	2008	161
175 5/8	176 7/8	34 3/8	38 4/8	14 5/8	15	8 7/8	9 1/8	21 5/8	18	Park Co., MT	James B. Rose	James B. Rose	2007	162
175 3/8	175 6/8	36 4/8	36 7/8	15 1/8	15 1/8	8	8 3/8	23 1/8	19 5/8	Sanders Co., MT	William R. Mitchell	William R. Mitchell	2004	163
175 3/8	175 6/8	37 3/8	38 4/8	13 4/8	13 3/8	10 3/8	10 4/8	21 6/8	15 4/8	San Miguel Co., NM	Lori J. Ginn	Lori J. Ginn	2007	163
175 3/8	175 6/8	38 2/8	36 1/8	14 5/8	14 5/8	8 5/8	8 6/8	19 6/8	15 5/8	Missoula Co., MT	Philip W. Ramsey	Philip W. Ramsey	2007	163
175 3/8	176	38 4/8	38 1/8	15 2/8	15 1/8	7 2/8	7 1/8	20 4/8	20 5/8	Blaine Co., MT	Unknown	Ernest Shotton	2007	163
175 2/8	175 2/8	36 6/8	39 2/8	14 6/8	14 6/8	8 1/8	8 1/8	23 7/8	20	Taos Co., NM	Stanley R. Miller III	Stanley R. Miller III	2007	163
175 1/8	175 7/8	37 5/8	37 6/8	16	15 7/8	7 4/8	7 6/8	22 4/8	22	Okanogan Co., WA	John D. Hammer	John D. Hammer	2008	167
175 1/8	175 2/8	37	35 3/8	14 5/8	14 4/8	9 1/8	9 1/8	20 6/8	19 4/8	Park Co., WY	Paul A. Pearson	Paul A. Pearson	2009	168
206 3/8 *	206 6/8	45 3/8	45 4/8	15 4/8	15 5/8	12 2/8	12 2/8	22 5/8	21 2/8	Cadomin, AB	Picked Up	AB Fish & Wildl. Div.	2008	
206 *	206 4/8	45 2/8	46 6/8	15 7/8	15 7/8	11 4/8	11 4/8	23	23	Sphinx Creek, AB	Chad A. Meropoulis	Chad A. Meropoulis	2007	
202 2/8 *	202 5/8	44 2/8	43 6/8	16 1/8	16 1/8	10 7/8	10 6/8	24	19	Fergus Co., MT	Patrick L. White	Patrick L. White	2009	

Final score subject to revision by additional verifying measurements.

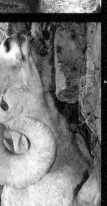

BIGHORN SHEEP
FINAL SCORE: 184
HUNTER: Terry J. Fricks

BIGHORN SHEEP
FINAL SCORE: 181 1/8
HUNTER: John E. Legnard

BIGHORN SHEEP
FINAL SCORE: 180 1/8
HUNTER: William E. Wilson

BIGHORN SHEEP
FINAL SCORE: 181 1/8
HUNTER: John C. Krueger

DESERT SHEEP

Ovis canadensis nelsoni and certain related subspecies

Minimum Score 165   World's Record 205 1/8

Final Score	Gross Score	Length of horn R.	Length of horn L.	Circumference of Base R.	Circumference of Base L.	Circumference at Third Quarter R.	Circumference at Third Quarter L.	Greatest Spread	Tip to Tip Spread	Locality	Hunter	Owner	Date Killed	Rank
179	179 4/8	39	36 4/8	15 4/8	15 3/8	8 3/8	8 3/8	25 4/8	25	Brewster Co., TX	Walter O. Ford, Jr.	Walter O. Ford, Jr.	2006	1
178 7/8	179 7/8	39	39 1/8	14 5/8	14 4/8	9 3/8	9 2/8	19 1/8	20 6/8	Pima Co., AZ	Sarah M. Dawe	Sarah M. Dawe	2007	2
177 6/8	177 7/8	39 6/8	39 6/8	14 4/8	14 4/8	9	9	26 7/8	26 7/8	San Bernardino Co., CA	Jay A. Kellett	Jay A. Kellett	2007	3
177 4/8	177 4/8	35 6/8	35 4/8	15 2/8	15	9 5/8	9 5/8	23 6/8	23 2/8	Pinal Co., AZ	Mark L. Walter	Mark L. Walter	2007	4
176 4/8	177	37 2/8	36 6/8	14 6/8	15	9 1/8	9 2/8	22 7/8	22 3/8	Yuma Co., AZ	Timothy Parrish	Timothy Parrish	2006	5
176 4/8	176 7/8	36 3/8	36 3/8	15 2/8	15 4/8	9 1/8	9 1/8	22 2/8	21 7/8	Clark Co., NV	Loren A. Pribyl	Loren A. Pribyl	2006	5
176 3/8	176 3/8	41 4/8	35 5/8	15 2/8	15 2/8	7 3/8	7 3/8	23 7/8	23 4/8	Baja Calif., MX	Robert E. Speegle	Robert E. Speegle	2008	7
176 2/8	178 7/8	37 2/8	36 4/8	15 4/8	15 2/8	9 5/8	8 2/8	24 4/8	22 7/8	Churchill Co., NV	Cindy D. Jackson-Miller	Cindy D. Jackson-Miller	2006	8
176 2/8	177 1/8	32 4/8	32 4/8	16	16 2/8	10	10 3/8	16 4/8	16 5/8	Sonora, MX	Walter O. Kirby	Walter O. Kirby	2006	8
176 1/8	176 3/8	37 2/8	36 3/8	15	14 7/8	9 2/8	9 1/8	20 5/8	17 5/8	Culberson Co., TX	Jerry M. Baker	Jerry M. Baker	2007	10
175 7/8	178 1/8	36 1/8	36	15 1/8	15 2/8	10 4/8	9	21 2/8	15 5/8	Tiburon Island, MX	Guinn D. Crousen	Guinn D. Crousen	2007	11
175 6/8	176 1/8	36 5/8	37 1/8	15 2/8	15 2/8	8 6/8	8 7/8	24 6/8	24 6/8	Nye Co., NV	Ben B. Hollingsworth, Jr.	Ben B. Hollingsworth, Jr.	2008	12
175 5/8	176 6/8	35 6/8	35 7/8	16 2/8	16 3/8	9	8 6/8	19 4/8	18 4/8	Baja Calif. Sur, MX	Bret C. Dolph	Bret C. Dolph	2009	13
175 3/8	176	36 2/8	36 1/8	16	16	8 4/8	8 5/8	21 1/8	17	Baja Calif., MX	Gordon Studer	Cabela's, Inc.	1962	14
174 5/8	175 2/8	35 4/8	35 5/8	15 4/8	15 3/8	8 6/8	8 5/8	22 5/8	21 6/8	Hudspeth Co., TX	Daniel F. Boone	Daniel F. Boone	2008	15
174 3/8	174 4/8	36 6/8	36 1/8	14 4/8	14 4/8	9 6/8	9 6/8	25	24	Nye Co., NV	William R. Balsi, Sr.	William R. Balsi, Sr.	2006	16
174 3/8	174 4/8	36 2/8	36 5/8	14 4/8	14 4/8	9 6/8	9 6/8	24 1/8	23 4/8	Nye Co., NV	David D. Elizondo	David D. Elizondo	2007	16
174 1/8	174 4/8	35 3/8	35	14 7/8	14 7/8	10 1/8	9 7/8	20 7/8	17	Clark Co., NV	Benjamin T. Himel	Benjamin T. Himel	2008	18
173 7/8	173 7/8	37 4/8	36 1/8	15 2/8	15 2/8	7 7/8	7 7/8	23 4/8	22 1/8	Clark Co., NV	Allen W. Campbell	Allen W. Campbell	2008	19
173 5/8	174	37 7/8	36 2/8	14 2/8	14 2/8	9 5/8	9 4/8	20	17 6/8	La Paz Co., AZ	David E. Combs	David E. Combs	2006	20
173 3/8	173 6/8	36 4/8	36 1/8	15 2/8	15 2/8	8 3/8	8 3/8	27 5/8	27	Nye Co., NV	David D. Stoker	David D. Stoker	2008	21
173 1/8	173 5/8	34 2/8	36 1/8	14 5/8	14 6/8	9 7/8	9 7/8	22 5/8	21 1/8	San Bernardino Co., CA	Picked Up	CA Dept. of Fish & Game	1987	22
173	173 4/8	35 5/8	36 1/8	14 5/8	14 6/8	8 7/8	8 6/8	21 4/8	18	Yuma Co., AZ	Anthony Wagner	Anthony Wagner	2006	23
173	174 6/8	36 3/8	37 5/8	15 6/8	15 6/8	7 5/8	8 1/8	21 3/8	21 3/8	Gila Co., AZ	Manuel O. Bercovich	Manuel O. Bercovich	2007	23
172 7/8	172 6/8	36 1/8	36 4/8	15 1/8	14 6/8	9 2/8	8 6/8	19 7/8	19 7/8	Carmen Island, MX	Jerry R. Tyrrell	Jerry R. Tyrrell	2009	25
172 4/8	172 6/8	35 2/8	36 6/8	14 7/8	14 7/8	8 3/8	8 3/8	23 2/8	23 6/8	Nye Co., NV	Vern E. Tranberg	Vern E. Tranberg	2006	26
172 2/8	172 5/8	37 4/8	37 2/8	14 4/8	14 5/8	8 4/8	8 3/8	28 2/8	28	Nye Co., NV	James D. Peterson	James D. Peterson	2006	27
172 3/8	172 3/8	38 1/8	36 3/8	14 4/8	14 4/8	8 3/8	8 3/8	19 4/8	18	Tiburon Island, MX	Douglas J. Leech	Douglas J. Leech	2008	28
172	172 2/8	36 6/8	37 1/8	15 3/8	15 2/8	8 2/8	7 5/8	21 6/8	20 6/8	Baja Calif. Sur, MX	Jerry R. Tyrrell	Jerry R. Tyrrell	2007	29
171 7/8	172 2/8	35 4/8	34	15 6/8	15 6/8	8 3/8	8 4/8	22 2/8	22	Nye Co., NV	John H. Parker	John H. Parker	2006	30
171 6/8	172 2/8	35	36 2/8	14 5/8	14 6/8	9 1/8	9 1/8	20 5/8	16 2/8	Culberson Co., TX	Rex Baker	Rex Baker	2008	30
171 6/8	172 3/8	35 4/8	35	15 5/8	15 5/8	8 2/8	8 2/8	24 2/8	16 1/8	La Paz Co., AZ	Michael W. DeWees	Michael W. DeWees	2008	30

Score	Gross Score	Length of Horn R	Length of Horn L	Circumference of Base	Circ. Third Quarter R	Circ. Third Quarter L	Tip to Tip Spread	Greatest Spread	Locality	Hunter	Owner	Date Killed	Rank
171 6/8	171 7/8	34 3/8	34 7/8	15 4/8	8 4/8	8 3/8	22 7/8	21 2/8	Brewster Co., TX	Steven S. Bruggeman	Steven S. Bruggeman	2009	30
171 4/8	171 1/8	36 5/8	35 7/8	14 5/8	8 5/8	8 4/8	22	17 2/8	La Paz Co., AZ	Scott M. Zeller	Scott M. Zeller	2008	34
171 3/8	173	35 6/8	36 5/8	14 1/8	10	10	20 6/8	19 4/8	La Paz Co., AZ	Ignacio Beltram	Ignacio Beltram	2007	35
171 2/8	172 1/8	37 1/8	37 1/8	14 2/8	8 1/8	8 7/8	24 1/8	23 7/8	Clark Co., NV	Jerry Crowe	Gary W. Crowe	1958	36
171 2/8	172 3/8	37 6/8	38	14 2/8	8 2/8	8 4/8	26	26	Mohave Co., AZ	Peter J. Kenney	Peter J. Kenney	2007	36
171	171 4/8	33 3/8	33 3/8	14 4/8	9 1/8	9	21 1/8	15	Culberson Co., TX	William M. Lauer	William M. Lauer	2009	38
170 7/8	171 6/8	36 2/8	34 5/8	14 7/8	9 1/8	8 6/8	24	23 4/8	Nye Co., NV	Robin L. Sutherland	Rob L. Sutherland	2006	39
170 6/8	171 5/8	34 4/8	34 6/8	15	8 5/8	8 7/8	22 4/8	22	Churchill Co., NV	Evan F. Pritchett	Evan F. Pritchett	2006	40
170 3/8	170 5/8	36 6/8	36 3/8	15 6/8	7 3/8	7 5/8	30	30	Mohave Co., AZ	Arthur Samora	Arthur Samora	2008	41
169 6/8	170	34 6/8	33 6/8	16	8	8 1/8	25 4/8	25	Nye Co., NV	Eddie L. Booth	Eddie L. Booth	2008	42
169 6/8	170 4/8	36 2/8	36	14	9 3/8	9	20 4/8	19 6/8	Nye Co., NV	Blake L. Sartini	Blake L. Sartini	2008	42
169 5/8	171 1/8	34	34 1/8	15 1/8	9 2/8	9 5/8	21 2/8	20 4/8	Pima Co., AZ	Darrel M. Lippert	Darrel M. Lippert	2007	44
169 4/8	170 4/8	34	34 2/8	15 2/8	8 3/8	8 4/8	19 5/8	17 6/8	Sonora, MX	E. Ann Kulp	E. Ann Kulp	2006	45
169 3/8	170 5/8	36 3/8	36	14 2/8	9 3/8	9 2/8	23 1/8	22 1/8	Nye Co., NV	Rick G. Duggan	Rick G. Duggan	2009	46
169 2/8	170	33	32 4/8	15 4/8	9 2/8	8 7/8	19 6/8	19 3/8	Churchill Co., NV	D. Ronald Jones	D. Ronald Jones	2007	47
169 1/8	169 7/8	33 5/8	33 4/8	14 4/8	10	10 2/8	19	18 5/8	Maricopa Co., AZ	Douglas M. Dreeszen	Douglas M. Dreeszen	2006	48
169 1/8	170 7/8	31 2/8	32 1/8	15 6/8	9 6/8	9 6/8	25	22 1/8	Nye Co., NV	John P. Simmons	John P. Simmons	2006	48
169 1/8	170 3/8	36 1/8	36	14 7/8	8 3/8	8 2/8	22 4/8	22 4/8	San Bernardino Co., CA	Brian E. McClintock	Brian E. McClintock	2007	48
169 1/8		34 6/8	34 7/8	15 1/8	8 2/8	8 3/8	22 4/8	19 6/8	Culberson Co., TX	Mark D. Nuessle	Mark D. Nuessle	2008	48
169	169 5/8	32 2/8	34	14 7/8	9 2/8	9 5/8	21	16	Sonora, MX	Shawn R. Andres	Shawn R. Andres	2007	52
168 7/8	169 3/8	35 1/8	34 2/8	14 6/8	8 2/8	8 2/8	19 7/8	13 4/8	Sonora, MX	J. Michael Goodart	J. Michael Goodart	2006	53

DESERT SHEEP
FINAL SCORE: 171
HUNTER: William M. Lauer

DESERT SHEEP
FINAL SCORE: 168 2/8
HUNTER: Roger D. Cook, Jr.

DESERT SHEEP
FINAL SCORE: 179 1/8*
HUNTER: John C. Marsh
* Final score subject to revision by additional verifying measurements.

DESERT SHEEP
FINAL SCORE: 175 6/8
HUNTER: Ben B. Hollingsworth, Jr.

Ovis canadensis nelsoni and certain related subspecies

Final Score	Gross Score	Length of horn R.	Length of horn L.	Circumference of Base R.	Circumference of Base L.	Circumference at Third Quarter R.	Circumference at Third Quarter L.	Greatest Spread	Tip to Tip Spread	Locality	Hunter	Owner	Date Killed	Rank
168 6/8	169 3/8	36 2/8	35 2/8	15 2/8	15 2/8	7 6/8	8	21 1/8	18 3/8	Baja Calif. Sur, MX	John R. Thodos	John R. Thodos	1999	54
168 6/8	169 4/8	33	35 2/8	15 1/8	15 2/8	9	8 5/8	20 7/8	17 2/8	Pima Co., AZ	Michael D. Aleff	Michael D. Aleff	2008	54
168 5/8	168 6/8	36 5/8	34 6/8	14 5/8	15 2/8	8 3/8	8 3/8	22 5/8	22 5/8	Mohave Co., AZ	Kyle R. Randall	Kyle R. Randall	2006	56
168 5/8	169 4/8	37 7/8	37 6/8	14	13 6/8	8 6/8	8 4/8	25 4/8	25 1/8	Clark Co., NV	Steven J. Reiter	Steven J. Reiter	2006	56
168 4/8	169 3/8	33 5/8	36 1/8	14 4/8	14 4/8	8 5/8	9 1/8	19 3/8	18 4/8	Clark Co., NV	Joseph R. McMullen	Joseph R. McMullen	2007	58
168 3/8	170 5/8	35 3/8	34 6/8	14 4/8	14 5/8	9 6/8	8 5/8	23	18 7/8	Graham Co., AZ	Bryant S. Harrison	Bryant S. Harrison	2007	59
168 3/8	170 2/8	32 7/8	35	14 5/8	14 5/8	8 6/8	9 5/8	20 5/8	18 1/8	La Paz Co., AZ	Phillip A. McCreary	Phillip A. McCreary	2008	59
168 2/8	168 6/8	35 3/8	36 3/8	14 1/8	14 2/8	8 4/8	8 5/8	20 2/8	19 4/8	Clark Co., NV	Tim S. Murray	Tim S. Murray	2006	61
168 2/8	168 7/8	36 1/8	35 5/8	14 7/8	14 6/8	7 4/8	7 5/8	20 1/8	16	Sonora, MX	F. Michael Parkowski	F. Michael Parkowski	2006	61
168 2/8	170 1/8	35 2/8	36 4/8	14 5/8	14 5/8	8 4/8	9	19	16 6/8	Pima Co., AZ	Roger D. Cook, Jr.	Roger D. Cook, Jr.	2007	61
168 1/8	168 7/8	34 3/8	32 4/8	14 6/8	14 5/8	9 2/8	9 3/8	23 6/8	23 2/8	Clark Co., NV	Robert T. Omiecinski	Robert T. Omiecinski	2006	64
168 1/8	168 3/8	34 3/8	33 6/8	14 6/8	14 6/8	8 5/8	8 4/8	21 4/8	19 6/8	Maricopa Co., AZ	Steven T. Melton	Steven T. Melton	2008	64
168 1/8	168 5/8	34 3/8	33 2/8	14 6/8	14 6/8	9	9 3/8	19 2/8	16 2/8	Pinal Co., AZ	James P. Walter	James P. Walter	2008	64
168	168 1/8	31 5/8	32 3/8	14 7/8	14 7/8	8 7/8	9	23 7/8	23 1/8	Garfield Co., UT	Paul C. Anderson	Paul C. Anderson	2008	67
168	168 5/8	34 2/8	34 5/8	14 3/8	14 3/8	8 4/8	9	24	24	Inyo Co., CA	Kenneth A. Wilson, Jr.	Kenneth A. Wilson, Jr.	2009	67
167 1/8	167 6/8	34 6/8	34 5/8	14 7/8	15	7 6/8	7 7/8	23 3/8	23	Churchill Co., NV	Roger A. Heath	Roger A. Heath	2007	69
167	167 5/8	34 2/8	33 2/8	14 4/8	14 6/8	8 4/8	8 6/8	20 6/8	19 4/8	Hudspeth Co., TX	Monty L. Davis	Monty L. Davis	2008	70
166 5/8	167	34 4/8	34 5/8	14 7/8	14 7/8	8 2/8	8	22 2/8	15 6/8	Clark Co., NV	James A. Algerio	James A. Algerio	2005	71
166 4/8	167 1/8	34 7/8	35 7/8	14 6/8	14 6/8	7 5/8	7 2/8	22 1/8	22 1/8	Kane Co., UT	Mark D. Butler	Mark D. Butler	2009	72
166 3/8	167 2/8	33 5/8	34	14 3/8	14 4/8	9 2/8	9	22 1/8	19 3/8	San Bernardino Co., CA	Douglas C. Imhoff	Douglas C. Imhoff	2007	73
165 5/8	165 7/8	34 5/8	34 6/8	14 5/8	14 4/8	8 2/8	8 2/8	22 3/8	21 5/8	Nye Co., NV	Thomas P. Ryan	Thomas P. Ryan	2007	74
165 3/8	165 7/8	33 5/8	32 6/8	14 4/8	14 3/8	9	8 6/8	21 5/8	22 4/8	Yuma Co., AZ	Gerald W. Backhaus	Gerald W. Backhaus	2008	75
165 2/8	169 2/8	36 4/8	37	14 2/8	14 2/8	9 1/8	9 4/8	21 3/8	20 6/8	Clark Co., NV	Blake L. Sartini	Blake L. Sartini	2006	76
165 1/8	166 3/8	32 3/8	34 2/8	16	16	7 7/8	7 2/8	19 6/8	19 4/8	Sonora, MX	Edward A. Petersen	Edward A. Petersen	2006	77
165	165 5/8	34 1/8	33 1/8	14 4/8	14 4/8	8 6/8	8 3/8	20	16 3/8	Yuma Co., AZ	John I. Hudson	John I. Hudson	2007	78
165	166 2/8	34	34	14 1/8	14	8 6/8	9 3/8	21 7/8	20 7/8	Nye Co., NV	Kenneth R. Peterson	Kenneth R. Peterson	2008	78
165	165 1/8	33 2/8	34	13 2/8	13 2/8	9 4/8	9 4/8	20 2/8	20 2/8	Coconino Co., AZ	Anthony R. Matthews	Anthony R. Matthews	2009	78
184 *	184 3/8	39	38 6/8	15 5/8	15 6/8	9	9 1/8	23 5/8	22 1/8	Culberson Co., TX	Stephanie Altimus	Stephanie Altimus	2007	
182 2/8*	183	37 1/8	37 1/8	15 5/8	15 5/8	10 1/8	10 2/8	21 6/8	20 7/8	Nye Co., NV	Joseph L. Maslach	Joseph L. Maslach	2008	
181 6/8*	182 4/8	36 4/8	36 2/8	16 4/8	16 6/8	9 2/8	9	21 2/8	17 3/8	Tiburon Island, MX	Donald W. Snyder	Donald W. Snyder	2006	
179 2/8*	179 4/8	38 5/8	38 5/8	15 1/8	15 1/8	9 1/8	9 1/8	23 3/8	22 3/8	Pima Co., AZ	Robert E. Wingle, Jr.	Robert E. Wingle, Jr.	2006	
179 1/8*	180	37	36 3/8	16	16	8 7/8	9 3/8	20 5/8	20 1/8	Baja Calif, MX	John C. Marsh	John C. Marsh	2007	

Final score subject to revision by additional verifying measurements.

DALL'S SHEEP

Ovis dalli dalli and *Ovis dalli kenaiensis*

Minimum Score 160   World's Record 189 6/8

Final Score	Gross Score	Length of horn R.	L.	Circumference of Base R.	L.	Circumference at Third Quarter R.	L.	Greatest Spread	Tip to Tip Spread	Locality	Hunter	Owner	Date Killed	Rank
173 4/8	173 7/8	42 4/8	42	14	14 1/8	6 2/8	6 2/8	30 3/8	30	Brooks Range, AK	Frank M. Chapman	Frank M. Chapman	2009	1
172 7/8	173 3/8	39 4/8	39 7/8	15 1/8	15 1/8	6 4/8	6 5/8	26 5/8	26 5/8	Moraine Lake, YT	John Beecher	John Beecher	2007	2
170 3/8	171 3/8	43 2/8	44 1/8	13 7/8	13 4/8	6	6	29 2/8	29	Wrangell Mts., AK	James L. Morrow	DLJM Collection	1972	3
169 4/8	169 5/8	41 3/8	42 7/8	13 5/8	13 4/8	6	5 7/8	27	27	Rainy Pass, AK	William N. Beach	Shelburne Museum	1926	4
167 7/8	168	40 4/8	40 5/8	13 2/8	13 2/8	6 3/8	6 3/8	24	23 7/8	Arkell Creek, YT	Alan Klassen	Alan Klassen	2009	5
167 6/8	168 4/8	41 2/8	42 4/8	13 4/8	13 4/8	5 6/8	6 2/8	26	26	Bonnet Plume Lake, YT	Garth K. Carter	Garth K. Carter	2008	6
167 1/8	167 6/8	38 4/8	38 7/8	15	15	6 1/8	6 2/8	30	29 7/8	Hawkins Glacier, AK	Jefferson A. Rogers	Jefferson A. Rogers	2008	7
166 7/8	166 7/8	39 3/8	40 6/8	13 3/8	13 3/8	6 3/8	6 3/8	27 6/8	27 6/8	Big River, AK	Roger S. Sambueso	Roger S. Sambueso	2007	8
166 5/8	166 7/8	42 3/8	42 2/8	13 4/8	13 5/8	5 4/8	5 4/8	24 3/8	24 2/8	Arctic Red River, NT	Jerrell F. Coburn	Jerrell F. Coburn	2008	9
166 2/8	166 4/8	41	40	13 2/8	13 2/8	5 7/8	6	30	29 6/8	Chugach Mts., AK	James D. Pex	James D. Pex	2007	10
165 2/8	165 7/8	40 1/8	39 7/8	13 4/8	13 6/8	6 2/8	6	25 7/8	25 6/8	Tok River, AK	Steve D. Adams	Steve D. Adams	2007	11

DALL'S SHEEP
FINAL SCORE: 166 5/8
HUNTER: Jerrell F. Coburn

DALL'S SHEEP
FINAL SCORE: 163 7/8
HUNTER: David L. Hussey

DALL'S SHEEP
FINAL SCORE: 162 5/8
HUNTER: Jedediah L. Konsor

DALL'S SHEEP
FINAL SCORE: 162 4/8
HUNTER: Matthew J. Jurad

DALL'S SHEEP

Ovis dalli dalli and Ovis dalli kenaiensis

Final Score	Gross Score	Length of horn R.	L.	Circumference of Base R.	L.	Circumference at Third Quarter R.	L.	Greatest Spread	Tip to Tip Spread	Locality	Hunter	Owner	Date Killed	Rank
165 2/8	165 3/8	41 1/8	39 3/8	13	12 7/8	6 6/8	6 6/8	24 2/8	23 7/8	Brooks Range, AK	Mark E. Renner	Mark E. Renner	2009	11
164 4/8	165 1/8	40 5/8	39 7/8	13 1/8	13 4/8	6	5 6/8	25 2/8	25	Alaska Range, AK	Arthur E. Goodrich	Arthur E. Goodrich	2007	13
164 2/8	164 5/8	39 6/8	39 2/8	13 6/8	13 7/8	5 7/8	5 7/8	26	26	Mackenzie Mts., NT	Roger W. Faulkingham	Roger W. Faulkingham	2007	14
163 7/8	164 3/8	40 2/8	40 3/8	12 6/8	12 5/8	6 2/8	6 3/8	23	22 5/8	Mackenzie Mts., NT	David L. Hussey	David L. Hussey	2006	15
163 7/8	164 1/8	39 4/8	39 5/8	13 7/8	13 7/8	5 7/8	5 6/8	22	22	Chugach Mts., AK	Scott B. Wayment	Scott B. Wayment	2007	15
163 7/8	164 2/8	40 6/8	40 3/8	13 5/8	13 6/8	5 6/8	5 6/8	26 4/8	26 4/8	Chugach Mts., AK	C. Kay Neitsch	C. Kay Neitsch	2009	15
163 3/8	163 5/8	36	42 3/8	13 1/8	13	6 2/8	6 2/8	22 2/8	22 2/8	Mackenzie Mts., NT	Judd M. Stauss	Judd M. Stauss	2008	18
162 5/8	163 2/8	37 7/8	41	13 6/8	13 6/8	5 4/8	5 7/8	24 6/8	24 3/8	Brooks Range, AK	Jedediah L. Konsor	Jedediah L. Konsor	2009	19
162 4/8	163 1/8	39 6/8	40 6/8	13 3/8	13 3/8	5 4/8	5 6/8	26 4/8	26 3/8	Dry Pass, YT	Matthew J. Jurad	Matthew J. Jurad	2009	20
162 2/8	162 3/8	38	40 4/8	13 4/8	13 4/8	5 3/8	5 4/8	26 6/8	26 6/8	Chugach Mts., AK	Michael S. Perchetti	Michael S. Perchetti	2007	21
162 2/8	162 3/8	37	37 2/8	14 1/8	14 1/8	6	6 3/8	25 2/8	25 2/8	Takhini River, BC	Ronny Bohrmann	Ronny Bohrmann	2009	21
162	162 3/8	36 2/8	35 4/8	13 1/8	13 3/8	8 1/8	8 2/8	19	18 4/8	Nahanni River, NT	Victor A. Engel	Victor A. Engel	2005	23
161 6/8	162	39 7/8	39 4/8	13	13	5 4/8	5 5/8	30 4/8	30 4/8	Primrose Lake, YT	Tony J. Grabowski	Tony J. Grabowski	2006	24
161 6/8	161 6/8	39 6/8	39 4/8	12 7/8	12 7/8	5 5/8	5 5/8	19 6/8	17 4/8	Chugach Mts., AK	George F. Garrison III	George F. Garrison III	2009	24
161 4/8	162	38 6/8	39	13 3/8	13 5/8	5 3/8	5 3/8	25 3/8	25 5/8	Talkeetna Mts., AK	Raymond N. Andersen	Raymond N. Andersen	2009	26
161 2/8	161 7/8	34 5/8	35 7/8	13 6/8	13 6/8	7 6/8	7 5/8	20	17	Philip Smith Mts., AK	Bronko A. Terkovich	Bronko A. Terkovich	2006	27
160 7/8	161 3/8	39 7/8	40	13	13 1/8	5 3/8	5 4/8	22 2/8	22	Chugach Mts., AK	Geofrey S. Moss	Geofrey S. Moss	2007	28
160 4/8	160 7/8	39 3/8	39 7/8	13 6/8	13 7/8	5	5 1/8	22 4/8	22 2/8	Kenai Mts., AK	Craig J. Weaver	Craig J. Weaver	2009	29
160 3/8	160 4/8	39	39 1/8	13 2/8	13 2/8	5 7/8	6	27 6/8	27 6/8	Rockslide Creek, YT	Warren T. Kinniburgh	Warren T. Kinniburgh	2005	30
160 2/8	160 2/8	38 5/8	39 3/8	12 4/8	12 4/8	6 5/8	6 5/8	23 4/8	23 4/8	Tonzona River, AK	William N. Beach	Shelburne Museum	1926	31
180 7/8*	181	43 6/8	43 5/8	14 1/8	14 1/8	7 5/8	7 4/8	27 3/8	27 3/8	Quill Creek, YT	James B. Anthony	James B. Anthony	2007	
177 4/8*	177 7/8	41 4/8	41	14 4/8	14 4/8	7 4/8	7 4/8	22 3/8	22 1/8	Chugach Mts., AK	Daniel H. Smith III	Daniel H. Smith III	2006	
176 3/8*	177 2/8	42 7/8	45 6/8	14 3/8	14 3/8	6 3/8	5 6/8	27 2/8	27	Chandalar River, AK	Louis R. Lacher, Jr.	Louis R. Lacher, Jr.	2007	
174 1/8*	174 5/8	44 3/8	40 2/8	14 3/8	14 3/8	6 2/8	6 3/8	27 2/8	27	Alaska Range, AK	Mark R. Stiller	Mark R. Stiller	2007	
173 7/8*	174 7/8	43 1/8	42 4/8	14	13 7/8	6 1/8	6 6/8	25 4/8	25 4/8	Chugach Mts., AK	Boyd L. Mothe, Jr.	Boyd L. Mothe, Jr.	2007	

* Final score subject to revision by additional verifying measurements.

STONE'S SHEEP

Ovis dalli stonei

Minimum Score 165 World's Record 196 6/8

Final Score	Gross Score	Length of horn R.	L.	Circumference of Base R.	L.	Circumference at Third Quarter R.	L.	Greatest Spread	Tip to Tip Spread	Locality	Hunter	Owner	Date Killed	Rank
180 4/8	180 7/8	44 5/8	45 3/8	13 6/8	13 7/8	6 5/8	6 6/8	29 2/8	29 2/8	Stikine River, BC	Don South	Don South	2008	1
177 2/8	177 3/8	40 3/8	42 3/8	14 7/8	14 7/8	6 5/8	6 4/8	24 2/8	23 6/8	Stikine River, BC	R. Terrell McCombs	R. Terrell McCombs	2007	2
174	176 4/8	44 1/8	46 5/8	14 2/8	14	4 7/8	5 7/8	27 2/8	27 2/8	Pelly Mts., YT	Donald W. Snyder	Donald W. Snyder	2007	3
173 4/8	174 2/8	42	41 4/8	14 4/8	14 6/8	6	6	27	27	Richard Creek, BC	Eugene K. Foisy	Eugene K. Foisy	2008	4
173 3/8	173 6/8	41 1/8	40 2/8	15	15	6	5 6/8	26 2/8	26	Tuchodi Lakes, BC	Thomas R. Martini	Thomas R. Martini	2007	5
173 1/8	173 2/8	39 6/8	39 3/8	15 4/8	15 4/8	6	5 7/8	26 6/8	26 6/8	Richards Creek, BC	Michael D. Schauer	Michael D. Schauer	2007	6
171 7/8	172 4/8	44 3/8	45	13	12 6/8	6 2/8	6 2/8	25 3/8	25 3/8	MacMillan Plateau, YT	James L. Fisher	James L. Fisher	2009	7
170 4/8	171 1/8	40 3/8	36 5/8	15 2/8	15 4/8	6 3/8	6 5/8	25 5/8	23 4/8	Prairie Creek, BC	James P. Wilson	James P. Wilson	2008	8
170 4/8	170 7/8	38 4/8	37	15 2/8	15 2/8	6 7/8	6 7/8	23 5/8	20 1/8	Muskwa Area, BC	Greg A. Strait	Greg A. Strait	2009	8
170 1/8	170 3/8	41 5/8	41 2/8	14 2/8	14 2/8	6 1/8	6 2/8	29 2/8	29 2/8	Telegraph Creek, BC	James P. Stager	James P. Stager	2007	10
167 6/8	167 6/8	39 3/8	39 2/8	13 6/8	13 7/8	6 6/8	6 6/8	24 6/8	24 6/8	Ogilvie Mts., YT	Peeler G. Lacey	Peeler G. Lacey	2009	11 COLOR
166 6/8	167 4/8	40	39	13 4/8	13 6/8	7 2/8	7 6/8	26 2/8	25 7/8	Cassiar Mts., BC	Unknown	DLJM Collection	PR 1982	12
166 2/8	167	35 7/8	38 1/8	13 6/8	13 6/8	7 3/8	7 6/8	19 4/8	16 5/8	Tuchodi River, BC	Jeffrey S. Shoaf	Jeffrey S. Shoaf	2007	13
165 3/8	166	39 5/8	38	14 1/8	14 2/8	6 2/8	6 2/8	20 7/8	19 2/8	Rabbit Creek, BC	Jeffrey Dejax	Jeffrey Dejax	2008	14
165 3/8	165 6/8	39 6/8	39 5/8	13 6/8	13 7/8	6	6 1/8	24 5/8	24 4/8	Ogilvie Mts., YT	L. Victor Clark	L. Victor Clark	2009	14 COLOR
174 5/8*	175 5/8	41 4/8	41 1/8	14 3/8	14 4/8	6 6/8	6 3/8	25 7/8	25 7/8	Anvil Range, YT	Tim Parker	Tim Parker	2008	
174 3/8*	174 6/8	41	38 1/8	15 1/8	15	6 3/8	6 2/8	24 5/8	24 5/8	Kechika River, BC	Daniel M. Plamondon	Daniel M. Plamondon	2009	

* Final score subject to revision by additional verifying measurements.

OFFICIAL SCORE CHARTS FOR NORTH AMERICAN BIG GAME TROPHIES

250 Station Drive
Missoula, MT 59801
(406) 542-1888

BOONE AND CROCKETT CLUB®
OFFICIAL SCORING SYSTEM FOR NORTH AMERICAN BIG GAME TROPHIES

BEAR

MINIMUM SCORES	AWARDS	ALL-TIME
black bear	20	21
grizzly bear	23	24
Alaska brown bear	26	28
polar bear	27	27

KIND OF BEAR (check one)
- ☐ black bear
- ☑ grizzly
- ☐ Alaska brown bear
- ☐ polar

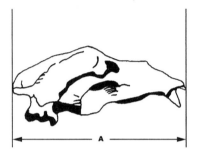

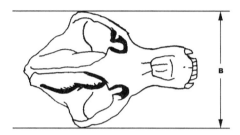

SEE OTHER SIDE FOR INSTRUCTIONS	MEASUREMENTS
A. Greatest Length Without Lower Jaw	16 13/16
B. Greatest Width	10 6/16
FINAL SCORE	27 3/16

Exact Locality Where Killed: **Spring Camp Creek, Unalakleet River, Alaska**

Date Killed: **5/23/2009**   Hunter: **Rodney W. Debias**

Trophy Owner: **Rodney W. Debias**   Telephone #:

Trophy Owner's Address:

Trophy Owner's E-mail: Guide's Name:

Remarks: (Mention Any Abnormalities or Unique Qualities)

I, **Robert Boutang** _____ , certify that I have measured this trophy on **8/15/2009**
PRINT NAME   MM/DD/YYYY

at **Fairbanks, Alaska** _____
STREET ADDRESS   CITY   STATE/PROVINCE

and that these measurements and data are, to the best of my knowledge and belief, made in accordance with the instructions given.

Witness: _____   Signature: _____   I.D. Number ☐☐☐☐
B&C OFFICIAL MEASURER

INSTRUCTIONS FOR MEASURING BEAR

Measurements are taken with calipers or by using parallel perpendiculars, to the nearest **one-sixteenth** of an inch, without reduction of fractions. Official measurements cannot be taken until the skull has air dried for at least 60 days after the animal was killed. All adhering flesh, membrane and cartilage must be completely removed **before** official measurements are taken.

- **A. Greatest Length** is measured between perpendiculars parallel to the long axis of the skull, without the lower jaw and excluding malformations.
- **B. Greatest Width** is measured between perpendiculars at right angles to the long axis.

MATERIALS RELEASE FORM FOR ALL NON-HUNTER-TAKEN TROPHIES

I certify by my signature that the information I have provided on this form is accurate and correct. I also understand that all my entry materials, including photographs, as well as any additional photographs taken by Boone and Crockett (our representatives or agents) during Awards Programs or Judges Panels, or likenesses rendered from these photographs become the property of the Boone and Crockett Club and may be used to promote the Club, and its records-keeping activities.

Date: _____ Signature of Trophy Owner: _____

ENTRY AFFIDAVIT FOR ALL HUNTER-TAKEN TROPHIES

For the purpose of entry into the Boone and Crockett Club's® records, North American big game harvested by the use of the following methods or under the following conditions are ineligible:

- I. Spotting or herding game from the air, followed by landing in its vicinity for the purpose of pursuit and shooting;
- II. Herding or chasing with the aid of any motorized equipment;
- III. Use of electronic communication devices to guide hunters to game, artificial lighting, electronic light intensifying devices (night vision optics), sights with built-in electronic range-finding capabilities, thermal imaging equipment, electronic game calls or cameras/timers/motion tracking devices that transmit images and other information to the hunter;
- IV. Confined by artificial barriers, including escape-proof fenced enclosures;
- V. Transplanted for the purpose of commercial shooting;
- VI. By the use of traps or pharmaceuticals;
- VII. While swimming, helpless in deep snow, or helpless in any other natural or artificial medium;
- VIII. On another hunter's license;
- IX. Not in full compliance with the game laws or regulations of the federal government or of any state, province, territory, or tribal council on reservations or tribal lands;

Please answer the following questions:

Were dogs used in conjunction with the pursuit and harvest of this animal?
☐ Yes ☐ No

If the answer to the above question is yes, answer the following statements:

1. I was present on the hunt at the times the dogs were released to pur
☐ True ☐ False

2. If electronic collars were attached to any of the dogs, rece
☐ True ☐ False

To the best of my knowledge the answers to the above statements are tru
separate sheet.

I certify that the trophy scored on this chart was not taken in vi
information provided on this entry is found to be misrep
1) all of my prior entries are subject to deletion from fu
accepted. I also certify by my signature that the info
materials, including photographs, as well as any a
Programs or Judges Panels, or likenesses rende
to promote the Club, and its records-keeping

FAIR CHASE, as defined by the Boone a
wild, native North American big game

The Boone and Crockett Club® may
conditions deemed inappropriate

Date: _____

(LIC.)

Date: _____

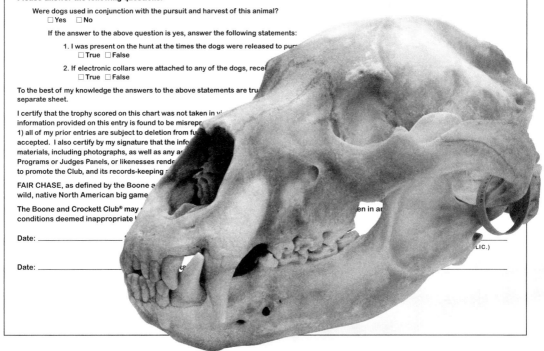

Records of
North American
Big Game

250 Station Drive
Missoula, MT 59801
(406) 542-1888

BOONE AND CROCKETT CLUB®
OFFICIAL SCORING SYSTEM FOR NORTH AMERICAN BIG GAME TROPHIES

COUGAR AND JAGUAR

	MINIMUM SCORES		
	AWARDS	ALL-TIME	
cougar	14 - 8/16	15	
jaguar	14 - 8/16	14 - 8/16	

KIND OF CAT (check one)
☑ cougar
☐ jaguar

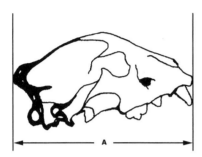

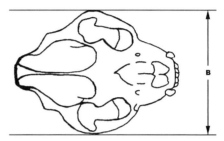

SEE OTHER SIDE FOR INSTRUCTIONS	MEASUREMENTS
A. Greatest Length Without Lower Jaw	9 4/16
B. Greatest Width	6 10/16
FINAL SCORE	15 14/16

Exact Locality Where Killed: **Lochsa River, Idaho County, Idaho**

Date Killed: **12/13/2007**   Hunter: **Rodney E. Bradley**

Trophy Owner: **Rodney E. Bradley**   Telephone #:

Trophy Owner's Address:

Trophy Owner's E-mail: Guide's Name:

Remarks: (Mention Any Abnormalities or Unique Qualities)

I, **Ryan Hatfield** , certify that I have measured this trophy on **2/17/2008**
PRINT NAME   MM/DD/YYYY

at **Eagle, Idaho**
STREET ADDRESS   CITY   STATE/PROVINCE

and that these measurements and data are, to the best of my knowledge and belief, made in accordance with the instructions given.

Witness: _____ Signature: _____ I.D. Number
                                          B&C OFFICIAL MEASURER

INSTRUCTIONS FOR MEASURING COUGAR AND JAGUAR

Measurements are taken with calipers or by using parallel perpendiculars, to the nearest **one-sixteenth** of an inch, without reduction of fractions. Official measurements cannot be taken until the skull has air dried for at least 60 days after the animal was killed. All adhering flesh, membrane and cartilage must be completely removed **before** official measurements are taken.

A. Greatest Length is measured between perpendiculars parallel to the long axis of the skull, without the lower jaw and excluding malformations.

B. Greatest Width is measured between perpendiculars at right angles to the long axis.

MATERIALS RELEASE FORM FOR ALL NON-HUNTER-TAKEN TROPHIES

I certify by my signature that the information I have provided on this form is accurate and correct. I also understand that all my entry materials, including photographs, as well as any additional photographs taken by Boone and Crockett (our representatives or agents) during Awards Programs or Judges Panels, or likenesses rendered from these photographs become the property of the Boone and Crockett Club and may be used to promote the Club, and its records-keeping activities.

Date: _____ Signature of Trophy Owner: _____

ENTRY AFFIDAVIT FOR ALL HUNTER-TAKEN TROPHIES

For the purpose of entry into the Boone and Crockett Club's® records, North American big game harvested by the use of the following methods or under the following conditions are ineligible:

I. Spotting or herding game from the air, followed by landing in its vicinity for the purpose of pursuit and shooting;
II. Herding or chasing with the aid of any motorized equipment;
III. Use of electronic communication devices to guide hunters to game, artificial lighting, electronic light intensifying devices (night vision optics), sights with built-in electronic range-finding capabilities, thermal imaging equipment, electronic game calls or cameras/timers/motion tracking devices that transmit images and other information to the hunter;
IV. Confined by artificial barriers, including escape-proof fenced enclosures;
V. Transplanted for the purpose of commercial shooting;
VI. By the use of traps or pharmaceuticals;
VII. While swimming, helpless in deep snow, or helpless in any other natural or artificial medium;
VIII. On another hunter's license;
IX. Not in full compliance with the game laws or regulations of the federal government or of any state, province, territory, or tribal council on reservations or tribal lands;

Please answer the following questions:

Were dogs used in conjunction with the pursuit and harvest of this animal?
☐ Yes ☐ No

If the answer to the above question is yes, answer the following statements:

1. I was present on the hunt at the times the dogs were released to pursue this animal.
☐ True ☐ False

2. If electronic collars were attached to any of the dogs, receivers were not used to harvest this animal.
☐ True ☐ False

To the best of my knowledge the answers to the above statements are tr___ ___ __ ___ please explain on a separate sheet.

I certify that the trophy scored on this chart was not taken i___ ___ ___rstand that if the information provided on this entry is found to be misrepr___ ___ram and 1) all of my prior entries are subject to deletion from fu___ ___ accepted. I also certify by my signature that the info___ ___ ___ materials, including photographs, as well as any a___ ___ Programs or Judges Panels, or likenesses rende___ to promote the Club, and its records-keeping ___

FAIR CHASE, as defined by the Boone a___ wild, native North American big game ___

The Boone and Crockett Club® may ___ conditions deemed inappropriate by th___

Date:_____ Signature ___

Date:_____ Signature ___

250 Station Drive
Missoula, MT 59801
(406) 542-1888

BOONE AND CROCKETT CLUB®
OFFICIAL SCORING SYSTEM FOR NORTH AMERICAN BIG GAME TROPHIES

	MINIMUM SCORES	
	AWARDS	ALL-TIME
Atlantic	95	95
Pacific	100	100

WALRUS

KIND OF WALRUS (check one)
☐ Atlantic
☑ Pacific

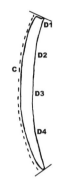

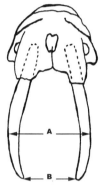

SEE OTHER SIDE FOR INSTRUCTIONS		COLUMN 1	COLUMN 2	COLUMN 3
A. Greatest Spread (If possible)	N/A	Right	Left	
B. Tip to Tip Spread (If possible)	N/A	Tusk	Tusk	Difference
C. Entire Length of Loose Tusk		34 2/8	34 5/8	3/8
D-1. Circumference of Base		9 4/8	9 4/8	0
D-2. Circumference at First Quarter	Location of First Quarter Circumference: 8 21/32	9 6/8	9 5/8	1/8
D-3. Circumference at Second Quarter	Location of Second Quarter Circumference: 17 5/16	8 1/8	7 7/8	2/8
D-4. Circumference at Third Quarter	Location of Third Quarter Circumference: 25 31/32	6 3/8	6 2/8	1/8
	TOTALS	68 0/8	67 7/8	7/8

ADD	Column 1	68	Exact Locality Where Killed: **Platinum Creek, Alaska**
	Column 2	67 7/8	Date Killed: 1963 Hunter: **Picked Up**
	Subtotal	135 7/8	Trophy Owner: **Richard Van Blaricom** Telephone #:
	SUBTRACT Column 3	7/8	Trophy Owner's Address:
FINAL SCORE		**135**	Trophy Owner's E-mail: Guide's Name:
			Remarks: (Mention Any Abnormalities or Unique Qualities)

I, __Larry C. Lack__ , certify that I have measured this trophy on __4/28/2010__
PRINT NAME   MM/DD/YYYY

at __Reno, Nevada__
STREET ADDRESS   CITY   STATE/PROVINCE

and that these measurements and data are, to the best of my knowledge and belief, made in accordance with the instructions given.

Witness: _____ Signature: _____ I.D. Number ☐ ☐ ☐
                                                  B&C OFFICIAL MEASURER

INSTRUCTIONS FOR MEASURING WALRUS

All measurements must be made with a 1/4-inch wide flexible steel tape to the nearest one-eighth of an inch. Enter fractional figures in eighths, without reduction. Tusks **should** be removed from mounted specimens for measuring. Official measurements cannot be taken until tusks have air dried for at least 60 days after the animal was killed.

- **A. Greatest spread** is measured between perpendiculars at a right angle to the center line of the skull. **Greatest spread does not add into the final score.**
- **B. Tip to Tip Spread** is measured between tips of tusks. **Tip to tip spread does not add into the final score.**
- **C. Entire Length of Loose Tusk** is measured over outer curve from a point in line with the greatest projecting edge of the base to a point in line with tip.
- **D-1. Circumference of Base** is measured at a right angle to axis of tusk. **Do not** follow irregular edge of tusk; the line of measurement must be entirely on tusk material.
- **D-2-3-4. Divide length** of longer tusk by four. Starting at base, mark **both** tusks at these quarters (even though the other tusk is shorter) and measure circumferences at these marks.

MATERIALS RELEASE FORM FOR ALL NON-HUNTER-TAKEN TROPHIES

I certify by my signature that the information I have provided on this form is accurate and correct. I also understand that all my entry materials, including photographs, as well as any additional photographs taken by Boone and Crockett (our representatives or agents) during Awards Programs or Judges Panels, or likenesses rendered from these photographs become the property of the Boone and Crockett Club and may be used to promote the Club, a̶̶̶̶̶̶rds-keeping activities.

Date: _____ Signature of Trophy Owner: _____

ENTRY AFFIDAVIT FOR ALL HUNTER-TAKEN

For the purpose of entry into the Boone and Crockett Club's® records, North American big game _____ use of the following methods or under the following conditions are ineligible:

- I. Spotting or herding game from the air, followed by landing in its vi_____ urpos_____ shooting;
- II. Herding or chasing with the aid of any motorized equipment;
- III. Use of electronic communication devices to guide hunters to ga_____ ghting_____ intensifying devices (night vision optics), sights with built-in electronic range-finding capab____ l imag_____ electronic game calls or cameras/timers/motion tracking devices that transmit images a_____ mation____
- IV. Confined by artificial barriers, including escape-proof fenced e_____
- V. Transplanted for the purpose of commercial shooting;
- VI. By the use of traps or pharmaceuticals;
- VII. While swimming, helpless in deep snow, or helpless in any oth_____ artificia_____
- VIII. On another hunter's license;
- IX. Not in full compliance with the game laws or regulations of th_____ ernmen_____ province, territory, or tribal council on reservations or tribal lands;

I certify that the trophy scored on this chart was not taken in violation of t_____ isted abo_____ is statement, I understand that if the information provided on this entry is found to be misrepresented or fraud_____ spect, it w_____ ed into the Awards Program and 1) all of my prior entries are subject to deletion from future editions of **Re_____ th Ameri**_____ 2) future entries may not be accepted. I also certify by my signature that the information I have provid_____ n is accura_____ I also understand that all my entry materials, including photographs, as well as any additional photographs ta_____ e and Croc_____ entatives or agents) during Awards Programs or Judges Panels, or likenesses rendered from these photograp_____ e property _____ d Crockett Club and may be used to promote the Club, and its records-keeping activities.

FAIR CHASE, as defined by the Boone and Crockett Club®, is the ethica_____ like and law_____ d taking of any free-ranging wild, native North American big game animal in a manner that does not _____ ter an impro_____ e over such game animals.

The Boone and Crockett Club® may exclude the entry of any animal that _____ have been ta_____ hical manner or under conditions deemed inappropriate by the Club.

Date: _____ Signature of Hunter: _____
(SIGNATURE MUST ____ED BY AN OFFIC____ R OR A NOTARY PUBLIC.)

Date: _____ Signature of Notary or Official Measurer: _____

250 Station Drive
Missoula, MT 59801
(406) 542-1888

BOONE AND CROCKETT CLUB®
OFFICIAL SCORING SYSTEM FOR NORTH AMERICAN BIG GAME TROPHIES

TYPICAL
AMERICAN ELK (WAPITI)

MINIMUM SCORES
AWARDS   ALL-TIME
360   375

Detail of Point
Measurement

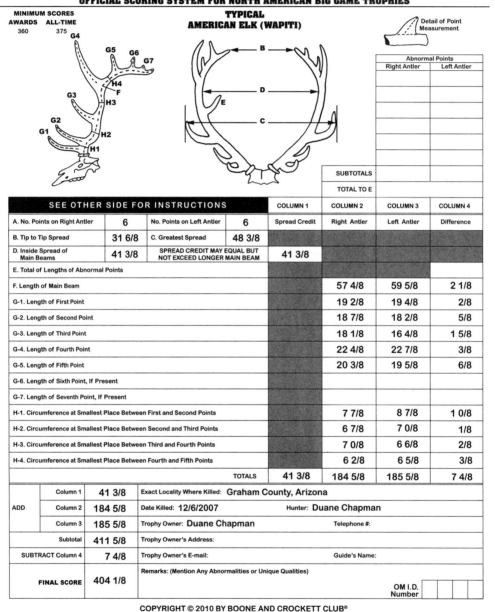

	Abnormal Points	
	Right Antler	Left Antler
SUBTOTALS		
TOTAL TO E		

SEE OTHER SIDE FOR INSTRUCTIONS			COLUMN 1	COLUMN 2	COLUMN 3	COLUMN 4
A. No. Points on Right Antler	6	No. Points on Left Antler	6	Spread Credit	Right Antler	Left Antler	Difference
B. Tip to Tip Spread	31 6/8	C. Greatest Spread	48 3/8				
D. Inside Spread of Main Beams	41 3/8	SPREAD CREDIT MAY EQUAL BUT NOT EXCEED LONGER MAIN BEAM	41 3/8				
E. Total of Lengths of Abnormal Points							
F. Length of Main Beam				57 4/8	59 5/8	2 1/8
G-1. Length of First Point				19 2/8	19 4/8	2/8
G-2. Length of Second Point				18 7/8	18 2/8	5/8
G-3. Length of Third Point				18 1/8	16 4/8	1 5/8
G-4. Length of Fourth Point				22 4/8	22 7/8	3/8
G-5. Length of Fifth Point				20 3/8	19 5/8	6/8
G-6. Length of Sixth Point, If Present						
G-7. Length of Seventh Point, If Present						
H-1. Circumference at Smallest Place Between First and Second Points				7 7/8	8 7/8	1 0/8
H-2. Circumference at Smallest Place Between Second and Third Points				6 7/8	7 0/8	1/8
H-3. Circumference at Smallest Place Between Third and Fourth Points				7 0/8	6 6/8	2/8
H-4. Circumference at Smallest Place Between Fourth and Fifth Points				6 2/8	6 5/8	3/8
		TOTALS	41 3/8	184 5/8	185 5/8	7 4/8

ADD	Column 1	41 3/8	Exact Locality Where Killed: Graham County, Arizona
	Column 2	184 5/8	Date Killed: 12/6/2007 Hunter: Duane Chapman
	Column 3	185 5/8	Trophy Owner: Duane Chapman Telephone #:
	Subtotal	411 5/8	Trophy Owner's Address:
SUBTRACT Column 4		7 4/8	Trophy Owner's E-mail: Guide's Name:
FINAL SCORE		404 1/8	Remarks: (Mention Any Abnormalities or Unique Qualities)

OM I.D.
Number

COPYRIGHT © 2010 BY BOONE AND CROCKETT CLUB®

I, _____ Clay Goldman _____ , certify that I have measured this trophy on ___ 04/07/2008 ___

PRINT NAME   MM/DD/YYYY

at   Payson, Arizona

STREET ADDRESS   CITY   STATE/PROVINCE

and that these measurements and data are, to the best of my knowledge and belief, made in accordance with the instructions given.

Witness: _____   Signature: _____   I.D. Number ☐☐☐

B&C OFFICIAL MEASURER

INSTRUCTIONS FOR MEASURING TYPICAL AMERICAN ELK (WAPITI)

All measurements must be made with a 1/4-inch wide flexible steel tape to the nearest one-eighth of an inch. (Note: A flexible steel cable can be used to measure points and main beams only.) Enter fractional figures in eighths, without reduction. Official measurements cannot be taken until the antlers have air dried for at least 60 days after the animal was killed.

A. Number of Points on Each Antler: To be counted a point, the projection must be at least one inch long, with length exceeding width at one inch or more of length. All points are measured from tip of point to nearest edge of beam as illustrated. Beam tip is counted as a point but not measured as a point. **Point totals do not add into the final score.**

B. Tip to Tip Spread is measured between tips of main beams. **Tip to tip spread does not add into the final score.**

C. Greatest Spread is measured between perpendiculars at a right angle to the center line of the skull at widest part, whether across main beams or points. **Greatest spread does not add into the final score.**

D. Inside Spread of Main Beams is measured at a right angle to the center line of the skull at widest point between main beams. Enter this measurement again as the Spread Credit if it is less than or equal to the length of the longer main beam; if greater, enter longer main beam length for Spread Credit.

E. Total of Lengths of all Abnormal Points: Abnormal Points are those non-typical in location (such as points originating from a point or from bottom or sides of main beam) or pattern (extra points, not generally paired). Measure in usual manner and record in appropriate blanks.

F. Length of Main Beam is measured from the center of the lowest outside edge of burr over the outer side to the most distant point of the main beam. The point of beginning is that point on the burr where the center line along the outer side of the beam intersects the burr, then following generally the line of the illustration.

G-1-2-3-4-5-6-7 Length of Normal Points: Normal points project from the top or front of the main beam in the general pattern illustrated. They are measured from nearest edge of main beam over outer curve to tip. Lay the tape along the outer curve of the beam so that the top edge of the tape coincides with the top edge of the beam on both sides of point to determine the baseline for point measurement. Record point length in appropriate blanks.

H-1-2-3-4. Circumferences are taken as detailed in illustration for each measurement.

MATERIALS RELEASE FORM FOR ALL NON-HUNTER-TAKEN TROPHIES

I certify by my signature that the information I have provided on this form is accurate and correct. I also understand that all my entry materials, including photographs, as well as any additional photographs taken by Boone and Crockett (our representatives or agents) during Awards Programs or Judges Panels, or likenesses rendered from these photographs become the property of the Boone and Crockett Club and may be used to promote the Club, and its records-keeping activities.

Date: _____   Signature of Trophy Owner: _____

ENTRY AFFIDAVIT FOR ALL HUNTER-TAKEN TROPHIES

For the purpose of entry into the Boone and Crockett Club's® records, North American big game harvested by the use of the following methods under the following conditions are ineligible:

I. Spotting or herding game from the air, followed by landing in its vicinity for the purpose of pursuit and shooting;

II. Herding or chasing with the aid of any motorized equipment;

III. Use of electronic communication devices to guide hunters to game, artificial lighting, electronic light intensifying devices (night vision optics), sights with built-in electronic range-finding capabilities, thermal imaging equipment, electronic game calls or cameras/timers/motion tracking devices that transmit images and other information to the hunter;

IV. By any artificial barrier, including escape-proof fencing enclosures;

V. Transplanted for the purpose of commercial shooting;

VI. By the use of traps or pharmaceuticals;

VII. While swimming, helpless in deep snow, or helpless in any other natural or artificial medium;

VIII. On another hunter's license;

IX. Not in full compliance with the game laws or regulations of the federal government or of any state, province, territory, or tribal council on reservations or tribal lands.

I certify that the trophy scored on this chart was not taken in violation of the conditions listed above. In signing this statement, I understand that if the information provided on this entry is found to be misrepresented or fraudulent in any respect, it will not be accepted into the Awards Program and 1) all of my prior entries are subject to deletion from future editions of **Records of North American Big Game** 2) future entries may not be accepted. I also certify by my signature that the information I have provided on this form is accurate and correct. I also understand that all my entry materials, including photographs, as well as any additional photographs taken by Boone and Crockett (our representatives or agents) during Awards Programs or Judges Panels, or likenesses rendered from these photographs become the property of the Boone and Crockett Club and may be used to promote the Club, and its records-keeping activities.

FAIR CHASE, as defined by the Boone and Crockett Club, is the ethical, sportsmanlike, lawful pursuit and taking of any free-ranging wild, native North American big game animal in a manner that does not give the hunter an improper advantage over such game animals.

The Boone and Crockett Club® may exclude the entry of any animal that it deems to have been taken in an unethical manner or under conditions deemed inappropriate by the Club.

Date: _____   Signature of Hunter: _____

                       (MUST BE WITNESSED BY AN OFFICIAL MEASURER OR A NOTARY PUBLIC.)

Date: _____   Signature of Notary or Official Measurer: _____

Records of North American Big Game		250 Station Drive Missoula, MT 59801 (406) 542-1888

BOONE AND CROCKETT CLUB®
OFFICIAL SCORING SYSTEM FOR NORTH AMERICAN BIG GAME TROPHIES

NON-TYPICAL AMERICAN ELK (WAPITI)

MINIMUM SCORES	
AWARDS	ALL-TIME
385	385

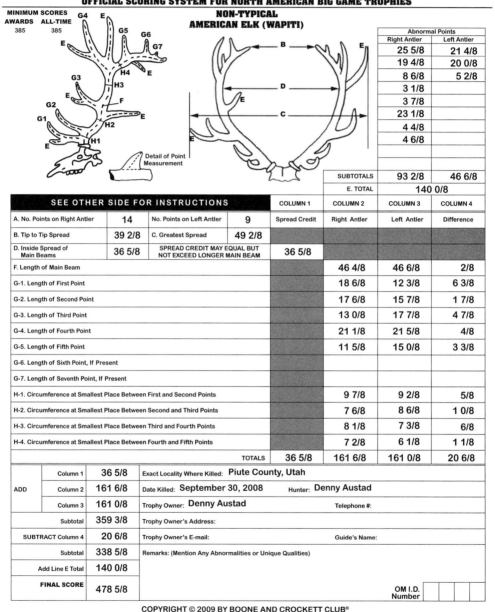

Detail of Point Measurement

Abnormal Points	
Right Antler	Left Antler
25 5/8	21 4/8
19 4/8	20 0/8
8 6/8	5 2/8
3 1/8	
3 7/8	
23 1/8	
4 4/8	
4 6/8	
SUBTOTALS 93 2/8	46 6/8
E. TOTAL 140 0/8	

SEE OTHER SIDE FOR INSTRUCTIONS				COLUMN 1	COLUMN 2	COLUMN 3	COLUMN 4
				Spread Credit	Right Antler	Left Antler	Difference
A. No. Points on Right Antler	14	No. Points on Left Antler	9				
B. Tip to Tip Spread	39 2/8	C. Greatest Spread	49 2/8				
D. Inside Spread of Main Beams	36 5/8	SPREAD CREDIT MAY EQUAL BUT NOT EXCEED LONGER MAIN BEAM	36 5/8				
F. Length of Main Beam					46 4/8	46 6/8	2/8
G-1. Length of First Point					18 6/8	12 3/8	6 3/8
G-2. Length of Second Point					17 6/8	15 7/8	1 7/8
G-3. Length of Third Point					13 0/8	17 7/8	4 7/8
G-4. Length of Fourth Point					21 1/8	21 5/8	4/8
G-5. Length of Fifth Point					11 5/8	15 0/8	3 3/8
G-6. Length of Sixth Point, If Present							
G-7. Length of Seventh Point, If Present							
H-1. Circumference at Smallest Place Between First and Second Points					9 7/8	9 2/8	5/8
H-2. Circumference at Smallest Place Between Second and Third Points					7 6/8	8 6/8	1 0/8
H-3. Circumference at Smallest Place Between Third and Fourth Points					8 1/8	7 3/8	6/8
H-4. Circumference at Smallest Place Between Fourth and Fifth Points					7 2/8	6 1/8	1 1/8
			TOTALS	36 5/8	161 6/8	161 0/8	20 6/8

ADD	Column 1	36 5/8	Exact Locality Where Killed: Piute County, Utah
	Column 2	161 6/8	Date Killed: September 30, 2008 Hunter: Denny Austad
	Column 3	161 0/8	Trophy Owner: Denny Austad Telephone #:
	Subtotal	359 3/8	Trophy Owner's Address:
SUBTRACT Column 4		20 6/8	Trophy Owner's E-mail: Guide's Name:
	Subtotal	338 5/8	Remarks: (Mention Any Abnormalities or Unique Qualities)
	Add Line E Total	140 0/8	
FINAL SCORE		478 5/8	OM I.D. Number

COPYRIGHT © 2009 BY BOONE AND CROCKETT CLUB®

I, _____**Buck Buckner**_____, certify that I have measured this trophy on ___**01/02/2009**___
PRINT NAME   MM/DD/YYYY

at **Ammon, Idaho**
STREET ADDRESS   CITY   STATE/PROVINCE

and that these measurements and data are, to the best of my knowledge and belief, made in accordance with the instructions given.

Witness: _____ Signature: _____ I.D. Number [ ][ ][ ]
                                                              B&C OFFICIAL MEASURER

INSTRUCTIONS FOR MEASURING NON-TYPICAL AMERICAN ELK (WAPITI)

All measurements must be made with a 1/4-inch wide flexible steel tape to the nearest one-eighth of an inch. (Note: A flexible steel cable can be used to measure points and main beams only.) Enter fractional figures in eighths, without reduction. Official measurements cannot be taken until the antlers have air dried for at least 60 days after the animal was killed.

- **A. Number of Points on Each Antler:** To be counted a point, the projection must be at least one inch long, with length exceeding width at one inch or more of length. All points are measured from tip of point to nearest edge of beam as illustrated. Beam tip is counted as a point but not measured as a point. **Point totals do not add into the final score.**
- **B. Tip to Tip Spread** is measured between tips of main beams. **Tip to tip spread does not add into the final score.**
- **C. Greatest Spread** is measured between perpendiculars at a right angle to the center line of the skull at widest part, whether across main beams or points. **Greatest spread does not add into the final score.**
- **D. Inside Spread of Main Beams** is measured at a right angle to the center line of the skull at widest point between main beams. Enter this measurement again as the Spread Credit if it is less than or equal to the length of the longer main beam; if greater, enter longer main beam length for Spread Credit.
- **E. Total of Lengths of all Abnormal Points:** Abnormal Points are those non-typical in location (such as points originating from a point or from bottom or sides of main beam) or pattern (extra points, not generally paired). Measure in usual manner and record in appropriate blanks.
- **F. Length of Main Beam** is measured from the center of the lowest outside edge of burr over the outer side to the most distant point of the main beam. The point of beginning is that point on the burr where the center line along the outer side of the beam intersects the burr, then following generally the line of the illustration.
- **G-1-2-3-4-5-6-7. Length of Normal Points:** Normal points project from the top or front of the main beam in the general pattern illustrated. They are measured from nearest edge of main beam over outer curve to tip. Lay the tape along the outer curve of the beam so that the top edge of the tape coincides with the top edge of the beam on both sides of point to determine the baseline for point measurement. Record point length in appropriate blanks.
- **H-1-2-3-4. Circumferences** are taken as detailed in illustration for each measurement.

MATERIALS RELEASE FORM FOR ALL NON-HUNTER-TAKEN TROPHIES

I certify by my signature that the information I have provided on this form is accurate and correct. I also understand that all my entry materials, including photographs, as well as any additional photographs taken by Boone and Crockett (our representative or agents) during Awards Programs or Judges Panels, or likenesses rendered from these photographs become the property of the Boone and Crockett and may be used to promote the Club, and its records-keeping activities.

Date: _____ Signature of Trophy Owner: _____

ENTRY AFFIDAVIT FOR ALL HUNTER-TAKEN TROPHIES

For the purpose of entry into the Boone and Crockett Club's® records, North American big game harvested by the use of the following methods under the following conditions are ineligible:

- I. Spotting or herding game from the air, followed by landing in its vicinity for the purpose of pursuit and shooting;
- II. Herding or chasing with the aid of any motorized equipment;
- III. Use of electronic communication devices to guide hunters to game, use of electronic light intensifying devices (optics), sights with built-in electronic range-finding capabilities, electronic game calls or cameras /timers/motion tracking devices that transmit images and other information to the hunter, electronic;
- IV. Confined by artificial barriers, including escape-proof fenced enclosures;
- V. Transplanted for the purpose of commercial shooting;
- VI. By the use of traps or pharmaceuticals;
- VII. While swimming, helpless in deep snow, or helpless in any other natural or artificial medium;
- VIII. On another hunter's license;
- IX. Not in full compliance with the game laws or regulations of the federal government or of any state, province, territory, or tribal council on reservations or tribal lands;

I certify that the trophy scored on this chart was not taken in violation of the conditions listed above. In signing this statement, I understand that if the information provided on this entry is found to be misrepresented or fraudulent in any respect, it will not be accepted into the Awards Program and 1) all of my prior entries are subject to deletion from future editions of **Records of North American Big Game** and 2) future entries may not be accepted. I also certify by my signature that the information I have provided on this entry is accurate and correct. I understand that all my entry materials, including photographs, as well as any additional photographs taken by Boone and Crockett (or our representatives or agents) during Awards Programs or Judges Panels, or likenesses rendered from these photographs become the property of the Boone and Crockett Club and may be used to promote the Club, and its records-keeping activities.

FAIR CHASE, as defined by the Boone and Crockett Club®, is the ethical, sportsmanlike and lawful pursuit and taking of any free-ranging wild North American big game animal in a manner that does not give the hunter an improper advantage over such game animals.

The Boone and Crockett Club® may exclude the entry of any animal that it deems to have been taken in an unethical manner, or in a manner deemed inappropriate by the Club.

Date: _____ Signature of Hunter: _____
                                                    (SIGNATURE MUST BE WITNESSED BY AN OFFICIAL MEASURER)

Date: _____ Signature of Notary or Official Measurer: _____

Records of
North American
Big Game

250 Station Drive
Missoula, MT 59801
(406) 542-1888

BOONE AND CROCKETT CLUB®
OFFICIAL SCORING SYSTEM FOR NORTH AMERICAN BIG GAME TROPHIES

ROOSEVELT'S AND TULE ELK

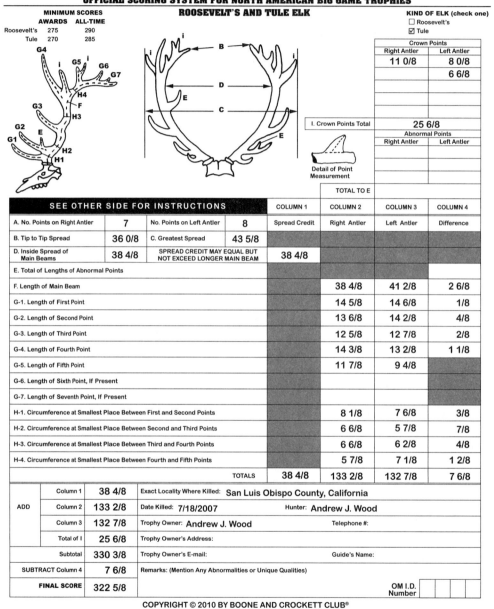

MINIMUM SCORES		
	AWARDS	ALL-TIME
Roosevelt's	275	290
Tule	270	285

KIND OF ELK (check one)
- ☐ Roosevelt's
- ☑ Tule

Crown Points	
Right Antler	Left Antler
11 0/8	8 0/8
	6 6/8

I. Crown Points Total	25 6/8

Abnormal Points	
Right Antler	Left Antler

Detail of Point Measurement

TOTAL TO E	

SEE OTHER SIDE FOR INSTRUCTIONS			COLUMN 1	COLUMN 2	COLUMN 3	COLUMN 4
A. No. Points on Right Antler	7	No. Points on Left Antler: 8	Spread Credit	Right Antler	Left Antler	Difference
B. Tip to Tip Spread	36 0/8	C. Greatest Spread: 43 5/8				
D. Inside Spread of Main Beams	38 4/8	SPREAD CREDIT MAY EQUAL BUT NOT EXCEED LONGER MAIN BEAM	38 4/8			
E. Total of Lengths of Abnormal Points						
F. Length of Main Beam				38 4/8	41 2/8	2 6/8
G-1. Length of First Point				14 5/8	14 6/8	1/8
G-2. Length of Second Point				13 6/8	14 2/8	4/8
G-3. Length of Third Point				12 5/8	12 7/8	2/8
G-4. Length of Fourth Point				14 3/8	13 2/8	1 1/8
G-5. Length of Fifth Point				11 7/8	9 4/8	
G-6. Length of Sixth Point, If Present						
G-7. Length of Seventh Point, If Present						
H-1. Circumference at Smallest Place Between First and Second Points				8 1/8	7 6/8	3/8
H-2. Circumference at Smallest Place Between Second and Third Points				6 6/8	5 7/8	7/8
H-3. Circumference at Smallest Place Between Third and Fourth Points				6 6/8	6 2/8	4/8
H-4. Circumference at Smallest Place Between Fourth and Fifth Points				5 7/8	7 1/8	1 2/8
TOTALS			38 4/8	133 2/8	132 7/8	7 6/8

ADD	Column 1	38 4/8	Exact Locality Where Killed: San Luis Obispo County, California
	Column 2	133 2/8	Date Killed: 7/18/2007 Hunter: Andrew J. Wood
	Column 3	132 7/8	Trophy Owner: Andrew J. Wood Telephone #:
	Total of I	25 6/8	Trophy Owner's Address:
	Subtotal	330 3/8	Trophy Owner's E-mail: Guide's Name:
SUBTRACT Column 4		7 6/8	Remarks: (Mention Any Abnormalities or Unique Qualities)
FINAL SCORE		322 5/8	OM I.D. Number

COPYRIGHT © 2010 BY BOONE AND CROCKETT CLUB®

630

I, _____ **Harrel Wilson** _____, certify that I have measured this trophy on ___ 06/06/2008 ___
　　　　　　 PRINT NAME 　　　　　　　　　　　　　　　　　　　　　　　　　　　　　　 MM/DD/YYYY

at _**Oroville, California**_____
　 STREET ADDRESS 　　　　　　　　　　　　　　　　　　　　　　CITY 　　　　　　　　　　　　　　　 STATE/PROVINCE

and that these measurements and data are, to the best of my knowledge and belief, made in accordance with the instructions given.

Witness: _____ Signature: _____ I.D. Number ☐☐☐☐
　　　　　　　　　　　　　　　　　　　　　　　　　　　　　　　　B&C OFFICIAL MEASURER

INSTRUCTIONS FOR MEASURING ROOSEVELT'S AND TULE ELK

All measurements must be made with a 1/4-inch wide flexible steel tape to the nearest one-eighth of an inch. (Note: A flexible steel cable can be used to measure points and main beams only.) Enter fractional figures in eighths, without reduction. Official measurements cannot be taken until the antlers have air dried for at least 60 days after the animal was killed.

A. Number of Points on Each Antler: to be counted a point, the projection must be at least one inch long, with length exceeding width at one inch or more of length. All points are measured from tip of point to nearest edge of beam as illustrated. Beam tip is counted as a point but not measured as a point. **Point totals do not add into the final score.**

B. Tip to Tip Spread is measured between tips of main beams. **Tip to tip spread does not add into the final score.**

C. Greatest Spread is measured between perpendiculars at a right angle to the center line of the skull at widest part, whether across main beams or points. **Greatest spread does not add into the final score.**

D. Inside Spread of Main Beams is measured at a right angle to the center line of the skull at widest point between main beams. Enter this measurement again as the Spread Credit if it is less than or equal to the length of the longer main beam; if greater, enter longer main beam length for Spread Credit.

E. Total of Lengths of all Abnormal Points: Abnormal Points are those non-typical in location or pattern occurring below G-4. Measure in usual manner and record in appropriate blanks. Note: do not confuse with Crown Points that may occur in the vicinity of G-4, G-5, G-6, etc.

F. Length of Main Beam is measured from the center of the lowest outside edge of burr over the outer side to the most distant point of the main beam. The point of beginning is that point on the burr where the center line along the outer side of the beam intersects the burr, then following generally the line of the illustration.

G-1-2-3-4-5-6-7. Length of Normal Points: Normal points project from the top or front of the main beam in the general pattern illustrated. They are measured from nearest edge of main beam over outer curve to tip. Lay the tape along the outer curve of the beam so that the top edge of the tape coincides with the top edge of the beam on both sides of point to determine the baseline for point measurement. Record point length in appropriate blanks.

H-1-2-3-4. Circumferences are taken as detailed in illustration for each measurement.

I. Crown Points: From the well-defined Royal out to end of beam, all points other than the normal points in their typical locations are Crown Points. This includes points occurring the Royal, on other normal points, on Crown Points, and on the bottom and sides of main beam after the Royal. Measure and record in appropriate blanks provided and add to score below.

MATERIALS RELEASE FORM FOR ALL NON-HUNTER-TAKEN TROPHIES

... on I have provided on this form is accurate and correct. I also understand that all my entry materials, including photographs, ... Boone and Crockett (our representatives or agents) during Awards Programs or Judges Panels, or likenesses rendered from these photographs by ... of the Boone and Crockett Club and may be used to promote the Club, and its records-keeping activities.

Date: _____ ... by Owner: _____

... FOR ALL HUNTER-TAKEN TROPHIES

For the purpose ... t Club's® records, North American big game harvested by the use of the following methods ... are ineligible:

... he air, followed by landing in its vicinity for the purpose of pursuit and shooting;

... of any motorized equipment;

... on devices to guide hunters to game, artificial lighting, electronic light intensifying devices (night ... it-in electronic range-finding capabilities, thermal imaging equipment, electronic game calls or ... cking devices that transmit images and other information to the hunter;

... iers, including escape-proof fenced enclosures;

... urpose of commercial shooting;

... or pharmaceuticals;

... elpless in deep snow, or helpless in any other natural or artificial medium;

... 's license;

... ce with the game laws or regulations of the federal government or of any state, province, territory, or tribal ... ions or tribal lands;

... d on this chart was not taken in violation of the conditions listed above. In signing this statement, I understand that if the info... entry is found to be misrepresented or fraudulent in any respect, it will not be accepted into the Awards Program and 1) all ... e subject to deletion from future editions of **Records of North American Big Game** 2) future entries may not be accept... my signature that the information I have provided on this form is accurate and correct. I also understand that all my entry material ... aphs, as well as any additional photographs taken by Boone and Crockett (our representatives or agents) during Awards Programs ... or likenesses rendered from these photographs become the property of the Boone and Crockett Club and may be used to promote... records-keeping activities.

... Boone and Crockett Club®, is the ethical, sportsmanlike and lawful pursuit and taking of any free-ranging ... me animal in a manner that does not give the hunter an improper advantage over such game animals.

... clude the entry of any animal that it deems to have been taken in an unethical manner or under ... he Club.

... ture of Hunter: _____
　　　　　　　　　　　(SIGNATURE MUST BE WITNESSED BY AN OFFICIAL MEASURER OR A NOTARY PUBLIC.)
... ture of Notary or Official Measurer: _____

Records of
North American
Big Game

250 Station Drive
Missoula, MT 59801
(406) 542-1888

BOONE AND CROCKETT CLUB®
OFFICIAL SCORING SYSTEM FOR NORTH AMERICAN BIG GAME TROPHIES

TYPICAL
MULE DEER AND BLACKTAIL DEER

MINIMUM SCORES	AWARDS	ALL-TIME
mule deer	180	190
Columbia blacktail	125	135
Sitka blacktail	100	108

KIND OF DEER (check one)
☐ mule deer
☐ Columbia blacktail
☑ Sitka blacktail

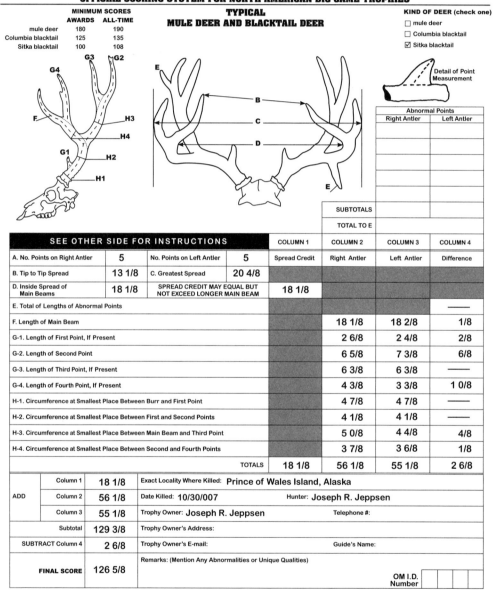

Detail of Point Measurement

Abnormal Points	
Right Antler	Left Antler

| SUBTOTALS | |
| TOTAL TO E | |

SEE OTHER SIDE FOR INSTRUCTIONS				COLUMN 1	COLUMN 2	COLUMN 3	COLUMN 4
				Spread Credit	Right Antler	Left Antler	Difference
A. No. Points on Right Antler	5	No. Points on Left Antler	5				
B. Tip to Tip Spread	13 1/8	C. Greatest Spread	20 4/8				
D. Inside Spread of Main Beams	18 1/8	SPREAD CREDIT MAY EQUAL BUT NOT EXCEED LONGER MAIN BEAM	18 1/8				
E. Total of Lengths of Abnormal Points							——
F. Length of Main Beam					18 1/8	18 2/8	1/8
G-1. Length of First Point, If Present					2 6/8	2 4/8	2/8
G-2. Length of Second Point					6 5/8	7 3/8	6/8
G-3. Length of Third Point, If Present					6 3/8	6 3/8	——
G-4. Length of Fourth Point, If Present					4 3/8	3 3/8	1 0/8
H-1. Circumference at Smallest Place Between Burr and First Point					4 7/8	4 7/8	——
H-2. Circumference at Smallest Place Between First and Second Points					4 1/8	4 1/8	——
H-3. Circumference at Smallest Place Between Main Beam and Third Point					5 0/8	4 4/8	4/8
H-4. Circumference at Smallest Place Between Second and Fourth Points					3 7/8	3 6/8	1/8
			TOTALS	18 1/8	56 1/8	55 1/8	2 6/8

ADD	Column 1	18 1/8	Exact Locality Where Killed: **Prince of Wales Island, Alaska**
	Column 2	56 1/8	Date Killed: **10/30/007** Hunter: **Joseph R. Jeppsen**
	Column 3	55 1/8	Trophy Owner: **Joseph R. Jeppsen** Telephone #:
	Subtotal	129 3/8	Trophy Owner's Address:
SUBTRACT Column 4		2 6/8	Trophy Owner's E-mail: Guide's Name:
FINAL SCORE		126 5/8	Remarks: (Mention Any Abnormalities or Unique Qualities)

OM I.D. Number

I, _____ **James F. Baichtal** _____ , certify that I have measured this trophy on _____ **1/3/2008** _____
PRINT NAME   MM/DD/YYYY

at **Thorne Bay, Alaska**
STREET ADDRESS   CITY   STATE/PROVINCE

and that these measurements and data are, to the best of my knowledge and belief, made in accordance with the instructions given.

Witness: _____ Signature: _____ I.D. Number [ ][ ][ ]
                        B&C OFFICIAL MEASURER

INSTRUCTIONS FOR MEASURING TYPICAL MULE AND BLACKTAIL DEER

All measurements must be made with a 1/4-inch wide flexible steel tape to the nearest one-eighth of an inch. (Note: A flexible steel cable can be used to measure points and main beams only.) Enter fractional figures in eighths, without reduction. Official measurements cannot be taken until the antlers have air dried for at least 60 days after the animal was killed.

A. Number of Points on Each Antler: To be counted a point, the projection must be at least one inch long, with length exceeding width at one inch or more of length. All points are measured from tip of point to nearest edge of beam. Beam tip is counted as a point but not measured as a point. **Point totals do not add into the final score.**

B. Tip to Tip Spread is measured between tips of main beams. **Tip to tip spread does not add into the final score.**

C. Greatest Spread is measured between perpendiculars at a right angle to the center line of the skull at widest part, whether across main beams or points. **Greatest spread does not add into the final score.**

D. Inside Spread of Main Beams is measured at a right angle to the center line of the skull at widest point between main beams. Enter this measurement again as the Spread Credit **if** it is less than or equal to the length of the longer main beam; if greater, enter longer main beam length for Spread Credit.

E. Total of Lengths of all Abnormal Points: Abnormal Points are those non-typical in location such as points originating from a point (exception: G-3 originates from G-2 in perfectly normal fashion) or from bottom or sides of main beam, or any points beyond the normal pattern of five (including beam tip) per antler. Measure each abnormal point in usual manner and enter in appropriate blanks.

F. Length of Main Beam is measured from the center of the lowest outside edge of burr over the outer side to the most distant point of the Main Beam. The point of beginning is that point on the burr where the center line along the outer side of the beam intersects the burr, then following generally the line of the illustration.

G-1-2-3-4. Length of Normal Points: Normal points are the brow tines and the upper and lower forks as shown in the illustration. They are measured from nearest edge of main beam over outer curve to tip. Lay the tape along the outer curve of the beam so that the top edge of the tape coincides with the top edge of the beam on both sides of point to determine the baseline for point measurement. Record point lengths in appropriate blanks.

H-1-2-3-4. Circumferences are taken as detailed in illustration for each measurement. If brow point is missing, take H-1 and H-2 at smallest place between burr and G-2. If G-3 is missing, take H-3 halfway between the base and tip of G-2. If G-4 is missing, take H-4 halfway between G-2 and tip of main beam.

...Y AFFIDAVIT F...R ALL HUNTER-TAKEN TROPHIES

For the purpose of ...to the Boone and ...ckett Clu...s® records, North American big game harvested by the use of the following methods or under th... ...wing conditions are ...ligibl...

 I. Spotting or her... ...me... ...m the air, f... ...by landing ...vicinity for the purpose of pursuit and shooting;
 II. Herding ...sing ...id of any m... ...ed equipm...
 III. Use of e... ...sion devic... ...to game, artificial lighting, electronic light intensifying devices (night vision op... ...with... ...elec... ...ng capabilities, thermal imaging equipment, electronic game calls or cameras/t... ...transmit images and other information to the hunter;
 IV. Confined b... ...pe-proof fenced enclosures;
 V. Transplante... ...hooting;
 VI. By the use of trap...
 VII. While swimming ...in any other natural or artificial medium;
 VIII. On another...
 IX. Not in full... ...the federal government or of any state, province, territory, or tribal

...onditions listed above. In signing this statement, I understand that if the ...t in any respect, it will not be accepted into the Awards Program and ...future editions ...ecords of **North American Big Game** 2) future entries may not be ...nformation I have provided on this form is accurate and correct. I also understand that all my entry ...y additional photographs taken by Boone and Crockett (our representatives or agents) during Awards ...ndered from these photographs become the property of the Boone and Crockett Club and may be used ...ng activities.

...one and Crockett Club®, is the ethical, sportsmanlike and lawful pursuit and taking of any free-ranging ...me animal in a manner that does not give the hunter an improper advantage over such game animals.

...y exclude the entry of any animal that it deems to have been taken in an unethical manner or under ...by the Club.

...gnature of Hunter: _____

(SIGNATURE MUST BE WITNESSED BY AN OFFICIAL MEASURER OR A NOTARY PUBLIC.)

...Signature of Notary or Official Measurer: _____

Records of
North American
Big Game

250 Station Drive
Missoula, MT 59801
(406) 542-1888

BOONE AND CROCKETT CLUB®
OFFICIAL SCORING SYSTEM FOR NORTH AMERICAN BIG GAME TROPHIES

NON-TYPICAL
MULE DEER AND BLACKTAIL DEER

MINIMUM SCORES	AWARDS	ALL-TIME
mule deer	215	230
Columbia blacktail	155	155
Sitka blacktail	118	118

KIND OF DEER (check one)
- ☑ mule deer
- ☐ Columbia blacktail
- ☐ Sitka blacktail

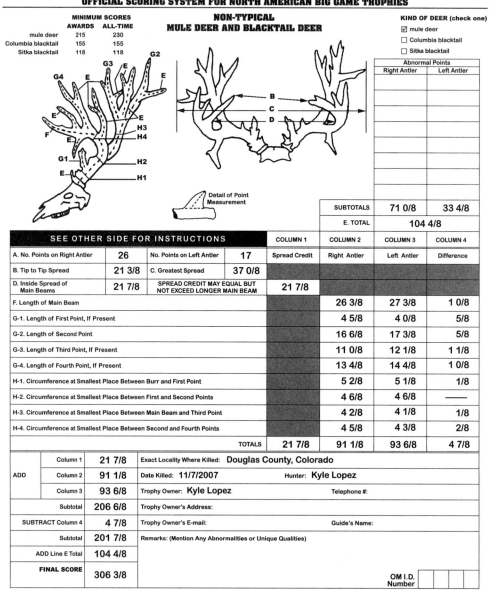

Abnormal Points	
Right Antler	Left Antler

SUBTOTALS	71 0/8	33 4/8
E. TOTAL	104 4/8	

SEE OTHER SIDE FOR INSTRUCTIONS		COLUMN 1	COLUMN 2	COLUMN 3	COLUMN 4
		Spread Credit	Right Antler	Left Antler	Difference
A. No. Points on Right Antler	26	No. Points on Left Antler **17**			
B. Tip to Tip Spread	21 3/8	C. Greatest Spread **37 0/8**			
D. Inside Spread of Main Beams	21 7/8	SPREAD CREDIT MAY EQUAL BUT NOT EXCEED LONGER MAIN BEAM	21 7/8		
F. Length of Main Beam			26 3/8	27 3/8	1 0/8
G-1. Length of First Point, If Present			4 5/8	4 0/8	5/8
G-2. Length of Second Point			16 6/8	17 3/8	5/8
G-3. Length of Third Point, If Present			11 0/8	12 1/8	1 1/8
G-4. Length of Fourth Point, If Present			13 4/8	14 4/8	1 0/8
H-1. Circumference at Smallest Place Between Burr and First Point			5 2/8	5 1/8	1/8
H-2. Circumference at Smallest Place Between First and Second Points			4 6/8	4 6/8	——
H-3. Circumference at Smallest Place Between Main Beam and Third Point			4 2/8	4 1/8	1/8
H-4. Circumference at Smallest Place Between Second and Fourth Points			4 5/8	4 3/8	2/8
	TOTALS	21 7/8	91 1/8	93 6/8	4 7/8

ADD	Column 1	21 7/8	Exact Locality Where Killed: **Douglas County, Colorado**	
	Column 2	91 1/8	Date Killed: **11/7/2007**	Hunter: **Kyle Lopez**
	Column 3	93 6/8	Trophy Owner: **Kyle Lopez**	Telephone #:
	Subtotal	206 6/8	Trophy Owner's Address:	
	SUBTRACT Column 4	4 7/8	Trophy Owner's E-mail:	Guide's Name:
	Subtotal	201 7/8	Remarks: (Mention Any Abnormalities or Unique Qualities)	
	ADD Line E Total	104 4/8		
	FINAL SCORE	306 3/8		

OM I.D. Number

COPYRIGHT © 2010 BY BOONE AND CROCKETT CLUB®

BOONE AND CROCKETT CLUB'S

I, _____ **Roger Selner** _____ , certify that I have measured this trophy on _____ **1/26/2008** _____

                PRINT NAME   MM/DD/YYYY

at **Denver, Colorado**

   STREET ADDRESS   CITY   STATE/PROVINCE

and that these measurements and data are, to the best of my knowledge and belief, made in accordance with the instructions given.

Witness: _____ Signature: _____ I.D. Number ☐☐☐

                                              B&C OFFICIAL MEASURER

INSTRUCTIONS FOR MEASURING NON-TYPICAL MULE DEER AND BLACKTAIL

All measurements must be made with a 1/4-inch wide flexible steel tape to the nearest one-eighth of an inch. (Note: A flexible steel cable can be used to measure points and main beams only.) Enter fractional figures in eighths, without reduction. Official measurements cannot be taken until the antlers have air dried for at least 60 days after the animal was killed.

  A. Number of Points on Each Antler: To be counted a point, the projection must be at least one inch long, with length exceeding width at one inch or more of length. All points are measured from tip of point to nearest edge of beam as illustrated. Beam tip is counted as a point but not measured as a point. **Point totals do not add into the final score.**

  B. Tip to Tip Spread is measured between tips of main beams. **Tip to tip spread does not add into the final score.**

  C. Greatest Spread is measured between perpendiculars at a right angle to the center line of the skull at widest part, whether across main beams or points. **Greatest spread does not add into the final score.**

  D. Inside Spread of Main Beams is measured at a right angle to the center line of the skull at widest point between main beams. Enter this measurement again as the Spread Credit if it is less than or equal to the length of the longer main beam; if greater, enter longer main beam length for Spread Credit.

  E. Total of Lengths of all Abnormal Points: Abnormal Points are those non-typical in location such as points originating from a point (exception: G-3 originates from G-2 in perfectly normal fashion) or from bottom or sides of main beam, or any points beyond the normal pattern of five (including beam tip) per antler. Measure each abnormal point in usual manner and enter in appropriate blanks.

  F. Length of Main Beam is measured from the center of the lowest outside edge of burr over the outer side to the most distant point of the main beam. The point of beginning is that point on the burr where the center line along the outer side of the beam intersects the burr, then following generally the line of the illustration.

  G-1-2-3-4. Length of Normal Points: Normal points are the brow tines and the upper and lower forks as shown in the illustration. They are measured from nearest edge of main beam over outer curve to tip. Lay the tape along the outer curve of the beam so that the top edge of the tape coincides with the top edge of the beam on both sides of point to determine the baseline for point measurement. Record point lengths in appropriate blanks.

  H-1-2-3-4. Circumferences are taken as detailed in illustration for each measurement. If brow point is missing, take H-1 and H-2 at smallest place between burr and G-2. If G-3 is missing, take H-3 halfway between the base and tip of G-2. If G-4 is missing, take H-4 halfway between G-2 and tip of main beam.

MATERIALS RELEASE FORM FOR ALL NON-HUNTER-TAKEN TROPHIES

I certify by my signature that the information I have provided on this form [is] accurate and correct. I also understand that all my entry materials, including photographs, as well as any additional photographs taken by Boone and Crockett [Club or its representatives or agents] during Awards Programs or Judges Panels, [or likenesses] rendered from these photographs become the property [of] Boone [and] Crockett Club and may be used to promote the Club, and its records-[keeping activities].

Date: _____ Signature of Tro[phy Owner]: _____

ENTRY AFFIDAVIT FOR ALL HUNTER-TAKEN TROPHIES

For the purpose of entry into the Boone and Crockett Club's records, North American big game harvested by the use of the following methods or under the following conditions are [ineligible:]

  I.   Spotting or herding game from [the air, followed by] landing in [its] vicinity for the purpose of pursuit and shooting;

  II.   Herding or chasing with the aid [of any] motorized equipm[ent;]

  III. Use of electronic communication[devices to guide hunters to [game], artificial lighting, electronic light[s, or electronic relaying devices (night vision optics), sights with built-in electronic range-finding [capabilities], [the]rmal imaging equip[ment, electronic game] calls or cameras/timers/motion tracking devices that transmit ima[ges and]information to [the hunter];

  IV. Confined by artificial barriers, including escape-proof fenc[ed enclosures];

  V.   Transplanted for the purpose of commercial shooting;

  VI. By the use of traps or pharmaceuticals;

  VII. While swimming, helpless in deep snow, or helpless in any other [natural or artificial medium];

  VIII. On another hunter's license;

  IX. Not in full compliance with the game laws or regulations of the feder[al government or any state], province, territory, or tribal council on reservations or tribal lands;

I certify that the trophy scored on this chart was not taken in violation of the cond[itions listed above. In signing this statement, I understand that if the] information provided on this entry is found to be misrepresented or fraudulent in [any respect, it will not be accepted, and further understand that] 1) all of my prior entries are subject to deletion from future editions of Records [of North American Big Game and future entries may not be] accepted. I also certify by my signature that the information I have provided on th[is entry is accurate and correct, and that all my entry] materials, including photographs, as well as any additional photographs taken by Bo[one and Crockett Club or its representatives or agents] during Awards Programs or Judges Panels, or likenesses rendered from these photographs become the [property of the Boone and Crockett Club and may be used] to promote the Club, and its records-keeping activities.

FAIR CHASE, as defined by the Boone and Crockett Club®, is the ethical, sportsmanlike [and lawful pursuit and taking of any free-ranging] wild, native North American big game animal in a manner that does not give the hunter an[improper advantage over such game animals.]

The Boone and Crockett Club® may exclude the entry of any animal that it deems to have bee[n taken under conditions, or] conditions deemed inappropriate by the Club.

Date: _____ Signature of Hunter: _____

                                      (SIGNATURE MUST BE WITNESSED BY AN OFFIC[IAL MEASURER OR A NOTARY PUBLIC.])

Date: _____ Signature of Notary or Official Measurer: _____

Records of
North American
Big Game

250 Station Drive
Missoula, MT 59801
(406) 542-1888

BOONE AND CROCKETT CLUB®
OFFICIAL SCORING SYSTEM FOR NORTH AMERICAN BIG GAME TROPHIES

MINIMUM SCORES		
	AWARDS	ALL-TIME
whitetail	160	170
Coues'	100	110

TYPICAL
WHITETAIL AND COUES' DEER

KIND OF DEER (check one)
☐ whitetail
☑ Coues'

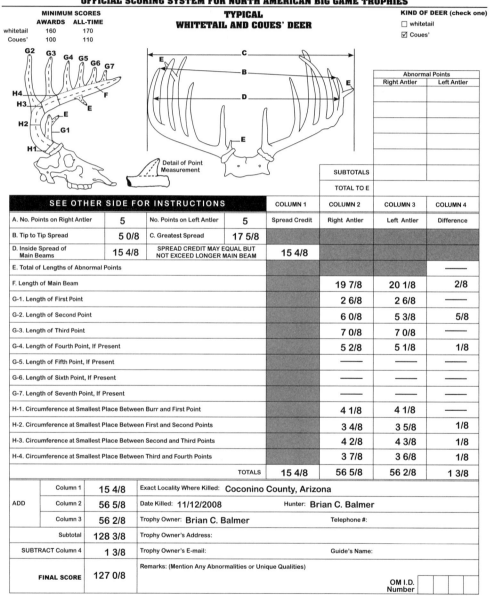

Abnormal Points	
Right Antler	Left Antler

SUBTOTALS	
TOTAL TO E	

SEE OTHER SIDE FOR INSTRUCTIONS				COLUMN 1	COLUMN 2	COLUMN 3	COLUMN 4
A. No. Points on Right Antler	5	No. Points on Left Antler	5	Spread Credit	Right Antler	Left Antler	Difference
B. Tip to Tip Spread	5 0/8	C. Greatest Spread	17 5/8				
D. Inside Spread of Main Beams	15 4/8	SPREAD CREDIT MAY EQUAL BUT NOT EXCEED LONGER MAIN BEAM	15 4/8				
E. Total of Lengths of Abnormal Points							——
F. Length of Main Beam					19 7/8	20 1/8	2/8
G-1. Length of First Point					2 6/8	2 6/8	——
G-2. Length of Second Point					6 0/8	5 3/8	5/8
G-3. Length of Third Point					7 0/8	7 0/8	——
G-4. Length of Fourth Point, If Present					5 2/8	5 1/8	1/8
G-5. Length of Fifth Point, If Present					——	——	——
G-6. Length of Sixth Point, If Present					——	——	——
G-7. Length of Seventh Point, If Present					——	——	——
H-1. Circumference at Smallest Place Between Burr and First Point					4 1/8	4 1/8	——
H-2. Circumference at Smallest Place Between First and Second Points					3 4/8	3 5/8	1/8
H-3. Circumference at Smallest Place Between Second and Third Points					4 2/8	4 3/8	1/8
H-4. Circumference at Smallest Place Between Third and Fourth Points					3 7/8	3 6/8	1/8
			TOTALS	15 4/8	56 5/8	56 2/8	1 3/8

ADD	Column 1	15 4/8	Exact Locality Where Killed: Coconino County, Arizona
	Column 2	56 5/8	Date Killed: 11/12/2008 — Hunter: Brian C. Balmer
	Column 3	56 2/8	Trophy Owner: Brian C. Balmer — Telephone #:
	Subtotal	128 3/8	Trophy Owner's Address:
	SUBTRACT Column 4	1 3/8	Trophy Owner's E-mail: — Guide's Name:
FINAL SCORE		127 0/8	Remarks: (Mention Any Abnormalities or Unique Qualities)

OM I.D. Number

COPYRIGHT © 2009 BY BOONE AND CROCKETT CLUB®

I, _____ **Clay Goldman** _____ , certify that I have measured this trophy on ___ **2/8/2009** ___
PRINT NAME   MM/DD/YYYY

at **Payson, Arizona** _____
STREET ADDRESS   CITY   STATE/PROVINCE

and that these measurements and data are, to the best of my knowledge and belief, made in accordance with the instructions given.

Witness: _____ Signature: _____ I.D. Number
                                               B&C OFFICIAL MEASURER

INSTRUCTIONS FOR MEASURING TYPICAL WHITETAIL AND COUES' DEER

All measurements must be made with a 1/4-inch wide flexible steel tape to the nearest one-eighth of an inch. (Note: A flexible steel cable can be used to measure points and main beams only.) Enter fractional figures in eighths, without reduction. Official measurements cannot be taken until the antlers have air dried for at least 60 days after the animal was killed.

A. Number of Points on Each Antler: To be counted a point, the projection must be at least one inch long, with the length exceeding width at one inch or more of length. All points are measured from tip of point to nearest edge of beam as illustrated. Beam tip is counted as a point but not measured as a point. **Point totals do not add into the final score.**

B. Tip to Tip Spread is measured between tips of main beams. **Tip to tip spread does not add into the final score.**

C. Greatest Spread is measured between perpendiculars at a right angle to the center line of the skull at widest part, whether across main beams or points. **Greatest spread does not add into the final score.**

D. Inside Spread of Main Beams is measured at a right angle to the center line of the skull at widest point between main beams. Enter this measurement again as the Spread Credit if it is less than or equal to the length of the longer main beam; if greater, enter longer main beam length for Spread Credit.

E. Total of Lengths of all Abnormal Points: Abnormal Points are those non-typical in location (such as points originating from a point or from bottom or sides of main beam) or extra points beyond the normal pattern of points. Measure in usual manner and enter in appropriate blanks.

F. Length of Main Beam is measured from the center of the lowest outside edge of burr over the outer side to the most distant point of the main beam. The point of beginning is that point on the burr where the center line along the outer side of the beam intersects the burr, then following generally the line of the illustration.

G-1-2-3-4-5-6-7. Length of Normal Points: Normal points project from the top of the main beam. They are measured from nearest edge of main beam over outer curve to tip. Lay the tape along the outer curve of the beam so that the top edge of the tape coincides with the top edge of the beam on both sides of the point to determine the baseline for point measurements. Record point lengths in appropriate blanks.

H-1-2-3-4. Circumferences are taken as detailed in illustration for each measurement. If brow point is missing, take H-1 and H-2 at smallest place between burr and G-2. If G-4 is missing, take H-4 halfway between G-3 and tip of main beam.

MATERIALS RELEASE FORM FOR ALL NON-HUNTER-TAKEN TROPHIES

I certify by my signature that the information I have provided on this form is accurate and correct. I also understand that all my entry materials, including photographs, as well as any additional photographs taken by Boone and Crockett (our representatives or agents) during Awards Programs or Judges Panels, or likenesses rendered from these photographs become the property of the Boone and Crockett Club and may be used to promote the Club, and its records-keeping activities.

Date: _____ Signature of Trophy Owner: _____

ENTRY AFFIDAVIT FOR ALL HUNTER-TAKEN TROPHIES

For the purpose of entry into the Boone and Crockett Club's® records, North American big game harvested by the use of the following methods or under the following conditions are ineligible:

    I. Spotting or herding game from the air, followed by landing in its vicinity for the purpose of pursuit and shooting;
    II. Herding or chasing with the aid of any motorized equipment;
    III. Use of electronic communications devices, to guide hunters to game, artificial lighting, electronic light intensifying devices (night vision optics), sights with built-in range-finding capabilities, thermal imaging equipment, electronic game calls, cameras/timers/motion tracking, transmit images and other information to the hunter;
    IV. Confined by artificial barriers, including escape-proof fenced enclosures;
    V. Transplanted for the purpose of commercial shooting;
    VI. By the use of traps or pharmaceuticals;
    VII. While swimming, helpless in deep snow, or helpless in any other natural or artificial medium;
    VIII. On another hunter's license;
    IX. Not in full compliance with the game laws or regulations of the federal government or of any state, province, territory, or tribal council on reservations or tribal lands;

I certify that the trophy scored on this chart was not taken in violation of the conditions listed above. In signing this statement, I understand that if the information provided on this entry is found to be misrepresented or fraudulent in any respect, it will not be accepted into the Awards Program and 1) all of my prior entries are subject to deletion from future editions of **Records of North American Big Game** and 2) future entries may not be accepted. I also certify by my signature that the information I have provided on this form is accurate and correct. I understand that all my entry materials, including photographs, as well as any additional photographs taken by Boone and Crockett (our representatives or agents) during Awards Programs or Judges Panels, or likenesses rendered from these photographs become the property of the Boone and Crockett Club and may be used to promote the Club, and its records-keeping activities.

FAIR CHASE, as defined by the Boone and Crockett Club®, is the ethical, sportsmanlike, and lawful pursuit and taking of any free-ranging wild, native North American big game animal in a manner that does not give the hunter an improper advantage over such game animals.

The Boone and Crockett Club® may exclude the entry of any animal that it deems to have been taken in an unethical manner or under conditions deemed inappropriate by the Club.

Date: _____ Signature of Hunter: _____
                                     (SIGNATURE MUST BE WITNESSED BY AN OFFICIAL MEASURER OR A NOTARY PUBLIC.)

Date: _____ Signature of Notary or Official Measurer: _____

Records of North American Big Game

250 Station Drive
Missoula, MT 59801
(406) 542-1888

BOONE AND CROCKETT CLUB®
OFFICIAL SCORING SYSTEM FOR NORTH AMERICAN BIG GAME TROPHIES

NON-TYPICAL
WHITETAIL AND COUES' DEER

MINIMUM SCORES	AWARDS	ALL-TIME
whitetail	185	195
Coues'	105	120

KIND OF DEER (check one)
☑ whitetail ☐ Coues'

Abnormal Points	
Right Antler	Left Antler
6 7/8	7 1/8
7 4/8	1 2/8
4 0/8	3 4/8
7 2/8	9 6/8
2 3/8	1 4/8
	1 6/8
	6 2/8
	1 2/8

SUBTOTALS	28 0/8	32 3/8
E. TOTAL	60 3/8	

SEE OTHER SIDE FOR INSTRUCTIONS			COLUMN 1	COLUMN 2	COLUMN 3	COLUMN 4
A. No. Points on Right Antler*	13	No. Points on Left Antler*	15	Spread Credit	Right Antler	Left Antler	Difference
B. Tip to Tip Spread*	20 0/8	C. Greatest Spread*	29 5/8				
D. Inside Spread of Main Beams	24 0/8	SPREAD CREDIT MAY EQUAL BUT NOT EXCEED LONGER MAIN BEAM	24 0/8				
F. Length of Main Beam				26 1/8	27 1/8	1 0/8
G-1. Length of First Point				5 3/8	6 7/8	1 4/8
G-2. Length of Second Point				9 7/8	11 3/8	1 4/8
G-3. Length of Third Point				11 7/8	8 4/8	3 3/8
G-4. Length of Fourth Point, If Present				10 4/8	11 5/8	1 1/8
G-5. Length of Fifth Point, If Present				9 0/8	7 7/8	1 1/8
G-6. Length of Sixth Point, If Present				6 0/8	4 1/8	1 7/8
G-7. Length of Seventh Point, If Present				2 4/8	——	2 4/8
H-1. Circumference at Smallest Place Between Burr and First Point				5 1/8	5 1/8	——
H-2. Circumference at Smallest Place Between First and Second Points				4 5/8	4 6/8	1/8
H-3. Circumference at Smallest Place Between Second and Third Points				7 5/8	7 4/8	1/8
H-4. Circumference at Smallest Place Between Third and Fourth Points				6 0/8	6 3/8	3/8
		TOTALS	24 0/8	104 5/8	101 2/8	14 5/8

ADD	Column 1	24 0/8	Exact Locality Where Killed: **Jackson County, Iowa**
	Column 2	104 5/8	Date Killed: **10/16/2008** Hunter: **Kyle M. Simmons**
	Column 3	101 2/8	Trophy Owner: **Kyle M. Simmons** Telephone #:
	Subtotal	229 7/8	Trophy Owner's Address:
SUBTRACT Column 4		14 5/8	Trophy Owner's E-mail: Guide's Name:
	Subtotal	215 2/8	Remarks: (Mention Any Abnormalities or Unique Qualities)
ADD Line E Total		60 3/8	
FINAL SCORE		**275 5/8**	OM I.D. Number

*A, B, and C do not add into the score.

COPYRIGHT © 2010 BY BOONE AND CROCKETT CLUB®

I, _____ **Loren D. Miller** _____ , certify that I have measured this trophy on _____ **1/10/2009** _____
PRINT NAME   MM/DD/YYYY

at **Spragueville, Iowa**
STREET ADDRESS   CITY   STATE/PROVINCE

and that these measurements and data are, to the best of my knowledge and belief, made in accordance with the instructions given.

Witness: _____   Signature: _____   I.D. Number

B&C OFFICIAL MEASURER

INSTRUCTIONS FOR MEASURING NON-TYPICAL WHITETAIL AND COUES' DEER

All measurements must be made with a 1/4-inch wide flexible steel tape to the nearest one-eighth of an inch. (Note: A flexible steel cable can be used to measure points and main beams only.) Enter fractional figures in eighths, without reduction. Official measurements cannot be taken until the antlers have air dried for at least 60 days after the animal was killed. If the trophy was bleached, frozen, or boiled, it must dry for 60 days after it is bleached or removed from the freezer or boiling pot.

A. Number of Points on Each Antler: To be counted a point, the projection must be at least one inch long, with the length exceeding width at one inch or more of length. All points are measured from tip of point to nearest edge of beam as illustrated. Beam tip is counted as a point but not measured as a point. **Point totals do not add into the final score.**

B. Tip to Tip Spread is measured between tips of main beams. **Tip to tip spread does not add into the final score.**

C. Greatest Spread is measured between perpendiculars at a right angle to the center line of the skull at widest part, whether across main beams or points. **Greatest spread does not add into the final score.**

D. Inside Spread of Main Beams is measured at a right angle to the center line of the skull at widest point between main beams. Enter this measurement again as the Spread Credit if it is less than or equal to the length of the longer main beam; if greater, enter longer main beam length for Spread Credit.

E. Total of Lengths of all Abnormal Points: Abnormal Points are those non-typical in location (such as points originating from a point or from bottom or sides of main beam) or extra points beyond the normal pattern of points. Measure in usual manner and enter in appropriate blanks.

F. Length of Main Beam is measured from the center of the lowest outside edge of burr over the outer side to the most distant point of the main beam. The point of beginning is that point on the burr where the center line along the outer side of the beam intersects the burr, then following generally the line of the illustration.

G-1-2-3-4-5-6-7. Length of Normal Points: Normal points project from the top of the main beam. They are measured from nearest edge of main beam over outer curve to tip. Lay the tape along the outer curve of the beam so that the top edge of the tape coincides with the top edge of the beam on both sides of the point to determine the baseline for point measurement. Record point lengths in appropriate blanks.

H-1-2-3-4. Circumferences are taken as detailed in illustration for each measurement. If brow point is missing, take H-1 and H-2 at smallest place between burr and G-2. If G-4 is missing, take H-4 halfway between G-3 and tip of main beam.

MATERIALS RELEASE FORM FOR ALL NON-HUNTER-TAKEN TROPHIES

I certify by my signature that the information I have provided on this form is accurate and correct. I also understand that all my materials, including photographs, as well as any additional photographs taken by Boone and Crockett (our representatives or agents) during Awards Programs or Judges Panels, or likenesses rendered from these photographs become the property of the Boone and Crockett Club and may be used to promote the Club, and its records-keeping activities.

Date: _____   Signature of Trophy Owner: _____

ENTRY AFFIDAVIT FOR ALL HUNTER TAKEN TROPHIES

For the pur_____ _ _ ntry into the Boone and Crockett Club's® records, North Amer___ _ig_ ame harvested by the use of the following methods o_ __de_ _e following conditio_ s are ineligible:

I.   Sp___ _ _ herding g__ _e from __e air, followed by la_ding in_ts vicin__ for ____ose of pursuit and shooting;
II.   Her__ _ _ chasing_ ith the aid_ f any motorized eq_ pment;
III. Use ___ tronic_ommunicatio_ devices to guid_ h_nters to_ ame, _tif__ _ _ electronic light intensifying devices (night visio_ __es), __ghts with bui__-i_ _lectronic range fi__ ing cap__ lit__ _ th_ a __ _ g equipment, electronic game calls or cam__ __ __/motion tra_k_ _g_ evices that tran__ _ images a__ _er__ _ o the hunter;
IV.   Conf__ __tificial barrie_ __uding escape-p_ __ _nced e_ __ _ _ur__;
V.   Transp___ _r the purpose_ _ommercial sho__;
VI.   By the us__ _ _pharma__ _icals;
VII. While swimmi__ _ _ _ snow, or helpl_ _n any oth__ __tificial medium;
VIII. On another hu__ _ _ _
IX.   Not in full comp___ __ _ _ _s or re_____ _e federal government or of any state, province, territory, or tribal _ __n reserv__

_____ __ _ _cored_ _____ _ion of the conditions listed above. In signing this statement, I understand that if the _ __ _ _ _fraudulent in any respect, it will not be accepted into the Awards Program and _ _ _s of **Records of North American Big Game** and 2) future entries may not be _ _ _ _ e provided on this form is accurate and correct. I also understand that all my entry __aphs taken by Boone and Crockett (our representatives or agents) during Awards __ _ _ _ _graphs become the property of the Boone and Crockett Club and may be used

_____ _ _ _ ethical, sportsmanlike and lawful pursuit and taking of any free-ranging _ _ ner that does not give the hunter an improper advantage over such game animals.

_ _ry of any animal that it deems to have been taken in an unethical manner or under

__re of Hunter: _____
(SIGNATURE MUST BE WITNESSED BY AN OFFICIAL MEASURER OR A NOTARY PUBLIC.)

Signature of Notary or Official Measurer: _____

250 Station Drive
Missoula, MT 59801
(406) 542-1888

BOONE AND CROCKETT CLUB®
OFFICIAL SCORING SYSTEM FOR NORTH AMERICAN BIG GAME TROPHIES

MOOSE

MINIMUM SCORES		
	AWARDS	ALL-TIME
Canada	185	195
Alaska-Yukon	210	224
Shiras	140	155

KIND OF MOOSE (check one)
- ☐ Canada
- ☒ Alaska-Yukon
- ☐ Shiras

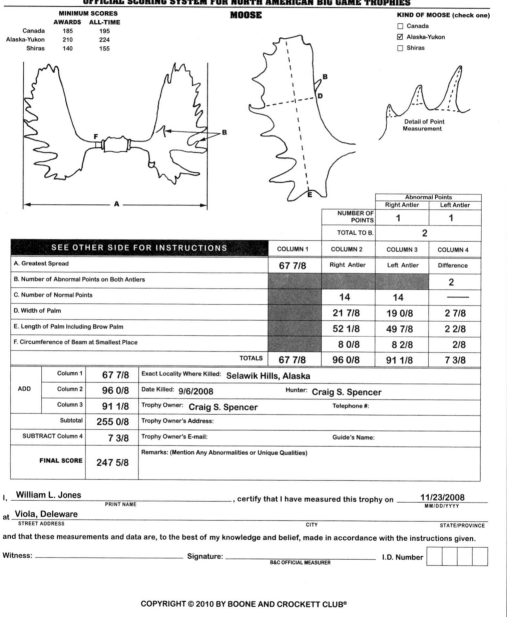

Detail of Point
Measurement

	Abnormal Points	
	Right Antler	Left Antler
NUMBER OF POINTS	1	1
TOTAL TO B.	2	

SEE OTHER SIDE FOR INSTRUCTIONS	COLUMN 1	COLUMN 2	COLUMN 3	COLUMN 4
A. Greatest Spread	67 7/8	Right Antler	Left Antler	Difference
B. Number of Abnormal Points on Both Antlers				2
C. Number of Normal Points		14	14	——
D. Width of Palm		21 7/8	19 0/8	2 7/8
E. Length of Palm Including Brow Palm		52 1/8	49 7/8	2 2/8
F. Circumference of Beam at Smallest Place		8 0/8	8 2/8	2/8
TOTALS	67 7/8	96 0/8	91 1/8	7 3/8

ADD	Column 1	67 7/8	Exact Locality Where Killed: **Selawik Hills, Alaska**	
	Column 2	96 0/8	Date Killed: 9/6/2008	Hunter: **Craig S. Spencer**
	Column 3	91 1/8	Trophy Owner: **Craig S. Spencer**	Telephone #:
	Subtotal	255 0/8	Trophy Owner's Address:	
SUBTRACT Column 4		7 3/8	Trophy Owner's E-mail:	Guide's Name:
FINAL SCORE		247 5/8	Remarks: (Mention Any Abnormalities or Unique Qualities)	

I, __William L. Jones__
PRINT NAME
, certify that I have measured this trophy on __11/23/2008__
MM/DD/YYYY

at __Viola, Deleware__
STREET ADDRESS   CITY   STATE/PROVINCE

and that these measurements and data are, to the best of my knowledge and belief, made in accordance with the instructions given.

Witness: _____ Signature: _____ I.D. Number ☐☐☐☐
B&C OFFICIAL MEASURER

INSTRUCTIONS FOR MEASURING MOOSE

Measurements must be made with a 1/4-inch wide flexible steel tape to the nearest one-eighth of an inch. Enter fractional figures in eighths, without reduction. Official measurements cannot be taken until antlers have air dried for at least 60 days after animal was killed.

- **A. Greatest Spread** is measured between perpendiculars in a straight line at a right angle to the center line of the skull.
- **B. Number of Abnormal Points on Both Antlers:** Abnormal points are those projections originating from normal points or from the upper or lower palm surface, or from the inner edge of palm (see illustration). Abnormal points must be at least one inch long, with length exceeding width at one inch or more of length.
- **C. Number of Normal Points:** Normal points originate from the outer edge of palm. To be counted a point, a projection must be at least one inch long, with the length exceeding width at one inch or more of length. Be sure to verify whether or not each projection qualifies as a point.
- **D. Width of Palm** is taken in contact with the undersurface of the palm, at a right angle to the inner edge of palm. The line of measurement should be taken from the inside edge of the palm to a dip between bumps or points at the widest outside edge of the palm. If there are no bumps or points, the width measurement is taken at the widest part of the palm. The line of measurement should begin at the midpoint of the inner edge of the palm and end at the midpoint of the edge of the palm between points or bumps, which gives credit for the desirable characteristic of palm thickness.
- **E. Length of Palm,** including brow palm, is taken in contact with the undersurface of the palm, parallel to the inner edge, from dips between bumps or points at the top edge of the palm to dips between qualifying points (if present) on the brow palm. If a bay is present, measure across the open bay if the proper line of measurement is parallel to the inner edge and follows this path. The line of measurement should begin and end at the midpoint of the palm edges, which gives credit for the desirable characteristic of palm thickness.
- **F. Circumference** of Beam at Smallest Place is taken as illustrated.

MATERIALS RELEASE FORM FOR ALL NON-HUNTER-TAKEN TROPHIES

I certify by my signature that the information I have provided on this form is accurate and correct. I also understand that all my entry materials, including photographs, as well as any additional photographs taken by Boone and Crockett (our representatives or agents) during Awards Programs or Judges Panels, or likenesses rendered from these photographs become the property of the Boone and Crockett Club and may be used to promote the Club, and its records-keeping activities.

Date: _____ Signature of Trophy Owner: _____

ENTRY AFFIDAVIT FOR ALL HUNTER-TAKEN TROPHIES

For the purpose of entry into the Boone and Crockett Club's® records, North American big game harvested by the use of the following methods or under the following conditions are ineligible:

- I. Spotting or herding game from the air, followed by landing in its vicinity for the purpose of pursuit and shooting;
- II. Herding or chasing with the aid of any motorized equipment;
- III. Use of electronic communication devices to guide hunters to game, artificial lighting, electronic light intensifying device vision optics), sights with built-in electronic range-finding capabilities, thermal imaging equipment, electronic game cameras/timers/motion tracking devices that transmit images and other information to the hunter;
- IV. Confined by artificial barriers, including escape-proof fenced enclosures;
- V. Transplanted for the purpose of commercial shooting;
- VI. By the use of traps or pharmaceuticals;
- VII. While swimming, helpless in deep snow, or helpless in any other natural or artificial medium;
- VIII. On another hunter's license;
- IX. Not in full compliance with the game laws   s of the federal government or of any state, province, council on reservations or tribal la

I certify that the trophy scored on this chart   on of the conditions listed above. In signing   s state information provided on this entry is found t   fraudulent in any re   will not be acce   d into 1) all of my prior entries are subject to dele   of **Records of No   an Big G   ** futur accepted. I also certify by my signature that   provided on this f   a   so   y entry materials, including p   otographs, as well as   h taken by B   during Aware Programs or Judges Pa ls, or likel   a   s bec   an   ub and may be to promote the Club, and   records-ke

FAIR CHASE, as defin   rsuit   ing of any   e-r   g wild, native North A   erica big g   ls.

The Boone and Cro kett   der conditions deemed in   pro

Date:_____   er:_____
                              (SIGNATURE M   EASURER OR A NOTARY PUBLIC.)

Date:_____ Signature of Notary or Official M_____

Records of North American Big Game

250 Station Drive
Missoula, MT 59801
(406) 542-1888

BOONE AND CROCKETT CLUB®
OFFICIAL SCORING SYSTEM FOR NORTH AMERICAN BIG GAME TROPHIES

CARIBOU

MINIMUM SCORES	AWARDS	ALL-TIME
mountain	360	390
woodland	265	295
barren ground	375	400
Central Canada barren ground	345	360
Quebec-Labrador	365	375

KIND OF CARIBOU (check one)
- ☐ mountain
- ☐ woodland
- ☐ barren ground
- ☑ Central Canada barren ground
- ☐ Quebec-Labrador

Detail of Point Measurement

SEE OTHER SIDE FOR INSTRUCTIONS		COLUMN 1	COLUMN 2	COLUMN 3	COLUMN 4
A. Tip to Tip Spread		27 2/8	Spread Credit	Right Antler	Left Antler	Difference
B. Greatest Spread		43 2/8				
C. Inside Spread of Main Beams	41 2/8	SPREAD CREDIT MAY EQUAL BUT NOT EXCEED LONGER MAIN BEAM	41 2/8			
D. Number of Points on Each Antler Excluding Brows			11	11	——
Number of Points on Each Brow			7	1	
E. Length of Main Beam			54 3/8	55 2/8	7/8
F-1. Length of Brow Palm or First Point			21 4/8	19 2/8	
F-2. Length of Bez or Second Point			22 5/8	25 5/8	3 0/8
F-3. Length of Rear Point, If Present			1 5/8	——	1 5/8
F-4. Length of Second Longest Top Point			11 3/8	12 2/8	7/8
F-5. Length of Longest Top Point			17 2/8	18 0/8	6/8
G-1. Width of Brow Palm			17 3/8	11 1/8	
G-2. Width of Top Palm			3 6/8	3 0/8	6/8
H-1. Circumference at Smallest Place Between Brow and Bez Point			5 0/8	5 1/8	1/8
H-2. Circumference at Smallest Place Between Bez and Rear Point			4 7/8	4 4/8	3/8
H-3. Circumference at Smallest Place Between Rear Point and First Top Point			4 2/8	4 4/8	2/8
H-4. Circumference at Smallest Place Between Two Longest Top Palm Points			5 6/8	5 5/8	1/8
	TOTALS	41 2/8	187 6/8	176 2/8	8 6/8

ADD	Column 1	41 2/8	Exact Locality Where Killed: Thonokied Lake, Northwest Territories
	Column 2	187 6/8	Date Killed: 9/3/2006 Hunter: Nyla K. Swast
	Column 3	176 2/8	Trophy Owner: Nyla K. Swast Telephone #:
	Subtotal	405 2/8	Trophy Owner's Address:
SUBTRACT Column 4		8 6/8	Trophy Owner's E-mail: Guide's Name:
FINAL SCORE		396 4/8	Remarks: (Mention Any Abnormalities or Unique Qualities)

OM I.D. Number

I, _____ **Ed Defibaugh** _____ , certify that I have measured this trophy on _____ **8/27/2008** _____
PRINT NAME   MM/DD/YYYY

at **Venus, Pennsylvania** _____
STREET ADDRESS   CITY   STATE/PROVINCE

and that these measurements and data are, to the best of my knowledge and belief, made in accordance with the instructions given.

Witness: _____ Signature: _____ I.D. Number
B&C OFFICIAL MEASURER

INSTRUCTIONS FOR MEASURING CARIBOU

All measurements must be made with a 1/4-inch wide flexible steel tape to the nearest one-eighth of an inch. (Note: A flexible steel cable can be used to measure points and main beams only.) Enter fractional figures in eighths, without reduction. Official measurements cannot be taken until the antlers have air dried for at least 60 days after the animal was killed.

A. Tip to Tip Spread is measured between tips of main beams. **Tip to tip spread does not add into the final score.**

B. Greatest Spread is measured between perpendiculars at a right angle to the center line of the skull at widest part, whether across main beams or points. **Greatest spread does not add into the final score.**

C. Inside Spread of Main Beams is measured at a right angle to the center line of the skull at widest point between main beams. Enter this measurement again as the Spread Credit if it is less than or equal to the length of the longer main beam; if greater, enter longer main beam length for Spread Credit.

D. Number of Points on Each Antler: To be counted a point, a projection must be at least one-half inch long, with length exceeding width at one-half inch or more of length. Beam tip is counted as a point but not measured as a point. There are no "abnormal" points in caribou.

E. Length of Main Beam is measured from the center of the lowest outside edge of burr over the outer side to the most distant point of the main beam. The point of beginning is that point on the burr where the center line along the outer side of the beam intersects the burr, then following generally the line of the illustration.

F-1-2-3. Length of Points are measured from nearest edge of beam over outer curve to tip. Lay the tape along the outer curve of the beam so that the top edge of the tape coincides with the top edge of the beam on both sides of point to determine the baseline for point measurement. Record point lengths in appropriate blanks.

F-4-5. Length of Points are measured from the tip of the point to the top of the beam, then at a right angle to the bottom edge of beam. The Second Longest Top Point cannot be a point branch of the Longest Top Point.

G-1. Width of Brow is measured in a straight line from top edge to lower edge, as illustrated, with measurement line _____ right angle to main axis of brow.

G-2. Width of Top Palm is measured from midpoint of lower edge of main beam to midpoint of a dip between points, at widest _____. The line of measurement begins and ends at midpoints of palm edges, which gives credit for palm thickness.

H-1-2-3-4. Circumferences are taken as illustrated for measurements. If brow point is missing, take H-1 at smallest point between burr and bez point. If rear point is missing, take H-2 and H-3 measurements at smallest place between bez and first top point. Do not depress the tape into any dips of the palm or main beam.

MATERIALS RELEASE FORM FOR ALL NON-HUNTER-TAKEN TROPHIES

I certify by my signature that the information I have provided on this form is accurate and correct. I also understand that all my entry materials, including photographs, as well as any additional photographs taken by Boone and Crockett (our repr_____ of agents) during Awards Programs or Judges Panels, or likenesses rendered from these photographs become the property of the Boone and Crockett _____ and may be used to promote the Club, and its records-keeping activities.

Date: _____ Signature of Trophy Owner: _____

ENTRY AFFIDAVIT FOR ALL HUNTER-TAKEN TROPHIES

For the purpose of entry into the Boone and Crockett Club's® records, North American big game harvested by the use of the following methods or under the following conditions are ineligible:

I.   Spotting or herding game from the air, followed by landing in its vicinity _____ the purpose of pursuit and shooting;

II.   Herding or chasing with the aid of any motorized equipment;

III.   Use of electronic communication devices to guide hunters to game, art_____ lighting electronic light intensifying devices (night vision optics), sights with built-in electronic range-finding capabilities, thermal imag_____ equipment, electronic game calls or cameras /timers/motion tracking devices that transmit images and other in_____ation to t_____

IV.   Confined by artificial barriers, including escape-proof fenced en_____res;

V.   Transplanted for the purpose of commercial _____ting;

VI.   By the use of traps or pharmaceuticals;

VII.   While swimming, helpless in deep snow, or hel_____ss in any o_____al or artifi_____

VIII.   On another hunter's license;

IX.   Not in full compliance with the game laws or regula_____ of th_____ gover_____ state, province, territory, or tribal _____ on reservations or tribal lands;

I certify that the trophy scored on this chart was not taken in violation o_____ ment, I understand that if the information provided on this entry is found to be misrepresented or fra_____ny r_____ he Awards Program and 1) all of my prior entries are subject to deletion from future editions of _____ tries may not be accepted. I also certify by my signature that the information I have pro_____ nd that all my entry materials, including photographs, as well as any additional photographs _____ ts) during Awards Programs or Judges Panels, or likenesses rendered from these photogra_____ nd may be used to promote the Club, and its records-keeping activities.

FAIR CHASE, as defined by the Boone and Crockett Club®, is the ethical, spo_____ ing wild, native North American big game animal in a manner that does not give the hunter an im_____

The Boone and Crockett Club® may exclude the entry of any animal that it de_____ conditions deemed inappropriate by the Club.

Date: _____ Signature of Hunter: _____
(SIG_____ TNESSED BY AN O_____ C.)

Date: _____ Signature of Notary or Official Measu_____

27TH BIG GAME AWARDS   643

250 Station Drive
Missoula, MT 59801
(406) 542-1888

BOONE AND CROCKETT CLUB®
OFFICIAL SCORING SYSTEM FOR NORTH AMERICAN BIG GAME TROPHIES
PRONGHORN

MINIMUM SCORES	
AWARDS	ALL-TIME
80	82

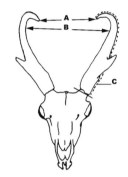

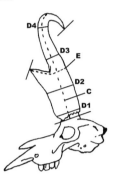

SEE OTHER SIDE FOR INSTRUCTIONS		COLUMN 1	COLUMN 2	COLUMN 3
A. Tip to Tip Spread	2 1/8	Right Horn	Left Horn	Difference
B. Inside Spread of Horns	8 0/8			
C. Length of Horn		17 2/8	17 2/8	——
D-1. Circumference of Base		7 4/8	7 3/8	1/8
D-2. Circumference at First Quarter	Location of First Quarter Circumference: 4 5/16	7 7/8	7 3/8	4/8
D-3. Circumference at Second Quarter	Location of Second Quarter Circumference: 8 5/8	4 4/8	4 4/8	——
D-4. Circumference at Third Quarter	Location of Third Quarter Circumference: 12 15/16	2 6/8	2 7/8	1/8
E. Length of Prong		6 5/8	6 4/8	1/8
	TOTALS	46 4/8	45 7/8	7/8

ADD	Column 1	46 4/8	Exact Locality Where Killed: **Harding County, New Mexico**
	Column 2	45 7/8	Date Killed: **8/27/2006** Hunter: **Larry J. Landes**
	Subtotal	92 3/8	Trophy Owner: **Larry J. Landes** Telephone #:
SUBTRACT Column 3		7/8	Trophy Owner's Address:
FINAL SCORE		91 4/8	Trophy Owner's E-mail: Guide's Name:
			Remarks: (Mention Any Abnormalities or Unique Qualities)

At the time of official measurement, were the sheaths reattached to the cores by the use of some type of filler or adhesive? ☐ Yes ☒ No

I, __Clay Goldman_____, certify that I have measured this trophy on _____1/1/2007_____
          PRINT NAME   MM/DD/YYYY

at __Payson, Arizona_____
      STREET ADDRESS   CITY   STATE/PROVINCE

and that these measurements and data are, to the best of my knowledge and belief, made in accordance with the instructions given.

Witness: _____ Signature: _____ I.D. Number ☐☐☐☐
                                                                B&C OFFICIAL MEASURER

INSTRUCTIONS FOR MEASURING PRONGHORN

All measurements must be made with a 1/4-inch wide flexible steel tape to the nearest one-eighth of an inch. Enter fractional figures in eighths, without reduction. Official measurements cannot be taken until horns have air dried for at least 60 days after the animal was killed.

- **A. Tip to Tip Spread** is measured between tips of horns. **Tip to tip spread does not add into the final score.**
- **B. Inside Spread of Horns** is measured at a right angle to the center line of the skull, at widest point between horns. **Inside spread does not add into the final score.**
- **C. Length of Horn** is measured on the outside curve on the general line illustrated. The line taken will vary with different heads, depending on the direction of their curvature. Measure along the center of the outer curve from tip of horn to a point in line with the lowest edge of the base, using a straight edge to establish the line end.
- **D-1. Circumference of Base** is measured at a right angle to axis of horn. Do not follow irregular edge of horn; the line of measurement must be entirely on horn material.
- **D-2-3-4. Divide measurement C** of longer horn by four. Starting at base, mark both horns at these quarters (even though the other horn is shorter) and measure circumferences at these marks. If the prong interferes with D-2, move the measurement down to just below the swelling of the prong. If D-3 falls in the swelling of the prong, move the measurement up to just above the prong.
- **E. Length of Prong:** Measure from the tip of the prong along the upper edge of the outer side to the horn; then continue around the horn to a point at the rear of the horn where a straight edge across the back of both horns touches the horn, with the latter part being at a right angle to the long axis of horn.

MATERIALS RELEASE FORM FOR ALL NON-HUNTER-TAKEN TROPHIES

I certify by my signature that the information I have provided on this form is accurate and correct. I also understand that all my entry materials, including photographs, as well as any additional photographs taken by Boone and Crockett (our representatives or agents) during Awards Programs or Judges Panels, or likenesses rendered from these photographs become the property of the Boone and Crockett Club and may be used to promote the Club, and its records-keeping activities.

Date: _____ _____ re of Trophy O_____

____NTRY AFFIDAVIT F__ ALL HUNTER-TAKEN TROPHIES

For the purpose of ent___ ___to the Boone and Crockett Club__ ___cords, North American big game harvested by the use of the following methods or under the ___ ___owing conditions are ineligible:

- I. Spotting or H___ ___ng game from the air, followed b___ ___ding in its vicinity for the purpose of pursuit and shooting;
- II. Herding or c___ ___ng with the aid of any motoriz___ ___pment;
- III. Use of electr___ ___communication devices to gu___ ___ters to game, artificial lighting, electronic light intensifying devices (night vision optics)___ ___ts with built-in electronic ra___ ___ding capabilities, thermal imaging equipment, electronic game calls or cameras/time___ ___otion tracking devices that___ ___s and other information to the hunter;
- IV. Confined by ___ ___ial barriers, including esc___ ___ced enclosures;
- V. Transplan___ ___ ___e purpose of commerci___ ___ ___;
- VI. By the us___ ___r pharmaceuticals;
- VII. While sw___ ___less in deep sno___ ___ss in any other natural or artificial medium;
- VIII. On anoth___ ___ense;
- IX. Not in full___ ___h the o___ ___ regulations of the federal government or of any state, province, territory, or tribal council on ___

I certify that the trophy___ ___ot taken in violation of the conditions listed above. In signing this statement, I understand that if the information p___ ___nd to be misrepresented or fraudulent in any respect, it will not be accepted into the Awards Program and 1) a___ ___e subject to deletion from future editions of **Records of North American Big Game** 2) future entries may not be___ ___y by my signature that the information I have provided on this form is accurate and correct. I also understand that all m___ ___luding photographs, as well as any additional photographs taken by Boone and Crockett (our representatives or agent___ ___ms or Judges Panels, or likenesses rendered from these photographs become the property of the Boone and Crock___ ___o promote the Club, and its records-keeping activities.

FAIR CHASE, as define___ ___t Club®, is the ethical, sportsmanlike and lawful pursuit and taking of any free-ranging wild, native North Am___ ___ manner that does not give the hunter an improper advantage over such game animals.

The ___ ___d Cro___ ___e the entry of any animal that it deems to have been taken in an unethical manner or under ___lub.

___e of Hunter:_____

(SIGNATURE MUST BE WITNESSED BY AN OFFICIAL MEASURER OR A NOTARY PUBLIC.)

___ure of Notary or Official Measurer: _____

250 Station Drive
Missoula, MT 59801
(406) 542-1888

BOONE AND CROCKETT CLUB°
OFFICIAL SCORING SYSTEM FOR NORTH AMERICAN BIG GAME TROPHIES

MINIMUM SCORES	
AWARDS	ALL-TIME
115	115

BISON

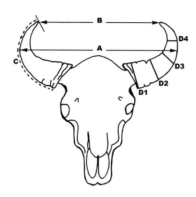

SEE OTHER SIDE FOR INSTRUCTIONS		COLUMN 1	COLUMN 2	COLUMN 3
A. Greatest Spread		34 5/8	Right Horn	Left Horn	Difference
B. Tip to Tip Spread		26 5/8			
C. Length of Horn			17 6/8	18 5/8	7/8
D-1. Circumference of Base			15 1/8	15 7/8	6/8
D-2. Circumference at First Quarter	Location of First Quarter Circumference: 4 21/32		13 7/8	13 6/8	1/8
D-3. Circumference at Second Quarter	Location of Second Quarter Circumference: 9 5/16		11 5/8	11 6/8	1/8
D-4. Circumference at Third Quarter	Location of Third Quarter Circumference: 13 31/32		8 4/8	8 3/8	1/8
		TOTALS	66 7/8	68 3/8	2 0/8

ADD	Column 1	66 7/8	Exact Locality Where Killed: Teton County, Wyoming
	Column 2	68 3/8	Date Killed: 9/18/2007 Hunter: Edward D. Riekens, Jr.
	Subtotal	135 2/8	Trophy Owner: Edward D. Riekens, Jr. Telephone #:
	SUBTRACT Column 3	2 0/8	Trophy Owner's Address:
FINAL SCORE		133 2/8	Trophy Owner's E-mail: Guide's Name:
			Remarks: (Mention Any Abnormalities or Unique Qualities)

I, ___David A. Pawlicki_____, certify that I have measured this trophy on ___12/10/2007___
　　　　　　　PRINT NAME　　　　　　　　　　　　　　　　　　　　　　　　　　MM/DD/YYYY

at ___Cheyenne, Wyoming_____
　　STREET ADDRESS　　　　　　　　　　　　　　　　　　CITY　　　　　　　　　STATE/PROVINCE

and that these measurements and data are, to the best of my knowledge and belief, made in accordance with the instructions given.

Witness: _____   Signature: _____   I.D. Number ☐☐☐☐
　　　　　　　　　　　　　　　　　　　　　　　B&C OFFICIAL MEASURER

INSTRUCTIONS FOR MEASURING BISON

All measurements must be made with a 1/4-inch wide flexible steel tape to the nearest one-eighth of an inch. Wherever it is necessary to change direction of measurement, mark a control point and swing tape at this point. Enter fractional figures in eighths, without reduction. Official measurements cannot be taken until horns have air dried for at least 60 days after the animal was killed.

A. Greatest Spread is measured between perpendiculars at a right angle to the center line of the skull. **Greatest spread does not add into the final score.**

B. Tip to Tip Spread is measured between tips of horns. **Tip to tip spread does not add into the final score.**

C. Length of Horn is measured from the lowest point on underside over outer curve to a point in line with the tip. Use a straight edge, perpendicular to horn axis, to end the measurement, if necessary.

D-1. Circumference of Base is measured at right angle to axis of horn. Do not follow the irregular edge of horn; the line of measurement must be entirely on horn material.

D-2-3-4. Divide measurement C of longer horn by four. Starting at base, mark both horns at these quarters (even though the other horn is shorter) and measure the circumferences at these marks, with measurements taken at right angles to horn axis.

MATERIALS RELEASE FORM FOR ALL NON-HUNTER-TAKEN TROPHIES

I certify by my signature that the information I have provided on this form is accurate and correct. I also understand that all my entry materials, including photographs, as well as any additional photographs taken by Boone and Crockett (our representatives or agents) during Awards Programs or Judges Panels, or likenesses rendered from these photographs become the property of the Boone and Crockett Club and may be used to promote the Club, and its records-keeping activities.

Date: _____ Signature of Trophy Owner: _____

ENTRY AFFIDAVIT FOR ALL HUNTER-TAKEN TROPHIES

For the purpose of entry into the Boone and Crockett Club's® records, North American big game harvested by the use of the following methods or under the following conditions are ineligible:

I. Spotting or herding game from the air, followed by landing in its vicinity for the purpose of pursuit and shooting;

II. Herding or chasing with the aid of any motorized equipment;

III. Use of electronic communication devices to guide hunters to game, artificial lighting, electronic light intensifying devices (night vision optics), sights with built-in electronic range-finding capabilities, thermal imaging equipment, electronic game calls or cameras/timers/motion tracking devices that transmit images and other information to the hunter;

IV. Confined by artificial barrier, including escape-proof fenced enclosures;

V. Transplanted for the purpose of commercial shooting;

VI. By the use of traps or pharmaceuticals;

VII. While swimming, helpless in deep snow, or helpless in any other natural or artificial medium;

VIII. On another hunter's license;

IX. Not in full compliance with the laws or regulations of the federal government or of any state, province, territory, or tribal council on reservations or t...

I certify that the trophy scored on this ... that if the information provided on this e... Awards Program and 1) all of my prior ent... future entries may not be accepted. I also cer... also understand that all my entry materials, includi... representatives or agents) during Awards Programs or ... of the Boone and Crockett Club and may be used to promote the C...

FAIR CHASE, as defined by the Boone and Crockett Club®, is th... ny free-ranging wild, native North American big game animal in a manner that d... game animals.

The Boone and Crockett Club® may exclude the entry of any anim... nner or under conditions deemed inappropriate by the Club.

Date: _____ Signature of Hunter: _____
(SIGNATURE MUS... ...RER OR A NOTARY PUBLIC.)

Date: _____ Signature of Notary or Official Measure...

250 Station Drive
Missoula, MT 59801
(406) 542-1888

BOONE AND CROCKETT CLUB®
OFFICIAL SCORING SYSTEM FOR NORTH AMERICAN BIG GAME TROPHIES

MINIMUM SCORES	
AWARDS	ALL-TIME
47	50

ROCKY MOUNTAIN GOAT

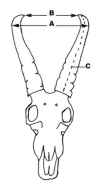
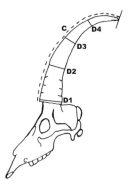

SEE OTHER SIDE FOR INSTRUCTIONS		COLUMN 1	COLUMN 2	COLUMN 3
A. Greatest Spread	7 3/8	Right Horn	Left Horn	Difference
B. Tip to Tip Spread	6 7/8			
C. Length of Horn		11 0/8	11 1/8	1/8
D-1. Circumference of Base		5 7/8	6 0/8	1/8
D-2. Circumference at First Quarter	Location of First Quarter Circumference: 2 25/32	4 7/8	5 0/8	1/8
D-3. Circumference at Second Quarter	Location of Second Quarter Circumference: 5 9/16	3 2/8	3 2/8	——
D-4. Circumference at Third Quarter	Location of Third Quarter Circumference: 8 11/32	2 0/8	2 0/8	——
	TOTALS	27 0/8	27 3/8	3/8

ADD	Column 1	27 0/8	Exact Locality Where Killed: **Kalum Lake, British Columbia**
	Column 2	27 3/8	Date Killed: **11/22/2008** Hunter: **A.C. Smid**
	Subtotal	54 3/8	Trophy Owner: **A.C. Smid** Telephone #:
	SUBTRACT Column 3	3/8	Trophy Owner's Address:
FINAL SCORE		54 0/8	Trophy Owner's E-mail: Guide's Name:
			Remarks: (Mention Any Abnormalities or Unique Qualities)

I, **Clint Walker**
_____
PRINT NAME
, certify that I have measured this trophy on **1/21/2009**
MM/DD/YYYY

at **Telium, British Columbia**
_____
STREET ADDRESS   CITY   STATE/PROVINCE

and that these measurements and data are, to the best of my knowledge and belief, made in accordance with the instructions given.

Witness: _____ Signature: _____ I.D. Number ☐☐☐☐
B&C OFFICIAL MEASURER

COPYRIGHT © 2010 BY BOONE AND CROCKETT CLUB®

INSTRUCTIONS FOR MEASURING ROCKY MOUNTAIN GOAT

All measurements must be made with a 1/4-inch wide flexible steel tape to the nearest one-eighth of an inch. Wherever it is necessary to change direction of measurement, mark a control point and swing tape at this point. Enter fractional figures in eighths, without reduction. Official measurements cannot be taken until horns have air dried for at least 60 days after the animal was killed.

- **A. Greatest Spread** is measured between perpendiculars at a right angle to the center line of the skull. **Greatest spread does not add into the final score.**
- **B. Tip to Tip spread** is measured between tips of the horns. **Tip to tip spread does not add into the final score.**
- **C. Length of Horn** is measured from the lowest point in front over outer curve to a point in line with tip.
- **D-1. Circumference of Base** is measured at a right angle to axis of horn. Do not follow irregular edge of horn; the line of measurement must be entirely on horn material.
- **D-2-3-4. Divide measurement C** of longer horn by four. Starting at base, mark both horns at these quarters (even though the other horn is shorter) and measure circumferences at these marks, with measurements taken at right angles to horn axis.

MATERIALS RELEASE FORM FOR ALL NON-HUNTER-TAKEN TROPHIES

I certify by my signature that the information I have provided on this form is accurate and correct. I also understand that all my entry materials, including photographs, as well as any additional photographs taken by Boone and Crockett (our representatives or agents) during Awards Programs or Judges Panels, or likenesses rendered from these photographs become the property of the Boone and Crockett Club and may be used to promote the Club, and its records-keeping activities.

Date: _____   Signature of Trophy Owner: _____

ENTRY AFFIDAVIT FOR ALL HUNTER-TAKEN TROPHIES

For the purpose of entry into the Boone and Crockett Club's® records, North American big game harvested by the use of the following methods or under the following conditions are ineligible:

- I.   Spotting or herding game from the air, followed by landing in its vicinity
- II. Herding or chasing with the aid of any motorized equipment;
- III. Use of electronic communication devices to guide hunters to game, artificial
  vision optics), sights with built-in electronic range-finding capabilities, therma
  cameras/timers/motion tracking devices that transmit images and other inform
- IV. Confined by artificial barriers, including escape-proof fenced enclosures;
- V.   Transplanted for the purpose of commercial shooting;
- VI. By the use of traps or pharmaceuticals;
- VII. While swimming, helpless in deep snow, or helpless in any other natural or a
- VIII. On another hunter's license;
- IX. Not in full compliance with the game laws or regulations of the federal govern
  council on reservations or tribal lands;

I certify that the trophy scored on this chart was not taken in violation of the conditions liste
that if the information provided on this entry is found to be misrepresented or fraudulent in any
Awards Program and 1) all of my prior entries are subject to deletion from future editions of Reco
future entries may not be accepted. I also certify by my signature that the information I have prov
also understand that all my entry materials, including photographs, as well as any additional photog
representatives or agents) during Awards Programs or Judges Panels, or likenesses rendered from th
of the Boone and Crockett Club and may be used to promote the Club, and its records-keeping activities

FAIR CHASE, as defined by the Boone and Crockett Club®, is the ethical, sportsmanlike and lawful pursuit and
wild, native North American big game animal in a manner that does not give the hunter an improper advantage

The Boone and Crockett Club® may exclude the entry of any animal that it deems to have been taken in an unet
conditions deemed inappropriate by the Club.

Date:_____ Signature of Hunter:_____
(SIGNATURE MUST BE WITNESSED BY AN OFFICIAL MEASU

Date:_____ Signature of Notary or Official Measurer: _____

250 Station Drive
Missoula, MT 59801
(406) 542-1888

BOONE AND CROCKETT CLUB®
OFFICIAL SCORING SYSTEM FOR NORTH AMERICAN BIG GAME TROPHIES

MINIMUM SCORES	
AWARDS	ALL-TIME
105	105

MUSK OX

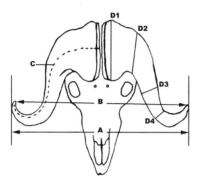

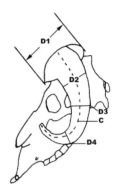

SEE OTHER SIDE FOR INSTRUCTIONS		COLUMN 1	COLUMN 2	COLUMN 3
A. Greatest Spread	28 6/8	Right	Left	Difference
B. Tip to Tip Spread	26 4/8	Horn	Horn	
C. Length of Horn		29 1/8	29 1/8	——
D-1. Width of Boss		11 2/8	10 6/8	4/8
D-2. Width at First Quarter	Location of First Quarter Width: 7 9/32	6 3/8	6 0/8	3/8
D-3. Circumference at Second Quarter	Location of Second Quarter Circumference: 14 9/16	10 7/8	11 1/8	2/8
D-4. Circumference at Third Quarter	Location of Third Quarter Circumference: 21 27/32	6 4/8	6 3/8	1/8
	TOTALS	64 1/8	64 1/8	1 2/8

ADD	Column 1	64 1/8	Exact Locality Where Killed: **Kugluktuk, Nunavut**
	Column 2	64 1/8	Date Killed: 3/28/2007 Hunter: **Ben L. Mueller**
	Subtotal	128 2/8	Trophy Owner: **Ben L. Mueller** Telephone #:
	SUBTRACT Column 3	1 2/8	Trophy Owner's Address:
	FINAL SCORE	127 0/8	Trophy Owner's E-mail: Guide's Name:
			Remarks: (Mention Any Abnormalities or Unique Qualities)

I, **Homer Saye**
PRINT NAME
, certify that I have measured this trophy on **10/24/2007**
MM/DD/YYYY

at **Cypress, Texas**
STREET ADDRESS   CITY   STATE/PROVINCE

and that these measurements and data are, to the best of my knowledge and belief, made in accordance with the instructions given.

Witness: _____ Signature: _____ I.D. Number ☐☐☐☐
B&C OFFICIAL MEASURER

INSTRUCTIONS FOR MEASURING MUSK OX

All measurements must be made with a 1/4-inch wide flexible steel tape and adjustable calipers to the nearest one-eighth of an inch. Enter fractional figures in eighths, without reduction. Official measurements cannot be taken until horns have air dried for at least 60 days after the animal was killed.

- **A. Greatest Spread** is measured between perpendiculars at a right angle to the center line of the skull. **Greatest spread does not add into the final score.**
- **B. Tip to Tip Spread** is measured between tips of horns. **Tip to tip spread does not add into the final score.**
- **C. Length of Horn** is measured along center of upper horn surface, staying within curve of horn as illustrated, to a point in line with tip. Attempt to free the connective tissue between the horns at the center of the boss to determine the lowest point of horn material on each side. Hook the tape under the lowest point of the horn and measure the length of horn, with the measurement line maintained in the center of the upper surface of horn following the converging lines to the horn tip. A flexible steel cable may be substituted for the 1/4-inch steel tape for this measurement only.
- **D-1. Width of Boss** is measured with calipers at greatest width of the boss, with measurement line forming a right angle with horn axis. It is often helpful to measure D-1 before C, marking the midpoint of the boss as the correct path of C.
- **D-2-3-4. Divide measurement C** of longer horn by four. Starting at base, mark both horns at these quarters (even though the other horn is shorter). Then, using calipers, measure width of boss at D-2, making sure the measurement is at a right angle to horn axis and in line with the D-2 mark. Circumferences are then measured at D-3 and D-4, with measurements being taken at right angles to horn axis.

MATERIALS RELEASE FORM FOR ALL NON-HUNTER-TAKEN TROPHIES

I certify by my signature that the information I have provided on this form is accurate and correct. I also understand that all my entry materials, including photographs, as well as any additional photographs taken by Boone and Crockett (our representatives or agents) during Awards Programs or Judges Panels, or likenesses rendered from these photographs become the property of the Boone and Crockett Club and may be used to promote the Club, and its records-keeping activities.

Date: _____ Signature of Trophy Owner: _____

ENTRY AFFIDAVIT FOR ALL HUNTER-TAKEN TROPHIES

For the purpose of entry into the Boone and Crockett Club's® records, North American big game harvested by the use of the following methods or under the fol_____ _____ditions are ineligible:

I. Spot_____ ir, followed by landing in its vicinity for the purpose of pursuit and shooting;

II. H_____ __otorized equipment;

III. _____ ___uide hunters to game, artificial lighting, electronic light intensifying devices (night _____ __e-finding capabilities, thermal imaging equipment, electronic game calls or _____ images and other information to the hunter;

_____ fenced enclosures;

_____ ;

_____ any other natural or artificial medium;

_____ ns of the federal government or of any state, province, territory, or tribal

_____ n of the con___itions listed above. In signing this statement, I understand _____ ____ented or ____udulent in any respect, it will not be accepted into the _____ n from f____e editions of **Records of North American Big Game** 2) _____ that ___ ___ormation I have provided on this form is accurate and correct. I _____ ___ as any additional photographs taken by Boone and Crockett (our ___s ranels, or likenesses rendered from these photographs become the property ___he Club, and its records-keeping activities.

_____ e ethical, sportsmanlike and lawful pursuit and taking of any free-ranging _____ oes not give the hunter an improper advantage over such game animals.

_____ mal that it deems to have been taken in an unethical manner or under

___URE MUST BE WITNESSED BY AN OFFICIAL MEASURER OR A NOTARY PUBLIC.)

___al Measurer: _____

Records of
North American
Big Game

250 Station Drive
Missoula, MT 59801
(406) 542-1888

BOONE AND CROCKETT CLUB®
OFFICIAL SCORING SYSTEM FOR NORTH AMERICAN BIG GAME TROPHIES

SHEEP

MINIMUM SCORES		
	AWARDS	ALL-TIME
bighorn	175	180
desert	165	168
Dall's	160	170
Stone's	165	170

KIND OF SHEEP (check one)

☑ bighorn
☐ desert
☐ Dall's
☐ Stone's

PLUG NUMBER
_____

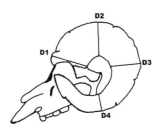

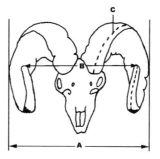

Measure to a
Point in Line
With Horn Tip

SEE OTHER SIDE FOR INSTRUCTIONS		COLUMN 1	COLUMN 2	COLUMN 3
A. Greatest Spread (Is Often Tip to Tip Spread)	25 1/8	Right Horn	Left Horn	Difference
B. Tip to Tip Spread	25 1/8			
C. Length of Horn		44 4/8	44 2/8	
D-1. Circumference of Base		16 4/8	16 4/8	———
D-2. Circumference at First Quarter — Location of First Quarter Circumference: 11 1/8		16 0/8	16 0/8	———
D-3. Circumference at Second Quarter — Location of Second Quarter Circumference: 22 2/8		14 5/8	14 5/8	———
D-4. Circumference at Third Quarter — Location of Third Quarter Circumference: 33 3/8		10 5/8	10 6/8	1/8
TOTALS		102 2/8	102 1/8	1/8

ADD	Column 1	102 2/8	Exact Locality Where Killed: **Fergus County, Montana**
	Column 2	102 1/8	Date Killed: **9/21/2008** — Hunter: **Toni L. Sannon**
	Subtotal	204 3/8	Trophy Owner: **Toni L. Sannon** — Telephone #:
	SUBTRACT Column 3	1/8	Trophy Owner's Address:
	FINAL SCORE	204 2/8	Trophy Owner's E-mail: — Guide's Name:
			Remarks: (Mention Any Abnormalities or Unique Qualities)

I, **Brad Zundel** _____, certify that I have measured this trophy on _____ **11/25/2008**
PRINT NAME   MM/DD/YYYY

at **Billings, Montana** _____
STREET ADDRESS   CITY   STATE/PROVINCE

and that these measurements and data are, to the best of my knowledge and belief, made in accordance with the instructions given.

Witness: _____ Signature: _____ I.D. Number [ ][ ][ ][ ]
                                                              B&C OFFICIAL MEASURER

COPYRIGHT © 2009 BY BOONE AND CROCKETT CLUB®

INSTRUCTIONS FOR MEASURING SHEEP

All measurements must be made with a 1/4-inch wide flexible steel tape to the nearest one-eighth of an inch. Enter fractional figures in eighths, without reduction. Official measurements cannot be taken until horns have air dried for at least 60 days after the animal was killed.

A. **Greatest Spread** is measured between perpendiculars at a right angle to the center line of the skull. **Greatest spread does not add into the final score.**

B. **Tip to Tip Spread** is measured between tips of horns. **Tip to tip spread does not add into the final score.**

C. **Length of Horn** is measured from the lowest point in front on outer curve to a point in line with tip. Do not press tape into depressions. The low point of the outer curve of the horn is considered to be the low point of the frontal portion of the horn, situated above and slightly medial to the eye socket (not the outside edge). Use a straight edge, perpendicular to horn axis, to end measurement on "broomed" horns.

D-1. **Circumference of Base** is measured at a right angle to axis of horn. Do not follow irregular edge of horn; the line of measurement must be entirely on horn material.

D-2-3-4. **Divide measurement C** of longer horn by four. Starting at base, mark both horns at these quarters (even though the other horn is shorter) and measure circumferences at these marks, with measurements taken at right angles to horn axis.

MATERIALS RELEASE FORM FOR ALL NON-HUNTER-TAKEN TROPHIES

I certify by my signature that the information I have provided on this form is accurate and correct. I also understand that all my entry materials, including photographs, as well as any additional photographs taken by Boone and Crockett (our representatives or agents) during Awards Programs or Judges Panels, or likenesses rendered from these photographs become the property of the Boone and Crockett Club and may be used to promote the Club, and its records-keeping activities.

Date: _____ Signature of Trophy Owner: _____

ENTRY AFFIDAVIT FOR ALL HUNTER ⸺ EN TRO

For the purpose of entry into the Boone and Crockett Club's® records, North Ame⸺⸺⸺⸺ harv⸺⸺ methods or under the following conditions are ineligible:

I. Spotting or herding game from the air, followed by landing in its vicinity for ⸺⸺⸺⸺⸺⸺
II. Herding or chasing with the aid of any motorized equipment;
III. Use of electronic communication devices to guide hunters to game, artificial li⸺⸺⸺⸺⸺g devices vision optics), sights with built-in electronic range-finding capabilities, therma⸺⸺⸺me calls cameras/timers/motion tracking devices that transmit images and othe⸺⸺
IV. Confined by artificial barriers, including escape-proof fenced ⸺⸺
V. Transplanted for the purpose of commercial shooting;
VI. By the use of traps or pharmaceuticals;
VII. While swimming, helpless in deep snow, or helpless in ⸺⸺
VIII. On another hunter's license;
IX. Not in full compliance with the game laws or regulati⸺⸺⸺⸺⸺tory, or tribal council on reservations or tribal lands;

I certify that the trophy scored on this chart was not taken in ⸺⸺⸺⸺⸺⸺tatement, I understand that if the information provided on this entry is found to be m⸺⸺⸺⸺⸺e accepted into the Awards Program and 1) all of my prior entries are subject to ⸺⸺⸺⸺erican Big Game 2) future entries may not be accepted. I also certify by my signa⸺⸺⸺curate and correct. I also understand that all my entry materials, including photogr⸺⸺⸺⸺ographs taken⸺⸺ and Crockett (our representatives or agents) during Awards Programs or Judge⸺⸺s, ⸺⸺es⸺⸺om these photogra⸺⸺come the property of the Boone and Crockett Club and may be used to promote⸺⸺ub, a⸺⸺s re⸺⸺ee⸺⸺activities.

FAIR CHASE, as defined by the Boone and Crockett Club®, i⸺⸺ethical, sports⸺⸺ and⸺⸺ful pursuit and taking⸺⸺ny free-ranging wild, native North American big game animal in a manner th⸺⸺oes not give th⸺⸺er⸺⸺n i⸺⸺per advantage over su⸺⸺ game animals.

The Boone and Crockett Club® may exclude the entry of any⸺⸺imal that it deem⸺⸺⸺⸺ taken in an unethical m⸺⸺er or under conditions deemed inappropriate by the Club.

Date: _____ Signature of Hunter: _____

(SIGNATURE MUST BE WITNESSED BY AN OFFICIAL⸺⸺ (ARY PUBLIC.)

Date: _____ Signature of Notary or Official Me⸺⸺

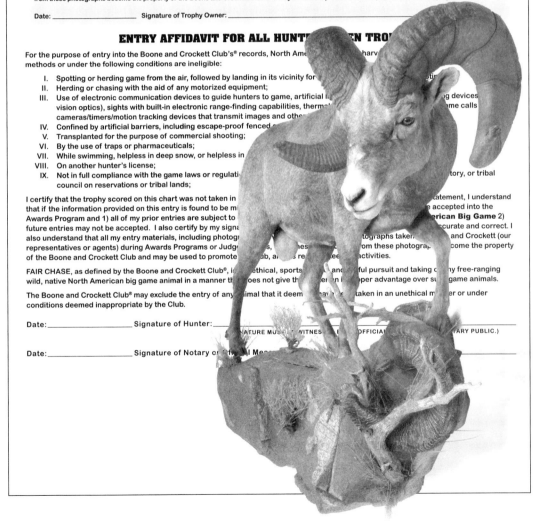

FIELD PHOTOGRAPHS COURTESY OF THE TROPHY OWNERS

TROPHY FIELD PHOTOS FROM THE 27TH BIG GAME AWARDS PROGRAM 2007-2009

27th Big Game Awards Program Sponsors

ABOVE: typical whitetail deer

SCORE: 162 $^7/_8$

LOCATION: Mahoning Co., OH — 2007

HUNTER: Adam J. Bouch

LISTING ON PAGE: 533

TOP LEFT: black bear
SCORE: 21 $^{10}/_{16}$
LOCATION: Garrett Co., MD – 2007
HUNTER: Coty L. Jones
LISTING ON PAGE: 451

TOP RIGHT: bighorn sheep
SCORE: 181 $^3/_8$
LOCATION: Wallowa Co., OR – 2005
HUNTER: Russell S. Holcomb
LISTING ON PAGE: 609

BOTTOM: Shiras' moose
SCORE: 164 $^1/_8$
LOCATION: Jackson Co., CO – 2009
HUNTER: Brad A. Knutson
LISTING ON PAGE: 570

TOP LEFT: bison

SCORE: 116 $^6/_8$

LOCATION: Teton Co., WY – 2007

HUNTER: Eric H. Boley

LISTING ON PAGE: 599

TOP RIGHT: pronghorn

SCORE: 83 $^4/_8$

LOCATION: Yavapai Co., AZ – 2007

HUNTER: Mike P. Landgren

LISTING ON PAGE: 587

BOTTOM: non-typical American elk

SCORE: 391 $^4/_8$

LOCATION: Apache Co., AZ – 2009

HUNTER: Robert L. Hudman

LISTING ON PAGE: 482

ABOVE: typical Coues' whitetail deer
SCORE: 111 $^6/_8$
LOCATION: Pima Co., AZ — 2007
HUNTER: Jane A. Beck
LISTING ON PAGE: 560

TOP LEFT: typical whitetail deer
SCORE: 170 3/8
LOCATION: Loon Lake, SK – 2008
HUNTER: Derek J. Wade
LISTING ON PAGE: 523

TOP RIGHT: mountain caribou
SCORE: 411 3/8
LOCATION: Arctic Red River, NT – 2009
HUNTER: Gregory Menzies
LISTING ON PAGE: 574

BOTTOM: grizzly bear
SCORE: 24 15/16
LOCATION: Norton Sound, AK – 2009
HUNTER: Frank S. Noska IV
LISTING ON PAGE: 466

BOONE AND CROCKETT CLUB'S

ABOVE: Stone's sheep
SCORE: 167 3/8
LOCATION: Ogilvie Mts., YT — 2009
HUNTER: Peeler G. Lacey
LISTING ON PAGE: 617

ABOVE: typical mule deer
SCORE: 183 $^1/_8$
LOCATION: Bow River, AB — 2006
HUNTER: Douglas C. Murray
LISTING ON PAGE: 494

TOP LEFT: Alaska brown bear

SCORE: 28 3/16

LOCATION: Aliulik Pen., AK – 2008

HUNTER: Luke A. Terkovich

LISTING ON PAGE: 468

TOP RIGHT: non-typical whitetail

SCORE: 193 1/8

LOCATION: Frio Co., TX – 2007

HUNTER: David O. Traylor

LISTING ON PAGE: 553

BOTTOM: bison

SCORE: 125

LOCATION: Coconino Co., AZ – 2007

HUNTER: Patrick J. Cooley

LISTING ON PAGE: 598

TOP LEFT: desert sheep

SCORE: 169 $^1/_8$

LOCATION: San Bernardino Co.,
CA – 2007

HUNTER: Brian E. McClintock

LISTING ON PAGE: 613

TOP RIGHT: Alaska brown bear

SCORE: 26 $^5/_{16}$

LOCATION: Kiliuda Bay, AK – 2009

HUNTER: James R. Trull

LISTING ON PAGE: 470

BOTTOM: mountain caribou

SCORE: 373 $^5/_8$

LOCATION: Rabbit River, BC – 2006

HUNTER: Kanina M. Fulton

LISTING ON PAGE: 575

ABOVE: pronghorn
SCORE: 82 $^6/_8$
LOCATION: Colfax Co., NM — 2008
HUNTER: Brian A. Hauck
LISTING ON PAGE: 589

ABOVE: non-typical whitetail deer

SCORE: 199

LOCATION: Leavenworth Co., KS— 2006

HUNTER: Jim W. Slapper, Jr.

LISTING ON PAGE: 548

TOP LEFT: Canada moose

SCORE: 198 $1/8$

LOCATION: Tuya River, BC – 2008

HUNTER: Bradley R. Jackle

LISTING ON PAGE: 564

TOP RIGHT: typical Sitka blacktail

SCORE: 111 $3/8$

LOCATION: Kosciusko Island, AK – 2008

HUNTER: Spencer P. Richter

LISTING ON PAGE: 509

BOTTOM: grizzly bear

SCORE: 24

LOCATION: Kirbyville Creek, BC – 2006

HUNTER: Brian M. McDonald

LISTING ON PAGE: 467

TOP LEFT: typical mule deer

SCORE: 190 $5/8$

LOCATION: Johnson Co., WY – 2008

HUNTER: Jason O. Burns

LISTING ON PAGE: 491

TOP RIGHT: mountain caribou

SCORE: 369 $2/8$

LOCATION: Mackenzie Mts., NT – 2007

HUNTER: William D. Eshee, Jr.

LISTING ON PAGE: 575

BOTTOM: pronghorn

SCORE: 82 $6/8$

LOCATION: Coconino Co., AZ – 2006

HUNTER: Robert B. Andersen

LISTING ON PAGE: 589

ABOVE: Shiras' moose

SCORE: 156 $^6/_8$

LOCATION: Flathead Co., MT— 2007

HUNTER: James L. Friske

LISTING ON PAGE: 571

TOP LEFT: Alaska brown bear

SCORE: 26 ^{5}/$_{16}$

LOCATION: Bering River, AK – 2007

HUNTER: Vincent L. Hazen

LISTING ON PAGE: 470

TOP RIGHT: pronghorn

SCORE: 81 ^{4}/$_8$

LOCATION: Lassen Co., CA – 2009

HUNTER: Terri L. Mankins

LISTING ON PAGE: 593

BOTTOM: typical mule deer

SCORE: 185

LOCATION: St. Mary River, AB – 2007

HUNTER: James M. Tardif

LISTING ON PAGE: 494

ABOVE: desert sheep
SCORE: 176 $\frac{1}{8}$
LOCATION: Culberson Co., TX— 2007
HUNTER: Jerry M. Baker
LISTING ON PAGE: 612

ABOVE: typical whitetail deer
SCORE: 185
LOCATION: Jackson Co., IL— 2008
HUNTER: Craig D. Ahlers
LISTING ON PAGE: 511

TOP LEFT: non-typical Coues' deer
SCORE: 120 3/8
LOCATION: Santa Cruz Co., AZ –
2008
HUNTER: Audria L. Dolan
LISTING ON PAGE: 562

TOP RIGHT: bison
SCORE: 122 2/8
LOCATION: Custer Co., SD – 2006
HUNTER: David R. Lautner
LISTING ON PAGE: 598

BOTTOM: non-typical American elk
SCORE: 386 5/8
LOCATION: Gila Co., AZ – 2008
HUNTER: James P. Mellody III
LISTING ON PAGE: 483

TOP LEFT: desert sheep

SCORE: 182 2/8*

LOCATION: Nye Co., NV – 2008

HUNTER: Joseph L. Maslach

LISTING ON PAGE: 614

* Final score subject to revision by additional verifying measurements.

TOP RIGHT: pronghorn

SCORE: 80

LOCATION: Sioux Co., NE – 2009

HUNTER: Kerry G. Keane

LISTING ON PAGE: 597

BOTTOM: Alaska brown bear

SCORE: 26 12/16

LOCATION: Johnson River, AK – 2008

HUNTER: Terry B. Neely

LISTING ON PAGE: 470

ABOVE: bison
SCORE: 118
LOCATION: Teton Co., WY — 2007
HUNTER: Jerrell F. Coburn
LISTING ON PAGE: 599

ABOVE: typical mule deer

SCORE: 192 ⁴/₈

LOCATION: Great Sand Hills, SK — 2007

HUNTER: Jim Clary

LISTING ON PAGE: 490

TOP LEFT: Stone's sheep
SCORE: 174 5/8*
LOCATION: Anvil Range, YT – 2008
HUNTER: Tim Parker
LISTING ON PAGE: 617

* Final score subject to revision by
additional verifying measurements.

TOP RIGHT: typical American elk
SCORE: 379 7/8
LOCATION: Sevier Co., UT – 2006
HUNTER: Gerald S. Laurino
LISTING ON PAGE: 478

BOTTOM: pronghorn
SCORE: 83 4/8
LOCATION: Natrona Co., WY –
2009
HUNTER: Glen H. Taylor
LISTING ON PAGE: 588

ABOVE: bighorn sheep
SCORE: 184 2/8
LOCATION: Columbia Co., WA — 2008
HUNTER: Chris A. Dianda
LISTING ON PAGE: 608

TOP LEFT: cougar

SCORE: 14 $^{11}/_{16}$

LOCATION: Carbon Co., WY – 2008

HUNTER: Jack L. Morey, Jr.

LISTING ON PAGE: 475

TOP RIGHT: mountain caribou

SCORE: 394 $^{2}/_{8}$

LOCATION: Whitehorse, YT – 2007

HUNTER: Thomas J. Little

LISTING ON PAGE: 574

BOTTOM: typical whitetail deer

SCORE: 175 $^{3}/_{8}$

LOCATION: Eagle Creek, SK – 2008

HUNTER: William T. Longman

LISTING ON PAGE: 516

TOP LEFT: Alaska brown bear

SCORE: 28 $^3/_{16}$

LOCATION: Olga Bay, AK – 2009

HUNTER: Fred J. Fanizzi

LISTING ON PAGE: 468

TOP RIGHT: mountain caribou

SCORE: 424 $^2/_8$*

LOCATION: North Lakes, YT – 2008

HUNTER: Mike E. Broadwell

LISTING ON PAGE: 575

* Final score subject to revision by
  additional verifying measurements.

BOTTOM: Stone's sheep

SCORE: 165 $^3/_8$

LOCATION: Ogilvie Mts., YT –
  2009

HUNTER: L. Victor Clark

LISTING ON PAGE: 617

ABOVE: non-typical whitetail deer
SCORE: 234 $^1/_8$
LOCATION: Delaware Co., OH — 2008
HUNTER: Gregory S. Hunt
LISTING ON PAGE: 540

ABOVE: typical American elk
SCORE: 375
LOCATION: Golden Valley Co., MT — 2008
HUNTER: Brendan V. Burns
LISTING ON PAGE: 478

TOP LEFT: typical Coues' deer
SCORE: 108
LOCATION: Sonora, MX – 2008
HUNTER: Gary A. Hayden
LISTING ON PAGE: 561

TOP RIGHT: pronghorn
SCORE: 80 $^6/_8$
LOCATION: Sioux Co., NE – 2007
HUNTER: Jina L. Nemnich
LISTING ON PAGE: 595

BOTTOM: typical whitetail deer
SCORE: 172 $^5/_8$
LOCATION: Buffalo Co., WI – 2007
HUNTER: Corinne L. Brenner
LISTING ON PAGE: 519

TOP LEFT: Alaska brown bear

SCORE: 27 5/16

LOCATION: Manby Stream, AK – 2008

HUNTER: George E. Miller

LISTING ON PAGE: 469

TOP RIGHT: Dall's sheep

SCORE: 165 2/8

LOCATION: Brooks Range, AK – 2009

HUNTER: Mark E. Renner

LISTING ON PAGE: 616

BOTTOM: bighorn sheep

SCORE: 181 4/8

LOCATION: Park Co., WY – 2008

HUNTER: Kirk C. Clinkingbeard

LISTING ON PAGE: 609

ABOVE: typical mule deer
SCORE: 181 $^2/_8$
LOCATION: Grand Co., CO — 2008
HUNTER: Gary A. Durfee
LISTING ON PAGE: 496

ACKNOWLEDGEMENTS
Boone and Crockett Club's
27th Big Game Awards, 2007-2009

Data compiled and book assembled with the able assistance of:
Eldon L. "Buck" Buckner – Chairman, Boone and Crockett Club's Records Committee
Howard P. Monsour, Jr. – Chairman, Boone and Crockett Club's Publications Committee
Kyle C. Krause – Deputy, Boone and Crockett Club's Publications Committee
Tony Schoonen – Chief of Staff, Boone and Crockett Club
Jack Reneau – Director of Big Game Records, Boone and Crockett Club
Justin Spring – Assistant Director of Big Game Records, Boone and Crockett Club
Julie T. Houk – Director of Publications, Boone and Crockett Club
Karlie Slayer – Assistant Graphic Designer, Boone and Crockett Club
Sandra Poston – Office Manager, Boone and Crockett Club
Wendy Nickelson – File Clerk, Records Program Assistant, Boone and Crockett Club
Keith Balfourd – Director of Marketing, Boone and Crockett Club
Abra Loran – Assistant Controller, Boone and Crockett Club
Janice Krueger – Controller, Boone and Crockett Club
Jodi Bishop – Development Program Manager, Boone and Crockett Club
Amy Hutchison – Customer Service, Boone and Crockett Club

Copy Editing by:
Jack Reneau – Director of Big Game Records, Boone and Crockett Club
Justin Spring – Assistant Director of Big Game Records, Boone and Crockett Club
Julie Cowan – Missoula, Montana

Desert sheep painting on the cover by:
Chris Lacey – Sparks, Nevada

Special Trophy Handling:
Scott Bergan – Robert M. Lee Trust – Sparks, Nevada
John Capurro – B&C Official Measurer – Sparks, Nevada
Don Child – Robert M. Lee Trust – Sparks, Nevada
H. Hudson DeCray – B&C Regular Member – Bishop, California
Brian Jensen – Nevada Bighorns Unlimited, Reno, Nevada
Kyle C. Krause – B&C Official Measurer – Arlington, Texas
Chris Lacey – B&C Official Measurer – Sparks, Nevada
Robert M. Lee – B&C Regular Member – Sparks, Nevada
Dan E. McBride – B&C Regular Member – Burnet, Texas
Randy Moeller – Cabela's – Sidney, Nebraska
Bill Sparrow – Robert M. Lee Trust – Sparks, Nevada
Ken Tavener – ITS Logistics – Sparks, Nevada
Jeff Yahn – Cabela's – Sidney, Nebraska

Printed and bound by:
Sheridan Books – Chelsea, Michigan

Limited Editions binding by:
Roswell Book Binding – Phoenix, Arizona